HISTORICAL COMMENTARY ON THE OLD TESTAMENT

* * *

1 Kings

Volume 1: 1 Kings 1-11

HISTORICAL COMMENTARY

ON THE OLD TESTAMENT

Editorial team:

Cornelis Houtman
(Kampen, The Netherlands)

Willem S. Prinsloo †
(Pretoria, South Africa)

Wilfred G.E. Watson
(New Castle, UK)

Al Wolters
(Ancaster, Ontario, Canada)

1 Kings

by

Martin J. Mulder

Volume 1: 1 Kings 1-11

PEETERS - LEUVEN

The translation was made possible due to the financial assistance of NWO, the 'Nederlandse organisatie voor wetenschappelijk onderzoek'*.

Translated from the Dutch by John Vriend.

Dr. M.J. Mulder
1 Kings: Vol. 1 Kings 1-11
(Historical Commentary on the Old Testament)
Cover design by Dick Prins
NUGI 632
ISBN 90-429-0678-2
D. 1998/0602/296

© 1998 — Peeters, Bondgenotenlaan 153, B-3000 Leuven (Belgium)

All rights reserved. No part of this publication may be reproduced, stored in a retrieval system, or transmitted, in any form or by any means, electronic, mechanical, photocopying, recording, or otherwise, without the prior written permission of the publisher.

---

* The Dutch Organisation for Scientific Research.

CONTENTS

Editorial Preface (I) ix
Editorial Preface (II) xi
Abbreviations xii
Bibliography xxi

INTRODUCTION

§1 Name, division, place in the canon 1
§2 The masoretic text 1
§3 The Ancient Versions
   3.1 The Septuagint 2
   3.2 Other Greek Versions 5
   3.3 The Latin Versions 6
   3.4 The Peshitta 7
   3.5 The Targum 9
§4 Parallels to the books of Kings
   4.1 The books of Chronicles 10
   4.2 Josephus 11
§5 Time of origin, sources, and authorship of Kings 11
§6 Content and character of 1 Kgs. 1-11 18
§7 Linguistic aspects of Kings 21
§8 The Solomonic temple and its significance 22
§9 Bibliographic pointers 26

1 KINGS 1:1-4
Translation 32
Introduction 32
Exegesis 32

1 KINGS 1:5-53
Translation 38
Introduction 41
Exegesis 41

1 KINGS 2:1-46
Translation 83

Introduction 86
Exegesis 87

1 KINGS 3:1-3
Translation 130
Introduction 130
Exegesis 130

1 KINGS 3:4-15
Translation 136
Introduction 136
Exegesis 137

1 KINGS 3:16-28
Translation 153
Introduction 153
Exegesis 154

1 KINGS 4:1-6
Translation 161
Introduction 161
Exegesis 162

1 KINGS 4:7-19
Translation 169
Introduction 169
Exegesis 171

1 KINGS 4:20-5:8
Translation 187
Introduction 187
Exegesis 188

1 KINGS 5:9-14
Translation 198
Introduction 198
Exegesis 199

1 KINGS 5:15-32
Translation 206
Introduction 207
Exegesis 207

1 KINGS 6:1-38

Translation	226
Introduction	228
Exegesis	230

1 KINGS 7:1-12

Translation	284
Introduction	284
Exegesis	285

1 KINGS 7:13-51

Translation	300
Introduction	302
Exegesis	302

1 KINGS 8:1-13

Translation	375
Introduction	375
Exegesis	377

1 KINGS 8:14-61

Translation	400
Introduction	403
Exegesis	404
Introduction to vss. 22-30	409

1 KINGS 8:62-66

Translation	450
Introduction	450
Exegesis	451

1 KINGS 9:1-9

Translation	460
Introduction	460
Exegesis	461

1 KINGS 9:10-28

Translation	471
Introduction	472
Exegesis	473
Introduction to vss. 15-23	479

1 KINGS 10:1-29

Translation	505
Introduction	507
Exegesis	510

1 KINGS 11:1-13

Translation	546
Introduction to chapter 11	546
Introduction to vss. 1-13	548
Exegesis	549

1 KINGS 11:14-25

Translation	563
Introduction	563
Exegesis	565

1 KINGS 11:26-43

Translation	579
Introduction	580
Exegesis	581

HISTORICAL COMMENTARY ON THE OLD TESTAMENT 603

EDITORIAL PREFACE (I)

The *Historical Commentary on the Old Testament* is a commentary series written by an international team of contributors. The operative word in the title is 'historical,' by which the editors mean to convey a specific perspective on the writings of the Old Testament.

In contrast to the ahistorical approach of much of contemporary reader-oriented exegesis, in which it is mainly the interaction between the modern reader and the final text that matters, the editors of the *HCOT* are committed to an approach which takes seriously the historical embeddedness of the message of the Old Testament. As itself the product of a long and complex process of transmission, and as part of the sacred Scriptures which have been embraced by both Judaism and Christianity, the Hebrew Bible or Old Testament is rooted in the concreteness of human history, and cannot be properly understood apart from that historical rootedness.

The editors are committed to the view that the Old Testament was and is a vehicle of the knowledge of God – a knowledge that was originally imparted at specific times and places within the bounds of human history. In order for people today to recognize and accept the permanent validity of that knowledge, they must realize that the Old Testament originated in a human society which, with respect to the basic realities of the human condition, was not so very different from our own. It was in the context of a fundamentally similar society, in the concreteness of ordinary human history, culture, and language, that the revelation of God was received over the centuries. It is only by concentrating on the specificity of that thoroughly historical revelation (often brought into focus by comparing the traditions of Israel with those of its neighbours), that we can hope to grasp the uniqueness of the faith of ancient Israel.

In connection with this emphasis, the editors aim at producing a commentary on the Old Testament that devotes explicit attention to the history of interpretation, both as this can be discerned within the Hebrew canon itself, and as it has continued subsequent to the close of the Old Testament canon.

As the term 'Old Testament' indicates, the commentary stands in the Christian exegetical tradition. The contributors, representing a wide range of denominational affiliation, will treat the history of both Jewish and Christian interpretation with due respect, but will also be free to take their own stand on controversial issues.

The commentary will seek to be both up-to-date with respect to contemporary scholarship and in touch with the centuries-long tradition of exegetical reflection on the Old Testament. On the one hand, it is impossible nowadays to present a fully argued exegetical case without referring constantly to the flood of new information which is constantly being made available in such disciplines as archaeology and philology. The wealth of information on any biblical text is so overwhelming that a good commentary nowadays will often need to be more extensive than its predecessors. On the other hand, theological exegesis cannot afford to write off previous scholarship in its field. There is a wealth of largely untapped exegetical wisdom that is available in the history of biblical interpretation.

Since the commentary is intended to serve not only the guild of Old Testament scholars, but also pastors and the educated laity, its format is designed to serve a wide readership. The discussion of every pericope of the biblical text will consist of a new translation of the pericope in question, a relatively brief non-technical section entitled 'Essentials and Perspectives,' and a longer, technical section entitled 'Scholarly Exposition.' The translation will be a new rendering based directly on the Hebrew or Aramaic text. Under the heading *Essentials and Perspectives* the authors will summarize the results of their exegesis in non-technical language. In this section, a knowledge of the biblical languages will not be assumed, and the exegetical exposition will be based primarily on the final shape of the text. However, if various strata can be discerned in the growth of the present text, it will be appropriate to elucidate the meaning of every stratum in its own historical setting. Related passages elsewhere in the Old Testament may also be adduced in this section, especially those that can be regarded as later applications or actualizations of the text in question. This will also be the place for the treatment of significant exegetical insights from the history of Jewish and Christian interpretation outside of the Old Testament itself, especially those found in the New Testament. Although there is an emphasis in this section on the history of interpretation, the authors are free to bring forward their own insights with respect to the contemporary relevance of the text.

The exegetical summary will constitute an invitation to the reader to consult the subsequent section of *Scholarly Exposition*, which will contain the more detailed and technical treatment of the exegetical issues. Here the commentator, though under no editorial constraints with regard to questions of authorship, dating, or method, is expected to deal with the full range of issues raised by modern critical scholarship. However, in accordance with the goal formulated above, the authors are expected to pay due attention to the meaning of every historical stage which they discern in the formation of the text, including its final canonical stage. Tradition-historical and redaction-critical analyses should not become ends in themselves, but should be subservient to an understanding of the inner-canonical history of interpretation.

If the historical context cannot be defined precisely (as is the case with many parts of the book of Proverbs), the historical background of the genre as such (in the case of Proverbs the proverbial wisdom literature of the Ancient Near East) can provide the appropriate historical context in terms of which the text should be understood.

Generally speaking, everything that brings the concrete historical world of the text closer to the modern reader – whether that be specific data regarding climate, geology, geography, minerals, flora and fauna, or whatever – should be treated extensively in the scholarly exposition. Where appropriate, due attention should also be paid to scribal conventions and the physical aspects of the transmission of ancient texts.

EDITORIAL PREFACE (II)

The present volume is a translation of Martin J. Mulder's exegesis of 1 Kings 1-11 in Dutch. It is based on Mulders commentary on 1 Kings 1-7, published in 1987 in the Dutch series Commentaar op het Oude Testament, and on the manuscript of his commentary on 1 Kings 8-11, finished some month before his death in 1994. For this translation the Dutch text was checked through and the bibliographical material brought up to date.

The Dutch Organization for Scientific Research (NWO) was kindly willing to bear the costs of translation. The translation was made by John Vriend. The text was prepared for publication by Bart Diemer, Dr. Willem van der Meer and Dr. Klaas Spronk. The editors are grateful for their dedication.

Kampen, January 1998   THE EDITORS

Cornelis Houtman
Willem S. Prinsloo†
Wilfred G.E. Watson
Al Wolters

ABBREVIATIONS
OF PERIODICALS, REFERENCE WORKS, AND SERIES

AASOR	Annual of the American Schools of Oriental Research
AB	The Anchor Bible
ABD	*The Anchor Bible Dictionary*
AbrN	*Abr Nahrain*
AfO	*Archiv für Orientforschung*
AHw	W. von Soden, *Akkadisches Handwörterbuch*, Wiesbaden 1965-1981
AION	*Annali del' Instituto Universario Orientale di Napoli*
AJSL	*American Journal of Semitic Languages and Literatures*
AnBib	Analecta Biblica
ANEP	*The Ancient Near East in Pictures relating to the Old Testament*, ed. J.B. Pritchard
ANET	*Ancient Near Eastern Texts relating to the Old Testament*, ed. J.B. Pritchard
AnOr	Analecta Orientalia
AOAT	Alter Orient und Altes Testament
ARM	Archives royales de Mari
ARTU	J.C. de Moor, *An Anthology of Religious Texts from Ugarit*, Leiden 1987
ArOr	Archiv Orientální
ARW	*Archiv für Religionswissenschaft*
ASTI	*Annual of the Swedish Theological Institute*
ASV	American Standard Version
ATD	Das Alte Testament Deutsch
AThANT	Abhandlungen zur Theologie des Alten und Neuen Testaments
Aug	*Augustinianum*
AUSS	Andrews University Seminary Studies
AV	Authorized Version (King James Version)
BA	*Biblical Archaeologist*
BARev	*Biblical Archaeology Review*
BASOR	*Bulletin of the American Schools of Oriental Research*
BBB	Bonner biblische Beiträge
BC	Biblischer Commentar über das Alte Testament (Keil & Delitzsch)
BDB	F. Brown, S.R. Driver, C.A. Brigges, *A Hebrew and English Lexicon of the Old Testament*, corrected impression, Oxford 1952
BeO	*Biblia e Oriente*
BetM	*Beth Mikra*
BETL	Bibliotheca Ephemeridum Theologicarum Lovaniensium
Bg.	G. Bergsträsser, *Hebräische Grammatik*, I-II, Leipzig 1918-1929 (repr. Hildesheim 1962)
BH	*Bijbels Handboek* (ET: *Bible Handbook*, Vol. I, *The World of the Bible*, Grand Rapids 1986; Vol. II [Dutch edition IIa], *The World of the Old Testament*, Grand Rapids 1989)
BHHW	*Biblisch-historisches Handwörterbuch*, ed. B. Reicke and L. Rost

BHK	*Biblia Hebraica*, ed. R. Kittel
BHS	*Biblia Hebraica Stuttgartensia*
Bib	*Biblica*
BiLe	*Bibel und Leben*
BiOr	*Bibliotheca Orientalis*
BIOSCS	*Bulletin of the International Organization for Septuagint and Cognate Studies*
BiTr	*Bible Translator*
BJRL	*Bulletin of the John Rylands Library*
BK	Biblischer Kommentar
BL	H. Bauer, P. Leander, *Historische Grammatik der hebräischen Sprache des Alten Testaments*, Halle 1922 (repr. Hildesheim 1962)
BN	*Biblische Notizen*
BNV	Die Bybel. Nuwe Vertaling, Bybelgenootskap van Suid-Afrika, Kaapstad 1983
BOT	De Boeken van het Oude Testament
BR	*Biblical Research*
BRL[1,2]	*Biblisches Reallexikon*, ed. K. Galling, Tübingen 1937[1], 1977[2]
BrSynt.	C. Brockelmann, *Hebräische Syntax*, Neukirchen 1956
BRW	G.B. Winer, *Biblisches Realwörterbuch*, I-II, Leipzig 1847f.[3]
BS	*Bibliotheca Sacra*
BTB	*Biblical Theology Bulletin*
BW	*Bijbels Woordenboek* (ed. A. van den Born), Roermond 1966-1969
BWANT	Beiträge zur Wissenschaft vom Alten und Neuen Testament
BWL	W.G. Lambert, *Babylonian Wisdom Literature*, Oxford 1960
BZ	*Biblische Zeitschrift*
BZAW	Beihefte zur Zeitschrift für die alttestamentliche Wissenschaft
CAD	*The Assyrian Dictionary of the Oriental Institute of the University of Chicago*, ed. L. Oppenheim et al., Chicago 1956-
CAH	Cambridge Ancient History
CAT	Commentaire de L'Ancien Testament
CBCNEB	The Cambridge Bible Commentary on the New English Bible
CBSC	Cambridge-Bible for Schools and Colleges
CBQ	*Catholic Biblical Quarterly*
CeB	The Century Bible
Coll	*Collationes*
ConB	Coniectanea Biblica
COT	Commentaar op het Oude Testament
CTA	A. Herdner, *Corpus des tablettes en cunéiformes alphabétiques découvertes à Ras Shamra-Ugarit de 1929 à 1939*, Paris 1963
CTJ	*Calvin Theological Journal*
DB	*Dictionary of the Bible*, ed. J. Hastings
DBAT	*Dielheimer Blätter zum Alten Testament*
DBS	*Dictionaire de la Bible, Supplément*
DCH	*The Dictionary of Classical Hebrew*, ed. D.J.A. Clines, Sheffield 1993-
DDD	*Dictionary of Deities and Demons in the Bible*, ed. K. van der Toorn et

	al., Leiden 1995
DISO	C.F. Jean, J. Hoftijzer, *Dictionnaire des inscriptions sémitiques de l'Ouest*, Leiden 1965
DJD	*Discoveries in the Judean desert*
DLU	G. del Olmo Lete, J. Sanmartiń, *Diccionario de la lengua ugarítica*, I (Aula Orientalis Supplementa 7), Sabadell 1996
DOTT	*Documents from Old Testament Times*, ed. D.W. Thomas, London 1958
EA	J.A. Knudtzon, *Die El-Amarna Tafeln*, I-II, Leipzig 1915
EAEHL	*Encyclopedia of Archaeological Excavations in the Holy Land*
EchB	Echter-Bibel
EH	Exegetisches Handbuch zum Alten Testament
EJ	*Encyclopaedia Judaica*
EncMiqr.	אנציקלופדיה מקראית (Encyclopaedia Biblica), I-VIII, Jerusalem 1955-1982
ERE	*Encyclopaedia of Religion and Ethics*
ErIs	*Eretz-Israel*
EstBib	*Estudios Bíblicos*
ET	*Expository Times*
EThL	*Ephemerides Theologicae Lovanienses*
EvQ	*The Evangelical Quarterly*
EvTh	*Evangelische Theologie*
FAT	Forschungen zum Alten Testament
FJB	*Frankfurter Judaistische Beiträge*
FO	*Folia Orientalia*
FRLANT	Forschungen zur Religion und Literatur des Alten und Neuen Testaments
FzB	Forschungen zur Bibel
GAG	W. von Soden, *Grundriß der Akkadischen Grammatik* (AnOr 33/47), Roma 1969
GD	J.C.L. Gibson, *Davidson's Introductory Hebrew Grammar – Syntax*, Edinburgh 1994
GELS	J. Lust et al. (eds.), *A Greek – English Lexicon of the Sepuagint*, Stuttgart 1992-
Ges.[18]	*Wilhelm Gesenius' hebräisches und aramäisches Handwörterbuch über das Alte Testament*, 18th ed., ed. R. Meyer and H. Donner, Berlin 1987-
Ges-B	W. Gesenius, F. Buhl, *Hebräisches und aramäisches Handwörterbuch über das Alte Testament*, Leipzig 1921[17]
Ges-K	W. Gesenius, E. Kautzsch, *Hebräische Grammatik*, Leipzig 1909[28] (ET: A.E. Cowley, Oxford 1910[2])
GLAJJ	M. Stern, *Greek and Latin Authors on Jews and Judaism*, I-III, Jerusalem 1976-1984
GNB	*Groot Nieuws Bijbel*, vertaling in omgangstaal, Haarlem 1983
GoodNB	*Good News Bible. Today's English Version* (British Edition), 1976
GThT	*Gereformeerd Theologisch Tijdschrift*
HAL	W. Baumgartner et al., *Hebräisches und aramäisches Lexikon zum Alten Testament*, Leiden 1967-1996
HAT	Handbuch zum Alten Testament
HBT	*Horizons in Biblical Theology*

HCOT	Historical Commentary on the Old Testament
Hen	*Henoch*
HK	Handkommentar zum Alten Testament
HR	*History of Religions*
HSAT	Die heilige Schrift des Alten Testaments (Kautzsch)
HSchAT	Die heilige Schrift des Alten Testaments (Feldmann & Herkenne)
HThR	*Harvard Theological Review*
HTS	*Hervormde Teologiese Studies*
HUCA	*Hebrew Union College Annual*
IB	The Interpreter's Bible
ICC	The International Critical Commentary
IDB(S)	*The Interpreter's Dictionary of the Bible (Supplementary Volume)*
IEJ	*Israel Exploration Journal*
Int	*Interpretation*
JAAR	*Journal of the American Academy of Religion*
JANES	*Journal of the Ancient Near Eastern Society of Columbia University*
JAOS	*Journal of the American Oriental Society*
JB	The Jerusalem Bible, New York 1966
JBC	Jerome Biblical Commentary
JBL	*Journal of Biblical Literature*
JCS	*Journal of Cuneiform Studies*
JE	The Jewish Encyclopedia
JEA	*Journal of Egyptian Archaeology*
JEOL	Jaarbericht van het Vooraziatisch-Egyptisch Genootschap Ex Oriente Lux
JETS	*Journal of the Evangelical Theological Society*
JJS	*Journal of Jewish Studies*
JNES	*Journal of Near Eastern Studies*
JNSL	*Journal of Northwest Semitic Languages*
JPOS	*Journal of the Palestine Oriental Society*
JQR	*Jewish Quarterly Review*
JSem	*Journal of Semitics*
JSJ	*Journal for the Study of Judaism*
JSOT	*Journal for the Study of the Old Testament*
JSOTSup	Journal for the Study of the Old Testament Supplement Series
JSP	*Journal for the Study of the Pseudepigrapha*
JSS	*Journal of Semitic Studies*
JThS	*Journal of Theological Studies*
Jud	*Judaica*
KAI	H. Donner, W. Röllig, *Kanaanäische und aramäische Inschriften*, I-III, Wiesbaden 1966-1969²
KAT	Kommentar zum Alten Testament
KBL	L. Koehler, W. Baumgartner, *Lexicon in Veteris Testamenti Libros*, Leiden 1953
KBS	*De Bijbel* uit de grondtekst vertaald (= Willibrord Vertaling), Katholieke Bijbelstichting, Boxtel 1975
KEH	Kurzgefasstes exegetisches Handbuch zum Alten Testament

KHC	Kurzer Hand-Commentar zum Alten Testament
KJV	Authorised King James Version
KK	Kurzgefaßter Kommentar zu den heiligen Schriften Alten und Neuen Testamentes (Strack & Zöckler)
KöWB	E. König, *Hebräisches und aramäisches Wörterbuch zum Alten Testament*, Leipzig 1922^{2+3}
KP	*Der kleine Pauly: Lexikon der Antike*, ed. K. Ziegler and W. Sontheimer
KS	*Kleine Schriften*
KTU	M. Dietrich et al. (eds.), *Die keilalphabetischen Texte aus Ugarit*, I, Neukirchen-Vluyn 1976
KuD	*Kerygma und Dogma*
KVHS	Korte Verklaring der Heilige Schrift
LÄ	*Lexikon der Ägyptologie*
LCL	*The Loeb Classical Library*, London/Cambridge Mass.
Leš	*Lešonēnu*
LThK	*Lexikon für Theologie und Kirche*
LV	Leidse Vertaling, vertaling en aantekeningen van de hand van A. Kuenen, I. Hooykaas, W.H. Kosters en H. Oort, Leiden 1900f.
MGWJ	*Monatsschrift für Geschichte und Wissenschaft des Judentums*
MIOF	*Mitteilungen des Instituts für Orientforschung*
Mm	Masora Magna (G. E. Weil, *Massorah Gedolah*, I, Rome 1971).
MNAW.L	Mededelingen der Kon. Ned. Adademie van Wetenschappen. Afdeling Letterkunde
MTZ	*Münchener theologische Zeitschrift*
NCeB	New Century Bible
NEB	The New English Bible
NEchB	Die Neue Echter Bibel
NedThT	*Nederlands Theologisch Tijdschrift*
NGTT	*Nederduits Gereformeerde Teologiese Tydskrif*
NICOT	The New International Commentary on the Old Testament
NIV	New International Version
NEB	The New English Bible, Oxford 1970^2
NJB	The New Jerusalem Bible, New York 1985
NJPS	The New Jewish Publication Society of America, Translations to the Holy Scriptures
NRTh	*Nouvelle Revue Théologique*
NV	Nieuwe Vertaling (Nederlands Bijbelgenootschap 1951)
OBO	Orbis Biblicus et Orientalis
Olsh.	J. Olshausen, *Lehrbuch der hebräischen Sprache*, Braunschweig 1861
OLZ	*Orientalistische Literaturzeitung*
Or	*Orientalia*
OrAnt	*Oriens Antiquus*
OrChrP	*Orientalia Christiana Periodica*
OTE	*Old Testament Essays*
OTL	Old Testament Library
OTP	*The Old Testament Pseudepigrapha*, ed. J.H. Charlesworth

OTS	Oudtestamentische Studiën
O(u)TW(SA)P	Papers read at die Ou-testamentiese Werkgemeenskap in Suid-Afrika
PCV	De Heilige Schrift. Vertaling van de Apologetische Vereniging 'Petrus Canisius,' Amsterdam 1936-1939
PEQ	Palestine Exploration Quarterly
PG	J.P. Migne, *Patrologiae cursus completus. Series Graeca*
PJ	Palästinajahrbuch
PL	J.P. Migne, *Patrologiae cursus completus. Series Latina*
POT	De Prediking van het Oude Testament
PRU	Le Palais royal d'Ugarit
PW	Pauly-Wissowa, *Realencyclopädie der klassischen Altertumswissenschaft*
Qad	Qadmoniot
1QS	see E. Lohse, *Die Texte aus Qumran*, Darmstadt 1964 (='Die Gemeinderegel')
1QH	idem ('Die Loblieder')
RA	Revue d'Assyriologie et d'Archéologie Orientale
RAAM	H. Gese et al., *Die Religionen Altsyriens, Altarabiens und der Mandäer* (Die Religionen der Menschheit 10,2), Stuttgart 1970
RAC	Reallexikon für Antike und Christentum
RB	Revue Biblique
RdQ	Revue de Qumrân
RE	Realencyclopädie für protestantische Theologie und Kirche
REJ	Revue des Études Juives
RGG	Die Religion in Geschichte und Gegenwart
RHPhR	Revue d'Histoire et de Philosophie Religieuses
RHR	Revue de l'Histoire des Religions
RhW	Rondom het Woord
RIDA	Revue Internationale des Droits de l'Antiquité
RLA	Reallexikon der Assyriologie
RSO	Rivista degli studi orientali
RSP	Ras Shamra Parallels, I-III, ed. L.R. Fisher et al., Roma 1972-1981
RSPhTh	Revue des sciences philosophiques et theologiques
RSP	Ras Shamra Parallels
RSR	Recherches de Science Religieuse
RSV	Revised Standard Version
RTAT	W.Beyerlin(ed.), *Religionsgeschichtliches Textbuch zum Alten Testament*, Göttingen 1975 (1985^2) (ET: *Near Eastern Texts Relating to the Old Testament*, Philadelphia 1978)
RThPh	Revue de Théologie et de Philosophie
SAT	Die Schriften des Alten Testaments (Gunkel & Gressmann)
SBBS	The Soncino Books of the Bible
SBJ	La Sainte Bible traduite en français sous la direction de l'École Biblique de Jérusalem
SBLMS	SBL Monograph Series
SBOT	The Sacred Books of the Old Testament
SBPC	La Sainte Bible, Paris (Pirot & Clamer)

SBS	Stuttgarter Bibelstudien
SBT	Studies in Biblical Theology
SEÅ	Svensk Exegetisk Årsbok
SEI	Shorter Encyclopaedia of Islam, Leiden 1953
Sem	Semitica
Semeia	Semeia
SJOT	Scandinavian Journal of the Old Testament
SJTh	Scottisch Journal of Theology
SOTSMS	Society for Old Testament Study Monograph Series
SS	C. Siegfried, B. Stade, Hebräisches Wörterbuch zum Alten Testament, Leipzig 1893
Str-B	H.L. Strack, P. Billerbeck, Kommentar zum Neuen Testament aus Talmud und Midrasch, I-IV, München 1922-28
StTh	Studia Theologica
SV	Statenvertaling
SVT	Supplements to Vetus Testamentum
SVTP	Studia in Veteris Testamenti Pseudepigraphia
TBC	Torch Bible Commentaries
TDNT	Theological Dictionary of the New Testament, ed. G. Kittel and G. Friedrich
TE	Theologica Evangelica
TeT	Tekst en Toelichting
TeU	Tekst en Uitleg
THAT	Theologisches Handwörterbuch zum Alten Testament, ed. E. Jenni and C. Westermann
ThB	Theologische Bücherei
ThLZ	Theologische Literarturzeitung
ThQ	Theologische Quartalschrift
ThZ	Theologische Zeitschrift
TOB	Traduction Oecumenique de la Bible. Ancient Testament, Paris 1976
TQ	Theologische Quartalschrift
TRE	Theologische Realenzyklopädie
ThR	Theologische Rundschau
ThSt	Theologische Studien
ThZ	Theologische Zeitschrift
TOTC	Tyndale Old Testament Commentaries
TS	Theological Studies
TSSI	J.C. Gibson, Textbook of Syrian Semitic Inscriptions, I- III, Oxford, 1971-1982
TT	Theologisch Tijdschrift
TThZ	Trierer Theologische Zeitschrift
TUAT	Texte aus der Umwelt des Alten Testaments, ed. O. Kaiser
TvT	Tijdschrift voor Theologie
TWAT	Theologisches Wörterbuch zum Alten Testament, ed. G.J. Botterweck and H. Ringgren
TynB	Tyndale Bulletin

UF	*Ugarit-Forschungen*
VT	*Vetus Testamentum*
WBC	Word Biblical Commentary
WC	Westminster Commentaries
WbMyth	*Wörterbuch der Mythologie*, ed. H.W. Hausig
WdO	*Welt des Orients*
WMANT	Wissenschaftliche Monographien zum Alten und Neuen Testament
WThJ	*Westminster Theological Journal*
WO	*Die Welt des Orients*
WOC	B.K. Waltke, M. O'Connor, *An Introduction to Biblical Hebrew Syntax*, Winona Lake 1990³
WV	Willibrordvertaling (see KBS)
ZÄS	*Zeitschrift für ägyptische Sprache und Altertumskunde*
ZA	*Zeitschrift für Assyriologie*
ZAH	*Zeitschrift für Althebraistik*
ZAW	*Zeitschrift für die alttestamentliche Wissenschaft*
ZBK	Zürcher Bibelkommentare
ZDMG	*Zeitschrift der deutschen morgenländischen Gesellschaft*
ZDPV	*Zeitschrift des deutschen Palästina-Vereins*
ZKTh	*Zeitschrift für katholische Theologie*
ZRGG	*Zeitschrift für Religions- und Geistesgeschichte*
ZS	*Zeitschrift für Semitistik*
ZThK	*Zeitschrift für Theologie und Kirche*
ZWTh	*Zeitschrift für wissenschaftliche Theologie*

FURTHER ABBREVIATIONS

Akkad.	Akkadian
a.l.	ad locum
Aq.	Aquila
Arab.	Arabic
Aram.	Aramaic
BT	Babylonian Talmud (cited by tractate and folio)
cons(a).	consecutivum, consecutiva
cstr.	constructus
dtr.	deuteronomist(ic)
dtrH	the deuteronomistic historical work
dtrN	the nomistic redaction of the deuteronomistic work
dtrP	the prophetic redaction of the deuteronomistic work
et al.	and others
Eth.	Ethiopic
fem.	feminine
ff.	the two following pages (as a rule)
Fs	Festschrift
Hebr.	Hebrew
hiph.	hiphil

ABBREVIATIONS

hitp.	hitpael
hoph.	hophal
imper.	imperative
impf.	imperfect
inf.	infinitive
$k^e tib$	as written in MT
LXX	Septuagint (^{A}: codex Alexandrinus; ^{B}: Codex Vaticanus; $^{Hex.}$: Hexaplaric recension; $^{Luc.}$: Lucian recension; *: 'original' Septuagint)
M	Mishnah
masc.	masculine
MS(S)	manuscript(s)
MT	Masoretic text
n.	note
niph.	niphal
p.	page/person
par.	parallel
part.	participle
pers.	personal
Pesh.	Peshitta
pf.	perfect
Phoen.	Phoenician
pi.	piel
pl.	plural
prep.	preposition
pron.	pronoun
pronom.	pronominal
PT	Palestinian (Jerusalem) Talmud
pu.	pual
$q^e re$	what is to be read
Sem.	Semitic
sing.	singular
st. cstr.	status constructus
s.v.	sub voce
Symm.	Symmachus
textcr. app.	textcritical apparatus
Tg.	Targum
TAT	Theologie des Alten Testaments
Theod.	Theodotion
Ugar.	Ugaritic
Vet.Lat.	Vetus Latina
vs(s).	verse(s)
Vulg.	Vulgate

In the translation

[ ]	inside these brackets MT has to be viewed as secondary text or gloss
( )	inside these parentheses are words intended to clarify the MT

BIBLIOGRAPHY

Abel, *GP*	F.M. Abel, *Géographie de la Palestine*, Paris 1967³
Ahlström, *Admin.*	G.W. Ahlström, *Royal Administration and National Religion in Ancient Palestine*, Leiden 1982
Aistleitner	J. Aistleitner, *Wörterbuch der ugaritischen Sprache*, Berlin 1963
Albright, *ARI*	W.F. Albright, *Archaeology and the Religion of Israel*, Baltimore 1953³
Alt, *KS*	A. Alt, *Kleine Schriften zur Geschichte des Volkes Israel*, I-II, München 1953-1959
Baer	S. Baer, *Liber Regum*, Leipzig 1895
Barrois	A.G. Barrois, *Manuel d' Archéologie biblique*, I-II, Paris 1939-1953
Barthélemy	D. Barthélemy, *Critique textuelle de l'Ancien Testament*, I. Josué-Esther (OBO 50/1), Göttingen 1982
Bartlett 1976	J.R. Bartlett, "An Adversary Against Salomon: Hadad the Edomite," *ZAW* 88 (1976), 205-226
Benzinger, *Arch.*	I. Benzinger, *Hebräische Archäologie*, Leipzig 1927³
Berlinger	I. Berlinger, *Die Peschitta zum 1. (3.) Buch der Könige und ihr Verhältnis zu MT, LXX und Targ.*, Berlin 1897
Bertheau	E. Bertheau, *Die Bücher der Chronik erklärt*, Leipzig 1854
Bochart, *Hieroz.*	S. Bochartus, *Hierozoicon, sive Bipertitum Opus de Animalibus S. Scripturae*, etc. (ex recensione Joh. Leusden), Lugduni Bat./Trajecti ad Rhen. 1692³
Böttcher	F. Böttcher, *Ausführliches Lehrbuch der hebräischen Sprache*, I-II, Leipzig 1866-1868
Böttcher, *Neue Aehrenlese*	idem, *Neue exegetische Aehrenlese zum Alten Testament*, 2. Abteilung (Regum-Psalmi), Leipzig 1864
Van den Born	A. van den Born, *Koningen* (BOT), Roermond-Maaseik 1958
Brettler 1991	M. Brettler, "The Structure of 1 Kings 1-11," *JSOT* 49 (1991), 87-97
Brockelmann, *LexSyr.*	C. Brockelmann, *Lexicon Syriacum*, Halle 1928²
Brockelmann, *VG*	idem, *Grundriß der vergleichenden Grammatik der semitischen Sprachen*, I-II, Berlin 1908-1913
Brockington	L.H. Brockington, *The Hebrew Text of the Old Testament*, Oxford 1973
Brongers	H.A. Brongers, *I Koningen* (POT), Nijkerk 1967
Brown, *Lebanon*	J.P. Brown, *The Lebanon and Phoenicia*, I. *The Physical Setting and the Forest*, Beirut 1969
Buber-Rosenzweig	*Bücher der Geschichte*, verdeutscht von M. Buber in Gemeinschaft mit F. Rosenzweig, Köln 1956
Buis	P. Buis, "Livre des Rois," *DBS*, X, 695-740
Burney	C.F. Burney, *Notes on the Hebrew Text of the Books of*

	Kings, Oxford 1914
Busink	Th.A. Busink, *Der Tempel von Jerusalem*, I. Der Tempel Salomos, Leiden 1970; II. Von Ezechiel bis Middot, Leiden 1980 (referred to as 'Busink II')
Cheyne, *CB*	T.K. Cheyne, *Critica Biblica*, London 1903/4 (= Amsterdam 1970)
Conrad 1973	J. Conrad, "Der Gegenstand und die Intention der Geschichte von der Thronfolge Davids," *ThLZ* 108 (1973), 162-176
Crüsemann, *Widerstand*	F. Crüsemann, *Der Widerstand gegen das Königtum* (WMANT 32), Neukirchen-Vluyn 1978
Dalman, *ANH*	G.H. Dalman, *Aramäisch-Neuhebräisches Handwörterbuch zu Targum, Talmud und Midrasch*, Frankfurt/Main 1922^2
Dalman, *AuS*	idem, *Arbeit und Sitte in Palästina*, I-VII, Gütersloh 1928-1942 (reprint: Hildesheim 1964-1971)
Delitzsch, *LSF*	F. Delitzsch, *Die Lese- und Schreibfehler im Alten Testament*, Berlin 1920
Dever 1982	W.G. Dever, "Monumental Architecture in Ancient Israel in the Period of the United Monarchy," Ishida, *Studies*, 269-306
Dhorme	E. Dhorme et al., *La Bible. Ancien Testament* (Bibliothèque de la Pléiade), Paris 1956
Driver	S.R. Driver, *A Treatise on the Use of the Tenses in Hebrew and some other Syntactical Questions*, Oxford 1969^3
Driver, *Samuel*	idem, *Notes on the Hebrew Text and the Topography of the Books of Samuel*, Oxford 1913^3 (=1960)
Edelkoort	"Koningen," *Commentaar op de Heilige Schrift* (ed. J.A. van der Hake), Amsterdam 1956
Ehrlich	A.B. Ehrlich, *Randglossen zur hebräischen Bibel*, VII, Leipzig 1914
Eißfeldt	O. Eißfeldt, *Das erste Buch der Könige* (HSAT), Tübingen 1922
Eißfeldt, *KS*	idem, *Kleine Schriften*, I-VI, Tübingen, 1962-1979
Ellenbogen, *Foreign Words*	M. Ellenbogen, *Foreign Words in the Old Testament*, London 1962
Eusebius, *Onom.*	Eusebius, *Das Onomastikon der biblischen Ortsnamen* (ed. E. Klostermann), Leipzig 1904 (repr. 1966)
Ewald	H. Ewald, *Ausführliches Lehrbuch der hebräischen Sprache des alten Bundes*, Göttingen 1870^8
Ewald, *GVI*	idem, *Geschichte des Volkes Israel*, I-IV, Göttingen 1864^3
Faber van der Meulen	H. Faber van der Meulen, *Das Salomo-Bild im hellenistisch-jüdischen Schrifttum*, Kampen 1978
Fokkelman	J.P. Fokkelman, *Narrative Art and Poetry in the Books of Samuel*, I: King David (II Sam. 9-20 & I Kings 1-2), Assen 1981
Fritz, *Tempel*	V. Fritz, *Tempel und Zelt. Studien zum Tempelbau und zu dem Zeltheiligtum der Priesterschrift* (WMANT 47), Neukir-

	chen 1977
Gaster, *Myth*	Th.H. Gaster, *Myth, Legend, and Custom in the Old Testament*, New York/Evanston, 1969
Van Gelderen	C. van Gelderen, *De Boeken der Koningen* (KVHS), I, Kampen 1937²
Gesenius, *Thesaurus*	G. (= W.) Gesenius, *Thesaurus philologicus criticus Linguae Hebraeae et Chaldaeae Veteris Testamenti*, I-III, Leipzig 1829-1842 (with *Indices, Additamenta et Emendationes* by Ae. Roediger, Leipzig 1858)
Gibson, *CML*	J.C.L. Gibson, *Canaanite Myths and Legends*, Edinburgh 1978²
Ginzberg, *Legends*	L. Ginzberg, *The Legends of the Jews*, I-VII, Philadelphia 1909-1938
Görg, *Gott-König-Reden*	M. Görg, *Gott-König-Reden in Israel und Ägypten* (BWANT 105), Stuttgart 1975
Goettsberger	J. Goettsberger, *Die Bücher der Chronik oder Paralipomenon* (HSAT), Bonn 1939
Gooding 1965	D.W. Gooding, "Pedantic Timetabling in 3rd Book of Reigns," *VT* 15 (1965), 153-166
Gooding 1967	idem, "Temple Specifications: A Dispute in Logical Arrangement Between the MT and the LXX," *VT* 17 (1967), 143-172
Gooding 1969	idem, "Text-sequence and Translation-revision in 3 Reigns IX 10-X 33," *VT* 69 (1969), 448-463
Gooding, *Relics*	idem, *Relics of Ancient Exegesis. A Study of the Miscellanies in 3 Reigns 2*, Cambridge 1976
Gordis	R. Gordis, *The Biblical Text in the Making. A Study of the Kethib-Qere*, New York 1971 (=1937)
Gordon, *UT*	C.H. Gordon, *Ugaritic Textbook*, Rome 1965
Gray	J. Gray, *I and II Kings* (OTL), London 1970²
Greßmann	H. Greßmann, *Die älteste Geschichtsschreibung und Prophetie Israels* (SAT II,1), Göttingen 1921²
Greßmann, *Lade*	idem, *Die Lade Jahves und das Allerheiligste des Salomonischen Tempels*, Berlin 1920
De Groot, *Altäre*	J. de Groot, *Die Altäre des Salomonischen Tempelhofes* (BWAT NF 6), Berlin 1924
Guthe, *KBW*	H. Guthe, *Kurzes Bibelwörterbuch*, Tübingen/Leipzig 1903
Haran, *Temples*	M. Haran, *Temples and Temple Service in Ancient Israel*, Oxford 1978
Hentschel	G. Hentschel, *1 Könige* (NEchB.AT), Würzburg 1984
Herrmann 1953	S. Herrmann, "Die Königsnovelle in Ägypten und Israel. Ein Beitrag zur Gattungsgeschichte in den Geschichtsbüchern des Alten Testaments," *Wissenschaftliche Zeitschrift der Karl Marx Universität* 3. geschichtlich-sprachwissenschaftliche Reihe. Heft 1 (Fs A. Alt), Leipzig 1953, 51-62

Hochberg-Rosenberg	R. Hochberg, A.J. Rosenberg, ספר מלכים א / *Kings* (מקראות גדולות), New York 1980
Hölscher 1923	G. Hölscher, "Das Buch der Könige, seine Quellen und seine Redaktion," *Eucharisterion* (Fs Gunkel, ed. H. Schmidt; FRLANT 36), I, Göttingen 1923, 158-213
Hoftijzer	J. Hoftijzer, *The Function and Use of the Imperfect Forms with Nun Paragogicum in Classical Hebrew* (Studia Semitica Neerlandica 21), Assen 1985
Hoogewoud	F.J. Hoogewoud, "Moderne benaderingswijzen van Salomo's Tempel," J.F. van Agt et al., *De Tempel van Salomo*, 's-Gravenhage 1976
Houtman, *Himmel*	C. Houtman, *Der Himmel im Alten Testament. Israels Weltbild und Weltanschauung* (OTS 30), Leiden 1993
Hulst, *OTTP*	A.R. Hulst, *Old Testament Translation Problems*, Leiden 1960
Ishida, *Studies*	*Studies in the Period of David and Solomon and Other Essays* (ed. T. Ishida), Winona Lake 1982
Jastrow	M. Jastrow, *A Dictionary of the Targumim*, 1903 (repr. New York 1950)
Jellicoe, *Septuagint*	S. Jellicoe, *The Septuagint and Modern Study*, Oxford 1968
Jenni, *Pi'el*	E. Jenni, *Das hebräische Pi'el*, Zürich 1968
Jepsen, *Quellen*	A. Jepsen, *Die Quellen des Königsbuches*, Halle 1956²
Jeremias, *ATAO*	A. Jeremias, *Das Alte Testament im Lichte des Alten Orients*, Leipzig 1930⁴
Joüon	P. Joüon, *A Grammar of Biblical Hebrew*. Translated and Revised by T. Muraoka (Subsidia Biblica 14), Roma 1993
Kamphausen	A. Kamphausen, *Die Bücher der Könige*, Tübingen 1896²
Katzenstein, *Tyre*	H.J. Katzenstein, *The History of Tyre*, Jerusalem 1973
Keel, *Bildsymbolik*	O. Keel, *Die Welt der altorientalischen Bildsymbolik und das Alte Testament. Am Beispiel der Psalmen*, ZürichNeukirchen 1972
Keel, *OLB*	O. Keel, M. Küchler, C. Uehlinger, *Orte und Landschaften der Bibel*, Göttingen 1984-
Keil	C.F. Keil, *Die Bücher der Könige* (BC), Leipzig 1876²
Kennicott	B. Kennicott, *Vetus Testamentum Hebraicum, cum Variis Lectionibus*, I, Oxonii 1776
Klostermann	A. Klostermann, *Die Bücher Samuelis und der Könige* (KK), Nördlingen 1887
Kittel	R. Kittel, *Die Bücher der Könige* (HK), Göttingen 1900
Kittel, *SHARG*	idem, *Studien zur Hebräischen Archäologie und Religionsgeschichte*, Leipzig 1908
König	F.E. König, *Historisch-kritisches Lehrgebäude der hebräischen Sprache*, I-III, Leipzig 1881-1897
König, *Stil.*	idem, *Stilistik, Rhetorik, Poetik in Bezug auf die biblische Literatur*, Leipzig 1910

KP	Der Kleine Pauly. Lexikon der Antike (ed. K. Ziegler, W. Sontheimer), I-V, Stuttgart 1964-1975
Krauss, GLL	S. Krauss, Griechische und lateinische Lehnwörter im Talmud, Midrasch und Targum, I-II, Berlin 1898f. (repr. Hildesheim 1964)
Krauss, TA	idem, Talmudische Archäologie, I-III, Leipzig 1910-1912
Krautwurst, Studien	G. Krautwurst, Studien zu den Septuagintasätzen in 1.(3.) Könige und ihren Paralleltexten, diss. Mainz 1977
Krinetzki, Bibelhebräisch	G. Krinetzki, Bibelhebräisch. Eine Einführung in seine grammatischen Charakteristika und seine theologisch relevanten Begriffe, Passau 1981
Langlamet 1976	F. Langlamet, "Pour ou contre Salomon," RB 83 (1976), 321-379; 481-528
Lemaire	A. Lemaire, Inscriptions hebraïques, I, Les Ostraca, Paris 1977
Letteris	M.H. Letteris, Biblia Hebraica, London 1944
Lettinga	J.P. Lettinga, Grammatica van het Bijbels Hebreeuws, Leiden 1976[8]
Levy	J. Levy, Neuhebräisches und Chaldäisches Wörterbuch über die Talmudim und Midraschim, I-IV, Leipzig 1876-1889 (+ Nachträge und Berichtigungen, Berlin 1924)
Lewis-Short	C.T. Lewis, C. Short, A Latin Dictionary, Oxford 1966 (=1879)
Liddell-Scott	H.G. Lidell, R. Scott, A Greek-English Lexicon, Oxford 1968[9] (=1940; with a Supplement 1968)
Lisowsky	G. Lisowsky, Konkordanz zum hebräischen Alten Testament, Stuttgart 1958[2]
Long	B.O. Long, 1 Kings, with an Introduction of Historical Literature (The Forms of the Old Testament Literature), Grand Rapids 1984
Mauchline	J. Mauchline, "Kings," Peake's Commentary on the Bible, London 1962
Mettinger, King	T.N.D. Mettinger, King and Messiah. The Civil and Sacral Legitimation of the Israelite Kings (ConB OT 8), Lund 1976
Mettinger, Officials	idem, Salomonic State Officials. A Study of the Civil Governments of the Israelite Monarchy (ConB OT 5), Lund 1971
Metzger, Königsthron	M. Metzger, Königsthron und Gottesthron. Thronformen und Throndarstellungen in Ägypten und im Vorderen Orient im dritten und zweiten Jahrtausend vor Christus und deren Bedeutung für das Verständnis von Aussagen über den Thron im Alten Testament (AOAT 15:1-2), Neukirchen-Vluyn 1985
Von Meyenfeldt, Het hart	F.H. von Meyenfeldt, Het hart (leb, lebab) in het Oude Testament, Leiden 1950
Meyer	R. Meyer, Hebräische Grammatik, I-IV, Berlin 1966-1972[3]

Michel, *Grundlegung*	D. Michel, *Grundlegung einer hebräischen Syntax. Teil I: Sprachwissenschaftliche Methodik, Genus und Numerus des Nomen*, Neukirchen-Vluyn 1977
Montg.-Gehman	J.A. Montgomery, H.S. Gehman, *A Critical and Exegetical Commentary on the Books of Kings*, Edinburgh 1951
Mulder, *Ba'al*	M.J. Mulder, *Ba'al in het Oude Testament*, 's-Gravenhage 1962
Mulder, *Kanaän. goden*	idem, *Kanaänitische goden in het Oude Testament* (Exegetica 4.4-5), Den Haag 1965
Mulder, 1989	idem, "Solomon's Temple and YHWH's Exclusivity," *OTS* 25 (1989), 49-62
Mulder 1991	idem, "Die Partikel אן als Konjunktion und Interjektion im biblischen Hebräisch," *Studies in Hebrew and Aramaic Studies* (Fs J. Hoftijzer, ed. K. Jongeling), Leiden 1991, 132-142
Muller	F. Muller, *Grieksch Woordenboek*, Groningen 1933³
Myres 1948	J.L. Myres, "King Solomon's Temple and Other Buildings and Works of Art," *PEQ* 80 (1948), 14-41
Naslaan-Bybel	*Die Naslaan-Bybel*, Kaapstad 1957 (revised edition)
Niemann, *Herrschaft*	H.M. Niemann, *Herrschaft, Königtum und Staat. Skizzen zur soziokulturellen Endwicklung im monarchischen Israel* (FAT 6), Tübingen 1993
Noth	M. Noth, *Könige I* (BK IX/1), Neukirchen-Vluyn 1968
Noth, *GI*	idem, *Geschichte Israels*, Göttingen 1969⁷
Noth, *IPN*	idem, *Die israelitischen Personennamen im Rahmen der gemeinsemitischen Namengebung*, Stuttgart 1928
Noth, *ÜGS*	idem, *Überlieferungsgeschichtliche Studien*, Darmstadt 1967³ (=1943¹)
Noth, *Welt*	idem, *Die Welt des Alten Testaments*, Berlin 1962⁴
Nowack, *Arch.*	W. Nowack, *Lehrbuch der hebräischen Archäologie*, I-II, Freiburg/Br./Leipzig 1894
Oort	*Textus Hebraici Emendationes quibus in Vetere Testamento* (ed. H. Oort), Leiden 1900
Ouellette 1969	J. Ouellette, "Les vestibule du temple de Salomon était-il un *bit ḥilâni?*," *RB* 76 (1969), 365-378
Payne Smith	*A Compendious Syriac Dictionary*, ed. J. Payne Smith, Oxford 1903
Pedersen	J. Pedersen, *Israel, Its Life and Culture*, I-IV, London 1926-1940
Pedersen, *Eid*	idem, *Der eid bei den Semiten* (Studien zur Geschichte und Kultur des islamischen Orients 3), Strassburg 1914
Von Rad, *TAT*	G. von Rad, *Theologie des Alten Testaments*, I-II, München 1962-1965⁴
Rahlfs, *SSt.*	A. Rahlfs, *Septuaginta-Studien*, I-III, Göttingen 1965² (=1904-1911; these studies are sometimes cited according to

	the consecutive pagination of the second edition, sometimes also according to the pagination of the individual studies I-III; see esp. no. I, *Studien zu den Königsbüchern*, Göttingen 1904, =1965², 17-104; and no. III, *Lucians Rezeption der Königsbücher*, Göttingen 1911, =1965², 361-658)
Rehm	M. Rehm, *Das erste Buch der Könige*, Würzburg 1979
Rehm, *Untersuchungen*	M. Rehm, *Textkritische Untersuchungen zu den Parallelstellen der Samuel-Königsbücher und der Chronik* (Alttestamentliche Abhandlungen 13.3), Münster 1937 (repr. 1970)
Richter 1918	G. Richter, "Die Kesselwagen des salomonischen Tempels," *ZDPV* 41 (1918), 1-34
Riesener, *Der Stamm* עזב	I. Riesener, *Der Stamm* עזב *im Alten Testament* (BZAW 149), Berlin 1979
Ringgren, *IsrRel.*	H. Ringgren, *Israelite Religion*, London 1966
Robertson Smith, *Religion*	W. Robertson Smith, *The Religion of the Semites*, New York 1894²
De Rossi	J.B. de Rossi, *Variae Lectiones Veteris Testamenti*, I, Parma 1784 (= Amsterdam 1969)
Rost, *Überlieferung*	L. Rost, *Die Überlieferung von der Thronnachfolge Davids*, Stuttgart 1926
Rudolph	W. Rudolph, *Chronikbücher* (HAT), Tübingen 1955.
Šanda	A. Šanda, *Die Bücher der Könige* (EH), I, Münster 1911
Schleusner	I.F. Schleusner, *Novus Thesaurus Philologico-criticus sive Lexicon in LXX ... Veteris Testamenti*, I-V, Leipzig 1820f.
Schmitt, *Zelt und Lade*	R. Schmitt, *Zelt und Lade als Thema alttestamentlicher Wissenschaft*, Gütersloh 1972
Schneider	W. Schneider, *Grammatik des biblischen Hebräisch*, München 1976²
Segal	M.H. Segal, *A Grammar of Mishnaic Hebrew*, Oxford 1927
Simons, *Jerusalem*	J. Simons, *Jerusalem in the Old Testament*, Leiden 1952
Simons, *GTTOT*	idem, *The Geographical and Topographical Texts of the Old Testament*, Leiden 1959
Skinner	J. Skinner, *I and II Kings* (CeB), Edinburgh 1904
Slotki	I.W. Slotki, *Kings* (SBBS), London 1950
Smit, *Planten*	D. Smit, *Planten uit de bijbel, hun herkomst en gebruik*, Amsterdam 1990
Snaith	N.H. Snaith, R.W. Sockman, R. Calkins, *The First and Second Books of Kings* (IB III), New York 1954
Snaith, *HOT*	N.H. Snaith, *Hebrew Old Testament*, London 1962
Stade	B. Stade, *Lehrbuch der hebräischen Grammatik*, Leipzig 1879
Stade, *GVI*	idem, *Geschichte des Volkes Israel*, I-II, Berlin 1887f.
Stade 1901	idem, "Die Kesselwagen des Salomonischen Tempels. I Kö. 7, 27-39," *ZAW* 21 (1901), 145-190
Stade-Schwally	B. Stade, F. Schwally, *The Books of Kings. Critical Edition of the Hebrew Text printed in Colors*, Leipzig 1904

Swete, *Introd.*	H.B. Swete, *An Introduction to the Old Testament*, New York 1968³
Talstra, *Solomon's Prayer*	E. Talstra, *Solomon's Prayer. Synchrony and Diachrony in the Composition of I Kings 8, 14-61* (Contributions to Biblical Exegesis and Theology 3), Kampen 1993
Taylor, *Sun*	J.G. Taylor, *Yahweh and the Sun. Biblical and Archaeological Evidence for Sun Worship in Ancient Israel* (JSOTSup 111), Sheffield 1993
Thackeray, *Grammar*	H.St.J. Thackeray, *A Grammar of the Old Testament in Greek*, I, Cambridge 1909
Thenius	O. Thenius, *Die Bücher der Könige* (KEH), Leipzig 1849, 1873², 1898³ (ed. by M. Löhr)
Vanoni, *Literarkritik*	G. Vanoni, *Literarkritik und Grammatik. Untersuchungen der Wiederholungen und Spannungen in I Kön 11-12* (Arbeiten zu Text und Sprache im Alten Testament 21), St. Ottilien 1984
De Vaux	R. de Vaux, *Les Livres des Rois* (Sainte Bible), Paris 1958
De Vaux, *Inst.*	idem, *Les institutions de l'ancient testament*, I-II, Paris 1958-1960 (ET: *Ancient Israel: its Life and Institutions*, New York 1961)
Veijola, *Dynastie*	T. Veijola, *Die ewige Dynastie. David und die Entstehung seiner Dynastie nach der deuteronomistischen Darstellung*, Helsinki 1975
Veijola, *Königtum*	idem, *Das Königtum in der Beurteilung der deuteronomistischen Historiographie*, Helsinki 1977
Vincent, *Jérusalem*	L.-H. Vincent, *Jérusalem de l'Ancien Testament*, II, Paris 1956
De Vries	S.J. de Vries, *I Kings* (WBC 12), Waco 1985
De Vries, *Yesterday*	idem, *Yesterday, Today, and Tomorrow. Time and History in the Old Testament*, Grand Rapids 1975
Weber	*Biblia Sacra iuxta Vulgatam Versionem* (ed. R. Weber), Stuttgart 1975²
Wehr-Cowan	H. Wehr, J.M. Cowan, *A Dictionary of Modern Written Arabic*, New York 1976³
Weinfeld, *Deuteronomy*	M. Weinfeld, *Deuteronomy and the Deuteronomistic School*, Oxford 1972 (1983²)
Wellhausen, *Hexateuch*	J. Wellhausen, *Die Composition des Hexateuch und der historichen Bücher des Alten Testaments*, Berlin 1899 (1963⁴)
Wellhausen, *Prolegomena*	idem, *Prolegomena zur Geschichte Israel*, Berlin 1905⁶
Wiener, *Altars*	H.M. Wiener, *The Altars of the Old Testament*, Leipzig 1927
Willi, *Chronik*	T. Willi, *Die Chronik als Auslegung* (FRLANT 106), Göttingen 1972
Williams	R.J. Williams, *Hebrew Syntax. An Outline*, Toronto 1967
Wonneberger, *LBH*	R. Wonneberger, *Leitfaden zur Biblia Hebraica Stuttgartensia*, Göttingen 1986²

Würthwein	E. Würthwein, *Die Bücher der Könige. 1. Das erste Buch der Könige, Kapitel 1-16* (ATD 11,1), Göttingen 1985² idem, *Die Bücher der Könige. 2. 1.Kön. 17 - 2.Kön. 25* (ATD 11,2), Göttingen 1984
Würthwein, *Thronfolge*	idem, *Die Erzählung von der Thronfolge Davids. Theologische oder politische Geschichtsschreibung* (ThSt 115), Zürich 1974
Van Zijl, *Baal*	P.J. van Zijl, *Baal. A Study of Texts in Connection with Baal in the Ugaritic Epics* (AOAT 10), Neukirchen-Vluyn 1972
Zorell	F. Zorell, *Lexicon Hebraicum et Aramaicum Veteris Testamenti*, Roma 1940-1984 (with Aramaic section by E. Vogt, Roma 1971)

INTRODUCTION

§ 1 *Name, division, place in the canon*
In LXX and Vulg. the books of Kings, along with the books of Samuel, are incorporated as a single whole. The LXX speaks of Βασιλειων, '(the books of) kingdoms'; the Vulg., more correctly, of *regum*, in accordance with the מלכים, 'kings.' These versions therefore refer to our books of Kings as 3 and 4. In the Jewish canon, like the books of Samuel, the books of Kings were originally a single book. It was not until the end of the 15th century that the division of Kings into 2 books entered the Hebrew canon via the Vulg. (see R. Bach, *RGG*³, III, 1703). But – as is evident from his *prologus* to the 4 books of Kings – Jerome already knew of this division when, after mentioning Joshua, Judges/Ruth and (the 2 books of) Samuel, he wrote: *Quartus Malachim, id est Regum, qui tertio et quarto Regnorum volumine continetur; meliusque multo est Malachim, id est Regum, quam Malachoth, id est Regnorum dicere, non enim multarum gentium regna describit, sed unius israhelitici populi qui tribubus duodecim continetur* (Weber, 364). This quotation not only shows that Jerome was critical of the designation of our books in the LXX but also that the possibility exists of using the designation *Liber Malachim* instead of *Regum*, which, accordingly, is what is done in R. Weber's recent edition of the Vulg.

In the Jewish division of the Old Testament designated as *TeNaCH*, i.e. *Torā* (Pentateuch), *Nebi'îm* (Prophets) and *Ketûbîm* (Writings), our books belong to the 'early prophets' (נביאים ראשונים) to which also Joshua, Judges, and Samuel belong. In the LXX, however, one finds another principle of division of the canonical books of the OT, one which, thanks to the Vulg., can also be found in our Bibles. In this connection, by comparison with the Jewish division of the canon, the place of our books is not that different, although in our Bibles the books of Samuel are preceded by the little book of Ruth and the books of Kings are followed by the books of Chronicles, which in the Jewish division of the canon are even the last books of the 'Writings.'

§ 2 *The masoretic text (MT)*
As the basis for the translation and interpretation of the books of Kings we have taken the *Biblia Hebraica*, of which the third edition of Rud. Kittel (1937) was still prepared for the press by Kittel himself and M. Noth, and which in the new edition of the *Biblia Hebraica Stuttgartensia* was prepared by A. Jepsen (1974). This masoretic text is that of the so-called *Codex Leningradensis* B19ᴬ, a transcription, completed in 1008 CE, with masoretic notes and comments by Aaron ben Moshe ben Asher. For the *BHS* G.E. Weil issued a handy edition of the *Massorah Gedolah* (1971) on this codex. For our research

we were not able to use the carefully vocalized and edited codex of Aleppo, which is now published in Jerusalem by *The Hebrew University Bible Project*. In *BHK* (in 2 parts) and in *BHS* (in a single rubric) the text-critical apparatus is intended for students rather than for specialized scholars, though the latter, as indeed the former (can) make cautious use of it. In many cases, however, the text-critical apparatus is incomplete, unreliable, and/or superfluous. This last term certainly applies to the proposed conjectures, etc., which are frequently more exegetical than text-critical in nature. The well-known variant-collections of Kennicott (1776-1780), De Rossi (1784-1788), and C.D. Ginsburg (1926^2), as well as the independent use of the ancient versions, continue to be commendable.

Every translator and interpreter of MT needs to be aware that MT is merely one − be it an authoritative − version, or represents merely one tradition or recension. Studies by F.M. Cross of Hebrew fragments of the books of Samuel found in the Dead Sea caves ($4QSam^a$) have brought to light that $4QSam^a$ often agrees with the Lucian recension of LXX ($LXX^{Luc.}$) against MT as well as LXX^B (the codex Vaticanus of LXX). Aside from the fact that such comparisons raise interesting problems for the relations between recensions within the LXX, they are also of importance for our MT.[1] Divergencies in translation of the LXX in relation to MT are not 'translation idiosyncracies' but above all a confirmation of the fact that in the historical books of the OT LXX faithfully followed its 'Vorlage' which, however, did diverge from what we usually find in the MT now.[2] This means, not only that LXX has to be a unique instrument for OT textual criticism, but that MT itself must continually be approached critically as well, especially where, textually as well as contextually, serious criticism is possible. In the part of 1 Kings we will deal with in this volume, this stance we take toward MT will be regularly apparent.

§ 3 *The Ancient Versions*

3.1 *The Septuagint*

Within the confines of this short introduction to the books of Kings we can only briefly comment on the ancient translations and their value for the history and criticism of the text of MT. This certainly holds true for the ancient Greek translation we know as the Septuagint (= LXX). This translation, despite the

---

[1] See, e.g., F.M. Cross, "The History of the Biblical Text in the Light of Discoveries in the Judaean Deser," *HThR* 57 (1964), 281-299; esp. 288f.

[2] F.M. Cross, *The Ancient Library of Qumran and Modern Biblical Studies*, New York 1961^2, 180. See now also E. Ulrich, F.M. Cross et al, *Qumran Cave 4/IX. Deuteronomy, Joshua, Judges, Kings* (DJD 14), Oxford 1995, esp. p. 183: '4QKgs agrees with MT Kgs (and Chr) against LXX in all the frequent and substantial variants which give to the *Vorlage* of the Old Greek its very strong character and which reflect an intensive editorial activity.'

legend of its birth, the so-called Aristeas letter (cf. Swete, *Introd.* 531-606), is anything but a unified whole. This is certainly true of the Pentateuch but all the more emphatically of the books of Samuel and Kings. Even within a specific book, diversity of style and diction may suggest the hand of several translators. Thackeray, *Grammar*, 10, for example, divided the books of Samuel and Kings as follows: 'early parts' K. α (= 1 Sam.); K. ββ (= 2 Sam. 1:1-11:1); K. γγ (= 1 Kgs. 2:12-21:43); 'later parts' K. βγ (= 2 Sam. 11:2-1 Kgs. 2:11); K. γδ (= 1 Kgs. 22:1-2 Kgs. end). According to him, the parts K. βγ and K. γδ (together K. βδ) are probably the work of one hand, which bears much resemblance to Theod. K. γγ is said to be more paraphrastic and idiomatic than the rest (cf. J. Trebolle, *RB* 87 [1980], 89f. and n. 5).

Aside from these technical translation problems of LXX, there is the diversity of traditions or recensions. We may assume the reader knows how the church father Jerome, in his prologue to the books of Chronicles, wrote: *Alexandria et Aegyptus in Septuaginta suis Hesychium laudat auctorem, Constantionopolis usque Antiochiam Luciani martyris exemplaria probat, mediae inter has provinciae palestinos codices legunt, quos ab Origene elaboratos Eusebius et Pamphilius vulgaverunt, totusque orbis hac inter se trifaria varietate conpugnat* (Weber, I, 546). Of these 3 recensions the Hexapla of Origen is probably the best-known (see e.g. Jellicoe, *Septuagint*, 134-146). It is generally assumed that the basic exemplar of his Greek text was Alexandrian (codex A), which is more extensive that the codex Vaticanus (B).

This 'Alexandrian group' or 'Origen group' is assumed to be represented by (among others) the MSS A, c, x^3 and supported by the Syro-Hexapla and the Armenian translation. The Hesychian recension is more disputed, even occasionally repudiated, but currently again recognized, though not yet identified for certain parts of LXX (cf. J.W. Wevers, *IDB*, IV, 275; Jellicoe 1968, 146-156). More clearly discernible in our books is the Lucian recension or group, which is primarily represented by the MSS b, o, c_2 and e_2, and, in addition to this, also a 'sub-Lucian' group which exhibits connections with the Hebr. text of Chronicles, some fragments found in the Dead Sea caves, and also in some instances with the *Antiquitates* of Josephus (cf. Wevers, 275f.; Jellicoe, 157-171). Besides these 'recensions,' which have all sorts of connections or raise questions (e.g. the question concerning the pre-Lucian text's relation to the pre-hexaplaric), one can distinguish in the books of Samuel-Kings a 'Vaticanus group' as well, whose main representative is Codex B (= Vaticanus). Most LXX MSS belong to this group, the MSS y, a_2, and the Ethiopian among them

---

[3] For a more detailed description and use of the sigla, see A. Rahlfs, *Verzeichnis der griechischen Handschriften des Alten Testaments* (Mitteilungen des Septuaginta-Unternehmens 2), Göttingen 1914.

(cf. Wevers, *ZAW* [1945/8], 46f.). In 2 Sam. 11:2-1 Kgs. 2:11 this group underwent a noticeable change in the direction of a 'literal' reproduction of the Hebr. text. Inasmuch as a striking example of this change – against Greek usage – is the translation of גם(י) by καί γε, there is occasional reference to the *Kaige*-group. This group is also discernible in other books of the LXX.[4] The Lucian recension of the books of Kings has been thoroughly and extensively examined by Rahlfs in 1911. In our commentary we make grateful use of it as well.[5]

The LXX text on Kings used in this commentary is the large 'Cambridge Edition' of A.E. Brooke, N. McLean, H.St.J. Thackeray (Vol. II, Part II, Cambridge, 1930), from which also the sigla of the above MSS have been derived. The basis for this edition is LXX^B, as also the small 'Cambridge Edition' of H.B. Swete (1887 and later editions). The books of Kings have not (yet) been published in the Göttinger-project of the 'Septuaginta Unternehmen'; they have, however, in the wellknown pocket edition of Rahlfs (1935 and later editions). In the present edition no particular MS was selected as the basis for the text, but it is based in the main on 3 – very well known – MSS: the *codex Vaticanus* (4th century); the *codex Sinaiticus* (4th century) which, however, was not preserved in the case of our books; and the *codex Alexandrinus* (mid-5th century). For the books of Kings and especially 1 Kings Rahlfs used LXX^B; in addition O=LXX^A with the Syrohexapla, and supported here and there by the Armenian translation, and up to 15:7 a 12th century MS. which agrees with the hexaplaric reading; finally there is L, i.e. the Lucian recension, supported mainly by the sigla b and o in the edition of Brooke-McLean.

For a long time scholars have been struck by the large differences which exist between the Hebr. and the Greek text of Kings. As early as 1713 B. de Montfaucon already pointed this out in his Hexapla-edition, and since then this observation has only been confirmed in countless studies (cf. Krautwurst, *Studien*, 12). Also in the different LXX-text traditions, when compared to each other (e.g. LXX^A to LXX$^{Luc.}$), one encounters striking textual differences and divergences.[6] Further, LXX has a number of additions in its translation which are lacking in MT: LXX 3 Kgs. 2:35^{a-k}, 46^{a-l}; 12:24^{a-z} (Jeroboam tradition); 16:28^{a-h} (Jehoshaphat traditions; cf. 1 Kgs. 22:41-51 MT) and 4 Kgs. 1:18^{a-d} (Joram tradition; cf. 2 Kgs. 3:1-3 MT). The additions in 1 (3) Kgs. 2 have been especially examined by Krautwurst with respect to their form, value, and

---

[4] See D. Barthélemy, *Les devanciers d'Aquila* (SVT 10), Leiden 1963.

[5] See now also the edition by N. Fernández Marcos and J.R. Busto Saiz, *El Texto Antioqueno de la Biblia Griega*, II, 1-2 Reyes (Textos y estudios Cardenal Cisneros 53), Madrid 1992.

[6] Burney, pp. xx-xxxi, furnishes comprehensive, though somewhat dated, lists which are still based on Paul de Lagarde's problematic edition of the Lucian recension: *Librorum Veteris Testamenti canonicorum*, I, Göttingen 1883.

provenance; cf. also Stade-Schwally, 64ff. In addition, both in the details (e.g. in 1 Kgs. 4-7) but also in larger sections (e.g. 1 Kgs. 20ff.), LXX often has a different division of verses or chapters than MT (cf. Swete, *Introd.* 232). Also among themselves, however, the LXX-recensions differ in arrangement and text. Šanda already correctly observed that LXX^A, because it translates virtually all the Hebr. passages omitted by LXX^B, 'nachträglich einmal dem Hebräischen adaptiert worden (ist)' (p. XIII).

These summary statements clearly bring out the importance of LXX for the determination of the Hebr. text. In this connection it must be said in advance that MT need not necessarily be the best or predominant text for the translation and exegesis of 1 Kings.[7]

3.2 Other Greek Versions

In considering the other ancient Greek translations we have in mind primarily the familiar trio Aquila, Symmachus, and Theodotion. These 3 Greek versions, incorporated in the *magnum opus* of the Alexandrian theologian Origen (ca. 235 AD), known by the name of the *Hexapla*, are only fragmentarily known to us, one reason being that in its original form the *Hexapla*, too, has been lost. Aquila, who lived at the time of the emperorship of Hadrian (117-138), was a proselyte and, according to Jewish tradition, a pupil of R. Eliezer and R. Joshua or of R. Akiba (Swete, *Introd.* 32; cf. also Jellicoe, *Septuagint*, 77f.). Up until the end of the 19th century, our knowledge of (the translation of) Aquila was limited to a number of citations in patristic or talmudic literature and marginal or textual notes in LXX MSS. Along with all other hexaplaric fragments, then known, they were collected by Field, after scholars like J. Crusius (1622) and B. de Montfaucon (1713) had published collections earlier.[8]

Aquila's work is incorporated in the so-called 'third column' of the *Hexapla*. In 1897 F.C. Burkitt published a number of fragments from the books of Kings in Aquila's translation. This concerns a palimpsest fragment from the genizah of Cairo from the 6th century CE, which contains 1 Kgs. 20:9-17 and 2 Kgs. 23:12-27 (cf. S.P. Brock, *TRE*, VI, 169),[9] while in 1900 C. Taylor published still other parts of (the Hexaplaric) Aquila. Often, however, new studies no

---

[7] On the LXX version of Kings see now also Z. Talshir, "The Image of the Edition of Kings Reflected in the Septuagint," *Tarbiz* 59 (1989f.), 249-302 (Hebr.); N. Fernández Marcos, *Scribes and Translators: Septuagint and Old Latin in the Books of Kings* (SVT 54), Leiden 1994; W.M. Schniedewind, "Textual Criticism and Theological Interpretation: The Pro-Temple *Tendenz* in the Greek Text of Samuel-Kings," *HThR* 87 (1994), 107-116; and Ph. Lefebvre, "Le troisième livre des Règnes," M. d'Hamontville et al., *Autour des livres de la Septante* (Le centre d'études du Saulchoir 4), Paris 1995, 81-122.

[8] F. Field, *Origenis Hexaplorum quae supersunt; sive veterum interpretum graecorum in totum Vetus Testamentum fragmenta*, Oxford 1874² (repr. Hildesheim 1964).

[9] Cf. also P.E. Kahle, *The Cairo Geniza*, Oxford 1959², 28.

longer speak of a (new) translation by Aquila but of a revision of the above-mentioned *Kaige*-recension (Brock, a.l.).

Also of the translation of Symmachus – whom Epiphanius situates in the time of Severus (193-211) and calls a Samaritan who converted to Judaism, but whom Eusebius describes as Ebionite (Jellicoe, 95) – only small fragments remain. In contrast to Aquila's 'monstrosities' (Thackery; cf. Jellicoe, 94) Symmachus displayed an elegant style, though in fact he did base his work on his predecessors Aquila and Theodotion (cf. Barthélemy, SVT 10, 261-265).

Theodotion, according to Irenaeus, was a proselyte from Ephesus. Barthélemy, however, considers him the author of the *Kaige*-recension who worked in the 2 centuries around the beginning of our calendar and placed him on a par with Hillel's pupil Jonathan Ben Uzziel. Others assume the existence of 2 correctors who bore the name Theodotion, one of whom is said to have lived at the beginning of the first century, the other in the second. According to Brock, Theodotion's work has been transmitted best in those books in which the *Kaige*-recension shapes the main stream, hence especially in βγ and γδ of the books of Kings.

Although in patristic commentaries and *catenae*, for example, there have been Greek readings of ὁ Σύρος or ὁ Ἑβραῖος, here we will leave these translations alone (see Brock, 169f.) Aside from the above-mentioned work of Field, the hexaplaric readings (the *quinta* of Origen and the readings of Aquila, Symmachus, and Theodotion respectively, as well as the 'others') have also been noted in the work of Brooke-McLean-Thackeray.[10]

3.3. *The Latin Versions*

Although for this commentary, Jerome's Latin translation, the Vulg., in the edition produced by Weber and published by the *Württembergische Bibelanstalt* (1969), has been of primary importance, we do not wish to ignore that before this translation – one generally used in the Latin church in the 7th century – there were old-Latin translations, relatively few of which have been preserved for us (see e.g. Brock, 177f.) and then usually only in fragments. It is possible that many of these old-Latin versions are based on Greek MSS (cf. J. Gribomont, *IDBS*, 528ff.). The most significant material of the *Vetus Latina* was published at the time by Sabatier.[11] Since 1949, under P.B. Fisher at Beuron, scholars have begun to publish the remnants of the old-Latin Bible in a large critical edition, but it is not yet available on the books of Kings. Available are the readings from different old-Latin fragments incorporated in the above-

---

[10] Cf. also the very useful work of Primus Vannutelli, *Libri Synoptici Veteris Testamenti seu Librorum Regum et Chronicorum Loci Paralleli*, Romae, 1931.

[11] P. Sabatier, *Bibliorum sacrorum latinae versiones antiquae seu Vetus Itala*, Rheims 1739-1743, Paris 1751.

mentioned edition of Brooke-McLean-Thackeray (see their prefatory notes on the books of Samuel and Kings). Because the old-Latin Bible translation is not uniform, one often finds different text types in the same Bible books. In the books of Kings the *Vetus Latina* sometimes follows the Lucian recension of LXX (cf. Rahlfs, *Sst.* III, 152ff.; Burney, XXXVI-XXXIX), but caution remains imperative.[12]

In most books of the Vulg. we are dealing with a direct translation by Jerome (ca. 347-420 AD) from a Hebr. original, also in the case of the books of Kings. Just as this is usually the case with the other ancient versions, so also the Vulg. MSS have a tumultuous history.[13] Initially the old-Latin translations and Jerome's translation influenced each other. Around the end of the 8th century and the beginning of the 9th, the revision of Alcuin of Tours and other scholars at Charlemagne's court became important. Similarly significant was the decree of the Council of Trent dated April 8, 1546, in which the Vulg. was declared the authentic translation of the Catholic church. It still took a half century before the official text edition of Sixtus V (the *Sixtina*) made its appearance, but because it was too imprecise and incomplete, it was replaced some years later (in 1592, reprinted in 1593 and 1598) by the edition of Clemens VIII (the *Clementina*). Because the latter could not claim either to provide an integral reproduction of Jerome's text, MSS research continued. In progress since 1926, a large-scale Vulg. edition, still started by Pius X, is becoming available, of which already many volumes, including the books of Kings (1945), have appeared.[14] The text does not reproduce the *Clementina* – like that of M. Hetzenauer (1914), which we consulted occasionally as well – but is a scientific recension according to the MSS (Weber, XII). One of the best-known and most ancient MSS is the *codex Amiatinus* (siglum: A), dating from the 8th century and copied in Northumbria. Another is the *codex Cavensis* (siglum: C), from the 9th century and copied in Spain.

3.4 The Peshitta

The Peshitta, the 'simple' translation, is no more a unified whole than LXX; but, like LXX, Pesh. can be viewed as a direct translation (in Syriac) from a

---

[12] See now also N. Fernández Marcos, *Scribes and Translators: Septuagint and Old Latin in the Books of Kings* (SVT 54), Leiden 1994; and his "The *Vetus Latina* of 1-2 Kings and the Hebrew," *VIII Congress of the International Organization for Septuagint and Cognate Studies. Paris 1992* (ed. L. Greenspoon et al., SBL Septuagint and Cognate Studies 41), Atlanta 1995, 153-163.

[13] See the 'Vorwort' in the edition of Weber; J.O. Smit, *De Vulgaat*, Roermond/Maaseik 1948; J. Gribomont, *IDBS*, 530ff.

[14] *Biblia Sacra iuxta Latinam Vulgatam versionem ad codicum fidem ... cura et studio monachorum abbatiae pontificiae S. Hieronymi in urbe ordinis S. Benedicti edita*, I-XVI, Roma 1926-1981.

Hebr. 'Vorlage.' This at once establishes its value for the history and criticism of the text.[15] Precisely when the Syriac translation of the OT came into being and by whom it was brought into being is still a disputed question. We may assume that it originated in a Jewish or Jewish-Christian circle in Edessa not too long after the beginning of the Christian era. Specialized studies of each OT book are needed, however, and over the last 2 centuries they have in fact appeared. Though one's judgment has to be qualified from book to book, it may in general be concluded that Pesh. was translated from a Hebr. text which differs only slightly from MT. It may be concluded further that some influence of the Jewish tradition is discernible, as also in LXX and in the Tgs. The most ancient Bible MSS of Pesh. stem from the 5th century and later, while the Syriac was handed down in 3 different script types: *Estrangelā*, *Sertō* or Jacobitic, and the Nestorian (also Chaldean). Pesh. is not the only known Syriac translation: the Syrohexaplaric of Paul, bishop of Tella (613-617), a translation of Origen's *Hexapla*, is at least equally well-known and an important help for the reconstruction of Origen's work. There have been other translations as well (cf. Brock, 181-189; A. Vööbus, *IDBS*, 848-851).

In the critical edition *The Old Testament in Syriac according to the Peshitta Version*, furnished by the Peshitta Institute of the State University of Leiden, *The Books of Kings*, prepared by H. Gottlieb in collaboration with E. Hammershaimb, was published in 1976 (Part II, fasc. 4). Like almost all Old Testament books in this edition, the basic text was taken from *MsB.21 Inferiore* of the Ambrosian library at Milan according to the facsimile edition of Ceriani,[16] in connection with which the original was consulted in Milan. Along with this MSS many others were collated as well. The intent of this edition is that the (basic) text will be consistently used along with the second apparatus. Generally speaking, the manuscript tradition in Pesh. proves to be quite uniform, but the Ambrosianus (siglum: 7a1) is not per se better than a 9th or 12th century MS. In 1897 Berlinger examined the Pesh. of 1 Kings on the basis of the edition of the Pesh. text as it is found in the London Polyglot of Brian Walton (6 vol., 1657); the London edition of S. Lee (1823) and the Urmia edition (1852). This last edition follows the Nestorian tradition, as does the Mosul edition (1887-1891), which Berlinger did not consult. Ongoing Pesh.-research has shown that Pesh. has greater independent value for the history and criticism of the OT text than was formerly thought, which is also why we have consistently consulted it.

---

[15] See my "The Use of the Peshitta in Textual Criticism," *La Septuaginta en la Investigación Contemporánea* (V. Congreso de la IOSCS; ed. F. Fernández Marcos), Madrid 1985, 37-53.

[16] A.M. Ceriani, *Translatio Syra Pescitto Veteris Testamenti ex codice Ambrosiano des. fere VI photolithograpice edita*, Milan 1876-1883.

Burney, xxxii-xxxv, who characterizes the Pesh. as 'a close and accurate, though not too servile, representation of the original' (p. XXXIII), has summed up a number of characteristic deviations from MT (along with consistent reference to Pesh. in his *Notes*). What these deviations come down to are especially what he calls 'paraphrases' (on 1 Kgs. 1:36, 50; 2:42; 3:16, 18 etc.) and 'additions' (on 1:10f., 21, 39 etc.). In addition, there are a number of similarities with Tg. The number of 'corruptions' in the Pesh. text, according to him, is very small, and can usually be traced to the confusion or transposition of letters in proper names.[17]

3.5 The Targum

Just as the Tg. Onqelos is considered an 'official' Aramaic translation of the Pentateuch, the Tg. Jonathan is so considered for the earlier and later prophets. Also the Tg. Jon. originated in Palestine and was subjected, between the 3rd and 5th century in Babylonia, to a uniformizing redaction. Along with the Tg. Jon. – referred to in our commentary simply as Tg. – fragments of possibly lost Tgs. are known to exist as well (cf. P. Schäfer, *TRE*, VI, 223). These are currently being published, through 'The Institute for the History of Jewish Bible Research' of the Bar-Ilan university, by M. Goshen Gottstein and his fellow workers. Part I, titled *Fragments of Lost Targumim*, was published in 1983.

For the continuing Tg. we have made use of the critical edition of A. Sperber, *The Bible in Aramaic*, II, Leiden 1959, in connection with which we incidentally consulted P. de Lagarde, *Prophetae Chaldaice*, Leipzig 1872 (reprint 1967).

This is not the place to discuss the character (etc.) of Tg. because we have already repeatedly done this elsewhere.[18] We will confine ourselves to again referring to Burney, XXXIf., who describes a number of characteristics of our Tg. on Kings with good examples. This Tg., also, has an anti-anthropomorphic bias where it concerns God and a tendency to 'haggadic digressions' (e.g. in 5:13). This does not, however, alter the fact that Tg. is a fairly faithful reproduction of MT as well.

We wish to conclude this section on the 'ancient versions' by reminding the reader that there are still other, frequently valuable, translations of OT. We are referring to the Ethiopic, Arabic, Coptic, Armenian, and Syro-Palestinian version. In part these translations are only fragmentarily familiar to us, in part

---

[17] See also P.B. Dirksen, "Some Remarks in Connection with the Peshitta of Kings," *OTS* 25 (1989), 22-28; and D.M. Walter, "The Use of Sources in the Peshitta of Kings," *The Peshitta as a Translation: Papers Read at the II. Peshitta Symposion. Leiden 1993* (ed. P.B. Dirksen et al., Monographs of the Peshitta Institute Leiden 8) Leiden 1995, 187-204.

[18] See a.o. *Het meisje van Sodom*, Kampen 1970, 10-18; *De Targum op het Hooglied*, Amsterdam 1975, 8-11 (with litt.).

they are also strongly dependent on LXX, and in part they are written in languages to which the present author has no access (cf. Mont.-Gehmann, 14ff.). For a meticulously detailed account of the text – something the scope of this commentary does not permit – they would have to be fully honoured. Now we only make incidental use of them.

§ 4 Parallels to the books of Kings

4.1 The books of Chronicles

With respect to the text (and its history) as well as to the (history of the) exegesis of the books of Kings we have the good fortune of having at our disposal a piece of parallel Hebr. literature which stems from a later period as well as from another circle: the books of Chronicles which are for a substantial part based on the books of Samuel and Kings. We already referred earlier (§ 3.2) to the work of Vannutelli – indispensable for textual criticism and exegesis – which offers a clear overview of the parallel passages. We can further mention here the smaller but handy work of Bendavid, in which the parallels between Samuel/Kings and Chronicles constitute the 'pièce de resistance'.[19] It does not make much sense for us to repeat here what is clearly furnished in the way of parallels in these works, and is often reported in our commentary as well.

Although this is not the place for us to discuss at length the sources of the books of Chronicles, we may, along with Rudolph, X, and other exegetes, observe that, especially in the narrative sections, the reproduction of Chronicles often so precisely corresponds to the text of the books of Samuel and Kings – right down to the diction and textual errors – that there hardly needs to be any doubt that the Chronicler had these books before him, though in theory it is also possible that both versions are traceable to a third source. The idea that all deviations and additions in the books of Chronicles, as compared to the text of Kings, 'seinem eigenen Geist entsprungen sind,' as Rudolph believes, seems less plausible inasmuch as in a later period in Judaism, hence before the closing of the official canon of OT, a midrash-like tradition was already developing, which further continued in rabbinical Judaism. In addition, linguistic developments or changes may have occurred which are reflected in a new or different word usage of Chronicles (see, e.g., below, under 5:23). In connection with the first eleven chapters of Kings which we are treating in this volume, not many other 'sources' need initially to be considered for Chronicles, because this book is based almost exclusively on our story in Kings. Apart from all this, one must not lose sight of the goal which the Chronicler pursued in reproducing the history. That goal was certainly different from that of the

---

[19] A. Bendavid, *Parallels in the Bible*, Jerusalem 1972.

author(s) of the books of Kings. With the Chronicler the figure of David, the temple and its cultic institutions — which become pledges of the right relation to YHWH[20] — come to be central, so that his 'history' can rightly be called a 'philosophy of history,' with all the advantages and disadvantages of the same.

4.2 *Josephus*

Although the work of Flavius Josephus was already characterized by older exegetes like Thenius, XXXI, as a 'second-rank witness' for the textual criticism of OT, and considered totally worthless for historical criticism, the work he has left behind is today again given a more positive appraisal, though Josephus remains an author about whom the last word has not yet been said.[21] Rahlfs, *Sst.* II, 80-111, who gave a lot of attention to the place of Josephus in his relation to LXX$^{Luc.}$ and to MT, came to the conclusion that as far as the books of Samuel are concerned Josephus tends to follow the Lucian recension, while as it concerns the books of Kings he is more likely to follow MT and only then LXX. In the case of the last-mentioned, no distinction must be made between LXX* and the Lucian recension. Rahlfs, 94, correctly points out that with respect to agreements in the details one has to be very careful and constantly remember that, in addition to the books of Kings, Josephus used the books of Chronicles as well. To this may be added that with Chronicles Josephus stands in a later Jewish midrash-tradition. This means that when he deviates from the text of Kings, he need not simply be fantasizing, but is drawing from an ancient Jewish tradition. In addition — and even Thenius does not deny this — Josephus has value for the determination of the text of Kings. In our commentary we have therefore frequently referred to the works of Josephus, especially to his reproduction — in *Ant.* VII and VIII — of the parts which parallel our chapters from the book of Kings.[22]

§ 5 *Time of origin, sources, and authorship of Kings*

In general, the time of origin of the books of Kings does not present insurmountable difficulties: at the conclusion of 2 Kgs. 25 there is mention of the favours bestowed on Jehoiachin, one of the last kings of Judah. That happened after the death of Nebuchadnezzar II under his successor Evil-Merodach (Awil-Marduk), who governed the Babylonian empire from 562-560 BCE. One can say, therefore, that in any case 560 is the earliest date *post quem* for the origin

---

[20] See a.o. Th.C. Vriezen, A.S. Van der Woude, *De literatuur van oud-Israel*, Wassenaar 1973⁴, 299f.; cf. H.H. Grosheide, *BH*, IIA, 353ff.

[21] See A. Schalit, *Zur Josephus-Forschung* (WdF 84), Darmstadt 1973, VII and elsewhere in this collection.

[22] See now also V. Spottorno, "Josephus' Text for 1-2 Kings (3-4 Kingdoms), *VIII Congress of the International Organization for Septuagint and Cognate Studies. Paris 1992* (ed. L. Greenspoon et al., SBL Septuagint and Cognate Studies 41), Atlanta 1995, 145-152.

of our books. Presumably the date *ante quem* for the origin of our books is the beginning of the Chronistic tradition which evidently made use of our books and which Jepsen, *Quellen*, 4, puts at 400 BCE. So we are looking at a time span of approximately 150 years within which the books in their present form can have originated.

Nor does the view that the author(s) of the books of Kings must have drawn their materials from various sources and other documents present any difficulties. In Kings itself there is repeated reference to this, as in 1 Kgs. 11:41: 'the book of the Acts of Solomon,' and then, over and over, in formulaic phrases, after the mention of Judean or Israelite kings: 'the Book of the Annals of the kings of Judah' and 'the Book of the Annals of the kings of Israel.' By these statements the author(s) refer the attentive reader, who wants to know more about the persons in question, to these sources (Van Gelderen, 10, speaks, rather aptly, about a negative implication). Conversely, the authors do not tell us where they found their material. Still it is clear that they may have utilized documents, lists, annals, even volumes of poems. This last possibility seems to be confirmed by LXX when in 8:53a it describes what occurs in MT 8:12f. as 'written in the Book of the Song.'

In addition, there are clearly identifiable narrative cycles in our books:

(1) The end of the period of David's life and rule in 1 Kgs. 1 and 2. This at the same time forms the conclusion of what began in 2 Sam. 9-20, described by Rost 1926 as 'Die Überlieferung von der Thronnachfolge Davids.' Many scholars have followed him in this. In style and content the bulk of these 2 chapters indeed belongs to the subject matter in Samuel, though 2:13-46 constitutes a transition to the intrigues surrounding Solomon's accession to the throne.[23]

(2) The Elijah-cycle which is located in 1 Kgs. 17-19; 21 and 2 Kgs. 1. This is a prophetic narrative from Northern Israel which in the present edition of Kings is interrupted by other narratives concerning Ahab. In LXX, chap. 20 follows immediately after chap. 21 so that the connection is more natural. 2 Kgs. 1 seems less like the preceding and is a suitable transition to the narratives in the Elishah-cycle.

(3) The Elishah-cycle covers 2 Kgs. 2-13 and, though from a literary as well

---

[23] Cf. O. Eißfeldt, *The Old Testament, An Introduction*, London 1965, 286. See now also D.A. Knight, "Moral Values and Literary Traditions: The Case of the Succession Narrative (2 Samuel 9-20: 1 Kings 1-2)," *Semeia* 34 (1985), 7-23; *Studies in the Succession Narrative* (Old Testament Essays from the 27th Congress [1984] and the 28th Congress [1986] of the OTSSA; ed. W.C. van Wyk) Pretoria 1986; G. Keys, "The So-called Succession Narrative: A Reappraisal of Rost's Approach to Theme in II Samuel 9-20 and I Kings 1-2," *IBS* 10 (1988), 140-55; O. Kaiser, "Beobachtungen zur sogenannten Thronnachfolgeerzählung Davids," *EThL* 64 (1988) 5-20.

as a religious perspective, it is separate from the Elijah-cycle, there are remarkable parallels between the two.[24] This fact may suggest that the 2 cycles perhaps derive from the same surroundings and the same hand (cf. also Hölscher 1923, 188-195).

(4) An 'Ahab-source.' The information concerning king Ahab which, in chapters 20 and 22:1-38 clearly interrupts the flow of the Elijah-cycle, by its anti-Syrian attitude and connection with prophetic circles (20:35-43; 22:5-28), prove to be linked with Northern prophetic traditions.

(5) One can call 2 Kgs. 18:13-20:19 the 'Isaiah-source' because this section (aside from 2 Kgs. 18:14-16) parallels or duplicates what we find in Isa. 36-39. As a rule scholars assume that these legends have been transferred from the books of Kings to Isaiah. According to S. Szikszai, *IDB*, III, 33, 'this source represents the coalescence of historical narratives and the prophetic legends'. It is evidently from the south (hence from Jerusalem).

Alongside these more or less isolable sources, the books of Kings also here and there contain prophetic narratives and/or legends. It may be that the author(s) found these stories in other available sources or were familiar with them in some form from the oral tradition (e.g. 1 Kgs. 11:29-39; 14:1-18: prophecies of Ahijah, the Shilonite; 12:21-24: prophecy of Shemaiah; 12:32-13:34: a nameless prophet, etc.).

From the perspective of this overview of 'sources' – to which in the course of our commentary on Kings we hope to return in greater detail – the conclusion is more or less inescapable that one really has to speak of an editor or redactor of Kings (or of these persons in the plural) rather than of author(s). Particularly if one looks at the framework in which all sorts of sources, fragments, legends, etc. have been put, the judgments concerning kings which have been subjoined in fixed formulas and the considerations on which these judgments are based, not surprisingly the conclusion has been drawn that these judgments breathe the spirit of 'deuteronomistic theology.' The question is: must we look for this deuteronomistic (=dtr.) element in widely scattered remarks, interpolations or revisions – a kind of cement between the building blocks called 'sources' – or are we dealing with a dtr. history which has rendered its sources uniform in scope and ideology?[25] In 1943 M. Noth published his *Überlieferungsgeschichtliche Studien*, having the subtitle: *Die sammelnden und bearbeitenden Geschichtwerke im alten Testament*. In it he refers – in addition to 2 other collections (the pentateuch and the chronistic history) – to the dtr. history, by which he means that in this work we are not

---

[24] See, already, E. Renan, *Histoire du people d'Israel*, Paris 1887-1893, II, 284; H.C. Schmitt, *Elisa*, Gütersloh 1972, 183-187; my *De Naam van de afwezige god op de Karmel*, Leiden 1979, 6.

[25] See also J.A. Soggin, *Introduction to the Old Testament* (OTL), London 1989³, 179.

dealing with a dtr. redaction but with a deliberately composed historical work which begins with Deuteronomy and continues to the end of the books of Kings. This implies that the Deuteronomist has deliberately selected his fragments, pieces, and sources and the like, molding them in accordance with his theological insights. Thus, according to Noth, often all he did was 'die ihm als literarische Unterlagen zur Verfügung stehenden Quellen zu Worte kommen (lassen) und verknüpfte (er) nur die einzelnen Stücke durch einen verbindenden Text' (p. 11). But he also made this selection deliberately, as is evident from his account of the time of the kings (pp. 74ff.). His theological interpretation of the period he covered and described, particularly of the − in his view − crucial points in history, comes to expression either in the speeches of the dominant personalities (e.g. Josh. 1; 23; 1 Sam. 12 and 1 Kgs. 8), or in the summaries he himself formulated (e.g. Josh. 12; 2 Kgs. 17, etc.). Especially in these sections one can track down the 'theologische Leitgedanken' (pp. 100-110) in which the theme of the 'Gottesverehrung' − admittedly especially from the perspective of the recurrently arising 'false roads' taken − is central and in which an emphatically negative attitude to the cult comes to expression. The question to which 'geistige Welt' the Deuteronomist ultimately belongs Noth can only answer in negative terms (pp. 109f.): his work has no official stamp; it did not spring from the sphere of the priesthood; neither is it rooted in the realm of ideas characteristic of the official life of the state; nor is it imbued with the future ideology of the so-called national prophets. All these negative features the Deuteronomist shares with the book of Deuteronomy. 'Wir haben es also wohl mit der aus eigener Initiative unternommenen Arbeit eines Mannes zu tun, in dem die geschichtlichen Katastrophen ... die Frage nach dem Sinn dieses Geschehens geweckt hatten und der nun ... eine Antwort auf diese Frage zu geben suchte' (p. 110).

Although Noth's interpretation was widely accepted and the term 'deuteronomistic history' is almost universally employed to describe the books of Joshua and Kings, a further study of Noth's hypothesis has shown that he has oversimplified the problems of these books and fails to take sufficient account of the 'Vielschichtigkeit und Komplexität der Überlieferungen und ihrer Bearbeitung'.[26] Independently of Noth, Jepsen, in the work referred to above, had already shown that there is discernible in the books of Kings a plural redaction which he distinguishes as follows: a 'priestly,' a 'nebiistic' or 'prophetic,' and a 'levitical' redaction, the second of which (the prophetic) can be equated with Noth's Deuteronomist. Cross assumes the existence of 2 Dtr's, viz. Dtr^1, which refers to the 7th-century author of the dtr. history, and Dtr^2, which is applicable to the exilic editor of the work. In contrast to Noth (as well

---

[26] R. Rendtorff, *Das Alte Testament. Eine Einführung*, Neukirchen-Vluyn 1983, 195.

as to Jepsen) he therefore considers a large part of the dtr. history pre-exilic (the 'Josian redaction').[27] Even before Cross, scholars like Kuenen, Wellhausen, and others, reckoned with a pre-exilic and an exilic or post-exilic redaction.[28] Along with Smend and his pupils Dietrich and Veijola, 3 consecutive literary redactions have come to be accepted.[29] Analysis of the texts, according to these and other scholars, shows that DtrH, which from a historiographic and literary viewpoint is the first work, was expanded and transformed by a 'prophetically-oriented' redactor. This redactor was given the siglum DtrP. Finally a nomistic redactor oriented to the Mosaic law gave the work its present form DtrN. In addition, of course, post-dtr. supplementary material can repeatedly be found in the text as well.[30] W. Roth, *TRE*, VIII, 543-552, describes the dtr. opus as an encyclopedic work, 'das sich auf mehreren Ebenen zugleich bewegt.' In a succinct but comprehensive summary of the dtr. history, he characterizes the work (1) as historiography which encompasses more than 600 years (from the entry to the rehabilitation of Jehoiachin in 562 BCE), in which different aspects spring into view, like the building of the temple and the institution of the 2 dynasties; periods of wellbeing and disaster, etc; (2) as spatially and topographically defined, with Canaan as the land 'flowing with milk and honey' at the center; (3) as institutionally and sociologically charac-

---

[27] F.M. Cross, *Canaanite Myth and Hebrew Epic*, Cambridge Mass. 1973, 274-289); cf. also R.D. Nelson, *The Double Redaction of the Deuteronomistic History* (JSOTSup 18), Sheffield 1981.

[28] For a 'Forschungsgeschichte' of the dtr. history see also E. Jenni, *ThR* 27 (1961), 1-32; 97-146; A.N. Radjawane, *ThR* 38 (1974), 177-216; H. Weippert, *ThR* 50 (1985), 213-249; S.W. Halloway, *ABD*, IV, 70-73; H.D. Preuß, *ThR* 58 (1993), 229-264, 341-395; see now also C. Westermann, *Die Geschichtsbücher des Alten Testaments. Gab es ein deuteronomistisches Geschichtswerk?*, Gütersloh 1994; and on the books of Kings E. Noort, "Omgaan met Koningen. Tendenzen in de exegetische literatuur," *GThT* 88 (1988), 66-81; G.N. Knoppers, *Two Nations under God: The Deuteronomistic History of Salomon and the Dual Monarchies*. Vol. 1: *The Reign of Salomon and the Rise of Jerobeam;* Vol. 2: *The Reign of Jerobeam, the Fall of Israel, and the Reign of Josiah* (HSM 52 and 53), Atlanta 1993 and 1994; S.L. McKenzie, "The Books of Kings in the Deuteronomistic History," *The History of Israel's Tradition. The Heritage of Martin Noth* (ed. S.L. McKenzie, M.P. Graham; JSOTSup 182), Sheffield 1994, 281-307; G.N. Knoppers, "The Deuteronomist and the Deuteronomic Law of the King: A Reexamination of a Relationship," *ZAW* 108 (1996), 329-346; and *Israël construit son histoire* (ed. A. de Pury et al., Le monde de la Bible 34), Geneva 1996, esp. the contribution by T. Römer and A. de Pury, "L'historiographie deutéronomiste (HD): Histoire de la recherche et enjeux du débat," pp. 9-120.

[29] See now on 1 Kgs. 1-11 the dissertation (guided by Veijola) by P. Särkiö, *Die Weisheit und Macht Salomos in den israelitischen Historiographie. Eine traditions- und redaktionskritische Untersuchung über 1 Kön 3-5 und 9-11* (Schriften der Finnischen Exegetische Gesellschaft 60), Göttingen 1994.

[30] See, e.g., R. Smend, *Die Entstehung des Alten Testaments*, Stuttgart 1978, 110-139; W. Dietrich, *Prophetie und Geschichte* (FRLANT 108), Göttingen 1972; and Veijola, *Dynastie* and Veijola, *Kingdom*.

terized, a view in which 3 intermediaries of the divine presence are in the foreground: (a) the place of the temple; (b) the word of YHWH; and (c) the book of the law of Moses.

The above analysis of dtr. history is based on the literary criticism of the individual pericopes, verses or verse-parts. This method is often categorized as 'redactionsgeschichtlich.' But, as Rendtorff has correctly pointed out (op. cit., p. 195), the text in its present arrangement is not itself made the object of the exegesis.

Hoffmann, who does do this, comes to the conclusion that in the dtr. historiography there is discernible a substantial unity and that more material can be attributed to the single author of Dtr. than is done by the above-named authors.[31] He describes his work as 'überlieferungsgeschichtlich,' which means that the text we now have before us in its definitive final phase is the product of the consciously and deliberately planned work of the composer(s) of Dtr. Its central theme is the history of cultic reformations, culminating in the complete dtr. composition of 2 Kgs. 22-23 (Josiah's reformation), which accords with all the previous reports concerning the reformation of the cult without, however, being itself a more comprehensive contemporary source.

It is clear that the 2 briefly sketched methods can only be combined with difficulty. Add to this that it has become evident, as a result of investigation by Brekelmans[32]; N. Lohfink (cf. *TRE*, VIII, 541) and other scholars, that so-called dtr. elements exist in the pentateuch and elsewhere as well, so that the dtr. history cannot be considered in isolation but that also these 'proto-dtr.' or 'early dtr.' elements need to be explained. Rendtorff is of the opinion that the book of Deuteronomy must have been known and exerted influence before the time of its 'discovery' under Josiah; there is much to be said for the view 'daß sowohl die Entstehung des Deuteronomiums als auch die Anfänge, deuteronomistischer Arbeit in der Zeit Hiskijas und Manasses anzusetzen sind' (p. 197). He further views Deuteronomy as the 'connecting link' between the 4 preceding books of the Pentateuch and the following dtr. history. Along with Cross et al., Rendtorff finds the end of the dtr. history in the report on Josiah's reformation, to which later a conclusion was added along dtr. lines, ending with Jehoiachin's rehabilitation, which opened the door to the future of the Davidic dynasty (cf. J.D. Levenson, *JBL* 103 [1984], 353-361).

Along with Rendtorff we are of the opinion that the question needs to be further examined whether 'sich diese Datierung halten läßt und welche exegeti-

---

[31] H.D. Hoffmann, *Reform und Reformen. Untersuchungen zu einem Grundthema der deuteronomistischen Geschichtsschreibung* (AThANT 66), Zürich 1980. Cf. Long, 21: '... there is no *necessary* reason to accept the multiple redaction to 1-2 Kings (and the dtr. history ...)'.

[32] C. Brekelmans, "Die sogenannte deuteronomistische Elemente in Gen.-Num.," SVT 15 (1966), 90-96.

schen Folgerungen daraus im einzelnen zu ziehen sind' (p. 198). First a precise exegesis of both books will have to be completed before we can come to a well-rounded position of our own. However, as a working hypothesis for the section we will treat in this volume it must be assumed that 1 Kings 1-11 which must doubtlessly have made use of ancient lists (4:2-6, 7-19) and other archival information (building of the temple: chap. 6; Jachin and Boas 7:15-22; the 'wheeled stands': 7:27-39, etc.), was composed by one or more authors or redactors. Along with, for instance, Würthwein, 489, we are prepared to describe this section as 'die dtr Grundschrift von Kön.' For a study of this section does not make it likely that these lists or technical cultic particulars, which are mentioned nowhere else in the OT and clearly have Canaanite backgrounds, were deliberately created by a later or late author with a preconceived plan designed for its message. It cannot be denied, however, that especially in the so-called archival documents some later adaptations have occurred. This can often be easily established from glosses and other textual expansions and also by comparison with the ancient *versiones*. Accordingly, when Würthwein, 490, states that 'Die meisten Texte, die wir in 1. Kön. 3-11 über Salomo lesen, wurden von späteren Dtr oder in nachdtr Zeit eingestellt' then, to our mind, this applies less to 1 Kings 3-7 than to the sequel. Especially the 'report' about the building of the temple – which from a philological and literary perspective seems chaotic, as a result of which the details only with difficulty become clear – argues more for an ancient and early reportage than for a later time. If the latter were the case, why would people make it so obscure?[33]

Just where DtrH came into being is also a disputed question, one which is linked to the time of its origin. There are scholars,[34] who think that it is Babylon in the time of the exile; others, a majority, prefer Palestine, among the survivors of the destruction of Jerusalem. Arguments can be advanced for both positions. Accordingly, there are also scholars,[35] who consider the question of DtrH's place of origin insoluble. If, however, one is prepared, on the basis of literary analysis, to distinguish the hands of several earlier and later redactors, one can also assume that sections from different localities have been joined

---

[33] See now also S.L. McKenzie, "The Prophetic History and the Redaction of Kings," *Hebrew Annual Review* 9 (1985), 203-220. In his opinion the contribution of the Prophetic historians are the gathering of many of the traditions now found in 1 Kgs. 3-10, reaching a climax in 1 Kgs. 11. According to M.A. Sweeney, "The Critique of Solomon in the Josianic Edition of the Deuteronomistic History," *JBL* 114 (1995), 607-622, DtrH presents Solomon as a foil to Josiah, insofar as Solomon causes the fundamental problems that Josiah attempts to set aright.

[34] E.g., Soggin, *Introduction*, 164; E.W. Nicholson, *Preaching to the Exiles*, Oxford 1970, 117ff.

[35] Cf. P.R. Ackroyd, *Exile and Restoration. A Study of Hebrew Thought of the Sixth Century B.C.*, London 1968, 68.

together. This, of course, renders the establishment of the place where DtrH originated difficult.

Although, in view of the above, it is impossible ever to establish who the author(s) of the books of Kings is (are), it is of interest to note that the Babylonian Talmud, in listing the authors of the different Bible books, mentions Jeremiah as author of the books of Kings (Baba batra 15a, cf. also Ginzberg, *Legends*, VI, 387, n. 15). While this mention will not hold up under scientific scrutiny, it does show that the ancient Jewish tradition had a keen sense that the books of Kings were 'prophetic' history, viewed from the time of the end of the pre-exilic Davidic kingdom. Bewer called the dtr. opus 'a religious philosophy of Hebrew history'[36] and Soggin, 231, even speaks of 'a theology of history.' These characterizations indicate that in speaking of 'Jeremiah' the ancient Jewish tradition had a good sense of the deepest aims of the books of Kings.[37]

§ 6 *Content and character of 1 Kgs. 1-11*

As stated above, chaps. 1 and 2 are viewed as the conclusion of the history of the succession to David's throne, in which not the advanced age and death of David are first of all central, but primarily the question who will succeed him and, hence, how the Davidic dynasty will take shape. Although there is agreement about the high literary character of 2 Sam. 9-20 and 1 Kgs. 1f., opinions are divided when it comes to answering the question what the intention is of these 2 concluding chapters concerning the succession to the throne which form the beginning of Kings. We are struck, for example, by the alternately congenial and uncongenial traits of David (cf. K.W. Whitelam, *JSOT* 29 [1984], 61-87). No less contrasting are some important features in the image of his successor Solomon, in connection with which one only need to recall the pitiless harshness with which he treated people who opposed him (2:13-46), even though in the case of the executions of Joab and Shimei he is to be viewed as the executor of the will of his father David (2:5-9). Still in itself it is very well possible that 2:5-9 is a later addition by someone who had difficulty with Solomon's measures and sought to exonerate him (cf. Würthwein, *Thronfolge*, 16; Crüsemann, *Widerstand*, 182f.; Conrad 1973, 174, n. 14). On the basis of this consideration many scholars today make a (redactional) distinction between the original historical account and one or more later versions of it (cf. Veijola, *Dynastie* and Langlamet 1976 [with extensive biblio-

---

[36] J.A. Bewer, *The Literature of the Old Testament*, New York 1962³, 280.

[37] See now also R.R. Wilson, "The Former Prophets: Reading the Books of Kings," *Old Testament Interpretation* (Fs G.M. Tucker, ed. J.L. Mays et al.), Nashville 1995, 83-96. In his opinion the book's final edition has a viewpoint close to that found in the book of Isaiah.

graphy]). An objection against this layered view of the construction of our chapters, however, is that, though 1 Kgs. 1 and 2 indeed contain inconsistencies, not many linguistic or stylistic arguments can be conceived which support this layered character (so, e.g., Conrad, 163). Conrad – basing himself on a study by Seebass, who rejects the idea that at issue in these narratives is a positive versus a negative posture toward David and Solomon, but thinks that what is at stake is the new role of the power embodied in them[38] – rejects the term 'Thronfolgegeschichte' as 'inappropriate' and believes that the new balance of power under David and Solomon is the source of inspiration for the account of the history and the criticism: 'Diese Macht erscheint geradezu als eine selbständige Größe, die denen, die sie ausüben, ihre eigenen Gesetze aufzwingt, Gesetze, deren Nichteinhaltung schwere Schäden zur Folge hat' (p. 168). Precisely the fact that under David's kingship a new centralized political order over *all* of Israel came in the place of the – up until then prevailing – order of the tribes occasioned this crisis of and struggle for power which plays out in a narrow circle of a few individuals. This power struggle is described 'mit kühler Objectivität' (E. Meyer) so that it is a mistake to characterize this history as a 'Tendenzschrift' (p. 169). The author of this history breathes the spirit of the later 'prophets of doom' in his criticism of the foundation – laid under David and Solomon – of the future 'Klassengesellschaft' (p. 170) and also in the clear indication of the problem of individual guilt which may have consequences for an entire nation (pp. 171f.). However, in distinction from the later prophets of doom, who make their indictments and announce the destruction of the existing order, the author of our history is concerned to secure 'die königliche Macht mit allen Mitteln' (p. 172). Theologically this acceptance of the royal power is confirmed by showing how YHWH has pronounced himself in favour of David's and Solomon's rule. Despite the rebuke of the misuse of power it is YHWH's will to save Israel. In contrast to Würthwein, Conrad characterizes the work of the author of this history as 'theologische Geschichtsschreibung' (p. 173).

At the end of a study of the recensions and the history of 1 Kgs. 2 Trebolle states that the sentence καὶ ἡ βασιλεία κατωρθοῦτο ἐν Ιερουσαλημ, preserved in LXX on 2:35, indicates that the so-called 'succession history' consists of a cycle of 'romances,' grouped around a central core of narratives of greater scope and a theme which can be defined as 'history of the consolidation of royal power in the new dynasty and the court of Jerusalem.'[39] Even maintaining the layered construction and attending to the textual differences provided by comparison of MT, LXX[B, Luc.] etc., one can, as it concerns the main theme

---

[38] H. Seebass, *David, Saul und das Wesen des biblischen Glaubens*, Neukirchen-Vluyn 1980.
[39] J. Trebolle, "Testamento y Muerte de David," *RB* 87 (1980), 87-103; esp. p. 103.

of our chapters, arrive at similar outcomes. We can for the time being still leave out of consideration the stylistic and structural analysis of 2 Sam. 9-20 and 1 Kgs. 1f., as Fokkelman offers it in the first of 4 volumes on the books of Samuel.

If – as commentator on the books of Kings – one considers 1 Kgs. 1 and 2 as more or less separate from the conclusion of Samuel, one is inclined – along with Seebass, Conrad, Trebolle, and others – with research based on text-critical and literary-critical analysis, to find the central meaning of the chapters 1 and 2 in 'the consolidation of the power of the Davidic dynasty'.[40]

Following the overture in chaps. 1 and 2, the actual history of the kingship of Solomon which runs through chap. 11 begins in chap. 3. The beginning of chap. 3, like the beginning of chap. 9, contains a vision or dream of Solomon. Chaps. 3-8 as it were constitute the one side of Solomon's administration, the side which is bathed in a favourable light – the words of YHWH to Solomon in the dream are all favourable – and culminate in the building of the temple and the 'temple-prayer'; chaps. 9-11 constitute the other side, the side in which Solomon's mistakes and deficiencies come up, and which are introduced by a 'threatening' dream.[41] But one of the core words which unites the 2 parts and in which the narratives about Solomon are as it were embedded is the word חכמה, 'wisdom' already prepared for in 2:6 (also 3:28; 5:9 *et passim*; 10:4 *passim*; 11:41) and presupposed in the dialogic dream in chap. 3. While the 2 panels (3-8; 9-11) hinge on 'wisdom,' the center of the triptych is formed by the construction of the temple and the dedicatory prayer of the temple (6-8). The temple is not only the high point of Solomon's 'wise' government but also the high point of the history of kings: 'la suite de l'histoire des rois, et déjà celle de Salomon lui-même, ne peuvent plus être que des degradations' (correctly states Buis, 697). Solomon's era of government is the period of 'wisdom' in which even the voices of prophets are silent. Their voice is again

---

[40] Cf. Whitelam, *JSOT* 29 (1984), 76ff.; see also J.W. Whedbee, "On Divine and Human Bonds: The Tragedy of the House of David", *Canon, Theology, and Old Testament Interpretation* (Fs B.S. Childs, ed. G.M. Tucker et al.), Philadelphia 1988, II, 147-65; J.S. Ackermann, "Knowing Good and Evil: A Literary Analysis of the Court History in 2 Samuel 9-20 and 1 Kings 1-2," *JBL* 109 (1990), 41-60; G.G. Nicol, "The Death of Joab and the Accession of Solomon: Some Observations on the Narrative of 1 Kings 1-2," *JSOT* 7 (1992), 134-151.

[41] See now also K.I. Parker, *Wisdom and Law in the Reign of Solomon*, Lewiston 1992, about Solomon as the ideal (chaps. 3-8) and apostate (chaps. 9-11) king. J.T. Walsh, "The Characterization of Solomon in First Kings 1-5," *CBQ* 57 (1995), 471-493, also finds a negative point of view underlying the positive characterization on the surface in the first chapters. Cf. also C. Schäfer-Lichtenberger, *Josua und Salomo. Eine Studie zur Autorität und Legitimität des Nachfolgers in Alten Testament* (VTS 58), Leiden 1995, 225-355: Solomon was a failure because he conformed neither to what was exemplary in his father nor to the Torah which David had specifically commanded to him.

heard only when Solomon's wisdom has vanished (11:29).[42]

Alternating with stories about Solomon's wisdom in administering justice (3:16-28) and his lifestyle (4:21-34) one finds ancient reports on divisions of the land and names of high officials (4:1-20) as well as the organization of the work (chap. 5). Also the reports on the building of the temple and palace (6 and 7) and the miscellaneous notes on the wealth of Solomon in chap. 9 are not only based on probably ancient archival documents but are undoubtedly ancient citations, considering their fragmented stylistic construction, their frequently no longer understood technical terms and glossarial additions scattered throughout these sections, apart even from the sometimes chaotic sequence of the phrases. In chap. 7 we encounter descriptions of temple instruments and ornaments ('Jachin and Boaz,' the 'wheeled stands,' etc.) which most likely derive from the Canaanite cultic sphere which must certainly have been present before the establishment of the Davidic kingship in Jerusalem and probably still persisted for a long time afterward. Why would a 'dtr. redactor,' who intended to write a theological history in the 'Yahwistic' pattern, nevertheless maintain these linguistically difficult fragments which are hard to interpret theologically as well? Despite these hard-to-interpret passages, however, the author succeeded in injecting a dimension of theological interest: YHWH − and not the priestly king with his palace-temple complex − has a 'home' among his people.[43]

§ 7 Linguistic aspects of Kings

Although it is still too early in this volume to discuss in detail the linguistic aspects of the books of Kings, and although one will generally *not* find a separate section devoted to this part especially in the case of the books of Kings inasmuch as these books exhibit little unity on this level (cf. Buis, 725-728), it is nevertheless desirable to pay some attention to it here, in part because Buis has done this so creditably in his article. In it he has pointed out, among other things, that a comparison of the so-called dtr. terms in Kings with those in Deuteronomy brings out that between the 2 works there is scarcely ever any identity in formulas (p. 727). His research shows that, though Kings has a number of words which also occur in Deut., the usage frequencies differ and the words occur in different groups. The limited number of stylistic affinities between the books of Kings, Deuteronomy and in this connection also

---

[42] See now also A. Lemaire, "Wisdom in Solomonic Historiography," *Wisdom in Ancient Israel* (Fs J.A. Emerton, ed. J. Day et al.), Cambridge 1995, 106-118.

[43] See on the structure of these chapters also K.I. Parker, "Repetition as a Structuring Device in 1 Kings 1-11," *JSOT* 42 (1988), 19-27; M. Brettler, "The Structure of 1 Kings 1-11," *JSOT* 49 (1991), 87-97; and A. Frisch, "Structure and Significance: The Narrative of Solomon's Reign (1 Kings 1-12.24)," *JSOT* 51 (1991), 3-14.

Jeremiah can perhaps be explained by the fact that all of them belong to the same theological tradition.

In addition to more theologically-focused interest in linguistic usage in Kings there is the question concerning the specific usage in the various genres Kings presents, in this volume especially in the first eleven chapters of these books. For instance, here, in chaps. 6 and 7, in connection with the building of the temple and the palace and the material used for that purpose, we encounter, aside from a difficult, obviously defective and sometimes even chaotic sentence structure (things which in themselves argue for the use of authentic but ancient documents and for the growth of glosses and the like on the original reports), technical terms which not only boggle the minds of modern interpreters and translators but already presented insurmountable difficulties to the ancient versions and – as is evident here and there – to the author(s) of the parallel books of Chronicles. In our commentary we will discuss these problems further *in loco,* but we can say here that, based on detailed analysis of words like צלע and יציע in 6:5-10, we had to infer a construction of the temple without small built-on rooms and 3 floors. In the case of the most difficult technical construction items (e.g. in the case of the 'wheeled stands' in 7:27-37) we have practically no parallels at our disposal which could help in interpretation and translation. Consequently, the commentator has to rely on 'internal evidence,' 'logical inference,' and sometimes on etymology or indications which can be found in the ancient versions.

The diversity of genres in our chapters alone renders it impossible to bring this section linguistically under a single heading, except that, dispersed throughout this part, one can find dtr. cement between the broken fragments. This linguistic observation alone argues against the view that the books of Kings flowed from the pen of a single author who himself, in the interest of the theological purpose for which he designed this historical work, molded or even created his material. The construction of these books, also from the perspective of the linguistic constructs used, has been much more complex. In the commentary we will, wherever necessary, pay attention to the linguistic aspects of the text, including – following especially the older commentaries – grammar, syntax, and word study.

§ 8 *The Solomonic temple and its significance*
Although the section of Kings which is found in the first eleven chapters does not resonate much in the NT,[44] still the temple of Solomon has been of great

---

[44] In *Novum Testamentum Graece*, Stuttgart 1993[27], 780f., the editors only list 1:48; 2:10, 26; 5:10, 25; 6:1f.; 8:1, 6, 10f., 20, 27, 39, 41f.; 9:7f.; 10:1, 4ff., 18; 11:14, 40 as *loci citati vel allegati*.

significance, also in its cosmic symbolism, within and outside of Judaism as well as in Christianity. Van Pelt devoted his Leiden dissertation to this subject.[45] In this work the author deals with the history, character, and influence of the cosmic speculations surrounding the temple. While in this section we cannot comment in detail on all these aspects, in the abovementioned book they are treated adequately enough. But it is of interest to point out that, according to Van Pelt, the form and description of Solomon's temple need not lead to the assumption 'that this sanctuary was an 'Abbild,' a representation of the world, an *imago mundi*' (p. 43). Indeed, the temple definitely possessed cosmic symbolism, something he refers to in the term *'recapitulatio mundi'* (ibid.). This concept does justice 'to the essence of the symbolism of a temple designed on the basis of a mythical cosmology.' This symbolism, according to the author, is not dependent on the rite, nor on the shape of the whole, 'but on the meaning of the place where the sanctuary was built' (p. 46). 'Just as the world encompasses heaven, earth, and underworld, so the holy site was the place where heaven, earth, and underworld came together' (p. 47). Ultimately heaven and earth coincide in the earthly temple and the temple is experienced and understood as *recapitulatio mundi* (p. 50).

In our discussion of chaps. 6 and 7 we find not only the influence but above all the rudiments of Canaanite culture and religion. The Canaanite world was still ordered according to myth. Van Pelt refers to this connection as well (p. 51). It cannot be denied that the choice of 'Mount Zion' on the one hand sanctioned for Israel the installation of the ark in a new cult center, 'and at the same time upheld the adoption by Israel of features borrowed from the cult of El-'Elyon'.[46] According to the Canaanites the supreme deity dwelt in a tent or temple on a 'holy' mountain and that the earthly temple was a copy of the heavenly; and this was the case not only in Canaan but we encounter these ideas also in Ugarit, Egypt, and Babylonia.[47] Even in Israel this idea was known at a later time: Moses was shown a model of the tent on the mountain (Exod. 26:30; cf. 25:9, 40; 27:8 and Num. 8:4). One may call it − with Clifford − an 'ancient religious principle' of 'like is like' when Moses had to work in this fashion.[48] Clifford, accordingly, correctly points out that in the case of the temple of Solomon one can demonstrate a similar correspondence, even though, according to him, the interpretation of the individual elements remains difficult

---

[45] R.J. van Pelt, *Tempel van de Wereld; de cosmische symboliek van de tempel van Solomo*, Utrecht 1984.

[46] R.E. Clements, *God and Temple*, Oxford 1965, 50.

[47] See, e.g., J.C. De Moor, *The Seasonal Pattern in the Ugaritic Myth of Ba'lu* (AOAT 16), Neukirchen-Vluyn 1971, 60f.

[48] R.J. Clifford, *The Cosmic Mountain in Canaan and the Old Testament*, Cambridge Mass. 1972, 123.

(p. 177). In this connection he refers among other things to a cosmic symbolism as one can find it in the interpretation of the pillars Jachin and Boaz by Albright, *ARI*, 142-153 (see also our commentary on 7:21). He describes these suggestions as 'conjectural' though at the same time he keeps the door open for the possibilities 'that individual elements of the Solomonic Temple are cosmic in the sense that they represent elements of the temple in the heavens' (p. 178; cf. also Clements, 67, who, like Clifford, distances himself from the opinion of De Vaux, *Inst.* II, 169ff., who denied that the symbolism of the temple had any meaning to Israel).[49]

According to many scholars (Clements, 79-99; Haran, *Temples*, 132-148; Van Pelt, 94ff.[50]), a fundamental reinterpretation of the meaning as well as the function of the temple occurred in the 8th and especially in the 7th century BCE, when the prophets reacted against the − in their view − Canaanized and Baalized Israelitisch temple worship and religion, a reaction which prompted the deuteronomistic reformation. 'In Israel ... mythical conceptions and, by implication, the basis for the mystical worldview were considered debatable' (Van Pelt, 94). The norms were shifted from the 'mystical temple of Solomon' to the 'Utopian new temple, from the past to the future' (p. 96). The temple lost its meaning as *recapitulatio mundi* and was at best still an *imago mundi* which at most offered a structure for the worship of God 'which results in a drawing near to God.'

However, the fact that the tabernacle was made according to the design or model shown by God to Moses on the mountain, and that in the later theological reflection of Israel also Solomon's temple is a project of YHWH, provided a sort of code enabling people, by means of an analysis of the measurements and dimensions of the temple, to visualize a plan of God. In this manner the creation of the tabernacle and the temple becomes an allegory for the creation of the world by God. 'The way in which the Bible presents the image of the temple therefore suggests that this image had to be interpreted like a code' (p. 100). Philo of Alexandria is the source of the most ancient preserved philosophical speculation which has 'as its startingpoint an architecture which has become a theoretical model' (p. 103). In this respect Philo's influence extends as far as the philosophical activities of Spinoza. In the world-image of post-antiquity, the temple and the tabernacle played a large role as cognitive model (p. 104). Since the beginning of the 19th century, under the heading of 'symbolism,' alongside the cosmic symbolism of the Solomonic temple, a

---

[49] See now also S. Frolov, V. Orel, "The House of YHWH," *ZAW* 108 (1996), 254-257, interpreting the temple of Solomon as an architectural and religious reminiscence of the house of Baal, as described in the Ugar. myth of Baal (*KTU* 1.1-6): the house decorated with gold, silver and lapis lazuli, the house without windows, the house of cedar.

[50] Cf. also H.W. Turner, *From Temple to Meeting House*, The Hague 1979, 65ff.

number of works have been published which can better be designated as 'archaeologies.' We have especially in mind here the work of Bähr.[51] In this work, to be sure, there is no express mention of the Solomonic temple (in 1848 Bähr wrote a work on it in the course of a polemic with F. Friederich; see Van Pelt, 336-340), but it addresses particularly the basic form, the oriental character, the representation of the creation and the tabernacle, etc. Still the implications of the study apply also to the temple: the whole (of the tabernacle but also of the temple) is designed and built according to a specific principle; everything, down to the details, serves a single goal; everywhere precise connections and rigid consistency prevail (Bähr, I, 117). Bähr combats the opinion of Von Bohlen and Vatke who want to deduce the tabernacle from the Solomonic temple, or even declare the tabernacle to be a pure fiction and the Solomonic temple the original. Especially Vatke pointed out that the Solomonic temple was not only a product of Phoen. style and supervisors, but that also the symbols found in it were of Phoen. origin, and adopted in the course of history by the Israelites.[52] Although Bähr says of this: 'An Beweisen für diese Behauptung fehlt es natürlich gänzlich' (p. 118), we can say, on the basis of our exegesis of certain elements in 1 Kgs. 7, that Vatke in his day already had a keen sense of this influence and that in the course of time the evidences have emerged. The pillars Jachin and Boaz, the 'Bronze Sea,' the 'wheeled stands' and perhaps still more elements can be traced to the Canaanite 'Umwelt,' even though in the Israelite cult they (later) received another function and symbolism. This is not the place to explore these questions. We only wish to point out that the placing of the 'Bronze Sea' and the 'wheeled stands' in relation to Solomon's temple may have continuing symbolic impact in Ezekiel's vision of the 'temple river' (Ezek. 47), where the lifegiving water also flows from under the temple. However, anyone venturing to explore the symbolism of the temple (or tabernacle) must know what he or she is doing. In any case, there is an example in Heb. 9:1-10 in which there is mention of an earthly as well as a heavenly sanctuary and in Rev. 21:9-22:5 where it is said that there will be no temple in the future of 'the Lamb,' 'for its temple is the Lord God the Almighty and the Lamb' (21:22) but that 'a river of the water of life, bright as crystal' flows 'from the throne of God and of the Lamb,' on either side of which again there are trees growing. But a Sea was no more (21:1). Whatever the Canaanite symbolism of the temple may have been, the Jewish tradition and subsequently

---

[51] K.Chr.W.F. Bähr, *Symbolik des Mosaischen Cultus*, I-II, Heidelberg 1837-39. In this work the typology 'in Coccejanischer Form und Methode' (I, v) is dismissed, but the author does follow the work of the romantic G.Fr. Creuzer, *Symbolik und Mythologie der alten Völker, besonders der Griechen*, Leipzig 1819-1823².

[52] J.K.W. Vatke, *Die biblische Theologie, I, Die Religion des Alten Testaments*, Leipzig 1835, 323, 335f. (succeeding volumes have not appeared).

the NT have employed and interpreted it in their own way (see now also Mulder 1989).

§ 9 *Bibliographic pointers*
In this section we want to give some information about the way in which in this commentary we have used the almost boundless literature on our subject.

Alongside of the modern dictionaries (Ges-B, Zorell, *KBL,HAL,* and *Ges.*[18]), we regularly looked up Gesenius's *Thesaurus Philologicus Criticus,* I-III, 1829-1858, as well as J. Simonis-G.B. Winer, *Lexicon Manuale Hebraicum et Chaldaicum,* 1828[4], in order if necessary to track down the older studies. Other dictionaries which we consulted are J. Fürst-V. Ryssel, *Hebräisches und Chaldäisches Handwörterbuch über das Alte Testament,* 1876[3]; C. Siegfried-B. Stade, *Hebräisches Wörterbuch zum Alten Testament,* 1893 and E. König, *Hebräisches und Aramäisches Wörterbuch zum Alten Testament,* 1922[2,3] (=1936[6,7]). Although the modern dictionaries keep the user abreast of the state-of-the-art philology, the older dictionaries, aside from helping one to track down the older literature, are also useful for gaining insight into the history of the development of word meanings.

Much attention is devoted in our commentary to the grammatical and syntactic side of the Hebr. language. A basic work, despite its being in certain respects, seriously out-of-date, is Böttcher's *Ausführliches Lehrbuch der Hebräischen Sprache,* alongside of which his *Exegetisch-kritische Aehrenlese* (1849) and especially his *Neue exegetisch-kritische Aehrenlese,* 2 Abt. (1864; like his grammar, it was edited after his death by F. Mühlau) open up significant perspectives. Another important grammar is that of W. Gesenius, *Ausführliches grammatischkritische Lehrgebäude der Hebräische Sprache* (1817), which was a companion volume to his *Hebräisches Elementarbuch* (1813), and finally culminated in his still deservedly widely used grammar of Gesenius-Kautzsch, *Hebräische Grammatik.* Other much used and still useful grammars from the 19th century were written by Ewald, Olshausen, Stade, König (frequent reference is made in this commentary to the important third volume, which treats the Syntax), Davidson, and S.R. Driver.

The more modern 20th-century grammars consulted are from Bauer-Leander, Joüon, Bergsträsser (intended as a new revised edition of Ges-K[28] but unfortunately not completed), Meyer, Brockelmann, and R.J. Williams. Even though they are primarily intended for academic or undergraduate instruction, there are nevertheless grammars which, because they have a unique approach or perspective on one or more themes, are worth consulting on the text of the OT. We will mention: the grammar by Schneider; J. Blau, *A Grammar of biblical Hebrew,* 1976; J.F.A. Sawyer, *A Modern Introduction to Biblical Hebrew,* 1976; and for the Dutch language-area J.P. Lettinga, *Grammatica van het Bijbels Hebreeuws,* 1976[8] (1936[1], by J. Nat, under another title); for the

Afrikaans language area B. Gemser-C.J. Labuschagne, *Hebreeuse Spraakkuns*, 1968³.

In addition to the abovementioned more general works, there are countless monographies and individual works in the area of grammar and syntax which have been consulted and referred to wherever possible and/or necessary. For word study we used *THAT* and the more broadly conceived *TWAT*. Also very useful, among other things for the Greek, *TDNT*.

Aside from the lexicons and grammars also the commentaries are important. For this volume a number of them were used not only because they happened to be available and could therefore be consulted but especially because they permitted a discussion of several aspects arising from the design we chose.

For the ancient Jewish aspect of the exegesis, alongside of an edition of the מקראות גדולות (Schocken edition, 1519), we took into account especially the commentary by Hochberg-Rosenberg, in which, besides the reproduction of MT and Tg. and the commentaries by Rashi, Kimchi, also a translation of Rashi's commentary is provided as well as parts of commentaries of other ancient authoritative Jewish rabbis. Somewhat comparable as a modern Jewish commentary, thoug not as detailed, is the commentary by Slotki.

The *Critici sacri sive annotata doctissimorum viorum in V. ac N.T.* (8 vol. in the Amsterdam edition of 1698) yielded *annotata* – still worth reading and pondering – on our chapters by older scholars such as Münster, Vatablus, Clarius, Drusius, Hugo Grotius and others. As annotations in the modern sense, viz. as notes of various kinds, but especially of the text-critical, philological and exegetical kind, can be viewed: Stade-Schwally, Ehrlich, and especially Burney. Also to be mentioned here is Cheyne, *Critica Biblica*, in the 4th volume of which can be found critical linguistic, literary, and historical comments on the books of Kings. The work *Old Testament Translation Problems*, published in 1960 and edited by Hulst and others, which offers directions for the translation of difficult verses, has a sequel, as it were, in *Preliminary and Interim Report on the Hebrew Project*, 2 (1976, publication of United Bible Societies) and recently in D. Barthélemy, *Critique Textuelle de l'Ancien Testament*, 1 (1982), a very comprehensive work. But, as is evident from the last 2 titles alone, comments in these publications deal particularly with text-critical problems.[53]

As commentaries in the more traditional sense of the word we especially consulted those written by Thenius, Keil, Klostermann, Benzinger, Kamp-

---

[53] Most of the recent literature on the study of the MT and the Versions is surveyed in *Mikra. Text, Translation, Reading and Interpretation of the Hebrew Bible in Ancient Judaism and Early Christianity* (ed. M.J. Mulder, Compendia Rerum Iudaicarum ad Novum Testamentum 2.1), Assen 1988.

hausen, Skinner, Kittel, Šanda, Greßmann, Eißfeldt, Van Gelderen, Montgomery-Gehman, Snaith, Van den Born, Gray, Brongers, Noth, Robinson, Würthwein, and Rehm.

Annotations further occur under Bible translations, or sometimes in separate publications. In *La Sainte Bible* (traduite en français sous la direction de l'École Biblique de Jérusalem, 1956) De Vaux furnished valuable notes on the books of Kings (see now the entirely new and expanded edition under the title *La Bible de Jérusalem*, 1979). Dhorme annotated these books in *La Bible*, I, 1956 (Bibliothèque de la Pléiade). A third new annotated French translation is *Traduction Oecuménique de la Bible, Ancien Testament*, 1976, in which many scholars collaborated. No special names are associated, in this ecumenical translation, with the translation and annotation of the books of Kings.

This takes us to the use of translations, always an excellent tool for tracking down textual problems by comparing the different renderings. In preparing our translation and commentary we have checked the usual Dutch versions, like the Statenvertaling, the Nieuwe Vertaling of the Dutch Bible Society (NV), the so-called Leidse Vertaling (LV), the Petrus Canisius Vertaling (PCV), the Willibrordvertaling (WV), the translation by Obbink-Brouwer (to the extent it was translated for 1 Kgs. 1-11), and in addition also the (ecumenical) new Frisian translation (1978). Use was made as well of the South-African translation of 1933 (*Naslaan-Bybel*), followed in 1983 by "Die Bybel. Nuwe vertaling." We collaborated in a supervisory role in the production of the Groot Nieuws Bijbel (GNB).

As for other translations, in the preceding we have already mentioned a number of them from the French-language area. To these we can add the translation by Louis Segond. From the German-language area we can list, alongside of the Luther Bible, also in its revised form (1964), the Zürcher Bibel (1931) and the well-known translation by M. Buber-F. Rosenzweig. In addition we consulted the Jewish translation edited by H. Torczyner and others (1937), the Catholic translation edited by P. Riessler and R. Shorr (1952) and the so-called Pattloch-Bibel (1956). From the English-language area we used, besides the King James Version and the Revised Standard Version (1952), also the New English Bible (NEB), as well as the Good News Bible (GoodNB). The private Bible translation of J. Moffatt (OT 1924) was consulted incidentally. In 1978 the Jewish Publication Society of America published a (new) translation of the (early and late) Prophets.

Several of the above translations have brief or more extensive annotations or marginal notes. In connection with the LV (cf. Oort) in which textual changes in the LV were scientifically accounted for, and in connection with the NEB, Brockington 1973.

For the exploration of the literary, geographic, cultural, social, and other backgrounds of the OT texts, various standard works are available. For the mores, customs, and practices in Bible Dalman's standard work, *Arbeit und Sitte in Palästina*, which is based on study as well as personal observation, is still of special importance. Life in the countryside, in summer and winter, but also the life of plants and animals, is given thorough attention. A work of a different kind but one that is no less important, is that of Pedersen, *Israel, its Life and Culture*, which still consistently deserves to be consulted in exegetical work. Further we consulted BRL^{1+2}, the handbooks of De Vaux, Nowack, Benzinger, Barrois, and Krauss.

For the study of the history of Israel there are various handbooks and textbooks. I will take the liberty of referring to my article in *BH*, II A, 7-140 in which, on pp. 15f., the literature consulted also for this commentary is listed. This list can be supplemented with Ewald, *GVI*, esp. vol. III, *Geschichte Davids und der Königsherrschaft in Israel* (1866). Also the work of E. Renan, *Histoire du peuple d'Israel*, I-V, Paris 1887-1893, needs to be mentioned, as well as B. Stade, *Geschichte des volkes Israel*, I-II, Berlin 1887-1888.

For the geography of Palestine, see Abel, *GP* and especially Simons, *GTTOT* and *Jerusalem*. Incidental use was made also of A. Neubauer, *La Geographie du Talmud*, Paris 1868 (repr. Amsterdam 1965).

For the literature, religions, and the history of the nations surrounding Israel various handbooks are available. We mention the following: Donner-W. Röllig, *Kanaanäische und Aramäische Inschriften*, I-III, Wiesbaden 1962-1964 (and later reprints) (=*KAI*); J.C.L. Gibson, *Textbook of Syrian Semitic Inscriptions*, I-III, Oxford 1971, 1975, 1982 (=*TSSI*). For the Ugaritic C.H. Gordon, *Ugaritic Textbook*, I-III, Rome 1965; G.R. Driver, *Canaanite Myths and Legends*, 1956, a new edition by J.C.L. Gibson, Edinburgh 1978 (=*CML*); A. Caquot, M. Sznycer, A. Herdiner, *Textes Ougaritiques*, I, Paris 1974; II, 1989; J.C. de Moor, *An Anthology of Religious Texts from Ugarit*, Leiden 1987 (see also the "select bibliography" in Gibson, *CML*, XIII-XX). The Ugaritic texts are cited according to the edition in *KTU* in the second, enlarged edition (M. Dietrich, O. Loretz, J. Sanmartín, *The Cuneiform Alphabetic Texts*, München 1995). Generally speaking one finds many texts which can be related to the OT translated in J.B. Pritchard (ed.) *Ancient Near Eastern Texts relating to the Old Testament*, Princeton 1955^2 (=*ANET*), with the companion volume from the same publisher: *The Ancient Near East in Pictures*, Princeton 1954 (=*ANEP*) and followed by a supplementary volume for both, 1969. We also used W. Beyerlin (ed.), *Religionsgeschichtliches Textbuch zum Alten Testament*, Göttingen 1975 (=*RTAT*), and K. Galling (ed.), *Textbuch zur Geschichte Israels*, Tübingen 1979^3. See now also *Texte aus der Umwelt des Alten Testaments* (ed. O. Kaiser), Gütersloh 1982ff. (=*TUAT*).

A good supplementary volume to these works is K.R. Veenhof (ed), *Schrijvend Verleden*, Leiden 1983, in which a number of documents from the ancient Near East rarely printed elsewhere have been translated and explained.

Unfortunately this work lacks an index of texts. Ringgren, *Israelite Religion*, lists much modern literature, especially in the "Nachtrag" to the second edition, 1982, 319-338. In order not to make this easily expandable survey too long we again mention the *Bijbels Handboek* (ed. A.S. van der Woude, vol. I, II a and b, 1981 ff. (=*BH*).

To conclude this account of bibliographic references we will still mention a number of dictionaries — not directly bearing on the OT — which we consulted, as well as a few general encyclopedias or handbooks, which we found useful in our research: M. Jastrow, *A Dictionary of the Targumim*, I-II, 1903 (reprint 1950); G. Dalman, *Aramäisch-Neuhebräisches Handwörterbuch*, 1922²; J. Payne Smith (Mrs. Margoliouth), *A Compendious Syriac Dictionary*, 1903 (and later repr.); C. Brockelmann, *Lexicon Syriacum*², 1928; C.F. Jean-J. Hoftijzer, *Dictionnaire des Inscriptions sémitiques de l'Ouest*, 1965 (=*DISO*); J. Aistleitner, *Wörterbuch der ugaritischen Sprache*, 1963.[54] In connection with the Ugaritic the following are useful: L.R. Fisher (ed), *Ras Shamra Parallels*, I-II, 1972, 1975, and III (ed. S. Rummel), 1981 (=*RSP*). For the Akkadian we used W. von Soden, *Akkadisches Handwörterbuch*, I-III, 1965, 1972, 1981, (=*AHw*).

H.G. Liddell-R. Scott, *A Greek-English Lexicon* (With a Supplement, 1968), 1968, was used for the Greek as well as F. Muller, *Grieksch Woordenboek*, 1933³; and esp. for LXX: I.F. Schleusner, *Novus Thesaurus Philologico-criticus*, I-V, 1820-1821. For the Latin, C.T. Lewis-C. Short, *A Latin Dictionary*, 1966; and J. van Wageningen-F. Muller, *Latijnsch Woordenboek*, 1929⁴.

In addition to the more general (theological) encyclopedias like the *RE*³, *RGG*¹⁻³, *TRE*, and *DBS*, the following works were used: *The Interpreter's Dictionary of the Bible*, 4 vol. + Suppl. Volume, 1962-1976 (=*IDB[S]*); B. Reicke-L. Rost, *Biblisch-Historisches Handwörterbuch*, I-IV, 1962-1979 (=*BHHW*); אנציקלופדיה מקראית (*Encyclopaedia Biblica*), I-VIII, 1972-1982 (=*EncMiqr.*); *The New Bible Dictionary*, 1962 (=*NBD*); A. van den Born, *Bijbels Woordenboek*, 1966-1969³ (=*BW*); W.H. Gispen et al., *Bijbelse Encyclopedie*, I-II, 1975²; *Der Kleine Pauly* I-V, 1964-1975 (=*KP*); *Woordenboek der Oudheid*, I-III, 1976-1986 (=*WdO*). See now also the *Anchor Bible Dictionary*, 1992 (=*ABD*). Incidentally also older reference works were consulted, a.o. G.B. Winer, *Biblisches Realwörterbuch*, I-II, 1833-1838² (1847f.³); E.C.A. Riehm, *Handwörterbuch des Biblischen Altertums*, I-II, 1884; and H. Guthe, *Kurzes Bibelwörterbuch*, 1903.

Much literature that was consulted, especially that pertaining to a single word, verse, pericope or chapter, is only mentioned in the part concerned. In

---

[54] See now G. del Olmo Lete, J. Sanmartín, *Diccionario de la lengua Ugarítica*, Sabadell 1996-.

most cases articles are cited not by title but by periodical, the year of publication and page number.

1 KINGS 1:1-4

1:1 *Now King David was old and advanced in years, and although they covered him with bedclothes, he just could not get warm.*
 2 *So his servants said to him: 'Let us find a young girl for my lord the king, who can wait on the king and be his deputy. Also, she can lie in your bosom, so that my lord the king can get warm.'*
 3 *So they searched for a beautiful girl throughout all the territory of Israel, and found Abishag the Shunammite, who was brought to the king.*
 4 *Now the girl was exceptionally beautiful, and became the king's deputy and served him, but the king did not have intercourse with her ...*

INTRODUCTION

This pericope, with which the books of Kings open and which is a concluding part of what is generally considered 'the Davidic Succession' (cf. Rost, *Überlieferung*), is as it were the 'overture' to what follows in chaps. 1 and 2. David's age, the search for a 'deputy,' the finding of an exceptionally beautiful girl, and the old king's impotence, are not merely items of information from the private sector of the royal palace but have consequences for country and nation, indeed for the future of the whole of Israel as well.

EXEGESIS

1:1 *Now King David was old and advanced in years, and although they covered him with bedclothes, he just could not get warm.*
The *waw copulativum* at the beginning of our book closely links the following with the preceding. One similarly finds the *waw copulativum* at the beginning of the books of Exodus and Ezra. Several other books, such as Leviticus, Numbers, Joshua, etc., begin with an impf. cons. Job and Daniel have an independent beginning (cf. Ges-K §49b).

Joüon §159f takes the first half of our verse to be a nominal clause which is used more or less independently of the context. BrSynt. §142 considers the first 3 words appositional to the following 2 inasmuch as the second of 2 consecutive verbs explains and describes the first. זקן can be qal pf. 3 p. masc. sing. or an adjective (Meyer §92.1; cf. §98.1a). *HAL* and others opt here for the verb form. This is also likely because in Josh. 23:2, immediately following the same expressions, the author has Joshua continue with באתי בימים. זקנתי This also implies that בא here, as in the 3 other places in the OT where this formula occurs (aside from Josh. 23:1 also in Gen. 24:1 and Josh. 13:1; see Mm 159), can be a form of the pf. of the verb. The first 5 words of our verse, because it is a somewhat independent statement, can be read as a motto over the story which now follows. The sequence המלך דוד is the usual in 2 Samuel (with the exception of 13:39). This simultaneously indicates that this episode is closely connected with the preceding.

It is natural to assume that David was covered with bedclothes because he was unable to get warm, not because he was very old. Besides יֵחַם (*BHK*, *BHS*) the form יָחַם occurs as well (Letteris, Baer, Snaith; cf. Ewald §136b; Stade §490a). This is a so-called Aramaizing form (qal. impf.) of חמם (cf. Ges-K §67g; Bg. II §27o) alongside of יָחֹם (Isa. 44:16; cf. 2 Kgs. 4:34). Often (but not always by far) an impf. vowel /o/ (/u/) denotes a transitive, an impf. vowel /a/ an intransitive verb. BrSynt. §35b points out that physical and psychic impressions are usually expressed by the body parts which experience the feelings as subject. But such a subject is also often lacking as in our verse (cf. Ewald §346b; König §§157 and 186b). In BT Berachot 62b the fact that David could not get warm is attributed to his contempt for clothing when he cut off a corner of Saul's cloak (1 Sam. 24:5; cf. Seb. Münster; also K.-M. Beyse, *TWAT*, II, 1046).

The 3 p. pl. of ויכסהו denotes a general subject ('they') (cf. Ges-K §144l, Joüon §155b), though we may by anticipation think here of the king's servants mentioned in the following verse. In בבגדים the MT uses the article because this is suggested by the preceding verb (as Burney correctly comments).

1:2 *So his servants said to him: 'Let us find a young girl for my lord the king, who can wait on the king and be his deputy. Also, she can lie in your bosom, so that my lord the king can get warm.'*

What is said by the servants in this verse is said to the king (לו). Many MSS of LXX (except LXX[Luc]; cf. Rahlfs, *Sst.* 523) leave it untranslated, so that the reader gets the impression that the servants were talking about the king among themselves (see vs. 3). In some MSS of LXX the Hebr. text is adjusted to this line of thought (לאדני [2x] in place of לאדני and למלך [2x] in place of המלך). An attempt is made as well to retouch the possible offensiveness of this verse by substituting κοιμηθήσεται μετ' αὐτοῦ for ושכבה בחיקך. We see no reason to follow LXX, however, all the less since the other ancient versions support MT. Admittedly one would have expected לו after instead of before עבדיו. Perhaps המלך is to be taken as vocative but can be viewed equally well as apposition with לאדני. ל, in turn, can, on the basis of its use in certain cases in Ugar. but also occasionally in Hebr., be considered as vocative (cf. among others M. Dahood, *VT* 16 (1966), 299ff.; T. Penar, *VD* 45 (1967), 32-46; M.H. Pope, *UF* 20 (1988), 201-207; but cf. also P.D. Miller, *UF* 11 (1979), 617-

639). Here, on account of the construction of בקש with ל and of the conclusion of this verse by which וחם would come to hang in the air, this is improbable.

יבקשו, 'search' in the sense of 'select' (cf. S. Wagner, *TWAT*, I, 757), pi, 3 p. masc. pl., here functioning as jussive, is continued with a pf. cons. (3 p. fem. s.; cf. Driver §113.2; Joüon §119k). The apposition בתולה alongside of נערה indicates that the young woman must still be *intacta*, at least unmarried (cf. Lev. 21:3; Judg. 21:12; further Lev. 21:14; Ezek. 44:22). The combination of the 2 words can also be found elsewhere in OT (Deut. 22:15, 20, 23, 28; Esth. 2:2f.). It needs to be said that the word בתולה, which also occurs in other Sem. languages (Akkad.: *batultu*, 'young, marriageable woman'; Ugar.: *btlt*, epithet for the goddess Anath; further Aram. and Arab.) does not primarily mean 'virgin' but rather – also in OT (cf. Joel 1:8) – 'young marriageable woman' (cf. further J. Bergman, H. Ringgren, M. Tsevat, *TWAT*, I, 872-877; and B. Becking, *DDD*, 1678ff.). In Hebr. as well the word underwent development, but here the combination of the 2 words as also the context prompt the suspicion that only a 'virgin' can be intended. The relation between the substantives in the combination is that of *genus* to *species,* the special following the general (cf. Cf. Ges-K §131b; Burney; differently, Ewald §287e). עמד לפני here and elsewhere (Deut. 10:8; 1 Sam. 16:22; 2 Kgs. 5:16, etc.) means 'wait on,' i.e. 'take care of,' though it can also simply mean 'to position oneself before' (so 2 Kgs. 5:15). This brings with it that the word סבנת, which only occurs in the fem. form in our pericope, must mean something other than 'nurse' or 'attendant' as one finds it in most translations. In an extensive inquiry into the meaning of this word which we undertook some time ago and to which we refer here (see *VT* 22 [1972], 43-54) we believed we were able to demonstrate that the word had to mean 'agent,' or 'deputy' (see now also O. Loretz, *ZAW* 94 [1982], 126f.). In certain ways the girl had to take the place of the old queen, especially in those matters in which Bathsheba no longer had the resources to meet the demands made on a queen at that time. The young woman had to be beautiful, pure, and fertile, while at the same time she was going to occupy a high position at the court (cf. A.A. Wieder, *BIJS* 2 [1974], 103ff.). In addition, both with a view to the well-being of the kingdom (see the sequel) and with an eye to the geriatric complaint of the king, his chronic coldness (cf. Josephus, *Ant.* VII §343, who in this connection refers to *medical* advice to David), she was to share the king's bed: ושכבה בחיקך (cf. G. André, *TWAT*, II, 912-915).

Though up until now the king had been addressed in the third person, now the suffix, 2 masc. sing. is used with חיק. Incongruency or change in person or number occurs more frequently in the case of sentences with אדני (cf. Gen. 23:6a; 43:20; 44:9 etc.; König §344i). The expression 'lying' or 'sleeping' in the king's 'bosom,' despite its obvious purposes, has a somewhat euphemistic, endearing sound. This is how the little ewe lamb sleeps in the 'bosom' of its owner (2 Sam. 12:3), how the living and the dead baby were laid in the 'bosom,' or at the breast, of the (other) mother (1 Kgs. 3:20), and the beloved wife is sometimes described as 'she who lies in your bosom' (Mic. 7:5; cf. Deut. 28:54, 56: the 'woman he embraces' or 'the man she embraces'). The author describes the king in terms both of endearing and of decrepit old age.

This atmosphere of almost disarming innocence is even fortified – though the reader of course suspects there is more to it – by the conclusion: 'this will keep my lord the king warm.' But is this really a strictly private matter without any consequences for the country and the nation?

1:3 *So they searched for a beautiful girl throughout all the territory of Israel, and found Abishag the Shunammite, who was brought to the king.*
We are not told whether the king gave a positive reply, but we learn that his servants do begin the search for a girl. This may have prompted the opinion of some who say that in the previous verse the servants were talking among themselves, not to the king (cf. לו). But this is not correct: the rest of the story indicates that the court was acting in accordance with a specific traditional Canaanite custom (see after vs. 4).

גבול means 'boundary' as well as 'a bounded territory' (M. Ottosson, *TWAT*, I, 896-901). Although the word occurs frequently in the pentateuch, Joshua, and Ezekiel, it is used rarely in Kings (1 Kgs. 5:1; 2 Kgs. 3:21; 10:32; 14:25; 15:16; 18:8). In Samuel (1 Sam. 5:6; 6:12; 7:14; etc.) the word occurs with greater frequency, sometimes in connection with a search action in the entire territory of Israel (cf. 1 Sam. 11:3; 7; 27:1). The expression indicates that the stated problem extends to the boundaries of Israel. The description of the purpose of the search has changed a little: instead of looking for 'a young woman of marriageable age' (נערה בתולה) they are now searching for 'a beautiful girl' (נערה יפה) but practically this does not make any difference of course.[1] At last they find (no mention is made of the way in which the search was conducted, but it does not matter in the story) Abishag, the Shunammite. After David this is the second proper name mentioned at the beginning of the book. In the OT only one woman bears this name (again in 1 Kgs. 1:15; 2:17, 21f.). Only a few MSS of LXX deviate both from MT and somewhat from each other in the manner of writing the name (A: Ἀβισαγ; B: Ἀβεισα; Luc: Ἀβισακ, etc.) while Josephus (*Ant.* VII §344; VIII §§5, 8f.) prefers Ἀβισάκη. Noth, *IPN*, 15, 234, considers the meaning of the name as a

---

[1] According to W. Schottroff, "Der Zugriff des Königs auf die Töchter," *EvTh* 49 (1989), 268-285, Abishag should probably be understood as one of the unmarried daughters referred to in 1 Sam. 8:13; see also M. Häusl, *Abishag und Batsheba: Frauen am Königshof und die Thronfolge Davids im Zeugnis der Texte 1 Kön 1 und 2* (Arbeiten zu Text und Sprache im Alten Testament 41), St. Ottilien 1993.

'Satzname,' the first element of which describes a relation to a male relative but whose second element cannot be easily explained (?? שוג, ישׁי). E.S. Hartom, *EncMiqr.* I, 33, s.v., suspects the root is שׂגא, 'to be great,' so that the meaning of the name would be 'My father (i.e. my God) is great.'

The woman is called a 'Shunammite.' The clan name refers to Abishag's place of origin. Shumem (Josh. 19:18; 1 Sam. 28:4; 2 Kgs. 4:8) was situated in the tribal territory of Issachar, in the valley of Jezreel about 5 km E of present-day Afula and about 15 km SSE of Nazareth. The place is already mentioned on a list of pharaoh Tuthmose III (*ANET*, 243) and the name also occurs in the El Amarna literature (*ANET*, 485). Eusebius mentions the place in his *Onomasticon* (ed. E. Klostermann, 158, 11f.) and, aside from indicating its location in Issachar, informs us that in his days Shunem was called Shulem and lay 5 miles to the south of Mount Tabor. Although the identification of Shunem with Shulam is still current on most maps of Israel (cf. also Alt, *KS*, III, 169ff.) and in the exegetical literature from ancient times the Shulammite (Cant. 6:13; cf. LXX a.l.) was frequently equated with the girl mentioned in our pericope, particularly this last-mentioned identification is problematic.[2] Admittedly, examples of a transposition of /l/ and /n/ in the Semitic languages can be demonstrated (cf. J.A. Montgomery, *JAOS* 43 (1923), 50f.: H.H. Rowley, *AJSL* 56 (1939), 84ff.). Some ancient versions as well indicate a transposition of consonants. LXX^A: Σουμανιτιν; LXX^B: Σωμανειτιν; Pesh.: *šilomāytā*.

Abishag was brought to the king. That is saying more than that she was brought to his palace. The phrasing implies that she was brought into a sexual relation to the king (cf. Judg. 12:9).

1:4 *Now the girl was exceptionally beautiful, and became the king's deputy and served him, but the king did not have intercourse with her ...*
At the end of the overture of the story of David's age and succession the whole focus is on the beautiful young girl, in order all the more starkly to highlight the impotence of the old king and so to effect the transition to what follows. The girl is now described as 'exceptionally beautiful' (though BT Sanhedrin 39b does not consider her as beautiful as Sara, of whom in Gen. 12:14 it is said יפה הוא מאד, an 'inclusive' addition), a fact which can also be conveyed by phrases like יפת־מראה (Gen. 12:11) or יפת־תאר (Gen. 29:17) (cf. Ges-K §128x). Some ancient versions translate as though these last phrases occurred in their 'Vorlage' (so LXX^Luc. and a number of more recent MSS; Pesh.; except 9 al *fam*), and they are materially correct. As for her appearance, the girl is

---

[2] Cf. A. Robert, R. Tournay, A. Feuillet, *Le Cantique des Cantiques* (Études Bibliques), Paris 1963, a.l.

exceptionally attractive; she is a 'deputy administrator' who meets the demands (vs. 2); finally, she is at the service of the king in everything. She apparently combines external beauty with good inner and mental attributes. In distinction from vs. 2 it is no longer the words עמד לפני and שכב בחיק that are used before and after סבנת but שרת pi., 'to serve' (according to F. Perles, *OLZ* 22 [1919], 111f., derived as loan-word from the Akkad. *šarrūtu*, 'kingship'). The משרת, in distinction from the עֶבֶד, 'servant,' is the staff member with a serving task.³ The concept עבד is broader and can be used for persons from high to low (cf. Riesener, *Der Stamm* עבד; H. Ringgren, U. Rütersworden, H. Simian-Yofre, *TWAT*, V, 982-1012). In LXX שרת is rendered by λειτουργεῖν in a non-cultic context (cf. H. Strathmann, *TDNT*, IV, 219). שרת is approximately the same as עמד לפני but it also includes the שכב בחיק. In LXX^Luc. למלך סבנת is rendered by τῷ βασιλει συγκοιτος. Although this cannot be the correct translation of MT (see above, vs. 2), it does reproduce the essential meaning of this part. Abishag shared the king's table and bed. Josephus, too, clearly brings out this aspect in his account (*Ant.* VII, §344): she slept with the king in one bed and kept him warm. His words are a little too colorless, however, when he construes the end of our verse by saying that on account of his advanced age he was too weak to experience sexual pleasure or to have sexual intercourse with the woman. Of course, in the general plan of the story this is correct, but the words והמלך לא ידעה are not only the anticlimactic description of the Abishag-David relation but also the introduction to the drama which follows.

---

³ For an analysis of the two words, see L.A. Snijders, *NedThT*, 6 (1961), 344-360; N.N. Reeves Jr., שר- *in the Pre-Christian Hebrew Literature*, Diss. Univ. of Southern California, 1969.

1 KINGS 1:5-53

1:5 *Now Adonijah, the son of Haggith, was feeling ambitious and said: 'I will be king.' He provided himself with a chariot, and horsemen, and fifty men to run before him.*

6 *At no time in his life had his father ever corrected him by saying: 'Why are you behaving like that?' Add to this that he was extremely handsome! To him (his mother) had given birth after Absalom.*

7 *He discussed his plans with Joab, the son of Zeruiah, and with Abiathar the priest, so that they offered their support and rallied to his cause.*

8 *But neither Zadok the priest, nor Benaiah, the son of Jehoiada, nor the prophet Nathan, nor Shimei and Rei, nor David's champions joined Adonijah.*

9 *Then Adonijah sacrificed sheep, oxen, and fatted cattle at 'Snake Rock' by the spring of Rogel, and invited all his brothers, the king's sons, and from among all the (distinguished) men of Judah the king's servants.*

10 *But he had not invited Nathan the prophet, or Benaiah, or the champions, or Solomon his brother.*

11 *Then Nathan said to Bathsheba, Solomon's mother: 'Have you not heard that Adonijah son of Haggith has become king and our lord David does not know it?*

12 *Now, then, let me give you good advice, so that you may save your life and the life of your son Solomon.*

13 *Go and enter with king David and say to him: "My lord the king, did you not swear to me your servant: Surely Solomon your son will be king after me and* he *will sit on my throne but why then is Adonijah king?"*

14 *Then, while you are still speaking with the king, I will come in after you and complete your story.'*

15 *So Bathsheba went to see the king in his room. Now the king was very old and Abishag the Shunammite was attending him.*

16 *Bathsheba knelt and bowed down before the king, and the king said: 'What do you want?'*

17 *She said to him: 'My lord, you swore by YHWH your God to your servant saying: "Surely, Solomon your son will be king after me, and* he *will sit on my throne."*

18 *But now look, Adonijah has become king and you my lord the king do not know about it.*

19 *He has made a sacrifice of oxen, fatted cattle, and sheep in great quantities and invited all the king's sons, the priest Abiathar and Joab the commander of the army, but he has not invited your servant Solomon.*

20 *As for you, my lord the king, the eyes of all Israel are on you to tell them* *who will sit on the throne of my lord the king after him.*

21 *I fear that when my lord the king is laid to rest with his fathers, I and my son Solomon will be the losers.'*

22 *While she was still speaking with the king, look, Nathan the prophet came in.*

23 *They told the king: 'Nathan the prophet is here.' When he came in before the king he bowed down before the king with his face to the ground.*

24 *Then Nathan said: 'My lord the king, have you said: "Adonijah shall be king after me and he shall sit on my throne?"*

25 *For today he has gone down and has made a sacrifice of oxen, fatted cattle, and sheep in great quantities. He has invited all the kings' sons, the commanders of the army, and the priest Abiathar. Right now they are eating and drinking with him and shouting: "Long live king Adonijah."*

26 *But me, your servant, Zadok the priest, Benaiah son of Jehoiada, or your servant Solomon, us he has not invited.*

27 *Can it be that this thing was brought about by my lord the king and that you have not told our servants who would sit on the throne of my lord the king after him?'*

28 *Then King David answered and said: 'Ask Bathsheba to come in' and she came into the king's presence and stood before him.*

29 *The king swore this oath: 'As YHWH lives, who has delivered me from all adversity,*

30 *just as I swore to you by YHWH, the God of Israel: "Surely Solomon your son will be king after me and will sit on my throne in my place," so I swear I will bring it about this day.'*

31 *Then Bathsheba knelt with her face to the ground and, bowing down before the king, said: 'May king David live yet for a very long time.'*

32 *Then king David spoke up: 'Call in Zadok the priest, Nathan the prophet and Benaiah the son of Jehoiada.' When they came in before the king,*

33 *the king said to them: 'Take with you the servants of your lord and have my son Solomon ride on my own mule, and bring him down to (the spring) Gihon.*

34 *There let the priest Zadok and the prophet Nathan anoint him king over Israel. Blow the trumpet and shout "Long live king Solomon!"*

35 *Then you are to go up with him and he is to come in and sit on my throne. He will be king in my place, for he is the one I have appointed to be ruler over Israel and over Judah.'*

36 *Benaiah, the son of Jehoiada, answered the king and said: 'Amen! May YHWH, the God of my lord the king, speak thus as well.*

37 *As YHWH has been with my lord the king, so may he be with Solomon; indeed, may he make his throne greater than the throne of my lord king David.'*

38 *Then Zadok the priest, Nathan the prophet and Benaiah the son of Jehoiada, along with the Cherethites and the Pelethites, went down and had Solomon ride on king David's mule and brought him to (the spring) Gihon.*

39 *There the priest Zadok took the horn of oil from the tent and anointed Solomon. Then they sounded the ram's horn and all the people shouted: 'Long live king Solomon!'*

40 *And all he people went up after him, playing flutes and shouting for joy, so that the ground split by their sound.*

41 *Then Adonijah and all the guests who were with him and had finished eating heard it. But Joab heard the sound of the ram's horn and asked: 'Why is the city in an uproar?'*

42 *While he was still speaking, Jonathan the son of Abiathar the priest came in. Adonijah said: 'Come on in, you are a reliable fellow and surely you bring good news.'*

43 *Jonathan answered and said to Adonijah: 'You bet ...! Our king David has made Solomon king.*

44 *The king sent with him the priest Zadok, the prophet Nathan, and Benaiah the son of Jehoiada, as well as the Cherithites and the Pelethites and they had him ride on the king's mule.*

45 *Then the priest Zadok and the prophet Nathan anointed him king at (the spring) Gihon, and from there they went up shouting for joy so that the city is in an uproar. That is the noise you heard.*

46 *And Solomon also sits on the throne of the kingdom.*

47 *Also, the king's servants have come to congratulate king David with the words: "May your God make the name of Solomon more glorious than yours and his throne greater than yours." At this the king bowed down upon his bed.*

48 *And the king also said as follows: "Praise be to YHWH, the God of Israel, who today has granted someone to sit on my throne and permitted me to witness it".'*

49 *At this, all Adonijah's guests got up trembling and everyone went his way.*

50 *Adonijah, too, was afraid of Solomon. He got up and went to grasp the horns of the altar.*

51 *It was reported to Solomon: 'Look, Adonijah is afraid of king Solomon; in fact, he is clinging to the horns of the altar, saying, "Let king Solomon first swear to me that he will not put his servant to death with the sword".'*

52 *Then Solomon said: 'If he is really a reliable fellow, then not one of his hairs will fall to the ground; but if disloyalty is found in him he will die.'*

53 *Then king Solomon sent (messengers) to have him brought down from the altar. He came and bowed down before king Solomon. And Solomon said: 'Go to your home.'*

1 KINGS 1:5-53

INTRODUCTION

The rest of chap. one (vss. 5-53) offers a classic description of a court intrigue, that is to say: the style is lively, the story is fascinating, the scenes are clear. Any effort of the commentator to clarify the story threatens to obscure it, even though for a modern reader the distance in time and place, as well as the actions whose motivation is so different, require some explanation. This and the next chapter, as well as the entire narrative of the 'Thronnachfolge', betray the masterful hand of the author whose work may rightly be counted among the greatest classics of all times.

According to ancient Canaanite ideas, the impotent and decrepit old king is a threat to the nation's existence. It is not surprising, therefore, that Adonijah who was viewed by many as *the* successor of David rose up and prepared himself for kingship. He was supported in this undertaking by an 'upper ten' which had not for a moment considered supporting Absalom in his day. We are masterfully shown how the projected 'coup d'état,' which seemed such a sure thing, was frustrated in favour of Solomon by the ingenious game played by Nathan and supported by Bathsheba and the head of the Zadokite priesthood. Noth correctly comments that everything is 'sehr weltlich-menschlich geschildert' (p. 39). The narrator nowhere states that YHWH brought about the Davidic succession. But in this chapter even Solomon himself, like the senile David, remains a figure in the background. The antagonists seem to be especially the vain Adonijah and the crafty court prophet Nathan, each with his own group of supporters. It is a fine specimen of narrative technique, in which a once-given promise concerning Solomon is the apple of discord thrown into the midst of the circle, both for the listener of long ago as well as for the scholarly investigator now ...

For a discussion of the 'layeredness' of our narrative, currently frequently defended, we refer to Introd. §6 and to the detailed discussion of the text which follows.

EXEGESIS

1:5 *Now Adonijah, the son of Haggith, was feeling ambitious and said: 'I will be king.' He provided himself with a chariot, and horsemen, and fifty men to run before him.*

According to 2 Sam. 3:4 (1 Chr. 3:2), Adonijah the son of Haggith is David's 4th son born at Hebron. David's first-born Amnon the son of Ahinoam, and Absalom the son of Maacah, the third, had already died (2 Sam. 13 and 18). Of Chileab, David's second son, whom he had by Abigail, Nabal's former wife (1 Sam. 25), nothing is known. In the parallel verse 1 Chr. 3:1 his name is listed, however, as *Daniel* (cf. also the ancient versions). It is possible that this son died at a very young age. Of Haggith, Adonijah's mother, nothing is known either. According to Noth, *IPN*, 222, her name means something like 'born on a feast day (חג).' To describe a prince whose father possessed a harem the name of the mother is frequently mentioned (2 Sam. 3:2-5; 1 Kgs. 2:13; 14:31 etc.; C. Kühne, *UF* 5 [1973], 180).

The name Adonijah is spelled 2 ways: אדניה and אדניהו; the latter spelling occurs most often and exclusively in Kings. אדון is a theophoric element which frequently occurs in personal names in Western Sem. languages (Noth, *IPN* 114) and as such is also widespread in Israel (pp. 117f.). The meaning of the longer form of the name is possibly 'YHWH is Lord,' but originally the word 'Lord' was presumably the appellative of a Canaanite deity whose name in antiquity was widely known as Adonis (cf. K. Spronk, *DDD*, 994-998). In place of 'Αδωνείας, LXX[Luc.] reads Ορνια, as LXX has in 2 Sam. 3:4, which assumes ארניה as 'Vorlage' (Rahlfs, *Sst.* III, 183; for a possible explanation of these and similar deviations of LXX[Luc.], see 184ff.). We see no reason to diverge here from MT (as, e.g., Stade-Schwally do here).

The part. hitp. masc. sing. of נשא has a durative aspect (Joüon §121f), is stronger than a niph. (Ewald §124a) and functions as predicate in a nominal sentence (Ges-K, §116o). The temporal aspect of the verb in our sentence is determined by the context. The part. is followed by an impf. cons. (Bg. II, §13f), so that it can be taken as an indication of an act or state of Adonijah which manifested itself in specific momentary achievements: directly in an idea, in the long run in the acquisition of status symbols. נשא, which occurs approx. 600x in qal-forms and is found repeatedly in other Semitic languages as well ('to raise, to raise up' etc.), occurs some 10x in the hitp. (Num. 16:3; 23:24; 24:7; Ezek. 17:14; 29:15; Prov. 30:32; Dan. 11:14; 1 Chr. 29:11; 2 Chr. 32:23) in the sense of 'elevating oneself,' 'rising up against,' 'being exalted,' in connection with which the intended nuance of meaning definitely need not be unfavourable. Neither are we required here to immediately attach an unfavourable shade of meaning to the word. Adonijah wished to make a career for himself and expected on good grounds to be able to bring it off. After all, following the death of Absalom, he was expected to become king. But even if initially the idea of 'elevating himself' was legitimate, the immediately following statement 'I will be king,' with the emphasis on the personal pronoun 'I,' which is demonstratively put at the beginning of the sentence, is a hint that the author does not wish to absolve Adonijah from egoistic motives in this ambition (cf. H. Grotius, who advances examples from the classics of sons who could not wait for their father's death to become king). The stereotypical לאמר (inf. cstr. of אמר) 'namely' or merely a colon, can perhaps mean 'thinking' here, a meaning of אמר which occurs more frequently in OT (Gen. 17:17 etc.). For the rest the use of לאמר in OT is quite differentiated (cf. S. Wagner,

TWAT, I, 359f.). On the other hand, as is evident from what follows, the possibility exists that Adonijah frequently *spoke* about his future kingship with his friends and in his social circle. In his words but also in his conduct he assumed the status of a future king.

He 'prepared for himself' or 'had others prepare for him' רכב ופרשים, words which occur repeatedly in conjunction (e.g. 1 Kgs. 10:26; 1 Chr. 19:6; 2 Chr. 1:14; cf. Exod. 14:28; 1 Kgs. 9:19 etc.), and are translated by 'chariots and horsemen' by LXX, the Vulg., and many other versions. פרש can, however, be 'horseman' (1 Sam. 13:5; 2 Sam. 8:4, etc.) as well as 'riding horse' (Ezek. 27:14; Joel 2:4 etc.). Galling, *BRL*[1], 426, is of the opinion that the word, certainly when it is linked with רכב ('chariot'), must be taken to mean 'team' and not 'horsemen.' The preference for 'a team of horses' over 'horsemen' is based in part on the consideration that before the 8th century there were hardly any 'cavalry' and hence 'horsemen' in Israel (*ibid.*, 425). But among surrounding nations like Egypt (cf. Löhr, *OLZ* 31 [1928], 923-928) and Mesopotamia (see further H. Weippert, *BRL*[2], 250-255) horses and horsemen were known long before that date, and in an Aram. inscription (the so-called Zakir-inscription, early 8th century, *KAI* 202B,2; *ANET*, 501f.), פרש is mentioned next to רכב as well.

The 'fifty men who run before him' are members of the bodyguard (cf. 1 Sam. 22:17; 2 Sam. 15:1; 1 Kgs. 14:27f. etc.). In 2 Sam. 15:1 the same is said in connection with Absalom.[1] The number fifty is not arbitrary; cf. e.g. in Kings 1 Kgs. 18:4, 13; 2 Kgs. 1:9, 11; 2:16f. etc. The part. pass. qal of חמש means 'arrayed (for battle) in 5 sections' (Ex. 13:18; Josh. 1:14; 4:12; Judg. 7:11); apart from a central core, there was a vanguard, a rear guard, and 2 flanks. An officer commanding such a detachment was called שַׂר־חֲמִשִּׁים (e.g. Isa. 3:3).

By instituting such a royal bodyguard, Adonijah, like his brother Absalom, was arrogating something to which he was not entitled (Cf. Benzinger, *Arch.* 161; and Rashi referring to BT Sanhedrin 21b).

1:6 *At no time in his life had his father ever corrected him by saying: 'Why are you behaving like that?' Add to this that he was extremely handsome! To him (his mother) had given birth after Absalom.*
One reason for Adonijah's arrogant behavior lay, in the first place, in the attitude of his father: ולא־עצבו אביו. The verb עצב II can describe a physical (Eccl. 10:9) as well as a mental (Isa. 54:6) form of injury (Burney). Here it has

---

[1] See now also G.R. Stone, "Running at the Wheel," *Buried History* 26 (1990), 244-248: the runners accompanying the chariots of David's sons Absolom and Adoniah represented a claim to their father's throne.

the meaning of 'troubling' or 'tormenting' in a mental sense. The LXX reads ἀπεκώλυσεν, from ἀποκωλύειν, 'to restrain,' which has prompted some to assume that the LXX read עצר in the 'Vorlage.' But this is not very likely. LXX^{Luc.} reads ἐπετίμησεν, from ἐπιτιμᾶν, 'to reprimand,' a translation of נער which is not unusual in LXX (e.g., Gen. 37:10; Ruth 2:16 etc.). Materially this reading is also close to our MT. Also, 'to restrain' would be in conflict with the following statement as to why Adonijah had done 'thus or so' (cf. G.R. Driver, *JBL* 55 [1936], 115f. for a possible Arab. background for עצר). Along with LXX^{Luc.}, also the Vulg., Tg. and Pesh. materially support MT which therefore need not be altered. מימיו in this form, occurring only here, by the use of the מן-partitive (Ges-K §119w; cf. König §81) does indicate a certain period (cf. BrSynt. §111e), but then one of longer duration (cf. also Segal §297). David's lenience toward his son is underscored by a vague but telling time designation (Noth; Burney, among others, opts for an 'indefinite period'). The particle מדוע (approx. 70x), in distinction from the reproachful למה, usually introduces questions asking for information.[2] The interrogative sentence is asyndetically linked to this particle (cf. BrSynt. §133d; König §412: 'ein im semitischen Casus adverbialis, d.h. im. Acc. gedachtes Äquivalent von *quo cognito*'). כָּכָה (in Hebr. a stressed long /ā/ > ô; an unstressed /a/ or one with a secondary stress remains unchanged; cf. Br. *VG*, I, 142) is a doubling of *ka* = *kô* and occurs approx. 35x in OT. The little word seems to reinforce כה (Joüon §102h), but this can be described, with König §318b, as a more recent form which intensifies the fading meaning of כה.

A second reason for Adonijah's arrogance, for which his father David was not responsible, nor attributable to himself but which did contribute to his rebellion, were his exceptional good looks. The וגם, when placed up front, adds another argument to the preceding: 'moreover' (Ewald §352b; cf. F. Langlamet, *RB* 83 [1976], 482f.). But one who knows the whole story of David's sons is aware that such exceptional good looks had already played a negative role in the life of a son before, viz. in the case of Absalom who in 2 Sam. 14:25 is praised for his exceptional beauty (cf. Ehrlich), though the word תאר is not mentioned here. The word occurs 15x in OT and is used in an esthetic sense not only of people but, for example, of cattle as well (Gen. 41:18f.). There is disagreement over whether the word comes from ראה (so, among others, Ges-B, Montg.-Gehman) or from תאר (Zorell, *BDB*), 'to twist.' Grounds can be cited for both possibilities, so that we will refrain from taking a position on this point. The emphasis here falls on Adonijah's exceptionally fine figure. A (future) king is identifiable among the people by his figure (cf.

---

[2] A. Jepsen, in *Das ferne und nahe Wort* (Fs L. Rost; BZAW 105), Berlin 1967, 106-113; W. Schotroff, *THAT*, I, 685.

e.g. Judg. 8:18). The word יפה, though used in vss. 3f. and of Absalom and already of Joseph (Gen. 39:6) and Rachel (Gen. 29:17, in both cases with תאר) is lacking here and 'replaced' by טוב, meaning 'good,' 'fitting.' The idea is not so much the beauty as such, therefore, but the goal which can be attained by means of a very good figure, one that befits a king.

The verse ends with the statement that he 'had been borne' after Absalom. In vs. 5 we had already been told that Haggith had given birth to him. Here we find the impersonal fem. ילדה, which occurs also in Num. 26:59 and 1 Chr. 7:14 (Böttcher §935; Ewald §294b). The subject is omitted (Joüon §155e) and Haggith cannot grammatically be viewed as such (versus König §324f; Stade-Schwally a.o.). LXX$^{Luc.}$ reads ἐγέννησε as though its 'Vorlage' read הוליד, but in view of the other ancient versions this reading cannot be preferred. Montg.-Gehman, along with others, read ילד, a 3 p. masc. sing., therefore, in the sense of 'procreation' (cf. Ps. 2:7), but this is not necessary either. Perhaps it is best, with Burney, to speak of 'a semi-impersonal use of the verb.'

The structure of this short sentence puts the accent on 'him,' i.e. Adonijah who was born next *after* Absalom, and could therefore make claims to the succession. This is evident from the prominence given to the object אתו (Driver §208, 1). Absalom, as is well known, played the main role in an earlier palace revolution (2 Sam. 13-19). In this 'subsequent history' in 1 Kings his name, besides here, occurs only still in passing in 2:7 and 28. Ehrlich goes too far when, based on the first half of this verse, he states that David had designated Adonijah as his successor. What is implicitly conceded in this verse is that Adonijah's succession to the throne was in line with the people's expectation in general.

1:7 *He discussed his plans with Joab, the son of Zeruiah, and with Abiathar the priest, so that they offered their support and rallied to his cause.*
This verse marks a new stage on the road to Adonijah's kingship: the process of gaining the support of powerful and influential persons in Israelite society. 'His words were with' is reminiscent of Abner's negotiations with the elders of Israel concerning David's kingship (2 Sam. 3:17; cf. K.-H. Bernhardt, *TWAT*, II, 405). These 'negotiations' or 'dealings' need not per se have been malicious (cf. Judg. 18:7), though it must be admitted that what follows clearly suggests a conspiracy. The 2 prominent men with whom Adonijah is taking his chances are Joab, the son of Zeruiah and the priest Abiathar. Joab is the (oldest?) son of Zeruiah (2 Sam. 2:18), who in turn is mentioned in 1 Chr. 2:16, along with Abigail, as David's sister. But in 2 Sam. 17:25 Abigail, though Zeruiah's sister, is the daughter of Nahas. On this basis there is some reason for doubting whether Joab was in fact David's (full) nephew. Zeruiah may have become a half sister of David after her mother (cf. however, Driver, *Samuel*, 326) married Jesse. It has also been thought that Zeruiah was a clan name later

interpreted as a woman's name (see *BW*, s.v.), but this is probably going too far. In the war stories of David Joab himself plays, if not always a starring role, at least a striking one. In Absalom's rebellion he was unconditionally on David's side and, against the express will of the king, killed the unfortunate rebel. This time he will react differently.

Abiathar the priest, similarly a faithful adherent to David, was the only priest who escaped Saul's bloodbath at Nod and, taking the so-called 'ephod' with him, chose the side of David (1 Sam. 22:20-23; 23:6; 30:7). A son of Ahimelech and of the family of Ithamar, he was David's 'personal priest' but later had to share this position with Zadok (2 Sam. 8:17; cf. 15:24-36; 20:25). This Zadok is virtually without genealogy,³ which has led to the assumption that he was at one time a member of the Canaanite priesthood in Jerusalem. As a result of this, despite the 'collaboration' of the 2 priests, tensions are said to have arisen between them which emerge more clearly later on in this story (cf. e.g. Ringgren, *IsrRel.* 210f., R. Meyer, *TDNT*, VII, 35-54 on the Sadducees). However this be, Joab and Abiathar decided to help Adonijah in the realization of his plans. Perhaps the pl. דברי (in contrast to 2 Sam. 3:17 where the sing. is used) suggests that Adonijah had to use considerable pressure. The expression ויעזרו אחרי indicates they were prepared to help him by taking his side (cf. Benzinger who mentions as a second possibility a reciprocal niph.: יעזרו. This is not necessary; cf. LXX^Luc.; αντελαμβανοντο αυτου). In 1 Chr. 12:22 עזר עם is used, which denotes a certain simultaneity or equivalence. In any case the narrator hints that the 2 old allies of David believe that by joining Adonijah they are on the right, i.e. the legitimate, road.

1:8 *But neither Zadok the priest, nor Benaiah, the son of Jehoiada, nor the prophet Nathan, nor Shimei and Rei, nor David's champions joined Adonijah.*
Other 'citizens,' however, dissociate themselves from this party formation. This does not mean that they immediately or upon further reflection saw something illegitimate in Adonijah's endeavor. Their not joining may have been based on, say, personal considerations. This is perhaps especially true for Zadok, the other priest, who was not only Abiathar's colleague but also his rival. About him we already said a few things in the previous verse. Later, after Abiathar's fall under Solomon, he became the only recognized priestly leader and eponym of the priestly family of Zadokites (Ezek. 40:46; 44:15f.; 48:11; cf. R.W. Corney, *IDB*, IV, 928f.; M.D. Rehm, *IDBS*, 976f.). In place of Σαδὼκ LXX^Luc. here and later reads Σαδδουκ and instead of Ἰωδαε for יהוידע: ιωαδ. This Zadok is the father of Benaiah who in the past had frequently distinguished himself by his heroic deeds (2 Sam. 23:20-23; 1 Chr. 11:22-25) and was said

---

³ See also M.D. Goulder, *Psalms of the Sons of Korah* (JSOTSup 20), Sheffield 1982, 66-71.

to come from Kabzeel, a place in the south of Judah. He was in charge of the royal bodyguard, the Cherethites and the Pelethites (2 Sam. 8:18; 20:23; 23:23; 1 Chr. 18:17). Nathan is a court prophet who, aside from this episode, twice before made his appearance at decisive moments in the stories around David, viz. on the occasion of the promises concerning the Davidic dynasty (2 Sam. 7:1-17) and in connection with David's adultery with Bathsheba (2 Sam. 12:1-15). In 2 Sam. 12:25 we are told that Nathan contributed to the namegiving of Solomon, Jedidiah. In Chronicles there is reference to a history of David by Nathan (1 Chr. 29:29) and to a history of Solomon (2 Chr. 9:29), while a role in the development of the music of the temple is attributed to him as well (2 Chr. 29:25).

The following names are Shimei and Rei. As to who this Shimei is, is not known. Sometimes he is identified with Solomon's governor in Benjamin referred to in 1 Kgs. 4:18 but this is most uncertain (cf. T.M. Mauch, *IDB*, IV, 331). Rei is almost even less known, because he is mentioned nowhere else in the OT. LXX here reads Σεμεεὶ and ʽΡησεὶ but LXX$^{Luc.}$ has Σαμαιας και οι εταιροι αυτον, a reading which is supported by Josephus (*Ant.* VII §346; see Delitzsch, *LSF* §8b): Σιμούεις ὁ Δαυίδου φίλος. This may create the impression that instead of רעי we should perhaps read רעיו, 'and his friends' (or sing., see Ehrlich, who mentions Hushai [2 Sam. 15:37; 16:16]). Klostermann, taking a further step, reads Solomon instead of Shimei. This last proposal is totally without support and does not deserve to be followed, anymore than the older suggestion (taken over by Ehrlich) of Thenius, who, following Josephus, wants to read 'and Chusai, the friend of David.' In view of the other ancient versions it does not seem warranted to diverge from MT. We consider Shimei and Rei courtiers whom we cannot identify any further.

David's 'champions' are listed elsewhere as well: 2 Sam. 10:7; 16:6; 20:7; 1 Chr. 19:8; 28:1; 29:24; Cant. 4:4. In 2 Sam. 23:8-39 (// 1 Chr. 11:11-47) the most important are mentioned by name (cf. B. Mazar, *VT* 13 [1963], 310-320). The word גבור, an intensive form (cf. BL §479j), denotes a particularly strong person and becomes an honorary title for 'a member of David's elite corps'(cf. H. Kosmala, *TWAT*, I, 909-11). In the interest of avoiding the st. cstr., especially in the case of proper names, one finds here the construction of ל + אשר (cf. Burney). Now of all these men it is stated that they did not join Adonijah. LXX and Pesh. translate עם as if their 'Vorlage' had אחרי. Some Hebr. MSS confirm this possibility. LXX$^{Luc.}$, however, reads μετά. There is, accordingly, no reason whatever to alter the text here. The conclusion of vs. 7 may perhaps have prompted this reading (Thenius).

1:9 *Then Adonijah sacrificed sheep, oxen, and fatted cattle at 'Snake Rock' by the spring of Rogel, and invited all his brothers, the king's sons, and from among all the (distinguished) men of Judah the king's servants.*

After recording the existence of the 2 parties, the author relates what Adonijah starts to do to execute his plans. To that end he first of all prepares a (sacrificial) meal at a precisely indicated location. זבח, which occurs frequently in OT (cf. J. Bergman, H. Ringgren, B. Lang, *TWAT*, II, 509-531) usually has the concrete meaning of 'slaughter,' 'sacrifice'(cf. also C. Westermann, *THAT*, I, 680). But this 'slaughter' was not performed 'neutrally' but 'ritually,' and the meal was not 'a common meal' but in many cases a cultic or ritual ceremony. Originally a small group of people performed a private sacrifice on special occasions, such as a thankoffering, an offering for a firstborn, etc., to which a meal was joined. One finds an extensive festival ritual in 1 Sam. 1 and 2 which may also be assumed on other occasions, such as is mentioned here (cf. for festivals in whose context a king was acclaimed: 1 Sam. 11:15; cf. 9:12f.; 16:3, 5; 2 Sam. 15:12 etc.). The 'material' for this festive slaughter is small stock, oxen, and fatted cattle[4]. מריא, which occurs also in Ugar. (Gordon, *UT*, 1544) and Akkad., according to 2 Sam.6:13 as well as what follows (1 Kgs. 1:19, 25; cf. further Isa. 1:11; 11:6; Ezek. 39:18 and Am. 5:22) is a reference to fat healthy animals for slaughter, a reference which frequently served to highlight a sacrificial meal. Because they are here (cf. vss. 19, 25) distinguished from oxen as well as from small stock one can best take the word to refer to 'other prime quality animals of slaughter' (cf. Vulg.: *immolatis ... universis pinguibus*; LXX, which is less precise). The place of slaughter is אבן הזחלת, located next to the spring of Rogel. זחלת can be derived from the verb זחל I (*HAL*, s.v.) which means 'to crawl' (said of a snake): Deut. 32:24; Mic. 7:17. In addition some have thought they could establish another זחל II (cf. GB, *HAL*, s.v.) 'to fear,' 'to be afraid' (Job 32:6). Often, however, the word is derived from the first-mentioned stem so that the reference here is to 'a snake rock.' The ancient versions do not help very much: LXX[A]: παρα τον λιθον του ζωελεθ; LXX[B]: μετὰ Αἰθὴ τοῦ Ζωελεθεὶ; LXX[Luc.]: του εν σελλαθ; Vulg. *iuxta lapidem Zoheleth;* Pesh. is even more vague and speaks of a *k'p' rbt'*, 'a large rock.' Josephus (*Ant.* VII §347) simply states that Adonijah prepared a meal 'outside the city by the spring in the royal garden.' Rashi views it as a high rock on which young people tested their powers. Tg. speaks of אבן סכותא, 'the Sakkuth-rock.' Sakkuth, vocalized as סִכּוּת in Am. 5:26, is a Babylonian god sometimes identified with Saturn. This gives us a point of contact with the Arab. Zuhal (Saturn), which Wellhausen associates with our rock .[5] R. Eisler (*OLZ* 16 [1913], 397-402) links up the 'snake rock' and the spring of Rogel

---

[4] Cf. R. Rendtorff, *Studien zur Geschichte des Opfers im Alten Testament* (WMANT 24), Neukirchen-Vluyn 1967, 148f.; 161f.

[5] J. Wellhausen, *Reste Arabischen Heidentums*, Berlin/Leipzig 1927², 146; see on Sakkuth now also M. Stol, *DDD*, 1364f.

with a tradition concerning a 'snake rock' near Kadesh which yielded water (Nu. 20:8, 11). The spring of Rogel is said to derive its name from foot stamping on the rock so that water gushed from it (cf. Rashi, Kimchi). According to the Koran (*surah* 38:42), Job must have done this, hence the name 'Job spring' *(bīr Eyyub)* used today for the old Rogel spring. Sometimes Snake Rock is related to the Snake Spring of Neh. 2:13 (עין התנים; cf. H. Niehr, *TWAT*, VIII, 719f.). In pre-Israelite times a cult for a snake-god is said to have been practiced here (cf., e.g., Kittel, *SHARG*, 178ff.; E.S. Hartom, *EncMiqr.* I, 47; G.A. Barrois, *IDB*, IV, 291: Montg.-Gehman 73f.). This connection is far from sure, however, especially since the word זחלת does not per se have to be translated by 'snake'. G.R. Driver, *ZAW* 52 (1934), 51f. translates it by 'the rolling stone.' Furthermore, the topography of the spring in Neh. 2:13 and in our text does not completely agree (cf. *EncMiqr.* VI, 209). It is possible that הזחלת has to be viewed as an attributive with 'rock' (BrSynt. §60a), not a st.cstr.-combination (see Noth). But this does not help either to give us the precise location of the rock. Vincent, *Jérusalem*, I, 134ff., thought that the entire rocky area between the Gihon and Rogel Spring is denoted by this name. This suggestion has as much value as that of others mentioned above or not mentioned here (cf. Simons, *Jerusalem*, 160f.; see now also J. Briend, *DBS*, X, 691-695). One may indeed assume that the rock by which the cattle were slaughtered was not far removed from the Rogel spring and, in view of the sacrificial meal, was possibly an ancient shrine.

Some attention must be given the prepositions עם and אצל. עם often indicates the place next to which or by which an action was performed (e.g., Gen. 25:11; 35:4 etc.), but אצל also frequently expresses this proximity (Gen. 39:10, 15; Deut. 11:30, etc.). In the one case one could perhaps very well translate 'by' the stone (cf. BrSynt. §§113, 117c) in the other 'next to' the spring.

As noted above, many scholars (cf. also S. Achituv, *EncMiqr.* VI, 212f.) consider the Rogel spring to be the present Job spring south of Jerusalem where the valleys of Kidron and Ben Hinnom merge. In Josh. 15:7; 18:16 this spring marks the boundary between Judah and Benjamin. At this spring Jonathan and Ahimaaz waited for news from the city at the time of the Absalom rebellion (2 Sam. 17:17). In Josh. 15:7 the boundary between the 2 tribes mentioned above is fairly precisely indicated: from En-Shemesh to En-Rogel. Between these 2 there is no other spring. The latter, now called the Job Spring, in earlier times was also called the Joab Spring (cf. Kittel, *SHARG*, 164-169). The spring is about 33 m deep, of which only the lowest part has been hewn out in the rock. Burney, however, identifies it with the modern 'Fountain of the Virgin,' called *'Ain Umm ed-Deraj* which provides the pool of Siloam with water. Tg. and Pesh.: *qṣr'* = 'fuller.' We already referred to the dubious etymology above.

Adonijah invited all his brothers – except of course, Solomon. The reference 'king's sons' or 'princes' feels somewhat redundant. Except for LXX^Luc., these words are therefore omitted in the LXX tradition. It is not easy to tell whether this is an ancient gloss. Remarkable, further, is that, according to many, קרא is here construed with 2 different prepositions, at least if one does not wish – as we, with Noth, do – to translate: 'Adonijah invited his brothers and *from among* (or: as it concerns) the Judean men, the servants of the king' (for this, cf. also Ewald §310a). The verb קרא in fact *can* be construed with 2 prepositions (with ל, e.g., in Gen. 12:18, 20:8f., etc.), and this is how LXX, Vulg., and Pesh. probably understood this. Because of the close kinship between Hebr. and Aram., Tg. could adhere closely to MT. Pesh. and some MSS put an 'and' between 'men of Judah' and 'servants of the king' implying that the invitation was addressed to 3 categories of people. This is superfluous. Sometimes it is assumed that LXX and Vulg. (and Pesh.) must have had ואת־כל etc., instead of לכל־אנשי יהודה in their 'Vorlage' but this is not at all certain, though some MSS support this suspicion (see, e.g., BHS). Noth rightly calls this 'eine Glättung und Erleichterung' (of the problem). On the other hand, from a syntactical point of view, it is not so obvious that the so-called *nota accusativi* have been omitted before עבדי המלך. Noth again perhaps offers a solution here by pointing out that the unusual frontal placing of the 'Zugehörigkeitsbezeichnung' (ל) was conducive to the omission of those *nota accusativi*. It is possible that 'the men of Judah' constitute a group of prominent men. Many MSS of LXX (except LXX^Luc., Hex.) bring this to expression in the words τοὺς ἁδροὺς Ἰούδα. On the other hand, כל suggests that the reference is to *all* Judean men, of whom the servants of David then formed a special group. This is the most plausible assumption.

1:10 *But he had not invited Nathan the prophet, or Benaiah, or the champions, or Solomon his brother.*
It is natural that those who had not joined Adonijah's party did not get an invitation: Nathan, Benaiah, the 'champions' and Adonijah's brother Solomon. In contrast to vs. 8, Zadok, Shimei and Rei are not mentioned here. Nor is Benaiah designated as the son of Jehoiada. However, because of this, and the omission of the *nota accusativi,* we need not – with Ehrlich – delete his name from our verse. Appearing for the first time in this verse is the name of one who is more or less central in all that follows: Solomon. See for the meaning of his name esp. Noth, *IPN*, 165; J. J. Stamm, *ThZ* 16 (1960), 285-297; E. Lohse, *TDNT*, VII, 459-465; and now also the articles on Solomon by J. Briend, Ph. Abadie, J. Brière, in *DBS*, XI. In 2 Sam. 12:24f. we learn of his naming following his birth as son of Bathsheba and David. We are further informed that through the agency of Nathan his name was called Jedidiah, 'beloved of Yahweh.' Folk-etymologically and in the manner of the later rabbinical midrash, there is some playing with his name and the 'peace and

quiet' (שלום) he was to bring in 1 Chr. 22:9. In LXX^Luc. Σαλωμὼν is reproduced as Σολομων, according to Rahlfs (*Sst.* III, 184) along with Σομοηλος, 'volkstümliche Aussprachen.' Montg.-Gehman comment: 'without further explanation.'

The question why Zadok was omitted from this verse is hard to answer. A pure *argumentum e silentio* would be the notion that though he was invited in view of his position in the old Jerusalem, he chose to disregard the request as coming from the other 'party.' There is also a suspicion (thus Noth for example) that the text here was not transmitted whole. A third possibility is that the author simply listed a few people from the other camp and then mentioned Solomon to indicate that these were the people who would belong to the 'Solomon party.'

1:11 *Then Nathan said to Bathsheba, Solomon's mother: 'Have you not heard that Adonijah son of Haggith has become king and our lord David does not know it?*

This new episode in which steps are taken on the part of David and his adherents to elevate Solomon to the kingship begins rather abruptly. LXX^Luc. here reads και ἐλθε ... και εἰπεν (followed by Burney, Klostermann et al.). W.L. Morag, *Bib* 46 (1965), 385 (review of Noth) prefers this reading over that of MT because (1) in 1:1-2:46 there are 43 cases of אמר followed by a direct quotation and about 17 of לאמר without a preceding form of אמר; (2) the introduction of Nathan is certainly somewhat too abrupt here. This latter point is not too convincing because elsewhere in this narrative as well – and in the narrative style of the ancient Israelites in general[6] – the unexpected and incomplete is a characteristic phenomenon. There is more to be said in favour of the first argument. A contrary argument, however, is that LXX^Luc. sought to smooth out the unevenness it felt to be present in its 'Vorlage.' In the textcr. app. of *BHS* the comment of *BHK* is therefore no longer cited – correctly, in our opinion.

Nathan has already been adequately introduced in vss. 8 and 10; similarly Solomon in the immediately preceding verse; now his mother Bathsheba comes to the fore. Noth, *IPN*, 147, n. 2, explains this name as 'die Üppige, Volkommene'; J.A. Montgomery, *JQR* 25 (1935), 262, as 'daughter of the seventh day.' In 1 Chr. 3:5 she is called Bathshua, daughter of Ammiel, and her 4 children here are Shimea, Shobab, Nathan, and Solomon. In 2 Sam. 11:3 the components of her father's name are reversed: Eliam. On the basis of 2 Sam. 12:24 it is likely that we must assume that also (a part of) the list of sons must

---

[6] Cf. among others E. Auerbach, *Mimesis. Dargestellte Wirklichkeit in der abenländische Literatur*, Bern 1964³, 5-27.

be read in chronologically reversed order. The element שׁוע in the name Bathshua is theophoric and a Sem. adaptation to a Hurrian word *sew(e)* (cf. I. Yeivin, *EncMiqr*. II, 380), which frequently occurs in other Hurrian names as well. This would mean that also the element שׁבע in the name Bathsheba would be a further adaptation, so that the explanation of this name by Noth and others cannot be maintained (cf. also Yeivin, pp. 379f.).

Meanwhile Bathsheba is sufficiently familiar to the reader of this passage from the story of 2 Sam. 11f. From these chapters also Nathan's involvement in David's marriage to the wife of Uriah the Hittite and in the birth and naming of Solomon is evident. Accordingly, the question Nathan here poses to Bathsheba is not unusual: 'Have you not heard that Adonijah, the son of Haggith, is becoming king?' שׁמעת has a *taw* with *dageš*. According to Bg. I, §18a) the spirantization is left out after a vowel in a form of the 2 p. fem. sing. pf. of a verb III laryngeal; according to Meyer, I, §17.1, following P. Kahle, we are dealing here with a 'Mischform,' in which case both the given pronunciation as *šama't* can be used. מלך, 'being king,' 'becoming king' (see a.o. *HAL*, s.v.) here precedes Adonijah (cf. also 2 Sam. 15:10; 2 Kgs. 9:13) and cannot be equated with the familiar formula יהוה מלך (cf. further (with litt.) J.A. Soggin, *THAT*, I, 917f.; K. Seybold, *TWAT*, IV, 933-956).[7] In contrast to 2 Sam. 15:10 (Absalom) and 2 Kgs. 9:13 (Jehu) we are not dealing with a general proclamation: 'X has become king,' but with a private question which is not designed to note a fact but only makes an inquiry into this (possible) fact. The translations of LXX, Vulg. and Pesh., like Tg. which is closely tied in with MT, take the verb as a past tense: Adonijah has become king. In this connection it must be noted that LXX[Luc.] has βεβασίλευκεν instead of ἐβασίλευσεν. 'The son of Haggith,' despite its omission in the majority of good Syrian textual witnesses, is to be maintained.

The first part of Nathan's question has a sequel in the second: 'Our lord David knows nothing about this?' Both perfects not only express something ironic (so Noth) but also something unreal. The second harks back to vs. 6a where David was depicted as the ever-indulgent father to Adonijah. In English, after such a question, one could expect something like: 'Come on now!' The 2 parts are chiastically constructed in order to position 'becoming king' over against 'know' and Adonijah, the son of Haggith, over against lord David.

1:12 *Now, then, let me give you good advice, so that you may save your life and the life of your son Solomon.*
In this verse Nathan urgently recommends countermeasures. The sentence begins with ועתה, which, like its equivalent in, say, the Aram. (Tg.: וכען)

---

[7] See now also J.C. de Moor, *The Rise of Yahwism* (BEThL 91), Leuven 1990, 101-222.

frequently introduces a very pertinent viewpoint.⁸ The following לכי functions as an interjection and reinforces the ועתה (cf. Bg. §10p; Joüon §§105e; 177f: 'come on'). The following *figura etymologica* (cf. Ges-K §117p) יעץ (qal) + עצה is frequently found (e.g. 2 Sam. 16:23; 17:7; 12:8, 13) in the sense of: giving *good* advice (see also H.-P. Stähli, *THAT*, I, 748, 753). The form איעצך נא indicates a cohortative (cf. Bg. II §10d; for the /ā/ in place of the /a/, see Meyer, II, §184.2). This good advice is calculated to enable Bathsheba to secure the safety of her life and that of her son. The cohortative is here continued with an imperative (according to Joüon §116f an indirect imper., cf. also König §364i). An imperative need not only indicate a command but can also indicate promises, threats, warnings and the like (cf. BrSynt. §3; Ewald §347a, who speaks of an *imperativum futuri*; and Driver §65). Burney here considers the continuation of the cohortative by the imper. the *purpose* of the action described by the previous verb. It is not impossible also to view this imper. as the *result*. Probably both nuances can be defended. LXX^Luc. prefers οπως σωσης (instead of LXX*: καὶ ἐξελοῦ). מלט (pi.) + נפש signifies – depending on the pers. pron. added – 'to save someone's life' (cf. 1 Sam. 19:11; Isa. 48:6 etc.). The verb is closely related to פלט and is discussed in conjunction with this word by E. Ruprecht, *THAT*, II, 420-427, and G.F. Hasel, *TWAT*, VI, 589-606. Nathan is here suggesting that even Bathsheba's and Solomon's life was at risk. Whether this was really so is uncertain. In the following story this statement has effect as a result of the magnanimity shown by Solomon, and therefore, from a literary viewpoint, belongs here.

1:13 *Go and enter with king David and say to him: "My lord the king, did you not swear to me your servant: Surely Solomon your son will be king after me and he will sit on my throne but why then is Adonijah king?"*
Nathan's advice consists in urging Bathsheba to go to David in order, with a view to an oath he once swore concerning the kingship of Solomon, to inquire into the reason for Adonijah's kingship now. לכי linked by ו to באי (König §357i) probably means 'go' here (cf. also R. Tournay, *VT* 25 [1975], 545). נשבע is usually construed with כי when the oath is positive in content (Joüon §165b), even though, as here, this כי is separated from נשבע by other words, like לאמר. There is no reason (with Ehrlich for example) to delete the לאמר (cf. vs. 30). Nor is it necessary (with Burney) to take the כי here as a kind of recitative (ὅτι). even though the particle frequently functions as such. As Keller has demonstrated נשבע need not per se be translated by 'to swear an oath', but the word can simply mean 'ein feierliches, unwiderufliches

---

⁸ H.A. Brongers, "wᵉ'attah im Alten Testament," *VT* 15 (1965), 289-299; esp. pp. 294f.; see also A. Lauretin, *Bib* 45 (1964), 168-197.

Versprechen' by which one obligates himself 'etwas unter allen Umständen zu tun bzw. nicht zu tun.'⁹

אמה is sometimes used alongside of שפחה in the same sense which has given rise to a tendency to equate the two (see e.g. *KBL*, s.v. שפחה) or to an argument for distinguishing different sources.¹⁰ Jepsen has demonstrated, among other things, that there is a definite distinction between the 2 words. In this connection, as it concerns אמה, he refers to the woman's lack of freedom, whether as the concubine of the free man or as the wife of a slave, whereas, according to him, the שפחה tends more to describe the still virginal young woman serving her mistress. Here and in a number of other texts אמה is a kind of courtly formula by which a woman indicates that she is seeking protection and help.¹¹ LXX^Luc. reflects the understanding that the promise of which David has to be reminded by Bathsheba was made κατα κυριου του θεου. The 'Vorlage' of this recension perhaps anticipated vs. 17. That the author omitted it *here* is probably due to it not being recorded anywhere, that there ever was such a promise and to his wish to build a climax by not mentioning the name of YHWH in the first instance and by later mentioning it *expressis verbis*. True, 1 Chr. 28:5 mentions Solomon as the legitimate successor to David, but there we are dealing with a later expanding tradition which in the community of Israel assumed the 'sure promises to David'¹² and became part of Israel's *credo*. It is purely speculative to venture an answer to the question whether and, if so, when David ever promised anything to that effect. The literary framework in which this statement occurs and which is preceded by 2 Sam. 6-20 has worked toward this moment. Why else do we have 2 Sam. 7, a chapter which, in virtue of 2 Sam. 7:1, is chronologically decidedly incongruous, and why the elaborate stories concerning David's 'sin with Bathsheba'? Accordingly, we are dealing with a literary *topos* which in this framework rightly gives numerous commentators the impression that David had promised nothing and that the wish is father to the promise whose realization the author unfolds in a fascinating story. The author suggests that David, old and senile, not only remembers nothing of what he might possibly have promised at some time in the past, but is also very amenable to being influenced. This is the

---

⁹ C.A. Keller, *THAT*, II, 858; cf. also G. Giesen, "Semantische Vorfragen zur Wurzel שבע 'schwören'," in: *Bausteine biblischer Theologie* (Fs G.J. Botterweck, ed. H.J. Fabry; BBB 50), Bonn 1977, 127-143; id., *Die Wurzel šbʻ* (BBB 56), Bonn 1981; I. Kottsieper, *TWAT*, VII, 974-1000.

¹⁰ Cf. O. Eißfeldt, *Einleitung in das Alte Testament*, Tübingen 1956², 243.

¹¹ A. Jepsen, "*Amah* und *Shiphalah*," VT 8 (1958), 293-297, 425; esp. p. 295. See on אמה now also É. Lipiński, *ZAH* 7 (1994), 12-16.

¹² Cf. a.o. S. Amsler, *David, Roi et Messie. La tradition davidique dans l'Ancient Testament*, Neuchâtel 1963, 32-38.

circumstance which Nathan, along with his helper Bathsheba, exploits. He offers his – literary – perspective on a historical process in which in the end not Adonijah but Solomon became king.

The word כסא, 'throne', occurs 135x in OT, 34 of which in 1 Kings. One also finds the word in Phoen. (e.g. *KAI* 24, 9: *yšbt 'l ks' 'by*: 'I sat on the throne of my father'; cf. Y. Avishur, *UF* 8 (1976), 11), Ugar., Aram. and Akkad. in the last-mentioned of which it is a borrowing from Sumerian (cf. Ellenbogen, *Foreign Words*, 89; *AHw*, s.v., *kussû(m)*). The 'throne' denotes the power of the ruler. In this chapter and the next the expression '(sitting) on the throne' occurs repeatedly (vss. 17, 20, 24, 27, 30ff.) and therefore evidently plays a large role from a literary viewpoint (cf. further M. Görg, *TWAT*, III, 1023f. and especially H.-J. Fabry, *TWAT*, IV, 247-272 with bibliography).

The content of David's promise is linked with and opposed to the personal question: 'Why is Adonijah now becoming king?' That promise itself is stated as direct discourse, as so often elsewhere (Gen. 24:7; Judg. 21:1 etc.) Preceding מדוע (see vs. 6) is the ו (Joüon §§115c; 177m), which confers a special emotive value on this 'why.'

1:14 *Then, while you are still speaking with the king, I will come in after you and complete your story.'*
But Nathan's plan has still not been completely unfolded. The climax is still to come. While Bathsheba is still speaking with the king, Nathan 'drops by' to add a little to her words. הנה is supplemented in numerous MSS as well as by almost all MSS of the ancient versions with a preceding ו (cf. vs. 22). The construction of this sentence, in which the durative (Joüon §121c) as well as the periphrastic nuance (Böttcher §997, 2c) of the part. comes to expression, by the emphatic positioning of the pers. pron. אני conveys also in a literary sense the unexpectedness (Ewald §341d) of the second part of the sentence (see Driver §§166-169; Ges-K §116u): the planned moment of surprise. The verb מלא here has the meaning: 'complete,' 'confirm,' 'corroborate' (L.A. Snijders, *TWAT*, IV, 880f.; further M. Delcor, *THAT*, I, 897-900; cf. also Burney; Benzinger; F. Langlamet, *RB* 83 (1976), 333 n. 20; D. Pardee, *BASOR* 239 (1980), 47f.).

1:15 *So Bathsheba went to see the king in his room. Now the king was very old and Abishag the Shunammite was attending him.*
Whereas in the preceding Nathan's intent was sketched in bare outline, in the following the execution of the plan is depicted in vivid detail. Bathsheba enters the king's private room. In this locative Ges-K §90c sees a rudiment of an original accusative, whereas Meyer, II, §45.3c denies it. The חדר is especially the dark inner room (cf. G.R. Driver, *JThS* NS 7 [1956], 19f.); in certain cases it can even denote 'the hiding place' (cf. Y. Zakovitch, *Leš* 37 (1972/3), 13f.;

R. Mosis, *TWAT*, II, 755-759).

The author masterfully meshes the 'overture' of our story (vss. 1-4) into what is about to take place now (similarly Benzinger et al., against Klostermann). Again the reader is reminded of the king's advanced age and the mediating position of Abishag the Shunammite who is present to serve the king. David in his old age is really no match for what is coming! משרת is a contraction of *משרתת (Ewald §188b; Stade §276a; Ges-K §80d; cf. Burney). In place of 'served the king,' some MSS of LXX, Pesh., and the Vulg. have 'served him,' which of course makes no material difference.

1:16 *Bathsheba knelt and bowed down before the king, and the king said: 'What do you want?'*

At length, almost with a touch of irony, but in any case slowing the momentum of the story to heighten the tension, the author now reports the greeting ceremony. In the presence of Abishag as silent witness in the background, the still vigorous spouse bows before the age-stricken king. The verbs קדד and *שחה, *שחו (cf. Olsh. §272b) or *חוה in this kind of context often appear in conjunction (cf. Gen. 24:26; Ex. 34:8; 1 Sam. 24:9 etc.). קדד (approx. 15x in OT) means 'to bow,' 'to kneel' (10x κύπτειν in LXX) whereas the verb השתחוה can be rendered 'to prostrate oneself' (in LXX προσκυνεῖν). In the past the last-mentioned verb was often derived from *שחה, of which it is a hitp. form. Since the discovery of the Ugar. tablets, the tendency is now to derive it from *חוה (root ḥwy), although this derivation had also already been proposed in the previous century (see, e.g., König, II, p. 383 Anm. [for the form König, I, pp. 565ff.]; J.A. Emerton, *OTS* 20 (1977), 41-55; S. Kreuzer, *VT* 35 (1985), 35-60, all of whom refer to M. Hartmann, *Die Pluriliteralbildungen in den semitischen Sprachen*, 1875, 17; further Meyer, II §83.5c; H.D. Preuss, *TWAT*, II, 784-794). Often השתחוה was linked to ארצה 'to earth' or אפים ארצה, 'with the face down to earth' (also in some MSS, see Thenius), and combined with other words like נפל or כרע etc. (cf. H.P. Stähli, *THAT*, I, 530-533) or with prepositions. Representations of such 'bowing down' can be found a.o. in *ANEP*, 45f., 355. The reference is to a show of 'Huldigung' (Kreuzer) to superiors or in the cult to *proskynesis* before the deity.

Various MSS of MT, as also some MSS of recensions of the ancient versions add לה after ויאמר which, though it fits materially, is unnecessary in view of the following לך.

1:17 *She said to him: 'My lord, you swore by YHWH your God to your servant saying: "Surely, Solomon your son will be king after me, and he will sit on my throne."'*

In this verse Bathsheba repeats what Nathan said in vs. 13. There are only a few minor text-critical variants. After 'lord' LXX^A, Pesh., and various MSS add 'the king'; LXX^{Luc.} similarly reads 'Bathsheba' in place of 'she' and 'God' in place of 'your God.' One MS adds לאמר to 'your servant' (see also Stade-Schwally). But none of these variants need modify the MT.

1:18 *But now look, Adonijah has become king and you my lord the king do not know about it.*
The second ועתה, which *Sebir* and many MSS of MT and most MSS of the ancient versions want to read as ואתה, constitutes a text-critical problem (see already Kimchi; further, Stade-Schwally, Barthélemy etc.) Roberts counts this form among 'the aural errors' (cf. vs. 20).[13] Gutturals indeed are at times interchanged, either by an aural error or by the later copyists' inattention (cf. Delitzsch, *LSF* §136a). On the basis of the numerous textual witnesses we follow the modification of the ancient MSS and versions, though also a second 'but now' as a 'sign of excited speech' can be understood (Noth).
The second part of this verse can be read as a question (Ehrlich views it as a later addition).

1:19 *He has made a sacrifice of oxen, fatted cattle, and sheep in great quantities and invited all the king's sons, the priest Abiathar and Joab the commander of the army, but he has not invited your servant Solomon.*
While in vs. 9 there was mention of צאן, and בקר and מריא, here (and in vs. 25) we read שור, מריא, and צאן. Aside from the change in sequence בקר has been replaced by שור. This last word refers to the male specimen of the ox: bull (see the dictionaries). To indicate that the reference is not to a few animals, there is now (and in vs. 25) the addition of רב לרב or רוב 'multitude' is often construed with ל to indicate abundance (cf. Gen. 30:30; Deut. 1:10, etc.). Hence our translation: 'in great quantities.'
In the list of the guests Adonijah invited to his coronation feast, whose names were already familiar from the preceding, Joab is now described as 'the army commander,' a designation which also occurs elsewhere (11:15, 21; cf. 2 Sam. 24:2: שר־החיל) and which of course applied to others as well (e.g. Sisera [Judg. 4:7] or Abner [1 Sam. 17:55; 26:5 etc.]). Although LXX^{Luc.} omits mention of Adonijah's not inviting Solomon, there is no reason to follow this omission (see following verse).

1:20 *As for you, my lord the king, the eyes of all Israel are on you to tell them who will sit on the throne of my lord the king after him.*
Numerous MT MSS, as well as a number of editions and MSS of Tg. and Vulg., along with a number of commentators (cf. vs. 18: Roberts and

---

[13] B.J. Roberts *The Old Testament Text and Versions*, Cardiff 1951, 97.

Delitzsch), insist at this point on reading ועתה in place of ואתה. Thenius and Burney, who follow this reading, argue that Bathsheba is now coming to a conclusion (cf. Gen. 3:22; 1 Sam. 25:26f. etc.). This is true. But it is equally true that a pron. pers. can be stated first to give emphasis (cf. Ehrlich), especially when it precedes an object linked to a preposition (cf. Ges-K §135g; König §§19 and 341b), in this case עליך. The entire first half of this verse is preceded in LXX[Luc.] and partially replaced by the first half of vs. 27: 'If this has happened at the direction of my lord the king because the eyes of all the people are upon you ...' According to Rahlfs (*Sst.* III, 175), this change has also crowded out the conclusion of vs. 19 in LXX[Luc.] and resulted in other changes as well.

In OT having one's eyes set on a person often occurs in the sense of 'concentrated attention to' (Gen. 44:21 and frequently; cf. E. Jenni, *THAT*, II, 263). There is some exaggeration here: 'the eyes of Israel,' with the omission of Judah. The inf. cstr. hiph. of נגד is used here in place of a conjugated tense, in connection with which the preceding context indicates the subject as well (for this cf. Joüon §124s). Bathsheba now poses the question which of the two – Solomon on the basis of the (secret) oath, or Adonijah on the ground of public reality – will be David's successor. If one takes the conclusion of vs. 18 as an ironic question, Bathsheba is delicately accusing David of a kind of double morality in order thereby to make the senile old king even more unsure of himself but all the more sure with regard to Solomon's appointment.

1:21 *I fear that when my lord the king is laid to rest with his fathers, I and my son Solomon will be the losers.'*

As a climax, and not as something incidental, Bathsheba points out the ultimate consequence of David's ambivalence for her son and her after his death. 'Resting with one's forefathers' (cf. B. Alfrink, *OTS* 2 [1940], 106-118; A. de Bondt, *GThT* 47 [1947], 78-87; W.A.M. Beuken, *TWAT*, VII, 1312ff.) occurs repeatedly in OT (Gen. 47:30; Deut. 31:16; 2 Sam. 7:12), and especially in the books of Kings and Chronicles, where it concerns the death of kings, and is a euphemism for 'dying' (De Bondt). Despite the problem in the case of Ahab's death (1 Kgs. 22:40; cf. also C.F. Whitley, *VT* 2 [1952], 148), the expression is used as a rule in the case of peaceful or 'natural' death (cf. E. Jenni, *THAT*, I, 11, and Alfrink). The 'burial' must be distinguished from this as a separate act (H. Ringgren, *TWAT*, I, 10). The allusion to David's death serves to make clear the danger that Bathsheba and Solomon will become חטאים. In contrast to the many translations which use words like 'as,' 'be counted,' etc.,[14] in the MT

---

[14] We can note here, quite arbitrarily, a number of translations of this passage: AV: '... that I and my son, Solomon, shall be counted offenders'; the Dutch 'Statenvertaling': '... dat ik en mijn

there is a simple identity between 'Solomon and I' on the one hand and חטאים on the other: they *are* or *will be* that. Words and verbs based on the stem חטא are frequent in OT (cf. R. Knierim, *THAT*, I, 542; K. Koch, *TWAT*, II, 857-870). Derivations of this word can denote actions contrary to the understanding of community, whether against one's next of kin, say a brother (Gen. 42:22; 50:17), or against one's (own) king (Gen. 40:1; 1 Sam. 24:12; 26:21); or the reverse, an action by a king against his subjects (1 Sam. 19:4f.; cf. Koch, 860) etc. The marginal comment in LV rightly relates the adj. חטא, which occurs some 20x in OT, to the end of vs. 12, where danger threatens the life of Bathsheba and Solomon if events were really to unfold further in the direction in which they appeared at that moment to be moving. It is clear that here the word does not mean 'sinner' in a cultic or ritual sense, but refers to people who were on the 'wrong side' of an issue and are therefore 'criminal' or 'wrong' (Buber-Rosenzweig; cf. Rashi). Although it is nowhere openly stated that Adonijah knew of Solomon's aspirations to kingship, the author proves ever more clearly to give relief and grimness to the opposition between Adonijah and his group on the one hand and Solomon and his circle on the other. Accordingly, a translation by 'counting as' is too weak by comparison with the use of היה plus adj. as well as the actual situation as Bathsheba expects it for her son and herself (cf. Joüon §§146c, 148d on the resumptive pronoun). There is therefore no reason, with Ehrlich, to consider this verse a later addition.

1:22 *While she was still speaking with the king, look, Nathan the prophet came in.*
Here we see happen what was projected in vs. 14 as the plan: Nathan reports. The part. is continued with a pf. (Lettinga §73d). The fact that והנה apparently does not occur in Pesh. and Vulg. does not mean that it was not present in their 'Vorlage.'

1:23 *They told the king: 'Nathan the prophet is here.' When he came in before the king he bowed down before the king with his face to the ground.*
Nathan's coming to the king is stated in a few words. Only the main point is reported. It is a secondary thing, for example, that Bathsheba was obviously

---

zoon Salomo [*als*] zondaars zullen,' with a.o. a reference to Gen. 43:9; 44:10; and Josh. 2:19, remarking that they would be regarded guilty because they wrongfully tried to become king; NV: '... als opstandelingen zullen gelden'; LV: '... als misdadigers gerekend worden' with a marginal note to the effect that they 'sought to take over the government,' with reference to vs. 12 and 2:22-46. WV: '... vallen ... in ongenade'; TOB: '... nous serons traitées comme des coupables'; RSV: '... will be counted offenders'; NEB: 'shall be treated as criminals'; Zürcher Bibel: '... so müssen ... büßen'; Buber-Rosenzweig: '... werden ... fehlsein.'

not present at this conversation (cf. vs. 28) because her audience with the king had ended. The author is still leaving the reader in the tension of waiting for an answer ... This tension is heightened by this verse. Strictly speaking, vs. 24 could have immediately followed vs. 22 because what vs. 23 says is self-evident and could have been filled in by the reader or hearer himself. For that matter the reader already knows the content of what Nathan is about to say. The pericope vss. 22-27 slows down the story to heighten the climax. At the same time it shows how the senile king is psychologically manipulated to pronounce his oath regarding Solomon's kingship. Ehrlich, accordingly, calls Nathan a schemer.

BrSynt. §110a correctly notes that בוא differs in meaning depending on whether it is construed with the prep. על or לפני. The king is now seated on a throne so that Nathan approaches him horizontally. Often people sat on the ground so that a person walking in stood 'above' the others (cf. Gen. 18:8; 2 Sam. 12:17). By contrast with vs. 16 the word קדד is not used now as a sign of esteem, only וישתחו but now with the expression על־אפיו ארצה (according to König §402h an *accusativus specificationis* or *modi*).

1:24 *Then Nathan said: 'My lord the king, have you said: "Adonijah shall be king after me and he shall sit on my throne?"*
Not only is there a difference in the manner in which Bathsheba and Nathan approach the king. Bathsheba goes to the king in his private room; Nathan, on the other hand, steps forward and stands before the king, possibly in his official receiving room (while this is not stated, on the basis of vs. 28 this is not imaginary). There is a difference as well in the way 'the problem' is approached. Bathsheba – as woman – is first given permission to speak and then reminds the king of an oath once (if ever) sworn to Solomon; Nathan comes straight to the point, be it with a 'my lord the king' (only in Jer. 37:20 does this occur again on the lips of a prophet; so Ehrlich), and refers to a reality – at least, so it seems – implying that the king has designated Adonijah as his legitimate successor. And, meanwhile, the poor senile old king knows of nothing! What Nathan says is intended as a question (Rashi; Meyer §111.2a), but has the character of a pure statement (Klostermann; Benzinger; W.T. Claassen, *JNSL* 11 [1983], 40) inevitable. In Hebr., too, it is the tone which makes the music (cf. BrSynt. §54a; Ges-K §150a; Joüon §161a; König §353b). Ewald §324b (cf. also Stade-Schwally) thinks that in the case of 'mit einem hauche anfangenden Wörtern' the interrogative particle is absent, but against this see Ges-K §150b.

1:25 *For today he has gone down and has made a sacrifice of oxen, fatted cattle, and sheep in great quantities. He has invited all the kings' sons, the commanders of the army, and the priest Abiathar. Right now they are eating*

and drinking with him and shouting: "Long live king Adonijah."
Again the story of Adonijah's feast of sacrifices and a summing up of the invited parties is repeated, but now in fuller detail than in Bathsheba's speech. In place of the 'army commanders' LXX$^{Luc.}$ reads τον αρχιστρατηγον Ιωαβ as Bathsheba did as well (vs. 19). Many scholars believe they should also follow this version here, with the following argumentation (Burney; see also Oort): (1) it is improbable that Nathan would have omitted mention of Joab; (2) mention of the 'commanders of the army' could also implicate Benaiah. Still this argumentation is not strong because in the preceding the description was more global and less specific (vs. 9). Furthermore, in the following verse. Nathan does mention Benaiah as a member of Solomon's party. Along with the ancient versions we maintain the reading of MT here (cf. also Barthélemy).

The new details are now that everyone is eating and drinking and shouting: 'Long live Adonijah!' This blessing (Bg. II §10h) is repeatedly called out when a new king comes forward (1 Sam. 10:24; 2 Sam. 16:16 etc.). According to P.A.H. de Boer, *VT* 5 (1955), 225-231, the jussive indicative means: the king lives = has power; cf. G. Gerleman, *THAT*, I, 552; Mettinger, *King*, 134ff.

1:26 *But me, your servant, Zadok the priest, Benaiah son of Jehoiada, or your servant Solomon, us he has not invited.*
Those who have not been invited to the feast are described as ולי אני־עבדך. This either indicates special emphasis (Burney; Ges-K §135g; cf. GD §1d), or no more than a designation of persons (Ehrlich; Joüon §146d), but in any case a placing first of Nathan himself followed by the others (cf. BrSynt. §68a).

In place of 'your servant Solomon' LXX$^{Luc.}$ reads 'your son Solomon' (followed by Klostermann et al.). Benzinger (et al.) correctly comments that though this would not be completely in keeping with etiquette, 'servant' is still more appropriate than Adonijah's being 'lord' (cf. Stade-Schwally).

1:27 *Can it be that this thing was brought about by my lord the king and that you have not told our servants who would sit on the throne of my lord the king after him?'*
The most important question in this verse is whether one should read *(k^{e}tib)* 'your servants' or with numerous MSS and the ancient versions *(q^{e}re)* 'your servant.' The latter only applies of course to Nathan. Usually the sing. is taken as an expression of impatience and blame (Thenius; Benzinger et al.), the pl. as being more in keeping with the context as an invitation as yet to disclose the actual state of affairs (see Stade-Schwally). These considerations are legitimate. Still one must not lose sight of the fact that as court prophet Nathan believed he had a right at least to be consulted in important matters such as the succession to the throne and the associated oath pertaining to the successor. Merely his role in matters pertaining to the cult in and around the palace alone became

clear in 2 Sam. 7, whatever one's view of the historicity of this chapter.[15] The succession to the throne, after all, also had a cultic dimension. In our opinion, therefore, it is not certain whether the pl. is to be preferred over the sing.

The verse opens with אם as interrogative particle (cf. König §353g; GD §152). According to Ges-K §150f, this is one of those rare cases in which a simple question is actually based on the omission of the first member of a double question (other examples Isa. 29:16; Job 6:12; 39:13). In precisely this case, according to Ewald §324c, the second member has been omitted 'wie aus bescheidenheit oder aus eile.' Benzinger too thinks of modesty. Joüon §161d thinks אם comes from an indirect question (cf. Latin: *an venit?*). The somewhat less frequent introduction of this direct question is integral to the scheme of Nathan's whole story, which is a question rather than a statement of fact (cf. vs. 24). The question of vs. 24, after the parenthetical sentences of vss. 25ff., is simply continued with: If this has proceeded from the king ... , then you have ... The word מאת is a more idiomatic expression than the usual מן (Burney). נהיה niph. of היה construed with מאת also occurs in 12:24 (par. 2 Chr. 11:4). Somewhat ceremoniously one could translate it by 'has come to pass.'

The pericope of vss. 22-27 shows how Nathan's 'addition' was conceived in vs. 14. The 'why' of Adonijah's kingship (vs. 13) and the questioning eyes of 'all Israel' (vs. 20) find their climax in the non-involvement in and unfamiliarity with the issue of the court prophet who evidently has first rights to this information. This is the final flourish. Now the king *has* to answer.

1:28 *Then King David answered and said: 'Ask Bathsheba to come in' and she came into the king's presence and stood before him.*
On the basis of this verse and of vs. 32 the impression is reinforced by the narrator that David received Bathsheba as well as Nathan individually, and therefore that Bathsheba was not present to hear the preceding conversation with Nathan. At the same time the narrator underscores the impression that, as a result of the seeming 'independence' of his informants Bathsheba and Nathan, the aged king became convinced of his neglect or forgetfulness of an oath or promise he had once made. In some ancient versions the twice recurring לפני המלך with a preceding המלך David has led to another reading either because of the perceived tautology or because of another reading in the 'Vorlage'. Thus LXX[B, Luc.] omit the first המלך; LXX[Luc.] also the second, while the other MSS of LXX prefer to omit the third, followed in this by Vulg. and a number of important MSS of Pesh. (7 al and 9 al *fam*). Other Pesh. MSS are approximately parallel to LXX[Luc.]. However, this is of no material significance for the exegesis. Montg.-Gehman rightly comment that 'Semitic rhetoric is

---

[15] Cf. among others J. Lindblom, *Prophecy in Ancient Israel*, Oxford 1976[6], 76f.

repetitive.' Ehrlich views ותבא לפני המלך as a gloss, but this is unnecessary.

1:29 *The king swore this oath: 'As YHWH lives, who has delivered me from all adversity,*
The king now swears an oath in Bathsheba's presence. This and the following verse contain the content of the oath. חי־יהוה, an oath formula, occurs 43x in OT. חי in this connection is a substantive: 'By the life of YHWH.' When an oath is sworn 'by the life of a man' the *nomen regens* reads: חֵי (cf. M. Greenberg, *JBL* 76 [1957], 34-39; G. Gerleman, *THAT*, I, 552; H. Ringgren, *TWAT*, II, 892f.). This formula is followed by a relative clause. After YHWH this is very rare (cf. Ehrlich). The verb פדה occurs 58x in OT, by far the majority in qal. In Kings it occurs only in our verse, though in most other Sem. languages the verb is customary. In Hebr., however, the – in some respects – synonymous verb גאל occurs more frequently (cf. J.J. Stamm, *THAT*, I, 383-394; H. Ringgren, *TWAT*, II, 884-890). In legal usage the word usually means 'ransom,' 'redeem' and the substantive פדיון 'ransom'; in cultic regulations it frequently means 'the redemption of the firstborn.' In religious usage YHWH is the subject of the act of 'redemption' and the act does not imply the payment of a countervalue. Along with 2 Sam. 4:9, where precisely the same formulation is put on David's lips, this doxological addition to David's actual oath is counted as one of the most ancient instances of this formula. For פדה, cf. J.J. Stamm, *THAT*, II, 389-406; esp. 398f.; H. Cazelles, *TWAT*, VI, 514-522; also O. Procksch, *TDNT* IV, 332-336. Meyer has demonstrated that פדה stands in opposition to injustice and death, and denotes a 'release' from a circumstance (not from a person or place) by a redeemer aside from any motive or responsibility on his part.[16] When this relates to YHWH this view is correct. YHWH has delivered David 'from all adversity.' צרה, like פדה, only occurs here in Kings. The word refers to the distress and oppression David often had to suffer.

1:30 *just as I swore to you by YHWH, the God of Israel: "Surely Solomon your son will be king after me and will sit on my throne in my place," so I swear I will bring it about this day.'*
The oath is introduced as well as continued here by the particle כי (cf. Joüon §§165b; Lettinga §80n; Meyer §122, 5b), because here 2 clauses are coordinated by כאשר + pf. + subordinate clause on the one hand and by כן + impf. on the other (for this kind of construction, see M.J. Mulder, *OTS* 21 [1981], 202-227 and E. Talstra, *OTS* 21 [1981], 228-239). In the previous as

---

[16] W.F. Meyer, *Semantic Significance of Padah in Old Testament Hebrew*, Wisconsin 1974; cf. *ZAW* 87 (1975), 232.

well as the present verse the emphasis is put on swearing an oath by YHWH, here supplemented by 'the God of Israel.' The content of the oath is virtually the same as the formulation in vs. 13, with the addition of תחתי 'in my place' following כסאי. This differs from אחרי 'after me' (cf. *KAI* 24, 13f.; Avishur, *UF* 8 (1976), 18).

Even if the oath had not been sworn earlier, it is now final and no longer open to appeal, as it were.

1:31 *Then Bathsheba knelt with her face to the ground and, bowing down before the king, said: 'May king David live yet for a very long time.'*
Remarkable here is the second mention of a *proskynesis* and bowing to the ground of Bathsheba, just as in vs. 16, but now as a sign that her audience with the king has ended. In vs. 28, in the intervening entrance of Bathsheba, there was no such act of obeisance. Added to ותקד we now find אפים ארץ. Though it is not so strange that *Sebir* and various MSS have ארצה in place of the last word, still ארץ as an 'accusative of direction' (cf. König §330b [cf. §402h]; Joüon §125n, Ges-K §156c) can indeed be maintained (cf. Isa. 49:23). As Ges-K §156c indicates, אפים ארץ is actually a nominal circumstantial clause: 'while her face was inclined to the earth.' In this audience with the king Bathsheba has the last word: 'May my lord king David live forever!' Here the writer creates a contrast to the conclusion of vs. 25, where 'people' call out (but without the לעלם) this blessing to 'king' Adonijah (cf. Bg. II §10h and above by vs. 25). In the Hebr. OT לעולם occurs no fewer than 181 out of a total of 446x of עולם, but only 4x in 1 Kings (2x in 2 Kings). In the wish addressed to the king, we encounter a certain courtly style of address which is also found outside of Israel, from the Amarna letters to Greek literature (cf H. Sasse, *TDNT*, I, 208 and n. 4). Perhaps this formula originally related to the deification of the king but in Israel it is no more than a hyperbole of the courtly style of speech (cf. E. Jenni, *THAT*, II, 228-243; esp. 237f.; H.D. Preuß, *TWAT*, V, 1150). One must not overlook the fact that, as it concerns David, the author here emphatically brings out the עולם (cf. also 2:35, 45): we are talking a long time! It goes beyond the language of the court. The name of the king is mentioned (Ehrlich).

1:32 *Then king David spoke up: 'Call in Zadok the priest, Nathan the prophet and Benaiah the son of Jehoiada.' When they came in before the king,*
Now, aroused from the impotent slumber of senility, the king proceeds to act. The author imperceptibly allows the king to 'revive' and once again, like Samson, to reach his old level of decisiveness, insight and courage. The king orders the priest Zadok, the prophet Nathan, and Benaiah the son of Jehoiada to be summoned before him in order to execute the final counter-move on the chessboard of intrigues. There is little more to be said about this verse, except

that the word 'David' is lacking in LXX^Luc. and in many MSS of the Pesh. (rightly, according to Stade-Schwally).

1:33 *the king said to them: 'Take with you the servants of your lord and have my son Solomon ride on my own mule, and bring him down to (the spring) Gihon.*
First 'the servants of your lord' are mobilized, a sovereign and remarkable detachment, which also occurs in 2 Sam. 20:6. In vs. 38 it turns out that the reference is to the Cherethites and Pelethites. Second, Solomon has to mount the king's personal mule and ride around. פרדה (only here and in vss. 38 and 44) is the fem. form of פרד which occurs 14x in OT. A mule is a cross between a male donkey and a mare (cf. S. Achituv, *EncMiqr*. VI, 567ff.; J. Feliks, *BHHW*, II, 1177); a hinny is a cross between a female donkey and a stallion. Though in Lev. 19:19 there is a prohibition against the breeding of such hybrids, hence of mules, they do occur in Israel's stories from the time of David and his sons (2 Sam. 13:29; 18:9). A mule looks like its mother (a horse) but at the same time has the clear marks of his father (a donkey), among other things as it pertains to head and ears.

The construction 'the mule which belongs to me,' הפרדה אשר לי describes somewhat more emphatically the idea of personal property than a suff. poss. pron (cf. Ewald §292b; König §282I; Joüon §130c; GD §36, rem. 3(3); Burney). Aberbanel has commented that a horse is the symbol of war, a donkey the symbol of peace. Adonijah prepared for war but Solomon did not allow himself to be intimidated by this.

A third assignment is to be immediately added to the second: let him go down to the spring Gihon. Both Tg. and Pesh. here read שילוחא (similarly in vss. 38 and 45). They identify the spring with the well-known 'pool of Siloach' or 'Siloam' (Isa. 8:6; Joh. 9:7), but that seems incorrect. According to *HAL*, גיחון is related to גיח: 'to break forth,' 'to bubble up' (cf. also BL, 476vß) and can only mean 'spring.' Aside from this chapter, the name occurs also in 2 Chr. 32:30; 33:14 (not to be confused with the paradisal river by the same name [cf. Gen. 2:13]). The reference is to a spring at the foot of the W slope of the Kidron valley southeast of the present walled city of Jerusalem, currently called *ēn Sittī Maryan*, 'spring of Mary' or *ēn Umm ed-Dereğ*, 'spring of the mother of the steps' (cf. Simons, *Jerusalem*, 163f.; M. Avi-Yona, *EncMiqr*. II, 482f.; H. Donner, *BRL*², 157f.; G.A. Barrois, *IDB*, II, 396 etc.). This spring lay outside the city wall and from the late bronze age on could be reached from within the city by a 15m. long vertical, and a 30m. long slanted shaft. Later a tunnel cut by Hezekiah and about half a kilometer in length conducted spring water under the southeast hill to the 'pool of Siloach' (*ēn Silwān, el-Birke*; cf. *ANEP*, 744; Barrois, *IDB*, IV, 353). Even before Hezekiah's activities there was a channel which conducted water from an overflow basin ('upper pool') situated by the Gihon spring down to the later King's Pool (Neh. 2:14) or Pool of Shelah (Neh. 3:15). This aqueduct was sealed off by Hezekiah for defensive reasons. MT has the preposition אל (but read by many MSS as על): 'above' (cf. vs. 38). Klostermann mentions the possibility that the text originally read תעלת (נחון), the 'aqueduct of ...' In this connection, based on the prep. ב in vs. 45 before Gihon, the possibility of a place designation has to be considered. Referring to Isa. 7 and 36 he thinks an 'aqueduct' is a better place for a public proclamation than a hidden spring. An additional advantage is that this offers a better explanation for the ancient tradition found in Pesh. and Tg. Still we cannot concur with this view. It is striking that both Adonijah's coronation ceremony and that of Solomon take place by a spring. Possibly this has to do with a pre-Israelite, Canaanite coronation ritual which was performed by a 'sacred' spring (with the possibility of purifications) and thereby acquired cultic-religious status (cf. Gaster, *Myth*, 489f.). There is, accordingly, no reason whatever, with Thenius, to read, 'Gibeon' instead of Gihon and to have Solomon's coronation ceremony take place there.

1:34 *There let the priest Zadok and the prophet Nathan anoint him king over Israel. Blow the trumpet and shout "Long live king Solomon!"*
The difficulty in this verse is to decide whether the subject of ומשח is only the priest Zadok or also Nathan the prophet. MSS of LXX and Pesh. support the pl., but very often, mainly however when the subject is an animal or thing, the predicate preceding pl. subjects is in the sing. (cf. e.g. Ges-K §145o; BrSynt. §50a). Delitzsch, *LSF* §19c thinks of a scribal error for ומשחו. In vs. 45 this pl. in fact occurs, but in vs. 39 only Zadok is mentioned as the subject of the anointing of Solomon. The anointing of kings occurs 32x in OT, mostly in the books of Samuel and Kings (cf. J.A. Soggin, *THAT*, I, 913f.; K. Seybold, *TWAT*, V, 46-59[17]); but also prophets (1 Kgs. 19:16; Isa. 61:1) and priests (Ex. 28:41; 29:7 etc.) could be anointed. This anointing has a sacral meaning and can probably be viewed as one of the most important acts during the enthronement of a king (cf. H. Grotius: *Apud Hebraeos, Reges extra controversiam regni heredes ungi non solebant, sed exortis controversiis adhibita unctio ad majorem cautionem*). From 2 Sam. 4:7; 5:3 etc. one may infer that – at least in Judah – it was not a specific person who performed the anointing, though in practice this anointing may well have been carried out by one man on behalf of the community. In our verse Zadok is primarily responsible for the anointing, but is assisted by the court prophet Nathan. Stade-Schwally (cf. also *BHK* and

---

[17] See also E. Kutsch, *Salbung as Rechtakt im Alten Testament und im Alten Orient* (BZAW 87), Berlin 1963.

BHS) think that Nathan has been added by mistake here. It is remarkable that the Chronicler, who ignores the court intrigues surrounding Solomon's enthronement, has the 'community' anoint Solomon as king as well as Zadok as priest (cf. also F. Hesse, *TDNT*, IX, 499, n. 32). In the ancient Near East a royal anointing occurred (among others) among the Hittites.[18] It must already have taken place in Palestine before Israelite times, in the El-Amarna period, as well (Kutsch, pp. 34f.).

The order is to the effect that Solomon is to be anointed king over Israel (LXX[Luc.]: + 'and Judah' [cf. vs. 35], but this seems to be a secondary adaptation), at the Gihon spring by Zadok and Nathan, in connection with which the author presumably had the undivided kingdom in mind. At the same time the ram's horn must be blown (G. Wallis, *BHHW*, II, 749; H.P. Rüger, *BRL*[2], 235), to be clearly distinguished from the חצצרה 'trumpet,' which was probably made of metal (Num. 10:2; cf. G. Friedrich, *TDNT*, VII, 76f.) and mentioned in the later parts of OT. It is clear from 2 Kgs. 11:14 (par. 2 Chr. 23:13) that also trumpets were used at coronation ceremonies probably to supplant the (cheaper) ram's horns. The blowing on the ram's horn is denoted by the verb תקע. It is a matter of 'thrusting' on this instrument or on the trumpet (cf. *TDNT*, VII, 78, and H.-J. Zobel, *TWAT*, VIII, 755), but the verb can have objects other than 'horns' or 'trumpets,' for example, 'fastening a tentpin' (Gen. 31:25), or 'clapping hands' (Ps. 47:2; Nah. 3:19).

The third order in this verse is to call out or raise the cry, 'Long live king Solomon!' (cf. vs. 25).

1:35 *Then you are to go up with him and he is to come in and sit on my throne. He will be king in my place, for he is the one I have appointed to be ruler over Israel and over Judah.'*
In this verse the *perfecta consecutiva* are still dependent on the *imperativa* of vs. 33: 'you must then go up after him to the city above and he must go into the palace and sit on my throne.' Some LXX MSS, including LXX[B], omit the first 3 words of this verse but, despite objections (cf. F. Langlamet, *RB* 83 [1976], 494ff.) there is no reason to follow these MSS (cf. vs. 46). Nor is there good reason to read, along with some LXX MSS, ואני in place of ואתו.

David here states that he has instructed Solomon to be נגיד over Israel and Judah. From the books Samuel on, the word occurs 44x in OT (in Kings only again in 1 Kgs. 14:7; 16:2 and 2 Kgs. 20:5; cf. esp. G.F. Hasel, *TWAT*, V, 203-219; as well as the interpretive explanation of our verse in 1 Chr. 29:22).

---

[18] Kutsch, op. cit., 36f.; R. de Vaux, *Mélanges E. Tisserant* (= Studia e Testi 231), Città del Vaticano, I, 1964, 133, note 68; cf. 129f.; K.R. Veenhof, *BiOr* 23 (1966), 311f.; Mettinger 1976, 185-232.

Alt, *KS*, II, 23, offers as his opinion that Saul's being נגיד implies that, though he was designated by YHWH, the acclamation of the people made him מלך (1 Sam. 9:16; 10:1; 13:14; cf. 11:15). So, according to him, the נגיד was the designated future king at the time of Saul (and David). W. Richter (*BZ* 9 [1965], 71-84) thinks that in the books of Samuel and Kings the word especially describes the essential religious component, the bond between YHWH and the kind, in the royal titulature, a component which was later lost (except in the late reprinstinations, as in Isa. 55:4; Dan. 9:25f.; 11:22; cf. C. Westermann, *THAT*, II, 34f.). Sometime ago Mettinger, *King*, 151-184, rejected this view. He believes that precisely our text is the oldest witness for the title as a secular term for the crown prince, appointed by the ruling king.[19] He further points out that this verse is a response to vs. 20 in which Bathsheba asked David to say (להגיד) who should be David's successor on the throne. נגיד, according to him, is a part. pass. qal of נגד (see also Alt, *KS*, II, 23, n. 2): 'the designated,' 'the one proclaimed (king).' This concept then underwent 'theologization,' the results of which occur in Samuel and elsewhere in OT. But this view, which is opposed to that of Alt, is not certain either (cf., e.g., H.G.M. Williamson, *VT* 28 [1978], 499-509; S. Shaviv, *VT* 34 [1984], 112). Ishida takes an intermediate position. He believes that נגיד was originally a title for a person who was intended to be king either on the part of YHWH or of the ruling king. The title is used only in connection with the designation of the following 6 kings: Saul (1 Sam. 9:16; 10:1); David (1 Sam. 25:30; 2 Sam. 5:2; 6:21 etc.); Solomon (our verse); Jeroboam (1 Kgs. 14:7); Baasha (1 Kgs. 16:2) and Abijah (2 Chr. 11:22). Hezekiah (2 Kgs. 20:5) is said to be a special case.[20] Still we think (along with Liver and Mettinger) that one is asking too much of the word if one assigns a charismatic meaning to it. As is evident from other texts (a.o. Jer. 20:1; Neh. 11:11), נגיד is an ordinary ('secular') word for 'ruler' or 'leader' and is parallel to 'king' (e.g. Ps. 76:13). Hasel, 212, considers the original meaning as 'Erhöhter,' 'Hoher,' which was first a 'Funktionsbezeichnung' and then ('den verschiedenen at.lichen Gebrauchsweisen entsprechend') became a special title for a high government official. J. van Seters, *Or* 50 (1981), 153, takes still a further step. According to him, the term נגיד does not belong to any particular primitive source, nor does it reflect a special conception of the monarchy, but is a special term of the Deuteronomist. The entire history of the royal court is a post-deuteronomistic addition to the history of David with an anti-messianic thrust. However this may be, it is not clear from

---

[19] Contra L. Schmidt, *Menschlicher Erfolg und Jahwes Initiative* (WMANT 38), Neukirchen-Vluyn 1970, 159; cf. also É. Lipiński, *VT* 24 (1974), 497ff.

[20] T. Ishida, "נגיד, A Term for the Legitimation of Kingship," *Annual of the Japanese Biblical Institute* 3 (1977), 35-51; cf. idem, *The Royal Dynasties in Ancient Israel* (BZAW 142), Berlin 1977, 50f.; J. Liver, *EncMiqr*. V, 753ff.

David's words that YHWH had first designated Solomon to be king. It is similarly hard to prove that the word 'originally' meant crown prince. In extrabiblical literature the word is hardly ever used. It occurs in an Aramaic inscription from Sefire (*KAI* 224, 10; *DISO*, 174; Gibson, *TSSI*, II, 48, 54; G.F. Hasel, *TWAT*, V, 203ff.; J.W. Flanagan, *JSOT* 20 [1981], 67f.; further D. Michel, *TRE*, II, 502f.). There it means something like 'officer' or 'commander.'

David meant Solomon to be successor to the throne over Israel and Judah, hence over both kingdoms. The midrash in 1 Chr. 29:22 even makes this 'the second time' that Solomon was elevated to the kingship (see 1 Chr. 23:1). Mettinger, *Kings*, 160 and n. 26, correctly points out that in this verse the personal union is stressed by David and that LXX$^{Luc.}$ already read 'Israel and Judah' in the previous verse as well. Textcritically as well as materially, therefore, the mention of the 2 little states is indisputable (so also Thenius a.o.).

1:36 *Benaiah, the son of Jehoiada, answered the king and said: 'Amen! May YHWH, the God of my lord the king, speak thus as well.*

In this and the following verse Benaiah, son of Jehoiada, as the spokesman for all those loyal to David and Solomon, offers a solemn response which publicly confirms the royal oath as well as the royal instructions. Although the word 'amen' is customarily used in OT as response to a curse that has been pronounced (cf. H. Wildberger, *THAT*, I, 194f.), here perhaps a more general usage predominates, one that is possibly found also in an inscription of Yavne-Yam (*KAI* 200, 11), although this reading is disputed. Wildberger, 195, here characterizes the 'amen' as a 'verpflichtendes Ja.' A. Jepsen, *TWAT*, I, 345, views 'amen' as introducing a wish that God would give his blessing on David's plans. BrSynt. §56b characterizes the word as a 'bejahende Interjektion': 'truly.'[21] In any case, by the use of this word the speaker agrees with David's words (cf. Rashi; A. Weiser, *TDNT*, VI, 186; J. Jeremias, *TRE*, II, 386f.).

In view of the ancient versions, the rest of this verse occasions some difficulty. In place of יאמר LXX reads the word πιστώσαι: 'May YHWH confirm ...,' which Hatch-Redpath mistakenly regard as a 'translation' of יאמר. One could sooner (cf. *BHK* and *BHS*) think of יאמן, although the preceding אמן may have influenced this translation as well. LXX$^{Luc.}$ considerably expands the translation of LXX and reads: γενοιτο ουτως πιστωσαι ο θεος τους λογους του κυριου μου του βασιλεως ουτως ειπε κυριος ο θεος σου κυριε μου

---

[21] See now also K. Seybold, "Zur Vorgeschichte der Liturgischen Formel 'Amen'," *ThZ* 48 (1992), 109-117.

βασιλευ. This looks very much like a double reproduction of the text, viz. the Masoretic and the LXX version (cf. Rahlfs, *Sst.* III, 171). Aq. and Symm., by contrast, adhere almost literally to the MT. The Pesh. which after the אמן continues as follows: *hkn' n'bd mry' 'lhk*: 'May the Lord your God do so' as though MT read כן יעשה, is deviant. There are indeed a few Hebr. MSS which follow this reading (cf. Stade-Schwally, Burney, Montg.-Gehman), but opposed to this is that the important 9 al *fam.* of Pesh., in place of *n'bd* etc., reads *nhw'*, therefore (with the preceding): 'Truly, let it be so.' The latter again comes more or less close to the translation of Tg.: 'Truly, may the will of YHWH, the God of my lord the king, be so.'

The above survey of the translations of a number of ancient versions does not give us sufficient reason to modify MT (thus, correctly, Burney). It is of course understandable that MT presented somewhat of a problem. This is probably due to the word יאמר. But the narrator also has Benaiah utter the wish that YHWH, the God of David, may act in precise accordance with what David now has in mind. יאמר, therefore, is not some kind of historical present (cf. also König §159) but a wish which is intended to confer a divine sanction on the human action of the preceding verses. The author indirectly indicates that the preceding was not primarily a plan of YHWH but the product of human – sometimes cunning – calculation.

1:37 *As YHWH has been with my lord the king, so may he be with Solomon; indeed, may he make his throne greater than the throne of my lord king David.'*
This verse conveys the elaboration of the wish as well as the endorsement of Benaiah and his party. The idea of wish is expressed by the $k^e tib$ יהי, supported by LXX and Vulg. Opposed to this is that various MSS of MT; *DJD*, III and LXX$^{Luc.}$ support the $q^e re$ יהיה. With Montg.-Gehman, the indicative form must be considered 'a theological rectification of the jussive' and the jussive form is to be preferred (Stade-Schwally; Noth; Ehrlich et al.).

According to Noth, Benaiah's wish is not tactless but should be understood in terms of the atmosphere in which a human being continues to live in his descendants, particularly the outstanding ones. YHWH's 'being with Solomon' is a particularization of a formula which occurs more than 100x in OT: 'YHWH is with someone.' According to H.D. Preuß, *ZAW* 80 (1968), 138-173, a fundamental structure of OT belief comes to light in this formula. Originally these words referred to the idea of nomads that the deity travelled with them and their flocks and protected them. From the time of David on the formula more generally refers to the assistance of YHWH. The formula, says Noth, rarely occurs in Israel's 'Umwelt' so that it would describe a piece of typical Israelitisch piety.

1:38 *Then Zadok the priest, Nathan the prophet and Benaiah the son of Jehoiada, along with the Cherethites and the Pelethites, went down and had Solomon ride on king David's mule and brought him to (the spring) Gihon.*
The order formulated in vs. 33 by David is now carried out. For the first time in Kings the 'Cherethites and Pelethites' are mentioned (cf. vs. 44). The group-name כרתי (pl.: כרתים) further occurs in 2 Sam. 8:18; 15:18; 20:7, 23 (q^ere); Ezek. 25:16; 1 Chr. 18:17. Also גוי כרתי (Zeph. 2:5) and נגבה כרתי (1 Sam. 30:14). 'Pelethite' is linked to the former in 2 Sam. 8:18; 15:18; 20:7, 23 and 1 Chr. 18:17. In 1 Sam. 30:14; Ezek. 25:15 and Zeph. 2:5 the Cherethites are mentioned in tandem with the Philistines and possibly refer to 'Cretans.' In the case of the 'Cherethites and Pelethites' we are dealing with David's bodyguard. Though its organization is not very clear, Benaiah, son of Jehoiada, must have been its commander. Whereas the Cherethites are often identified with the Cretans and thereby with the 'Sea Peoples,' the Pelethites are often equated with the Philistines (the /š/ must have been absorbed by the /t/). The Greek tradition views כרת (Zeph. 2:6) as Crete and the Cherethites as the 'inhabitants of Crete' (cf. Montg.-Gehman 85f.). Accordingly it is very probable that both the 'Cretans' and 'Philistines,' both of whom can be counted as having originally been part of the 'Sea Peoples,' are at the root of the name of David's bodyguard.[22] The notion that Pelethite is a 'nichtssagende Anreimung' with Cherethites (Noth) is improbable. It is more likely that the 2 groups of people were related to each other in rhymes. It is striking that, possibly from an aversion to the idea that David – by tradition, an authentic Judean and Israelite – would have had foreigners serving as his bodyguard (this aversion is still present as well in Thenius, Keil [*ad* 2 Sam. 8:18] a.o.), Tg. translates קשתיא וקלעיא as 'archers and slingers,' followed in this by Pesh. which speaks elsewhere of 'freemen and peasants' (*h'r' wplh'*). LXX and Vulg. adhere, be it with variations in orthography, to proper names. It still needs to be remarked that in 2 Kgs. 11:4, 19 (and in the k^etib of 2 Sam. 20:23) there is mention of כרי 'Carites' who presumably constituted queen Athaliah's bodyguard. Especially on the ground of the k^etib-q^ere question in 2 Sam. 20:23 they are sometimes identified with the Cretans; others prefer to think they are mercenaries from the region of Caria, S.W. Asia Minor (NE of Crete; cf. E. Höhne, *BHHW*, II, 934; Montg.-Gehman, etc.). Herodotus (*Hist*. III, 154) already contains a clear indication that Carites entered foreign military service as mercenaries, and in another passage (*Hist* I, 171) makes a connection with 'mainlanders' and Crete, though according to him the Carites themselves deny

---

[22] Cf. also H.J. Stoebe, *BHHW*, II, 1003; J.C. Greenfield, *IDB*, I, 557; E.R. Dalglish, *IDB*, III, 709f.; S.E. Loewenstamm, *EncMiqr*. IV, 332ff.; and now also M. Delcor, *VT* 28 (1978), 409-422; E. Noort, *Die Seevölker in Palästina* (Palestina Antiqua 8), Kampen 1995, 37.

this connection. Both on this point and on the connection between Cherethites and Carites in OT, there is much that awaits clarification. It is certainly striking that after the mention of Cherethites and Pelethites in this pericope, we never encounter them again in the OT. The reference was to a specific and utterly loyal bodyguard of David. It is also striking that David frequently employed foreigners in his army (for example, the Gittites: 2 Sam. 15:18; 18:2; or Uriah the Hittite: 2 Sam. 11:3ff.).

The end of the verse reports the implementation of the king's order to take Solomon on his own mule to the Gihon spring. Only the words differ somewhat by comparison with vs. 33, which has led to a number of understandable but not necessarily to-be-adopted variants in certain Hebr. MSS and ancient versions (cf. *BHK* and *BHS*; also Burney with examples of על after a verb of motion).

1:39 *There the priest Zadok took the horn of oil from the tent and anointed Solomon. Then they sounded the ram's horn and all the people shouted: 'Long live king Solomon!'*

This verse describes the anointing performed by Zadok (cf. also 1 Chr. 23:1 and 29:21ff.). It is expressly stated that Zadok took a horn of oil from the 'tent' (which, according to Rashi, had been made by Moses in the wilderness). Montg.-Gehman correctly point out that ויקח expresses a succession of ideas, not of time (with reference to Driver §76). This implies of course that Zadok already had the horn with him when the procession left to go to the spring. We could also translate: 'Zadok took with him ...' There is also mention of a horn of oil for the anointing of a king (Saul) in 1 Sam. 16:1, 13. In the case of a royal anointing, besides the קרן השמן there is also the פך השמן (1 Sam. 10:1; 2 Kgs. 9:1, 3): 'the flask of oil,' as well as the צפחת השמן (1 Kgs. 17:14, 16), but not for the anointing of a king. The ointment could be preserved, transported and used in various containers (cf. P. Welten, *BRL*^{2}, 260-264). Here we are told it came from the 'tent.' The author undoubtedly had in mind the cult sanctuary of YHWH (cf. 2:28), in which, according to the tradition, David had placed the ark (2 Sam. 6:17; cf. Eißfeldt, *KS*, VI, 6f.; Rashi and Aberbanel). Precisely what this 'tent' or 'hut' (cf. Alt, *KS*, III, 240) looked like is hard to reconstruct but that in this sanctuary, as in all others, 'holy' oil was kept for use in certain ceremonies is plausible (Ex. 30:22-32 [P] may be of a later date but the core of it indicates the 'holy' character of the oil). It is hardly plausible that this tent was identical with the 'tabernacle' (cf. Von Rad, *TAT*, I, 237, n. 108).

The statement that 'all the people' now raised the cry, 'Long live king Solomon!' constitutes an expansion of vs. 34. In light of, for instance, vs. 35, the author intends to underscore both the quantity involved in this event (the overwhelming majority over against a handful of Adoniah-adherents) and the quality (both Judah and Israel).

1:40   *And all he people went up after him, playing flutes and shouting for joy, so that the ground split by their sound.*
This verse serves to highlight the hubbub. Solomon is proclaimed king to the accompaniment of so much exuberance and festive music that the ground shakes (see also 1 Chr. 19:21f.). Textcritically especially מחללים (cf. Bg. II §17h) בחללים produce the usual problems. Must one read the verb (with, e.g., *HAL*; Noth, Stade §154d) as a pi. of חלל III, a denominative of חליל 'flute'? Or are we dealing with a pil'el form of the verb חול (מחללים) 'dancing in the round'? The latter view finds support in LXX^B ἐχόρευον ἐν χοροῖς. LXX$^{Luc.}$ (cf. Rahlfs, *Sst.* III, 171), however, again has a double translation here in which it supports LXX^B on the one hand and on the other follows the former which is also shown by Vulg. *(canentium tibiis)*. Pesh. has *rb'yn brby"*, 'beating on the tambourines.' This last word is also a translation for מחלה (round dance) in Ex. 15:20; Judg. 11:34, so that it is not entirely clear what Pesh. may have read in MT. Tg. reads משבחין בחנגא, 'rejoicing with choral dances (or: musical instruments).' The word חנגא can denote the dance as well as a musical instrument (cf. Dalman, *ANH*; Burney, n. 1, etc.), so that Tg. also fails to give us a sure solution. Are Tg. and Pesh. (again) concurrent here? In any case there is nothing against maintaining MT, the more since – as Burney correctly notes – the stress is especially on the *noise* and not on the very retardant effect of a dance procession (as Thenius rightly remarks). The 'flute' (1 Sam. 10:5; Isa. 5:12; 30:29; Jer. 48:36; cf. Sir. 40:21; 1 QS X, 9; 1 QH XI, 23) is an aerophonic instrument of wood in the form of a tube with a mouthpiece in which a reed can vibrate, hence a kind of oboe (or double oboe). This instrument was not used in the temple cult.[23] The instrument was usually played in the case of a dirge or in sad circumstances (cf. G. Stählin, *TDNT*, III, 844, n. 96), but there are also examples of the opposite as in our text. The *figurae etymologicae* used in this verse underscore this point (cf. König §329g; BrSynt. §99a). The noise and shaking are so intense that the earth began to split (בקע niph.). In Num. 16:31 the word is used to indicate the consequences of an earthquake. Perhaps LXX$^{Luc.}$ ἤχησεν (instead of LXX* ἐρράγη) and Vulg: *insonuit* have sought to weaken somewhat the bold imagery of MT, which for that matter is supported by Pesh. (Ethpe'el of *ṣr'*: 'split in two') and to a lesser degree by Tg. (וזעת ארעא). Thenius's proposal to read ותתקע in place of ותבקע need not be followed. In the case of the passive form of the

---

[23] Cf. also Dalman, *AuS*, VI, 242; H.P. Rüger, *BRL*², 235; *HAL*; further H. Seidel, *Musik in Altisrael* (Beiträge zur Erforschung des Alten Testaments und des antiken Judentums 12), Frankfurt a.M. 1989, 113, 221.

verb the prep. בּ indicates 'la cause instrumental' (Joüon §132e).

1:41 *Then Adonijah and all the guests who were with him and had finished eating heard it. But Joab heard the sound of the ram's horn and asked: 'Why is the city in an uproar?'*
Now begins the pericope which tells the story of Adonijah's fall. The first thing he and his party notice of David's counter-measures to make Solomon king is the noise, the sound. Immediately after they had finished the meal Adonijah and his guests heard 'something.' Ehrlich does not regard this as a time indication — they continue to eat! — but rather an indication of Joab's characteristic attitude: Joab is alert while the others are unconcerned. The text here uses a subordinate clause with a pf. and a subject which is placed first (GD §137c; Driver §§16 and 160; Bg. II §6d). After the 'something' (not reproduced in MT) Joab hears the sound of a ram's horn and poses the far from rhetorical question: 'why is the city in an uproar?' The construction of the last words of this verse is rather striking (König §349a; Ges-K §146a; Stade-Schwally; Joüon §127a; BrSynt. §124a). The predicate of the genitive-connection is pointed to the *rectum* in pl. of the *regens* (Joüon: 'attributive accusative of state'). Nevertheless we need not immediately think here of textual corruption and propose emendations (contra Ges-K et al.), even though LXX$^{Luc.}$ deviates from the other LXX: τις η φωνη της βοης ηχει μεγα. But LXX$^{Luc.}$ must have read קריאה instead of קריה (cf. Jonah 3:2) (Šanda; Montg.-Gehman; etc.). Now קריה (30x in Hebr. part of OT), 'city,' by comparison with עיר, is rare, especially in prose texts (cf. aside from another occurrence in vs. 45, only in Deut. 2:36; 3:4). One encounters the word more frequently in poetic and prophetic sections (Num. 21:28; Isa. 1:21, 26; 22:2; 24:10; 25:2f. etc.) and as a an element in place names (e.g. Kiriath-Arba in Gen. 23:2 etc.; Kiriath-Baal in Josh. 15:60 etc.). The word frequently refers to Jerusalem (Isa. 1:21, 26; 29:1, etc.), but also to other cities (Damascus in Jer. 49:25; Gilead in Hos. 6:8 etc.). The word also occurs in the Aram. part of OT (9x in Ezra; cf. *DISO*, 266). On the well-known Mesa-stone one finds קר, pl. קרן (*KAI* 181, 11f., 24, 29), which is again related to the Hebr. קיר 'wall.' But already in Ugar. one encounters *qrt, qryt* (Aistleitner, 2462). It is not certain whether the word comes form the root קרה and may mean a 'meeting place of men' (*BDB*; cf. Ges-B and Zorell; *civitas*). It is better to assume a connection with the abovementioned קיר, so that the word can refer to the 'walled' or 'fortified city' (cf. also A.R. Hulst, *THAT*, II, 268; and now *HAL* as well), in our case Jerusalem *inter muros*, the city from which — though they were some distance away from it — the noise reached the Adonijah-group. המה indicates the noise of a city, e.g. also in Isa. 22:2 (cf. Ps. 46:7), but it can convey all sorts of sounds and noise (cf. A. Baumann, *TWAT*, II, 444-449), in connection with which the meaning often implies a negative qualification (cf. also the roots נהם

and הםם). The words of Joab certainly have this ominous nuance, even reinforced by the question: 'why,' what is the reason for all this? Something must have gone wrong ...

1:42 *While he was still speaking, Jonathan the son of Abiathar the priest came in. Adonijah said: 'Come on in, you are a reliable fellow and surely you bring good news.'*

While he is still speaking the dénouement of the riddle comes in the form of a 'Botenspruch.' The messenger is Jonathan, son of Abiathar the priest. One meets him also in 2 Sam. 15:27, 36 and 17:17, 20 where, during Absalom's uprising, he chose the side of David and functioned as a courier. Here, too, we find him performing this function, though it is not explicitly stated that he is now on the side of Adonijah. MT creates the impression that Jonathan comes in amidst the situation which Joab had depicted as alarming (LXX[Luc.] leaves בא untranslated), whereupon Adonijah, prompted more by wishful thinking than by the actual situation, invites him to bring him a 'good message,' because he is undoubtedly a 'reliable man.' איש חיל in the sing., or אנשים in the pl., in 17 out of 23 cases denotes a military man (cf. H. Eising, *TWAT*, II, 905). In other cases, also in other combinations with חיל[24] the basic meaning of חיל, 'power,' 'might' comes through one way or another, whether one wishes to translate it by 'wealthy' or by 'strong' in the sense of 'formidable,' 'sincere,' 'valiant,' 'trustworthy' (cf. Burney). The verb בשר pi. occurs 23x in OT (cf. Jenni, *Pi'el*, 246) and means 'report,' 'convey a message' (R. Ficker, *THAT*, I, 903f.). It has a neutral meaning which is often used (esp. in Deut.-Isa.) *in bonam partem:* 'bring a joyful message' (cf. G. Friedrich, *TDNT*, II, 707-710). Here (cf. Isa. 52:7 and 2 Sam. 18:27) טוב is added to bring out the 'good' content of the message. In 2 Sam. 18:27 as well as here the 'psychische Hochspannung der Adressaten' is indicated and the addition 'good' describes the expectation of a 'joyful message' (O. Schilling, *TWAT*, I, 847). It needs further to be stated that in 2 Sam. 18:27 there is mention of a איש טוב in place of a איש חיל by which not so much the 'martial' as the 'trustworthy' character of the messenger is communicated.

1:43 *Jonathan answered and said to Adonijah: 'You bet ...! Our king David has made Solomon king.*

The content of Jonathan's message (vss. 43-48) is a restatement of what has already been related in the preceding. On the one hand, it is a 'good news' for all who are kindly disposed toward the Davidic dynasty in the Solomonic line;

---

[24] See my article "*Hayil* in het boek Ruth, een vertaalprobleem," *Verkenningen in een Stroomgebied* (Fs M.A. Beek, ed. M. Boertien et al.), Amsterdam 1974, 120-131.

and that includes all possible readers of the author of his story. On the other hand, as vss. 49ff. teach, it is bad news for Adonijah and his party.

In some important LXX MSS Adonijah is not mentioned (it is in LXX[Luc.], Aq., Symm., and Theod.), but that has no material significance for the story. The meaning of אבל is disputed: 'Ach' (Noth); 'leider' (Ehrlich); 'Nay but' (Burney); 'Indeed' ('in ironic contradiction,' in Montg.-Gehman; cf. Thenius) etc. If the word is related to בל, בלתי and essentially has a negative undertone (cf. BrSynt. §56b), then, with a dose of irony, it underscores the meaning of the following statement (*HAL*; König §351a): 'You bet ...!' (cf. M. Kilwing, *BN* 11 [1980], 23-28).

1:44 *The king sent with him the priest Zadok, the prophet Nathan, and Benaiah the son of Jehoiada, as well as the Cherithites and the Pelethites and they had him ride on the king's mule.*
The only striking element in this text is that the *nota accusativi* before Zadok and Nathan are not repeated before Benaiah and the Cherethites and Pelethites (Ewald §339b; König §319l). We can agree with König (against Ewald) that this need not *per se* point to the 'secondary rank' of Benaiah, since in Hebr. the repetition of particles is omitted more often.

1:45 *Then the priest Zadok and the prophet Nathan anointed him king at (the spring) Gihon, and from there they went up shouting for joy so that the city is in an uproar. That is the noise you heard.*
Aside from the fact that LXX[Hex.] and LXX[Luc.] read וישמחו as sing. (cf. vs. 34) and some Hebr. MSS omit Nathan from Adonijah's anointing, especially ותהם is interesting in this verse (cf. 1 Sam. 4:5; Ruth 1:19). The form is a niph. of הום (cf. *HAL* etc.) in the sense of 'being beside oneself' (cf., however, Ges-K §72h and 67n). Bg. II §31f rightly comments that one would rather expect a form of המה 'to be in an uproar' (cf. vs. 41; cf. also Driver, *Samuel*, ad I 4:5; Ehrlich, who reads וַתֵּהֹם, etc.). *HAL* then adds to this 'confusion' by listing the form found at the palaces mentioned once more under המם I niph., for that matter with the same translation as was given by הום and with reference to this verb. It seems to us that the analogy with vs. 41 would favour a form of the verb המה, also in view of the ancient versions like LXX and Vulg. Tg. here (and in vs. 41) has a form of the verb שׁגשׁ, 'confuse'; Pesh. has this verb only in vs. 41 but here it has a form of *hd'*, 'rejoice' (except MSS 9 al *fam* which have *w'štgšt*). Apparently the meaning of this form was not entirely clear to (the translators of) the ancient versions either. For הקריה LXX[Luc.] reads ἡ κραυγή, 'the noise.'

1:46 *And Solomon also sits on the throne of the kingdom.*
This verse and the 2 following verses each time begin with וגם, which not only

suggests a hasty, somewhat fragmented way of telling a story (Benzinger) – it certainly does that too – but also a step-by-step process of leading to a climax. The particle in question has an 'emphasizing' character.²⁵

A peculiarity in this verse is that Jonathan relates that Solomon is seated on 'the throne of the kingship.' מלוכה, which out of 24x in OT occurs more than half of the time in Samuel and Kings (cf. 1 Kgs. 2:15-22). It is a fem. *qatûl*-form of מלך with an abstract meaning (BL, 472vα; K. Seybold, *TWAT*, IV, 940f.). This is the only time (of a number that is already small) that the 'throne of the kingship' in the sense of 'royal throne' is so used in the OT. Elsewhere one also finds כסא ממלכתו (Deut. 17:18; 2 Sam. 7:13) or הממלכה (2 Chr. 23:20); כסא המלכים (2 Kgs. 11:19; 25:28) or something similar (cf. Hag. 2:22; Est. 2:1; 5:1 etc.) Strikingly, the expression 'throne of David' (cf. vs. 37; 2:12, 24 [*qᵉre*]; Isa. 9:6 etc.), or 'throne of Israel' (cf. 2:4; 8:20, 25; 9:5; 10:9 etc.) is not used here. Is it perhaps the author's implicit intent, by way of Jonathan's words, to refer to the undivided kingdom (of Judah *and* Israel)? In the formulation adopted, is he expressing a hidden criticism of the 'throne of Israel'? In 1 Chr. 29:23 there is mention of על־כסא יהוה (also cf. vss. 24ff.; 1 Chr. 28:5). Here we are already in a later stage in history. 'Throne of Israel' nowhere occurs in the 'Thronfolgegeschichte' except in 2:4, but here we are probably dealing with a redactional interpolation (see below under 2:2ff.).

1:47 *Also, the king's servants have come to congratulate king David with the words: "May your God make the name of Solomon more glorious than yours and his throne greater than yours." At this the king bowed down upon his bed.*

In Jonathan's account there is now a falling back on Benaiah's congratulations in vs. 36f. The author expands this to 'the king's servants' and uses the word 'bless' (ברך pi.) (cf. J. Scharbert, *TWAT*, I, 808-841; C.A. Keller, G. Wehmeier, *THAT*, I, 353-376). The word, both in the form of a verb and in that of a substantive, occurs almost 400x in OT, of which 233x in pi. (even apart from the biblical Aram.). Genesis, Deuteronomy, and Psalms most frequently show a form of the root ברך; 1 Kings, 12x; 2 Kings, only 5x. In the narrative sections of OT, forms of the word tend to occur in connection with congratulations or greetings, as in our verse. Usually a superior person 'blesses' an inferior one, but ברך is also used conversely, be it somewhat rarely, as in our vs. in which David's servants express to God the wish that Solomon may become even greater than his father.

A *kᵉtib-qᵉre* issue is אלהיך *kᵉtib* and Pesh., which (except in 9 al *fam*) has

---

²⁵ Cf. C.J. Labuschagne, "The Emphasizing Particle *GAM* and its Connotations," *Studia Biblica et Semitica* (Fs. Th. C. Vriezen), Wageningen 1966, 193-203.

mry' precede *'lhk*, where the *qᵉre,* supported by a number of MSS, LXX, Vulg. and Tg., reads אלהים. On the basis of vs. 36 one is inclined to give priority to the *kᵉtib* form (Thenius, Stade-Schwally et al., opposed: Burney). Interesting from a textcritical viewpoint is the expansion of LXX^Luc. after לאמר: και εισεληλυθασι μονοι και ειπον, which is probably not based on a MT-'Vorlage' (but cf. Burney). To be mentioned also is that LXX^Luc., along with a number of MSS of LXX (minus B), adds 'your son' to 'Solomon.' The form ייטב is a jussive hiphil of the verb יטב or טוב, a so-called 'mixed' form (BL, 402u"; Bg. II §26h, cf. also Ges-K §70e, who thinks that here an impf. is used for the form יטיב; cf. further Böttcher §956g), which brings out the wish-form of Jonathan's quotation. Jonathan further brings out that the 'servants of the king' wish that in many respects Solomon will surpass his father (cf. BrSynt. §111g). An element he adds to his report is that David bowed down upon his (cf. Joüon §137f) bed. The word משכב occurs only here in 1 Kings. The question is for whom David actually bowed on his bed (for the verb, see under vs. 16). As a rule it is assumed that he bowed down in worship before God but, aside from the fact that bowing as a rule takes place in the cult and in the presence of a cult object, this is not a bowing before God but before people who pronounced a blessing. Accordingly, we believe, with Thenius (cf. Gen. 47:31; 48:12, also 37:7ff.), that the reference here is to a grateful bowing, a gesture of acknowledgment toward those who have spoken good words and wishes.

1:48 *And the king also said as follows: "Praise be to YHWH, the God of Israel, who today has granted someone to sit on my throne and permitted me to witness it".'*

This thought is reinforced by the fact that in this verse Jonathan adds a fresh statement by saying that today God has granted a successor on the throne. This is a new element, not immediately connected with the preceding, the bowing down on his bed, though there is of course a logical connection between this argument and all the preceding ones. But the new element in this communication is even reinforced by the use of a 'cataphoric' כבה (for the term, cf. Schneider, §52.6), a doubling of *ka = kô (cf. also Ewald §105b and the above remarks at vs. 6). Textcritically it is a question whether, following נתן היום, with a number of MSS and certain ancient versions or MSS of the same, בן or מזרעי must be inserted (cf. LXX ἐκ τοῦ σπέρματός μου; many MSS of Tg.: בר; Pesh. *br'*). It is of course possible that originally the text read 'son' or 'of my descendants,' but when this is omitted, as in MT, the meaning of the statement remains unchanged, because of course David intends to say: a descendant of mine. We therefore maintain the reading of MT and regard the additions in the ancient versions as clarifications of the text. Noth correctly comments that the true weight of the verse lies in the end: David, though very old, still saw the day when the succession to the throne was definitely settled. According to the author this was in accordance with a once-given promise. The formula ברוך יהוה אלהי ישראל is also found in 1 Sam. 25:32; 1 Kgs. 8:15; Ps. 41:14; 106:48; 1 Chr. 16:36; 2 Chr., 2:11; 6:4 (cf. 1 Chr. 29:10).

1:49 *At this, all Adonijah's guests got up trembling and everyone went his way.*
In the preceding the author led Jonathan's statements toward a climax and it would seem to be his intent to link especially the fear of Adonijah's guests and of Adonijah himself to Jonathan's concluding statement. Inasmuch as a promise has been fulfilled by God it no longer makes sense for Adonijah and his friends to continue to pursue the 'natural' line of succession. As if they knew about the promises in 2 Sam. 7 and about Nathan's intrigues! There is no sign of resistance on the part of Adonijah and his group. Here we see the evidence of the 'stylization' of the story by the narrator. There is no indication of the actual course of events because at least some resistance on the part of Adonijah and his adherents was to have been expected. The verb חרד (A. Baumann, *TWAT*, III, 176-182) occurs in the qal 23x and in the hiph. 16x in OT (cf. also H.-P. Stähli, *THAT*, I, 768) and is usually translated by 'tremble,' 'shudder.' The word is frequently emotionally charged so that it can mean 'fall into panic,' often in reaction to a theophany (cf. Baumann, 177, and the LXX-translation ἐξίστημι: A. Oepke, *TDNT*, II, 454f.). In Kings the word only occurs again in 2 Kgs. 4:13 (Baumann, 181).

1:50 *Adonijah, too, was afraid of Solomon. He got up and went to grasp the horns of the altar.*
The entire focus is on Adonijah, who is filled with understandable fear of Solomon. He does what in such circumstances other people in Israel apparently did as well (cf. 2:28): he fled to the sanctuary and grasped one of the horns of the altar, seeking asylum. H. Grotius, in this connection, rightly comments: *Ad aram confugit, non ex Legis instituto, sed ex gentium more ...* In Ex. 21:14 there is mention only of altars, not of horns. But it is known from OT (cf. Ex. 29:12; 30:10; Lev 4. *passim,* etc.) as well as from excavations (cf. A. Reichert, *BRL*², 28f.) that altars sometimes had horn-shaped extensions at the 4 corners. Evidently, under certain conditions, these horns – and probably these sanctuaries as a whole – offered a certain protection until the king had pronounced justice (cf. J. de Vaulx, *DBS,* IX, 1489-1492; Ch. Dohmen, *TWAT,* IV, 799f.).[26] In our verse and in 2:28ff. the reference is to political asylum, not to

---

[26] On the right of asylum connected with the altar, see also J. de Groot, *Die Altäre des Salomonischen Tempelhofes* (BWAT 6), Stuttgart 1924, 76-88; B. van Oeveren, *De vrijsteden in*

unintentional homicide. The right of asylum associated with sanctuaries and their appurtenances is known not only from Israel (cf. also 1 Macc. 10:43), but from the entire Near East (numerous examples are given by De Vaulx, 1483-1489; see also Herodotus, *Hist.* VI, 108; Tacitus, *Ann.* 3, 60.1; Strabo 5, 230; 16, 750, etc.). In addition there were in Israel 6 so-called 'cities of refuge' as well for those involved in accidental manslaughter (ערי מקלט: Num. 35:6-34; Deut. 4:41ff.; 19:1-13; Josh. 20; cf. M. David, *OTS* 9 [1951], 30-48; A.G. Auld, *JSOT* [1978], 26-40; De Vaulx, 1492-1499). It is not clear specifically to what the horns originally corresponded. Some, e.g., Benzinger, *Arch.*, 320, think of the (waxing) moon.[27] De Groot sees a connection with the crowns of horns worn by gods and kings and attributes apotropaic significance to them; often, however, they were linked to the bull-cult (cf. Dohmen, 800). Similarly uncertain is the original background of this custom. Adonijah's act, however, is clear. In our vs. it is not explicitly stated where Adonijah went to grasp the horns of the altar. In 2:28 we do read this (אל־אהל יהוה) and LXX[Luc.] also has this clarifying addition in our vs. The reference here is the tent which David must have placed before the ark. The altar with horns must have been located by this tent (cf. Galling, *BRL*², 325).[28] This tent was located on Mt. Zion (cf. LXX on 3:15; Thenius; Rashi, however, thinks of Gibeon). But the idea that Adonijah as God's protégé had become inviolable to anyone seeking his life (thus Benzinger) is incorrect (this is evident from 2:28ff. alone).

1:51 *It was reported to Solomon: 'Look, Adonijah is afraid of king Solomon; in fact, he is clinging to the horns of the altar, saying, "Let king Solomon first swear to me that he will not put his servant to death with the sword".'*

Naturally the report of Adonijah's flight does not remain unknown to Solomon. Not only is he told of Adonijah's fear and flight to the altar but also of the request he makes to the king. There is indeed a fine distinction in the first half of our vs. by comparison with the previous vs. Whereas there use was made of the verb חזק hiphil (cf. *DBS*, IX, 1490) as it concerns the horns of the altar, here the verb אחז is used, a word which to our mind is virtually synonymous (cf. also H.H. Schmid, *THAT*, I, 108f.; A.S. van der Woude, *THAT*, I, 538ff.). Perhaps the first means 'to catch hold of,' the second 'to hold onto.'

---

het Oude Testament, Kampen 1968, 130ff.; 151f.; L. Delekat, *Asylie und Schutzorakel am Zionheiligtum*, Leiden 1967, 6, n. 1; 208ff.; 272; see now also C. Houtman, "Der Altar als Asylstätte im Alten Testament: Rechtsbestimmung (Ex. 21,12-14) und Praxis (1 Reg. 1-2)," *RB* 103 (1996), 343-366.

[27] Cf. also G. Ryckmans, *L'Ancien Testament et l'Orient* (Orientalia et Biblica Lovaniensia 1), Louvain 1957, 102, for ancient Arabia.

[28] Cf. also H.M. Wiener, *The Altars of the Old Testament*, Leipzig 1927, 12ff.

The content of Adonijah's oath seems to us logical, but the form of it occasions some comments. In the first place there is the textcritical question whether one must read כיום or ביום, 'today,' the latter especially on the basis of LXX σήμερον, Pesh. *(ywmn')* and Vulg. *(hodie)*. Tg. however, does have כיומא. Though materially there is not much difference between the 2 readings, one can in fact translate כיום by 'first' (cf. e.g. Gen. 25:31; 1 Sam. 2:16 etc.), because in this adverb of time the concept of 'day' has receded into the background and the present is especially contrasted with the future (thus correctly Driver, *Samuel*, on I Sam. 2:16; cf. also BrSynt. §109b; De Vries, *Yesterday*, 51f. n. 77.). In addition, אם is here used in the oath of denial, in our language 'if not'; conversely אם לא, 'if'; GD §156b; BrSynt. §170c; Ges-K §149c and esp. C. van Leeuwen, *OTS* 18 (1973), 34-38.

1:52 *Then Solomon said: 'If he is really a reliable fellow, then not one of his hairs will fall to the ground; but if disloyalty is found in him he will die.'*
Solomon is not indisposed to grant Adonijah's request but does lay down a condition. If he will be a בן־חיל, not a hair will be injured, but if רעה is found in him, he will die. In vs. 42 we encountered the expression איש־חיל, which does not always serve to describe a military man but can mean the 'reliable, valiant' man. Here too the word has reference to peaceful circumstances: the man must prove himself capable of being described with the concept of 'faithful,' 'reliable' in relationship (cf. H. Eising, *TWAT*, II, 904f.), and not with the concept of 'evil,' 'wicked,' 'unreliable.' בן here indicates the possessor of a quality ('genitival phrases,' Joüon §129j; G. Fohrer, *TDNT*, VIII, 345ff.).

After יהיה a small number of MSS add לי, but even without the addition the text is clear. Asyndetically, לא־יפל is added to the preceding because as a rule no *waw apodosis* is added before particles (Joüon §176n, Driver, §136, p. 175, n. 1). משערתו is formed by מן + שערה + suff. שערה (also Judg. 20:16; 1 Sam. 14:45; 2 Sam. 14:11; Ps. 40:13; 69:5 and Job 4:15) refers especially to a single hair (the so-called *nomen unitatis,* indicated by the fem., cf. Ewald §176a; Ges-K §122t), in contrast to שער, the 'shock of hair.' מן in a partitive sense as 'part of' (cf. Ges-K §119ʷ, note 1; BrSynt. §34ᵃ) or, as Driver, *Samuel*, ad I 14:45, calls it 'starting from' (also cf. Burney), emphatically singles out the one of all the others. For parallels in Arab., see Driver, Burney.[29] This מן as it were functions as the subject of the clause (BrSynt. §105ᵇ): not one of the hairs will fall. Tg. and Pesh. add with LXX^Luc. 'from his head,' as though the 'Vorlage' read משערת ראשו as in 1 Sam. 14:45. But even then no textual modification is needed. We still need to refer to the different constructions of the 2 sentences

---

[29] Cf. also W. Wright, *Grammar of Arabic Language*, Cambrigde 1967³, §48f, Rem. b.

which start with אם. In the first Adonijah is the subject: if he turns out to be a reliable man, then ... he will have every chance in the world. In the second 'wickedness' is the subject. Adonijah is as it were the 'passive' object, with wickedness as 'subject.'

1:53 *Then king Solomon sent (messengers) to have him brought down from the altar. He came and bowed down before king Solomon. And Solomon said: 'Go to your home.'*
So with respect to Adonijah, Solomon gives him the benefit of the doubt, sent to have him brought down from the altar and lets him go home (1 Chr. 29:24 merely alludes to this event). It makes little difference whether with MT one reads the pl. or with some ancient versions (LXX minus Luc.; Pesh. Vulg.) the sing. as subject of the verb ירד. In both cases Solomon will have ordered his servants. The expression מעל המזבח prompts the suspicion that Adonijah had climbed up on a high altar and had to be brought down from there. Also from 2:34 (עלה) one gets the impression that the altar had to be 'ascended' (cf. also 12:32f.; 2 Kgs. 16:12; 23:9 etc.). Ex. 20:26 prohibited steps alongside the altar but there are traditions which in any case testify of a perhaps sloping ascent in the form of a spiral or the like (cf. Ezek. 43:17; further Burney and A. Reichert, *BRL*[2], 9f.), or otherwise one can hardly speak of 'going up' or 'down.' In Mishna Middoth III, 3 there is a description of the altar in the second temple and we read that on the south side there was a 'walk-up,' a kind of rampart (כבש) 32 cubits long and 16 cubits wide; and from III, 4 one can conclude it was made of stone (from the valley of Bet Kerem). Josephus (*Bell*. V §225) also refers to this walk-up from the south: ἄνοδος ἠρέμα προςάντης ὑπτίαστο, 'the passage up to it was very gradual.' Although this altar is of a late date, along with the large altars found in Palestine it does provide us with insight into the height and size of it. It is not impossible that the author had some such altar in mind.

1 KINGS 2:1-46

2:1 *When David was about to die, he gave his son Solomon a statement of his last will, saying:*

2 *'I am about to go the way of all the earth. Be strong. Show yourself a man.*

3 *Watch over the charge which YHWH, your God, has given you to keep: walking in his ways, keeping his statutes, his commandments, his ordinances, and his testimonies, as recorded in the law of Moses, so that you may be successful in everything you do and undertake,*

4 *and that YHWH may fulfill the word he has spoken concerning me: "if your sons watch their conduct by walking faithfully before me with their whole heart and soul, (then), as far as you are concerned, no one will ever be cut off from the throne of Israel."*

5 *Further, you know too what Joab son of Zeruiah did to me and what he did to the two commanders of the army of Israel, Abner son of Ner and Amasa son of Jether. He killed them, shedding the blood of war in time of peace, thus spattering the blood of war on the belt around his waist and the sandals on his feet.*

6 *Act therefore according to your wisdom and do not let his gray head go down to the underworld in peace.*

7 *As regards the sons of Barzillai of Gilead, treat them as friends, let them sit among those who eat at your table, for they were as kind to me when I had to flee from your brother Absalom.*

8 *You also have with you Shimei son of Gera the Benjaminite from Bahurim, who cursed me with an offensive curse on the day I went to Mahanaim, but when he came down to meet me at the Jordan I swore to him by YHWH: "I will not put you to death with the sword."*

9 *But now, do not consider him innocent; you are a wise man; you know what you have to do; you must bring his gray head, bloodied, down into the underworld.'*

10 *So David went to rest with his ancestors and was buried in the city of David.*

11 *The period in which David was king over Israel lasted forty years – seven years in Hebron and thirty-three in Jerusalem.*

12 *Then Solomon sat on the throne of his father David and his royal rule was very stable.*

13 *Then Adonijah son of Haggith came to Bathsheba, Solomon's mother. She said: 'Does your coming mean peace?' He answered: 'Peace!'*

14 *Then he added: 'There is something I have to discuss with you.' 'Go on,'* *she replied.*

15 *'You know,'* he said, *'that I had title to the crown and that all Israel had looked to me to be king. But the crown switched (persons) and went to my brother, since it was YHWH's will to give it to him.*

16 *But now to the point: I have one request to make of you, and please do not refuse me.'* *'Go on,'* she said.

17 He continued: *'Please speak with king Solomon — for he will not refuse you — and (ask him) to give me Abishag the Shunammite as wife.'*

18 *'Very well,'* answered Bathsheba, *'I myself will speak to the king about you.'*

19 *So Bathsheba went to king Solomon to speak to him about Adonijah. The king rose to meet her and bowed before her; then he sat down on his throne, and had a chair brought in for the king's mother so that she was seated at his right.*

20 *She said to him:* *'I have one small request to make of you; please do not refuse me.'* *The king answered:* *'Just say it, mother; I cannot refuse you.'*

21 *She said:* *'Please may Abishag the Shunammite be given to your brother Adonijah as wife?'*

22 *Then king Solomon answered and said to his mother:* *'Now why do you ask me to give Abishag the Shunammite to Adonijah? You might as well ask me to give him the crown. After all, he is my older brother and Abiathar the priest and Joab the son of Zeruiah are (undoubtedly) on his side.'*

23 *Then king Solomon swore by YHWH:* *'May God deal with me, yes even worse, if Adonijah did not dream up this scheme at the cost of his life.*

24 *And now listen: As surely as the Lord lives who has established me (in my office as king) and has set me on the throne of my father David and who, as he promised, has started a dynasty for me, so surely will Adonijah be put to death still today.'*

25 *So king Solomon gave orders to Benaiah son of Jehoiada who struck him (Adonijah) down so that he died.*

26 *Then the king said to Abiathar the priest:* *'Go to Anathoth to your estate, for you deserve to die. Now, however, I will not put you to death because you have carried the ark of the Lord YHWH before my father David and you shared all my father's hardships.'*

27 *So Solomon discharged Abiathar from his position as priest of YHWH, thus fulfilling the word of YHWH which he had spoken at Shiloh concerning Eli's family.*

28 *When word reached Joab — for Joab had joined Adonijah and his party though (earlier) he had not joined Absalom — Joab fled to the tent of YHWH and took hold of the horns of the altar.*

29 *When king Solomon was told that Joab had fled to the tent of YHWH and was evidently by the altar, he sent Benaiah son of Jehoiada, charging him:*

'Go, strike him down.'

30 When Benaiah arrived at the tent of YHWH, he said to him: 'The king says: "Come out".' But he said: 'No, I will die here.' So Benaiah sent word back to the king: 'So Joab has spoken and so I have answered.'

31 Then the king said to him: 'Do as he has said. Strike him down and bury him. So clear me and my father's house of responsibility for the blood which Joab has shed without cause.

32 And YHWH will bring his blood down on his own head because without the knowledge of my father David, he (fatally) struck down and killed with the sword two people who were more righteous and better than he, Abner son of Ner, commander of the army of Israel, and Amasa son of Jether, commander of the army of Judah.

33 May their blood come down on the head of Joab and his descendants for ever, but may David, his descendants, his dynasty, and his throne for ever have peace from YHWH.'

34 Then Benaiah son of Jehoiada went up, struck him and so killed him. He was buried on his estate in the wilderness.

35 The king appointed Benaiah son of Jehoiada in his place as head of the army and the priest Zadok in place of Abiathar.

36 The king also sent for Shimei and said to him, 'Build yourself a house in Jerusalem, live there but do not leave it to go anywhere else.

37 On the day you leave it and cross the Kidron Brook, be very clear that you will die. Your blood will then be on your own head.'

38 'Very well,' Shimei answered the king. 'Your servant will do as my lord the king has explained.' So Shimei lived in Jerusalem for a long time.

39 But about three years later two of Shimei's slaves ran away to Akish son of Macah, king of Gath. Shimei was told: 'Look, your slaves are in Gath.'

40 Shimei got up, saddled his donkey, and went to Akish at Gath to track down his slaves. So Shimei went and brought his slaves back from Gath.

41 When Solomon was told that Shimei had gone from Jerusalem to Gath and back,

42 the king sent for Shimei and said to him: 'Did I not make you swear by YHWH and very clearly warn you: "On the day you leave from here and go anywhere else, be very sure you will die," to which you even responded by saying, "Very well; I have heard you."

43 But why then have you not kept the oath to YHWH and the order I gave you?'

44 The king then said to Shimei: 'You must bring to mind all the wickedness you did to my father David; now may YHWH bring your wickedness down on your own head.

45 But may king Solomon be blessed and may the throne of David be kept secure before YHWH for ever.'

46 *On orders from the king, Benaiah son of Jehoiada, then stepped forward and struck Shimei down so that he died. So the kingship was solidly in Solomon's power.*

INTRODUCTION

This chapter seems to be less unified than the preceding one, despite the fact that, connected with it as this chapter is, it belongs to the conclusion of the succession-narrative. It is therefore significant that LXX$^{Luc.}$ for example, starts the book 3 Kingdoms at vs. 12, and so it creates a 'natural' ending to David's life and the beginning of Solomon's rule.

Striking is the 'revival' of David, by which his 'last words' before he dies acquire a grim and vengeful quality, even aside from the dtr. coloring of some verses. Splendidly told, again, is the tale of Adonijah's public conduct which indeed is not as innocent as it seems and that of Solomon's alertness in seeing through the plot. Looming behind Adonijah – who has to pay for his 'small' request with his life – Solomon espies the figures of Abiathar and Joab. The removal of Abiathar from the priestly service in favour of Zadok legitimatizes the Zadokite priesthood but has also furnished some scholars the understandable suggestion that Abiathar may have been the (sulking) author of this section. An air of anti-Davidic and anti-Solomonic feelings unmistakably clings to this entire chapter. The stability of the Davidic dynasty is purchased at the price of blood and tears, a fate in which even Shimei has to share. But despite stories which to people of 'modern sensitivities' are revolting,[1] the final editor has whipped them into fascinating shape.

This chapter begins with a 'farewell speech' by king David (vss. 1-9), which does not seem to be all of one piece[2]. Generally vss. 3f. are viewed as a dtr. addition to which vs. 2 can serve as introduction. But also vss. 5-9, in which the recommended elimination of Joab is somewhat differently motivated than its execution in vss. 28ff. and also the lauded wisdom of Solomon (vss. 6 and 9) have a premature 'feel' in light of the following chapter (thus Noth), suggest that the section of vss. 1b-9 has been added to the story from another source. This surmise also confirms the beginning of LXX$^{Luc.}$: και εγενετο etc.

---

[1] Cf. B.E. Scolnic, "David's Final Testament: Morality or Expediency?," *Jud* 43 (1994), 19-26.

[2] For this aspect, see, e.g., E. Cortès, *Los Discursos de Adíos*, Barcelona 1976; and L.G. Perdue, *ZAW* 93 (1981), 122ff. The unity of vss. 1-10 is defended by W.T. Koopmans, "he Testament of David in 1 Kings ii 1-10," *VT* 41 (1991), 429-449, but again questioned by R. de Hoop, "The Testament of David: A Response to W.T. Koopmans," *VT* 45 (1995), 270-279; cf. also M. Anbar, "Un 'mot en vedette' et une 'reprise' introduisant une promesse conditionelle de l'éternité de la dynastie davidique," *VT* 44 (1994), 1-9.

(see also Stade-Schwally). This does not have to mean that the entire pericope is dtr. (contra Jepsen, *Quellen*, 19).³ For the final composition of his narrative the author may have utilized other (ancient) traditions. In any case Noth's view would seem plausible, i.e. that this farewell speech, despite David's senility, is here put on his lips in part to render Solomon's heavy-handed conduct in the beginning period of his rule acceptable by means of a final 'will and testament' from his father. It is understandable that the Chronicler wants no part of any last words of David with such content. There is therefore considerable difference between David's final word in our passage and that in 1 Chr. 29:20. Similarly, there is a big difference between our pericope and 1 Chr. 22:6-16, in which David's last words to Solomon concern the command to build a temple. That fits the Chronicler's framework.

EXEGESIS

2:1 *When David was about to die, he gave his son Solomon a statement of his last will, saying:*
The beginning of this verse, a construction of ל + קרב (cf. König §399w; Bg. II §11k), occurs also in Gen. 47:29, but then with Israel as proper name (cf. also Deut. 31:14). ויצו is used here, as in Gen. 49:29, 2 Sam. 17:23 and 2 Kgs. 20:1/Isa. 38:1, in the sense of 'giving his final testament' (cf. also G. Liedke, *THAT*, II, 533; and for the addition from vs. 10 in LXX^Luc.; Montg.-Gehman, 97f.; Rahlfs, *SSt.* III, 283f.).

2:2 *'I am about to go the way of all the earth. Be strong. Show yourself a man.*
As in Josh. 23:14, so here the person who is about to die announces his forthcoming death as 'going the way of all the earth.' As in other languages, so the Hebr. הלך is a euphemism for 'dying'⁴, which in the present case is supplemented and clarified by the words 'the way of all the earth.' In OT there are various expressions for 'to die' which are linked with various views of the Hebr. person concerning the afterlife (cf. F. Hauck, S. Schulz, *TDNT*, VI, 571f. and Tromp, 167-175). For the future meaning of the ptc. הֹלֵךְ, see GD §76c; Ges-K §116lo and Bg. II §13h*; the immediately following perfect consecutives serve to introduce a command or wish (cf. Ges-K §112aa and

---

³ See now also J.S. Rogers, "Narrative Stock and Deuteronomistic Elaboration in 1 Kings 2," *CBQ* 50 (1988), 398-413. In his opinion this chapter is composed of an basic pre-dtr. narrative and a subsequent dtr. elaboration.
⁴ Cf. N.J. Tromp, *Primitive Conceptions of Death and the Nether World in the Old Testament* (Biblica et Orientalia 21), Rome 1969, 167f.

Driver §119).

The phrases 'being strong' and 'a man' are expressions which play a role in the genre ('Gattung') characterized by Lohfink as 'Amtseinsetzung'.[5] Elements of this 'Gattung' are: a 'formula of encouragement' (חזק and אמץ), a task description, and a statement that YHWH will help (יהוה עמך). Compare Deut. 31:23, where this formula occurs in its simplest form and which can also – as McCarthy correctly points out – be found outside of the Deuteronomy and Joshua complex, as in our text (cf. also 1 Chr. 28:10, 2 Chr. 19:5-7; 32:6-8; further Hag. 2:4; Ezra 10:4). According to McCarthy, the formula cannot be traced to the 'holy war' but to the cult in the royal sanctuary (cf. Ps. 27:14; 31:25). Although the formula has been characterized as dtr., that does not describe its source.

חזק, 'be strong'(cf. A.S. van der Woude, *THAT*, I, 538-541; F. Hesse, *TWAT*, II, 846-857) is an encouragement with which 'being a man' is linked. In Tg. this last expression is understood as a גבר דחל חטאין, 'a man who fears (committing) sins.' LXX [Luc.] speaks of an ανδρα δυναμεως. A.D. Crown, *VT* 24 (1974), 110f., points out that in the remainder of the story nothing is said about Solomon's courage or manliness; according to him, the expression simply means 'and become king.' In support of this he refers to parallels in the El-Amarna literature, particularly to the meaning of *amelū*, 'man,' in the sense of 'ruler,' 'king.' Still it is a question whether we should adopt Crown's opinion, because the reference here is to a more or less fixed formula, as has already been shown. Further, the virtual par. 1 Sam. 4:9, for example, points in the direction of 'strong,' 'forceful men,' who are not afraid in battle. The idea that חיל was omitted after איש however, is doubtful. With Burney we prefer to think of periphrastic additions in different MSS of the ancient versions.

Finally we still wish to mention the unusual rendering of אנכי by εγω ειμι in LXX, according to Thackeray, *Grammar*, 10, one of the characteristics of the translator of the 2 parts of the books of Kings which he designates as βγ and γδ (or together as βδ). This εγω ειμι is then followed by a finite verb as here (cf. also Rahlfs, *SSt*. III, 259).

2:3 *Watch over the charge which YHWH, your God, has given you to keep: walking in his ways, keeping his statutes, his commandments, his ordinances, and his testimonies, as recorded in the law of Moses, so that you may be*

---

[5] N. Lohfink, "Die deuteronomistische Darstellung des Übergangs der Führung Israels von Moses auf Josue," *Scholastik* 37 (1962), 32-44; cf. D.J. McCarthy, *JBL* 90 (1971), 31-41, and now also C. Schäfer-Lichtenberger, *Josua en Salomo: Eine Studie zu Autorität und Legitimität des Nachfolgers im Alten Testament* (SVT 58), Leiden 1995.

successful in everything you do and undertake,
For this verse and the following scholars have repeatedly pointed to the parallels which also occur in Deuteronomy and in the dtr. redaction of other books of OT.[6] Thus one finds ושמרת (את) משמרת in Deut. 11:1, but also repeatedly outside of it (Gen. 26:5; Lev. 8:35; 18:30; 22:9, etc.), be it with a slightly different shade of meaning. ללכת בדרכיו also occurs in Deut. (8:6; 10:12; 11:22, etc.); לשמר חקתיו etc. occurs repeatedly in various combinations (cf. Deut. 4:2, 40; 5:29 etc.); למען תשכיל etc. in Deut. 29:8; למען יקים etc. in Deut. 9:5; לכל־לבבם ובכל־נפשם in Deut. 4:29, 6:5, etc. Of course, ככתוב בתורת משה only occurs outside the Pentateuch (Josh. 8:31; 2 Kgs. 14:16; Ezra 3:2; 2 Chr. 23:18 etc.), but the expression relates to a time when the text of the 'law' or the 'book of the law' of Moses must have been fixed and that certainly means at least the time of the exile or later. Accordingly, in this passage we are dealing with a passage along dtr. lines which was put on David's lips. These verses are reminiscent of 1 Chr. 22:12f., in which the Chronicler has David pass on to Solomon similar instructions concerning his plans for the building of a temple. The commitments made there reach beyond the fact of building the temple to the period of Solomon's reign. Possibly the author or interpolator of our verses (so Thenius) had also Deut. 17:18ff. before him (see further on in the commentary on this verse).

שמר משמרת, like מִשְׁמָר, can mean 'to stand guard' in a military or general sense. מִשְׁמָר or מִשְׁמֶרֶת is also a technical cultic term for the 'service' in a sanctuary performed in Israel especially by Levites. Finally the substantive, often again in conjunction with the verb שמר (468x in OT) as here, serves in an ethical-religious sense to denote obedience to the commandments of YHWH (Gen. 26:5; Lev. 8:35; 18:30, etc.; cf. G. Sauer, *THAT*, II, 982-987; G. Bertram, *TDNT*, IX, 238). That which follows these words is more or less intended as a material summary of what must be understood by Hebr. In the first place it is 'walking' in the 'ways' of YHWH (cf. Sauer, *THAT*, I, 459f.). The laws, commandments, etc., serve as it were as markings of that way. The verb is introduced with inf. ל, which serves to refine the preceding description of the action (cf. Joüon §124o; Ges-K §114o). It is not necessary, with various Hebr. MSS (Kennicott) or with those of some ancient versions, to place the copula ו before לשמר. The ordinances and commandments are divided into 4 categories: (1) the חקות, that is, 'statutes' (cf. G. Liedke, *THAT*, I, 632; H. Ringgren, *TWAT*, III, 149-157); (2) the מצות, i.e. the 'commandments' (cf. Liedke, *THAT*, II, 532ff.; B. Levine, *TWAT*, IV, 1085-1095); (3) the משפטים

---

[6] Cf., e.g., Burney; S.R. Driver, *An Introduction to the Literature of the Old Testament*, Edinburgh 1913[9], 200, and now also J.S. Rogers, "Narrative Stock and Deuteronomistic Elaboration in 1 Kings 2," *CBQ* 50 (1988), 398-413.

or 'guidelines' (cf. Liedke, *THAT*, II, 999-1009; B. Johnson, *TWAT*, V, 93-108); and (4) the עדות or 'testimonies' (cf. C. van Leeuwen, *THAT*, II, 217-220; H. Simian-Yofre, *TWAT*, V, 1125-1128). Especially in such summaries they are to be regarded as virtually synonymous, although older exegetes like Münster, Vatablus, Clarius, and others, attempt to make sharp distinctions between them. As for the last word: this is a pl. form of עֵדוּת (for this see Ges-K §95u). In many cases the עֵדוּת is a religious symbol (so, correctly, also Ehrlich): in OT it often denotes the content of the ark, a kind of 'witness-symbol'.[7] In formulas such as occur in our text the more concrete original meaning of the word has of course been lost.

The term 'the תורה of Moses,' which is characteristic for the dtr. and chronistic literature, is the written instruction or the scripturally recorded will of YHWH which sometimes coincides with the entire range of the present Pentateuch (cf. also G. Liedke, C. Petersen, *THAT*, II, 1041). G. von Rad, *TAT*, I, 351f., has pointed out that the Dtr. assumes in his 'theology of history' that the revelation of YHWH to Moses had been handed down to the kings of Israel as a divine mandate, indeed even in the form of a written book (cf. also 2 Kgs. 10:31; 14:6; 17:13, 37; 21:8; 22:8, 11; 23:24f.), posits a clear connection between king David and Moses (law of YHWH) which runs programmatically through his entire historical work. The 'torah' is the norm for the moral religious conduct of kings and is evidently mentioned in our verse as universally applicable, also for all the succeeding kings of Judah and Israel. Viewed in this light the 'torah of Moses' or the 'book of the torah of Moses' is a fixed normative entity. But its scope is not such that we can simply identify it with the Pentateuch in its present form. With Noth, *ÜGS*, 86, n. 2, we might even limit its reference to the book of Deuteronomy. In this connection, for the concept of ספר, 'book,' cf. J. Kühlewein, *THAT*, II, 162-173.

The following purpose is introduced by the particle למען. According to H.A. Brongers, *OTS* 18 (1973), 84-96, this particle occurs in OT 268x, 16x in 1 Kings and 9x in 2 Kings. In a paranetic context like the present one the word occurs with a final meaning. The verb שׂכל, which in OT always – except for once in qal – occurs in the hiph. (cf. M. Saebø, *THAT*, II, 824-828) can mean 'to have insight,' but also 'to act sensibly' and so 'to have success' (cf. Deut. 29:8; Josh. 1:7f.; 1 Sam. 18:5, 14f.; 2 Kgs. 18:7; Isa. 52:13; Jer. 10:21; Prov. 17:8). We could perhaps best translate the combination of 'to act sensibly' and 'to have success' by the expression 'to have had a fortunate hand in.'

תשׂכיל is followed by 2 object clauses, first את כל־אשׁר תעשׂה, second –

---

[7] Cf. L. Koehler, *TAT*, Stuttgart 1966[4], 198f.: 'memorial sign'; see now also N. Lohfink, "'*d(w)t* in Deuteronomium und in den Königsbüchern," *BZ* 35 (1991), 86-93.

with a 'slight zeugma' (Burney) — ואת כל־אשר תפנה שם. On the basis of LXX^(A, B), this latter clause is sometimes altered into בכל־אשר אצוך (κατὰ πάντα ὅσα ἂν ἐντείλωμαί σοι), but LXX^(Luc.) rather supports the version of MT: πανταχη ου εαν επιβληφης εκει. The other ancient versions support MT as well, so that there is no reason to follow the smoother translation — one that is even more adapted to dtr. usage — of the LXX. Ehrlich proposes that we take שם, not locally but materially in the sense of אליו and to proceed from פנה אל, 'to turn your attention to.' The translation would then approximately be: 'in everything to which you turn your attention.' In Prov. 17:8 where the same expression is used, it has this same meaning. 'Materially,' therefore, Ehrlich has the right idea. In OT פנה occurs in qal with relative frequency in the sense of 'turning' (transitively or intransitively). It is a question, however, whether the translation 'at every place to which you turn' has to be rejected in favour of the more objective translation of Ehrlich. A more or less concrete-sounding expression is used here to denote a somewhat abstract idea.

2:4 *and that YHWH may fulfill the word he has spoken concerning me: "if your sons watch their conduct by walking faithfully before me with their whole heart and soul, (then), as far as you are concerned, no one will ever be cut off from the throne of Israel."*
It is plain, and also generally recognized, that the promise to which the beginning of our verse refers harks back to what was promised in 2 Sam. 7:12-16. The hiph. of קום (as S. Amsler correctly remarks in *THAT*, II, 639ff.) is used in Deuteronomy and in the dtr. theology to convey 2 aspects of YHWH's action in history: (1) YHWH raises up persons in order to lead his people by them; (2) history itself is the work of YHWH who so leads events that the promises are fulfilled, as is the case in our verse (cf. also 2 Sam. 7:25 and the par. 1 Chr. 17:23, where in place of הקם, יאמן is used). Whether we have to read 'his word' (so MT and LXX) or 'his words' (so LXX^(Luc.); Pesh., Tg., Vulg.) makes no material difference. Somewhat more important is the reading עלי (MT) or עליו (some MSS of the Hebr. text). But MT is supported by the ancient versions, except by LXX^B, which omits both. Originally the promise was also effectively addressed to David as a spoken word.

A number of dtr. formulas follow, which, as Burney a.o. correctly comments, are characteristic for the books of Kings, especially הלך לפני יהוה (3:6; 8:23, 25; 9:4; see also F. Hauck, S. Schulz, *TDNT*, VI, 571). First comes the expression שמר דרך. It is a textcritical question whether, with LXX^(Luc.), Pesh., and a few MSS of the Vulg., we have to read 'their ways' in place of 'their way.' We prefer MT. In other places in OT as well there are references to 'observing' or 'keeping the ways of God' (Gen. 18:19; 2 Sam. 22:22; cf. G. Sauer, *THAT*, I, 459f.; II, 985). The prep. ל of ללכת, according to König §406e, simultaneously has a modal as well as a consecutive nuance. The word

אמת, which occurs 127x in MT, appears only 7x in the books of Kings (3:6; 10:6; 17:24; 22:16; 2 Kgs. 20:3, 19; cf. H. Wildberger, *THAT*, I, 177-209, esp. 181f. and A. Jepsen, *TWAT*, I, 333, who lists 126x for OT). The word, rooted in the radical אמן,[8] has several shades of meaning, varying from 'reliability,' 'faithfulness' to 'constancy,' 'truth.' For a wide-ranging discussion, see next to Wildberger, 201-208; Jepsen, 333-341; and *HAL*, s.v., also G. Quell, R. Kittel, *TDNT*, I, 233-8, 240f. God as well as man can be marked in their conduct by אמת (Van Dorssen, 108f.). In our verse the reference is to an honest, trustworthy, upright attitude toward that which God has prescribed as the way, further defined by the well-known words 'with all your heart and all your soul:' (cf. Deut. 4:29; 6:5; 10:12, etc.). The second לאמר is either omitted or deleted from our verse by a Hebr. MS (Kennicott; cf. De Rossi), LXX^Luc., Vulg. and, following in their footsteps modern commentators like Thesius and Benzinger; but along with Burney, Montg.-German et al. we believe that – on the basis of comparison with other places – this is not necessary. The words לא־יכרת etc. now continues the עם-clause, which is further described by ללכת etc. If the condition in question is met, no one will be cut off from the throne of Israel 'for you.' This is sometimes referred to as an 'Unaufhörlichkeitsformel' which among others also occurs in Josh. 9:23 (cf. J. Halbe, *VT* 25 [1975], 613-641). This emphatically positioned לך, coupled with the verb כרת, as Joüon §130g remarks, indirectly expresses 'the genitival relationship of possession.' In 'eradication-formulas' the expression כרת (niph.) is customarily employed in announcements of misfortune, but also occurs in 'non-eradication-formulas' (cf. E. Kutsch, *THAT*, I, 857-860, esp. 858); further 1 Kgs. 8:25 (par. 2 Chr. 6:16); 9:5 (par. 2 Chr. 7:18) and Jer. 33:17.[9] It is expressly and personally promised to David that he will never see the day that one of his descendants will be torn from the throne of David. In other words: the dynasty will last conditionally. The preposition מעל occurs more frequently to indicate 'sitting on something' (cf. 1 Sam. 25:23; Gen. 24:64; further Burney). Only here there is reference to the 'throne of Israel' to describe the davidic dynasty. Otherwise the reference is usually to 'the throne of David' (cf. O. Schmitz, *TDNT*, III, 162).

2:5 Further, you know too what Joab son of Zeruiah did to me and what he did to the two commanders of the army of Israel, Abner son of Ner and Amasa son of Jether. He killed them, shedding the blood of war in time of peace, thus spattering the blood of war on the belt around his waist and the sandals on his

---

[8] Cf. J.C.C. van Dorssen, *De derivata van de stam* אמן *in het Hebreeuwsch van het Oude Testament*, Amsterdam 1951, 44-76.

[9] Cf. E.W. Nicholson, *Preaching the Exiles*, Oxford 1970, 92.

feet.
Following the dtr. introduction we now encounter a section that is very different in content and form. It is hard to tell whether these words have merely been put on the lips of a 'dying' king David in order to justify the cruel actions of Solomon (who is depicted in a later tradition [1 Chr. 22:9] as a 'man of peace'), or that David himself could still be so rancorous. Skinner, 69f., has pointed out that on *historical* grounds alone vss. 5-9 cannot be completely ignored, nor on *moral* grounds, because of David also other than solely chivalrous character traits are known to us (cf. 2 Sam. 21). This does not alter the fact that a person can still have objections against such 'last words' of David on *literary* grounds, i.e. on the basis of a difference in style and motive.

The וגם, as in 1:46ff., introduces a new thought unit. It is also possible that his וגם combines parts which originally were not connected. Accordingly, this composite particle is either something introduced by the author/redactor, or original; but then it is a combination of 2 parts the first of which is unknown to us. David reminds Solomon of what Joab son of Zeruiah has done to him. One may ask whether this לי refers to anything other than what follows in this verse after the second אשר; in other words, is David, before he noted Joab's misdeeds against Abner and Amasa, looking back at some harm done to him personally? The copula ו, which some Hebr. MSS, LXX$^{Luc.}$, and Pesh. place before the second אשר, may suggest an affirmative answer to this last question. Rashi, for example, thinks that in this connection the ancient rabbis thought of the fact that Joab, to save his own life after the death of Uriah, publicly read David's letter concerning Uriah to the furious officers. Rabbi Levi Ben Gerson thinks here of Joab's killing Absalom in defiance of David's orders. Still it is probable that, even if in the 'Vorlage' of the ancient versions there really was a copula before the second אשר, this was a *waw epexegeticus;* i.e. David experienced what Joab did to Abner and Amasa as an attack on him personally (so Thenius et al.).

We encountered Joab already in an earlier chapter (see vs. 7). Now 2 of his murders of army commanders are mentioned: (1) Abner son of Ner, and (2) Amasa son of Jether. Abner had had a long military career in Saul's army and is introduced in 1 Sam. 14:50 as Saul's nephew. After Saul's death Abner put Saul's son Ishbosheth on the throne and made Mahanaim the capital. After countless clashes with David and the Judeans, and after falling in disfavour with Ishbosheth, he crossed over to David's camp. The final agreement concerning the union of the 2 little kingdoms was to be made in Hebron (2 Sam. 3). But Abner was not to see this anymore: Joab and his brother Abishai craftily murdered him at Hebron, thereby avenging the death of their brother Asahel (see 2 Sam. 3:22-29; cf. 2:18-23). From 2 Sam. 3:37 one might get the impression that the people initially suspected that David was behind the murder, but his lament over Abner cleared him.

Amasa was Joab's cousin, his mother Abigail a sister of Zeruiah (2 Sam. 17:25; 1 Chr. 2:17). His father was an Ishmaelite (1 Chr. 2:17; cf. 2 Sam. 17:25: Israelite). He was made commander of the army by Absalom in place of Joab who remained loyal to David (2 Sam. 17:25). Later, after Absalom's defeat, David for political and tactical reasons, made Amasa commander also of his army, thus replacing Joab (2 Sam. 19:13). As a result of this political decision of David, Israel felt it rated second to Judah, David's homeland (2 Sam. 19:41ff.). The resulting dissatisfaction crystallized into a rebellion under the leadership of the Benjaminite Sheba, which threatened the national unity (2 Sam. 20). When Amasa failed in his mission to mobilize Judah's army in 3 days, David charged Abishai, Joab's brother, with that mission, ordering him to crush the revolt before the rebels managed to get fortified cities into their hands. In Gibeon Amasa joined Abishai's (and Joab's) troops, but was treacherously slain there by Joab. Both of these murders witness to Joab's fierce, jealous nature but in view of David's own misguided actions they hardly seem to us so grave that, after Joab's many years of service, they should again be avenged in his old age. In any case, that was something David could have done earlier.[10]

In 1 Sam. 14:50 Abner is called Abiner (cf. LXX in our verse: Abenner); in 2 Sam. 17:25 Jether is also called Ithra. This latter form may serve to underscore Amasa's Ishmaelite origin (for details, cf. Montg.-Gehman). The *waw* before ויהרגם is epexegetical (Burney, Montg.-Gehman) and continues the thought already indicated in the preceding עשה (cf. Jouön §118j; GD §78; Driver §76a). The expression 'to shed the blood of war in (time of) peace' – and what follows – is intended as the well-motivated reason for this late act of revenge against Joab. The expression as such, then, does not leave in doubt what is meant here. Still a correct translation – and explanation – of what we read here gives rise to difficulties. Do we have here a summary of what Joab had done to the 2 military commanders, or does the first clause have special reference to Abner, and the second to Amasa? On the basis of LXX$^{Luc.}$ καὶ εξεδικησεν, וישם is sometimes taken to be a mistaken transcription of ויקם (qal of נקם = to avenge; cf. Klostermann, Stade-Schwally, Burney, Ehrlich et al.), but LXX really does not give sufficient ground for this suspicion (καὶ ἔταξεν; cf. Vulg. *effudit* [וישפך]). Tg. describes this part as follows: ודמי דיתחשיב דמהון עלוהי כדם תבירי קרבא, 'and it seemed that their blood was viewed by him as that belonging to those who had fallen in war,' and then

---

[10] See now also M.L. Geyer, "Stopping the Juggernaut: A Close Reading of 2 Samuel 20:13-22," *Union Seminary Quarterly Review* 41 (1987), 33-42. He suggests that in 1 Kgs. 2 we find David's reaction to Joab's coup in taking charge of the army.

continues: 'and he responded to their peace with ambushes.' Pesh., though more succinctly, has a similar translation: *wḥšb 'nwn 'yk dbqrb'*, 'and he counted them as being in battle.' We will nevertheless have to maintain MT, in connection with which we can (with Noth) refer to Deut. 22:8, where שׂים דמים ב means 'to incur blood-guilt.' H.J. Van Dijk (*VT* 18 [1968], 16-30) has argued that in certain circumstances the verbs שׂים, נתן and שׁית are synonymous and can mean to 'shed,' or 'bring upon.' He translates vs. 5b as follows: 'And he shed the blood of war in time of peace, and he let spatter the blood of war upon the girdle about his loins and on the sandals of his feet' (22). It is his opinion (with Dhorme, I, 1029f.) that the Hebr. text is completely clear. Accordingly, Joab's error was that he transposed blood that had been shed in war to a time of peace and so, whether to his mind justly or unjustly, he acted as an avenger of blood. Although B. Kedar-Kopfstein (*TWAT*, II, 258) is inclined to accept the emendation of וישׂם into ויקם, he nevertheless rightly comments that in Israel the different acts of blood were differently valued, so that one who killed amidst the violence of war was judged differently than one who killed in time of peace. Joab, at least in David's (invented) opinion, had become so integrally interwoven with war that he could no longer see a distinction between blood shed in war and blood shed in time of peace. The remainder of this verse works this idea out further. Compared with LXX[Luc.] and Vet. Lat., however, all 3 p. sing. suffixes are changed into 1 p. sing. suffixes, as though the reference was to the belt around David's waist and the sandals on his feet, and not to these items of clothing of Joab (cf. Stade-Schwally; also Barthelemy). There are exegetes (e.g., Montg.-Gehman) who very definitely opt for this emendation. The mistakes originally made by Joab had been attributed to David, and that had to be avenged now.

Moreover, in this part, in particular versions or MSS, there are still other changes or omissions as well. We mention LXX[B], which leaves the words בשׁלם ויתן דמי מלחמה untranslated, whereas LXX[A] and many other MSS of LXX, Luc. among them, do have them. Instead, a number of MSS of LXX read αἷμα ἀθῷον, 'unavenged blood' (דמי מלחמה) which in Hebr. can also be read דם נקי (cf. e.g. Deut. 27:25; 1 Sam. 19:5, etc.; cf. Vet. Lat.: *innocenticum*). But it is also possible that — aside from the possibility of another Hebr. 'Vorlage' — we are dealing with a smoothing out of textual difficulties. As it concerns the conclusion of this verse, Tg. and Pesh. are in remarkable agreement: 'He shed their blood with the sword (Tg.: אספניקי; Pesh.: *syp'*), which was in his belt and trampled (on them) with the shoes (Tg.: טלריתא; Pesh.: *msn'* [pl].) which were on his feet.' These last-mentioned translations simplify MT in a striking way. Vulg. remains closer to MT: *et posuit cruorem proelii in balteo suo qui erat circa lumbos eius et in calciamento suo quod erat in pedibus eius*. The word *cruor*, 'blood,' occurs relatively rarely in Vulg.

(Exod. 7:19; Num. 35:33; Deut. 21:9; 32:42; 2 Kgs. 24:4; and here), and has a more restricted meaning than *sanguis*. It refers especially to blood which gushes from a wound (cf. Lewis-Short, 485).

Still we believe that, despite these possibilities of emending MT on the basis of these variants in the ancient versions, we must maintain MT. We view the part of the sentence which begins with ויתן as a further explication of the perhaps idiomatic expression וישם דמי־מלחמה בשלם. 'Warblood' means: blood which in war (unfortunately) flows with impunity, yet profusely, that is to say, for which blood-vengeance need not or ought not go into effect. This 'blood' works in 2 directions: in the direction of Joab because he had shed blood as though it had been war, or perhaps: because, in the background, belief in the magical operation of blood was in effect (cf. V. Kubáč, *VT* 31 [1981], 225f.); further, in the direction of Abner and to a lesser degree toward Amasa, because in wartime they had killed a relative of Joab on whom, precisely because it was war, blood vengeance could not legitimately be applied. 'War blood' thus tends to get a double meaning (cf. also vv. 31, דם חנם). This aspect is reinforced by the reference to 'the belt around his waist' (cf. F.I. Andersen, *AbrN* 3 [1961]/2], 69, n. 8; J.M. Sasson, *RSP*, I, 396 [III, 18g]) and 'the shoes on his feet.' In connection with these expressions one need not immediately think of military clothing. If that were intended, David's reproach would be less understandable. In these expressions one should rather see a parallel with בשלם. After all, in peace time one can still wear a belt and shoes. חגורה also occurs in Gen. 3:7 where it is sometimes translated as 'apron,' further in 2 Sam. 18:11; 2 Kgs. 3:21 and Isa. 3:24. In addition one finds חגור in 1 Sam. 18:4; 2 Sam. 20:8 and Prov. 31:24. Even more frequent is the occurrence of the verb חגר ('to gird'). (Exod. 12:11; 29:9; Lev. 8:7 [2x], 13; 16:4, etc.; cf. B. Johnson, *TWAT*, II, 744-748). On the basis of these places and also on the basis of the discussions of Dalman, *AuS*, V, 232-246; Nowack, I, 120f.; Benzinger, *Arch,* 76ff. et al.[11], one cannot say that the belt has special reference to military clothing. Even in 2 Kgs. 3:21, where the RSV translates 'armour,' this nuance is not warranted because 'to gird oneself' means 'to get ready to travel' rather than 'to get ready to fight,' even when one girds oneself for war. Interesting in this connection is the passage in 2 Sam. 20:8ff., in which precisely Joab's murder of Amasa is described. Also this verse is to be viewed as a *crux interpretum* on which many have tried their skills (see, a.o., Driver, *Samuel*, a.l.). For example there has been discussion on the question whether Joab had one or 2 swords. Clear, in any case, is that Amasa, whatever the case may have been with the sword(s), was

---

[11] Cf. also H.W. Hönig, *Die Bekleidung des Hebräers. Eine biblisch-archäologische Untersuchung*, diss. Zürich 1957, 76f.

not the least bit suspicious of Joab wearing a belt around his waist (cf. also Rashi, who suspects that Joab held the opening of the sheath of the sword downward so that it could easily slip out and could pick it up again without arousing suspicion on the part of Amasa). מתנים denotes the area of the loins, the hips, the crotch (Gen. 37:34, etc. approx. 45x in all in OT). Even less than 'belt' does 'footwear' refer to military gear, though the word נעל is relatively rare in OT (approx. 22x; the verb is נעל in the sense of 'to bolt shut' [6x] and 'to put on shoes' [2x]). נעל is the sandal strapped to the foot, and was along with the belt, part of one's normal clothing (cf. Dalman, AuS V, 296f).

2:6 *Act therefore according to your wisdom and do not let his gray head go down to the underworld in peace.*
This verse begins with a pf. cons., although the last syllable is not stressed. This pf. cons. has a precative or imperative meaning and, though it is almost independent here, is in a sense on a level with the preceding pfa. consa. of the vss. 2ff. (cf. also Böttcher, 981; König §367y; Driver §119d; Bg. II §9i and Lettinga §72f). Also striking in this verse is that the negation of the jussive form תורד is not אל but לא (cf. Böttcher, 964; Ewald §345a; König §191g; GD §67, rem. 2; Driver §50 [cf. 174]). Though rare, it also occurs in Gen. 24:8 and 1 Sam. 14:36 etc. (see Burney). Ges-K §109d and Joüon §114l think the jussive form may have resulted from a *scriptio defectiva* of the form of the verb; in this connection Bg. II §10n refers to 'mixed modes of expression': alongside of forms of the jussive with לא there are also indicative forms with אל. But also the latter believes that we are here dealing with errors in vocalization because in the first category we have a defective, in the second a complete spelling.

In this verse David appeals to Solomon's 'wisdom.' Although the word חָכְמָה here and in vs. 9 rather means 'cunning,' even 'slyness' (cf. G. Fohrer, *TDNT*, VII, 484), Solomon is already being introduced here as a 'wise' man. This is a qualification which will stay with him throughout his life and far beyond it (1 Kgs. 3:12, 28; 5:9ff., 14, 21, 26; 10:4, 6ff., 23ff.; 11:41 etc.). The word חכם occurs as verb 27x, as חָכָם 138 and as חָכְמָה even 149x in OT (cf. M. Saebø, *THAT* 1, 557-567; H.-P. Müller, M. Krause, *TWAT*, II, 920-944, and G. Fohrer, *TDNT*, VII, 476-496). After Proverbs (39x) and Ecclesiastes (28x) the word חכמה occurs more than 10x in a single Bible book also in Job (18x) and 1 Kgs. (17x). According to Müller, 929, the earliest texts in which the root חכם can be found only reflect an unspecified use, a judgment in which he includes also our verse (and vs. 9). Indeed the word here is still ambiguous. On the other hand, it is self-evident that the author, by putting these words on David's lips, is letting Solomon's reputation for wisdom already start in his youth.

The expression, 'letting' or 'not letting someone's grey hairs go down in peace,' occurs in almost the same way, apart from vs. 9, also in Gen. 42:38; 44:29, 31. שֵׂיב or שֵׂיבָה occurs 20x in OT and refers to very advanced age, the state of 'greyheadedness.' *šbt*, 'grey hair,' is already found in Ugar. as well (cf. Aistleitner, 2573). Here, among other things, there is mention of *šbt dqnk*, 'the grey colour of your beard' (*KTU* 1.3: V. 2, 25; 1.4: V. 4; 1.18, 12). The intent of the expression is to say that someone whose hair has turned grey as a result of much work and anxiety will fall asleep forever at an advanced age. This is not the death David wants for his loyal old comrade-in-arms. Remarkable is the explanation of Rashi (cf. also *Yalkhut Shimoni*) that David added: 'and let him go down to Gehinnom (the "fire of purgation").' Thus David's good intentions would become clear: a severe punishment in this world, a chance at 'purgation' in the next. Again, as in the previous verse, the author uses בשלם. Because Joab shed the blood of war 'in time of peace,' there should be no such time of peace for him even in his old age. Again the reproach that he had joined Adonijah's cause is absent. E. Jacob, *TDNT*, IX, 624, notes that the head is one of the places of the body in which — it was thought — the life of a human being is concentrated. For that reason, in blessing someone, one puts his hands on someone's head.

The usual technical term for the underworld in OT is the word שאל, which is found there approx. 65x (G. Gerleman, *THAT*, II, 837-841; L. Wächter, *TWAT*, VII, 901-909).[12] In the books of Kings it occurs only here and in vs. 9. The etymology of the word is still very controversial, but it is assumed that it is related to the stem שאה 'to be waste' (with the form element ל). There is no doubt that it was understood as a place, sometimes as the parallel opposite to 'heaven.' The fact that the word has almost evolved into a kind of proper name is evident, according to König §292c, from its occurrence as a noun without an article. In Gen. 42:38; 44:29, 31, it occurs with a local ה (Delitzsch, *LSF*, 21c, but not, for example, in 1 Sam. 2:6. Grammatically it is possible in our verse to take בשלם שאל as a st. cstr.: 'in the peace of the underworld,' but both בְּיָגוֹן (Gen. 42:38; 44:31, etc.) and בדם (vs. 9), as well as the parallelization of בשלם in the previous, as well as the present verse make such a construction unacceptable here.

2:7 *As regards the sons of Barzillai of Gilead, treat them as friends, let them sit among those who eat at your table, for they were as kind to me when I had to flee from your brother Absalom.*

---

[12] Cf. also S. Jellicoe, "Hebrew-Greek Equivalents for the Netherworld, its Milieu and its Inhabitants in the Old Testament," *Textus* 8 (1973), 1-19, esp. 1; Tromp, *Primitive Conceptions*, 21ff.

After the order to execute one person comes the order to do good to another. Barzillai, whose name is linked with the usual Semitic name for 'iron' (cf. Noth, *IPN*, 225), was one of the influential men from across the Jordan, from Rogelim in Gilead. On the occasion of David's flight from Absalom to Mahanaim, Barzillai provided him with an abundance of goods (2 Sam. 17:27ff.) and, after Absalom's defeat, as honourable escort for himself and his company to the Jordan (2 Sam. 19:32ff.). On account of his advanced age he refused to accompany David to his court in Jerusalem, but instead let his son Chimham go with David.[13]

In our verse there is mention of the sons of Barzillai. This, among other things, is a reason for Ehrlich to emend the text. He reads 'son' and changes קָרְבוּ to קֵרְבוֹ. He takes the latter to mean that Barzillai 'recommended him (i.e. his son) to me (i.e. David) for companionship.' But to us it seems definitely unnecessary to change the vocalization. Neither has it been proved that Barzillai had only one son, nor is it impossible that among Barzillai's בנים his grandchildren were included. For the word חסד see on 3:6, further, H.-J. Zobel, *TWAT*, III, 52.

The part. in the st. cstr. here has the function of a substantive: 'those eating from the table' (cf. Ewald §288a; König §241e; Ges-K §116h), i.e. those cared for by the king (for 'table guests,' cf. 2 Sam. 9:10ff.; thus, correctly, Thenius). The expression may be intended to convey that Chimham was 'endowed' with a piece of crown property, to which – as Alt, *KS*, III, 358f. (cf. also Ewald [in Thenius] et al.) has tried to demonstrate – the name Geruth Chimham, a caravansary or inn close to Bethlehem (mentioned in Jer. 41:17), may refer. Although, on the basis of Pesh., Tg., and Vulg., it has been proposed that, in place of כי־בן, the words כי על כן be read (Hitzig et al.) MT should be maintained also here (thus, correctly, Stade-Schwally; Burney). קרב אל is used here, as J. Kühlewein, *TWAT*, II, 676, rightly comments, in the figurative sense of 'coming out to meet,' i.e. to 'pay tribute.' The verb ברח, which occurs almost 60x in OT, must be distinguished form the related word נוס, 'to run from danger' (cf. S. Schwertner, *THAT*, II, 47f.; J. Gamberoni, *TWAT*, I, 779). The first verb mentioned means 'to flee from familiar surroundings (to live as an emigrant in another area).'

2:8 *You also have with you Shimei son of Gera the Benjaminite from Bahurim, who cursed me with an offensive curse on the day I went to Mahanaim, but when he came down to meet me at the Jordan I swore to him by YHWH: "I will not put you to death with the sword."*

---

[13] See now also I.W. Provan, "Why Barzillai of Gilead (1 Kings 2:7)?: Narrative Art and the Hermeneutics of Suspicion in 1 Kings 1-2," *TynB* 46 (1995), 103-116.

The third man listed by David is again one on whom Solomon has to execute vengeance. Shimei son of Gera is a Benjaminite belonging to the family of Saul. During David's flight from Absalom Shimei had met him by Bahurim on the way to the land across the Jordan, and cursed David as a scoundrel and a shedder of blood (2 Sam. 16:5-14). When David returned, Shimei offered apologies which were accepted by David after a fashion (2 Sam. 19:17-24). He swore, in fact, that he would not kill Shimei, but the curse remained on his house. Now David wished to pay him back by ordering Solomon to insure that the dynasty would be protected from threats on the part of Shimei and the other members of his tribe. In Ehrlich's opinion, nothing can be done with עמך and proposes to read עוד: 'And then there is the case of Shimei ...' But MT offers a good meaning for והנה (cf. also D. J. McCarthy, *Bib* 61 [1980], 334). The words 'with you' can also be taken as 'among your subjects' or 'not far from you.' Bahurim (2 Sam. 3:16; 16:5; 17:18; 19:17; 23:31; corrected in accordance with 1 Chr. 11:33) is a village E of Jerusalem, frequently identified with *Rās et-ṭamim* (Simons, *GTTOT* 750; *EncMiqr.* II, 46; O.R. Sellers, *IDB*, I, 340), NE of the Mount of Olives, also identified earlier with *Abu dīs*, situated somewhat to the SE of Jerusalem (Thenius); Z. Weisman, *VT* 31 (1981), 449f., translates the place name by 'warriors' village.' David recalls the curses mentioned earlier. This is indicated by a *figura etymologica*: *qll* pi. with a noun of the same stem furnished with an attributive adjective (König §329g). The verb form (without *dageš*: Bg. II §17h) has 2 objects and occurs in pi. 40x in OT (C.A. Keller, *THAT*, II, 641-647). The basic meaning of the word, which is almost generally Sem., is 'to be light,' which has developed in 2 different directions: (1) 'to be swift,' etc.; and (2) 'to be insignificant, contemptible.' In the pi. the word has both a declarative and factitive function: declaring someone contemptible is simultaneously to make him a contemptible person. Just as ברכה works, so also קללה works the 'curse.' It has magical power which can be disastrous for a person's descendants and needs to be averted. 2 Sam. 16:5-14 in fact shows how Shimei pronounced the curse from the bottom of his heart and how the radical occurs in this section.

The word נמרצת further qualifies the curse. Aside from the present instance, the niph. of the word also occurs in Mic. 2:10 and Job 6:25 (and as hiph. in Job 16:3). The word means 'to be sick' and is related to the Arab. *mrd* (cf. L. Kopf, *VT* 8 [1958], 163; Burney). From there it becomes 'to be painful' and 'to be offensive' (cf. F. Stolz, *THAT*, I, 568, and *HAL*, s.v.). Noth, however, takes the word to mean 'to be powerless,' because as part. niph. it can in his view hardly have a causative meaning (but see Burney). LXX translates ὀδυνηρά (cf. G. Bertram, *TDNT*, V, 631); Vulg. *pessima,* Tg. and Pesh. speak of 'bitter curses.' Thenius rejects all these translations in favour of the translation 'disastrous' or 'horrendous,' proceeding here from the basic meaning 'to be sick.' Interesting is that — according to the hermeneutic rules

followed by the rabbis – they saw the word as a *notarikon* (i.e.: acronym) for
נוֹאֵף (adulterer), מַמְזֵר (illegitimate child), רוֹצֵחַ (murderer), צוֹרֵר (enemy) and
תּוֹעֵבָה (horror, i.e. idolater).[14] Rashi links the word with Job 6:25; 16:3 and
translates it by 'clear'.

Mahanaim is a place across the Jordan (Gen. 32:3; Josh. 13:26, 30; 21:38;
2 Sam. 2:8, 12, 29; 17:24, 27; 19:33; 1 Kgs. 4:14; 1 Chr. 6:65), not far
either from the Jordan or the Jabbok (cf. also LXX and Vulg.). Although the
precise location of this place can no longer be determined, Simons, *GTTOT*,
415 (232), suspects, with De Vaux, that *Tell-Ḥeǧǧāǧ*, S of *Tulūb ed-ḏahab*,
could be the ruins of this town (cf. Stoebe, *BHHW*, II, 1123f.; *HAL*, s.v.;
Abel, *GP*, II, 373f., refers to an ancient tradition which identifies the town
with Chirbet Mahne, N of the Jabbok and SE of Jabesh in Gilead).[15] According to reports in 2 Sam. David, fleeing Absalom, found a temporary residence
here.

The double use of והוא indicates that David, speaking from personal experience, conveys 2 important things about Shimei: (1) his cursing; (2) his excuses
('it was he who ...'), which function parenthetically. The oath which David
swore is reported in 2 Sam. 19:23. This verse does not say that Shimei had to
be killed with the sword, but neither is this in conflict with what is said here.
What is striking is that in the preceding verse the sons of Zeruiah, who wanted
to kill Shimei on the spot, are told twice that *today* (היום) this was David's
decision, a subtle way of alluding to 'a delayed execution' (cf. also vs. 21).

2:9 *But now, do not consider him innocent; you are a wise man; you know
what you have to do; you must bring his gray head, bloodied, down into the
underworld.'*

With a reference to his 'wisdom,' David's successor is requested to deal with
Shimei as he was asked to deal with Joab (vs. 6). As before, so here too there
is a difference in the various versions concerning the reading ועתה (cf. 1:20).
LXX[Luc.] and Vulg. seem to have read ואתה, 'and you.' The fact that this συ is
lacking in LXX[B] et al. is attributable, according to Montg.-Gehman, to a
haplology with the following ου (see also Noth). But Tg. and Pesh. do not
support this view; MT, which we (with Burney against Thenius and Klosterman et al.) continue to support, does. ועתה can very well introduce a summarizing conclusion, which is the case here.

The pi.-form of נקה occurs 18x in OT, 5 of them as inf. abs., 25x in the
niph., and once in the qal (cf. C. van Leeuwen, *THAT*, II, 101-106). The
adjective נָקִי occurs even more frequently (43x). In Kings we encounter the

---

[14] For this, see S. Lieberman, *Hellenism in Jewish Palestine*, New York 1961², 69.
[15] See now also R.A. Cooghanour, "A Search for Mahanaim," *BASOR* 273 (1989), 57-66.

verb only here. In OT the word belongs especially in the sphere of jurisprudence and in the pi. means especially 'to leave unpunished.' In LXX this word is often, as here, translated by ἀΘῳοῦν. One almost always finds the verb – again as here, but then with לא – in statements of negation. Whereas elsewhere YHWH is always used as subject, here it is Solomon. Because Solomon is 'wise' (for this, see vs. 6) he will certainly find an opportunity to eliminate Shimei legally, as a potential threat to the dynasty (Cf. Josephus, *Ant.* VII, 388; further Rashi and H. Grotius).[16]

Appendix
In the case of vss. 8 and 9, LXX (including Luc.) have a par. text in 2:35l-o as well[17], which according to Montgomery, conveys an earlier translation. A number of striking differences are: (1) the term 'son of the seed' by Shimei after son of Gera in LXX[B] (not in LXX[Luc.]), i.e. בן זרע; (2) in LXX[B] the name of the place given is Hebron (in place of Bahurim) (in LXX[Luc.]: ΓαβαΘα); (3) ἀνὴρ φρόνιμος in place of ἀνὴρ σοφός; (4) καὶ νῦν μὴ ἀΘῳώσῃς (35o) in place of καὶ οὐ μὴ ἀΘῳώσῃς (9); see further under v. 35.

2:10 *So David went to rest with his ancestors and was buried in the city of David.*
The vss. 10-12 belong to the chronological-redactional framework in which information about the kings is regularly reported in the book of Kings. In 1 Chr. 29:26-30 one finds a similar statement, in part in identical language. This and other statements like it are based, in part as it would seem, on notes recorded in annals or other documents.

Our verse tells us that David 'went to sleep with his fathers' and was buried in 'the city of David.' The expression שכב עם־אבתיו already occurred in 1:21 (see there). According to 2 Sam. 5:7, 9, 'the city of David' is the מְצֻדַת צִיּוֹן (cf. 1 Chr. 11:7), the location of which is disputed. In the past this was often equated with the SW ridge extending from the temple mount; today it is equated with the SE ridge. The first-mentioned opinion is based on a tradition which originated around the first centuries of the Christian era, the latter is the view of many modern scholars (cf. Driver, *Samuel,* on 2 Sam. 5:7; Simons, *Jerusalem,* 35-39; B. Mazar, *EncMiqr.* III, 808-812). Another question is whether the 'stronghold of Zion' and 'the city of David' are completely identical or if the stronghold of Zion as the center of government only covers

---

[16] See on this verse now also E. Talstra, "Hebrew Syntax: Clause Types and Clause Hierarchy," *Studies in Hebrew and Aramaic Syntax* (Fs J. Hoftijzer, ed. K. Jongeling et al.), Leiden 1991, 180-193.

[17] Cf. J.A. Montgomery, "The Supplement at the End of 3 Kingdoms 2," *ZAW* NF 9 (1932), 124-129.

the N part of the E hill (Mazar, 810f.). On small maps (cf. *ibid.*, 809f.; *BRL*^{1}, 301f.; *BRL*^{2}, 159; Simons, *Jerusalem*, a.l.) 'the city of David' is often identified with the most ancient Jebusite Jerusalem, as it must have looked in the bronze age and the beginning of the iron age. Toward the N the elevation of the city rose — the Ophel — and finally reached its highest point on the later temple mount. According to H. Donner, *BRL*^{2}, 158ff., this city, which was then restricted to the SE hill, was no larger than 44,000 square meters. The most ancient necropolis, one that was also in use in later years, must have been located in the Kidron valley on the W side of the Mount of Olives.

Now we must not lose sight of the fact that the information in our verse stems from a later time, in which much was attributed to David which had not been made or built by him. This renders a more precise identification difficult. Zion later expressly becomes the mount on which the temple stands (1 Macc. 4:37f.; 7:33; cf. Isa. 8:18; 60:14; Ps. 2:6, etc.; see Burney). In David's time, however, there was neither a temple as YHWH-sanctuary there, nor any human habitation. It was a settlement on the SE hill. We will therefore have to accept that 'the city of David' is identical with the part conquered by David that may afterward have been extended, and that his tomb was located here. It is possible that he was buried in an inhabited area (for this, see also Noth). In connection with excavations made since 1913-14, the tombs of the 'sons of David' have been found on the SE hill (Simons, *Jerusalem*, 194-225; Donner, *BRL*^{2}, 161f. and fig. 42:a). These tombs were not far from the pool of Siloam. Whether David's tomb was actually included is uncertain because the Romans utilized this area as a stone quarry. Even the remnants of the tombs are heavily damaged.[18] Simons (*Jerusalem*, 234f., fig. 30) believes the 'stronghold of Zion' was a location on the SE edge of the SE hill, a bit to the W of the Gihon spring, and that Jerusalem stretched out behind it. This theory as such is not impossible. The SE hill in its entirety is said to have had the name Ophel, which was originally the area of Jebus. Simons, 201-204, also offers a list of OT passages in which there is mention of the royal necropolis. Kings is compared with Chronicles and the differences are noted. That an ancient tradition knew of royal tombs in 'the city of David,' i.e. on the SE hill, is clear.

In this connection it is interesting to note that Josephus (*Ant.* VII, 392ff.; cf. XIII, 249 and *Bell* 61) records that Solomon buried David with such a profu-

---

[18] Cf. D.R. Ap-Thomas, "Jerusalem," *Archeology and Old Testament Study* (ed. D. Winton Thomas), Oxford 1967, 277-295, esp. 287; concerning the difficulties, indeed virtual impossibility, of identifications in the case of the excavation results of the southeastern hill, cf. K.M. Kenyon, *Digging up Jerusalem*, London 1974, 129-171. See now also W.H. Shea, "The Tomb of David," *AUSS* 34 (1996), 287-293, identifying the largest tomb of the group as the tomb of David, on the basis of remnants of a relief decifered (with the 'rebus principle') as the name of David.

sion of riches that centuries later (Josephus talks of 1300 years, but it is no more than 800) Johannes Hyrcanus (135-105 BCE), at the siege of the city by Antiochus VII Euergetes, opened one of the chambers in David's tomb (ἕνα οἶκον τῶν ἐν τῷ Δαυίδου μνήματι) and took out 3000 talents [of gold] of which he offered a part to Antiochus for the raising of the siege of the city. Many years later Herod is said to have done something similar (cf. *Ant.* XVI, 179-182). But, adding to these stories, Josephus notes that no one touched the crates of the kings because they had been so skillfully (μηχανικῶς) concealed under the ground, rendering them invisible to anyone entering the tomb. Theodoretus (in Thenius) has Josephus add to this that these tombs were located near Siloam. The extent to which this is correct and whether anyone in Josephus's — and in Peter's (Acts 2:29) — time still knew the exact location of the royal tombs, and of David's tomb in particular, is at least problematic. Even today the tombs of David, Absalom, and others in Jerusalem, are marked by memorials which have no greater value than as attractions for pilgrims and tourists.

2:11 *The period in which David was king over Israel lasted forty years — seven years in Hebron and thirty-three in Jerusalem.*
In 2 Sam. 5:5 the time of his reign over Judah in Hebron is put at 7 years and 6 months. Somewhat more precisely the phrase 'over all Israel and Judah' is added in connection with the 33 years in Jerusalem. Josephus (*Ant.* VIII, 389) also mentions the 7½ years of Hebron and refers to his age as 70 years. The number 40 plays a certain role in OT (cf. H. Balz, *TDNT*, VIII, 136f.). It is a 'round' number which is probably connected with the succession of the generations. It is often clear, therefore, that 40 cannot be viewed as a chronometrically exact designation but has rather a typical-symbolic meaning (examples in Balz, a.l.) It is hard to tell whether in the case of the reported 40 years of David's reign (and later also of his son Solomon, cf. 11:42) we are dealing with chronologically reliable data in a modern sense, because one may surmise the presence of dtr. redactional work in these time measurements, as also in regard to the round number 30 for David's age at the time of his accession (cf. 2 Sam. 5:4). On the other hand, the reference to the 7½ years of kingship in Hebr. (2 Sam. 2:11; 5:5) does sound exact (see also Noth, *ÜGS*, 66, n. 1). According to these figures, then, David could have been 70 years old at the time of his death.

With this verse the life of David and the time of his reign ends. In LXX[Luc.] this fact is also indicated by inserting before vs. 12 the heading '3 Kingdoms' as the beginning of a new book (cf. textcr. app. of Brooke-McLean-Thackeray; H.St.J. Thackeray, *JThS* 8 [1907], 262-278; idem, *Grammar*, I, 10f.). It has to be admitted that this ending of the second book seems less artificial than the one we now as a rule follow traditionally. 1 Chr. 29:28 further embellishes the end of David's life by commenting that he died 'in a good old age, full of days, riches, and honour,' after which the author adds a reference to further literature about David's life history.

2:12 *Then Solomon sat on the throne of his father David and his royal rule was very stable.*
This verse can be viewed as the beginning of the Solomon-narratives, with which (from the viewpoint of the annalistic and schematic historiography) the vss. 46bf. are closely connected and in which the outcome of the narrative cycle about the struggle over the succession finds a place which is warranted from a compositional point of view. It is emphatically stated that Solomon (on him, see also E. Lohse, *TDNT*, VII, 459-465) occupies the throne of his father David, a statement which highlights both the hereditary dynastic succession and the so-called 'messianic' line of David. In LXX[A] and a few other MSS of LXX (but not B and Luc.) there is the addition that Solomon was then 12 years old. For the rabbinic tradition, cf. Ginzberg, *Legends*, IV, 125 and VI, 277; Josephus, *Ant*. VIII, 211, has Solomon become king at age 14; cf. also Eupolemos in Eusebius, *Praep. Evang.* IX, 30, 8; Rahlfs, *SSt*. III, 113.

The hereditary dynastic line of succession is further justified by the statement that the kingship was very firmly established. מלכות, an abstract form of the noun (cf. G. von Rad, *TDNT*, I, 570), occurs 91x in OT, only one of which (here) in the book of Kings (cf. J.A. Soggin, *THAT*, I, 910; K. Seybold, *TWAT*, IV, 941f.). As is evident from the statistical spread, one finds the word — as is to be generally expected in the formation of abstract nouns — in the later OT books (Esther, Daniel and the Chronistic opus including Ezra-Nehemiah: 78x). According to Von Rad, the word in the first place means 'kingship', only later 'kingdom.' Here too the word denotes political kingship, the 'kingdom.' This kingship's being 'firmly established,' 'firmly anchored,' is indicated by the niph. of כון (cf. 1 Sam. 20:31; 2 Sam. 78:16, etc), often used concretely but applicable also to abstractions (cf. E. Gerstenberger, *THAT*, I, 812-817; K. Koch, *TWAT*, IV, 95-107). The word מאד further underscores this firm anchorage (cf. B. Kedar-Kopfstein, *TWAT*, IV, 611ff.). Consequently, this brief sentence is important not only for the description of the assault on this kingship which immediately follows this verse but also for the entire account of the kingship of David's house which follows in the books of Kings. From this viewpoint it seems to me more correct to view this verse as an independent statement, a kind of heading, than — as is often done (e.g. by Montg.-Gehman) — as a subordinate clause leading into a main clause: 'After Solomon occupied the throne ..., and the kingship was established, (13) it happened that ...' etc. It is not for nothing, after all, that LXX[Luc.] starts a new Bible book with this verse (see end of preceding verse).

2:13 *Then Adonijah son of Haggith came to Bathsheba, Solomon's mother. She said: 'Does your coming mean peace?' He answered: 'Peace!'*

The thread of the Adonijah narrative, which seemingly ended at the close of chap. 1, is now resumed and taken, in a rather lengthy story, to his death in vs. 25. This episode is a first phase in the 'establishment' of the Davidic dynasty and is followed by similar stories whose inner connectedness consists solely in the motif of making the throne of David secure. Solomon's wisdom is manifest especially in that he – though this is never directly stated – manages to eliminate all potential enemies of the throne on grounds other than the charge that they were attempting to bring about the immediate overthrow of the newly formed dynasty. The assault on the throne comes most directly to the fore on the occasion of Adonijah's execution. In all this we westerners of the modern age must never forget that these stories, which as such may be based on historic facts, were enacted in the ancient Near East, the Near East in which even today very different customs and practices are current than we are familiar with.

In this verse we are told that Adonijah paid a visit to Bathsheba. In *BHS*, which follows the codex Leningradensis, one reads חַגִּית in place of חַגִּית (similarly *BHK*), a difference in nuance which is of no importance for the exegesis. LXX^B and a few other MSS of the Greek translation as well as the Ethiopic translation completely omit any reference to the mother of Adonijah. Textcritically a more important question is whether Adonijah, when he came to Solomon' mother, also bowed before her (καὶ προσεκύνησεν αὐτῇ), as LXX has it. In vs. 19 – so MT – Solomon indeed does this when his mother calls on him, and Solomon was her own child! Ehrlich believes that there was a high degree of familiarity between Adonijah and Bathsheba and that therefore the word וישתחו is not used here. But this explanation does not seem meaningful. Was there no familiarity between Bathsheba and Solomon, just as between Bathsheba and David (cf. 1:16)? The act of bowing is a form of deference which in the courtly etiquette of the Jerusalem palace seems to have had nothing to do with familiarity but everything with intrigue. The craftier the questions the deeper the curtsies. The author after all sprinkles the acts of deference in his story with deliberate care. We, accordingly, follow MT.

The question-and-answer game of the 2 plotters in this part of our chapter starts out with a more or less customary greeting: 'Is your coming prompted by peaceful intentions?' The substantive שלום functions in this question as predicate and has the value of an adjective (Joüon §§141a, 154g and several examples in Burney).

2:14 *Then he added: 'There is something I have to discuss with you.' 'Go on,' she replied.*
Many MSS of LXX, B among them, omit the initial ויאמר, so that Adonijah's

answer after the repetition of שלום, which can be taken to mean 'yes,' is continuous (Stade-Schwally et al. consider this correct). To heighten the tension, as it were, Adonijah does not immediately state his request but says: 'I have a message for you.' Repeatedly this is an introduction to an important message or, rather, to an act (cf. Judg. 3:19f.; 2 Kgs. 9:5). Bathsheba then asks him to reveal the matter. Some MSS, along with LXX, Pesh. and Vulg., still add: 'to him.'

2:15 *'You know,' he said, 'that I had title to the crown and that all Israel had looked to me to be king. But the crown switched (persons) and went to my brother, since it was YHWH's will to give it to him.*

This verse recalls a piece of history, viewed from Adonijah's perspective. Words such as לי and עלי are given an emphatic position so as to highlight Adonijah's claim to the kingship and the people's expectations for him. He is far from having unlearned the habit of 'self-promotion' (1:5), despite the lesson he has been taught. The word מְלוּכָה (see on 1:46) recurs a couple of times in this passage, here even as the subject of a sentence: ותסב המלוכה ותהי לאחי. KBL translate סבב והיה ל: 'in jmds Besitz übergehen,' a combination of 'turning away' and 'beginning to belong to.' In place of אין שים ל (see on 1:20) the words פנים שים ל are used (A.S. van der Woude, *THAT*, II, 440), followed by an inf. cstr., the purpose of which is to indicate that Adonijah should really be king (so Joüon §124s; cf. Burney). The inf. cstr. need not be changed into the substantive מֶלֶךְ, as certain Hebr. MSS (De Rossi) and also the ancient versions propose. Along with Thenius et al. we opt for the reading of MT. It is remarkable that the author has Adonijah say: 'The kingship turned away and became my brother's, for it was his from the Lord.' There is not a word here about the intrigues which preceded this 'turning away' both on his part and on the part of David (and Solomon). The 'primary author' referred to is YHWH. This is clearly the opinion of the author who puts this pronouncement on the lips of his main character in this episode. For all the parties involved there has evidently been an act of intervention from above, the intent of which is not clear at the moment. Adonijah uses this 'confession' as a cover-up for the real purposes of his unexpected visit to Bathsheba. Indeed, a clever *captatio benevolentiae* (Thenius).

2:16 *But now to the point: I have one request to make of you, and please do not refuse me.' 'Go on,' she said.*

Again (see 1:12, 18 etc.) the ועתה introduces a new subject, and this time a question. The verb שאל occurs 171x in the OT, especially in the historical books (21x in Kings). The abstract verbal noun שאלה occurs 14x (Cf. G. Gerleman, *THAT*, II, 841-844). Here the word-play between the verb and the noun applies rather to a modest request than to a brazen desire. The modest nature of the request is underscored even more intensely in LXX^Luc. and certain Hebr. MSS by the addition, after אחת, of 'small' (Kennicott; De Rossi; cf. v. 20). The part. practically denotes a present (cf. Driver §135(2), also Burney). Still the question itself is not posed until after an affirmative answer. חשב את פנים (cf. vss. 17, 20; 2 Kgs. 18:24 [par. Isa. 36:9]; Ps. 132:10 [par 2 Chr. 6:42]) means 'to turn away someone's face' by 'rejecting someone,' 'not accepting his request' (cf. A.S. van der Woude, *THAT*, II, 441). The Hebr. text has 'my face,' LXX 'your face,' while also in vss. 17 and 20 it diverges at this point. MT deserves preference.

By this elaborate manner of telling the story and presenting the request as very minor, the author raises the tension to a maximum. No wonder Bathsheba gives her permission. Her name is not mentioned in MT, but it is in LXX.

2:17 *He continued: 'Please speak with king Solomon – for he will not refuse you – and (ask him) to give me Abishag the Shunammite as wife.'*
Adonijah's question, or rather his request, speaks for itself and also *seems* to be completely innocent. But in the ancient Near East the taking of a concubine from the royal harem implied the acquisition of a claim on the throne (H. Grotius; see also M. Tsevat, *JSS* 3 [1958], 237ff.); cf. 2 Sam. 3:6-10 (Abner and Rizpah); 16:20-23 (Absalom and David's concubines); possibly also 1 Sam. 25 (David and Abigail; see also J.D. Levenson, *CBQ* 40 [1978], 22-18). The title המלך here follows Salomon, but this is even more frequently reversed (cf. Ges-K §135g; Joüon §131k; König §333x).

2:18 *'Very well,' answered Bathsheba, 'I myself will speak to the king about you.'*
Bathsheba accepts the request and is prepared to submit Adonijah's plans of marriage with the beautiful Abishag from Shunem to her son Solomon. With a certain emphasis the pers. pron. *separatum* is positioned up front (cf. Ges-K §135a; Joüon §146a; cf. Driver §160, n. 1 on pp. 201f.).

2:19 *So Bathsheba went to king Solomon to speak to him about Adonijah. The king rose to meet her and bowed before her; then he sat down on his throne, and had a chair brought in for the king's mother so that she was seated at his right.*
For all the difference, there is also a certain resemblance between Bathsheba's 'coming' to Solomon and her coming to David in 1:15f. Whereas in the latter case it was Bathsheba who did obeisance to David, now it is Solomon who honours his mother. The core of the issue, however, is again Adonijah, the personalization of an illegitimate claim on the throne of David, and Abishag whose presence then was also expressly mentioned, though in a parenthetical sentence. The 2 narratives are interconnected. They even suggest something of

a chiasm at the center of which, at the point where the lines intersect, Abishag is the silent but controlling point of interest. Whereas in 1:15f. Bathsheba in a sense pleaded against Adonijah and for Solomon, she now pleads for Adonijah and by implication against Solomon. While in 1:15 Abishag was the serving object, she is now the subject dominating the conversation.

Of some textcritical interest in our verse is the divergent translation of וישתחו לה in LXX: καὶ κατεφίλησεν αὐτήν, which in Hebr. could have been וישקה derived from נשק 'to kiss,' 'to embrace.' But with Thenius, Stade-Schwally, Burney, Barthelemy and numerous others I see no reason to deviate from MT. The reading in LXX (and also in Josephus, *Ant.* VIII, 7: περιπλακέντος) is possibly connected with the opinion of the Alexandrine Jews that it was inappropriate for a king to bow to someone else. Gray, however, mentions a Ugar. letter, in which a king says to his mother: 'I bow down before you' (*KTU* 2.13:5f.). [19] Our verse enters at length upon the honour shown to Bathsheba. This has to do with the position of the גְּבִירָה, the 'queen mother' in Israel. Not always (cf. e.g. Gen. 16:4; 8f.; 2 Kgs. 5:3, etc.) but in fact quite often this word was practically an official title for the queen mother (1 Kgs. 15:13 [par. 2 Chr. 15:16]; 2 Kgs. 10:13; Jer. 13:18; 29:2; cf. Isa. 47:5, 7; cf. H. Kosmala, *TWAT*, I, 909; J. Kühlewein, *THAT*, I, 176; A.S. van der Woude, *THAT*, II, 943.). Now it is true that the title is not used here, but both from the above-mentioned example in OT in which the title *is* used, and from the extrabiblical data from countries outside of Israel, e.g., from the Hittites (cf. A.A. Kampman, *JEOL* 7 [1940], 432-442), it is clear that she received much honour and had much influence both on the ruling monarch and on his subjects. Respect for Bathsheba on the part of Solomon is also evidenced by the placement of a throne for his mother at his right hand (it is unnecessary with Stade-Schwally to interpret וישם passively). Sitting or standing (cf. Ps. 45:10 and 110:1) at someone's 'right hand' implies deep respect (cf. W. Grundmann, *TDNT*, II, 37ff., and Strack-Billerbeck, I, 835f.).

2:20 *She said to him: 'I have one small request to make of you; please do not refuse me.' The king answered: 'Just say it, mother; I cannot refuse you.'*
Bathsheba proposes that she now make her 'small' request. The form אל־תשב, with retracted stress, gets much attention in the grammars (cf. Olsh. §229c; Ewald §224b; König I §38, 5 (p. 466); Bg. II §28m; BL, 56u (p. 405); Driver §70; Joüon §§47a n. 2; 80n; 114i; Burney, etc.). 'Normally' the form should have been תָּשֵׁב.

In the etiquette of the court the question-and-answer game goes so far that

---

[19] On this element in Ugar. letters, see J.-L. Cunchillos, "Correspondance," *Textes Ougaritiques*, II, Paris 1989, 239-421, esp. 249ff.

Solomon even tells his mother that 'he will not turn away her face,' that he will not refuse her request. Although the implications of the refined eastern courtly nuances escape us today, these words do not seem to mean more than a polite encouragement to go on and make known the 'small' request.[20]

2:21 *She said: 'Please may Abishag the Shunammite be given to your brother Adonijah as wife?'*
Bathsheba proceeds to the core of the issue. יֻתַּן is a passive form of the verb נתן in connection with which the object of the active construction remains that of the passive construction as well (Ewald §295b, Ges-K §121b; Joüon §128b; Burney). In this connection the passive form of the verb is 'impersonal.' In the (older) lexicons this form is often cited as hophal of נתן. There is also a line of thought which views this (and similar) form(s) as a passive qal based on the sound consideration that the verb in question only occurs in the qal (cf. König II, §121, 2 (p. 384); Lettinga §§41h, 53hj). Like certain other Northwestern Sem. languages, the Hebr. must originally also have had a passive qal stem modification, which has been suppressed by the niph. Accordingly, the above form is a rudiment of his passive qal stem.

2:22 *Then king Solomon answered and said to his mother: 'Now why do you ask me to give Abishag the Shunammite to Adonijah? You might as well ask me to give him the crown. After all, he is my older brother and Abiathar the priest and Joab the son of Zeruiah are (undoubtedly) on his side.'*
Solomon immediately sees through Bathsheba's question and Adonijah's intention. He latches on to the 'small' request – Abishag as wife for Adonijah – by asking why Bathsheba does not immediately come up with the 'big' request: the kingship for Adonijah! The ו before למה, according to Burney, has a sarcastic nuance. The same is true for the ו before the imperative שאלי, which conveys an aspect of irony (cf. König §371a; GD §66; Ges-K §154b; Joüon §§114m, 177m): "you may as well ask for ..." After Abishag, LXX omits the 'Shunammite' but is not followed in this by other ancient versions. Against MT, then, there is no objection whatever. A harder issue concerns what follows after הגדול ממני. As MT now reads, Solomon suggests to his mother that she ask the kingship for him (i.e. Adonijah), and *for* Abiathar the priest, and *for* Joab son of Zeruiah. Vulg. and Pesh., however, offer translations which read approximately as follows: 'On his side are Abiathar ... and Joab ...' (cf. also Barthelemy). Tg. paraphrases: 'Were not he, and Abiathar ..., and Joab ... involved in one and the same plan,' which more or less comes down to the same thing as the translations of the other ancient versions.

---

[20] See now also H. Barilqo, "One Small Question," *BetM* 30 (1984f.), 305-311 (Hebr.).

Moreover, this paraphrase materially conveys the intent of the Hebr. text best, because it adds a second argument to the first: the first, remember, was that Adonijah was older than Solomon; the second that in addition he had 2 powerful allies in the high priest and the supreme commander of the army (thus, already, Thenius; also Burney, Benzinger et al., cf. Ehrlich). Especially LXX supports this idea by adding ὁ ἀρχιστράτηγος ἑταῖρος after 'Joab son of Zeruiah.' ἑταῖρος indicates the character of an *alliance* (cf. Klostermann, though his text emendation does not have to be followed). The addition 'commander of the army' in LXX (and a number of MSS of Pesh.), though not necessary, is understandable (cf. 1:19). For למה with the accent on the final syllable, see Stade §372b.

2:23 *Then king Solomon swore by YHWH: 'May God deal with me, yes even worse, if Adonijah did not dream up this scheme at the cost of his life.*

Following these venomous words of Solomon, in which he seemingly 'did not turn away the face of his mother' (cf. v. 20) and in which he did not formally abandon his courteousness, the other side of the coin is clearly shown to the listener and reader. He swears an oath the content of which is that Adonijah has introduced this matter against his own life. According to the text Solomon swears by YHWH, but refers to אלהים (one MSS of LXX has the word κύριος in place of Θεός; see also Montg.-Gehman). This may indicate that the author lived in a time in which saying the name YHWH was already avoided. The formula itself already occurs a number of times in the books of Ruth, Samuel and Kings (1 Sam. 3:17; 14:44; 20:13; 25:22; 2 Sam. 3:9, 35; 19:14; Ruth 1:17; 2 Kgs. 6:31; and with a pl. verb on the lips of the 'pagan' Jezebel, 1 Kgs. 19:2 and Benhadad 1 Kgs. 20:10; cf. Joüon §165a [1]). The verbs in this formula (impf.) are used here in an imperative or jussive sense (cf. Bg. II §10m). After the 'formula of self-malediction' here follows כי (Ges-K §149d; cf. Ewald §330b), elsewhere אם or כי אם (cf. Burney). The ב in בנפשו can be viewed as a *bet pretii* (cf. König §332o; Burney; BDB, s.v. ב [III 3a]), which can be translated by 'at the cost of his life,' i.e. 'at his own expense' (Joüon §146k).

2:24 *And now listen: As surely as the Lord lives who has established me (in my office as king) and has set me on the throne of my father David and who, as he promised, has started a dynasty for me, so surely will Adonijah be put to death still today.'*

Just as in 1:29 (see the commentary a.l.) David swears by YHWH when his throne and the legitimate succession are being threatened, so Solomon now swears as the throne and the 'legitimate' succession are being threatened. Thus Adonijah's death sentence is subtly placed in the context of the preservation of the Davidic dynasty.

The hiph.-form of כון (see above on vs. 12) often denotes an 'establishment,' or 'confirmation' of the throne or the successor to the throne in the line of David (2 Sam. 5:12; 7:12; Ps. 89:5; 1 Chr. 14:2 etc.) Here also the nuance 'to prepare' (cf. LXX ἑτοιμάζειν and W. Grundmann, *TDNT*, II, 704f.) is present. The throne has been prepared for Solomon but Solomon has also been prepared for the throne! Then comes the 'sitting' on the throne. As to the form of the verb, it concerns a k^etib q^ere question. In the written form one expects: וְיוֹשִׁיבֵנִי, but in the spoken form it is: וְיוֹשִׁיבָנִי. Although in the case of an imperfect with suffix the 'connecting vowel' /e/ is more in keeping with the rule, there are exceptions (cf. Olsh. §231c; Ewald §249d; Böttcher §869; Stade §636b; Bg. II §5g; BL, 337n; 384c). But the text tradition in the Hebr. MSS, as is already clear from a comparison of *BHK* with *BHS* and their critical apparatuses, is not exactly unambiguous on this point (cf. also Thenius, Montg.-Gehman; Delitzsch, *LSF* §34b et al.).

More important is the question what is meant by 'made me a house.' Thenius is of the opinion that 'house' here cannot mean 'posterity' because Rehoboam (cf. 14:21 with 11:42) cannot have been born yet. The word is said to refer to the 'succession of regents,' for which the foundation was laid by Solomon's accession to the throne. Also in 2 Sam. 7:11, 16, 26f. בית is said to have this meaning. But it is not necessary to propose such a rationalistic interpretation, nor to modify לי into לו, as is often done (cf. Klostermann, Benzinger, Stade-Schwally, Ehrlich and the textcr. app. in *BHK*.) בית can also – figuratively – mean 'family,' 'generation,' 'dynasty' (cf. H.A. Hoffner, *TWAT*, I, 636f.; O. Michel, *TDNT*, V, 120). In this sense there is in our verse an allusion to 2 Sam. 7:11 as well (cf. Burney; on היום see De Vries, *Yesterday*, 224).

2:25 *So king Solomon gave orders to Benaiah son of Jehoiada who struck him (Adonijah) down so that he died.*
The king leaves the act of carrying out the death sentence to Benaiah son of Jehoiada who both now and in the future will discharge such lugubrious duties punctually. ב+פגע 'to fall upon somebody' (in a hostile sense) recurs in this chapter (vss. 29, 31f., 34, 36; cf. S. Amsler, *THAT*, II, 682). The construction שלח ביד is more highly charged than this verb with 'a self-evident object' (cf. BrSynt. §127b).

2:26 *Then the king said to Abiathar the priest: 'Go to Anathoth to your estate, for you deserve to die. Now, however, I will not put you to death because you have carried the ark of the Lord YHWH before my father David and you shared all my father's hardships.'*
In this and the following verse judgment is pronounced over the priest Abiathar who was also mentioned earlier (cf. 1:7). On account of his loyal parti-

sanship to David and perhaps especially on account of his 'spiritual office,' the death sentence also threatening him is converted into banishment. The king orders him to go to his estate in Anathoth although he was 'a man of death.' We must, however, mention that Levi had no 'inheritance' in Israel (Deut. 12:12; 18:1 and Num. 18:24), so that a priest who owned an estate does not sound exactly 'orthodox' (but see *GLAJJ*, I, 32f.).

Aside from this passage Anathoth is also mentioned as a 'city of Levites' in Josh. 21:18 (par. 1 Chr. 6:45); in Isa. 10:30; and in Jer. 1:1; 32:7ff. as Jeremiah's hometown; and in Neh. 11:32, while 'the men of Anathoth' occur also in Jer. 11:21, 23; Ezra 2:23 and Neh. 7:27. The city is located a couple of kilometers NNE of Jerusalem in the tribal area of Benjamin (cf. Eusebius, *Onomastikon*, 26, 27). Today, according to Noth, the name is *Rās el-Ḥarrūbe*, near *'Anāta*. But others (for instance, Simons, *GTTOT*, §337, 12) are not so sure of this localization. König (§262p) thinks that Anathoth is probably the pl. of the name of the goddess Anat, describing the בית ענת, the temple of Anat. As is well known, this goddess plays a large role as sister and spouse of Baal in the mythological texts which have emerged since 1929 as a result of the excavations at Ugariti (Ras Shamra). Also in the Elephantine papyri her name, combined with Bethel and Yahô, plays a role.[21] König's suggestion, therefore, is not unacceptable, even though her name occurs only incidentally in OT (see my *Kanaän. goden*, 52ff., and now also the survey by P.L. Day, *DDD*, 62-77).

It is noteworthy that the accusative of direction, Anathoth, here precedes the imperative, which puts the emphasis on the place where Abiathar has to go (Joüon §§125n, 155s; Ges-K §118f). The word שָׂדֶיךָ is only an apparent pl. and therefore has to be translated in the sing. (Ges-K §93ss; Joüon §96Ce), as also numerous MSS with the ancient versions suggest.

Apart from the field, שׂדה, a word which occurs approx. 320x in OT (cf. *KBL*, s.v.), LXX[Luc.] (with Theod.) adds the phrase 'and to your house,' an expansion which may have been intended materially but cannot, strictly speaking, be inferred from the available Hebr. text. As we noted above, Anathoth was a 'city of Levites' and – after the priests of Nob had been slaughtered by Doeg, among whom was Abiathar's father Ahimelech – this city may have been assigned to the only remaining priest, later David's faithful ally, as place of residence. Haran, *Temples*, 120, however, is of the opinion that the landed estate had accrued to him by way of his ancestors. For the rest, על need not be replaced here by אל (Burney).

---

[21] Cf. A. Vincent, *La religion des Judéo-Araméens d'Éléphantine*, Paris 1937, 622-653; see now also K. van der Toorn, "Anat-Yahu, Some Other Deities, and the Jews of Elephantine," *Numen* 39 (1992), 80-101.

Abiathar is called an אִישׁ מוֹת. This is a 'genitival phrase' (Joüon §129j; cf. Ges-K §128t; König §306n), to which one may compare an expression like בֶּן־מָוֶת (1 Sam. 20:31; 2 Sam. 12:5 and 1 Sam. 26:16; 2 Sam. 19:29 [pl.]; cf. also A. Phillips, *VT* 16 [1966], 243f.). In these cases Phillips considers the possibility of the translation 'the deadly man,' the 'arch-villain,' a person who is surely morally worthy of death (cf. D. Winton Thomas, *VT* 3 [1953], 219ff.; S. Rin, *VT* 9 [1959], 342f.). Although in ancient Hebr. this nuance may have been part of the expression, we do not find this translation compelling here (see also D.W. Thomas, *VT* 18 [1968], 123, n. 5).

In contrast to MT, LXX, by the transposition of the *waw-copulativum*, has the phrase 'on this day' refer to the preceding, by which the meaning of Solomon's words is considerably modified: 'today you may be a child of death, but you will not die, because ...' etc. The meaning of MT may be: 'You are a child of death, but you will not die today.' This would not, then, exclude a later execution. In view of the 'enlightened despotism' of ancient oriental rulers such an argument is of course far from impossible. A change along the lines of Ehrlich וְעִם זֶה, 'nevertheless,' is therefore not necessary. Perhaps LXX aimed at presenting Solomon as being less capricious than MT?

The reason for Solomon's pardon is clear: Abiathar's participation in David's hardships. The phrasing, however, is somewhat surprising. There is reference to carrying the אֲרוֹן, the so-called 'ark of the covenant' (cf. LXX: τὴν κιβωτὸν τῆς διαθήκης), the box which was 125 cm. long and 75 cm. wide, covered with gold and adorned with cherubim, which served as a cult object and of which there are stories saying that long ago, at YHWH's command, it was made on Mount Sinai (cf. H.-J. Zobel, *TWAT*, I, 391-404). Thenius already pointed to the difficulty involved in the carrying of the ark by Abiathar, a chore usually performed by Levites, referring to verses like 1 Sam. 2:28; 14:3 (cf. also vs. 18) in order to present the proposal – later taken over by others – to read אֵפוֹד here in place of 'ark' (see, e.g., Stade-Schwally). In 1 Sam. 23:6 there is mention of this cult object, which is somewhere between a priestly garment and an image or depiction of a god, and was often used when seeking an oracle (cf. W. Dommershausen, *TWAT*, I, 995f.; *HAL*, s.v. etc.). Josephus, *Ant.* VIII, 10, interprets our verse as follows: 'Abiathar owes his life to the hard times he shared with David and to the ark which he brought up (to Jerusalem) along with him.' This is a reference to 2 Sam. 6:12ff. In 2 Sam. 15:24, in connection with David's flight from Absalom, there is also mention of the transport of the ark and even Abiathar's name is mentioned, be it in passing. Still, neither Josephus's line of thought, nor the last-mentioned text, are concrete indications for a relation to our verse. On the other hand, there are a couple of reasons to maintain MT (cf. also Haran, *Temples,* 79): (1) none of the ancient translations deviates from the MT; (2) the *ephod* never appears with the addition Adonai, Elohim, or YHWH (Burney). One gets the impression that the author or possibly the redactor who introduced this argument into the text viewed 'carrying the ark of YHWH (of God, etc.)' as a figurative description for 'functioning as (high) priest.' Montg.-Gehman are of the opinion that later editors, because of the ark's great importance, wished to insert it in place of an ancient instrument of divination.

Some MSS, as well as LXX and Pesh., omit אדני. Now — as Mm 1553 demonstrates — the ark in combination with YHWH or with 'the God of Israel' occurs rather frequently. The combination with אדני could be a late insertion in this passage (cf. O. Eißfeldt, *TWAT*, I, 66-78, esp. 69f. and comments on 3:10). Some MSS read אלהים after YHWH, which, though understandable, is unnecessary.

For the hardships which Abiathar experienced in David's company the Hebr. uses the word ענה in hitp., which apart from this use (2x) occurs 4 more times in this stem-modification (Gen. 16:9; Ps. 107-17; Dan. 10:12 and Ezra 8:21; cf. R. Martin-Achard, *THAT*, II, 341-350; E.S. Gerstenberger, *TWAT*, VI, 247-270). To distinguish it from ענה I, 'to answer,' this root is sometimes designated as II, from which also adjectives like עָנָו and עָנִי, or a substantive like עֳנִי, are derived. Quite often the factitive pi. is used in the sense of 'to oppress,' 'to treat badly,' 'to humiliate.' LXX uses the word κακουχέω, 'to torment,' 'to vex' (cf. Hebr. 11:37 and 13:3). By the use of this verb his active participation in David's suffering is indicated (cf. also W. Michaelis, *TDNT*, V, 907, n. 21).

2:27 *So Solomon discharged Abiathar from his position as priest of YHWH, thus fulfilling the word of YHWH which he had spoken at Shiloh concerning Eli's family.*
This verse, along with the second half of the previous verse, leaves the impression of being a redactional (dtr.?) expansion, for the purpose of adding still more valid reasons for replacing Abiathar as high priest by Zadok. Solomon 'banishes' Abiathar from his function. In the books of Kings the word גרש pi. is only used here (cf. H. Ringgren, *TWAT*, II, 72ff.). A comment like this shows the extent to which the (high) priesthood was essentially a royal affair (so already H. Grotius).

This measure by Solomon is described by the dtr. redactor as a 'fulfillment' of the word of YHWH (Ehrlich has another opinion). He employs the verb מלא pi., preceded by ל (M. Delcor, *THAT*, I, 899f.; see also Joüon §124l). For 'fulfill' (מלא) LXX, here and approx. 7x elsewhere, has πληρόω (G. Delling, *TDNT*, VI, 287f.). The object is the 'word of YHWH,' 'the decisive force in the history of Israel' (O. Procksch, *TDNT*, IV, 96). According to the redactor this 'word' relates to what we read in 1 Sam. 2:27-36 and esp. in vss. 31-33 concerning the judgment over the priest Eli in the sanctuary at Shiloh. On the basis of other information about Abiathar in the OT we do not make this immediate connection. According to 1 Sam. 22:20, Abiathar was the son of Ahimelech, the son of Ahitub (2 Sam. 8:17, in the reading of MT, is not correct and will have to be corrected; see the commentaries a.l.). 1 Sam. 14:3 mentions Ahitub, Ichabod's brother, son of Phinehas, Eli's son, but as Ahitub's son it mentions Ahijah, not Ahimelech. There are strong indications, however, based on the strange location of this genealogy and the highly unusual form (a brother is included), that this verse is a gloss. Further, the identification of Ahijah with Ahimelech is incorrect. Perhaps the intent of this later gloss is to link the priesthood under Saul with the 'bad' house of Eli and so to speak in favour of the Zadokites. Nowhere in OT do we find clear evidence of a genealogy of Eli. Josephus mentions one (based on tradition?) in *Ant.* V, 361: Eli is said to descend from the house of Ithamar, one of the sons of Aaron (cf. also 1 Chr. 24:6), but this genealogy is not convincing either. Perhaps Eli's family was the ancient priesthood of Shilo (thus a.o. R.W. Corney, *IDB*, II, 85). In later times it became important to link every priest or Levite with Aaron.[22]

Viewed in this light our text clearly gives the impression of being a later addition and adaptation, intended to furnish extra relief to Abiathar's 'judgment' (on the 'sons of Eli,' cf. J. Liver, *EncMiqr.* 6, 231ff.). The redactor unconditionally places Abiathar, if not in the genealogy, then certainly in the priestly tradition of Eli, the (high) priest of Shiloh. This town, today called *ḥirbet Selūn* (Simons, *GTTOT*, §641) is situated about half way, and somewhat to the E of, the road from Jerusalem to Nablus, closer to the latter than the former. According to tradition, 'the tent of meeting' was set up in Shiloh under Joshua (Josh. 18:1). As is evident from the history of Eli, the sanctuary functioned for a time for the Israelites. That it was destroyed by the Philistines and that Jeremiah makes allusions to this event (Jer. 7:12, 14; 26:6, 9) is a possibility but hard to prove. According to the excavations made at the site there is no direct evidence of a destruction in the so-called Iron Age I-period. It *is* true that the city has known its ups and downs (cf. S. Holm-Nielsen, *IDBS*, 822f.)

2:28   *When word reached Joab — for Joab had joined Adonijah and his party though (earlier) he had not joined Absalom — Joab fled to the tent of YHWH and took hold of the horns of the altar.*

This and the following verses (concluding with vs. 34) describe the sentence carried out in the case of Joab. Even at greater length than in the Abiathar

---

[22] Cf. also the argument of M.D. Goulder, *The Psalms of the Sons of Korah* (JSOTS 20), Sheffield 1982, 65-84, about the dual priesthood, in which that of Dan played an important role.

case, we are given the motivation for it. In vs. 35 we then get the factual information, perhaps derived from some chronicle, about whom Solomon replaced by whom. The expansive and elaborative sections in these verses are probably commentaries on the facts as he knew them or as they were handed down to him.

The word שמעה comes first, so occupying an emphatic position (cf. 2 Sam. 13:30). Twice more it occurs in Kings (10:7; 2 Kgs. 19:7) and denotes 'what was heard,' 'the rumor,' which, however, often does contain a clear core of truth (Vulg. reads: *nuntius*). In our pericope this is the case, as the sequel shows. Following the first mention of Joab, LXX[B, Luc.] read 'the son of Zeruiah,' but this addition is omitted by LXX[A] as well as a large number of MSS of LXX (even Lucas Brugensis and Amama already occupy themselves with the textcritical issues which the translations raise). That Joab had joined Adoniah's camp is sufficiently well known. That the text expressly adds that he had not joined Absalom's camp seems completely superfluous. LXX[Luc.] has the reading 'Solomon' in place of 'Absalom.' This reading is supported by Pesh. and the majority of the MSS of Vulg. Josephus (*Ant.* VIII, 13) also shares this opinion and it is not surprising that exegetes like Thenius et al. consider this reading the correct one. Still it cannot be said that this reading offers much that is new, unless one were to inject into it the nuance 'not yet' in the sense that 'even after David's death he had still not yet become a loyal supporter of Solomon' (cf. Ehrlich's solution to the problem). Then the reading 'Absalom' – also in light of the misery (mentioned above) which Abiathar had shared with David – is more logical, so that the ancient versions, to the extent they depart from MT, need not be followed here; cf. aside from Stade-Schwally, also W.T. Claassen, *JNSL* 11 (1983), 41, who calls the כי-clause 'parenthetical.'

As Adonijah had done earlier (see 1:50), Joab flees to 'the tent of YHWH' and grasps the horns of the altar. It is evident that the 'the tent of revelation' was equipped with various cultic attributes such as an altar (see O. Eißfeldt, *KS*, VI, 6f.). According to A. Alt, *KS*, III, 240 n. 7, what we are dealing with here is more like a 'hut' (see above, 1:39). The LXX translates the word by σκήνωμα, which serves approx. 46x as the translation for אֹהֶל (cf. W. Michaelis, *TDNT*, VII, 370f., and 385).

2:29 *When king Solomon was told that Joab had fled to the tent of YHWH and was evidently by the altar, he sent Benaiah son of Jehoiada, charging him: 'Go, strike him down.'*

In this verse, in LXX, besides a few smaller additions, there is one large insertion. Or, if you will, MT, either by *homoeoteleuton* or *homoeoarcton*, omitted a significant part of a sentence. The smaller additions a.o. are τῷ Σαλωμων λέγοντες in place of למלך שלמה, while it reads κατέχει τῶν κεράτων τοῦ Θυσιαστηρίου in place of אצל המזבח. Also Pesh. has something similar: 'he sought refuge by the horns of the altar.' But after וישלח שלמה comes a long insertion (see the Hebr. reproduction in the textcr. app. of *BHK*): '(And Solomon) sent Joab the message: 'What is the matter with you that you have fled to the altar?' To which Joab answered: 'Because I am afraid of you I have fled to the Lord.' Thereupon Solomon sent …' etc.

None of these insertions or additions proves that our MT is corrupt, or that LXX was arbitrary. The LXX, after all, may have followed another 'Vorlage.' Burney correctly comments that אצל המזבח occurs with a very common meaning (cf., e.g., Lev. 1:16; 6:3). The ground around the altar is 'holy ground.'

Although נתן occurs here without suffix or personal pronoun, we are not left in doubt as to who is meant (Burney; but cf. Montg.-Gehman). The insertion in LXX, the verbal exchange between Solomon and Joab, really does not introduce much that is new in the story and the omission of this addition, accordingly, is at least as meaningful as the full reading of LXX. Perhaps Montg.-Gehman are right when they speak (also) here of 'another case of uniformity.' At most Solomon's astonishment at Joab's flight could be considered a new aspect.

Benaiah is again commissioned to perform the bloody execution and, according to LXX, to bury him.

2:30 *When Benaiah arrived at the tent of YHWH, he said to him: 'The king says: "Come out".' But he said: 'No, I will die here.' So Benaiah sent word back to the king: 'So Joab has spoken and so I have answered.'*

Benaiah goes to the 'tent of YHWH.' LXX still adds 'son of Jehoida.' He conveys to Joab the order of the king to come along, but Joab is on to him and says: 'I want to die here.' Some Hebr. MSS read לו in place of לא. LXX and the other versions supplement the לא as though the 'Vorlage' had לא אצא (cf. Thenius). But the text is clear as it stands. The לא is an absolute 'no' (König §352f; cf. also Ewald §320b, n.) separated from the preceding ויאמר by a *paseq* (Olsh. §43; Bg. I §10u) by which the delivery is slowed down a bit and no one will read ויאמר לו: 'and he said to him.' The כי is adversative (cf. Ges-B, *BDB*, Montg.-Gehman et al.). Inasmuch as Benaiah shrinks from shedding Joab's blood on holy ground, and respects the right of asylum, he will not act without (new) instructions from the king.

2:31 *Then the king said to him: 'Do as he has said. Strike him down and bury him. So clear me and my father's house of responsibility for the blood which Joab has shed without cause.*

Benaiah receives permission from the king to kill Joab on holy ground. In this connection the king refers to Joab's own wish. In addition he gives orders that he should be buried, presumably with a view to his dignity (cf. 2. Kgs. 9:34; the contrast being 2 Kgs. 9:10; Jer. 22:19; 26:23; Ehrlich; Burney). In 2 MSS the word והסירת is read in the 1 p. sing. in place of the 2 p. sing., but this change is not necessary since even without it, it is clear that what Benaiah does is ultimately the work of the king. סור occurs 134x in the hiph. in the sense of 'remove,' 'eliminate,' etc. (S. Schwertner, *THAT*, II, 148ff.). Striking here is the penultimate stress, where the reader expects the accent to be on the last syllable (cf. Böttcher §974 [p. 202]). According to Olsh. §255i, what we have here is a brief pause which shifts the accent; see further BL, 404; Bg. II §4c; Driver §110, 5; and Burney.

In vs. 5 there was mention of דמי־מלחמה here we read of דמי חנם. Because adverbs and particles can in certain cases function as nouns, one can in such a case obtain a st. cstr. combination (GD §24, n. 4; BrSynt §71c; Meyer §97, 3a). Ges-K §128w views the adverb as an epexegetical genitive (cf. also Joüon §§129l, 132c; König §318c; and Ewald §287d). In 1 Sam. 25:31 there is mention of לְשָׁפָּךְ־דָּם חִנָּם, hence of the sing., though חנם can be taken here as a direct adverb with שפך. The reference is to blood shed without a specific juridical ground (Noth). LXX often renders the word with δωρεάν, an adverbial accusative also used here: 'without ground' and 'without purpose' (cf. in NT, e.g., John 15:25 and Gal. 2:21). The murders (pl.!) of Joab are described as senseless. Although basically also Vulg. *(sanguis innocens)*, Tg. (דאשר יואב מָ גָּן +דם זכי), 'which Joab shed without cause') and Pesh. (approximately the same as Tg.) mean this, 'innocent blood' is still misleading, for חנם is not an adjective, but being rather adverbial, it also says something about the shedding of the blood; the man himself need not be innocent (cf. דם נָקִי, 2 Kgs. 21:16, etc.). Naturally our text refers to what in vs. 5 had been noted in other words by David on his deathbed. There, remember, David twice spoke of 'the blood of war.' This blood was shed מעלי ומעל בית אבי, that is, this blood as it were flowed *on* Solomon and *on* the house of his father. Here again a reference to vs. 5 is possible, since the words את אשר־עשה לי יואב closely link Joab's deeds to David's life (cf. also Burney).

2:32 *And YHWH will bring his blood down on his own head because without the knowledge of my father David, he (fatally) struck down and killed with the sword two people who were more righteous and better than he, Abner son of Ner, commander of the army of Israel, and Amasa son of Jether, commander of the army of Judah.*
The story (see vs. 5) is again related at length so that Joab becomes increasingly worse (טבים ממנו) and David increasingly more innocent (דוד לא ידע). Instead of 'causing the blood to return upon his own head,' LXX has 'the blood of injustice' (τὸ αἷμα τῆς ἀδικίας αὐτοῦ) and Tg.: יַת חוֹבַת קְטוּלָה. This is also the intent of the Hebr. expression: the blood shed by Joab returns to his

own head (cf. 1 Sam. 25:39; Judg. 9:57; Burney).[23]

LXX (except LXX[Luc.]) adds 'their blood' to 'David did not know.' This, too, is a further explication of MT (for the emphasis on 'my father David,' cf. Joüon §155m).

2:33 *May their blood come down on the head of Joab and his descendants for ever, but may David, his descendants, his dynasty, and his throne for ever have peace from YHWH.'*

With respect to Joab and his posterity, we get to an all-time low; and to an all-time high as regards David and his dynasty: retribution on Joab's head (see the Egyptian parallels to this expression: J.J. Rabinowitz, *VT* 7 [1957], 398f.; R. Yaron, *VT* 8 [1958], 432f.; Rabinowitz, *VT* 9 [1959], 209f.) and on his descendants 'forever,' but to David, his 'house' and his 'throne,' peace from the Lord forevermore. The retribution is rooted in 2 Sam. 3:28f. where David pronounces a judgment on Joab. This retribution is negative; in contrast is the 'positive retribution' from the side of YHWH, שלום (cf. G. Gerleman, *THAT*, II, 927ff.) which is a gift from YHWH (G. von Rad, *TDNT*, II, 403f.). This שלום can be called the condition or the existence of the Davidic government and dynasty (M. Metzger, *UF* 2 [1970], 158).

2:34 *Then Benaiah son of Jehoiada went up, struck him and so killed him. He was buried on his estate in the wilderness.*

The execution of Joab by Benaiah is reported as factual information. The latter 'climbs on' the altar (see above, 1:53). We are further informed that he buried Joab 'at his own house in the wilderness.' In place of 'house' LXX[Luc.] and Pesh. (except the MSS 9al*fam*) have 'grave.' Joab, a relative of David, probably came from Bethlehem (cf. the burial of his brother Asahel in Bethlehem, 2 Sam. 2:32). Since this city is situated on the edge of the 'wilderness of Judah,' it is not excluded that Joab was buried there, by his family, in the 'wilderness.' Rabbinical exegetes, Rashi among them, explain Joab's residence in the wilderness in a sense that is favourable to him. Ehrlich's suggestion that we reed 'in Tadmor' in place of 'in the wilderness' (במדבר) (cf. comments on 9:18) must be considered unfounded.

2:35 *The king appointed Benaiah son of Jehoiada in his place as head of the army and the priest Zadok in place of Abiathar.*

The 'changing of the guard' is now legitimated in a way which can no longer astonish us. Benaiah becomes the supreme commander of the army and Zadok succeeds Abiathar. Following the statement of Benaiah's appointment LXX

---

[23] See now also J.M. Babut, "Que son sang soit sur sa tête," *VT* 36 (1986), 474-480.

adds: καὶ ἡ βασιλεία κατωρΘοῦτο ἐν Ιερουσαλημ. This addition resembles the conclusion of vs. 46 in MT, with the understanding that 'by the hand of Solomon' has been replaced by 'in Jerusalem.'

Following our verse, LXX has a very extensive elaboration usually marked in our LXX editions as 35a-35o. As to the first addition, it is possible that in former times the end of vs. 46 followed our verse, inasmuch as the stabilization of Solomon's kingship rested primarily on the reliability of the army and the priesthood. The following story about Shimei is not of essential importance to this stabilization (see a.o. Burney). Zadok is appointed as priest. LXX expressly adds 'as high priest' (ἱερεύς πρῶτος; cf. G. Schrenk, *TDNT*, III, 266; W. Michaelis, *TDNT*, VI, 865). This seems to us only an explanatory addition. There are scholars who deem the entire addition about Zadok to be secondary (for instance, J.A. Montgomery, *ZAW* 50 [1932], 124f.; cf. idem. *JBL* 49 [1930], 311-319). It is true that this information as such does not add much that is new, because we had already been told earlier that Zadok was priest (cf. 2 Sam. 8:17; 20:25b, so Noth). But as a way of underscoring the stabiliy of David's dynasty, the statement need not be superfluous. The term הכהן הגדול is post-exilic; the term כהן הראש (2 Kgs. 25:18) was used for the last 'high priest' before the exile: Seraiah (see K. Koch, *BHHW*, II, 737ff.).

Opinions are divided about the nature and value of the lengthy addition after our verse in LXX. Although it is not of direct importance for the exegesis of our verse in MT, we will nevertheless reproduce this section in translation:

35a *The Lord gave understanding to Solomon and very much wisdom and largeness of heart as the sand by the sea,*

35b *so that the wisdom of Solomon exceeded that of all the ancients and that of all the wise men of Egypt.*

35c *He took Pharaoh's daughter and brought her into the city of David until he had finished building the house of the Lord and the wall of Jerusalem round about. In seven years he built and finished them.*

35d *Solomon had 70,000 bearers of burdens and 80,000 hewers of stone in the mountain.*

35e *And Solomon made the sea, and its bases, and the large lavers, and the pillars, and the foundation of the court, and the brazen sea, whereupon he built a jutting defense. He dug (a tunnel) through the city of David.*

35f *After the daughter of pharaoh went up out of the city of David to her house which he had built for her, he built the citadel.*

35g *And three times a year Solomon brought burnt offerings and peace offerings on the altar which he had built for the Lord; he also burnt incense before the Lord; and he finished the house.*

35h *The chief persons appointed to preside over the works of Solomon* *numbered 3600. They supervised the people who performed the work.*

35i *He also built Assur (= Hazor), Magdo (= Megiddo), Gezer, Upper-Baithoron and Ballath.*

35k *True: he built these cities after he had built the house of the Lord himself and the wall of Jerusalem round about.*

35l *When David was still alive he charged Solomon saying: 'Look, there is with you Shimei son of Gera, of the family of Jemeni of Hebron.*

35m *On the day of my departure to the battle positions (= Mahanaim), he cursed me with a bitter curse.*

35n *And (afterward) he came to meet me at the Jordan where I swore to him by the Lord: "you will not be slain by the sword."*

35o *But you must not hold him guiltless. You are a wise man and so you will know what you have to do to him. You will bring down his gray hairs with blood to the underworld.'*

As may be evident, this section is composed of 2 main parts: (1) 35a-k, in which, along with Solomon's 'wisdom,' particularly his building activities, are reported; then (2) 35l-o, in which David's 'last words' about Shimei again come up, words which tie in with what follows in MT (see also V. Peterca, *Rivista Biblica* 30 [1982], 175-196). Swete, *Introduction*, 247, offers a sort list of passages in MT and LXX (as does Montgomery, 126ff.) which correspond to the above verses. Still, in these 2 parts there is an assortment of glosses, interpolations, and midrash-like elaborations which make the text (and the translation) murky and which in part read differently in other MSS of the LXX (see Montgomery). A comparison with the 'real' LXX further shows that the Greek translation of these segments has to be from another hand. Gooding, having made a special study of these segments (Gooding 1976; also 2:6a-l), speaks of a careful ordering of these segments which are designed to serve the midrash and clearly bear the imprint of the debates in the rabbinical schools in Palestine as well as in Alexandria. In addition, there is the recent dissertation by Krautwurst (1977) on the problems presented by the additions in LXX (see our *Introduction* 3.1).

2:36 *The king also sent for Shimei and said to him, 'Build yourself a house in Jerusalem, live there but do not leave it to go anywhere else.*

Finally, as a kind of 'bonus,' there is the report of Shimei's unfortunate fate which relates to the 'curse' addressed to him according to the dying David (vss. 8f.). By itself it is not impossible that, as a descendant of Saul, Shimei was a potential danger to the Davidic dynasty and therefore put under 'house arrest,' so that the authorities could more easily keep an eye on him. David, as we learn from 2 Sam. 9, had already brought Mephibosheth as a descendant of Saul within his reach in Jerusalem. The way both earlier (vs. 8f.) and here the Shimei-case is treated by Solomon or his father raises questions. Did the redactor perhaps again insert the Shimei-case into the record to temper Solomon's reputation as a wise man and to disparage his fame? Those of the modern exegetes who think this is the case have the Bible text on their side.

The expression אָנֶה וָאָנָה, used here and in vs. 42, occurs also in 2 Kgs. 5:25 (cf. Ewald §104d; Olsh. §§130d, 222e; König §318h; Ges-K §§80i, 90i; BL, 216o, 529u, 631f). The unaccented affix /ā/ has been placed after the quite frequently occurring אָן, 'where?', as this is also the case with the ה-local, after which dissimilation of the vowel must have occurred (cf. BL, 529x, but also Stade §132).

In place of the king's 'sending' for Shimei, LXX in B and other MSS only has: καὶ ἐκάλεσεν ὁ βασιλεὺς ..., while LXX^Luc. again indicates, after Shimei, that he is the 'son of Gera.'

2:37 *On the day you leave it and cross the Kidron Brook, be very clear that you will die. Your blood will then be on your own head.'*
The categorical command to Shimei to live in Jerusalem is followed by the lethal threat not to leave the city, more specifically, not to cross the brook Kidron, because if he does no redress will be possible. In this dependent clause, an inf. cstr. with suff. (צֵאתְךָ) is followed by a pf. cons. with future significance (Bg. II §9f; cf. §9i; Joüon §§119o, 124q; Meyer §§101.6b, 103.5a; cf. also Burney).

The 'brook' Kidron is designated as the boundary of an area within which Shimei has freedom of movement. This is the deep valley between Jerusalem and the Mount of Olives to the E. Among the Arabs it is called *Wādi Sitt Mirjām*, further S *Wadi Silwān,* still further *Wadi en Nār* and, finally, *Wadi Mar Sāba,* which in the end empties into the Dead Sea. In the rainy season this brook has water which has earned it the qualification נחל, a word which in OT occurs 141x (*KBL*; L.A. Snijders, *TWAT*, V, 361-366). 'Kidron' occurs much less frequently in OT (2 Sam. 15:23; 1 Kgs. 2:37; 15:13; 2 Kgs. 23:4, 6 (2x), 12; Jer. 31:40; 2 Chr. 15:16; 29:16; and 30:14) and is also mentioned in NT (John 18:1). Etymologically the name has been related to קדר, 'being dark' or 'dirty' (cf. *KBL*: 'Trübbach'; further Abel, *GP*, I, 400f.; H. Kosmala, *BHHW*, II, 946f.; *HAL*, s.v.). Now Kidron only seals off one side of the area Shimei might not leave. This is probably linked to Shimei's original hometown (viz. Bahurim), a small town − as we saw above − to the NE of the Mount of Olives (vs. 8). It is particularly in this area, apparently, that Shimei was no longer allowed to be seen (Thenius, Noth). This does not alter the fact that other limits had clearly been set for Shimei as well, as the sequel shows.

The formula of 'blood guilt': 'your blood come down on your own head' is derived from the legal world and serves to establish the guilt of someone condemned to death. At the same time it indicates the 'non-culpability' of the one carrying out the death sentence. See H. Reventlow, *VT* 10 (1960), 311-327, esp. 316-320: 'eine kultrechtliche Funktion'; K. Koch, *VT* 12 (1962), 396-416, esp. 413: the formula aims 'bei gewaltsamer Tötung die Übertragung der Blutsphäre aus(zu)schließen'; see further G. Gerleman, *THAT*, I, 449f.

Because in vs. 42 there is mention of an oath sworn by Solomon with regard to Shimei, LXX adds to the words of MT the following: the king swore it to him on that day (see also the textcr. app. of *BHK*; Thenius, Burney a.o.). Again it is hard to tell whether LXX here gives an explanatory expansion or followed a Hebr. 'Vorlage' in these words. Burney is not wrong when he thinks that the swearing of an oath may well be *implied* in the account of the vss. 37 and 38a.

2:38 *'Very well,' Shimei answered the king. 'Your servant will do as my lord the king has explained.' So Shimei lived in Jerusalem for a long time.*
Shimei assents to the king's decree. The word באשר, as related to the following כן (see our study on the particle כן, *OTS* 21 [1981], 210), is better suited here than the *nota relationis* אשר read by LXX, Pesh., and a number of Hebr. MSS. In this connection also the difference in tense 'past future' ('pf. impf.') in the Hebr. text is clear (see Böttcher 945 [beginning] and Bg. II §6b).

The end of our verse, ימים רבים, which indicates a long period of indefinite length, is further defined in LXX as 'three years,' a possible anticipation of the following verse (so also others, like Thenius and Burney).

2:39 *But about three years later two of Shimei's slaves ran away to Akish son of Macah, king of Gath. Shimei was told: 'Look, your slaves are in Gath.'*
After 3 years 2 of Shimei's slaves take off for Gath in the land of the Philistines. Ehrlich suspects — rather nicely — that this occurred to establish Shimei's guilt. The circumscription of the genitive by the preposition ל may indicate the necessity of maintaining the indefiniteness of the first word, hence not *the* 2 slaves of Shimei but 2 of Shimei's slaves (cf. GD §36, rem. 35; Burney). Vulg. only refers to 'slaves' without indicating the number. Shimei, therefore, was clearly not a man without means. The phenomenon of runaway slaves was a frequent occurrence in those days (cf. 1 Sam. 25:10). Shimei's slaves ran off to Achis son of Maacah of Gath. We encounter his name also in 1 Sam. 21:10-25; 27:2-12; 28:1f.; 29:2-9). These passages show that David, in fleeing Saul, sought and found shelter with this king. According to the tradition even a very friendly relationship had developed between the two. In 1 Sam. 27:2 Achis is called the son of Maoch (מעוך) (but Pesh. has our form there). LXX reads Αμησα in our verse, at least in MS B, but most MSS of LXX, have Maacah or something like it.

The question arises in how far we have information here which relates to a factual situation. Along with Thenius et al. one can say that around that time — though in David's early years he must already have been king — Achis may still have been alive. One could further assume that he — though subject to David's and Solomon's 'sovereignty' — still remained king over Gath, though in those days the Philistines no longer had much power. But is it the intention of the author to convey all this with precision or is it to sketch a situation in which Shimei left the area assigned to him but in precisely the *opposite* direction from that in which the brook Kidron flowed? And were we told in the previous verse only of an E boundary in order to keep the W boundary — which was seemingly much more innocent — open for him? This view does not seem improbable to us. Achis's name proves to be almost traditionally linked to hospitality (think of David) and to loyalty to the Davidic dynasty.

Gath, as a capital city in the country of the Philistines, is mentioned repeatedly in OT, especially in the books of Joshua, Samuel, and Kings. There is some uncertainty about the question whether, when OT refers to Gath as other than a Philistine city, we are always dealing with the same city. The true location of this historic city is somewhat controversial (cf., e.g., Simons, *GTTOT* §1633 with §§325, 328, 659, and 753; K. Elliger, *BHHW*, I, 515; and also *HAL* [with additional bibliography]).

2:40 *Shimei got up, saddled his donkey, and went to Akish at Gath to track down his slaves. So Shimei went and brought his slaves back from Gath.*
This is the core of the first part of the episode; Shimei takes to the road to get his slaves back, without having obtained the king's permission. For the locative form גתה, in which oddly enough the *taw* has not been doubled (cf. Böttcher §§299, 837 [no. 62]; Olsh. §§130b, 147e; Ewald §§90, 216c; BL, 559k, 563x; Ges-K §90i). LXX[Luc.], following the second mention of Shimei in this text, reports that the latter left Jerusalem — as though to put extra stress on this fact. Some MSS of LXX and the Vulg. modify the somewhat redundant-seeming conclusion of our verse so that it only reads: 'and he brought them with him from Gath.' Still MT yields good sense, because it underscores especially Shimei's *going*.

Some have cited this passage as proof that in antiquity there already existed extradition treaties pertaining to slaves (cf. de Vaux, *Inst*, I, 135). In fact such clearly defined treaties have been found, among other places, at Alalach (see *ANET*, 531ff.). Also in ancient Ugarit the 'extradition treaty' seems to have been known (F.B. Knutson, *RSP*, II, 128f.). If at the time of Solomon's accession to the throne and later Gath was still relatively independent, such a treaty would not have been impossible (cf. also O. Eißfeldt, *KS*, II, 459). In addition, at least according to Deut. 23:16f., slaves could (later on) no longer be extradited in Israel (Noth). Nevertheless we doubt that on the basis of these statements one can and may draw such stringent conclusions. As the text in the end once more clearly indicates, the key issue is Shimei's וילך from Jerusalem. His motive is plain: to personally secure his property, believing that this is less serious than to cross the Kidron to the city of his birth. But the sequel shows otherwise.

2:41 *When Solomon was told that Shimei had gone from Jerusalem to Gath and back,*
Solomon learns what has happened after everyone has returned safe and sound to Jerusalem. The explanation of LXX: 'and he brought his slaves back' is unnecessary.

2:42 *the king sent for Shimei and said to him: 'Did I not make you swear by YHWH and very clearly warn you: "On the day you leave from here and go anywhere else, be very sure you will die," to which you even responded by saying, "Very well; I have heard you."*
Shimei, summoned by Solomon, is reminded of his command and his oath. After the word צאתך LXX has 'from Jerusalem,' undoubtedly a clarifying expansion which, while materially correct, is not necessary textually. LXX[B] and [Luc.] (along with some other MSS) omit the conclusion of our verse.

As we saw earlier (see vs. 37) nothing is said there about an oath (except by LXX). But here it is expressly mentioned, supplemented with ואעד etc. For the form of the verb here, cf. Ges-K §72aa; Delitzsch, *LSF*, §80; Bg. II §5d. The verb עוד usually occurs in the hiph.-form, as here, of which there are only a couple of instances in the books of Kings (cf. C. van Leeuwen, *THAT*, II, 209-221, esp. 211 and 216f.). The verb belongs to the terminology of law and justice and, among other things, means 'to invoke as witness.' When God is witness, a person may, upon a failure to keep the oath, bring down the malediction upon himself. He may also call forth God's punishment as a threat upon himself. Van Leeuwen thinks that from this line of thought the meaning 'to warn,' 'to admonish' can be developed (cf. Rashi, Burney; H. Strathmann, *TDNT*, IV, 510, n. 1). This meaning is perhaps somewhat too weak here. We prefer: 'to state under oath.' Striking, further, is that Solomon again (here and in vs. 36) uses the extremely indefinite phrase 'to any place whatever,' without any further description of the boundaries (LXX now has: 'to the right and to the left'). One might almost say: in this way a person can always be caught in the juridical meshes of the royal net. That net is shut tight with the last words Solomon quotes from Shimei. Ehrlich views שמעתי as meaning 'I will obey.'

2:43 *But why then have you not kept the oath to YHWH and the order I gave you?'*
No answer to this question can possibly exonerate Shimei. The שבעת יהוה is

an objective genitive: the oath sworn by YHWH (cf. Ges-K §128h; Joüon §129g; König §336tß; further Ex. 22:10; 2 Sam. 21:7).

2:44 *The king then said to Shimei: 'You must bring to mind all the wickedness you did to my father David; now may YHWH bring your wickedness down on your own head.*
Shimei's misconduct toward the fleeing David is again brought up (above: vs. 8). Klostermann — and following him, others as well (cf. textcr. app. *BHK* and *BHS*) — has corrected the beginning of the text as follows: 'Now I have gained insight into all your malice that your heart was conscious of having perjured yourself before YHWH ...' Still these and other more or less radical text-modifications are unnecessary. Thenius already pointed out that the first ידע is a 'mere reference' (cf. also W. Schottroff, *THAT*, I, 682-701, esp. 686f.: to perceive, note, discern, observe, experience; G.J. Botterweck, *TWAT*, III, 486-512), although in our opinion the diction of our verse by no means runs smoothly. The heart is often mentioned in OT as the seat of memory (cf., besides F. Stolz, *THAT*, I, 861-867, and H.-J. Fabry, *TWAT*, IV, 413-451, also Von Meyenfeldt, *Het hart*). Certainly in his memory Shimei's 'malice,' i.e. his misconduct, must live on. This is what YHWH will cause to return upon his own head. Remarkably enough, the ancient versions (LXX, Vulg., Pesh., and some MSS of Tg.) read, instead of the future sense of the pf. cons., the preterite of the pf. with copula or of the impf. cons. As a rule scholars suspect the latter (וישב) but in our opinion the former is equally well possible, all the more because the pf. cons. definitely need not be linked to the preceding verb from which it gained its special meaning (cf. Driver, §119; GD §60, rem. 1; Böttcher §981; König §367y). The ancient versions may have mistakenly understood this form as a pf. (with *waw*).

2:45 *But may king Solomon be blessed and may the throne of David be kept secure before YHWH for ever.'*
As earlier in vs. 33b, there now follows a laudatory expansion in favour of the Davidic and Solomonic dynasty. Here and in the following verse the niph. of כון is again used to emphasize the 'stability' of Solomon's kingship and throne (see above, vs. 12). Here it is a part. with a form of היה which gives a modal nuance to the meaning; in the following verse it is a pf. (Meyer §104.2g; cf. Joüon §121e).

Josephus, *Ant.* VIII, 17-20, relates this story at even greater length than we find it in MT. In his expansions he does his utmost to exhibit Solomon's wisdom, while at the same time attempting to vindicate the king in the matter of the admittedly late execution of Shimei.

2:46 *On orders from the king, Benaiah son of Jehoiada, then stepped* *forward and struck Shimei down so that he died. So the kingship was solidly in Solomon's power.*

Again Benaiah is ordered to perform the execution. After this statement, from which LXX^B omits the words 'and he died,' LXX* again has a number of verses (46a-l), which are lacking in MT and other versions (also in LXX^A, the Armenian version and in the Syro-Hexapla). Again we will give a translation of this part:

46a *King Solomon was very intelligent and wise. And Judah and Israel were very numerous like the sand by the sea in multitude as they ate and drank and delighted themselves.*

46b *Now Solomon was first in all the kingdoms and they were accustomed to bring him gifts and served Solomon all the days of his life.*

46c *And Solomon began to open the natural resources of the Lebanon.*

46d *He built Thermae in the wilderness.*

46e *And this was Solomon's breakfast: 30 measures of fine wheat flour and 60 measures of finely ground flour; 10 choice oxen and 20 cattle from the pastures; 100 sheep, aside from deer, gazelles and choice birds from the pastures.*

46f *Was he not the ruler over everything on the other side of the river from Raphi to Gaza, over all the kings across the river?*

46g *He had peace with all the divisions of his (sphere of influence); and Judah and Israel lived securely each under his own vine and fig tree as they ate and drank from Dan to Beersheba all the days of Solomon.*

46h *These were Solomon's chief men: Azariah son of Zadok was priest; Ornias son of Nathan was chief of the officers; Edramen was appointed over his house; Suba was the scribe and Basa son of Achithalam was secretary; Abi son of Joab commander-in-chief; Achire son of Edrai was superintendent over the bearers of burdens; and Benaiah son of Jehoiada was over the royal court and the title works; and Kachur son of Nathan was counselor.*

46i *Solomon had 40,000 brood mares for the chariots and 12,000 horses.*

46k *He also reigned over all the kings from the river to the land of the foreigners (= Philistines), even to the borders of Egypt.*

46l *So Solomon son of David reigned in Jerusalem over Israel and Judah.*

Without entering in depth on a discussion of these interesting 'additions' in LXX[24], we wish to say that also here one can point to an assortment of

---

[24] Cf. J.A. Montgomery, *ZAW* 50 (1932), 124-129; D.W. Gooding, *JSS* 13 (1968), 76-92; M. Rehm, "Die Beamtenliste der Septuaginta in 1 Kön 2, 46h," *Wort, Lied und Gottesspruch* (Fs J. Ziegler; Forschung zur Bibel 1), Würzburg 1972, 95-101; Gooding 1976; and Krautwurst, *Studien*.

parallels to the Hebr. text, be it in other chapters. Nevertheless, there are items of information here which are hard to match with MT (e.g. 46c,d). Perhaps in the case of vs. 46d we can think of MT 9:18b where there is mention of Tamar (Tadmor, according to others) (see exegesis on this verse).

The word δυναστεύμα in vs. 46c is unique and its translation uncertain (cf. Montgomery, 128). In the list of Solomon's officers in vs. 46h there are a number of noteworthy deviations as compared to similar lists in MT (cf. Rehm). It is therefore possible that Benaiah, of whom we said in the translation that he was 'over the royal court and the tile works,' was still called head of the Cherethites and the Pelethites but that the possible Hebr. 'Vorlage' of our LXX prompted the translators to translate as they did. It is similarly possible that in vs. 46i we must read ἱππέων in place of ἵππων in line with the Hebr. in 5:6; פָּרָשִׁים. All in all these Greek additions, compared with MT and the remaining text of LXX, furnish material for further analysis of LXX itself, as also of the text of our Hebr. Bible and the composition of the narratives concerning Solomon.

The last 4 words of our verse seem to be the conclusion of the preceding text. But Klostermann, Stade-Schwally et al. are of the opinion that the pf. נכונה indicates that this short statement forms the introduction to the story which follows. In that case the purpose would be to describe the situation which made it possible for Solomon to become the son-in-law of Pharaoh. LXX[Luc.] and Symm., among others, seem to support this viewpoint. But here the one possibility need not exclude the other. Schulte considers it very well possible that the Yahwist did not conclude his work with our verse, but incorporated in it a number of other histories of Solomon which, according to him, stem from the family of Abiathar and originated in Anathoth.[25]

---

[25] H. Schulte, *Die Entstehung der Geschichtsschreibung im Alten Testament* (BZAW 128), Berlin 1972.

1 KINGS 3:1-3

3:1 *Solomon allied himself with Pharaoh king of Egypt: he married Pharaoh's daughter and brought her into the 'city of David' until he had finished building his own house and the house of YHWH and the wall around Jerusalem.*
  2 *The people, however, were sacrificing on the high places, because no house had yet been built for the name of YHWH.*
  3 *Solomon loved YHWH (and showed it by) walking in the statutes of his father David. Only he offered sacrifices and burned incense on the high places.*

INTRODUCTION

The rounding off of the narratives around the succession to the throne of David and particularly the confirmation of the kingship in Solomon's hands is followed by a portrayal of Solomon's kingship which continues to the end of chap. 11. It is composed of various narratives, documents, traditions, and redactional adaptations, with Solomon's building of the temple occupying a central position. Chap. 3 consists of 2 narrative parts: (1) Solomon's dream at Gibeon (vss. 4-15) and (2) related to this, a sample of Solomon's wisdom (vss. 16-27). This is preceded by a few introductory verses of which the literary composition is rather complex. These verses are clearly tailored to what follows. An attempt is made in the verse-by-verse analysis to elucidate the compositional problems. It is evident, certainly in the view of the final redactor, that our chapter is the 'overture' to the later actions − actions which are marked by 'wisdom' − of Solomon as king. The composition of the first verses, which has a somewhat chaotic feel to it, along with the noteworthy structure of LXX mentioned earlier, indicate that some preliminary redactional work must have preceded the definitive form in which the MT has come down to us.

EXEGESIS

3:1 *Solomon allied himself with pharaoh king of Egypt: he married pharaoh's daughter and brought her into the 'city of David' until he had finished building his own house and the house of YHWH and the wall around Jerusalem.*
In LXX the initial statement is missing at this point and occurs after 5:14 along with what is said in 9:16f. about Solomon's relation to the Egyptian king (LXX^A does follow the sequence of MT; cf. Stade-Schwally). Many exegetes

rightly suspect that this verse is misplaced here, but differ over where it should be located. From a compositional viewpoint, however, the reference to the royal marriage following the ascension to the throne is not strange (thus Montg.-Gehman), although the alliance with pharaoh, king of the Egyptian 'house of bondage,' would hardly seem – especially from a religious perspective – to be a point in Solomon's favour. We will observe that here, as in the preceding, certain pro- and anti-Solomonic tendencies can be discerned in the composition of the narratives. The notice as such seems to be historical, a point which we will revisit later.

The hitp. of חתן, which occurs in this stem-modification 9 more times in OT (this is the only occurrence in the books of Kings) means 'to ally oneself with a person by marriage' and is also in Hebr. a denominative of חָתָן 'son in law,' 'bridegroom'. For the meaning and the development of the word in and outside Israel, cf. E. Kutsch, *TWAT*, III, 288-296 (with bibliography). It is construed both with ב and את (Ewald §124b). Ehrlich views what follows as epexegetical of the first clause of our verse: Solomon married – for that is the meaning of לקח here – the daughter of the pharaoh. Had this not been added one might think of a 'distant relation.' Accordingly Ehrlich wants to place the *atnaḥ* under the second 'pharaoh' of our verse. Still this relocation is unnecessary. We have in this verse a buildup of information: first the statement concerning an alliance by marriage with the royal house of Egypt; then the statement that it concerns a daughter of pharaoh; and finally some further information on the place where this woman will reside.

פרעה is the title of the Egyptian king and (according to *HAL*) occurs 274x in OT. Sometimes, as here, the title is further explicated: 'king of Egypt.' The Egyptian equivalent from which the Hebr. word is derived is *pr. '3*, 'the Great House,' a word which from the 18th dynasty on referred not only to the royal palace but to the king himself. Only rarely does one find in OT a further designation of the pharaoh; e.g. in Jer. 44:30: 'pharaoh Hophra' and in Jer. 46:2: 'pharaoh Neco.' Sometimes pharaohs are also referred to by name without the preceding title, especially in the case of Lybian, Ethiopian, and Saitic pharaohs who are mentioned also in Egyptian texts as 'pharaoh such and such' (see B. Reicke, *BHHW*, III, 1445ff.). Because in our case a name is lacking as well, the question has often been raised who then Solomon's father-in-law may have been. Many interpreters think of Sheshonk I, the founder of the 22nd – or Lybian – dynasty which must have ruled approx. from 946-925 B.C. and whose name is also found in 14:25. This Sheshonk or Shishak – was the ruler of the city-state Herakleopolis and, as the leader of a group of Lybian soldiers, elevated Tanis and Bubastis in the eastern Nile delta to the main seats of this dynasty.¹

There are also exegetes, however, who think of an earlier pharaoh: Psusennes II of the 21st dynasty, for example, or one of his predecessors, Siamun (Netercheperre), who around 979-960 ruled as the last ruler of the house of Smendes (cf. A. Malamat, *JNES* 22 [1963], 11f.; and J. von Beckenrath, *LdÄ*, V, 921). This would conform more closely to the chronology of Solomon, the beginning of whose reign must be put at about a quarter of a century before that of Sheshonk. Still, aside from this uncertainty, it is equally uncertain when Solomon may have married this Egyptian woman, because the chronological locus of this information is by no means certain. What is certain is that the Egyptian self-assurance, which was still reflected in the words of Amenophis III: 'From ancient times the daughter of an Egyptian king is given to no one,'² was a thing of the past in the time of Solomon (see also Montg.-Gehman; Noth).

Whereas the names of the pharaoh and his daughter thus remain in the dark, it is clear that Solomon took her 'as wife,' though אשה (as it occurs e.g. in Gen. 25:1) is omitted here. Then there is the building-related statement in which mention is made of the 'city of David' where the Egyptian princess was to reside until the completion of the palace, the temple, and the wall around Jerusalem. This brings up the problems of 'the history of the construction of Jerusalem' about which there is considerable difference of opinion among the experts. We are extensively informed on this by Busink, 96-111, to which we refer the reader for further information (on the city in the time of David, cf. 77-96).³ In 2 Sam. 5-7 (cf. 1 Chr. 11:5) the stronghold of Zion is equated with the 'city of David' (cf. above, on 2:10; also G. Fohrer, *TDNT*, VII, 294, n. 3). The reference here is to the so-called eastern hill to the east of which the Kidron-valley is situated and on top of which the city of the Jebusites was built which was later captured by David and named after him (J.M. Miller, *ZDPV* 90 [1974], 115-127, denies the identification of Jebus with Jerusalem). Still later this hill, at least a part of it, was also called Ophel (see Busink, 77ff.) Our note puts Solomon's marriage even before his building activities at the beginning of his reign.

The construction of the wall around Jerusalem probably refers to the part that still had to be walled in after the expansion of the city, and further to the

---

¹ See further J. von Beckenrath, *Abriß der Geschichte des alten Ägypten*, Oldenbourg 1971, 48f.; and M.L. Bierbrier, "Scheschonq," *LdÄ*, V, 585f.

² J.A. Knudtzon, *Die El-Amarna-Tafeln*, Leipzig 1915, IV, 6f. On the possible motivation of the Egyptian king, see now also Y. Freud, "The Marriage and the Dowry," *The Jewish Biblical Quarterly* 23 (1995), 248-251.

³ See now also F.G. López, "Construction et destruction de Jérusalem: Histoire et prophétie dans les cadres rédactionels des Livres des Rois," *RB* 94 (1987), 222-232.

fortification and superstructure of the existing walls. The word סביב (cf. 5:11; 6:5f.; 7:12, etc.) is put here to accentuate the walling in of Jerusalem, both the older and the newer part, on all sides. The new part is probably the southwestern hill.

3:2 *The people, however, were sacrificing on the high places, because no house had yet been built for the name of YHWH.*
רק, with which this verse begins, prompts one to think that perhaps something is amiss in the logical order of the verses. In addition it is odd that while vss. 1 and 3 have Solomon as subject, in our verse 'the people' is the subject. It is further noteworthy that again in vs. 3 a sentence occurs beginning with רק. Along with Benzinger, Burney, Noth, Montg.-Gehman et al.[4], we therefore think that this verse is a later redactional note which was added to the dtr. redaction of Solomon's dream at Gibeon. If one wished to assign some meaning to this redactional notice or gloss in the context, one would expect this verse rather after vs. 3 (see Ehrlich). The gloss, as also vs. 3b, is completely understandable because it must serve to give status to the later detested practice of 'offering sacrifices on the high places' which is being performed by Solomon in the now following narrative. On the basis, for example, of Deut. 12:13f., the offering of sacrifices at places other than the central sanctuary was described as highly suspect. In the books of Kings we therefore frequently find such dtr. touchups (e.g. 15:14; 22:44; 2 Kgs. 12:4, etc.).

An attempt is sometimes made to give our text a meaning in the context of the whole. For example, B. Jongeling, *OTS* 18 (1973), 104, paraphrases it as follows: 'True: the people sacrificed ..., but one could hardly blame them, because...' – a line of thought one can also apply to Solomon in the following verse. Despite this ingenious solution, our verse nevertheless remains strange within this context. LXX, too, had difficulties with it, as is evident from the different MSS. LXX[Luc.] begins the sentence as follows: καὶ ὁ λαὸς ἦσαν Θυμιῶντες, while LXX[B] simply starts with Θυμιῶντες and LXX[A] and many other MSS begin with πλὴν ὁ λαὸς ἦσαν etc. (cf. Vulg.: *et tamen* [in some MSS: *attamen*]).

The part. מזבחים, in this and similar contexts in which a statement of information is handed down from the past, often signifies a frequentative act (Driver §135, 2o; Joüon §121f; BrSynt. §44c). The word במה occurring (with slight variations) in all Semitic languages, means 'back' (Deut. 33:29), 'ridge,' 'high places' (Deut. 32:13, etc.) and especially 'cult high places,' 'cult places,' as in our verse and in about 80 other locations in OT. Finally also the meaning

---

[4] See now also E. Eynikel, *The Reform of King Josiah and the Composition of the Deuteronomistic History* (OTS 33), Leiden 1996, 52-60.

'burial mound' is found (Isa. 53:9 etc.;cf. K.D. Schunck, *TWAT*, I, 662-667; Haran, *Temples*, 18-25). In Canaanite and early-Israelite times these cult places, sometimes constructed on natural, sometimes on man-made elevations, were built and utilized throughout Palestine. Excavations have uncovered various 'high places.' They usually consisted of a place for sacrifice with wooden poles and stone pillars and were furnished with an assortment of smaller cult objects, such as water basins and libation plates. Criticism of these cult places, which among the older Israelites hardly occasioned any problems, is attributable to the attitude of prophets who feared the dangers of syncretistic practice, as well as to the growing attempts at centralization by the (later) YHWH cult in Jerusalem. This critical attitude, therefore, is of a late date; in Solomon's time the במה was not yet in any way a problem. Hence the critical touchup of our late glossarist.

Dtr., also, is the reference to the 'name of YHWH' (cf. H. Bietenhard, *TDNT*, V, 255f.). This expression almost becomes an alternative form of YHWH's name itself, indeed, as it were, an independent revelatory form of YHWH (cf. Exod. 23:20f.). The Dtr. has YHWH live in heaven but choose a place on earth where 'his name may dwell' (Deut. 12:11; 14:23; 16:11 etc.). The 'name of YHWH' is then almost literally present and palpable, and capable of dwelling in a house (2 Sam. 7:13; 5:17, etc., also our text). Cf. Bietenhard, 254-258, and A.S. van der Woude, *THAT*, II, 935-963, esp. 953-958, who rejects 'eine specifische dtn. Namenstheologie' (955) but emphasizes שׁם יהוה as having become 'besonders in der Kultsprache zum Wechselbegriff für Jhwh.' While acknowledging the possibility developed by Van der Woude, it nevertheless seems to us that the expression also marks a certain theologically-coloured phase of development which is usually described today by the term 'deuteronomistic.'

Finally the expression עד הימים ההם points to a rather late date at which this notice was inserted. LXX reads ἕως νῦν, but in any case it has no support in the other ancient versions, so that one must follow the MT.

3:3 *Solomon loved YHWH (and showed it by) walking in the statutes of his father David. Only he offered sacrifices and burned incense on the high places.* This verse takes us back to what vs. 1 conveyed in the way of biographical particulars of Solomon, although this verse, too, gives the impression that it serves as commentary and introduction to what follows. It probably flowed from the pen and the insight of a redactor.

It speaks of Solomon's love for YHWH by his walking in the statutes of his father David (for LXX προστάγματα, cf. W. Michaelis, *TDNT*, V, 51). Here again the point of gravity lies in the 'dtr. theology' (cf. E. Jenni, *THAT*, I, 70ff.; G. Wallis, *TWAT*, 1, 124ff.). Solomon proves this love 'by walking' in the statutes of his father David. Here the inf. cstr., preceded by the preposition

ל, fulfills the function of the Latin gerundive ending with *-ndo* (cf. Lettinga, §73b4; Burney calls this construction a 'D phrase'; see Deut. 10:12; 11:22; 19:9 etc.). The חקות are the 'legal statutes,' the 'commandments,' plural of the word חֻקָּה, a relatively late formation of the noun חֹק viewed as a substantival infinitive. The first-mentioned word occurs 104x in OT; the last-mentioned 129x (G. Liedke, *THAT*, I, 626-633; H. Ringgren, *TWAT*, III, 149-157). One could perhaps view it as a retrospective dtr. reference to what was brought up, for example, in vss. 2:2ff. There, too, these notices functioned as a kind of link between the various parts of the narrative. It is stated, somewhat as a 'whitewash,' that Solomon used to offer sacrifices on the high places and to burn incense (cf. Meyer §104.2d: 'Durativ der Vergangenheit'). Nowack, II, 246ff., was of the opinion that קטרת and the word קטר (pi.) used in an older phase of the language could only mean 'smoke,' 'sacrificial fragrance' or something of that nature, and that the meaning '(an offering of) incense' only gained currency later, a meaning which also applied to the verb in the hiph. According to him, this happened in or after the 8th century when a penchant for the 'pagan' cult and mores had grown stronger in Israel. M. Haran, *VT* 10 (1960), 113-129, viewed the use of קטר (pi.) – according to *HAL*, s.v. used for the legitimate cult only in Amos 4:5! – as a form of bringing a 'meal offering,' and he indicates how 'incense' was 'presented' in 3 different ways. There is not much against dating the use of 'incense' by Israelites and Canaanites earlier than the 8th century, even apart form the 'late' redaction of our verse. Y.M. Grintz, *Leš* 39 (1974f.), 172f., (cf. Montg.-Gehman) has mentioned a possible Egyptian origin of or kinship with this word. Perhaps the verb קטר (hiph.), which occurs 7 more times in Kings, can be appropriately translated by 'letting (an offering) go up in fragrance and smoke.'

1 KINGS 3:4-15

3:4 *One time the king went to Gibeon to sacrifice there since the principal high place was located there. On that altar Solomon presented a thousand burnt offerings.*

5 At Gibeon YHWH appeared to Solomon in a dream by night; and God said: 'Ask what I should give you.'

6 Solomon said: 'You have dealt very graciously with your servant David. Because he walked before you in faithfulness, in uprightness, and integrity of heart, you have continued this most faithful love to him: you have given him a son to sit on his throne today.

7 Now, then YHWH, my God, you have made our servant king in place of my father David, but I am only a little fellow who does not know the first thing about this business.

8 Your servant finds himself in the midst of your people whom you have chosen, a powerful people, a people so numerous that its number can neither be estimated or counted.

9 So give your servant a heart to understand how to govern your people, able to discern between good and evil; otherwise, who could govern this great people of yours?'

10 Now it pleased the Lord that Solomon had above all asked for this.

11 God said to him: 'Since you have asked not for a long life, or riches, or for the life of your enemies, but for discernment in the administration of justice,

12 therefore I will now act according to your words and give you such a wise and understanding heart as no one has had before and no one will have after you.

13 Moreover, I will also give you what you have not asked for: both riches and honour so that in your lifetime no other king will compare with you.

14 Now if you will walk in my ways, keeping my statutes and my commandments, as our father David did, I will prolong your days.'

15 Then Solomon woke up and realized it had been a dream. He returned to Jerusalem, where he positioned himself before the ark of the covenant of the Lord, sacrificed burnt offerings and peace offerings, and arranged a banquet for all his servants.

INTRODUCTION

Now follows the story of Solomon's dream at Gibeon on the occasion of the sacrificial ceremony (vss. 4-15). G. Fohrer, *TDNT*, VIII, 350, and others view this event as a legitimation of Solomon's kingship after he had become king without selection by or a treaty with the people. In 2 Chr. 1:2-13 one finds an interesting parallel to this section. It is shorter and devoid of the parts which seem to have been added in our chapter by a redactor. On the other hand, 2 Chr. 1 has other additions. A study of these expansions and/or omissions furnishes insight into the motives which may have prompted the enrichment of the basic narrative. Burney, among others, offering an extensive study of this comparison, rightly states: 'Probably the original form of the narrative was very near that of Kings, with omission of the insertions of R^D.'[1] In our analysis of the individual verses we will, if necessary, refer to the parallels.

EXEGESIS

3:4 *One time the king went to Gibeon to sacrifice there since the principal high place was located there. On that altar Solomon presented a thousand burnt offerings.*

In our verse we are told that Solomon went to Gibeon and made a great sacrifice there. Thenius infers from an addition of LXX (that the king 'rose up': ויקם) that the now following pericope must have been derived from a larger unit and relocated here. Though not impossible this suggestion is hard to prove.

Gibeon, often identified with *el-ġib* (but cf. Simons, *GTTOT*, §327 II/1), is situated approx. 10 km NW of Jerusalem. The name of the place occurs a number of times in OT. Thus the 'ruse of the Gibeonites,' which is said to have been enacted in the time of Joshua, is not unfamiliar (Josh. 9 and 10). In the time of David Gibeon is referred to as the scene of bloody events (2 Sam. 2:12-17; 20:8 also cf. 2 Sam. 21). Gibeon also occurs in extrabiblical sources, for instance, in a list of the Egyptian king Sheshonk I (*ANET*, 242). The identification of Gibeon with *el-ġib* seems confirmed by the discovery of earthen pots bearing the inscription 'Gibeon' (see J.B. Pritchard, *IDB*, II, 393; but also cf. Simons, a.l.). In this city of Gibeon, a city belonging to the tribe of Benjamin, Solomon proceeds to present a sacrifice on the highest במה (the article before the adjective gives superlative meaning to 'big'; BrSynt. §60c). The word כי indicates the reason why Solomon went to Gibeon: here was the

---

[1] Cf. also H.A. Kenik, *Design for Kingship: The Deuteronomistic Narrative Technique in 1 Kings 3:4-15* (SBL Diss. Ser. 69), Chico 1983; A.G. Auld, "Solomon at Gibeon: History Glimpsed," *Avraham Malamat Volume* (eds. S. Ahituv et al.; Eretz Israel 24), Jerusalem 1993, 1*-7*; idem, "Salomo und die Deuteronomisten – eine Zukunftsvision?," *TZ* 48 (1992), 343-355.

largest (in a spatial sense; so, correctly, Ehrlich) 'high place' in the kingdom. LXX translates: 'because this high place was the highest and very large' (cf. W. Foerster, *TDNT*, V, 480f. and n. 76). Rashi – and following him Vatablus et al. – believes that the bronze altar made by Moses was located there and that therefore a greater sanctity was present in Gibeon. Just where this large and high cult place has to be localized is a subject of discussion. Some think of a high place with a sanctuary that is still present today, namely *en Nebi Samwil* to the S of the place; others, to the contrary, of a ridge located somewhat to the N of the place (see Noth et al.). The statement that Solomon went to the high place at Gibeon may in itself be a historical indication of its importance at the time (cf. J. Dus, *VT* 10 [1960], 353-374; Busink 597f.). It is further stated that Solomon had a thousand burnt offerings presented on the altar (Haran, *Temples*, 24, n. 21, thinks that 'high place' and 'altar' are identical here).[2] The impf. יעלה indicates a longlasting act in the past (cf. Ges-K §107b; Bg. II §7d). It is likely that those thousand sacrifices were made rather in a long series than simultaneously (cf. König §157). Burney rightly comments that אלף need not literally mean a 'thousand' but be a round number for the many sacrifices offered there.

Whereas in our verse one discerns a veiled justification for Solomon's going to Gibeon (because the largest sanctuary built on a high place was there), in 2 Chr. 1 we encounter extensive commentary on this deed. At the outset we are told that Solomon summoned all the leaders, high and low, ordering them to go with the whole 'community' to Gibeon because 'God's tent of meeting' was there 'which Moses, YHWH's servant, had made in the wilderness.' With a single brush stroke all the offensiveness was removed from the story and, with the help already given by 1 Chr. 21:29, the Dtr. redactor was vindicated! And because this explanatory statement could possibly provoke further critical questions on the part of his readers, the Chronicler continues by saying that, though the ark of God had indeed been brought up by David from Kiriath-Jearim to Jerusalem (cf. 1 Chr. 13; 15:1-24; 25-29; 16:1-3), where he had pitched a tent for it, he had placed the bronze altar, the product of Bezalel's skillful workmanship (cf. Exod. 31:2), before the משכן of YHWH at Gibeon (cf. Rashi's explanation mentioned above). On that bronze altar of the 'tent of meeting' Solomon sacrificed his hecatombs. Accordingly, the attributes belonging to the 'tabernacle' of YHWH were geographically spread: the ark in Jerusalem, the rest in Gibeon. Meanwhile, Solomon is blameless! His sacrifices are legitimate.

---

[2] See now also W. Boyd Barrick, "On the Meaning of בֵּית־הַ/בָּמוֹת בָּמוֹת and בָּתֵּי־הַבָּמוֹת and the Composition of the Kings History," *JBL* 115 (1996), 621-642. In his opinion בָּמָה in 1 Kgs. 3:4 'denotes a built cult place' (p. 642).

3:5 *At Gibeon YHWH appeared to Solomon in a dream by night; and God said: 'Ask what I should give you.'*
YHWH appears – immediately, without the intervention of a prophet (cf. 9:2-9; 11:11-13) – to Solomon in a dream (LXX: ὔπνος; Pesh.: 'vision'; cf. A. Oepke, *TDNT*, V, 221; W. Michaelis, *TDNT*, V, 333; H. Balz, *TDNT*, VIII, 550f.). The word חלום occurs approx. 60x in OT, only 2 of them in the books of Kings, both in this pericope (also in vs. 15). The verb חלם, which occurs 24x in qal and twice in hiph., has parallels in Ugar., Aram., Arab., and Eth. The dream narratives in OT are concentrated especially in Genesis and Daniel (cf. J. Bergman, M. Ottosson, G.J. Botterweck, *TWAT*, II, 986-998; A. Oepke, *TDNT*, V, 228-234). Because Solomon has himself proved he had visited the sanctuary of Gibeon, this dream is sometimes counted among the incubation dreams; thus, among others, M. Ottosson, *TWAT*, II, 993; cf. H. Balz, *TDNT*, VIII, 550, n. 39; Businck, 598: 'Tempelschlaf'.[3] Our narrative does not tell us, however, that Solomon expressly went there to receive an oracle, although this intention is not excluded. It is noteworthy that the parallel story in Chronicles omits the mention of the word 'dream.' This may indicate that in a later period this kind of 'dream-receptions' was interpreted negatively (even Maimonides, *More Nebûkim*, II, 45, believes that Solomon never attained to the level of a 'true prophet').[4] The space between our verse and the previous one in MT is an attempt to show that Solomon's sacrifice and YHWH's appearance are 2 different things. LXX and Pesh. (cf. Vulg.) draw the phrase 'in Gibeon,' with which our verse begins, into the previous verse, so as to create a closer connection between the 2 events. The following נראה seems to have preceded in the form of וירא (with a copula); in Pesh. only by the MSS of the 9al *fam*.[5]

From Israel's 'Umwelt' dreams are known as the consequence of incubation rites or as indications to establish or visit a sanctuary. In the case of Egypt one can point to the so-called Sphinx Stela, which relates how the god Harmakhis asked Thutmose IV (±1421-1413 BCE) in a dream to restore his great image before assuming the reins of government (*ANET*, 449). Here too the young king finds himself on holy ground and the god addresses him in a dream. From the Mesopotamian region we have to mention the hymn of the building of the

---

[3] See now also C.L. Seow, "The Syro-Palestinian Context of Solomon's Dream," *HTR* 77 (1984), 141-152; and A. Jeffers, "Divination by Dreams in Ugaritic Literature and in the Old Testament," *Irish Biblical Studies* 12 (1990), 167-183.

[4] Cf. D. McLain Carr, *From D to Q: A Study of Early Jewish Interpretation of Solomon's Dream at Gibeon* (SBLMS 44), Atlanta 1991.

[5] Cf. M. Delcor, "The Selloi of the Oracle of Dodona and the Oracular Priests of the Semitic Religion," *Wort, Lied und Gottesspruch* (Fs J. Ziegler; Forschung zur Bibel 1), Würzburg 1972, 31-38; esp. 35f.

temple of Gudea of Lagash.⁶ This hymn relates (in Sumerian) how in a dream the city-ruler Gudea receives the command of Ningirsu, the chief god of the city, to rebuild his sanctuary Eninnu. Additional information concerning its construction is provided in a dream. Blessings and prosperity are promised upon carrying out that which was requested in the dream. These and other dream experiences of kings, princes, or prominent persons in the ancient literature of the Near East have prompted the suspicion that there is a close connection between Solomon's dream referred to here and his building of a temple (cf. a.o. Herrmann 1953, 33f.; A.S. Kapelrud, *Or* 32 [1963], 56-62; and Weinfeld, *Deuteronomy*, 244-260). It has to be said that the form in which the 'incubation ritual' is presented and the framework in which the dream is confined (vss. 3f. and 16) form a close link between the extrabiblical material and our narrative (cf. Herrmann, a.l., Görg, *Gott-König-Reden*, et al.). On the other hand, the contents of the dream prove to be filled 'deuteronomistically' (Weinfeld). Weinfeld thinks that Solomon went to Gibeon to acquire 'technical wisdom' pertaining to the building of a temple. In a lengthy study Zalevsky has attempted to show that the narrative of God's revelation in a dream to Solomon at Gibeon has to be of ancient origin and gives an authentic report.⁷

It is expressly stated that the dream occurred at night (cf. Gen. 20:3; 31:24; Job 33:15). In the Sphinx Stela the dream is received during the day (*ANET*, 449). Does this added time designation of the dream perhaps indicate a deliberate position against extrabiblical (Egyptian?) material and consequently – implicitly – a close relationship? In the dream it is God who speaks. In connection with the appearance, there is mention of YHWH; in the case of the question asked (at least in MT) there is mention of אלהים, for whom LXX reads κύριος (cf. Tg.). Vulg. omits this unit (Ehrlich wants to read אליו in place of אלהים). Also in vs. 11 the speaker is אלהים, while in vss. 10, 15 אדני is used; also cf. Stade-Schwally. To quote Thenius: this is probably not accidental. מה, as sometimes elsewhere in OT as well, is used without an antecedent (Ewald §331b; Burney).

3:6 *Solomon said: 'You have dealt very graciously with your servant David. Because he walked before you in faithfulness, in uprightness, and integrity of heart, you have continued this most faithful love to him: you have given him a son to sit on his throne today.*

In these ('dtr.' expanded) words of Solomon there is first a backward glance at the favours of God to David. In this verse alone one encounters the word

---

⁶ A. Falkenstein, W. von Soden, *Sumerische und Akkadische Hymnen und Gebete*, Zürich 1953, 137-182.

⁷ Z. Zalevski, "The Revelation of God to Solomon in Gibeon," *Tarbiz* 42 (1972f.), 215-258 (Hebr.).

יִשְׁרָה*, of which יֹשֶׁר is the st. cstr. and which is introduced by lexicons such as Ges-B and *HAL* as a distinct lemma. Older grammarians like Olsh. §245d and Ewald §238a classify the form under the heading of the infinitives, but one can also view it as the fem. form of the much more frequently occurring יֹשֶׁר (cf. BL §21k), which functions as an abstract noun (cf. G. Liedke, *THAT*, I, 791).

The following expressions have been characterized as deriving from dtr. phraseology (cf. Weinfeld, *Deuteronomy*): שׁמר הברית והחסד (Deut. 7:9, 12; 1 Kgs. 8:23); הלך לפני יהוה בישרת לבב (cf. 2:4; 8:23, 25; 9:4); כיום הזה (Deut. 2:30; 4:20, 38; 6:24; 8:18; 10:15; 29:27 and 1 Kgs 8:24, 61). Now some of these expressions are not specifically Israelitish but also occur, for example, in Akkad. texts. In this connection Weinfeld, 75f., mentions a gift from king Asshurbanipal to his Servant Baltaya of whom it is said: '... his heart is devoted (lit. is whole) to his master, served me (lit. stood before me) with truthfulness and acted perfectly (lit. walked in perfection) in my palace ...' In a Phoen. inscription from around the middle of the 10th century BCE we find something similar. On this inscription it is said of Yehimilk, king of Byblos, that he was a righteous and honest king before the holy gods of Byblos (*mlk ṣdq wmlk yšḥr lpn 'l gbl qdšm*, KAI 4, 6f.; cf. Y. Avishur, *UF* 8 [1976], 7f.). The so-called 'dtr.' expressions as such need not yet be proof that in the early period of the kings, for example in Solomon's time, they could not have been used in approximately the same form or that the scribes of the royal court could not have employed a similar terminology with respect to their king. But it must be granted Görg, 27, and others that the כאשר clause does expand the first part of our verse 'in unnötig breiter Weise.' It may therefore very well be additional commentary after which he continues with ותתן־לו.

Of the 245x that the word חסד is used in OT (cf. H.J. Stoebe, *THAT*, I, 600-621; H.-J. Zobel, *TWAT*, III, 48-71), it occurs by far the most frequently (127x) in the Psalms and only 5x in Kings (aside from the 2x in our verse, also in 2:7; 8:23 and 20:31). The word denotes 'goodness' in varying nuances. Zobel (56) finds that 3 elements are constitutive for the concept: its deed character, its community character, and its steadiness. The evidences of 'goodness' toward David have a distinct place in OT (Zobel, 64ff.) which e.g. in Isa. 55:3; 2 Chr. 6:42 end with the expression חסדי דוד. The word כאשר here, as more often (cf. the lexicons), indicates the reason why something is the way it is: 'because,' 'considering that.' This all the more gives to the clause beginning with כאשר and ending with the (second) החסד הגדול the character of an intermediate clause in which the first חסד is explained by the adjective גדול. Accordingly, the par. in 2 Chr. 1:8 entirely omits this parenthetical material. The great חסד which God showed David found its counterpart in David's 'walking' before the face of God in אמת; צדקה, and ישרת לבב. אמת (see also on 2:4) occurs more often in the semantic field of חסד (Zobel,

56) and indicates its 'steadfastness,' its 'faithfulness.' צדקה occurs in Kings, besides here, only still in 8:32 and 10:9 as well. The stem צדק, for that matter, is relatively rare in our books (cf. K. Koch, *THAT*, II, 511). The word is hard to 'translate' in our Western languages and cultural patterns (see Koch, esp. 514-518). Our word 'righteousness' says too much because we hear in it the idea of conforming to a 'norm.' The word צדקה, as well as its masc. pendant צדק, convey more than merely the idea of 'moral' conduct. Implied in it is also a condition of wholesome, undisputed, salvific existence (Koch, 516). Often צדקה denotes faithful conduct in response to or in consequence of the 'goodness' of YHWH. Thus David manifested 'the right kind of conduct' in his life (cf. also J.J. Scullion, *UF* 3 [1971], 347). Mentioned, alongside David's 'wholesome attitude' and 'right conduct,' is the third element: his ישרת לבב. This is an inward matter: his heart was in the right place (before God; cf. G. Liedke, *THAT*, I, 790-794; also L. Alonso Schökel, *TWAT*, III, 1065). Burney points out that the expression הלך עם יהוה is very unusual (found also in Mic. 6:8). Usually one finds הלך לפני in such cases.

It would seem that the LXX did not read ותתן־לו בן as a new sentence – as we do – but that it read something like לתת בנו (δοῦναι τὸν υἱὸν αὐτοῦ), which would seem to make the end of our verse dependent on 'and you have preserved steadfast love for him.' Now, from a objective viewpoint, the continuation of the Davidic dynasty in Solomon's kingship is in fact a proof of God's 'favour,' but that is not how MT puts it.

3:7 *Now, then YHWH, my God, you have made our servant king in place of my father David, but I am only a little fellow who does not know the first thing about this business.*
In this verse the distinction emerges between the steadfast love of God who tangibly preserves the dynasty and the 'smallness' of the bearer of that dynastic dignity. Especially the conclusion of our verse is a reason for Weinfeld, *Deuteronomy*, 251f., to consider the material kinship between the Egyptian 'Königsnovelle' and our story dubious, because in the former the 'election motif' is so clear (against Hermann 1953, 54f.).

Solomon considers himself still a 'young fellow' who does not know 'how to go out or to come in.' The last 2 inf. cstr. are to be viewed as object of the verb ידע (cf. GD §105c; Ges-K §114c; Joüon §124c; Bg. II §11d*; Lettinga §73b.I; also Ewald §285c; H.P. Müller, *UF* 2 [1970], 238, n. 86). The expression 'going out and coming in' occurs frequently in OT (E. Jenni, *THAT*, I, 266),[8] but this does not mean that scholars have been able to point to a special

---

[8] Cf. J.G. Plöger, *Literarkritische, formgeschichtliche und stilkritische Untersuchungen zum Deuteronomomium* (BBB 26), Bonn 1967, 174-184; and now also A. van der Lingen, *"bw' - ys'*

'Sitz im Leben' for it. In our verse it does refer to the discharge of special duties related to the royal office (thus also Burney). Although some Hebr. MSS and the ancient versions read the copula ו before לא, this is not necessary because an asyndetic combination of a sentence which indicates the 'circumstance' with a preceding one which has already alluded to it is fairly common in ancient Hebr. (cf. Ehrlich). The self-designation 'little fellow,' put on Solomon's lips, clearly indicates his inexperience in government affairs, though to our ears it sounds somewhat exaggerated (cf. Thenius; Benzinger). There has been and still is much speculation about Solomon's age at the time of his accession. Josephus, for example, assumes (*Ant.* VIII, 211) that Solomon must have been 14 years old; the later Jewish tradition mentions the number 12 (Ginzberg, *Legends*, IV, 125 and VI, 277), and Rashi also (like Münster and Clarius) refers to this tradition in his marginal notes on this verse. Also outside of this Jewish tradition calculations have been made concerning Solomon's age at the time of his accession. Thus, on the basis of a comparison with data in the books of Samuel, Stade thinks (*GVI*, I, 297) that Solomon must have been no younger than 20. Benzinger a.o. concurs with him. For the rest, this speculation is quite irrelevant to our text because this hyperbole is a (literary) convention and in the rest of OT there is no clear indication as to how old Solomon really was at the time of his accession.

3:8 *Your servant finds himself in the midst of your people whom you have chosen, a powerful people, a people so numerous that its number can neither be estimated or counted.*
This verse, closely linked to the following, mentions the 'great people' and the wisdom needed to govern it. Stylistically the 2 verses have sometimes been termed an 'envelope construction' in which a parallelism functions 'at a distance': in vs. 8 the words עם רב and in vs. 9 the words עמך הכבד. The 2 word combinations, joined to the words which follows the first combination, have prompted J.S. Kselman (*VT* 29 [1979], 112) – not incorrectly – to assume a poetic substratum in this royal prayer. Alongside of stylistic features such as 'parallel pairs' and 'inclusion' one can also point to repetition and chiasmus.

In vs. 8 there is mention of the fact that God has chosen his people. The verb בחר occurs here for the first time in Kings and, except for 1 Kgs. 18:23, 25, also has Israel's God as subject (1 Kgs. 8:16, 44, 48; 11:13, 32, 34, 36; 14:21; 2 Kgs. 21:7; 23:27). The object in Kings – apart from 'the people' in our verse – is especially Jerusalem and David. This mode of expression has a strong 'dtr.' feel to it, the reason being that also in the book of Deuteronomy the verb is often found with God as subject (see H. Wildberger, *THAT*, I, 275-

---

('to go out and to come in') as a Military Term," *VT* 42 (1992), 59-66.

300; H. Seebass, *TWAT*, I, 592-608). According to the statistic in Wildberger, after Deut. (30x), Kings is the book in which בחר is most frequently used in the 'theological' sense (12x)! It is further remarked that this theological use is more recent than, say, its use in J and E and its point of gravity is said to be found in the dtr. history. In OT בחר became a kind of technical term for 'election'. The election of a king by a deity is an idea which Israel shares with the nations surrounding it; the election of a people, however, is something new in the history of religion of the ancient Near East (Wildberger, 283f.). The *locus classicus* of the 'election of Israel' in OT is Deut. 7:6-8. In the dtr. historiography, however, the 'election of the people' is only mentioned in our verse. Viewed against the background of our texts in Kings as well as that of the overall import of the books in which Judah and Israel are especially regarded as peoples who lacked 'the fear of the Lord,' it is a question whether our verse can simply be called 'dtr.,' even aside form the stylistic-poetic structure of our verse. It *is* the case – something Seebass, 605, has pointed out – that our verse forms an apparent contrast to Deut. 7:7f. Our verse, however, must not be viewed in isolation from the following verse which speaks in the idiom of international wisdom: the king wants the people to be an example to all peoples. The people whom YHWH has chosen for himself live out their life in full view of the surrounding nations.

The people are described as עם רב, so that because of its numbers it can neither be 'estimated or counted' (for this translation, cf. Ges-K §166b; Meyer §118.2). The last part of our verse is not reproduced in LXX. Instead LXX[Luc.] reads: 'You have chosen a great people for yourself, which is like the sand of the sea which can neither be counted or described.' Theod. translates this part in the same way. The par. report in 2 Chr. 1:9 has the following: '... for you have made me king over a people as numerous as the dust of the earth.' The verb מנה further occurs in the niph. in 8:5; Gen. 13:16; Isa. 53:12; Eccl. 1:15 and 2 Chr. 5:6 (also 12x in qal; in pi. and pu. it has a somewhat different meaning). The verb means 'to count' and is synonymous with the other verb used here: ספר (cf. J. Kühlewein, *THAT*, II, 164f.) which in qal and niph. is found resp. 27 and 8x in OT (in niphal also in 8:5 and 2 Chr. 5:6; further: Gen. 16:10; 32:13; Jer. 33:22; Hos. 2:1 and 1 Chr. 23:3). The hyperbole of the 'young fellow' is continued in the 'innumerable people.'

3:9 *So give your servant a heart to understand how to govern your people, able to discern between good and evil; otherwise, who could govern this great people of yours?'*
Solomon prays for a 'hearing heart' so that he may be able to govern the great people (cf. Wisdom 7:1-8:1). In a sense this is the (delayed) response to the question posed in vs. 5b. The answer is further shaped in terms of 2 considerations: (1) 'the judging' of the people and (2) 'the ability to discern' between

good and evil. According to Görg, *Gott-König-Reden*, 28, however, the first motive is superfluous because it returns in almost identical form at the end of our verse. Others, like Šanda and Montg.-Gehmann, are not entirely persuaded of this superfluity – despite the fact that Görg, in stressing that doublets can serve as an excellent criterion for literary criticism, is essentially correct.

Textcritically it can be said in connection with this verse that LXX, Pesh., and Vulg. unite the 2 'reasons' with the copula 'and' and that LXX adds to 'judging the people' the phrase ἐν δικαιοσύνῃ. Aside from the fact that the other versions lack this addition, it is a question whether we do not have here an adaptation to the expression שפט בצדק which occurs for example in Ps. 9:9; 96:13; 98:9. Grammatically of interest is that between טוב and לְ רע occurs where one would expect לְ. According to Joüon §103c the vowel /ā/ was probably avoided when it could be mistaken for that of the article. Along with בן ... בן one finds here the combination לְ ... בן which also occurs frequently (König §319n; cf. also I. Höver-Johag, *TWAT*, III, 330: 'Rechts-terminologie').

The expression לב שמע may be rooted in Egyptian ideas (cf. Noth; H. Brunner, *ThLZ* 79 [1954], 697-700 et al.). Noth refers to a line in the wisdom teaching of Ptahhotep: 'It is the heart which can make a human being become a listener or a non-listener.' Vs. 11 mentions as object of שמע the word משפט. In this sense the word could mean 'to understand,' 'to grasp,' rather than 'to hear.' The verb שמע occurs no less than about 1160x in OT, especially in its narrative parts (cf. H. Schult, *THAT*, II, 974-982). As well as denoting the physical capacity for acoustic perception, the word is also used idiomatically. In vs. 11, according to Schult (977), it refers to 'die Fähigkeit zur Urteilsfindung durch Anhörung von Parteien and Zeugen.' In conjunction with לב, 'heart' (cf. F. Stolz, *THAT*, I, 861-867; H.-J. Fabry, *TWAT*, IV, 413-451), it relates here both to 'justice' and to 'wisdom' (לשפט and להבין). It seems to us quite consistent, therefore, when vs. 12 simply speaks of a לב חכם. In connection with the verb 'to hear' Noth further wants to think of 'die jeweils rechte innere Eingebung' behind which in Egypt the ordering principle of Ma'at, in OT the rule of YHWH, is said to be operative.

The שפט of the people which occurs twice in our verse (cf. שפט: G. Liedke, *THAT*, II, 999-1009) refers, *inter alia*, to an act by which the disturbed order in a (legal) community is restored and a state of שלום again prevails. The verb need not always relate to a judicial verdict but in the practice of royal government this nuance is bound to have a certain emphasis. Also the 'ability to discern' between 'good and evil' (cf. 2 Sam 14:17; 15:3) has a legal background (cf. W.M. Clark, *JBL* 88 [1969], 266-278; for the meaning of 'to discern,' cf. H. Ringgren, *TWAT*, I, 625; for בין: H.H. Smid, *THAT*, I, 305-308).

The 2 reasons why in the preceding Solomon has prayed for a 'hearing heart' are finally motivated in the form of a rhetorical question. There is mention here of a עם כבד while the par. text in 2 Chr. 1:10 speaks of an עם גדול. Thenius qualifies this as 'explicative.' Kselman views רב and כבד as parallels and has the beginning of vs. 8 and the end of our verse form 'an attractive inclusion'.[9] The stem כבד, which is found in many Semitic languages, often occurs in the Hebr., both in a nominal and a verbal form (cf. C. Westermann, *THAT*, I, 794-812, esp. 795; further Ch. Dohmen, P. Stenmans *TWAT*, IV, 13-23). The adjective generally denotes that which in our language would be called 'weighty.' This weightiness is not only or even in the first place due to 'weight' but especially to its 'effect,' its function (in our language, cf. the phrase: financial 'burdens'). That which is 'weighty' can be experienced negatively as well as positively ('to lend weight to'). Thus people refer to a 'weighty army' (e.g. 1 Kgs. 10:2; 2 Kgs. 6:14; 18:17) and here to a 'weighty people.' This underscores the parallelism with רב on this point. Allow me still to note that Tg. and Pesh. (cf. also Vulg.) repeat the word 'people' after 'your people.'

3:10 *Now it pleased the Lord that Solomon had above all asked for this.*
In the impf. יטב is the by-form of טוב and occurs 44x in the qal, 73x in the hiph. (cf. I. Höver-Johag, *TWAT*, III, 315-339, esp. 323; H.J. Stoebe, *THAT*, I, 652-664, esp. 653ff.). Here it means that 'the matter' was right in the eyes of the Lord (cf. e.g. Gen. 41:37; Josh. 22:33). Of textcritical interest in this verse is the use of YHWH in place of אדני in LXX and in many Hebr. MSS. The use of this divine name, which occurs also in vs. 14, has prompted Noth et al. to advance it as an argument against the originality of vs. 10. Another weighty argument, moreover, is that the content of this verse actually eliminates the tension from the narrative and betrays in advance what the rest of it will tell the reader. This unevenness may certainly point to the secondary character of our verse. Klostermann wants to resolve this tension by including this verse in the content of Solomon's prayer. It seems to us that this verse is part of the (later) redactional work and can therefore be considered parenthetical (cf. Görg, *Gott-König-Reden*, 29). The divine designation אדני is rather rare in Kings (1 Kgs. 2:26; 3:10, 15; 8:53; 2 Kgs. 7:6; 19:23) and in general in the narrative parts from Genesis through 2 Kings (cf. O. Eißfeldt, *TWAT*, I, 66-78). It occurs approx. 450x in OT, 134x by itself and 315x in combination with YHWH (esp. in Ezek.). Although, according to Eiszfeldt (75), this divine name must already have been known and used in the first half of the tenth century, it only reemerged and was used intensively much later in the case of prophets like Amos, Isaiah, and Ezekiel, first alongside of YHWH, later even in

---

[9] J.S. Kselman, "RB//KBD: A New Hebrew-Akkadian Formulaic Pair," *VT* 29 (1979), 110-114, esp. 112.

the place of the 'ineffable' name.

3:11 *God said to him: 'Since you have asked not for a long life, or riches, or for the life of your enemies, but for discernment in the administration of justice,*
This verse begins with the (positive) answer of YHWH to Solomon's request, an answer which runs to the end of vs. 14. The vss. 11 and 12 clearly belong together, but have been divided to avoid an overly long verse (so, correctly, Joüon §15e). On the basis of ancient versions like LXX (cf. Pesh. and Vulg.), there has been a tendency also here to replace אלהים (which is also found in the par. text 2 Chron. 1:11) by YHWH (cf. comments on vs. 5). This is not necessary. The second לך is lacking in LXX and at the par. place in 2 Chr. 1:11, but Montg.-Gehman rightly point to the effect of the frequent use of the second person in our verse. The verb שאל dominates, and is even accentuated by the so-called *dativus commodi* (Burney). The final pf. with the copula (ושאל) is not so frequent but can be explained from the adversative meaning of ו which as a result gains added emphasis (Joüon §172a; Burney; cf. GD §84; Driver §130; Bg. II §9n). This, accordingly, is not based on a textual error (Ges-K §112tt; Stade-Schwally think of a gloss in connection with v. 11b). Burney correctly observes that a ו *simplex* presupposes a coordination with the preceding and that a form of the impf. cons. וַתִּשְׁאַל would not have been fitting here.

The particle יען, expanded in many cases (as here) with אשר or even כי, introduces a so-called 'Begründungssatz' which occurs above all in prophetic pronouncements of weal or woe. It can perhaps be viewed as a technical term originating from prophetic circles.[10] The part. indicates the reasons why a given action will or will not take place. This indication of grounds occurs formally here in an accumulation of pf. forms of שאל. Stylistically this is a means to bring the narrative tension to a climax and a reason for considering vs. 10 secondary. Görg, *Gott-König-Reden*, 45, diagrams the structure of this sentence in an orderly scheme: שאל occurs 5x in this verse, preceded the 2nd, 3rd, and 4th time by לו; the 2nd, 3rd, and 5th time by לך. The 4th member can do without לך because it concerns איביך. There is also an implicit climax in the things Solomon has not asked for: 'many days' (2 Chr. 1:11 has this as the last of the 3 things), i.e. a long life; riches; or 'the soul of your enemies,' because for a king of the ancient Near East riches counted for more than a long life; but being the victor over one's enemies counted for more than riches. Aside

---

[10] See my article on יען in *OTS* 18 (1973), 49-83; further D.E. Gowan, "The Use of *ya'an* in Biblical Hebrew," *VT* 21 (1971), 168-185; W. Dietrich, *Prophetie und Geschichte* (FRLANT 108), Göttingen 1972, 68.

from here and in vs. 13 the word עֹשֶׁר occurs in Kings only again in 1 Kgs. 10:23 (37x in the whole of OT). In the par. text 2 Chr. 1:11 the word is further explicated by the synonyms נְכָסִים[11] and כָּבוֹד, 'wealth and honour.' In the case of the נפש of the enemies (in pl. of אֹיְבֶיךָ 2 Chr. 1:11 has שֹׂנְאֶיךָ, 'haters,' here) one should think of their 'life' (cf. C. Westermann, *THAT*, II, 71-96).[12]

The inf. הבין functions here as object (Bg. II §11d), but the translation of the word is somewhat more nuanced than in vs. 8 (cf. H. Ringgren, *TWAT*, I, 625). Whereas there it was possible to translate it by 'discern,' here one would perhaps do better rendering it by 'the capacity to discern (in listening)' (so also Thenius: 'Einsicht, um Gericht zu halten'); cf. also Isa. 56:11: לא ידעו הבין. The word מִשְׁפָּט, which derives from the root שפט, is no more solely juridical in character than the verb (cf. G. Liedke, *THAT*, II, 1004f.; B. Johnson, *TWAT*, V, 93-107). Here the word denotes a certain ethical quality enabling one to discriminate between good and evil; in this connection, certainly in the case of a king, juridical considerations play a role as well (see V. Herntrich, *TDNT*, III, 927). The הבין לשמע משפט belongs to being חכם (see following verse) and is concretely demonstrated in the second half of our chapter.

3:12 *therefore I will now act according to your words and give you such a wise and understanding heart as no one has had before and no one will have after you.*

After the 'Begründung' of the previous verse, this verse announces the 'saving gift' Solomon will receive: 'wisdom.' The pf. which follows הנה is translated – as it concerns the tense – by a future (Böttcher §947b: pf. *affirmativum*; cf. also Ewald §135c; Bg. II §6e: 'konstatierendes Perfectum'; my article in *OTS* 18 [1973], 79: 'pf. *confidentiae*'; Burney: 'perfects of certitude'; cf. also Görg, 46, n. 110). אשר serves as a conjunction introducing sentences which indicate a sequel: 'so that' (cf. Ges-K §166b; Meyer, §118, 2; Schneider, §53.4.4.2). Instead of the first 3 words of our verse LXX[BL] reads: ἰδοὺ πεποίηκα τὸ ῥῆμά σου. Instead of כדבריך one would only surmise דברך. Although this is only a formal difference, Montg.-Gehman, for example, would give preference to the second reading. The first words of our verse relate the promises to Solomon's prayer. According to Görg, 46, the formal structure of our verse corresponds to this actual aspect: the verb in the pf. is positioned between the element והנה and the expression of relation כדבריך. The second verbal sentence has a similar structure. Here that which was requested by Solomon is summed up in the words לב חכם ונבון. חכם occurs in the speech of God as a pivotal and ex-

---

[11] Cf. R. Polzin, *Late Biblical Hebrew* (HSM 12), Missoula 1976, 146: a late Hebrew word of Aramaic origin.

[12] Cf. also J.H. Becker, *Het begrip nefesj in het Oude Testament*, Amsterdam 1942, 19.

tremely important word (so also Noth), although it was already implied in vs. 9. The word נָבוֹן clearly refers back to בִּין in that verse. True: Burney is right when he says that the 2 adjectives occur also in Deut. 1:13 and 4:6 – a work of the dtr. redactor, according to him – but this dtr. redactor does not refrain from introducing these words at a crucial moment and letting them determine, thematically as it were, all of Solomon's further conduct (as a 'prelude,' cf. 2:6, 9; further 3:28; 5:9-11, 14, 21, 26; 10:4, 6-8, 23f.; 11:41; also G. Fohrer, *TDNT*, VII, 481ff.). In the par. text 2 Chr. 1:12, as in the preceding verse, there is mention again of חָכְמָה and מַדָּע, which now function in a passive construction (נָתוּן לָךְ).

The wisdom given to Solomon surpasses that of any other. This is expressed by the 2 sentences introduced by אֲשֶׁר and, in addition, structured chiastically in relation to each other. Such incomparability-statements occur also elsewhere in Kings (2 Kgs. 18:5; 23:25), and they are often attributed to the dtr. redactor (thus, e.g., Burney). In the following diagram Görg illustrates the contrary tendency which is manifest in all parts of the 2 corresponding sentences:

```
אַחֲרֶיךָ          כָּמוֹךָ
לֹא יָקוּם   ✕   לֹא הָיָה
כָּמוֹךָ          לְפָנֶיךָ
```

Striking here is that, at the exact point where the 3 dotted lines intersect, the figure of Solomon 'in all his wisdom' can be put at an absolute summit which has never before him been reached in the past (הָיָה) and which can never be reached after him in the future (יָקוּם) (for the form, cf. BL §651x-z).[13]

3:13 *Moreover, I will also give you what you have not asked for: both riches and honour so that in your lifetime no other king will compare with you.* Though Solomon is 'incomparable' in wisdom, he will be that in other respects as well, be it, according to our text, within a more limited time frame. Nevertheless the words כָּל־יָמֶיךָ present a problem, especially in a textcritical sense, because most MSS of LXX, including B and Luc. omit them. 2 Chr. 1:12 even renders them: 'such as no king before you ever had and no king after you will have.' This clearly contradicts MT in our verse. If one omits the last 2 words, the text only says that before Solomon there never had been kings as rich as he. Nothing is said about the future. Montg. Gehman comment that the 2 words referred to – as gloss – are intended to be no more than an interpretation of the past in which the future life of the king is now also included. It is certainly not necessary, along with Klostermann, Benzinger et al., to change הָיָה into יְהוָה. It does seem to us that the words כָּל־יָמֶיךָ do not help to make the text more

---

[13] See now also G.N. Knoppers, "»There was None Like Him«: Incomparability in the Book of Kings," *CBQ* 54 (1992), 411-431.

clear and therefore need to be considered a gloss (along with Stade-Schwally, Montg.-Gehman; otherwise: Ehrlich). To this must be added that in the following verse the days of Solomon's life are more 'naturally' integrated in the narrative. Ehrlich and Noth, however, think that the words in question really belong to the main sentence, so that the אשר-clause through במלכים is a subordinate clause. Still, this solution seems too artificial. It certainly makes sense not to accord such high status to Solomon as it concerns his 'riches' and 'honour' − this word pair occurs here for the first time, later several times more in Chronicles (C. Westermann, *THAT*, I, 800f.) − though in these respects his position is still high enough! − as to him in regard to his 'wisdom.' The author had probably heard, seen, or experienced in his days that kings could be richer and more glorious than Solomon, but certainly not wiser, at least in his view of things.

3:14 *Now if you will walk in my ways, keeping my statutes and my commandments, as our father David did, I will prolong your days.'*
Here Solomon is again promised a long life but this time on condition that he will be pleasing to YHWH. In this connection Ehrlich points to Prov. 16:31 and Ps. 21:4. Because Solomon did not meet the stated condition, Münster and Clarius do not find 52 years all that long (cf. comments on vs. 7).

Benzinger (and others) consider the first half of this verse a dtr. interpolation. Here we encounter the same phraseology as, for instance, in 2:3f. References to David regularly occur in the dtr. redaction (e.g. the vss. 3 and 6 above; further 9:4; 11:4, 6, 33, 38 etc.; see Burney, 31). The hiph. of ארך with YHWH as subject is found only in this verse. For the rest, the hiph. of this verb with, for instance, the Israelites as subject is quite normal in Deut. (e.g. 4:26, 40; 5:16, 33; 6:2 etc.). In our verse the expression stands for 'giving (someone) a long life'; in Akkad.: *urruku ūmē* (cf. *HAL*, s.v.; also Ewald §122d on the causative significance of the hiph. of this verb). It is striking that our verse has no par. in 2 Chr. 1. For ארך hiph. LXX (minus Luc.) uses πληθυνῶ; Luc.: μακρύνω. According to G. Delling, *TDNT*, VI, 281, n. 12, πληθύνειν ἡμέρας is a late slavish translation.

3:15 *Then Solomon woke up and realized it had been a dream. He returned to Jerusalem, where he positioned himself before the ark of the covenant of the Lord, sacrificed burnt offerings and peace offerings, and arranged a banquet for all his servants.*
Following the words of YHWH in the dream Solomon wakes up. This verse belongs to the later framework in which the dream-revelation has been incorporated. Moreover, it moves the scene from Gibeon to Jerusalem, to the sanctuary which in a later period was considered the only true one. It is strange that Solomon went to Jerusalem to make a sacrifice after the dream, though we had

just been told in vs. 4 that he went to Gibeon to do it there (see Burney a.o.). Whether it is true that vs. 5a replaced another introduction to the dream, as e.g. Görg, *Gott-König-Reden*, 30, suggests, is hard to prove. It is in fact clear that this 'postscript' following the dream displays a number of dtr. redactional traits. This is all the more conspicuous when one compares with our verse. the LXX which some scholars (like Thenius, Klostermann, and Šanda) wish to follow. Thus for ויבוא LXX reads: καὶ ἀνέστη, and after ויעמד through אדני: κατὰ πρόσωπον τοῦ Θυσιαστηρίου τοῦ κατὰ πρόσωπον κιβωτοῦ διαθήκης Κυρίου ἐν Σειών while it further makes משתה 'great,' both for himself and for all his servants. These additions indicate that in the course of time the text has been tinkered with, probably especially to retouch somewhat the 'offensiveness' of sacrificing on the 'high place' at Gibeon. Some scholars want to remove from this text the words ויבוא ירושלם (Görg, 31), some even through אדני. On the basis of the beginning of our verse it does not seem impermissible to view vs. 5a (with Görg) as an addition, as in our verse at least 'the coming to Jerusalem.' The dream and the sacrifice took place in Gibeon (cf. the par. text in 2 Chr. 1:13).

The verse opens with ויקץ (for the varying forms of *qof* with or without *dagesh* in the MSS and editions, cf. *inter alia* Böttcher §500.9; Olsh. §242a; Ges-K §71; Delitsch, *LSF* §80). The verb יקץ occurs 11x in OT (once more in Kings I 18:27; cf. G. Wallis, *TWAT*, III, 849-855). In Gen. 41:7 one finds a similar beginning. The word 'behold, a dream' implies that the preceding is viewed as a revelation of God by means of a dream. And in the Israelite view dreams are not illusions but realities (Pedersen, I-II, 134f.). On the other hand, this implies that initially the preceding may have been experienced as 'sleep.' This is possibly assumed when LXX uses ὕπνος in vs. 5 and ἐνύπνιον in our verse (the latter is customary for 'dream' in LXX: A. Oepke, *TDNT*, V, 221).

The text then reports Solomon's going to Jerusalem where he positioned himself before 'the ark of the covenant of Adonai.' Still aside from the transfer of the scenario from Gibeon to Jerusalem, there is the striking reference to the 'ark.' True, the ark is mentioned in 1 Kgs. 6:19; 8:1-21 and already in 2:26 above (which see), but here the mention of the ark – and in LXX of the altar of the ark of the covenant – underscores the legitimacy of Solomon's sacrifices at the 'right place' (reinforced in LXX by 'in Zion'). As in vs. 10, so here again many mss as well as LXX have YHWH in place of Adonai. Mentioned as sacrifices which Solomon is said to have made here in Jerusalem are עלות, 'burnt offerings' which totally go up in smoke and fire, and שלמים, 'peace offerings.' The 2 kinds of sacrifices frequently occur together in OT. עלה occurs 287x in OT (cf. G. Wehmeier, *THAT*, II, 274, 280f.) and is first mentioned in Kings in vs. 4 above. It is the 'entire offering,' the gift which totally goes up in flames before the deity. The *plurale tantum* שלמים (in the sing. only in Amos 5:22) occurs only 87x, 6 of which in our books Kings (aside from our verse also 3x in 1 Kgs. 8:63; 9:25 and 2 Kgs. 16:13; G. Gerleman, *THAT*, II, 920f.; 931f.). The importance, function and meaning of these various kinds of sacrifices are in dispute (see also T. Seidl, *TWAT*, VIII, 101-111), but it is clear from Leviticus, as well as from the parallelization עלה and שלמים that the two are to a high degree alike. Only the latter is not consumed altogether, only the fat parts, while we may assume that the other parts were eaten in the course of a sacrificial meal. Gerleman suspects that the עלה was a part of the שלמים. The pl., in which this word is nearly always found, is said to relate to the pieces of the sacrifice which were offered separately. These pieces, which were intended for YHWH, are said to be 'payments' substituting for the whole. De Moor[14] draws a parallel between Ugar. and Hebr. שלמים and thinks that these were offered up in the cult as a kind of payment to a god to prevent him from carrying on against his devotees. Thus the sacrifices were thought to guarantee a peaceful existence for the people. One could therefore, with a measure of caution, reproduce the word in our language as 'peace offerings.'

Finally, Solomon provided a משתה, the only time this word occurs in our books. This 'verbal abstractum' (G. Gerleman, *THAT*, II, 1024) usually means a 'drinking bout' or a 'feast'; in a later phase of the language it also occasionally means 'drink' (Dan. 1:10 etc.). Solomon involves all his servants in this event. Only now the servants – who, according to 2 Chr. 1, had been involved even before Solomon's going to Gibeon – joyfully share in the event of God's special investiture of their 'new' king on David's throne. The question is whether we must understand these 'servants' in a restricted sense or whether the entire population of Jerusalem and Judah were included. A variant in Josephus, *Ant.* VIII, 25, permits both possibilities: καευώχει τοὺς ἰδίους ἅπαντας; or: τοὺς Ἰουδαίους ἅπαντας.

---

[14] J.C. de Moor, "The Peace-Offering in Ugarit and Israel," in *Schrift en Uitleg* (Fs W.H. Gispen), Kampen 1970, 112-117.

1 KINGS 3:16-28

3:16 *Once upon a time two prostitutes came to the king and stood before him.*

17 *One of the women said: 'If it pleases you, my lord, this woman and I lived in the same house and, while I was with her in the house, I gave birth to a child.*

18 *The third day after I had given birth this woman also gave birth to a child. We were alone together; no on else was in the house with us; there were just the two of us.*

19 *Now one night this woman's child died because she had lain on him.*

20 *So she got up in the middle of the night and took my son from beside me while your servant was sleeping; she laid it at her breast while she laid her dead child at my breast.*

21 *And when in the morning I got up to nurse my child, it was dead. When in the morning light I looked at him more closely, he was not the child that I had borne.'*

22 *Then the other woman spoke up: 'Absolutely not! My son is the live one; your child is the dead one.' But she said: 'Absolutely not! Your child is the dead one but my son is the live one.' And so they wrangled before the king.*

23 *The king observed: 'One says: "My son is the live one and yours is the dead one," and the other says, "Absolutely not! Your son is the dead one and mine is the live one".'*

24 *Then the king said, 'Get me a sword.' And they brought the king a sword.*

25 *And the king said, 'Cut the living child in two, and give half to the one and half to the other.'*

26 *At this the woman who was the mother of the living child spoke to the king, for she was filled with intense pity for her child, and said, 'Please, my lord, give her the living baby. Don't kill him!' But the other woman said, 'Neither I nor you should have him. Cut him in two!'*

27 *Then the king answered and said: 'She (who said): 'Give her the living baby; don't kill him,' she is the mother.'*

28 *When all Israel heard the verdict the king had pronounced, they held the king in awe because they saw that he had wisdom from God to settle legal cases.*

INTRODUCTION

Here starts the 'the Solomonian judgment' which continues to the end of this chapter. Along with Noth et al. we can regard this story as a unit without particular editorial adaptations. It is evident that the story serves to demonstrate the wisdom promised to Solomon (vs. 12; cf. Benzinger). The story has a folkloristic rather than a historical character. Gaster, *Myth*, 491-494, mentions numerous examples of the legendary world literature of ancient date in which one finds similar stories, many of which came from India and China. Although the particle אז is temporal, in this connection it is almost the equivalent of 'once upon a time' in English, and can introduce a fairy tale. In any case, in these and similar stories it is not the historicity but the motif or import which is important.[1]

EXEGESIS

3:16 *Once upon a time two prostitutes came to the king and stood before him.*
On אז, followed by an impf., as the beginning of a story see König §137 (with an explication in 140); Ges-K §107c; Joüon §113i; Bg. II §7g; GD §62, rem. 2; Schneider §48.4.3.4; and Lettinga §72d2 ('impf. with past meaning'). The persons who play a large role in our story are described as 'two prostitutes,' literally: 'two women,' with the word 'prostitutes' in apposition (Joüon §131b; cf. GD §46a; for the use of the numeral: Joüon §142c; BrSynt. §83b). The word זנה, which occurs in qal 83x in OT and the substantival forms זונה 33x, in by far the greatest number of cases denotes 'committing fornication' by a woman, whether this fornication relates to illicit sex between a woman and a man, or relates metaphorically to the infidelity of the people of Israel over against its God (cf. J. Kühlewein, *THAT*, I, 518ff.; S. Erlandsson, *TWAT*, II,

---

[1] See on this pericope now also A.M. Dubarle, "Le jugement de Salomon: un coeur à l'écoute," *Revue de Sciences Philosophiques et Théologiques* 63 (1979), 419-427; C. Fontaine, "The Bearing of Wisdom on the Shape of 2 Samuel 11-12 and 1 Kings 3," *JSOT* 34 (1986), 61-77; S. Lasine, "Solomon, Daniel, and the Detective Story: The Social Function of a Literary Genre," *HAR* 11 (1987), 247-66; K.A. Deurloo, "The king's Wisdom in Judgement: Narration as Example (1 Kings iii)," *OTS* 25 (1989), 11-21; E. and G. Leibowitz, "Solomon's Judgment," *BetM* 35 (1989-90), 242-44 (Hebr.); W.A.M. Beuken, "No Wise King Without a Wise Woman (I Kings III 16-28)," *OTS* 25 (1989), 2-10; Hugh S. Pyper, "Judging the Wisdom of Solomon: The Two-Way Effect of Intertextuality," *JSOT* 59 (1993), 25-36; A. Reinhartz, "Anonymous Women and the Collapse of the Monarchy: A Study in Narrative Technique," *A Feminist Companion to Samuel and Kings* (ed. A. Brenner), Sheffield 1994, 43-65; and E. van Wolde, "Who Guides Whom? Embeddedness and Perspective in Biblical Hebrew and in I Kings 3:16-28," *JBL* 114 (1995), 623-642.

612-619).² In the national life of Israel the 'harlot' was a familiar figure, as she is in most nations in antiquity and the present (cf. F. Hauck, S. Schulz, *TDNT*, VI, 585f.). 'Cultic prostitution' is another issue, but that is not what is going on in our story. It is remarkable that in a number of MSS of LXX the word πόρναι has been replaced by the word πονηραι, 'oppressed,' which may suggest the social distress which comes to light through such practices (cf. Amos 7:17). Extenuating also is the translation of Tg.: פונדקין, 'inn-keepers,' 'hostesses' or 'women traders,' a fem. form of the Greek πάνδοκος (cf. Krauss, *GLL*, II, 428f.). Josephus somewhat describes the 'function' of these women by calling them δύο γυναῖκες ἑταῖραι τὸν βίον (*Ant.* VIII, 27), while the rabbinical exegetes similarly attempt to 'clean up' the profession of these women.

These 2 women now come to Solomon in his capacity as judge.

3:17 *One of the women said: 'If it pleases you, my lord, this woman and I lived in the same house and, while I was with her in the house, I gave birth to a child.*

בי אדני is an 'opening signal' (Schneider §54 1.4), the etymological origin of which has prompted much discussion. Ewald §101c (cf. his *GVI*, I, 195) considers the particle an abbreviation of אבי; *BDB*, Burney et al. think of the root ביי; others again of the root באה; Montg.-Gehman refer to an article by A.M. Honeyman, *JAOS* 64 (1944), 81f., who stands by the root אבה 'to will.' Joüon §105c is probably right when he regards בי, almost always combined with אדני, as a 'an entreating interjection in the special sense of *Pardon!, Excuse me!*' (cf. Gen. 43:20; 44:18; Exod. 4:10, 13 etc.) LXX again reproduces the beginning as Ἐν ἐμοί (cf. Vulg.: *obsecro mi*; Tg. בבעו רבוני; Pesh. *b'y' 'n'*). From this overview it is clear that LXX, Vulg. and Pesh. heard in בי a 1 p. sing. which they sought to honour in the translation. The numeral אחד after בית indicates that the reference is to one and the same house (Joüon §147a). Ehrlich calls the following ואלד עמד בבית 'good English' but 'bad Hebrew'! However, in Esth. 7:8 one finds another construction like it. We will leave Ehrlich's opinion for what it is worth (cf. Joüon §132a). LXX omits עמה in the translation. The intent of the text is to say that the speaker gave birth to a child while another woman was also in the house.

3:18 *The third day after I had given birth this woman also gave birth to a child. We were alone together; no on else was in the house with us; there were just the two of us.*

---

² See now also H. Schulte, "Beobachtungen zum Begriff der *Zônâ* im Alten Testament," *ZAW* 104 (1992), 255-262.

It is striking that Josephus, *Ant.* VIII, 27, has it occur the same day and even the same hour. The function of the preposition ל is that of the description of the genitive, a formation by which the preceding construction is not changed (Joüon §130d; cf. Ewald §292a; Konig §281d; Ges-K §129f; GD §36, rem. 3; Burney). The resulting sense is: 'on the third day after my delivery.' The word הזאת after גם־האשה conveys a measure of contempt (Joüon §143d). LXX[Luc.] expressly adds that 'that woman' gave birth to a 'son.' The plaintiff further points out that they were together in the house. יחדו, which occurs approx. 90x in OT, is viewed by Joüon (§146i) as a form with a 'vague' suffix, by Ges-K (§135r) as a form with an 'ossified' suffix. J.C. De Moor, *VT* 7 (1957), 350-355, has attempted to show that it concerns an ancient locative ending added to the word יחד, a 'unit,' an 'enclosed whole,' later in use as adverb. The local as well as the temporal aspect can be indicated by the use of the word. Here the idea is to indicate that they were home alone and therefore that no one else was there. This is again underscored by what follows. LXX simply says: 'there was no one by us': καὶ οὐκ ἔστιν οὐθεὶς μεθ'ἡμῶν, leaving בבית untranslated. But MT speaks of a זר, a word that occurs about 70x in OT, 56x as substantive and 14x as adjective. The basic meaning of the verb זור is 'to distance oneself,' 'to deviate.' Often the word is translated by 'stranger,' an 'outsider,' and this in various senses (cf. L.A. Snijders, *TWAT*, II, 556-564; R. Martin-Achard, *THAT*, I, 520ff.). Here the word serves especially to report that there was no one else in the house and by implication that no other witness can be summoned to appear at the following trial (Josephus, *Ant.* VIII, 29. As though to once more underscore this point, there follows the sentence beginning with זולתי, a preposition (cf. e.g. *HAL*, s.v.) which denotes an exception: 'except,' or as Burney prefers: 'but only.' This אנחנו which follows שתים can be viewed as an apposition (BrSynt. §67a; but cf. §144).

3:19 *Now one night this woman's child died because she had lain on him.*
The baby of the other woman dies. Cause: she lay on him while asleep. This, at least, is the reason the one woman cites (the idea that there is an allusion here to 'sleeping with another,' in view of her profession, is not likely since, after all, there was no one else in the house). The conjunction which indicates the reason here is אשר, one of the possibilities the Hebr. offers to indicate causal connections (cf. Joüon §170e; Ewald §353a; Schneider §53.4.4.1; also my article in *OTS* 18 [1973], 80, 82). This particle here conveys especially the 'objective causality': because this has happened, the following logically happened as well. We are not told what proof this woman had for her assertion, but in the framework of the story this is in no way important.

3:20 *So she got up in the middle of the night and took my son from beside me while your servant was sleeping; she laid it at her breast while she laid her*

dead child at my breast.
Now comes the switching of the babies. The story does not say how soon after the birth of the 2 babies this drama occurred. In his version Josephus is slightly 'more exact' by informing his reader that this already occurred 'on the third day' (*Ant*. VIII, 28). Our verse, like the previous verse, only says 'in the night.' Perhaps the idea is to say that the death of the second child and exchange of the first child still took place during the night in which the second baby was born.

In place of מאצלי LXX reads ἐκ τῶν ἀγκαλῶν μου, 'out of my arms,' which in Hebr. could be the word אֱצִיל (Jer. 38:12; Ezek. 13:18 etc.). This version finds no support in other ancient translations, however, nor is it required by our context. Moreover, LXX[B, Luc.] and still other MSS, as well as Vet.Lat., omit the parenthetical clause 'while your maidservant slept.' But we do not have to follow this reading.

3:21 *And when in the morning I got up to nurse my child, it was dead. When in the morning light I looked at him more closely, he was not the child that I had borne.'*

By the use of the hitp. the following word אתבונן (derived from the verb בין) expresses very well how the mother made her sad discovery: back and forth, turning the baby this way and that! (Thenius). There is no reason whatever to omit the second בבקר (as Stade-Schwally, textcr. app. of *BHK* et al. propose). This is not so much because of 'feminine repetitiousness' (Montg.-Gehman) but above all because it was only by the clear light of the morning that the woman could be sure that this was not her own child. This the Vulg. sensed very well: *quem diligentius intuens clara luce*.

3:22 *Then the other woman spoke up: 'Absolutely not! My son is the live one; your child is the dead one.' But she said: 'Absolutely not! Your child is the dead one but my son is the live one.' And so they wrangled before the king.*
The ping-pong game of 'yes!' 'no!' 'It is!' 'It isn't!' begins. What can they expect when there are no witnesses and the true mother could barely tell in broad daylight that the dead baby was not her own ...?

The one woman says: 'No, but my son is alive,' etc. This לא, reinforced by כי (cf. Ewald §320b; König §352f.) conveys an emotional denial. This does not in any way alter the fact that the other woman too sticks to her guns: וזאת אמרת (Driver §135.1). Being without any witnesses they keep arguing before the king on the basis of their own trustworthiness and authority (ותדברנה). Textcritically, on this verse, it needs to be added that there are quite a few MSS – especially of LXX (except B and Luc.) as well as Vulg. – which have the women change places in what is said. In addition, LXX omits the words of the first speaker who contradicts her rival. This omission as such makes some sense but the chiastically-structured redundancy of MT brings out better the endless back-and-forth 'It is!' 'It is not!' argument before the king.

3:23 *The king observed: 'One says: "My son is the live one and yours is the dead one," and the other says, "Absolutely not! Your son is the dead one and mine is the live one".'*
The endless back-and-forth is underscored by having the king repeat the hopelessly repetitive words of the women: זאת ... זאת: the one woman ... the other (woman) (König §48; Joüon §143c; GD §5). LXX leaves the impression the king himself addressed the women: 'You say this and you say that' but this is 'scarcely so good as MT' (Burney).

3:24 *Then the king said, 'Get me a sword.' And they brought the king a sword.*
In this impasse the king renders judgment, decisively, but to our minds very rigorously. Actually this is not even a verdict but an order which seems to have nothing to do with the issue. It does, however, all the more heighten the tension in the story; 'Bring me a sword'. For the article, cf. Meyer §96; Joüon §137f; H. Grotius cites examples of this from classical antiquity.

3:25 *And the king said, 'Cut the living child in two, and give half to the one and half to the other.'*
The verb גזר, 'to cut,' 'to slaughter' also occurs in other Sem. languages (M. Görg, *TWAT*, I, 1001-1004). Görg (1003) points out that the consequence of this 'cutting' is 'deciding,' a (later) semantic nuance of this Hebr. word (Job 22:28; Esth. 2:1). To the mention of the child LXX (except Luc.) adds that it was τὸ Θηλάζον, 'a nursing child.' And LXX[Luc.] adds to the conclusion: 'similarly cut the dead child in pieces and give it to the 2 women.' This is an addition Josephus also assumes in his version (*Ant.* VII, 31). In Exod. 21:35 one encounters the latter procedure in the case of 'goring oxen' (Klostermann; Burney). Rahlfs, *SSt.* III, 101f., 284, thinks this correspondence is not accidental but part of the (written or oral) Jewish tradition because 'die eigentümliche Verbalhornung des weisen Urteils Salomos offenbar' belongs to 'der jüdischen Haggada'(p. 102). Ginzberg, *Legends*, IV, 130f., however, nowhere states that this haggada occurs in other rabbinical traditions.

3:26 *At this the woman who was the mother of the living child spoke to the king, for she was filled with intense pity for her child, and said, 'Please, my lord, give her the living baby. Don't kill him!' But the other woman said, 'Neither I nor you should have him. Cut him in two!'*
Both women react to the king's command but their reactions are very different. The mother of the baby that is still alive speaks first and pleads that, given this

fate, the living baby had better be given to the other woman. The reason given is: כי־נכמרו רחמיה על־בנה. The verb כמר only occurs 4x – and that in the niph. – in OT (Gen. 43:30; Hos. 11:8; and Lam. 5:10). It is probably closest to its 'basic meaning' in Lam. 5:16: 'being burning, hot' (see the lexicons s.v.). The remaining times (after emendation in Hos. 11:8) the pl. of רחם ('womb') is subject and the expression means something like 'being stirred up, excited.' The abstract pl. רחמים, after all, conveys 'compassion,' and refers to the seat of this emotion in one's inmost (cf. H.J. Stoebe, *THAT*, II, 761ff.). Since psychic and physical emotions and disturbances lie close together, it is sometimes hard to tell whether it refers to a feeling by itself or to a feeling somewhere in the body (Pedersen I-II, 525).

In her words to the king the mother now uses the word ילוד, the qal pass. part.: the 'new-born' (cf. vs. 27 and Job 14:1; 15:14; 25:4; 1 Chr. 14:4). As nuance of ילד this word is understandable and fitting (otherwise a.o. Stade-Schwally; Delitzsch, *LSF*, §§58b; 103, n. 2; Ehrlich). She urgently requests the king to please! not kill the child – indicated in MT by a *figura etymologica*, an inf. abstr., *plus* a finite verb of the hiph. of מות (for the inf. abstr. followed by a negation, cf. Joüon §123o; Bg. II §12c).

The reaction of the other 'mother' is totally different, a fact which also comes to expression in the language used. In place of the imploring prohibitive with אל we now have the almost commanding לא, followed by an imper. which is unambiguous. In MT the first words are addressed to the other woman, the final command to the soldiers. In LXX it is presented as if she directs all her words to the king (and the soldiers): 'May it belong neither to me nor to *her*.'

3:27 *Then the king answered and said: 'She (who said): 'Give her the living baby; don't kill him,' she is the mother.'*
Now follows the point of the preceding: the king administers justice, not by way of oracles or ordeal, but on purely rational grounds. The text itself, however, contains a problem. As it now reads, one could draw the (mistaken) conclusion that the king awarded the living baby to the woman who spoke last. In various ways exegetes have attempted to solve the problem, e.g. by assuming that the king gestured in the direction of the first woman (so Burney et al.). LXX still has another solution. It translates: 'The king answered: "Give the baby to her who said: »Give her the (living baby)«".' An even simpler solution – launched already by Klostermann (and Delitzsch, *LSF* §132b) and recently given new life by E. Ruprecht, *ZAW* 88 (1976), 415-418 – is to assume that between ויאמר and תנו the word האמרת fell out as a result of haplography. This is then picked up again at the end by היא. In that way the text flows naturally and gains a logical ending. We have taken over this emendation of the text.

3:28 *When all Israel heard the verdict the king had pronounced, they held the king in awe because they saw that he had wisdom from God to settle legal cases.*

Our verse needs to be viewed as a summary conclusion from the preceding. Strictly speaking, it not only belongs to the immediately preceding tale of 'the Solomonian judgment' but also to the material which preceded that story, and hence flowed from the pen of the final redactor. Twice we encounter in our verse the word משפט, each time with a slightly different nuance. The LXX shows a good appreciation of this difference when it translates κρίμα and δικαίωμα respectively (for the latter cf. G. Schrenk, *TDNT*, II, 221ff.). Again the core of the matter is 'wisdom,' described here as a חכמת אלהים. This is not so much 'enormous wisdom' as 'divine wisdom.' If the latter were not the case, why would it be expressly stated that the people 'stood in awe' of the king? It is with 'awe' and a 'reverent modesty' that humans enter into contact with persons, places, etc., that are especially associated with God (Exod. 34:30; Josh. 4:14; 1 Sam. 12:18, etc.; cf. Luke 4:36; 8:25; G. Wanke, *TDNT*, IX, 197f.; H.-P. Stähli, *THAT*, I, 765-778). We can perhaps best describe this attitude with 'standing in awe.'

Mont.-Gehman further point out that in keeping with the Arab. word, 'wisdom' here could mean 'a judicial judgment.' Although in the present context the word can have this as its primary meaning and this may conform to the intent of the context, we still think a broader meaning is not excluded.

1 KINGS 4:1-6

4:1 *So King Solomon became king over all Israel.*

2 *And these were his high officials: Azariah son of Zadok, priest;*

3 *Elihoreph and Ahijah sons of Shisha, secretaries; Jehoshaphat son of Ahilud, herald;*

4 *Benaiah son of Jehoiada, commander of the army; [Zadok and Abiathar, priests];*

5 *Azariah son of Nathan, chief administrator; Zabud son of Nathan the priest, friend of the king;*

6 *Ahishar, master of the palace, and Adoniram son of Abda, in charge of forced labour.*

INTRODUCTION

In this chapter and in the first 8 verses of the following one we are introduced to Solomon's government apparatus. Based on the form and character of the following statements it is rather generally assumed, especially since the researches of A. Alt ("Israels Gaue unter Salomo" = *KS*, II, 76-89), that in this section we encounter not just very ancient material from administrative sources but also material of considerable historical value. This material has been located here by a (or the) redactor of our books after 3:28 concluded with the word 'wisdom' – a keyword for Solomon – and before 5:9 continues with it.

The chapter division of MT differs from that in our translations: MT chaps. 4 and 5 through vs. 14 = RSV 4:1-34. The latter chapter and verse division also occurs already in Vulg. and LXX, although these versions contain a fair number of deviations from the order of MT. One can look these up in various editions. They are the following:

LXX	=	MT
4:17, 18, 19	=	4:18, 19, 17
4:20-21, 22-24, 25-30	=	4:7-8, 2-4, 9-14
5:1-16, 17	=	5:15-30, 32b
6:2-3	=	5:31-32a

Similar shifts occur also in chaps. 6, 7, 10 and 11, while chaps. 20 and 21 are even completely switched around (cf. Swete, *Introd.* 232). In our commentary we follow the verse division of MT.

EXEGESIS

4:1 *So King Solomon became king over all Israel.*
In vss. 2-6, after in our verse it has been observed that Solomon had become king over all Israel, we first encounter a list of high officials (cf. also 2 Sam. 8:15-18; 20:23-26). In a number of MSS of LXX there is a deviant opinion concerning whether the first-mentioned מלך actually has to be read (so also Pesh.) and whether כל belongs before Israel. It deserves to be noted that in our verse 'Israel' is expressly mentioned while 'Judah' is not referred to at all. Our verse is a redactional introduction to the list which now follows (Thenius, Benzinger, Noth et al.).

4:2 *And these were his high officials: Azariah son of Zadok, priest;*
Although this list cannot be readily dated, the general view is that it stems from the royal chancellery in Jerusalem (so Noth et al.). If this view is correct, it has to stem from a somewhat later period in Solomon's reign and not from its earliest beginning, because mention is made at the very outset of a son of Zadok the priest. The latter, as we learned from the first 2 chapters, actively participated in Solomon's accession to the kingship and replaced Abiathar the priest (2:26f.).

The sentence begins with the statement that the now following persons were שרים in the king's service (for the description of the genitive, see Ewald §292b; Joüon §130e, et al.). The word שר, which we first encountered in our books in 1:19, occurs no less than 420x in OT, is related to the Akkad. word *šarru*, 'king,' 'ruler' (*AHw*, 1188) and also in Hebr. frequently denotes a high official. Begrich believes that at the end of David's reign this term began to replace the older term עבדים. According to him, this change effected an adaptation to the Egyptian terminology where *sr.w* also denotes 'high officials'[1]; cf., however, Mettinger, *Officials*, 3 with n. 10, and H. Niehr, *TWAT*, VII, 859.

By comparison with the 2 lists of David referred to in 2 Sam. 8 and 20, this list begins by mentioning the priest, though this addition is deliberately omitted in very important MSS of LXX (B and Luc. among them). From this version one gets the impression that this Azariah, of whom we do not know anything else, was a ספר, along with Elihoreph, Ahijah and Shisha mentioned in the following verse. But this is not likely, partly because the office of (high) priest, apart from vs. 4b (which we will discuss later), would not have been men-

---

[1] J. Begrich, "Sofer und Mazkir. Ein Beitrag zur inneren Geschichte des davidisch-salomonischen Großreiches und des Königreiches Juda," *ZAW* 58 (1940f.), 1-29 (= *Gesammelte Studien zum Alten Testament*, München 1964, 67-98), esp. 13f. (81f.).

tioned. With Benzinger et al. we stand by MT here (otherwise: Delitzsch, *LSF* §98d et al.) and share the opinion that the article before כהן denotes precisely the function which the head of the priests would later perform: the high priest. Later on this 'first priest' would sometimes be called כהן הראש (2 Kgs. 25:18 etc.) or הכהן הגדול (2 Kgs. 12:11 etc.; cf. Benzinger, *Arch.* 347f.; H.-P. Müller, *THAT*, II, 706; W. Dommershausen, *TWAT*, IV, 74ff.). The express mention of the high priest at the top of the list indicates that he was first of all an official of the king or, if you will, of the state.

In 1 Chr. 5:36 (6:10 RSV) we read that Azariah son of Amasiah son of Zadok was the (first) priest who functioned as high priest in the newly built temple of Solomon. It is in fact almost generally assumed (e.g. by Thenius; Burney; Rudolph) that 1 Chr. 5:36 should have been in the place of the preceding verse. If the shift of this original marginal gloss to vs. 35 is correct, then Azariah was not the son but the grandson of Zadok, and we can conclude that this list originated at the earliest in the second half of Solomon's reign.

4:3 *Elihoreph and Ahijah sons of Shisha, secretaries; Jehoshaphat son of Ahilud, herald;*
This verse, in all its simplicity, nevertheless still contains a number of text-critical problems relating especially to the names handed down. For example, the name אליחרף which occurs here is read in LXX^B as Ἐλιάφ and in LXX$^{Luc.}$ as Ἐλιάβ. J.A. Montgomery (*JBL* 49 [1930], 311-319; cf. his commentary) has proposed the reading עַל הַחֹרֶף '(appointed) over the year'. This would mean that the word relates to Azariah, mentioned in the previous verse, which according to LXX, is the true reading (hence omitting 'the priest') and the son of Zadok would be an 'eponym of the year.' This text modification, however, is as ingenious as it is improbable (similarly Noth). If we maintain 'Elihoreph' as the proper name of a person (about whom we know nothing else), the pl. 'sons' of MT need not be changed into the singular, even though in many of its MSS LXX has Ahijah as the only son of Shisha.

There is reason why the name Shisha is even more disputed, even aside from the – again deviant – orthographies in the recensions of LXX. In 1 Chr. 18:16 the reading is שַׁוְשָׁא; in 2 Sam. 8:17 – if at least we are dealing with the same person: שְׂרָיָה (LXX minus Luc.: Ἀσά) and in 2 Sam. 20:25: שִׁיא (k^etib) or שׁוא (q^ere; cf. LXX$^{Luc.}$: Σουσά and the targum editions). Accordingly, considering the possibilities of interchange between *yod* and *waw* in the ancient Hebr., the reading שׁושׁא is not impossible (so Burney et al.), but by no means certain (so Benzinger et al.). We think that – also as it concerns the other divergencies of the ancient versions from our MT – in our text we can continue to follow the latter integrally.

It follows from the above that Elihoreph and Ahijah, like their father, were 'secretaries' and Jehoshaphat (2 Sam. 8:16; 20:24) a מזכיר. The ספר is the royal secretary par excellence (see Begrich, a.l.; Mettinger, *Officials*, 42ff.; J. Kühlewein, *THAT*, II, 164; H. Niehr *TWAT*, V, 926f.). R. de Vaux, *RB* 48 (1939), 394-405, and Begrich have pointed out – and many more recent commentators follow them in this – that סופר has its Egyptian equivalent in the word *sš*, 'secretary' of the king, and מזכיר in the word *whm.w*, 'speaker' or also 'herald' (of the king; cf. also Ahlstrom, *Admin.* 28). The Egyptian secretary is not merely an archivist or recorder (of the minutes) but a secretary in charge of correspondence with foreign powers. The 'speaker,' furthermore, is the official who handles relations between the court and the people, the public-relations man who makes known the will and decisions of the king and at the same time furnishes information about and in matters of state. The מזכיר (aside from this instance, also in 2 Sam. 8:16 and 20:24; also in 2 Kgs. 18:18, 37 [par. Isa. 36:3, 22], 1 Chr. 18:15 and 2 Chr. 34:8) is described in LXX in this place as ὑπομιμνῄσκων, elsewhere with words of the same import. His function as 'herald' of the king is sometimes questioned, among others by H. Graf Reventlow, *ThZ* 15 (1959), 161-175, and *ZThK* 60 (1963), 300f., who views him rather as a more juridical functionary: a 'public prosecutor'; cf. מזכיר עון, G. von Rad, *TDNT*, II, 73f.[2] Still his function can be illustrated both from Egyptian and Mesopotamian (*nāgiru*) parallels (Mettinger, 57-60), so that the word 'herald' in our translation probably corresponds best to the Hebr. word. Further cf. Schottroff, op. cit., 253-260 (with litt.); 395; idem, *TWAT*, I, 508f.; H. Eising, *TWAT*, II, 584f.; J. Liver, *EncMiqr.* IV, 782f.). Since in the lists reported in 2 Samuel David already had these high functionaries, one can raise the question whether Egyptian or Mesopotamian models were used in the organization of the Judean-Israelite court under David and Solomon. A. Cody, *RB* 72 (1965), 381-393, holds the view that the 'strange' name שׁישׁא in our text and its varying orthography is an (early) attempt to reproduce the Egypt. title *sš š't*, 'composer of documents.' This title also occurs in the El-Amarna literature as *šaḫšiḫa* (*EA* 316, 16). If this parallelization is correct, there is not much to object to in the suspicion that the organization of the new state betrays an Egyptian origin (cf. R.J. Williams, SVT 28 [1975], 235f.; otherwise, É. Lipiński, *TRE*, III, 592). Even though one need not immediately think of the presence of Egyptian 'advisors' in the construction of the new state – the names of the persons are, generally speaking, too 'Hebrew' for that – nevertheless it is not too farfetched to believe that a king seeking to surpass the status of a ruler of a city state looked for models in the government of the great powers surrounding him. Nor is the only or even the primary motive a hankering for 'status,' but rather a matter of finding an answer to certain organiza-

---

[2] Cf. also W. Schottroff, *"Gedenken" im Alten Orient und Alten Testament* (WMANT 15), Neukirchen 1967², 262-270.

tional problems which a state with a rather heterogeneous population simply forced on him.

4:4 *Benaiah son of Jehoiada, commander of the army; [Zadok and Abiathar, priests];*
The first half of this verse is lacking in LXX^B. What is said in this verse can also be found in 2:35. In vs. 6, however, LXX^B does have: καὶ Ἐλιὰβ υἱὸς Σὰφ ἐπὶ τῆς πατριᾶς, where πατριᾶς is presumably an error for στρατιας (see Rahlfs, *SSt*. III, 201 n.). In LXX^B on 2:46h we read: καὶ Ἀβεὶ υἱὸς Ἰωὰβ ἀρχιστράτηγος. On this ground Noth, for example, assumes that in vs. 6 after Ahishar (who was set 'over the house') MT must have read: 'and Eliab son of Safath was appointed commander of the army,' while in our verse there is nothing like this. Another possibility – according to him – is that MT omitted precisely this passage in vs. 6, because vs. 4 already had some of this information. Along with Benzinger we believe that it is not easy to decide which text was the original and which was not. Precisely the statement in 2:35 argues for the originality of vs. 4a in our MT. On the other hand, the difficulty of finding an explanation for LXX^B 2:46h and 4:6 argues for a more original reading in the 'Vorlage' of LXX^B than we now possess in MT. Benzinger nevertheless has the scales tip in favour of MT, based on considerations concerning the antiquity of the list.

The second half of our verse – though text-critically not debatable – is materially not only a repetition of 2 Sam. 20:25 but also in conflict with 1 Kgs 2:27. Numerous commentators – rightly – view it as a late redactional addition or gloss (Stade-Schwally; Benzinger; Burney; Delitzsch, *LSF* §160b; Noth).

4:5 *Azariah son of Nathan, chief administrator; Zabud son of Nathan the priest, friend of the king;*
The list continues with the mention of עזריהו son of Nathan who was set over the נצבים. LXX here reads either Ὀρνειὰ or Ὀρνια. Some commentators relate this again to the LXX naming of Adonijah in chap. 1 (Benzinger; Burney et al.). There is no reason to depart from MT. Nathan may have been the well-known 'court prophet' of David and Solomon, though this cannot be proved. The word נצב also occurs in vs. 7; 5:7, 30; 9:23; 22:48 and 2 Chr. 8:10. The form is a part. niph. of the verb נצב and indicates that someone has been set over something or someone: 'viceroy' or 'governor' (cf. et al. Ges-B, *HAL*, s.v. נצב I, and now also J. Reindle, *TWAT*, V, 555-565, esp. 559: 'governor of a province'). This meaning sometimes also has the *qᵉtîl*-form of this root: נציב (cf. vs. 19; 2 Sam. 8:6, 14; see Ges-B, s.v.; and *HAL* which in a number of cases also considers possible the meaning 'poet' or 'garrison'). In some MSS, e.g. in vs. 7, this last form is sometimes interchanged with the first. Mettinger, 124, holds the view that the North Israelite equivalent of נצבים is the term

שרי המדינות (20:14-19; cf. further Mettinger, 111f.; Y. Aharoni, *EncMiqr.* V, 914ff.). In the present case the reference is to the head of the prefects of the 12 districts in which the land was divided in Solomon's time, a list of which follows in vss. 7-19.

Zabud, also a son of Nathan, is mentioned next, and that as 'friend of the king.' The name זבוד is passed on by some Hebr. MSS (Kennicott) as זכור; in LXX^{Luc.} as Ζαχουρ or Ζακχουρ; in Pesh.: *zbwr.* The qualification כהן is attributed to Nathan but in the most important MSS of LXX it is omitted (cf. also Barthélemy). It is not clear whether the 2 persons mentioned in our verse are both sons of the same Nathan or whether the word כהן is deliberately added to the second time Nathan occurs to distinguish him from the former. Nor is it likely that this second Nathan is a son of David (cf. 2 Sam. 5:14), although according to 2 Sam. 8:18 David's sons were 'priests.' It is also possible that כהן does not refer to Nathan but to Zahud who was priest friend of the king. Ewald, *GVI*, III, 366f., already pointed out that a king, besides having a chief priest, could also elect to have 'einen ihm besonders zusagenden Haus-Priester als seinem "Freund",' who assisted him as a sort of 'minister for spiritual affairs' (Montg.-Gehman refer to a 'court title'). Ewald expressly refers to our text. However this may be, there is little reason, along with Noth et al., to delete כהן in our verse.

There is mention of a רעה המלך exclusively in the time of David and Solomon (2 Sam. 15:37 [LXX also 15:32]; 16:16v.; 1 Chr. 27:33; cf. 2. Sam. 16:17). The form רעה in st. cstr. here and elsewhere is rather striking (cf. Böttcher §§459; 824; Olsh. §166b; Ewald §211e; Ges-K §93ll; Stade §205b; Bg. I §17I; Joüon §96Ce). LXX generally reproduces this title by ἑταῖρος τοῦ βασιλέως; 1 Chr. 27:33; however, by πρῶτος φίλος τοῦ βασιλέως, an honorific title in use at the court of the Ptolemaics (cf. W. Michaelis, *TDNT*, VII, 738 n. 10; for additional connections, also with NT: *TDNT*, II, 697f.; VI, 310ff.; IX, 151-156). The Hebr. title, also familiar from the El-Amarna letters (*EA* 228, 11; see Ahlström, *Admin.* 28) was held rather exclusively by just one person at a time. In view of the character of this list it must have designated an official function: a kind of councillor, perhaps later replaced by the term יועץ.[3] Perhaps this term too was taken from the Egyptian court where, inter alia, a *rh nsw.t*, 'a friend of the king' was known at the time of the Middle Kingdom (cf. H. Donner, *ZAW* 73 [1961], 272; A. van Selms, *JNES* 16 [1957], 118-132; Haran, *Temples*, 81 and n. 30). Elsewhere in the Near East there are indications for this function as well (Donner, 269-277; further R. de Vaux, *RB* 48 [1939], 403ff.; Penna; Mettinger, 63-69; R.J. Williams, SVT 28 [1975], 236).

---

[3] Otherwise: A. Penna, "Amico del Re," *Rivista Biblica* 14 (1966), 459-466, who questions whether this is an official title.

4:6 *Ahishar, master of the palace, and Adoniram son of Abda, in charge of forced labour.*

The name Ahishar is the only one in this list to appear without the name of his father (aside, that is, from the dubious vs. 4b). Instead of what we find in the first part of our verse, LXX^B reads: Καὶ ᾿Αχεὶ ἦν οἰκονόμος, καὶ ᾿Ελιὰβ υἱὸς Σὰφ ἐπὶ τῆς πατριᾶς. LXX$^{Luc.}$ has a different reading, in the first place, by reading Ahiel in place of Achei; further, by omitting what is said about Eliak; and by letting Eliab be a son of Joab who was επι της στρατ(ε)ιας (cf. the discussion in Barthélemy). The same phrase occurs also in LXX$^{Luc.}$ in 2:46h where LXX^B reads Abei (cf. also Rahlfs, *SSt.* III, 201). On the basis of this difference in reading in the recensions of LXX and further on the basis of mutual deviations in the different LXX MSS, the commentators are disposed to make various text emendations or additions bearing on the first half of our verse. Thenius – to mention a couple of examples – omits the statement that Eliak was 'master of the house' as a useless variant of LXX^B but considers the end which says that Eliab son of Saph had been appointed ἐπὶ τῆς πατριᾶς an indication that – on the basis of 1 Chr. 11:25, where LXX also uses πατριὰ – we must read משמעת. According to him, in MT a sentence like 'and Eliab son of Saph (or: Saphath) was over the bodyguard' probably fell out. This view is also held by a recent commentator like Noth who cites as one of the probable reasons for the omission in MT 'Rücksicht auf 4a.' But even before Thenius and Noth, Ewald (*GVI*, III, 369 n. 2) already referred to the probability of this addition in MT. Burney assumes that precisely the beginning of MT has been corrupted and, with the help of LXX-variants, reads: 'And Eliab son of Zer(iah) was appointed over the house.' Montg.-Gehman finally translate: 'And Ahiel was over the house,' without supplementing MT. The other ancient versions, except LXX, move along the same (last-mentioned) line. In view of the deviant division and the unexpected, long elaborations of LXX in the case of some MT texts, we are inclined to agree with Montg.-Gehman's statement that there is no reason 'to reconstruct H from the frail G' (p. 119).

The title (אשר) על הבית also occurs elsewhere in OT (16:9; 18:3; 2 Kgs. 18:18 etc.; 12x in all). It also occurs outside OT: an example is a tomb inscription in Silwan by Jerusalem (*KAI* 191, 1; Gibson, *TSSI*, I, 23f.), which indicates that a certain Sebaniah(?) held this title. The title also occurs on a seal found at Lachis and was held by a certain Gedahiah, probably the same person mentioned in 2 Kgs. 25:22ff., Jer. 40 and 41 (Gibson, *TSSI*, I, 62 [no. 18]). LXX often speaks about the οἰκονόμος (O. Michel, *TDNT*, V, 149f.) and in the supplement on 2:46 about 'him who was in charge of his house.' Mettinger, *Officials*, 70-79, who also gave a lot of attention to our title, has come to the conclusion that the function of the person permitted to hold this title was, or could be, both a kind of major domo and an administrator of the royal possessions. He points to the similarity of this function to that of the

Egyptian *mr pr wr* (so also Ahlström, *Admin.* 32) and not to the Akkad. title bearers *ša pān ekalli* (R. de Vaux, *RB* 45 [1936], 98f.; Montg.-Gehman) or *ša muḫḫi bīti* (S. Morenz, *ThLZ* 84 [1959], 412 n. 25b). These latter functions did not correspond to the Israelitisch (and Egyptian) ones (R.M. Good, *RB* 86 [1979], 580ff., however, refers also to a Ugar. parallel [*KTU* 4.755]).

Finally Adoniram son of Abda is mentioned as being in charge of forced labour. In 2 Sam. 20:24 this Adoniram is called Adoram but there it is most likely a variant of Adoniram, as in 1 Kgs. 12:18 (cf. 5:28 and 2 Chr. 10:18). The name of Adoniram's father is variously handed down in the LXX-tradition: Ephra (LXX^B), but also Edra (m), Esdram, Addo, Sabdo, etc. Combining the data about Adoniram, one could conclude that he already fulfilled this function under David and was still active after Solomon's death. He was in charge of the מס (Mettinger, 128-139), a term which occurs 5x in OT (2 Sam. 20:24; 1 Kgs. 5:28; 12:18; 2 Chr. 10:18; see S.J. North, *TWAT*, IV, 1006-1009). The word מס, moreover, occurs an additional 18x in OT, usually rendered in LXX (14x) by φόρος. The Hebr. word indeed has a forerunner in the Akkad. *massu*, but is of unknown origin there. On the Alalach tablets (so *AHw*, 619a) it means 'a labourer obligated to perform forced labour' (see Mettinger, 129ff.) and in Hebr. it is therefore something like 'mandatory' or 'forced labour'. J.A. Wainwright, *ET* 91 (1979f.), 137-140, takes the word to mean something like 'unskilled' labour; cf. also N. Avigad, *BetM* 27 (1981f.), IV, who mentions a scarab-shaped seal from the 7th century bearing the inscription אשר על מם; idem, *IEJ* 30 (1980), 170ff. It is significant that it is only said of Adoniram that he was in charge of these mandatory labour services and that in the days of Rehoboam he was murdered in Shechem. Neither his work nor he himself is likely to have left behind a positive memory among the common people. Mettinger thinks that this mandatory labour was of Canaanite origin (p. 139) and that also Adoniram and his father were of non-Israelite origin (p. 133). It seems to us hazardous to infer such conclusions solely from the names of the persons in question. But it can be said with some certainty that, in view of his long record of service, Adoniram must have been a good organizer. Though ironfisted, he was of value for the construction and glory of the new state and dynasty.

1 KINGS 4:7-19

4:7 *Solomon had twelve officials over all Israel who regularly supplied food for the king and his palace; each one had to make provision for one month of the year.*

8 *These are their names: Ben-Hur in the hill country of Ephraim;*

9 *Ben-Deker in Makaz, in Shaalbim, Beth-Shemesh, Elon, and Beth-Hanan;*

10 *Ben-Hesed in Arubboth; to him belonged Socoh and the whole region of Hepher;*

11 *Ben-Abinadab the entire Dor mountain ridge. Taphath, Solomon's daughter, was his wife.*

12 *Baana son of Ahilud (was in charge of) Taanach and Megiddo and (the whole region of) Beth-Shean[, which is next to Zarethan below Jezreel; and from Beth-Shean to Abel-Meholah to beyond Jokmeam].*

13 *Ben-Geber in Ramoth-Gilead; to him belonged the tent villages of Jair son of Manasseh which are in Gilead; to him belonged (also) the region of Argob which is in Bashan: sixty large cities, walled-in, and provided with bronze bars.*

14 *Ahinadab son of Iddo, over Mahanaim.*

15 *Ahimaaz over Naphtali. He too had married a daughter of Solomon, Basemath.*

16 *Baana son of Hushai, over Asher and Bealoth;*

17 *Jehoshaphat son of Paruah over Issachar;*

18 *Shimei son of Ela over Benjamin;*

19 *Jeber son of Uri over the region of Gilead, the territory of Sihon king of the Amorites and of king Og of Bashan. [There was also one garrison in the field(?)].*

INTRODUCTION

Now follows a second ancient list (vss. 8-19) which, as we shall see in some detail, probably stems from the last years of Solomon's reign and sums up the 12 districts with their administrators. Solomon divided his little kingdom in these districts for political and economic reasons. This division into districts or provinces coincides in part with what we know from other sources about the ancient tribes; partly, however, the boundaries of the provinces are different. A. Alt, *KS*, II, 76-89, believes that Solomon strictly maintained the ancient tribal boundaries wherever possible, so that people can attribute 'der ganze Gaueinteilung eher übertriebenen Konservatismus als übertriebene Neuerungssucht den

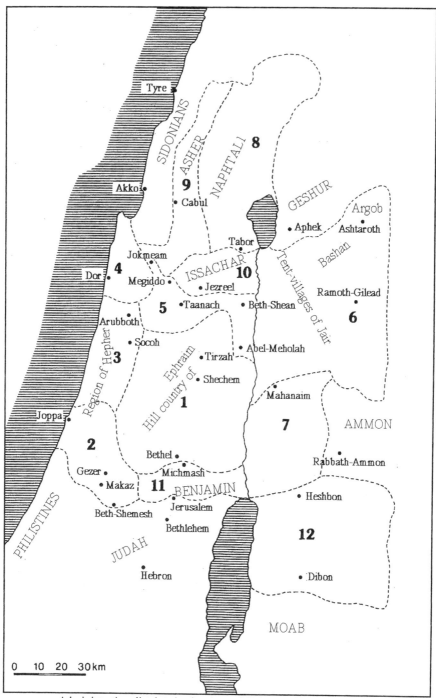

Administrative districts in the time of Solomon (1 Kings 4:8-19)

älteren Verhältnissen gegenüber' (p. 88). Wright on the other hand, argues against Alt 'that the rearrangement in Israel into provinces was a far more radical shift from the tribal system, and that the new provinces were fixed as administrative entities of approximately equal economic capacity'.[1] Alongside of these 2 main views there are others, of which we mention that of Pintore.[2] He does not think in this connection of a provincial system but of an organically shaped system for the collection of excise duties and taxes in the N part of Solomon's kingdom and of a kind of postal network for official trips. Still another view is that of Mettinger, *Officials*, 111-127, who especially stresses Solomon's political motives for this division into districts. Wherever Solomon could maintain the ancient tribal boundaries without risk to the unity of the new kingdom, he did so. But to maintain a firm grip on the growing political power of Ephraim and Manasseh (the 'house of Joseph') in the N, he divided that region in such a way that Ephraim's power bloc would be broken, for example by linking the Canaanite cities immediately to the court and not to the ancient tribal areas.[3]

EXEGESIS

4:7 *Solomon had twelve officials over all Israel who regularly supplied food for the king and his palace; each one had to make provision for one month of the year.*

Both in our verse and in the entire list the position of Judah is exceptional: its name is not mentioned. Several explanations have been given for the absence of this prominent partner in the 'united kingdom.' They come down to saying that either Judah as the 'ancestral land' of the offspring of David occupied a privileged position or its territory must have been hidden somewhere in this list. We will come back to this question. In any case it is clear that our verse speaks of 12 prefects over 'all Israel,' a formula which is identical with that in vs. 1 and can readily be viewed as an addition. Now it is a question whether our entire verse belonged to the original text of the list or was added to it as a later redactional statement. The form in which our verse and also vs. 8a has been cast departs appreciably from the following list and prompts the suspicion that in any case the list is older than its heading. The final redactor of our chapter possibly found the list and the heading in his archival records. For an

---

[1] G.E. Wright, "The Provinces of Solomon," *ErIs* 8 (1967), 58*-68*; esp. 59*.

[2] F. Pintore, "I dodici intendenti di Solomone (1 Re 4, 7-19)," *RSO* 45 (1970), 177-207.

[3] See now also V. Fritz, "Die Verwaltungsgebiete Salomos nach 1 Kön 4,7-19," *Meilenstein* (Fs H. Donner, ed. M. Weippert, S. Timm; Ägypten und Altes Testament 30), Wiesbaden 1995, 19-26.

answer to the question why then in our chapter a provincial division of 'all Israel' but not one of 'all Judah' is given, Noth et al. refer to Josh. 15:20-62. We do find one there, dating from the time after Solomon. Depending on the position one takes with regard to whether or not Judah can be found in vss. 8-19, one will have to decide whether or not the phrase 'in all Israel' came into our text as a gloss. Determining one's position in this matter is difficult in part because in different periods the word 'Israel' was variously conceived.

The pilpal-form of the verb כול (see *HAL*, s.v.): כלכל (see Bg. II §20c; Meyer §72.3), meaning 'to provide with food,' 'to provision,' occurs not only in our book (5:7; 17:4, 9; 18:4, 13), but also elsewhere in OT (see A. Baumann, *TWAT*, IV, 93f.). The pf. cons. after a nominal clause in the past (Joüon §119f) here has a frequentative or iterative character, brought out in our translation by the adverb 'regularly' (cf. Böttcher §981 and n. 3; König §367h; Driver §120; Ges-K §112l; Bg. II §9g). The statement implies that the heading only indicates the economic motives for the following division and remains silent about the political. Or does 'provisioning' imply something more than 'supplying food products'? Even the word 'food products' has to be broadly interpreted. The 'provisioning' of royal courts is also known from Israel's 'Umwelt' (cf. R.P. Dougherty, AASOR 5 [1925], 23-65). Of the areas mentioned not one could possibly have produced exactly the same products because each area is geologically and climatologically different and its products must therefore differ from the others as well. From our verse it is not clear what a given area had to produce and how the division among the provinces was arranged. The one thing that is clear is that there was an annual assessment for all 12 provinces: every month a different province. This division is based on a lunisolar system (Noth). The choice between אחד and האחד (cf. Böttcher §603) is a matter of $k^e tib$-$q^e re$. This is one of 13 cases in which the ה, though missing at the beginning of a word (cf. Weil, Mm no. 1856; Gordis, 147 [List 77]) is expected (Burney; otherwise: Stade-Schwally).

Although our verse (see on vs. 5 above) refers to נצבים, Josephus, who in contrast to the previous list did include the following one (*Ant.* VIII §§35ff.), describes these 'district administrators' as στρατηγοὶ καὶ ἡγεμόνες. He apparently suspects a political and especially a military motive behind Solomon's division into provinces, though he may also have in mind the הַשָּׂרִים of vs. 2a.

4:8 *These are their names: Ben-Hur in the hill country of Ephraim;*
One of the questions occurring in the case of several names in this list is that it only states that someone is called 'the son of Y' (see vss. 9a, 10a, 11a, 13a). It has often been assumed that a marginal strip containing the proper names had been lost from this list (so Böttcher, Thenius et al.). However, some time ago Alt, *KS*, III, 198-213, pointed out that it is evident from the El-Amarna letters

and material from Ugarit that, alongside of lists of people with proper names, people are also frequently simply described by their patronymics. According to him, these people were members of the subservient nobility who were only described by their family name. If this was a Canaanite practice, this would be very fitting in our list because in it also (formerly?) Canaanite areas are called provinces. Now it is difficult to document this conclusion, though as such it is quite attractive. However, the widespread view that in a number of cases the proper names have been lost as a result of damage to the list is at least debatable: (1) the LXX, for example, considering its reproduction of the names, offers no ground for this suspicion; (2) Alt's article has made clear that in Israel's 'Umwelt' the designation 'son of X' etc. was very common in archival lists; (3) it is striking that in vss. 12a, 14a, etc., the proper name has not dropped out or been omitted. Granted: here and there in the LXX-tradition it is precisely these names that are unclear, but that need not take us back to the widespread position that the list was damaged (as Noth thinks).

As with many other persons on this list, we have no further information on Ben-Hur. Elsewhere the OT does indeed mention names of people who were 'sons' of Hur, among them the well-known Bezalel son of Uri son of Hur (Exod. 31:2; 35:30 etc.), also Rephaiah son of Hur, a rebuilder of Jerusalem's walls in the days of Nehemiah (Neh. 3:9). LXX^B and $^{Luc.}$ render the name as Βαιώρ and Josephus as Οὔρης. Only LXX^A has Βὲν υἱὸς Ὤρ (cf. Vulg. *Benhur*).

The area over which someone is prefect is preceded by the preposition ב, except in vss. 11, 12, 14. In our verse this is 'the hill country of Ephraim,' which naturally is not the same as 'the tribe of Ephraim' (so also Wright, 60*f.; Mettinger, 113; Noth; et al.). It is certainly generally admitted that the reference is to the area which primarily encompasses Ephraim and is defined to the W by the area which covers district III (vs. 10; cf. Y. Aharoni, *Tel Aviv* 3 [1976], 6; see the map above; cf. also the maps in Aharoni, 8f., and Wright, 60*). It is also evident from Josh. 17:14ff. that the tribes of Ephraim and Manasseh inhabit 'the hill country of Ephraim.' Even in antiquity this area was very fertile. G.B. Winer, *BRW*, I, 333, already asserted that this mountainous region belonged in antiquity 'zu den cultivirtesten Districten Palästinas' and added: 'wie denn auch noch jetzt der Ertrag des Bodens bedeutend ist.' The reason for or the principle behind the order of the districts as we now find them in our list is not altogether clear. Thenius suspects it is the order in which the officials must provide for the royal table. Perhaps it was in fact the economic aspects which determined the order.

Striking, further, is that after our verse as well as after vss. 9, 11-13, 15f. LXX puts the numeral 'one.' This practice is also familiar from MT (Josh. 12:9-24; Ezek. 48:23-27) and is subjected by Rahlfs, *SSt*. III, 235-239, to an extensive discussion. The numerous variants in LXX have even prompted

Rahlfs to make precisely this part in Kings 'eine Probe eines textkritischen Kommentars' (see 224-239, esp. 225), as it should actually be done for the whole LXX.

4:9 *Ben-Deker in Makaz, in Shaalbim, Beth-Shemesh, Elon, and Beth-Hanan;* In contrast to the previous verse this verse and the following verses mention a number of areas for which the prefect was responsible – naturally with the adjacent areas. According to Alt, *KS*, II, 86, the reference is to former Canaanite city states 'deren politische Unterordnung erst kürzlich stattgefunden hat.' The prefect of district II is called Ben-Deker – an unknown person – rendered in LXX[B] as υἱὸς 'Ρῆχας, in LXX[Luc.] as 'Ρηχαβ. Before the place names Makaz and Shaalbim the preposition ב is used. This has led Wright, 58*, n. 5, to assume that the following place names are additions to the first two. As far as these place names are concerned, there is no unanimity in the tradition, especially in that of LXX. LXX[B] has Μαχεμὰς, which is reminiscent of Michmas (cf. 1 Sam. 13:2, 5; 14:31), but this cannot be correct because the latter is situated only a few km to the NE of Jerusalem, and because this town has to be much farther to the W, in the ancient tribal territory of Dan. Βηθαλαμεὶ is the rendering of Shaalbim, also mentioned in Judg. 1:35 and as Shaalabin in Josh 19:42 (the 'inheritance of Dan'). Βαιθσάσμυς is Beth-Shemesh named Ir-Shemesh in Josh. 19:41, a border city (Josh. 15:10), today called *Tell Rumeileh* (Simons, *GTTOT* §336.3; cf. also Y. Tsafrir, *ErIs* 12 [1975], 44f.). Ἐλὼμ, though a correct rendering of MT אילון, is often read as Aijalon, amongst others on the basis of LXX[A] and because the town is said to be closer to the preceding one (Stade-Schwally, Wright, Mettinger, Noth et al.; cf. also Barthélemy). But it is evident from Josh. 19:43 that there must also have been an Elon in Dan (cf. B. Maisler, *EncMiqr*. I, 266f.), so that there is no immediate need for emendation of the text (cf. also Aharoni [6f.], who raises the possibility that the reference is to Elon of the family of Hanon). In place of Elon Beth-Lanan (asyndetically connected in MT), LXX reads: Ἐλὼμ ἕως Βαιθλαμάν, a reading which some commentators take over via an inserted עד in MT (Stade-Schwally; Burney; cf. Simons, *GTTOT* §874.I.5). It is a question where precisely Beth-Hanan is to be located (cf. Simons, a.l., Abel, *GP*, II, 81). Noth in any case views the location proposed by Abel (ביתענו) – approximately 9 km to the E of *Jalo* – as highly uncertain. Josephus mentions Diokleros as prefect of district II and as the only town he refers to Bithiemes, a variant of Bethlehem. It seems to us best to maintain MT both in spelling and in syntactical construction. In this connection we would (in contrast to Aharoni) resolve the asyndeton between Elon and Beth-Hanan by putting 'and' in the translation.

Along with Noth, Wright, Aharoni, et al. we would look for district II in the ancient tribal territory of Dan (viewed in light of Judg. 1:29, 34f.), whose border runs from the seacoast around Jafo in a SE direction, enclosing a part of the W hill country.

4:10 *Ben-Hesed in Arubboth; to him belonged Socoh and the whole region of Hepher;*
The district of which Ben-Hesed was prefect, is the subject of much discussion among scholars. Alt has succeeded in *not* identifying the Socoh mentioned in our verse with similarly-named towns in the Judean tribal territory (Josh. 15:35, 48 etc.), but with *ḥirbet Šuweikat Errās,* approximately 3 km NW of *Ṭūl Karm,* situated today at about one-third of the distance of the road which runs from the well-known coastal town Nataniah to the central Palestinian town of Nablus (in ancient times: Shechem; cf. Alt, *KS,* II, 77ff.; Mettinger, 113f.; Noth, Aharoni etc.). This identification has been generally accepted so that district III can be geographically located with a degree of certainty. It naturally remains uncertain precisely what the boundaries of the district looked like. This is best made clear by comparing the maps in the articles of Wright and Aharoni. This is connected with the location of the other town mentioned in our verse: Arubboth and 'all the land of Hepher.' Arubboth – in light of the redaction of our verse – would seem to have been the main town of the district. Wright (p. 63*) – following W.F. Albright, *JPOS* 5 (1925), 28 – links the name with present-day *'arrābeh,* approx. 17 km ENE of the Socoh mentioned earlier. This suggestion has been taken over, et al., by Mettinger (p. 114). Alt (*KS,* II, 81) initially did not know where to locate the town but later proposed *Tell el-Asāwir* as a possible site (*Palästinajahrbuch* 28 [1932], 31ff., a view also adopted by Noth). This last-mentioned town is situated about 10 km ESE of Caesarea-by-the-Sea and is therefore much closer to the coast than *'arrābeh.* A. Zertal (*Qad* 14 [1981], 112-118) considers identification with *ḥirbet el-Ḥammam* (Narbata) a possibility. A decision in this matter is difficult, though archeological investigations do not point clearly in the direction of *Tell al-Asāwir.* Mettinger, 114 and n. 20, situates the third district N of Manasseh, bounded to the NW by district IV, to the S by district I (cf. also Lemaire, 62). Even more difficult is the identification of 'all the land of Hepher.' Some scholars think of *Tell Ibšār (el-Afšār)* in the curve of the *Nahr Iskanderūneh* in the coastal plain, not far from the Mediterranean seacoast (so Simons, *GTTOT* §§510.18; 874.III,3; Noth). Wright (p. 63*), relying on the observations of Albright, F.M. Cross, *BASOR* 163 (1961), 12-14, Lemaire, 287ff. et al., occasioned by Samaritan ostraca, looks for the land of Hepher in the W tribal territory of Manassah N of Nablus (cf. Num. 26:33; 27:1; Josh. 17:3). But Aharoni, 5f., has pointed out the speculative nature of the proposed location. Along with Alt, Aharoni, et al. we believe that also the 'land of Hepher' must be sought in the coastal plain and that therefore the third district probably covered the coastal plain between present-day Tel Aviv and the area S of Mt.

Carmel: the plain of Sharon. Wright advances as his objection to this relatively narrow coastal strip considered as a separate district that in antiquity it could not possibly have been able to produce the things needed to maintain the life of the court for a month. It is only in the recent past, after all, that this plain, especially the part which used to consist of swamps and woods, has been made ready for construction by colonists. Mettinger, 116f., has correctly pointed out that this argument is unconvincing because (1) it has not been proved that, economically speaking, goods and taxes did not have to be furnished proportionally by the districts and (2) that also in antiquity a number of important towns were situated between the coastal strip and the hill country, a fact reported also in extrabiblical sources (cf. the list of cities compiled by Thutmose III, *ANET*, 242f.). Moreover, in the Phoenician Esmun'azar-inscription on a sarcophagus there is reference to 'Dor and Jaffa, splendid grain fields' or 'lands of Dagan' (*KAI* 14, 19). This is precisely the area in which our district must have been located. A part of the population of this district, finally, may have lived from the fishing industry. Aside from these considerations – as we again readily grant Mettinger – also political motives played a role in the division into districts.

In LXX, as it concerns B and Luc., our verse shows strongly divergent readings which Rahlfs, *SSt*. III, 227ff., has subjected to lengthy analysis. He rightly comments that in the words Βηρνεμαλουσαμηνχὰ καὶ ʿΡησφαραχεὶν we are not dealing with a translation but a transcription 'wie wir sie in der LXX öfter finden, wo die Übersetzer mit dem hebräischen Texte nichts anzufangen wußten' (p. 228; cf. also the Hebr. translation in Burney). In any case one is bound to fail in attempting to shed more light on a vague text (MT) with the aid of an unclear text (LXX). Josephus completely skipped our verse.

4:11 *Ben-Abinadab the entire Dor mountain ridge. Taphath, Solomon's daughter, was his wife.*
District IV is less troublesome to the interpreters. Ben-Abinadab was responsible for כל־נפת דאר. We only hear of Ben-Abinadab in this verse. He was Solomon's son-in-law, being married to his daughter Taphath. Also in vs. 15 a daughter of Solomon who was married to a prefect is mentioned by name: Basemath. Both names have a fem. ending, as do other women's names in OT (cf. Gen. 26:34; 28:9; 2 Chr. 11:18, etc.). Burney has pointed out that many of these names were non-Israelite. One encounters these *ath*-endings especially in Phoenician and Aramaic inscriptions, so that Burney suspects that both women were daughters of Solomon's Canaanite spouses. This is possible, of course, but hard to prove on the basis of the names alone (cf. Noth, *IPN*, 226). We can agree with Noth that here and in vs. 15 the additions in the list have a strange 'feel'. For example, a verb with a personal form is used, though the list itself contains only names and substantive clauses. On the other hand, the mention of

these women by name does point to a certain authenticity, so that the details here and in vs. 15 may stem from around the time of Solomon. The special mention of Solomon's daughters may be indicative of the great value the king – for political reasons – attached to a sound administration of this seaport area. But what the redactor, writing a couple of centuries later, had in mind when he so conspicuously recorded these particulars, is a question.

Dor is generally identified with *El-Burğ*, some distance to the N of Ṭanṭūrah, on the coast of the Mediterranean Sea W of the Carmel mountain range (cf. Simons, *GTTOT* §510.29). The city is mentioned in OT (Judg. 1:27; Josh. 12:23; 17:11; cf. 1 Chr. 7:29) as well as in extrabiblical sources. An example is the well-known story of the so-called Wen-Amon journey from the 11th century BCE in which Dor is called a town of Tjeker, one of the 'Sea Peoples' (*ANET*, 26, n. 5; cf. further *GLAJJ*, III, 11f.). According to M. Ben-Dov, *Tel Aviv* 3 (1976), 70-73, precisely the word נפה, which in our verse and also in Josh. 12:23 (in Josh. 11:2: נפות דאר) is linked with Dor, has to do with those 'Sea Peoples.' It is said to be a geographical term used by the Sea Peoples to mean a 'wooded area.' The Sem. equivalent is the word Sharon, which in OT is especially a designation for the coastal plain between Haifa and Caesarea but is in more ancient times probably applied to a much larger area. The older interpretation of נפה is usually 'mountain range' (so e.g. *KBL*; cf. *HAL*); 'hilly area' (Simons et al.) or 'height' (Noth). D.W. Thomas (*PEQ* 67 [1935], 89f.) translates Nephat Dor by 'height of encircling,' a sanctuary on a hill where ritual dances were performed around an altar or a holy object. Although there is no proof for this ingenious translation, it is nevertheless remarkable that from the Maccabean period a priestly seal of a priest from Dor has surfaced that was inscribed on both sides: (a) *lsdq bn mk'*; (b) *lzkryw khn d'r* (N. Avigad, *Qad* 8 [1975], 118f.). Ben-Dov's view is attractive because we know from antiquity that the area around Dor must have been heavily wooded. Accordingly, the district נפת דאר covers the Sharon area, Dor being the main city.

For LXX and its variants we again refer the reader to Rahlfs. LXX^B includes the beginning of our verse in the previous one. All traditions of LXX are clear on the point that they speak of Solomon's daughter as of the wife of the prefect. Josephus says that Dor and the coast (τὴν παραλίαν) were under Abinadab, while he omits reference to the name of Solomon's daughter.

4:12 *Baana son of Ahilud (was in charge of) Taanach and Megiddo and (the whole region of) Beth-Shean[, which is next to Zarethan below Jezreel; and from Beth-Shean to Abel-Meholah to beyond Jokmeam].*

The fifth district is not hard to localize either, because place names occur in it which are known also from other OT passages as well as from extrabiblical literature. Again the MT of our verse, however, prompts many exegetes – with good reason – to propose textual modifications and transpositions.

For the first time this list does not confine itself to just naming the patronymics but offers also a proper name: Baana. Although this name also occurs in vs. 16 and elsewhere in OT (2 Sam. 4:2-9; 23:29; 1 Chr. 11:30; Ezra 2:2 etc.) we know nothing about this man nor about his father who is mentioned already in vs. 3. We do not know if this Ahilud is in fact the same person and whether therefore Jehoshaphat and Baana were brothers. Noth, *IPN*, 40, and Montg.-Gehman suspect that the name Baana was a hypocorism, the first element of which was בעל. LXX – in its various recensions – has deviant readings of this name and of the other names, for which we refer the reader to Rahlfs, *SSt.* III, 229-232.

Taanach and Megiddo are cities which already occur together in the song of Deborah (Judg. 5:19). Taanach (*Tell Ta'annek*) and Megiddo (*Tell el-Mutesellim*), which lies about 8 km to the NW, are situated on the SW side of the 'Plain of Jezreel' or the 'Great Plain of Esdrelson,' while Beth-Shean (*Tell el-Ḥoṣn*) is on the E side of it, immediately NW of *Beisan* not far from the Jordan (cf. et al. Simons, *GTTOT* §874 and Map IIa). Jezreel itself lies between the 2 cities (*Zirʿīn*) while Jokmeam (*Tell Qaimūn*), which is also mentioned in our verse, is located on the SE side of the Carmel mountain range, some 20 km SE of the port city Haifa. The somewhat less well-known places Zarethan and Abel-Meholah occur in our verse as well. The first-mentioned town (here furnished with the so-called ה locale, though preceded by a preposition; see Ewald §216b; Ges-K §90i). also occurs in 7:46 and in Josh. 3:16 (cf. Judg. 7:22b and 2 Chr. 4:17). According to Josh. 3:16, this town was located near Adam not far from the Jordan and also 1 Kgs 7:46 suggests that the town lay in the Jordan area. Simons (*GTTOT* §565f.), accordingly, suspects that the reference is to *Qarn Sarṭabeh* in the plain of the Jordan about 20 km SW of present-day Nablus (cf. Abel, *GP*, II, 450f.), but the exact determination of the location is difficult. N. Glueck (AASOR, XXV-XXVIII [1951], 334-347), for example, identifies the town with present-day *Tell es-Saʿīdiyeh,* about 18 km N of Adam E of the Jordan, approx. 15 km S of *Tell Abu Ḥaraz* and approximately 10 km SE of *Tell Abu Sifri.* These are 2 tells which, being a hill of ruins, have been held to be Abel-Meholah (see Noth et al.). The last-mentioned town also occurs in Judg. 7:22 and 1 Kgs. 19:16 (birthplace of Elisha) but archaeologically the site of the city is hard to determine (cf. Simons, *GTTOT* §567f.; Noth; Wright, p. 59*, n. 7 et al. Aharoni (pp. 10f.), however, considers the identification of Abel-Meholah with *Tell Abū Ṣūs*, 15 km S of Beth-Shean, as rather certain. He and some others regard Jokmeam as one of the Levitical cities mentioned in 1 Chr. 6:53 (RSV 6:68), tentatively linking it with *Tell el Mazār* some km to the N of the abovementioned *Qarn Sartabeh,* hence in a totally different area than the Jokmeam mentioned in our verse. The Jokmeam of our verse (cf. 1 Chr. 6:53), as suggested above, is usually identified with the Jokmeam of Josh. 12:22; 19:11; 21:34. This last-mentioned town, as described in Joshua, is situated in the border area of the tribe of Zebulun by the Carmel mountain range and is known also from extrabiblical sources (e.g. as *'nqn'm*, a city occurring as 113th on the list of cities conquered by Thutmose III; cf. G.W. Van Beek, *IDB*, II, 963). Also Taanach (Josh. 12:21; 17:11; 21:25; Judg. 1:27; 5:19; 1 Chr. 7:29) and Megiddo (Josh. 12:21; 17:11; Judg. 1:27; 5:19; 1 Kgs. 9:15; 2 Kgs. 9:27; 23:29f.; Zech. 12:11; 1 Chr. 7:29; 2 Chr. 35:22) are mentioned there and elsewhere. The difficulty arises particularly in the question where – on account of the references to a number of hard-to-identify places – the borders of the area actually ran. Some, Noth and Wright among them, do not consider it problematic to assume that the boundaries of this district also crossed over the Jordan. It is after all only in wartime that the Jordan is a 'trennende Grenze' (Noth). Others, Aharoni among them, consider such a border-crossing over the Jordan less likely. He locates Jokmeam on the W bank of the Jordan in the neighbourhood of *Wādi Far'ah*. He does modify the text with reference to Jezreel: 'And all of Beth-Shean below Jezreel,' in which case Jezreel itself need not be included in the fifth district but in the tenth. He then continues: 'and from Beth-Shean to Abel-Meholah to beyond (*'d my'br*),' to which he adds: 'which is beside Zarethan.' Similar transpositions are found also in other exegetes (see e.g. the conjectures in *BHK* and *BHS*). We agree with Noth that the actual nucleus of our text consists in the statement that 'Taanach, Megiddo and all of Beth-Shean' belonged to Baana. The material which follows are early or late secondary 'marginal notes' which have gradually crept into the text, and perhaps not always at the proper place (see also Stade-Schwally). W.F. Albright, *JPOS* 5 (1925), 26, has proposed the reading: 'Taanach and Megiddo to beyond Jokmeam and all of Beth-Shean below Jezreel from Beth-Shean to Abel-Meholah close to Zarethan,' but this transposition, too, remains uncertain (cf. Gray, 134).

Josephus in his account of this passage tells us that the 'great Plain' was under the supervision of Benaiah, προσεπῆρχε δὲ καὶ τῆς ἄχρι Ἰορδάνου πάσης, 'being governor over the entire area as far as the Jordan.' Though this comment reduces the difficulties of MT to a minimum, it does offer an approximate determination of the boundaries of the district.

Beth-Shean, spelled both as בית שן (1 Sam. 31:10, 12; 2 Sam. 21:12) and as בית שאן (Josh. 17:11, 16; Judg. 1:27; 1 Chr. 7:29), is the later Scythopolis. Not only is it mentioned frequently in extrabiblical sources but it is also known as a result of archaeological investigations which have clearly demonstrated the presence of Egyptian influence in the city (see R.W. Hamilton, *IDB*, I, 397-401; M.W. Prausnitz, *IDBS*, 97f.). Jezreel, which repeatedly occurs in OT, particularly in Kings (18:45f.; 21:1, 23, etc.), was in antiquity a strategically located city in the plain named after it, in which the road from E to W and N to S intersected (G.W. Van Beek, *IDB*, II, 906f.). With Burney, Aharoni, et al., the expression עד מעבר ל is to be understood to mean 'as far as the other side of,' i.e. viewed from the point of view of the speaker or writer.

4:13 *Ben-Geber in Ramoth-Gilead; to him belonged the tent villages of Jair son of Manasseh which are in Gilead; to him belonged (also) the region of Argob which is in Bashan: sixty large cities, walled-in, and provided with bronze bars.*

With Ben-Geber at the head of district VI we come into the region across the Jordan. Nothing is known to us about this prefect. The name Geber occurs also in vs. 19. Ramoth in Gilead occurs with relative frequency in OT. The orthography is somewhat uncertain: ראמות/ראמת/רמת/הרמה/רמ(ו)ת גלעד (Deut. 4:43; Josh. 20:8; 21:38; 1 Kgs. 22:3-29; 2 Kgs. 8:28f.; 9:1, 4, 14, etc.). In place of רמות LXX – as here – reads רמת, hence a sing. form. Here as well as elsewhere 'Gilead' is added to the name to distinguish the city from Rama at the right side of the Jordan. Along with Glueck, Noth and other scholars look for this Ramoth at *Tell Ramīt,* about 7 km S of the village *Remteh* at the Jordan-Syrian border (Simons, *GTTOT* §337.45). The city was one of the 3 so-called 'cities of refuge' on the E side of the Jordan (cf. S. Cohen, *IDB*, IV, 10; H.M. Jamieson, *IDBS*, 726). Generally speaking, in OT Gilead is a geographical name, the precise location of which cannot be determined because it can serve as designation for a city, a tribe, as well as a region. In the broadest sense, it was practically the entire area across the Jordan to which Israel thought it could rightfully lay claim. Especially the N part of this area, in which Ramoth must have been located, had a permanent settlement from the 23rd century BCE on. The Bashan mountain range is known for its fertility (cf. S. Cohen, *IDB*, II, 397f.; Simons, *GTTOT* §93). Gilead as 'tribe' is sometimes the same as 'Gad' (cf. Judg. 5:17), at other times it embraces more than a tribe.

Two clauses beginning with לו ('he was in charge of') are added to the name of the city and the district. The first clause is lacking in the LXX tradition. But it is not certain this is an indication that MT should be emended. In the first clause there is reference to חות יאיר. The question is whether this is a place name or whether it is better to reproduce them as we have done in our translation. Num. 32:41 and Deut. 3:14 are an indication that we may view the word חוה (with *HAL* et al.) as 'tent-village,' 'a host of tents' (cf. H. Bauer, *ZDMG* 71 [1917], 413). For the meaning of this word Arab. (cf. also Pedersen, I-II, 50, n. 1) and Ugar. parallels are adduced, though not everyone is in agreement (cf. *AHw*, 339b, s.v. *hēja,* 'Wachtturm'?; also Noth, 57). Jair is called the son of Manasseh, who occupied the tent-villages in Gilead in the region of Argob (Num. 32:41; Deut. 3:14; Josh. 13:30; cf. 1 Chr. 2:22; his father is called Segub – a descendant of Judah – and his grandmother a daughter of Machir, the father of Gilead). His name is also used as eponym or gentilic in 2 Sam.

daughter of Machir, the father of Gilead). His name is also used as eponym or gentilic in 2 Sam. 20:26. One gets a strong impression that in the name Jair we are dealing with the designation of a separate tribe or clan which is later joined to that of Manasseh. In 2 Kgs. 15:25, we are told, the term 'tent-villages of Jair' fits better in MT than what we read there now (see there). In any case, we are looking at a fairly large area in which as many as 60 tent-villages once flourished (cf. Deut. 3:4). Furthermore, the name Jair is probably related to the judge by that name (Judg. 10:3, 5) who had 30 sons, who in turn possessed 30 villages, also called the 'tent-villages of Jair.' About these striking villages (perhaps organized for defense?) there was an ancient tradition which is reflected in the present name. This latter point prompts the idea that our supplementary sentence may be a secondary addition by a (later) reader or glossator. The localization of these villages is the area S of the Yarmuk, the *'Aǧlūn* (B. Mazar, *EncMiqr.* III, 66f.; Abel, *GP*, II, 71).

The second nominal clause tells us that the prefect of this district also had charge of the חבל Argob. The first word is frequently used in OT in the sense of 'rope,' 'snare,' 'tape' but in Zeph. 2:5f. and in combination with Argob (Deut. 3:4, 13f.) the meaning must be something like 'region,' 'strip of land' or perhaps 'a piece of land measured off with a surveyor's tape' (Noth; cf. the comparison with the Ugar. *Yrgb*: M.C. Astour, *RSP*, II, viii 48, 291f.). According to Simons (*GTTOT* §21), the region of Argob covers practically the whole S part of Bashan from the E rim of *El-Leǧa* to approximately the *Nahr er-Ruqqād* (cf. map Vbis in his work). This is roughly an area which begins E of the Golan heights – E of the lake of Gennesareth – and ends before the W spurs of the *Haurān*-mountain range, the present border area between Jordania and Syria. But we do not have absolute certainty (cf. also S.E. Loewenstamm, *EncMiqr.* I, 528). Tg. terms this area טרכונא פלך, the 'district of Trachonitis' (cf. Luke 3:1). In later times the W border region of this landscape was called Gaulanitis, a mountain plateau immediately E of the Jordan. Now Josephus calls precisely this last area a part of district VI together with all 'Galaditis,' that is, the entire territory in which the Gileadites lived 'up to the Lebanon.' One gets the strong impression that both Tg. and Josephus, in localizing the region of Argob, went by what they in their day saw as the roughly corresponding territory, without having a sharply delineated sense of the geography of the Solomonic district. LXX reads σχοίνισμα Ἐρεταβάμ, an area of land measured with a σχοῖνος, 'a line' or 'tape.' The word σχοίνισμα only occurs in LXX.

Our MT localizes Argob in Bashan. For the time of OT, this area also is hard to describe with precision. Sometimes one gets the impression it has to do with the fruitful, stone-free plain (Arab. *batanat*), then again that also a part of the former kingdom of Og is included in this word. Generally speaking, one can say that the area is bounded by Mt. Hermon in the N, the *ǧebel Druz* or

Haurān in the E, the hills of the lake of Gennesaret in the W, and (approximately) the course of the Yarmuk river in the S. Parts of this area, therefore, must have been called the 'tent-villages of Jair' and the 'region of Argob,' if the 2 nominal additions in our verse in fact refer to 2 different regions and are not totally or partly identical (cf. Josh. 13:30!). Generally, this area is the fertile, sometimes even very fertile, highland of volcanic origin, and on the average between 500 and 800 m above sea level (Simons, *GTTOT* §33).

The addition which refers to 60 strong walled-in cities equipped with bronze bars (for these appositional combinations, cf. Driver §28, rem. 4; König §380c; Ges-K §128c; Joüon §131m) seems to have been borrowed from Deut. 3:4f.; 13f. and is therefore redactional (Benzinger; Stade-Schwally). In Deut. 3 one finds a 'dtr.' redaction of the story of the victory over Og, king of Bashan (cf. Num. 21:23ff., etc.). This story is then linked, associatively, by the redactor to Bashan (see also Noth).

4:14 *Ahinadab son of Iddo, over Mahanaim.*
In this verse, as in vs. 12, an ה locale is used after the place name Mahanaim. According to Ges-K §90d, this ה locale also occurs 'in etwas abgeschwächter Bedeutung,' 'um einen Ort zu bezeichnen wo sich etwas befindet oder geschieht' (cf. also König §330g). Ahinidab son of Iddo, the prefect of district VII, had his administrative territory and presumably his post in Mahanaim, a city in Gilead in the territory of the tribe of Gad, not far from the tribe of Manasseh. The name of this city (meaning 'double camp') occurs, aside from the texts (Josh. 13:26, 30; 21:38) describing the division of the land, also in other narratives, such as that of the patriarch Jacob (Gen. 32:3; 2 Sam. 2:8, 12, 29; 17:24, 27; 19:33; 1 Chr. 6:65). We already encountered the name above (2:8) and noted there that some scholars (Simons, Noth, De Vaux) identify the location of the ancient city in *Tell Ḥeǧǧāǧ* (cf. Aharoni). It is not hard to localize the 7th district in the central part of the country E of the Jordan. According to the tradition, Mahanaim was the temporary capital of Israel in the days of Esbaal, Saul's son, and at the time of David's flight from Absalom. The N boundary of this district must have coincided more or less with the river Jabbok, while the S boundary was dependent on the – still to be discussed – district XII. In conclusion, let it be said that Josephus combines this and the following district into a single district.

4:15 *Ahimaaz over Naphtali. He too had married a daughter of Solomon, Basemath.*
In our comments on vs. 11 we already noted that Ahimaaz was Solomon's son-in-law. That he was the son of Zadok, though it is not stated here, is in fact assumed. Ahimaaz son of Zadok, as David's friend, rendered services to David (2 Sam. 15:27, 36; 17:17, 20; 18:19, 22f., 28f., 1 Chr. 5:34f.; 6:38). He cannot

that, in contrast to the other names in this list, there is no בן connected with this name. This has prompted the suspicion that also before this name still another name plus 'son of' has dropped out, so that the governor would have been the son of Ahimaaz who, in turn, would have been a son of Zadok (cf. also E.R. Dalglish, *IDB*, 1, 69). However, we cannot do more than cite 'suspicions.'

In our verse as well as in the following, ancient tribal names are used to describe a district. Naphtali covers the territory of E Galilee from Mt. Tabor and the Plain of Jezreel in the S to Coele-Syria or the Litani river in the N. The Jordan along with the lake of Gennesaret presumably was the boundary to the E and in the W district IX (cf. also K. Elliger, *IDB*, III, 508f.; 4, 706f. and Z. Kallai, *IDBS*, 920ff.). Josephus extends Naphtali's borders to Sidon (cf. also Josh. 19:32-39).

4:16 *Baana son of Hushai, over Asher and Bealoth;*
The following tribe mentioned as the 'prefecture' of Baana, son of Hushai, is Asher. Of the prefect nothing more can be said and of district IX only that it must have been located W of Naphtali (again see Josh. 19:24-31). The W boundary was washed – in small part – by the Mediterranean Sea, in so far as the coastal region N of the Carmel mountain range was not the territory of the Tyrians and Sidonians. K. Elliger (*IDB*, IV, 707) suspects that Asher's dreams hardly went farther N past *Ras en-Nāqūra*, the present boundary at the coast between Israel and Lebanon. In 1 Kgs. 9:12f., we are told that, in exchange for help in his building activities from Hiram of Tyre, Solomon had given the land of Cabul. Presumably also this area, situated in the neighbourhood of Acco, was no longer a part of district IX (see below by these verses). This area, therefore, cannot have been very large. However, aside form Asher there is also mention of בעלות. This name is a problem (see e.g., Stade-Schwally), because it cannot of course be a reference to Bealoth in Judah (Josh. 15:24). On the basis of the reading 'Maala' in the LXX, scholars (e.g. Thenius and Kittel) have sometimes thought of מעלות (the reading of LXX^A!), the 'steps,' the so-called κλίμαξ Τύρου/Τυρίων (cf. 1 Macc. 11:59; Josephus, *Ant.* XIII, 146), the 'ladder of Tyre,' the coastal strip between Tyre and Acco-Ptolemais which is transected and divided by mountain spurs (e.g. *Ras en-Nāqūra;* cf. also H. Guthe, *RE*, XIV, 558, and Simons, *GTTOT* §1178). But this is not very likely either if a part of this territory had been given by Solomon to Hiram, as we noted above. Even if one takes the ב before עלות as a prep. (cf. Noth) – apart from the fact that the prop. בְּ before ב often coincides in Hebr. – that is no help at all in localizing Aloth, if such a city ever existed. In any case, Vulg. and Pesh. (except MS 7a1) do read Baalot (cf. Tg.).

Still remaining is a suggestion from Alt (*KS*, II, 84, n. 1) who suspects that in place of an unknown place, what we have here is a correct or mutilated form of the name of an area occupied by Zeblun. Wright (p. 59*, n. 8), at the suggestion of his colleague F.M. Cross Jr., takes a further step by even reading Zebulun here, a suggestion taken over by Aharoni (p. 12). Although on the basis of MT all this is extremely uncertain, this proposal is in fact quite appealing because either 'the tribe of Zebulun' falls out of the picture or has to subsumed elsewhere. G.W. Ahlström (*BASOR* 235 [1979], 79f.) however, points out that an interchange of בעלות and זבולון is not – textcritically – obvious.

4:17 *Jehoshaphat son of Paruah over Issachar;*
Issachar, district X, an area described in Josh. 19:17-23, is subject to the administration of Jehoshaphat son of Paruah. It is clear that a large part of the Plain of Jezreel – perhaps including the city itself – extending to the Jordan, must have belonged to it. The Jordan must have been approximately the boundary from the S point of the lake of Gennesaret to Beth-Shean. The S border area must have virtually coincided with the N boundary of district V (see vs. 12). In the NW Mt. Tabor was perhaps a boundary marker (see Z. Kallai, *IDBS*, 921; Aharoni). The name 'Issaschar,' as in conformity with the k^e*tib perpetuum* in MT, is often written and, as a result of the q^e*re perpetuum* and LXX, is pronounced as Issachar (and so written; see Gen. 30:18 and *HAL*, s.v.). In the OT tradition Issachar and Zebulun are usually closely connected. Perhaps the 2 tribes had a common shrine on Mt. Tabor (cf. Deut. 33:19). This close connection, however, need not be a reason – assuming now one does not find an explanation given in the preceding verse persuasive – for uniting Zebulun with Issachar in this one district.

4:18 *Shimei son of Ela over Benjamin;*
The next-to-the-last district is Benjamin of which Shimei son of Ela (cf. Lemaire, 49) was the chief administrator. Some MSS of LXX here omit the proper name. That Shimei here is the same person as the one mentioned in 1:8, though this is often assumed, is extremely uncertain. The territory of Benjamin is rather extensively described in Josh. 18:11-28. The reference is to a narrow area stretched from E to W directly N of Jerusalem, with the Jordan as the E boundary and in the W the SE boundary of district II. Cities such as Jericho and Bethel may have belonged to the district.

4:19 *Jeber son of Uri over the region of Gilead, the territory of Sihon king of the Amorites and of king Og of Bashan. [There was also one garrison in the field(?)].*
The twelfth district is mentioned here, but the verse confronts us with substantial difficulties. In the first place there are the deviances of $LXX^{B, Luc.}$, such as the omission of Geber at the beginning of our verse or the spelling Adai for

the omission of Geber at the beginning of our verse or the spelling Adai for ארי, Gad or Gilead and – not to be overlooked – Judah after בארץ (cf. also Rahlfs, *SSt*. II, 234f.). In the second place, this verse also seems to have been augmented over time with a number of additions, such as the reference to Sihon and Og and the concluding words.

With Noth (against Albright, Van den Born et al.) one can assume that the beginning of our verse in MT will be approximately the right text, provided one may change Gilead into Gad (with LXX but along with the objections which Noth [74] advances!). In any case it need not be incorporated in vs. 13a or be viewed as a variant of this verse. The twelfth district is the territory which, described as Gad, covers the SW part of the land E of the Jordan, bounded to the W by the Dead Sea, to the S by the Arnon and to the N by the S boundary of district VII. It covers a larger part of the (earlier) tribal territories of Gad and Ruben. However, since the term 'the land of Gilead' (cf. Num. 32:1, 29; Josh 17:5f.; 22:9, 13, 15, 32, etc.) can denote this area, there is nothing against maintaining this designation of MT (cf. also A. Lemaire, *VT* 31 [1981], 41-46). Probably because this was a vague concept, a glossator added to this the traditional description: Sihon king of the Amorites (Num. 21:21, 23, 29, 34; Deut. 1:4; 2:24, 26, 30ff.; 3:2, 6, etc.), who had his capital in Heshbon (a place which LXX apparently wants to read instead of 'the Amorites'). Perhaps unnecessarily – because his name was probably often mentioned in one breath with Sihon – the glossator further added: king Og of Bashan (Num. 21:33; Deut. 1:4; 3:1, 3, 11, etc.), despite the fact that his territory is situated in a much more N direction – in Bashan (district VI). From time immemorial, at least for the glossator, Sihon had been connected with Heshbon, as the ancient ballad recalls (Num. 21:27). That was the territory of district XII.[4] According to Noth (Numeri [ATD], 1966, 145), the story of Og is solely based on the dtr. literature and subsequently, via that literature, connected with Sihon. Heshbon appeared to be concealed under *Tell Hesbân*, about 26 km SW of Amman, capital of Jordan (cf. S.H. Horn, *BA* 32 [1969], 27ff.), to which archaeological expeditions have been made. But these expeditions have not succeeded in demonstrating that the capital of Sihon has to be localized here (cf. Horn, *IDBS*, 410f.).

A second addition to our text would seem to be the conclusion where it is stated that there was still one more 'prefect' (or 'garrison', *HAL*) in 'the land.' This is a meaningless comment unless, with Mettinger (p. 12), one views vs. 19a as 'a historical footnote containing the information that formerly ... all of Transjordan formed one administrative unit headed by a certain »Geber ben

---

[4] For Sihon and Og, see: J.R. Bartlett, "Sihon and Og, Kings of the Amorites," *VT* 21 (1970), 257-277, and now also G. del Olmo Lete, "Og עוג," *DDD*, 1204-1207.

Uri«', and incorporates this into the districts VI and VII. This leaves still one more district, namely Judah, which according to Mettinger was not included in the original list. According to him Judah was governed directly from Jerusalem. A case can be made, however, that LXX (which draws Judah, with which vs. 20 begins, into this verse) is right. The intent, then, would be to say that also in Judah, as 13th district, there was a prefect in charge. But even with this concession this is nothing more than a (late) gloss which was probably intended to accentuate the unity of the little states Israel and Judah. The addition does not make much sense, however, because vs. 7 makes express mention of 12 prefects and not of 13. Josephus seems to think that over these 12 prefects there was still a senior prefect: ἐπὶ δὲ τούτων εἷς πάλιν ἄρχων ἀποδέδεικτο. This too is based on a misunderstanding of MT and resembles a conjecture already proposed by Klostermann (cf. also Burney; Benzinger et al.).

On the basis of the above interpretation of vss. 8-19 it is plausible to state that the ancient list itself must have been short, probably containing no more than the 12 names of the prefects and the brief indication of their prefecture by means of reference to one (or more) capital(s), a region or a tribal name. If this is true, the many redactional or secondary glosses are easy to explain. Verses like vss. 8, 14-18 and to a lesser extent also vss. 9 and 10 leave the impression that they are authentic and without additions. In other verses one clearly encounters additional material.

1 KINGS 4:20-5:8

4:20 *Judah and Israel were as numerous as the sand by the sea(shore); they ate and drank and were happy.*
5:1 *Solomon ruled over all the kingdoms from the River to the land of the Philistines, even to the border of Egypt; they brought tribute and served Solomon throughout his entire life.*
  2 *For Solomon's provisions the daily requirement was: thirty cors of fine flour and sixty cors of meal,*
  3 *ten fat cattle, twenty pasture-fed cattle, hundred sheep; besides a deer, a gazelle, a roebuck, and fatted geese.*
  4 *For he had dominion over all the region 'on the other side of the river' from Tiphsah to Gaza, over all the kings 'on the other side of the river.' He kept peace around him on all sides.*
  5 *During Solomon's lifetime Judah and Israel lived securely, each under his vine and under his figtree, from Dan to Beersheba.*
  6 *Solomon had four(fourty) thousand horse stalls for his chariot park and twelve thousand horsemen.*
  7 *The above officials, each in his month, supplied king Solomon and all who were admitted to king Solomon's table; they saw to it that nothing was lacking.*
  8 *They also brought to the proper place barley and straw for the chariot horses and race horses, each in accordance with the guideline set for him.*

INTRODUCTION

From LXX it is already evident, that the verses following these lists (4:20-5:8) follow a different order than MT. Literarily, and in content, the material attached to the lists is not uniform (so, correctly, Noth), though it is hard to tell how then the correct order must have been. Are the changes in LXX really 'Erleichterungen' in a textcritical sense? In any case we must assume that 5:7ff. has been placed immediately after the list of district officials, because these verses not only tie in well with it but also with 4:7. Noth further reconstructs the rationale by saying that mention of the horses in 5:8 led to the prior positioning of 5:6 which was derived from 10:26a. The statements about the wealth of the royal court led to the statement about Israel's prosperity in general (4:20). 5:4 again depends on vs. 5:1 and presumably originated in the postexilic period. 5:5 serves as still another repetition concerning the overall prosperity. The most recent element in this complex must be vss. 2ff.

EXEGESIS

4:20 *Judah and Israel were as numerous as the sand by the sea(shore); they ate and drank and were happy.*
In the form as we now have it in MT the addition begins with a statement concerning Israel's size and prosperity. This verse plus 5:1, 5f. are lacking at this place in LXX but they do occur in the additions attached to 2:46 (see there). In the exegesis of vs. 19 we already mentioned that one must not rule out the possibility that 'Judah' belongs in that verse rather than here, unless one accepts a haplography of 'Judah.' The expression כחול אשר־על־הים לרב also occurs in 2 Sam. 17:11. In addition the expansion על־שפת הים similarly occurs elsewhere (Judg. 7:12; cf. 1 Sam. 13:5; 1 Kgs. 5:9). Some Hebr. MSS and Pesh. also want to read this expansion in our verse. But this is not necessary. חול, 'sand,' which occurs 22x in OT, like עפר, 'dust,' is often used as a simile for 'multitude' and 'abundance' (see G. Wanke, *THAT*, II, 354; cf. A.S. Kapelrud, *TWAT*, II, 803-806). The participles 'eating, drinking, and being happy' denote an ongoing state of affairs in the past, an ever-repeated (possible; cf. Ehrlich) act (BrSynt. §44c).

5:1 *Solomon ruled over all the kingdoms from the River to the land of the Philistines, even to the border of Egypt; they brought tribute and served Solomon throughout his entire life.*
This verse describes the area over which Solomon ruled. The first half of this verse has a par. in 2 Chr. 9:26 which in turn coincides with LXX on 2:46k. Aside from the fact that in 2 Chronicles ושלמה היה reads ויהי, the latter has המלכים in place of הממלכות, and between 'the River' and 'the land of the Philistines' the word ועד, which corresponds, resp., to LXX ἐν πᾶσιν τοῖς βασιλεῦσιν and καὶ ἕως. It has to be admitted that, from the viewpoint of congruence, the part. מנשים fits better with the masc. מלכים 'kings' than with the fem. ממלכות 'kingdoms.' On the other hand, a sing. or pl. part. can include an indefinite subject (König §324n; also cf. Böttcher §997.4A; Ges-K §144i, who regard the text as being 'corrupt' here). It is even possible that in the case of fem. antecedents the construction of the participles is nevertheless masc. (cf. König §§412i and 249a-c). It is well-known that in a later time the participle could be construed with היה – a construction which frequently occurs in the Aramaic (cf. also Ewald §§168d: a second היה in case of several participles; 200a; Driver §135.5).

As far as the saying מן־הנהר ארץ פלשתים is concerned, according to König §330b (see Ewald §281d; Burney; also H. Grotius). it is possible to view such a construction as 'landward,' 'toward the land.' One therefore need not read 'the river of the land of the Philistines' (so Pesh., Tg., Vulg.), nor insert ועד

(so 2 Chr. 9:26; Ehrlich; Delitzsch, *LSF*, §92). In the land of the Philistines there are no rivers of importance. 'The River' here is no other than the 'Great River' (Gen. 15:18; Deut. 1:7; 11:24; Josh. 1:4), the Euphrates (cf. Gen. 31:21; 36:37, etc.; Simons, *GTTOT* §81). The other boundary of Solomon's kingdom extended to the territory of Egypt, along the side of, or over the land of the Philistines. In essence the reference is to the ideal land of Israel, in line with the ideal image people gradually formed of it (also cf. Exod. 23:31). It is not clear precisely where the border with Egypt lay. Some suggest the *Wādi el-'Ariš* S of Gaza, identified in OT with the 'wadi of Egypt' (Num. 34:5 etc.; cf. Simons, *GTTOT* §70). Though 'the land of the Philistines' in our verse can be explained, its mention feels syntactically somewhat forced. It is no wonder that Noth views these words as a marginal gloss, later absorbed into the text (Stade-Schwally refer to a 'restrictive explanation'). However this may be, Solomon undoubtedly inherited from David a position, in which peoples from beyond the ancient boundaries had been made subject to him (cf. 2 Sam. 8:1-14). The verb משל occurs in OT in qal 77-79x, in hiph. 3x; in 43 places the part. act. masc. qal occurs with the meaning 'to rule' (see J.A. Soggin, *THAT*, I, 930-933; H. Groß, *TWAT*, V, 73-77).

The hiph. of נגש is used to describe those who bring tribute (H. Ringgren, *TWAT*, V, 232-237). The word מנחה here means 'tribute.' Of the approx. 210x the word occurs in OT, it is used 37x in the ordinary 'civilian sense' (*KBL*) of 'gift,' 'present,' to express gratitude, homage, or veneration. A few times it obviously also means 'tribute' (Judg. 3:15, 17f.; 2 Sam. 8:2, 6, etc.; also cf. K. Weiss, *TDNT*, IX, 81; H.-J. Fabry, M. Weinfeld, *TWAT*, IV, 987-1001). The word in OT is by far most frequently used in the sense of 'offering,' esp. 'meal offering' (see *HAL*, s.v.). The tribute possibly consisted of natural products. The 'servitude' referred to may have consisted in forced labour for the king. Josephus, *Ant*. VIII, 4 §39, reproduces the verse as follows: 'The king also had other officials who ruled over the land of the Syrians and of the foreigners (οἵ τῆς τε Σύρων γῆς καὶ τῶν ἀλλοφύλων), which stretched from the river Euphrates to the land of the Egyptians, and who also collected the tributes for him from among the nations (ἐκλέγοντες αὐτῷ φόρους παρὰ τῶν ἐθνῶν).'

5:2 *For Solomon's provisions the daily requirement was: thirty cors of fine flour and sixty cors of meal,*
Vs. 1 is separated from vs. 4 by an intermezzo in which we are informed about the provisioning of Solomon's court. In LXX these verses – more correctly – follow vss. 8 and 9. Solomon with his royal household daily consumed 30 cors of fine flour and 60 cors of coarse meal. ליום אחד is here used distributively (cf. GD §48, rem. 2) and it is not necessary for us, with LXX before us, to change this into ביום.

A כר is a measure equated in Ezek. 45:14 with a homer. The word itself is derived from the Akkadian which in turn borrowed it from the Sumerian: GUR = Akkad. *kurru(m)*. From there it found its way into the Aram., Hebr., and other Sem. languages, and even into the Greek: κόρος (cf. *AHw*, 511b). Besides here and in vs. 25 the word occurs in Ezek. 45:14; 2 Chr. 2:9 and 27:5. This measure is used both for dry and liquid substances (see Nowack, I §35, who, however, considers our text 'corrupt'; Benzinger, *Arch.* §40; G. Schmitt, *BRL*², 204ff.; M. Stern, *EncMiqr*. IV, 852-858; De Vaux, *Inst.* I, 303-309; Noth et al.). Precisely what the capacity of this measure was, is uncertain. On the one hand, the contents varied from land to land and from time to time; on the other hand, the state of the economy frequently played a role in this regard. In addition, there is a difference between dry and liquid substances. For the *cor* Benzinger indicates 364,4 liters; Stern, 220 liters; Noth, between 350 and 400 liters; Barrois, II, 250, 393, 84 liters; O.R. Sellers (*IDB*, IV, 835), 55 gallons, etc. The 'fine flour' is called סלת, a word which occurs esp. in Leviticus and Numbers (in Kings also in 2 Kgs. 7:1, 16, 18), 'wheat flour,' in Akkad. *siltu* (*AHw* 1044a), LXX: σεμίδαλις, in Arab. *smīd* The difference between this flour and the following קמח, 'ordinary flour' (Gen. 18:6; Num. 5:15; Judg. 6:19; 1 Sam. 1:24; 28:24; 2 Sam. 17:28; 1 Kgs. 17:12, 14, 16; 2 Kgs. 4:41; Isa. 47:2; Hos. 8:7; 1 Chr. 12:41), which occurs also in other Semitic languages, in LXX: ἄλευρον, is that the latter kind is probably more coarse, as Dalman *AuS*, III, 284f.; 290-296[1] Lemaire, 158; and K. Galling, *BRL*², 3) has explained. Necessary for סלת is repeated siftings, though, despite this process the flour is still among the coarser constituents of the materials ground (Dalman, 293).

On the basis of the numbers given here, people have often made an estimate of the number of staffers Solomon's court must have had. Estimates vary from 14,000 to 32,000 (see Thenius; Šanda; Montg.-Gehman). Now, though antiquity boasted also other courts at which fantastic numbers of people were fed (see Noth), it is likely that our verses speak in superlative terms about Solomon's riches and greatness, so that these and other numbers must certainly be taken with a grain of salt. That is, unless the provisioning applies to a broader group of people than only the royal household, for example, a group that included also the members of the families of court officials, the soldiers, and the attendants of Solomon throughout the land.

5:3 *ten fat cattle, twenty pasture-fed cattle, hundred sheep; besides a deer, a gazelle, a roebuck, and fatted geese.*

---

[1] Cf. also his "Die Mehlarten im Alten Testament. Ein Beitrag zur biblischen Archäologie," A. Alt, et al., *Alttestamentliche Studien* (Fs R. Kittel), 1913, 61-69.

This verse supplies information about the meat that was consumed: 10 head of fat cattle open the series. ברִיא is used both for animals and humans (cf. Gen. 41:2-20; Judg. 3:17; Ezek. 34:3; 20; Hab. 1:16; Zech. 11:16; Ps. 73:4; Dan. 1:15) and means 'fat' or 'healthy.' This need not be intended as a contrast (otherwise: Ehrlich). In a sense these cattle are indeed contrasted to the pasture-fed cattle mentioned next.

The word רְעִי, 'pasture,' which occurs only here in OT, stands in apposition to בקר (cf. Ewald §287h; König §333p; Ges-K §131c) and in opposition to בראים which, as attribute, is in the plural (cf. König §334i). It is by no means necessary, with Ehrlich, also to read רָעִים and to compare Gen. 18:7 with it. One gets the impression that the so-called 'fat cattle' had been in the stalls while the 'pasture-cattle' were arbitrarily selected (good) cows from the open field (cf. LXX μόσχοι ἐκλεκτοί... βόες νομάδες). In addition, 100 'units' of small stock came to the royal table as well, even aside from (לבד מן, cf. Exod. 12:37; Num. 29:39 etc.; HAL, s.v. בד I, 105a) a number of separate delicacies. איל (Deut. 12:15, 22; 14:5; 15:22; Isa. 35:6; Ps. 42:2; S. of S. 2:9; 17; 8:14; also the fem. form אַיָּלָה occurs a number of times in OT) is the 'fallow deer' (*cervus capreolus*, see *HAL*, s.v.), and צבי (Deut. 12:15, 22; 14:5; 15:22; 2 Sam. 2:18; Isa. 13:14; Prov. 6:5; S. of S. 2:9, 17; 8:14; cf. S. of S. 2:7; 3:5; 4:5; 7:4 and 1 Chr. 12:9) the 'gazelle,' which – as the cited texts show – are often mentioned together. A third animal, also mentioned in Deut. 14:5 along with the 2 preceding ones, is יחמור, 'roebuck,' a word which also occurs in the Aramaic and is therefore conveyed in that form by Pesh. and Tg. LXX omitted the word here, but in Deut. 14:5 calls the animal βούβαλος, an 'African antelope' (cf. Liddell-Scott, s.v.). Josephus does use the word in this location. Bochart, *Hieroz.* lib. III, cap. 22, 909-915, already devoted generous attention to the animal and its identification.

The following word ברבר also gives us the usual translation problems. As pass. part. qal אבם only occurs twice in OT (also in Prov. 15:17) and means 'to fatten,' cf. אבום 'feedtrough' (Isa. 1:3; Job 39:9; Prov. 14:4). The word ברבר only occurs in our verse and is sometimes translated by 'cuckoo' (see e.g. *KBL*, s.v., *HAL*, s.v.[2]) which was considered a delicacy in antiquity and still is in countries surrounding the Mediterranean (cf. Plinius, *Nat. Hist.*, X, 9). Eißfeldt (*KS*, II, 413; III, 89-91) has suggested, however, that the reference here is to 'fatted geese,' representations of which have been found on ivory from the 13th and 12th century BCE. LXX concludes our verse by mentioning (ἐκτὸς) ὀρνίθων ἐκλεκτῶν ... and also the Pesh. reads *w'wp' mptm'*, like Tg. ועופא ופטימא and Vulg.: *et avium altilium*. Hence the reference is either to fine or to fatted birds. Josephus expands all this by speaking of 'birds and fishes'

---

[2] Cf. also L. Köhler, *Kleine Lichter: fünfzig Bibelstellen erklärt*, Zürich 1945, 27-30.

(τῶν πετεινῶν καὶ ἰχθύων). G.R. Driver, *PEQ* 87 (1955), 133f., considers the Arab. *birbir*, 'young fowl' a possible description of the bird. For various earlier views, cf.: Bochart, *Hieroz.* II, lib. I, cap. 19, 127-135, of which the statement – rejected by Bochart as anachronistic – that there is a connection between the Hebr. word and the Latin *vivarium* is odd. Although we are inclined to follow Gesenius (*Thesaurus,* 246) and Eißfeldt – also in translating these words – we do not wish to rule out other possibilities.

5:4 *For he had dominion over all the region 'on the other side of the river' from Tiphsah to Gaza, over all the kings 'on the other side of the river.' He kept peace around him on all sides.*
This verse again picks up the thread that had been broken off in vs. 1 after vss. 2ff. had been inserted by a redactor. Actually one can say that though this verse states in other words precisely the same thing as vs. 1, it came from a different author. The twice-repeated עבר הנהר 'on the other side of the River' (viz. the Euphrates) prompts the suspicion that the author resided E of the river in Babylon and that this comment stems from the time of or after the exile (cf. Ezra 4:10f. etc.) Two cities are mentioned: (1) Tiphsah and (2) Gaza, names which are missing in some Hebr. MSS and also in LXX[B, Luc.]; either by *homoioteleuton* or because it concerns an even later addition in certain Hebr. MSS LXX does have this addition in 2:46f. The first-mentioned city is read there as Ῥαφεὶ; in the addition of LXX[A] and Origin as Θαψα. Tiphsah is the Θάψακος in Greco-Roman literature, a city on the western bank of the Euphrates, important as a river port and at the same time as a 'crossing place' over the river (see also H. Grotius). The name תפסח (root: פסח) also means 'ford.' At this location Cyrus, for example, crossed the Euphrates (Xenophon, *Anabasis*, I, 4, 11, 17ff.) and also Darius forded the stream (Arrianus, *Anabasis*, II, 13, 1; cf. W. Röllig, *KP*, V, 649f.). Although these witnesses come from the time after the exile, one has to assume that in antiquity there always was a settlement by this ford. This mention of the place as the farthest border city of Solomon's kingdom, however, points in the direction of a late dating of the statement (cf. Simons, *GTTOT* §292).

Gaza is a well-known Philistine city, both in OT (Gen. 10:19; Deut. 2:23 etc.) and today. Of the Philistine cities it is the most southern and the nearest to Egypt. It is said that Solomon ruled over all the kings who resided between these 2 cities, the reference being especially to Philistine and Aramaic kings. From 11:23-25 it is clear, however, that this view is at least exaggerated. The verb רדה (aside from Joel 4:13 where it literally means 'to tread') occurs 21 times in OT in the sense of 'to rule' (J.A. Soggin, *THAT*, I, 932), which is less frequently than the related word משל. In our book we also find it in vs. 30 and in 9:23.

As if to underscore the condition of peace in Solomon's kingdom once more, it is said that he enjoyed peace on all sides. There are several Hebr. MSS which read עבדיו here in place of עבריו (cf. Stade-Schwally; Montg.-Gehman; differently but mistakenly: Burney). Both readings indeed make sense in the framework of this verse, also the reading of our MT, which is further supported by the ancient *versions* and preferable (so, correctly, Stade-Schwally).

5:5 *During Solomon's lifetime Judah and Israel lived securely, each under his vine and under his figtree, from Dan to Beersheba.*
In a kind of chiastic structure with 4:20, Solomon's kingdom of peace is further depicted, in an ironic way,[3] as beneficent for all his people when the ideal state of Judah and Israel is sketched here. It is a state in which every citizen can live securely under his vine and his figtree. To this picture LXX adds in 2:46g: 'eating and drinking (from Dan to Beersheba) ...' Sitting under one's figtree against which the vine can climb up and which suggests a measure of prosperity, is a topic which recurs in OT (Mic. 4:4; cf. Zech. 3:10 and 2 Kgs. 18:31; C.-H. Hunzinger, *TDNT*, VII, 752f.; Brueggemann). Also the phrase 'from Dan to Beersheba' is a kind of fixed expression in certain parts of OT for designating the territory of Israel from N to S (Judg. 20:1; 1 Sam. 3:20, etc.; in reverse sequence 2 Chr. 30:5; cf. Simons, *GTTOT* §289).

5:6 *Solomon had four(fourty) thousand horse stalls for his chariot park and twelve thousand horsemen.*
In terms of content, vss. 6-8 again belong to what was stated in 4:7ff. about the prefects and their districts. In this connection our verse, with an eye to the following verses, contains information about the king's horses-and-chariot park (Noth). There is a par. to our verse in 2 Chr. 9:25a but also 1 Kgs. 10:26 and 2 Chr. 1:14 can be compared with it. Our verse says that Solomon had 40,000 ארות horses for his מרכב. There are a fair number of uncertain factors in this statement (see esp. Barthélemy). In the first place, there is the number 40,000. The par. verse in 2 Chr. 9 mentions 4,000, as does LXX[B] in 1 Kgs. 10:26. Vulg., Pesh., Tg. and LXX[Luc.] etc. in 10:26, as well as Josephus (*Ant.* VIII §41) opt for the 10x larger and more exaggerated figure of 40,000. Thenius, Noth et al. tend to favour the smaller number. If one reads the first half of our verse in light of the second, in which there is mention of 12,000 'horsemen,' then, given a ratio of 3 horsemen per team of horses (plus chariot), the lower number is the more obvious. Even then, at this late date it is hard to check whether the figures really tally.

---

[3] Cf. W. Brueggemann, "»Vine and Fig Tree«: A Case Study in Imagination and Criticism," *CBQ* 43 [1981], 188-204.

What is the meaning of אֻרְוָה*? It is a word which does not occur in this form in OT but does in the plural (aside from our verse and 2 Chr. 9:25, also in 2 Chr. 32:28), be it orthographically somewhat variable. *HAL* gives as its meaning the word 'stable,' 'stall' (see e.g. W. Rudolph on 2 Chr. 9:25). We are dealing here with an Akkad. loan word, *urû(m)*, which Von Soden (*AHw*, 1435) enters under 2 lemmas: I 'Stall' and II 'Gespann'. In Akkad. the word can also mean 'horses' or 'stallions.' Pesh. and Tg. leave the word virtually untranslated: *'wrwn.* In Syriac *'ûryā* means 'manger,' 'stall.' J. Payne Smith, s.v., here supplies as root the Arab. or (or Aram.?) *'ry*, 'to stable an animal.' In the Aram. of the Tg. the word means 'crib' (cf. Isa. 1:3) and Vulg. renders it by *praesepia*, which has the same meaning. Josephus, in the passage cited above, says: ὡς τέσσαρας εἶναι μυριάδας φατνῶν τῶν ὑποζευγνυμένων ἵππων, which can be translated by 'cribs' or 'feeding-troughs' (cf. M. Hengel, *TDNT*, IX, 51-54). LXX[B]'s rendering in 10:26 (cf. 2 Chr. 9:25) is peculiar: τέσσαρες χιλιάδες θήλειαι ἵπποι (εἰς ἅρματα), 'female horses,' i.e. 'mares'. Cf. Bochart, *Hieroz.* II, IX, 157: 'In *Graeca* versione ארות, vel אריות סוסים, absurde redditur Θήλειαι ... , quasi הרות et הריות legerint, quod *foetas*, significa ret'. Now the translation 'stall' or 'manger' and the like hinges somewhat on the translation of פרש in the second half of our verse. Are we dealing here with 'horsemen' or with 'horses'? The word after all can have both meanings, as we demonstrated in our comments on 1:5 above.[4] It is important in this connection to bring 1 Kgs. 10:26 and (the par.) 2 Chr. 1:14 to bear on the question. There, we may assume without much exaggeration, the reference is to 1,400 chariots of Solomon, in connection with which 4,000 teams of horses would not be excessive. For every team of horse, whether 2, 3 or 4 horses per team, there would then be 3 horsemen, assuming one opts for 'horsemen' as the translation of פרש. But one may equally well opt for the translation 'steed,' or 'horse,' in which case our verse speaks of '4,000 stalls for the chariot park with 12,000 steeds.' The new element in our verse, then, is that one can add mention of 4,000 stalls to the 1,400 chariots and 12,000 steeds. S. Yeivin (*Tarbiz* 40 [1970f.], 395f.) considers the statement in 2 Chr. 9:25a, where there is mention of 4,000 'stalls' for horses *and* chariots, a clarification of the report in our verse, because the number 40,000 can only apply to the stalls and not to the chariots. He therefore sticks to 4,000 chariots and, based on a statement of Salmanassar III (858-824; cf. *ANET*, 278f.), substantiates the credibility of this number by referring to Ahab's contribution in the battle by Qarqar at the Orontes (853): 2,000 chariots and 10,000 foot

---

[4] See now also G.I. Davies, "'*Urwōt* in 1 Kings 5:6 (EVV. 4:26) and the Assyrian Horse Lists," *JSS* 34 (1989), 25-38, who translates in 1 Kgs 5 and 2 Chr. 9 'teams (of horses)' and in 2 Chr. 32:28 'stables.'

soldiers. Even then this would still be only half of Ahab's entire chariot park (cf. 1 Kgs. 16:9). He then explains the difference between the 4,000 and the 1,400 by applying the one item to the beginning of Solomon's reign and the other to the end.

However this may be, it seems best to us to construe the word ארות as a st. cstr., meaning 'stable' (cf. H. Weippert, *BRL²*, 317) and to construe the word מרכב, which may elsewhere mean 'saddle' (Lev. 15:9; S. of S. 3:10), to mean 'chariot park' (so also *HAL*). In that case it is still perhaps best to render the ambiguous word פרש as 'horseman.' We also wish to abandon the possibility of taking אר(י)ות as st. abs., in which case סוסים למרכבו, as apposition, would be an explicatory note in the sense of 'teams,' viz. 'horses for the chariot park' in distinction from the 'steeds', which in that case would not be used specifically for the chariots, though this interpretation is not totally excluded.

In the above-mentioned par. verses to ours we are further told where the horses, chariots and/or horsemen were stationed (cf. further comments on 10:26). In this connection reference has sometimes been made to the stables at Megiddo (see, for example, the pictures in *ANEP*, pl. 741f.) but strong voices are currently being raised to view these as storage rooms (Weipert, op. cit., for 'horse' in OT; cf. also O. Michel, *TDNT*, III, 336f.).

5:7 *The above officials, each in his month, supplied king Solomon and all who were admitted to king Solomon's table; they saw to it that nothing was lacking.*
This and the following verse form the logical continuation of the list of governors (see 4:19; אלה refers to the immediately preceding) as is also clear from the order in LXX. In terms of content our verse ties in very well with 4:7, to which we can refer also for the form and meaning of כלכל (cf. the frequentative or iterative character of the pf.). Besides taking care of the king, the prefects were also obligated to take care of כל־הקרב to the king's table. The קרב is 'one who approaches' (cf. Num. 1:51; 3:10, 38, etc.). LXX^B translates the term by πάντα διαγγέλματα; LXX$^{Luc.}$ by: τὰ διηγγελμένα; cf. Vulg. *necessaria mensae*. From these translations one gets the sense that the reference is not so much to persons as to the materials the king has ordered: the (necessary) goods on order. Still it is better to view the Hebr. text as referring to the persons who made use of the royal table. This is how Pesh. and Tg. view the word. We can, however, make a further distinction between the court personnel, who were regularly supplied from the king's table, and the (incidental) guests, who were literally table companions of the king. Thenius, for example, thinks only of the former category because the reference here is to 'the regular palace household' and also Montg.-Gehman move in this direction: 'one who has *entrée*, regular guest.' Nevertheless we do not think it possible to make such a sharp distinction. We are further told that 'each in his

month' was responsible for provisioning the court and that 'they saw to it that nothing was lacking.' The verb עדר occurs in pi. only here: 'letting it fail'; further in niphal (1 Sam. 30:19; 2 Sam. 17:22; Isa. 34:16; 40:26; 59:15; Zeph. 3:5): 'be missing.'

5:8 *They also brought to the proper place barley and straw for the chariot horses and race horses, each in accordance with the guideline set for him.*
This verse first lists 2 products which are of importance to the royal cavalry. שערים and the sing. שערה, associated with שֵׂעָר ('hair growth,' etc.), denotes 'barley,' a well-known grain also in the West, identifiable by its long-awned spikes. According to Deut. 8:8, this is the second cereal crop with which Palestine is blessed and which, accordingly, is mentioned more than 30 times in OT (cf. J. Feleks, *BHHW*, I, 553f.). תבן (Exod. 5:7-18; Gen. 24:25 etc.) is 'chopped straw,' a product of the threshing floor. According to Dalman, *AuS*, III, 133f., distinctions were made among the various kinds of chopped stalks. The most important one, certainly, is *tibn*, 'fine chop.' This kind of 'chop' which contained the most tender parts of the blade, the pieces of which varied in length from 3 to 12 mm, served as fodder for horses, mules, and donkeys. Horses are the animals mentioned here. Next comes the word רכש which also occurs in Mic. 1:13 and Esth. 8:10, 14. LXX reads ἅρματα; Vulg.: *iumenta*, while Pesh. renders barley and straw as *lrkš'* (pl.) *wlswsyt'* (pl.) which Tg. reads in the reverse order. In Syriac *rakšā* means 'horse,' which also fits in the other OT texts. In the Elephantine papyri the word also occurs with this meaning (cf. *DISO*, s.v.). In New-Egyptian, it can mean 'horse' but also 'team' (Noth). The latter need not specifically mean that the reference is to a team of horses. The word may in fact refer to racehorses (so already Thenius).

Now all these provisions were brought to a specific location. The construction of this sentence, however, is not overly clear. What is meant by אשר יהיה שם? LXX and Vulg. take the subject of this verb to be the king. This suggests that the king was often on tour. Though this certainly is not the correct view, it has found considerable support (Kittel, Šanda, Noth). Nor is the following איש subject, though grammatically this is a possibility. But it does not make sense to assume that each time the prefects had to be at a different location (so, correctly, Noth). One can also supply an indefinite subject in the sentence: 'wherever it was required,' i.e. the barley and the straw (so Klostermann, De Vaux, Van den Born). The impf. conveys a dependent indeterminacy which in English is sometimes expressed by 'may' (cf. Driver §38). The fodder was brought where it was needed. The 'it' as subject refers back to the whole supply of barley and straw (so also Burney, Benzinger et al.). This is also the most logical line of thought because it was especially the (race)horses which might speedily move from location to location. Now every prefect performed the work he was charged to do כמשפטו, 'according to his guideline' (cf. comments on 2:3). The question is: to whom does the 3 p. sing. suffix apply, to Solomon (sub. gen.) or to the prefect (obj. gen.)? The question is clearly answered by Vulg. *iuxta constitum sibi*: 'according to the guideline given him.'

An ostracon, inscribed in ancient Hebr. and found in Samaria (C1101) between 1931 and 1935, somewhat illustrates the kind of provisioning described in our verse. The ostracon reads as follows in translation: 'Baruch has carried out ... Baruch: give them their provision and they will return ... he will weigh out 3 ephahs of barley' (cf. A. Lemaire, 246; idem, *RB* 79 [1972], 566-703). As such this sort of transaction is not unfamiliar.

1 KINGS 5:9-14

5:9 *God gave Solomon wisdom and immense insight, and breadth of vision like the sand on the seashore.*
10 *Solomon's wisdom surpassed the wisdom of all the people of the East and all the wisdom of Egypt.*
11 *He was wiser than anyone else, than Ethan the Ezrahite, than Heman, Calcol and Darda the sons of Mahol. His name was mentioned (with deep respect) among all the surrounding nations.*
12 *He uttered three thousand proverbs and composed one thousand five songs.*
13 *He discoursed on trees, from the cedar of Lebanon to the hyssop growing on the wall; he also discoursed on animals, on birds, on reptiles and on fish.*
14 *People came from every nation to listen to Solomon's wisdom, (being delegated by) all the kings of the earth who had heard of his wisdom.*

INTRODUCTION

The vss. 9-14 again concentrate particularly on the wisdom of Solomon, an account of which was interrupted in 4:1-5:8 by a summary of organizational measures the king had undertaken relative to the administration of his kingdom. In connection with our verses A. Alt has referred to the so-called Onomasticon of Amen-em-opet, an Egyptian document dating back approximately to 1100 B.C. (*KS*, II, 90-99), in which entire series of proverbs and information about a wide range of topics concerning nature are summarized. This so-called 'Listenwissenschaft' was also known in Mesopotamia and, according to Alt, the influence of the 2 cultural regions on the rise and development of Israel's own (literary) culture must have been considerable. For 'the teaching of Amen-em-opet,' cf. *ANET*, 421-425; further Alt, *KS*, I, 231f.; on various types of wisdom: G. Fohrer, *TDNT*, VII, 476-496; R.J. Williams, *TRE*, I, 500.

The section that follows is composed as narrative and constitutes a relative unity in which there are no (discernible) indications that a dtr. redactor has introduced changes in it. The focus is Solomon' wisdom with regard to nature, a wisdom which differs from the juridical wisdom of 3:4-28 or the practical wisdom we encounter in proverbs (etc.). This part possibly dates back to a relatively late post-exilic time when the greatness and worldwide fame of Solomon had found a place in the narratives concerning this wise king. Still, as Noth asserts, it is very difficult to date this piece. In any case, there is in our verse no reference whatever to 3:4-14, where we already learned that Solomon received wisdom from God.

EXEGESIS

5:9 *God gave Solomon wisdom and immense insight, and breadth of vision like the sand on the seashore.*
As word for God we again find אלהים in place of יהוה (cf. however, LXX and Tg.) Along with חכמה there is mention here of תבונה, a word which occurs more than 40x especially in the chokmatic parts of OT (also cf. 7:14; also H.H. Schmid, *THAT* 1, 306). It denotes 'insight' into or 'understanding' of the nature and coherence of things (cf. also 3:12). The adverbial הרבה, here used attributively (cf. König §318e; Ges-K §131e), along with the following מאד accentuate the exceptional nature of Solomon's 'wisdom and insight'.[1] Added to this as a third element is the expression רחב לב, 'largeness of heart.' The word רחב frequently occurs in OT in describing the breadth of a thing (Gen. 6:15; 13:17; Exod. 25-29 *passim*, etc.). Along with לב (cf. Isa. 60:5; Ps. 25:17; 119:32), it presumably denotes 'breadth of vision' here, or 'broad knowledge' (Noth; cf. also Pedersen, I-II, 149). Burney here takes 'heart' to mean 'the seat of the intellect,' and Von Meyenfeldt, *Het hart*, 35f., translates it by 'broad (universal) giftedness ...,' and thus attempts to distinguish it from the preceding words 'insight' and 'understanding,' to which it is in fact related (cf. G. Fohrer, *TDNT*, VII, 476, n. 88). Still these last 2 suggestions are problematic in that they put too much emphasis on the intellect and mental ability, while the Hebr. text intends especially to indicate the encyclopedic scope of the subjects the king has described or celebrated in song (thus already Amana). Compare also the 2 versions in LXX (on 2:35b): πλᾶτος καρδίας and (on our verse): χύμα καρδίας. To this still somewhat abstract qualification the text adds that this outlook was as spacious 'as the sand by the seashore,' a comparison which seems better suited to concrete numbers, as in 4:20. Noth suspects that for this very reason Pesh. perhaps omitted it. Pesh. 9al *fam*, however, does have this addition, without its having to be a later attempt to bring the Syrian text into harmony with MT (Kimchi states that sand is not subject to being measured but to being counted). In the second place, Pesh. reads, instead of 'breadth', *rabbût lebbā*, 'largeness of heart,' 'largeheartedness, courage' (Payne Smith). In any case, the idea of this addition is to further highlight Solomon's enormous wisdom.

---

[1] See now also B. Gosse, "La Sagesse et l'Intelligence de Salomono en 1 Rois 5,9," *BN* 65 (1992), 12-14.

5:10 *Solomon's wisdom surpassed the wisdom of all the people of the East and all the wisdom of Egypt.*
A similar intent comes through in this verse in which it is said that the king's wisdom was even greater (impf. cons. qal of the verb רבה) than the wisdom of the people of the East and of the Egyptians. The בני־קדם are referred to by Josephus (*Ant.* XIII, II.5 §42) and LXX as ἀρχαῖοι ἄνθρωποι, the 'people of prehistoric times,' the 'ancients,' thereby taking up one of the meanings of קָדֶם in OT (cf. 2 Kgs. 19:25; Isa. 23:7, etc.). Here, we assume, the reference is to the other meaning 'east,' which combined with 'sons,' means 'Eastlanders' (Gen. 29:1; Judg. 6:3, 33; 7:12 etc.; also cf. E. Jenni, *THAT*, II, 587ff.). Now 'east' is a broad term and dependent on the point of reference. In Gen. 29:1 the term is interpreted to apply to Mesopotamia, but in Judg. 6:3, 33, for example, the reference is to tribes living immediately to the E of the Jordan valley, tribes inhabiting the Syrian-Arabian desert (cf. Grotius: '*Arabia autem ad Orientem Judaeae*'). Eißfeldt, *KS*, III, 297ff., in an article in which he describes inscriptions from Safa (the first 6 or 7 centuries B.C.), also discusses 'the people of the east.' This Safa region is the NW part of the Syrian-Arabian desert around the mountains ǧebel Ḥaurān and ǧebel Sēs and the Ḥarrat ir-Rādšil. In this area Eißfeldt also localizes the 'sons of the east' of Old Testament times. Here, as tentdwellers, they lived with their camels, raising and herding sheep and goats. In this area, which may include the more western 'Vorland,' lived a people who were known for their wisdom. According to Eißfeldt, Gen. 29:1 also relates to this area, a view which is supported by Noth. We also subscribe to this view. The reference is to tribes which lived in the deserts even farther to the E than Moab, Ammon, and Edom, and whose tribal wisdom was apparently proverbial.

More familiar to us is the wisdom of the Egyptians. The priestly soothsayers of Egypt, the חַרְטֻמִּים, are also mentioned in OT (Gen. 41:8, 24; Exod. 7:11, 22, etc.; for Babylonia, cf. also Dan. 1:20; 22) and allusions to the wisdom of Egypt are made as well (cf. e.g. Isa. 19:11; also Acts 7:22; see further comments on vs. 9 above).

5:11 *He was wiser than anyone else, than Ethan the Ezrahite, than Heman, Calcol and Darda the sons of Mahol. His name was mentioned (with deep respect) among all the surrounding nations.*
In this verse there is mention of a number of 'wise men' whom Solomon is said to have surpassed. But prior to this it is stated that he was wiser 'than all other men.' חכם, used as verb esp. in Proverbs and Ecclesiastes and only here in the books of Kings, by the succeeding preposition מן, gives expression to a quantitative or qualitative difference (BrSynt. §111g). Noth correctly comments that the following אדם in the plural refers to human individuals, some of whom are then mentioned by name. It is therefore not necessary, with Šanda,

Greßmann, Montg.-Gehman, a.o., to change the word into 'Edomites,' although in the OT tradition this people too were said to be 'wise' (cf. Jer. 49:7; Obad. 8).

Of the following specifically listed wise men we do not know anything beyond what is said here. Ethan as a name occurs also in Ps. 89:1, again with the addition 'the Ezrahite'; in 1 Chr. 2:6 he is referred to, along with the others mentioned in our verse, as descendants of Judah; in 1 Chr. 6:42 as a descendant of Levi among the 'temple musicians.' In 1 Chr. 15:17 and 19 he is again 'incorporated' in the tribe of Levi and among the temple musicians. It is understandable that, on the basis of 1 Chr. 2:6, where Ethan and the other sons of Zerah, son of Judah by Tamar (Gen. 38:30), are mentioned, Tg. interprets 'Ezrahite' as 'son of Zerah.' This solution, though followed by Ges-B, *KBL*, *HAL* et al., is not well-founded. Pesh. calls Ethan 'the Easterner' (*madnᵉhāyā*), undoubtedly because it linked the stem זרח with the Syrian *dnh* (the 'rising' of the sun). It is natural to consider אזרחי a *nisbe*, a gentilic, so that 'Ezrahite' deserves preference. Albright, *ARI*, 127, 210, n. 95, and S. Mowinckel, *VT* 5 (1955), 19, think that the meaning is indigenous and that Ethan as well as the following persons we are dealing with are 'pre-Israelite types of wise men' (Mowinckel). Now this last comment is certainly true but the question is whether 'Ezrahite' expresses this. It is more likely that this is the translation of אזרח (Exod. 12:19, 48f.; Lev. 16:29; 17:15 etc.). It is probable that Thenius and Noth are correct in saying that occurrences of the word in Chronicles and in the headings of Pss. 88 and 89 probably hark back secondarily to our verse, and that the reference is to an unknown wise man from the 'classical' antiquity of Israel. Montg.-Gehman indeed think that names like Ethan and Heman have Arabian backgrounds but, according to Noth, this can only be proved 'mit Hilfe sehr dürftigen und ragwürdigen Vergleichsmaterials.'

The name Heman in part occurs as parallel to that of Ethan, in part along with other 'singers' such as Jeduthun (Ps. 88:1; 1 Chr. 2:6; 6:18; 15:17, 19; 16:41f.; 25:1, 4-6; 2 Chr. 29:14; 35:15). It is not said of him and of the persons following that they were Ezrahites, though this is what Ps. 88:1 has secondarily concluded from the data. He, Calcol and Darda – variously spelled in the LXX and other translations – are called 'sons of Mahol.' Albright, *ARI*, 127 and n. 96,[2] reads מחול as 'dance' (thus, already, Rashi). The 'sons of the dance' are said to be connected with a guild of dancers or singers. Because the name Calcol occurs on various ivory objects found at Megiddo, and in the form of *Kurkur* or *Kulkul* in hieroglyphs (13th century), it is said to be the name of a female singer for the god Ptah-ruler-of-Ashkelon. Because male and female names are regularly interchanged in the Canaanite and Hebrew, accord-

---

[2] See also his *Yahweh and the Gods of Canaan*, Garden City 1968, 219.

ing to Albright, 'the difference of sex need arouse no surprise.' However ingenious Albright's suggestion may be, there is no evidence of any kind that he is right (cf. Grotius, who suggests it is a name of a *femina erudita!*). Calcol and Darda – written as דרע in MT – occur also in 1 Chr. 2:6. Apuleius, *Apologia*, 90, mentions Darda alongside of Moses; see Josephus, *Ant.* VIII §43; *GLAJJ*, II, 203f.). מחול, as the name of a person, occurs only here; in the sense of 'choral dance' it occurs more frequently in OT (Jer. 31:4, 13; Ps. 30:12; 149:3; 150:4 and Lam. 5:15; cf. H. Eising, *TWAT*, II, 800f.). From the mention of these names we can only conclude (as Noth observes) that 'at one time' – we cannot even say where (see G. Fohrer, *TDNT*, VII, 480 and n. 125) – there were 'wise men' whose wisdom must have been proverbial among people (like the 'righteousness' of Job, Noah, and Daniel in the days of Ezekiel; cf. Ezek. 14:14, 20). But Solomon surpassed even these men. It therefore need not surprise us either that his name became proverbial among the surrounding nations (cf. Pedersen, I-II, 247). This conclusion, which is the logical sequel to the first half of our verse, is omitted by LXX. It *may* be a later redactional gloss (so Stade-Schwally, et al.).

5:12 *He uttered three thousand proverbs and composed one thousand five songs.*

Now that in the preceding section Solomon's wisdom has been profiled against the background of the wisdom of other mortals, it is also materially quantified. In the first place he uttered 3,000 proverbs. The word משל occurs here in the singular and is usually regarded, like the following שיר, as a collective (Ewald §176a; König §255b; GD §21; 17; Lettinga §24j; see also Delitzsch, *LSF* §18d). After figures like 'hundred' and 'thousands,' however, various words occur in the singular (cf. GD §47 rem. 1: to be viewed as a class or genus; Ges-K §134g; see also Noth, 79, on our verse). Aside from 9:7, the word משל occurs only here in the books of Kings of the approximately 40x it occurs in OT. In LXX, the word, as it is here, is often translated by παραβολή. The reference is to proverbs of various kinds: a 'saying,' a 'wisdom saying' (as here), a parable, even a 'taunt song' (cf. F. Hauck, *TDNT*, V, 744-751; H. Gese, *RGG*³, VI, 1577ff.; E. Jenni, *THAT*, I, 452; K.-M. Beyse, *TWAT*, V, 69-73).[3] Of the wisdom sayings, according to the tradition, he uttered 3,000. But the tradition concerning the number of 'songs' is less consistent because LXX and a number of Vulg. MSS read 5,000 instead of 1,005. Josephus (*Ant.* VIII §44) still uses the MT numbers but reverses the order and speaks of 'the books of odes and songs' (βιβλία περὶ ᾠδῶν καὶ μελῶν) and of 'the books of

---

[3] Cf. also O. Eißfeldt, *Der Mashal im Alten Testament* (BZAW 24), Gießen, 1913; and E. Sellin, G. Fohrer, *Einleitung in das Alte Testament*, Heidelberg 1969¹¹, 339 (litt.).

proverbs and similitudes' (παραβολῶν καὶ εἰκόνων βίβλους), a remarkable heightening of Solomon's greatness and wisdom which can also be found in the remainder of Josephus' argument. After all, in our text we only read that Solomon 'uttered' this number of proverbs and songs, which, to be sure, is no small achievement (Grotius cleverly refers to the *collection* by Solomon *ex historicorum et poetarum scriptis*).

The word שיר occurs only here in the books of Kings. One often finds it especially in the Psalms and even then in the headings (42 out of 77x; cf. R. Ficker, *THAT*, II, 895). In addition the fem. form שירה also occurs 13x (but not in Kings) and finally the verb (87x, but not in Kings). The stem שיר is used especially in connection with the cult. In the main, שיר denotes cultic song (for this and for the relation to מזמור, cf.: Ficker, 896f.) be it originally perhaps above all 'Sprechgesang' (recitative). In view of what comes up in the following verse, it is not likely that the author here thought of cultic songs. It is hard, for that matter, to say whether the author or redactor of our verse even knew about the proverbs which are attributed to Solomon in the book by that name. Conversely, this book was probably attributed to Solomon by the existing wisdom tradition to which our verse witnesses (Sellin-Fohrer, *Einleitung*, 347). In our book of Psalms only 2 are attributed to Solomon: Ps. 72 and Ps. 127, while also the Song of Songs was attributed to him by the late tradition. It remains difficult – even assuming that the numbers in our verse are inflated – to determine where the core of truth is located. Perhaps in the designation of Solomon as a promoter of music and the fine arts, among which poetry?

5:13 *He discoursed on trees, from the cedar of Lebanon to the hyssop growing on the wall; he also discoursed on animals, on birds, on reptiles and on fish.*

With the word וידבר this verse continues the quantification begun in the previous verse by introducing further specification. What follows is a division of animate nature into a plant and animal kingdom. The latter is again subdivided into quadrupeds, birds, reptiles, and fish. It is not said here that the animal and plant kingdom form the content of the proverbs and songs referred to in the previous verse. The reference in our verse is rather to a separate 'discipline,' the discipline of the king's nature studies, from which no plant or animal was excluded. This, too, is part of the king's wisdom. Besides being a poet, the king was a student of nature (thus, correctly, Thenius; cf. G. Fohrer, *TDNT*, VII, 481, and n. 133). On the other hand, when a poet undertakes to study nature, one cannot say that one thing totally excludes another. That in the mention of a certain kind of systematic study of nature there can be reference to Egyptian onomastica, we have already stated in vs. 9 above.[4]

Noth takes the pl. of עֵץ to be broader than 'tree.' One could also translate the word by 'plant,' although this translation is not common (cf. J.A. Soggin, *THAT*, II, 356-359). This is not entirely the translation suggested by the word ארז which, though often translated by 'cedar,' rather denotes a 'tall conifer' (cf. my articles in *TWAT*, III, 783 and IV, 465f.; also *EncMiqr*. I, 553 ff.; but see Busink, 223f. and n. 193) as also by אזוב, a word usually translated by 'hyssop.' In *ZAW* 94 (1982), 410ff., we have undertaken a more detailed study of Noth's view and the words עֵץ and אזוב, a study to which we take the liberty to refer the reader. It turns out that though עֵץ has a number of fine shades of meaning in Hebrew it cannot mean 'plant' in general. The 'hyssop' is probably the *Majorana syriaca* or *Origanum maru L,* a plant which can hardly be called a 'tree' either, so that we face the dilemma that the translation 'plants' is saying too much and 'trees' is saying too little. We must indeed note that עצים almost immediately precedes 'cedar,' a fact which may have influenced the choice of words.

The genitive construction 'cedar of Lebanon' is referred to in our verse as אשר ב (Joüon §130f; cf. BrSynt. §82e). Also hyssop אשר יצא is noteworthy alongside of the more usual הַיֹּצֵא (Joüon §158e).

The word בהמה occurs approximately 185x in OT, 4x in the books of Kings (18:5; 2 Kgs. 3:9; 3:17) and may denote wild as well as tame animals (cf. G.J. Botterweck, *TWAT*, I, 523-536). In an expression like 'man and beast,' which occurs about 45x, the reference is to the totality of humans and animals, and also in our verse one gets the impression that in this word we are dealing with the totality of the animal world, just as in עצים it seemed we were dealing with the totality of the plant world. This implies that the word ועל which follows 3 more times in our verse, either indicates a further differentiation of that animal world or an addition to it. The latter is the more likely because also elsewhere in OT a distinction is made in any case between 'animals' and 'birds' (cf. e.g. Gen. 2:20), and at the same time other distinctions occur (cf. Gen. 1:24f.; further Botterweck, a.l.). The problem arises from the fact that in Israel and the surrounding world, people held a different view of the biological functions of man and animal than we, who, though accustomed to divide fauna in strict categories, do not distinguish animals psychologically as was done in ancient times: animals, birds, fish, reptiles ('creeping things') (cf. also Pedersen, I-II, 480ff.). For the word רֶמֶשׂ and the verb רמשׂ which means 'to creep,' or 'to swarm' (esp. in Gen. 1:21-30; 7:8, 14, 21; 8:17, 19; 9:2; further: Lev. 11:44, 46; 20;25; Deut. 4:18; Ezek. 38:20; Ps. 69:35; 104:20), refers to a wide

---

[4] Cf. also J.M.A. Janssen in *L'Ancien Testament et l'Orient* (ed. G. Ryckmans), Louvain 1957, 38f., who expressly refers to our verse.

assortment of creeping or stalking animals. It may refer to snakes but also to insects and beetles. Only here the word רֶמֶשׂ occurs in our books (further esp. in the above-mentioned contexts of the verb). But 'insects' can also be classified under עוֹף to the extent that they fly. The classification points especially to the elements in which the animals live: land, air, and water.

5:14 *People came from every nation to listen to Solomon's wisdom, (being delegated by) all the kings of the earth who had heard of his wisdom.*
The fact that many nations heard rumours of this wise king and wanted to learn from his wisdom is the consequence of the preceding. In what follows we will encounter examples of this: among other things, that of the visit by the queen of Sheba.

By comparison with other ancient versions, our MT is somewhat divergent. Thus LXX reads that 'all the nations' came to listen and not, as MT says, that 'men from every nation' came to listen. In any case MT offers good sense and does not need modification. A second difference is the addition in LXX[Luc.] and Pesh. of 'he received gifts' from all the kings of the earth who heard of his wisdom. This addition is taken over by Klostermann, Noth, and others, and is materially in agreement with, say, 2 Chr. 9:23f. On the other hand, Burney has proposed to read מאת as 'deputed by' (cf. 2 Sam. 15:3), hence as 'delegated by the kings' (see Barthélemy; but cf. Ewald §219a: accentuation of the preposition). This seems to us a plausible interpretation of MT. The kings themselves did not come but sent their envoys (so, already, Thenius).

In the third place, as we have already pointed out earlier, the sequence of what follows in our vs. is different in LXX. The latter continues with what was said in MT in 3:1 and adds the vss. 9:16, 17a. It is worthy of note that Josephus (*Ant.* VIII §§45ff.) makes extensive reference to Solomon's knowledge of exorcism and his ability to compose incantation formulas against diseases. Josephus even describes a feat of exorcism by means of Solomon's prescriptions, performed in his time by a certain Eleazar in the presence of Vespasian and his court. In this manner the greatness of Solomon's name is still being demonstrated in Josephus's days (cf. E. Lohse, *TDNT*, VII, 460-463).

1 KINGS 5:15-32

5:15 *Now Hiram, king of Tyre, sent his servants to Solomon, for he had heard that they had anointed him king in place of his father. Hiram, you must know, had always been on friendly terms with David also.*

16 *Then Solomon sent to Hiram (a message):*

17 *'You know that my father David could not build a house for the name of YHWH, his God, on account of the warfare with which his enemies surrounded him, until YHWH put them under the soles of his feet.*

18 *But now YHWH my God has given me peace on every side: there is neither adversary nor misfortune any more.*

19 *Moreover, I am thinking of building a house for the name of YHWH, my God, as YHWH said to my father David: "Your son, whom I will put on the throne in your place, will build the house in honor of my name."*

20 *Now then, give orders that cedars of Lebanon be cut for me, a project in which my servants will work together with your servants, and I will pay you for your men such wages as you set. For you know very well that among us there is no one so skilled in felling timber as the Sidonians.'*

21 *When Hiram heard these things from Solomon he was very pleased and said: 'Praised be YHWH today that he has given David such a wise son to rule over this great nation.'*

22 *Hiram sent word to Solomon, saying: 'I have heard the message which you have sent me and will do all you want in the matter of the cedar and cypress timber.*

23 *My servants will haul them down from the Lebanon to sea and I will float them in rafts by sea to the place you direct. There I will break them up so that you can take them further. You can fulfill my wish by providing food for my household.'*

24 *So Hiram supplied Solomon with all the cedar and cypress he desired,*

25 *while Solomon give Hiram twenty thousand cors of wheat as food or his household, and twenty cors of beaten oil. Solomon did this for Hiram year after year.*

26 *YHWH gave wisdom to Solomon as he had promised him. There was peace between Hiram and Solomon: and they made a treaty between them.*

27 *King Solomon raised a levy of forced labour from all of Israel, which numbered thirty thousand men.*

28 *He sent ten thousand men to the Lebanon in monthly relays; they spent a month on the Lebanon and two months at home. Adoniram was in charge of the forced labour.*

29 *Solomon had seventy thousand carriers and eighty thousand stonecutters* *in the hills,*

30 *aside from the three thousand three hundred supervisors of the governors who were over the project, who had charge of the people who carried out the work.*

31 *At the king's command, they quarried out large blocks of quality stone to lay the foundation of the house of dressed stone.*

32 *Solomon's craftsmen and those of Hiram (the Giblites) cut and prepared the timber and the stone for the building of the house.*

INTRODUCTION

5:15 marks the beginning of a large unit in which the preparations for building the temple and the construction itself are described. Vss. 15-26 are designed to reflect the negotiations between Solomon and the Tyrian king Hiram and give the impression of being a single whole. This in contrast to vss. 27-32 which, though they clearly follow upon 15-26, are much more heterogeneous in structure. Vss. 15-26 contain so-called dtr. phrases (e.g. vss. 17, 19: 'a house for the name of YHWH') and seem in any case adapted by dtr. if they have not been composed by him on the basis of 'dispersed items of information' (thus, for example, Noth). In any case our pericope is more than an arid summary of exact data. The impression that it is a composed narrative rooted in traditional materials is probably correct. Already in 2 Sam. 5:11 (cf. 1 Chr. 14:1) the cordial relationship between David and Hiram is noted. Still the story also contains information which fits well with the transports – doubtlessly enormous for that time – which were organized for the purpose of the temple construction, as well as for the building of the palace (which is not mentioned in our chapter).[1]

EXEGESIS

5:15 *Now Hiram, king of Tyre, sent his servants to Solomon, for he had heard that they had anointed him king in place of his father. Hiram, you must know, had always been on friendly terms with David also.*

Our verse introduces the story of the negotiations and as such gives an impres-

---

[1] Cf. F.C. Fensham, "The Treaty Between the Israelites and Tyrians," SVT 17 (1969), 71-87, esp. 73ff.; J. Priest, "The Covenant of Brothers," *JBL* 84 (1965), 400-406; H. Donner, "Israel und Tyrus im Zeitalter Davids und Salomos. Zur gegenseitige Abhängigkeit von Innen- und Außenpolitik," *JNSL* (1982), 43-52; and now also J.K. Kuan, "Third Kingdoms 5.1 and Israelite-Tyrian Relations During the Reign of Solomon," *JSOT* 46 (1990), 31-46.

sion of being independent. Also aside from the following story our verse could have functioned as a statement of information. The exchange of envoys and pleasantries on the occasion of a royal succession is also reported in 2 Sam. 10:2 (cf. Montg.-Gehman, 133). In our verse the king of Tyre is called Hiram (Chirām), in vss. 24, 32 Hirom (Chirôm). This difference is the result of shifts in the Phoen. system of vocalization (cf. Ewald §37a).[2] The name is probably a contraction of אחירם, 'my brother is exalted,' a statement in which the element אח is presumably theophoric (cf. Noth, *IPN*, 71-75). The rendering of the name as 'the brother of the exalted one' (cf. Burney) is to be regarded as less correct. The name of this king occurs especially in our chapter, and in the chaps. 9 and 10. Josephus calls him Εἴρωμος. His rule must be dated in the middle of the 10th century BCE (for the dates, cf. Montg.-Gehman, 133).[3] Phoe. influence was extended around the Mediterranean Sea by trade and colonization. Josephus, *Ant.* VIII §§144ff. (cf. *c.Ap.* I §§116ff.; *GLAJJ*, I, 123ff.) in this connection cites Menander and also Dios who are said to have translated Tyrian stories into Greek. These stories furnish details about the work done by Hiram (cf. also R.W. Corney, *IDB*, II, 606f.). He is to be carefully distinguished from his namesake who was the chief architect for the construction of Solomon's temple (7:13, 40, 45; 2 Chr. 4:11, 16, etc.). There is some reason to doubt whether the Hiram referred to in 2 Sam. 5:11 is the same as the Hiram in our pericope. Is not this Hiram's father who is called Abibalos by Menander in Josephus (§44; thus Thenius et al.)? But this is not certain.

LXX, following the statement that Hiram sent his servants to Solomon, reproduces MT as follows: χρίσαι τὸν Σαλωμὼν ἀντὶ Δαυεὶδ τοῦ πατρὸς αὐτοῦ, an abbreviation of the text which is not an improvement (so also Stade-Schwally). MT makes good sense as it stands. אתו is emphatic by position as though Hiram, too, was familiar with the events of chap. 1 (cf. Burney). Besides this reason for sending envoys to Solomon (viz. the report that Solomon had succeeded David), there was a second motive, introduced by כי: Hiram was a close friend of David. In the first place, the verb אהב is used here (cf. J. Bergman, A. Halder, G. Wallis, *TWAT*, I, 105-128; E. Jenni, *THAT*, I, 60-73). which in this case clearly refers to a friendly alliance between 2 heads of state (cf. also J.A. Thompson, *VT* 29 [1979], 200). In the second place, the genitive is here circumscribed by ל. This circumscription is often used to indicate greater indefiniteness than usual (cf. comments on 2:39 and Burney, a.l). Sometimes this *lamed* is called 'the dative of the possessor' (cf. König

---

[2] Cf. also Z.S. Harris, *A Grammar of the Phoenician Language*, New Haven 1936, §11.
[3] J. Liver, לבעית הכרונולוגיה של הירם מלך צור, *Studies in Bible and Judean Desert*, Jerusalem 1971, 189-197, thinks he became king in 979/8 and assisted in the construction of the temple in 968/7.

§286c). It does not state the object of the verb.⁴ A final addition states that this friendship lasted כל הימים, i.e. all his (David's) life (cf. 12:7; 14:30 etc.). Following these words Pesh. has still another addition: 'thus Hiram sent envoys to David and blessed him.' This addition seems to find some support in Josephus's rendering of the text: καὶ πέμψας πρὸς αὐτὸν ἠσπάζετό τε καὶ συνέχαιρεν ἐπὶ τοῖς παροῦσιν ἀγαθοῖς. It is likely that this addition, if one does not wish to attribute it to a later expansion of the tradition, is based on a deviant 'Vorlage.' It is not necessary to augment MT with these words.

5:16 *Then Solomon sent to Hiram (a message):*
To this brief sentence Josephus (*Ant.* VIII §50) adds that the message was a letter (γράμματα) which Solomon returned to Hiram. In *c.Ap.* I §111 he reports that the 2 kings exchanged numerous letters which 'up until now' have been preserved in Tyre (σώζονται δὲ μέχρι νῦν παρὰ τοῖς Τυρίοις πολλαὶ τῶν ἐπιστολῶν ἃς ἐκεῖνοι πρὸς ἀλλήλους ἔγραψαν). Eusebius, *Prep. Evang.*, IX, 31ff., mentions Solomon's letters as well. The source of this information is Eupolemus, a Hellenistic Jewish historian who wrote his Περὶ τῶν ἐν τῇ Ἰουδαίᾳ βασιλέων in Palestine in the middle of the second century BCE. In this correspondence Hiram is called Σούρων. The letter referred to in our verse and the next differs somewhat in content from what we find in Josephus (cf. Eusebius, IX, 33, 1; and also 2 Chr. 2:2ff., where one finds another version of Solomon's letter to Hiram).

5:17 *'You know that my father David could not build a house for the name of YHWH, his God, on account of the warfare with which his enemies surrounded him, until YHWH put them under the soles of his feet.*
In this verse and the next the request for help in building a temple is introduced by Solomon. These verses contain a fair amount of dtr. material (see also comments on 3:2 above) based on amongst others 2 Sam. 7. The position of the personal pronoun (2 p. sing.) is emphatic. Next 'David my father' is placed proleptically before כי (Ewald §336b; König §414c; Ges-K §117h; Jouon §157d), so that the subject of the subordinate clause becomes the object of the main clause. This construction occurs especially in the case of the so-called *verba sentiendi*. The word מלחמה 'war' occurs approximately 320x in OT (cf. A.S. van der Woude, *THAT*, II, 502ff.; H.D. Preuß, *TWAT*, IV, 914-926). On account of the rather difficult construction, text modifications have been proposed. One of these is that, in imitation of the ancient versions, some scholars want to read the pl. of מלחמה (cf. Stade-Schwally). It has correctly been pointed out (Ewald §317b; Burney) that the grammatical sing. of a word

---

⁴ So F. Giesebrecht, *Die hebräische Präposition Lamed*, Halle 1876, 37.

can indicate a pl. Thus, in our case, one could speak of 'the state of warfare' or of 'enemies'.[5] It is a question, however, whether a pl. form or idea really helps the sense of the immediately following words. One can indeed say that 'wars surrounded him,' but then how does one explain the אתם which follows next? It is not wars, after all, but enemies which are put under the feet of the conqueror. It is better, therefore, and more natural, to assume that סבב is construed with 2 accusatives, one of which is the so-called *nota relationis* אשר (cf. GD §90a; König §327q; BrSynt. §152d; also Kittel, Benzinger, Šanda, Noth). The subject of the subordinate clause – 3 p. pl. – is the indefinite subject 'people' (BrSynt. §36c): people surrounded him (David) with war, i.e. with a state of constant fighting, until YHWH put 'them' under the soles of his feet (cf. P. Ackroyd, *TWAT*, III, 451). As for the last word, there is a difference between $k^e tib$ and $q^e re$ (see Delitzsch, *LSF*, §42a). The $k^e tib$, with Pesh., reads 'his foot'; with a number of MSS $q^e re$ reads 'my feet.' According to LXX, Vulg., Tg. and many Hebr. MSS, a third possibility is 'his feet.' The first or third option is undoubtedly the best because the suffix can logically apply only to David. Further, the pl. form is to be preferred, also because the suffix ו more frequently indicates a pl. For the rest, according to the Mm, there are no fewer than 48 cases in which a *waw* is written at the end of a word but *yod* is read (Weil, no. 3811). Putting enemies under the feet of their conqueror is repeatedly depicted in antiquity, as is clear from pls. 296 and (esp.) 417 in *ANEP* (cf. also Ps. 110:1 and Mal. 3:21). The expression also occurs outside OT (e.g. *KAI* 26A I, 16f.; *KAI* 18, 6f.) in Phoen. inscriptions, where the verb שית is used in place of נתן (cf. Y. Avishur, *UF* 8 [1976], 9). The expression, accordingly, has a literal as well as a symbolic meaning (cf. Josh. 10:24 and K. Weiss, *TDNT*, VI, 626).

As the reason why David could not build a temple for 'the name of YHWH' (cf. also Pedersen, I-II, 245 and H. Bietenhard, *TDNT*, V, 254ff.) our verse (and the sequel) states that as yet there was no state of peace or rest. In 2 Sam. 7 (cf. also 1 Kgs. 8:17ff.) the building of a temple was expressly reserved for David's son.[6] In 1 Chr. 22:8ff. and 28:2ff. this objection is motivated by the addition that David was a warrior whose hands had shed blood which would have made the sacred work on the temple impossible.[7] A similar motivation occurs in Eupolemos (Eusebius, *Prep. Evang.*, IX, 30, 5). It is indeed clear that – according to the core information in these versions – David must have had or made plans to begin the building of a temple, but that for some reason – his

---

[5] Thus also C.F. Burney, *The Book of Judges*, London 1930³, 115, n.

[6] For a discussion of Nathan's motives in 2 Sam. 7, cf. R.E. Clements, *God and Temple*, Oxford 1965, 56-59.

[7] See now P.B. Dirksen, "Why was David Disqualified as Temple Builder? The Meaning of 1 Chronicles 22:8," *JSOT* 70 (1996), 51-56.

age perhaps? – he failed to achieve his goal. Donner, *JNSL* 10 (1982), 51f., regards 2 Sam. 5:11 and 24:5ff. as late ('nachgeformte') texts. At that time David would no longer have had connections with Tyre.

5:18 *But now YHWH my God has given me peace on every side: there is neither adversary nor misfortune any more.*
Solomon now points to the 'rest' he and his kingdom enjoy. The so-called hiph. I of the verb נוח occurs 33x in OT – in Kings only here – and generally means 'to let rest.' In many cases, as also here, it is YHWH who furnishes rest to his people or his beloved, a connection in which also the noun מְנוּחָה is used. Frequently forms of the stem נוח occur in connection with public speeches on the entry into the 'Promised Land,' in which – again as in our verse – the conquest of the enemies of Israel constitutes a part. Such speeches, moreover, often have a dtr. stamp (cf. F. Stolz, *THAT*, II, 43-46; also H.D. Preuß, *TWAT*, V, 297-307). In these dtr. layers one can make a further distinction between 'rest' in the sense of a secure dwelling place for Israel on both sides of the Jordan (Deut. 3:20; Josh. 1:13, 15; 10:40-43; 11:16-20 etc.) or in 'having time for God' (Josh. 23; 2 Sam. 7:1, 11, our verse, etc.).[8]

The word שטן occurs 27x in OT (see G. Wanke, *THAT*, II, 821ff.), several of them in Job 1 and 2, and in our book 3x in chap. 11 (vss. 14, 23, 25), where Solomon's 'adversaries' come up. Via the 'copulative-distributive' אין...ואין (König §371e) פגע רע is joined to the former. The reference in this term is to that which 'strikes' a person (cf. S. Amsler, *THAT*, II, 682f.). Here it means that which a person experiences in the way of misfortune (cf. Prov. 9:11, the other instance of this noun in OT; the verb פגע occurs much more frequently; cf. 2:25, 29, 31f., 34, 46). LXX[B] translates פגע by ἁμάρτημα in place of the more natural and more commonly followed (in the LXX-MSS) word ἀπάντημα (cf. G. Bertram, *TDNT*, I, 288: 'the obstacle to building the temple'). Schleusner suspects that ἁμάρτημα is another rendering of a commentator who, instead of פגע, read the word פֶּשַׁע.

5:19 *Moreover, I am thinking of building a house for the name of YHWH, my God, as YHWH said to my father David: "Your son, whom I will put on the throne in your place, will build the house in honor of my name."*
The verb אמר, here as so often, means 'to think,' 'to plan' (cf. Exod. 2:14; 1 Sam. 30:6; 2 Sam. 21:16 etc.). In this verse the 'temple-building' plan is unfolded which already surfaced in 2 Sam. 7 in the case of David. הנה is often construed with a pronom. suffix and a part. with the pronom. suffix occurring

---

[8] Cf. W. Roth, "The Deuteronomic Rest Theology: A Redaction-Critical Study," *BR* 21 (1976), 5-14; and M. Metzger, *UF* 2 (1970), 157 n. 50.

125x in 1 p. sing., as here.[9] No fewer than 118x YHWH is the subject of it, in which case the formula presupposes a response to a summons. Here the situation is somewhat different: Solomon is the subject; his plan to build a temple is the response to the 'rest' in which his God and he may live.

It is evident (so also Thenius et al.) that 2 Sam. 7:12f. is foundational to our verse. But there, too, scholars consider the addition post-dtr. (Benzinger et al.). Benzinger even supposes that in place of our vss. 17-19 there must originally have been a sentence having the following content: 'I am planning to build a palace and a temple.' Whether we have to go this far is hard to prove. It is more natural to attribute both 2 Sam. 7:12f. and our verse to a (dtr.) adaptor. Entirely within the expanding framework of Chronicles, a theological motivation, or perhaps better: a theologically rounded *apologia* for the building of a temple and the Tyrian assistance given to that end, occurs in 2 Chr. 2:2-6. Striking there is that David is mentioned (vs. 3) as the recipient of Hiram's cedars for use in the construction of his palace. Benzinger and others are therefore right in saying that the fact of Solomon's negotiations with Hiram must, in the course of time, have undergone all sorts of expansions and embellishments.

5:20 *Now then, give orders that cedars of Lebanon be cut for me, a project in which my servants will work together with your servants, and I will pay you for your men such wages as you set. For you know very well that among us there is no one so skilled in felling timber as the Sidonians.'*
With the word ועתה a new idea or a new subject is introduced. Now comes the actual request for help and the delivery of wood. The imperative which follows this particle with ו can be called a 'voluntative' (cf. Driver §62; Joüon §177j; Burney), which can be reproduced by 'in order to' or by 'that they ...' 'They' as 'impersonal' 3 p. pl. here applies to Hiram's workmen. 'Cedars' have to be cut for the construction of a temple. Earlier we saw (under vs. 13 above) that in general the word ארז denotes 'tall coniferous trees.' In vs. 22, in Hiram's response to Solomon, our word is further specified as the 'wood of cedars' and the 'wood of cypresses.' Also in the par. verse 2 Chr. 2:8 there is mention of these kinds of woods as well as of algum timber (אלגומים). The LXX simply refers to ξύλα (cf. Pesh.: 'wood of cedars') but this is no reason for modifying MT. The concept of ארז is itself a summary of the different kinds of wood suited for the building of a temple and palace (cf. H. Mayer, *BZ* NF 11 [1967], 53-66; also *RSP*, I, 397 [litt.]). From antiquity, thanks to the work of Theophrastus of Eresos (± 372-287 BCE), we possess rather accurate descriptions of woods and plants, also in the area of the Eastern Mediterranean. He speaks,

---

[9] Cf. P. Humbert, *Opuscules d'un hébraïsant*, Neuchâtel 1958, 54-59.

amongst others, of the homogeneity of 'cedar woods' but also clearly about the different kinds of 'cedars' which already existed in his time (cf. Brown, *Lebanon*, 140-147).

Sometimes, as in our verse, the Lebanon is linked with the article (cf. König §295c), as is also the case with certain other names (e.g. Bashan). Ehrlich clarifies the collaboration of Solomon's servants with those of Hiram by saying that there it is a matter of the former helping the latter. To us it also seems logical that Solomon would pay the wages of the labourers. The word שכר occurs almost 30x in OT, combined sometimes with נתן (Gen. 30:18; Exod. 2:9). LXX^B, however, reads δουλείας, where LXX$^{Luc.}$ has και τον μισθον των δουλων, which ties in closely with our MT. We encounter another text-critical difficulty in the word בכל. Some Hebr. MSS and *Sebir* read בבל; Pesh. reads as though MT simply read כל. But MT offers good sense and does not need to be changed.

The conclusion of the text states that the 'Sidonians,' in contrast to Solomon's subjects, were good woodcutters. They had knowledge of the right kind of trees, of the best time to fell them, and of the further treatment and processing of the timber (thus Thenius). Their knowledge was probably not limited to these aspects of timber processing (contra Thenius). Also from 1 Chr. 22:4 and Ezra 3:7 we learn of the name and fame of the inhabitants of the Lebanon region with respect to woodproducts and as wood suppliers. These inhabitants were called 'Sidonians' after the city of Sidon, which in certain periods of antiquity was even more powerful than Tyre. 'Sidonian' can often mean the same thing as 'Phoenician.' Thus Homer (*Iliad*, 23, 743) also uses 'Sidonians' but in the next line he speaks of 'Phoenicians': ... ἐπεὶ Σιδόνες πολυδαίδαλοι εὖ ἤσκησαν. Φοίνικες δ' ἄγον ἄνδρες ἐπ' ἠεροειδέα πόντον ... (cf. also 6, 290f., *Odyssey* 4, 84; 6, 18 etc.). In our text, however, it is not certain whether this identity can be maintained. Cf. also the above-mentioned texts 1 Chr. 22:4; Ezra 3:7 (cf. Van Gelderen, a.l., and my *Ba'al*, 27, n. 4). The present-day *Saidā*, smaller than the once-mighty Sidon, situated in and by the sea, is located approximately halfway between Tyre and Beirut.

5:21 *When Hiram heard these things from Solomon he was very pleased and said: 'Praised be YHWH today that he has given David such a wise son to rule over this great nation.'*

Hiram happily accepts Solomon as colleague on the throne of his southern neighbour. He expresses his joy, amongst others, by saying: ברוך יהוה (cf. also Exod. 18:10 and 1 Kgs. 10:9 in the mouth of non-Israelites). It is probable that underlying the curse or blessing addressed to a deity there is the primitive idea that by them the deity's power can be either weakened or strengthened (cf. amongst others J. Hempel, *ZDMG* 79 (1925), 20-110, and *RGG*^{2}, V, 391f.; more generally: H.W. Beyer, *TDNT*, II, 761ff.), so that even the utterance of a malediction or a blessing to the deity is efficacious and irresistible. It may seem unlikely that Hiram 'blessed' Israel's God in that way; still it was not unusual in the ancient Near East for rulers to acknowledge and bless the presence and power of the gods of neighbouring countries (cf. De Vries, *Yesterday*, 225 n. 276). The Chronicler (2 Chr. 2:10f.) expands Hiram's answer (aside from the fact that he has it conveyed by means of a letter) as follows: 'Blessed be YHWH, the God of Israel, who made heaven and earth.' Such a confession of faith is certainly more than Hiram would have made. Admittedly, in our verse LXX$^{Luc.}$ reads 'the Lord, the God of Israel,' which Klostermann et al. would find more fitting on Hiram's lips. But the abbreviated form is no less fitting. We do not even have to follow LXX here, which reads ὁ θεός in place of YHWH.

The word היום, omitted in one Hebr. MS and in LXX$^{Luc.}$, presents a small difficulty. It is indeed rather strange to limit this word to 'today' as if Solomon had become king that very day. Ehrlich proposes putting היום by נתן and translating: 'Blessed by YHWH, who has *now* given to (ל as designation of the genitive) David a wise son to be king over this great people.' But it is hard to see how this would actually solve the problem. In the case of commandments, promises, blessings, and imprecations the word 'today' has a deeper meaning than solely as a designation of (measurable) time. It has a certain 'theological' weight (cf. Deut. 26:17-19) as 'charged time,' which is often decisive for God and people (for this cf. E. Fuchs, *TDNT*, VII, 269f.; also. De Vries, 225). In this formula of blessing (cf. Deut. 1:10; 6:24; 11:26 etc.) 'today' can therefore be fittingly maintained. It would seem that Hiram is citing a liturgical formula.

5:22 *Hiram sent word to Solomon, saying: 'I have heard the message which you have sent me and will do all you want in the matter of the cedar and cypress timber.*

Hiram agrees to Solomon's request. אני is emphatically placed up front (cf. Joüon §146a); Solomon's wish will be fulfilled. The noun חפץ occurs 38x in OT, 8 of them in the dtr. historiography (cf. G.J. Botterweck, *TWAT*, III, 102). Here the meaning is 'wish' (cf. Botterweck, 108; further, G. Schrenk, *TDNT*, III, 53). Aside from the 'cedars' which will be cut for Solomon, there is now also mention of ברושים. This word is much less frequent in OT than ארז; it occurs only 20x, 6 of them in our books (vs. 24; 6:15, 34; 9:11; 2 Kgs. 19:23). It was often translated by 'cypresses' (*Cupressus sempervirens)*, but no stork made its home in these trees (cf. Ps. 104:17). It must have been a tree indigenous to Lebanon, not so much to Palestine. It is probably a coniferous tree, perhaps the *Juniperus excelsa* (M. Zohary, *IDB*, II, 292f.) or the *Juniperus phoenicea* (*HAL*, s.v.). The former resembles the 'cedar' in sturdiness and height and emits a strong fragrance. In addition its wood is very well-suited for construction. Perhaps 'juniper wood' or 'juniper berry wood' best conveys the meaning of the word here. The LXX translates ξύλα κέδρινα καὶ πεύκινα. In LXX the last-mentioned word can also convey the hard-to-track-down 'algum wood' (2 Chr. 2:8; 9:11). But Josephus (*Ant.* VIII §54) speaks of ξύλα (πολλὰ καὶ μεγάλα) κέδρου τε καὶ κυπαρίσσου. LXX's πεύκινα are 'pine trees,' a genus of plants belonging to the family of conifers of which there are many kinds (cf. Schleusner, s.v.; for the manufacture and supply of wood, see Laetus [2 century BCE], *GLAJJ*, I, 129).

5:23 *My servants will haul them down from the Lebanon to sea and I will float them in rafts by sea to the place you direct. There I will break them up so that you can take them further. You can fulfill my wish by providing food for my household.'*
A few details about the transport of the material follow. First the wood must be hauled down from the mountains to the sea. This Hiram's servants will do. It is not necessary to think especially of Solomon's servants for this job as *BHK* et al. still suggest. It is still a question whether as a result of haplography of the *mem* a suffix (3 p. pl.) has dropped out after ירדו (for this, cf. Böttcher §296; Ehrlich; Delitzsch, *LSF* §8a et al.). We think, with Montg.-Gehman, that such an emendation, which is natural in a translation (cf. LXX), is unnecessary.

A second phase of the process is the further transfer of the wood. A well-tested way is to bind the logs together into rafts and to float them to their destination. In our text the word for 'rafts' is the *hapax legomenon* דברות. In the parallel vs. 2 Chr. 2:15 the word רפסדות is used, similarly a *hapax legomenon*. One arrives at the given translation on the basis of the context and the ancient versions, such as LXX, Pesh., and Vulg. Montg.-Gehman further refer to the stem דבר, 'to conduct,' 'to guide,' but such an etymological explanation tends not to shed much light. Just as both marine and navigational terms in OT were derived from other peoples (for this, cf. M. Wüst, *BRL*², 276f.), that may be the case with this term as well. It is usually imagined that the timbers, bound together into rafts, were pulled by ships to their destination. A question which arises in this context is whether Hiram had control over all the timber resources of the Lebanon or only over the part within his jurisdiction. That territory was not larger than the area between Beirut and Tyre. Biologists, basing themselves on the woods available in antiquity and information from classical literature, believe that no timber could be cut below Tyre, so that Hiram must have had control if not over the whole Lebanon, then at least over a large part of it (cf. Brown, *Lebanon*, 206f.).

The transport of the rafts occurred up to a specifically agreed-upon place where they were again taken apart. For this concise construction we need not revise MT by, for instance, replacing בים with וַאֲבִיאָם (cf. *BHK*). In 2 Chr. 2:16 Joppa is mentioned as the final destination, an instance of specific information which may be based both on tradition and the actual state of affairs at the time of the Chronicler (cf. Ezra 3:7). For the breaking up of the rafts MT uses the verb נפץ pi., but only here in Kings.

A third point discussed in this verse is the arrangement for paying for all this work, consisting in supplying food to Hiram's household. The reference is specifically to this, and not to providing for all of Hiram's workmen. This last point will come up later. Thenius rather nicely comments that as long as the Tyrians and Sidonians were working on this project they could not go shopping elsewhere, and that Solomon therefore had to take over this responsibility from them. לתת is here used as a gerundive (cf. GD §108; further also König §400c). Josephus, *Ant.* VIII §54, explains the request for food by pointing out that Hiram was living 'on an island.' This economic dependence of the Tyrians and Sidonians is evident in a later period as well (cf. Acts 12:20). To all this Josephus adds that right up to his own time the Tyrians still possessed copies (ἀντίγραφα) of these letters (cf. *c.Ap.* I §§106ff.). He notes this especially to drive home to his readers the fact that he did not make up anything, but that all his claims rested on verifiable information.

5:24 *So Hiram supplied Solomon with all the cedar and cypress he desired,*
Hiram starts with the implementation of his promise. The part. plus a form of the verb היה denotes the regular, ongoing nature of the action (cf. König §239b; Bg. II §13i*). We believe, with Noth, that כל־חפצו is in apposition with the preceding objects, so that one need not, for instance, with LXX$^{Luc.}$, emend the text. LXX^B and other LXX MSS omit the 'cypress trees' here.

5:25 *while Solomon give Hiram twenty thousand cors of wheat as food or his household, and twenty cors of beaten oil. Solomon did this for Hiram year after year.*
Now Solomon's *quid pro quo* is considered. The pf. qal נתן, in contrast to the construction with ויהי ... נתן in the preceding verse, seems to denote a single once-for-all event. Still this is not the case, as is evident from the conclusion of our verse: כה יתן. According to König §157a, this impf. expresses an event in the past, which on account of its repetition and duration has to appear to be incomplete (cf. also Bg. II §7d: 'tend to ...'). Driver §160, moreover, has pointed out that the kind of construction as that with which our verse begins, indicates a circumstantial clause: 'while Solomon gave Hiram ...' If it had really been a new sentence it would have begun with ויתן (cf. also Burney; Montg.-Gehman). What Solomon gave Hiram is first of all 20,000 cors of wheat. For בר, cf. vs. 2 above. חטה, 'wheat,' occurs approx. 30x in OT but in the books of Kings only here (cf. Dalman, *AuS* 2, 243ff.). Wheat is a costly and precious grain, gladly used also in antiquity for baking (cf. W.L. Reed, *BASOR* 146 [1957], 6-10). It is not surprising that this wheat is referred to as food for Hiram's household. מכלת (mistakenly called 'wohl Schreibfehler' by

Bg. I §15bd) originated, with assimilation of the *'aleph,* from מַאֲכֹלֶת (cf. Isa. 9:4, 18; Ewald, §§ 79b, 160d; Stade §112a; Ges-K §23^f; Delitzsch, *LSF* §14a; *BR* 493a; cf. for the Syriac, Pesh. on Ezek. 48:18, where most MSS read *m'kwlt'* but 7h2 *mkwlt'!*). In the par. verse 2 Chr. 2:9, the text even reads מַכּוֹת, which, just as e.g. LXX^B μαχεὶρ or LXX^A μαχαλ etc., shows that the translators did not clearly understand the Hebr. word. Only Aquila noted διατροφή as a gloss in LXX MS 71 after μαχιλ. This 'transcription' of the Hebr. word from our verse into the different MSS of the LXX as well as into the parallel verse in 2 Chr. 2, is all the more remarkable since the other ancient versions simply translate the word by 'food.'

In the second place he supplies 20 *cors* of beaten oil. As far as the amount is concerned, LXX, 2 Chr. 2:9, Pesh. and also Josephus, *Ant.* VIII §57, diverge from our text by writing 20,000. In addition 2 Chr. 2:9, LXX, and Josephus also speak of בַּת in place of כר, where it concerns the oil. A בת is especially a liquid measure, occurs 12x in OT, and is mentioned in Kings in 7:26, 38. In Ezek. 45:14, 10 בת is said to be equal to one חֹמֶר, but it is very much a question whether this proportion is valid for all the periods of Israel's history. In that case a בת would equal about 40-45 l (cf. *HAL,* s.v.; Barrois, II, 248 [איפה=], 250 [=39, 38 l.]; De Vaux, *Inst.* I, 306ff.; G. Schmitt, *BRL*^{2}, 205). Josephus tells us as a matter of interest that the *bath* contained 72 *sextarii,* i.e. 72 *log* (ὁ δὲ βάτος δύναται ξέστας ἑβδομήκοντα δύο). ξέστης is usually taken to be a corruption of the Lat. *sextarius* (cf. Krauss, *GLL,* II, 293, 535) and is the equivalent of about half a liter. In NT the word occurs in the sense of 'vessel,' 'bar,' 'cup' (Mark 7:4). In our verse the reference is not to 'ordinary' oil but to שֶׁמֶן כָּתִית (Exod. 27:20; 29:40; Lev. 24:2; Num. 28:5 and our verse), that is 'beaten' oil (cf. the verb בתת, i.e. the oil gained from olives under very light pressure from the initial crushing). This oil was 'clear' or 'pure' (זַךְ, Exod. 27:20; Lev. 24:2), hence of the best quality and expensive. It was used, for example, for the lamps in the sanctuary and the daily food offering, hence for those actions which required the absolute best. By heightening the pressure or by heating one could obtain a second yield but of a lower quality oil (for oil and its preparation, cf. Dalman, *AuS,* IV, 153-290; D. Kellermann, *BRL*^{2}, 238ff.). In antiquity apparently only wealthy people could afford to purchase the precious oil (cf. 2 Kgs. 20:13 and Amos 6:6). The question now is whether our MT is correct or whether we should follow LXX et al. A problem in our text is, first of all, that for a liquid the *cor* is used, which is equal to about 10 *baths,* hence a volume of almost 400 l. In the second place, the number 20 seems particularly small by comparison with 20,000. Still we are not inclined to modify MT on the basis of LXX or 2 Chr. 2:9. In the first place, LXX – and also Chronicles – has a tendency, wherever possible, to inflate Solomon's position. J.W. Wevers, *OTS* 8 (1950), 308f., has correctly pointed out the possibility that the LXX translator reduced the size of the measure (from *cor* into *bath*) but exaggerated the number. In the second place, the *cor* as liquid measure cannot be completely ruled out. In that case we would be talking about 8000 l of high quality oil – no small amount. Noth, furthermore, makes the point that, given the soil conditions of Phoenicia, while olive trees could produce oil, the land was not well-suited for agriculture, so that agricultural products might well be imported in quantity from Israel.

2 Chr. 2:9, continuing the tendency to exaggerate, also reports 20,000 *cors* of barley and 20,000 *baths* of wine as items of export from Israel to Phoenicia under Solomon (Josephus also mentions wine in this quantity). Our text does not report this at all, but does say that Solomon annually organized a transport of the kind described above (cf. Lev. 25:53; Deut. 15:20). And we know from 9:10-13 that Solomon had to pay a good deal more than the natural products cited. In how far a statement such as we find in our verse stems from ancient 'archival material' is hard to determine.

5:26 *YHWH gave wisdom to Solomon as he had promised him. There was peace between Hiram and Solomon: and they made a treaty between them.*
Here we encounter a 'dtr.'-sounding connective sentence (cf. Burney et al.), which can nevertheless be considered integral to the narrative. Also the agreements made with Hiram are traced to Solomon's proverbial חכמה, so that the existence of שלום, the 'relationship of friendly alliance' (cf. G. von Rad, *TDNT*, II, 402), even a ברית, a 'covenant' (a 'commercial treaty' according to G. Quell, *TDNT*, II, 112, n. 31) between Solomon and the 'Canaanite' city of Tyre, escapes the criticism of circles zealous for YHWH. The 'wisdom of Solomon,' after all, is a gift from the same YHWH. The word ברית occurs – in the sing. alone – 287x in OT; in Kings already in 3:15 above in connection with the 'ark.' Though the word is usually translated by 'covenant', a better translation perhaps is 'obligation' (according to E. Kutsch, *THAT*, I, 339-352,[10] but cf. also M. Weinfeld, *TWAT*, I, 781-808).

Especially in Israel's religion (idea of covenant) the word plays a large role (cf. W. Eichrodt, *TAT*, I-III, Leipzig 1933-1939). Pedersen, *Israel*, I-II, 285, has pointed out that the words שלום and ברית are often interchangeable (Gen. 26:28f.; Ps. 55:21). In any case there is a close connection between the 2 words and associated concepts. Josephus reports that the 'friendship' (φιλία) between Solomon and Hiram continued to grow, but this is an interpretation of 2 Hebr. words in an emotional interhuman sphere, which can at best be surmised, but not proved from the words of our verse.

---

[10] Cf. also his "Gottes Zuspruch und Anspruch" in: *Questions Disputées d'Ancient Testament*, Leuven 1974, esp. p. 81.

5:27 *King Solomon raised a levy of forced labour from all of Israel, which numbered thirty thousand men.*
Though it may have been 'peace' between Solomon and Hiram, our verse betrays the hard measures which are going to cause plenty of difficulties later in the life of Solomon's successor, when the people complain about the heavy burdens Solomon had laid on them (12:4). In 4:6 we already encountered the word מס. It is usually translated by 'forced labour,' though Wainwright argues for 'unskilled labour.' From our verse he draws the conclusion, that only volunteers desiring to take part in public projects did so for a few months a year.[11] But it is a question whether such modern 'humaneness' can be attributed to Solomon with respect to the use of labour.[12] Admittedly there is a difference between מס and מַס עֹבֵד (Gen. 49:15; Josh. 16:10; 1 Kgs. 9:21), while in addition the word סֵבֶל (cf. 1 Kgs. 11:28; Ps. 81:7; Neh. 4:11) is used. מס and סבל were in fact viewed as periodic forced labour to which every inhabitant of the kingdom was subject, whereas מס עבד was rather a condition of 'state slavery' to which only the Canaanites were subject (cf. A.F. Rainey, *IEJ* 20 [1970], 191-202; Ahlström, *Admin.* 36 and n. 61). In any case Solomon, as the first to do so, imposed this corvée on all Israel (cf. also I. Mendelsohn, *BASOR* 167 [1962], 33), whether we are dealing here with an old Canaanite system (Mendelsohn, *BASOR* 143 [1956], 17-22), or whether he was following Egyptian models (cf. Pedersen, *Israel*, III-IV, 67). There is indeed some discrepancy between this and 9:9, 15a + 20-22 where the reference is only to the Canaanite population as subject to this forced labour (Noth, *GI*, 193: 'sachlich korrekt' contra Mendelsohn, *BASOR* 167 [1962], n. 15: 'obviously an attempt by a later editor to remove the stigma from Solomon as the initiator of the hated corvée'). It is clear from our text that Israelites were spared the affliction of lifelong slavery (C. Hauer, *JSOT* 18 [1980], 66). On the other hand, Israel, to the exclusion of Judah, is accentuated in our verse, whether with MT one reads מכל or with a number of MSS על־כל. This is bound to have been regarded in Israel as an infringement on its liberty,[13] inasmuch as it is wrong to include Judah in 'all Israel.'

It is said that Solomon raised this levy of forced labour (ויעל); in LXX we read ἀναφέρω φόρον, while Josephus (§58) speaks of ἐπέταξε παντὶ τῷ λαῷ φόρον as if the king imposed the payment of a kind of tribute on all the people(!). According to K. Weiss, *TDNT*, IX, 80, if the context did not make it

---

[11] J.A. Wainwright, "Zozer's Pyramid and Solomon's Temple," *ET* 91 (1979f.), 137-140.

[12] Cf. W. Dietrich, "Das harte Joch (1 Könige 12,4). Fronarbeit in der Salomo-Überlieferung," *BN* 34 (1986), 7-16, and D. Jobling, "»Forced Labor«: Solomon's Golden Age and the Question of Literary Representation," *Semeia* 54 (1991), 57-76.

[13] Thus, correctly, J.A. Soggin in J.H. Hayes-J.M. Miller, *Israelite and Judaean History*, London 1977, 378.

completely clear to him that it concerned forced labour, a Greek might easily think of payments of tribute. The second מס has the article, because the word is now 'relatively familiar' (König §298b). The levy is said to consist of 30,000 men.

5:28 *He sent ten thousand men to the Lebanon in monthly relays; they spent a month on the Lebanon and two months at home. Adoniram was in charge of the forced labour.*
The purpose for which this levy of forced labour is to be used is now stated: it is for work in the Lebanon. The text can be understood to mean that every month there were 10,000 men on the Lebanon, who were then relieved by 10,000 other men, in order to spend 2 months at home (cf. also Rashi). This would explain the number 30,000. This would imply a relatively early form of working in relays, which every so often relieved each other. Also LXX understands the text this way. חליפה occurs in various meanings in OT: (1) '(a change of) garment' (Gen. 45:22; Judg. 14:12f.; 2 Kgs. 5:5, 22f.); (2) 'what has been' (Sir. 42:19); 'agreement' (Ps. 55:20), at least according to *KBL* and *HAL*; 'change' (S. Tengström, *TWAT*, II, 1000); 'relief' (Job 14:14; cf. 10:17). It is indeed possible in our verse to translate the word by 'relief' (e.g. *HAL*), but one can also take it as an adverb: 'alternating every month' (*HAL* refers to Ges-K §118 [*accusativus temporis*]; idem, Tengström, a.l.). The last-mentioned seems the most probable (Burney thinks of an accusative of manner or condition: 'in relays').

The question is now whether these labourers, after working a month in the Lebanon, could rest 2 months at home (so Josephus et al.),or had to work on the temple or elsewhere. The suffix (3 p. sing.) after בית in our verse can be taken to mean 'his,' i.e., Solomon's house (or temple), but LXX speaks of 'their homes,' and according to König §348u a pl. can frequently be represented by a sing. pronoun (cf. Stade-Schwally; textcrit. app. *BHS*; Burney). If Noth is right and vss. 27f. are a late adaptation, there is nothing against the view that Solomon acted with great humaneness toward the Israelites by letting them 'rest' 2 months after one month of 'forced labour.' According to R.J. Williams, SVT 28 (1975), 237 (also *TRE*, I, 501), Solomon's division of labour into 3 groups was 'also an Egyptian custom.' For the conclusion of our verse, see 4:6, where it was already reported that Adoniram was in charge of the forced labour. Vss. 27 and 28 constitute an independent report which (despite vs. 23a, to which Noth refers) need not be unreliable. In vs. 20 Solomon had already committed himself to provide help from his men, something that is nowhere rejected by Hiram.

5:29 *Solomon had seventy thousand carriers and eighty thousand stonecutters in the hills,*

The independent little block of vss. 27f. is now followed by another report, probably from another source. One sometimes gets the impression that all sorts of items of information about Solomon's organization of labour have been incorporated randomly. Having been told of the 30,000 men of the forced-labour group, we now learn of 70,000 carriers and 80,000 stonecutters, numbers which approach – if they do not cross – the boundaries of the probable. סבל, a *qattāl*-form, which in Sem. languages frequently denotes someone who performs the work indicated by the root of the verb, is a 'burden bearer' (Neh. 4:4; 2 Chr. 2:2, 18; 34:13). In the nearly parallel vs. 2 Chr. 2:18 the word is therefore used by itself as self-explanatory. For נשׂא can also mean 'carrier.' We are dealing here with an appositional addition of a noun which must be taken as explanatory (BrSynt. §63a; cf. Ges-K §131b; also Ewald §287e; König §306r). Along with the LXX and Vulg. there are those (E.g. Burney; cf. Ehrlich),[14] who in place of סָבָל want to read the word סֵבֶל, 'burden,' but this is unnecessary. In addition there were 80,000 men who cut stones 'on the mountain.' חצב is 'to cut (out)' and חֹצֵב is 'stonecutter,' sometimes followed, sometimes not, by the word אֶבֶן (2 Kgs. 12:13; Ezra 3:7; 1 Chr. 22:2, 15; 2 Chr. 2:1, 18; 24:12). Is the mountain or mountain range referred to in our verse the Lebanon (e.g. Thenius) or a Palestinian mountain range (Noth)? Or is it simply an indication that we are talking about stonecutters 'in the mountains'? This last option is quite logical because stone quarries are usually found in mountainous areas. Noth thinks it is unlikely that the reference here is to the Lebanon, because Palestine, too, has a fair number of stonequarries. But could not the reference be especially to the mountain or mountains on which Solomon's palace and temple would be built? There, and in that context, after all, a lot of breaking and cutting had to be done (cf. vs. 31).

5:30 *aside from the three thousand three hundred supervisors of the governors who were over the project, who had charge of the people who carried out the work.*
The introduction with מן לבד (see vs. 3 above) indicates an exception and makes this verse into a marginal comment (Noth). The resemblance of this verse to 9:23, aside from the precise number, is striking. *There* mention is made of 550 men. Who are these people? Are they the 'head supervisors,' 'superintendents,' the 'chiefs of the foremen' or just 'the supervisors of the governors' whom Solomon had appointed at the time of the organization of the abovementioned districts? It makes sense to assume that נצב in our verse does not refer to something other than what it means in 4:5, 7; 5:7, etc., viz.

---

[14] Cf. also M. Held, "The Root ZBL/SBL in Akkadian, Ugaritic and Biblical Hebrew," *Essays in Memory of E.A. Speiser* (= *JAOS* 88/1), New Haven 1968, 90-96, esp. 94f.

Solomon's district governor. In addition one has to grant Thenius (et al.), that if indeed there is mention here of a 'head supervisor,' where is the 'assistant supervisor'? We are evidently dealing with the directors of the (public) works who worked under Solomon's governors. Whether, and if so in what way, these offices were involved in the special labour force for the building of the palace and the temple, is not clear from this side comment. Perhaps the regular 550 men of 9:23 have been considerably augmented for this special purpose (thus Noth). But the numbers are unverifiable for us (so, correctly, Benzinger). This is confirmed by the comparison of our 3,300 men with the number mentioned in 2 Chr. 2:2, 18. Not only is there mention here of 3,600 men, but 2 Chr. 2:2 stresses that these persons were also appointed to oversee the burden bearers and stonecutters mentioned in vs. 29.

Chr. also avoids the words שרי הנצבים and speaks of מְנַצְּחִים. Josephus, too, thinks that the reference here is precisely to the overseers of the artisans mentioned, but gives the number of our text as 3,300. In the LXX one finds a variety of numbers: LXX^B has 3,600; LXX$^{Luc.}$ has 3,700; LXX^A et al. have 3,500. Vulg., Pesh. and Tg., however, remain in line with MT. This is an argument in favour of keeping MT as the original reading, at least in this verse. It does not make much sense, as is sometimes done in commentaries, to look for explanations for each of the numbers in MT and the variant readings (cf. e.g. Rashi; Šanda; Thenius), precisely because they are unverifiable. Admittedly, Benzinger is right when he points out that, by comparison with the number of labouring men used by the pharaohs for pyramid construction and the like, the numbers cited in our chapter need not be considered out of line.

Of these supervisors it is said that they were 'in charge of the people' (for רדה, see vs. 4 above). Thenius picks up in this word the notion of 'driving' ('Treibvögte'), 'coercing' to work. Perhaps he is not totally wrong in this, but it is not necessary to assume this on the basis of word usage. It may, and likely does, point equally well to the flawless organization of the project. LXX^B omits בעם, but this hardly helps to convey the meaning of the text more accurately, certainly not where in MT there is the clause adjoining 'the people' which reads: 'who carried on the work,' literally: 'occupied themselves with the work.' Twice in our verse the word מלאכה occurs, i.e. of the total number of 166 or 167x it occurs in OT (10x in 1 Kings and 6x in 2 Kings). In Ugar. the verb *l'k* means 'to send' and in OT the word 'messenger' (מלאך) occurs as often as 213x. The primary meaning of our word is 'mission,' 'project' and so 'cause,' 'work,' 'labour,' especially in the younger texts (cf. R. Ficker, *THAT* 1, 900f.). In our verse it refers to 'skilled' labour, the specialized work involved in building a temple and a palace and everything associated with it, a kind of 'public works' (cf. J. Milgrom, D.P. Wright, *TWAT*, IV, 905-911; cf. Haran, *Temples*, 191, n. 4: 'as it required special skill').

5:31 *At the king's command, they quarried out large blocks of quality stone to lay the foundation of the house of dressed stone.*

If vss. 29f. bear a secundary character (Noth), the now following verses merit the same valuation. Noth, for example, suspects that these verses are made with an eye to 7:10f. or evolved from them, because all the key words there occur here as well. It is also possible to view vs. 30 as a later insertion in this secondary text and to link vs. 31 directly with the 'stonecutters' of vs. 29. For in any case the reference in vss. 31f. is to the work of these men. That the order of the verses was already uncertain in antiquity, is evident from LXX[B, Luc.], where our verses were placed after 6:1 (along with 6:37 and 38a).

The subject in our verse is the laying of the foundations of 'the house,' i.e. of 'the temple,' at Solomon's command. For this purpose large stones are used which are also יקרות. In Kings and also elsewhere the adjective יקר occurs especially in connection with stones (2 Sam. 12:30; 1 Kgs. 7:9-11; 10:2, 10f.; Ezek. 27:22 etc.). As a rule the word is translated by 'costly' from a root *yqr* (*wqr*) which is also well-known in other Sem. languages. In OT the root occurs 73x in the form of a verb, adjective, and substantive, especially in younger, post-exilic texts (cf. S. Wagner, *TWAT*, III, 855f.). The reference in texts like 2 Sam. 12:30; 1 Kgs. 10:2; 2 Chr. 9:1, 9, etc., is to 'precious stones.' That, of course, is not the meaning of the word in our verse; the reference is rather to qualitatively good stones, suited for foundations, especially these of a costly building like the temple (Noth; Wagner, 858), because not every stone quarry would have yielded high-quality stone (cf. J. Jeremias, *TDNT*, IV, 269, n. 5). This semantic nuance for the word יקר is more natural than that suggested by Gray: 'split stones,' even though the Arab. *waqara* can mean 'to split' (see also Montg.-Gehman). The idea of 'breaking out' or 'splitting' stones from a mountain is expressed by the hiph. form of the verb נסע, which in this stem-modification occurs in only 7 other places in OT (Exod. 15:22; 2 Kgs. 4:4; Ps. 78:26, 52; Ps. 80:8; Job 19:10; Eccl. 10:9), more often in qal., especially in Numbers, like 'to pull up (tentpins),' 'to break up'. For the construction of the connection of the clause, cf. König §369k: 'eine brachylogisches Übergehung des Objectssatzes.' The object is the laying of the foundation conveyed by יסד (pi.). But also in qal יסד can mean 'to lay a foundation.' The verb occurs 41x in OT (20x in qal, 10x in pi. and 6x in pu.) and is then used especially, as here, in a technical sense related to construction; in addition also in the terminology of creation (cf. W.H. Schmidt, *THAT*, I, 736ff.; R. Mosis, *TWAT*, III, 668-682). It is presumably the intent of our verse to indicate that the entire building complex of temple and palace was constructed on a solid foundation of high quality heavy blocks of stone, which could aid in the creation of a level terrain (cf. also Thenius). The word גזית (also in 6:36; 7:9, 11f.; Exod. 20:25; Isa. 9:9; Ezek. 40:42; Amos 5:11; Lam. 3:9; 1 Chr. 22:2), which may or may not follow אבני, is the block of stone which was hewn from the mountain, a 'block of natural stone,' which is different from tiles or paving stone (cf. Amos 5:11; H. Weippert, *BRL²*, 210f., and below on 6:36). These blocks, which were sawn to measure, were probably marked in such a way that, when they were fitted on site (cf. also 7:6), they could simply be laid on top of each other. It is not necessary, therefore, to view the words אבני גזית, with which our verse ends, as a gloss (with Montg.-Gehman) on the אבנים יקרות because the concepts are not the same (cf. Josephus).

5:32 *Solomon's craftsmen and those of Hiram (the Giblites) cut and prepared the timber and the stone for the building of the house.*
The verb פסל (also Exod. 34:1, 4; Deut. 10:1, 3; Hab. 2:18), from which the more familiar word פֶּסֶל (the 'image of god' cut from stone or wood, or cast in metal) is derived, here presumably means 'to hew out,' or 'to hew.' This is what the 'builders' of Solomon and Hiram, i.e., the craftsmen, were doing. LXX reads the text as if it read בְּנֵי instead of בֹּנֵי, and translates it by 'the sons of Solomon' and 'the sons of Hiram.' This joint labour of Israelite and Phoen. workers was apparently supported by the assistance of the Giblites or the 'inhabitants of Byblos,' an ancient and familiar Phoen. harbour city. As to the form of the word, גבלי, this is a so-called *nisbe* or gentilic (Ges-K §86h) and can therefore be understood as 'inhabitants of' גבל, Byblos (Ezek. 27:9; also cf. Josh. 13:5) (cf. M.A. Beek, *BHHW*, I, 293f.). In Ugar., as the probable designation for this place, one finds *gbl* (cf. *RSP*, II, 272), *Gubla* in cuneiform, and *kpn(y)* in Egyptian, etc. (cf. *HAL*, s.v.). It is sometimes conjectured that the name is connected with the Arab. word *ǧubail* or *ǧbēl*, 'little mountain.' And indeed the town is situated on a promontory of the Lebanon which extends into the Mediterranean Sea. The Greeks called the place 'Byblos' (cf. our word 'Bible'). What, with respect to the Giblites, tends to make the text suspect, is in the first place, the question why the inhabitants of Byblos have to be mentioned again alongside of the builders of Hiram. Did they not belong to his little kingdom or were they extraordinarily skilled workers in stone? In the second place, LXX has something very different here; LXX^B: καὶ ἔβαλαν (LXX^Luc.: ἐνέβαλον) αὐτούς, which means the LXX assumed that Solomon's and Hiram's builders also laid down the stones they had hewn out (laid them down, i.e. on the correct place; see Stade-Schwally: 'a meaningless corruption of M'). Neither do Pesh. and Tg. here read 'the inhabitants of Byblos,' but *'argôblayyā*, 'stonecutters' (cf. Krauss, *GLL*, II, 126). Vulg. alone has the Giblites in mind, but draws them into the second part of our verse: *porro Biblii praeparaverunt ligna et lapides ad aedificandam domum*. Josephus neglects to mention the inhabitants of Byblos. Thenius already suggested the reading ויגבלום (cf. Klostermann: והגבילום) and was followed in this by many other scholars (see *BHK*, textcr. app.). The meaning would then become: 'to border,' 'to furnish the stone blocks with grooved edges,' by which they could be made

to fit precisely (for the גבל in the hiph., cf. Exod. 19:12, 23; also *HAL*, s.v. גבל I). It cannot be denied that this is an ingenious conjecture, which Thenius supports with weighty arguments. Still, despite this proposed text emendation, we still do not find the arguments for a correction of MT strong enough (with Noth et al.). We prefer to think here of an explanatory gloss, which crept into our text at an early stage. To a later reader or copyist the builders of Hiram the Phoenician were especially Byblians, 'skilled artisans' (cf. Ezek. 27:9). In that case the Giblites alone need not have dressed the wooden beams and stone blocks for the temple (and the palace), as the Vulg. would have it, but all the craftsmen together.

In LXX vs. 32b still precedes 6:1, and comes immediately after vs. 30. It is noteworthy that in LXX the last 2 words of MT have been omitted, but instead it reads: τρία ἔτη (LXX$^{Luc.}$: τρισὶν ἔτεσιν εἰς τὴν οἰκοδομὴν τοῦ οἴκου). LXX obviously applies the 3 years to the time of preparation for the building of the temple, which, according to 6:1, is said to have begun in the 4th year of Solomon's reign. But here again it is unnecessary to deviate from MT (so also Burney).

1 KINGS 6:1-38

6:1 *In the four hundred and eightieth year after the exodus of the Israelites from the land of Egypt, in the fourth year of Solomon's reign over Israel, in the month of Ziv – which is the second month – he began to build a house for YHWH.*

2 *Now the house which king Solomon built for YHWH was sixty cubits long, twenty cubits wide, and thirty cubits high.*

3 *The front hall before the main hall of the house was twenty cubits long across the width of the house, and ten cubits was its width in front of the house.*

4 *In front of the house he made windows provided with frames and latticework.*

5 *He also built a layer against the wall of the house, right around the wall of the house, the holy place, and the shrine. He made supporting structures all around.*

6 *The bottom layer was five cubits wide, the middle six cubits, and the third seven cubits. So he made offsets on the outside of the house without (especially) reinforcing the walls of the house (with beams).*

7 *During its construction the house was built with rough-hewn stones from the quarry; no sound of hammers, pick, or any iron tool was heard while the house was being built.*

8 *The door of the middle structure gave access to the right-hand corner of the house and spiral-shaped decorations ran toward the middle and from the middle to the third (layer).*

9 *So he built the house and completed it, and covered it with drain pipes and eavestroughs made of cedar.*

10 *[He built a layer against the whole house, five cubits high, and reinforced the house with cedar wood.]*

11 *Now the word of YHWH came to Solomon:*

12 *'As for this house which you are building: if you will walk in my statutes and obey my ordinances, and faithfully keep all my commandments, I will fulfill the promise which I made about you to your father David;*

13 *Then I will live among the Israelites and not forsake my people Israel.'*

14 *So Solomon built the house and completed it.*

15 *He lined the interior walls of the house with cedar boards by covering the inside of the house with wood from the floor to the ceiling. He covered the floor of the house with planks of cypress.*

16 *He built twenty cubits of the rear walls of the house with planks of cedar from floor to ceiling [and built the inside into a shrine, viz. the 'holy of* holies'].

17 *The (temple) house [that is 'the holy place'] in front of the shrine was forty cubits.*

18 *The cedar wood of the interior was carved with gourds and rosettes. Everything was cedar; not a stone was showing.*

19 *Inside the house he prepared the shrine to put the ark of the covenant of* YHWH *in it.*

20 *The shrine was twenty cubits long, twenty cubits wide, and twenty cubits high, and he overlaid it with gold leaf. He also made an altar of cedar wood ...*

21 *[Solomon also overlaid the inside of the house with pure gold and he drew chains of gold] ... in front of the shrine and overlaid it with gold.*

22 *[Next he overlaid the whole house with gold to perfect the whole house; even the whole altar in front of the shrine he overlaid with gold.]*

23 *In the shrine he made two cherubim of oleaster, ten cubits high.* (see verse 26)

24 *One cherub's wing was five cubits long and the other cherub's wing was five cubits long – ten cubits from wing tip to wing tip.*

25 *The other cherub also measured ten cubits; the two cherubim were identical in size and shape.*

26 (after verse 23) *The height of each cherub was ten cubits.*

27 *He placed the cherubs in the innermost part of the house; the cherubs extended their wings so that the wings of the one touched the wall just as the wing of the other touched the other wall, while their other wings, the ones that pointed toward the center of the house, were also touching.*

28 *He also overlaid the cherubim with gold.*

29 *As for the walls of the house, he carved them all around with carved engravings, cherubs, palm ornaments, and rosettes, from inside to outside.*

30 *He also overlaid the floor of the house with gold, from inside to outside.*

31 *He similarly provided the door of the shrine with door wings of oleaster. The portal (in front of the shrine) had posts with five indented sections.*

32 *On the door wings of oleaster he carved wood engravings, cherubs, palm ornaments and rosettes and overlaid them with gold; he also overlaid the cherubs and palm ornaments with gold.*

33 *For the door of the holy place he also made doorposts of oleaster with four indented sections.*

34 *The two doors were of cypress wood; each door had two leaves which turned in sockets.*

35 *He carved cherubs, palm ornaments, and rosettes on them, overlaying them with gold hammered evenly over the carved work.*

36 *He further built the inner court with three rows of hewn stone plus one row of cedar beams.*

37 *In the fourth year the foundation of the house of YHWH was laid, in the month of Ziv.*

38 *And in the eleventh year, in the month of Bul — which is the eighth month — the house was finished in all its details and according to all its specifications. He was seven years in building it.*

INTRODUCTION

Introduced and concluded by a chronological reference to the time and duration of the construction and interrupted (vss. 11ff.) by a dtr. digression, this chapter primarily contains technical information about the construction of Solomon's temple, with a focus on measurements and materials. About the exact location where the temple was built not a word is said. An objective, almost dry, summary of quantifiable materials is glued together by verbs, among which the verbs 'to build,' 'to make,' and 'to join' are predominant. It is not surprising, therefore, that some scholars (e.g., Noth; Dhorme, XXXVI)[1] trace the basic substance of our chapter to official notes from the royal chancellory in Jerusalem. The core of the chapter is nothing other than a verbal blueprint of the building of the temple. It remains a question, however, whether in our chapter we are dealing with the original building plan and the execution of that plan at the time of Solomon himself, or with a reflection from the later history of the construction of the temple.[2] Rupprecht is of the opinion, among other things, that from a literary viewpoint the annex described in vss. 6-8 is a later addition so that the lateral structures attached to the temple date from a later period. This suggestion is not one we should simply reject. It is and remains hard, however, to demonstrate categorically which elements in our chapter are very old, i.e. belonged to the original temple construction plan of Solomon, and which date from a later time.[3] What *is* clear is that the entire chapter, in

---

[1] Cf. also J. Ouellette, "The Basic Structure of Solomon's Temple and Archaeological Research," *The Temple of Solomon. Archaeological Facts and Medieval Tradition in Christian, Islamic and Jewish Art* (ed. J. Gutmann), Missoula 1976, 1-20; esp. 2.

[2] Thus, for example, K. Rupprecht, "Nachrichten von Erweiterung und Renovierung des Tempels in 1. Könige 6," *ZDPV* 88 (1972), 38-52; cf. also C.L. Meyers, "The Elusive Temple," *BA* 45 (1982), 33-41; and T. Roger, "»Our Holy and Beautiful House«: When and Why was 1 Kings 6-8 Written?" *JSOT.* 70 (1996), 33-50 (according to Roger between 597 and 587 BCE).

[3] See now also J. Van Seters, "Solomon' Temple: Fact and Ideology in Biblical and Near Eastern Historiography," *CBQ* 59 (1997), 45-57. He concludes: The story is basically a composition of the Deuteronomistic Historian to which a number of later additions have been made. The description of the temple and its furnishings in 1 Kings 6-7 is not a historical witness to the temple in Solomon's time but is rather an attempt to establish an ideological continuity between the beginning of the monarchy under David and Solomon and its end, and to suggest the

the form in which we now have it, was composed *during* if not *after* the exile. Did the author really have available to him documents from the royal archives or did he reconstruct a 'building report' from memory or from what he was able to find out about the preexilic temple? In how far did the later version of the temple of that first period really resemble the original temple which Solomon built? In how far can this temple construction be called really new?.[4] In other words, did Solomon perhaps renovate an ancient (El- or YHWH-) temple? In any case, it seems indisputable that, assuming that Solomon's (house) temple stood next to his palace on the hill N of the ancient 'city of David,' the present-day Ḥaram eš-Šarīf (which is not questioned by anyone; cf. Simons, *Jerusalem*, 344), there must have been a Canaanite or Jebusite sanctuary in that location earlier. In the OT tradition this spot is sometimes known as the 'threshing floor of Araunah' (2 Sam. 24:18; cf. 16). We will, however, abstain here from a detailed study concerning a possible continuation or a comparison with other Canaanite sanctuaries. For such a study of the many aspects of the temple of Jerusalem, its building materials and techniques, in addition to a virtually complete bibliography, we would refer to the work of Busink, 1970; cf. also Fritz, *Tempel*.[5]

---

possibility of restoration and a new beginning, perhaps under a restored Davidic ruler.'

[4] For this question, cf. also K. Rupprecht, *Der Tempel von Jerusalem. Gründung Salomos oder jebusitischen Erbe?* (BZAW 144), Berlin 1977.

[5] See also V. Fritz, "Der Tempel Salomos im Licht der neueren Forschung," *MDOG* 112 (1980), 53-68.

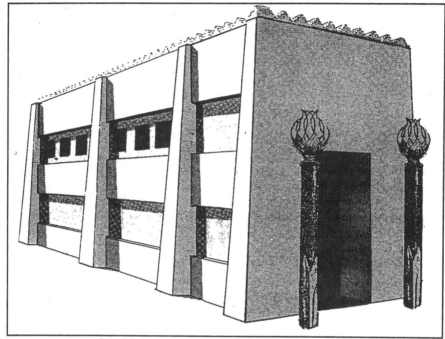

Possible reconstruction in outline of the temple of Solomon, according to 1 Kgs. 6, drawn by A.P. van Weezel, conservator of the Bijbels Museum, Amsterdam

EXEGESIS

6:1 *In the four hundred and eightieth year after the exodus of the Israelites from the land of Egypt, in the fourth year of Solomon's reign over Israel, in the month of Ziv – which is the second month – he began to build a house for YHWH.*

Noth et al. consider this verse a borrowing from the end of our chapter (vss. 37f.), where mention is also made of the 4th year of Solomon's reign and of the month of Ziv, the second month after the beginning of the spring new year. That vss. 37f. are older than our verse is proved, among other things, by the use of the word ירח for 'month' in contrast to the word חדש used here. The first word is Canaanite and refers to the 'moon month'; the second word, which came into vogue later, means 'new moon' (cf. De Vaux, *Inst.* I, 279; Ehrlich: 'on the new moon day'). In addition vss. 37f. fit better at the end of the technical statements about the construction than they do here.

The word שנה, placed after the number, is repeated after the designation of the number (cf. König §314e; Ges-K §134h,o; Joüon §142o). The number 480 can be found in LXX^Luc. but not in the other LXX-MSS, the important LXX^A and B among them. These read 440 (cf. the NT in Acts 13:20: ὡς ἔτεσιν τετρακοσίοις καὶ πεντήκοντα, hence approx. [=ὡς] 450 years). Josephus even had 592 years (*Ant.* VIII §61), a figure based on the count from Joshua to David's conquest of Jebus (515 years) plus 40 years for Moses, 33 years for David in Jerusalem and 4 years for Solomon (cf. *Ant.* VII §68). Josephus, nevertheless, lacks a consistent system for the calculation of his biblical chronology (cf. *Ant.* XX §230 and *c.Ap.* II §19), since he also speaks of 612 years between the exodus from Egypt and Solomon's building of the temple. According to Noth (cf. his *ÜGS*, 18-27), these 480 years are part of the overall chronology of dtr. But he rejects the view, supported by several scholars, which holds that these 480 years may also have to do with the period from the construction of Solomon's temple to the building of the so-called 'second temple' after the exile (but see De Vaux; Van den Born and others). Still this view cannot simply be rejected. Burney and also Stade, *GVI*, I, 89f., furnish a calculation from Solomon's temple construction to the time after the return from exile, which makes a period of 480 years after the building of the temple credible for a post-exilic dtr. glossator. Along with Burney we assume that our verse is the work of a post-exilic editor. Aside from the use, mentioned above, of the 'newer' word for 'month,' it is also striking that LXX inserts our verse before 5:31, 32a, followed by vss. 37f. But actually these verses occupy the place of our verse. Accordingly, LXX did not read our verse in our MT form. Wellhausen, *Hexateuch*, 264f., correctly drew from this fact the conclusion that in this case we may assume that LXX has the original. If we now assume that the author of our verse lived a fairly long time after the return from exile, it is clear that he not only viewed the building of Solomon's temple as a kind of terminus of the period between the exodus and Solomon, but as a climax, in relation to which the 'second temple' was simultaneously a terminal point and the new beginning of a new era. That 480 is a round number here hardly needs saying. At the same time it is clear that it makes little sense to count back 480 years from the moment Solomon began to build the temple to get an exact determination of the date of the exodus. Nor can it be clearly demonstrated that 12 x 40 would have to refer to 12 periods (after the 12 tribes?) of 40 years each (a human generation?), on the analogy of Matt. 1:17.

To be noted in לְצֵאת is an exceptionel vocalisation of the ל (Joüon §124g; cf. also König §281d,f). One would have expected לָצֵאת here (according to Mm no. 1028 also in Exod. 19:1 and Num. 33:38). According to Joüon, our form presupposes the genitive.

Both here and in vs. 37 there is express mention of the 4th year of Solomon's reign. The accentuation of special events in the 4th year of a king is a recurrent feature (cf. Jer. 25:1; 28:1; 36:1; 46:2; 51:59; Zech. 7:1, etc.). The name of the month is called Ziv, one of 4 still familiar ancient names of months. It may mean 'blossom month' or 'month of flowers' and falls in April/May. The other ancient-Hebr. names which are still known, are Bul (vs. 38), the 'rain' month in October/November; also Ethanim, the month of 'everflowing streams' (Sept./Oct., 1 Kgs. 8:2) and finally Abib, the month of the 'fresh ear of grain' (March/April, Exod. 13:4; 23:15; Deut. 16:1). The counting of months probably began in the fall, while later new year's day was fixed in the spring. In the (later) period of the kings it became a custom, probably under foreign influence, to describe the months numerically. After the exile the Babylonian-Assyrian names of the months found increasing acceptance. Beginning in the spring, the name of the first month was Nisan, that of the second Iyyar, etc. (cf. A. Strobel, *BHHW*, II, 1233f.). Josephus, accordingly, reports that the 'Macedonians' called the 4th month Artemisios and the Hebrews Iyyar (... ὃν Μακεδόνες μὲν Ἀρτεμίσιον καλοῦσιν Ἑβραῖοι δὲ Ἰάρ). The 'glossator's sentence' (König §357f): 'this is the second month,' can certainly not be regarded as redundant in a later time. The par. verse 2 Chr. 3:2 adds here that Solomon started building on the second day of the second month, but there the 'second day' is text-critically rather doubtful (cf. also Rudolph, a.l.). The fact that Chronicles is rooted in a still later tradition than our chapter, is also apparent from the statement in 2 Chr. 3:1 that the temple was built by Solomon on Mount Moriah, the place David had designated for this purpose. Here the tradition forges a link with the 'sacrifice of Isaac' by Abraham, the so-called *Aqeda* (Gen. 22). Also in Gen. 22:2 the MT, as we now have it, alludes to Mount Moriah. Our text does not mention it and only states that Solomon built 'the house' for YHWH.

6:2 *Now the house which king Solomon built for YHWH was sixty cubits long, twenty cubits wide, and thirty cubits high.*
A start is now made in giving the dimensions of 'the house': 60 cubits long, 20 cubits (to be so taken with LXX, Pesh. and certain MSS of the Hebr. OT) wide and 30 cubits high. It is not made clear, however, whether the reference is to outside or to inside measurements. It is most natural to think of outside measurements. Then there is the question what precisely is meant by 'house': the whole temple complex or only the main temple, the היכל (cf. vs. 3; also Acts 7:47). Next there is the divergence, in the measurements cited, from the specifications of LXX. LXX[B, Luc.] have 40 cubits for the length and 25 for the height (the width is the same as in MT). Various explanations have been given for these differences (cf. Gooding 1967, 143ff., as well as his own explanation: 168ff.; see also Barthélemy). According to Gooding, the divergent measurements in LXX are based on another (mistaken?) interpretation of the data still to be reported in our chapter (cf. vss. 16f.). Josephus also shows some divergence in the measurements. He prefaces his specification of these

measurements with a full description of the foundation of the temple (*Ant.* VIII §§63f.). His account is possibly based in part on what he still knew from his own time and from experience. He also relates that the building, which rested on a heavy, deep-set foundation, was constructed of white marble right to the roof: ἀνήγαγε δ'αὐτὸν ἄχρι τῆς ὀροφῆς ἐκ λευκοῦ λίθου πεποιημένον. He then gives the measurements: 60 cubits in length and height and 20 cubits in breadth. 2 Chr. 3:3, finally, omits mention of the height but holds to the measurements of MT in Kings, although it speaks of the 'cubit' as מדה ראשונה, 'the old measure.' Apparently during the time when Chronicles was written, the measure was changed. From Ezek. 40:5; 43:13 it is evident that a 'handbreadth' had to be added to the old cubit to have a 'new measure.' The 'normal cubit' can be put at approx. 45 cm; the larger cubit, in use also in Egypt and Babylon, at approx. 52,5 cm (cf. G. Schmitt, *BRL*², 204). The word בית must probably be understood as the space in which the 2 parts, the היכל and the דביר, were located, 30 m long, 10 m wide and 15 m high. The building to a certain extent paralleled the design and arrangement of other ancient sanctuaries, like those of the temple found at Arad,[6] but now in oblong form. As the result of the addition of the אולם, mentioned in the following verse, it acquired the tripartite temple form also known from Syria (cf. Alt, *KS*, II, 100-115). In the measurements furnished in MT we are dealing with standard measurements, which do not include technical information such as the thickness of the stone outer walls, which Ezek. 41:5 does mention. Perhaps the author is interested in the value of the numbers of היכל, the 'house,' to which in this case also דביר belongs. The temple's interior space is only described in what follows.

6:3 *The front hall before the main hall of the house was twenty cubits long across the width of the house, and ten cubits was its width in front of the house.*
In front of the actual temple space there was a front hall which was probably attached to the main building and which, compared to the older temples found in Palestine like the one in Arad, formed a new element. The word אולם, also spelled אילם, occurs almost 50x in OT, especially in the next chapter and in Ezek. 40-46, as the term for a 'front hall.' The etymology of the word is disputed and uncertain (in addition to *KBL* and *HAL*, cf. also Busink, 164 n. 14; Noth; Hoogewoud, 75f.).[7] As will become clear from 7:6-8, the word אולם

---

[6] Cf. Y. Aharoni, "The Solomonic Temple, the Tabernacle and the Arad Sanctuary," AOAT 22, Neukirchen-Vluyn 1973, 1-8; see also J. Ouellette, *IDBS*, 872f.
[7] Cf. also M. Görg, "Weiteres zur Gestalt des Tempelbaus," *BN* 13 [1980], 22-25, who derives it from the Egyptian *wrmt*, 'covered space'.

has no special religious significance, since such a front hall can also be built in front of a palace. The same is true for the word היכל which occurs no fewer than 78x in OT and can denote a 'palace' or a 'temple' as well as, as we saw above, the 'main space' of a palace or temple. The word stems from the Sumerian where *e-gal* means a 'large house' and via the Akkad. *ēkallu* one also finds the word in other Sem. languages, such as the Ugar. *hkl,* the Syr. *hayklā* or the Arab. *haikal* (see M. Ottosson, *TWAT*, II, 408-415). The distribution of the word over OT is greater than that of אולם, for, besides its occurrence in our chapter and the next, as well as in Ezek. 8:41f., we also find it frequently in the book of Psalms (5:8; 11:4; 18:7; 27:4; 29:9 etc.), and in prophetic books (Isa. 13:22; 39:7; 66:6 etc.). The height of the אולם is not indicated. This is done in the par. verse, 2 Chr. 3:4, where the height indicated is no less than 120 cubits, which cannot possibly be true for the front hall of Solomon's temple. Josephus, too, speaks of a height of 120 cubits but applies it to the whole temple, on top of which, according to him, there was a superstructure of the same height as the actual temple. The אולם, designated by him as προναϊον, was of the same height. Josephus possibly misinterpreted the data in Kings and Chronicles.

Our text indicates that the length of the front hall equals, and probably connects with, the width of the actual temple, and the width of the front hall therefore connects with the length of the actual temple. A. Kuschke (*BRL*[2], 340) points out that there is a strong possibility that the front hall had no front wall. If one assumes that Solomon's temple, like its successors, faced the east, then the temple had no E wall; the first wall (plus entrance), then, was that of the היכל, a view which agrees pretty much with the data of our chapter. If this is correct, Solomon's temple must have been a so-called 'Antentempel,' a temple in oblong form whose walls on the longest sides, the N and S wall, would have run on past the היכל. Accordingly, he rejects the comparison of Solomon's temple with the so-called Migdal-temples of Shechem (Middle Bronze II[B]) and Megiddo (Middle Bronze II[B], Late Bronze II[A]), as Noth proposed in his commentary. In the case of Solomon's temple the ratio of length to width is 3:1. The 'openness' of the front hall to the east, according to Kuschke, is not affected by Ezek. 40:48, because these pillars do not prove anything for the temple of Solomon. Precisely, the discovery of temples at Tell Mardikh (Middle Bronze II[A]), Mumbaqat (Middle Late Bronze) and Meskene (Late Bronze II[B]) form a connection between the discovery of the Early Bronze 'Antentempel' of *Tell Elḥuwēra* and of the temple of *Tell Ta'yīnāt* (often advanced in this connection) and Solomon's temple. This tradition has persisted as far as the Roman temples in Syrian territory. It cannot be denied that Kuschke's hypothesis has much that is appealing, although in this regard, as a result of the sketchiness of the information given in this chapter, not much can be proven (cf. also Busink).

In place of היכל הבית, LXX[B, Luc.] only reads τοῦ ναοῦ, cf. Vulg. *ante templum*. But textual modification is no more needed here than in the sequel of our verse, where LXX[B, Luc.] in part has a divergent reading, because the width of the front hall has been omitted and where, in addition, LXX inserts vs. 14 (cf. vs. 9a): καὶ ᾠκοδόμησεν τὸν οἶκον καὶ συνετέλεσεν αὐτόν. The expression באמה, 'in cubits,' has a par. in the Akkad. *X ina ammitim* (Von Soden, *GAG* §139i; also cf. Ewald §317c).

6:4 *In front of the house he made windows provided with frames and latticework.*

This verse, like the other verses in this and the following chapter, presents difficulties for the precise determination of the meaning of the technical terms used. חלון occurs approx. 30x in OT and can usually be translated by 'window.' These windows were often large open rectangles, in some cases perhaps made of wood, through which light and air could enter houses – if indeed they had windows – and buildings (cf. K. Galling, H. Rösel, *BRL*², 79f.). Also in the Ugar. the word occurs (cf. *DLU*, 176). The word שקפים occurs in this form only again in the following chapter (7:4) and in the following verse. שֶׁקֶף, which seems to be related, as well as the more frequently occurring verb שקף (in niph. and hiph.) which means 'look down' and 'bend forward to look' (cf. *KBL*, s.v.). As the translation for this word *KBL* tentatively proposes: 'appearance windows.' Galling (*BRL*¹, 164) sees a connection here with the Assyrian word *sakkapu*, resp. *askuppatu*, the 'lintel' or the 'threshold' of a door (cf. W. Michaelis, *TDNT*, V, 815, n. 7). This last-mentioned Akkad. word is rendered by Von Soden (*AHw*, 74) as 'Steinplatte,' 'Türschwelle' (cf. the Hebr. מַשְׁקוֹף, 'lintel' in Exod. 12:7, 22f.), and in later Judaism (cf. Krauss, *TA*, I, 37f.) the word occurs as well. אטמים, finally, is sometimes (cf. *HAL*, s.v.) derived as pass. part. from the verb אטם 'stop,' 'close' (cf. Isa. 33:15; Ps. 58:5; Prov. 17:28; 21:13). Linked with חלון we also find the pass part. in Ezek. 40:16; 41:16, 26. According to Galling/Rösel (*BRL*², 80), the חלוני שקפים אטמים are to be viewed as '(high) lattice-windows made of stone,' in which case the authors are adopting Noth's view. These lattice-windows, installed especially in harems (cf. Judg. 5:28; Prov. 7:6; S. of S. 2:9), were presumably made of wood and could not be opened.[8] Ouellette has suggested that אטם is a word of Dravidic origin and in those languages – still spoken primarily in India – would mean 'upper story,' 'loft of a building,' or 'raised platform'.[9] In our

---

[8] Cf. also K. Galling, "Miscellanea Archaeologica (1. Steinerne Rahmenfenster)," *ZDPV* 83 (1967), 123-135.

[9] J. Ouellette, "*'Atumim* in 1 Kings VI,4: A Dravidian Origin," *Bulletin of the Institue of Jewish Studies* 2 (1974), 99-102.

verse the word would mean something like a 'turret,' while the preceding word שְׁקֻפִים could be either an explanatory gloss or an architectural term. To us this suggestion does not sound particularly plausible, in the first place because the link between the Dravidic and our word remains obscure and, in the second place, because אטם, though it does not occur frequently, is nevertheless intelligible. For this reason the view of *BRL*[1], 165 (*atmānu* = 'Wohnraum'), a view now apparently abandoned by Galling/Rösel, is less appealing to us (cf. also Noth). Another proposal by Ouellette 1969 contains the reading *bīt hilāni* for (ל)בית חלוני) of our text. A *bīt hilāni* is a palace with 2 long and rather narrow spaces, the main axis of which runs par. to the front of the building. The first space, then, is the entrance hall (cf. A. Kuschke, *BRL*[2], 244 and depictions of such palaces in *Tell Ta'yīnāt*, p. 243, fig. 62[4,5]). Now for Solomon's palace the *bīt hilāni* type can certainly not be ruled out, considering also the spread of this type in the ancient Near East, but it is going too far to read into our verse that, in front of the *bīt hilāni*, in this case doubtlessly in front of the temple, Solomon had a series of arcade-like portals made. It is a question whether the word *bīt hilāni*, which occurs more frequently in Akkad., was known in that form in Hebr. (cf. also *AHw*, 345, s.v. *hilāni, hill/tlāni*). LXX[B, A] speaks of θυρίδας παρακυπτο μένας κρυπτάς, in LXX[Luc.] δεδικτυωμένας, which according to Burney may be a corruption of διακυπτομένας which occurs in some other MSS. According to Schleusner, III, 393, the reference in LXX is to *fenestras, per quas aliquis inclinans se prospicere poterat*. In the LXX translation of C. Thomson-C.A. Muses, the text refers to windows which were 'wide within and narrow without' ('windows which as they bend forward become hidden'). Liddell-Scott, s.v. παρακύπτω: 'prob. *out of which people look*.' The intent of the translation of LXX is not altogether certain, because it probably did not have a good grasp of the Hebr. text either (see Burney for the other Greek translations). Vulg. reads *fenestras obliquas*, which is a substantial simplification of MT. Pesh. more or less agrees with this: 'windows wide within and narrow without' (Payne Smith, s.v. *štp*). Tg. calls them: 'windows opened within and closed without.' Montg.-Gehman, in this connection, resignedly comment: 'moderns know little more than the ancients' (cf. also Amama). An overview of the very divergent views of moderns on this verse can be found also in Busink, 193ff. His view comes down to saying that in words like שְׁקֻפִים and אטמים we are only dealing with the details of the windows in question. The first word denotes the frame, the lower, upper, and side jambs of the window; the second refers to the lattice-work inside the window opening (cf. Busink, 196, fig. 59). This view resembles that of Noth, who translated the phrase by 'vergitterte Rahmenfenster.' Our translation 'windows provided with frames and latticework' accords with that, although it still contains uncertain elements.

6:5 *He also built a layer against the wall of the house, right around the wall of the house, the holy place, and the shrine. He made supporting structures all around.*

This verse, too, contains a number of architectural terms whose meaning can only be roughly approximated. Consequently the mental picture one can form of the 'surrounding structure' around the temple remains clouded, even aside from the possibility that what is said here and in the following verses was inspired by annexes of a later period. We already encountered the word קיר in 5:13 of our book. Especially in our chapter but also elsewhere (e.g. 14:10; 16:11 etc. and in Ezekiel) the word frequently occurs in the sense of 'partition,' 'wall.' We read here that Solomon installed or 'built' a יציע (q^ere) or יצוע (k^etib) on and all around the wall of the temple. In the first place we face a choice between the *pa'ûl* or the *pa'îl* form of the word (cf. Gordis, 117). Gordis suspects that the k^etib form in the sense of 'bed' or 'couch' is normal here, but that the divergent q^ere form is intended to colour also the meaning of the word: 'the lower projecting story of the Temple' (p. 176, n. 153). יצוע in the sense of 'bed' or 'couch' also occurs in Gen. 49:4; Ps. 63:7; 132:3; Job 17:13 and 1 Chr. 5:1; Sir 34/31:18; 47:20; יציע occurs only here and in the vss. 6 and 10. The meaning 'couch' obviously does not fit here. LXX here translates the word by μέλαθρα, a word which already occurs in Homer for 'ceiling beams,' hence also for 'ceiling.' In 7:4 LXX uses this word as the translation of the שקפים and in 7:20 as the translation of the כתרת. It is striking that the LXX$^{A, B}$ renders ויבן by ἔδωκεν and LXX$^{Luc.}$ by ἐποιησεν. Vulg. takes the words: *et aedificat super parietem templi tabulata per gyrum*, to mean 'joisting.' Tg. renders the word by זיזא, which, according to Dalman, *ANH*, means a 'cornice' or 'extension' (cf. Krauss, *TA*, I, 54f.). Both for יציע and for צלעות (which occurs here) Pesh. has the single translation *ḥdrt'* (pl.), 'surrounding outer walls,' or 'annexes.' Symm. uses the word καταστρώματα (also in vs. 10): 'covers' or 'roofs.' Most modern commentators (see already Rashi with 3 words for 'room': יציע, תא and צלע), take יציע to mean an 'annex' surrounding a house (cf. e.g. Thenius, Benzinger, also Busink, 212). Ouellette proceeds from יצוע in Gen. 49:4 and refers to the Akkad. words *bīt eršī*, 'bed space' in a palace or temple (*AHw*, 133) and *bīt majjāle*, 'bedroom' (a.l.).[10] He takes our word to mean an administrative area alongside the temple. S. Yeivin, *Leš* 32 (1967-68), 8, continues in this direction by pointing out that in Ezek. 41:5-9 the words בית הצלעות, refer to the 'side chambers' of the temple but that Ezekiel does not use our word. He suspects that our word is a Phoen. building term *or* related to the Arab. and means a 'low-ceilinged room.'

---

[10] J. Ouelette, "The *yāsīa'* and *s^elā'ōt*: Two Mysterious Structures in Somolon's Temple," *JNES* 31 (1972), 187-191.

In the determination of the meaning of our word one can clearly see the influence of the description of the temple buildings in Ezekiel. So Josephus (*Ant.* VIII §65) states: περιῳκοδόμησε δὲ τὸν ναὸν ἐν κύκλῳ τριάκοντα βραχέσιν οἴκοις, οἳ συνοχή τε τοῦ παντὸς ἔμελλον ἔσεσθαι διὰ πυκνότητα καὶ πλῆθος ἔξωθεν περικείμενοι, i.e. 'around the temple he built thirty small rooms which, by surrounding it on the outside, had to hold it together by their closeness and number.' In Ezek. 40:17 there is in fact mention of 30 rooms, but there they are referred to with the word – one which occurs frequently in Ezek. 40ff. – לשכות. Still, we believe that Noth rightly expressed himself cautiously when he spoke of a 'Schicht,' a 'layer' around the temple, although he interprets this layer as 'in any case something horizontal' and thinks in that connection of a 'leveling of the surfaces of the masonry,' a necessary ingredient when using natural stone (see vs. 7), and a condition for making a good roof construction. He does indeed point to the difficulties of the terminology used in connection with יציע in our verse and in vs. 16 (על־קירות־הבית), but he nevertheless – rightly – rejects the idea of an annex or of side wings. He too much narrows the semantic field of the prefix על in this context when he wants to use it exclusively in the sense of 'on top of.' על can also have the meaning 'before' (cf. Gen. 18:8) or 'around' (Gen. 37:23). Moreover it cannot be proved that יציע denotes a horizontal layer. Why could there not have been a vertical layer of durable wood or some other material put around the temple, reinforced with beams as buttresses to give the temple both greater sturdiness and greater beauty? For now, we see no reason to go beyond the translation 'layer'.[11]

In stating that this 'layer' was put all around the temple the text is redundant. LXX[B, Luc.] as well as a number of Tg.-MSS leave the words את־קירות הבית סביב untranslated so that the first סביב, by means of the prep. ל, is immediately connected with the היכל and the דביר. But Noth even considers the mention of these 2 words premature here and even omits them as being an explanatory gloss on the difficult word יציע. It is a question, however, whether one should go that far. It is clear that, as the text now stands, the first סביב seems labored with את, a subject on which grammarians differ (cf. Böttcher §516 with König §288m,n; Ewald §277d: indication of general *casus obliquus* and can therefore occur with סביב; cf. also König §319q). But Driver has rightly pointed out that את often indicates a following gloss: 'viz.,' for example.[12] In this light the divergent reading of LXX[B, Luc.] and

---

[11] See also our "Exegetische Bemerkungen zum Tempelgebäude I Könige 6:5-10," *JNSL* 10 (1982), 83-92.

[12] G.R. Driver, "Glosses in the Hebrew Test of the Old Testament," in: *L'Ancien Testament et l'Orient* (ed. G. Ryckmans), Leuven 1957, 127.

of certain Tg.-MSS becomes understandable; he built a layer against the wall of the house, joining it to היכל and דביר. קירות הבית סביב is an apposition (gloss) with קיר, but להיכל etc. is not directly a genitive of apposition by 'walls' (as, e.g. King §280e proposes). In any case, this redundancy is proof that also the original readers had, or at least could have, difficulty with this presentation.

Both היכל and דביר are mentioned in our text. We already discussed the first word above, vs. 3. דביר recurs 7x in our chapter (16, 19-23, 31), further in 7:49; 8:6, 8; Ps. 28:2; 2 Chr. 3:16; 4:20; 5:7, 9; Sir. 45:9. From what follows in our chapter it is evident that the דביר was not simply a separate room in the temple, but rather a cubiform object set in a wood-paneled space, a part of the temple's inventory itself.[13] For this kind of object Schult points to Egyptian parallels which date from the 21st and 22nd dynasty. In the Egyptian the term is a loanword from the Canaanite and denotes a kind of shrine, which is then identified in vs. 16 with the 'holy of holies.' But there the addition is possibly an explanatory gloss from a later time (see further under this verse). Also S. Terrien (*VT* 20 [1970], 322) points out the probable kinship of our word with the Egyptian ('back room'). This relation is more plausible than the derivation of *dbr* 'speak,' 'act,' from which the traditional 'oracle' is then derived (cf. SV: 'aanspraakplaats (place of address)'; see Hoogewoud, 78, who sees a connection here with Arab. *dabara*, 'turning one's back on someone'). It is striking that LXX nearly always transliterates דביר (not in Ps. 28:2; 1 Kgs. 8:6 and Sir. 45:9): δαβείρ or something similar. Vulg. sometimes translates the Hebr. word as *oraculum* but, as is clear from such verses as Ezek. 25:18, 20; 37:6 and 40:18 (according to numbering followed by Vulg.), this is also the translation of כפרת, for which the word *propitiatorium* is used as well (Exod. 37:6!). Apparently this translator did not think of a separate space. Tg. renders the word by בית כפורי and Pesh. by *byt ḥwsy'*, i.e. 'the house of reconciliation.' Later traditions concerning the nature and function of the 'holy of holies' come together in these renderings, but they do not help in the determination of the character of דביר. Ouellette also supports the view that the דביר was a room built within the structure of the temple and separated from the היכל by a wooden screen, so that this room was not architecturally distinguishable from the היכל.[14] In the only one of 4 places in 2 Chronicles where דביר is not immediately dependent on the par. places in Kings, 2 Chr. 3:16, we are possibly dealing with a corrupt text (cf. Curtis, Goettsberger,

---

[13] So H. Schult, "Das Debir im Salomonischen Tempel," *ZDPV* 80 (1964), 46-54; cf. also A. Kuschke, "Der Tempel Salomos und der »syrischen Tempeltypus«," *Das ferne und nahe Wort* (Fs L. Rost; BZAW 105), Berlin 1967, 124-132.

[14] J. Ouellette, "The Solomonic *dᵉbir* according tot the Hebrew Text of I Kings 6," *JBL* 89 (1970), 338-343.

Noordtzij and Rudolph a.l.), so that this verse also fails to help us in determining the exact translation of the word (cf. also S. Yeivin, *Leš* 32 [1967-8], 10f.). It is not impossible that the word דביר is a Phoen. loanword (Yeivin), which was not only (temporarily) known during the Solomonic age in Israel, but also in Egypt. However this may have been, around these parts of the temple a 'layer' was constructed.

The 3 concluding words of our verse are lacking in LXX^B. In the MSS of Pesh., used in the text-critical Leiden edition, they do occur (*contra* the textcr. app. of *BHK* and *BHS*). The word צלע occurs approx. 40x in OT, especially in Exod. 25-27, 30, 36-38, Ezek. 41 and in our chapter and, according to the lexicons, has many meanings: 'rib' (Gen. 2:21f.); 'side' (especially in Exod.); 'plank' (1 Kgs. 6:15f.); 'door leaf' (1 Kgs. 6:34); 'side chamber' (Ezek. 41 and 1 Kgs. 6:8); 'supporting beam' (1 Kgs. 7:3). In this and the next chapter alone the word occurs in 4 different senses, and that in a section abounding with technical terms. We have demonstrated elsewhere that such diversity in technical meanings for a single word is not only exceedingly confusing for the present reader, but must have been so for the original reader as well.[15] Along with Noth we therefore start from the 'basic' meaning of צלע 'rib,' 'side' (2 Sam. 16:13; of a mountain). As in 7:2 (see also Burney in that location), we translate the word by 'beams,' or, even better, by 'buttresses.' Also in other Sem. languages the word occurs meaning 'rib,' 'side,' for instance, in Akkad. (cf. *AHw*, 1090). In our opinion our verse intends to say that the whole temple, the holy place with the דביר, was surrounded by 'layers' (wood or stone?) and that upright beams or buttresses furnished additional support and sturdiness to the walls and the 'layers.' As we hope to show, this viewpoint is confirmed by what follows.

6:6 *The bottom layer was five cubits wide, the middle six cubits, and the third seven cubits. So he made offsets on the outside of the house without (especially) reinforcing the walls of the house (with beams).*

Against virtually all modern commentators (cf. also Hulst, *OTTP*, 36f.) who, based on the LXX translations, supported by Tg., wish to change היציע of our MT into הצלע, we stand by the (more difficult) reading of MT. One of the (strongest) arguments advanced by commentators for going along with LXX is the consideration that יציע is only fem. here and masc. in the other places in our chapter. Böttcher (§658 [no. 13]) already seems to be swayed by this argument, though in the §§656-658 he himself cites many examples of 'Ambigua,' words which in Hebr. can be both masc. and fem. (but cf. Ewald

---

[15] M.J. Mulder, "Einige Bemerkungen zur Beschreibung des Libanonwaldhauses in I Reg 7,2f.," *ZAW* 88 (1976), 99-105, esp. 103ff.; see now also H.-J. Fabry, *TWAT*, VI, 1059-1064.

§174d). In our view 3 layers or strips have been added to the temple walls for embellishment and reinforcement, and that from the bottom to the top. These layers or ledges, from the bottom to the top, were 5, 6 and 7 cubits wide, respectively. If one assumes that the lowest offset layer begins on ground level and the top layer ends against the edge of the roof, one gets 2 recessed middle strips of 6 cubits. The total height (vs. 2), remember, was 30 cubits (2x6+5+6+7). If this is correct, it also explains the word מגרעות. In OT the word occurs only here and, according to *HAL*, s.v., means 'Absatz,' 'Verkürzung (d. Mauer).' We would translate the word by 'recession,' 'offset,' 'indentation.' The verb גרע, aside from 'trim (a beard)' (Jer. 48:37; Isa. 15:2), also means 'diminish' (Exod. 21:10, etc.), 'take away' (Deut. 4:2, etc.) or similar acts of reduction. Projecting and receding sections then alternate around the temple, reinforced by buttresses or beams. LXX[B] here reads διάστημα, 'intervening space,' also used in Ezek. 41:6 but then for באות, a somewhat obscure form (as to meaning) of בוא. In this text the word is צלעות, which in this section is generally translated by 'rooms,' of which there were some 30. In form and content the above verse resembles our verse and scholars (W. Zimmerli, for example) suspect that it is a technical term which materially coincides with מגרעות. Besides, Zimmerli has a rather negative view of the value of the LXX translation. He even thinks that in LXX we have 'einen farblosen Verlegenheitsausdruck' (BK XIII/2, 1030), which serves to translate the most divergent Hebr. words. On this last point he is not altogether wrong, as a glance at Hatch-Redpath shows in the blink of an eye (10 Hebr. words in 12 OT places; also cf. Schleusner). In our opinion the translation of LXX nevertheless deserves more confidence. The Vulg. in its translation does not clearly bring out the primary meaning of the Hebr.: *trabes autem posuit in domo per circuitum forinsecus.* Concretely it had in mind 'beams.' Tg. has the word נפקתא, 'projections,' 'ledges'; Pesh: *gᵉdānᵉpē,* with approximately the same meaning (cf. Payne Smith, s.v.). Also B. Eshel, *Lešˇ* 37 (1972f.), 5ff., thinks of a 'frame' or 'ledge' along the wall at the ends of which the joists or ceiling of an adjacent house were laid. Still the interpretation of our verse is frequently too much determined by what people think they are reading in Ezek. 41:6, viz. that there were projections on the walls of the temple, which could serve as supports for the little side rooms. Still, it is a question whether one may assume the presence of such a construction already in the case of Solomon's temple. K. Galling, *BRL*[1], 517ff.[16] firmly places such construction in a later period and explains the מגרעות-supports merely as an interpretation 'von einem nachträglichen 'Anlehnen' des Anbaus' (cf. also Busink, 211f.). Busink believes that מגרעות can only be translated by 'offsets' ('Absätze'). As

---

[16] Cf. also A. Bertholet, K. Galling, *Hesekiel* (HAT I,13), Tübingen 1936[2], 143.

architect he points out that in view of the relatively great height of the temple a 'surround' was needed to prop up the construction. To back up his point he refers to Josephus's comment (*Ant.* VIII §65), cited above, which stated that the 'rooms' (along with other features) served by their compactness and number to hold the temple walls together. He believes that the 'surround' was part of the original design of Solomon's temple. To us, too, it seems plausible to trace the 'surround' (but not then consisting of a series of little chambers) to the first phase of the project. It does, however, remain a question how we must understand the last 4 words of our verse.

The word לבלתי (according to König §406g) introduces a 'verneinte Consequenz,' here followed by an inf. cstr. of אחז. In OT the verb rather frequently occurs in the sense of 'grab' or 'hold onto.' *HAL* subsumes our verb under אחז I, whereas for אחז II it offers the meaning 'cover', which would fit in the case of ויאחז in vs. 10. It is questionable, however, whether in a section which, like the present one, is loaded with technical terms one may assume 2 distinct meanings for a single verb. In the Elephantine-papyri edited by Kraeling,[17] there is the odd occurrence of the word אחד or אחז in a construction-related technical sense, as in papyrus 3 (dating from 437 BCE), line 5: אחד ונשרן לא, 'and beams it does not have' (p. 155; cf. pap. 4:8f.; 9:12f; 10:2f.). Kraeling even proposes as a possible – though ultimately not very likely – translation: 'with beams it is not held' (p. 160; also cf. *DISO*, 10 [s.v. אחז]). Kraeling is right when in this connection he also refers to our verse for the meaning of this technical word. It seems possible to us that אחז may mean 'hold together' or 'hold onto' by means of beams. Walls could then, and can today, especially in mountainous regions, be reinforced by having beams inserted into or joined to them. Our verse merely says that no extra beams were used *in* (ב) the temple walls. It is also clear that as a result of the use of the word מגרעות there is reference to 'outward offsets' (חוצה). On the basis of statements made here one can visualize how there were 3 layers of wood, 5, 6, and 7 cubits wide respectively, lying on top of each other and against the wall, with 2 layers of stone (מגרעות) in between, each of them 6 cubits wide, within which the (wooden) layers fitted precisely and which, by their 'compactness' and 'number' (Josephus), gave the necessary sturdiness and embellishment to the outer walls of the temple. There is no mention in our verse of a 'surround' embracing a series of little rooms. Also the par. places in Chronicles are silent on this point. This idea probably arose only later, as this kind of construction came into vogue, and was subsequently virtually everywhere read back into our text.

---

[17] E.G. Kraeling, *The Brooklyn Museum Aramaic Papyri. New Documents of the Fifth Century B.C. from the Jewish Colony of Elephantine*, New Haven 1953.

6:7 *During its construction the house was built with rough-hewn stones from the quarry; no sound of hammers, pick, or any iron tool was heard while the house was being built.*

In this verse we are told of what material the exterior of the temple was composed. This verse is viewed by many scholars (Thenius, Benzinger, Burney, et al.) as an 'intruder,' which came from somewhere else, or as an editorial note from a time other than that in which our report was written. Noth thinks that our verse forms the concluding sentence of the report about the 'basic construction' of stone. We also consider this a possibility, at least as far as vs. 7a is concerned. Vs. 7b is to be considered, with many scholars, Noth now among them, as secondary.

The first part of our verse contains a verb, בנה, in the passive (niph.) form. In such a case the second object of the verb remains in the accusative (cf. Ewald §284c; Joüon §128c). The word מסע, which in this form occurs again only in Job 41:18, but then in a very different sense, is related to the verb נסע, 'quarry out (stone).' The word indicates the place from which the natural stone was taken, viz. the quarry (so *HAL*; Noth). Before this, however, we read that this is 'whole stone.' The adjective שלם occurs 27x in OT, some of these also in Kings (1 Kgs. 8:61; 11:4; 15:3, 14; 2 Kgs. 20:3), but then as adjective modifying לב, another favorite substantive (see also G. Gerleman, *THAT*, II, 920, 926f.). Gerleman considers the basic meaning of שלם to be 'paying,' i.e. 'willing to submit,' 'ready,' but comments on this place: 'eine überraschende Bedeutungserweiterung ins Sinnliche hin' (p. 927; cf. also K.-J. Illman, *TWAT*, VIII, 99f.). Also in Josh. 8:31 there is mention of 'whole' stones, and that in relation to the altar, for which stones were used that had not been worked on with iron. According to Gerleman, the added word מסע further defines the requisite quality of the temple stones: already when they are broken out of the quarry, without having been treated with (metal) tools, the stones have to be 'fittable' ('nachgiebig, fügsam'). In essence Gerleman is right. The stones arrived unhewn from the quarry at the work area of the temple and were there fitted together, not as hewn into square or dressed blocks of stone. Nevertheless we prefer to take שלם in this technical sense as meaning 'unhewn.' The stones were in the state in which they were, when they were taken from the quarry or the mountainside. From ancient times unhewn stone were customary in Palestine for building the walls of buildings (cf. H. Weippert, *BRL* ², 210f.; Busink, 220f.). H. Schult, *ZDPV* 88 (1972), 53f., however, thinks – on the basis of vs. 7b – that since quiet had to prevail on the temple square, the expression אבן־שלמה מסע now means that the hewn stones had already been 'prepared' in the quarry (cf. also P. Wernberg-Møller, *JSS* 11 [1966], 256). Though this kind of procedure is entirely conceivable as such, it is not the intent of our expression. One can also draw this conclusion from the translation of LXX: λίθοις ἀκροτόμοις ἀργοῖς ᾠκοδομήθη. Ἀκρότομος means 'cut off on top' in the sense of 'rough' and ἀργός seems only to confirm this meaning here, as Schleusner (s.v.) makes plain: '*lapides non politi et elaborati, integri, quales advecti sunt. Dicitur autem* ἀργός *de lapide rudi nec caeso.*' Vulg. has a somewhat different translation: *lapidibus dedolatis atque perfectis.* A correct translation of the Hebr. is further made difficult by the grammatical construction of the 3 words. König (§277q), for example, takes מסע to be an *accusativus relationis* (in §328k he speaks of an *acc. specificationis*) with the 2 preceding words ('with respect to the quarry') in order thus to stress a certain distinction with regard to the *altar* stones in Exod. 20:25; Deut. 27:6 and Josh. 8:31. He rejects every form of *acc. appositionis,* as well as the duplication of the מ for מסע 'from the quarry,' as, for example, Klostermann and also Ges-K §131c propose. Ges-K §131c, however, does think of a 'Nominal-Apposition' (cf. also GD §39e). Noteworthy is the view of Ewald (§289a), who points out that adjectives can sometimes 'force' their way between 2 closely connected nouns (stat. cstr.) instead of being placed (with an article) after such a construction. Noth (following BrSynt. §81) understands the word as an accusative of further specification. Despite these grammatically diverse explanations, the meaning is clear: the quarry further defines the unhewn stone (cf. Burney).

The second part of our verse contains material parallels to the above-mentioned verses from Exod. 20, Deut. 27 and Josh 8 (cf. also Burney) which only pertain to the altar. Here the dread of iron and metal rooted in ancient-Israelitish ideas regarding the altar has been transferred to the construction of the whole temple, which, as a result, virtually acquired the status of a miracle. These 'miracle stories' surrounding the building of the temple can later be found in the works of the ancient rabbis who claimed that Solomon, by employing a miracle-working worm named *šāmîr*, had cut the stones to measure (Talmud Sota, IX, 12; and Aboth, V, 6), while Theodoretus claimed that the temple was built up out of stones, which under divine guidance had been shaped in advance and deposited in a stone quarry. מקבת (Judg. 4:21; Isa. 44:12; Jer. 10:4) is a 'hammer,' especially the hammer of the stonemason and the blacksmith, and the mallet (for driving tent-pegs down) of the nomads (H. Weippert, *BRL*[2], 133f.). The word גרזן also occurs in Deut. 19:5; 20:19 and Isa. 10:15; cf. in the Siloah inscription (*KAI* 189, 2.4) גרזן ('pick axe'). It is an axe or pick axe. In Palestine various kinds of picks and axes have surfaced as a result of (archeological) discoveries and also the OT has varying names for them (cf. H. Weippert, *BRL*[2], 23-26). All these implements are summed up in and subsumed under the expression 'all objects of iron.' ברזל, which occurs repeatedly in OT and also in Kings, has its equivalents in other Sem. languages as well, e.g. *parzillu* in Akkad. and *brdl* in Ugar. This word is of non-Sem. origin (cf. M. Weippert, *BRL*[2], 219f.). The metal itself has been known in the Near East since the ancient-Assyrian texts (end of 3rd millennium). Many Hebr. MSS and also the ancient versions read the copula before the כל. Still, this is definitely unnecessary, because this asyndetic connection sums up all the possibilities of the class (Burney; cf. also Ewald §349a). Grammatically irregular is the joint occurrence of 2 words מקבות and הגרזן, of which only the second has the article. Noth regards the latter as perhaps a later addition. That the verb is in the sing., though the subject is pl., while strange, is not impossible (see Ewald §339c). However, as we noted above, vs. 7b is to be viewed as a later addition which perhaps also underwent a 'period of development.' It is hard to imagine how the construction of the temple could be accomplished without any noise, even if no objects or tools of iron were used. Josephus (*Ant.* VIII §69) paraphrased our entire text. He says that the temple was built so ably, that a spectator could not but get the impression that no hammer or any other tool had been used, but that all the materials came together naturally, so that the process of joining and fitting things seemed to have occurred automatically without the use of any tool. The formation of legends continues.

6:8 *The door of the middle structure gave access to the right-hand corner of the house and spiral-shaped decorations ran toward the middle and from the middle to the third (layer).*
Certainly in the case of this verse the outcome of the exegesis determines one's picture of what the verse really and literally says. If — like the majority of exegetes — one starts from the assumption that in the preceding account one not only finds a description of the sanctuary as such, but also of a number of additional little rooms attached to the sanctuary, then one believes he has found here a further description of the entrance to these little rooms. This viewpoint requires, among other things, the assumption of a modification of the text as well as the assumption of an etymological uncertainty (לולים). It cannot be denied that in its present form the verse creates the impression of being a torso and that the omission of the entire verse helps rather than hinders the flow of the report as far as its intelligibility is concerned. But this can be said of other verses too. We must therefore try to picture what it is this verse intends to say and why it is located here.

As for vs. 8a it is striking that in the masoretic pointing it forms a nominal sentence. Though in LXX and Pesh. the word פתח is occasionally preceded by a copula, this does not mean that the Hebr. 'Vorlage' also had it. The word צלע, a fem. noun here (cf. vs. 34; König §252b), is followed by התיכה. תיכון refers to the 'middle one' (Exod. 26:28; 36:33 etc.; cf. vs. 6), but on the basis of LXX and Tg. many exegetes here read התחתנה, 'the lowest one' (cf. also Barthélemy). If one assumes that צלע also means '(a row of) little room(s)' he almost has to adopt such a modification of the text to give 8a some meaning. Aside from the fact that Vulg. and Pesh. read 'middle,' also Noth has pointed out that a textual modification is unnecessary. In his view of the 'surround' of the temple, in which he assumes a system of galleries open to the outside, 'middle' is also quite defensible, because, of course, an 'open' lowest level needed no entrance at all. Also in our view of צלע as 'buttress,' maintaining the word תיכון does not present any problem. Next there is reference to the 'right' (or 'south'?) כתף of the house. The word כתף means 'shoulder,' sometimes combined with the 'upper arm' (Exod. 28:12 etc.) and so frequently becomes a technical term for 'side' or 'side piece' of an architectural construction (cf. 7:39; Ezek. 40:18, 44 etc.; see H.-J. Zobel, *TWAT*, IV, 403f.).[18] Hence 8a means that an opening in the middle buttress gave access to the right hand side of the house. Which house? The temple or perhaps another house, say, the royal palace? In an unvocalized text one might in the case of פתח, think of a form of the verb, though a masc. form by a fem. word is highly unusual, unless one posits Solomon as the subject of the sentence: he opened the middle buttress to the right side of the palace. In other words, Solomon would have made a (royal) passageway from his palace to the temple via an entrance placed in or by the middle buttress of the temple. In any case, in our opinion there is no mention in vs. 8a either of a series of little side rooms. This part of the verse does fit in the context, because it is still speaking of the outside construction of the temple.

But how are we to understand vs. 8b? The beginning of this part, ובלולים, is a real *crux interpretum*. Usually, and with an assortment of arguments, exegetes view ב as a preposition with לולים, which for that matter is a *hapax legomenon* in OT. LXX here reads: ἑλικτὴ ἀνάβασις; Aquila has: (καὶ ἐν) κοχλίαις; Vulg. *per cochleam* (also in Ezek. 41:7); Tg.: מסבתא, a word which also occurs in Ezek. 41:7 (Tg.) and is presumed to occur there for MT (*HAL*, s.v. מסבה; Zimmerli, a.l.). Also the Mishnah Middoth, IV, 5 speaks of a מסבה, a winding ascent which 'ran up' (עולה) from the NE corner to the SW corner and which is then connected with the 38 'cells' (תאים) alongside the temple building. In the case of the translations of LXX, Aq., and Vulg., most exegetes think of 'winding stairways' as the equivalent of לולים. It remains a question, however, whether this is the correct translation of LXX. It is more correct to speak here of a 'winding ascent.' There is no reference to a stairway or a ladder. Pesh., remarkably, translates the word by *qātaraqtā*, which comes from the Gr. καταρράκτης, 'downward-plunging,' 'steep' and as substantive is used for 'trapdoor' (Muller, s.v.). The meaning 'trapdoor,' for לול, also occurs in the lexicon of Siegfried-Stade (B. Stade, *ZAW* 3 [1893], 136ff., develops his view there). Also *HAL*, s.v. לול*; Gray and Noth think of 'trapdoor', but most modern lexicons and commentators stick to 'winding stairs' (but cf. I. Löw, *OLZ* 15 [1912], 558, who also defends the meaning 'trapdoor'). Montg.-

---

[18] Cf. also R.D. Haak, "The 'Shoulder' of the Temple," *VT* 33 (1983), 271-278.

Gehman offer an overview of the etymology of the word לול* and, inspired by R. Dozy, relate it to the Arab. *lawlawa*, 'winds', which is said to underscore the origin of the present biliteral form of לוה. E. Qimron (*Lešׁ* 38 [1973f., 225ff.), however, rightly questions the correctness of this etymology and the biliteralness of the word in general (cf. also Y. Bin-Nun, *Lešׁ* 38 [1973/4], 317). Among other things he points out that in many MSS (in the Leningradensis,[19] but not in *BHK* and *BHS*!) the word is ובלולים, hence with a dagesh in the second ל. In the second place there are important Mishnah-MSS which, in Middoth IV, 5 read ובלולין etc., in place of היו פחוחין בעליה ולולים etc. This section of Midd. tells us, that in the top floor there were 'openings' through which workmen were let down in boxes, so that they could not feast their eyes in the 'Holy of Holies.' Accordingly, ancient and good *miqra* and *mishna* traditions confirm that the ב is part of the root. The root בלל occurs in several Sem. languages and means, among other things, 'mix up,' 'confuse' (Gen. 11:7, 9!). Granted, this is not enough to yield the correct meaning of the word בלול. Qimron himself thinks it means 'spiral-shaped stairs.' As such this is possible, because 'winding stairs' (against Stade) were also known already in antiquity (cf. also Busink, 215ff.). But the meaning of a word also derives from its context. In that context ובלולים is no longer a substantive with a preposition, which indicates the means by which *people* could climb up, but the בלולים which themselves ascend. The verb, rare in this verse, in its impf. form indicates the character of maintaining a condition (Bg. II §7b; Driver §30). Now it says that the בלולים went up to the middle and then from the middle to the third. Both times the fem. form התיכנה is used (again), while a number of Hebr. MSS, a number of ancient versions and the majority of modern commentators read השלשית (cf. also Delitzsch, *LSF* §129b) in place of השלשים. But what is the substantive here? Is it צלע? If one translates this word by 'story' or '(a series of) little rooms,' that is indeed a possibility. The sentence construction suggests that the reference is to layers superimposed on each other. But then what is more natural than the suspicion that not צלע, but the word יציע has been omitted (cf. vs. 6)? Also in vs. 6 – though this was questioned by many – it was a fem. noun. That in this framework בלולים would mean 'trapdoors' or the like is rather unlikely. One wonders further whether, in the absence of floors with cells or rooms, 'winding stairs' built onto the temple are all that meaningful. It is most natural to think in this connection of spiral-shaped structures, embellishments, or possibly 'niches' (see Levy, s.v. לול), which gave the outside wall of the temple a well-cared-for appearance and at the same time served to fortify the entire building, since they ran from the bottom to the middle and subsequently to the third layer (cf. vs.

---

[19] Cf. C.D. Ginsburg, *The Early Prophets*, London 1926, a.l.

6). The 'third' was very likely the top layer (cf. LXX: τριώροφα). Josephus (*Ant.* VIII §70) stresses the esthetic and artistic nature of the 'access' to the 'top part': ἐφιλοτέχνησε δὲ ὁ βασιλεὺς ἄνοδον εἰς τὸν ὑπερῷον οἶκον διὰ τοῦ εὔρους τοῦ τοίχου. But in that connection he probably does think of little rooms or the like, although he also again here stresses the value of the technical constructions for the reinforcement and strength of the building (ὥστε ἀντ' ὀχυρωμάτων καὶ ῥώμης τοῦτο εἶναι).

Surveying the whole of this somewhat fragmentary verse one can say that – despite its fragmentary character – it does make 2 statements about the exterior of the temple building.

6:9 *So he built the house and completed it, and covered it with drain pipes and eavestroughs made of cedar.*
In this verse as well we are still dealing with the exterior of the temple building, even though vs. 9a is almost literally repeated in vs. 14. It has at times been said (Stade, Benzinger and others) that this verse, being a late gloss, has ended up in the wrong place. While this may be true for vs. 9a, vs. 9b does mention the construction of the roof cover at precisely the right moment, though the technical terms used, again confront us with the usual problems of translation and interpretation (see Burney, Noth et al.). This somewhat untidy vs. 9a shows at this location that the composer of this part was not overly thoughtful ('wenig überlegt' – Noth) in going about his work.

The verb ספן occurs, aside from here and in 7:3, 7, also again in Jer. 22:14 and Hag. 1:4 in the sense of 'cover (with wood)' (*HAL*, s.v.). In Deut. 3:21 the word, if correctly reproduced there, means 'preserve.' In vs. 15 the word סִפֻּן occurs in the sense of 'ceiling' and the ship mentioned in Jonah 1:5, ספינה, was furnished with a 'deck.' We may therefore assume with confidence that in vs. 9b the reference is to the construction of the roof covering of the temple. The verb is construed with a double object (so, correctly, Ewald §283b; König §327o). The words גבים וּשְׂדֵרֹת have not been translated by LXX[B, Luc.], but by LXX[A] and its supporting MSS by φατνώμασιν καὶ διατάξεσιν, 'with panels and rows.' The verb that is used is κοιλοσταθμέω, which can mean 'cover with panels (of a ceiling)' (so Liddell-Scott). In vs. 15 the verb occurs once more in LXX, while the subst. κοιλόσταθμος occurs in Hag. 1:4. Pesh. translates vs. 9b as follows: 'and he covered the house with sawed cedar beams' (*bgwb'* [pl.] *nsyrt'* [pl.] *d'rz'*). *gwb'* can also mean 'well' or 'hole.' Vulg.: *texit quoque domum laquearibus cedrinis*. *Laquear* is a ceiling with squares. So in a slightly different form Vulg. reads the same as LXX[B, Luc.]. Somewhat more extensively the Tg. has: 'and he covered the house with beams (הנתוכין) and above them were a series of cedar boards joined together' (סדרא דרכפת דמפריש אעי ארזיא). In *HAL* גב' is distinguished by a 'II' from 'I' which means a 'pool' or 'water pit' (2 Kgs. 3:16; Jer. 14:3; 39:10). What then the precise meaning of גב II is, is not stated. Klostermann, Van Gelderen and others thought of 'stories' or 'pits' (for still other nuances, cf. Busink, 185f.). Busink himself considers it most unlikely that the word refers to the space between the beams. He himself thinks of a 'flat earthen roof' ('Erddach'), possibly equipped with 'eaves' which served to drain off the water from the flat roof in the rainy season (cf. also K. Galling, H. Rösel, BRL^2, 54). In any case he rejects the meaning 'domes' (so, e.g., SV). De Geus follows somewhat the same line as Busink, by taking גבים to mean a 'series of water basins.' He derives the word from יגב which means 'to work irrigated fields'.[20] A very different line of thought is that of Görg, who derives גבים ושדרת from the Egyptian and thinks of 'side buildings and pillared halls.'[21] But we consider this translation highly improbable, if only because this fails to give any meaning to our text. A translation which Busink (186, n. 85) does not totally reject, is that of the LV: '... en dekte hem met kromhouten en rijen cederen balken (and covered it with dwarf pine and rows of cedar beams).' LV comments in the margin: 'On the slightly arched beams which spanned the building, approx. 12 m long cedar beams, lay firmly together and over the entire length, and probably resting on them was a flat stone roof, with presumably a handrail or balustrade all around.'

Now what does שדרת mean? Aside from here the word also occurs again in 2 Kgs. 11:8, 15; 2 Chr. 23:14. KBL flatly says: 'ungedeuteter Bauausdruck,' but whether this also applies to 2 Kgs. 11:8, 15 has to be looked at there. In those verses (and 2 Chr. 23:14), B. Eshel, Leš 37 [1972f.], 8f., thinks of the narrow passage between the temple and the wall of the outer court. But this does not fit here. Noth suggests the possibility of linking the word with סדר, 'order,' 'set in rows,' even though, according to him the alternation of /š/ and /s/ is remarkable. Similarly remarkable is the combination of this word with the following 'cedars' by means of the preposition ב. Burney suggests that this could be a ב essentiae or at least a variant of it: consisting of cedar. NV translates: He roofed 'het huis bij wijze van vakken en rijen met cederhout (the house by way of squares and rows of cedarwood).' In Hulst, OTTP, 37, the dubious nature of this translation is conceded, though he adds: 'it is clear that the verse is concerned with roof construction.' In regard to 2 Kgs. 11:8, 15, the meaning 'row' was assumed for שדרות, and the comment was made that this word perhaps refers to 'the all-important ceiling joists or beams that are stretched out in parallel 'rows' from one wall to the opposite side,' so that the

---

[20] C.H.J. de Geus, "The Importance of Archaeological Research into the Palestinian Agricultural Terraces, with an Excursus on the Hebrew Word $gbî$," PEQ 107 (1975), 65-74; cf. also J.B. Gottlieb, PEQ 109 (1977), 53f., who cites passages from rabbinic litterature for 'water basins'.

[21] M. Görg, "Zwei bautechnische Begriffe in 1 Kön 6,9," BN 10 (1979), 12-15 (reprinted in M. Görg, Aegyptiaca – Biblica (Ägypten und Altes Testament 11), Wiesbaden 1991, 50-55.

beams uniting the other 2 walls cross each other. In that case the גבים are the 'squares' (cf. Montg.-Gehman) which result. Clear in all this is the conjecture, which is made on the basis of etymology and the meaning of the context. Noth, with all due reservation, translates: 'in Balken und Brettern.' Ehrlich ('Balken und Bohlen aus Zedernholz') does the same, with reference to Gen. 7:21.[22]

We are of the opinion that the peculiar feature of the roof covering of the temple is not so much that it was covered with beams. This is already assumed by the reading ויספן ... בארזים. The 2 words at issue in between indicate something special, which possibly has something to do with the collection of water and drainage: 'water basins and drain pipes.' This too is only a conjecture, though, as far as the first word is concerned, it is based on a known meaning of the word.

6:10 *[He built a layer against the whole house, five cubits high, and reinforced the house with cedar wood.]*
What is the new information which this verse adds to the preceding verses? In vss. 5a and 6a it was already stated that a 'layer' was built against the wall of the temple and that the 'lowest' was 5 cubits wide. Now we read that *the* layer against the wall was built 5 cubits high. One who thinks יציע is an annex (with rooms) can now follow the suggestion of Stade, Burney and others who read 15 instead of 5. The difference between this and vs. 6a would then be that there the width, while here the height, was referred to. Noth here distinguishes the meaning of the word יציע from that in the previous verses: here, he says, the reference is to a layer which was applied to the entire house, measuring 5 m(!) high (p. 117). To our deficient knowledge of the situation of those days he attributes the fact that we cannot conceive how this woodwork (for according to him the construction was of wood) was applied. But it would be very confusing if the same word all of a sudden had to mean something else. LXX here speaks of a plurality: τοὺς ἐνδέσμους δι'ὅλου τοῦ οἴκου πέντε ἐν πήχει τὸ ὕψος αὐτοῦ and then continues: καὶ συνέσχεν τὸν σύνδεσμον ἐν ξύλοις κεδρίνοις. Here we read ἔνδεσμος, 'joint' and σύνδεσμος, 'fastening.' For this last word LXX[Luc.] has the pl. of the first word, which is therefore read twice in this verse (LXX[A] has the sing.). The word ἔνδεσμος occurs only rarely in LXX (Prov. 7:20; Ezek. 13:11 and 3 Macc. 3:25); σύνδεσμος, on the other hand, occurs somewhat more frequently (1 Kgs. 14:24; 2 Kgs. 11:14; 12:20(21); Job 41:6(7); Isa. 58:6, 9; Jer. 11:9; Dan. [Theod.] 5:6, 12; also in the NT), but in each case for different Hebr. equivalents. Whether it is really

---

[22] See now also M. Görg, "Noch einmal zu śdrt in 1 Kön 6,9," *BN* 57 (1991), 14-16, and "*Sdbt* staat *śdrt*: eine Revision zu BN 57, 14-16," *BN* 60 (1991), 24-26.

the rendering here of בית (as e.g. Hatch-Redpath suggests) is doubtful. Striking is that Noth takes the preposition על to be purely local: 'on top of,' while LXX translates it by 'throughout': 'fastenings throughout the entire house' (G. Fitzer, *TDNT*, VII, 855, accordingly, overstates the case when he views the word as translation of יצוע, 'outhouse'). LXX stresses the connections within and the entire coherence of the house by means of cedar beams and woodwork, but nowhere suggests an 'annex.' Vulg., however, does think of a 'superstructure': *et aedificat tabulatum super omnem domum quinque cubitis altitudinis* (cf. Pesh. and Tg.). It is a question, however, whether the preposition על has to be taken and translated so strictly. The use of this preposition in OT shows that an entire spectrum of translation nuances is permissible, e.g. Josh. 10:5: 'and they camped against (על) Gibeon,' without always having to think of a local 'above.' Just as in vs. 5, we here translate 'against the house,' omitting 'the wall.' But because it had been so clearly stated there, it is – also from a literary viewpoint – superfluous here. In addition it is incomplete, if one does not wish to go along with Stade's suggestion. We already knew that the lowest layer had to be 5 cubits wide or high. To that extent this gloss confirms that in vs. 5 we can substitute 'height' for 'width.' That, then, is the advantage of the gloss.

The second half of our verse reminds us of the rather negative ending of vs. 6 (for the form of ויאחז, cf. BL, 353b; Bg. II §24b). We here stand by the explanation given there. It says that the exterior walls of the house were reinforced by cedar beams, etc. It is a question, however, who the subject of ויאחז is, the יציע, king Solomon, or his workmen. A large number of commentators (e.g. Klostermann, Stade, Benzinger, and Burney) favour the first possibility. Benzinger, for example, writes: 'Mit Cedernbalken greift der Seitenbau ... in "das Haus" ein ...' The ancient versions and other commentators (see e.g. Noth) rightly refer to Solomon and his labourers. Like 10a, we consider also 10b a further and later gloss.

6:11 *Now the word of YHWH came to Solomon:*
Most commentators are agreed that vss. 11-13 are a later interpolation in the structure of the 'temple building' report. Many (such as Stade, Benzinger et al.; cf. Pedersen, III/IV, 587, n. 1) think it is a dtr. addition, but Burney offers a rather detailed analysis in which he demonstrates that the expressions used are more reminiscent of P than of D, a view in which the Holiness Code (H) gets special attention. It is striking that the original LXX also omits the vss. 11-14 as an awkward and inopportune interruption in the structure of the narrative. Although we too consider the vss. 11-14 a late addition, we nevertheless wish to take a look at these verses, because they are now a part of the final redaction of our chapter (and book). They belong to the 'thematic framework' of Kings (J. Van Seters, *Or* 50 [1981], 167-170).

Keil, among others, correctly comments that the form of vs. 11 points to a prophetic report. According to G. Gerleman (*THAT*, I, 439), דבר יהוה occurs as subject, with as predicate היה אל, no fewer than 118x in OT (cf. W. Zimmerli, BK XIII/1, 89f.; W.H. Schmidt, *TWAT*, II, 119-122 [litt. 89ff.].).[23] We are dealing here with the so-called 'Word-Event formula' ('Wortereignisformel') which is not used by the older 'writing prophets,' such as Amos, Hosea, Isaiah, and Micah. Later prophets such as Jeremiah and Ezekiel do use it frequently (about 30 and 50x resp.) and in the reports about the earlier prophecy it also occurs frequently. Our verse (along with Gen. 15:1; 1 Kgs. 18:31, says Zimmerli, 89) seems somewhat removed from this prophetic region, but this is only appearance. The 'word of YHWH,' here and elsewhere, is an objective entity, on the way to a hypostatization which was to play a role in later Judaism. The formula originated in prophetic circles during or perhaps just before the exile (see also Schmidt, 121) and reflects something of the 'prophetic view of history' (O. Procksch, *TDNT*, IV, 96). By whom the 'word of YHWH' came is – naturally – not stated.

6:12 *As for this house which you are building: if you will walk in my statutes and obey my ordinances, and faithfully keep all my commandments, I will fulfill the promise which I made about you to your father David;*
Ehrlich rightly comments that הבית הזה is, as it were, the main subject of this and the following verse, to which reference is made in vs. 13a, though not by a subject as is usually the case. One can also call this *casus pendens* (Burney and others). Burney attempts to localize the phrases which now follow in the sources familiar to us. For חקות, cf. 3:3 above; and for this and the following words like משפט, שמר etc., see also 2:3ff. We are concerned here with several phrases which frequently occur in the dtr. literature. The only one which calls attention to itself in this verse, is the fact that YHWH fulfills his word (hiph. of קום)[24] אתך, *with* Solomon, a word which is omitted in a large number of MSS of the hexaplaric recension of LXX and incorporated in the Syrohexapla sub* (as already noted in connection with vs. 11, LXX[B, Luc.] do not have these verses at all). In 2:2ff. David spoke the words to Solomon, but in 2 Sam. 7 words of like import are immediately addressed to David. It is possible that the word in question is a later gloss, but there is no reason not to maintain it here.

6:13 *Then I will live among the Israelites and not forsake my people Israel.*

---

[23] Cf. also O. Grether, *Name und Wort Gottes im Alten Testaments* (BZAW 64), Berlin 1934, 67f.

[24] Cf. E.W. Nicholson, *Preaching to the Exiles. A Study of the Prose Tradition in the Book of Jeremiah*, Oxford 1970, 89.

If Solomon will meet the condition stated in the previous verses, YHWH will dwell in Israel's midst and not forsake it. Of the 111x the verb שׁכן occurs in the qal, it only occurs here and in 8:12 in the books of Kings (cf. A.R. Hulst, *THAT*, II, 904-909). In religious parlance it is fitting that God should *dwell* in Israel (cf. Exod. 25:8; 29:45f.; Num. 35:34 and Ezek. 43:9). The idea here is one of concrete residence. In the discussion of the previous verse it was already noted, that in place of the word to be expected בתוכו, viz. 'in the midst of the house,' we read בתוך בני ישראל. According to G. Gerleman, *THAT*, I, 783, this last expression occurs 21x in 1 Kings and 11x in 2 Kings. 'Children of Israel' is used especially in the books of Exodus (123x) and Numbers (171x), much less frequently in Deut. (only 21x) and hardly at all in the 'major' and 'minor' prophets (of whom Ezekiel uses this expression most often: 11x). This summary reinforces Burney's view that the expression stems not so much from D as from P.[25] 'Israel' is used in this verse as a term for 'the people of God,' not as the word for a political entity.

6:14 *So Solomon built the house and completed it.*
This verse is virtually par. to vs. 9a and, as it now stands in the final redaction, again picks up the thread of the story. Materially, however, vs. 15 is linked to vs. 10, as LXX[B, Luc.] demonstrates. LXX transposes this brief sentence to the end of vs. 3 (MT), without mentioning Solomon, whose name does not occur again in the further description of the building activities (so Stade).

6:15 *He lined the interior walls of the house with cedar boards by covering the inside of the house with wood from the floor to the ceiling. He covered the floor of the house with planks of cypress.*
The description of the interior of the temple building begins with this verse. The indefinite ויבן (see vss. 5a, 9a, 10a, 14, 16a, and 36a) again serves here to introduce the account. That we are here dealing with the interior of the house, is evident from the locative מביתה, which is additionally construed with the preposition מן. Of the 13x such a construction occurs in OT, this is the only occurrence in Kings.[26] The LXX in its translation omits an equivalent for the word. There is no reason for this, however, not even when further on in this verse one encounters the spelling מבית. The word צלעות again means 'beams', as in vss. 5, 8, but now on the inside. Görg in this connection points to a strange word in Egyptian, *dr't*, which means 'plank' and is said to have

---

[25] Cf. A. Besters, ""Israël" et "Fils d'Israël" dans les livres historiques (Genèse - II Rois)," *RB* 74 (1967), 5-23.

[26] Cf. J. Hoftijzer, *A Search for Method. A Study in the Syntactic Use of the H-locale in Classical Hebrew*, Leiden 1981, 60, 200, 231ff.

possibly been derived from the West-Sem.[27] Tg. consistently clings to the translation מחזא, 'division,' 'chamber,' which is followed by none of the modern commentators (nor by other ancient translations). The interior was lined with beams of cedar from the floor to the roof. The word קרקע also occurs in Num. 5:17; Amos 9:3 and in this (vss. 16, 30) and the following chapter (7:7).

The expression קירות הספן occasions more difficulties. The last-mentioned term occurs only here (see on vs. 9) and is usually taken to mean 'ceiling.' The first word would have to mean 'walls', but they do not get attached to ceilings. LXX[B, Luc.] reads: ... καὶ ἕως τῶν δοκῶν καὶ ἕως τῶν τοίχων. On this basis the second part of this quotation is viewed as a doublet, while the first part of it suggests the reading קורות in place of קירות. The word קורה (Gen. 19:8; 2 Kgs. 6:2, 5; S. of S. 1:17 and 2 Chr. 3:7) does not occur in our chaps. 6 and 7. LXX here omits the word for 'ceiling' (cf. further down in this verse). Vulg. reads ... *usque ad summitatem parietum et usque ad laquearia* ... On the other hand, the Pesh. reads simply: *w'dm' lšmwhy*, 'up to the highest parts,' i.e. the ceiling. Tg. on this point is again somewhat more complex: 'to the walls up to the top of the beams.' From this little survey it is clear that the translations do agree materially, but that it is not easy to determine what the masoretic 'Vorlage' actually read. Perhaps קירות ועד קורות (*BHS*)? The proposal made by Thenius, Stade, Burney, Noth and others that we here simply follow the suggestion of the first part of the above citation from the LXX*, cannot altogether be dismissed (with Thenius) with the comment, that Vulg. and Tg. try in vain to overcome the difficulties. For then the same is true for LXX. The only ancient translation, which could most easily brush it off, is Pesh. It is not impossible that the 'Vorlage' of LXX, Vulg. and Tg. was more extensive at this point than the present MT. On the other hand one has to reckon with the fact, that errors in writing *yod* as *wāw* (and the reverse) could very easily occur in the ancient versions (see Delitzsch, *LSF* §40b). In that case, even if we do not involve the ancient versions, the reading קורות is very well possible. Every proposal to solve the problem is bound to retain unsatisfactory aspects (cf. also the following, and Barthélemy).

Many scholars (Stade and Noth among others) view the following words צפה עץ מבית as a gloss which got into the text later, but LXX reads: ἐκοιλοστάθμησεν συνεχόμενος ξύλοις ἔσωθεν. According to Liddell-Scott, the verb κοιλοσταθμέω means: 'provide with a covered ceiling or panels' (cf. vs. 9), a word by which LXX has *now* translated what it did not reproduce in the previous words, viz. the word we have translated by 'ceiling.' This makes

---

[27] M. Görg, "Ein Fachausdruck israelitischer Architektur," *BN* 3 (1977), 14ff. See now also H.-J. Fabry, *TWAT*, VI, 1059-1064.

it very likely that LXX not only had the MT reading הסִפָּן before it, but also the words which follow. In this rendering, however, there are certain difficulties: for example, the question of what word συνεχόμενος(-α) is the 'translation.' Is it צפה (so, e.g. Gooding 1967, 167) or is it without a Hebr. 'Grundlage' (so H. Köster, *TDNT*, VII, 879f.). Also from the other ancient versions it is not apparent, that they did not have the 3 last-mentioned words as 'Vorlage'. The only issue is how these words were divided. With Burney (cf. also Šanda, Noth), we regard the clause from מקרקע to בית as a 'circumstantial clause', in which a pf. of the verb is used (on this point cf. Driver §163). This gives good sense to MT: in general he built the interior of the house with 'cedar beams,' while especially overlaying that interior from the bottom to the top with wood. The verb צפה II occurs in the piel, especially in Exod. 25ff., in our chapter (and par. passages in Chronicles), and in 10:18; 2 Kgs. 18:16 (44x in all, according to Jenni, *Pi'el*, 289) and can be translated by 'overlay,' 'cover' (for the construction with a double noun, cf. König §327o).

The rest of our verse presents no difficulties, either textcritically or grammatically. It is said that the floor of the temple (Haran, *Temples*, 190, n. 2, only lets בית apply to the 'holy place,' without דביר) was covered with beams of cypress. In 5:22 above we have already considered the word ברושים, also frequently translated by 'cypress wood,' which must have spread a pleasant fragrance (cf. Busink, 224).[28]

6:16 *He built twenty cubits of the rear walls of the house with planks of cedar from floor to ceiling [and built the inside into a shrine, viz. the 'holy of holies'].*
Also this verse, which describes the covering of a part of the temple interior, is so awkwardly constructed, that the thought of textual corruption is unavoidable. Readily explicable, however, is the so-called *nota objecti* before the numeral (Ewald §277d; König §228f; Joüon §125h; Ges-K §117d), designating these specific cubits. Then, alongside of מירבותי (*k*^{e}*tib*), one finds the reading מירכתי (*q*^{e}*re*), which occurs more often (Jer. 6:22; 25:32; 31:7; 50:4; Ezek 38:15; 39:2), also construed with other prepositions or with no preposition (Exod. 26:22; 36:27; Judg. 19:1, 18, etc.), and which means 'the farthest extreme' (cf. e.g. Amos 6:10; 1 Sam. 24:4 etc.). The reference is often to virtually 'inaccessible' areas (Jer. 31:7; Ezek. 38:15 etc.). According to *HAL*, ירכה* is the 'backside,' related to ירך, 'hip,' 'seat,' 'upper leg' and connected with the Akkad. *(w)arkû* and *(w)arkatu(m)* or *urkatu(m)* (cf. *AHw*, 1467f.; 1470f.). The

---

[28] See on vss. 14f. now also A. Ruderman, "King Solomon's Wealth," *The Jewish Bible Quarterly* 19 (1990f.), 136-138, comparing this description with claims made by other ancient rulers.

pl. form in the k^etib only occurs here in OT, but that is no reason to ignore it. The fem. pl. or dual form has also been a subject of discussion in the various grammars (Böttcher §679; Olsh. §113a; Stade §§339b; 340a; König §258a; Delitzsch, *LSF* §54d). With Böttcher and Noth, and against many MSS and interpreters, we opt for the pl. form. The form is designed to indicate that the reference is to the 'backsides' of the house, the 3 walls which, viewed from the entrance, form the end and from there or to there are calculated at 20 cubits. Also the 20 cubit-wide back wall (cf. vs. 2) belongs to the 'rear of the house.'

Against these 3 walls beams of cedar were built from the floor to the 'rafters.' Here, as possibly also in the preceding verse, one must read קורות in place of קירות, a construal that is supported by LXX (cf. Vulg.: *usque ad superiora*; and Pesh.). With a minimal change in the text one achieves a clear picture: the back walls were paneled with wooden beams. Noth (and others) believe that the reference is to a partition of cedar in the main temple hall, which would separate a back space from a front space (דביר from היכל). Later, in Ezek. 41:3, this wooden partition would then be replaced by a wall. It cannot be denied that the statement can be read that way, although in that case the unique form מירכותי (which we have maintained) would become less urgent and intelligible. Schult, *ZDPV* 80 (1964), 46-54 (see also above under vs. 5]), proposes that we translate the first half of our verse as follows: 'Und er baute die zwanzig Ellen, von der Hinterseite des בית (gerechnet), mit Zedernbrettern, von Boden bis an die Balken (sc. der Decke) ...,' and then continues: '... und er baute es ihm innen zum דביר, zum Allerheiligsten.' He rightly does not view the 20 cubits as the place where a partition between the 2 parts of the temple would run, but the entire space before and between the back walls, and takes בנה to mean 'extend.'

Accordingly, the cube of 20 cubits built of cedar beams is a space, a shrine, in the היכל. It would seem this line of thought is only being confirmed by the following words of our verse: he built it for him from within for a דביר, a 'holy of holies.' In place of 'he built' LXX and Vulg. read: 'and he made.' This suggestion need not be followed, however, anymore than that of Noth and others, which would be to read the word ויבדל 'and he partitioned it off' in place of ויבן לו. The following לו can possibly be understood as a *dativus commodi* (Burney) (also cf. König §28; Ehrlich has it refer back to בית in the first half of our verse), hence: 'he extended it for himself ...' מבית means 'within.' In this connection the following ל before דביר must be linked, not with this word, but with בנה (otherwise: BrSynt. §120a: 'innerhalb des Allerheiligsten'). Although LXX (cf. Vulg.) does not translate this לו, Tg. (cf. Pesh.) has less difficulty with this ל (more frequent in Aram.) as indication for the accusative with the proleptic pronominal suffix: 'and within the house he built the house of atonement ....' But in a later period in Hebr. the ל is often indication for the accusative (Ges-K §117a). In that case the translation: 'so within he built the דביר' is natural.

The following 'holy of holies' (cf. 7:50; 8:6) further describes דביר (cf. vs. 5 above) and is a term for the innermost part of the sanctuary also in P (Exod. 26:33f.; Num. 4:4, 19). The word can also refer to certain gifts (Lev. 21:22) or to 'holy' places (Num. 18:10; Ezek. 43:12) other than the 'holy of holies.' Often the 'most holy offerings' are designated by these words (Num. 18:9; Ezek. 42:13; 44:13, etc.; cf. also H.P. Müller, *THAT*, II, 604f.). In P the words are applied to 'the bronze altar,' 'the altar of incense,' the twelve 'showbreads' and the parts of the offering intended for the priests. In other places where the word occurs, as in Ezekiel, Chronicles, Ezra, etc., it is influenced by P (Burney). It is therefore not surprising that Burney (and others) regard the words here as a later gloss on דביר. Burney rightly points out, however, that in that case the gloss must have originated prior to LXX. It seems to us that not only the last words of our verse but the whole of vs. 16b from ויבן on is a later explanatory gloss on the preceding words. The formulation in late biblical Hebr. (ל as indication for the accusative; the use of the proleptic suffix) and the material repetition in other words of what has already been said in the first half of our verse, confirm this suspicion: along 20 cubits of the back walls a shrine was built. It is not stated in this verse how it was closed off in front and how it was covered on top, except that it reached to the 'rafters.' Josephus (*Ant*. VIII §71) mentions partitioning (διελὼν) the temple in 2 parts, the 'most holy' (LXX: δαβεὶρ) part of which is called ἄδυτον. This is 20 cubits, the rest 40 cubits. Also the LXX translation diverges rather markedly from MT: 'And he built the 20 cubits from the 'top' (or 'end,' LXX: ἀπ' ἄκρου [Luc.: 'from the house']), the one side (perhaps: the partition distinguished from the 3 other wall planes) from the floor to the rafters ... etc.'(cf. Gooding 1967, 168-172). In any case LXX by no means contradicts the possibility of the דביר existing *in* the temple, indeed it confirms it even (cf. the 40 cubits for the length of the entire temple according to LXX* in vs. 2 above).

6:17 *The (temple) house [that is 'the holy place'] in front of the shrine was forty cubits.*

Virtually all modern commentators are agreed that there is something wrong with MT of this and the following verses. A mere glance at LXX[B, Luc.] surely conveys an impression of a more logical progression of our verse than what we find there now: viz. the hard-to-explain לפני (D.W. Gooding, *VT* 15 [1965], 409f., criticizes LXX and its imitators). True, some older grammarians (Ewald §164a; Stade §301b; cf., however, Olsh. §§217b; 223m ['wenn anders der Text richtig']) have pointed out the more or less customary nature of the *ay*-ending following nouns, but more recent ones (e.g. BL, 588[1]) do not hesitate to point to the impossibility of this form as such (cf. Segal §§269 and 393, and Barthélemy, who defends the reading of MT on the basis of Aq. and Theod.).

Combined with the beginning of vs. 20, the text virtually precisely yields what we may expect from it: the house was 40 cubits long in front of the דביר. This is in fact also the translation of LXX. We are therefore justified in suspecting, that the vss. 18 and 19 are a later interpolation, which breaks the natural sequence. How did this text corruption originate? We will only mention 2 of several views here. In the introduction to his commentary Benzinger (XVIff.) calls the vss. 16-21 'ein sehr schönes Beispiel für die Entwicklung, welche der Text durchmachte, bis er die Form des jetzigen Hebr. erhielt.' He distinguishes an 'Urtext,' a second and a third 'Stufe', to which the 'allerspäteste Veränderungen' are then again said to have been added. Noth, 100, offers a more logical explanation by pointing out the possibility that in the (original?) MS לפני was the last word of a column, which was inadvertently repeated at the beginning of the following column. A note was written in the margin beneath the first column and later unthinkingly taken over by a copyist (now vs. 19). LXX[B, Luc.] reproduces this stage in a somewhat adapted form. Later on vs. 18 was inserted before vs. 19.

To us, too, the most natural connection seems to be between the end of our verse and vs. 20 (Vulg., by its translation *pro foribus oraculi*, also supports this connection). In our verse we read that the space in front of the דביר amounted to 40 cubits. Only the younger MSS of Pesh. here read 20 (this is certainly not the case for all of them, as the textcr. app. in *BHS* suggests). Another textcritical question is whether the words הבית הוא belonged to the original substance of the text. LXX[A] did translate these words, but in LXX* and also in Vulg. a clear translation is lacking. It *is* the case that the Greek word ναός in LXX can be the translation of different Hebr. words (cf. also O. Michel, *TDNT*, IV, 882, n. 7), but the absence of a complete translation of the 2 words, as LXX[A] does present them, supports the suspicion that LXX* did not have the words of our MT in its 'Vorlage'.

6:18 *The cedar wood of the interior was carved with gourds and rosettes. Everything was cedar; not a stone was showing.*
This verse is a totally 'lost' notation on the embellishment of the interior wall (presumably) of the space of the temple building without the shrine. This notation strongly resembles what we read in vs. 29 of this chapter and from there might have been put in the margin here by a diligent reader of the text, at least if the theory of Noth does not yield an even better explanation of this 'transposition' (see previous verse). It is truly significant that LXX* does not translate our verse. Again it is stated that the interior of the house was overlaid with cedar. The preposition אל has a strange feel to it. The Vulg. reads *et cedro omnis domus intrinsecus vestibatur*, which inspires the textcr. app. of *BHS* to make the – at least not impossible – conjecture כל in place of אל. But the question mark behind this conjecture also indicates that the composer of the

textcr. app. himself was not certain. Pesh. and Tg., accordingly, do not support this proposal. The word פנימה 'within' occurs 12x in OT, 4 of which in this chapter, 3x in Ezekiel (40:16 [2x]) and 41:3). The word מקלעת (also in vss. 29, 32 and 7:31) of which the verb can be found in the vss. 29, 32, and 35, means 'wood carving' or at least 'carving,' one of the forms of woodworking which was already known in antiquity (cf. H. Weippert, *BRL*², 147ff.). Some Hebr. MSS here read a pl. (cf. also Vulg.), but it is not necessary to follow this reading. פקעים are 'gourd-like ornamentations' (cf. also 7:24; cf. 2 Chr. 4:3), a form of which (פַּקֻעת) occurs in 2 Kgs. 4:39, the *colocynthis vulgaris,* a cucumber-like plant whose fruit, when eaten, apparently has a strong purgative effect (cf. also Dalman, *AuS,* I, 343). In conjunction with the following word the reference is to carvings of flowers, inflorescence, or plants which gave the cedar walls a cared-for and pleasing appearance.

The word פטורי צצים again confronts the researcher with the customary uncertainties. The *nomen regens* of this st. cstr.-combination is a pl. pass. part. of the qal of the verb פטר, which means 'escape,' 'release,' 'remove' (cf. the word פֶּטֶר, 'first-born,' 'that which opens the womb'). In combination with the following word it occurs again in the vss. 29, 32, and 35 of this chapter. Noth translates the word, together with the *nomen rectum,* as 'Blumenkelche' ('aufgespaltene Formen von Blumen'). In *KBL* one finds the possible translations listed as 'Blumengehänge,' 'Knospen,' both of them followed by a question mark. This again leans on what Ges-B describe as '(ausgebreitete) Gehänge, Guirlanden v. Blumen, od. Rosetten' (cf. also *BDB*: '*usually outspread* (garlands) *of flowers*'; Burney: 'open flowers,' etc.). That in practically all translations there is mention of 'flowers' arises from the use of the word צצים. (For the form with *dagesh,* cf. Ewald §118a; Olsh. §83c; BL, 534 ['quantitative metathesis'].) The word ציץ can denote the 'flower' or the 'rosette' on the highpriest's turban (Exod. 28:36; 39:30; Lev. 8:9; Sir. 40:4).[29] More often it refers to 'blossom' (Num. 17:23; Ps. 103;15; Job 14:2; Isa. 28:1; 40:6-8), 'the opening flower.' The verb צוץ is usually translated in Ezek. 7:10 (qal) by 'blossom,' in Num. 17:23; Isa. 27:6; Ps. 72:16; 90:6; 92:8; 103:15 (hiph.) by 'putting forth blossoms,' 'blossom.' The combination of the words פטורי צצים probably means the just opened flower in its freshness and beauty. The whole complex of plants and flowers had been crafted on the wall in or on the wood. Among experts there is also a difference of opinion about the technique involved in this fine woodcarving work. Busink (258) believes that for technical reasons the so-called 'relief en creux' is the most probable for walls and doors; Noth, on the other hand, thinks of 'Flachrelief' (cf. Thenius who associates מקלעת with a kind of bas-relief, such as can be seen on

---

[29] Cf. also A. de Buck, "La fleur au front du grand-prêtre," *OTS* 9 (1951), 18-29.

Egyptian monuments). It is striking that Vulg., Pesh. and Tg. read 3, instead of 2, kinds of ornamentation in our text: Vulg.: *habens tornaturas suas et iuncturas fabrefactas et celaturas eminentes;* Pesh.: '... which were carved out with gourds (?, *hēqlē*), ornaments (?, *bātlē*) and lilies (*šûšānē*) ...'; Tg. '... things that looked like eggs and garlands and lilies had been carved out ...' For the reproduction of Tg. it is interesting to compare 2 Chr. 3:5, where there is mention of תמרים ושרשרות, 'palms and chains.' This last-mentioned word occurs, aside from 2 Chr. 3:5, 16, also in Exod. 28:14 (conjectured in vs. 22 as well) and in 1 Kgs. 7:17; it is a word occurring in the Akkad. ((*šeršerratu[m]*; Assyrian: *šaršaratu[m]*; cf. *AHw*, 1218), which means 'chain.' Tg. and the chronicler probably hark back to the more recent garland motifs on the walls of the temple after the exile (cf. also Rudolph, 203). In the ancient Near East, especially in Mesopotamia, it was not unusual for people to embellish temples and shrines with gold, precious stones and the like (cf. Busink, 258).

Our 'displaced notice' is concluded with the general comment that 'all' was cedar and that not a (single) stone was visible. נראה is a part. (not a pf., as Ewald §321a mistakenly assumes), which is negated by אין (GD §113d; Joüon §160i; cf. König §409c). This construction (with the undefined noun) can have either a predicative or an attributive meaning. In English one can translate it thus: 'not a stone was visible,' but also 'there was not a stone to be seen.' Joüon correctly translates: 'il n'y avait pas de pierre qui parût (there was no stone that was visible).'

6:19 *Inside the house he prepared the shrine to put the ark of the covenant of YHWH in it.*
This addition states the purpose of the shrine in the temple: the 'ark of the covenant of YHWH' was placed here. Noth has pointed out that in this addition (which must be older than vs. 18) there are a number of formulations which will not be found in the rest of this chapter: מפני ימה (also again in the secondary vs. 21); הכין (only here); 'the ark of the covenant of YHWH' (in place of the probably older 'ark of YHWH'); and then also the peculiar form לתתן, the inf. cstr., preceded by the preposition of ל, of the verb נתן. To start with this last word, often the form תתן, which also occurs in 17:14 (*kᵉtib*), is viewed as a mistake or a (deliberate) misspelling for לתת or לתתו (cf. König §396h; Ges-K §66i; BL, 368l; Olsh. §245d; Delitzsch, *LSF* §58b). Older grammarians were generally not so sure of this here. Böttcher (§1162d) and Ewald (§238c), for example, think here of a kind of reduplication **tntn,* while also Bg. II §25d has in mind a second form of the inf. alongside the usual one from **tint,* in both verses 'mit Umstellung erhalten'. Also cf. König, I, §33, 5 who, like Böttcher before him, comments that this form cannot twice in a row have been written wrong by accident. His proposal for the solution of the problem (*nun* as 'parasitical addition') is not very convincing (cf. Segal §169: '*forma mixta*' of

the 'colloquial' לתן and the 'literary' לתת; and Burney). In our judgment also this unusual form of the inf. cstr. must not be changed, because this form either existed as a 'second form' alongside the first or we are dealing with a 'dialectical' distinction. The preposition ל before this inf. has the force of a conjunction (Olsh. §224d; König §381f).[30]

It is not so strange that the verbal form הכין is lacking in LXX[B, Luc], considering the differing construction of the section vss. 17-19, in which vs. 18 has not been processed. We also already encountered the hiph. of כון in 2:24 and 5:32 (see there). This word, combined with בתוך־הבית, confirms Schult's view (see above under vs. 16) that the דביר is a structure, a shrine, *in* the temple, in the היכל. This does not yet mean that דביר and היכל can now be equated, as Schult remarkably enough has it, be it that he himself has the right reading: 'denn der היכל ist nichts weiter als derjenige Teil des בית, den der דביר ubrigläßt' (op. cit., p. 51). 'In the middle' can also be 'in the middle of the rear,' hence the innermost part of the היכל as seen from the front hall.

Already in 2:26 we encountered the 'ark' in our books of Kings (see there), just as in 3:15 the 'ark of the covenant' of אדני (see there), and we will still frequently meet it especially in chap. 8. This does not alter the fact that we wish to pause for a moment here to reflect on the specific expression ארון ברית יהוה (also cf. Busink, 276-285, with litt. on the ark). This expression is characteristic for the dtr. and the traditions influenced by him. This description of the ark describes its function as the place where a copy of the decalogue was stored. For J and E the 'ark' was still only a symbol of divine leadership to the Israelites departing from Sinai (cf. e.g. Num. 10:33-36). It belonged to the military side of Israel's life as a war palladium. For the rest it cannot be totally ruled out that Deuteronomy and dtr. were following older traditions in their view of an 'ark,' a 'chest' which could contain something (cf. H.-J. Zobel, *TWAT*, I, 399ff.).

6:20 *The shrine was twenty cubits long, twenty cubits wide, and twenty cubits high, and he overlaid it with gold leaf. He also made an altar of cedar wood ...*

As already noted under vs. 17, this verse ties in with the conclusion of that verse (cf. also Barthélemy). As is evident from the measurements given here, the shrine was a cube: the length, width, and height were all 20 cubits. In the later MSS of Pesh. the length is given as 40 cubits, but the older MSS (7a1 among them) agree with MT. The comment of *BHK* and *BHS* on this point, which suggests that *all* Pesh. MSS have this deviation, is therefore mistaken.

---

[30] Cf. the contrived view of F.E.C. Dietrich, *Abhandlungen zur hebräischen Grammatik*, Leipzig 1846, 192f.

Why the later Pesh. MSS deviate is not clear: did they perhaps collapse the דביר into the היכל? In the par. vs. 2 Chr. 3:8 an indication of height is lacking, but it does say that the length of the דביר corresponded to the width of the house. Older commentators, such as Thenius, refer to the symbolism of the cube: '... zur Symbolisirung der *Vollkommenheit* des Göttlichen die *vollkommenste* Gestalt des Parallelopipedon, die des *Kubus* ...' Another question is whether the remaining height, viz. 10 cubits (cf. vs. 2), was left 'open' or that one must imagine that the shrine was placed on an elevation of 10, cubits so that the top of the דביר would coincide with the top of the היכל. Still another possibility, found especially in the older exegetes, is the view that the דביר, as seen from the outside, was lower than the היכל (see Busink, 199, n. 112). But then the assumption is that the main building and the adytum were 2 separate 'rooms,' clearly separated also when seen from the outside. Many scholars (Galling et al.) are inclined to assume a *podium adytum*, based in part on discoveries of Canaanite temples in Beth-shean (see Busink, 200-203). But Busink (203ff), believing that the grounds advanced for such a *podium adytum* are not adequate, stands by an *adytum* on the same level as the היכל. Noth also finds the assumption of an elevation of the דביר less than compelling. We agree with this view. An empty space of 10 cubits above a large shrine does not seem abnormal to us. On the other hand, while the idea of a podium need not be absolutely rejected, there is not enough proof for it in the text.

Added to the measurements of the דביר is a statement saying that the shrine was overlaid with 'gold leaf.' Stade, 140-143, has attempted at length to show that this is a later addition, but Burney has stamped Stade's various arguments (among other things, that there were insufficient skilled workmen for ornamentation in gold) as 'not entirely convincing.' צפה (pi., see vs. 15 above), correctly says Burney, may not necessarily denote heavy gold plating (as probably in 2 Kgs. 18:16), but can also refer to a thin gilding with liquid gold. LXX reads: καὶ περιέσχεν αὐτὸν χρυσίῳ συνκεκλεισμένῳ, 'is overlaid with pure gold' (O. Michel, *TDNT*, VII, 744). This phrase undoubtedly has to do with the expression זהב סגור, described in 2 Chr. 3:8 as זהב טוב. As the most usual word for gold, זהב occurs about 385x in OT (also in Sir. and the Qumran texts). Its synonyms (חרוץ, כתם, פז and also סגור) occur substantially less often (cf. B. Kedar-Kopfstein, *TWAT*, II, 534-544). According to Kedar-Kopfstein, it is difficult to precisely determine the meaning of all these words, which often occur in combination with other words. Perhaps זהב סגור is identical with the סגור mentioned in Job 28:15, and a form of the Akkad. *ḫurāṣu sagru*. According to Von Soden (*AHw*, 1003) *sagru* is 'eine Goldlegierung.' The Hebr. סגר 'close,' under which סגור is sometimes adduced as a part. pass. (cf. Ges-B: 'gediegenes [verschlossenes] Gold'), probably has less to do with the supposed pass. ptc. than the Akkad. equivalent. Therefore *KBL* correctly advances סגור as an independent lemma for our verse and the following verse as 'Press-oder Blattgold, für Vergoldung ganz dünn gehämmerte Blättchen aus lauterstem Gold'; for 7:49f.; 10:21; 2 Chr. 4:20, 22; 9:20 as 'pure gold' (so now also *HAL*). It is hard to derive technically responsible distinctions from the etymology of the words used, but in the context of our narrative the term 'gold leaf' seems to be most satisfactory (cf. also Benzinger, who refers to the vocational designation מסגר in 2 Kgs. 24:14, 16).

The final addition to our verse has, with good reason, puzzled many an exegete. What altar is meant and how can one cover or overlay with cedar an altar on which something is sooner or later going to burn up? It is very tempting to follow the reading of LXX and to adapt our text and vs. 21 along those lines: καὶ ἐποίησεν θυσιαστήριον (21) κατὰ πρόσωπον τοῦ δαβεὶρ καὶ περιέσχεν αὐτὸν χρυσίῳ: 'he made an altar in front of the דביר and overlaid it with gold.' Benzinger, Noth, and others follow this reading and, in my opinion, with good reason. By the altar in front of the adytum is meant (with Noth; Nowack, II, 39f. and n. 1; Benzinger, *Arch.* 330; Montg.-Gehman; Busink, 288, n. 466; 291) the table on which 'the bread of the presence' is laid (Lev. 24:6; Exod. 25:23-30; see also by 7:48 below). An altar of wood is not only less-well suited for burning materials on it; it can also be equated with the 'golden altar' mentioned in 7:48. In contrast with LXX, the word ארז in our verse can be maintained (cf. also Ezek. 41:22). The material intended for it in Exod. 25:33 is עצי שטים (שלחן), sometimes translated by 'acacia wood' (in Ezek 41:22 simply by 'wood').

6:21 *[Solomon also overlaid the inside of the house with pure gold and he drew chains of gold] ... in front of the shrine and overlaid it with gold.*
As we already noted in connection with the previous verse, we are here dealing – aside from the last 4 words of this verse – with a later addition or gloss. In any case the words from ויצף to the second זהב are misplaced here, perhaps because as doublet they were written in the margin of the following verse and ended up in the wrong place in the text (Benzinger; cf. Noth). This does not alter the fact that this displaced gloss still tells us something. In the first place we learn that Solomon overlaid the whole house, hence the whole temple, with 'gold leaf.' This statement may of course belong to the custom, which arose in a later time, of inflating in value and wealth everything that Solomon did by making extravagant claims. It is striking – as Stade and others point out – that 'Solomon,' contrary to the habit of the narrator, is here mentioned by name. On the other hand, it cannot technically be ruled out that in Solomon's day the practice of overlaying walls and objects with gold could occur; cf., for instance, a building inscription by Amen-hotep III (ca. 1400 BCE) which mentions 'the great shrine of fine gold' (*ANET*, 375). Even in Ugar. texts we find indications that the 'resting place' of El was of gold (cf. A. van Selms, *UF* 7 [1975], 475).

In the second place, there is mention of golden רתוקות or רתיקות depending on one's preference either for the q^ere or the k^etib. One also finds רתוק in Ezek. 7:23 and a pl. רתקות in Isa. 40:19. The stem רתק occurs in the pu. in Nah. 3:10 as 'bound in fetters' and as niph. in the q^ere in Eccl. 12:6 (k^etib: ירחק). In Isa. 40:19 this word is taken to mean 'chains' while, as it concerns the meaning of this word, Ezek. 7:23 is rather disputed (cf. W. Zimmerli, BK XIII/1, 165). Lexicons like Ges-B and *KBL*, accordingly, hesitate when it comes to determining the meaning of this word in our verse (cf. also the comments regarding the shifting vocalization and pl. form in the older grammarians: Olsh. §§120a, 183d, 185a, 186a; Bg. I §25d), though Ges-B, for example, thinks here of a 'fetter' or 'chain' (cf. also *BDB*, 958; Zorell, etc.). The question often asked among those who wish to maintain our text integrally is: what are we to make of 'with chains (or fetters) before the דביר'? Among the ancient versions only the hexaplaric recension of LXX has the translation of MT, viz. LXX^A: (... καὶ παρήγαγεν ἐν) καθηλώμασιν (χρυσίου ...). The noun καθήλωμα, in contrast to the verb, occurs in Greek only here in LXX and is taken to mean 'nail'. Cf. Liddell-Scott, s.v.: 'that which is nailed on, revetment'; Schleusner, s.v.: *clavus*, while he translates LXX^A as follows: '*ubi catenarum aurearum loco, quarum usum non intellexit, melius clavos aureos posuit, e quibus velum, quod adytum a sancto separabat, suspendebatur*'. Vulg. translates the entire second part of our verse thus: *et adfixit lamminas clavis aureis*, 'he fastened the plates with nails of gold.' The word *lammina* or *lamina* is often used by Vulg. in OT or other Hebr. words (Exod. 26:29; 27:6, 17; 28:36; 38; 29:6; 36:34; 37:28; 38:2, 6; 39:29; Lev. 8:9; Num. 16:38f.; 2 Chr. 3:5, 7f.; Job 19:24; 40:13; Isa. 30:22; 40:19; and in our books in our chapter vs. 35 and 10:16, and 2 Kgs. 18:16) and usually denotes a sheet of metal, plate (of silver or gold). Pesh. translates the conclusion of our verse: 'and he made a portal (or doorpost, syr.: *prwstd*') for the sanctuary and overlaid it with gold.' Tg. has: 'And he installed golden chains in front of the most holy place and covered it with gold.' All these translations are based on the MT redaction as we now have it (except, of course, LXX$^{B, Luc.}$), and this determines the translation and interpretation. Similarly determinative for the interpretation is ויעבר, a pi.-form of the verb עבר which is very rare (cf. Job 21:10 and *KBL* and *HAL*, s.v.). In Job 21:10 the verb, like the pa'el of the Aram. עבר, means 'make pregnant.' In our verse *KBL* translates (with a [?], for that matter), 'darüberziehn'. Cf. also Noth and *HAL*: 'durchziehen mit'; Jenni, *Pi'el*, 140, n. 161: 'enthält einen technischen Ausdruck, der wohl faktitiv als "durchzogen machen" zu verstehen ist'. Older Jewish commentators like Rashi and Kimchi take the verb to mean something like 'close off,' 'cordon off,' by means of chains, and so the opinion has taken root that the 'inner sanctuary' was sealed off from the 'sanctuary' by means of chains. On the basis of 2 Chr. 3:14, Thenius believes that an object must have dropped out and that the פָּרֹכֶת is the 'curtain.' But such emendations (cf. Klostermann, Burney; Busink, 206, n. 132, et al.) are not necessary if one follows the hypothesis we support, viz. that we are here dealing with a later gloss which has ended up in the text independently of the context. What is said in our text is probably – because in view of the fragmentary and sometimes dubious character of this gloss no certainty can be achieved – that the 'house' was 'pervaded' with golden chains. But how, where, and to what end they were installed – supposing now that they were installed during the time of the building of the temple itself – is far from clear. It may have been ornamental chains; it may also have been 'directional chains' such as one finds in museums and the like.[31]

6:22 *[Next he overlaid the whole house with gold to perfect the whole house; even the whole altar in front of the shrine he overlaid with gold.]*
This verse, too, is obviously an addition, since it again repeats what had been stated earlier. That the end of our verse is omitted in LXX[B, Luc.] will therefore not be surprising. The repetitions in our chapter are simply not of a literary character, but are especially due to the fact that in a later time people had difficulty gaining a clear picture of the early temple building. A second reason is that people sought to ascribe to Solomon more power, honour, and wealth than he ever had. Striking in this connection is the word תם in our verse, an inf. of the verb תמם (cf. Jer. 36:23), which in this combination can mean 'complete' and refers to the final completion of the temple building, prompting the impression that both the exterior and the interior of the temple were overlaid with gold (for תמם, cf. also K. Koch, *THAT*, II, 1045-1051). This word confers a certain 'completeness,' 'perfection' on the temple (cf. also the LXX: συντελεία and G. Delling, *TDNT*, VIII, 66). For this reason alone, this verse must be viewed as a (much later) gloss. One must assume that by the 'altar' in the second part of our verse, the 'table of the showbreads' is meant (cf. Busink, 291ff.).

6:23 *In the shrine he made two cherubim of oleaster, ten cubits high.* (see verse 26)
The vss. 23-28 deal with the placing and measurement of the כרובים in the 'most holy place,' the shrine. Again the author is apparently especially interested in the dimensions, the material and 'position' of the 2 cherubim without being concerned about their appearance and function. The scant statements given here and elsewhere about the cherubim have given rise to many a commentary, article or study in which various conjectures are

---

[31] See now also M.C.A. Korpel, "Soldering in Isaiah 40:19-20 and 1 Kings 6:21," *UF* 23 (1991), 219-221.

expressed.³² The word כרוב, which we encounter for the first time here in Kings, occurs almost 90x in OT, 19 of which in our chapter and in 7:29, 36, and 8:6 (further in 2 Kgs. 19:15; Gen. 3:24; Exod. 25:18-22; 26:1, 31; 36:8, 35; 37:7-9; Num. 7:89; 1 Sam. 4:4; 2 Sam. 6:2; 22:11; Isa. 37:16; Ezek. 9:3; 10:1-20; 11:22; 28:14, 16; 41:18-25; Ps. 18:11; 80:2; 99:1; 1 Chr. 13:6; 28:18; 2 Chr. 3:7-14; 5:7f.). From this it is evident that the cherubim played a role in the description of sanctuaries (Exodus, Kings, Ezekiel), but also in mythologically tinted passages (cf. Gen. 3:24; Ezek. 28:14, 16; Ps. 80:2; 99:1, etc.). Usually a connection is made between the Hebr. word and the Akkad. *kurību*, which especially occurs in the New Assyrian and Late-Babylonian and which, according to Von Soden, means 'ein Genius' (cf. *AHw*, s.v., and also *HAL*; K. Jaroš, *ZAW* 92 (1982), 211f.; and in general Metzger, *Königsthron*, 309-319, and T.N.D. Mettinger, *DDD*, 362-367). The verb *karābu(m)* means 'pray,' 'consecrate,' 'bless,' 'greet,' (cf. *AHw*), but it is a question whether this Akkad. derivation helps very much to clarify the identity and function of the Hebr. cherub (for this and other etymological derivations, cf. also J. Trinquet, *DBS* 5, 161-186, esp. 162ff.; D.N. Freedman, P. O'Connor, *TWAT*, IV, 323-326). ᵈ*Kuribi*, according to Frankena, is the word for the bull colossi at the entrance of a sanctuary, such as Assarhaddon built in front of the sanctuary of Assur.³³ To this he adds, among other things, that both materially and linguistically they would presumably be called cherubim in Israel. Others, however, think that the name is 'the typical Assyrian expression for the gods of intercession, the genii'.³⁴ If we were compelled to accept a strong material dependence of the Hebr. cherubim on the Akkad. *kurību* we might be inclined to view the Hebr. כרוב as late, i.e., as belonging to the period of the exile. In that case the cherubim in Solomon's temple could hardly be considered authentic. But we can agree with Vriezen, op. cit., p. 115, that the OT representation 'shows a totally different type.' From OT one gets the impression that the cherubim frequently function as (mythical) beings in the form of angels (Gen. 3:24, where they guard the garden of Eden). In Ezek. 28, the 'lament over the king of Tyre,' one finds a mythical description which offers some details. There is mention here of a כרוב הסוכך, 'a protective cherub,' placed on the 'holy mountain of the gods,' and 'walking among stones of fire.' From there this cherub was removed by God himself. Although there is kinship to the tradition in Gen. 3:24, there is a clearly different development here (for this cf. M.D. Cassuto, R.D. Barnett, *EncMiqr*. IV, 238-244; see also

---

³² See now also O. Keel, "»Mit Cherubim und Serafim«. Ein Exegetenstreit und seine theologische Hintergründe," *Bibel heute* 28 (1992), 171-174.

³³ R. Frankena, *Tākultu. De sacrale maaltijd in het Assyrische ritueel*, Leiden 1953, 100.

³⁴ Cf. also Th.C. Vriezen, *Onderzoek naar de paradijsvoorstelling bij de oude semietische volken*, Wageningen 1937, 113ff.

TWAT, IV, 326f.). The cherubim perform a striking function in carrying the chariot throne of God (Ezek. 10). YHWH, accordingly, is sometimes called he 'who is enthroned on the cherubim' (1 Sam. 4:4; 2 Sam. 6:2; 2 Kgs. 19:15; Isa. 37:16; Ps. 80:2; 99:1; 1 Chr. 13:6; cf. Hebr. 9:5, the only time cherubim are referred to in NT). YHWH is later represented as 'speaking from between the 2 cherubim' (Exod. 25:22; Num. 7:89, etc.). From 1 Sam. 4:4 it is clear that, within a certain period, place, or circle in ancient Israel, there was a connection between YHWH, the ark, and the cherubim (cf. E. Lohse, *TDNT*, IX, 427f.; also for the representation of cherubim in post-biblical Judaism).

It is clear that in our verses and also later in our chapter we are dealing with representations of cherubim which were made of wood, overlaid with gold or carved out in relief, and put on walls or the like. Josephus (*Ant.* VIII §73), in reproducing our verse, rightly comments: τὰς δὲ Χερουβεῖς οὐδεὶς ὁποῖαί τινες ἦσαν εἰπεῖν οὐδ' εἰκάσαι δύναται; that is: 'As for the cherubim, no one can tell or imagine what they looked like.' Although in this statement scholars see an attempt on the part of Josephus (and ancient Jewish exegesis) to soften the theological difficulties arising from Solomon's neglect of the second commandment of the decalogue[35] one can also take it very realistically: the modern literature on our subject demonstrates the quandary, even though scholars can point to objects resembling cherubim which have come to light through archeological research. Representations from Israel's 'Umwelt' sometimes depict these beings in human form, than again furnished with wings, finally as hybrid beings with the body of an animal and a human head (see the literature cited in *TWAT*, IV, 322f., and *DDD*, 366f.). Busink further explores the question how the cherubim, which the text only describes as having wings, may have looked in the eyes of others, e.g. winged sphinxes (W.F. Albright, *BA* 1 [1938], 1-3, Barnett, Parrot, et al.). Iconographically there are 3 types of these winged sphinxes: the resting ones; those with a standing animal body; and the sphinx with his animal body standing upright like a human (cf. Noth, 123f. and *DBS*, V, 171), but there are also cherubim in human form (so Busink himself, 268). Now sphinx-like figures have been found throughout the whole ancient Near East over a large territory: from the Mitanni king Šaušattar, Cyprus, Athens, Ugarit, to the graffito from the royal quarry by Jerusalem (Noth, 124), which De Vaux claims was inspired by the cherubim in Solomon's temple.[36] The winged cherubim alongside the ark in the shrine may have been reminiscent of familiar representations of the sphinxes-throne, as it

---

[35] Cf. H.St.J. Thackeray et al., *Josephus*, London 1926-1965, V, 611, n. c.

[36] R. de Vaux, "Les chérubins et l'arche d'alliance, les sphinx gardiens et les trônes divins dans l'ancient Orient," *Mélanges de l'Université Saint-Joseph* 37 (1960f.), 91-124 (reprinted in *Bible et Orient*, Paris 1967, 231-259), esp. 117f.

is depicted on the sarcophagus of Ahiram (Byblos, 10th century) (cf. e.g. *ANEP*, pls. 456-458). The description in our vss. 23-28, however, gives us no reason to think of such a throne, though it cannot be denied that OT expressions like יהוה צבאות ישב הכרובים (1 Sam. 4:4) may contribute to such a view (also cf. M. Görg, *TWAT*, III, 1028: Metzger, *Königsthron*, 309-351). Kuenen sought to derive from the expressions 'YHWH, who is enthroned,' or 'who rides upon the cherubim' (2 Sam. 22:11; Ps. 18:11) the idea, that originally the cherubim represented the dark thunder clouds, which conceal the thundering god from the eyes of humans[37], a derivation which can also be found later with H. Torczyner and H. Schmidt (cf. Busink, 287). Especially the cherubim's wings were viewed as clouds or 'veils', which shield the eyes of humans from the כבוד of YHWH (cf. 1 Chr. 28:18). Also YHWH is said to 'rise up' on these 'clouds' (cf. Ezek. 10; Ps. 18:10 [par. 2 Sam. 22:11]; Ps. 104:3f.; cf. *DBS*, V, 169ff.). But also these ideas, which have undoubtedly been derived from mystical representations and can be found in Ugar. texts in the description of Baal as 'cloud-rider' (cf. my *Kanaän. goden*, 26),[38] offer no decisive explanation for the form of the cherubim in the shrine nor of their function. Did they function as the 'keepers' of the ark (F. Landsberger, *HUCA* 20 [1947], 233; cf. K. Jaroš, *ZAW* 92 [1980], 211f.), who had to ward off unauthorized or unholy intruders, or are they rather the representatives of the heavenly court (Busink, 287)? It is clear, in any case, that, in the placing of cherubim in the shrine above and by the ark, Israel introduced a part of a mythical worldview into the practice of its own piety, filling it with a content of its own. Something of the contours of this view and practice is discernible in other OT texts, which speak of YHWH and the cherubim, but the essence of the intent of these beings as they were depicted in the temple, indeed of the representations themselves, escapes us.

Our verse states that the 2 cherubim in the shrine were made of עצי שמן, a detail missing in LXX[B].[39] This wood is also mentioned in vss. 31f. and further in Isa. 41:19; Neh. 8:15 and Sir. 50:11; in Neh. 8:15 it is clearly distinguished from עֲלֵי־זַיִת. The reference, therefore, is not to the wood of the olive tree, nor in all likelihood to that of the olive willow (though many modern investigators suspect this), the *Elaeagnus angustifolia*, a relative of our sea buckthorn, but to the wood of the 'oleaster,' the wild olive tree, oil-bearing wood that is also of

---

[37] A. Kuenen, *De godsdienst van Israël tot de ondergang van den joodschen staat*, Haarlem 1896, I, 234.

[38] See now also M.C.A. Korpel, *A Rift in the Clouds. Ugaritic and Hebrew Descriptions of the Divine*, Münster 1990, 598-605.

[39] G. Hentschel, "Zum Bau des Tempels und seiner Ausstattung," *Dein Wort Beachten* (ed. J. Reindl and G. Hentschel), Leipzig 1981, 16-32, believes that initially there was only one cherub in the *adytum*.

sufficient hardness and size.⁴⁰ Expert opinion on the correct definition of the kind of wood referred to here, however, is not unanimous (cf. Dalman, *AuS*, IV, 163f., with Noth, 101; also R. Stieglitz, *JNES* 29 [1970], 56). In the par. vs. 2 Chr. 3:10 we read that the cherubim were מַעֲשֵׂי־צַעֲצֻעִים, an expression which only occurs here and is translated by *KBL* and *HAL* as 'Guss, Gegossenes'; by e.g. Rudolph with 'Plastiken'; by J. Trinquet, *DBS*, V, 172, with 'oeuvre de sculpture en métal, de fondeurs?' The last-mentioned scholar sees here an unmistakable ('sans doute') harmonization with Exod. 25:18. Also S. Yeivin, *Leš* 38 (1973/4), 38-43, devotes special attention to the expression from 2 Chr. 3:10, stressing, on the basis of an Arab translation, the connection (also noted by *KBL* and others) with the Arab *ṣāga*, 'form,' 'mould,' 'cast' (cf. also Wehr-Cowan, s.v.). He observes, that the matter at issue is the method of production, aside from any reference to the material. In any case, 2 Chr. 3:10 neither contradicts nor refutes the 'wild olive wood' of our verse.

The conclusion of our verse is more difficult. To what does the 3 p. masc. suffix of קוֹמָתוֹ refer? Any number of solutions have been proposed for this *crux*, as a glance at the commentaries and grammars shows. Still, it is less than satisfactory simply to observe that a pl. is represented here by a sing. pron. (König §348u; cf. Ewald §319a). Nor are we satisfied when Thenius 'resolves' the puzzle by reading קוֹמָה מְתֻכֶּנֶת, 'in aufrechter Statur,' on the basis of LXX: μέγεθος ἐσταθμωμένον. But Stade already correctly pointed out that תִּכֵּן can only mean 'establish.' His own solution, followed by many, is to insert vs. 26 between 23a and 23b: 'so ist alles in Ordnung.' And it is true: this is a rather plausible solution if one does not wish to delete vs. 23b as a superfluous gloss (a possible solution suggested by Kittel). Noth thinks that between vss. 23a and b there must have been a masc. sing. as antecedent of the suffix of קוֹמָתוֹ. This lost word would then have been a 'platform' (10 cubits high) supporting the cherubim. But the context never mentions it again. If one does not wish to delete the last 3 words, then Stade's alternative seems to us the most natural, despite the redundancy of such a text. But this is a defect we have already encountered several times in our chapter. Rather striking is that Josephus (*Ant.* VIII §72) mentions a height of 5 cubits for the cherubim. Is he perhaps confusing the wingspread of a cherub with its height?

6:24 *One cherub's wing was five cubits long and the other cherub's wing was five cubits long – ten cubits from wing tip to wing tip.*
In this verse there is mention of the wingspread of the cherubim which amounted to 5 cubits per wing. Aside from here, the word קצוה* also occurs in 12:31; 13:33; 2 Kgs. 17:32 and Jdg. 18:2; Ps. 19:7; Sir. 16:17. Here and in Ps.

---

⁴⁰ F.J. Bruijel, *Bijbel en Natuur*, Kampen 1939, 159.

19:7 the end means the 'tip.' More frequent in OT, however, is the form קצה. In *BHK* and *BHS* the pl. suffix in the form כנפיו is sometimes stated in the textcr. app. as sing. in some (or all) translations, but the reproduction in the translations can also be based on the narrative technique (and not on another 'Vorlage'). If each wing was 5 cubits long, the entire shrine must have been connected from wall to wall by the 2 pairs of wings, which must also have touched eachother at shoulder level.

6:25 *The other cherub also measured ten cubits; the two cherubim were identical in size and shape.*
Here it is stated that the 'other' cherub was also 10 cubits. This must be a reference to height. Since mention of הכרוב האחד is missing here, one could also have expected this statement in vs. 23b. The problem, then, is that both statements have been interrupted by vs. 24. Even now, however, the statement feels somewhat out of place in this location.

מדה means 'extent,' 'measure,' 'size,' and occurs 53x in OT (J. Kühlewein, THAT, II, 164). קצב, on the other hand, occurs here and in 7:37 in the sense of 'form' or 'configuration,' and in Jonah 2:6 and Sir. 16:19 rather as 'foundation' (H. Wildberger, *THAT*, II, 558; *HAL*: 'Zuschnitt'). The verb קצב means 'cut off' (2 Kgs. 6:6; S. of S. 4:2). Vs. 25b indicates the complete identity of the 2 representations.

6:26 (after verse 23) *The height of each cherub was ten cubits.*
In our discussion of vs. 23 we already commented that this verse can be inserted between vs. 23a and b, if the sequence is to be meaningful *there* and it not seem a meaningless repetition *here*.

6:27 *He placed the cherubs in the innermost part of the house; the cherubs extended their wings so that the wings of the one touched the wall just as the wing of the other touched the other wall, while their other wings, the ones that pointed toward the center of the house, were also touching.*
In a sense this verse also reports what we already knew from the preceding verses, viz. that the cherubim were located 'in the innermost part of the house,' i.e. the shrine, and that they were positioned with their wings spread out so that one of their wings touched the N and S wall, respectively – so, explicitly, says Josephus *Ant.* VIII §73 –, and the other touched the wing of his partner. It is striking that our verse does not speak of the דביר, but about the 'innermost part of the house' (cf. also 7:50, where the term 'holy of holies' is added; also Ezek. 41:17, etc., and 1 Kgs. 6:36 and 7:12, where the reference is to the 'inner court'). This expression suggests the work of an author other than the one who composed the section with the דביר. The expression does confirm the concept – mentioned above – of the shrine *within* the temple building itself

and not that of a separate building or section behind the היכל.

On the basis of some ancient translations, mainly LXX, some minor textual modifications are made in our verse. Still the most obvious is the replacement of the words כנפי הכרובים by כנפיהם (cf. LXX, textcr. app. *BHK* and *BHS*). It does not seem necessary to us, on the basis of LXX and Pesh., to replace the pl. ויפרשׂו by a sing. One can indeed argue, that as a result one achieves greater coordination with the sing. p. form at the beginning of our verse (ויתן). On the other hand, these 'wooden' cherubim can radiate a certain 'animation' by extending their wings themselves. The verb פרשׂ can also be used, for example, for the cherubs which extend their wings in Exod. 25:20; 37:9, where their posture is then further described by the statement that in that fashion they cover 'the mercy seat' while facing one another. In the par. notice in 2 Chr. 3:11-13 also, there is reference to the touching of the walls and of each other's wingtips. Our verse is clarified by the statement — also made earlier — that each cherub, with its wings extended, measured 10 cubits, together 20 cubits. A supplementary comment occurs in vs. 13, where we read that the cherubim 'stood on their feet' and 'faced the house.' On what these particulars are based is not altogether clear; in any case they differ from Exod. 25:20. Perhaps we can read the details of Chronicles as supplementary information to the rather scant statements in our verses: the cherubs were winged wooden images with human or animal legs and their wings formed 'a covering for the ark that had been placed between them' (Josephus, *Ant.* VIII §73).

6:28 *He also overlaid the cherubim with gold.*
According to Benzinger, this simple statement is a later interpolation.

6:29 *As for the walls of the house, he carved them all around with carved engravings, cherubs, palm ornaments, and rosettes, from inside to outside.*
This as well as the following verse speak of the decorations applied to the interior of the house. Stade, Benzinger, Burney and others are of the opinion that originally these verses do not belong here. It is true that our verse shows kinship with vs. 18 and that, after vs. 22, vs. 30 feels redundant. In addition there is kinship with Ezek. 41:18, so that, as far as these verses are concerned, it is not surprising that Benzinger for one speaks of their being 'am denkbar ungeschicktesten Platz.' But from a stylistic viewpoint this chapter is somewhat fragmentary in any case and it is therefore hard to say with certainty that these verses are an *additamentum*. They do after all add a certain amount of new information to what has been said earlier. Turning this around we can also say, that what vs. 18 reports (see above) actually belongs here, a transposition resulting in a more logical sequence after vs. 17.

Our verse begins with the copula and the *nota accusativi*. According to König §341p this is an absolute accusative: 'and as it concerns ...' (cf. Böttcher

§516: adverbial accusative of place; Meyer §92.4b: object which can syntactically count as subject). The reference here is obviously to the walls of the entire temple interior. That all the walls are in view is expressed by מסב which Klostermann, Burney, Ehrlich, Delitzsch, *LSF* §89a, and others (cf. textcr. app. of *BHK* and *BHS*) all erroneously wish to change into מְסָבִיב. מֵסַב is a substantive which among other things can mean 'surroundings' (cf. 2 Kgs 23:5; Ps. 140:10; Job 37:12; and S. of S. 1:12 [here perhaps a 'round table']) and may here be an adverbial noun (cf. BL, 632¹; *HAL*; Montg.-Gehman; Noth) meaning 'round about.' The verb קלע II was already mentioned in vs. 18 in the discussion of the derivative מקלעת. It means 'engrave' (cf. LXX: ἔγραφεν; G. Schrenk, *TDNT*, I, 743). Also the word פתוח, in the pl. here, means something like 'woodcarving' (cf. M. Görg, *BN* 13 [1980], 22-25, who assumes kinship with the Egyptian *pth*, 'engrave'; Delitzsch, *LSF* §153b, considers it a gloss on the previous word) and occurs repeatedly in OT (Exod. 28:11, 21, 36; 39:6, 14, 30; Zech. 3:9; Ps. 74:6; 2 Chr. 2:6, 13 and the verb פתח II: 1 Kgs. 7:36; Exod. 28:9, 11, 36, etc.). These engravings can in general be done in stone, ivory, metal, and wood. Noth suspects that here it concerns 'Flachrelief,' reliefs carved into or 'laid on' wood. Examples of artistic woodcarvings and engravings in ivory can be found in *ANEP*, pls. 122ff. (cf. also H. Weippert, *BRL*², 147ff.).

Whereas the מקלעות are more or less general and – according to Busink, 258, n. 351 – both possibly 'laid on' and 'en creux,' the כרובים and תמרת are somewhat more specific. In appearance and form the cherubim are the same as the beings in the shrine discussed in vs. 23. The תמרה (cf. BL, 476wß, n.) is 'a palm ornament' (vss. 32, 35; 7:36; Ezek. 40:16, 22 *(qᵉre)*, 26, 31 *(qᵉre)*, 34 *(qᵉre)*, 37*(qᵉre)*; 41:18, 19, 20, 25, 26; 2 Chr. 3:5), a diminutive of תמר, 'date palm' (Exod. 15:27; Num. 33:9 etc.), found for example in a palace in Mari[41] (cf. *ANEP*, 654 and Busink, 272ff.). For פטורי צצים, a word combination omitted here by LXX^(B, Luc.), we refer the reader to vs. 18. It is hard to decide whether these words are the result of a later interpolation or belong here. The latter seems to us more likely. The following word מלפנים is often changed – something with a reference to the following verse – into לפנימה (cf. Benzinger; *KBL*; *HAL*; Delitzsch, *LSF* §10a; the textcr. app. of *BHK* and *BHS*). Also לפנימי is sometimes proposed (cf. Burney; Montg.-Gehman, and others). Noth, however, does not simply wish to reject the text form, though he does not consider the relation between a noun פנים (but cf. also פנימה, 'to the inside,' etc.) and פנים clear. But on the basis of a presumed original unity between the vss. 29 and 30, he opts for the above-mentioned emendation of our word. However much this last position can be defended and is

---

[41] Cf. A. Parrot, *Mission archéologique de Mari*, II, Paris 1958, 53ff.

understandable, we nevertheless want to take a further step and maintain the text form (in this connection cf. also the remarks of Olsh. §146a). It is not altogether certain whether the Masoretic vocalization can be maintained, though the form מלפנים (Isa. 41:26) is used only once and then in reference to time ('from of old'; cf. also Segal §393). In our verse the word, in combination with the following ולחיצון (according to Ehrlich to be changed here and in the following verse into לחוצה, because according to him חיצון cannot be used adverbially), indicates that these ornamentations have been worked into the walls 'from the inside to the outside.' Accordingly, one must not take the statement to mean that the ornamentations were applied both to the interior and the exterior walls of the temple, but it should be seen as an indication that they were applied both around the shrine and around the 'sanctuary' of the house (possibly with the front hall) to the interior walls, hence from the inside to the outside. Granted: חיצון (which in Kings occurs again in the following verse and in 2 Kgs. 16:18; further esp. in Ezek. 40-46, approx. 25x in OT) as adjective denotes the 'outermost' (with פנימי as contrast), but in our verse it is clearly used independently (Ehrlich's objection therefore no longer applies). This expression, which occurs in our verse as well as the following, probably belongs to the Hebr. idiom. According to the Masoretic pointing, this direction 'from inside to outside' bears on all the preceding ornamentations. On the basis of the unvocalized and unpointed text (as Noth correctly observes), this expression could apply solely to 'opening flowers.' Along with MT we stick with the first reading.

6:30 *He also overlaid the floor of the house with gold, from inside to outside.*
This is an addition, which by its excessiveness virtually proves how little credit it deserves. In vs. 15 it had already been stated that the floor of the temple was made of cypress. If then this costly wooden floor was to be overlaid with gold, why select this costly wood? The idea that it possibly concerned only the edges of the floor, as Noth assumes for a moment, is improbable. As an alternative we prefer his opinion, that we are here dealing with a 'Stichwortglosse', where לפנימה ולחיצון may have been the 'Stichwort' in the margin, while the rest of the marginal text was later also incorporated in the text (cf. also Noth, *Welt*, 315). In any case we are here clearly dealing with an exaggeration, which in a later time was designed to make Solomon's temple appear even more splendid than it must have been in reality before.

6:31 *He similarly provided the door of the shrine with door wings of oleaster. The portal (in front of the shrine) had posts with five indented sections.*
The vss. 31-35 are concerned with the doors in the temple. These verses, too,

match the fragmentary character of the majority of verses in our chapter. Our verse and the following verse deal especially with the entrance to the shrine. Again the expositor is confronted with difficult exegetical issues, which surface especially in the second part of our verse. In the first part we read, that an entrance to the shrine was made with door wings of oleaster (for this word cf. vs. 23). The verb עשה is here construed with 2 accusatives, where, according to König §327y, the second accusative indicates 'ein Mittelding von Effect und Material'. According to Montg.-Gehman: *ad sensum* as it concerns ואת פתח etc. There is no reason to change this beginning into ולפתח on the basis of various ancient translations (so, correctly, Stade and Burney). The word דלת occurs no fewer than 87x in OT (cf. A. Baumann, *TWAT*, II, 244-248) and is also known in other Sem. languages as 'door wing' (cf. also K. Galling, H. Rösel, *BRL*[2], 348). Sometimes a sharp distinction is made in OT between פתח and דלת (e.g. in Gen. 19:6-11). The first indicates the door opening in which there may be 'wings' (second word).

The information given in the first part of our verse is couched in very general terms, so little can be inferred concerning the shape of the doorway and the doors ('wings'), except the material of which they were made. Does the second part yield greater clarity? A look at both ancient and modern translations and into the commentaries shows that we are here facing a *crux interpretum* (cf. esp. Busink, 204-208). While LXX[B], as a result of *parablepsis* or *per homoeoteleuton* (as is generally assumed), omitted the conclusion of this verse up until almost the end of vs. 33, also LXX[A, Luc.] and Vulg. have not (clearly) reproduced the word איל. איל III (cf. *HAL*) occurs, aside from here, also 21x in Ezek. 40:10-41:3 and is translated by *HAL* as 'Torpfeiler.' Zimmerli (BK XIII/2, 1002) thinks it is a partition between 2 alcoves; Noth thinks of 'Türgewände'; Montg.-Gehman of 'upper lintel' or 'gable' (with Kim i, etc.); Pesh. translates the last 3 words of MT by 'supporting and reinforcing the doorposts'; the word *prwstd'* is used, which is a Syrian version of the Greek προστάς, 'porch,' 'vestibule' or παραστάς 'doorpost.' Tg., though it probably saw the word in its 'Vorlage', did not translate it or had a hard time with it (Sperber אלהי, but cf. Burney and Montg.-Gehman). The second word מזוזות is clearer. In OT it occurs several times (Exod. 12:7, 22f.; 21:6; Deut. 6:9; 11:20; Judg. 16:3; 1 Sam. 1:9; Isa. 57:8; Ezek. 41:21; 43:8 [2x]; 45:19 [2x]; 46:2; Prov. 8:34 and in our book also in vs. 33 and 7:5) and is probably related to the Akkad. *manzāzu(m)* or *mazzāzu(m)* (cf. *AHw*, 638), 'post,' 'stand.' The word denotes the doorpost and is known, especially in postbiblical Judaism, as the little cylinder containing passages from Deut. 6 and 11, which had to be attached to the doorpost. The third word חמשית can mean 'a fifth part' (e.g. in Gen. 47:24; Lev. 27:15, 19) and corresponds to רביעית in vs. 33 (also cf. BL, 629a). But, with Benzinger and others, one is prompted to ask: of what is it a fifth part? In vs. 33 LXX reads: τετραπλῶς and in our verse LXX^(A, Luc.) etc. read: φλιὰς πενταπλᾶς. This has led most modern exegetes to read, in place of חמשית, the form חֲמֻשׁוֹת here, a passive part. of the denominative verb חמש, which could then mean an 'order,' a 'step-by-step ascent' in 5 parts (Noth: 'gefünftet'; also cf. Thenius following Böttcher: 'fünfwinkelig'; Benzinger; Burney; Montg.-Gehman et al.). Vulg. translates the phrase: *postesque angulorum quinque.*

But how are we to understand the last 3 words of our verse? Stade proposed that we read והמזוזות (cf. Burney, *BHK* textcr. app.), so that 'the wall- (or: door-)opening and the doorposts' could be 'pentagonal.' In that case it is better to read 'pillar' for איל. But Noth has rightly reminded us, that it is risky 'in einem schwer verständlichen Text stärkere Konjecturen anzubringen' (p. 102), though he is here opposing De Vaux, who wanted to read מזוזות עצי־שמן האיל חמשות. His own translation – be it with reservations, as his exegetical notes show – comes down to offering 'das Türgewände (bestand) aus gefünfteten Pfosten' as his reproduction of MT. He pictures this as 'eine nach hinten enger werdende Fünf-Staffelung des Türgewändes' (p. 127). In that case האיל is the 'doorwall' itself, which is of cedar according to vs. 16 and therefore needed no further description.

Nevertheless, this view keeps a lot of uncertainty. In our opinion Businck proposes an explanation highly worth considering, who comes to an understandable translation through a small and explainable change of text. He assumes, that in front of the shrine there could have been a porch (אילם or אולם) (on the basis of 2 Chr. 29:7a) and that therefore in the original text אילם instead of איל had been written (haplography of the מ). His translation is:'(das) Ulam (hatte) gefünftete Pfosten' (p. 207f.). On the pictures 48, 50 and 56 in his book one can see how he imagines the step-like posts. This translation, too, offers no absolute certainty, naturally, although the syrian *prwstdwhy* (pl.) can give some support. In Greek αἱ παραστάδες can denote an 'arcade', a kind of fronthall.

6:32 *On the door wings of oleaster he carved wood engravings, cherubs, palm ornaments and rosettes and overlaid them with gold; he also overlaid the cherubs and palm ornaments with gold.*

This verse deals with the ornamentations of the door wings mentioned in vs. 31. The somewhat peculiar beginning of this verse, viz. a *nomen absolutum* before the conjunction and the predicate, which now functions as a *casus pendens,* has led some expositors, partly on the basis of the content of this verse, to delete it as a superfluous gloss or to transpose it (cf. Stade, Benzinger, Burney, et al.). Thenius makes the beginning of our verse dependent on עשה in the preceding verse, but this solution only makes the matter more complicated. Even though we are of the opinion that many exegetes are right in viewing our verse as a gloss or as redundant (but cf. Noth), still the beginning can well be considered as a *casus pendens* (so Burney; König, §341m, also §294f, n. 1) serving to give extra attention to the 2 wings of these doors. And considering the ornamentations worked into them, they were worth it (cf. in that sense also Noth).

The form וקלע has drawn special attention in commentaries and grammars because of its irregularity (Böttcher, §982; Ewald §342b; Bg. II §9r; Driver §133). The pf. here presumably denotes the iterative or frequentative aspect of the verb, which in English can be conveyed by the addition of the particle 'also' (cf. Böttcher). The idea that the construction of this 'isolated irregularity' (Driver) is characteristic for the style of the postexilic interpolator, as Burney suggests, is going a little too far for us. Although no new forms are added to the ornamentations listed earlier in vs. 29, they are described in greater detail as far as the treatment is concerned. Grammatically noteworthy is the masc. suffix by the fem. antecedent in עליהם (cf. König §14; M.G. Slonim, *JQR* 29 [1939], 397-403; Montg.-Gehman, 160 and 213 under 9:13). The form וירד is generally derived from the verb רדד (hiph.). While it is true that this verb occurs in hiph. only in this verse, and in qal only in Isa. 45:1 and Ps. 144:2 ('subdue'), there is no need to reduce this somewhat 'more difficult' form to the more 'common' one of ירד, as Ehrlich, for example, wants (cf. also LXX[Luc.]). It is presumably a technical term, as also the Targum: וְנְסָךְ (cf. Burney) suggests, and may be approximately equivalent to רָקַע, 'hammer out,' 'inlay,' 'overlay' (Exod. 39:3; Num. 17:4; Isa. 40:19). From a technical viewpoint there must be a distinction between צִפָּה and רדד (hiph.). The first (see vs. 15 above) means more generally 'overlay' and the second refers to a certain artistic inlay of gold leaf, and that particularly with respect to the cherub figures and the palm ornaments. Noth suspects that the flower motifs were not included in this process, because they had been worked especially into the margins, but this is hard to prove. In any case the conclusion of our verse need not directly clash with the immediately preceding description, which may be confirmed also by the paraphrased conclusion of vs. 35. Nor does a temple covered over with beaten metal have to be incompatible with the content of 2 Kgs. 18:16, because there the reference may very well be to renovation, if not to restoration.

6:33 *For the door of the holy place he also made doorposts of oleaster with four indented sections.*
Our verse now proceeds to a consideration of the doors of the temple building itself. The Chronicler, however, adds to the preceding text that a פָּרֹכֶת was made: a 'curtain' of blue and purple, crimson fabric and fine linen, into which cherubim were worked (2 Chr. 3:14). This word occurs further only in the Pentateuch and especially in Exodus to denote the 'cloth' between the temple building and the shrine (cf. also vs. 21 above). Although Rudolph in his

commentary a.l. does not seem to consider this curtain a 'Chronistic invention,' it is nevertheless not clear on what basis this statement is made other than on a parallelization of the wilderness sanctuary. In any case the author or redactor of our piece is silent on the subject.

The problem in our verse is especially the end where the text seems to speak about the form of the doorposts of the sanctuary. What is the meaning of מאת רבעית? Ewald (§219a) believes that it concerns an architectural term, which simply denotes an ordinal number (as in Latin: *ex aequo*). But usually (based on LXX: στοαὶ τετραπλῶς; Vulg. *quadrangulatos*) exegetes follow commentators like Thenius, Stade, Benzinger, Kittel (cf. also *BHK* textcr. app.), who read: מזוזות רבעות, a term for which one can also refer to Ezek 41:21. Montg.-Gehman propose that we delete מאת (cf. *BHS* textcr. app.) and view the last word of our verse as analogous to the last word of vs. 31, which materially comes down to the emendation adopted by Thenius and most others (Thenius: 'und zwar vierwinkelige Pf[osten]'; Montg.-Gehman: 'a tetragon'). Along with Noth and Busink, 186ff., we are of the opinion that here again we must speak of 'vierfach gestaffelte' doorposts, hence posts which ran up in 4 indented stages (cf. in Busink the figs. 48-50 and 58), examples of which have been found also in Israel's 'Umwelt', e.g. the entrance to the main hall of the temple in *Tell Tainat* (Busink, 188). Also Noth deletes מאת as a 'Textfehler.'

6:34 *The two doors were of cypress wood; each door had two leaves which turned in sockets.*

This as well as the following verse deal further with the doors of the היכל, while in our verse special attention is devoted to the construction of the door wings. In the first place we are told that these door wings were of cypress wood (see 5:22 above). The reason, why in their selection of the material for these door wings the builders deviated from the door wings mentioned earlier, must be technical. Thenius, for example, suspects that posts and planks of this kind of wood are longer and stronger and could also meet the required width. Noth, on the other hand, believes that these doors could be made of wood that was less costly and durable, because they were a kind of 'outside' doors. But if they were nevertheless furnished with all kinds of embellishments (cf. next verse), it is not clear, why the material, which would be more vulnerable to conditions of weather and climate than the door wings mentioned above, would be made of less durable material. The opposite, rather, is the case and Thenius is probably closer to the truth, because the doors of the היכל were simply larger than those for the דביר.

What follows in this verse has repeatedly occasioned discussion among the experts. Generally speaking, they concur with the ancient versions and some MSS of the Hebr. Bible by changing the word קלעים into צלעים (Thenius; Stade; Klostermann; Burney; Delitzsch, *LSF* §99a; etc.). Noth, however, again pursues his own course by proposing the opposite procedure, hence of reading, in place of צלעים, the word קלעים, which he translates by 'Einschnitzungen.' His objection concerns the masc. pl. of צלע, which only occurs here. Already under vs. 6 (above) we pointed to the *Ambigua* and many grammarians adopt the double pl. ending of צלע, even with a difference in meaning (Olsh. §117; Ewald §152e; Stade §310c; Joüon §90e; cf. König §252b; as well as the argumentation in Barthélemy). As a result the double meaning (which we did not accept) of the word could not come to expression in 'side room,' 'beam' and 'wing.' קלע II means 'screen' or 'curtain' and occurs, besides here, only in Exod. 27-39 and Num. 3:26; 4:26 (15x in all). Perhaps Böttcher, *Neue Aehrenlese,* 43, is right when he considers קלעים a writing error 'vom Vorausblick auf קלע V. 35 her.' With that Noth's translation (and interpretation) collapses, which says that the one as well as the other door wing was embellished with circular engravings; that is: the issue is not a technical detail pertaining to the door, but its ornamentation.

HAL and many exegetes take the word גליל I to mean 'pivoted,' others 'hinge' (cf. also S. of S. 5:14 and Esth. 1:6) Dalman, *AuS*, VIII, 69, even considers it something very special that the doors had double wings, 'aus je zwei drehbare Teilen,' and also refers to Ezek. 41:23f. It was assumed that the reference was to 2 folding door wings. Each wing again had 2 leaves of equal width, which were so tied together vertically, that they could be folded over each other (Thenius). Sometimes the 2 parts of a wing were pictured horizontally, so that people had double door wings, such as one still finds on Dutch farms (Ewald, Merz in Thenius). But Galling, supported in this by H. Gese (see in Busink, 190f.), thinks that, among other things on archeological grounds, objection needs to be made against folding doors on hinges, because these do not occur until Roman times.[42] Busink, however, has noted that this assumption is not well founded, because iron hinges of the tenth century BCE, if they did exist, would no longer be extant (pp. 190f.). Technically, he considers swinging doors a possibility. But the text itself possibly points in the same direction. The construction of the vss. 34b and 34c, however simple at first blush, is nevertheless rather obscure. So König §285c has rightly commented in connection with הדלת האחת that this has to be predicative, a statement to which he – always the cautious one in such matters – added: 'und sieht wie Glosse aus.' Usually people here translate as if the Hebr. reads: צלעי הדלת etc., hence a st. cstr. combination. If one omits 'the one door' as well as 'the other door' (or 'door wing') for a moment, it reads: '2 beams were pivoted' and again '2 beams were pivoted.' Whether or not one takes the

---

[42] In G. Fohrer, *Ezekiel* (HAT 13), Tübingen 1955, 233ff.; cf. also W. Zimmerli, BK XIII/2, 1052.

phrases הדלת האחת and הדלת השנית to be a gloss or not, a fact is that there were 4 pivoted beams available for the door wings. The question is now, whether one must picture this, as though the entrance to the temple had a double gate in which 2 door wings could swing in front and 2 door wings could swing in back, so that a kind of portal was formed, or that in fact we are dealing with swinging doors with a double set of wings. The latter is the idea of Busink, 192, who comments that for lack of a technical term for 'swinging door' this is the description that had to be used. Aside from the word גלילים, also the word צלעים (which occurs twice in the improved text) is hard to explain. Often this last word is translated 'door wing' (so already Ewald §152e), but Gese (among others) has correctly pointed out the contradiction because also דלת is said to mean this.[43] He associates the word with the 'front' or 'reverse' side of a double door. But this is not likely (see Busink, 191f.). In our opinion צלעים means nothing other than the צלעות mentioned several times before in our chapter (see vs. 5 above). Now our text can say that the door wings (the sing., after all, can be taken as a collective) could swing by means of 2 beams. It remains undecided, then, whether in the end we are dealing with a 'folding door' with 4 beams and wings, aside from the doorposts mentioned in vs. 33, or with 2 sets of 2 door wings, placed one behind the other, which together formed a double entrance from the front hall into the sanctuary and could turn 180 degrees. A third possibility which Busink lists is a main door, in which 2 small doors had been constructed for daily use, while the main gate (cf. Ps. 24:7) only opened on feast days (192f.).

6:35 *He carved cherubs, palm ornaments, and rosettes on them, overlaying them with gold hammered evenly over the carved work.*
As in vs. 32, so here there is a description, in virtually the same phrases, of the final artistic workmanship on the doors. For the form וקלע, see under vs. 32. Busink (270f.) points out that especially in Mesopotamia the cherubim, here carved into the doors of the temple, were placed, as apotropaic figures, in the form of bulls and snakes, etc. in front of the main temples (Babel, Borsippa etc.). At stake in our verse is, as it were, the continuation of the ornamentations with the motifs mentioned earlier in connection with the sanctuary. With Montg.-Gehman, among others, one could describe these data 'as literarily secondary' and immediately add 'and yet the data have authentic colour.' The secondary character of these additions and others like it can perhaps be attributed to the Mesopotamian influence, which the glossator underwent and place him in the exile.

Again there is reference to the gold overlay upon these ornamentations (see

---

[43] H. Gese, *Der Verfassungsentwurf des Ezechiel (Kap. 40-48)*, Tübingen 1957, 183.

vs. 20 above), to which is now added מִישַׁר עַל־הַמְחֻקֶּה. This is the only time that the verb ישׁר occurs in pu. In pi. it occurs more frequently in the sense of 'level,' 'make smooth' (Isa. 40:3; 45:2, 13; Ps. 119:28; Prov. 3:6; 9:15; 11:5; 15:21; 2 Chr. 32:30). Here it refers to the 'hammering out' of the gold leaf, which was applied to reliefs or in carvings (cf. L. Alonso Schökel, *TWAT* 3, 1062). מְחֻקֶּה is a pu. part. of חקה, which according to *HAL* is a subsidiary form of חקק and means 'be carved in' (also in Ezek. 8:10 and 23:14). The word is here used substantively (cf. Böttcher §1036: 'die Sculptur'; König §305b; Bg. II §31f, 173). The procedure, therefore, is the same as in vs. 32. As Noth points out, it is hard to tell how things were done precisely, because we lack archaeological material for comparison. Noth himself wonders if it was like 'cloisonné' work, as that can still be observed in ivory art. In this art form the contours of figures are indicated by thin strips of metal. Thenius thinks of very thin gold, which is cut out in the form of the figure and fixed with a stylus or pen in the figures, which have been engraved in the wood. For this process he refers to Jer. 10:4 and Isa. 41:7 and notes that the weight of the nails is expressly mentioned in 2 Chr. 3:9. But aside from the value of this statement in Chronicles, nothing can be inferred from this concerning the gold overlay in our text.

Josephus, *Ant.* VIII §75, adds here that the outside doors, like the inside doors, were provided with curtains. This comment has some kinship with an addition, which LXX[B, Luc.] places at the end of the following verse (see following verse), even though Josephus concludes with the words: ἡ δὲ τοῦ προναίου πύλη τούτων οὐδὲν εἶχε.

6:36 *He further built the inner court with three rows of hewn stone plus one row of cedar beams.*

In a sense this verse concludes the account of the building of the temple by referring to a court, a delimited space, a forecourt. The word חצר occurs approx. 145x (so *BDB*) in OT, both in the masc. and the fem. form (and with masc. or fem. pl.). Some scholars have assumed 2 different protosemitic roots, the one meaning 'settlement,' 'village,' the other 'enclosure' or 'court' (cf. *HAL*, s.v. חצר* III), but V. Hamp, *TWAT*, III, 141, rightly considers a primitive semitic root meaning 'enclose' the most likely. In other Sem. languages (Ugar.; Phoen.; Aram.) the word is usually also found in the meanings cited (Hamp. 141ff.). In the Hebr. of OT the meaning 'settlement,' 'farmstead' occurs about 47x.[44] When the word refers to 'court' the gender changes. According to Orlinsky, 30, it is masc. 15x and then refers exclusively to the forecourt of the temple and is limited to exilic and post-exilic sections. In our

---

[44] See H.M. Orlinsky, "*Ḥāṣēr* in the Old Testament," *JAOS* 59 (1939), 22-37; esp. 28.

verse the reference is to the 'inner court' which is also mentioned in 7:12; Ezek. 8:16; 10:3; 40:19 etc., in distinction from the 'great court' (1 Kgs. 7:9, 12), which according to some scholars enclosed the temple precincts as a whole as well as the royal palace (Noth; Hamp, 144f.). In the history of the kingdom of Judah which has come down to us, there is repeated reference to 'going up' and to 'going down,' to the temple court and to the palace respectively (Jer. 22:1; 26:10; 36:11f.). In 7:8 there is also mention of a third court, 'an other court' which lay 'back of the אולם.' Opinions are rather divided over the location of these 3 courts, especially over the 'great court' and 'the other court.' A good overview – with illustrations – of the main positions can be found in Busink, 143-149. He offers a well-considered situation plan of the Solomonic fortress, in which he starts with the 3 courts, viz. the temple court, the 'great court' around the royal buildings minus the temple, and an 'inner court' (p. 160). In this design the temple court lies outside of the great court around the royal palace. Now on the basis of later information we must consider it likely, that the original temple forecourt, which was none too big, was expanded. So in Isa. 1:12 there is reference to the 'courts' of the temple and in 2 Kgs. 21:5 and 23:12 to the '2 courts of the house of the Lord.' In 2 Chr. 20:5 we are told that Jehoshaphat stood in the house of YHWH before the 'new court.' If this translation is reliable, this expansion must have occurred in the time of Jehoshaphat or somewhat earlier. In post-exilic times we usually read simply of the 'courts' of the temple (Isa. 62:9; Zech. 3:7; Neh. 8:16; 13:7; cf. Pedersen, III-IV, 254).

The reason why the author mentions this inner court, is to be found in the statement of how it was enclosed. The word טור occurs approx. 25x in OT (primarily in Exod. 28 and 39; Ezek. 46:23 and 2 Chr. 4:3, 13), 11x in this and the following chapter (7:2-4, 12, 18, 20, 24, 42) and is usually translated by 'layer' or 'row' (cf. *HAL*). Outside the OT, in the Nabatean, one also finds the meaning 'wall' (cf. *DISO*, טור II, a meaning which also occurs in *DJD*, III, 247, no. 95). In our verse the reference is to 3 טורי גזית. We already encountered this word in 5:31. There we learned that it can denote stone quarried from rocks, natural stone as opposed to 'tiles.' It does need to be noted here (as Noth correctly points out), that there is a difference between the roughly quarried natural stone used in the building of the temple, and the more polished natural stone mentioned here. Noth links these stones, which were worked on with iron tools, with the lesser 'holiness' of the court as compared to that of the temple itself. This suggestion seems to us somewhat plausible.

A 4th טור is formed by כרתת of cedars. This word occurs only here and in 7:2 and 12. Relating it to the root כרת, some scholars (Noth, *HAL*) think it means shorter 'beams' cut from tall trees. As a rule the picture drawn is that of 3 layers of hewn stone plus a layer of cedar beams piled on top of each other, which then made up the enclosure of the court (cf. e.g. Thenius, Benzinger,

Noth and others) But Noth betrays some uneasiness when he asks how things went on top of the layer of beams, 'die schwerlich den oberen Abschluss bildete, weiterging.' We have pointed out in *ZAW* 88 (1976), 102f., that the author certainly meant to say more than that something was left uncompleted. Our position is (cf. also Šanda; C. van Gelderen, *AfO* 6 [1930/1], 106), that the enclosure of the court consisted of 3 upright rows of hewn stone, one immediately behind the other, against which, as a 4th row, an additional row of cedar beams was placed. As a result the wall not only became exceptionally sturdy, but also gained a very pleasing appearance. To this LXX further adds (but this helps to support both views) that the layer of beams went around (κυκλόθεν), a pragmatic note which can just as well be omitted. The further addition of the LXX$^{B, Luc.}$ is more interesting: καὶ ᾠκοδόμησε καταπέτασμα τῆς αὐλῆς τοῦ αἰλὰμ τοῦ οἴκου τοῦ κατὰ πρόσωπον τοῦ ναοῦ. Some scholars (Burney et al.) make a connection between this addition and the difficult ending of 7:12, for which Stade, Burney and others propose the necessary emendations (see below under 7:12). The reference here is to the 'building' of a καταπέτασμα a 'veil' or 'curtain'[45]; in LXX it is usually the translation of the word פָּרֹכֶת, the 'rug' between the 'holy of holies' and the 'holy place' and between the temple and the court, sometimes also the translation of the word מָסָךְ, the 'veil' hanging before the so-called 'tabernacle' (also in Sir. 50:5; 1 Macc. 1:22; 4:51; the epistle of Aristeas 86 etc.; cf. in NT Matt. 27:51; Mark 15:38; Luke 23:45, etc.; see C. Schneider, *TDNT*, III, 629f.). Now a curtain need not be 'built' (so, correctly, Burney). On the other hand, it is striking that amidst the variety of phrases, this notice in LXX$^{B, Luc.}$ shows some resemblance to Josephus, *Ant.* VIII §75, which we cited at the conclusion of the previous verse (cf. also his detailed description of the curtain in *Bell.* V §212). It is possible that both the Lucian recension of LXX (plus B) and Josephus are based on another 'Vorlage' of the Hebr. text, of which we can find fragments in the ending of 7:12. It is also possible that both texts draw from a tradition which attempts to equate the temple exterior with a reconstructed 'tabernacle exterior.' Finally and similarly it is not impossible that — certainly on special occasions — hanging rugs were used on the exterior of sanctuaries. But to have a rug there permanently was probably not possible for climatological reasons.

6:37 *In the fourth year the foundation of the house of YHWH was laid, in the month of Ziv.*
This verse and the following, which tie in closely with vs. 1 (see there),

---

[45] Cf. S. Légasse, "Les voiles du temple de Jérusalem. Essai de parcours historiques," *RB* 87 (1980), 560-589.

indicate the time it took to build the temple. In its phrasing our verse only slightly deviates from vs. 1. Here the older word ירח is used for the name of the month Ziv. At the same time the passive form יֻסַּד (pu.) is used in place of the active יִסַּד (cf. 5:31 above), a form which is not entirely consistent with the retention of the consonants of the Hebr. text, but is also presupposed by LXX (6:4): ἐθεμελίωσεν. Noth is of the opinion – and he may be right – that our notice is 'certainly' based on 'amtlichen Unterlagen.'

6:38 *And in the eleventh year, in the month of Bul – which is the eighth month – the house was finished in all its details and according to all its specifications. He was seven years in building it.*
Just as Ziv indicated the 'blossom month' in the pre-exilic nomenclature of Hebr. months, so Bul meant the 'rain month' in the fall (see under vs. 1 above; Meyer §61:1), the 8th month, later called מַרְחֶשְׁוָן in the Babylonian nomenclature. Just as in vs. 1, as a kind of note from the author (or copyist?), there is added to the old name of the month the statement, that Bul is the 'eighth month.' In place of כלה (qal) Ehrlich, with a view to the following ויבנהו, prefers to read the pi. He views הבית as then being a 'selbstredend Objekt.' Nevertheless it is not necessary here to read the piel of כלה in place of the qal, unless in the previous verse one wants to read יִסַּד in place of יֻסַּד. הבית is the subject: the house was finished, just as in the previous verse its foundation was laid. Does the punctuation make visible here the respect which the Masoretes fostered with respect to YHWH, the 'occupant of the house'? The following word כל־דבריו here refers to 'things,' 'particulars' (cf. Noth: 'Bewandtnisse'; W.H. Schmidt, *TWAT*, II, 112f.). LXX and Vulg. both have the word in the sing. (εἰς πάντα λόγον αὐτοῦ and: *in omni opere suo*), but this does not prove that their *Vorlage* also had that reading. The word משפטו in the *k*ᵉ*tib*, as for that matter also in LXX (πᾶσαν διάταξιν), has the sing., but many Hebr. MSS and also the other ancient versions read pl. Probably the word here means 'requirement' (cf. Noth: 'Erfordernisse'; G. Liedke, *THAT*, II, 1005: 'das, was einem zukommt,' 'Anspruch'). Vulg. here thinks of 'utensils' (*in universis utensilibus*), but that is less correct.

The last 3 words convey the impression of being a later addition. They are also lacking in LXX[A, B and Luc]. Thenius points out that 'actually' it is 7½ years, but that, compared to other great building projects in antiquity, the construction proceeded quite smoothly. This could perhaps be an indication that – despite the great splendor and costliness of this temple in the eyes of many contemporaries – it was not exceptionally large. As a royal sanctuary it definitely did not surpass the other building projects of Solomon, as the following chapter may show.

1 KINGS 7:1-12

7:1 *Solomon built his own house in thirteen years, in which he (also) finished his entire house.*

2 *He built the 'Lebanese Forest House' one hundred cubits long, fifty cubits wide and thirty cubits high: four rows of cedar pillars with cedar paneling covering the pillars.*

3 *From the top down it was covered with cedar against the supporting beams which lay on the (interior) pillars: fourty five (that is) fifteen to a row.*

4 *There were also three rows of window-frames: three feet from opening to opening.*

5 *And all the doors with their posts ran to a point in four stages as far as the doorframes were concerned [and across from them the openings were three feet apart].*

6 *He made the Hall of Pillars fifty cubits long and thirty cubits wide. [The front hall was in front and the pillars as well as the canopy were in front.]*

7 *He also made the Hall of the Throne, where he would pronounce judgment, the Hall of Justice, which was covered with cedar from floor to ceiling.*

8 *Now the house in which he would reside, in the other court back of the front hall, was of the same construction. Solomon also made a house like this hall for Pharaoh's daughter whom he had taken in marriage.*

9 *All these buildings, from the court of the temple to the great courtyard, and from the foundation to the coping, were of costly stone, cut to size, and trimmed with a saw on the inside as well as the outside.*

10 *The foundations were of costly stone, huge stones, some measuring ten cubits and some eight.*

11 *And above these were high-grade stones, cut to measure, and cedar wood.*

12 *The great court had three courses of dressed stone around it and one course of cedar beams, (as was also the case) with the inner courtyard of the house of YHWH and the front hall of the palace.*

INTRODUCTION

This chapter, which in form corresponds to the previous chapter and in content clearly links up with it, has 2 main sections: (1) the construction of king Solomon's complex of palaces (vss. 1-12); and (2) the construction of the various things needed in, or in connection with, the temple (vss. 13-51). Just as in the previous chapter, so also here it was perhaps 'official notes' from the royal chancellery (Noth; see also introduction to chap. 6) which were used, linked together by 'narrative' sections from the pen of the author or redactor of the material. LXX^(B, Luc.) puts vss. 1-12 after vss. 13-51, so that the manufacture of the temple accessories ties in with the temple construction detailed in chap. 6. The book of Chronicles omits the entire section about the building of the palace, so that there too (2 Chr. 2) there is a direct connection between chap. 6 and 7:13ff. Josephus places his rendering of 7:1-12 at the very end of his rendering of chap. 8 (*Ant.* VIII §§130ff.). The question arises whether LXX, Josephus, and Chronicles did this on theological grounds (essentially only the temple is important) or for systematic reasons. In the case of Josephus one may find it easiest to assume the latter, although LXX may have served as his model. Even though in the book of Kings the theological interest of the events described and therefore the construction of the temple is central, in the context of statements concerning Solomon's greatness and wisdom something also had to be said about the complex of palaces that adjoined the 'royal temple.' It is not necessary, as e.g. Klostermann did, to derive the pericope of vss. 1-12 from another source. It is possible that several versions of our book were in circulation and that their structures differed.

EXEGESIS

7:1 *Solomon built his own house in thirteen years, in which he (also) finished his entire house.*
This verse is an introductory redactional comment in which we learn that Solomon built his 'house,' i.e. his complex of palaces, over a period of 13 years. LXX^(B, Luc.) only has the first half of the verse (in LXX 7:38), while the second half concludes our chapter in LXX (LXX 7:50). Noth suspects that the 2 halves are not even from the same hand. The somewhat jerky and redundant character of our verse is resolved by Thenius (among others) as follows: Solomon built his house in 13 years, so that (in this timespan) he brought to completion everything that pertained to that house. But this translation exegetically smoothes over more than the Hebr. text permits. Our verse only intends to convey that Solomon built his palace complex over 13 years, even 6 more years than it took him to build the temple (but cf. Montg.-Gehman). Josephus and other Jewish commentators have attempted to explain the 'offensiveness' of this longer duration of palace construction. Among other things Josephus says (*Ant.* VIII §§130ff.) that the palace was not built with the same zeal as the temple. The temple was even finished before the time appointed, since God so obviously cooperated with the builders. This was not the case with the construction of the palace, while also the material used was of an inferior quality, because the building was only intended for kings, not for God. This motive is further elaborated in later Jewish legends (cf. Ginzberg, *Le-*

gends, IV, 155f.; VI, 294f.). The truth, of course, is that the complex of palaces was larger and more beautiful than the temple and therefore took more time.

The statement in our verse, when combined with the conclusion of the previous chapter, yields the number 20, which in 9:10 is in fact the time given for the construction of the 2 'houses.' But the relation between these 2 verses is hard to determine. In our opinion, Noth is correct when he says that the sequence of the construction: first the temple and then the palace, is improbable and that it is better to picture the construction as simultaneous.

7:2 *He built the 'Lebanese Forest House' one hundred cubits long, fifty cubits wide and thirty cubits high: four rows of cedar pillars with cedar paneling covering the pillars.*

In this verse the description of the 'Lebanese Forest House' begins and continues to vs. 5.[1] The reserve, which the author of this part displays toward the palace construction of Solomon (so Noth), does not apply to the description of the 'Lebanese Forest House,' of which relatively many details are related. The basis for this may have been, that this part of the palace was more of a public nature and was accessible to many. In addition it may have enjoyed considerable renown both for its kind and its forms of construction. Busink, 136ff., proposes a number of hypotheses for the original purpose of the building. One of them points in the direction of an 'armoury.' This hypothesis finds support in OT (Isa. 22:8; Neh. 3:9; cf. 1 Kgs. 10:17, 21 and the par. 2 Chr. 9:16, 20). But the later use of the building tells us little about its original purpose. As far as that is concerned, scholars like Busink may be right in thinking it was to serve as a 'royal reception hall'.[2] Also in Altintepe the Turkish archeologist Özgüç found a building which showed a strong resemblance to the 'Lebanese Forest House' (Ussishkin, 94). According to Josephus (*Ant.* VIII §133), the function of the building was to admit large groups of people to public trials and judgments and to provide room for people who wanted to come together for lawsuits.

The name 'House of the Forest of Lebanon' is striking. Proper names for buildings are not customary in OT. We are possibly dealing here with a popular name for a striking building. Noth and many others think that the building owed its name to the number of cedar pillars, with which the *interior*

---

[1] Besides mentioning the commentaries and literature cited there, the 'archaeologies' of among others Nowack, *Arch.* I, 255ff. and Benzinger, *Arch.* 211ff., we can refer the reader for further details to Busink (I, 129-140) and my "Einige Bemerkungen zur Beschreibung des Libanonwaldhauses in I Reg 7, 2f," *ZAW* 88 (1976), 99-105, to which Busink, II, 747, n. 59, again responds at some length.

[2] Cf. also D. Ussishkin, "King Solomon's Palaces," *BA* 36 (1973), 78-105, esp. 92ff.

of the house was furnished (Busink, 133). On the basis of the vss. 9ff. it is assumed that the *exterior* of the building must have been made of stone (so, e.g., C. van Gelderen, *AfO* 6 [1930/1], 105). But the vss. 2-5 differ in form and content from the vss. 6-8, so that one cannot simply apply the term בל־אלה in vs. 9 to vss. 2-5. The striking fact about the 'Lebanese Forest House' must have been that it was completely built of cedar (so, correctly, H. Kosmala, *BHHW*, II, 838; cf. Josephus, *Ant.* VIII §133), both inside and outside. Both to contemporaries and later generations it was a showpiece of Solomonic 'wisdom.'

Along with many other scholars we assume that the 'Lebanese Forest House' must have been a detached building (otherwise, e.g. Van Gelderen, 101), 100 cubits long, 50 cubits wide, and 30 cubits high. This last part is omitted by LXX[B, Luc.], but one cannot think of a reason for this other than an omission in the 'Vorlage' of LXX*. The construction of this building on the *outside* was on top of 4 rows of cedar pillars. There is no reason at all for changing 4 into 3, as LXX does (cf. now also Barthélemy). In general a detached building has 4 sides. The reading of LXX is to be viewed as an anticipation of vs. 3, where there is mention of 3x15 pillars. Accordingly, most exegetes do not follow the textual alteration proposed in *BHK* and *BHS*. In this connection, what does טורים mean? Already in 6:36 (see there) we encountered this word as well as the term כרתות. There we were of the opinion that the enclosure of the court consisted of 3 consecutive vertical rows of dressed stones against which, as a 4th row, a row of cedar beams had been placed. עמודים occurs approx. 100x in OT and always refers to vertical pillars. Also in our verse the reference is to 4 rows of cedar pillars which together make up the outer wall or perimeter of the building, against which a layer of cedar is applied as panelling. Just as in the case of the enclosure in 6:36, this panelling of cedar suggests a special and costly form of ornamentation of the exterior of the building. The second על in our verse can also mean 'against' (cf. Ch. Yalon, *Leš* 31 (1966f.), 283-286; K. Aartun, *BiOr* 28 [1971], 125; and on 6:5 above). Hence the construction is not 'on top of' the pillars. The first על can also be taken as 'against,' although – to put it in Noth's words – 'die Einführung von 2b mit על seems 'ungeschickt.' In English one could say: 'on 4 rows of pillars there was cedar panelling against the pillars.' In our language the preposition 'on' can mean: 'as it concerns,' while the ו before כרתות is intensive, the so-called *waw concomitantiae* (Ges-K §154, n. 1b): 4 rows of cedar pillars *with* panelling of cedar against the pillars (see also the translation of 6:36).

7:3 *From the top down it was covered with cedar against the supporting beams which lay on the (interior) pillars: fourty five (that is) fifteen to a row.*
Now the description of the 'Lebanese Forest House' pertains to the interior. סָפֻן is to be regarded as a pass. part. qal (see Böttcher §994[6]) of ספן (see on

6:9) which relates to the בית יער הלבנון in the previous verse: the building was covered with cedar. But Ehrlich and Noth suspect that the original word here was סֻפָּן, which we already encountered in 6:15 (see there): 'ceiling.' In the unvocalized and unpunctuated text that is certainly possible. There is even a third possibility, namely, to read סָפַן (cf. Böttcher, a.l.) and to take it actively: 'he covered it ...'; cf. LXX: καὶ ἐφάτνωσεν τὸν οἶκον ἄνωθεν ... In any case it is clear what is meant in the first 4 words of our verse: from the top down, the covering consisted of cedar. Now what does הצלעת mean here? In our discussion of 6:5 (above) we have already pointed to the wide spectrum of meanings ascribed to this word in lexicons and commentaries. There we proceeded from the basic meaning 'side' and 'rib' and so arrived at the meaning 'buttress' (see for this and the following also my remarks in *ZAW* 88 [1976], esp. 103ff.). Also in the present context the meaning 'buttress' or 'supporting beam' works well (cf. also Noth), so that there is no need to think of 'chambers' here either. The reference here is to supporting beams set against (על) the pillars, whether in part they 'leaned' against the pillars from a position in the roof or in large part or for the entire length (height) lay against the pillars. The word ממעל points toward this manner of reinforcement 'from above.

In virtue of the steep slope of the 'supporting beams' the roof construction, which must have consisted of heavy cedar, was considerably reinforced. The 'pillars' mentioned in our verse differ from the 'interior pillars' mentioned in the previous verse. 'The number of these pillars' — so literally reproduced in the LXX as well — is 45; 15 for each row. Hence these pillars were arranged in 3 rows in the interior of the 'Lebanese Forest House' (cf. also Busink, 132f.), so that the building must have consisted of a space with 4 distinct areas. This building with its 45 pillars, which undoubtedly were also of cedar — though that is not stated here — must have made a powerful impression (cf. also A. Parrot, *BiOr* 30 [1973], 81).

7:4 *There were also three rows of window-frames: three feet from opening to opening.*
This verse tells us something about the interior illumination of the building. In our exegesis of vs. 6:4 we already discussed the word שקפים. With Noth and Busink we too — be it with some hesitation — came to the conclusion that the word tends especially to refer to the framing of the actual windows. It is therefore said in the first place that there were 3 rows of window openings in the building. The word מחזה only occurs here and in the following verse and is translated by *HAL* as 'Lichtöffnung,' 'Durchblick,' a translation based on that of Eißfeldt and Noth. The LXX renders it by χώρα, '(seating) space,' which shows little connection between the Hebr. and the Greek word (cf. also Schleusner, who refers to a conjecture made by Michaelis: ὥρα from ὁράω). In

our verse Vulg. only has *contra se invicem positas,* which depends on the *columnas* of the previous verse and therefore sheds no light on the Hebr. text at all. Pesh. translates as follows: 'There were 3 balconies (or: halls: *'ksdr'* [pl.]) and they were positioned over against each other 3 times over.'' 3 times' is our translation of *tlt zbnyn* (pl.). The root חזה 'see' seems to us clearly present in the nominal *miqtal*-form (cf. BL 492p), which justifies the translation 'light opening' or 'window' (see also Busink, 134ff.; differently Barthélemy on vs. 5). Finally there remains the question what שלש פעמים means here (and in the following verse). This expression occurs no fewer than 17x in OT, in Kings except here also in 9:25; 17:21; 2 Kgs. 13:18f., 25 (see especially E. Lipiński, *RSO* 44 [1970], 93-101). Lipiński basically thinks it means 'efficacement,' but believes he can translate it in our verses by '3 paces,' in accordance with the etymological sense of the word פעם. He, too, assumes the 'effectiveness' ('la grande efficacité') of the '3 times.' Of the 118x פעם occurs in OT, approximately 100x it means 'times' (E. Jenni, *THAT*, II, 378), but the other times it can also mean 'foot,' 'stride,' 'push,' or even 'anvil.' The instances in which פעם can mean 'foot' are among others Ps. 57:7; 58:11; Prov. 29:5; S. of S. 7:2(1); Isa. 26:6 (cf. vs. 30 below). As a linear measure 'foot' *is* used in Israel's 'Umwelt' (cf. e.g. Benzinger, *Arch.* 190f.; *AHw,* s.v. *šepu(m)),* but there is no clear instance of it in Hebr.; the word פשע occurs once (1 Sam. 20:3; cf. פסיעה, Krauss, *TA,* II, 391). The usual measure of length was the cubit (אמה), while smaller units were indicated by 'span' (זרת), 'handbreadth' (טופח) and 'finger breadth' (אצבע) (see G. Schmitt, *BRL*², 204). It is not surprising that E. Stern for one (*EncMiqr.* IV, 849) finds it strange that the 'foot' (רגל), which did occur among the neighbouring nations as well as in later Hellenistic Israel, is not mentioned in the Bible. But we believe that Lipinski was on the right track when he viewed פעם here as a kind of measure of length, which raises the question whether this word does not convey the *pace* length of the feet rather than the *foot.* It is not impossible, in my opinion, that the first line in the Punic inscription *KAI* 80, which Donner-Röllig translate: 'Diese Schlachtopferstelle mit *Füßen* erneuerten und stellten her die zehn Männer ...,' could be much better translated as follows: 'The men in charge renewed and made this place of sacrifice of 10 paces (in length)' etc.[3] Based on the linear measure in our text, the last part states that 'from viewing opening to viewing opening' the distance had been measured at 3 paces. On this assumption the first words say that in the Lebanese Forest House 3 rows of window frames had been fashioned, in which at regular

---

[3] See further my "*pa'am* as a Measure of Length in 1 Kings 7:4 and KAI 80:1," *Text and Context, Old Testament and Semitic Studies* (Fs. F.C. Fensham, ed. W. Claassen; JSOTSup 48), Sheffield 1988, 177-181.

intervals of 3 'feet' or 3 'paces,' 'see-through openings,' that is, light- and air-openings had been made. Especially the 'regular interval' in the provision of illumination is important, as Busink, 136, underscores. We disagree with him – and with others – that our verse has fallen into disarray. It goes without saying that we also reject the view of especially the older commentators (e.g. Thenius, Van Gelderen and others), that there were floors with little chambers around or in the 'Lebanese Forest House.' On the basis of this understanding the various elements of our verses are then 'bent' into the direction of this viewpoint.

7:5 *And all the doors with their posts ran to a point in four stages as far as the doorframes were concerned [and across from them the openings were three feet apart].*
This verse continues the schematic description of the interior of the building by at least in the beginning telling us something about the doors. The last 5 words of our verse are literally identical with those of the previous verse, so that the suspicion of dittography (so, correctly, also Noth) is natural unless these words, viewed in context, can yield new and useful information. We therefore first want to study the first part of our verse. The reference here is to *all* the doors of the building. This suggests, but by no means proves, that there must have been *many* doors in that building. It is likely that the reference to the doors relates solely to their striking or important design and workmanship. The word מזוזות already occurred in 6:31 (see there) and 33, and denotes 'doorposts.' Many exegetes (Thenius, Stade; cf. also Noth), however, believe they have to follow LXX here, which reads αἱ χῶραι, which is the translation of מחזה in the preceding verse. But by itself it is not impossible to speak of 'doors with posts which converged to a point in 4 stages' (see on 6:33 above), where we must assume that רבעים in our verse means what the emended רבעות meant there: 'vierfach gestaffelt' (Busink, 188). In that connection what are we to think of שקף, which somewhat comes limping behind, and which in this form only occurs in our verse? In 6:4 we already encountered the word שקפים, which there, however, was vocalized by many scholars as a pl. of our word שקף (see above). In that case the word means 'surround with a frame,' a meaning we too have adopted. In our verse also the word can hardly mean anything else. LXX reads: μεμελαθρωμέναι, a word which is directly related to μέλαθρα, the translation of שקפים in the preceding verse, where it denotes the frame (of wood or stone) surrounding a window or door opening. The word שקף can, with Noth, be viewed as an adverbial accusative 'Näherbestimmung' of רבעים: doors and doorposts which, as far as the framing was concerned, narrowed to a point in 4 stages. The strange thing is that the word שקף is in the singular, but it is also quite possible that it was once written as שקפים, if one assumes that the following ומול, which is now the start of the second part of our verse, at one time came out in *scriptio continua* as follows:

שקפימימחזה (see Noth, 131). An error in writing from *yod* into *waw* is not unusual in the old script. True, some (e.g. Stade; see also Delitzsch, *LSF* §153b; textcr. app. of *BHK* and *BHS*) – on the basis of the reading of LXX: ἀπὸ τοῦ θυρώματος ἐπὶ θύραν – want to emend MT into: ומפתח אל־פתח or something like it (cf. Vulg.: *et super columnas quadrangulata ligna in cunctis aequalia*), but it is a question whether this change corresponds to the original reading of the Hebr. text. In our opinion, the best assumption is that our verse ended with the word שקפים and the rest ended up here as a dittography or a gloss (a possibility rightly suggested by Noth) and must therefore be viewed here as meaningless. The word מול, which as substantive means 'front' (Exod. 26:9; 28:25, 27, 37, etc.), often functions as a preposition meaning 'over against' (BrSynt. §116f), but that does not yield any sense here. That is the reason why LXX tried to give this word a better meaning by translating it as though it read מן. It is difficult to reason back to the 'Vorlage', but it is useful to point to a third possibility for explaining our gloss (or dittography): viz. the reading of the end of our verse: שקפים ולמחזה. This allows us to think that the redactor added something about the מחזה which, however, was mistakenly replaced (at an early stage) by a copyist by the conclusion of vs. 4. But this idea, too, remains hypothetical, just like the beautiful reconstruction of a 3-story building. These stories were furnished with little openings overlooking the atrium of the building, as well as other useful arrangements (so Thenius; also cf. Benzinger) about which there is not a word in the text. Even Josephus did not understand much of our text – at least if he had the MT as 'Vorlage' – as Marcus correctly comments in his translation of Josephus, *Ant.* VIII §133: ἰσομέτροις δὲ φλιαῖς καὶ θυρώμασι τριγλύφοις ἀσφαλῆ τε ὁμοῦ καὶ κεκαλλωπισμένον: '(the building was) at once firm and ornamental having doorposts of equal length and door wings fluted with 3 grooves.'

7:6 *He made the Hall of Pillars fifty cubits long and thirty cubits wide. [The front hall was in front and the pillars as well as the canopy were in front.]* This and the following verse speak of 2 'front halls.' The word אולם was also used for the front hall of the temple (in 6:3 above). Our verse mentions 'the front hall of the pillars' (for the retention of /ā/ in st. cstr., cf. Ewald §213c; BL, 563x; Ges-K §92g). These pillars, according to Noth, who alludes to vs. 2, were of cedar. This is possible, of course, but not certain. In the first place it is not as certain as Noth (among others) seems to think (against Thenius and many others), that this אולם was an integral part of the Lebanese Forest House described earlier. In the second place there is here no explicit statement saying that the pillars were of cedar wood. One could conceive an independent structure, perhaps in the immediate vicinity of the Lebanese Forest House (cf. Myres 1948, 35: 'it had one side open as a colonnade, with pillars supporting the roof'). The measurements given are 50 cubits in height and 30 cubits wide.

If one considers this building as immediately adjacent to the preceding one (so, e.g., C. van Gelderen, *AfO* 6 [1930f.], 103), the length of the front hall of pillars must be equal to the width of the Lebanese Forest House. Although this is a possibility, it is not likely (so, correctly, Busink, 140). While LXX[B] reads 50 cubits also for the width, by which the text is said to link up better with vs. 2, this reading has little support in the other LXX mss and the other ancient versions. The omission of עשה can be found, aside from LXX[B], also in LXX[Luc.], but this seems textcritically too weak to adopt it here. Klostermann (supported, among others, by Benzinger and Montg.-Gehman), with a view to vs. 7, wants to read עֹמְדִים (the front hall of 'the awaiting'), in place of עמודים.

The second half of our verse presents insurmountable difficulties in interpretation. Noth, Šanda, and others, with good reason find here a conglomerate of doublets with the first half of our verse, which for that matter also gives the impression of being rather a loose interjection than a well-considered literary composition. Does one have to picture a situation in which there is another 'front hall' in front of 'the front hall of pillars' and in front of that structure still more pillars, plus an עב (but cf. Busink, 140)? This last word is cited e.g. in KBL and *HAL* as עב I and occurs, aside from here, also in Ezek. 41:25f. Although *KBL* describes the word as an obscure architectural term, it suggests the word 'canopy'; *HAL*: 'ein hölzerner Bauteil im Palast' (cf. H. Weidhaas, *ZA* 45 [1939], 115, n. 2: the canopy in front of the אולם). Montg.-Gehman suggest a 'cornice'; Klostermann a 'threshold.' Tg. with the word סקופתא, also refers to this, followed by Thenius, Stade, and others ('schwellenartige Vorlage'; 'Auftritt'). Pesh. has the word *dārtā*, 'court' (for אולם it has: 'estwā: 'portico'); Vulg.: *epistylia*, 'architraves' which rest on the capitals of the pillars and carry the cornice. LXX[B, Luc.] renders it with πάχος, the 'thickness,' a 'thick beam' (Schleusner). Siegfried-Stade suspect a 'Schutzdach,' 'Vordach,' but scholars are generally agreed that we are dealing with an obscure term (also cf. *HAL* and Busink). H. Cazelles (*VT* 19 [1969], 505) recently proposed 'a kind of podium' in connection with the Ugar. *gb*, but J.C. de Moor, *UF* 2 (1970), 320, n. 98, energetically rejects this linkage and continues to regard עב in our verse as an 'unexplained architectural term.' Görg thinks it means a 'passageway'.[4] An explanation based on Ezek. 41:25f. also remains difficult (see W. Zimmerli, BK XIII/2, 1052f.), while it is striking that of the ancient versions Tg. maintains his view ('threshold').

The question arises to what the 3 masc. pl. suffix of the twice-occurring

---

[4] M. Görg, "Lexikalisches zur Beschreibung des salomonischen Palastbezirks (1 Kön 7,1-12), *BN* 11 [1980], 7-13, esp. 10ff.; cf. also G. Garbini, "Note linguistico-filologiche (Cantice 6,9; Salmo 20,6; 1 Re 7,6), *Hen* 4 (1982), 163-174: 'sacred wood.'

על־פניהם (cf. *HAL* and A.S. v.d. Woude, *THAT*, II, 445, for the meaning 'over against' or 'in front of') applies. It seems most natural to apply it to the 'pillars' (so, correctly, also Noth). But in view of all this, much is demanded of the imagination of the reader, who wants to construct something useful from these disconnected statements. Furthermore, if we are only dealing with secondary glosses torn from their original context, which to be sure must have gotten into the text at an early stage, there is not much point to an attempt at reconstruction.

Josephus offers his version of the tradition (*Ant.* VIII §134). According to him, there was another 'house,' rectangular in character, which extended along the entire width of the first house (i.e. the Lebanese Forest House): ἄντικρυς ἔχων ναὸν παχέσι στύλοις ἀνατεταμένον, 'opposite a temple built on top of massive pillars.' This, then, is either a very free rendering of the second half of our verse or the translation of the 'Vorlage' or tradition which is closer to the original notice. Striking, too, is that LXX still adds to our text the words τοῖς αἰλαμμείν.

7:7 *He also made the Hall of the Throne, where he would pronounce judgment, the Hall of Justice, which was covered with cedar from floor to ceiling.*
In this verse the reference is to a 'throne hall,' which is distinguished from the 'hall of pillars' mentioned in the previous verse, though Josephus already suggested that the former, the throne hall, was located inside the latter (Busink, 140, assumes that the Hall of Pillars and the Throne Hall are identical). Our text, however, scarcely allows any notion other than that we are dealing here with a separate 'entrance hall', in which the royal throne (further described in 10:18-20; cf. 2 Chr. 9:17-19) was located. Although LXX[B, Luc.] leaves out the part from עשה to the end of the verse, this does not mean this part is to be regarded as secondary. LXX[A] and the other ancient versions support MT, albeit that in Pesh. the second הקרקה is taken to mean *šᵉmayyā*, ceiling, and in the Vulg. *summitas,* the Hebr. 'Vorlage' of which is sometimes thought to be הקורות, 'beams' (so, among others, Thenius, Stade, Burney; also see comments on 6:15 above). But neither this reading (see, e.g., Klostermann with his equally defensible הרקיע), nor the necessity for emendation are certain (LXX[A] and Tg., for example, support the reading of MT). If one does not, with Noth for example, wish to speak of an curious kind of roof with a 'double bottom' ('eine mehrschichtige Bedeckung'), one can agree with Montg.-Gehman, that the idea of 'from floor to floor' as well as 'from bottom to top' is by no means to be ruled out (cf. also Böttcher, *Neue Aehrenlese,* 46). In any case, the second half of our verse is a technical statement, added to the more general statement, that the reference is to a throne hall which is simultaneously the 'Hall of Judgment.' These terms only occur here in OT. A link is made here between the throne as the seat of the king and the justice administered by him

or in his name. שפט (see G. Liedke, *THAT*, II, 999-1009) occurs here in the impf., because the administration of justice is viewed as something (Böttcher §949δI; Driver §39b; GD §64a; Bg. II §7k) which would occur later. The pass. part. ספון preceded by the copula *waw*, though the construction is infrequent, must be viewed as the description of a state of affairs (Driver §161.1; Ges-K §118p; Burney) and need not be altered (cf. e.g. Noth who here, as in vs. 3, wants to change into סְפוּן). The intent is to say that the throne hall was covered with cedar (for ספן, see comments on 6:9 above), and this certainly applies not only to the roof construction (against Noth), but to the whole interior 'from the bottom to the top.' In view of the statement in this verse, there is no reason to assume (with Montg.-Gehman) that the word אולם in this verse would have to mean something different than in the preceding verse ('Gate, Porte of Justice' versus 'Pillared Portico'). Deserving of mention here is Thenius's comment that when people walked from the throne hall into the court, the hall as it were constituted the gateway of the court, 'und in den Thoren ihrer Paläste pflegen ja die orientalischen Fürsten Gericht zu halten und Audienz zu geben ...'

7:8 *Now the house in which he would reside, in the other court back of the front hall, was of the same construction. Solomon also made a house like this hall for Pharaoh's daughter whom he had taken in marriage.*
In this verse we read about Solomon's own living quarters as well as those of his Egyptian princess. In the first part of this verse a number of grammatical forms occur which are not usual. For example, יסב, an impf. which can be explained like יספט of the previous verse, and in the second part – יעשה, which also bears an 'exceptional character' (so Driver §27b; cf. further König §§158; 368k; Bg. II §7b). Also striking is the article before אחרת after the noun without the article (cf. vs. 12 but also vs. 9). Ewald (§300a; cf. §293a) considers this construction possible ('in kurzer Baubeschreibung') in classical Hebr. (cf. also König §33p; Driver §209; Joüon §138c; BrSynt. §60a; Burney) and so Delitzsch's suggestion (*LSF* §90a and *BHK* – no longer adopted in *BHS*) of making it החצר does not merit adoption (cf. H.M. Orlinsky, *JAOS* 59 [1939], 31). Another matter is whether, on the basis of LXX αὐλὴ μία, one should read חצר האחת here. Other ancient translations (Pesh. and Tg.) do not support this reading while Vulg., which for that matter deviates from MT (*et domuncula in qua sedetur ad iudicandum erat in media porticu simili opere*), does not support the translation of LXX either. In 6:36 (see the commentary there) there was mention of the 'inner court' which in 7:12 is distinguished from the 'great court.' Along with Busink (see his discussion of the 'courts,' 143-149, fig. 47, 160) and others, we assume that the 'other court' was a court intended for Solomon's private residence and for that of his Egyptian wife, while the 'great court,' in distinction from the 'inner court' or the 'temple court,' surrounded the more public buildings of his palace, such as the

Lebanese Forest House and the Hall of Justice. Perhaps the 'other court' is practically identical with the 'middle court' mentioned in 2 Kgs. 20:4 (cf. *in 'media' porticu*, Vulg.). For the rest it remains difficult to reconstruct, from the unrelated items of information provided, the precise location of the courts (and the buildings). This was also the background of the obscure rendering of these words in LXX: καὶ ὁ οἶκος αὐτῶν, ἐν οἴκῳ καθήσεται ἐκεῖ, αὐλὴ μία ἐξ ἑλισσομένης(!) τούτοις κατὰ τὸ ἔργον τοῦτο ('and the house of these (two), along with the house in which he was going to live, had one court – which was connected with those houses – of the same workmanship'(?). Does LXX view the 'great court' and the 'other court' as one single court? In any case, it is best to take מבית לאולם as 'set farther back of the אולם' (cf. also *HAL*, 120a, no. 3). This last-mentioned 'hall' is the 'Throne Hall' (so Thenius and others), though Noth questions this and believes that following this word, on account of an abbreviation, an additional term has fallen out. Although in this connection we do not wish to rule out the possibility of a mutilation of the text, the assumption of such a possibility does not make it any easier to interpret the statement of the text. 'This workmanship' presumably refers to the construction mentioned earlier, which was realized in the Lebanese Forest House and the halls. Particularly in the vss. 17-33 of our chapter the word מעשה occurs as a term describing the products of the technical skill of the builders. Although there is no textcritical basis for it – the contrary is true – a reading כאולם הזה, as at the end of our verse, would not seem to us an impossibility here in the original text.

In the second part of our verse, there is mention of the palace of pharaoh's daughter, which was also constructed like the buildings referred to earlier. For Solomon's marriage to pharaoh's daughter, see comments on 3:1. Thenius thinks that this residence as well as the other buildings of Solomon's palace must have been erected on the model of very ancient Egyptian royal palaces. Although this makes sense in order to create an Egyptian atmosphere for an Egyptian princess, it cannot be inferred from the text. Stade, Benzinger, Noth, and others have good reason to believe that the intermediate clause אשר לקח שלמו is to be regarded as an (early) gloss. It need not be deleted but can be put in parentheses or between dashes.

Josephus, besides speaking of 'the house of the queen,' also mentions the other buildings for meals and rest periods after the exertion of public activities.

7:9 *All these buildings, from the court of the temple to the great courtyard, and from the foundation to the coping, were of costly stone, cut to size, and trimmed with a saw on the inside as well as the outside.*
This verse and the following verses are descriptions of the materials and building methods used in the construction. 'All these structures' were made of 'costly' stones, i.e. 'suitable' stones (cf. comments on 5:31 above) as it

concerns quality and durability (see also S. Wagner, *TWAT*, III, 858f.). About that quality there is an additional statement: במדת גזית. Actually the reference is to 'measure' (cf. comments on 6:25 above; also see vs. 11), i.e. the size which is similar to that of the blocks of stone cut from the mountains (see comments on 5:31 and 6:36; also Wagner, 859: 'nach Quadermaß'; cf. Ehrlich: 'von der Grösse von Quadern'). LXX[B, Luc.] lack this detail and Noth, among others, thinks these words are a secondary addition based on vs. 11, but this is not certain. A further quality of the stones is that they are מגררות במגרה. מגרה is a 'stone saw' and further occurs in 1 Chr. 20:3 and 2 Sam. 12:31, although some scholars also read מגזרה, 'axe,' in these places (see *HAL*, s.v. מגרה and *מגזרה). The word comes from the root גרר, which only occurs in the po'al here. In qal (Hab. 1:15; Prov. 21:7) the verb means 'drag along or away' or (Lev. 11:7; conj. Deut. 14:8) 'chew.' Accordingly, the blocks had been sawn to measure with a stone saw, and that מבית ומחוץ, 'on the inner and outer sides.' The word ומחוץ is lacking in LXX[B, Luc.]. The textcr. app. of *BHK* and *BHS* have erroneously reported this point concerning the second מחוץ occurring in this verse (cf. Barthélemy and Noth who relies on this mistaken textcritical comment). The intent of our text is to say that the stone blocks have been dressed on both sides, a fact which LXX interprets as follows: κεκολαμμένα ἐκ διαστήματος ἔσωθεν, 'engraved' (or 'sawn') 'on the inside over the (whole) surface.'

The third peculiarity reported about the 'suitable' stones (cf. König §259, who points to the 'pluralization' of אבנים in reference to an interest in the elaboration of detail) is that they extended from מסד to the טפחות. The first word occurs only here in OT and means 'foundation' (derived from יסד; cf. Böttcher §415 ['Kunstwort']; Olsh. §197a; Ewald §160c; Stade §269b; Delitzsch, *LSF* §64a: מסדו). The second is the pl. of טפח, 'handbreadth' (Exod. 25:25; 37:12; 1 Kgs. 7:26; Ezek. 40:5, 43; 43:13; Ps. 39:6; 2 Chr. 4:5 [cf. Böttcher §719]) of *טפחה (II in *HAL*, s.v.), which is an unfamiliar technical term, sometimes related to the Akkad. *adappu* I or *dappu* I, 'horizontal crossbeam' (*AHw*). LXX translates it by γεῖσον, 'lean-to,' 'cornice (extending outside of the wall)'; Vulg.: *(usque ad) summitatem parietum;* Pesh. simply: *'dm' l'l*, 'to the top,' while Tg. describes this part as וּמְשַׁכְלְלָן בְּפָשְׁבַיָּא, 'which (i.e. the stones) they founded with handbreadths.' Jastrow, s.v. פּוֹשְׁבָא, translates the word by 'projections,' 'eaves' (= the lowest edges of the roof), but this translation of Tg. is based too much on the conjectured meaning of the Hebr. The meaning 'projecting cornice' or 'coping' is accepted by many scholars, from as far back as Gesenius, *Thesaurus*, s.v. טפח. Thenius understands the word to mean 'die *zinnen*artige Schutzwehr der flachen Dächer'; Noth: 'Auflage,' a meaning he attempts to derive from the Akkad. *ṭappu*: and M. Görg, *BN* 11 (1980), 7-10, who relates the word to Egyptian and translates it by 'roof' (cf. De Vaux, *Inst.* II, 153: the brick superstructure encased in wood). It is clear – despite all the uncertainty about the correct meaning of the word – that the reference is to a vertical construction (composed of large natural stones), which ran up from the foundations to a certain height, be it to the coping, or to 'the tin-like breastwork of the roof,' or to a (first?) protruding story.

The second ומחוץ, with which the concluding words of our verse are introduced, again gives us problems. True, the ancient versions, except for Pesh., have approximately what we read in MT (in place of 'the great court,' Pesh. reads 'the court of the house' [i.e. of the temple]), but the indeterminacy of this ומחוץ suggests, that the text is not in order (so, correctly, Noth). Noth himself, but also Burney and others, suggest the reading ומחצר בית יהוה, i.e. from the temple court to the great court. This, they say, better corresponds with what is said in vs. 12. The intent of these somewhat enigmatic words would then be to say, that the wall of the temple court to the wall of the great court, and along with these walls all the intervening buildings, had been built of these dressed stones (so also Benzinger). But the selection of the correct reading as well as the determination of the correct meaning in large part remain obscure. It is also hard to tell whether one must picture the temple with its court inside or outside 'the great court.' V. Hamp, *TWAT*, III, 145, for example, thinks that the 'great court' encompassed the royal palace as well as the temple area (so also Noth; Pedersen, *Israel*, III-IV, 252; and others). Busink among others (cf. K. Galling, *BRL*[1], 411f.) thinks that this is not the case. As already indicated in our discussion of the previous verse, we believe that this last view is most deserving of support. It remains possible, however, that the entire area – known today as the 'temple mount' – on which the palaces- and temple-complex was located, was again surrounded by a fortified wall. But that is not something we can infer from the text. Laperrousaz, however, has attempted to trace the alternation in the placing of the stone blocks and in the technique of it in the E wall of the former Jerusalem temple complex – an alternation already observed by M. Dunand and K.M. Kenyon – to the Solomonic era.[5] These deviations could point to the substructures (or: the SE corner) of the Solomonic buildings described in our verses. The construction technique of the stone blocks, still visible today, later found throughout the Syrian-Palestinian region, may very well stem from the time of Solomon. The present SE wall would be a vivid illustration of what is described in our verses (9-12).

7:10 *The foundations were of costly stone, huge stones, some measuring ten cubits and some eight.*

---

[5] E.-N. Laperrousaz, "A-t-on dégagé l'angle sud-est du »Temple de Salomon«?" *Syria* 50 [1973], 355-399, esp. 385-392.

In this verse we are further informed about the substructure with stone blocks. The foundation is indicated by the pu'al masc. part. ומיסד of יסד (see comments under 5:31 and 6:37). Actually what we have here is a nominal sentence (with a plusqperfect meaning, according to Böttcher §997.2), which is incomplete, i.e. without a clear subject (so Noth; cf. Burney). It is nevertheless clear that the reference has to be to the substructures mentioned in vs. 9. As measurements for the massive blocks of stone we read of 8 and 10 cubits (for the st. cstr. אבני Driver §192.1). Josephus only mentions stones of 10 cubits.

7:11 *And above these were high-grade stones, cut to measure, and cedar wood.*

Here we read of the superstructure which gives even greater relief to what is stated in vs. 9. מלמעלה, which occurs approx. 25x in OT and twice more (7:25 and 8:7) in our book, means 'from top to bottom,' or simply 'above' (see *HAL*, s.v. מעל II). On top of the foundation of the wall 'suitable' and durable stones were placed 'of the size of the blocks of natural stone' (see comments on vs. 9). Mentioned also are cedar beams which either complete the structure or cover the (upper) walls. Josephus, *Ant.* VIII §135, emphasizes especially the ornamentation and the splendid appearance of the buildings.

7:12 *The great court had three courses of dressed stone around it and one course of cedar beams, (as was also the case) with the inner courtyard of the house of YHWH and the front hall of the palace.*

What is said in 6:36 of the 'inner court,' the wall around the forecourt of the temple, is applied here to the wall around the 'great court.' Beginning with ולחצר the verse is actually superfluous and accordingly, is not mentioned in LXX[B, Luc]. If one nevertheless wishes to maintain the second half of our verse, the preposition ל must be taken as a means of stressing a noun in the sentence (Ewald §310b; cf. König §271a): 'this also pertained to ...'. Ewald §315d and König §375b point to the incompleteness and brevity of vs. 12b, apparently without thinking of a gloss (Böttcher, *Neue Aehrenlese*, 47, on the other hand, *does* think so). In the context, however, especially the last 2 words of our verse, ולאולם הבית, are illogical. Stade and others here prefer, with good reason, to read ולחצר אולם הבית, because this reading not only accords better with LXX[B, Luc] in 6:36 (see above), but also because it runs better with the word חצר (already mentioned twice in our text). In this connection 'house' can only mean 'palace' (so, among others, also Burney, Van Gelderen, Benzinger), while the אולם probably refers back to the 'Throne Hall' referred to in vs. 8. The reference then is to the wall of the so-called 'other court.' The suspicion of Šanda (supported by Noth) that the last 2 words of our verse (without the *waw*) have fallen out after the first word of vs. 15 and have been transferred to this verse, seems to us too uncertain.

Deserving of mention is Josephus's (*Ant.* VIII §§136ff.) exuberant account of the buildings and the outstanding workmanship of the builders, of which we do not read a word in the Hebr. text. Thackeray-Marcus, with a reference to Weill, suspect that Josephus derives his expansion from the design of Herod's palace. Noth, however, refers to the undeniable reserve with respect to the palace displayed by the author of MT. Is it the case that Josephus in his tradition had more information at his disposal than we now know?

Finally it is also worthwhile, with Thenius, to bring up here the interrelated position of the temple and the palace buildings. Thenius sought Solomon's palace in another area than the temple, viz. at the N corner of the SW hill, where, in their opinion, also the Hasmoneans resided. Stade, *GVI*, I, 315f., not only correctly pointed out that the temple and the palace buildings must be located on one and the same hill, the E hill, but also that the temple was situated N of the palace complex. The layout, as Stade (fig. between pp. 314 and 315) reproduced it, exerted great influence (see Busink, 157). K. Galling, *BRL*[1], 411; H. Donner, *BRL*[2], 160; Busink, 156-161; and numerous other scholars in any case assume that the palace complex must have been situated S of the temple, though about the disposition of the buildings relative to each other there are differences of opinion. This is not surprising in view of the scarce and incomplete items of information given in the OT text. We agree with the view of Busink, 160, fig. 47, because it is archaeologically and architecturally well thought-through, with the understanding, however, that we do not equate the 'Hall of Pillars' with the 'Throne Hall' referred to in the vss. 6 and 7 and are also skeptical about the 'stalls' reported by Busink in the way of augmentation.

1 KINGS 7:13-51

7:13 *King Solomon sent a message and brought Hiram from Tyre.*

14 *He was the son of a widow from the tribe of Naphtali; his father was a man of Tyre, a worker in bronze. He was full of wisdom, insight, and skill for making any work in bronze. He came to King Solomon and did all his bronze work.*

15 *He cast two pillars of bronze. The height of one pillar was eighteen cubits, while a line twelve cubits long measured its girth. The other pillar was the same.*

16 *And he made two capitals of molten bronze to set upon the tops of the pillars; the height of the one capital was five cubits and five cubits was the height of the other capital.*

17 *Then (he made) chain work – network, twisted cords, work of chains – for the capitals surmounting the pillars, seven for each capital.*

18 *He also fashioned pomegranates (for one capital), two rows around over the chain work, (which served) to cover the capitals surmounting the pillars. He did the same for the other capital.*

19 *And the capitals surmounting the pillars (he fashioned) after the pattern of the lilies (in the front hall): four cubits.*

20 *As for the capitals surmounting the pillars, also above the rounded projection which was on the one side, there was chain work. There were also two hundred pomegranates in rows around about on the (one capital as well as the) other.*

21 *He set up the pillars before the front hall of the temple. He set up the pillar on the right and called its name Jachin; and he set up the pillar on the left and called its name Boaz.*

22 *Upon the tops of the pillars was a pattern of lilies. Thus he completed the work of the pillars.*

23 *Then he made a basin of cast metal, ten cubits from rim to rim; it was altogether round; it was five cubits high and a line of thirty cubit measured its circumference.*

24 *Under its rim were gourd-like ornamentations (ten cubits all around the basin). The gourd-like ornamentations were cast in two rows when the casting took place.*

25 *(The basin) rested on twelve oxen, three facing north, three facing west, three facing south, and three facing east. The basin was mounted on top of them, while the hindquarters of all (oxen were turned) inward.*

26 *Its thickness was a handbreadth, and its rim was like the rim of a cup, an open lotus flower. It held two thousand baths.*

27 He also made ten wheeled stands of bronze; each stand was four cubits long, four cubits wide, and three cubits high.

28 A wheeled stand was designed as follows: they were made of (vertical) panels and of (vertical) panels between the (horizontal) crosspieces.

29 On the vertical panels between the crosspieces were lions, oxen, and cherubim, similarly on the crosspieces above. Below the lions and the oxen were wreaths of hammered metal.

30 Each wheeled stand had four bronze wheels and bronze axles. Its four pedestals had shoulderings under the basin, cast over against each of the wreaths.

31 Its opening was within a crown which projected upward a cubit and a half. This opening was round: it was like a rest for a vessel [a cubit and a half]. At this opening also there were carvings [square, not round, were the panels (of the stand)].

32 Four wheels were underneath the panels and the supports of the wheels were of one piece with the stand. The height (diameter) of each wheel was a cubit and a half.

33 The construction of the wheels was like the construction of a chariot wheel: their axles, rims, spokes, and hubs were all of cast metal.

34 [And the four shoulderings rested on the four corners of each stand; the shoulderings and the stand (were all of a piece).]

35 [At the top of the stand there was a round (opening) half a cubit high. At the top of the stand were supports and panels which were of one piece with them.]

36 On the surfaces of its handholds and its panels he engraved cherubim, lions, and palm motifs [on every one of its open spaces with wreaths] on all sides.

37 In this way he made all ten stands: they were all cast in the same mold and were all the same size and shape.

38 He then made ten bronze basins, each holding forty baths. Each of the basins was four cubits across, one basin per stand and (so) for (all) ten stands.

39 He placed five of the stands on the right side of the house and five on the left side, and the (great) basin he placed at the right side of the house eastward over against the south.

40 Now Hiram made the basins, the scoops, and the sprinkling bowls, and Hiram finished all the skilled work he did for king Solomon in the house of YHWH:

41 the two pillars and the two moldings of the capitals surmounting the pillars; the two sets of network to cover the two moldings of the capitals surmounting the pillars;

42 the four hundred pomegranates for the two grids, two rows of pomegranates per grid, to cover the two basins of the capitals surmounting the pillars;

43 *and the ten stands plus the ten basins on the stands;*
44 *and the one basin with the twelve oxen under the basin;*
45 *the cooking pots, the scoops, and the sprinkling bowls [and all these objects which Hiram made for king Solomon for the temple of YHWH were of burnished bronze].*
46 *The king had them cast in clay molds in the Jordan flats between Succoth and Zarethan.*
47 *Solomon put all these objects (on a scale): but on account of their enormous quantity the weight of the bronze could not be determined.*
48 *Solomon also made all the furnishings for the house of YHWH: the golden altar and the golden table on which was the Bread of the Presence;*
49 *and the lampstands, five to the right and five to the left before the shrine, of leaf gold; similarly the floral work, the candelabra and the snuffers were of gold;*
50 *also the basins, the knives, the sprinkling bowls, incense boats, and firepans were of leaf gold, as were the sockets of the door wings of the interior of the Holy of Holies (of the doorwings of the temple).*
51 *When all the work which King Solomon had done for the house of YHWH was completely finished, he brought in the things his father David had consecrated: the silver and the gold and the (other) objects, and placed them in the treasury of the house of YHWH.*

INTRODUCTION

From vs. 13 to the end of the chapter this section in the main — though interrupted by later 'narrative' elements (Noth) like the vss. 13f., 21, 40, 46 — describes which objects were made of which metal or which material for the temple and by what techniques. This section ties in directly with the end of the previous chapter, and LXX, accordingly, places it before vss. 1-12. Its entire focus is the temple; the royal palace, although bigger and more richly furnished, is merely a matter of secondary importance.

EXEGESIS

7:13 *King Solomon sent a message and brought Hiram from Tyre.*
This verse reports the appointment of a Tyrian foundry man and metal worker, who has the same name as king Hiram, king Solomon's friend, and is mentioned also in vs. 40 (here also spelled חירום once) and vs. 45. In the more or less par. section in 2 Chr. 2:10ff., where mention is made of a letter from king Hiram of Tyre to Solomon, his name is reproduced as חורם אבי (vs. 12, also

vs. 4:16, but without אבי in 4:11).[1] Older exegetes (Bertheau, Thenius, and others) but also Rudolph, who refer among other places to Gen. 45:8, take this addition 'my father' (so LXX and Vulg.) to mean 'master,' a title which immediately distinguishes the man from the king with the same name. This man, who came from Tyre, was by that token a subject of king Hiram.

In this (later) report it is admitted, that certainly the skilled labour of metal casting, but also the further construction of the temple was work done under the supervision of non-Israelite technicians. Although in the ancient Near East this was by no means an uncommon phenomenon, one may wonder, with Noth, whether the relatively late statement of our verse is 'true.' Montg.-Gehman offer a number of examples, which show that also at the courts of 'great kings' it was common practice to hire foreign experts for construction purposes. Implicitly, perhaps, the non-Israelite origin of the following objects is also suggested here.

7:14 *He was the son of a widow from the tribe of Naphtali; his father was a man of Tyre, a worker in bronze. He was full of wisdom, insight, and skill for making any work in bronze. He came to King Solomon and did all his bronze work.*
As if to soften somewhat the foreign character of this building- and metal-expert, this verse refers to his half-Israelite origin: his mother was a widow of the tribe of Naphtali, his father a Tyrian. Of the 55x the word אלמנה, 'widow' occurs in OT, one finds 5 in our books of Kings (also 11:26; 17:9f., 20; cf. Krinetzki, *Bibelhebräisch*, 86 for the apposition of the 2 words). Especially the negative aspect of widowhood comes to the fore in OT: the loss of social and economic security as a result of the death of her husband (see further: J. Kühlewein, *THAT*, I, 169-173; H.A. Hoffner, *TWAT*, I, 308-313). While this circumstance as such already helps us to understand that she was married to a Tyrian, the genealogy of the man is made even more complicated, when LXX inserts the copula *before* הוא and reads as if not the widow, but Hiram himself was a member of Naphtali's tribe, so that the Tyrian to whom his mother was married was his stepfather. Rashi (commenting on 2 Chr. 2:13), for example, refers to this possibility and also Josephus, *Ant.* VII §76, asserts that Hiram is a full-blooded Israelite. This opinion has also been shaped by the divergent report in 2 Chr. 2:13, where it is said that Hiram 'was the son of a woman of the daughters of Dan, but his father was a man of Tyre.' Some (e.g. Rashi, Kimchi, and other rabbinical scholars) attempt to harmonize these contradictory statements by assuming, that our verse states that Hiram, and not his mother,

---

[1] See on the differences between 2 Chr. 2:12f. and 1 Kgs. 7:13f. now also T. Lorenzin, "2 Cr 2, 12-13: un derash del Cronista?" *BeO* 32 (1990), 156-161.

came from Naphtali. It is further assumed that Hiram's father had gone to live in Tyre (cf. Bertheau, Thenius, Keil, and others).

It must be clear to the reader that these subtle attempts to resolve the contradictions are not convincing. While acknowledging the fact that the addition (at a later time?) of the word 'widow' implies a tendency to 'save' Hiram as an Israelite, we cannot draw from our text any conclusion other than that, both in terms of his name and country of birth, Hiram was a Tyrian. Of his mother it is said that she came from the tribe of Naphtali. Of the approx. 250x the word מטה occurs in OT one finds it only here and in 8:1 in Kings. Usually it means 'stick,' 'staff' and is used especially in P for 'tribe' (another word is שֵׁבֶט; cf. K.-D. Schunck, *BHHW*, II, 1851f.; H. Simian-Yofre, *TWAT*, IV, 818-826). Naphtali is mentioned in Gen. 30:8 and 35:25 as the son of Jacob and Rachel's maid Bilhah. Naphtali's tribal territory laid on the E side of the Galilean mountains and the headwaters of the Jordan up to the Sea of Tiberias (cf. Josh. 19:32-39; 21:32; Judg. 1:33) and was bounded by Issachar, Zebulon, Asher and Dan. In 4:15 Naphtali is mentioned as an administrative region under Solomon (see there). By itself it is not at all unusual for people from neighbouring areas to marry each other.

Hiram is called a technician in bronze (חרש נחשת), a colleague of Tubal-Cain, for whom this word is also used in Gen. 4:22. חרש I (cf. *HAL*) is 'plow,' 'engrave,' but also 'work upon.' According to the lexicons, e.g. *HAL*, there is kinship with the more frequently occurring חָרָשׁ, 'craftsman.' But H.-P. Müller (*UF* 1 [1969], 80) believes that our word should rather be derived from חרש III: 'magic,' 'practice magic' (cf. Isa. 3:3: חֲכַם חֲרָשִׁים, 'those who are skilled in [magical] craftsmanship'). One who is skilled in working with metal also knows how to manage the magical forces which lodge in it. In the ancient Near East, manual-technical labour without accompanying magic was meaningless. Although Müller's opinion is certainly not improbable, it remains a question whether our חֹרֵשׁ can be explained in this way.

As a term for (an object of) metal נחשת occurs approx. 140x in OT and was mentioned in our book for the first time in 4:13. The word is usually translated by 'bronze,' sometimes by 'brass.' In antiquity this metal was not merely an alloy of tin and copper, but also a copper alloy which contained no tin but lead, antimony, or other metals (cf. R.J. Forbes, *JEOL* 8 [1942], 747-756; idem, *BHHW*, I, 273; M. Weippert, *BRL*^{2}, 219-224; H.-J. Fabry, *TWAT*, V, 397-408). Although bronze originated in even more northern regions of Syro-Phoenicia, there must already at an early time have been a flourishing and well-known bronze industry (cf. Brown, *Lebanon*, 90-97).

Although it is logical to apply the addition 'technician in bronze' to Hiram, it is also possible – and done by some scholars – to take this apposition with Hiram's father. It could be that it has been given such an ambiguous position in our text to indicate, that we are here dealing with a 'bronze-technical' generation.

What follows in our text is a characterization, again derived from P, which occurs almost literally in Exod. 31:3 and 35:31, where it relates to Bezalel, the builder of the so-called 'tabernacle.' וימלא has static significance (Joüon §118b) and is construed with an accusative (with *verba copiae et inopiae*; Joüon §125d; cf. BrSynt. §96). The חכמה (for the determination, see BrSynt. §21c) is here connected with the (sacral) traditional activities of a craftsman (cf. also H.P. Müller, *TWAT*, II, 936; G. Fohrer, *TDNT*, VII, 484). In addition there is mention of תבונה (see comments on 5:9 above) and דעת. The last-mentioned word occurs in this form only here in the books of Kings and denotes 'technical' knowledge (for ידע and its derivatives, cf. esp. G.J. Botterweck, *TWAT*, III, 486-512; W. Schottroff, *THAT*, I, 682-701), however much upon this concept has been 'theologized' here (cf. e.g. Prov. 2:6, 10 in connection with 'wisdom'; see Botterweck, 496). Just as, on a macrocosmic scale, YHWH once founded the earth by his 'wisdom' and by his 'understanding' established the heavens and by his 'knowledge' cleaved the deeps (Prov. 3:19f.), so Hiram goes to work microcosmically to fashion the 'place for YHWH.' Although the רוּחַ אֱלֹהִים is not mentioned here (as in Exod.), he is still viewed as being implicitly present. (For the word מלאכה: see comments on 5:30 above.)

Of the conclusion of this verse we still need to say that, based on the reading in LXX, it is suggested that in place of ויבוא we read the passive וַיּוּבָא, while, on the basis of the readings of LXX and Pesh., the sing. masc. suff. of the last word is sometimes omitted. But neither of these emendations can be recommended.

7:15 *He cast two pillars of bronze. The height of one pillar was eighteen cubits, while a line twelve cubits long measured its girth. The other pillar was the same.*

The first bronze work, which deserved to be mentioned and was made by Hiram, are the pillars 'Jachin' and 'Boaz' (see comments on vs. 21). In our verse something is first said about the construction and height of the shafts. The form ויצר, with which the verse begins, is rendered in LXX as ἐχώνευσεν, which has prompted many exegetes and the textcr. app. of *BHK* (cf. the question mark in *BHS*) to change the form into וַיִּצֹק. Now it is true that forms of the verb יצק, 'cast', occur more often in this connection and even in our chapter (cf. vss. 16, 23f., 30, 33, 46), but this does not mean that on that account the verb has to be modified. As a rule (cf. *HAL*, s.v.) exegetes derive our form from the root צור III, 'form,' 'cast,' which also again occurs in 2 Kgs. 12:11 and Exod. 32:4 as a by-form of יצר. Bg., II §31h opposes the derivation from the root צור and views our form – if the consonants are correct – as an imperf. of יצר, but examples such as are given in Meyer (II, §80.3c) show that there is nothing that stands in the way of *HAL*'s opinion, so that MT can be maintained textcritically as well as grammatically.

Hiram cast (cf. P.L. Garber, *BA* 14 [1951], 8, on 'single castings of 'brass'') 2 pillars of bronze, MT tells us, followed by all the ancient versions except LXX. LXX[B] has: καὶ ἐχώνευσεν τὸ αἰλὰμ τοῦ οἴκου; most other and important MSS of LXX read: καὶ ἐχώνευεν τοὺς στύλους τῷ αἰλὰμ τοῦ οἴκου. 2 Chron 3:15 offers as the location of the 2 pillars לפני הבית, a description that is even more general and vague than that in LXX. But it is not until vs. 21 that there is mention of the place where the pillars were set up, so that in our verse there is as yet no need to be more specific (so also Benzinger and others). The height of the one pillar is said to be 18 cubits; the height of the other is not specified in our verse. The par. place in 2 Chr. 3:15 offers – exaggeratedly – a 'length' of 35 cubits, and that for both pillars. The height of 18 cubits is 'confirmed' by 2 Kgs. 25:17 and the par. Jer. 52:21, as well as by Josephus, *Ant*. VIII §77, who expressly mentions that this height applies to both pillars. In these and similar places (2 Kgs. 25:17, etc.), it is perhaps possible to take העמוד האחד to mean 'per pillar' (cf. Slotki). In our verse, however, this view is made rather difficult, because it is stated that a line 12 cubits long could measure its circumference. But there is considerable textcritical doubt about the correctness of this information.

Aside from the par. passage Jer. 52:21, חוט 'line' occurs also in Gen. 14:23; Josh. 2:18; Judg. 16:12; Eccl. 4:12 and S. of S. 4:3. The impf. יסב can very well be regarded as an indication of a *possibility* in the past (so, correctly, already Böttcher §§942, 949; otherwise GD §63, rem. 1; cf. also Burney). By itself the concluding sentence of our verse makes good grammatical-syntactic, and conceptual, sense but it is merely a small part of a larger literary whole. After all, what can be the sense of reporting only the height of the one pillar and the circumference of the other? The textual modifications which are being proposed are based in part on readings in the ancient versions, in part on par. places in MT. LXX, after stating the height, inserts the following: καὶ περίμετρον τέσσαρες καὶ δέκα πήχεις ἐκύκλου αὐτόν, τὸ πάχος τοῦ στύλου τεσσάρων δακτύλων τὰ κοιλώματα καὶ οὕτως στύλος ὁ δεύτερος. If one compares this long Greek quotation to Jer. 52:21b in MT, one finds a striking correspondence; only the circumference of the pillar is given by LXX as 14, while the conclusion is not found in the Hebr. text, while it is in Tg. and Pesh. (that is, as the translation of our verse). It is understandable, therefore, that many scholars (Ewald, *GVI*, III, 322, n.; Thenius, Stade, Benzinger, Burney, Noth, among them) want to change MT in line with these data (cf. also textcr. app. in *BHK* and *BHS*) so that (according to Jer. 52:21) we must add: 'and its (i.e. the bronze wall of which the pillar was made) thickness (עֳבִי, cf. comments on vs. 26) was 4 fingers; it (i.e. the pillar) was hollow (נָבוּב).' The conclusion then reads: 'and the same is true of the other.' Although one can grant, that the data of Jer. 52:21 fit well in our verse and yield a better insight than our verse (also Josephus supports this opinion), textcritically it remains a question whether this emendation is the correct one. Barthélemy points out that in any case the LXX of our verse cannot have borrowed [text] from the LXX on Jer. 52:21, but has processed in its translation material derived from MT on Jer. 52:21. He further rejects Noth's suggestion that Jer. 52:21b could hardly have drawn on any source other than the complete text of our vs. 15. Jer. 52:21b had its own traditions. Barthélemy maintains, that our vs. 15 has been preserved in its original form in our MT and cites Jewish exegetes, who applied the 19th exegetical-hermeneutic rule of R. Eliezer ben Jose, the Galilean: a statement made with a view to something also applies to something else.[2] Rashi, Kimchi, but also Tg. Pesh. and even Vulg., are said to have perfectly understood the import. This view of the situation, however, seems to us too easy a solution and a simplification of textcritical questions. In the overall text of our chaps. 6 and 7 in MT there are too many lacunae, fragmentary parts, glosses and addenda, in respect to which par. Hebr. texts as well as the ancient versions disagree, than that we could speak of a complete MT. It is certainly not impossible that the LXX reading is based on a 'better' 'Vorlage', certainly as it concerns the conclusion of our verse, in which LXX gets support from other ancient versions. Further, the symmetry present in the following verse suggests that it also applied to our verse. In any case, virtually everyone agrees, that what was true in terms of height and circumference of the one pillar was also true of the other. We consider a slight textual addition, such as the one *BHS* proposes under 'd' (the insertion of אתו ובן after the second את), both textcritically and exegetically entirely warranted. Ehrlich simply wants to delete השני as being a dittography arising from the following verse, but this seems unlikely.

Albright, *ARI*, 194, and – following him – also Busink, 302f., have raised their objections to the circumference and thickness of the pillars as indicated in our verse Albright wants to read 2 cubits in place of 12 cubits, which would come down to a diameter of 31 cm per pillar; Busink thinks that the number 12 refers to the combined size of the 2 pillars, which would come down to a diameter of approx. 95 cm per pillar. However acceptable it may be that in reality the pillars were rather thinner than indicated in our verse, the author wants us to believe – this much is textcritically rather certain – that they were 12 cubits in circumference. Given this fact, evidence to the contrary is hard to furnish.[3]

---

[2] Cf. H.L. Strack, *Einleitung in Talmud und Midrasch*, München 1982, 165.

[3] See now also M. Görg, "Die »ehernen Säulen« (I Reg 7,15) und die »eiserne Säule« (Jer 1,18). Ein Beitrag zur Säulenmetaphorik im Alten Testament," *Prophetie und geschichtliche Wirklichkeit im alten Israel* (Fs S. Herrmann, ed. R. Liwak et al.), Stuttgart 1991, 134-154.

7:16 *And he made two capitals of molten bronze to set upon the tops of the pillars; the height of the one capital was five cubits and five cubits was the height of the other capital.*

Textcritically this verse, which speaks of the 'superstructure' of the pillars, offers no special difficulties. LXX^B, for example, neglects to say that this part, too, was made of bronze, which for that matter is a piece of superfluous information in a section which expressly deals with bronze work. In our chapter, in the following section (and in the par. parts of other books), the word כתרת occurs several times and is usually (see, e.g., *HAL*) translated by 'pillar capital' and associated with כתר II, 'surround.' Noth, however, follows the LXX translation (ἐπίθεμα, which he renders by 'superstructure' (cf. Liddell-Scott, s.v., which here, in addition to a number of other meanings, 'cover' among them, translates, specifically in our verse, by 'capital of a column'; cf. also Schleusner, s.v.). Vulg. translates: *capitella*; Tg. uses the word קְרוֹנְתָא, from the Gr. κορωνίς, explained by Krauss, *GLL*, II, 565f., as 'capital,' whereas Pesh. views the word $k^e r\bar{a}mt\bar{a}$, rendered by Brockelmann, *Lex. Syr.*, s.v., as *epistylium, abacus*, rather as a cover over the capital or architrave. Already in 6:36 Pesh. used this word for בְּרוֹתִים (cf. 7:2). Krauss considers the Syrian word 'an ancient error in writing' in the place of the word in Tg., because they no longer knew what to do with the word. We would not want to rush into repeating this opinion. In the (more or less) par. place 2 Chr. 3:15 the word צֶפֶת is used, which only occurs in the OT in this verse and is also translated (in *HAL*) by 'capital.' This is also how כַּפְתֹּר (Amos 9:1; Zeph. 2:14; see L. Rost, *BHHW*, II, 932) is translated. It is clear from excavations and discoveries in Palestine that (stone) pillars with typical 'volute capitals' date from the so-called Iron II Age (see H. Weippert, *BRL*^{2}, 259f.; Y. Shiloh, *PEQ* 109 [1977], 39-52), and may even stem from an earlier period (so Shiloh). The part of the pillar which suggested the idea of 'capital' had thus been long familiar in Israel, wherever this architectural form may have originated (cf. *KAI* 10, 6, where in a Phoen. inscription from the 5th and 4th century such 'pillars' with 'capitals' probably also occur). With Busink, 305, n. 525a (cf. Klostermann, who already translates it by 'upper structures' and in his commentary points out correspondence with כפתר 'capital'!), it seems to us that there is every reason, and no objection, to continue translating our word by 'capital.' True, these capitals, like the pillars themselves, were cast in bronze (מצק, hoph. part. of יצק, serving here and in vss. 23 and 33 as a technical term) and were no longer made of stone, but it was probably a solid bronze, and they differed from the then current forms for capitals, as will be evident from what follows. Josephus, *Ant.* VIII §77, speaks about the 'cast lily-work' on top of each pillar (χωνευτὸν ... κρίνον), but like our text he estimates them at 5 cubits (2 Kgs. 25:17 speaks of 3 cubits in contrast to Jer. 52:22).

7:17 *Then (he made) chain work – network, twisted cords, work of chains – for the capitals surmounting the pillars, seven for each capital.*
This verse as well as the following ones, filled as they are with technical information, present great difficulties to our understanding and interpretation. Textcritically, too, there is a lot going on here. In the first place, LXX begins our verse with a verb which most interpreters have taken over. Noth considers that addition as 'eine Glättung des auch sonst stichwortartig nominal formulierten Textes.' Although – as we remarked several times before – these narrative chapters are very disjointed in their composition, in our opinion it is going too far to assume that the composer(s) of this section would not have used a verb (see the beginning of chap. 6 above). Our verse begins with the word שְׂבָכִים, a pl., the sing. form of which occurs almost immediately after in our verse and also elsewhere in our chapter (vss. 18, 20, 42) with a fem. pl. ending (vss. 41f.). The word is also found elsewhere in OT (2 Kgs. 1:2; 25:17; Jer. 52:22f.; Job 18:8 and 2 Chron 4:12f.), usually in texts that are virtually par. to our verse. The usual translation is 'lattice-work,' 'grating,' 'plaiting,' 'net' (cf. Job 18:8), for which in Arab. the word *šabaka*, 'interweave,' can be cited as etymologically cognate (*KBL*, Noth). To this somewhat general but not unclear expression, there is added, by way of explanation and probably, secondarily, a further description of the technical term, which is left out in LXX: 'a network of tassels; chain work.'

גְּדִל*, aside from here, also occurs in Deut. 22:12, both times in the pl. In Deuteronomy the reference is to a 'tassel' on a garment, for which Num. 15:38 uses the word צִיצָת, a braided cord. Now the statement in Deuteronomy need not be identical to that in Numbers (so, correctly, S. Bertman, *BA* 24 [1961], 119). From antiquity it is sufficiently well-known from words and images, however, that little tassels or other forms of appendages were worn on the (under) side(s) of a garment (see Bertman, 119-128), so that in our case also it is best to think of 'tassels' or 'braided cords.' This last idea is reinforced by a second 'secondary note' in which there is reference to שַׁרְשְׁרוֹת, 'chains.' This word occurs also in Exod. 28:14, 22; 39:15; and 2 Chr. 3:5, 16, and is related to the Akkad. *šeršerratu* (Assyr. *šaršarratu*) with the same meaning (*AHw*, s.v.). Accordingly, the 2 'explanatory notes', which later ended up in the text, speak of the word שְׂבָכִים, i.e. plaiting (with the added words): braided cords, (or) chain work. Also Tg. and Pesh. understand it in the sense of 'plaited work,' each of them in its own phraseology, and Vulg. does not diverge from this (*quasi in modum retis et catenarum sibi invicem miro opere contextarum*). LXX alone has: καὶ ἐποίησεν δύο δίκτυα περικαλύφαι τὸ ἐπίθεμα τῶν στύλων ... Whether the addition 'two' in LXX is to be explained in terms of the logical conclusion from the preceding statement (cf. beginning of vs. 16) or from another 'Vorlage' is no longer traceable. Along with the omission of the verb also the numeral may have disappeared. But even though this should be the case, it is nevertheless clear that the 'plaiting' referred to was intended for both capitals. Accordingly, it is not necessary, with LXX, to read the text as though the Hebr. text should have to read: לְבֻסּוֹת אֶת־הַכְּרָתוֹת, a phrase which was possibly moved here from the following verse, though many exegetes (Thenius, Benzinger and others; cf. also the textcr. app.) follow these emendations or proceed to reorganize the entire Hebr. text (so, e.g. Vincent, *Jérusalem*, II-III, 405, who, with the usual emendations, adopts the order 17a-18b-17b-18a-20c-18c-22a-20b-19-21-22b). The more or less par. 2 Chr. 3:16 refers to chains which were supposed to be בַּדְּבִיר. Usually exegetes emend the text to read בָּרְבִיד, 'like a necklace' (cf. Rudolph), or מִכְבָּר, 'trellis-work,' because it makes no sense here to think of the cella of the temple. Josephus, *Ant.* VIII §77, in his understanding of the text, moves in the direction of LXX, when he writes that the lily-work on the pillars, which was cast in massive bronze, was wound around with a network of bronze palm buds (... ᾧ περιέκειτο δίκτυον ἐλάτη χαλκέα περιπεπλεγμένον καλύπτον τὰ κρίνα), which in turn was said to cover the lilies.

The final difficulty presented by our text is the mention of the number 7, which is quite generally, also on the basis of LXX, changed into שְׂבָכָה (cf. Burney, but also Böttcher, Thenius, Stade, and others). The other ancient translations, however, support MT and so Noth, for example, wants – for good reason – to hold on to MT. In this Barthélemy (346f.) concurs with Noth. The former does not, like Thenius for example, wish, in exegeting the difficult vss. 17-20, to proceed from the less difficult vss. 41f. (cf. 2 Chr. 4:12f.) and to correct our verses in light of those verses. It is very well possible, after all, that the translator of LXX has already done this and has used the content of vss. 41f. to illumine our verse. According to Barthélemy, when correcting MT, extreme caution in the use of LXX is imperative. Along with Noth he maintains that when the beginning of our verse speaks clearly about שבכה, a corruption of שבעה into שבכה is easier to explain than the reverse. In addition, he cites Noth's view (already launched by Benzinger) that our verses convey the plan, whereas vss. 41f. convey the execution of it, but not altogether in keeping with the plan.

Along with Noth and Barthélemy, we too hold on to the textcritically certain number 7, although we are not as willing (as Barthélemy seems to be) to yield to the suspicion, that in its translation LXX has corrected the text in light of vss. 41f. We want to keep open the possibility that the translator(s) of LXX had another 'Vorlage' before them. The vss. 41f. demand an explanation of their own, one in which the data, now provided, will have to be discussed. Perhaps Noth in his interpretation is on target insofar as, in reference to the number 7, he pictures chain ornaments, one above the other and surrounding the capitals, which he calls permanent 'Aufsätze' ('superstructures'), be it '(ziemlich hohe) wulstartige Aufsätze.' But what is there against calling curved or bowl-shaped capitals 'capitals'? As for this last word, consider the suggestion by Görg relating כתרת to the Egyptian word *k,'t-rd, 'lotus-work' in vs. 19: מַעֲשֵׂה שׁוּשָׁן (also cf. vs. 22).[4] But even if there were this semantic connection between the 2 words, the translation 'capital' would still be defensible.

7:18 *He also fashioned pomegranates (for one capital), two rows around over the chain work, (which served) to cover the capitals surmounting the pillars. He did the same for the other capital.*
This verse is burdened by even greater textcritical and exegetical difficulties than the previous one. For in vs. 15 there already was mention of the making of the pillars. Here – as Ehrlich correctly remarks – we are dealing with the ornamentation of their top sections, their capitals. Along with Noth, we can view the first words of our verse ('and he made the pillars') as a misplaced marginal gloss, or we can – with a number of Hebr. MSS and a considerable series of exegetes (Böttcher; Thenius; Stade; Burney; Delitzsch, *LSF* §99b and others) – alter עמודים into רמנים and further down in this verse – with approx. 50 Hebr. MSS plus Pesh. – רמנים into עמודים. Barthélemy, 348, in light of what was said in connection with the previous verse, does not find this transposition textcritically very strong ('au niveau des conjectures') and agrees with Thenius that certainly the change of הרמנים into העמודים by copyists (on the basis of vs. 41) was made 'um in das völlig Sinnlose einen Sinn zu bringen ...' The conclusion of Barthélemy's argumentation is, that the text is too hopelessly corrupt for the witnesses to the text tradition still to enable us to restore it. But on that basis what is the value of his last sentence: 'Mieux vaut le préserver aussi intact que possible et laisser la critique littéraire essayer d'en tirer parti'? Literary-critical work, after all, follows the text-critical and not the reverse. If, in light of this, we proceed from what is textcritically the most certain part of our verse, then that is the conclusion where we read that he has done or made the same thing for the *other* capital. The text does not say that the preceding was done or made for the *one* capital. The text merely states that something was done or made 'to cover the capitals which surmounted the רמנים.' The word רמן occurs about 30x in OT and denotes a pomegranate tree (*Punica Granatum*), a low-growing tree or shrub with thorns, a grey trunk, leathery leaves, red blossoms, and apple-shaped fruits similar to oranges with numerous red pits (cf. Dalman, *AuS*, I, 60f., 377f.; F.M.Th. Böhl, *JEOL* 3 [1935], 151; M. Zohari, *EncMiqr*. VII, 375ff.). The Akkad. word for the tree and fruit is *nurmû* or *lurmû* (*AHw*, s.v. *nurmû*), to which the word *rummân* or *rimmôn*, which occurs also in other West-Sem. languages, is related. Görg, art. cit., on the basis of Egyptian, believes it means 'column' or 'pillar'. The fruit,

---

[4] M. Görg, "Zur Dekoration der Tempelsäule," *BN* 13 (1980), 17-21.

the pomegranate, is regarded as a fertility symbol, while the shrub itself is sometimes viewed as a sacred tree (cf. Hoogewoud, 96f.; D. Diringer, *DOTT*, 225, and 1 Sam. 14:2). The pomegranate was further a favourite theme among artists in the Near East[5] and is also mentioned outside our chapter as decoration (e.g. Exod. 28:33f.; 39:24ff.; Sir. 45:9).

It is clear that the pomegranates which served as decoration were not *under* the capitals. This would be contrary to vs. 16. One can picture them *on* the capitals, possibly attached to the chainwork mentioned earlier. To that extent the emendation proposed at the beginning of this verse, in which 'pillars' and 'pomegranates' are interchanged in the text, is not illogical. Do the words ושני טורים סביב על־השבכה האחת say that 2 rows of pomegranates, one for each chain, were attached to the capitals? Right up until the end of our verse, where the text literally agrees with MT, LXX has reproduced the text as follows: καὶ ἔργον κρεμαστόν, δύο στίχοι ῥοῶν χαλκῶν δεδικτυωμένοι, ἔργον κρεμαστόν, στίχος ἐπὶ στίχον ...', '(he made) a suspended work: 2 rows of network of bronze pomegranates, suspended work, row upon row ...' (cf. vs. 42). However LXX may have been adapted to vss. 41f., still it too has attempted not only to give meaning to the Hebr. text, but to convey its meaning, perhaps in accordance with its 'Vorlage'. With the aid of the textcritical data (however weak) and the fragmentary givens of the text and context, one must, if one is not simply to delete this entire verse as a hopeless conglomerate of glosses and errors, introduce a change in the text which, though conjectural, seems logically rather well-founded: (1) transpose עמדים and רמנים; (2) relate לבסות not primarily to שני טורים, but to שבכה; (3) assume a possible disappearance of לכתרת האחת (by haplography?; see also comments on vs. 41 below). As for point (2), we refer the reader to the expression אשר ל or also simply ל (as here), 'in order to give more precision or more emphasis' (Joüon §130e). The chainwork, in any case, served to cover the capitals. The *waw* before ושני serves to indicate emphasis or, at times, explication (Ges-K §154a, n.).

7:19 *And the capitals surmounting the pillars (he fashioned) after the pattern of the lilies (in the front hall): four cubits.*
LXX puts vs. 21 between the end of the previous verse and the beginning of this verse. Vs. 22 is altogether missing there. The beginning of our verse is a doublet of vs. 22a (so, among others, also Benzinger), be it in somewhat different wording. Stade, for example, and Burney want to declare this verse, along with vss. 20a and 22, a gloss. However much the fragmentary text

---

[5] See inter alia, next to the articles by Böhl and Zohari, O. Loretz, *Das alt-hebräische Liebeslied* (AOAT 14/1), Neukirchen-Vluyn 1971, 27, n. 10.

prompt such suspicions, as far as our verse is concerned there is no direct textcritical necessity for it. Our verse literally states, that the capitals surmounting the pillars were of 'lily' or 'lotus' work. The word שׁוּשַׁן occurs, aside from our chapter (vss. 22, 26) also in Hos. 14:6; Ps. 45:1; 60:1; 69:1; 80:1 (all Psalm headings); S. of S. 2:1f., 16; 4:5; 5:13; 6:2f.; 7:3 and 2 Chr. 4:5, be it sometimes in somewhat varying orthography or vocalization. The word is also found in other Sem. languages, though it comes from the Egyptian *sšn* (*zššn*), 'lotus'.[6] The word is translated variously as 'lily' or 'lotus flower.' The latter was the lotus water lily, sacred in Egypt (*Nymphaea lotus*), which grew by the shores of the Nile. The only lily which can be considered for this name in Palestine is *lilium candidum*. It is therefore assumed by many scholars that any beautiful flower, any flower resembling a lily, tulip, or iris, could be called שׁוּשַׁן (Dalman, *AuS*, I, 357-360; J.C. Trever, *IDB*, III, 133f.; *EncMiqr*. VII, 607ff.). According to Ewald §188f, n. 1, the word means 'sechsblättrige' and 'entstammt unstreitig dem zahlworte' (for the so-called suffix -*ôn*, cf. Olsh. §215b; König §255b), but in light of the Egyptian derivation mentioned above this does not seem likely, though in folk etymology this connection may exist (cf. J. Feliks, *BHHW*, II, 1093). The capitals of the pillars, as was often the case in Egypt, were presumably lotus-shaped (cf. Myres 1948, 23 and the index of *ANEP* for illustrations on which lotus flowers figure).

What is the meaning of the added word באולם? The masoretic punctuation, Rashi and many later exegetes link this word to the preceding context, so that the suggestion is made that there were 2 pillars in the front hall of the temple. A further point of contention is then whether they were structurally functionless there or served as weightbearing pillars in the building. Thenius at great length defends the latter viewpoint. In modern times this viewpoint is again being supported. Thus Myres 1948, 27ff., and J.L. Ouellette, *RB* 76 (1969), 365-378, the latter basing himself on the so-called *bit ḫilâni* (see comments on 6:4 above), explain – using our verse (and vss. 21, 41f.) as evidence – that Jachin and Boaz were actually weightbearing columns at the entrance of the front hall. However, most expositors today – basing themselves on analogies from the 4th millennium BCE and on information about or depictions of 'twin pillars' from the Phoen.-Palestinian region of a later time – assume that the pillars in question were in any case freestanding pillars (see e.g. Busink, 302, 320f.). In place of באולם LXX reads: κατὰ τὸ αἰλάμ, supported by a Hebr. MS: כאולם, which hardly facilitates a better understanding of the text (see Myres, 23f., who, as it concerns LXX, either considers a popular etymology for the Sem. *ailam* a possibility, or a Greek architectural term derived from Sem. builders). Often an emendation of Klostermann is followed, reading

---

[6] R.O. Faulkner, *Concise Dictionary of Middle Egyptian*, Oxford 1962 (repr. 1986), 248.

כלם ארבע מאת in place of the last 3 words of our verse and then transposing this phrase to the beginning of vs. 18. But this emendation is hardly satisfactory either (so Ehrlich, among others). Ehrlich thinks the word אולם is an artistic expression whose meaning is no longer traceable. The objection to this – one we have registered repeatedly in the interpretation of these chapters – is that a homonymous expression would stand for technically different terms, a circumstance which is far from enhancing the clarity of the material. Targum reads לְקִיט בְּאוּלָמָא, an expression explicitly listed and translated by 'zusammenhalten' by Dalman, *ANH*, s.v. לקט. But what can 'lily-work 'folded together' in the front hall' contribute to a better understanding of our text? Jastrow, s.v. לָקִיט II, has a more acceptable translation: 'pinched out, chiselled, in bass-relief.' Chiselled lilies may well have been worked into bronze work. It is also probably the intent of Tg. to say that. But the front hall remains problematic in this location. It seems to us most plausible to take the words באולם as a separate gloss, which ended up here at an early stage. A reader (or copyist) tried to say, that the reference was to the pillars 'in the hall' and to nothing else.

7:20 *As for the capitals surmounting the pillars, also above the rounded projection which was on the one side, there was chain work. There were also two hundred pomegranates in rows around about on the (one capital as well as the) other.*

The authors or glossators are not yet done speaking about the capitals surmounting the pillars, but especially as it concerns the first half of this verse, it is hard to tell what its precise meaning is from the often oddly concatenated words. It is not surprising that the textcr. app. of *BHK* and *BHS* warns that the first half of our verse is corrupt or that others (Noth for example) leave parts of it untranslated. This difficulty stems not so much from inadequate understanding of the technical terms used, but from the defective text.

The beginning of our verse refers to the capitals surmounting the top of the pillars. The *waw*, with which our verse begins, may be intended explicatively: 'as for the capitals ...' Pesh., Tg., and Vulg. support this reading, as they do virtually all the words in our verse. But LXX* does not. In LXX^B the beginning of our verse reads: καὶ μέλαθρον ἐπ' ἀμφοτέρων τῶν στύλων. In 6:5 the word μέλαθρον is used to render the Hebr. יָצוּעַ. It means 'top beam,' 'ceiling,' 'roof.' Accordingly, it is at least problematic whether in its 'Vorlage' LXX read בֹּתְרֹת or its singular.

Of the following words in MT מִמַּעַל means 'above,' 'on top of,' and sometimes 'from above.' It occurs almost 30x in OT (see *HAL*, s.v. מעל II). The word מלעמת is a combination of מִן and לְעֻמַּת. The latter occurs as preposition in OT in 2 main senses: (1) 'close by, beside'; (2) 'corresponding to' (see *HAL*, s.v. עֻמָּה*). The combination only occurs here and is also taken to mean 'near' etc. (cf. Stade §378a). The word עָמָּה* is read by Meyer §116.2, as 'Verbindung' (see also *HAL* s.v.). Gray, 184, n., suggests changing the second *mem* into a *beth* and reading מלעבת. This is no real improvement, however, and so Gray himself points out that our word only occurs in P. This could mean that our verse is a later (P) expansion (cf. also Burney and others). If one were to try to translate the word it would be best to stick to the meaning 'near(by).'

The word בטן, which also occurs in other Sem. languages, is often used in OT for 'belly.' The only time the word occurs in our books, it is a technical term which can be translated as a 'protuberance' or 'swelling' on a capital or pillar (*HAL*, s.v.). Where is this 'swelling' to be located? Montg.-Gehman, for example, translate 'globe-top' and, like many others (see e.g. Busink, 304ff.), see a connection with the word גֻּלֹּת in vss. 41f., which means 'basins,' 'bowls' (see there). W. Kornfeld, *ZAW* 74 (1962), 55, believes, that the temple pillars were crowned by 'horizontale Scheiben bzw. Becken' and this was the idea conveyed by the word גלת. Also Busink, 305, n. 525a, sees similarity between בטן and גלת, and translates the word by 'Wulst,' 'swelling,' 'bump.' Gray's view also deserves attention. He proposes linking בטן with בָּטְנִים, a kind of nuts: 'a nutlike bulbous protuberance above the lower part of the capital,' or – still another of his proposals – the flat dish which catches the ashes from above a grating. These 2 not very plausible suggestions tend towards what Robertson Smith, *Religion*, 487f., remarked about our bronze pillars: altar candleholders also represented on depictions.[7] All this, however, is hard to infer from the word בטן. Also dubious is Noth's remark that the execution in vss. 41f. fails to match the design in our verse. But whatever reconstruction people choose for בטן (see e.g. that of Vincent and Busink in Busink, 300f.; also Burney, 89), it will (presumably) pertain to a 'swelling' of (or between) the pillar and the capital.

But this is not the end of the difficulties. What is the meaning of אשר לעבר שבכה (*k*ᵉ*tib*) or השבכה (*q*ᵉ*re*)? As for the first 2 words, have they 'probably come down in an erroneous tradition' (Noth)? We already encountered the word עבר earlier (see 4:12; 5:4). It often means 'side,' 'rim,' 'shore.' But is it perhaps a technical term here (so, with a question mark, *HAL*, s.v.)? The ancient versions do not help us. Pesh., for example, translates מלעמת by *mn lwqbl* and our word by *dlwqbl*; it is followed, as far as the first word is concerned, by Tg., which in Aram. leaves the second practically untranslated. Vulg. has *iuxta* and *contra* respectively. LXX^(B*), finally, reads: καὶ ἐπάνωθεν τῶν πλευρῶν ἐπίθεμα τὸ μέλαθρον τῷ πήχει, where, on the basis of the MSS, πήχει can better be read as πάχει. LXX says something like this: above

---

[7] Cf. P.L. Garber, "Reconstructing Solomon's Temple," *BA* 14 (1951), 2-24; esp. 9f.

the sides (!, צָלְעוּחֹ in place of מלעמת?) was a capital which served as a cover by its thickness. LXX^A omits the last 2 words. Are the words τῷ πάχει, which occur in LXX^{B, Luc.} and some other MSS, really the translation of אשר לעבר? It is not likely. LXX presumably found another word in its 'Vorlage'. Did it perhaps find the word עבי in place of עבר, a word which is sometimes a translation of πάχος (cf. vss. 24, 26; 2 Chr. 4:17; Job 15:26; Jer. 52:21)? Even if this emendation were textcritically defensible, it would still not help much to bring clarity to the text. Noth cannot imagine what is meant by the words: 'also above (i.e. those capitals) there was by the swelling, which was on the one side, a network.' Every other combination of words – though grammatically permissible – in our opinion obscures the meaning even more. Our attempt at translation can at best be viewed as a confirmation of what had already been said in vs. 17. But by that very token vs. 20a makes itself a more concealing than revealing gloss. In combination with vss. 41f., Busink, 307ff., for example, assumes that the words refer to a 'swelling' of the capital, over which there has been laid a separate network (שְׂבָכָה), furnished with tiny hooks from which the pomegranates could be hung (cf. his reconstruction: p. 301). But he himself frankly acknowledges the hypothetical nature of this reconstruction.

The second part of our verse is missing in LXX*. It speaks of the 200 pomegranates which were hanging in rows around the capital. According to 2 Chr. 3:16 (also cf. Jer. 52:23), there were only 100 pomegranates which had been attached to the 'festoons.' Now the word טרים is as such rather strange in our verse. Pesh. inserts the numeral 'two' before 'rows' (except 9 a1*fam*), so that one gets 2 rows of 100 pomegranates each, a clear assimilation to what is reported in vs. 42. In addition, Pesh. makes our text less refractory by, after speaking about 'the one capital,' adding: 'and so also for the other capital.' But in this matter it is not supported by Tg. and Vulg. (plus LXX^A etc.). We must, accordingly, not follow this resolution of textcritical problems but note that also in this second part the hand of a glossator or compiler is visible. טרים need not, as has been proposed (see textcr. app. *BHK*), be deleted, but can be regarded as an independent pointer to quality. That we are finally dealing with *two* rows of pomegranates is also reported by Josephus, *Ant.* III §78.

Hoogewoud, 96, has rightly underscored the importance of the pomegranates. After all, they are among the characteristic fruits of Canaan (cf. Num. 13:23; Deut. 8:8). The fruit is one of the country's fertility symbols and the pillars adorned with these apples could be stylized pomegranate trees, Canaanite fertility symbols, set in an Israelite framework. In Israel's 'Umwelt' various portrayals have been found in which pomegranates are depicted. Rather well-known is the tripod from Ras Shamra with its rounded top on which pendants in the shape of pomegranates are hung (*ANEP*, pl. 588; also cf. pls. 30, 344, 589, 631 and 632). It is therefore unlikely that רמון in our verses, as M. Görg,

BN 13 (1980), 20f., suggests, is directly related to the Egyptian word *rmn*, 'pillar.' From a symbolic viewpoint, the 'pomegranates' are entitled to an important place on the pillars, whose names are made known in the following verse.

7:21 *He set up the pillars before the front hall of the temple. He set up the pillar on the right and called its name Jachin; and he set up the pillar on the left and called its name Boaz.*
Now follows mention of the placing (קום) of the 2 pillars לאלם ההיכל, by the front hall of the main sanctuary, the first one to the right called Jachin, the second to the left called Boaz. Aside from the fact that our verse again occupies a rather strange – and therefore from a literary-critical viewpoint suspect – place in our pericope as a whole, there is not much to say either about the text-critical aspects, nor about its historical reliability. Textcritically one can at most refer to the somewhat nuanced orthography of the names of the pillars in LXX and Josephus, *Ant.* VIII §78. The latter reads Ἰαχείν and Ἀβαίζ; for the former it is suggested the reader looks up (the textcr. app. of) Brooke-McLean-Thackeray. A striking feature, as far as LXX is concerned, is that the par., 2 Chr. 3:17, translates the names of the pillars by Κατόρθωσις and Ἰσχύς. In the course of time, despite the rather clear intentions of our verse, many authors have written about the place, significance, form, and background of these pillars. A comprehensive discussion of the theories developed would take a separate monography. We can refer the reader to the lengthy and thorough discussion of these facets by Busink, 309-321, Noth, and Meyers.[8]

With Noth we must assume that the pillars were freestanding and did not have a weightbearing function (see also comments on vs. 19 above). They were probably set up before the front hall. 2 Chron 3:17 reads על־פני in place of the preposition ל of our verse. The placement is 'to the right' and 'to the left.' Now these 2 concepts can also mean 'to the south' and 'to the north' in OT (see, e.g., *HAL*, s.v. יָמִין, 4; J.A. Soggin, H.-J. Fabry, *TWAT*, III, 661). These indications are naturally geographically determined and independent of the position of the spectator. But is this the intent of our verse? When we, with many other exegetes (Benzinger, Kittel, Volz, Barrois, Parrot, Albright; see L.A. Snijders, *OTS* 14 [1965], 214f.) assume a W-E orientation of the temple, then, from the point of view of a person standing in the front hall of the

---

[8] C.L. Meyers, "Jachin and Boaz in Religious and Political Perspective," *CBQ* 45 (1983), 167-178; see now also M. Görg, "Jachin und Boas. Namen und Funktion der beiden Tempelsäulen," *Aegyptiaca-Biblica. Notizen und Beiträge zu den Beziehungen zwischen Ägypten und Israel* (Ägypten und Altes Testament 11), Wiesbaden 1991, 79-97.

temple, and therefore looks E, 'right' coincides with 'to the south' and 'left' with 'to the north.' But was this the orientation of the temple (on this point, cf. Snijders, 214-234)? The strongest argument in support of this viewpoint could be derived from vs. 39 (see there). To Snijders, 220, and – following him – to Busink, 252, n. 320, it has to be granted that Jachin, for example, is no more than a pillar 'to the right,' 'c'est-à-dire vue de celui qui se trouve à la porte en regardant à l'extérieur, comme le bâtiment lui-même "regarde" dans une certaine direction.' Even if the temple were positioned, say N-S, one could still say about the placement of the pillars vis-à-vis the temple exactly what we now read in the text. Conversely, one may certainly not assume a N-S placement of the pillars in order to infer a W-E orientation of the temple, although this last feature is, in our opinion, probable. In other words: though it is probably correct to say that Jachin is the southern and Boaz the northern pillar, it cannot be directly inferred from the text. It is striking that LXX* abstains from mentioning the 'right' and the 'left' and only speaks of the 'one' and the 'other' pillar (cf. also Busink, 312).

Now what is the meaning of 'Jachin' and 'Boaz'?[9] Ewald (*GVI*, III, 323f.) was of the opinion that these pillars were named 'nach damals beliebten männern, vielleicht jungen Söhnen Salomos' and he is amazed (in an added note), that exegetes can look in these 2 pillars 'auf gut Rabbinisch' for a figurative sense (cf. also S. Yeivin, *PEQ* 91 [1959], 21f.). It is true that in antiquity buildings could be named after persons, but Ewald's opinion takes no account of the background and purpose of the pillars. Another opinion is that of another grandmaster of the historiography of Israel from the 19th century, Renan, who comments that it is not impossible that the 2 names were engraved upon the pillars by Phoenician metal workers 'comme des *graffiti* talismaniques': 'Que [Dieu la] fasse tenir droite par (sa) force'.[10] Now it is nowhere stated that the names were written on the pillars. Our text only says: 'he called its name ...' Still most scholars simply assume that the names were engraved. Scott thinks that the names were derived from 'the initial words of dynastic inscriptions like that of Gudea'. The first pillar may have borne an inscription like 'He will establish ($yāk\hat{\imath}n$) the throne of David forever,' the other an inscription like 'In the strength of ($b^{e\,}\bar{o}z$) YHWH shall the king rejoice'.[11] Others, be it with the usual corrections, have followed Scott (cf. in Busink,

---

[9] For an overview, cf. also H. Bergema, *De boom des levens in Schrift en historie*, Hilversum 1938, 452-458; also see my "Die Bedeutung von Jachin und Boaz in 1 Kön. 7:21 (2 Chr. 3:17)," *Tradition and Re-interpretation* (Fs J.C.H. Lebram, ed. J.W. van Henten et al.; Studia Post-Biblica 36), Leiden 1988, 19-26.

[10] E. Renan, *Histoire du peuple d'Israel*, II, Paris 1889, 143.

[11] R.B.Y. Scott, "The Pillars Jachin and Boaz," *JBL* 58 (1939), 143-149; cf. *IDB*, II, 781; cf. also Albright, *ARI*, 1953, 139.

311). The form יָכִין, and – according to some MSS of LXX – יָכוּן, is presumably an impf. qal of the verb כּוּן, 'he establishes,' 'he is established' (cf. K. Koch, *TWAT*, IV, 96f.), while בְּעֹז can mean 'in him is strength'. For the different interpretations cf. also W. Kornfeld, *ZAW* 74 [1962], 51f.; cf. esp. the possibility of reading Boaz as *Ba'al-'az* (so. Greßmann, *Lade*, 62, n. 72; J.A. Montgomery, *JQR* 25 [1935], 265, et al.). It is not surprising that these 2 names, which as such are not unclear, have prompted exegetes to think of either a combination of the 2 words or of 2 shorter or longer sentences of which the 2 words formed the beginning or the core. The door to speculation and frequently very divergent opinions is always open. Before ending with a *non liquet*, which however in such situations is never inappropriate, we do still wish to attend to a couple of aspects which arise from the text and the context.

In the first place, we must hold on to the accent which the phraseology of our text puts on the verbs קוּם and קרא, 'set up' and 'name,' perhaps even 'call upon' (cf. Ps. 86:5; 99:6, etc.). The reference could therefore be to cultic activity. In the second place, it is noteworthy that the pillars Jachin and Boaz occur only by the Solomonic temple and evidently served as pagan symbols (so, correctly, Busink, 317f.). If then we are dealing with 'pagan' symbols, we can hardly avoid thinking of Canaanite or Phoen. influence (Renan, with his comment, was on the right track). Or to put it in the words of Kornfeld, art. cit., p. 53: 'Die Geschichte Israels rollte aber nicht im luftleeren Raum ab, sondern zeigt vielfältige Wechselbeziehungen zu den übrigen Völkern und Kulturen des alten Orients.' The possibility of considering Egyptian influence (obelisks), or that of Mesopotamia (ziggurats) or Arabia (*ansâb*) or even the Egyptian *dd*-columns as symbols of 'durability' (Kornfeld, 56v.) remains. We, however, are inclined to look to an area closer to Canaan. De Groot thinks here of neutral 'entrance stones' (also in the case of 2 Kgs. 23:8).[12] But we agree with Kornfeld and others that our pillars, like the 'masseboth,' belong to the 'primary symbols of mankind' and in this connection are not as innocent as 'entrance massaboth.' In Israel and its 'Umwelt' the veneration of stones was practiced from ancient times (Cf. Stade, *GVI*, 456, 460; Robertson Smith, *Religion*, 200-212).[13] When Lucean of Samosata (± 120-185 CE), in his well-known little book *De dea Syra* (a work the authorship of which has often been denied him), in his usual lively manner describes the temple and worship of the 'Syrian goddess' at Hierapolis (Mabbugh) in NE Syria, he at a given moment also mentions: καὶ φαλλοὶ δὲ ἑστέασι ἐν τοῖσι προπυλαίοισι δύο κάρτα

---

[12] J. de Groot, *Palestijnsche Masseben (Opgerichte steenen)*, Groningen 1913, 42, 93.

[13] See now also T.N.D. Mettinger, *No Graven Image. Israelite Aniconism in Its Ancient Near Eastern Context* (ConB OT 42), Stockholm 1995; and J.C. de Moor, "Standing Stones and Ancestor Worship," *UF* 27 (1995), 1-21.

μεγάλοι, ἐπ' ὧν ἐπίγραμμα τοιόνδε ἐπιγέγραπται: 'Τούσδε φαλλοὺς Διόνυσος Ἥρῃ μητρυιῇ ἀνέθηκα.' He is obviously writing about 2 'very large' phalluses in the front hall of the temple, on which were inscribed the remarkable words: 'I, Dionysius, have erected these phalluses for my stepmother Hera.' Although in a much later period and in another area of the ancient Near East than Jerusalem's temple scholars have distrusted Lucian's playful comments, it is nevertheless remarkable that he wants to designate the 2 pillars in front of the Hierapolitan temple as phallic cult symbols. For that reason the comment by Eerdmans is not as reprehensible as it has seemed to many: 'The phallic nature of both pillars is expressed in this case by the names "he establishes" and "in him is force"'.[14] He does immediately add, that in Jerusalem they later probably had no other significance than stylistic ornaments (C.L. Meyers, *CBQ* 45 [1983], 178, thinks the pillars indicate 'the historic passage of Yahweh ... into the earthly counterpart of his cosmic dwelling'). On this point Eerdmans is bound to be right, though it is a question how this 'later' has to be interpreted. In any case, in the context of the erection of Solomon's temple, which was in part a reconstruction of an earlier shrine of Canaanite signature, the pillars had a more-than-stylistic value: they were cult symbols derived and taken over from Canaanite Phoenician cult practices (cf. Pedersen, III-IV, 243 and n. 2 [688f.]). Striking is the verbal content of our verse: he (the 3rd p. sing. presumably refers to the royal priest) set up, erected. This is repeated 3x, while it is twice emphatically stated: 'he called its name.' It is usually assumed that at that moment he *gave* the pillars their names, but the Hebr. expression equally permits the translation: he *called* its name, viz. the name the pillars already bore at that moment, although now the reference was to the newly fashioned pillars in front of the new temple (cf. for קרא with שֵׁם, C.J. Labuschagne, *THAT*, II, 671). The *names* of the pillars, which probably (originally) had a phallic significance, were Canaanite (Cheyne, *CB*, thinks they were consecrated to N Arabian gods). It is natural to maintain the originally phallic significance of the words Jachin and Boaz. As for יכין, it is important to note *KTU* 1.17.I:25f. (part of the Ugar. Aqhat-legend). Baal requests progeny for Danel from El, asking for the blessing of children in these words: *ykn bnh bbt šrš bqrb hklh*, 'that he may establish a son in his house, a root (scion) in the midst of his palace' (cf. ll. 43f.; Gibson, *CML*, 104f.). The form *ykn* of *kn* or *kwn*, in this shorter form (the longer form is *knn)*, is frequently taken as a generally Sem. word for 'be' (cf. Gordon, *UT* 19, 1096, and 1213; Aistleitner, *WUS*, no. 1335; *DLU*, I, 219), but can of course be equally well translated as 'establish' and even 'beget.' The latter rendering even yields better sense. The word בעז has a masoretic vocalization in MT.

---

[14] B.D. Eerdmans, *The Religion of Israel*, Leiden 1947, 64.

The word contains a preposition בְּ with a form of the verb עז. This verb, too, occurs in the Ugaritic; for example, KTU 1.6.VI:17, 20: mt. 'z.b'l, 'z, 'Mot is strong (potent), Baal is strong' (Gibson, 80). Underlying this word, too, is the longer root 'zz (Gordon, UT 19, 1835; DLU, I, 96). It is not improbable, therefore, that originally ykn and b'z were the opening words of a sentence which to us modern people voiced the salacious, to the then-living cultic person the phallic function of 'erecting' the 'pillars.' It is hard to trace whether Solomon (re)cited the literal text or a modified version of it when the pillars were 'erected.' Nor is it clear whether this text or the beginning words of it were inscribed on the pillars themselves. As reported above, Hoogewoud, 96, rightly referred to 'the pomegranates which were attached to the capitals in such impressive numbers.' The new feature present in the original phallic symbols may have been that as stylized pomegranate trees the pillars symbolized fertility in a more 'Israelite' manner. The original sentences beginning with ykn and b'z were then perhaps adapted to these circumstances. Fact is that the pillars did not survive the first temple anymore than, say, the 'bronze serpent' survived it. The Canaanite character of the fertility symbols was probably still too strong.

Concluding the discussion of our verse let us merely report that Busink, 317, following in the tracks of K. Galling, BRL^1, 518, views the pillars mentioned in our verse 'für die Standarten des Tempels, welche besagten, daß der Tempel das Haus Jahwes, nicht des Ba'al, Moloch, usw. war.' In the reconstruction of the capitals (see fig. 75, p. 301) he sees resemblance to a candelabrum, the later symbol of Judaism. With a reference to Zech. 4:1ff. by Möhlenbrink[15] he considers the pillars 'als stilisierte Leuchter' to be 'Symbole Jahwes.' The objection to this and similar views is, in our opinion, that later 'Yahwistic' interpretations are projected into the time when these pillars originated in front of this temple.

7:22 *Upon the tops of the pillars was a pattern of lilies. Thus he completed the work of the pillars.*
The first part of this verse, which is lacking in LXX*, is an almost literal repetition of vs. 19. The second part is an (editorial) comment to conclude the making of these 2 unique pillars, a comment which, according to Noth (and others), fits better after vss. 41f. than at this location. These people are probably correct. In any case the rather messy character of the diverse data contained in our chapters has once again been underscored (for the verb תמם, cf. comments on 6:22 above).

---

[15] K. Möhlenbrink, "Der Leuchter im fünften Nachtgesicht des Propheten Sacharja," *ZDPV* 52 (1929), 257-286.

7:23 *Then he made a basin of cast metal, ten cubits from rim to rim; it was altogether round; it was five cubits high and a line of thirty cubit measured its circumference.*

Corresponding to 2 Chr. 4:2-5, one finds in the vss. 23-26 of our chapter a description of the so-called 'molten sea,' a basin of cast bronze and considerable girth. Josephus, *Ant.* VII §79, thinks that this bronze basin was called a 'sea' on account of its large size and capacity: ἐκλήθη δὲ τὸ χαλκούργημα θάλασσα διὰ τὸ μέγεθος. The explanation of this name and the function of this basin, however, as we will see below (under vs. 26), must rather be sought on the symbolic-cultic level. It is striking that in 2 Chronicles, preceding the part that is par. to our verses, there is the statement that Hiram made a bronze altar 20 cubits in length, breadth, and height. Since this brief factual notice in 2 Chr. 4:1 is confirmed rather than contradicted by texts like 1 Kgs. 8:22, 64; 9:25 and 2 Kgs. 16:14, it would seem that Rudolph's conclusion is warranted, that this statement has dropped out in our book as a result, for instance, of *homoeoarcton* of ויעש. Wiener, *Altars*, 14, correctly comments that if the Chronicler had been free, based on the sources he employed, 'he would have made David's construction in Araunah's threshing floor the altar of burnt offering *par excellence* for the whole pre-exilic period in accordance with the view he takes in 1 Ch. xxi 26, xxii 1. That he has not done so is strong evidence that he found the altar of bronze in some document he was using.'

Here the 'bronze altar' need not detain us, because elsewhere in this commentary there will be an opportunity to revisit the subject. De Groot, *Altäre* even assumes the existence of two altars in the temple court (against this view, cf. Wiener, *Altars*, 31f.; Rudolph, 207, n. 1). In our verse, we read that the 'bronze sea' was made by Hiram in terms of specific measurements. The word מוצק, already mentioned in vs. 16 as a technical term meaning 'cast bronze,' can be taken as a hoph. part. (so, e.g. *HAL*, s.v. יצק), but it can also be viewed as a noun (cf. BL, 490d; vs. 37; Job 38:38; Sir. 43:4), although the first possibility is more obvious (cf. also König §334m). In LXX[A, B, Luc] this adjective is lacking. Calculated from rim to rim (שפה, cf. comments on 5:9 above) its length was 10 cubits, to which is added that the basin was round in shape. Apart from here in this verse (and in the par. 2 Chr. 4:2), עגל also occurs in vss. 31, 35 and 10:19. Noth and others assume, that we are dealing with a term for a round and 'flat bellied vessel,' 'also nicht zylindrisch' (Metzger, *Königsthron*, 300: 'ringsum abgerundeter, auch außen umgebörtelter Rand der Öffnung'). Added to this is that the height (or depth) of this basin amounted to 5 cubits, while finally a measure for the entire circumference is given. To this end the word קָו (*qᵉre*) or קָוֵה (*kᵉtib*) is given. As 'measure' or 'line' this word occurs 13x in OT (aside from here and 2 Chr. 4:2 also 2 Kgs. 21:13; Isa. 28:17; 34:11, 17; 44:13; Jer. 31:39; Ezek. 47:3; Zech. 1:16; Ps. 19:5; Job 38:5 and Lam. 2:8; cf. תִּקְוָה in Josh. 2:18, 21) and is sometimes considered a derivation from the Akkad. *qû* (but see C. Westermann, *THAT*, II, 619). Hence a line of 30 cubits gave the circumference of the basin. Before we enter further upon a discussion of the measurements, shape, and capacity of the basin, let us say that LXX (minus Luc.) reads συνηγμένοι (LXX^Luc.: συναγωγη) and that 33 cubits. The word συνηγμένοι (a pf. pass.) refers to that which is drawn together at the extremities (cf. Liddell-Scott, s.v. [1691f.]). Schleusner (V, 177) believes that the LXX translation is determined by the fact that *in mente habuerunt notionem primariam* coniunctionis *et* collectionis, *quam habet qāwā*.' In any case LXX clearly intends to give the dimensions of the circumference. Both Pesh. and Tg. use the word *ḥûṭ*, in MT used also in vs. 15 (see above), but in MT it is non-synonymous with קוה (otherwise: Montg.-Gehman). The words *ḥûṭ* of Pesh. and Tg. and *resticula*, 'little string,' of Vulg. create the impression that people thought the basin was really surrounded by a thread, though MT's intent is to indicate that the measurement of the circumference was 30 cubits.

Aside from commentaries, much has also been written in separate articles about the measurements, shape, and content of the basin.[16] Zuidhof proceeds from the 'royal' or 'temple cubit' (51.8 cm.) and not from the 'ordinary cubit' (44.4 cm.). He takes into account the 'handbreadth' of the metal mentioned in vs. 26. His calculations lead to the result 'that the molten sea was a circular cylindrical vessel with a volumetric quality equal to 7,200,000 cubic fingers for all practical purposes' (art. cit., p. 183). One of Zuidhof's conclusions (incidental to our commentary, but interesting nevertheless) is that π (the so-called Ludolphic number named after Ludolf van Ceulen) must have had a value of 3.136 in ancient Israel (today: 3.1415926536). Essentially, however, the result of Zuidhof's study is not that different from Noth's simple remark, that one has to assume that the number 30 (of MT) and 33 (of LXX) 'nur ein Annäherungswert an die Zahl π zu Grunde liegt.' The one difference from Zuidhof is that Noth, in the measurement of the circumference, is thinking of the 'belly' of the basin, whereas Zuidhof – because he assumes a cylindrical shape – can think of the rim (cf. also Busink, 326ff.).[17]

7:24 *Under its rim were gourd-like ornamentations (ten cubits all around the basin). The gourd-like ornamentations were cast in two rows when the*

---

[16] So B. Spinoza, *Tractatus Theologico-Politicus*, Hamburg 1670, II, 22, already noted the mathematical inaccuracies of Solomon. Of the recent students of the subject we will still mention S. Yeivin, "Weights and Measurements of Various Standards in the Biblical Period," *Leš* 31 (1966f.), 243-250 (Hebr.), and A. Zuidhof, "King Solomon's Molton Sea and (π)," *BA* 45 (1982), 179-184.

[17] See now also R.C. Gupta, "The »Molton Sea« and the Value of π," *JBQ* 19 (1990f.), 127-135.

casting took place.
The reference in this verse is to the ornamentation of the basin. The word פְּקָעִים already occurred in 6:18 above (see there) as a term for 'gourd-like ornamentations' (also cf. Myres 1948, 36, n. 1). It is striking that the par. 2 Chr. 4:3 speaks here of דְּמוּת בְּקָרִים 'a kind of oxen' (see H.D. Preuß, *TWAT*, II, 277) or, according to Rudolph, דְּמוּת בָּקָר. Rudolph suspects that the Chronicler changed his 'Vorlage' text because to him the oxen were essentially 'unheimlich': 'sie erinnerten allzusehr an die heidnischen Stierbilder.' But Willi thinks that the Chronicler did not base his version on theological objections, but that the word פְּקָעִים was as unclear to him as it is to many modern exegetes (this despite a passage, which he himself cites, of F.C. Movers who opposes this thesis on the basis of the occurrence of the word in Tg. and in the Rabbinical literature).[18] Whatever the Chronicler's reason may have been (Thenius refers to: 'in Folge *verwischter Schrift*:' similarly Böttcher, *Neue Aehrenlese*, a.l.), LXX speaks about: ὑποστηρίγματα, 'supports'; cf. Myres 1948, 37: 'the small bracket handles supporting the rim of a vessel'; Schleusner here also tailors the meaning of the Greek word too much to that of the Hebrew when he writes: 'h.l. [i.e.: our verse] *globi instar cucurbitarum*'. Tg. on צוּרַת בִּיעִין, 'the shape of eggs'; Pesh. on *pqy''* (pl.), which, according to Payne Smith, can also be translated by 'support.' Vulg. refers to '*scalptura,*' 'carving.' As is evident from the conclusion of our verse, we are talking about gourd-like representations which, being cast in bronze, cannot of course have been carved out. These figures were located under the rim around the basin.

But, in this connection, what does עֶשֶׂר בָּאַמָּה mean? In the previous verse this expression denoted the diameter of the basin. The circumference of the basin is 30 cubits. Böttcher already pointed, out that the expression cannot mean 10 per cubit, because, grammatically, עֲשָׂרָה would then have had to be read alongside a masc. subst. According to Barthélemy, the idea of 10 gourds per cubit already occurs in Abrabanel and after him in any number of other interpreters. Kittel, following Stade, has proposed both in his commentary and in *BHK*² the emendation of 10 into 30 in order thereby to gain agreement with the circumference as indicated in the previous verse (cf. Burney). This conjecture has rightly been abandoned in *BHK*³ and *BHS*, inasmuch as not only all the ancient versions, but also the par. in Chronicles read '10 cubits.' Lacking indeed in LXX[A, B] is the redundant מַקִּפִים אֹתוֹ חִים. Since in this verse and in the broader context usually some form of סבב is used for 'surround,' the word נקף (hiph.), which occurs only here in the book of Kings (for other instances, cf. *HAL*, s.v.), we can with other exegetes safely regard these words as a gloss. Must we also regard the words עֶשֶׂר בָּאַמָּה מַקִּפִים אֹתוֹ חִים סָבִיב as

---

[18] T. Willi, *Die Chronik als Auslegung* (FRLANT 106), Göttingen 1972, 139.

such, as *BHK*, *BHS*, Noth and others suggest? This suggestion, though attractive, is also the easiest way out. Rashi and Kimchi represent a tradition which is also found in tractate BT Erubin 14b, viz. that Rami B. Jehezqel taught that the bronze sea was 3/5 rectangular, and that on the bottom, while the upper part (2/5 of the whole) was round. Barthélemy, who refers to this, also mentions that archaeological discoveries (mentioned by Noth under vs. 28) of the late Bronze Age have brought to the surface a number of basins, of which the support-structure was square while the basin itself was round. According to him it is not impossible, that also the 'molten sea' was constructed in that fashion. The translation of the words under discussion could read: 'on panels of 10 cubits they surrounded the sea.' If we keep the circumference of the square part at 40 cubits, this hypothesis would work well. But this does not resolve the question whether later copyists, who knew the tradition preserved in Erubin 14b, already put this gloss by the text or whether the later tradition, from a desire to do justice to the written text, was born from this (early) gloss. In other words, with Noth and others we nevertheless opt for the idea that the words are a (later) gloss.

The second half of our verse is lacking in LXX[B, Luc.]. It is stated that there were 2 rows of ornamental gourds upon or attached to the bronze basin (for טורים as predicate, cf. König §333a). And, as a detail, that they were יצקים ביצקתו. The word יצקה only occurs here in OT and – with Noth – denotes the action of casting the metal while the word מוצק indicates the product of it. The gourd-like ornamentations, therefore, had immediately been cast in this form when the basin itself was cast: truly a fine technical achievement (for metal working, cf. M. Weippert, *BRL*², 221ff.) Böttcher assuming the '10 cubits,' thinks that with 2 rows of gourds there will be 2x5 of them to a cubit (one gourd figure for every 4 square inches [so daß auf 1 פקע 4 Zoll fallen]), but such precise measurements cannot be drawn from the text.

7:25 *(The basin) rested on twelve oxen, three facing north, three facing west, three facing south, and three facing east. The basin was mounted on top of them, while the hindquarters of all (oxen were turned) inward.*

It is definitely not illogical when LXX[B, Luc.] places this verse after vs. 26, because precisely the latter verse forms a natural continuation of the preceding one. Still the order of MT must be quite ancient, because the par. part in Chr. also has it (2 Chr. 4:4). For this reason we will stick with the order of MT. In this verse the reference is to the support structure on which the basin rests, viz. 12 oxen, concerning which H. Grotius comments: *Hoc erat contra legem*. He refers to Josephus, *Ant*. VIII §195, who views this as the beginning of Solomon's sins.

Böttcher (*Neue Aehrenlese*), Thenius, Benzinger and others are of the opinion that for עמד, with which our verse begins, one would expect a further indication of the basin הים. But this is not necessary. LXX reproduced the active aspect of the beginning of our verse passively: καὶ δώδεκα βόες ὑποκάτω τῆς θαλάσσης. According to a couple of Hebr. MSS and the Sebir, supported by the par. 2 Chr. 4:4, שְׁנֵי is to be read as שנים. Perhaps in the case of שנים (and שתים) we are dealing with a *qᵉre perpetuum* שְׁנֵי (or שְׁתֵּי) and a *kᵉtib* שָׁנַיִם (or שְׁתַּיִם) (Stade §362b; Meyer §17.2). The 12 oxen were positioned in groups of 3 toward the 4 points of the compass, while the basin itself rested on the hindquarters of the oxen. Again not illogically, LXX^(B, Luc.) transpose the translation of the words והים עליהם מלמעלה after the last 3 words of MT. For מלמעלה, see vs. 11 above, and for a preceding על cf. Exod. 25:21. ביתה means 'inward' (cf. Exod. 28:26; 2 Sam. 5:9). Accordingly, the heads of the oxen were visible, while, according to Josephus, *Ant.* VIII §80, the basin rested like a ἡμισφαίριον on their hindquarters. From 2 Kgs. 16:17 one could conclude that the oxen were made of bronze. This assumption is also obvious. Noth and others think that the oxen were cast in a lying down position with their heads raised up (see fig. L.H. Vincent in Busink, 329). Busink, 331, objects to the idea, that the 36-ton basin rested on the hindquarters of the oxen themselves. This may have *seemed* so from the outside, but in reality the colossal structure rested on a stone base set squarely underneath it (fig. 77, p. 329). He does not consider this idea incompatible with 2 Kgs. 16:17. He – with many an other scholar – thinks that the images were done in 'Rundplastik,' having only a wooden core which was covered with bronze (p. 332). All this is possible, of course, but cannot with any certainty be reconstructed from the written sources.

7:26 *Its thickness was a handbreadth, and its rim was like the rim of a cup, an open lotus flower. It held two thousand baths.*
As remarked above, in LXX^(B, Luc.) this verse precedes the previous one. Next follows the translation of ועביו טפח of the first part of the verse, while in addition, in LXX^(B, Luc.), the description of the contents of the basin is missing. All this indicates that MT did not come into being without the labour of redactors and/or glossators, even if one is not inclined to deny to LXX a tendency to smooth things out.

עבי* is a word which only occurs here and in the par. 2 Chr. 4:5 and further in Jer. 52:21; Job 15:26 and 2 Chr. 4:17 (also cf. 2 Chr. 4:17 with vs. 46 מעבה below; further, on vs. 20 above, and for the form עביו in our verse cf. Böttcher §821; BL, 583v), and indicates the basin's 'thickness.' Well, the thickness of the metal of the basin – which is clearly what our verse has in mind – is a 'handbreadth.' In vs. 9 above we already found a pl. form of this word, though with a different meaning (other instances were mentioned there as well). With A. Strobel, *BHHW*, II, 1159, one can put a 'handbreadth' at 1/6 of the regular cubit, i.e. approx. 7.5 cm. Since the 'handbreadth' is equal to 4 'fingers,' it has sometimes been said (so Thenius among others) that the thickness of the pillars and that of the basin must have been the same (see on vs. 15 above and Jer. 52:21). This is a possibility which deserves consideration.

The rim of the basin resembles the rim of a cup. Of the more than 30x that כוס occurs in OT it only occurs here in the books of Kings (and in 2 Chr. 4:5 in the books of Chronicles). One can find the word already in the Ugar. and in other Sem. languages (see *HAL*); it denotes a shell-shaped drinking cup (H. Bardtke, *BHHW*, I, 208), which under certain circumstances can also be used as a magical or fortune telling cup (for the shapes of, for instance, ceramic shells, see U. Müller, *BRL*², 170f., 176f.). The rim of the basin was פרח שׁושׁן. For the last-mentioned word, see on vs. 19 above. The word פרח, aside from here and in the par. 2 Chr. 4:5, occurs in the books of Kings also in vs. 49 (17x in all in OT). The meaning is 'bud,' the bud of an opening flower. In Exod. 25:31-34; 37:17-20 etc. it is an ornament on the lampstand (see e.g. vs. 49). In our verse the word, in conjunction with the following one, denotes the bud of a lotus flower. That is what the rim of the basin looked like: a rim in the shape of a large opening flower. The petals of a lotus, after all, fold outward like a chalice. The question certainly is whether this is a description which only aims to portray how the rim of the basin folded outward (cf. R.B.K. Amiram, *Antiquity and Survival*, II 2/3 [1957], 197, fig. 32, and Myres 1948, 36) or whether it was the author's intent to indicate that this 'unfolding' rim really resembled a large lotus. The latter shapes have, for example, actually been found in excavations at Megidda (see Busink, 330). Busink thinks it possible to picture the decoration with lotus ornaments above the 2 rows of gourds. Again, the representation conveyed by the text is open to a variety of interpretations, even though we conceive פרח שׁושׁן as a predicate with שׂפתו. We think, accordingly, that the 'bronze sea' had the external shape of a gigantic lotus flower.

The text ends by indicating the internal capacity: 2,000 baths; in the par. 2 Chr. 4:5: 3,000 baths (so also in Josephus). C.C. Wylie, *BA* 12 (1949), 86ff., attempts to explain this considerable difference from the fact, that the basin mentioned in our verse was a hemisphere ($2/3 \pi r^3$) mistakenly calculated by the Chronicler as a cylinder ($\pi r^2 h$). In the case of 2 Chr. 4:5, however, Rudolph has demonstrated that what is going on here is an error in writing in the Chronicler. Aside from in this verse and in the par. 2 Chr. 4:5 the measure of capacity בת is also mentioned in vs. 38 and Isa. 5:10; Ezek 45:10-14 and 2 Chr. 2:9. R.B.Y. Scott, *BA* 22 (1959), 29, sees some connection with the homonymous בת 'daughter' and, in that connection, comments: 'one can speculate that it was about the capacity of the water jars carried from the well by the daughters of the household' (cf. Gen. 24:15, and the comment of Bagnani: 'In Egypt water for my workmen was brought by girls from the canal about a mile away in four-gallon petrol tins ...'[19] The בת is used as the main fluid measure; the אֵיפָה, on the other hand, as a dry measure, for solids and for grain. According to Ezek. 45:11, the 'ephah' and the 'bath' indicated the same measure of capacity and Ezek. 45:11 suggests a measure that is 1/10 of a bath: '1/10 of a bath from each כֹּר (for the measure of capacity, see comments on 5:2 above). Josephus, *Ant.* VIII §57, puts the content of a bath at 72 *sextarii* or *xestai*, i.e. 72 לֹג (Lev. 14:10-24), the smallest measure for fluids. But this is doubtful (see G. Schmitt, *BRL*[2], 205). In *PEQ* 73 (1941), 106-109, C.H. Inge reported the discovery in Tell-ed-Duweir (Lachish) of a fragment of a jar bearing the inscription: בת מלך, which he had earlier mentioned in *PEQ* 70 (1938), 253. Also stamps with only the phrase למלך on jugs are assumed to have indicated this measure of capacity (see the overview by D. Diringer, *PEQ* 73 [1941], 91-98, 104f.). Inge thinks that the bath of the preexilic period must have been considerably larger than that of Josephus's time. He even suspects 10 gallons (p. 109), about 45 1.[20] This measurement of capacity shows substantial difference from the specifications of scholars who studied this question before that time. Nowack (*Arch.* I, 204f.) and Benzinger (*Arch.* I, 193ff.) deem it to be 36,44 l; Galling (*BRL*[1,] 367f.) 39.3 liters; Barrois (II, 251f.)[21] arrives at 22.99 l. In addition there are still other indications of the content (see in Scott, 31f.) of the bath. Also a comparison with, say, the translation of בת by LXX yields little positive result, because LXX presents different translations with strongly divergent content among themselves (cf. Scott, 30).[22] Along with De Vaux, *Inst.* I, 308, we are inclined to say: 'Il est difficile que cette chaîne d'hypothèses conduise à aucune certitude' (cf. J.L. Mihelic, *IDB*, IV, 253). We will have to be content with an estimate and furthermore remind ourselves, that at different times also the word בת meant a varying content in relation to our liter. In the later Jewish literature one finds the Rabbinical rule, that 2,000 baths of fluid is equal to 3000 baths in dry measure (Krauss, *TA*, II, 392f.). But which estimate is the most plausible? With Busink, 327, n. 611, we agree that Noth's remark that the 'molten sea' could not have contained 2,000 baths is not to the point (cf. Bagnani, 114-117, who thinks of a pool of which merely the surface and the edge with its ornamentation was visible). Busink, by assuming that a bath is 23 liters, arrives

---

[19] G. Bagnani, "The Molten Sea of Solomon's Temple (1 R 7,23ss; 2 Chron 4,2-5)," *The Seed of Wisdom* (Fs. T.J. Meek, ed. W.C. McCullough), Toronto 1964, 114-118; esp. 115.

[20] For these stamps, cf. further S. Moscati, *L'Epigrafia Ebraica Antica 1935-1950*, Rome 1951, 83-98.

[21] Cf. the critical remarks of W.F. Albright on the 'royal bath' in *The Excavations of Tell Beit Mirsim*, III, AASOR 21-22 (1943), 58, n. 7.

[22] See E.C. Dos Santos, *An Expanded Hebrew Index for the Hatch-Redpath Concordance of the Septuagint*, Jerusalem 1973, s.v.

at 46,000 l. In this connection he assumes that the cubit is 50 cm and π 3. From the rest of his argument it is evident, that there is little that can be said about the shape of the 'sea' (cf. S. Yeivin, *EncMiqr.* V, 342f., who arrives at approx. 33,400 l). Admittedly important is the comment, that as an architect he considers the cast metal basin to be 'eine technisch mögliche Schöpfung' which was possibly 'aus Stücken gegossen.' The deviant measure of content in the Chronicler is to be explained either as an error in writing (Rudolph) or a later exaggerating interpretation of the Chronicler.

Still to be noted is that the impf. יָכִיל indicates a permanent property (König §157a; Bg. II §7b; GD §63, rem. 1; Driver §30). It is striking that this form of the verb כּוּל (hiph.) 'hold,' 'contain' (see *HAL*, s.v.) occurs altogether superfluously in the par. text in 2 Chr. 4:5, after, in the last-mentioned text, a precedent מַחֲזִיק (see Rudolph, a.l.).

Although the content and measurements of the bronze basin cannot be exactly converted into our metrical system, it is clear that the structure as a whole must have been a large and high object. According to 2 Chr. 4:6, the basin was meant for the priests to wash themselves in (according to Rudolph: to wash themselves *from*), hence a kind of swimming pool. But aside from the fact that it may concern a later interpretation here, it is a question whether in the case of so high a structure it was easily accessible to would-be bathers (Yeivin, *EncMiqr.* V, 343, assumes the presence of a stairway). Benzinger, *Arch.* 329, who notes this as well, thinks the basin corresponds to the basins at Babylonian temples and represents the heavenly ocean. In this connection the Akkad. word *apsû(m)* is often mentioned. It is a Sum. loan-word denoting a subterranean sweet-waterlake, 'ground water' and hence the water basin in the temples (cf. *AHw*, s.v.). Frankena reports, that the water basin set up in the temple in Assyria occupied an important place in the cult.[23] It is intended as a symbolization – serving cultic purposes – of the great *apsû*, the subterranean water area, which reaches from E to W. In the temple of *É-sag-íla* in Babel, we also find such an *apsû*. In this connection Frankena refers to our 'molten sea' in the temple at Jerusalem (cf. also Jeremias, *ATAO*, 543, and n. 1). It is not right for Benzinger and others to apply *apsû* to the heavenly ocean (so, correctly, Albright, *ARI*, 149), possibly with the additional assumption that the 12 oxen represent the 12 signs of the zodiac. Albright considers it likely that the 12 bulls are partly symbolic and partly decorative. As is well-known, the bull is linked, among others in Ugar. texts, with the fertility and rain god Baal, but it also occurs in connection with the life-bringing water of rivers (see Albright, 150 and n. 76). Albright, too, links the function of the 'molten sea' with the Mesopotamian word *apsû* (cf. also Mihelic, *IDB*, IV, 253). Most

---

[23] R. Frankena, *Tākultu. De sacrale maaltijd in het Assyrische ritueel*, Leiden 1953, 32f.

scholars, Busink among them (pp. 335f.), rightly believe there is a symbolic meaning underlying the bronze basin. Busink simultaneously assumes a practical use of the object, since, given a solely symbolic purpose, it would have been made lower and smaller. According to him, the temple service required the use of much water which, besides being supplied by rain, possibly came from the spring of Gihon (cf. also Kittel, *SHARG*, 236). Montg.-Gehman also assume that water of the basin served practical ends, in part to fill 'kettle wagons' or 'wheeled stands' which come up in what follows. They can point to various temple complexes in the area around the Mediterranean Sea and Mesopotamia where water reservoirs must have been present. Still we are of the opinion that the bronze basin was primarily, if not exclusively, intended for symbolic purposes, and, like the pillars Jachin and Boaz, stood and functioned in the pre-Solomonic El-temple at Jerusalem. One need not immediately associate the water reservoir – as symbol for waters underneath or above the earth – with Mesopotamia or Egypt, because temples with large water reservoirs have also been found in the Palestinian Canaanite-Phoenician world. Lucian of Samosata, for example, in his book on the Syrian goddess reports: Ἔστι δὲ καὶ λίμνη αὐτόθι, οὐ πολλὸν ἑκὰς τοῦ ἱροῦ, ἐν τῇ ἰχθύες ἱροὶ τρέφονται πολλοὶ καὶ πολυειδέες (*De Dea Syra* §45). He is referring to the temple of Hierapolis (Mabbugh), which he described and of which he had earlier expressly stated that it was situated on a hill (§28), so that it refers here to an artificial and, according to him, deep pool of water. Even though he expatiates at some length on the remarkable fish which are said to flourish in the pool, it is nevertheless clear that these and similar pools located by temples must originally have had symbolic significance, even though later perhaps the practical use of it predominated.

7:27 *He also made ten wheeled stands of bronze; each stand was four cubits long, four cubits wide, and three cubits high.*
With this verse the description begins of what has been called 'kettle wagons' or 'rinsing wagons' (Van Gelderen, Brongers), a description which continues to vs. 39. Striking again is the elaborate detail with which these wagons, which consisted of an undercarriage and water basin set in it, are described. This movable stand is not mentioned in par. passages in Chronicles. In terms of diction, word usage, and occasionally opaque sentence construction, this pericope – in the almost universal consensus of the exegetes – is among the most difficult parts of this chapter, even though archaeological findings resembling bronze undercarriages are frequently cited to help explain them. Familiar are the bronze standards of Enkomi and of Larnaka (Cyprus) (see the depictions in Burney; Benzinger, *Arch.* 219; Stade 1901, 152f.; the finding in the Zeus cave on Crete (Richter 1918, 2; Busink, 339) and the 'stand from Megiddo' (*ANEP*, pl. 587). Ewald, *GVI*, III, 333, already calls it remarkable

'daß man in unsern Tagen auch an manchen Orten Europa's solche eherne Kesselwäglein hohen Alterthumes ausgegraben hat welche mit den Salomonischen eine unverkennbare Ähnlichkeit haben.' Later he himself, prompted by a bronze 'kettle wagon' found near Peckatel (Mecklenburg; depiction in Stade, *GVI*, I, 338). Stade 1901, 145-190; Richter 1918, 1-34; Kittel, *SHARG*, 189-242; and Vincent, *Jérusalem*, 416-20, to mention only a few, have studied the 'kettle wagon' in great detail.[24] We will attempt to understand MT.

The word ויעש with which also this section begins, indicates that, by means of the Tyrian Hiram, Solomon had the following objects made. The extraordinary technical details and length of the description of these objects may indicate that people viewed these 'kettle wagons' as something special for this time; and further that such ingenious objects were the product of Solomon's חכמה, a category in which also this description finds its place. The word מכונה, which occurs approx. 25x in OT, is found some 15x in our chapter alone (further 2 Kgs. 16:17; 25:13, 16; Jer. 27:19; 52:17, 20; Zech. 5:11; Ezra 3:3; 2 Chr. 4:14 (2x) and as well as in Sir. 41:1; 44:6). In LXX the word is usually left untranslated: μεχωνώθ, while Tg. and Symm. give preference to בסיסה, *basis,* and βάσις resp.; Aq. prefers ὑπόθεμα and Pesh. *'agānā,* 'a large bowl.' The translation can read 'place' (Zech. 5:11), 'foundation' (Ezra 3:3) and, as in our chapter, 'undercarriage,' or 'Fahrgestell'; 'Kesselwagen' (*HAL*, s.v.; G. Fohrer, *BHHW*, II, 944) or 'Wagenkasten' (Richter, 6), where it must be remembered that the accent is more on the 'wagon' than on the 'kettle' (see Kittel, 205; Richter, 5f., also wants to keep the word for the whole [stand]). The *GNB* translates 'spoelkar' ('rinsing cart'), while Josephus, *Ant.* VIII §81, has λουτήρων βάσεις.

Of these undercarriages Hiram made 10 and that of bronze (for numbers following a prescribed word, cf. Ewald §290f; Ges-K §1341; König §334u; BrSynt. §85c, and for נחשת as second accusative indicating the material: König §327x). Our text cites as measurements: 4 cubits long, 4 cubits wide and 3 cubits high. LXX has somewhat different measurements: 5 cubits long, 4 cubits wide and 6 cubits high, and is supported by Josephus, *Ant.* VIII §81. It is hard to explain the difference at this late date. Thenius, for example, points to the possibility of an error in writing or an incorrect reading of the 'original' figures (characters) of the Hebr. 'Vorlage', but precisely the result of such an error in writing or interpretation in Böttcher, *Neue Aehrenlese,* shows, that in that case one can also end up with a very different result. Montg.-Gehman (also cf. Burney) go into another direction by referring to vss. 31f., where the top part and the undercarriage together make for 2 times a cubit and a half,

---

[24] For a lengthier bibliography cf. Montg.-Gehman, 174ff. and Busink, 337-352. See now also W. Zwickel, "Die Kesselwagen im Salomonischen Tempel," *UF* 18 (1986), 459-461.

which LXX is said to have added to the 3 cubits of our text to come to a height of 6 cubits. But this, of course, does not explain the one cubit difference in length. Kittel works rather extensively with this problem (pp. 205ff.). He comes to the conclusion that the whole 'Fahrstuhl,' wheels and carriage included, can never have been 3 cubits, an argument in which he also involves vs. 32 and vs. 35. If we were to subtract the cubits mentioned here from the 3 cubits, we would be driven 'zu einer starken Annäherung an Miniaturfiguren.' As the total height he also assumes a figure of 5½ to 6 cubits, allowing 3 cubits for 'das durch die Leisten bezeichnete Viereck' (p. 206). In this connection he makes no explicit mention of LXX. Nor is it likely that LXX followed the same reasoning to arrive at its figure 6. The most plausible solution is the assumption that LXX proceeded from another Hebr. 'Vorlage' on this point, at least if one does not wish to assume intentional exaggeration in LXX. The shape and contents of the basin and the wagon will be discussed in what follows.

7:28 *A wheeled stand was designed as follows: they were made of (vertical) panels and of (vertical) panels between the (horizontal) crosspieces.*
The word מעשה, which occurs in our chapter with some frequency (see vs. 8 above), denotes the thing that has been made or the manner of making it. We can translate it by 'construction' or perhaps also by 'model.' The model of the wheeled water basin or reservoir is described in what follows. LXX[A, B] and Pesh. read the plural of המכונה, for which, in light of the pl. suffix להם, an argument can be made. But then certainly the masc. form of the pl. suffix is strange here (so, correctly, Noth). From a purely grammatical viewpoint the construction is not correct (but that is also the case in what follows, see Montg.-Gehman). The intent of the sentence construction, however, is not unclear (otherwise: Richter, 10f.). The basins had מסגרות of 2 kinds (so, correctly, Noth): (1) 'ordinary' or 'general' ones; and (2) 'between the שלבים.' The second part of our verse, to be sure, is lacking in Pesh., but this is to be explained rather from an anxious desire for a good translation, than from textcritical considerations supposedly based on the lack of the text in the Hebr. 'Vorlage.'

The word מסגרת, in the sense of 'stronghold,' occurs in Ps. 18:46 (par. 2 Sam. 22:46); Mic 7:17, but also in Exod. 25:25, 27; 37:12, 24; 2 Kgs. 16:17 and further in our chapter as 'frame,' 'edge.' In this connection it is a question whether there is a close relation between the 2 meanings (see *HAL*, s.v.; Richter 1918, 7). LXX here reads: συγκλειστός, translated by Schleusner as *conclusus, iuncturis connexus.* Tg. here reads גדנפא 'edge,' 'frame,' as does Pesh. Striking is the translation of the Vulg.: *et ipsum opus basium interrasile erat*, i.e. the 'kettle-wagons' were finished in bas-relief (*interrasilis*). Based in part on the occurrence of the word in Exod. 25:25, 27 in MT, scholars also think here of 'frame' or perhaps better still 'panel' in the frame (Richter, 7: 'Verschlußplatte'; 'Seitenfeld'; 'Schild'; Vincent, *Jérusalem,* 416: 'panneau'; cf. S. Yeivin, *EncMiqr.* V, 343). The picture one forms is also dependent on the meaning of the word שלבים (cf. Olsh. §147c and Ges-K §20m before the word form), which occurs only in this and the following verse in OT (in association with the verb שלב [Exod. 26:17; 36:22]) and is usually translated by 'rung' (of a ladder), 'crossbar' (*KBL*). *KBL* refers to the Akkad. word *šulbū*, 'Türverschluß,' but Von Soden (*AHw*, s.v. [1267a]) indicates that the word (which, incidentally, he translates by 'ein Teil eines Riegels') is of unknown origin. LXX translates the word by ἐξεχομένα rendered by Liddell-Scott (s.v. ἐξέχω) as 'projecting panels.' Schleusner reports that many scholars translate שלבים by *prominentiae gradatae,* but he modestly adds: *qua obscura voce eminentias nescio quas innuere voluisse videntur.* Tg. uses a word which is identical to the Hebr. שליבא, which means the 'rung' or 'step' of a ladder (cf. also Krauss, *TA*, I, 35 and n. 420). One gets the impression that Pesh. did not really know what to do with our word. As already stated, the second half of our verse was not translated in Pesh. but in the following verse where שלבים occurs 2 more times, it is variously translated: once by *hᵉzāqā,* 'girdle,' 'edge,' 'bond' and once by *kᵉsāyā,* 'roof,' 'cover.' Hence the reference is to horizontal and vertical 'paneling.' Vulg. has: *et scalpturae inter iuncturas.* These terse indications in the Hebr. Text and in the ancient versions of the construction technique employed in making the 'wagons' leave a good deal open to conjecture. So some (Stade, Benzinger; see also Myres 1948, 38f. and Busink, 341f.) think that the שלבים are the vertical posts, between which the closing panels have to be located. One can find other views with Kittel, who has studied these problems at great length (pp. 211-218), concluding that, in line with the model of the wagon found at Larnaka in Cyprus, מסגרות signify 'die wagrechten Verschlußleisten, die mit den Pfosten zusammen das Viereck auf den beiden cyprischen Wagen ausmachen' (p. 213; cf. Stade 1901, 162; Richter, 7-11). He does not view 2 Kgs. 16:17 as an objection because, according to him, this text is disordered. He translates שלבים by 'Leitersprossen' (p. 215; so also Stade), which he also attempts to clarify by an example. These שלבים, he says, are rods placed slant-wise. A reconstruction of such a wagon as Kittel conceives it is depicted on p. 237 (fig. 44; cf. also Busink, 342). But Busink, 342f., is critical of Kittel's view of things and thinks, that שלבים only concern horizontal bars (cf. Vincent, *Jérusalem,* 418, n. 3). Set within the metal frame of the wagon were panels furnished with crosspieces. He offers a reconstruction of his view in figs. 81 and 82 (pp. 347f.). In this connection scholars also frequently refer to Josephus's description (*Ant.* VIII §§81f.), who tells us that the object was chased on all sides (κατὰ μέρος τετορευμένον) and closed off as follows (συνεκέκλειστο): there were 4 rectangular uprights (κιονίσκοι) on every corner, while the sides (πλευρά) of the wagon fit into the 4 uprights (hence every column held 2 panels at right angles to each other): ἐξ ἑκατέρου μέρους ἐν αὐτοῖς ἔχοντες ἐξηρμοσμένα). These panels were in turn divided into 3 sections (ἦν δὲ ταῦτα τριχῇ διῃρημένα), while on each of these sections there was a dividing strip (ὅρος) which ran to the bottom (ὑπόβασις). Busink – as against Kittel's view – is probably correct in saying that Josephus is not referring to surfaces lying one above the other, but to surfaces lying next to each other. Josephus did not so much have in mind a wagon consisting of a metal frame but a wagon having closed sides. Still the reference is to a description of the *framework* of a wagon which was furnished with panels and uprights. Noth thinks that the שלבים refer to vertical crosspieces between the top and bottom bars of the framework, 'vergleichbar den Sprossen einer auf die Seite gelegten Leiter.' The second half of our verse, according to Noth, tells us that also between these שלבים there were horizontal panels.

So against Klostermann, Vincent and others, and with Stade, Benzinger, Kittel, Busink, Noth and others, we are of the opinion that the walls were made of a metal frame and therefore not closed. With Montg.-Gehman, who also point to the occurrence of שלב in the so-called 'Marseille table of sacrifices' (*KAI* 69, 4, 8, 10; cf. *DISO*, s.v. it is often translated there by 'rib') we hold מסגרת to be the word for the vertical pieces of the framework and the שלבים for the horizontal ones. Montg.-Gehman therefore correctly comment: 'The stand was open within this frame of upright- and cross-pieces.'

7:29 *On the vertical panels between the crosspieces were lions, oxen, and cherubim, similarly on the crosspieces above. Below the lions and the oxen were wreaths of hammered metal.*
This verse describes the ornamentation of the rather broadly conceived frames of the 'chassis' of the 'kettle wagon.' As was made clear in the discussion of the preceding verse, we, along with many exegetes, assume that the undercarriage supporting the basin was not a closed chest with side panels (so e.g. Thenius), but a frame of rather wide panels on which, according to MT, lions, oxen, and cherubim were depicted. The word ארי, which, aside from here and in vs. 36, also occurs in our book in 10:19f., denotes an African lion (*HAL*, s.v.). For בקר, see comments on 1:9 above, and for כרובים our comments on 6:23. Josephus, *Ant.* VIII §82, has 'eagle' in place of cherubim, a fact which R.S. Rappoport (in R. Marcus, *LCL*, Josephus, V, 615, n. h) attributes to the influence of Ezek. 1:10 (cf. H. Grotius). The different depictions of the kettle wagon in the authors, who have made a special and lengthy study of these objects, show how these scholars have conceived these ornamentations (e.g. in Busink, 342, 345, and 347 for the reconstructions of Kittel, Vincent, and Busink respectively). These and similar reconstructions naturally include many uncertain elements. Noth has also called attention to the

fact that the preposition על could also mean, that the reference is to freestanding flat bronze figures, which had literally been put 'upon' or, perhaps even better, 'against' the frames, an idea for which he refers to miniature bronzes found at Enkami and Megiddo and to the Cretan findings published by Kittel, 194 (fig. 38). Although this idea has much that is attractive, we cannot say with certainty that this is how it was.

What follows raises the question whether כן is the anaphoric part. here or a noun.[25] LXX, Vulg. and Pesh. opt for the former possibility; Tg. for the latter. The word כן, translated by *HAL* (s.v. כן III) as 'Gestell' (base) and that of כיור, 'the basin,' occurs a number of times in Exod. (30:18, 28; 31:9; 35:16; 38:8; 39:39; 40:11) and Lev. (8:11) as well as in a somewhat difficult passage in the sequel (vs. 31, below). The context of our verses might be an argument for the second possibility, and there are translations which go into this direction, e.g. the LV: '... en op de sporten was een voetstuk van boven' ('... and on the rungs there was a base ...'; cf. also Keil; Vincent, *Jérusalem*, 416, et al.). But many commentators opt for the particle כן, in part because it is not until vs. 31 that there is any reference to 'pedestal' or 'base' (Thenius, Burney, et al.). Usually the *atnah* is moved from ממעל, so that one can read: 'and also upon the שלבים.' The connecting *waw* is then placed before ממעל, so that a new clause is started, which runs to the end of our verse (cf. also textcr. app. *BHK*). Noth, who also follows this change in accentuation and punctuation, nevertheless believes, that ועל־השלבים כן is an 'obvious addition', and in his translation therefore puts these words in brackets. Busink, 343, n. 652, takes still a further step and wonders whether ממעל should not then also be considered part of the 'addition.' We, however, think that nothing in our verse needs to be modified, not even the punctuation (*atnah*). What is said is that the upper cross-frames of the metal undercarriage similarly contained depictions of lions, oxen, and cherubim like the frames on the sides, but that at the bottom, as far as the lions and oxen were concerned, there were מעשה מורד ליות. But what do these last 3 words mean? Benzinger was very pessimistic about the recovery of the correct meaning of these words and declined any attempt at interpretation. The word ליָה* only occurs in the plural in our verse and in vss. 29 and 36 in OT, and scholars (e.g. S. Yeivin, *EncMiqr.* V, 343) often relate it to the Arab. *lawā*, 'wind,' 'twist' etc.; *layya*, 'turn' etc. (cf. also L. Kopf, *VT* 8 [1958], 181f. and n. 1 on 182). Often scholars see a connection with the word לִוְיָה*, which occurs in Prov. 1:9; 4:9 (conj. in 14:24) and means 'wreath' (*HAL*, s.v.). Bg. I §17f n., even believes that the latter form must be vocalized like the former, because the vocalization *liwyā* is to be viewed as an 'Anglei-

---

[25] For this, cf. also my "Die Partikel כן im Alten Testament" *OTS* 21 (1981), 201-227; esp. 205.

chung' to *liwyātān,* the 'wreath beast' (otherwise: Noth). However this may be, the difficulty of arriving at a correct determination of the meaning of the word is reflected in the ancient translations as well as in the commentators. LXX translates the last 3 words of our verse by: χῶραι, ἔργον καταβάσεως; Vulg. by: *quasi lora ex aere dependentia;* Tg. by: עוֹבַד כְּבוּשׁ מְדַבַּק, 'a joining together of pointing' (cf. Jastrow, s.v. כִּיבוּשׁ), while Pesh. speaks very freely about *ḥzw' 'bd' špyr'*: 'the appearance of the work was splendid,' a translation which is suggestive of the end of vs. 30, of which the last 3 words also present substantial translation difficulties (see there). Of the Vulg. translation it can be said, that it approaches the above-mentioned etymological derivation: 'straps,' 'reins,' 'girdles' (*lora*). From this translation and that of LXX it is clear that מורד has been linked to ירד. *HAL* does this too, though it should be noted that here the reference is to an unknown technical term. מורד further occurs as 'mountain slope' in Josh. 7:5; 10:11; Jer. 48:5 and Mic. 1:4, but it is obvious that this meaning is not to the point here. Usually scholars construe the last 2 words as 'hanging work' (e.g. Vincent, *Jérusalem,* 416: 'des festons pendants'), but Kittel, 220f., has already commented that this view, though possible, is not certain. He proposes to punctuate the word as מוּרָד and to derive it from רדד. This verb, which also occurs a number of times in OT in qal and hiph. (Isa 45:1; Ps. 144:2 and 6:32 above), means to 'pound,' 'flatten' (see comments on 6:32 above). Hence the meaning of these 2 words becomes as follows: 'Arbeit des Stampfens, Dünnschlagens, also geschlagene Arbeit Metallplättchen' (p. 221). The first word ליות can mean 'rosette', but also a 'Strickornament' (p. 235). In Kittel's translation, the second half of our verse then reads as follows: 'the lions and oxen had wreaths-hammered work.' Other exegetes adopted his view (Šanda, Montg.-Gehman, Noth, Gray; Richter, 12f. is opposed) and we too are of a mind to accept it.

Only we believe we do not have to regard the preposition ל before 'lions' and 'oxen' as a possessive dative: 'the lions (etc.) had ...', but as a connecting ל between the preceding preposition and its genitive (the same, for example, as in Gen. 1:7; see *HAL,* s.v. ל, no. 16). Beneath the ornamental lions and oxen (the cherubim have been omitted for reasons unknown to us) there were, at the bottom of the wagon, wreaths of hammered metal.

7:30 *Each wheeled stand had four bronze wheels and bronze axles. Its four pedestals had shoulderings under the basin, cast over against each of the wreaths.*

This verse is focused on the wheeled part of the kettle wagon. The beginning of our verse is clear: 4 bronze wheels with bronze axles. The word אופן occurs also in Exod. 14:25; Isa. 28:27; Nah. 3:2; Prov. 20:26 and Sir. 33/36:5, and with particular frequency in Ezek. 1 and 10. The word סרן is found only in our verse in OT, but it also occurs in the sense of axle (of a wagon) in a number of Aram. dialects, Syrian among them (Pesh.) The following phrase וארבעה פעמתיו is fraught with more problems. In the first place, as a result of the quite general rule of 'Sem. polarity' (in the case of numerals from 3 to 10 the fem. form is used when what is counted is masc., and vice versa, see Lettinga §39h), one has to assume that פעם is masc. here, though grammarians have pointed out exceptions to this rule (see König §312a). It is also possible (with e.g. Böttcher §719; Stade §336 and Olsh. §117.4) to assume a gender switch of the word פעם, when as here the word acquires a metaphorical meaning (cf. Michel, *Grundlegung*, 56: 'die ot-Plurale [bezeichnen hier] Artefakte'). However this may be, this deviation from a rather general grammatical rule has, in the second place, given rise to emendations of these words. So, for example, in Böttcher (*Neue Aehrenlese*; repeated in his grammar: §719, p. 514, nt. 2): וארבע הפעמת היו: 'and 4 feet were (or better: had) ...' (also cf. textcr. app. of *BHK* and *BHS*). Noth goes even further and views these words as 'ursprünglich eine wenig sorgfältige Randbemerkung,' which in translation should at the very most be bracketed. We are nevertheless of the opinion, that these words can be maintained, on the ground that neither textcritically nor contextually there is anything to be said against them. The word פעמות is also used elsewhere for 'bases' (Exod 25:12; 37:3; see *HAL*, s.v. and in the case of the 'kettle wagon' from Larnaka mentioned by Noth and many others it is clear how one can picture the 'feet' of the stand mounted on the axles (cf. Richter 1918, 16). The remarkable feature is not that these 'feet' are mentioned (they are virtually self-evident and could for that reason be omitted), but they had (להם) כתפת . The word כתף denotes 'shoulder,' but it occurs some 25x in connection with architectonic expressions (see comments on 6:8 above and R.D. Haak, *VT* 33 [1983], 273-278). Not implausible is the suspicion of Noth and others, that the reference is to the slanted rods, which served to support and reinforce the stand and at the underside of the connecting feet blended into the axles.

It is harder for us to imagine what is meant by the concluding words of our verse. The word כיור, which occurs 23x in OT, is used among other things for the bronze basin in Exod. 30:18, 28; 31:9 etc.; for the kettle in 1 Sam. 2:14, and even for a podium in 2 Chr. 6:13. In the Akkad. one finds the word *kiūru* (*AHw,*496a), a 'metal basin' which, according to Albright and others, is even of Sum. origin (see A.M. Honeyman, *PEQ* 71 [1939], 82 and n. 3; cf. Ellenbogen, *Foreign Words*, 84). Honeyman (see his fig. 12) is of the opinion, that the shape of a כיור can be seen 'in the broad handleless cooking pot of Early Iron I,' a wide open dish with a diameter of about 25 cm. LXX here reads ὠμίαι, 'shoulders,' 'corners,' which are located under the basins (pl.!). The rest of this verse and the following verses up to 32 למסגרות in MT is omitted by LXX[B, Luc]. Vulg. translates as follows: *et per quattor partes quasi umeruli subter luteram fusiles contra se invicem respectantes,* 'and on 4 sides stood as it were the fused shoulders under the basin over against each other.' Pesh. translates: 'the 4 corners were attached to it and there were shoulders under them, shoulders of cast (bronze), beautiful work.' Tg., finally, rather carefully follows MT but, in place of פעמים, reads (as does Pesh.): 'corners' זוויתיה, but translates the last 3 words of our verse by מְכַבַּשׁ עוֹבַד דְּבוּק, which could mean something like 'hammered (metal) joinery.' However divergent the translations – especially with respect to the last past of our verse – may be, it is clear that, in its overall form and word sequence, MT can be maintained. The first part of the second half of our verse can read as follows: 'The supporting shoulders were cast under the basin' (cf. also Busink, 344; Noth). The last 3 words give much more trouble, as is evident not only from the ancient versions, but also from the space left open in Noth's translation (see also Kittel, Benzinger, Stade, Kamphausen, Eißfeldt, and Vincent), and from the comment he added. These words seem to be related to כמער-איש וליות (סביב) in vs. 36. Šanda even puts this verse immediately after vs. 29 and justifies this action in part by saying that 'in vs. 30 die aus v. 36 dahingeratene unverständliche und verderbte Dittographie מעבר איש ליות' (is present). But according to him also כמער איש is 'totally obscure,' since he cannot do anything with the explanation of מער for 'nakedness' (from ערה) (which was accepted by others) and hence for 'empty space' (cf. Nah. 3:5 and also *HAL*, s.v.). In this connection Kittel, 224, n. 3, refers to the tractate BT Yoma 54a (*not* 55a), where the story is told, that when the Israelites went to the Festival, someone rolled up the curtain before their eyes, showed them the cherubim intertwined with each other, and said to them: 'Look! You are beloved before God as the love between man and woman ...' A bit further down in this tractate a question is raised concerning the meaning of כמער איש וליות, to which Rabbi son of R. Shilah replies: 'Even as a man embraces (לוייה) his bride (מעורה)' (Yoma 54a,b). Along with Kittel we are of the opinion that this interpretation in the Babylonian Talmud must not be followed. In contrast to Šanda's opinion Noth says, that in the cited words in vs. 36 there is clearly present 'eine Variante zu מעבר איש ליות' from our verse, which he also left untranslated in vs. 36. We are inclined to view Noth's view as more plausible than that of Šanda, because the latter is more likely. But by merely expressing this suspicion, we have not yet made much progress toward a solution. Stade 1901, 173, assumed, that מעבר איש and כמער איש could be 'verschiedene graphische Varianten derselben Phrase.' But what these words mean he leaves (after correctly rejecting Kittle's translation 'über Manneshohe') unsaid (in *SHARG*, 223f.; Kittel agreed with Stade and withdrew his translation in his commentary of 1900). In this connection it is advisable to note, as far as this can be done, the translations of the 2 expressions in the ancient versions. In our verse LXX[B, Luc.] as we saw earlier, omitted the words in question. In vs. 36 it reads: ἐχόμενον ἕκαστον κατὰ πρόσωπον ἔσω καὶ τὰ κυκλόθεν, 'having (every connection) inwardly and round about.' In addition to the reading of Vulg. we gave above, vs. 36 has: ... (*Cherubin* etc.) *quasi in similitudinem stantis hominis ut non celata sed adposita per circuitum viderentur:* '... as in the likeness of a standing man so that they seemed not to be hidden [i.e. cemented in], but placed around it in a circle.' Tg. in vs. 36 reads כיבש חר ומדבק סחור סחור, 'a fitting that was hammered down all around.' This translation comes closest to MT and to the translation of MT in our verse. In vs. 36 Pesh. gives no translation (it does of סביב = *kd ḥdr'*) but, as we saw already in vs. 29 above, also in our verse: '*bd' špyr'*, i.e. 'splendid work.' On the basis of a comparison of these translations it can be concluded that in our verse and in vs. 36 – as far as the words in question are concerned – Vulg. and Tg. had before them a text which hardly differed from MT, but that for them too, to use Stade's words, the same graphic variants of these words were present. From LXX one can hardly escape the conclusion, that either they did not see the words in question (in this form) or would or could not translate them. Pesh. had them before it only in vs. 29 and 30, but hardly in the form in which we know them now. Josephus, *Ant.* VIII §84, however, had something before him in vs. 36, since he read ὡς σύμφυτα ταῦτ' εἶναι δοκεῖν τοῖς ὁρῶσι there: 'that those who saw them might think they had naturally grown out of one piece.'

It seems to us the words in question were in fact graphic variants of an expression and that originally they occurred only in our verse. But which variant can claim to be the most original? S. Yeivin, *EncMiqr.* V, 344, thinks that מער־איש means 'opened out,' 'à jour,' which might fit in vs. 36, but not so well in our verse. If we proceed from our verse, a possible translation of these difficult words could be: 'over against each of the wreaths.' The word איש can indicate close connectedness (BrSynt. §74b), and therefore need not per se relate to 'man' or 'human being.' In our opinion, the (mutilated) words in vs. 36 (see there) are a later gloss. The fact that, grammatically, one would have expected the fem. form in place of איש, need not be a counterargument against our view, in a piece in which departures from the prevailing grammatical rules are so frequent. Further, in a later phase of the Hebr. language מעבר איש could have been a fixed expression.

7:31 *Its opening was within a crown which projected upward a cubit and a half. This opening was round: it was like a rest for a vessel [a cubit and a half]. At this opening also there were carvings [square, not round, were the panels (of the stand)].*

In this verse the upper part of the wheeled stand is somewhat further described. The word פה 'mouth' here refers to the 'opening' in or on which the water basin rested. On this point there is no disagreement among modern interpreters familiar with the models from Cyprus and elsewhere. But what is problematic is the masc. suffix (3 p. sing.) joined to the word. This can hardly refer to בְּיֹר in the previous verse, more easily to מכונה, but that is fem. This is why many exegetes (cf. also the textcr. app. in *BHK* and *BHS*) propose a modification of the text here. This is certainly defensible grammatically and preferable, but considering the grammatical anomalies in our context it is not 'airtight.'

The word מבית (see comments on 6:16 above) means 'within.' We have translated the following word כתרת in vs. 16 (see above) and the sequel by 'capital.' In connection with that verse Noth already pointed out, that actually what we are dealing with is a 'top piece' or 'crown,' a meaning which of course fits better here (cf. Richter 1918, 28f.: 'Aufsatz, der den Kasten krönte wie ein Knauf die Säule'). Although since Ewald it became almost self-evident for many exegetes to alter כתרת into כתפת (Klostermann, Stade, Kamphausen, Burney and others), this change is unnecessary (Montg.-Gehman equate it with [or read?] בֶּתֶר, 'crown'). The reference is clearly to the cylinder-shaped opening at the top of the wheeled stand, in which the basin or 'kettle' could be placed. This ridge jutted out at the top (ומעלה), as corresponding depictions from Larnaka, Enkomi, etc., show. How far this ridge extended, is not stated in our text. The word באמה occurs but the preceding numeral is missing. Pesh. and Vulg. (our text, after all, is missing in LXX[B, Luc.]), like Tg., read 'one' or 'a' but this only means that they too followed a 'Vorlage' of MT, which did not deviate, or hardly deviated, on this point from ours. The number one supplies depends partly on how one wishes to regard the 1½ cubit (for the article before אמה after חצי, cf. König §299d). Stade 1901, 176f., Burney and others view that 1½ cubit as something which later crept into the text. But this does not yet explain why in our case we would have to read 'one cubit,' all the more since in vs. 35 there is again mention of 'a half cubit,' even though this is perhaps a notice which originally came from another pen. Noth, on the other hand, views precisely the beginning of our verse 'as an addition.' Still another view comes from S. Yeivin, *EncMiqr.* V, 344. He thinks that at the top of the wheeled stand there was a round form, whose diameter was equal to the length of the wall of the stand and whose height was half a cubit. On that circle rested a crown in the shape of a truncated cone, of which the upper ridge was a little narrower than the basis, in order to prevent the basin from sinking away, due to the weight of the water, in the top piece. This would be the מעשה־כן of our verse. The whole design was 1½ cubits. Because of the fact, that the ridge of the top piece was a little narrower than the diameter of the circle, the ridge of the basin, which was placed in the top piece, rose a cubit above it. Because further the height of the top piece and the circle beneath it was about 2 cubits, one can assume, that the whole basin (3 cubits in all) had been placed above the level of the framework of the wheeled stand. The basis of this basin rested upon the supporting pieces, which had been put to the corners.

Obviously, that Yeivin attempts to take into account all the facts in our text, along with the stated measures. For that purpose, he comes to a round circle of half a cubit (cf. vs. 35), in our verse: כתרת; and to a top piece, resembling to a truncated cone of one cubit long, in our verse: מעשהדבן. Although not as clearly, also Montg.-Gehman move in the same direction, though the numbers differ somewhat. It is a question, however, whether it is legitimate to use the givens of our text (and those of other texts) in this fashion, so one can present a clear and coherent blueprint of a 'kettle wagon.'

Our text continues by saying that the opening is round (the suffix is right this time!) and immediately thereafter with מעשהדבן. In contrast to vs. 29 כן is rather generally regarded here as a noun: 'stand,' 'platform,' 'base' (cf. HAL, s.v. III), although both LXX^A and Vulg. suppose it is the anaphoric particle (Pesh. did not translate the word). Stade 1901, 177, views these words as a second predicate with ופיה (the first is עגל) and translates: 'ihre Mündung war rund, Gestellarbeit.' Then follows the mention of 1½ cubit. Striking again is that this verse is a chain of nominal sentences and phrases. This construction alone makes it problematic whether we can 'add up' all the givens of the text. On the other hand, it is also hard to determine which part is 'original' and which is based on a later insertion. To us it seems most probable to keep the 1½ cubit, but to move it forward, so that the opening rises 1½ cubit above the stand and the כתרת is described as מעשהדבן. But every proposed solution contains elements of uncertainty. We will return to these measurements later.

On the opening of the wheeled stand there were מקלעות. Already in 6:18 (see above) and 32 we encountered the word which we translated by '(wood) carving.' Klostermann, Benzinger, Richter, and others have criticized the translation, which assumed there were figures 'on the opening' ('denn auf dem offenen Munde können doch keine Figuren schweben' [Klostermann]), and proposed emendations here, without, however, convincing anybody by this method. It is after all entirely conceivable, indeed even probable, that also the opening was furnished with 'figures,' even though they were either engraved in the metal or as 'metal figures' put 'on' the opening. We have taken מסגרות, which occurs rather frequently in our pericope (see on vs. 28 above), to mean vertical frames or panels. Here they are called 'square,' a pual part. of רבע (cf. Ezek. 40:47; 45:2), which is closely related to the pass. qal part. which occurred in 7:5 (and 6:33) above. To what does the 3 p. pl. masc. suffix after מסגרת refer? To that question various anwers have been given. So B. Stade, in his first article (ZAW 3, [1883], 166) comments that it relates to פה and ידות (vss. 32f.), but he puts vs. 30b and 31 after vs. 36. He considers it a better solution to read מסגרותיו, in which case the suffix refers back to כן. Kamphausen relates the suffix to the מכנות, but Benzinger again to כן, and views the *mem* as a dittography (so also Kittel, 230). In his second article (1901, 178f.) Stade comments, that if the opening of the wheeled stand consists of a round cylinder, there can be no מסגרת of the opening. It also seems unlikely to him that the suffix relates to מכנה. Therefore, according to him, the last 4 words are 'keinenfalls eine Fortsetzung der Angaben über den פה der מכונה.' His conslusion is, that our verse from ומסגריהם on, as well as the following verse, constitutes a par. of the vss. 28-30 and that the suffix in our word refers back to the main notice, which broke off in vs. 27 (so e.g. also Vincent, *Jérusalem*, 416). Hence the last 4 words have nothing to do with the opening for the basin. Kittel, 228ff., also regards these words as a 'postscript' to the account of the panels. In contrast to the שלבים, which according to him were probably round rods, these were square. It cannot be denied that the 'uncoupling' of the last 4 words of our verse from the immediately preceding words, solves a number of problems posed by the text. If in addition one also changes the text, say כן into קן 'nest,' as Richter 1918, 32f., does, and transposes a number of words, one gets this translation: 'Und innerhalb des Aufsatzes (כתרת) war eine mundartige, ringsum runde, 1½ Ellen tiefe Öffnung, gleichsam ein Nest. Wohlgemerkt: Seine (des Aufsatzes) Öffnung war rund, seine Wandungen dagenen viereckig, nicht rund. Und auf seiner Oberfläche waren ebenfalls Ornamente.' But in our opinion, this undoubtedly ingenious, but very hypothetical modification of the text does not lead to a solution of the problem the text poses. The 'round opening' contrasts with the 'non-round' – expressly so called – but 'square' panels. If the last 4 words are really from the author or redactor, he must have had the round opening in mind and linked the panels to it, even if we would then have expected ומסגרתיו (cf. Burney). If not, these words must certainly be viewed as a (transposed?) gloss, which in a translation can be put between brackets.

7:32 *Four wheels were underneath the panels and the supports of the wheels were of one piece with the stand. The height (diameter) of each wheel was a cubit and a half.*
This verse returns to the wheels and so augments what had been told in vs. 30. That the 4 wheels were under the panels, seems somewhat superfluous information, but it is still important, because this describes *how* the wagons, in combination with what follows, were constructed. In this connection also the word ידות is important. The word יד, 'hand,' which occurs about 1600x in OT, is very well-known. LXX[B, Luc.] and Pesh. keep this word 'hand'; Tg. has אַשְׁדְּתָא, 'axle'; Vulg. translates the beginning of our verse *quattor quoque rotae quae per quattor angulos basis erant coherebant subter basi*. HAL translates our word by 'Halter (= Achsen) d. Räder, d. Radachsen d. מְכוֹנָה.' Noth thinks of 'Handstücke' of the wheels, by which we are to understand the 'Halter' for the wheels, axles. Burney, too, thinks of 'wheel supports,' though he remarks: 'ידות seems to denote the diagonal stays ...' i.e. the slanted supports, which also the kettle wagons of Enkomi and Larnaka exhibit, but which we thought we recognized (vs. 30) in the word כְּתֵפֹת (cf. also Myres

1948, 39). Montg.-Gehman in their translation 'axle-trees,' follow the translation of Vulg. in the verse which follows: *axes*, 'wagon axles,' but it is not very likely that the word should be taken so generally. According to Kittel, 230, the 'feet' of the set from Enkomi end below in a round opening, resembling a hollow hand, by which the axles of the wheels are held. 'Diese Halter, nicht die schrägen Stützen des ganzen Gestells, sind die Hände oder Halter der Räder' (cf. E. Lohse, *TDNT*, IX, 416). NEB takes our word to mean 'wheel-forks,' which constitute a single unit with the 'trolleys,' an idea one can find already in Burney (and others). TOB speaks of 'les clavettes des roues,' a kind of bolts located in the frame of the wheeled stand. An added comment reads: 'Ce sont probablement des pièces destinés à maintenir les roues en place.' It is clear, also from the summary of the parts of the wheels listed in the following verse where our word is mentioned again, that we have here a technical term which has to denote the attachment or suspension of the wheels to the wagons. A few other translations reproduce the word as follows: LV: 'handles,' with the marginal note: 'grips,' and the comment that the axles of the front and rear wheels were not connected by a shaft, it seems, but 'the axle of each wheel was separately attached to the whole by a 'grip'; KBS translation: 'klemmen' ('clamps'); Dhorme: 'tenons'; Buber-Rosenzweig: 'Haltergriffe' (in the following verse 'Halter'); GNB: 'draagstukken' ('supports'). It is hard to find an accurate English word for these 'hands.' We prefer the translation 'supports.'

The size of the wheels is said to be a cubit and a half. But scholars again disagree about the placing of the wheels (see in Busink, 346). Stade, *GVI*, I, fig. 341; Benzinger and Kittel, 327, fig. 44, for example, put the wheels immediately under the panels; Richter 1918, 33, fig. 1, and others put the wagon on the axles; Vincent, *Jérusalem*, 419, fig. 130, puts the wheels a short distance outside the frame of the wagon and has this frame go down right to the axles. Stade 1901, 167, fig. 6 (followed by Busink, 347, fig. 81), is of the opinion that the bottom of the wagon frame must have been slightly above the wheels. But the text does not permit us to determine exactly how the situation was, even though we believe that, according to the text, the wheels were under the wagon, hence not jutting out at the sides (so also Šanda, Rehm, and others).

7:33 *The construction of the wheels was like the construction of a chariot wheel: their axles, rims, spokes, and hubs were all of cast metal.*
In this verse we are further told about the wheels of the carts. It is said, in the first place, that the construction of the wheels was like the construction of the wheels of chariots of war. In the second place, it is said of various parts of the wheels that they were of cast metal – a rather superfluous bit of information in this context.

The word מרכבה, which also occurs in other Sem. languages (e.g. Ugar. *mrkbt*), is found over 40x in OT. It may denote the travelling chariot (e.g. 2 Kgs. 5:21, 26, etc.), the ceremonial chariot (Gen. 41:43, etc.; cf. Tg. מרכבת יקרא), but also, as here, the chariot of war (see also J. Wiesner, *BHHW*, III, 2127-2130; H. Weippert, *BRL*², 253f.; *HAL*, s.v.). The comparison of the wheels of the 'kettle wagon' with those – in several ancient verisons it is pl. in place of sing. – of a chariot of war suggests both the solid and ingenious character of the wheels (cf. also Noth).

The first of the parts of the wheels to be mentioned is ידות, the 'supports,' though Businck, 347, is still inclined, on the basis of Vulg. and older translations like SV, the Luther Bible, etc., to translate it by axles, a par. to סרנים of vs. 30. Still this does not seem advisable to us. In vs. 30 it had already been clearly stated, that they were of bronze. In our verse the parts of the wheels are listed.

The following word גב is translated here and in Ezek 1:18 by 'rim,' though it can mean a 'bulge,' 'ridge,' or 'swelling' (*HAL*, s.v. I).[26] LXX translated the word by 'ridges', while Vulg. has *radii*, i.e. 'spokes.' Tg. (גביהון) and Pesh. (*gbyhyn* [pl.]) closely agree with MT. The following 2 words are *hapax legomena*. חשק is taken to mean 'spoke' (*HAL*), linked to חשק, 'hang on' (cf. also Burney); and חשר is taken to mean 'hub' (*HAL*, s.v.). Striking in these 2 words is the assonance, which prompts the idea that they form a fixed expression among those who use these technical terms. Is that perhaps the reason why LXX summed up the words in ἡ πραγματεία: 'things,' 'matters'? Pesh. translates the 2 words by: *sbthyn wšwprhyn*, 'their loveliness and comeliness,' also preserving the assonance. Tg. has חפיהון וכבושהון, 'bolts and rims' or '... hubs' (see Jastrow, s.v. II). Vulg. here has *canti et modioli*. *Cantus* or *canthus* is 'an iron ring around a wagon wheel,' 'rim,' and *moduli* are 'hubs.' The ancient verisons indicate the direction of the translation without being exact. For מוצק see vs. 16 above.

7:34 *[And the four shoulderings rested on the four corners of each stand; the shoulderings and the stand (were all of a piece).]*

Klostermann, Kittel and others take this verse (and also the following) to have come from another hand (Klostermann includes vs. 36). This view is not incomprehensible, not even totally impossible, because it states in other words the things which had come up earlier. In vs. 30, after all, there had already been mention of the כתפות, the 'supports,' which were attached to the פעמות, 'pedestals' which were 'of one piece' with the wheeled stand. Our verse seems to say pretty much the same thing, aside from a number of small differences.

---

[26] See now also D. Wolfers, "What is a *gab*?," *JBQ* 20 (1991f.), 17-23.

Here one speaks of פנות, 'corners.' The word פִּנָּה occurs only here and in 2 Kgs. 14:13 in the books of Kings, further some 20x in this sense in OT, while in addition it also occurs a few times in the sense of 'pinnacle' (Zeph. 1:16; 2 Chr. 26:15; Sir. 50:2) and 'chief' (Judg. 20:2 etc.) (*HAL*, s.v.). The '4 corners' of the altar are known as the bearers of 'horns' (Exod. 27:2; 38:2), but they also play a role in Ezekiel's altar design (Ezek. 43:20; 45:19). Is it the intent of vs. 34a simply to repeat vs. 30a (second part), this time underscoring the *4 corners*? Is the reference to 'shoulders', which are not constructed below, but at the top of the stand to give additional support to the basin? Or did the glossator or second 'hand' have still other intentions? It is not clear. What is clear is that in some Hebr. MSS the preposition אל is read as על (cf. comments on 6:18 above where על also functioned in a peculiar way.

Striking in the second part of our verse is the peculiar form כתפיה in place of the expected כתפותיה (for this cf. also Böttcher §734). Stade 1901, 182, thinks this discrepancy clearly shows 'daß verschiedene Hände schrieben.' The masc. and fem. form of the same word in this verse has even been expressed by LXX! Still Böttcher in his grammar has attempted by means of example to demonstrate, that this discrepancy in the *status conjunctus* need not immediately be attributed to 2 distinct 'hands', but that certain nouns have cast off the *-ôt* as 'minder nöthig', but did so 'nach erst späterm Missbrauch bequemer Abkürzung' (§718, b; also cf. *Neue Aehrenlese* and §719). We too are of the opinion that we are dealing here with a later (possibly post-exilic) addition, which states – and virtually all exegetes and translations agree on this – that the 'supports' were cast 'in one piece' with the stand. The preposition מן denotes 'a part of' (cf. e.g. BrSynt. §111a). Vulg. says it aptly: *ex ipsa basi fusiles et coniuncti erant*.

7:35 *[At the top of the stand there was a round (opening) half a cubit high. At the top of the stand were supports and panels which were of one piece with them.]*

In this verse we return to the top of the wheeled apparatus. One finds here a number of words which also came up earlier (e.g. vs. 31), but they hardly help make the text lucid. It is usually agreed that in the first half of our verse a subject of the masc. gender is lacking. Along with Stade, Benzinger, Šanda, Kittel (see also textcr. app. *BHK: fortasse*) and numerous others, one could think of כן. Stade himself also mentions פה as a possibility (cf. Burney) and Montg.-Gehman speak of 'another case of broken grammar.' Modern translations such as NEB, TOB, GoodNB, GNB convey the impression, that the text as it now reads makes sense: TOB: 'Au sommet de chaque base, il y avait un cercle d'une demi-coudée de haut ...'; NEB: 'At the top of the trolley there was a circular hand half a cubit high ...'; GoodNB: 'There was a 22 centimeter band round the top of each cart ...'; GNB: 'Aan de bovenkant van de spoelkar zat een cirkelvormige rand van 25 cm ...' ('At the top of the rinsing cart sat a circular ridge of 25 cm ...'). The words 'band,' 'ridge,' etc. must have been derived from עגל, 'round,' but this is still a glossing over of the problem posed by the text, though Vulg. already pointed in the direction of such a smoother translation: *In summitate autem basis erat quaedam rotunditas dimidii cubiti ita fabrefacta ut luter desuper possit inponi* ... If we do not wish to assume, that this verse consists of glosses and little fragments, but has some meaning, we need to follow Stade's suggestion. We must assume that פה is the subject which has fallen out. If the text is to be consistent with vs. 31a, then אמה may have been there in place of חצי האמה (Burney and others). But such an intervention has no support in the ancient versions. The addition of the cubit can more easily be explained than its omission. Stade 1901, 183, therefore rightly insists on maintaining the half cubit as another notice of the same matter. He considers a cart with an opening of half a cubit even more like the one of Larnaka (190). Presumably one must assume with most interpreters, that in place of קומה we must read קומתו (cf. comments on 6:2, 10, 20, 23; 7:2, 23, etc.; LXX*, Pesh. and textcr. app. in *BHK* and *BHS*).

The second part of our verse increases the number of translation and interpretation problems. As is evident from ועל ראש המכנה, with ידות and מסגרות we must again be at the top of the wheeled stand. As far as the last-mentioned word is concerned, that is certainly not impossible. They, remember, are the vertical panels (see vs. 28 above). In vs. 32, the ידות האופנים are the 'supports' of the wheels, hence located under the cart. A thing can hardly be simultaneously attached both to the top and to the bottom of a thing, unless one assumes that the function of the object is such that it is useful everywhere, or that in Hebr. the same name is given to 2 different objects having approximately the same function. But the latter option is particularly confusing, as we already remarked earlier in connection with other words in these chapters burdened with technical terms, and we must not begin with this assumption. In addition the fem. suff. make these words problematic. What is their antecedent? Is it מכנה or ראש (so Klostermann), or some other fem. word?

Solutions to these problems have been sought in dropping − for instance, as a gloss − the words ועל ראש המכנה (e.g. Stade 1901; Montg.-Gehman; Vincent, *Jérusalem* [dittography]; cf. textcr. app.), but then the following words of course end up hanging totally in the air, unless one opts for the solution which GNB has chosen. After translating the first half of the verse (see above): 'At the top of the rinsing cart sat a circular ridge of 25 cm,' it immediately goes on with 'handholds and partitions,' which is a not-terribly-lucid translation ... In that case it would be better, after the omission of the supposed dittography (in any case it is not a pure dittography, because בראש still means something specifically different from על ראש) to start a new sentence: 'Its supports and its panels were (of one casting) with it' (Kamphausen), although as such this is in no way new information, nor need this be expected from a gloss. Kittel (232) thinks, that one really has to assume a 'Gegenstück zu בראש: und *unten an der Mᵉkōna waren ihre Stützen*' (cf. also Eißfeldt; Zürcher Bibel), but in that case a wish – be it a good one – is father of the thought (Montg.-Gehman correctly speak of 'an arbitrary addition without fresh light,' and the textcr. app. of *BHS* has, also correctly, dropped this suggestion of *BHK*). NEB (cf. Brockington, a.l.) only omits ראש and translates: 'the struts and panels on the trolley were of one piece with it,' but even this translation tells us little more than we already knew. If we let the text stand as we now have it, it remains for us to translate that 'upon' the wheeled stand its ידות and its panels were of one casting with it. Noth, who had in vss. 32f. already translated this word by 'Handstücke' – whatever this may be –, can now remain faithful to his translation. In his explanation he felt 'an altogether vague intimation' that the missing word may have been כתרת (see vs. 31a). Perhaps our verse and vs. 31a belonged together. In this connection it needs to be remarked that, according to him, vs. 31a as well as vs. 35 are secondary and now a broken-up marginal comment is in a wrong sequence. He fails to furnish an explanation of the 'Handstücke', though he does consider them a part of the 'Aufsatz,' as he does the panels.

The above reflections make clear that either our segment says nothing new whatever and can be bracketed as a gloss, or in a somewhat confused form it furnishes us incomprehensible information. Neither do the ancient versions help us along here. We are inclined to opt for the first possibility: vs. 35b as a gloss in a piece of secondary text, unless it has to be assumed that attached *to* (על) the (round) opening there were supports and panels, which united it in one piece with the wheeled stand and which was a construction invisible from the outside, built to reinforce the base of the opening. But this is more speculation than can be permitted in light of the phrasing of the text.

7:36 *On the surfaces of its handholds and its panels he engraved cherubim, lions, and palm motifs [on every one of its open spaces with wreaths] on all sides.*

In this verse there is again mention of the ornamentation. The verb פתח II, derived from (or: from which has been derived) the word פִּתּוּחַ, 'engraving' (see 6:29 above), occurs also in Exod. 28:9, 11, 36; Zech. 3:9 and 2 Chr. 2:6, 13 and 3:7 (see *HAL*, s.v.; Jenni, *Pi'el*, 245). It denotes the engraving of various figures, and that on לחות. The word לוח occurs not only in OT (approx. 45x), but also quite frequently in other Sem. languages as a kind of technical term for 'tables,' i.e. boards or sheets of wood, stone, or metal on which people can make drawings or write ('writing desk'). In OT the word is used in most cases by far for 'the tables of the law' (17x in Exod., 16x in Deut.; cf. especially A. Baumann, *TWAT*, IV, 495-499). By itself it is a meaningful, perhaps even an essential statement that on metal sheets on, or attached to, the wheeled stand, figures – to be further identified in a moment – had been engraved. Only the word לחות has somewhat perplexed the exegetes (e.g. Stade 1901, 186f.; Burney, Kittel, and others), and they have seen in it a different name for terms used in the preceding section (e.g. for מסגרות [Kittel; Vincent, and others] or מסגרות and שלבים [Stade]). Noth finds it hard to place the sheets. According to him, what remains is only the triangular inserts ('Zwickel') between the round opening and the square surface of the wheeled stand (cf. also Myres 1948, 40), but he considers this unlikely. Following Kamphausen, Stade, Kittel and many others, he regards the words ידתיה ועל מסגרתיה as a dittography for the previous verse. This is not improbable, even though Busink, 346, in imitation of a number of Bible translations, wants to maintain the whole text. He takes לחת to be 'strips,' 'mittels deren die Halter an der oberen Leiste befestigt waren.' He refers to his sketches of them (figs. 81 and 82). But לחת has the definite article and this fact is not easily squared with the following genitive (so, correctly, Richter, Noth), even though also this grammatical anomaly need not throw us off too much. Richter 1918, 27, opts for the deletion of the article before לחת: 'Dann sind die Bilder auf den Haltern und Verschlußplatten des Aufsatzes, auf letzteren, soweit sie nicht durch die Halter verdeckt waren, auf ersteren, soweit sie ebene Flächen darboten.' But it is very much the question whether this is intended. In our opinion, הלחת must be maintained and the following words (cf. also the k^etib-q^ere-question מסגרתיהומסגרתיה; Delitzsch, *LSF* §135) are glosses from a later hand. LXX, on the one hand by the words: καὶ ἠνοίγετο ἐπὶ τέσσαρας ἀρχὰς τῶν χειρῶν αὐτῆς (end of vs. 35) and on the other by: καὶ τὰ συκλείσματα αὐτῆς illustrates the obscure situation facing it in its 'Vorlage'. Omitting only ידתיה (as e.g. NEB does) as a gloss, while maintaining ועל מסגרתיה as an epexegetical comment (e.g.: 'that is on the panels,' NEB), is clever and understandable, but not convincing. Our verse intends only to underscore that there were figures engraved on the panels, the smooth (metal) surfaces, whether these were found on the horizontal, on the vertical, or other frames, or on the supports. As stated at length under vs. 30, we consider the closing words of our verse, at least the words כמער איש וליות, to be a later gloss. Various attempts have been made by different commentators to give meaning to these words (cf. also BrSynt. §24e: 'nach dem Raum eines jeden'), but without much success. Making changes in terms of the closing words of vs. 30 does not make much sense here either. The word סביב indicates, that the figurations were done on all sides, wherever there were level parts or panels.

It is striking (something Noth has rightly called attention to) that this verse begins with a finite verb. We do not, with Noth, reject this verse as 'a later addition.' We even consider this verse essentially a redactional comment, following the preceding summing up of an assortment of technical terms and descriptions, to underscore the importance of the wheeled stands for the basins in the temple cult. As a kind of climax, after a rather wearisome recital of materials and parts, attention is focused on the figures as *symbols*, after this was done incidentally already in vs. 29. The difference between this verse and vs. 29 is, that now there is no longer any mention of בקר, but about תמרת (see comments on 6:29 above), the 'palm ornaments,' which had also been applied in the interior of the temple. Busink, 272ff., in our opinion, has rightly pointed out that not only in Israel's 'Umwelt', but also in the early cult of Israel the palm tree can symbolize the 'tree of life'.[27] Cherubim, lions, and palms: they need not be in conflict with the cherubim, lions, and oxen in vs. 29, because there the reference was more to the parts of the stands, while in our verse it is to the (remaining) larger surfaces. These motifs have been derived from pre-Israelite mythological representations. The flora and the trees point – almost paradisally – to fertility. Again we can agree with Hoogewoud, 97: 'It is possible that here again we are dealing with a borrowing of non-Israelite motifs, for both in Egypt and in Mesopotamia there were temple gardens.'

7:37 *In this way he made all ten stands: they were all cast in the same mold and were all the same size and shape.*
The grammars display considerable interest in the somewhat remarkable 3 p. fem. suffix in לכלהנה (Böttcher §873; Ewald §247d; Olsh. §98.6; Stade §352b; König §20 [cf. also §259a, n. 2]; Ges-K §91f; BL, 252p; 268j and Joüon §94h, to mention only these). Still one need not (with Klostermann and Benzinger) modify this 'irregular' suff. form (cf. also Ezek 16:53) into, say, לכל הנה. The words מדה and קצב occur in this combination also in 6:25 (see there). In LXX* the translation of קצב אחד is lacking, because for the second part of our verse it only has: τάξιν μίαν μέτρον ἕν πάσαις.

7:38 *He then made ten bronze basins, each holding forty baths. Each of the basins was four cubits across, one basin per stand and (so) for (all) ten stands.*
Information is now furnished about the basins which were placed on top of (or in) the stands. The capacity per basin was 40 baths and the diameter 4 cubits, at least if we have correctly understood the text. Thenius is correct when in connection with '4 cubits per basin' he comments, that in the case of a *round* object this can only apply to the diameter, a statement which also accords with the measurements given in vs. 27. How much is a bath? We have already discussed this question at length in connection with vs. 26 above. There we

---

[27] Cf. e.g. also Bergema, *De boom des levens in Schrift en historie*, Hilversum 1938, 450f., 491.

found that opinions about the precise capacity were divided, varying from 22 to 40 l per bath. In this way, the water contents per basin can therefore vary from 880 to 1600 l, but usually it ends up on the high side; Kittel, 238, for example coming to 1456 l; Benzinger to 1457.6 l; Šanda to 1575.36 or 1454.88 l; Rehm to 1560 or 880 l (the latter figure according to Albright); Würthwein to 920 l; Noth to approx. 1575 l; Busink, 348, to 920 l; TOB to approx. 1660 l, to mention only these few. LXX speaks of 40 χοεῖς, as does Josephus, *Ant.* VIII §85. The χοῦς is said to equal 3.43 l (cf. Muller, s.v.; but cf. *KP*, I, 1173, which shows that here too there are many variations) a particularly small measure which is undoubtedly based on a mistaken understanding of the word 'bath.' R. Marcus, *LCL*, a.l., points out that in *Ant.* III §197 Josephus was definitely aware of the content of a bath, i.e. 12 χοεῖς. One can safely assume that the metal cart, which in any case was not light and easily manipulable, would be even more awkward and heavy, with a basin containing approx. a ton of water, even aside from the metal weight of the basin itself. Josephus adds the information, that not primarily the diameter, but the *height* of a basin amounted to 4 cubits, καὶ τοσούτοις ἀπ' ἀλλήλων αὐτοῖς δι-ειστήκει τὰ χείλη, i.e. that the diameter of its rim was the same distance. In this way one would get a wheeled reservoir with a capacity of about 6,000 l water, an outcome which is certainly highly improbable. Busink, 348, who takes 40 baths to be 920 l, thinks that the kettle may have been a 'kugelsegmentförmige Schale', approx. one cubit deep, which in our view is a plausible estimate. Just *how* the basin was placed on top of or in the cylinder of the cart is not clear from the words used.

7:39 *He placed five of the stands on the right side of the house and five on the left side, and the (great) basin he placed at the right side of the house eastward over against the south.*
This verse describes the placing of the 'kettle wagons,' along with that of the 'Sea.' The verb used for the placing is נתן, 'give,' but construed with על it can also mean 'place' or 'set up' (cf. *HAL*, s.v. [no. 12]). The express statement that the ten stands, though furnished with wheels, etc., were *placed* somewhere is remarkable, and gives rise to the question whether they really functioned as mobile 'wash basins' or rinsing carts, as is often assumed, or whether one should rather assume they were put in a permanent location. We will return to this problem below. First a word about the localization. 5 stands were placed at the 'right shoulder' and 5 at the 'left shoulder' of the temple (as a result of a *homoeoteleuton* LXX* leaves out the statement about the right side; LXX[Luc.] even places all 10 on the left). We already encountered the word כתף, aside from our section on the 'kettle wagons' (vss. 30 and 34), in 6:8 (above) in which we also discussed the 'right shoulder' of the temple or the palace, which we construed as the 'side' of one of the buildings. According to R.D. Haak, *VT*

33 (1983), 277, כתף refers especially to the part of the entrance or gate, which extends outward from the corner of the opening to the following corner of the building. In our verse the 'kettle wagons' could have formed a kind of path to the temple entrance, hence be stationed in front of that entrance. A similar conclusion concerning the meaning of כתף had earlier already been reached by L.A. Snijders, *OTS* 14 (1965), 220f.: 'Les 'épaules' d'une maison sont sans aucun doute les parties courtes près de sa 'tête', l'entrée qui aux angles passe abruptement dans les murs de côté.' There is no reason to oppose the view of Snijders and Haak. Even if one, like Noth for example, thinks the 'kettle wagons' were lined up alongside the 2 long sides of the house, the preposition על would still allow us to picture this arrangement in continuity with the long sides. Since the temple entrance is thought to be on the short side, this does not even make much difference for the position of the 'kettle wagons.' In the first case, it is true, they do stand closer together, as a sort of aisle to the temple entrance. When one pictures the temple with its entrance facing E, the carts were also located N ('to the left') and S ('to the right'), a view held already by Josephus, *Ant.* VIII §86.

The localization of the 'Sea' is even more complicated. The words מכתף הבית הימנית occur also in Ezek. 47:1, where there is mention of the mysterious 'temple river' (cf. Ps. 46:5; 65:10, etc.). The reference is to the 'right,' i.e. the S side of the main temple building, whether one understands כתף to mean the S entrance side or the entire S side. The word קדמה refers to the E direction (cf. the 4 different points of the compass in Gen. 13:14; 28:14 and *HAL*, s.v. קדם*). 'On the S side in an E direction,' in our phraseology, already means 'SE ward.' The phrase ממול נגב has a somewhat redundant feel to it (also in the par. 2 Chr. 4:10). ממול (see also vs. 5 above) occurs 10x in OT and can geographically mean: 'in the direction of' or 'off ... from' (*HAL*, s.v. מול). Noth therefore correctly points out that from this further place reference 'in the direction of the S', it follows that in the preceding part of our verse the words 'left' and 'right' presumably have to be understood as points of the compass as well.

At the end of this detailed treatment of the 'kettle wagons' we are fascinated by the question what function these wheeled stands had. It is striking that in the par. 2 Chr. 4:6 only the basins (כיורים) are mentioned. They are to be *placed*, 5 to the right and 5 to the left, for the washings. In addition we are told, that in them the things used for the burnt offering (מעשה) were to be rinsed (cf. Rudolph). It is clearly the Chronicler's intent to assign a cultic function to the basins, while he obviously does not know what to do with the heavily-constructed mobile stands and hence does not even mention them. Also Josephus, *Ant.* VIII §87, reports that the 'kettle wagons' were intended for the cleaning of the intestines and legs of the sacrificial animals intended for the burnt offering. It is therefore not surprising, that many later exegetes have often simply accepted this function, and that this viewpoint is still held today. Other explanations have been sought as well (for this, see Busink, 348ff.; Noth and others). Kittel, 236-242, has (correctly, in our opinion; Richter 1918, 12, is not convincing on this point) referred to the weight and height of the 'kettle wagon' and comes to the conclusion: 'es spricht von allen Seiten die höhere Wahrscheinlichkeit dafür, daß sie nicht dem praktischen Gebrauche dienten, sondern der Verkörperung einer religiösen Idee.' Then with interspacing for emphasis, he writes the final sentence of his essay, the sentence which follows the preceding quotation: 'Sie sind die Symbole der regenspendenden Gottheit' (p. 242). Before him W.H. Kosters, *TT* 13 (1879), 445-476, had already pointed out the symbolic significance of the 'Sea' and the 'stands': things which in the books of Chronicles had been degraded to temple implements, holy things belonging to the sacrificial cult. Kosters looks for the characteristic feature of the מכנות (in distinction from the 'Sea'), not in the fact that the basins are water-bearing vessels – that is also true for the 'Sea' – but in something else: the main thing in the case of the מכנות is the movement: they are water-bearing vessels in *motion*. The cherubim on the wheeled stands are the motive forces, and he assumes that these stands depict the clouds which, borne up and driven by the winds, get their water from the subterranean sea; the cherubims which symbolize the motive force, represent not the clouds, but the *winds*. Also Nowack, *Arch.* II, 46, assumes that the mobile stands may originally have symbolized the clouds, while – in a note – he further adds that the figures on the stand – lions, oxen, cherubim – undoubtedly had mythological meaning. Kosters and apparently also Nowack in their reflections proceed from the assumption, that the contrivances had wheels and (on certain occasions) actually 'travelled.' Others, Benzinger, *Arch.* 329, for example, are very skeptical on this last point: it hardly needs saying, that the apparatuses for water transport in the forecourt were 'praktisch nicht brauchbar' (so Benzinger). In addition to those who only favour a practical or cultic use of the stands (Richter, but cf. also Šanda: 'Daß die großen Geräte wirklich praktischen Zwecken dienten, kann füglich nicht bezweifelt werden'; Vincent, *Jérusalem*, 422, et al.) and those who think exclusively of a symbolic function, there are exegetes who honour both aspects; e.g. Montg.-Gehman who attribute a symbolic function to the 'molten Sea,' but a practical one to the stands; or Busink, 349f., who does think of water transport by means of the wheeled stands, but on the other hand underscores the symbolic function especially of the undercarriages, a view by which he does not distance himself from Kosters' idea. One who does is Palache, who primarily accepts a practical function for the 'kettle wagons', but does not rule out the idea 'that later certain (mythological) conceptions became associated with them, but originally and in the first place they were certainly designed for practical temple service'.[28] Keel, *Bildsymbolik*, 124, presupposes, that if the 'molten Sea' represents the river (נהר), then the 'kettle wagons' might represent its 'branches' (fig. 188). Reymond on the other hand, finds it 'très difficile de préciser' what purposes the Sea and the stands served.[29]

The function of the 'kettle wagons' is undoubtedly bound up with the question of their origin (for this again see Busink, 350ff.). The 'kettle wagons' of Larnaka and Enkomi have proved to be important for the reconstruction of Solomon's 'kettle wagons.' Busink is of the opinion, that both the Cyprian and the Jerusalem type of 'kettle wagon' are of Phoenician origin. Fritz, *Tempel*, 26, on the other hand, thinks it cannot be very well determined, whether the 'kettle wagons' originated in the Mycenaean or in the Phoenician culture, although they were probably introduced into the Palestine region by way of the Phoenicians. To us it seems certain, in any case, that the 'kettle wagons,' certainly as it concerns the mobile undercarriages, come from the sphere of Canaanite-Phoenician religious culture and, just as this was the case with the pillars Jachin and Boaz, were in use in the so-called 'Jebusite,' hence pre-Solomonic, temple. It is remarkable that, just like those pillars, they were diminished or disappeared in the later cult of Israel. Kosters studied this issue, pointing among other things to the tendency of Ezekiel to replace the ancient symbols of the 'Sea' and the stands in the temple, and 'up to a point to make them unrecognizable' by making the cherubim the bearers of the throne of clouds and to add 4 wheels to the cherubim (art. cit., 456). Now one need not endorse all of Kosters' views to subscribe to the main thrust of his argument relative to the מכנות. He and other exegetes who stress the symbolic over the practical function of these carts, are correct, even though the original use of such carts in the pre-Solomonic sanctuary is hard to track down. From our text we get the impression, that the carts had a *static* function in the Solomonic sanctuary: they were stationed somewhere specific. They had their *cultic* place next to the entrance to the sanctuary, not far from the 'Sea.' Undoubtedly, in an earlier Canaanite temple they had a function in the myths and rites associated with vegetation and fertility. That the unwieldy carts actually moved around or even could move around seems excluded. In any case, if one takes seriously the measurements given and nevertheless assumes a practical purpose for these carts, one practically has to assume, as S. Yeivin, *EncMiqr*. V, 345, does, that to reach the basins the priests had to make use of 'portable ladders' (סולמות מיטלטלים), hardly a plausible idea. Also other self-conceived, but nowhere reported, draining systems are unacceptable. What remains is only the

---

[28] J.L. Palache, *Het heiligdom in de voorstelling der semietische volken*, Leiden 1920, 60, n. 2.
[29] P. Reymond, *L'eau, sa vie, et sa signification dans l'Ancient Testament*, Leiden 1958, 226.

symbolic function, of which Kosters' suggested 'cloud' function at least has attractive aspects to it (cf. also Keel's suggestion).

7:40 *Now Hiram made the basins, the scoops, and the sprinkling bowls, and Hiram finished all the skilled work he did for king Solomon in the house of YHWH:*
In the section which now follows (vss. 40-47) we find a summary of what Hiram is said to have made for Solomon and his temple. Sometimes additions (e.g. vss. 41f.) are furnished to what was described earlier, sometimes there is repetition of things said earlier or is reported elsewhere. One gets the impression, that the redactor of our chapter has added material which came in later, or has introduced supplementary material in the interest of offering a more or less complete picture of the building of the temple. Although Noth (and others) object to terms like 'recapitulation' or 'summary', because in the vss. 41-47 we find an 'Ausführungsvermerk' on the specifications given in the vss. 15-40a, still this section with its repetitions displays a secondary character in relation to the preceding one. It is conceivable, that later marginal comments on the original text, plus an account of material that was in fact present in the temple at a later date, were brought together here as a kind of rounding off of the technical information. But this does not detract from the possibility – this much we concede to Noth – that also the vss. 15-40a may contain 'sekundäre Umformulierungen.' In the par. section 2 Chr. 4, the transition between vs. 39 and vs. 40 is interrupted by statements, which are in part identical with other verses in our book (e.g. 2 Chr. 4:7 with 7:49; cf. 1 Chr. 28:15 and Jer. 52:19) and in part have no par. in our chapter (e.g. 2 Chr. 4:8a, the 10 tables). This too is indicative of the changing and secondary character of the tradition.

In our verse Hiram appears as the maker of the objects listed, objects which mainly relate to the ministry of sacrifice. For the variable orthography of the name Hiram, see comments on 5:15 above. The question arises whether, on the basis of the par. 2 Chr. 4:11, the identical summary in vs. 45 (below), the word usage in LXX* (λέβητας), Vulg. (*lebetas*) and a number of Hebr. MSS (Tg. supports MT; Pesh. uses 2 words: *lqn'* [pl.] *wqds'* [pl.]),[30] it would not be better to read הַסִּירוֹת in place of הַכִּירוֹת. Almost without exception commentators accept the first reading. The word סִיר, which occurs almost 30x in OT, denotes a cooking pot as well as a wash basin (see *HAL*, s.v.). The pot is used for cooking meat (Exod. 16:3; 2 Kgs. 4:38-41, etc.) or for storing ashes or waste (Exod. 27:3; 2 Kgs. 25:14, etc.). Accordingly, there is not much reason for not following the proposed emendation, surrounded as it is by such

---

[30] See now also, on the same reading in 4qKgs, against MT, E. Ulrich et al., *Qumran Cave 4* (DJD 14), Oxford 1995, 183.

a cloud of ancient and contemporary witnesses. We may well point out, however, that also the word כיור has meanings which, as we already showed above (in connection with vs. 30), come close to סיר (e.g. 1 Sam. 2:14, where a number of technical kitchen terms are summed up), so that a transposition of words, even by the use of the one word in the preceding section, is very understandable.

The following word היעים only occurs in the pl. in OT (aside from here and in vs. 45 also: Exod. 27:3; 38:3; Num. 4:14; 2 Kgs. 25:14; Jer. 52:18 and the par. 2 Chr. 4:11, 16). Scholars are not certain whether the sing. is יָע or יָעֶה (see *HAL*, s.v. יָע*), though they relate it to יעה which occurs once in the qal (Isa. 28:17), meaning 'wipe away,' 'sweep away.' The meaning would then be 'scoop' or 'shovel,' an implement for cleaning the altar (see also Dalman, *AuS*, VII, 207f.; Y.M. Grintz, *Leš* 39 [1974f.], 19f.). Especially hot ashes could be cleaned up by means of these implements; cf. LXX: θερμαστρεὺς, 'fire tongs' (Vulg., however, has *scutra,* 'flat pan'; Pesh. *'īrā,* 'pot'; and Tg. מַגְרוֹפְיָתָא, a kind of rake or hoe).

The third word המזרקות comes from מזרק, which in the pl. has both an *-ôt* and an *-îm* ending and means 'sprinkling bowl' (approx. 30x in OT) and was used for libation. Generally speaking, large quantities of fluid (e.g. blood) were caught in such bowls and poured out (see Burney).

In the second part of our verse the notice about Hiram's work seems to reach a conclusion (so, correctly, also Benzinger) and so it should also function. Many exegetes, however, take vs. 40b as a new beginning of what still follows (Thenius, Noth, Van Gelderen, etc.). Grounds for this can be advanced, for example the fact that otherwise what follows hangs more or less in the air – as a result of which the vss. 41f. can all the more readily be pulled forward (as Montg.-Gehman therefore have it) – or the fact that the second Hiram of our verse is spelled differently than in the first verse, which could indicate another 'hand.' By itself, however, the verb כלה (pi.) means conclusion, ending, even though in our chapters it is often used at the beginning (see 3:1; 6:9, 14; 7:1 above). Accordingly, one gets a strong impression that this second half of our verse is either secondary or – what, in our opinion, is more likely – should be located somewhere else at the end of the rather chaotic summaries. The vss. 41ff. depend on the first part of vs. 40, which starts with ויעש.

To judge by the pl. 'works' in LXX*, its 'Vorlage' may have had מלאכות. But this is not necessary, because Hiram's skilled artistic work can also be expressed by a sing. taken as a collective (for the word מלאכה, see comments on 5:30 above). Nor is it necessary – despite certain Hebr. MSS and Pesh. – to change למלך into המלך, because this is contrary to the entire structure of our chapters. בית יהוה, as LXX and many exegetes after it have correctly noted, is an accusative of place.

7:41 *the two pillars and the two moldings of the capitals surmounting the pillars; the two sets of network to cover the two moldings of the capitals surmounting the pillars;*
In this and the following verse the pillars Jachin and Boaz mentioned in vss. 15-22 again come up, but now in other words and with different information. Noth believes that the differences between vss. 15ff. and our verses can best be explained as the differences between 'design' and 'execution,' a framework in which our verses are then thought to indicate the final construction of the pillars. However, he is not able to offer an explanation of the reason for these differences. But to us this hypothesis seems unacceptable. If, as we have explained above, the pillars in essence stemmed from a pre-Israelitish sanctuary, then there was no 'design.' It seems better to assume that what follows in our verses was incorporated in the building report from another source (so e.g. Benzinger). We lean toward the assumption of an explanatory gloss from a later time, in connection with a bit of reportage, which then already presented problems for a right understanding of things, as became evident in the above discussion of the verses in question.

The abrupt beginning of our verse already reflects the fragmentary character of this 'redactional note,' although in the par. 2 Chr. 4:12 this entire construction has been taken over more or less unaltered. One can read עמדים etc. as accusative dependent on לעשות of the previous verse (Thenius and others), although, grammatically, dependence on יועש is also possible, especially if one regards vs. 40b as a secondary addition (from another location). It is stated that on top of the 2 pillars there were גלת הכתרת, distinguished in the par. 2 Chr. 4:12 as והגלות והכתרות. The word גֻּלָּה occurs a number of times in OT, but with different meanings. So *HAL* views it as a bowl or basin for oil (in Zech. 4:2f.) on the מנורה, which can also be made of gold (Eccl. 12:6). In Josh. 15:19 and Judg. 1:15 the word presumably refers to 'water basin.' In our verses (and the par. 2 Chr. 4:12f.) *HAL* sees it as 'Becken an Säulen.' Albright, *ARI*, 147, follows Robertson Smith, *Religion*, 488, saying the word גלה can be viewed as 'basin of a lampstand' (cf. also W.F. Albright, *BASOR* 85 [1942], 18-27: 'cresset' and H.G. May, *BASOR* 88 [1942], 19). The word is etymologically related to the Ugar. *gl*, 'bowl' and the Akkad. *gullu(m)* with the same meaning (*DLU*, I, 145; *AHw*, 297). Vincent, *Jérusalem*, 411, n. 5, has commented that this word and its many meanings can be derived from גלל, 'turn.' W. Kornfeld, *ZAW* 74 (1962), 55ff. – like *KBL*, s.v. II, earlier – thinks of the 'horizontale Scheiben' which the Egyptian Djed pillars also had. In Akkad. *gullatu* can mean '(an Bauten) schalenartige Basis' (*AHw*) and Noth, accordingly, thinks that based on the idea of a 'bulbous basin' one may suspect a transfer to 'einen wulstartigen Säulenteil.' Also Busink, 305, in considering our word, thinks of a 'swelling' or 'bulge' of the capital, which approximates the meaning of the word בטן in vs. 20 (see above). The exegesis of that verse has shown how hard it was to get a handle on the matter in question. We are here probably dealing with a gloss from a later period in which, under Akkad. influence, the word גֻּלָּה was introduced as a technical term for the word בֶּטֶן: the 'swelling' or 'bulge' or 'bowl-shaped projection' of the capitals on top of the shafts of the pillars (עמודים).

The second part of our verse mentions 2 networks (שׂבכות, see comments on vs. 17 above) which served to cover the 2 'capital swellings' on top of the pillars. Noth is right in commenting, that in this connection a good understanding of the word כסה (pi.) is desirable. Does it refer simply to a 'covering' of the exterior or should one rather think of 'capping' the top? The verb also occurred in vs. 18 (above), although there it referred to 'capping' the capitals on top of the pillars (actually: pomegranates). There we concluded, that the thrust of the difficult text was, that the chainwork ('network,' 'plaiting') served to finish the (bowl-shaped) capitals. In other words, and in a much more intelligible form, our verse, too, points in this direction.

7:42 *the four hundred pomegranates for the two grids, two rows of pomegranates per grid, to cover the two basins of the capitals surmounting the pillars;*

It is now stated that there were 400 pomegranates for the 2 sets of chainwork over the bowl-shaped capitals. While this squares with the number given in vs. 20 (i.e. 200), it does not agree with the number given in 2 Chr. 3:16 and Jer. 52:23. Especially the last-mentioned verse has a peculiar count, 96 רוחה, which has given commentators much to puzzle over, though it again adds up to 100 (cf. Busink, 306f.: 'eine Art arithmetische Spielerei').

The second part of our verse is virtually identical with the previous verse. Only now, in place of על־ראשׁ, the word על־פני is read. Along with a number of Hebr. MSS, Pesh. and Vulg. in fact presuppose the former reading, but Tg. supports MT. On the basis of the LXX reading, some scholars also think that in place of פני the word שׁני should be read. Materially these variant readings do not make much difference for the understanding of the meaning. Noth (cf. Delitzsch, *LSF* §88d) thinks that this 'abgekürzte Finalsatz 42bß' is probably based on a mistaken repetition of the same words from the preceding vs. Though this is possible, it is not necessary if one assumes that the whole of vs. 42 is again a later addition to the preceding gloss.

Grammatically we must still note the appositional combination טורים רמונים (König §333n; Burney).

7:43 *and the ten stands plus the ten basins on the stands;*

As cast metal temple implements, this verse lists the 10 stands with the 10 basins. Striking is that the par. place in 2 Chr. 4:14 reads עשׂה each time the numeral 10 occurs. See further vss. 27-37 above.

7:44 *and the one basin with the twelve oxen under the basin;*
Also the so-called 'molten Sea' is mentioned (see vss. 23-26 above), along with the 12 oxen standing under it (for the numeral, cf. Ewald §290f; GD §47e, and also the par. 2 Chr. 4:15).

7:45 *the cooking pots, the scoops, and the sprinkling bowls [and all these objects which Hiram made for king Solomon for the temple of YHWH were of burnished bronze].*
The beginning of this verse is virtually identical with the beginning of vs. 40 (see above) in listing the cultic implements, only this time the סירות are mentioned. Also the rest of the sentence would speak for itself, were it not that there are in it a number of textcritical difficulties, which require our attention. In the first place the par. 2 Chr. 4:16, in place of המזרקות, reads the word המזלגות which in the sing. in the form מַזְלֵג (*מִזְלָג) occurs a few times in OT (1 Sam. 2:13f.), in the pl. in Exod. 27:3; 38:3; Num. 4:14; 1 Chr. 28:17: the '3-pronged fork' for the preparation of meat (see K. Galling, *BRL*², 85). But, textcritically, the reading of our text is solid.

In the second place there is the *kᵉtib* האהל, i.e. הָאֹהֶל, 'tent,' 'tabernacle', but generally the *qᵉre* הָאֵלֶּה is followed (see Delitzsch, *LSF* §55). Still the Pesh. supports the *kᵉtib*-form with *tešmeštā*, 'worship service.' Also Gordis, 196, n. 481, makes a plea for the *kᵉtib*-form, arguing among other things, that the absence of the st. cstr.-form can be explained 'by assuming this as an example of apposition,' a position for which he then adduces the necessary support from practice and grammar. He thinks that perhaps the *kᵉtib* was changed because it was deemed an unbearable thought, that Hiram also made the cult-objects for the 'tent.' 'Yet the preceding verses *do* attribute to him all the Temple utensils.' On the other hand, B. Stade, *ZAW* 3 (1883), 166, already pointed out, that ו before the 4th ואת of our verse and the *qᵉre*-form exclude each other, because those utensils are introduced with the *waw* which had not yet been mentioned up until now, whereas האלה refers back to those which had been mentioned. He deletes the *waw* and (on the ground that it is also lacking in LXX and Vulg.) considers האלה superfluous. Tg. doet not take a decision and translates: '... and all the utensils, which are compatible with the construction of the utensils of the tabernacle, which Moses had made.' One has to grant Noth, however, that MT with the *qᵉre*-form has proposed 'eine leidlich möglich erscheinende, aber auch nicht recht passende Verlegenheitsauskunft,' and that we may be dealing here with a marginal gloss, which for that matter the par. passage in Chronicles has resolved by omitting not only the 'challenged' *kᵉtib-qᵉre* form, but also the following אשר, as a result of which the verse runs more smoothly.

That in the tradition of the Hebr. text of this verse there are differences, is also clear from LXX which, after the words: אשר עשה חירם למלך שלמה בית יהוה additionally reads: καὶ οἱ στύλοι τεσσεράκοντα καὶ ὀκτὼ τοῦ οἴκου τοῦ βασιλέως καὶ τοῦ οἴκου Κυρίου. πάντα τὰ ἔργα τοῦ βασιλέως ἐποίησεν Χειρὰμ χαλκᾶ ἄρδην: 'There were 48 pillars in front of the king's house and in front of the house of the Lord; Hiram made all the works of the king completely of copper.' At least this is how LXX^B reads. LXX$^{Luc.}$ has a number of minor deviations. This information furnished by LXX is important enough for us to pay some attention to it (so also Thenius, Benzinger, Burney and others), though not all commentators judge the value of this information alike. Keil (in a note) views it as 'apocryphal' (cf. J.W. Wevers, OTS 8 [1950], 308: 'tendency to enhance Solomon'; see Noth, 165), but Burney points out that this information does not, as happens in the preceding verses, refer back to something which had already been described in detail in the preceding account, and that it may therefore be 'a matter of great importance mentioned for the first time.' Even if one regards this addition in LXX as 'sehr spät' (Šanda), it is still valuable, because it presumably originated in the LXX from a Hebr. 'Vorlage'. It is clear that the compositor of the book of Kings omitted many points from the data available to him pertaining to the building activities of Solomon, because for his purpose they were of no interest. If Šanda is right, the words 'of the house of the Lord' are a doublet and the 48 pillars constitute a colonnade in the royal palace fortress. In any case, this makes clear why the final redactor was not interested in these 48 pillars.

But: is vs. 45b, as a marginal gloss still present in the text, not after all a rudiment of a much greater informational complex, which the redactor or author did not need, or was it his intention again to unite, with a *waw explicativum*, a summary with an immediately preceding 'short list,' as D.W. Baker, *VT* 30 (1980), 131, thinks? In our opinion, without our devaluing the explicative value of the *waw*, vs. 45b, united with את-*syntagma*, can be considered as a secondary rudiment of a larger informational complex, to which also – Noth seems to except them – the last 2 words נחשת ממרט belong. The word ממרט is a pu. part. of the verb מרט, which in qal can mean 'pull out' (of hair) (Isa. 50:6; Ezra 9:3; Neh. 13:25) and 'sharpen' (cf. a sword) (Ezek. 21:14, 16, 33) or 'polish,' 'rub bare' (Ezek. 29:18). In pu., alongside the longer form ממרט, also the shorter form מוֹרָט (Isa. 18:2, 7; see also Ezek. 21:15f.) occurs, which has led to the notion that the first-mentioned form is new (BL, 287o; Bg. II §15c) and based on a passive qal. Striking, further, is that נחשת here is apparently treated as masc. (König §251i). Probably the meaning is that it concerns polished bronze, something for which the ancient versions did not know the right word either. Pesh., for example, talks of 'bronze from Corinth'; Tg. of 'good bronze'; and Vulg. of '*aurichalcum*' (LXX^B: see above; LXX$^{Luc.}$ omits all further qualification of the bronze).

Still to be noted is that after this verse LXX continues with MT vs. 47 and then follows it up with MT vs. 46.

7:46 *The king had them cast in clay molds in the Jordan flats between Succoth and Zarethan.*
In this verse, in which we learn where the bronze came from, also others (than LXX) see a continuation of vs. 47, e.g. Burney, who offers detailed argumentation based on LXX for his transposition. Despite these arguments we hold to the order of MT, because it is not, after all, without meaning. Text-critically it is a question, whether המלך, omitted by LXX*, really belongs in the text. Essentially the author of Kings regards Solomon as the master builder of all the buildings in the capital, but Hiram nevertheless remains the artistic executor of all bronze and wrought-iron work. Noth has rightly called attention to the fact, that 'the king' is always in competition with the mention of Hiram's name (vss. 13, 40, 45 above). In place of במעבה האדמה the par. 2 Chr. 4:17 has בְּעֲבִי הָאֲדָמָה. G.F. Moore, ICC, on Judg. 7:22, already proposed, that instead of the 'meaningless' מעבה, we should read: במעברת (ה)אדמה, 'at the crossing (ford) of Adamah,' a suggestion followed among others by Abel, *GP*, II, 238. This Adamah is then assumed to have been located on or near present-day *tell ed-Dāmiye*, E of the Jordan, near the point where the Jabbok empties into this river. The word עבי* of 2 Chr. 4:17 is usually taken to mean 'thickness' (cf. Rudolph, a.l., who translates 'Verdickung des Bodens'). In Chronicles there is therefore no reason to conceive אדמה as anything other than 'earth,' since a place called Adam between Succoth and Zarethan can hardly be localized. Now modern investigators transfer this view to our verse as well. The word מעבה*, coupled with the following word, was interpreted by N. Glueck, *BASOR* 90 (1943), 2-23, as 'the earthen foundries,' a suggestion which is now followed by many other scholars. An example is Gray, who translates 'in clay moulds' and points out, that the location of a copper smelter was chosen on the basis of the thickness of the claybed, in which large moulds could be formed. In that case the word מעבה is identical with עבי. Noth goes into the same direction: 'in (den) Erdgruben,' as does J.G. Plöger, *TWAT*, I, 96). Support for this view is found in LXX (ἐν τῷ πάχει τῆς γῆς), Vulg.: *in argillosa terra;* Pesh. *bšwprh d'r'*, 'in the best of the land' (i.e. clay), and Tg.: 'in the thickness of the clay' (בְּעוֹבֵי נַרְנִישְׁתָּא). From excavations it has not only been shown, that in *tell Deir-'Allā* and surroundings there were many metal foundries, but also that clay-moulds were very common (for the processing of metals, cf. M. Weippert, *BRL*^{2}, 219-224 [with litt.]), so that there is no reason whatever to depart from the direction of translation already indicated by the ancient versions.

In our verse a couple of place references are mentioned. In the first place ככר הירדן, also הככר (cf. also Gen. 13:10-12; 19:17, 25, 28f.; Deut. 34:3; 2 Sam. 18:23; Neh. 3:22; 12:28 and the par. 2 Chr. 4:17). Often this area, actually 'surroundings' (see *HAL*, s.v. 4), is a reference to the S part of the Jordan valley (approximately from *qarn Sartabe* [=Alexandreion] to where the Jordan empties into the Dead Sea; see also J. Simons, *OTS* 5 [1948], 108-117), which is nowadays called *ġōr*, 'mit unbestimmter Ausdehnung nach N' (Noth; cf. Gray). Remarkable is Pesh.'s description of this area: 'In the *kikkar*, which lies in the gorge of Jericho next to the Jordan.' This is evidently an explicating comment from the translator to his readers.

Secondly, there is mention of the place name Succoth. A place in the Jordan valley called Succoth is also (besides here and in the par. 2 Chr. 4:17) mentioned in Gen. 33:17; Jos. 13:27; Judg. 8:5-16; Ps. 60:8; 108:8). Based on information in PT Šebi'ith, IX, 2, fol. 38d, scholars often identify Succoth with *tell Deir-'Allā* in Jordania, in the area where the Jabbok enters the Jordan (K. Elliger, *BHHW*, III, 1888; G. Sauer, *ZAW* 8, [1969], 150ff. [with litt.], etc.) but the excavator of this *tell*, H.J. Franken, has reservations with regard to this identification (see *VT* 11 [1961], 371f.; *VT* 14 [1964], 422). Simons, *GTTOT* § 415 (pp. 231f.) thinks of *tell el-Aḥṣāṣ,* as does Abel, *GP*, II, 470. However this may be, it has been clearly demonstrated that also this *tell*, as Gray puts it, was for many long periods in antiquity a center of metallurgy, because in every layer of the Iron Age metal slag and small blast furnaces have been found outside the city walls. But Franken has pointed out, that the same is true for other *tells* in the neighbourhood of *tell Deir-'Allā*.

Thirdly, there is mention of צרתן, on which we already commented in connection with 4:12 (for the form of this Hebr. word, cf. Böttcher §678; Ewald §180d; Olsh. §215c). There, too, it became clear, that the identification of this place with one of the many present-day *tells* was not a simple matter. Often the place is identified nowadays with *tell es-Saʿīdiyeh* (see Noth, Gray; also cf. R. Hestrin, *Qad* 2 [1969], 92-95, on the excavations there), located at the point where the *wādī Kufrinǧe* empties into the Jordan, E of that river. Assuming this localization of Succoth and Zarethan is correct, it is also evident that the identification of אדמה with *tell ed-Dāmiye* is incorrect, because there is no such place 'between' Succoth and Zarethan. Earlier in our chapter we already encountered forms of the verb יצק, 'casting (metal)' (cf. comments on vss. 15f., 23f., 33 above).

Still to be noted is that the par. 2 Chr. 4:17 has in mind not Zarethan, but צרדה, which according to 1 Kgs. 11:26 is the birthplace of Jeroboam I. It is assumed (see *HAL*, s.v.), that this is a reference to *'ēn Ṣerādā* (according S. Herrmann, *BHHW*, IV, 147: *dēr ġasanne*), some 30 km E of present-day Tell Aviv, in the Samaritan mountains. Usually – and for good reason – the reading of 2 Chronicles is considered an error (Rudolph).

The question has been posed why the bronze implements had to be cast in the surroundings of Succoth, when the main copper mines were and are located much farther to the S. Busink, 303, n. 518, in this connection refers to an article by Yadin, in which 2 Sam. 8:7-11 and 1 Chr. 18:7f. are mentioned.[31] In these passages there is mention of the golden objects and the copper which David had seized from Hadadezer. According to Yadin, David left this copper ore at Succoth, the ore from which Solomon later made the bronze implements for the temple (1 Chr. 18:8b, which does not occur in this form in the par. 2 Sam. 8, more or less prompts this suspicion). Although Busink believes that the implements were simply cast in Succoth, because it was there the well-developed metallurgical industries were located, it is very well possible, in our opinion, that also ore captured in war was processed in these industries. 1 Chr. 18:8b, according to Rudolph, gives the impression that it is original, all the more since this passage *does* have its equivalent in 2 Sam. 8:8b in LXX, though this verse fragment also has theological implications.[32]

7:47 *Solomon put all these objects (on a scale): but on account of their enormous quantity the weight of the bronze could not be determined.*
The intent of this verse is once more, perhaps unnecessarily, to make a contribution to the glorification of Solomon and his building projects. The word וינח, along with the following words including הכלים, which Montg.-Gehman (among others) view as a possible correction of the beginning of vs. 48 ('Solomon made ... etc.') and which are sometimes omitted in the translations (see, e.g. JB), present a great difficulty. Since LXX places our verse immediately after vs. 45, its translation of the beginning of our verse (on the basis of its 'Vorlage'?) takes another and more logical course: 'There was no weighing of the bronze of which he (i.e. Hiram), in virtue of its enormous quantity, made all these works:' But Pesh. (like the par. 2 Chr. 4:18; further cf. Ehrlich) reads the beginning of our verse as the beginning of the following verse, as though it read: ויעש. Tg. has the following solution (which accords with 2 Chr. 4:18): 'But Solomon hid (ואצנע) all the implements ...,' because he made more of them than were immediately needed. According to Rabbinical opinion, the remainder was stored in the temple for future use. Vulg. maintains MT: *et posuit Salomon omnia vasa.* If ויעש, as *lectio facilior*, must be put aside, one will, also when assenting to Montg.-Gehman, Noth, etc., as to the secondary character of the words in question, have to look for a solution for וינח, a so-called hiph. II of נוח, which (in hiph.) means 'deposit,' 'put' (*HAL*, s.v. II, 2e: 'bestehen lassen,' which applies to our verse). What does 'depositing' mean here? Does it mean that Solomon 'deposited' the implements

---

[31] Y. Yadin, "Some Aspects of the Strategy of Ahab and David (2 Kings 20; 2 Sam 11)," *Bib* 36 (1955), 332-351, esp. 346, n. 2.

[32] See now also M. Naor, "Who Poured What in the Jordan Valley?," *BetM* 37 (1991f.), 50-58 (Hebr.).

in the temple, in the sense of 'setting them up'? That comment, though not illogical, is rather superfluous. Rashi in his commentary comments on our verse in these words: 'without weighing the implements on account of their large quantity, and he refrained from calculating that weight' (also Kimchi takes this direction in his commentary). Later translations and commentators have followed this lead (cf. LV, NV, GNB, Keil, Thenius, et al.). It is a question, however, whether this artificial solution is really correct (so, correctly, also Noth).

But Noth himself sees no alternative solution and translates: 'Salomo ließ alle Geräte wegen sehr, sehr großer Menge offen.' One needs to consider the possibility of transposing the *atnaḥ* under the second מאד to כלים, so that the second half of our verse begins with מרב (Ehrlich, Gray, NEB). This second half can either be understood in immediate continuity with the first half, or as a completely independent sentence. In the latter case, the first half says no more than that Solomon put the implements in place, but the question remains: where? Then the first half is at best a rudiment of a larger whole we cannot recover, or an original marginal gloss which crept into the text at a later time. In the first case, the first half says something to which the second half reacts negatively. This could be that Solomon had all the bronze objects put on a scale, but that on account of the large quantity, weighting them all was out of the question. The word משקל, 'weight,' occurs numerous times (almost 50) in OT (see *HAL*). Especially foodstuffs were weighed but also money, and various handheld as well as standing scales have been found in Palestine and surroundings (see H. Weippert, *BRL*², 355). The niph. of חקר in qal, 'find out,' occurs, aside from here and in the par. 2 Chr. 4:18, only in Jer. 31:37 and 46:23, and then always with a negation: 'unfathomable,' 'impenetrable' (of the earth or a forest). As a result of their being 'very, very' many (cf. the inf. cstr. of רבב in Ewald §304a; Lisowsky takes רב to be a substantive; for the intensification of adverbs, cf. König §318f.) the weight of the bronze objects could not be determined. This hyperbole can also be found in 2 Kgs. 25:16 and the par. Jer. 52:20. The idea may be that, though people tried to determine the monetary value of the objects, they did not succeed, because it exceeded all human standards. If one takes the whole verse as a unit, then it states that Solomon did make an attempt to determine the value of all the objects, but did not succeed because of their enormous quantity. This statement strongly suggests that, like that in 2 Kgs. 25:16 and Jer. 52:20, it is a late notice inserted for the greater glory of Solomon.

7:48 *Solomon also made all the furnishings for the house of YHWH: the golden altar and the golden table on which was the Bread of the Presence;*
In this and the following verses separate mention is made of the golden objects

Solomon made (or caused to be made) for the temple.[33] It hardly seems possible to deny that we have here an addition to what has already been mentioned. The question is only whether it is a primary addition, i.e. an ancient one which reasonably corresponds to the actual situation, or a secondary addition, i.e. a late one which no longer corresponds to the actual situation. Exegetes such as B. Stade (*ZAW* 3 [1883], 168), Benzinger and others take the latter position. Skinner, in his commentary, sums up a number of grounds which seem to support this position: (1) the improbability that so much gold was used; (2) a golden altar in the temple, for which there is no historical evidence in pre-exilic times; (3) the discrepancy between our verse and 6:20ff.; (4) the odd circumstance, that the objects are listed without mention of their maker or description of their exterior. Nevertheless he also points to a number of aspects which argue for a greater originality of these additions, such as mention of the word דביר (vs. 49) and reference to the ten lampstands. He – rightly – considers it possible, that the person who added our verses had knowledge of such objects, objects which were present in the first temple. Noth, in his commentary, takes a further step. He not only minimizes some of the arguments reproduced above, but he also states, 'daß beim Ausziehen aus den amtlichen Vorlagen besonders zurückhaltend verfahren wurde,' though later on secondary material was added here and there. He includes especially the lengthy introductory sentence of our verse in such a later addition, and he may be right in this, because this sentence seems only to repeat what had been stated frequently before, viz. that Solomon made all these things for the house of YHWH.

Furthermore, as in the vss. 23 and 27, the object introduced by the *nota accusativi* ties in well with ויעש, though without the words את כל־הכלים אשר בית יהוה having to be per se mentioned here as in a parenthetical clause. Burney, Benzinger and others, following LXX (minus LXX[B], which reads ἔλαβεν), which translates by ἔδωκε, want to substitute ויתן from vs. 47: LXX* translates this parenthetical clause still somewhat 'more freely', than MT now offers us as 'Vorlage': τὰ σκεύη ἃ ἐποίησεν ἐν οἴκῳ (LXX[Luc.] plus κυρίου), a reading in which כל remains untranslated and the preposition ב seems to be present before בית, which is what also 12 Hebr. MSS have.

It is striking – a point various commentators have discussed – that in the first part of our verse Solomon is mentioned as the maker of the golden objects, and not Hiram. By itself, particularly in the case of a secondary addition, such a

---

[33] See on these objects now also J. Voss, "*Die Menora: Gestalt und Funktion des Leuchters im Tempel zu Jerusalem*" (OBO 128) Fribourg, 1993, and V.A. Hurowitz, "Solomon's Golden Vessels (I Kings 7:48-50) and the Cult of the First Temple," *Pomegrates and Golden Bells* (Fs. J. Milgrom, ed. D.P. Wright et al.), Winona Lake 1995, 151-164.

comment need not be given too much weight, because 'make' can also mean 'cause to make,' or because a later glossator wanted once more to highlight the exceptional wisdom and insight of Solomon. S. Rummel, *RSP*, III, 283f., has referred to the dangers of comparing Solomon's building of a temple with the building of a temple for Baal in the Ugar. texts. In both texts one can, upon comparison, point to, say, the ideology of the deity or the king himself as the builder of the temple, a view for which he cites a number of texts, our verse among them. Although the Ugar. texts can indeed contribute materially to an understanding of biblical texts, this in no way justifies, as Rummel rightly says, 'a reductionist approach to the structural interpretation of the texts.' The literary structure of our chapter has its interpretation and meaning.

Two of the objects made are mentioned in our verse. The first is the golden altar. Noth views the object as hardly belonging 'zum primären Bestand,' but as a secondary addition in line with Exod. 39:38; 40:5, 26; Num. 4:11 which is linked up with Exod. 30:1-10. De Langhe attempts to prove, that the word 'golden altar' owes its origin to a misunderstanding.[34] The word זהב (see also comments on 6:20 above) is said, on the basis of S-Arab. parallels, to mean 'spices' or 'herbs.' Accordingly, the reference is to an 'altar of incense.' We have to grant Noth, however, that it is unlikely that, in this section where 'gold' is the central point, the word זהב would be used in another sense. Already in connection with 6:21 Noth, 122, had voiced the suspicion, that the 'altar' of vs. 20 was the 'table' on which the bread of the Presence lay. By itself this suspicion is not implausible, but then the question arises, whether there could nevertheless be room also for a 'golden altar' and what its function must have been. We agree with Fritz, *Tempel*, 24, that, even if one regards our verse as an addition, the side-by-side mention of these 2 cult objects must have a objective basis. Fritz himself views the golden altar of our text and also the altar mentioned in 6:20, as an altar of incense inside the temple. In a certain sense this is also the position of De Langhe (and others). But to the question whether inside the temple there has been an altar of incense in pre-exilic times, various answers have been given. Wellhausen, *Prolegomena*, 66f., thinks, that originally the golden altar was nothing other than a golden table (with an appeal to Ezek. 41:21f.) and that in our verse this 'golden table' is something, that has slipped in. Of legitimate offerings of incense, according to him, ancient Israelite literature knows nothing up until the time of Jeremiah and Zephaniah (p. 63). Also B. Stade, *ZAW* 3 (1883), 169, holds this view. Eerdmans, on the other hand, is opposed to this view, demonstrating that

---

[34] R. de Langhe, "L'autel d'or du temple de Jérusalem," *Bib* 40 (1959), 476-494; and MNAW.L 14, 6 (1952), 3-23.

incense was offered in sacrifices long before the exile.[35] Others (e.g. I. Benzinger, *OLZ* 32 [1929], 28f.; Haran, *Temples*, 235, n. 11) similarly defend the view, that already in early times there could have been altars of incense in Israel (see also in Busink, 289). Busink, 290f., having weighed different positions is of the opinion that, though offerings of incense may have been made in the temple, this does not yet imply that there was also an altar of incense in the temple. A container full of incense, after all, could also have been standing on the table (of the 'showbread'). For the post-exilic period the existence of a golden altar is almost unanimously affirmed from the time of the Maccabees (e.g. 1 Macc. 1:21; 4:49) up until that of Josephus and the Mishnah. True, as evidence Josephus, *c.App.* I §198, cites Hecataeus of Abdera, who reports that the temple contained an altar (βωμός) and a lampstand. Nor is an altar of incense listed among the objects, which Pompey saw in the temple (*Ant.* XIV §72). But in *Bell.* I §152, a par. to the text just cited, there is mention of 'altars of incense' which were made of 'solid gold' (θυμιατήρια, ὁλόχρυσα πάντα). It is hard to prove, that also before the time of the Maccabees there were altars of incense in the temple,[36] but it is plausible (see also 1 Chr. 28:18; 2 Chr. 26:16), all the more because various small altars of incense have come to light in Israel from the beginning of the Iron Age (see M. Haram, *VT* 10 [1960], 119; Keel, *Bildsymbolik*, 128, 131; E. Lipiński, *RTAT*, 267). That in the interior part of the first temple offerings of incense were brought would seem certain (Isa. 6:6; see also H. Wildberger, BK X/1, 42, 253; Ch. Dohmen, *TWAT*, IV, 797). It is therefore not too farfetched – the more since we can assume the existence of a Jebusite-Canaanite shrine there, before the temple of Solomon – to consider as authentic the 'golden altar' as an altar of incense: the מִזְבַּח הַקְּטֹרֶת (e.g. Exod. 30:27; 1 Chr. 6:34, etc.; cf. Wiener, *Altars*, 23). In the Pentateuch (e.g. in Exod. 40:5) one finds a reflection of this ancient cultic practice. E. Neufeld, *BA* 34 (1971), 60f., informs us, that the smoke of incense and other aromas, widespread also in Egypt, Babylonia, and Canaan, served a twofold purpose: (1) protection against diseases; (2) use as insecticide. Although other reasons for burning incense can be cited (e.g. by Eerdmans: (1) to make pleasant the smell of sacrifices; (2) protection of the priests from the dangerous presence of the deity), the aspect of killing numerous insects, which might be attracted to sacrifices, is not altogether imaginary (on altars of incense and the term חמן, cf. also K. Galling, *IDB*, II, 669f.; G. Sauer, *BHHW*, III, 155ff.; J. Milgrom, *EncMiqr.* VII, 112-118). Depictions of 'altars of incense' can be found in *ANEP*, pl. 575, the

---

[35] B.D. Eerdmans, *Das Buch Leviticus*, Giessen 1912, 28-34.

[36] See also E. Schürer, *The History of the Jewish People in the Age of Jesus Christ* (rev. and ed. by G. Vermes et al.), Edinburgh, II, 1979, 296, and n. 17.

'horned' altar of Megiddo (further pls. 334, 493, 514, 579, 581, 624, often of smaller format). Also in the Mishnah (Joma, V, 5, 7; Chagiga, III, 8; Zebachim, V, 2 etc.) there is mention of מזבח הזהב, which is sometimes (e.g. in Joma, V, 5) equated with the 'outside' altar (Lev. 16:18). From descriptions of the altar of incense in Exod. 30:1-10; 37:25-28, where there is reference to a length and breadth of one cubit and a height of 2 cubits and other details, it must not be inferred, that these details will correspond to the dimensions and ornamentations of the 'golden altar' (so, correctly, C.von Orelli, *RE*³, XVI, 407).

The second object, which is mentioned in this connection and which therefore we (along with others) do not wish to identify with the first, is what is called 'the table of the bread of the Presence.' We already encountered the word שלחן, 'table,' earlier (in 2:7; 5:7 above). The par. place 2 Chr. 4:19 speaks of 'tables' on which lay he bread of the Presence, followed by Josephus, *Ant.* VIII §89, who then again marks one of them as 'a large golden table, on which was placed the bread of God' (καὶ μίαν μεγάλην χρυσέαν, ἐφ (ἧς ἐτίθεσαν τοὺς ἄρτους τοῦ θεοῦ). Undoubtedly this is again an illustration of the later tendency to 'scale' upward. The words לחם הפנים (Exod. 35:13; 39:36; 1 Sam. 21:7) are a variant of לחם פנים (Exod. 25:30), by which is meant that there must 'continually' (תמיד; cf. Num. 4:7 לחם התמיד) be bread before the face of God. A better translation would be 'face bread' (see W. Dommershausen, *TWAT*, IV, 543ff.). Further instructions for the number and quality of the loaves to be baked for a later period can be found in Lev. 24:5-8 (see W.H. Gispen, COT, a.l.). In Exod. 25:23-30; 37:10-16 details concerning the table are given. In Exod. 40:23 there is something about the 'arrangement' of the bread, עֵרֶךְ לֶחֶם. From the root ערך various expressions for the 'arrangement of the bread' have been derived (see 2 Chr. 13:11; or 1 Chr. 9:32; 23:29; Neh. 10:34; and also 1 Chr. 28:16; 2 Chr. 29:18). There is mention of 12 loaves of bread, something also known in Babylonia (see Jeremias, *ATAO*, 423) and explained by Josephus, *Ant.* III §182, as referring to the division of the year in 12 months (or the 12 constellations in the zodiac). There is no mention in OT of this cosmic meaning, but it is supposed that the reference is to the 12 tribes. The most ancient biblical witness to the 'showbreads' is certainly 1 Sam. 21:2-7, where in the sanctuary of Nob David and his men, against the rules which were even then in effect, in place of the priests ate the 'showbreads' (cf. Matt. 12:1-4 and par.). According to Ezek. 41:22, the table measured 2x2x3 cubits. That in the post-exilic temple there was also a table for 'showbreads', is evident not only from 1 Macc. 1:22; 4:49-51 and Josephus, *Bell.* VII §148, but also from the depiction of the so-called Arch of Titus above the forum in Rome (see, e.g. *IDB*, I, 464). Also in NT the cultic significance of the table is mentioned (Hebr. 9:2; cf. L. Goppelt, *TDNT*, VIII, 211). In the Mishnah (Menachot, XI, 5-7) there is a lengthy discussion of the correct preparation of the loaves (cf. also E. Schürer, op. cit., 298 and n. 19; Dommershausen, 544). The custom of putting food before the deity can be found among many peoples and serves not only to feed her, but especially to put her in a favourable frame of mind (cf. also Busink, 291f., for a description of tables found in the ancient Near East).

Finally we briefly revisit the question, which already came up earlier in connection with 6:20 (above). The 'altar' mentioned there was identified by Noth (and others) with the table of the bread of the Presence before the adytum, and not with the 'golden altar of incense.' After discussing this verse we think, that this identification seems probably the best option, though no one may draw from this the conclusion, that in the original Solomonic temple there was no altar of incense.

7:49 *and the lampstands, five to the right and five to the left before the shrine, of leaf gold; similarly the floral work, the candelabra and the snuffers were of gold;*

In this verse we encounter the lampstands or, in view of the singular הפרח in the section which follows, the lampstand (so Noth). The word מְנֹרָה or מְנוֹרָה occurs approx. 40x in OT and can denote an (ordinary) domestic lamp (2 Kgs. 4:10), but is more frequently a term for the illumination of the tabernacle or temple (Exod. 25:31-35; 26:35; 30:27; 31:8; 35:14; 37:17-20, etc.; Jer. 52:19; Zech. 4:2, 11, etc.; cf. C. Meyers, *TWAT*, IV, 981-987). Sometimes (Exod. 26:35; 40:4, 24) the word refers to the stand and the branches on which lights could be placed. Sometimes (e.g. Exod. 25:31-35) the word refers to the central part of the lampstand. Sometimes one also gets the impression, that a מנרה had only one light (e.g. Exod. 27:20). In our verse it is assumed, that in the Solomonic temple there were 10 golden lampstands, 5 on the S side and 5 on the N side in front of the adytum (דביר; for this word, see comments on 6:5 above). In Vulg. we are told, somewhat redundantly, that the 5 to the S were of gold and similarly the 5 to the N; in Pesh. this is said only once, in accord with MT, but immediately at the beginning (the comment in the textcr. app. of *BHS* is therefore incomplete, if not incorrect!). In the par. 2 Chr. 4:20 it is merely reported, that the lampstands 'and their lamps', which 'had to burn before the adytum as prescribed', were finished with goldleaf; in vs. 7 the statement of our verse had already been followed. In 2 Kgs. 25:14ff. there is no mention of the lampstands, but there is in the par. Jer. 52:19. It is remarkable that in 2 Chr. 13:11 there is mention of only one golden lampstand with its lamps, as for that matter is the case in the P-section Exod. 25:31; 40:24, etc. One can find the somewhat fluctuating tradition between one or (many) more lampstands in the temple also in Josephus. In *Ant.* VIII §90 he says that 10,000 lampstands were made, on instructions from Moses, of which only one was then placed in the temple, which, by law, burned every day (for the Mosaic origin of the lampstand, also cf. D. Sperber, *JSS* 16 [1965], 135-159). Later there is also mention of one lampstand (1 Macc. 1:21; 4:49f.; cf. also Hebr. 9:2 and Josephus, *c.Ap.* I §§ 198f.). On the Arch of Titus in Rome, which we mentioned above, there also occurs a lampstand as booty from the second temple, which in later times, especially in the first century A.D., was frequently in evidence in some such form (see Busink, 292ff., and cf. Josephus's description of the lampstand of the Herodian temple: *Bell.*, VII §§148f.).

The question has been raised whether, in view of the secondary character of our verses, at least in the opinion of many scholars, there ever was a 7-branched lampstand in the Solomonic temple. Busink, 296, and others with him think not, because according to him such a lampstand was no part of the temple furnishings until the Persian age. He does assume, that the Solomonic temple had lights and that, in the wake of the study by K. Möhlenbrink, *ZDPV* 52 (1929), 257-286, Zech. 4:1ff. can be of further aid, because מנרה only refers to the stand on which the lamps were mounted (Busink, 298f.). The shape of the stand, however, remains hypothetical. We too are of the opinion, that every (possible) reconstruction of the lampstand is based only on conjecture. Nor do we deem it certain, that there were more than one lampstand or even ten, as our verse has it, before the adytum, though the absence of reference to such a lampstand in 2 Kgs. 25, or in Ezekiel's design, need not yet be arguments against such lampstands. Meyers, art. cit., p. 986, is of the opinion, that the symbolic value of the one tree-shaped מנרה of the tabernacle was overshadowed by the functional value (as lightbearers) of the unbranched stand of the Solomonic temple, and that there was perhaps even some competition between the מנרה-symbolism and the pillars Jachin and Boaz. This last point holds water only if these pillars also functioned as lights, an assumption which, as we indicated above, we do not share.

For זהב סנור see comments on 6:20 above, and *HAL*, s.v. (p. 700). The reference is presumably to beaten gold, a kind of 'goldleaf' or 'refined gold.' Especially the element of refinement and great value comes to the fore in our verse. This value applies also to the technical terms pertaining to the lampstand our verse furnishes. We already encountered the word פרח earlier (see comments on vs. 26 above). It is a 'flower bud.' This word not only occurs in the description of the lampstand in Exod. 25:31ff. (vs. 31, but now in the pl.!), but other terms derived from the world of flora arrest one's attention as well. Perhaps, says Meyers, 983, this phenomenon points to the transition from the use of plant motifs in general to their use in architecture, as this can also be observed in Egyptian art. This in turn may point to what we have noted earlier: the image of fertility 'of life in abundance, of the garden of God' (Hoogewoud, 197). In our verse the word indeed seems to be purely technical, and the singular catches the eye. A form that crept in from Exod. 25?

The נרות are the 'lamps,' or 'wicks,' a derivative of נר, which occurs 45x in OT, but only here in the books of Kings. Often the word denotes the small earthen oil lamp, of which many have been found in the Near East (see *HAL*, s.v.). The מלקחים, finally, are the 'snuffers,' the scissors with which the wicks of the lamps are trimmed (Exod. 25:38; 37:23; Num. 4:6; Isa. 6:6 and the par. 2 Chr. 4:21): the wick made of fabric or threads was cut short with a sort of scissors (H. Weippert, *BRL*^{2}, 198). Also in a text found in ancient Ugarit (RS 1957, 701 rev.), 80 *nrt* (= 'lamps') occur alongside of 10 *mqht* (= 'snuffers').[37]

7:50 *also the basins, the knives, the sprinkling bowls, incense boats, and firepans were of leaf gold, as were the sockets of the door wings of the interior of the Holy of Holies (of the doorwings of the temple).*
What follows in this verse is a certain amount of technical data with an emphasis on their 'golden' character. The first word is ספות, the sing. of which is cited as סף I (*HAL*). The word *sp* (Ugar.) or *sappu* (Akkad.) also occurs in other Sem. languages (*AHw*, 1027) and there means 'measuring barrel' (Ugar.) or 'metal barrel' (Akkad.). In OT the word further occurs in Exod. 12:22; 2 Sam. 17:28; 2 Kgs. 12:14; Jer. 52:19 and Zech. 12:2, but is missing in 2 Chr. 4:22, while it is also lacking in 2 Chr. 25:15 (par. to Jer. 52:19). In Hab. 2:15 the reading סף in place of ספ is based on conjecture. *HAL* renders the word by '(kultische) Schale aus Metall,' and also Noth and others translate it by 'basin' or 'bowl' or something similar (cf. Montg.-Gehman). LXX, however, has 'doors' (πρόθυρα); Tg. קוליא 'bowls' (see Krauss, *GLL*, II, 504); Pesh. 'snuffers' (*mzmk'* [pl.]); Vulg. *hydrias* 'water jars.' Kimchi and other medieval commentators support the view of the Tg. Rashi, in considering this and the following word, thinks of musical instruments. On the basis of comparative Semitics we opt for the meaning 'bowls' or 'basins.'

מזמרת, in form a fem. part. of the pi. of the verb זמר II, 'prune,' is a (pruning) knife (also in 2 Kgs. 12:14; 25:14; Jer. 25:18 and the par. 2 Chr. 4:22) (see *HAL*). LXX takes this word to mean 'nails' (ἥλοι) (according to Böttcher, *Neue Aehrenlese*, 64, n. 1, this is an auditory error for מסמרות); Vulg., however, has '3-pronged forks' (*fuscinulas)*; Pesh: 'torches' (*nptr* [pl.]); and Tg. leaves the word untranslated. It is possible that these knives were also used as 'snuffers,' though a somewhat more general cultic use seems more likely.

We already called attention to the word מזרקות above, vs. 40. The reference is to basins for sprinkling or libations. According to Rashi, it is for 'collecting blood.' These objects also occurred in the Jewish sanctuary of Jeb (Elephan-

---

[37] See M. Dahood, in L.R. Fisher, *The Claremont Ras Shamra Tablets* (AnOr 48), Rome 1971, 33f.

tine).[38] Such a basin could serve both for 'sprinkling' and 'collection' (e.g. Num. 7:13; see A.M. Honeyman, *PEQ* 71 [1939], 83f.; M. Broschi, *EncMiqr.* IV, 785).

The כפות, derived from כף, the 'open, spread-out hand', (according to *HAL*, s.v. 5b) are the 'metal dishes' (Noth: 'Pfannen'). Other translations (see e.g. Montg-Gehman) render it by 'spoons.' W.F. Albright, *BASOR* 47 (1932), 15ff., identified them with incense burners or dishes, with holes in them (cf. also G.M. Crowfoot, *PEQ* 72 [1940], 150-153). That the כפות served for burning incense, is also the opinion of Rashi and Ralbag (= Rabbi Levi ben Gersham, 1288-1344), but they further take the word to mean 'spoons.' LXX translates the word by τρύβλια ('bowls'), as does Tg. (בזיכיא). Vulg. has *mortariola*, 'small vessels of mortar'; Pesh. uses the same word as MT. Also in the case of this word it is hard to indicate a specific use, but it suggests the idea of small hollow bowls, which could function as spoons.

The word מחתה occurs, aside from here and in the par. 2 Chr. 4:22 and the related vss. 2 Kgs. 25:15; Jer. 52:19, only in the Pentateuch (Exod. 25:38; 27:3; 37:23; 38:3; Lev. 10:1; 16:12; Num. 4:9, 14; 16:6, 17f.; 17:2ff., 11). *HAL* offers 3 shades of meaning: (1) a pail for carrying hot coals and ashes (e.g. our verse); (2) a coal pan for offering incense; (3) a small pan for use with a lampstand. Rashi rightly links this word with the root חתה, 'remove': the מחתות shaped like a hoe or a rake, mere instruments for removing ashes from the altar and for carrying coals from the outside altar to the inside altar for burning incense. In any case, they had to do with fire and burning incense, a view which the ancient versions seem to confirm.

All the objects mentioned are of the finest gold, something that is hardly confirmed by 2 Kgs. 25:14. The redactor of these and the preceding verses, a man who probably lived in exile, did his best to impress his readers with the overwhelming riches of even the smallest objects, which were naturally available in and around the temple. That there were hardly any limits to the exaggeration is evident from the description in Josephus, *Ant.* VIII, §§91-94, who passes on fantastic numbers from the temple inventory: 80,000 jugs, 100,000 bowls of gold and double that number of silver. And so it goes on: the high priests possessed 1,000 outer garments studded with scintillating gems, while there were 10,000 ordinary priestly garments with purple belts, and 200,000 linen robes for the Levite singers. Is this purely an invention of Josephus, as Thackeray and Marcus (*LCL*, 621, n. a) would have us think, or does he stand in a tradition, which already started in the exile and not only continued in the time since then, but grew in scope?

---

[38] A. Cowley, *Aramaic Papyri of the Fifth Century*, Oxford 1923 (repr. Osnabrück 1967), nos. 30, 12; 31, 11.

It seems to us, that also the second part of our verse (though formally one has to grant Noth and others, that it is 'schwerlich ursprünglich', because it should have been brought up already in chap. 6) is inspired by a strong desire for Solomonic up-scaling. The reference in this part of the verse is to the פתות, sing. פֹּת*, which occurs only twice in OT (aside from our verse, in Isa. 3:17). They belong to the door wings of the temple. About the meaning of the word there is no unanimity: *HAL*, partly on the basis of the Akkad. *pūtu(m) (AHw,* 884f.), opts for the meaning 'forehead,' 'front,' a line of thought in which it was preceded by G.R. Driver, *JThS* 38 (1937), 38, and is being followed by many interpreters (e.g. H. Wildberger, BK X, p. 139). For Isa. 3:17 the translation *pudenda muliebra* (e.g. Gesenius, *Thesaurus*, 1096f.) was not unusual in earlier years and is being defended by scholars to this day (cf. Mont.-Gehman).[39] It is clear that for our verse this last-mentioned meaning does not – or does at most figuratively (see Gesenius) – hold water. LXX translates it by θύρωμα, 'door wing'; Tg. מְגִלְסָיָא, 'bars' (from the Gr. μοχλός, see Krauss, *GLL*, 324); Vulg. *cardines,* 'hinges'; Pesh.: *qrm'* [pl.], 'sheets' or 'hinges,' or 'coverings.' Rashi is of the opinion that it refers to 'keys.' In the par. 2 Chr. 4:22 the word וּפֶתַח has been incorporated in place of וְהַפְּתוֹת. This time the notice we found in Kings in 6:31f. above was not taken over in Chronicles. In this connection A. van Selms, TeU, on 2 Chr. 4:22, comments, that the word in Kings must be understood in line with the view in the Talmud as a 'hole, in which the pivot of the door turns,' which is then understood to 'have some resemblance to the female sex organ,' which is 'enough' for the Chronicler 'to alter the text.' It seems questionable to us, however, that the Chronicler, driven by such modesty, changed our text. He probably no longer understood the word, which is a technical term. Dalman, *AuS* 7, 69f., explains the word סִיר (Prov. 26:14) as 'hinge pin' and the word פֹּת as the 'hinge hole' ('Angelpfanne'), in which the pin fits (see also Businck, 232ff.). He defends the link with the *pudenda muliebra* (this is not done by K. Galling, H. Rösel, *BRL*[2], 348f.). Although the interpretation is opposed by Dalman, Dietrich, and others, it seems to us that in Isa. 3:17 priority must be given, both from a contextual viewpoint and from that of a comparison with the Assyrian, to the translation 'forehead' for our word. For our verse this would mean that a translation like 'facing' or 'front' is preferable, and that actually nothing new would be added to 6:31f. Gray has rightly noted, that it would be 'impracticable' for the hinge sockets of the doors in the floor and the lintel to be of gold, and that therefore another part of the door must be intended. Galling/Rösel, 348, inform us, that both for the protection and the ornamentation of the door wing of a gate a kind of ribbon-shaped metal work

---

[39] See also W. Dietrich, *Jesaja und die Politik*, München 1976, 43, n. 23.

could be applied, which served to enhance the stability of the door wing. A depiction of such a door fitting in bronze from the late Bronze Age, found in Jaffa, can be seen in *EncMiqr.* III, 739. The translation could be: 'hinge strip' (see also fig. 88 [349] in the art. of Galling/Rösel and esp. *ANEP*, pls. 356-365: the bronze ribbons of Balawat [Salmanassar III]). The reference is to strips of material, applied to reinforce the door wings on which – possibly – ornamentation was crafted.

Concerning these strips the author expressly adds to the statement, that they were intended for the door wings (for this word see comments on 6:31 above) of the 'inner house,' i.e. the shrine (see comments on 6:27 above), here called the 'holiest' place (see comments on 6:16 and 6:5 above).

As we knew from 6:31f., these doors themselves were made of wood. The 4 concluding words of our verse, however, produce a secondary impression: are we dealing here with a (superfluous) gloss on the immediately preceding text, or are the words intended to convey new information? The latter is suggested by LXX*, Pesh. and Vulg., as does the par. 2 Chr. 4:22 which reads לדלתי in place of ודלתי. The idea then is, that all outside doors of the היכל (for this word see 6:3 above) were of gold instead of wood, hence a substantial enhancement of the radiance of Solomon's kingdom and the glitter of the temple. But if that is true, why could not the redactor say this at the outset? In fact, this is how LXX translates it. If the last 4 words are a gloss on the immediately preceding text, then they are a 'Verballhornung,' a worsening of a good intention. It seems to us, that what we have here is indeed an 'enhancing' gloss, but one of ancient date which in the ongoing tradition – beginning with 2 Chr. 4:22 – led to golden doors for the 'house' of the temple, an enhancement of splendour which also the unknown glossator already envisioned in his mind.

7:51 *When all the work which King Solomon had done for the house of YHWH was completely finished, he brought in the things his father David had consecrated: the silver and the gold and the (other) objects, and placed them in the treasury of the house of YHWH.*

Although our verse is 'unübersetzbar,' according to Ehrlich, its intent is clear: Solomon completes the work and brings the temple treasures his father had gathered from elsewhere, into the treasury of the temple. Thenius, Pedersen, III-IV, 238, Noth and others suspect, that the 'sacred' objects of David could easily be the captured objects mentioned in 2 Sam. 8:10-12. Ehrlich moves the first בית יהוה after אביו and then continues with ואת־הכסף which, along with the following substantives, then becomes the object of נתן (cf. Delitzsch, *LSF* §7b). In this way the sentence does in fact run more smoothly, but also the more difficult reading of the text yields good sense. The finite verb נתן, asyndetically connected with the preceding text, can in our translation, at least in our language, acquire the force of a part. (Driver, §163).

The verb שׁלם only occurs in qal here in the books of Kings of the approx. 10x, that it occurs in qal in OT (see *KBL*, s.v.). It is an intransitive verb, which here means 'be enough' (see G. Gerleman, *THAT*, II, 925), 'be finished.' Accordingly, the verb has an another nuance than 'end,' which we encountered earlier (see 3:1; 6:9, 14; 7:1, 40). In the Jewish tradition people associate the verb with שׁלום: during the entire period of construction not a single workman died or suffered illness. As soon as the work had been completed, the workmen died in peace ... (Yalkut Shimoni). The word קדשׁ, in the plural here, refers to things to which an aura of 'holiness' clings, the 'votive gifts' (see *HAL*, s.v. 3aβ), which had been brought to the temple (also cf. 15:15). We consider the silver, the gold, and the objects made of other metal to be a further specification of these votive gifts of David and not, as many scholars do, objects from Solomon's collection. Sometimes (e.g. by Noth) another division is made: the gold and the silver with the votive gifts of David, and the objects on the side of Solomon. But this division is not necessary, if one views the asyndetic נתן as dependent on ויבא as we did (with Driver). LXX expressly also mentions all the 'holy things of Solomon' alongside the 'holy things of David', before speaking of the silver and the gold. The latter precious metals were then stored in the treasuries. The word אוצר occurs approx. 80x in OT and means 'supply' (Neh. 12:44, etc.), 'storehouse' (Neh. 13:12f.), 'treasure' (see *HAL*), in LXX θησαυρός (see F. Hauck, *TDNT*, III, 136f.), and is used here of the treasures belonging to and deposited in the temple. Where the storehouse of the treasures was precisely located, is not stated. Josephus, *Ant.* VIII §95, speaks of the 'treasuries of God', where Solomon deposited his treasures. In the remainder of his account (§§95-98) he relates an assortment of details about the courts of the temple, which are not found in our books of Kings, but which are probably derived from his knowledge of Herod's temple.

1 KINGS 8:1-13

8:1 *Then Solomon assembled the elders of Israel [all the heads of the tribes and the heads of families of the Israelites before king Solomon] in Jerusalem to bring up the ark of the covenant of YHWH from the city of David, which is Zion.*

2 *So all the men of Israel assembled to king Solomon at the feast in the month Ethanim, which is the seventh month.*

3 *When all the elders of Israel had arrived, the priests took up the ark;*

4 *and they brought up the ark of the YHWH and the tent of meeting and all the sacred furnishings that were in it; the priests and the Levites brought them up.*

5 *King Solomon and the entire assembly of Israel which had joined him (went) with him before the ark, sacrificing so many sheep and oxen that they could not be estimated or counted.*

6 *The priests then brought the ark of the covenant of YHWH to its place, to the shrine of the house, the innermost sanctuary beneath the wings of the cherubim.*

7 *For the cherubim spread out their wings over the place of the ark so that the cherubim screened off the ark and its carrying poles from above.*

8 *These carrying poles were so long that their ends could be seen from the holy place in front of the shrine, but were not visible from the outside; they are there to this day.*

9 *There was nothing in the ark except the two tables of stone which Moses had placed in it at Horeb when YHWH had made (a covenant) with the Israelites on their journey from Egypt.*

10 *When the priests came out of the holy place, a cloud filled the house of YHWH.*

11 *The priests could not remain standing to perform their ministry because of the cloud, for the glory of YHWH filled the house.*

12 *Then Solomon said: 'YHWH has said he would dwell in darkness;*

13 *I have indeed built for you a princely house, a fixed residence for you to dwell in forever.'*

INTRODUCTION

Following the relatively lengthy treatment of the arrangement and some details of the sanctuary – details which in later times hardly any longer played a role – this chapter is devoted to the dedication of the temple, an event in which

Solomon plays a significant role. The 'dedication' mainly consists of an account of the transfer and placement of 'the ark of the covenant' (vss. 1-11), after which comes the 'temple-dedication saying' (vss. 12f.), which in LXX only occurs at the end of the chapter after vs. 53 (for the latter cf. also E. Tov, *JNSL* 13 [1987], 154f.). Then follows a long speech by Solomon, which has the character of a prayer (vss. 14-61), while the chapter ends with the dedicatory offerings and feasts customary on these occasions (vss. 62-66). In 2 Chr. 5:2-7:10 one finds a section which runs parallel to our chapter, with the usual modifications, additions, and omissions. As was to be expected, Josephus, *Ant.* VIII §99-123, also devotes considerable space to the things related in our chapter, following a description of (among other things) the temple courts which is nowhere to be found in the OT but seems to be based on Josephus's acquaintance with the temple of Herod (*Ant.* §§95-98; Thackeray-Marcus, *LCL*, 622, n. c; see also the comments on 7:50 above; and Faber van der Meulen, 126-143, for the arrangement of the temple according to Josephus).

Generally speaking, most modern scholars regard this chapter as dtr. with scattered but clear indications of a pre-dtr. 'Grunderzählung' (Hentschel).[1] The dtr. composition, however, is not a homogeneous whole either but sometimes shows clear evidence of additions or the influence of later hands (Noth, *ÜGS*, 70, and others; for the vss. 1-10, Wellhausen, *Hexateuch*, 265-268; and for the vss. 14-61: the study of Talstra, *Solomon's Prayer*. The expansions already show up, upon comparison of MT with LXX, in vss. 1-11. The LXX translation is not only shorter (in vss. 1-5) but the text also runs more smoothly (see Rehm, *Untersuchungen*, 88f.; Benzinger; Burney, etc.). The Hebr. text fragments of our segment of the text found at Qumran (4 Q Kgs^a) are, as far as we know now, in agreement with MT.[2] The narrative of the transfer of the ark is reminiscent of 2 Sam. 6 (Montg.-Gehman; cf. Hölscher 1923, 165f.), and is regarded by Hölscher as the conclusion of the 'Baubericht.' In a sense the beginning of this chapter *is* the close of the period of temple construction while the chapter as a whole is simultaneously the apotheosis of the opening of the (new or renovated) temple. At the end of this first part (vss. 1-11), in which many elements of P may be present, the 'temple-dedication saying' of Solomon (vss. 12f.) occupies a unique position.

---

[1] Cf. also F.K. Kumaki, "The Deuteronomistic Theology of the Temple – as Chrystallized in 2 Sam 7, 1 Kgs 8," *Annual of the Japanese Biblical Institute* 7 (1981), 16-52; see now also G.N. Knoppers, "Prayer and Propaganda: Solomon's Dedication of the Temple and the Deuteronomist's Program," *CBQ* 57 (1995), 229-254.

[2] Cf. S.L. Mckenzie, "I Kings 8. A Sample Study into the Text of Kings Used by the Chronicler and Translated by the Old Greek," *BIOSCS* 19 (1986), 15-34, esp. 21; see now also E. Ulrich et al., *Qumran Cave 4* (DJD 14), Oxford 1995, 171-183.

1 KINGS 8:1-13

EXEGESIS

8:1 *Then Solomon assembled the elders of Israel [all the heads of the tribes and the heads of families of the Israelites before king Solomon] in Jerusalem to bring up the ark of the covenant of YHWH from the city of David, which is Zion.*
LXX (minus A and a few more MSS) prefaces the MT text with an addition: 'It came to pass when Solomon after 20 years completed the construction of the house of the Lord and of his own house that he ...' etc., a combination of items one can also find in 6:37, 7:1f, and 9:1, 10 (cf. inter alia Stade-Schwally; the textcr. app. *BHS*; also Gooding 1965, 156f., who speaks of LXX's 'time-tabling'). Nevertheless one need not follow this expanded translation – even if one were to adopt the view (with Thenius e.g.). that the dedication of the temple occurred at the end of a 20-year building period – because אז frequently occurs at the beginning of a sentence or story (see comments on 3:16 above). It is grammatically striking that following this word there is the verb קהל in the jussive form of the impf. (see also König §140 [*Jaqtul elevatum*]; Ges-K §109k; Joüon §114l), which Ges-K seeks to explain on 'rhythmic grounds.' Böttcher (§973.4) sees אז as a 'sinn-verwandte Partikel' of the *waw* of the *fiens consecutivum*. This interpretation is plausible (but cf. Driver, *Tenses*, 77, n. 2 and XVI; GD §62, rem. 1). In the par. 2 Chr. 5:2 the Hebrew text has יקהיל, but the second vowel is read as /e/ (hence as a jussive) in place of /i/.

The verb קהל only occurs in the books of Kings here, in hiph. in 12:21, and in niph. in the following verse. In addition, primarily in this chapter, one finds the substantive קהל (vss. 14 [2x], 22, 55, 65, and 12:3; in the entire OT the word occurs 123x, translated by ἐκκλησία in approximately half of the cases in LXX) of which the verb is a denominative (see H.-P. Müller, *THAT*, II, 609-619; *HAL*; K.L. Schmidt, *TDNT*, III, 530-536).[3] As the primary meaning of the substantive *HAL* offers 'Aufgebot,' e.g. the summons to battle for which people gather. But there can be various reasons for assembling the people or the 'elders' (Müller, 613, 617), among other things – as in our verse – to a cultic assembly. The initiative in the case of this 'gathering' of the elders and tribal heads proceeds from Solomon. In these sacred rites the king functions in his palace temple, which has been elevated to the status of state temple (Pedersen, III-IV, 163) and from this fact he derives the right to convene the leaders of the people.

These leaders are called זקנים, a word derived from זקן, 'old,' which occurs

---

[3] Cf. also J.D.W. Kritzinger, *Qehal Jahwe: wat dit is en wie daaraan mag behoort*, diss. Vrije Universiteit, Amsterdam 1957.

frequently in OT (in Kings, in the sense of 'elders,' also in vs. 3; 12:8, 6, 13; 20:7, 8; 21:8, 11; II 6:32 (2x); 10:1, 5; 19:2; 23:1). J. Conrad, *TWAT*, II, 639-650, points out that elders as representatives of major social communities are well attested throughout the ancient Near East with the exception of Egypt. According to the Mari texts, for example, the elders functioned more as the king's negotiating partners than as his executive agents. Originally the institution of elders was perhaps an organ of nomadic tribal government. After the group had settled in one place the old system of government often for a long time continued to function with little change. This is evident, for example, from the extensive powers of the 'city elders' (e.g. Ruth 4:1-12), or of the elders of larger areas (e.g. the election of Jephthah to the role of leader: Judg. 11:5-11). In the time of the monarchy the elders of Jerusalem and later also those of Samaria became part of the upper stratum in the increasingly centralized government. In our verse the point of mentioning the 'elders' is presumably that the leaders of all the tribes of Israel were assembled to this special cultic manifestation (Conrad, 650; G. Bornkamm, *TDNT*, VI, 657; cf. Grotius: *seniores, ii sunt Senatores magni Synedrii*; Benzinger: 'der israelitische Adel'; cf. the same in *RE*, I, 224-227). Numerous Hebr. MSS (Kennicot and De Rossi) and virtually all (important) MSS of the ancient versions insert כל before זקן. It is possible that at one time this word was used in part of the text tradition, but its addition in our text (and in the translation) is unnecessary.

The words after the second את up to the second 'Solomon' are missing in LXX*. It has to be granted that the statement makes more sense when it is simply stated that Solomon assembled the elders of Israel to Jerusalem (called 'Zion' in LXX). The whole intermediate section seems to be a gloss or even a number of glosses whose omission would not have adversely affected the clarity of the statement (Stade-Schwally; Benzinger; Burney; Noth, etc.), though it has to be admitted that the Chronicler must already have seen (a large part of) this addition. The ראשי המטות and נשיאי האבות are to be taken as (later) explanations of the 'elders.' The first expression occurs, among other places, in Num. 30:2; 36:1 (cf. Num. 1:4; 32:28, etc.; see Burney). The word מטה (see comments on 7:14 above) which – according to Wellhausen and others – occurs especially in P and means 'tribe' (H. Simian-Yofre, *TWAT*, IV, 822; cf. W.H. Gispen, *Numeri* (COT), I, 23) . The expression נשיאי האבות is an abbreviation of נשיאי בית האבות; 'the princes of the ancestral house,' the family in a broader sense (Böttcher, *Neue Aehrenlese*, 67f.; König, *Stil.* 202f.; Noth; et al.). Aside from 11:34, נשיא, 'prince', occurs only here in the books of Kings (see F. Stolz, *THAT*, II, 110, 115f.; H. Niehr, *TWAT*, V, 647-657). The word occurs frequently in 'priestly' documents (Num. 62x; Ezek. 37x; Josh. 13x, so Stolz). Also Niehr, 653, points out that within the dtr. history the passage in which the word occurs needs to be attributed to the P-redactor. Although this possibility cannot be ruled out, it seems to us more likely that a glossator added this further clarification of the word 'elders' to the text, partly in connection with the following words. The first addition לבני ישראל can often be found after similar preceding st. cstr. combinations (Num. 30:2; 32:28 etc.; König §2811, n.). The second addition אל־המלך שלמה is redundant unless an attempt is made to explain it as a kind of substitute for a reflexive pronoun (Böttcher §852; cf. also Vatablus: *antecedens pro relatio*).

The purpose of the convocation of the elders by king Solomon is to transport the 'ark of the covenant' (on this subject see comments on 2:26; further [with bibliography] Busink, 276-285) from the old location to the new. The old location is here called 'the city of David.' This term, too, has occurred and been discussed earlier (see comments on 2:10 above). Here 'the city of David' – one of the relatively rare times in OT (G. Fohrer, *TDNT*, VII, 292, 297) – is expressly identified with 'Zion.' Of the 154x this name occurs in OT, it is mentioned 'independently' only here in the books of Kings (2 Kgs. 19:21, 31 are parallels of Isa. 37:22, 32). Especially in the case of prophets like Isaiah (47x), Jeremiah (17x) and in the Psalms (38x) the name often acquires a theological and cultic quality (see F. Stolz, *THAT*, II, 543-551; also Fohrer, 292, n. 1), but here it is no more than a term for a part of the old city with the acropolis (cf. 2 Sam. 5:7, 9; 6:10, 12, 16; E. Otto, *TWAT*, VI, 64f.). As already observed under 2:10, this 'fortress of Zion' must have been located on the S part of the E hill of Jerusalem. Solomon, by establishing his complex of palaces and court temple on the hill to the N of the city, undoubtedly created a connecting road or bridge between the 'old' Zion and the 'new' temple mount. Because the temple mount was on a higher elevation than the old part, a form of the verb עלה is appropriate here.

8:2 *So all the men of Israel assembled to king Solomon at the feast in the month Ethanim, which is the seventh month.*

Of this verse LXX* only reports the essential: the statement of the name of the month in which Solomon assembled 'all Israelites' (cf. Vulg.: *universus Israhel*) at Jerusalem. Here again the major part of this verse conveys the impression that it is glossarial or redactional. The difference between this and the previous verse is that now all the men of Israel, instead of only the 'elders,' have been summoned to Jerusalem. Perhaps the redactor or glossator intended, by means of this expansion, to underscore that the dedication of the temple ultimately had to be 'a feast of the Israelite people' for everyone. Josephus, *Ant.* VIII §99, combines the elements of the vss. 1 and 2 so as to say that the elders on their part carried out the organization involved in assembling the rest of the nation.

More important is the statement that the feast took place in the month Ethanim. Already in 6:1, 37f. there was mention of the ancient Canaanite month names Ziv and Bul. Ethanim is sometimes connected (by *HAL* for example) with איתן, 'permanent' as in 'an everflowing stream' (Deut. 21:4; Amos 5:24, etc.). This month name also occurs on Phoen. inscriptions (*KAI* 37, 1f.; 41,4), and here too scholars (e.g. *KAI*, II, 54; Gibson, *TSSI*, III, 126) refer to 'the ever-flowing stream' as explanation for the name of the month, which – as the 7th month – coincides with our month of September/October (in later Judaism the name Tishri is used for this month, see e.g. Josephus, *Ant.* VIII §100). Other explanations of the name Ethanim have been offered as well. Böttcher (*Neue Aehrenlese,* 68; cf. his grammar §697) points to a possible consideration of 'den Stillstand (cf. *solstitium*) der Nachtgleiche,' also because it is not until November and December that the 'everflowing streams' begin to flow. Thenius, who endorses Böttcher's criticism of the 'everflowing streams,' interprets Ethanim as '*Gaben-* oder *Frucht*monat.' But this suggestion, too, is no more than a hypothesis. A scholar like Noth similarly entertained doubts about the 'customary' explanation of Ethanim, without, however, offering a new explanation. Tg.'s translation is remarkable: 'In the month the ancients called the first month but which is now the 7th.' From this statement it would appear that the ancient Israelites began the (civil) year in the fall, and the later Jews in the spring. Pesh. speaks of $b^e jarḥa\ dallata$, 'in the month of the ingatherings (of the harvest).' This is the month in which 'the feast of tabernacles' is celebrated which, in the words of Josephus, is 'a particularly holy and important feast among the Hebrews.' Accordingly, it is the opinion of many scholars that the dedication of the temple coincided with the (beginning of the) feast of tabernacles, which is in fact the most important of the 3 great pilgrim feasts. On the older festival calendars this feast is called 'the feast of the ingathering,' especially of grain, oil, and wine (Exod. 23:16; 34:22); see also S. Aalen, *BHHW*, II, 1052f.). The 'tabernacles' are mentioned only in more recent festival calendars (Deut. 16:13; Lev. 20:34). The word חג in our verse must refer to this great harvest festival. The word occurs in the books of Kings also in vs. 65 and 12:32 (2x) and 33 of the 62x it is found in OT (B. Kedar-Kopfstein, *TWAT*, II, 703-744, esp. 734f.). The verb form חגג, on the other hand, occurs only 12x. Hrbek thinks that underlying חג there was originally a bilateral root חג, 'be round' from which the meaning 'describe a circle' and then 'dance' is said to have evolved.[4] Others prefer to think of the cycle of the year (cf. Kedar-Kopfstein, 731f.). In any case, the reference here is to a feast announced as a unique event.

As to the time of the celebration of the feast of dedication there is a peculiar difficulty. In 6:38 we are told that the temple was completed in the month Bul, which is the 8th month; in 12:32 we read that Jeroboam introduced his (new)

---

[4] I. Hrbek, "*ḥg* und verwandte Wurzeln in den semitischen Sprachen," *Wissenschaftliche Zeitschrift der Universität Halle* 17 (1968) (Fs C. Brockelmann), 95-104.

cultic service on the 15th day of the month Bul, with the express notation that it was 'like the festival held in Judah' (NIV). In our verse it is suggested, however, that the feast of dedication took place in the 7th month. Ewald, *GVI*, III, 334, thought that Solomon had advanced the feast, which lasted 2x7 days (see comments on vs. 65 below), by a month. Keil (also Šanda, Van Gelderen, Van den Born and others), on the other hand, believes that, after completing the construction of the temple in the 8th month, Solomon shifted the dedication to the 7th month of the following year 'um diese große Nationalfeier in den Sabbatmonat des Jahres zu verlegen, 8 Tage vor dem Laubhüttenfeste, an welchem das Volk mit Opfergaben von der Jahresernte beim Heiligtum zu erscheinen pflegte.' Thenius, basing himself on the 'prefatory statement' of LXX in vs. 1 (see above), believes it is possible that the dedication of the temple did not take place until the 13th year after its construction, something which the redactor of this part of MT had skillfully glossed over. Kittel, in turn, thinks that the author of our piece is a different as well as a later writer from the one who wrote 6:37f. From this assumption he then deduces a plausible point in time by which the 'second source' can be dated. At that point 'hatte man ein Interesse die Judäische Feier als durch Salomo geheiligt darzustellen,' and that in contrast to the 8th month of Ephraim. Benzinger considers the shift of the temple dedication from the month Bul, the actual month of the dedication, to the 7th month, which in later years was set aside for the great autumn festival, to be an accommodation to a custom which was already followed in the time of the Dtr. Noth (and, following him, Würthwein) thinks that originally a reference to a year had introduced the notice (vs. 1), which was later replaced by a dtr. redactor, as a result of which the time span between the completion of the construction and the transfer of the ark was obscured. Morgenstern claims that the beginning of the feast of dedication fell in the 7th month, and the climax in the 8th.[5] According to him, there was a change in the Israelite calendars, as a result of which the older calendar gave the 8th month as the highpoint of the feast, the later calendar the 7th (on this problem, see Montg.-Gehman and the lengthy note in Stade-Schwally). Gray adds that, in the Ugar. Baal myth, the completion of the 'house of Baal' also occurred on the eve of the rainy period in the fall.

Gaster, *Myth*, 494f., stresses that the time of the dedication of the temple was carefully considered because it followed an ancient custom in the course of which the rain and fertility goddess, after her disappearance in the realm of chaos, reappeared in fresh glory. This triumph and the enthronement of the deity took place annually and formed the central theme of the New Year's myths known to us from the Canaanite, Mesopotamian, and Hittite world. In

---

[5] J. Morgenstern, "The Three Calendars of Ancient Israel," *HUCA* 1 (1924), 13-78, esp. 67.

this connection especially the date chosen, the autumn equinox, is important in view of the importance of the sun.[6] De Moor also stresses the link between the New Year's festival and the feast of dedication of the Baal temple. In this connection he is of the opinion that Solomon delayed the dedication for almost a full year after the completion of the building of the temple, and that this dedication coincided with the feast of the king's own coronation.[7] Solomon's delaying the event, therefore, was not proof of idleness but an act of obedience to an ancient eastern tradition according to which sanctuaries must preferably be dedicated on a 'New Year's Day.'

In the views of these last-mentioned scholars there is well-warranted reference to the Ugar., or more broadly, the ancient oriental tradition concerning the coincidence of the feast of dedication of a sanctuary and the autumnal feast par excellence or perhaps also the New Year's festival preceding it. In our treatment of the preceding chapters about the construction of the temple we have more than once referred to the Canaanite background of the Solomonic temple. It may be assumed that also as it concerned the date of the dedication King Solomon adhered to this tradition. But we can no longer determine precisely to what the discrepancy in the texts between the 8th month of the completion and 7th month of the dedication is to be attributed. We agree with Montg.-Gehman that the solution to the problem presented by Morgenstern, is 'most attractive,' even though we definitely do not rule out the presence in the text of different redactional hands.

8:3 *When all the elders of Israel had arrived, the priests took up the ark;*
Only the second half of our verse occurs in LXX*. The fact that the 'elders of Israel' came is, after vs. 1., almost self-evident. Würthwein is of the opinion that in the old notice there was mention especially of the elders and not of the king and that the dtr. only afterwards attributed the initiative to the king. But in view of the temple's status as royal sanctuary this suggestion does not seem plausible to us. In our verse only the priests function as bearers of the ark, though in the following verse also the Levites are mentioned in MT (see there), and in the par. 2 Chr. 5:4 the word 'priests' has even been replaced by the word 'Levites.' In 2 Sam. 6:16, to which the narrator apparently tacitly orients himself, 'the city of David' is mentioned as the abode of the ark (cf. 2 Sam. 5:7 and comments on 2:10 above).

8:4 *and they brought up the ark of YHWH and the tent of meeting and all the*

---

[6] See also Th. H. Gaster, *Thespis*, New York 1961², 66ff.
[7] J.C. de Moor, *The Seasonal Pattern in the Ugaritic Myth of Ba'lu* (AOAT 16), Neukirchen-Vluyn 1971, 59f.; see also his *New Year with Canaanites and Israelites*, I, Kampen 1972, 18.

sacred furnishings that were in it; the priests and the Levites brought them up.
According to the shorter reading of LXX*, the priests mentioned in vs. 3 brought up the ark, as well as the 'tent of meeting' mentioned in our verse and all the sacred furnishings of that tent, after which the actions described in the vss. 5f. began. In the longer reading of MT we read that the priests 'brought up' these things, i.e. they brought them from the city of David, which was situated at a lower elevation, to the temple complex situated on a higher level. As a kind of gloss it is again reported at the end of the verse that the priests, but now in conjunction with the Levites (cf. 2 Chr. 5:4, which asyndetically joins 'Levites' to 'priests'; as do a few MSS – according to Kennicott – in our verse), brought up the furnishings (but Pesh. translates אתם by *'mhwn*, taking את as a preposition: 'with them'). As we commented earlier, the shorter reading of LXX seems to us more authentic. This does not alter the fact that our lengthier MT version *is* meaningful and at the same time already shows something of a later interpretation which is concluded in the text of Chronicles: not the priests, after all, but the Levites carried the ark and the sacred furnishings! Of the 354x that Levi or the Levites are mentioned in OT they occur in the books of Kings – excepting our verse – only in 12:31.

The long and complex history of the Levites in OT and in Judaism, especially since the late monarchy, is the history of the Israelite-Jewish cult as such (K. Koch, *BHHW*, II, 1077ff.; D. Kellermann, *TWAT*, IV, 499-521). There is a striking difference in the number of occurrences of Levites between Kings and Chronicles. While the name occurs twice in Kings, Chronicles has 113 occurrences or, if one includes the books of Ezra and Nehemiah as the 'chronistic history' as a whole, even 182. P, furthermore, mentions the Levites 66x and Deut. 26x (Kellermann, 502). On the meaning of the name לוי there is no unanimity, although today the tendency is to view it as a hypochoristic proper name meaning 'adherent, client, worshipper of the god X'.[8] Neither is there agreement, certainly, about the relation between the 'tribe' of Levi and the Levites, nor about the link between a 'secular' and a 'priestly' tribe, at least if there ever was a 'secular tribe' (on these problems, see Kellermann, 491ff.). Because of their close kinship to Simeon and Judah, the Levites are sometimes linked with the south of Judah or with the extra-Palestinian Kadesh. In Exod. 32:25-29 and Deut. 33:8-11 there is an emphasis on the Levites' special devotion to YHWH and on their performance of priestly functions (Kellermann, 493cf.). From Judg. 17 and 18 we may perhaps conclude that in ancient times the Levites could have an independent priestly function or at least be desired as

---

[8] Cf. M. Weippert, *Die Landnahme der israelitischen Stämme in der neueren wissenschaftlichen Diskussion* (FRLANT 92), Göttingen 1967, 48, n. 8 (ET: *The Settlement of the Israelite Tribes in Palestine* (SBT II, 21), London 1971, 43, n. 139).

priests ('umherziehende Priestergenossenschaft' [?], K. Koch, *BHHW*, II, 1078). In the time of the early monarchy there is little mention of 'Levites' because priests appealed to Zadok (Aaron). In Deuteronomy, however, priests are counted among 'Levites' ('levitical priests') but the cultic centralization occasioned by the Josian reforms over time made the Levites outside of Jerusalem into 'second-rate clergy.' Already in Ezek. 40-48, but especially in P (on this subject, see Burney among others) one finds Levites in this subordinate position vis-à-vis the priests: 'Aaroniden und Leviten zusammen bilden den Stamm Levi, die Aaroniden sind die Priester, die Leviten ihnen als Clerus minor unterstellt'.[9] In later times, therefore, there are 'priests who serve in the temple' and 'priests who serve at the altar' (Ezek. 40:45f.; cf. 42:13). In Num. 4, for example (but see also Deut. 10:8), the breaking up and transfer of the tent-sanctuary is mentioned as a 'service' of the Levites. These 'traces of priestly penmanship" also surface in our verse (so, correctly, Haran, *Temples*, 200), so that the word 'Levites' can appropriately be viewed as an accommodation to an exilic or postexilic idea concerning the task of priests and the Levites subordinate to them in the sanctuary, an accommodation which has no basis in Solomonic reality.

Another word one can only find here in the books of Kings is אהל מועד. This designation occurs in OT no fewer than 133x, 120x in P alone (see K. Koch, *TWAT*, I, 134; but cf. G. Sauer, *THAT*, 1, 743, who counts 146 occurrences in OT; further, see esp. Schmitt, *Zelt und Lade*, 175-255 [with lit.]). There are various translations for this desert tent: 'tent of meeting' (between YHWH and Moses, or Israel); 'tent of assembly' (of divine beings); 'tent of assembly' (for a festival; see also Koch, *TWAT*, IV, 750). Luther translated 'Stiftshütte' in accordance with the medieval distinction between 'parish churches and collegiate churches' (R. Kittel, *PE*³, XIX, 33; Koch, *TWAT*, I, 134). The attribute מועד proves to have been added to אהל later. In Exod. 33:7-11 we are told that Moses pitched a tent outside the camp to receive revelations or oracles there. He called this tent a 'tent of meeting' (cf. Num. 11:16-29; 12; Deut. 31:4f.; further also Exod. 34:4f.). A clear distinction can be demonstrated between this tent and the 'tabernacle' stemming from P (which possibly had the later temple as model; see also G. Sauer, *THAT*, I, 744f.; Haran, *Temples*, 262-269; esp. 269). According to Von Rad P is rooted in the 'Zeltradition,' the temple in the 'Lade-tradition').[10] P, however, later combines (and equates) the 'priestly' temple (tabernacle) with this 'non-priestly' but especially '(prophetic) tent of meeting.' This reality comes out,

---

[9] Cf. A.H.J. Gunneweg, *Leviten und Priester*, Göttingen 1965, 185.

[10] G. von Rad, "Zelt und Lade," *Gesammelte Studien zum Alten Testament* (ThB 8), München 1958, 109-129.

among other things, in the fact that the 'tent of meeting' is no longer pitched outside the camp as a mere 'oracle' tent but stationed in the center (see further Haran, 270-273; and esp. Schmitt, 256-303). In our redactional notice Solomon not only transferred the ark but also this tent to the renewed sanctuary (Schmitt, 193, thinks the reference here is only to 'David's tent'). But (with Wellhausen, Noth and many others; also cf. Pedersen, III-IV, 170, n. 2) we consider it unlikely that Solomon caused 'the tent,' which after all was a tent pitched by David (cf. 1:39; 2:28ff.; Schmitt, 193) to be moved along with the 'holy objects,' כלי הקדש in it (cf. also A. Reichert, *BRL*², 189-194; K.-M. Beyse, *TWAT*, IV, 184f.), though by itself it is conceivable that a certain selection of the older cult objects may have been given a function alongside the new. As an addition to our verses. Josephus, *Ant.* VIII §§104f., reports that the candlestick, the table and the golden altar were placed in the same position before the *adytum* which they occupied earlier in the tabernacle. According to him, the bronze altar was placed outside, across from the temple entrance.

8:5 *King Solomon and the entire assembly of Israel which had joined him (went) with him before the ark, sacrificing so many sheep and oxen that they could not be estimated or counted.*
Here again MT, by comparison with LXX^(B, Luc.), has a number of additions which are closely related to P. LXX* simply reads: 'and the king and all Israel in front of the ark sacrificed sheep and oxen without number.' The word עדה which (according to statements in *HAL* and *TWAT*, V, 1081) occurs 149x in various forms in OT is found in Kings only here and in 12:20. The greatest concentration (129x) occurs in the hexateuch; according to many exegetes in the form in which it is used here it is a typical and 'technical' (H. Ringgren, *TWAT*, V, 1092) word from the Priestly Codex, though it can also be used as a term for a 'swarm' of bees (Judg. 14:8) or 'birds' (Hos. 7:12). LXX very frequently translates the word by συναγωγή: hence the Hebr. word denotes the Israelitish judicial or cultic community. This 'younger' priestly word is said to have replaced the 'older' word from the dtr. school, קהל. That the עדת ישראל is viewed as a collective is evident from the following plural נועדים (for this phenomenon, cf. also König §334k; Ges-K §145c). This part. niph.-form of the verb יעד (G. Sauer, *THAT*, I, 742-746; M. Görg, *TWAT*, III, 697-706), which in qal (meaning 'determine time or place') occurs only 5x, in niph., on the other hand, 19x (but no more in the books of Kings), in the last-mentioned stem-modification usually means 'assemble (at the appointed place).' With the preposition על the verb frequently (except precisely the present verse) indicates opposition (see Görg, 703). It is no wonder, then, that some scholars (e.g. Delitzsch, *LSF* §150c, Ehrlich) view אתו as a variant of עליו. In the par. 2 Chr. 5:6 the former prepositional form has for that reason been omitted. Vulg. ingeniously saves both prepositions by inserting *gradiebatur* (*cum illo* ... etc.)

after *multitudo Israhel quae convenerat ad eum* (cf. also Pesh. which adds *qymyn 'mh*).

Our verse depicts king Solomon and the whole community of Israel sacrificing sheep and oxen as they walk before the ark (for the verb, see comments on 1:9 and 3:2 above). The verb זבח occurs in qal 113x, but only 22x in pi. (J. Bergman, *TWAT*, II, 513; cf Jenni, *Pi'el*, 205). According to Ewald §120b, the pi. – except again in our verse – relates to censurable actions in the sacrificial cult. In the above stem-modification of the verb Jenni (205ff.) sees an expression of the successive element, although it is often used for the illegitimate cult. He does not, however, think that our verse, along with the par. 2 Chr. 5:6 and 30:22, where the sacrifices are legitimate, is explained by a pi.-form of the verb.

The conclusion of our verse contains an expression we already encountered above in our discussion of 3:8 (cf. also Van Zijl, *Baal*, 271). Ges-K §119z thinks the preposition מן in מרב is used causatively in the sense of 'on account of.' LXX* reads ἀναρίθμητα for the entire dependent clause beginning with אשר, but we agree with Burney (against Stade-Schwally and others) that 'the translator's single word is intended to satisfy the whole expression in the Hebr.' The entire verse, as we now find it in MT, not only conveys the impression of being secondary but also of being written (by a later glossator) to give the feast of dedication, especially in the material sense, a dimension which will be virtually unsurpassable (cf. vs. 63; J. Conrad, *TWAT*, IV, 977f.; Benzinger, and others). Josephus, *Ant.* VIII §§102f., too, makes his contribution to the superlative degree by reporting, among other things, not only that the ground was soaked because of the many libations but that so much incense was offered that the sweet fragrance of it could be savored from a great distance. On the other hand, the use of a sacrificial feast by the king in conjunction with his people undoubtedly stems from an (early) time in which the priestly service had not yet been organized along the lines of P.

8:6 *The priests then brought the ark of the covenant of YHWH to its place, to the shrine of the house, the innermost sanctuary, beneath the wings of the cherubim.*

This verse highlights the transfer and placement of the ark in the shrine of the temple. As in 6:16, for example, so here too the phrase, 'the most holy [place],' is added. The ark, in accordance with dtr. usage (so Benzinger, Burney, Noth, etc.), is here called 'the ark of the covenant of YHWH' (see comments on 2:26 and 3:15 above), though LXX[B] only refers to the ark here (cf. also S.L. McKenzie, *BIOSCS* 19 [1986], 21). D. Sperber, *ZAW* 79 (1969), 80, has called attention to a tannaitic fragment of a *Beraitha de-Melechet Hammishkan*, in which our verse is cited as follows: 'The priests brought the ark of YHWH to the shrine of the house.' Both 'the covenant' and 'to its place' have been omitted in this Bible citation, a fact which could point to another Hebr. version, though only one of the MSS consulted by Kennicott shows the firstmentioned omission. This observation, accordingly, cannot be said to have much text-critical value. The designation of the 'place' מקום (see also J. Gamberoni, *TWAT*, IV, 1113-1124; esp. 1121) of the ark in the shrine דביר of the temple underneath the 'wings of the cherubim,' though it does not yet betray a 'technical use' of the word מקום (so H. Köster, *TDNT*, VIII, 197; cf. D.F. Murray, *VT* 40 [1990], 302f., and also the following verse), one does get the impression that the author used precisely this word intentionally. The 'deeper meaning' of the word seems to have escaped some of the later copyists of the Hebr. text.

In 6:23-28 the cherubim have already been treated at length. Here the discussion is continued particularly in connection with the location of the ark.

8:7 *The cherubim spread out their wings over the place of the ark so that the cherubim screened off the ark and its carrying poles from above.*
This verse indicates that the function of the cherubim in the shrine was to 'cover' the ark. The verb סכך is distinguished in *HAL* – in contrast to, say, *KBL* and Gesenius, *Thesaurus*, who assume a single root, and BDB, which assumes 2 roots – into 3 homonymous roots, of which I in qal (for the form see Bg. II §27d) has the meaning 'screen off protectively' (Exod. 25:20; 37:9; 40:3; Ezek. 28:14, 16; Ps. 140:8; Job 40:22; Lam. 3:44; 1 Chr. 28:18; further T. Kronholm, *TWAT*, V, 838-856, esp. 841ff.; Zorell, 553). In a number of the above-mentioned texts, as in our verse, this proves to be a special function of the cherubim (Exod. 25:20; 37:9; 40:3; 1 Chr. 28:18). In place of ויסכו the par. 2 Chr. 5:8 reads ויכסו, 'they covered,' and is supported in this by LXX. But this obvious simplification need not be taken over. In 2 Chr. 5:8 the preposition על would be more natural than אל after פרשים in our verse[11], but while אל indicates to what point the wings extended, על tells us that the wings extended *over* the ark. Keel, *Bildsymbolik*, 149, believes that the 2 cherubim must be viewed as the 'throne of YHWH,' because, especially in the psalms, there is mention of the 'throne of YHWH' (Pss. 9:5; 47:9; 93:2; 97:2; cf. also Isa. 6:1), and because the cube-shaped shrine could scarcely accommodate two 5 m high cherubim figures plus a throne. Figures in his book (pp. 149f.) show that in the early iron age such thrones cannot have been uncommon in the Phoen.-Canaanite area. Also Mettinger thinks that the cherubim were positioned side-by-side – hence did not face each other – with their faces toward the temple hall (see 2 Chr. 3:13) and that they thus formed a throne in the way such a throne is depicted on the sarcophagus of Ahiram of Byblos and

---

[11] So e.g. A. Noordtzij, *Het Hebreeuwse voorzetsel* אל, Leiden 1896, 104.

on a representation on an ivory plaque from Megiddo (14th to 12th century before our era).[12] With respect to the ark he agrees with De Vaux's view (cf. *Inst.* II, 127-133). The latter believed that the ark, as a box-shaped base and independently of a cherub throne, originally served the invisibly present deity. Later the ark acquired the function of a footstool in front of the cherub throne (cf. 1 Chr. 28:2). The ark and the footstool, according to Mettinger, are identical. Haran, *Temples*, 252f.) stresses that in this context the verb סכך may not mislead us, since it serves to indicate the position of the ark in relation to the cherubim: 'The symbol is not that of a covering but of a throne formed by the outspread wings.' Haran further points out (pp. 247-251) that the כפרת is actually the 'throne' and the ark a box which functions as a footstool before the throne. Greßmann, *Lade*, 64, believes, not that the cherubim were there to protect, still less to cover, the ark, 'sondern sie hatten einen anderen Zweck, der uns verschwiegen wird.' That mysterial purpose, according to him, was for them to screen off and cover a god-image with their wings. The image of the deity (and Greßmann, 63, posits that YHWH was conceived as Baal) was located in the ark. The ark, then, was a portable sanctuary in which the god-image was transported and on which it was occasionally exhibited. The ark came originally from Shiloh.

In a separate postscript after the vss. 1-13 of our chapter, Würthwein, 89ff., refers to what he considers the remarkably retiring role King Solomon played in the transfer of the ark to the temple. From this he deduces that Solomon preferred to view the cherubim as symbol of the presence of God in the temple. They were, according to 6:23-28, 'bearers of the deity.' In this preference scholars perceive a Canaanite background and this led to a 'Baalisierung des Jerusalemer Gottesbegriffes' (Maier). The tribes of Israel, however, especially the northern tribes, preferred to view the *ark* as symbol of the presence of God. Still according to Würthwein, there is perceptible, between the lines of our verses, a controversy between the king, who was open to Canaanite ideas, and the representatives of the ancient Israelitish traditions of faith − a controversy between the northern tribes and Jerusalem.

This is not the place for us to discuss the above theory and many other theories posited in this connection with respect to the essence and function of the ark (there is much material in the above-mentioned important study by Schmitt, *Zelt und Lade*; cf. also H.-J. Zobel, *TWAT*, I, 391-404; K. Galling, *BRL*[1], 343f.; *BRL*[2], 325f.; and Busink, 276-285, plus the literature cited there[13]). What is clear, however, is that in the (tradition and) religious history

---

[12] T.N.D. Mettinger, *The Dethronement of Sabaoth. Studies in the Shem and Kabod Theologies* (ConB OT 18), Lund 1982, 20-24.

[13] See now also C. Houtman, *Exodus* (COT), III, Kampen 1996, §4.5 (pp. 356-378).

of Israel, as this emerges in the literature left to us in the OT, the ark underwent a reduction and emptying of its function. As a result, in 1 Kgs. 8 one can hardly any longer find any trace of tension between the divine presence and the ark (cf. W. Seeber, *ThLZ* [1958], 723; Zobel, 402). The text only says that the cherubim 'stood protectively over' the ark and above the carrying poles (Pesh. reads 'in the holy place' instead of 'to the place of the ark'; it further translates the second הכרובים by 'with their wings,' a phrase which, according to Berlinger, is reminiscent of Exod. 37:9). How the cherubim were precisely positioned is not clearly indicated either in our verse or in 6:23-28 (only in 2 Chr. 3:13; against Würthwein). Partly on the basis of forms and representations of thrones in Egypt and the ancient Near East in the third and second millennium before our era, Metzger, *Königsthron*, 338-344, indeed suspects that the posture of the cherubim in the temple of Jerusalem was that they stood erect on their hind legs and extended their wings sideways. If the wings were attached to the back, they were probably spread out horizontally, but if they were attached to the upper arms, they were probably spread out obliquely. Metzger concludes from this that the formula ישב הכרובים in the case of YHWH may not be linked with the cherubim in the adytum because the cherubim themselves did not form the throne of the deity.

'Carrying poles,' ברים in Hebr., occur primarily in P as a reference to the carrying poles of the ark (Exod. 25:14f.; 35:12 etc.), of the altar (Exod. 27:6f., etc.), of the alter of incense (Exod. 30:4f., etc.) and of the 'table of the showbreads' (Exod. 25:27f., etc.). In addition the word occurs also in the sense of 'twig' (Ezek. 17:6; 19:14; cf., among others, *HAL*, s.v. בד II, to distinguish it from no fewer than 4 other homonyms). Busink, 282f., pictures our verse as saying that the ark was set on a stone socle (possibly covered by cedar and ornamented with flowers) which served as a pedestal (see also fig. 49 and 60 in his book). Partly based on 6:27, he assumes that the socle, as was customary in proto-Phoen. and Phoen. temples, was placed by itself in the middle of the shrine. He rejects the idea that there was a throne in the shrine on the ground that such a throne would certainly not have remained unreported in the account of the construction in Kings and/or Chronicles. This last comment fails to do justice to the not-to-be-underestimated quality of Greßmann's observation that the author or redactor of this section might have something 'to hide.' Metzger, 346ff., is also skeptical with regard to a throne erected in the shrine and ascribes a double function to the cherubim in the shrine: (1) they supported the 'firmament' conceived as the foundation of the throne; and (2) with their wings, which were directed inward, they protected the ark. Such a carrying and protecting function by lion-dragons is also depicted on an Assyrian cylinder seal (see Metzger, fig. 1333). It remains hard in this matter to move beyond − often well-grounded − conjectures.

8:8 *These carrying poles were so long that their ends could be seen from the holy place in front of the shrine but were not visible from the outside; they are there to this day.*
The author or redactor of this section continues for a bit longer his discussion of the remarkable position of the carrying poles of the ark which are said to have been observable 'to this day.' Wellhausen, *Hexateuch*, 266 (cf. also S.L. McKenzie, *BIOSCS* 19 [1986], 21) thinks that, since these words are missing in LXX*, they must be a later addition by which the 'imitirende Epigone' gives himself away. Benzinger already observes with some justification, however, that the older narrator may have made this comment, which may have erroneously been omitted in LXX. In fact, it would not have made much sense for an exilic or postexilic glossator to have referred 'to this day' if the ark had years earlier disappeared from the temple (see also Faber van der Meulen, 20). On the other hand, the time designation need not refer to the beginning of the time of the monarchy either, for then the description of our verse would have to apply to a real situation at the time of Solomon. Stade-Schwally, Van den Born, Noth (cf. textcr. app. in BHK and *BHS*) and others want to transpose the conclusion of our verse to vs. 9 where it would more easily apply to the 'stone tables' in the ark, but this suggestion would hardly make the function of this conclusion more meaningful. The author of our verse obviously attaches great value to the 'carrying poles' of the ark, although his motive for this remains for us a matter of conjecture (so also Würthwein). It is remarkable that LXX reads ἡγιασμένα (*sanctificata*, Schleusner, I, 21) for these poles in place of (as in 2 Chr. 5:9 LXX) the more usual ἀναφορεύς. Rehm, *Untersuchungen*, 55) thinks that LXX must have read הברים in place of הבדים. In the ancient Hebr. script a switch between a *reš* and a *dalet* is entirely possible. Similarly striking is that for the verb ראה in our verse LXX uses 2 different Greek verbs (see W. Michaelis, *TDNT*, V, 327).

We also earlier encountered the verb ארך in hiph. in 3:14. In our verse the meaning is 'to be long' (cf. LXX's translation by ὑπερέχω, 'to surpass'; G. Delling, *TDNT*, VIII, 524; Ehrlich, referring to Exod. 20:12, wants to read a qal but this does not look like an improvement). It is now stated that the length of the carrying poles of the ark was such that from 'the holy place,' i.e. from within the actual temple hall, the ends of these poles were visible on the front of the shrine. It is striking that the par. place 2 Chr. 5:9 does not read 'the holy place' but 'the ark'; this reading is undoubtedly based on the idea, which was circulating later, that even from the holy place nothing pertaining to the shrine should be visible.

A great deal has been written, also in the commentaries, about the position of the ark in the shrine, in the course of which various explanatory proposals have been made (see in Thenius, Keil, Šanda, Van Gelderen, Montg.-Gehman and many others). Without entering at length on all these suggestions we do want to point to an explanation which we can find already in the medieval commentator Rashi and which has also had influence on later exegetes. He believes that the ends of the carrying poles were visible in the curtains which hung against the entrance of the holy place in the אמה טרקסין (cf. Grotius: *non spectabuntur, intercedente velo*): This last-mentioned concept is understood to refer – on the basis of an explanation of 1 Kgs. 6:16 – to an empty space between the 2 cedar-covered parts of the temple building: the 'holy place' and the 'holy of holies.' This intermediate space is said to be one cubit wide. In the second temple this space was created by 2 separate curtains (Midd. IV, 7; BT Joma 51b, etc.). Josephus, *Ant.* VIII §72, following 2 Chr. 3:14 reports that there were curtains in front of the doors of the shrine also in Solomon's temple (cf. Faber van der Meulen, 126-131). According to Rashi, the ends of the ark caused the (outer) curtain to bulge outward like the breasts of a woman. Between the staves of the ark rested the Shekinah ('divine presence'), as 'between my breasts' (S. of S. 1:13). Münster and Clarius already assumed, that once a year the (high) priest placed the offering of incense between the staves (on the Great Day of Atonement). Moreover, according to Kimachi the staves were never removed from the ark (based on Exod. 25:15). In BT Joma 53b it is even asserted that, when the Jewish people were driven into exile, the ark with its carrying poles was hidden under the 'holy place.'

In the case of the 'tabernacle' (Exod. 26:31ff.) there is mention of a 'veil' in front of the 'holy of holies.' It is clear that Rashi as well as others believed this curtain to be present also in the Solomonic temple. The redactor of our verse himself supplies some ground for this view since he seems to appeal to a later situation. But this at the same time suggests that it becomes extraordinarily difficult to determine what the actual situation must have been in the Solomonic temple. Galling, for example, basing himself on the data of our text, has sought to present proof of an 'erhöhtes Adyton' in the 'Holy of Holies' of the temple.[14] Partly on the basis of 2 Chr. 29:7a, in which there is mention of the 'doors of the front hall,' Busink, 207f., believes (see also our commentary on 6:31) that the shrine must have had a kind of vestibule with door wings, outside of which the carrying poles (in the 'holy place') could not then be visible. A. Kamphausen, *Beilagen zu HSAT*, 1896², 23, already wanted to read מן־המקום in place of מן־הקדש, a reading by which he similarly suggests a (screened off?) space between the 'holy place' and the 'shrine.' But Eißfeldt, in *HSAT*⁴, has reservations about this idea. The carrying poles were visible only immediately before the 'room in the rear' but invisible further in. It is not clear to us how precisely one must picture this situation. Nor is it easy to form a precise idea of what the author or redactor meant by חוצה (for יראו [אל] as

---

[14] K. Galling, "Das Allerheiligste in Salomo's Temple," *JPOS* 12 (1932), 43-48.

jaqtul concomitans, see König §152f.; further Böttcher §949h; Ewald §346b; GD §63a; Driver §42). Greßman, *Lade*, 52f., believed the carrying poles were so long that they were visible (in the holy place) from within the 'holy of holies,' not, however, outside of this space (cf. also Galling, 44). Busink, 208, is of the opinion that, with a view to the considerable space of the temple house, this can hardly be assumed anyway. But when he asks: 'ist es nicht wahrscheinlich, daß "draußen" hier bedeutet "außerhalb des Ulam vor dem Dibir"?,' we are seeing a clear link with his exegesis of 6:31.

In our conception, one which agrees in a number of important features with that of Busink, the shrine is a cube-shaped chest with doors which could be opened and, along with the posts referred to in 6:31, form a kind of entrance to, or perhaps even a vestibule for, the inside of the shrine. Standing in the 'holy place' directly before these opened doors, one could (even) see the ends of the carrying poles. Outside of this location, however, one could no longer observe them. Though this explanation deserves consideration, there are still many uncertain elements in it. Again, one has to take account, after all, of a sketch of the situation that was colored by a redactor of a later period.

8:9 *There was nothing in the ark except the two tables of stone which Moses had placed in it at Horeb when YHWH had made (a covenant) with the Israelites on their journey from Egypt.*

This verse, too, still belongs to the redactional notes recorded in this pericope in connection with the ark. There were only 2 'stone tables' in the ark. We already encountered the word לוחות in 7:36. In our verse the word, combined with אבנים, has its special meaning as 'stone tables,' an expression found also in Exod. 34:1,.4 and Deut. 4:13; 5:22; 9:9ff.; 10:1 (cf. Exod. 24:12; 31;18). The reference, then, is to 'tables' which are said to have been inscribed at God's command or even with God's own finger (Exod. 31:18; Deut. 9:10) (see also A. Baumann, *TWAT*, IV, 498f.). These are the tables which Moses is said to have brought down from the mountain. People associated them with the ten words of the decalogue (Exod. 34:28; Deut. 4:13; 10:14; on this verse also cf. Tg., which adds: 'for on them [i.e. the 2 tables] the 10 words of the covenant were written that ...' etc.; Josephus, *Ant.* VIII §104). In the dtr. tradition these tables are also referred to as 'tables of the covenant' (Deut. 9:9, 11), which are then said to have been stored in an ark (Deut. 10:1, 3, 5). In P there is mention of 'tables of the testimony' (Exod. 31:18; 32:15; 34:29).

Striking in our verse is the word רק, 'only.' In any case our redactor as yet has no knowledge of a later Jewish tradition which surfaces in the NT in Heb. 9:4 and says that apart from the 'tables' the ark also contained a (golden) urn holding the manna and the rod of Aaron which budded (see K.G. Kuhn, *TDNT*,

Num. 17:4, in contrast, tell us that these objects were placed *before* the ark. Later Jewish scholars like Maimonides and Abarbanal, therefore, rightly held to this position. But then how are we to understand the word 'only' in our verse? Greßmann, *Lade*, 26, suspects that this little word is not as innocent as it looks because by it the author sought skillfully to camouflage the presence (or better: the absence in the present) of an idol image. Accordingly, רק has a polemical thrust (see also comments on vs. 7 above). This possibility cannot be ruled out, of course, but if we are here dealing with a late redactional note – and that is something we may indeed assume – one might also suppose that the later Jewish tradition concerning a number of special objects *in* the ark had already begun to take shape and that the redactor was intent on resisting it (so Noth; Hentschel; cf. also Benzinger: 'Der Vers sieht aus wie ein Protest gegen falsche Gerüchte, die im Umlauf waren'). Eißfeldt, *KS*, V, 79, thinks that in place of the inscribed stone tables the ark may have contained a 'holy stone' (say, from Mt. Sinai) – on the analogy of the black stone in the Kaaba in Mecca – which might suggest the veneration of ancient stones. In this respect, therefore, the statement of our text might strike a polemical note. Loretz is of the opinion that the tables of the law in the ark convey 'eine der brillantesten historischen Rekonstruktionen die im Buch Deuteronomium vereint sind. Ein Stück kanaanäischer Überlieferung über eine heilige Lade wurde hier ohne die sonst obligatorische Beschimpfung der früheren Bewohner Kanaans der neuen Gesetzreligion einverleibt.'[16] Anyone who has taken careful note of what we have written so far will have to admit that a great deal more of the Canaanite religious legacy was incorporated in the new temple without any of the usual polemics.

Tradition tells us that Moses put the tables in the ark on Horeb. Especially Deut. (1:2, 6, 19; 4:10, 15, etc.) refers to 'Horeb' instead of 'Sinai' (E. Lohse, *TDNT*, VII, 282 and n. 5; Pedersen, III-IV, 198f.). There God made a covenant with his people (Deut. 4:23; 5:2f.). Now the second אשר in our verse has given rise to a number of problems, especially if readers want to construe this word as a *nota relationis* (Burney and others). It is true that LXX, after mentioning the stone tables, adds as a kind of apposition: 'tables of the covenant' (cf. also Deut. 9:9f., 11, 15; 10:3), as a result of which – even if this expression had dropped out in MT – the reference to the 'making (of a covenant)' in the second half of our verse would acquire a clearer antecedent. What we now have, in a kind of '*positio absoluta*' (so König §209b), is the verb כרת with the usual object 'covenant.' But this somewhat strange position of אשר can be

---

[15] A. Sennertus already examined the subject in a *dissertatio 'de iis quae fuere in Arca Foed. ad 1 Reg VIII:9'*, see: *Thesaurus Theologico-Philologicus*, Amsterdam 1702, 465-468.

[16] O. Loretz, "Die steinernen Gesetzestafeln in der Lade," *UF* 9 (1977), 159-161, esp. 161.

the usual object 'covenant.' But this somewhat strange position of אשר can be well resolved by following the suggestion of König (§387g; cf. Pesh.: '*when the Lord made a covenant with ...*' and Vulg., '*quando pepigit foedus Dominus ...*') and to construe the verb in a temporal sense.

The verb כרת (see G.F. Hasel, *TWAT*, IV, 355-367; E. Kutsch, *THAT*, I, 857-860) is used as a formula for making a treaty – usually in conjunction with ברית – approximately 80x in OT and is possibly derived from a rite associated with covenant-making (Hasel, 364ff.; Kutsch, 858f.). The verb, as Barthélemy correctly notes, does not need a direct connection with ברית to nevertheless mean 'making a covenant (with).' The final 3 words of our verse are intended to convey that YHWH's making a covenant with his people took place during the journey known as 'the exodus from (the land of) Egypt.'

8:10 *When the priests came out of the holy place, a cloud filled the house of YHWH.*
Now that the ark, which is scarcely mentioned any longer in what follows, has been put in its place by the priests, a cloud fills the house of YHWH. Stade-Schwally correctly point out that the 'holy place' here, as in Lev. 16:2f.; Ezek. (not Exod.) 41:23, means the shrine or 'the holy of holies.' In place of the 'house of YHWH' LXX^B only reads 'the house' (cf. vs. 6).

The special feature in this statement is that the ark and the cloud, 2 distinct aspects of the presence of YHWH, have been brought together. Only in this and the following verse does the word ענן occur in the books of Kings of the 87x it is found in OT altogether (see D.N. Freedman, B.E. Willoughly, H.-J. Fabry, *TWAT*, VI, 270-275). The word occurs especially in the depiction of theophanies in the exodus- and wilderness-tradition (on 'clouds associated with theophanies,' see also E. Oepke, *TDNT*, IV, 907). In the so-called JE-material God appears to the Israelites in the 'pillar of cloud' alongside the 'pillar of fire' (Exod. 13:21f.; 14:19-24; Num. 12:5, etc.), which protects Israel from the Egyptians and leads it in the right direction. In P the כבוד of YHWH is combined with the 'cloud' so that the 'glory' of YHWH is present in the cloud (Exod. 16:10; also cf. Ezek. 10:3f.; Fabry, 273). Cloud and fire are both symbols of God's being and presence while simultaneously concealing his being (in this connection, also cf. the Ugar. expression: *rkb 'rpt*[17]). 'Der semitische Tempel ist Wohnsitz der Gottheit, nicht Versammlungssaal der Gemeinde,' correctly comments Benzinger.

In the par. 2 Chr. 5:11-13, between the statement that the priests came outside and the statement that a cloud filled the house, a long passage was inserted in which we are told that the priests had more or less informally

---

[17] Cf. Svi Rin, *Acts of the Gods. The Ugaritic Epic Poetry*, Jerusalem 1968, 68 (Hebr.).

'sanctified' themselves and that the 'Levitical singers Asaph, Heman, and Jeduthun' and their families formed a kind of orchestra along with 120 priests who blew on the trumpets. Temple music and the singing of hymns called in unison upon the Shekinah hidden in the clouds to descend to its place in the temple (Rudolph). We are here dealing with a post-exilic interpretive expansion of the narrative serving to underscore the importance people in that day assigned to the 'sound' of temple music and song for the realization of the presence of God.

8:11 *The priests could not remain standing to perform their ministry because of the cloud, for the glory of YHWH filled the house.*
What we read in the vss. 10f. corresponds in many respects to Exod. 40:34f. (also cf. Ezek. 43:1-4). What happens to Moses there as the cloud descended on the tabernacle happens to the priests in our verses. It hardly needs saying that one can agree with those interpreters who also discover the P element in our verses.

Although the priests have left the sanctuary (see vs. 10), our verse pictures the coming of the cloud in a way which suggests that the priests could not remain standing to do their work even if they were far from the temple in the temple court (so already the 18th-century Jewish commentator Altschuler in his *Mezudath David* on our verse). An older Jewish commentary, the *Yalkut Shimoni*, mentions that special angels who had been instructed to punish transgressors accompanied the cloud. For the expression 'remain standing' LXX[B] uses the verb (formed in Hellenism) στήκω which occurs only a few times in LXX (for this, see W. Grundmann, *TDNT*, VII, 635). LXX[A] and other MSS of the Origen-group have a form of στῆναι, 'come near to.' In fact the priests always performed their work standing (so, correctly, Thenius and others). We already encountered the verb שרת (pi.), which is used for 'doing this official work,' in a more 'secular' meaning in 1:4 and 15. The intimidating effect of the cloud kept the priests from performing these duties.

The explication of this fact is given in the second half of our verse: the כבוד of YHWH filled the temple. This word, too, is one we encountered earlier (in 3:13) but there it related to the king. The word occurs approx. 120x in OT (see C. Westermann, *THAT*, I, 794-812, esp. 802ff.; and M. Weinfeld, *TWAT*, IV, 23-40), but in the books of Kings only here and the other place mentioned. Among the many nuances of meaning one can assign to the word in translations that in 3:13 was especially the 'honour' of the king. Here the reference is to the 'glory' of YHWH. Especially in P כבוד יהוה acquires a pivotal meaning when it concerns the founding of the cult on and at the Sinai (Exod. 24:16f.; 40:34f.; Lev. 9:6, 23; see Westermann, 808f.). ''Glory' takes the form of a consuming fire surrounded by a cloud' (Weinfeld, 27). Perhaps on the basis of anti-anthropomorphistic tendencies Tg. has יְקָרָא instead (G.

Kittel, *TDNT*, II, 248f.; cf. also G. von Rad, *TDNT*, II, 238-242).

What is said in our verses serves to emphasize that, after the transfer of the ark, the Solomonic temple is the legitimate continuation of the dwelling of YHWH, who in the time of Moses dwelt in a wilderness sanctuary.

8:12 *Then Solomon said: 'YHWH has said he would dwell in darkness.*
8:13 *I have indeed built for you a princely house, a fixed residence for you to dwell in forever.'*

These verses constitute an independent unit and do not directly tie in with the preceding narrative, nor belong, from the viewpoint of literary style, to the following prayer of Solomon even though there is affinity in content (Goettsberger). These verses are usually – and with reason – described as a 'temple dedication saying.' LXX* not only has this saying at another location in our chapter (after Solomon's prayer, vs. 53; so, e.g., E. Tov, *JNSL* 13 [1987], 154f.), but – what is more important – it has an interesting expansion of the saying inasmuch as it begins with the words ἥλιον ἐγνώρισεν ἐν οὐρανῷ Κύριος and in addition also indicates the saying's place of origin: οὐκ ἰδοὺ αὕτη γέγραπται ἐν βιβλίῳ τῆς ᾠδῆς. Since Wellhausen, *Hexateuch*, 269, the Hebr. text has often been modified on the basis of LXX (so, e.g. LV and PCV), though the latter at certain points was again further corrected. So, among other things, ספר השיר, 'the book of the Song,' was changed into ספר הישר, 'the book of the Righteous' (so Josh. 10:13; 2 Sam. 1:18).[18] Wellhausen himself translated the modified saying as follows: 'Die Sonne am Himmel hat er geschaffen, Yahve, doch hat er wollen wohnen im Dunkeln und gesprochen: bau mir ein Haus, ein Haus meiner Heimstatt, dass ich dort ewiglich wohne – siehe es steht geschrieben im Buche des Redlichen.' But Rahlfs (*SSt.* III, 262), Thackeray[19], Burney, Mont.-Gehman, Gooding[20] – to limit ourselves to just these scholars – have pointed out that also the tradition in LXX is not uniform as far as its different recensions are concerned, and that MT cannot simply be emended on the basis of certain readings in LXX. Also Van den Born has demonstrated that certain Greek words in LXX, for instance, ἐγνώρισεν – LXX[Luc.] has εστησεν – can be interpreted differently in the Hebr.[21] He, for that matter, arrives at the following – sharply divergent – translation: 'Jahwe hat die Sonne an den Himmel gesetzt; Er hat (sie) ange-

---

[18] Cf. S. Mowinckel, "Hat es ein israelitisches Nationalepos gegeven?," *ZAW* 53 (1935), 130-138.

[19] H.St.J. Thackeray, *The Septuagint and Jewish Worship. A Study in Origins*, London 1923², 77f.

[20] D.W. Gooding, "Problems of Text and Midrash in the Third Book of Reigns," *Textus* 7 (1969), 1-29, esp. 21-25.

[21] A. van den Born, "Zum Tempelweihespruch (1 Kgs VIII 12f.)," *OTS* 14 (1965), 237-244.

wiesen, außerhalb des Dunkels zu wohnen: "Ich habe dir ein Haus zur Wohnung gebaut, eine Stätte zum Wohnsitz Monat für Monat" (p. 241).

It is not our intent to devote a lengthy discussion to all the proposed interpretations and translations of our verses. We do, however, wish to recall Josephus here (*Ant.* VIII §§106ff.; cf. with this Faber van der Meulen, 136ff.), who here and there expands the words of the text in his own special fashion. He describes at length the character and function of the 'thick cloud' and then the fact that Solomon rose up from his seat, after which he is said to have spoken approximately the following words: 'Thou, o Lord, possess, in the things thou hast created for thyself, an eternal dwelling, viz., the heavens, the air, the earth and the sea, in which thou dost move but by which thou canst not be fully contained. Now I have built for thy name this temple from which we, when we sacrifice and seek good omens, send up our prayers to thee. May everyone be persuaded that thou art nearby and not far removed.' Faber van der Meulen, 136-139, remarks in this connection that Josephus clearly brings out that God in his essence cannot be content with the temple alone, however much the divine presence is made tangible in the temple. R. Marcus, *LCL*, 630, n. a, recalls the Stoic terminology which Josephus often uses.

The ancient versions – except, of course, LXX – either closely agree with MT (like Vulg.), or at subordinate points diverge somewhat from MT (like Pesh. and Tg.). Tg. translates 'in the usual translator's style' (Burney) that YHWH 'delighted in having his Shekinah dwell in Jerusalem.'

If we now look at the Hebr. text, we are struck, after the introductory formula beginning with אז (see Böttcher §945; Bg. II §79), by the fact that YHWH as subject of the statement is at the beginning of the saying (cf. Joüon §155k). This may indicate that YHWH has been substituted here for something or someone else, e.g. for a stich in the manner of LXX or even for the name of another deity. In the OT, however, there is repeated mention of YHWH veiling himself in ערפל (see Exod. 20:21; Deut. 5:22). This word occurs 15x in OT (see our article on this word in *TWAT*, VI, 397-402); it generally means a 'dark cloud,' and has its 'Sitz-im-Leben' in the representation of a theophany. In the Pentateuch the word only occurs in the Sinai-Horeb theophany, sometimes, as in our verse, with the article. The ערפל is, as it were, the manifestation and representation of the hidden deity. Our verse as well bears witness in this manner to the paradoxically veiled manifestation of YHWH by which something of his original character becomes visible. This at the same time implies – a fact which is expressed also in what follows in our chapter (vs. 27) – that YHWH cannot be incarcerated in any earthly house (cf. also Isa. 66:1ff.). As we already remarked in connection with 6:13, the verb שכן occurs in the books of Kings only there and in our verse. In vs. 13 a form of the verb ישב is used. Scholars have sometimes seen a contrast between the two: the first verb refers to a 'permanent dwelling' (of God in heaven), the second to a 'dwelling in tents' in a nomadic sense. G. Fohrer rejects this contrast (*TDNT*, VII, 309, n. 95; see also Schmitt, *Zelt und Lade*, 219f.). Recently M. Görg, *TWAT*, VII, 1341-1345, has again referred to the semantic difference between the 2 verbs: according to him, ישב refers more to the process of consolidation in a fixed location, שכן the act of settling down without a permanent bond to a place (p. 1341). In our verses both verbs are connected with and applied to the divine presence of YHWH in the temple: 'Das kosmische *škn* JHWHs fügt sich hier zum *jšb*, Gottes im Tempelbau, eine Tendenz zugunsten einer Wohnidee, der u.a. die andere mit dem Gewicht auf der flexiblen Gegenwart Gottes in 2 Sam 7,5f. gegenüberstehen könnte ...' (p. 1345).

Thus, in the opening statement of this dedication saying, we perceive a bit of the tension which was not only felt but must also have been concretely present when an original Canaanite temple became 'a house for YHWH.' This radical intervention into one of YHWH's essential attributes is expressly ascribed to an act – and word – of Solomon. Ultimately we are dealing with more than a reference to YHWH's 'presence apart from images' as the 'key term for the *deus absconditus*' (G. von Rad, *TDNT*, II, 382); to the mind of the author he was dealing with a shift in the manifestation of YHWH which is as it were adapted to the new needs of the Davidic dynasty.

This tension between what YHWH has said – according to the old tradition (Pesh. translates 'YHWH has said,' with an eye to vs. 13 [Berlinger], by 'Lord, you have said...,' a translation mistakenly preferred by Thenius) – concerning his hiddenness and Solomon's initiative in localizing YHWH in the temple very clearly comes out in the form (weakened in the par. 2 Chr. 6:2), the *figura etymologica* or the *paronomasia*, with which vs. 13 begins: בנה בניתי. It is emphatically stated up front that 'I, Solomon, have built a temple for YHWH' (Goettsberger, however, sees no contrast with the preceding). The word זבל II, now translated by 'exalted dwelling' (*HAL*; cf. Zorelli: *Templum in monte Zion*), occurs also in Isa. 63:15; Hab. 3:11; Ps. 49:15, and in the par. 2 Chr. 6:2. Since the word *zbl* is often found also in the Ugar.[22], scholars nowadays often look at that language for the determination of the Hebr. word. For *zbl* I as verb the meaning given is 'honour,' exalt,' for *zbl* II it is 'rule' (see, among others, Van Zijl, *Baal*, 340). In that case our word זבול would mean 'exalted' (BDB[23]) or 'dwelling,' 'dwelling-temple' (Ges-B; L. Gaston, *ThZ* 18 [1962], 248), practically synonymous with 'heaven' (see also my *Baal*, 141), or also 'rule,' 'princely state' (Van Zijl; Gibson, *CML*, 146; M. Metzger, *UF* 2 (1970), 139 and n. 2: 'house of rule', cf. also M. Görg, *UF* 6 [1974], 56f.); or even

---

[22] Cf. R. E. Whitaker, *A Concordance of the Ugaritic Literature*, Cambridge 1972, 252.

[23] See also W.F. Albright, *JPOS* 16 (1936), 18; and D.W. Goodwin, *Text-Restoration Methods in Contemporary U.S.A. Biblical Scholarship*, Naples 1969, 109.

'zenith' (Gaster, *Myth*, 494, an allusion to the sun in its zenith).

It hardly seems disputable that 'exalted dwelling' is a good translation in our verse for the Hebr. word in question, the primary reference being no doubt to the Jerusalem temple, though Metzger is right in saying that in the sanctuary the boundaries between the 'heavenly' and the 'earthly' are suspended (*UF* 2 [1970], 144ff.). The concept of the throne of God which rises up from the sanctuary into heaven would in all probability be based on the idea of the divine mountain.

The word מכון, a derivative of כון occurs in OT 17x, 4 of them in our book, and that in our chapter alone (vss. 39, 43, 49 plus our verse) In the sing. the word relates especially to the 'holy place,' the place of YHWH's presence (see K. Koch, *TWAT*, IV, 96). As in other places in our chapter, this word is followed by the inf. cstr. qal, with a 2 p. masc. sing. suffix, of the verb יבש. In *RSP*, III, i, 192, M. Dahood offers a Ugar. parallel. The idea is to mark a fixed holy place for YHWH's residence as a parallel to the 'exalted house' of the first stich. It is clear from the remainder of our chapter that this place was also viewed as 'heaven' (see Metzger, 150f.). The free position of the accusative עולמים (Ges-K §118k) constitutes an answer to the question: how long? The word עולם, which occurs almost 440x in OT (see comments on 1:31; further H.D. Preuß, *TWAT*, V, 1144-1159) here has a pl. 'of extension' (König §260k) which serves to convey not only long duration but esp. the idea of 'forever' (see also Preuß, 1148).

Gaster, *Myth*, 494f., considers this little poem 'a sublime satire on the pagan rites, the implication being that the new temple of Yahweh is to enshrine him perpetually in a blaze of glory, whereas the sun can always be obscured by cloudmists!' Taylor, *Sun*, 142, rejects the notion that the statement that YHWH placed the sun in the sky has to be viewed as a polemic against an 'alien' solar deity. The passage must rather be regarded as a theological understanding which presupposes both continuity and discontinuity between Israel's God and the physical entity of the 'sun.' According to him, there was at Gibeon a more direct connection between the 'sun' and YHWH. This direct connection is rejected by the dtr. version in vs. 12 (MT)!

1 KINGS 8:14-61

8:14 *The king turned his face around and blessed the whole assembly, while the whole assembly of Israel stood there.*

15 *He said: 'Blessed be YHWH, the God of Israel who with his own hand has fulfilled what he promised with his (own) mouth to David my father:*

16 *Since the day I brought my people Israel out of Egypt, I have not chosen a city in all the tribes of Israel in which to build a house where my name might dwell; but I have chosen David to be over my people Israel.*

17 *Now my father David had it in his heart to build a house for the name of YHWH, the God of Israel.*

18 *But YHWH said to my father David: "Because it was in your heart to build a house for my name ... you did well to have this in your heart;*

19 *only: you will not build this house, but your son who shall be born to you will build the house for my name."*

20 *Now YHWH kept the promise he had made. I succeeded David my father and now I sit on the throne of Israel, as YHWH has promised and I built the house for the name of YHWH, the God of Israel.*

21 *I have provided a place there for the ark in which is the covenant of YHWH which he made with our fathers when he brought them up out of the land of Egypt.'*

22 *Then Solomon stood before the altar of YHWH in front of the whole assembly of Israel as he spread out his hands to heaven;*

23 *and he said: 'YHWH, God of Israel, there is no God like you in heaven above or on earth below, who keeps covenant and faithfulness toward your servants who wholeheartedly walk before your face;*

24 *you who have kept with your servant David, my father, what you promised him. With your (own) mouth you had promised it (to him) and with your (own) hand you have fulfilled it, as it is today.*

25 *Now therefore YHWH, God of Israel, keep with your servant David, my father, the promise you made to him, when you said: "You will never be without a man to sit on the throne of Israel if only your children are careful in what they do when they walk before me as you have walked before me."*

26 *Now then, God of Israel, let the word which you spoke to your servant, my father David, be confirmed*

27 *[But would God really settle on earth? Heaven, even the highest heaven, cannot contain you, how much less the house that I have built!].*

28 *And be pleased, YHWH, my God, to have regard for your servant's prayer and plea. Hear the cry and the prayer which your servant is praying before you this day,*

29 *so that your eyes may be open night and day over this house, the place of which you said "Let my name be there," so that you may hear the prayer which your servant offers toward this place.*

30 *Hear the pleas of your servant and of your people Israel, when they pray at this place. Hear in heaven, your dwelling place, and when you hear, forgive.*

31 *When a man wrongs his neighbour and (the latter) puts an imprecatory oath on him by placing him under a formula of imprecation, and he comes and swears the oath before your altar in this house,*

32 *then hear in heaven and act by pronouncing judgment over your servants, declaring the unrighteous man guilty, by bringing his conduct down upon himself and by vindicating the righteous by treating him according to his righteous conduct.*

33 *When your people Israel are defeated by an enemy because they would sin against you but they turn back to you, acknowledging your name, praying and making supplication to you in this house,*

34 *then hear in heaven and forgive the sins of your people Israel, and bring them back to the land which you gave to their fathers.*

35 *When heaven remains shut so that there is no rain because they sinned against you, but they pray at this place and acknowledge your name and turn from their sins because you have afflicted them,*

36 *then hear in heaven and forgive the sins of your servants and your people – you, after all, teach them the right way on which they must walk – and be pleased to send rain on your land, the land you gave your people as an inheritance.*

37 *Whenever there is famine in the land, or plague, or blight, or mildew, locusts or leaf-eaters; whenever his enemy besieges him in his cities; whatever plagues and diseases;*

38 *(and then) when any prayer, any supplication, is made by any of your people Israel, because everyone knows the affliction of his own heart and stretches out his hands toward this house;*

39 *then hear in heaven your dwelling place; be pleased to forgive, respond, and render to each according to all his ways, because you know his heart (for you alone know the hearts of all the children of men);*

40 *that they may fear you all the days that they may live in the land which you gave to our fathers.*

41 *Similarly, when a foreigner who does not belong to your people Israel comes from a far country for your name's sake;*

42 *– for they will hear of your great name and your strong hand and your outstretched arm – when he comes and prays in this house;*

43 *be pleased to hear in heaven your dwelling place, and act in accordance with everything for which the foreigner calls on you, that all the peoples of the earth may know your name and fear you as do your people Israel, and that* *they may know that your name has been proclaimed over this house which I have built.*

44 *When your people go to war against their enemy by whatever route you send them, and they pray to YHWH toward the city you have chosen and the house which I have built for your name;*

45 *then hear their prayer and supplication and settle their cause.*

46 *When they sin against you – for there is no one who does not sin – and you are angry with them and give them to an enemy who carries them away as captives to an alien land, far off or near;*

47 *but they have a change of heart in the land in which they are held captive, and repent and plead with you in the land of their captors, saying: "We have sinned, we have done evil, and have acted badly";*

48 *and they repent with all their heart and with all their soul in the land of their enemies who have taken them captive, and they pray to you toward the land which you gave to their forefathers, toward the city you have chosen and the house which I have built for your name;*

49 *then hear their prayer and their plea in heaven your dwelling place and adjudicate their cause.*

50 *Forgive your people who have sinned against you and all the transgressions which they have committed against you and grant them (to find) mercy in the eyes of those who have taken them captive so that they may show them mercy;*

51 *for, surely, they are your people and your inheritance which you brought out of Egypt from the midst of that iron-smelting furnace.*

52 *May your eyes be open to your servant's plea and to the plea of your people Israel, to listen to them whenever they call out to you.*

53 *For you separated them from all the peoples of the earth to be your own inheritance, as you have said through Moses your servant when you, Lord YHWH, brought our forefathers out of Egypt.'*

54 *When Solomon had finished the whole prayer to YHWH as well as this plea, rising up from before the altar of YHWH where he had been kneeling with his hands stretched out toward heaven,*

55 *he stood up and blessed the whole assembly of Israel in a loud voice saying:*

56 *'Blessed be YHWH, who has given a place of rest to his people Israel according to all that he promised. Not a single word has failed of all the good words he uttered by Moses his servant.*

57 *May YHWH our God be with us as he has been with our forefathers. May he not leave us or reject us,*

58 *so that our hearts may incline to him to walk in all his ways and to keep his commandments, his statutes, and his ordinances;*

59 *may these words of mine with which I have made supplication before*

YHWH *remain near to* YHWH *our God day and night, to adjudicate the cause of his servant and the cause of his people Israel according to each day's need,*

60 *so that all the peoples of the earth may know that* YHWH *and no one else is God.*

61 *May your heart be undivided before* YHWH *our God, as you walk in his statutes and keep his commandments, as is the case today.'*

INTRODUCTION

Following 'Solomon's dedication of the temple' described in the preceding section comes a – literarily somewhat complex – 'temple prayer by Solomon,' of which the vss. 31-51, as a complex of 7 special petitions, more or less form the core (for the following, cf. Talstra, *Solomon's Prayer*). These core petitions are as it were embedded in a double framework: (1) in the framework of the vss. 22-30 and 52f. in which Solomon asks God for open eyes with respect to his temple and the prayer of his people; and (2) in the framework of the vss. 14-21 and 54-61, in which Solomon turns to the assembled crowd to bless them, in the process reminding them of God's promises with respect to his dynasty and of the 'place of rest' he has given. Solomon is said to have pronounced his prayers with his hands stretched out to heaven (vss. 22 and 54) and (at least in part) in a kneeling posture.

The syntactic structure of the 7 core petitions follows a fixed pattern. First a 'case' is cited to which, by the use of *perfecta,* a sequel is added, and in which the prayer to God is subsequently formulated, often with an expansion.

The analysis of the composition of the vss. 14-61 led Talstra to the thesis that this composition, because in structure and thematization it is distinct from other dtr. speeches, is not serviceable to DtrH, as Noth described it in his *ÜGS* (cf. also Burney with the siglum R[D] and the opinion that the choice of subjects in the petitions had especially been suggested by the catalogue of curses in Deut. 28:15-68).[1] Because 'the prayer of Solomon' contains statements concerning the restoration of Israel, the forgiveness and renewal of the relation between God and Israel which have a post-dtr. 'feel' to them, it is even a question whether we can still speak here of a dtr. redaction.

The vss. 14-21, an address to the 'crowd' (Josephus, *Ant.* VIII §§ 109f.), which along with the vss. 54-61, a blessing, form (in Talstra's terminology) the 'second frame,' have as themes 'David' and 'temple building' but then supported, as vs. 21 (a later dtr. redaction – Talstra, 246) indicates, by the

---

[1] See further S. Wheeler, *Prayer and Temple in the Dedication Speech of Solomon, I Kings 8:14-61*, Diss. Columbia 1977 (*Dissertation Abstracts International* 38 [1977f.], 2860f.A.

themes 'exodus' and 'covenant.' Our verses may especially be viewed in the light of 2 Sam. 7, which they presuppose, but from which they also diverge in striking ways (see Talstra, 238-246, particularly the table of formal parallels, 238ff.).

EXEGESIS

8:14 *The king turned (his face) around and blessed the whole assembly, while the whole assembly of Israel stood there.*
At the beginning of 'Solomon's address to the people' (vss. 14-21; Skinner) the verb סבב is used. It had already been used in qal earlier (2:15; 5:17; 7:15, 23f.), but here it occurs in the hiph. with פנים as object. In certain cases one can translate this expression by 'turn away the face' (21:4; 2 Kgs. 20:2 // Isa. 38:2, etc.), but here it means 'turn the face about' (also Judg. 18:23) so that one can look a person in the face. The author's view is that, in the course of making his earlier statement, the king stood with his face turned to the holy place and now turned about eastward toward the people (so also Josephus, *Ant.* VIII §109; Thenius and others). On the other hand, it is not entirely impossible that – at least in the version and view of LXX – the king averted his face out of respect and for the purpose of worshiping (see E. Lohse, *TDNT*, VI, 771). Further, in this verse we for the first time encounter the term קהל ישראל. The verb was already used in vs. 2 (see above). As substantive קהל occurs only in this chapter in the books of Kings. The first time LXX leaves the word untranslated so that it speaks about 'all Israel'; the second time it translates it by ἐκκλησία which is the most usual Greek translation of the Hebr. word.

Our verse further relates how the king 'blessed' the whole assembly of Israel (ברך pi.; see comments on 1:47 above). This can be understood as 'greeting' (possibly with a blessing; Thenius, Goettsberger, et al.). Kimchi and other rabbinical scholars have wondered where then the blessing is in fact mentioned, aside from the laudation in the following verse and the blessing after the sacrifices (vv. 54ff.; cf. also Kittel, Šanda, and others). But Aberbanel calls the entire following prayer a form of blessings for Israel. The act of pronouncing a blessing by a father or by the head of a festive gathering cannot have been an unusual event in ancient Israel (see Pedersen, III-IV, 447f.). Nevertheless, in the case of our verse it seems to us best to look for the 'blessing' in the word of the following verse With some emphasis it is added in our verse that the people stood. Ralbag (Rabbi Levi ben Gerson [1288-1345]) points out in his commentary that it was forbidden to everyone but the king to sit in the temple court. Josephus already seems to have known of this rule (*Ant.* VIII §107), since he tells us that Solomon stood as he pronounced the benedictory saying, while he adds in passing: ἔτυχε γὰρ καθεζόμενος, a comment which can hardly be unintentional.

8:15 *He said; 'Blessed be YHWH, the God of Israel, who with his own hand has fulfilled what he promised with his (own) mouth to David my Father:*
The formula ברוך יהוה אלהי ישראל occurred earlier in 1:48 and 5:21. To this formula LXX adds σήμερον, an addition by which the statement of praise is linked to this special day, which can be viewed as a logical specification (Burney). The intent of this statement of praise is to assign to David's role in the building of the temple a special, even a divine, importance. It is observed that God spoke orally, and directly as it were, with David. Aberbanel, the medieval Jewish Bible exegete, sees here a distinction from God's indirect speech via Nathan, the court prophet. But in 2 Sam. 7:4-17 there is express reference to Nathan as the 'go-between' between God and David. One can point to tension between the 2 versions (for this, cf. Talstra, 241); but one can also apply the adverb 'orally' to the fact that God gave his promise with 'his own mouth,' regardless of whether the words were addressed to David directly or indirectly. This may also be what MT meant with the somewhat peculiar use of the particle את before David which may here be taken as a preposition ('with'). A number of Hebr. MSS here read אל (Kennicott). LXX (περι), Tg. (עם), Pesh. (*'am*) and Vulg. (*ad*), accordingly, have taken it to mean 'with,' 'to' (see also König §288k; further *Ges.*[18], s.v. את 2, [p. 115]).

In the remainder MT reads the sing. ידו, where the par. 2 Chr. 6:4 but also LXX, Tg., Vulg., and Pesh. (*not* the MSS of 9a1*fam*) read the pl. (cf. S.L. McKenzie, *BIOSCS* 19 [1986], 18). The reference here is to the hand of God who, as it were, with 'his own hand' and so 'in fact' completed the building of the temple. In this connection Rashi speaks somewhat enigmatically about God's 'good hand.' For the verb מלא (pi.), see comments on 1:14 and 2:17.

8:16 *Since the day I brought my people Israel out of Egypt, I have not chosen a city in all the tribes of Israel in which to build a house where my name might dwell; but I have chosen David to be over my people Israel.*
This verse highlights with a quotation what was referred to in the previous verse. The reference is to what can be found in 2 Sam. 7:5ff., especially in vs. 6 (for the parallelism of vss. 15-21 with 2 Sam. 7, cf. the overview in Talstra, 238ff.). In 2 Samuel YHWH's response to David's plan to build a temple sounds like an accusation which would put a stop to the idea; 'I have not dwelt in a house since the day I brought up the people of Israel from Egypt to this day, but I have been moving about in a tent for my dwelling.' This implies an ancient and serious criticism of the building of a temple (see Mulder 1989, 15; otherwise, H. Kruse, *VT* 35 [1985], 142-146). In our verse these words are now interpreted as a motivation for Solomon's building a temple.

Israel's liberation from Egypt as the comprehensive framework for the themes 'David' and 'temple building' is conveyed in our verse (see also vss. 21, 51, 53; 9:9 in 1 Kings) by the use of the hiph. of the verb יצא which can, be translated as 'cause to go out.' In addition there is the term 'cause to go up,' a hiph.-form of the verb עלה, e.g. in 2 Sam. 7:6 cited above. In this connection we are not dealing with 2 distinctive stylistic variants, as J. Wijngaards has tried to show in *VT* 15 (1965), 91-102, but with 2 different approaches to the exodus. The most ancient expression is that with עלה, a term which occurs 41x in OT in connection with the exodus.[2]

Since YHWH led his people out of Egypt he had not chosen a city in all the tribes of Israel to build a house, i.e. a temple, there. In 3:8 already we encountered the verb בחר. There the object of YHWH's election was his people, Israel. Now the reference is to the place where the temple should stand. In Hebr. the verb can be construed with an accusative as well as with the preposition ב.[3] The dtr. use of language in our verse is strongly reminiscent of Deut. 12:5, 11, 18, 21 etc., where the election of *one* place also already applied to Jerusalem, even though, understandably, this name is not yet mentioned there.[4]

In our verse one finds the negative formulation: 'I had not yet chosen a city' (cf. Talstra, 244). This city does exist now, following a history beginning with David and culminating in Solomon. The earlier non-tribal Jebus was incorporated in 'Israel' as Jerusalem (also cf. TOB). In 2 Chr. 6:5 something is added to this sentence: 'Nor had I chosen a man to be prince (= נגיד) over my people Israel,' but the Chronicler deliberately skips Saul here!

Added to the word עיר, 'city,' in MT is the phrase מכל שבטי ישראל, 'of all the tribes of Israel.' The word שבט, 'tribe,' occurs about 190x in OT, 16 of them in the books of Kings. Aside from the meaning 'stick,' or 'staff,' it means 'tribe' approx. 143x (concerning Israel, see also *KBL*, 941; Zorell, 816; further K. D. Schunck, *BHHW*, III, 1851f.). Less frequently in OT but having approximately the same meanings one also finds the word מטה (only in Kings in 7:14 and 8:1 [see above]). The 'clan' (משפחה) consists of 'tribes,' 2 words with the same meaning, which also denote the commander's staff and the royal sceptre. The tribe therefore embraced all those who obeyed the same chief (De Vaux, *Inst.* I, 22). It is the σκῆπτρον which is used in our verse in LXX for

---

[2] On the use of the two terms see at length: A. R. Hulst, C. van Leeuwen, *Bevrijding in het Oude Testament*, Kampen 1981, 20-29.

[3] Cf. Th. C. Vriezen, *De verkiezing van Israel, volgens het Oude Testament*, Amsterdam 1974, esp. 22-33; see now also *Ges.*[18], s.v. בחר (p. 137).

[4] For another opinion on the significance of Deut. 12 and the place of the *one* sanctuary, see also M. J. Paul, *Het Archimedisch punt van de Pentateuchkritiek. Een historisch en exegetisch onderzoek naar de verhouding van Deuteronomium en de reformatie van koning Josia (2 Kon 22-23)*, 's-Gravenhage 1988 (diss. Rijks Universiteit Leiden).

'tribe' (approx. 18x in LXX, as well as in Flavius Josephus and in the ancient Christian literature) but then in the phrase ἐν ἑνί σκήπτρῳ, 'in one tribe,' a more detailed or later explanation of 'of all the tribes' (of Israel) in MT, applied to Judah.

In 2 Chr. 6:6 (cf. also LXX) one finds a similar development inasmuch as 'and I have chosen Jerusalem that my name may be there' is added to our verse from Kings. Accordingly, we cannot support Böttcher (*Neue Aehrenlese*) when he postulates an original באחד in place of the מכל of MT. We do not share the opinion of Böttcher, Thenius, Ehrlich, Skinner, and many others (see Brockington, also the textcr. app. in *BHK* and *BHS*) that precisely these (or similar) words have dropped out in our verse, either by *parablepsis* of the writer, or on account of *homoeoarcton* of ואבחר or *homoeoteleuton* of שם (cf. Wonneberger, *LBH* §60). The addition in Chronicles and also in LXX^B is a deliberate augmentation of our verse (so also, correctly, Stade-Schwally; Šanda; cf. Talstra, 139).[5]

Before, in the second half of our verse, David is mentioned as Israel's chosen king and in the following verses there is further comment on David's intentions, the author adds that 'my name' will be in the temple. In our comments on 3:2 we have already mentioned the 'name-theology' of the Dtr. (see further Montg. Gehman and especially Talstra, 139ff. who advances linguistic arguments against the interpretations of Von Rad and others).

8:17 *Now my father David had it in his heart to build a house for the name of YHWH, the God of Israel.*
In this verse and the 2 following verses the author refers back to 2 Sam. 7. Solomon first recalls that it was in David's heart to build a temple (for the grammatical construction of the sentence, see König §397b; Bg. II §11m; for the use of the preposition עם in the place of לבב, see Burney; BrSynt. §113; Williams §337).

8:18 *But YHWH said to my father David: "Because it was in your heart to build a house for my name ... you did well to have this in your heart.*
In principle, David's plan to build a temple is not rejected by YHWH. In 2 Sam. 7:3, however, initially only Nathan was favorably disposed toward David's plan but later, at YHWH's direction, he had to correct the plan (for details regarding the differences in argumentation, see Talstra, 242f.). For the

---

[5] See now for a different opinion E. Ulrich et al., *Qumran Cave 4* (DJD 14), Oxford 1995, 1983: 'The most important reading of 4QKgs is the preservation of a substantial original reading of Kings, lost by homoioteleuton in 1 Kgs 8:16, but preserved in the parallel text of 2 Chr 6:5b-6a and partially preserved in the Old Greek text of 1 Kings 8:16.'

construction with יען אשר, see my article in *OTS* 18 (1973), esp. p. 66 and n. 2. In this note I have discussed at length the translation difficulties – of which many commentators are often unaware – which occur in connection with this verse. The problem is that, after the clause with 'whereas it was in your heart ...' etc., one can expect an *apodosis*, which never comes (König §145e, therefore, is not correct on this point). So we are dealing with an *anakoluton*, one which Kittel possibly spotted, to judge by his '-'. In many translations, partly quoted in the above note, the difficulty is either smoothed over or the particle יען is translated in an arbitrary fashion.

הטיבת is a hiph.-form of the verb טוב. Aside from in the par. 2 Chr. 6:8, this form also occurs in 2 Kgs. 10:30, in the sense of 'acting well, correctly' (*HAL*, s.v. 355a; cf. BL, 402n; Bg. II §28k). The form is related to the hiph. of the verb יטב and can be easily confused with it (BL, 402u; Bg. II §26h).

8:19 *only: you will not build this house, but your son who shall be born to you will build the house for my name."*
Earlier, in 5:17 [5:3; RSV], the fact of David's being prevented from building a temple for YHWH already came up but there a reason was cited (also cf. 1 Chr. 22:6-11). This time no reason for the fact is given. The word רק is not translated by LXX[B]. The word indicates a reservation which suggests that the fact of David's being prevented from building a temple is rooted in the unfathomable will of YHWH. The particle אם after כי is omitted in the par. 2 Chr. 6:9 but this omission does not have to alter the translation (König §372i). The word חלץ occurs 11x in OT – only in the dual – only one of which occurs in the books of Kings in this verse (V. Hamp, *TWAT*, II, 1008-1011). The word denotes the part of the body that is between the ribs and the hip bones: the loins (see also *HAL*, 309). Hence to 'come forth from his loins' means to 'descend from' (also Gen. 35:11). The word מחנים occurs more frequently in the sense of 'loins' in our books (2:5).

8:20 *Now YHWH kept the promise he had made. I succeeded David my Father and now I sit on the throne of Israel, as YHWH has promised and I built the house for the name of YHWH, the God of Israel.*
Solomon conceives his ascension to the throne as the realization of a promise made by YHWH and a mandate to build the temple. In contrast to the 1 p. sing. ואקם and ואשב (for these forms, cf. also Bg. II §5d), LXX[Luc.] has the forms ανεστησε με and εκαθισεν με, which even more clearly accentuates YHWH's initiative (Rahlfs, *SSt*. III, 262). So this form of presentation is somewhat more modest (Stade-Schwally). For the hiph.-form of קום, see comments on 2:4 and 6:12; for the word כסא, the comments on 1:13.

8:21 *I have provided a place there for the ark in which is the covenant of*

YHWH *which he made with our fathers when he brought them up out of the land of Egypt.'*
The object of the temple construction is here said to be the creation of a place for the ark in which the 'covenant with YHWH' can be kept (also see D.F. Murray, *VT* 40 [1990], 301ff.; 316ff.). In place of מקום לארון the par. 2 Chr. 6:11 reads את־הארון, which reading, though it is preferred by Stade-Schwally and others, as well as by the textcr. app. in *BHK*, is not so clearly supported by Pesh. as Berlinger suggests, since, after all, it also abbreviates our verse at other points (so, correctly, Montg.-Gehman). The 'covenant with YHWH' was inscribed on the tables of the law in the ark (see also vs. 9), and this must presumably be understood in a concrete sense, just as ברית 'bisweilen ganz konkret gebraucht werden (kann)' (Pedersen, *Eid*, 35). This is something other than a metonymy for 'the means of the covenant,' as König, *Stil.* 22 and 23, would have it. For the word ברית, see comments on 3:15 and 5:26, and for the 'stone tables' in the ark, above, on vs. 9.

The last part of our verse recalls the making of a covenant at Sinai, though the explicit reference is to the exodus from Egypt.

INTRODUCTION TO VSS. 22-30

As we already noted earlier, around the core of the 7 petitions (vss. 31-50) there are text segments which can be designated, respectively, as the 'first framework' (vss. 22-30; 52f.) and the 'second framework.' These are thoroughly analyzed, both synchronically and diachronically, by Talstra, 127-135; 226-237. In the vss. 23-26 Solomon prays for the continuation of the Davidic dynasty; in the vss. 27-30 the emphasis lies on YHWH's hearing the prayers of the king and people at the place where he dwells.

8:22 *Then Solomon stood before the altar of YHWH in front of the whole assembly of Israel as he spread out his hands to heaven.*
This verse tells us that Solomon subsequently positioned himself before the altar of YHWH (cf. vs. 54), over against, i.e. in front of (BrSynt. §116d) the whole assembly of Israel. In the preceding section there had as yet been no express mention whatever of a YHWH-altar in front of the temple. This altar only reappears at greater length in vs. 64, and then as a 'bronze (copper) altar.' This altar, which Solomon built, is mentioned again in 9:25. Kittel, *SHARG*, 50-53, is of the opinion that Solomon built the great altar before the temple at the same location where David built his (2 Sam. 24:25). Also De Groot, *Altäre*, 31, shares this view. But one cannot get beyond conjecture here (see also Noth, 191v.). The Chronicler, however, substantially expands the information given in our verse by stating (2 Chr. 6:13) that, in the midst of the court, Solomon

had made a bronze כיור 5 cubits long, 5 cubits wide, and 3 cubits high, where he first took a standing and then a kneeling position. In 1 Kgs 7:30ff. this word denoted a 'kettle' or a 'basin' but in the verse in Chronicles the reference is thought to be to a 'platform' (*HAL*, 450) or an 'elevation' (Zorell, 354). De Groot, 24, even believed that from this 'alte Notiz' one could derive the idea that 'daß es außer dem großen Altar noch ein Tempelgerät im Hofe gegeben hat, dessen Maße 5x5x3 Ellen waren.' These measurements, according to him, are the same as the measurements of the altar for burnt offerings in the old tabernacle (Exod. 27:1ff.; cf. also K. Galling, *BRL*[1] 20). Certain scholars are of the opinion that this statement from Chronicles has to be inserted after our verse in Kings (see among others, Rudolph), but with an array of arguments Böttcher (*Neue Aehrenlese;* cf. also Benzinger) already (contra Thenius) rejected the addition in Chronicles as a late gloss.

The citation in 2 Chr. (6:13) immediately distinguishes between praying in a standing posture and praying in a kneeling posture. The prayer posture was possibly one of standing, while the prostration or *proskynesis* presumably occurred at the beginning and at the end of the prayer (cf. Nowack, *Arch.* II, 260; Benzinger, *Arch.* 377; H.J. Boecker, *BHHW*, I, 521; further J. Herrmann, *TDNT*, II, 788f.). Our verse only mentions 'standing' while vs. 54, by contrast, creates the impression of 'kneeling' during the prayer but as such this need not be contradictory. During the prayer Solomon spread out his hands (Josephus, *Ant.* VIII §111 only mentions the 'right hand') to heaven (Pesh. [minus the MSS of 9a1*fam*] – redundantly – adds here: 'and he prayed,' cf. Tg.: 'in prayer'). From the time of Ach-en-Aton (approx. 1380-1362 BCE) there has been extant a representation of people who prayed in the direction of the sun with outstretched arms and hands (see T. H. Gaster, *IDB*, IV, 464, fig. 91). In this verse Taylor, *Sun*, 144f., sees a 'clear case' of the discovery of correspondence between YHWH who is both 'in heaven' and 'in the temple' and the sun which resides 'in the heavens' and is nevertheless 'in the temple,' as in the poem cited in the vss. 12f.

In 6:27 we encountered the verb פרש in connection with the Cherubim's wings 'spreading out'; here the reference is to hands spread out to heaven (for the directional accusative, see König §320c). Houtman, *Himmel*, 242, believes this gesture aims at giving expression to the longing for contact with the deity. The word 'heaven' in our verse in fact need not be inconsistent with, say, vs. 38, where the temple is mentioned as the place toward which praying people spread out their hands (contra: Stade-Schwally, Benzinger, and others).

8:23 *and he said: YHWH, God of Israel, there is no God like you in heaven above or on earth below, who keeps covenant and faithfulness toward your servants who wholeheartedly walk before your face.*
In the opening statement of his prayer Solomon asserts the incomparability of

God and his faithfulness with respect to his servants, in this case the dynasty. Often one finds a negative form of the expression for the incomparability of YHWH in songs and especially, as here, in prayers (see Ps. 86:8; Deut. 33:26; 1 Sam. 2:2; 2 Sam. 7:22; Jer. 10:6f.)[6]; we should also mention here the 'stoical' attribute of God, ἀπροσδεής (see also 1 Macc. 12:9; 2 Macc. 14:35; 3 Macc. 2:9), 'needing nobody,' in this connection in Josephus, *Ant.* VIII §111, who for that matter reproduces, expands, or sometimes abbreviates Solomon's prayer altogether arbitrarily and in accordance with his own insight (§§111-117). In the OT the unicity of God comes to expression also in another way, e.g. in Deut. 4:39, which shows a 'striking resemblance' to the statement in our verse (Labuschagne, op. cit., p. 122). Word pairs 'heaven and earth,' sometimes in conjunction with the prepositions 'above' and 'below,' occur frequently in OT (see, again, Deut. 4:39 and also Josh. 2:11; H. Traub, *TDNT*, V, 513, n. 119; Houtman, *Himmel*, 33-48). Böttcher, *Neue Aehrenlese*, 75, advances that אין in the expression אין־כמוך אלהים does not mean 'none' but a negative 'where' (?), 'der Sinn also zunächst: Wo (findet man), wie Dich, einen Gott?' (cf. Exod. 15:11; Ps. 86:8; further *Ges.*[18], s.v.). אין only means 'none' when אחר or איש is added. The prepositions ממעל and מתחת are lacking in the par. 2 Chr. 6:14, while ועל־הארץ is read as ובארץ.

The incomparability of God also comes out in the 'keeping of the covenant and of faithfulness,' an expression which occurs more often in these words (Deut. 7:9; Neh. 1:5; 9:32; Dan. 9:4; see comments on 3:6 above; further Burney; R. Bultmann, *TDNT*, II, 479; W. Zimmerli, *TDNT*, IX, 383; for the link between ברית and חסד also A. W. Argyle, *ET* 60 [1948f.], 26f.). As for those toward whom God maintains his covenant of faithfulness there is a difference to be noted between MT and LXX. In MT the reference is to servants (pl., all except a few MSS according to Kennicott) who wholeheartedly walk before God's face; in LXX to the servant (sing.). In the interest of clarity LXX[Luc] adds: 'David, my father.' Along with most commentators I believe that the reading of MT must be regarded as the correct one, because the reference is to a universally valid character trait of YHWH which is further defined in what follows. Despite this, Klostermann and Benzinger see a certain tension between vs. 23f. and 25f. But this tension need not lead to the judgment that the 2 parts are incompatible. In this general statement the words 'covenant' and 'faithfulness' need not especially apply to a possible 'covenant' with David, such as is intended in 2 Sam. 7, but this dtr. formulation may very well apply to, say, the 'Sinaitic covenant.'[7]

---

[6] Cf. C. J. Labuschagne, *The Incomparability of Jahwe in the Old Testament* (POS 5), Leiden 1961, 11f.; further G. Stählin, *TDNT*, III, 352.

[7] Cf. F.M. Cross, *Canaanite Myth and Hebrew Epic*, Cambridge 1973, 260, n. 180; differently:

In place of בכלליבם, expanded in line with 2:4, reads as follows: 'In sincerity, with their whole heart, and with their whole soul.'

8:24 *You, who have kept with your servant David, my father, what you promised him. With your (own) mouth you had promised it (to him) and with your (own) hand you have fulfilled it, as it is today.*
This verse is reminiscent of vs. 15. Here again LXX diverges from the reading of MT. In place of 15a LXX translates: 'what (= ἁ) you have kept for your servant David, my father.' It does not take אשר as a conjunction, therefore, but has it refer back to 'covenant and faithfulness' in the previous verse, as a result of which the words את אשר־דברת לו in a sense (only LXX^A still has them) become redundant. This is connected with the translation of the previous verse which similarly diverges from MT. The expression כיום הזה (Gen. 50:20; Deut. 2:30 etc., see König §402u) means: 'as this day shows,' 'the way things now are'; Thenius: 'um diese Zeit,' thereby rejecting the translation of the Vulg.: '*ut haec dies probat*' (cf. De Vries, *Yesterday*, 52, n. 77; idem, in his commentary, a.l.: 'this very day'). Further, the sing. 'hand' in our verse is rendered as a pl. in LXX in various Pesh. MSS (but not in 7a1) and in Vulg. Materially, of course, this makes no difference. For God to do something 'with his own hand' indicates that it is 'complete' (G. Delling, *TDNT*, VI, 287). Talstra, 228, correctly observes that our verse serves as the basis for the following verses.

8:25 *Now therefore YHWH, God of Israel, keep with your servant David, my father, the promise you made to him when you said: "You will never be without a man to sit on the throne of Israel if only your children are careful in what they do when they walk before me as you have walked before me."*
Here Solomon comes to the core of the prayer: the petition for the continuation of the dynasty. This petition starts with ועתה which introduces the relevant viewpoint (see comments on 1:12). In the remainder of the verse there is a backward reference to 2 Sam. 7, but in the terminology to 1 Kgs. 2:4 as well (also cf. 9:5; for כרת niph. in this connection, see comments on 2:4 above). Also in our verse A.D. Crown, *VT* 24 (1974), 111, translates איש, in an alternative manner, by 'a reigning monarch,' but there is no more reason for this here than elsewhere (see comments on 2:2 above).

The continuation of the Davidic throne is made dependent on the condition that his children will continue to walk in the right paths before God's 'face' (the par. 2 Chr. 6:16 has: 'in my law' [בתורתי]). This restrictive condition is introduced by רק אם (Ewald §270b; König §393g; Williams §393). The

---

M. Weinfeld, *Deuteronomy and the Deuteronomic School*, Oxford 1983², 75; further Talstra, 219.

question has been raised whether this restrictive condition indeed relates to the continuation of the Davidic throne as such and must not rather be limited to Solomon's obedience, on which the continuation of the throne over Israel as a whole is dependent (for this discussion and further literature on it, see Talstra, 228f.). An affirmative answer to that question removes the tension between statements such as that given in vs. 23 and the unconditional statements about the dynasty elsewhere (11:36; 15:4; 2 Kgs. 8:19). Talstra (et al.) consider the conditional statements about David's throne to have come from the hand of a pre-exilic redactor, a circumstance which may explain the difference between the material here and the following verses., which sound a somewhat different note.

8:26 *Now then, God of Israel, let the word which you spoke to your servant, my father David, be confirmed.*
Talstra, 229, cites a number of reasons why this verse must be attributed to another hand than the previous verses. One of the reasons is the repetition of ועתה which after the use of this expression in vs. 25 in fact feels redundant (many Hebr. MSS but also the versions add 'YHWH' in our verse on the analogy of the preceding verse). Also the entreaty formula נא יאמן נא (נא is omitted in the par. 2 Chr. 6:17) is not customary after an imperative. It is indeed striking, after the previous verse with its positive formulation, to be confronted here with this tentative wish-form. Accordingly, the verse has a parenthetical 'feel' to it. Although the tension in these petitions is palpable, the verse need not for that reason be a gloss.

The verb אמן, from which also the noun אמת (mentioned above in 2:4) has been derived, occurs only sporadically in our books (in niph. also in 11:38; in niphil in 10:7 and 2 Kgs. 17:14), and here means 'be fixed, certain, reliable' ('als Zeichen der Bewährung eines דבר angewandt,' so O. Procksch, *TDNT*, IV, 92; also cf. *Ges.*[18], 73f.; further cf. W. C. Kaiser, *JSOT* 45 [1989], 91-98). The pl. resp. the sing. of דבר(י)ך is a matter of k^etib resp. q^ere. The q^ere-form finds support in the par. 2 Chr. 6:17 but also in many Hebr. MSS (Kennicott; so also De Rossi, a.l.), LXX and Pesh. (also cf. König §258b, n. 1; Gordis 137). Although as a result of the sing. of דבר congruence in number with the predicate is created, deviation from this customary rule is quite normal (also) in biblical Hebr. (Ges-K §145a, o), so that a decision can hardly be made on the basis of grammatical considerations. Nevertheless, we prefer the q^ere-form (along with Thenius; Klostermann; Stade-Schwally and others; but Noth prefers the *lectio difficilior*). In place of דברת Pesh. translates: 'you have sworn,' which Berlinger views as 'sinngemäß.'

8:27 *[But would God really settle on earth? Heaven, even the highest heaven, cannot contain you, how much less the house that I have built!.]*

The second part of the 'first frame' (Talstra) of the 7 'petitions' contains, but now in the interrogative, a pronouncement on God (cf. vs. 23). Here a sharp contrast is indicated between the dwelling place of God, the heaven of heavens, and his earthly house, the temple. The word אמנם, sometimes reinforced by כי, is consistently combined with the interrogative particle ה. It has affirmative power and means 'really?', 'indeed?' (Gen. 18:13; Num. 22:37; Ps. 58:2; and the par. verse 2 Chr. 6:18; GD §116c; Burney; further Ges.[18], s.v.). A related form is אָמְנָם (with qames ḥatuf; 2 Kgs. 19:17; Isa. 37:18; Job 9:2, etc.) and both forms are related to the root אמן (see previous verse). 2 Chr. 6:18 further adds את־האדם, 'with humanity,' to the question whether God now really dwells on earth. LXX (and also Tg. though in paraphrase) supports this reading in our verse (μετὰ ἀνθρώπων). Many commentators (Thenius, Klostermann, Benzinger, De Vaux, et al.) consider this addition necessary in our verse; others (like Stade-Schwally, Montg.-Gehman, Barthélemy) reject it. Since the addition betrays the theological intentions of a later time, we join those who reject the addition here. The expression suggests an absolute contrast, which Kimchi already strikingly interpreted as follows: 'You are the place of the world, and the world is not your place.'

The fact of God's sublimity over all that is earthly is accentuated by what follows: Heaven, even 'the heaven of heavens' (6x in OT, according to Rehm: Deut. 10:14; Ps. 148:4; Neh. 9:6 and 2 Chr. 2:5; 6:18) cannot contain God. In Hebr. a superlative idea is expressed by the construction of 2 identical substantives (König §260b; GD §44, rem. 3; Joüon §141i). We already encountered the pilpal-form of כול in 4:7 in the sense of 'care for.' Here the verb means 'contain,' 'embrace,' 'incorporate' (similarly in Jer. 20:9; Mal. 3:2; Prov. 18:14; 2 Chr. 2:5; 6:18). The impf. here denotes a conative aspect: heaven cannot contain God (Driver §37; Burney). The following אף כי introduces what in the later rabbinical literature would be called the קל וחמר - rule, the conclusion from the minor to the major, or, vice versa: 'how much more,' or 'how much less'[8]; further König §353a; Ewald §354c; Williams §387; Burney; Ges.[18], s.v. אף 4°, 87; LXX[A, B] has: πλην και; LXX[Luc.]: πως; cf. Rahlfs, SSt. III, 201, a 'freie Änderung, um den Satz verständlich zu machen'). If the heaven of heavens cannot even contain God, 'how much less the temple which I, Solomon, have built.' To this LXX[B, Luc.] further adds: 'for your name,' according to Montg.-Gehman (correctly) 'again with theological restriction.'

It has struck many exegetes that this absolute pronouncement in our verse does not fit very well in the immediate context. Ehrlich, for example, writes: 'Der Übergang von V. 26 hierher ist aber zu abrupt; darum vermute ich, daß

---

[8] Cf. W. Bacher, *Die exegetische Terminologie der jüdischen Traditionsliteratur*, Darmstad 1965², I, 172ff.

dazwischen Worte ausgefallen sind.' Benzinger is even more clear when he posits that the dtr. does indeed take the position that God dwells on earth in the midst of his people (see 6:13), but that the writer of this verse betrays another mentality, the mentality of Deutero-Isaiah (cf. Isa. 40:12-26; 44:24ff.; 45:11-25, 66:1). Šanda aligns himself with this line of thought. He finds that the writer of this verse is 'bedeutend' removed from the Solomonic era. As the time of the origination of our verse he thinks of the exile, 'wo die Gefahr besonders nahe lag, Jahve nach Art der Heidengötter aufzufassen und die ehemalige Bundeslade als Fetisch anzusehen.' Other scholars as well argue along these lines; Gray, for example ('parenthetical, and perhaps a later theologizing interpolation'), and Würthwein ('eine Randbemerkung ..., die ... hierher versprengt worden ist'). Talstra, 231f., on the other hand, relates our verse to the conclusion of vs. 29 and to vs. 30. He does not think our verse is necessarily a gloss. The verses referred to concern praying in general and pertain 'to the relationship between praying, the temple, and heaven as God's dwelling place.'

It cannot be denied that, in its context and particularly in the framework of the following verses, our verse seeks to say that YHWH hears [human] prayers in heaven and not from within the temple (Ehrlich correctly pointed this out earlier). But in the background of this verse there is the additional factor of the frequently hidden polemic against the temple as the place where YHWH would and could dwell (see Mulder 1989, 15f.). Accordingly, we align ourselves with those who, because of its absolute and isolated character, consider our verse to be a gloss, possibly at one time recorded in the margin of this prayer by a fervent YHWH-worshipper but later incorporated in the text by a copyist. This assumption also facilitates a better linkage between vs. 28 and vs. 26 (or, better, vs. 25) than Böttcher (in his *Neue Aehrenlese*) proposed in his day.

8:28 *and be pleased, YHWH, my God, to have regard for your servant's prayer and plea. Hear the cry and the prayer which your servant is praying before you this day,*

Along with Talstra, 230, and others I am of the opinion that this verse, at least in substance, is a continuation of vs. 25 (Benzinger thinks of vs. 26), so that the pf. cons. ופנית with which this verse begins has to be taken as the continuation of the imper. שמר in vs. 25, a common construction in OT Hebr. In this verse Solomon pleads with God to have regard to his prayers. LXX[B, Luc.] abbreviates the phrase 'to the prayer and plea of your servant' (for this grammatical construction in Hebr. cf., among others, Jouön §129a; BrSynt. §70e) to ἐπὶ τὴν δέησίν μου; in place of 'my God' LXX reads 'the God of Israel' and the second אל־התפלה similarly omitted in LXX[B]. Further, in the par. 2 Chr. 6:19 the word היום is left out. There is no reason, however, for deviating from our MT.

The word תפלה, with the hitp. of the verb פלל occurs here in our chapter for the first time, remarkably enough concentrating itself in this chapter (see H.-P. Stähli, *THAT*, II, 427-432; E.S. Gerstenberger, *TWAT*, VI, 606-617). Forms of the verb – according to Stähli – occur 79x in OT, the substantive תפלה 77x. To 'pray' is the general meaning of the word, which, constructed with this root, hardly occurs outside the Hebr. in any other Sem. language. The word תפלה gained currency especially after the exile and especially reflects 'cultic, formalized prayer' (Gerstenberger). Often, therefore, תפלה denotes intercession.[9] But prayer frequently takes place in the framework of the cult or near a holy place, especially in the psalms, in which the one who is praying begs God to hear him, or in which he thanks God, because the Lord has heard him (Stähli, 430). Sometimes the congregation comes clearly to the fore as the subject of the prayer (Jer. 29:7; 12ff.; Ps. 32:6; 72:5; etc., see Gerstenberger, 615). This is also the case in our verse and in the context of our chapter: there is reference to the קהל (vss. 14, 22, 55, 65), which is gathered by the temple building as the liturgist stretches out his hands before the altar and utters the intercession. As components of, and substitutes for, this 'praying,' words like 'come' (vss. 31, 41f.), 'turn' (again or from) (vss. 33, 35, 47f.), 'acknowledge' (vss. 33, 35), 'make supplication' (vss. 33, 47) and 'stretch out hands' (vs. 38) are used.

Parallel to תפלה one finds in our verse, and in what follows (vss. [30], 38; 45, 49, 54; 9:3), the word תחנן (no fewer than 9x in our chapter and in 9:3 of the 25x in OT), which is derived from the root חנן, 'be gracious' (see H.J. Stoebe, *THAT*, I, 587-597; D.N. Freedman, J. Lundbom, *TWAT*, III, 23-40). Sometimes the word is virtually synonymous with the preceding תפלה. The reference is to a prayer of supplication, a prayer which God answers favorably or to which he will listen.

The third word which in our verse is only used here in this connection (Ehrlich therefore wants to replace this 'hochpoetisches Wort' here by תחנה) is רנה, often translated elsewhere in OT by 'shouts of rejoicing' (Isa. 14:7; 35:10; 44:23; 48:20 etc.). The word is derived from the verb רנן, 'rejoice,' which occurs 53x in OT (R. Ficker, *THAT*, II, 781-786; J. Hausmann, *TWAT*, VII, 538-545). The substantive is found 33x, almost half of the total in the Psalms. Essentially the reference, in the case of רנן is to 'loud cries,' the 'cry' that is directed to YHWH in an attempt to get through to him. Whether it is a cry for help or a cry of rejoicing depends on the circumstances (see N.E. Wagner, *VT* 10 [1960], 44).

---

[9] On the prayer of intercession, see also P.A.H. de Boer, *De Voorbede in het Oude Testament*, Leiden 1943; F. Hesse, *Die Fürbitte im Alten Testament*, Erlangen 1951; J. Scharbert, "Die Fürbitte im Alten Testament," *Festschrift für Dr. Atonin Hofmann*, Passau 1984, 91-109.

8:29 *so that your eyes may be open night and day over this house, the place of which you said "Let my name be there," so that you may hear the prayer which your servant offers toward this place.*
Solomon prays that YHWH's eyes may be continually open with respect to the temple and with respect to the prayer that is prayed in the temple. Although עניך is written defectively (on the other hand, cf. the par. 2 Chr. 6:20 but also numerous Hebr. MSS on this place according to Kennicott) the attribute ('open') is nevertheless in the pl. (essentially it is a dual form). In this connection, Baer, 100, and Mm, no. 1145, mention still 5 other places in which this phenomenon occurs (Deut. 15:18; 19:21; 25:12; Isa 37:17 and Job 14:3; cf. also Montg.-Gehman; further König §258b and Ges-K §91k). The usual (also in ancient Israel) sequence 'night and day' (cf. e.g. Gen. 1:5 etc.) is turned around in the par. 2 Chr. 6:20 and also in LXX (except for LXX^A) and in many MSS of Pesh. (but not in 9a1*fam*) (but see vs. 59 below). LXX repeats ἡμέρας καὶ νυκτός again at the end of our verse.

Also in our verse stress is put on the fact that the 'name' of YHWH dwells in the sanctuary (see comments on vs. 16 above and on 13:2). The words יהוה שמי שם are reproduced in the par. place in Chronicles as לשום שמך, that is, less absolutely, more conditionally. Benzinger observes that the expression of our verse (not literally, for that matter, but it is in Chronicles, MJM) agrees with Deut. 12:5, 11, and adds: 'wir haben also hier ein direktes Citat dieser Stelle und damit die feierliche Erklärung, daß der Tempel dem dort gemeinten Orte entspricht.' The final words: אל־המקום הזה, 'in the direction of the temple,' are understood by Keil (et al.) as meaning that Solomon prayed in the temple court in the direction indicated (also cf. vs. 22; Snijders points out that 'sending up prayers,' as, for example, NV suggests in its translation of our verse, creates a mistaken impression: it does not mean that people's eyes were directed upward toward heaven[10]).

Here and in the following verses the expression המקום הזה is used several times in reference to the temple at Jerusalem. H. Köster, *TDNT*, VIII, 197, n. 70, points out that, with a view to 2 Chr. 6:40 and 7:15, the phrase cannot simply be viewed as an adverb of place ('here'). Talstra, 231, n.20, correctly remarks that the futural translation of NV 'opzenden zal' ('will send up') is mistaken, because the future tense nullifies the intended universal validity of the statement.

8:30 *Hear the pleas of your servant and of your people Israel, when they pray at this place. Hear in heaven, your dwelling place, and when you hear,*

---

[10] L. A. Snijders, "Het gebed naar de tempel toe," *NedThT* 19 (1964f.), 1-14, esp. 4.

forgive.
This verse continues the line of thought developed in the preceding verses. In place of תחנת a number of Hebr. MSS have the reading תפלה, which is understandable but must not be taken over (also cf. the par. 2 Chr. 6:21: תחנוני). Along with BrSynt. §164a, אשר must be viewed as a 'Bedingungspartikel,' 'when' (otherwise: Ehrlich, among others).

The second part of our verse is introduced with urgency as a result of which the accent falls on the pers. pron.: ואתה תשמע (for the translation of ן, 'so' cf. Ewald §348a). To answer the question from where then YHWH must hear, the preposition אל is used twice where – considering the par. verse in 2 Chronicles (cf. also the ancient versions) – one would have expected מן. Nevertheless there is no reason to alter the text (cf. Ewald §217c; Ges-K §119g; also Burney, on 6:18), or to view the words from אל־מקום ... השמים as a gloss (so, e.g. Stade-Schwally). Heaven is here referred to as the dynamic place of YHWH's dwelling. H. Traub, *TDNT*, V, 521, strikingly refers to the functional determination of 'heaven' in his connection: 'Heaven is not defined as a place or state. It is a dynamic point of departure.' Houtman, *Himmel*, 230, construes the preposition in the sense of 'in the direction of,' that is, 'YHWH belongs in the direction of heaven.' He regards this as an elliptical way of saying: 'YHWH hears the prayer (uttered in the direction of the sanctuary) which rises to heaven (see also Snijders, art. cit, 11; and Talstra, 230ff.)

The concluding words of our verse ושמעת וסלחת are understood as a hypothetical sentence by Driver §149: 'and *when* you hear, forgive' (also cf. Vulg.: *et cum exaudieris propitius eris*). Consequently the form of the repeated verb שמע acquires a special function and is not meaningless. Pesh., however, omits ושמעת. LXX reads ποιήσεις in place of it, a translation which corresponds with ועשית in the vss. 32 and 43 (Stade-Schwally). Burney is – correctly – of the opinion that the reading of our text can be maintained here.

In OT the verb סלח occurs 33x in qal and 13x in niph., 5 of which in 1 Kings (in our chapter alone: vss. 30, 34, 36, 39 and 50) and 3x in 2 Kings (5:18 [2x] and 24:4). The basic meaning can be rendered by 'forgive' (see J. J. Stamm, *THAT*, II, 150-160; J. Hausmann, *TWAT*, V, 859-867; further Talstra, 192-201). The one who forgives sins is always YHWH. Other Hebr. words are used to designate mutual forgiveness among humans. OT does not know 'forgiveness' in the modern sense of the word as a spiritual event; 'es kennt sie vielmehr nur als einen konkreten, umfassenden, auch im Äußeren des Einzelnen oder der Gemeinschaft sich auswirkenden Vorgang' (Stamm, 152). It is evident from Lev. 4:20, 26, 31, 35; 5:10, 13 etc. and Num. 14:19f.; 15:25f., 28 etc., that the verb functions in the precepts for sacrifice, hence in the cult. Also in the prayers which take place in the cult the question of forgiveness comes up, 'und zwar so, daß die Vergebung in der Regel nicht nur die Aufhebung der Sünde, sondern damit zugleich die Abwendung der in einer Not erfahrenen Strafe umschließt' (Stamm, 155). Striking in our verse (and in vs. 39) is that סלח is construed without an object. Talstra, 200, believes that this specialized use of the verb is 'ad hoc, and can only be explained by the composition of text's final redaction.' The combination of the verbs שמע and סלח in our verse makes the following petitions penitential (so Noth).

8:31 *When a man wrongs his neighbour and (the latter) puts an imprecatory oath on him by placing him under a formula of imprecation and he comes and swears the oath before your altar in this house,*
In this verse begins the first of the 7 'petitions' which form the core of Solomon's prayer.[11] Talstra has analyzed at length the structure and interrelationship of these petitions (pp. 108-126, 174-225). In general, the 7 petitions consist of 2 protases and 2 apodoses. This first petition, however, differs from the following ones, because it refers, not to a situation of distress, but to what is usually called an 'oath of purification' (cf. e.g. Exod. 22:6ff. [RSV: 7ff.]); Num. 5:11-31; Deut. 17:8-13; 21:1-9). We are therefore dealing here with a special prayer in a specific case.[12] It is noteworthy, however, that the opening clause of the decrees in the Code of Hammurabi also concern testimonies the correctness or incorrectness of which has to be proven before the judges (*ANET*, 166).

The opening clause of this petition with the words את אשר already deviates from the opening of the other petitions and from the par. 2 Chr. 6:22, which begins with אם (so also Pesh. and Vulg.; but cf. LXX ὅσα ἄν, 'whichever'; Tg. supports MT). The words את אשר here introduces a conditional sentence and are usually translated by 'when' (Ewald §333a; Thenius), 'suppose that,' 'in the event that' (or 'when') (König §390d; cf. §384d; Williams §469; *Ges.*[18], s.v. אשר 10 [p. 112a]), 'as it concerns,' 'when' (Ehrlich). Burney rightly calls this beginning 'rather difficult' (also cf. the lengthy discussion of this question in Talstra, 109f.). Klostermann even speaks of 'ein unmöglichen Anfang' and reads אך אשר, 'nur wo (ein Mann ...),' which he then – as an exception – places after vss. 33f., though he does refer to a few cases in which אשר already by itself occurs in the sense of 'when,' etc. (e.g. vs. 33; Lev. 4:22; Deut. 11:27 etc.). It is his belief that the words were in the first place intended to indicate a *casus pendens* (so also J. Hoftijzer, *OTS* 14 [1965], 49), but that as a result of the length of the protases it was not completely worked out.

Next there is mention of the חטא of a person against his neighbour. We

---

[11] Cf. also my "I Koningen 8:31 en 32," *JNSL* 16 (1990), 107-114.
[12] It formed the basis for H. Schmidt's study *Das Gebet der Angeklagten im Alten Testament* (BZAW 49), Giessen 1928, see esp. pp. 1f.; cf. C. Kuhl, *OLZ* 32 (1929), 856; K. van der Toorn, *VT* 38 (1988), 427f.

already encountered the Hebr. word as an adjective in the more specialized sense of 'criminal' or as substantive ('loser') in 1:21. The verb (occurring 595x in OT with other forms of this root, R. Knierim, *THAT*, I, 542) which is not only found in the remainder of this chapter (vss. 33, 35, 46f., 50) but a number of times also later in our books (14:16, 22; 15:30 etc.), primarily means 'miss (a target)' (Judg. 20:16; Isa. 65:20; Job 5:24; Prov. 8:36), and more generally 'sink' 'injure,' i.e. do deeds which conflict with the experience of true fellowship with others, either with God, or with a fellow human being (for an extensive discussion of the word, cf. Knierim, 541-549; K. Koch, *TWAT*, II, 857-870). This fellow human being is here referred to by the word רע (in Kings also in 1 Kgs. 16:11; 20:35; 2 Kgs. 3:23; 7:3, 9) which is found numerous times in OT in the sense of 'friend,' 'colleague,' 'comrade' or 'companion' (Zorell, 779).

In our verse, then, a case is posited in which someone wrongs his neighbour, insults him, in brief, commits a 'crime.' From the words which follow it might be inferred that the person afflicted or wronged is possibly not – or perhaps not at all – certain who has wronged or injured him; at best he has a suspicion about it. Schmidt, op. cit., p. 1, however, assumes that the accused himself swears an oath before the altar. This idea is also current among other commentators and researchers.[13] In such a case, as here (cf. also Judg. 17:2), a curse was pronounced at a holy place to heighten the effect of that curse (see Petersen, I-II, 406, 441f.; III-IV, 448f.). Brichto refers to 'the exaction or imposition of an exculpatory oath.'[14] This is the procedure referred to in our text by the words ונשא־בו אלה.

The root אלה (only here in Kings) is represented in our verse by the noun and by a verb (in OT derivations from this root occur 43x: C. A. Keller, *THAT*, I, 149-152; J. Scharbert, *TWAT*, I, 279-285). אלה does not denote a 'curse' in general but a very specific curse 'which a person pronounces upon others or upon himself to protect legal rights or religio-ethical orders' (Scharbert, 280). Hence the word is a juridical term (Keller, 150). It concerns a legal but simultaneously dangerous (cf. Num. 5:11-31) judicial remedy against an aggressor who may be known but is more likely to be unknown, concerning whom one at best has certain suspicions (for the distinction between 'cursing' and 'swearing' see J. Schneider, *TDNT*, V, 460; further also Pedersen, *Eid*, 82v.).

Now נשא entails a textcritical difficulty. In *BHS* (but also already in *BHK*

---

[13] E.g. J. Krašovec, *La Justice (sdq) de Dieu dans la Bible Hébraïque et l'Interprétation juive et chrétienne* (OBO 76), Fribourg 1988, 186.

[14] H.C. Brichto, *The Problem of 'Curse' in the Hebrew Bible* (JBLMon. 13), Philadelphia 1963, 53.

and the editions of the *Biblia Hebraica* by Baer and Snaith) the word is reproduced with a *šin* (based, in part, on the readings of the *codex Leningradensis* and in the *Aleppo-Codex*) but in many Hebr. MSS and older editions of the *Biblia Hebraica* (already in the 'Bombergiana' but also in that of Joh. H. Michaelis, Halle, 1720; Joh. Simonis, Halle 1822³; C. G. G. Theile, Leipzig, 1902⁹, or in that of E. van der Hooght, A. Hahn [ed. 1834] and of Letteris [ed. 1944]) one finds a *śin* (see Barthélemy who calls the Masoretic situation 'extrêment complexe' but who, after having thoroughly weighed the textual witnesses, opts for the reading with *śin*). נשא I (with *šin*) in qal means, among other things, 'make a loan' (Deut. 24:11; Jer. 15:10 etc.). *HAL*, 687, here presents our verse as having the meaning 'jmdm e. Reinigungseid zuschieben,' in line with König, *Wörterbuch*, 290, but simultaneously refers in this connection to the lemma (נשא with śin, 685, no. 9) where 'e. Eid auferlegen, od. Fluch aussprechen' is given as the translation (with reference also to Noth). In an earlier stage, under the lemma אלה (p. 50), *HAL* had already opted for this form: 'Verfluchung aussprechen über.' The uncertainty of this lexicon at this point is also reflected in the commentaries and translations (see, e.g., Montg.-Gehman; Šanda; Rudolph, 212; also cf. Brichto, op. cit., 53f.; who opts for נשא as the *lectio difficilior*). LXX reads λάβῃ, which suggests נשא with *śin* (Barthélemy mistakenly judges otherwise), Tg., on the other hand, reads וירשי, an aphel-form of רשא, meaning 'making a loan,' but to be translated here as 'imposing (an oath)' (Dalman, *ANH*, 408), which again argues for the form with *šin* (somewhat along the same lines also Pesh.: *wnhybywhy [mwmt']*, 'he obligates him to an oath'). Vulg. paraphrases: *et habuerit aliquod iuramentum quo teneatur adstrictus,* 'and has to swear an oath to which he is held.'

A secondary difficulty is the question how בו needs to be understood. König §10, translates: 'damit er es (sein fehlerhaftes Wort etc.) bekräftige > "daß er ihn schwören lasse",' in the process referring to Thenius and Klostermann, which he calls 'pleonastisch zum Vorausg.' Now König is correct – in the section referred to he offers examples of it – in saying that in certain cases the pers. pron. of the 3rd p. can be used neutrally. But Barthélemy, citing Kimchi, remarks that the construction of נשא with the prep. ב, which introduces a person as complement in the case of the verb cited which he equates with נשא (see also the lexicon) is very common: this is how the person to whom one 'makes a loan' is introduced. The translation then has to be: 'et on lui soumettra un serment imprécatoire afin de la faire se lier par une imprécation.' The idea that בו should denote a reflexive pronoun is perhaps grammatically very well possible (see Lettinga §20a) and is sometimes also so rendered in (older) translations (see e.g. the translation of M. Luther of 1545: 'und nimpt des einen Eid auff sich' and, following Luther's version, the Deuxaes-Bible), but it is nevertheless improbably here.

But there is still another problem here, one which Talstra, 110f., has rightly signaled: in the transition from יחטא to ינשא is there perhaps a change of subject? A glance at various new(er) translations shows that the subject is changed. The SV, for example, already reads: 'wanneer iemand tegen zijnen naasten zal gezondigd hebben, en hij hem een eed des vloeks opgelegd zal hebben ...' ('If any man will have trespassed against his neighbour and he will have laid on him an oath of imprecation ...'), where in the marginal notes it is expressly stated with reference to 'he': the neighbour against whom the trespass has been committed (so, approximately, also LV, NV, PCV, WV, GNB, Torczyner [1937], Einheitsübersetzung [1980], Bible de Jerusalem, etc.). Also in various translations, the subject of the imposition of the oath is not the injured neighbour but an indeterminate 'they' (e.g. the Zürcher Bibel, Riessler-Storr in der Matthias-Grünewald-Bibel, Buber-Rosenzweig, Dhorme [Pléiade], TOB, Bible en Francais courant [1986], James Moffatt, NEB, Jew. Public. Soc. of America, etc.), or a passive translation is used to indicate that another imposes the oath (e.g.: 'und es wird ihm ein Fluch auferlegt,' Luther translation [1956]; 'and an oath he laid upon him,' KJV, etc.). The ones who impose the oath may then be judges or the priests, or the agents are not indicated.

Still another view is represented by Van den Born who translates: 'If anyone wrongs his neighbour and lays an oath on him by which he must call down a curse on himself ...' Accordingly, no change of subject occurs here. Citing 1 Sam. 2:25, Van den Born postulates that someone accuses his neighbour, 'but the latter has no way to assert his innocence other than an oath, i.e. a self-malediction in case he should speak untruth.' According to Talstra, 111, who supports Van den Born here, the reference is to 'an abuse of the procedure, as a device in an attempt "to place" an opponent "under the curse"...' In this manner also the inf. להאלתו would have a clear function. 'The function of the first petition in this view is not to ask God for effectuatio of the oath of self-malediction, but to remove its automatic effect by asking God himself to decide guilt and innocence.'

It cannot be denied that this last-mentioned viewpoint has much that is attractive. Nevertheless the question arises whether, in connection with אלה one can already in ancient Israel speak of 'automatism,' and whether it is not better, with Pedersen, *Eid*, 82, for example, to speak of 'Unglück als selbständige Größe, wie es in jemandem sitzt, und wie es auf seine Umgebungen einwirkt.' 'Es ist ein schädlicher, unheilvoller Stoff, der im Menschen seinen Sitz haben, *Num.* 5, der ein Land 'verzehren' kann, so dass die Äcker verdorren, *Jes.* 24,6; *Jer.* 23,10; cf. *Sach.* 5,3.' Only God can confirm or negate the numinosity of a 'curse,' just as he alone can unleash or undo wartime calamities, great drought, famines, etc., the things which come up in the following petitions. Brichto, op. cit., 54, voices this conditional viewpoint when he translates: 'If someone commits an offense against his fellow and the latter takes up an imprecation against him under the power of a curse, may (or and) that (conditional) imprecation come(s) before your altar in this temple ...' Furthermore, a quick change of subject is not uncommon in OT Hebr. (König, *Stil.* 257f.). Hence the subject of נשא is the aggrieved party who pronounces an imprecation over the (to him unknown) person who committed an offense against him, 'in order to curse him,' i.e. bring him under the power of the curse. This seemingly functionless repetition of the root אלה has the power of the (elsewhere so beloved) *figura etymologica* in the Sem. languages: a reinforcement of the basic idea. The verse-division of MT need not therefore (as Ehrlich and Noth would like, see below) be changed.

We have not yet faced all the difficulties presented by the text: after all, how must ובא אלה be understood? In this construction אלה is fem., and the verb is masc. Fact is that various grammatical solutions have been advanced for this phenomenon; for example, by referring to incongruence in relation to gender and number (König §§345a, 357e), or to an 'unreflected' verb in the case of a following sing. fem. (Ges-K §145o), but alongside of these suggestions one finds many proposals for changing the punctuation or the word sequence. The ancient translations already supply a basis for these proposals. LXX, for example, reads: καὶ ἔλθῃ καὶ ἐξαγορεύσῃ, a translation which, as far as the second verbal form is concerned, even suggests as 'Vorlage' a hitp. of ירה (cf. Lev. 5:5; further also vss. 33 and 35 of our chapter). Pesh. reads: 'he comes and he swears an oath.' Tg. goes in the same direction with וייתי יומיניה, while Vulg. reads *et venerit propter iuramentum.* These translations *may* have read the underlying text as בא ואלה: 'he comes and he swears an oath.' On this basis and also on the basis of Neh. 10:30 (cf. Ezek. 17:13) the reading בא באלה has been suggested: 'he comes in an oath,' 'they put (him) under oath' (Kamphausen; Montg.-Gehman; textcr. app. *BHK* and *BHS*; Talstra, 111, etc.; cf. also Stade-Schwally). However, Böttcher (*Neue Aehrenlese*; further §928, n. 2 [p. 130]) wants to punctuate אלה as an inf. abs. and view it as an adverb: 'he comes swearing an oath' (so also Thenius), a reading which he sees reflected in the ancient versions. In place of ובא אלה Ehrlich only reads באלה and links it with the preceding בהאלתי. He views these linked words (ignoring the dividing *atnaḥ* in MT) as 'Umstandssatz.' In his opinion the corruption arose as a result of dittography. Noth follows Ehrlich on this point and translates: '... um ihn mit einem Schwur schwören zu lassen vor deinem Altar in diesem Hause ...'

In this maze of emendations, translations, and opinions it is not easy for us to find a way out. From the preceding discussion it has become clear, and it is also evident from what follows, that in these verses especially the oath is a weighty matter, particularly the oath sworn before YHWH's face in the sanctuary. If the transgressor referred to in the opening clause is an unknown person; it is of course difficult to bring precisely this person before the altar unless one assumes that the person involved is a suspect known to the wronged party, a suspect who only needs to be 'cleared' (one finds this idea in the majority of the translations and commentaries we have consulted).

The question is, however, whether in this manner the intensity and scope of the 'curse' is not too much restricted. For the wronged party pronounces a curse 'an sich'; he curses a transgressor whom he does not know as such. At best he suspects one or more than one 'neighbour,' but via the sanctuary he lets the curse as it were do his work for him: ultimately God will have to decide. Viewing the text in this light, I would wish to leave it unchanged, at most adding a copula before אלה, and translate: 'he comes and utters a curse before the altar in this temple.' Accordingly, between נשא and בא there is no change of subject (against Talstra, 111); furthermore, בא and the following אלה, viewed as a pf. qal, may constitute an asyndetic combination (so, correctly, Keil; against Thenius).

8:32 *Then hear in heaven and act by pronouncing judgment over your servants, declaring the unrighteous man guilty by bringing his conduct down upon himself and by vindicating the righteous by treating him in accordance with his righteous conduct.*

Judgment is left, in trust, in the hands of YHWH. Here (and also in the vss. 34, 36, 39, 43, 45, and 49) שמים is construed without the preposition מן as this is found in the par. 2 Chr. 6:23 and in the ancient versions. One can speak here of an 'accusative of local determination' (Joüon §126h; also cf. Ewald §300a; König §330k; 'örtliche Sphäre' not on /a/; Ges-K §118g); one can also (with Stade-Schwally et al.) speak of 'a dogmatic correction made in the interest of the belief that YHWH dwells in the heavens, a belief which is, however, shared by this section.' The verb עשה hear means 'act,' 'react,' as e.g. also in Amos 3:6b (for the verb used absolutely, see my article in *VT* 34 [1984], 106ff.; further Burney). For שפט, see comments on 3:9.

In place of 'your servants' LXX translates 'your people Israel.' This probably happened with a view to the following petitions which generally speak also of 'the people (Israel).' This, we may assume, is what is intended. It is a question, in fact, whether one should apply 'servants' specifically to the 2 parties involved in the case (so, among others, Talstra, 112). In the preceding verse a general case was posited; in this verse a decisive verdict is expected from YHWH in favour of or over whomever in Israel has sworn an oath. Granted, a division will be manifest when God renders his judgment: evildoers will find their conduct coming down on their own head, while the righteous go free.

The nouns and verbs associated with the root רשע occur frequently in OT (according to C. van Leeuwen, *THAT*, II, 813-818, even 343x), but in our books they are only found in our chapter (in qal also in vs. 47; the hiph. only in our verse, as is the noun). Especially the books Ezekiel, Psalms, Job, Proverbs, and Ecclesiastes contains various words having this root, words which mean 'be guilty, criminal,' frequently the opposite in OT of the words formed from the root צדק, as in our verse. The רשע is the man who endangers the life of, or positive fellowship with, his fellow citizen, whether this person be the king or the wife of his neighbour. But also idolatry and oppression of the poor, fall under this heading. Both the evil deed *and* the guilt and punishment consequent upon such a deed are contained in this root (Van Leeuwen).

The petition is now that YHWH may cause the crime to fall back upon the head of the criminal. In place of the hiph. of the verb רשע the par. 2 Chr. 6:23 has להשיב ל, a clarification which weakens the reinforcing element contained in the paronomasia of our verse. In 2:32f., 37, 44, we already encountered the expression 'blood which returns upon someone's own head.' This or a related form of the expression occurs approx. 40x in OT.[15] Perhaps the expression, as used in our text, can best be understood as: causing the criminal to experience the consequences of his own deed (cf. Babut, op. cit., p. 479). The opposite of this is expressed in the following part of this verse in which the root צדק plays a role (see comments on 3:6 above; also B. Johnston, *TWAT*, VI, 898-924; further, Krašovec, OBO 76, 187). In this connection Krašovec comments that 'le verbe "justifier" les justes, en opposition avec la condamnation des injustes, signifie la reconnaissance de la fidélité des justes, pour qu'ils puissent bénéficier de la justice salvifique de Dieu.' According to him, it is not the works themselves which are the criterion for the verdict, but for the evildoers it is 'la corruption radicale de leur coeur,' and for the righteous it is 'leur fidélité' or 'leur amour pour la verité.' It has always been recognized that by perjuring oneself a person calls a curse down upon his or her head.

There is in our verse no mention of the manner in which a decision could come into being and how the divine judgment was executed. With Talstra, 112, we are of the opinion that we may assume the use of a certain ritual, about which, however, nothing specific has been handed down to us. Brongers assumes a decision came about by *urim* and *thummim,* but since the character of these fate-shaping means has by no means been established,[16] this suspicion is mere speculation. R. Press, *ZAW* 51 (1933), 138, already made a study of this question, proceeding from the assumption that the curse was pronounced

---

[15] See J.M. Babut, "Que son sang soi sur sa tête!," *VT* 36 (1986), 474-480.
[16] See C. van Dam, *The Urim and Thummim. A Study of an Old Testament Means of Revelation*, diss. Kampen 1986; also C. Houtman, "The Urim and Thummim: A New Suggestion," *VT* 40 (1990), 229-232.

by an accused person at a holy place and basically came down to being a formal self-malediction repeated after the officiant. In this connection he had in mind as examples cases from Exod. 22:7 and 10 but there the reference is to known persons who are under suspicion and attempt to clear themselves, whereas in our case the reference, in our opinion, is (mainly) to an unknown suspect.

8:33 *When your people Israel are beaten by an enemy because they sinned against you but turn back to you, acknowledging your name, praying and making supplication to you in this house,*
In the second petition we find a sketch of a distress situation caused by the circumstances of war (Pesh. explicitly refers to 'a war between enemies'). The conditional clause here is introduced (also cf. vs. 35) by means of an inf., preceded by the preposition ב. In the par. 2 Chr. 6:24 we find אִם־ (cf. König §404b; Driver, *Tenses* §118). The verb נגף occurs only here and in 2 Kgs. 14:12 in niph. in the books of Kings (49x in OT, 22 of them in niph. and 26 in qal, plus once in hitp., see H.D. Preuß, *TWAT*, V, 227-230). The word means 'beat,' and (in qal) YHWH is predominantly the subject of it. When Israel is 'beaten' (niph.) by its enemies, then it is as it were also struck by YHWH himself, who in this process uses 'enemies' as his means (Preuß). This idea, which is also found elsewhere in OT (e.g. in Deut. 28:25; 1 Sam. 4:3), is *expressis verbis* reproduced by LXX[Luc.] as follows: 'When your people Israel are beaten before your face and they fall before the face of their enemies ...' (according to Rahlfs, *SSt.* III, 193, we are here dealing with a doublet). Burney, accordingly, finds this reading 'very probably' correct because the eye of the copyist may have wandered from לפניך to לפני. Nevertheless MT also makes good sense.

The following אשר means 'when,' 'because' (Ewald §333a; cf. §353a; König §389a; cf. also Gray, who suspects the original was כאשר), and likewise, with the following impf. of a finite verb as the continuation of the inf. (König §413c), introduces a conditional clause (cf. 2 Chr. 6:24, which reads כי, as do a number of MSS in our verse). In MT שוב is construed with the prep. אל and a personal pronoun (2nd p.), which in OT often denotes a 'returning' to, a 'turning back to' YHWH or God (Deut. 30:10; 1 Sam. 7:3; Hos. 5:4; 7:10; Ps. 51:15 etc.). However, since LXX[B, Luc.] and the par. 2 Chr. 6:24 omit אליך and the resulting combination of שוב with והודו can mean 'again,' the 'conversion phase' is left out of this sequence. But to say with Stade-Schwally that אליך is 'unnecessary' and needs to be omitted as a probable 'scribal expansion' is going too far (so also Burney). In our verse conversion is distinctly mentioned but less emphatically than in vs. 35, and followed by 'acknowledgment of the name.'

Of the more than 100x it is used in OT the hiph. of ירה (II in distinction from I) occurs only here and in vs. 35 in the books of Kings, as well as 11x in hitpael (see C. Westermann, *THAT*, I, 674-682; G. Mayer, *TWAT*, III, 455-474). The verb includes 2 complexes of meaning: (1) 'praise,' 'sing a hymn to' and (2) 'acknowledge,' 'confess.' 'Thanksgiving' is a form of praise (Mayer, 428; Westermann, 675). In our context 'acknowledge (sins)' is appropriate, where 'the Name' is used again as substitute and hypostasis for YHWH (see comments on 3:2 above). This practice suggests a dtr. or post-dtr. time of origin (Mayer). According to Westermann, 681, ידה hiph., in only 6 places (viz. in our verses and the par. verses 2 Chr. 6:24, 26, further in Ps. 32:5 and Prov. 28:13), forms an independent group meaning: 'acknowledging (sins)'; for the rest, the hitp. is used in the later literature like the Priestly Code, Daniel and the books of Chronicles. The hitp. of פלל already came up in connection with vs. 28. There, too, the verb חנן was mentioned in connection with the noun תחנה. For the first time we find here the use of the hitp. of this verb in our books of Kings (further in the vss. 47, 59; 9:3 and 2 Kgs 1:13), of the 17x this form of the verb is found in OT. The meaning is 'beg for grace, mercy' (see also *HAL*, 321; Zorell, 254; further – next to the literature mentioned under vs. 28 – W. Zimmerli, *TDNT*, IX, 376-387).

The word אליך (which occurs twice) is similarly omitted by LXX[Luc.], whereas in the par. 2 Chr. 6:24 it is replaced by לפניך. Again, there is no reason here to modify the text in favour of LXX or Chronicles, the more since the last words of this verse ('in this house') present material problems in relation to the following verse, in which 'return' to the 'promised land' is requested. Stade-Schwally, accordingly, prefer to read אל הבית הזה, by which the direction of the prayer toward the temple is stressed. As such this is a meaningful change because one simply cannot be in 2 places at once. One could also read MT as praying 'to you who are present in the temple,' but this grammatical construction does not seem to be good Hebr.

8:34 *Then hear in heaven and forgive the sins of your people Israel, and bring them back to the land which you gave to their father.*
The end of the previous verse already suggested the problem connected with this verse. The question is what the word והשבתם means (for the form, cf. also Olsh. §255e; Bg. II §28m). Klostermann and Ehrlich vocalize this form as a hiph. of ישב, a construal in which אל has to be changed into על: 'let them continue to dwell in ...' Only a threat of deportation comes through here. In addition, one removes the tension observed between the previous and the present verse. Others (like Stade-Schwally, Gray) rightly maintain the masoretic vocalization: the form is that of a hiph. of the verb שוב, 'cause to return.' Talstra, 115, lists a number of analogous constructions and situations which can support the reading of the text. The reference in our verse is very much to an actual deportation, whether a partial (so Bertheau, Brongers, Gray et al.), or

a complete one (Van den Born).

YHWH is asked to forgive the 'sin' of the people and to cause the deportees to return to 'the land' which he 'has given to the fathers' (see also vss. 40 and 48; further, Burney). Although we here encounter the noun חטאת for the first of the 17x it occurs in 1 Kings, we did run into the verb earlier already (see comments on vs. 31 above). In OT we discover the word no less than 293x in 2 fundamental senses: 'sin' and 'sin offering.' The latter meaning occurs especially in books like Leviticus (82x, though also in the other sense) and Numbers (43x; see R. Knierim, *THAT*, I, 542).

We already encountered אדמה in 7:46 in the sense of 'land,' 'earth,' 'tillable land.' In OT the word occurs approx. 225x, 8 of them in Kings (H.H. Schmid, *THAT*, I, 57-60; O. Plöger, *TWAT*, I, 95-105). In our verse the word primarily refers to the hereditary possession of Israel which YHWH has sworn to give to 'the fathers' (cf. the word נחלה in vs. 36). We are dealing with a dtr. formula which is found rather frequently in OT (see the texts in Schmid, 59). Scholars (see the lengthy analysis in Talstra, 209-215) regard this (as well as the following) petition as dtr. or post-dtr., that is, as a composition from the time after the exile. 2 Chr. 6:25 inserts 'to them' before 'to their fathers,' which, according to Thenius, is 'willkürlich eingefügt,' but according to Bertheau the opposite is true. Noteworthy is that (according to Kennicott's listing) a few Hebr. MSS read: 'to Abraham' in place of 'to their fathers.'

Finally we note that in place of 'your people' (λαου σου) LXX$^{A, B}$ diverge from MT here – and also elsewhere (see vs. 36) – by reading δουλου σου (H. Strathmann, *TDNT*, IV, 33, n. 15; Barthélemy, on vs. 36).

8:35 *When heaven remains shut so that there is no rain because they sinned against you, but they pray at this place and acknowledge your name and turn from their sins because you have afflicted them,*
The third petition concerns a period of great drought for Israel as a result of which famine, a lack of essentials, with all its consequences, may arise. Certain aspects of these consequences, which may also be the result of other misfortunes, come up explicitly in the 4th petition, so that the emphasis in our verse is on the lack of rainfall (cf. Deut. 11:17; further Lev. 26:19; Deut. 28:23). In Israel, water is of course a matter of life and death.[17] In Ugar. texts as well the sending of rain is related to the well being of a temple, in that case the temple of Baal (cf. S. Rummel, *RSP*, III, iii, 1 [p. 284]).

The verb עצר means 'hold back, hold fast,' '(en)close' and occurs 36x in the qal, 10x in niph., only one of which in the books of Kings in this verse (see

---

[17] See, among others, P. Reymond, *L'eau, sa vie, et sa signification dans l'Ancien Testament* (VTS 6), Leiden 1958.

D.P. Wright, J. Milgrom, *TWAT*, VI, 333-338; further H. Köster, *TDNT*, VII, 877f.). Heaven is here viewed as the grammatical subject of the passive form of the verb but in reality YHWH is the subject. For it is he who supplies vivifying power to rain water but it is also he who can block this power and prevent heaven from fulfilling this function (see Houtman, *Himmel*, 185, who refers to similar ideas in the annals of Ramses II; *ANET* 257). The word שמים here, in contrast with 2 Chr. 6:26 (cf. Deut. 11:17), lacks the article, which prompts Ehrlich to make the suggestion that our verse must originally have read שמימה, 'als dadurch angedeutet würde, dass der Mangel an Regen nicht allgemein sein, sondern auf das Land der Israeliten sich beschränken wird, damit sie ihn als Strafe für ihre Sünden erkennen und empfinden.' But this conclusion need not follow from the lack of the article (cf. König §292b).

The word מטר (in our books also in vs. 36; 17:1; 18:1) generally means 'rain' but must often be distinguished from גשם which refers rather to (incidental) rain showers or thunder showers. The former occurs 38x in OT, the latter 35x (see H.-J. Zobel, *TWAT*, IV, 827-842). Rain can further be differentiated as 'early rain' (יורה) which occurs in the fall of the year and 'late rain' (מלקוש) which comes in the spring, both of them important periods in the fall and winter of Palestine because the absence of these rains can have disastrous consequences. The reason for YHWH's refusal to give rain (also cf. Jer. 3:3; 5:24f.) could again be the 'sin ' of the people. But if people would repent also in this case, and confess their sins 'at this place,' i.e. in this temple, then let there be hope. For the use and function of the so-called *nun paragogicum* in the form ישובון consult the standard work by Hoftijzer, esp. pp. 37, 39f.

The end of our verse presents problems because MT vocalizes the form תענם as a qal form with suffix of ענה I, 'answer,' whereas LXX here reads: ὅταν ταπεινώσῃς αὐτούς (cf. Vulg.: *propter adflictionem suam*), expressions for which a pi. form of ענה II, 'oppress,' 'humble' can serve, as indicated in the textcr. app. of *BHK* and *BHS*. Many exegetes follow this obvious emendation of the masoretic vocalization (Kamphausen, Benzinger, Burney, Stade-Schwally, Ehrlich, Skinner, Noth, and many others; Keil [cf. Van Gelderen] maintains the vocalization but translates as if the emendation is in force!). Nevertheless, the question is whether also MT does not make good sense and therefore – as *lectio difficilior* – needs to be upheld. According to C.J. Labuschagne, *THAT*, II, 339f.), in 62 out of 78 cases YHWH reacts as subject of ענה in response to human initiatives, i.e. human acts of 'calling' or 'seeking.' The reference here is to a group of people in the act of turning away from sin, to whom YHWH *can* respond. In this way the words כי תענם translated by 'when you will humble them,' do not hang from the sentence in isolation but gain emphasis, provided one reads them as an implicit appeal to YHWH's faithfulness in reaction to the repentance of sinners: 'for you *can* answer them' (also Talstra,

116 and n. 36, be it on somewhat different grounds, maintains the MT reading, which is supported by Pesh. and Tg. as well).

8:36 *then hear in heaven and forgive the sins of your servants and your people – you, after all, teach them the right way in which they must walk – and be pleased to send rain on your land, the land you gave your people as an inheritance.*

Again an appeal is made to YHWH's willingness to forgive. In place of עבדך (but cf. vss. 30 and 52), a number of Hebr. MSS (along with LXX and Tg.) read the sing. here. Barthélemy points out that throughout the prayer Solomon refers to himself in the 3rd p. (vss. 28ff., 52) but twice to 'your servant' (vss. 30 and 52). 3x in this prayer the MT uses the pl. form 'your servants' (vss. 23, 32, and 36), where LXX either uses the sing. or refers to 'your people Israel' (vs. 32). Against Stade-Schwally and others Barthélemy maintains the pl. of MT: 'il faut garder le pluriel qui peut ou bien désigner tous les rois futurs (comme au vs 23), ou bien être une redondance à l'égard de עמך qui suit comme c'est le cas par exemple en Ne 1, 10' (also cf. H. Strathmann, *TDNT*, IV, 33, n. 15, who believes that LXX is oriented here to the '*Ebed*-YHWH songs').

Next we are told about the instruction of YHWH concerning 'the right way.' Now the hiph. of the verb ירה III, 'instruct,' 'teach' is used, which occurs, aside from here, also in 2 Kgs. 12:3; 17:27f. in the books of Kings (in the whole OT, solely in the hiph. form, 45x; see S. Wagner *TWAT*, III, 920-930; also G. Liedke, C. Petersen, *THAT*, II, 1032, about the relation to the verb I and II). Wagner (345) points out that – in the dtr. framework – the meaning of 'instructing the people in the right way' implies that it pertains to 'worshipping Yahwe exclusively at the central sanctuary' (also cf. 1 Sam. 12:23). On the other hand, learning the 'way' or the 'path' need not always be understood in this specific sense, as for example Pss. 25:4; 32:8; 86:11 and 143:8 show (also cf. Talstra, 116f.). Although some exegetes (Stade-Schwally, textcr. app. *BHK*) consider the words from כי תורה through בה a gloss, the sense of this passage can very well be maintained (Montg.-Gehman; cf. also W. Rudolph, *ZAW* 63 [1951], 204, who thinks of a borrowing from Joel 2:23).

In our verse the pronominal suffix in ארצך, '*your* land,' calls attention to itself. LXX[B], accordingly, omits this pers. pron. from its translation, as does Pesh., which, however, speaks of 'your rain' (except in 9a1*fam* and 2 late MSS; not noted in the textcr. app. of *BHK* and *BHS*). But MT can be maintained at this point (cf. the par. pair *arṣ/mṭr* in Ugar. texts[18]). In the place

---

[18] See G. del Olmo Lete, in: *Mélanges bibliques et orientaux en l'honneur de M. Mathias Delcor* (AOAT 215, ed. A. Caquot et al.), Neukirchen-Vluyn 1985, 82.

of 'your people' LXX^B again has τῷ δούλῳ (see above).

In our verse we for the first time encounter the word נחלה (also in 1 Kgs. 8:51, 53; 12:16; 21:3f.; 2 Kgs. 21:14). In OT the word occurs 222x, no less than 50 of which in Joshua and 46 in Numbers (see G. Wanke, *THAT* II, 55-59; E. Lipiński, *TWAT*, V, 342-360; further, J. Herrmann, *TDNT*, III, 772). It means 'inheritance,' 'grundsätzlich unveräußerlicher, daher dauernder Besitzanteil vor allem an Boden' (Wanke, 56).

8:37 *Whenever there is a famine in the land, or plague, or blight, or mildew, locusts or leaf-eaters; whenever his enemy besieges him in his cities; all possible plagues and diseases;*

In the 4th petition (vss. 37-40) we encounter situations of distress which are also described elsewhere (Deut. 28 and Amos 4) in approximately the same words and order, so that they can be regarded as fixed expressions for all sorts of misery (for an extensive analysis of their use, see also Talstra, 186f.). Our verse heads its list with רעב (for examples in which the noun precedes the predicate see, aside from Burney, also König §341n), 'famine,' which even today not only ravages countries in the ancient Near East but also many other areas in the 'Third World.' In Kings the word occurs as well in 1 Kgs. 18:2; 2 Kgs. 4:38; 6:25; 7:4; 8:1; 25:3. Then there is mention of דבר, 'pestilence,' a word found in our books only in this place (also cf. G. Mayer, *TWAT*, II, 133ff.). This fatal disease, which can never be precisely identified, is always a divinely sent punishment for disobedience. Mayer points out that the word never appears alone but always as part of a sometimes long list of diseases and plagues, as, for example, the well-known 'Egyptian plagues' (Exod. 9:3, 15).

Pausing for a moment to consider the list of disasters in our verse, we encounter the words שדפון and ירקון (also combined in Deut. 28:22; Amos 4:9; Hag. 2:17 and 2 Chr. 6:28). The firstmentioned word (also cf. שדפה in 2 Kgs. 19:26) refers to the blighting of grain in the field (Vulg.: *corruptus aer,* 'toxic air'!), the second word (omitted in this place by LXX; ἐρυσίβη, 'mildew,' follows βροῦχος, 'locust'), though regularly translated by 'mildew,' is called 'Getreiderost' in German: grain rust. In Jer. 30:6 the word means 'paleness.' Mildew is a plant disease which, especially in humid summers, forms a whitish funguslike growth marked by black dots on the bottom leaves of wheat, the so-called *Erysiphe graminis*. The German 'Getreiderost' is a plant disease caused by *uredinales*. Dalman, *AuS*, I, 326, calls the disease a kind of 'jaundice,' 'das Blaßwerden der Spitzen des grünen Getreides infolge von "Würmerbildung" bei längerer Trockenheit.' In a note he points out, however, that his informants (i.e. Palestinians) also mentioned much rain as the cause of this disease. Elsewhere (*AuS*, II, 333) he writes of 'Braunrost' (caused by the fungus *puccinia glumarum, tricina, graminis*) by which, long before the harvest, the grain gets a brownish colour. The root ירק II is associated with 'pale,' 'silvery,' 'gold-coloured,' 'green.'[19]

Failures in badly-needed grain harvests can also be brought about by locusts (order: *Orthopetra*; family: *Acrididae*). Even today they constitute a plague in many African and Asiatic countries. In our verse 2 names are used: ארבה and חסיל. The former word occurs 24x in OT and is also the most common word for describing the locust in OT. It refers especially to the full-grown winged insect that can fly great distances; the second, on the other hand, which only occurs 6x in OT (aside from the par. 2 Chr. 6:28 also in Isa. 33:4; Ps. 78:46; Joel 1:4 and 2:25), relates to a locust's stage of immaturity (see Y. Palmoni, *IDB*, III, 144-148, esp. 145). Palmoni lists no fewer than 12 OT words for (different stages in the life of) the locust (cf. also Dalman, *AuS*, II, 346ff.). This shows how familiar and how dreaded the insect was in Palestine (cf. e.g. the context of Joel 1:4; 2:25). In the Ugar. KRT-text (e.g. *KTU* 1.14. II: 50; III: 1) one also finds the parallelization of *'irby* and *ḥsn*, in connection with which it is generally assumed that the latter word can be equated with our חסיל (M. Dahood, *RSP*, I, ii, 61; J. M. Sasson, idem, iii, 55).

At the end of our verse still 2 more words are used, the first of which can be regarded as a general expression for a God-sent plague: נגע. This word can be translated by ''blow' and of the 78x it is found in OT occurs no less than 61x in Lev. 13f. (in Kings alone only again the next verse; cf. L. Schwienhorst, *TWAT*, V, 219-226). In Lev. 13f. it is especially a more specific term for a skin rash or mildew on fabrics and houses, often translated by 'leprosy.' In our verse the meaning is more general, like the word מחלה (also in the par. 2 Chr. 6:28 and Exod. 15:26; 23:25; with different vocalization: Prov. 18:14; 2 Chr. 21:15) a secondary form of the much more frequently occurring חלי, 'disease,' 'sickness' (see K. Seybold, *TWAT*, II, 967; further F. Stolz, *THAT*, I, 567, 570).

Preceding these general words for 'plagues' and 'diseases' there is the statement – one which does not quite fit the series – that an enemy may close in on the land. The form יצר (Stade §499d; BL, 438; Bg. II §271) is a hiph. form of the verb צרר I which in this form means 'besiege,' 'close in on,' 'produce anxiety for' (also in Deut. 28:52; Jer. 10:18; Zeph. 1:17; Neh. 9:27; 2 Chr. 6:28; 28:20, 22; 33:12), derived from a qal 'be narrow,' 'be distressed' (see *HAL*, 990). An enemy can distress a land, and the population of a land, in its cities. Still, the construction 'in the land of its gates' sounds strange and unusual. It is not surprising, therefore, that, following LXX and Pesh., many exegetes (Thenius, Benzinger, Ehrlich, etc.; Noth, however, maintains MT: also Talstra, 119, 187f., leans that way) propose, in place of בארץ, the numeral באחר: 'in one of its gates,' i.e. 'in whatever gate,' while some (Thenius for

---

[19] Cf. A. Brenner, *Colour Terms in the Old Testament* (JSOTSup 21), Sheffield 1982, 100ff.

example) change שעריו into עריו, 'its cities.' This last emendation is not strictly necessary (so, correctly, Stade-Schwally) because 'gate' can be taken as a *pars pro toto* for city. The word שער occurs approx. 270x in OT (*KBL*, 1001; Zorell 871), in 1 Kings (aside from our verse) also in 22:10 (plus 18x in 2 Kings), and can be used metonymically for a city or its population (see Isa. 14:31; Obad. 13; Jer. 14:2; Zorell).

As to the first emendation, Barthélemy points out that in Deut. 28:52 the complement of the hiph. of צרר, 'in all your gates,' occurs twice, and that the second time this complement is further explained by the words 'throughout all your land, which YHWH your God has given you.' Accordingly, בארץ שעריו can very well be 'une expression concentrée de cela.' His proposed translation is: 'dans le pays qui est "ses portes",' although, in view of the textual witnesses, he insists there is distinction between our verse and the par. 2 Chr. 6:28. We, too, believe the expression can be maintained because it is not meaningless as such: the 'land of its gates' can be viewed as 'the land of its cities' (cf. also W. Rudolph, *ZAW* 63 [1951], 204, who, in part on the basis of Pesh. on 2 Chr. 6:28, wants to read 'in its land and in its cities'). Enemies are especially intent on besieging cities; the countryside can be trampled without extra effort.

8:38 *(and then) when any prayer, any supplication, is made by any of your people Israel, because everyone knows the affliction of his own heart and stretches out his hands toward this house;*
Burney rightly comments that the construction of this verse is somewhat involved, since its beginning ('any prayer and any supplication') reads more like the continuation of the plagues mentioned in the previous verse than like the cry to be delivered from certain forms of distress. Burney assumes that vs. 37 broke off with an *aposiopesis* (similarly Würthwein), so that the *apodosis*, with which the following verse begins ('then hear ...') is an answer to the *protasis*, which is formed by the second (and essentially different) category ('any prayer or supplication'). Ehrlich rather simply resolves the difficulty, which is certainly present here, by commenting that תפלה here refers to 'den Grund zum Gebet, die Not, um deren Abhilfe gebetet wird' (cf. Noth's translation: 'irgend ein Anlaß zu Gebet, irgend ein Anlaß zu Flehen'). Because it is not known *whether* something has been omitted after vs. 37, and if so, *what*, we follow this last-mentioned interpretation.

In what follows the general reference 'any man' is limited to 'all your people, Israel,' which is omitted by LXX[B, Luc.] (for this, see G. Bertram, *TDNT*, V, 890). Also in this construction there is a contradictory element (Ehrlich, with good reason, refers to the vss. 41-43, where there is mention of non-Israelites whose prayers are heard), so that we are inclined (along with many other exegetes, like Benzinger, Burney, Kittel) to follow LXX* at this point and view these words as a later insertion. The following אשר can better be construed as a conjunction in the sense of 'when' (e.g. Ewald §333a) than as *nota relationis* (so, for example, Talstra). The words נגע לבבו are described in the par. 2 Chr. 6:29 by נגעו ומכאבו, 'his own plague and his own sickness.' The combination in our verse occurs nowhere else in OT. Šanda explains this combination as something 'was innerlichen, geistigen Schmerz verursacht.' Kittel translates: 'wenn sie, jeder im eigenen Gewissen, sich getroffen fühlen'; Klostermann: 'den Biß seines Gewissens' ('denn Gott will durch das Unglück das demütige Sündenbewusstsein wecken'). Also Von Meyenfeldt, *Het hart*, 36, thinks here of conscience: the consciousness of sin of the Israelite as that is brought about by God's chastising hand; so also Van Gelderen; cf. Talstra, 188f.; further C. Maurer, *TDNT*, VII, 907). Thenius, however, wants to read the expression in a more objective sense: 'das, was der von Gott gefügte Unglücksfall ihm an Züchtigung bringen soll.' So also Rudolph, who in his commentary on Chronicles supports the description of the par. text in 2 Chr. 6:29: 'richtige Deutung der Vorlage, wo nicht Gewissensbisse gemeint sind.' Keil earlier already took the same track when he wrote: 'die Plage als ein das herz treffender Schlag gedacht, d.h. als eine von Gott über ihn verhängte Züchtigung.' The plague, that is, the illness strikes a human being in a way which threatens his heart, his very existence. The illness, after all, can take away his heart, i.e. his life. Consequently, every human being has to deal personally with his own cares and illness. Münster (and Clarius) therefore interpreted *plagam cordis sui* as follows: *Qui secretâ pressus infirmitate aut necessitate ad te cordium Scrutatorem clamaverit*. Hence this expression does not in the first place have much to do with conscience. For פרו כפיו, see comments on vs. 22 above.

8:39 *then hear in heaven, your dwelling place; be pleased to forgive, respond, and render to each according to all his ways, because you know his heart (for you alone know the hearts of all the children of men);*
This verse confirms the interpretation of לבב we proposed at the end of the previous verse. YHWH alone knows the heart of every human being (cf. 1 Sam. 16:7; Jer. 11:20; 17:10; Ps. 7:10; 1 Chr. 28:9; and in NT the word καρδιογνώστης, Acts 1:24, 15:8; see J. Behm, *TDNT* III, 613). He alone knows what it is that can threaten every human being existentially. He knows the 'life' of every person. This is more than the 'hidden motive of a person's action' (Von Meyenfeldt, *Het hart*, 36). It cannot be denied, however, that our verse has acquired a subjective element as a result of the words: 'render to each according to all his ways' (the change of 'according to all his ways' in 'according to all his needs (צרך),' as Ehrlich proposes, is unfounded). איש here means 'everyone' (Joüon §147d). One finds the last-mentioned expression, not only in the par. 2 Chr. 6:30, but also in Jer. 17:10 and 32:19 (cf. Ezek. 7:9).

Only in the verses in Jeremiah there are the additional words: 'and the fruit of his doings,' as a result of which (cf. Talstra, 190) they tie in with the word usage elsewhere in Jeremiah and Hoseah. In this connection Talstra rejects the idea of the literary dependence of our verse on the above-mentioned verses. He speaks of 'common ideas.' In any case, coming through in this expression there is something of divine retribution corresponding to the deeds of human beings, here described as בני אדם (cf. König §254g).

After 'heaven,' and in apposition with it, the beginning of our verse has מכון שבתך (also vss. 43 and 49; cf. vs. 30 above: מקום שבתך). In vs. 13 above we already encountered the word מכון. In a lengthy excursus Talstra deals, among other things, with this apposition (201-208). He assumes that this phrase is probably not dtr. (against Weinfeld), but even older. In the vss. 29f., he says, 'via מקום explicit statements are made about the function of the temple in relation to the place where God dwells ... But in Solomon's prayer one also finds expressions which rather reflect a standard – one might also say: pre-dtr – language and which do not involve a choice in the discussion about the temple and about the place where God dwells' (p. 205).

Striking in our verse is also the absolute use of סלח (cf. vs. 30), because nothing is said about the person whom something should be forgiven, nor why (cf. Talstra, 199). It is a question , of course, whether this verb originally belongs here (see also Talstra, 121). The following verb ועשת is lacking in the par. 2 Chr. 6:30. As elsewhere, so here too the meaning of עשה can be rendered by 'react' (also cf. our article in *VT* 34 [1984], 106ff.).

8:40 *that they may fear you all the days that they may live in the land which you gave to our fathers.*
למען, introducing an expansion, adds still another purpose of the preceding, as also in the following petition (cf. vs. 43). Talstra, 178, calls this a 'pedagogical' purpose, inasmuch as God's hearing the prayer may lead to people serving YHWH. We already encountered ירא, 'fear,' in 1:50f., and 3:28; cf. H.F. Fuhs, *TWAT*, III, 896-893; H.-P. Stähli, *THAT*, I, 765-778). The par. 2 Chr. 6:31 adds to this ללכת בדרכיך, 'by walking in your ways.' Although this is a 'beloved dtr. phrase' (Benzinger, following Böttcher and Thenius) the MT text of our verse needs nevertheless to be maintained at this point. In the remainder 3 Hebr. MSS (Kennicott) have left out פני (cf. also LXX*) but materially this omission does not make much difference.

8:41 *Similarly, when a foreigner who does not belong to your people Israel comes from a far country for your name's sake;*
With this verse the 5th petition begins (vss. 41-43). The beginning וגם אל־הנכרי is dependent on תשמע in vs. 43 (so, correctly, Thenius, Burney, Noth and others). The נכרי is the 'foreigner,' a person who is to be

distinguished from the גר. The word occurs 45x in OT, 4 of them in our book (further in vs. 43 and 11:1, 8; cf. B. Lang, *TWAT*, V, 454-462; R. Martin-Achard, *THAT*, II, 66ff.). According to Deut. 14:21, one may *give* carrion to a גר but *sell* it to a נכרי (see also M.A. Signer, *TRE*, XIX, 563f.). Josephus, *c.Ap.* II §210, also mentions that Jewish law makes a distinction between aliens who adopt the Jewish lifestyle and those who spend time incidentally among the Jews. This differentiation resembles the distinction made by Greek cities between μέτοικος and ξένος (see Lang, 456ff.). In our verse the 'foreigner' is not a fellow citizen ('is not of your people,' see Driver §198l), and comes 'from a far country.' He comes 'for your name's sake,' an expression which is further explained in the following verse He is on his way, as it were, to becoming a גר (cf. Isa. 56:6f.).

The end of our verse and the beginning of the following verse are missing in LXX[B, Luc.] probably because of the *homoeoarcton* ובא (Stade-Schwally).

8:42 – *for they will hear of your great name and your strong hand and your outstretched arm* – *when he comes and prays in this house;*
Because the foreigner 'from a far country' had learned of the great deeds of YHWH, he now comes to worship 'in this house.' Benzinger believes that our verse is a postexilic interpolation, because it does not fix its hope on the foreigner's worship in the future but assumes it as a present fact. Talstra, 208, also considers this 5th petition to be pre-dtr., stemming from 'the common cultic situations during the existence of Solomon's temple,' although, certainly in our verse, there is evidence of dtr. redaction. The question is what is meant by 'a far country' in the previous verse. Ehrlich, in this connection, referred to Deut. 20:15f. where a distinction is made between cities of the nations within the boundaries of Palestine and cities 'at a very great distance.' In our books of Kings we may think in this connection of the story of the queen of Sheba (1 Kgs. 10:1-13) or of that of Naaman the Aramaean (2 Kgs. 5:1-27). While the idea that foreigners will travel great distances to Jerusalem 'for the sake of the Name' gained strong currency in the postexilic era, this idea may already have been present in preexilic times as well.

The terminology into which this idea has been cast, however, can be called dtr. Burney and others furnish parallels to the phrase ואת ידך החזקה וזרעך הנטויה whether the 2 expressions occur in conjunction (Deut. 4:34; 5:15; 7:19; 11:2; 26:8; Jer. 21:5 [different order]; 32:21; Ezek. 20:34f.; Ps. 136:12), or whether יד חזקה stands by itself (Deut. 3:24; 6:21; 7:8 etc.). We already encountered חזק as a verb in 2:2, the word זרוע occurs only 3x in our books of Kings (also in 2 Kgs. 9:24 and 17:36) of the 92x it occurs in OT (A.S. van der Woude, *THAT*, I, 522ff.; cf. F.J. Helfmeyer, *TWAT*, II, 650-660). The word denotes the 'arm' or 'forearm' of a person but is then used metaphorically for 'power,' 'strength.' In our verse we are dealing with a stereotypical term for the great deeds of YHWH which were especially evident in the 'exodus from Egypt.' The verb נטה, 'stretch out' already occurred in 2:28 (for this word see H. Ringgren, *TWAT*, V, 409-415).

In the par. 2 Chr. 6:32 the first words of our verse כי ישמעון את־שמך are lacking so that the conclusion of our previous verse runs on: 'for the sake of your great name and your outstretched arm.' Some exegetes (e.g., Stade-Schwally, Rudolph) view this omission as a case of *homoeoteleuton* but it does not seem to us impossible that the Chronicler deliberately left them out.

8:43 *be pleased to hear in heaven your dwelling place, and act in accordance with everything for which the foreigner calls on you, that all the peoples of the earth may know your name and fear you, as do your people Israel, and that they may know that your name has been proclaimed over this house which I have built.*

On the basis of the reading in 21 Hebr. MSS (Kennicott), the par. 2 Chr. 6:33 and a number of ancient versions, the textcr. app. of *BHK* and *BHS* (with many commentators) propose to begin our verse with ועתה, hence with the copula ו. Bertheau already rightly commented that אתה in our verse has to be read without the copula because in our case the beginning of the verse stands in a special relation to the beginning of vs. 41 (see there). Here YHWH is petitioned to hear the prayer of the foreigner who 'out of fear' has approached the central sanctuary. Again (as in vs. 40) a more specific purpose is added: 'all the nations of the earth' must (1) know 'your name' to fear you, as your own people Israel ought to; and (2) that the name of YHWH has been proclaimed over this temple.

For the phrase כל־עמי הארץ Burney mentions, aside from the par. in 2 Chronicles, also Deut. 28:10, Josh. 4:24; Ezek. 31:12; Zeph. 3:20. The inf. ליראה also occurs several times in Deut. (see Burney). This form is the inf. of ירא with a so-called fem. ending (König §226c; BrSynt. §99b; BL, 317g; *HAL*, 413). 'To proclaim a name over a house or city' is a sign that this house or city is somebody's possession (cf. 2 Sam. 12:27f., according to Böttcher [*Neue Aehrenlese*] and Thenius). Here too Burney lists a number of places which primarily refer to the temple: Jer. 7:10f.; 14, 30; 32:34; 34:15; further, to 'the chosen people': Deut. 28:10; Jer. 14:9; Isa. 63:19; 2 Chr. 7:14; next, Jerusalem: Jer. 25:29 (cf. Dan. 9:18f.), etc.

8:44 *When your people go to war against their enemy by whatever route you send them, and they pray to YHWH toward the city you have chosen and the house which I have built for your name;*

With this verse begins the 6th petition (vss. 44f.) which some scholars view as the introduction to the 7th petition. Thenius, Šanda and other commentators as well consider the vss. 44-51 a later interpolation. Šanda offers a number of weighty arguments in support of this view: the fact that in the vss. 33f. already the topic of imprisonment has been dealt with; that in the present verses the name Israel is studiously avoided (though the name does appear in the immediately preceding vs. 43 and later again in vs. 52); that the style in these verses diverges from that of the preceding verses. In the discussion which follows we will see that especially the 7th petition may give rise to the assumption that the Babylonian captivity is here an actually existing situation.

The terminology of the 6th petition presupposes, at least in the opinion of some, the so-called 'holy war' (Montg.-Gehman, Brongers). Talstra, 217, points out that the emphasis in this petition is not so much 'on war, as destruction of the enemy, as in Deut. 20:16; Josh. 6:17; Josh. 7; 1 Sam. 15:3, 18 ..., as on obedience to the divine command' (בדרך אשר תשלחם). The 2 themes are not, however, mutually exclusive.

Both the 6th and the 7th petition begin with the particle כי, as a result of which the beginning of both petitions diverges from the earlier ones. The people of YHWH go to war against their enemy. In the par. 2 Chr. 6:34, as well as in a number of Hebr. MSS and the ancient versions, one finds there a pl.: 'enemies,' which is materially not very different. In our verse the emphasis is on the fact that YHWH sends them out on this warpath, hence approves of the war to be fought and – as Talstra, 217, correctly comments – demands obedience from his people. There is no mention of a specific war, though the author may have had in mind a specific 'holy war' such as is described, for example, in the book of Joshua.[20] R. Preß, *ZAW* 51 (1933), 232, considers the prayer 'to execute justice' the same as a prayer for victory.

Before going out to battle, the soldiers can direct prayers to YHWH, an activity during which they bring sacrifices (Von Rad, op. cit., p. 7). The words אליהוה of our verse are, more logically, rendered in the par. verse in Chronicles by אליך (Vulg.: *orabunt te*; but cf. LXX: 'in the name of the Lord'). Now it is said that the prayer is prayed דרך העיר, to which is added that YHWH has chosen this city (cf. comments on vs. 16 above) and built his temple (there) for his name (cf. comments on 3:2 above; for the defective form בנתי: Ges-K §75w). This second word דרך means 'in the direction of ' (*HAL*, 222; Burney). Thenius basing himself on the testimonies of Justin, Tertullian, and Epiphanius, reminds us that also the early Christians observed a prayer posture in the direction of the 'holy city.' Muslims to this day face their 'holy city,' Mecca, when they pray (the so-called *kibla*; for this cf. A. J. Wensick, *SEI*, 260f.), a custom which may been adopted from the Jews (as well as Christians) (cf. also Dan. 6:11). The fact that Jerusalem is meant here is even

---

[20] For a far-ranging discussion of this theme, cf. G. Von Rad's classic work, *Der Heilige Krieg im alten Israel*, Göttingen 1969[5].

more apparent from the par. 2 Chr. 6:34, where 'this' is added to 'the city' (see further J. Herrmann, *TDNT*, II, 790; W. Schrage, *TDNT*, VII, 824).

8:45 *then hear their prayer and supplication and settle their cause.*
The deviation of this (and the following) petition from the preceding ones is evident also from the (usual) continuation: in place of ואתה תשמע which was used in the preceding petitions, the continuation is now effected with a pf. cons. ושמעת. Also lacking in this petition is a second apodosis. The character of this petition is such that there is no need here to speak either of sin, or of conversion, nor of the knowledge of YHWH (see also Talstra, 123). People, after all, are walking 'on the way of YHWH,' though this does not alter the fact that his help must be concretely present and that he 'must execute justice (משפט).' This last expression occurs, aside from in the par. 2 Chr. 6, also in the vss. 49 and 59; Deut. 10:18; Mic. 7:9 and Ps. 9:5 (Burney). Press, as we noted earlier, considers the prayer 'to execute justice' identical with the prayer for victory. Talstra. 217, is of the opinion that precisely because of this expression 'the tone of this petition is different from that of the texts about the holy war,' because such a request is not present there. V. Herntrich, *TDNT*, III, 929f., correctly points out that the word מופט almost carries the meaning of 'grace,' or 'mercy' in this connection.

8:46 *When they sin against you – for there is no one who does not sin – and you are angry with them and give them to an enemy who carries them away as captives to an alien land, far off or nearby;*
One can view the 7th petition (vss. 46-51) as a climax, a high point, but at the same time also as a low point, because it enters so deeply into the backgrounds of the exile. Its cause is unambiguously indicated in the words: 'when they sin against you,' words which are continued in the innocent-sounding parenthesis: 'for there is no one who does not sin (cf. Eccl. 7:20). McConville for good reason describes this parenthetical statement as being 'heavy with irony in the mouth of the king who has recently established the dynasty promised to his father ...' The irony is that he – like his successors – will demonstrate the truth of this statement, as the remainder of this history teaches us. How can the dynasty endure if every person, even Solomon, sins? McConville, along with others, views this prayer 'as one of the indicators of a theology of hope beyond disaster in DtrH'.[21]

The verb אנף occurs, aside from the par. 2 Chr. 6:36, in qal also in Jes. 12:1; Ps. 2:12; 60:3; 79:5; 85:6 and Ezra 9:14. One finds the hitp.-form in 11:9

---

[21] J.G. McConville, "Narrative and Meaning in the Books of Kings," *Bib* 70 (1989), 31-49, esp. 36; cf. also his "1 Kings viii 46-53 and the Deuteronomistic Hope," *VT* 42 (1992), 67-79.

(further also in 2 Kgs. 17:18 and Deut. 1:37; 4:21; 9:8, 20). The verb, meaning 'be angry, wrathful,' is probably derived from the noun אף, 'nose,' through which a person may snort, after all, when he or she becomes angry (*Ges.*[18], 82; see further E. Johnson, *TWAT*, I, 379-389; G. Sauer, *THAT*, I, 220-224). Neither here nor in the preceding petitions are the sins which have been committed mentioned by name. But the development of the history, as described in our books, in fact makes clear what the author has in mind. Talstra, 124, accordingly, with good reason points out that 2 Kgs. 17:7f., where our verb is also used, designates 'worship of Baal and calves' as the concrete sins in question (for και επαξεις αυτους of LXX[B] and other variants, cf. Burney, textcr. app. of *BHK*). The wrath of YHWH delivers them up into the power of their enemy. The expression 'give them up before the face of' occurs frequently, especially in dtr. passages (for this expression, cf.: Deut. 1:8, 21; 2:31, 33, 36; 7:2, 23, etc.; Burney).

For deportation to a hostile country, 'far off or nearby,' the expression שבום שביהם אל־ארץ is used. The verb שבה occurs 29x in qal in OT, 2 of them in our chapter (also vs. 48), in the sense of 'carry away captive.' In addition the part. qal occurs separately 9x, a word which one can therefore view as a noun meaning 'captor,' 'deporter' (so Lisowsky: 3x in our chapter; aside from here also in the vss. 47 and 50). One further finds the niph. form of the verb 8x in OT (in Kings alone in the following verses; *KBL*, 939; Zorell, 814f.). It has been repeatedly pointed out that in this 7th petition verbs like שבה and שוב, 'return,' alternate several times (J. D. Levenson, *HAR* 6 [1982], 131-135; Talstra, 124f.; P. Welten, *TRE*, VII, 434f.).

It needs to be further noted that האיב is lacking in the par. 2 Chr. 6:36, as well as in LXX[B, Luc]. This omission could be original since a later glossator, either in the interest of clarity or to air his aversion to the enemy, could have added the word. Šanda calls 'a land nearby' 'sonderbar' because it could hardly bear on concrete relations. But could not the word-combination 'far off and nearby' be idiomatic (for the polarity רחוק and קרוב, cf. for example Deut. 13:8; Isa. 57:19; Jer. 23:23; 25:26; 48:24; Ezek. 6:12; 22:5; Prov. 27:10)?

8:47 *but they have a change of heart in the land in which they are held captive, and repent and plead with you in the land of their captors, saying: "We have sinned, we have done evil, and have acted badly";*
In this verse the accent is on the remorseful conversion, the contrition of Israel in captivity (here described as a future event). We translated the expression השיבו אל־לבם by 'coming to their senses' (cf. Deut. 4:39; 30:1). Literally the expression means: 'lay it to heart' (Thenius, Burney, Ehrlich, and others). Von Meyenfeldt, *Het hart*, 36f., understands it as the again laying to heart of God's punishments, which concerns religiously deepened perception. Whether the expression 'return to one's own heart' already aims to express this (rather

modern-feeling notion of) religious depth, may be doubted (but cf. the Vulg.: *et egerint paenitentiam in corde suo*). The reference is to a process of reflection on the situation of distress which has arisen 'in the land to which they have been carried captive.' For these last words the par. 2 Chr. 6:37 (cf. also LXX and Vulg.) reads the word שבים a derivative of שבי, 'that which has been carried away captive' (*KBL*, 941; *HAL*, 1293f.). There is no reason to change MT (otherwise: Burney).

In this place of exile they must call out 3 confessions of sin to YHWH: 'we have sinned,' 'we have acted badly,' and 'we have done evil.' The verb עוה, from which the word עון, '(human) evil' is derived, twice occurs transitively in hiph. in the sense of 'pervert' (Jer. 3:21; Job 33:27) and 7x intransitively ('innerlich-causativ,' R. Knierim, *THAT*, II, 243), in the sense of 'acting badly' (aside from here and in the par. 2 Chr. 6:37 also in 2 Sam. 7:14; 19:20; 24:17; Jer. 9:4; Ps. 106:6; cf. Knierim, a.l.; K. Koch, *TWAT*, V, 1160ff.). The verb רשע was already found in hiph.-form above in vs. 32 alongside the noun. Here we find it in the qal-modification, occurring, aside from the par. 2 Chr. 6:37, 7x (Lisowsky) and 8x if רשעה in Ezek. 5:6 is construed as inf. (so Mandelkern, Zorell, Van Leeuwen) in OT. The meaning is 'be unjust, guilty' (C. van Leeuwen, *THAT*, II, 813-818). In this trio we are dealing with an ancient form of the confession of sin (also cf. 2 Sam. 24:17 and Ps. 106:6; further G. Delling, *TDNT*, VIII, 223f. and n. 62; also R. Bultmann, *TDNT*, II, 477). It is possible, indeed even probable, that the 3 verb-forms were originally juxtaposed asyndetically (on this point cf. the differences between our verse and the par. 2 Chr. 6:37 as well as those between this verse and the ancient versions; see Burney and the textcr. app. in *BHK* and *BHS*), and were used as a liturgical exclamation in times of distress.

8:48 *and they repent with all their heart and with all their soul in the land of their enemies who have taken them captive, and they pray to you toward the land which you gave to their forefathers, toward the city you have chosen and the house built for your name;*

'Conversion' (ושבו from שוב) to YHWH 'with all their heart and with all their soul' is an expression which also occurs in Deut. 30:10 and 2 Kgs. 23:25 (cf. Jer. 3:10; Burney). E. Jacob, *TDNT*, IX, 626-628, n. 81, points out that the heart is mentioned first and then the soul. According to him, this means that love comes from within and is therefore not an impulse but a matter of deliberation. Now this conversion occurs in the land of the enemies 'who have taken them captive.' This (second) form שבו (from שבה, but now with another accent) is read by LXX[B, Luc.] as a 2 p. sing. Nevertheless, also with a view to the rest of the text tradition, MT can be maintained. Here again (see vs. 44 above) there is mention of prayer in the direction of the land which YHWH has given to the fathers and (the asyndetic position of העיר in our verse is linked in various Hebr. MSS and in the par. 2 Chr. 6:38 with the preceding material by means of the *copula*) of the city (Jerusalem) which YHWH has chosen for himself (cf. vss. 16, 44). In addition the temple is mentioned as the central point around which the city and land are situated in concentric circles. Kittel (also Skinner) recalls a midrash in Sifre (71b): 'those who stand outside the land of Israel must turn their face to the land of Israel when they pray; those who stand inside the land of Israel must turn their face to Jerusalem.'

A k^etib-q^ere problem occurs in the case of בנית. The question is: are we dealing here with the 1 p. sing., with the final *yod* lacking (for this problem, see the grammars of Böttcher §928, Olsh. §39d, Ewald §190d, Stade §458, Ges-K §44i; cf. also the textcr. app. *BHS*), or with the 2 p. sing.? The latter is what the k^etib-form aims to give. Delitzsch (*LSF* §20c) and others attribute the defective spelling of the 1 p. to Aram. influence. In any case, the par. 2 Chr. 6:38, but also many Hebr. MSS of our verse (Kennicott) and the ancient versions, have opted for the 1 p. sing. (cf. Gordis, 97 and n. 107). In this connection, the 1 p. sing. is indeed more logical than the 2 p. sing.

8:49 *then be pleased to hear their prayer and plea in heaven, your dwelling place, and adjudicate their cause.*
This verse again conveys a request to be heard (cf. vs. 45). The part beginning with את־תפלתם the end of this verse is lacking in LXX$^{B, Luc.}$ and is sometimes viewed as a gloss from vs. 45 here (see Burney).

8:50 *Forgive your people who have sinned against you and all the transgressions which they have committed against you and grant them (to find) mercy in the eyes of those who have taken them captive, so that they may show them mercy;*
Again the prayer for forgiveness resurfaces. 2 Chr. 6:39 only has the first 5 words of our verse (up to לך), after which there is no connection with the words of this section until vs. 52. LXX* reads the beginning of our verse thus: 'and forgive their transgressions which they have committed against you.' Accordingly, the part from לעמך to לך has not been translated in LXX. Talstra, 222, therefore wonders 'whether the וסלחת statement originally occurred in petition VII.' It would, after all, fit better in petitions 2 and 3. Comparing this statement with texts from Jer. 5, which in fact speak of 'not forgiving,' he writes that only later (Jer. 31 and 33) do we read of 'a new relationship between God and his people after the judgment has been executed, after the לא סלח.' What we have in the use of סלח in this verse is the 'post-dtr. incorporation of שוב from dtr. theology and of סלח from the theology of Jeremiah' (p. 223).

For the first time we encounter, in this verse, both the verb פשע and the noun derived from this root. The verb occurs 40x in qal (in Kings also in

12:19 and 2 Kgs. 1:1; 3:5, 7; 8:20, 22 [2x]) and once in niph. (Prov. 18:19). The noun occurs 93x in OT but in the books of Kings only in our verse R. Knierim, *THAT*, II, 488-495; see also *HAL*, 922ff.) is of the opinion that the translation 'protest,' 'rebellion,' prevalent since the study of L. Köhler, *ZAW* 46 (1928), 213-218, is no longer tenable for the noun, and proposes as a possible translation 'breach' > 'crime,' i.e. 'breaking with' a partner in the community or his possessions. But H. Seebass, *TWAT*, VI, 793-810, questions the tenability of Knierim's explanation and proposes 'legal violation' as basic translation. The word conveys 'einen Oberbegriff über verschiedene Delikte' (p. 799). This explanation fits our verse well.

Another word we encountered as noun in the sing. in 3:26 occurs here (only here in Kings of the 38x in OT) as an (abstract) pl.: רחמים, 'compassion,' 'pity' (cf. Ps. 106:4; Neh. 1:11; further Jer. 42:12). The verb of the same root occurs, aside from once in qal (Ps. 18:2), approx. 40x in pi. (further in Kings in 2 Kgs. 13:23), as well as 4x in pu. (H.J. Stoebe, *THAT*, II, 761-768; H. Simian-Yofre, *TWAT*, VII, 460-476). The meaning is 'have mercy,' 'have pity.' Burney and also Talstra, 219, have pointed out the connection between the terminology of the 7th petition and particularly Ps. 106. Especially Ps. 106:40-46 resembles our petition in structure. Talstra and other commentators as well have rightly commented that this petition must relate to the experiences of the (Babylonian) exile (Skinner for example: 'Such a prayer could hardly have originated except under actual experience of exile, without any prospect of immediate relief').

8:51 *for, surely, they are your people and your inheritance which you brought out of Egypt from the midst of that iron furnace!*
Not only the 7th petition but in a sense all the preceding petitions find their culmination in the wording of this verse. The verse recalls the fact that Israel is the people of YHWH and his inheritance (see comments on vs. 26 above; further, Deut. 9:26, 29; 32:9; Isa. 47:6; Ps. 106:5; etc.; Burney). He has brought it out of Egypt (cf. vss. 16 and 21 above), the 'iron furnace.' The word כור occurs also in Deut. 4:20; Isa. 48:10; Jer. 11:4; Ezek. 22:18, 20, 22; Prov. 17:3 and 27:21; further in Sir. 31[34]:26; 43:4, and refers to a small 'smelting furnace' (*HAL*, 445; cf. Ellenbogen, *Foreign Words*, 83, who considers the word as 'ultimately of Sumerian origin'). Added to it, in Deut. 4:20 and Jer. 11:4, is the word ברזל, 'iron' (for this word, see comments on 6:7 above). The mining industry, in which ore was won from rocks by means of smelting furnaces, was known from ancient times also in Palestine and surroundings (see M. Weippert, *BRL*², 42ff.).

8:52 *May your eyes be open to your servant's plea and to the plea of your people Israel, to listen to them whenever they call out to you.*

This and the following verse are counted by Talstra as part of the (concluding) first framework of the petitions. The opening of this verse is the same as that of vs. 29 but there the words עיניך להיות were in direct continuity with the preceding verse. In this case, however, there is a hiatus. Thenius and Stade-Schwally, for example, think that, if we skipped the vss. 44-51, our verse would tie in better with vs. 43. But Noth is not convinced of this and regards the vss. 52f. as a still more recent addition than the vss. 44-51. This addition seeks in part to reach back to the introduction of the Solomonic prayer and for that reason recalls the beginning of the prayer. Talstra, 134, lets our verse follow vs. 50, whereby we get the same construction as that between the vss. 28 and 29. It is indeed clear that the more or less par. 2 Chr. 6:40, with its words עתה אלהי יהוה־נא, has cleared up textual difficulties and created a much smoother transition, anyway with vs. 50a of our chapter (cf. LXX: καὶ ἔστοσαν ...). Talstra further points out in this connection that it is not, as in vs. 28, the position of the temple which is at issue but the position of Israel itself: prayer must find an open ear, not by way of God's attention to the temple, but by way of his attention to the prayer itself' (otherwise in the par. 2 Chr. 6:40).

In our verse the reference is again to 'opened eyes' (see vs. 29), to which 'attentive (קשֻׁבות) ears' are added in the par. 2 Chr. 6:40 (see also Ps. 130:2; 2 Chr. 7:15). LXX simply speaks of 'ears.' Burney believes this addition is probably a gloss, attributable to the idea that only eyes can be open to pleadings. For the inf. constr. בכל קראם אליך, cf. Deut. 4:7; also Gen. 30:41; 1 Chr. 23:31 (Burney and König §401p: the 'iterative simultaneity' of temporal clauses with infinitives).

8:53 *For you separated them from all the peoples of the earth to be your own inheritance, as you have said through Moses your servant when you, Lord YHWH, brought our forefathers out of Egypt.'*
The verb בדל, which we only find here in the books of Kings, occurs 10x in niph. and 31x in hiph. in OT. According to B. Otzen, *TWAT*, I, 518ff., it is probably a 'late' word in Hebr., in use especially in priestly circles. In hiph. the word means 'separate,' 'isolate,' 'distinguish' (see *Ges.*[18], 126a). The verb may indicate a distinction between 'clean' and 'unclean' (Lev. 10:10; 11:47 etc.), thereby giving it a sacral meaning. In our verse the verb expresses the idea of election (Otzen, 3), the separation between YHWH and his people on the one hand and all the other nations on the other. This separation is advanced as a promise to Moses (cf. e.g. Lev. 20:24, 26; also Burney for texts in which Israel is designated the נחלה of YHWH: on כל עמי הארץ, see comments on vs. 43).

Moses was mentioned earlier already in 2:3 and in vs. 9 above. Here there is mention of the 'hand of Moses, your servant' (also vs. 56; further Exod. 9:35; 34:29; 35:29; Lev. 8:36; 10:11; 26:46; Num. 4:37, 45, 49, etc.), which is to say, by his mediation, his action (Burney).

Striking is the continuation of the framework section of the petitions in 2 Chr. 6:40-42, which can scarcely still be called a parallel to our verse but which forms a wholly unique conclusion of the petitions and in turn shows par. features with Ps. 132:8-10. In translation, these verses in 2 Chr. 6 read as follows: 'Now then, my God, let your eyes be open and your ears attentive to prayer at this place. (41) And now arise, YHWH God, go to your resting place, you and the ark of your strength. Let your priests, YHWH God, be clothed with salvation and your friends rejoice in good things. (42) YHWH God, do not turn away the face of your anointed; remember the covenant faithfulness of David, your servant.'

8:54 *When Solomon had finished the whole prayer to YHWH as well as this plea, rising up from before the altar of YHWH, where he had been kneeling with his hands stretched out toward heaven.*

Just as vs. 22 formed the transition between the first praise utterance and the actual prayer, so this and the following verse form the transition between the prayer and the final praise utterance (vss. 56-61; Talstra, 142). The ויהי indicates the moment at which Solomon ended his (relatively long) prayer and plea (Joüon §166b, m), followed by the impf. cons. ויעמד, with which the following verse begins. As a kind of parenthesis between the report of the ending of this prayer and the giving of the blessing in what follows, it is said that he rose up before the altar of YHWH from a kneeling position and with hands outstretched toward heaven. In vs. 22, however, there is no mention of a kneeling position. The קם of our verse need not, as is sometimes (Böttcher, *Neue Aehrenlese*, Thenius, Montg.-Gehman and others; see textcr. app. *BHK* and *BHS*) proposed on the basis of LXX, be modified into ויקם, but can be understood as a pf. which introduces a dependent clause which is no part of the actual context: he had arisen (so, correctly, Talstra, 247) from (מן) a prone position (but cf. Vulg.: *utrumque enim genu in terram fixerat;* and also Pesh., which may perhaps have read כי). Presumably we are dealing with a later addition to the text.

The verb ברע, 'bow down,' occurs 30x in OT in the qal and 5x in the hiph., 4 of them (exclusively in the qal-form) in our books of Kings (1 Kgs. 19:18; 2 Kgs. 1:13; 9:24; H. Eising, *TWAT*, IV, 352ff.). As an expression of subservience one may 'bow' before another person, i.e. 'kneel' (2 Kgs. 1:13), but more often, as here, one 'bows down' before God. Kneeling, therefore, was a universally customary prayer posture (1 Kgs. 19:18; Isa. 45:23; Ps. 95:6; Ezra 9:5; Dan. 6:11). In our comments on vs. 22 we have already said that Solomon's (alternatively) 'standing' and 'kneeling' during this prayer need not be a contradiction, even though there was no mention of kneeling in that verse D.R. Ap-Thomas, *VT* 6 (1956), 226 (cf. Eising, 353), has pointed out, based on

Neh. 9:3ff., that 'change of posture had its place in the cultic prayers of the sanctuaries.' The alternations in the congregation probably took place later in response to vocal or musical cues from the liturgist. That 'bowing down' occurred on the 'knees' is again underscored by the dual-form of ברך, 'knee,' which, solely in this dual-form, occurs 30x (5 of which in Kings) in OT (*Ges.*[18], 179f.; the verb ברך I, 'kneel,' also occurs, be it very rarely [Gen. 24:11 in hiph.; Ps. 95:6 and 2 Chr. 6:13 in qal]). As in vss. 22 and 38, our verse in the end mentions the hands stretched out toward heaven.

In the context of the viewpoint of the Chronicler it is of interest to note that, in 2 Chr. 7:1-3, after mentioning the ending of Solomon's prayer, he continues with a report about an epiphany which legitimates the temple as YHWH's temple. As a result the blessing in our book of Kings is ignored: 'Fire came down from heaven and consumed the burnt offering and the sacrifices, and the glory of YHWH filled the house. (2) The priests could not enter the house of YHWH, because the glory of YHWH filled the house of YHWH. (3) When all the children of Israel saw the fire come down and the glory of YHWH upon the house, they kneeled with their faces to the earth on the pavement, and bowed down giving praise to YHWH, saying: 'Behold, he is good, for his steadfast love endures for ever.'

8:55 *he stood up and blessed the whole assembly of Israel in a loud voice saying:*
After Solomon had risen from his prayer posture, he 'positioned himself' (see Talstra, 142, with n. 31, but cf. his translation of this verse on p. 98) to pronounce the blessing over the assembled congregation (see comments on vs. 14 above). He did this with a 'loud voice' or 'out loud' (cf. Joüon §125s: 'accusative of the internal object'; cf. also Ewald §279d; GD §93, rem. 1). W. Weinberg, *ZAW* 92 (1980), 203, calls the expression קול גדול, 'a frequently occurring idiom, expressing emphasis, importance, urgency, and a variety of uninhibited emotions.'

8:56 *'Blessed be YHWH, who has given a place of rest to his people Israel according to all that he promised. Not a single word has failed of all the good words he uttered by Moses his servant.*
Central in this blessing pronounced here by Solomon (indicated by the word ברוך יהוה: see comments on vs. 15, where LXX* also added σήμερον) is the word 'rest' (מנוחה). In the books of Kings the word occurs only at this place. One can find the word, which is derived from the root נוח (see comments on 5:18 above) 21x in OT. The word denotes the 'place of rest' and hence also the 'rest' which people may enjoy in the turbulence of their life or at the end of an exhausting journey (cf. H.D. Preuß, *TWAT*, V, 304ff.; F. Stolz, *THAT*, II, 45f.). Living in the (promised) land and rest are connected in a special way

(e.g. Ps. 95:11). In our verse YHWH is praised because – after the gift of the land following the exodus, and after the time of Joshua who managed to ward off the attacks of the surrounding enemies – he finally, in the time of David and especially in that of Solomon who built the temple, gave 'rest' to his people (Preuß, 305). On redaction-critical grounds W. Roth, *BR* 21 (1976), 5-14, makes a distinction between the 'rest-theology' of the dtrH and that of dtrN. To dtrN, to which he assigns our vss. 56-61, 'rest' for Israel would consist especially in its being turned toward God, a fact in which the place (the 'promised land') or the existence of the temple played no special role. But the blessing, which is pronounced here, refers back, in word and intention, to Deut. 12:9f. (among other places), where there *is* mention of the gift of the land, and to Josh. 21:44f.; 23:14 ('not one thing has failed of all the good things ...'), where the ultimate 'rest' is the fulfillment of God's promises ('according to all that he promised'; Noth; Talstra, 248). Also in our verse there is backward reference to YHWH's promises which had been given by way of Moses.

8:57 *May YHWH our God be with us as he has been with our forefathers. May he not leave us or reject us,*
The actual blessing was restricted to the previous verse. Now follows a series of 3 wishes, the first of which is formulated here and in the following verse. Here the reference is to YHWH's 'Mit-Sein,' in this case with 'us,' as he had been 'with our fathers'.[22] This formula occurs approx. 100x in OT and expresses a basic structure of OT belief. Possibly playing in the background of this formula, there is, at least according to Preuß, the memory of the journey of a (nomadic) people who craved the accompaniment of the deity on its journeys. Talstra, 144f. (cf. p. 205), mentions that the formula is more frequently used 'in an application to individual persons' than to groups. He is further of the opinion that our verse 'uses standard liturgical idiom' (250). The expression יהוה אלהינו also occur in the vss. 59, 61, and 65; further in 2 Chr. 18:22 and 19:19; we found this expression, in 2 p. sing., in 1:17 and 2:3, and it also occurs in 10:9; 13:6, 21; 17:12; and 18:10. One can also find it in 2 p. pl. Burney interprets this expression as characteristically dtr.

The verb עזב 'leave' was already used in 6:13 and also occurs several times in the later chapters (9:9; 11:33; 12:8, 13; 14:10, etc.; H.-P. Stähli, *THAT*, II, 249-252; E.S. Gerstenberger, *TWAT*, V, 1200-1208). The verb נטש, 'forsake, abandon, cast away,' of the 33x it is found in the qal-form in OT, occurs only here and in 2 Kgs. 21:14 in our books of Kings (J. Lundbom, *TWAT*, V, 442).

---

[22] For this formula, cf. H.D. Preuß, "... Ich will mit dir sein," *ZAW* 80 (1968), 139-173, esp. 146.

8:58 *so that our hearts may incline to him to walk in all his ways and to keep his commandments, his statutes, and his ordinances.*
God's presence is desired in 2 specific cases. In the first place 'to direct our heart' (various Hebr. MSS, like LXX and Vulg. read: 'our hearts') 'to him' (cf. Josh. 24:23b; נטה hiph. also occurs in Kings in 11:2-4; 2 Kgs. 19:16; further see comments on vs. 42 above, and Talstra, 250), so that 'we walk in all his ways' (see comments on 2:3 above). This is a characteristic expression used in Deut. (8:6; 10:12; 11:22 etc.) and the dtr. literature. Also the second, 'keeping his commandments, his statutes, and his ordinances' belongs to this category. ומשפטיו is lacking in LXX.

8:59 *may these words of mine with which I have made supplication before YHWH remain near to YHWH our God day and night, to adjudicate the cause of his servant and the cause of his people Israel according to each day's need,*
The second wish Solomon utters concerns his own prayer (vss. 59f.) He wishes that 'these my words' (LXX[B, Luc.]: 'these words'; cf. König §334y), with which (= אשר; König §§57f.; Joüon §158i) he brings his pleas before YHWH (for the expression לפני יהוה, cf. also M.D. Fowler, *ZAW* 99 [1987], 388f.), may remain near to YHWH (cf. the contrast with קרוב in Ps. 22:2; Burney). In Deut. 30:14 we are told that YHWH's word is 'near' to Israel. That our verse can be called a reversal of this wish, as Talstra, 145f. (cf. also p. 250) asserts, is doubtful. One can also view these words along the lines of the observation expressed in Deut. as 'pleading on the promise.' At issue is the (legal) cause of 'his servant' and 'his people' ('the cause of the people' is omitted in LXX[B, Luc.]; the possessive pron. 'his' is replaced in LXX by 'your'). Striking, but not unusual, is the expression יום ביומו (Exod. 5:13, 19; 16:4; 2 Kgs. 25:30 [par. Jer. 52:34]; Dan. 1:4; Burney; König §288c, n. 1): 'according to the need of each day,' or 'each day its own' (so LV; in LXX[B] the words ἐν ἡμέρα αὐτου has been corrupted into ἐνιαυτοῦ, 'year': Stade-Schwally; Montg.-Gehman; textcr. app. *BHK*).

8:60 *so that all the peoples of the earth may know that YHWH and no one else is God.*
The purpose of this wish has also already been expressed in vss. 43 and 53: All the nations on earth must know that YHWH alone is God, a pronouncement one can also find in Deut. (4:35, 39) and elsewhere (e.g. in 18:39). We are dealing here with a fundamental confession of the dtr. and the later Israel. Talstra, 251, correctly comments that there is no longer any mention of the temple as in petition 5. A great many MSS, supported by LXX, Pesh. and Vulg., place the copula ו before אין. König, *Stil.* 216, however, points to the 'energisch protestierende' nature of the asyndetic אין עוד.

Noth (et al.) are of the opinion that the vss. 59f., are a later insertion, but

Talstra, 251, opposes this view.

8:61 *May your heart be undivided before YHWH our God, as you walk in his statutes and keep his commandments, as is the case today.*
The wish in this verse is an exhortation to the people to remain true to YHWH with an 'undivided heart.' We already encountered the word שלם in 6:7. One often finds this word, linked with לבב, also elsewhere in Kgs. 11:4; 15:3, 14; 2 Kgs. 20:3. This is one of those words which can hardly be rendered in English by just one word. KJ has 'be perfect with'; NIV: 'be fully committed to'; NJB: 'be wholly with'; NEB: 'be perfect in loyalty to'; RSV: 'be wholly true to.' Talstra translates it by 'true to,' SV and NV: 'volkomen' ('perfect'; cf. also Pedersen, I-II, 286: 'The one becomes "whole with" the other'; cf. 341, n. 1). All these nuances can be discerned in the word. This verse corresponds to vs. 58 (so, correctly, Noth). In place of the suffix 2nd p. pl., both LXX and Vulg. translate as if the 'Vorlage' read the 1 p. pl.: 'our hearts.' This reading as such is plausible because the 1st p. pl. is used also in the vss. 57ff. Nevertheless we maintain MT as the *lectio difficilior*.

1 KINGS 8:62-66

8:62 *Then the king, and all Israel with him, brought a sacrifice to YHWH.*
63 *Solomon offered peace offerings to YHWH. What he brought to YHWH as offering were twenty-two thousand oxen and a hundred and twenty thousand sheep. In this manner the king and all the Israelites dedicated the house of YHWH.*
64 *The same day the king consecrated the middle of the court that was before the house of YHWH; for there he had to offer the burnt offering and the cereal offering and the fat of the peace offerings, because the bronze altar that was before the Lord was too small to hold the burnt offering and the cereal offering and the fat of the peace offerings.*
65 *Around the same time Solomon and all Israel with him – a vast assembly coming from the entrance of Hamath to the Brook of Egypt – organized a feast for YHWH, our God, lasting seven days [and again seven days, fourteen days (in all)].*
66 *On the eighth day he sent the people away. They blessed the king and went to their tents, joyful and glad of heart for all the good things YHWH had shown David his servant and Israel his people.*

INTRODUCTION

The end of the story of (the building and) the 'actual' (cf. W. Dommershausen, *TWAT*, III, 21) dedication of the temple is divided in 2 parts (vss. 62-64 and 65f.). The first part (vss. 62-64) ties in with vs. 5, where the nature and number of the sacrifices are further specified, while in addition a comment is made about the altar in the court. Noth points out that the exaggeratedly high number of sacrificial animals is advanced by the dtr. as legitimation for the purity and uniqueness of worship at the temple in contrast to 'worship on the high places' at Gibeon (3:4). Furthermore – and this is something Mowinckel has called attention to – the situation is that the dtr. probably did not have access to contemporary reportage about sacrifices and feasts in the time of David or Solomon. 'Woher haben sie dann ihre Kunde über Einzelheiten des Festes? Etwa lediglich aus der Phantasie? Mit nichten. Sie haben hier dasselbe getan, wie so oft sonst, und was so viele andere Geschichtserzähler aus alter Zeit getan haben: sie werden die Feste nach den Gebräuchen geschildert haben, die zu ihrer eigenen Zeit üblich waren; diese Festgebräuche haben sie ganz unbefangen in die Zeit Davids und Salomos verlegt.'[1] In an incidental way a legitimation for the 'bronze altar' in the court is provided as well. Vs. 64, accordingly, looks like an addition from a later day.

The second part makes mention of 'the feast' which had already been mentioned as a fall festival in vs. 2. One gets the impression that dtr. here describes the 'feast of tabernacles' reported in Deut. 16:13ff. Both parts have their parallel (with the usual additions and omissions) in 2 Chr. 7:4-10.

EXEGESIS

8:62 *Then the king, and all Israel with him, brought a sacrifice to YHWH.*
This verse clearly ties in with vs. 5 (cf. also W. Rudolph, *ZAW* 63 [1951], 204). LXX reads 'all the children of Israel.' The verb זבח already occurred in 1:9; the noun, 'sacrifice,' 'bloody offering'; occurs here for the first time in the books of Kings. The verb זבח can also refer to an ordinary 'secular' killing of an animal (1 Sam. 28:24; 1 Kgs. 19:21), so that the expression לפני יהוה is certainly meaningful in this connection (so Böttcher, *Neue Aehrenlese*; Thenius). The part. (זבחים) sometimes replaces the finite verb and is continued in the following verse by an impf. cons. (König §239d; Bg. II §12f).

8:63 *Solomon offered peace offerings to YHWH. What he brought to YHWH as offering were twenty-two thousand oxen and a hundred and twenty thousand sheep. In this manner the king and all the Israelites dedicated the house of YHWH.*
The 'peace offerings' were already discussed in the course of our comments on 3:15 above. The par. 2 Chr. 7:5 omits השלמים ליהוה. It hardly needs further argument that the incalculable number of oxen and small stock slaughtered is based on the kind of exaggeration that serves to enhance Solomon's greatness and riches as well as to legitimate the central sanctuary as the unique sanctuary for YHWH (as also many a commentator has remarked over the years). LXX[B, Luc.] omits the large number of small stock with the result that the number in MT becomes more tolerable but is textcritically certainly no better warranted. Thenius in his commentary calculated that, if a day of sacrificing were put at 12 hours, some 262 oxen and 1430 sheep would have had to be offered up per hour. Greßman comes to 314 oxen and 1,714 sheep per hour; but Keil defends the high numbers by referring, among other things, to other hecatombs in antiquity (Josephus, *Bell.* VI §§423-426); Van Gelderen suggests that the numbers have presumably been rounded off but that suggestion does not help

---

[1] S. Mowinckel, *Psalmen-studien*, II, Oslo 1922 (repr. Amsterdam 1961), 109f.

much to reduce them either!

In the following the verb חנך, 'initiate,' 'use for the first time,' 'dedicate' is used, which occurs 4x elsewhere in OT (Deut. 20:5 [2x – said of a house]; Prov. 22:6 and the par. 2 Chr. 7:5). In addition one finds the substantive a few times as well (Num. 7:10f. [of an altar], 84, 88; Ps.230:1; Neh. 12:27 [2x – of a wall], and 2 Chr. 7:9; also in the Aram. part of OT: Dan. 3:2f.; Ezra 6:16f.; cf. W. Dommershausen, *TWAT*, III, 20ff. A temple dedication from the time of the Maccabees has gone down in history as the Feast of CHanukkah and is celebrated, for 8 days, from the 25th of Kislev (our month of December) (1 Macc. 4:36-59; 2 Macc. 10:1-8; De Vaux, *Inst.* II, 420-425). In our verse there is no mention of special consecration rites, but in the par. 2 Chr. 7:16 we read of priests who assisted and Levites with musical instruments made by David (cf. 1 Chr 23:5; cf. also 2 Chr. 5:11ff.). To this is added the further detail that, by their ministry, David offered praises to YHWH: 'for his steadfast love endures for ever.' Meanwhile the priests blew the trumpet and the people stood to listen. It is clear that this chronistic addition is a reproduction from a later liturgy.

The close of our verse has the following order: verb-object-subject, so that the accent falls on the subject: 'the king and all the children of Israel' (Driver §208.4; Williams §571).

8:64 *The same day the king consecrated the middle of the court that was before the house of YHWH; for there he had to offer the burnt offering and the cereal offering and the fat of the peace offerings, because the bronze altar that was before the Lord was too small to hold the burnt offering and the cereal offering and the fat of the peace offerings.*

In this verse the reader encounters a statement that is missing in the building account in the preceding chapters but included in 2 Chr. 4:1: the bronze altar (see comments on 7:23 above). True, this altar was mentioned in passing in the preceding verses (see vss. 22, 31, 54), but here the author pauses to consider it *expressis verbis*.

We are told in the first place that 'on that day' Solomon 'consecrated the middle of the court.' Apparently the numerous sacrifices mentioned in the previous verse occasioned this 'consecration' because a single altar could not process all those sacrifices in such a short time. Now 'on that day' does not mean 'for that day' alone (and perhaps the next few days), so that the 'consecration' would have been valid for only a limited period of time (so Noth). The use of the pf. after this temporal determination (cf. Jouön §176h) may have been intended by the author to indicate that this consecration was permanent, hence also for those periods in which no hecatombs were offered. Now the question arises whether the phrase 'the middle of the court' means that only a part of the inner court was 'consecrated' for this purpose. Many translations and commentators follow this view (SV, LV, PCV, NV, WV, RSV, Noth, et al.). But Ewald (§287g; his appeal to Isa. 66:17 is not convincing) expressed the opinion that the reference here is to the entire '*inner* court' (so also Thenius and the Luther-translation: 'den Mittelhof'). Earlier already (on 6:36) we addressed the problem of the temple and palace courts. There 'the middle court,' i.e. the temple court, was referred to by החצר הפנימית, so that it makes good sense to view אתתוך החצר here as 'the central part of the (inner) court.'

We translated the verb קדש pi. by 'consecrate.' It is distinct from the word חנן used in the previous verse. The word occurs many times in OT and in various stem-modifications (see W. Kornfeld, H. Ringgren, *TWAT*, VI, 1179-1204; H.-P. Müller, *THAT*, II, 589-609). In our book we encounter the verb only here and in the pi.-form in 2 Kgs. 10:20. Comparison of these 2 verses brings out that people could 'consecrate' certain things or feasts to YHWH as well as to Baal. People brought a given thing into the sphere of the sacred, that which was set aside for the deity, so as to withdraw it from 'profane' use. In our verse the act of 'consecration' by Solomon was possibly associated with rites unknown to us (W. Dommershausen, *TWAT*, III, 21). One *can* conclude that the author is of the opinion that this place was not meant for sacrifice before.

עלוה is the word for 'burnt offering,' the offering that was intended wholly for God. We also found it earlier in 3:4, 15 (see comments on 3:15 above; now also D. Kellermann, *TWAT*, VI, 105-124); מנחה, here and in most places elsewhere in OT, means 'offering,' in earlier times both of meat and of fruit or grains, later exclusively of grains. This offering is then especially called a 'cereal offering' (see comments on 5:1 above). The par. 2 Chr. 7:7 omits the last-mentioned offering; LXX* turns it into the pl., at least if one may regard the word θυσία here as a translation of מנחה (which Stade-Schwally call into serious question; see their explanation).

As a third kind of offering we read of חלבי השלמים. The word חלב occurs approximately 90x in OT, especially in the account of the sacrificial material in Lev. and Num. (54x) and means 'sacrificial fat' (G. Münderlein, *TWAT*, II, 951-958). Fat was regarded as one of the most precious parts of the sacrifice and, especially in the later legislation, became the part of the sacrifice that was brought to YHWH. Although originally also humans were allowed to eat the fat of animals (cf. Ps. 63:6), later such eating of fat by humans was considered a universal dietary prohibition (Lev. 3:17). In certain cases חלבים (for the pl., see König §259a) became the term for the fat parts of the offering or for the offerings themselves. In our verse too one could assign the word to this category (see Münderlein, 956). The reference is to the parts of the שלמים to be sacrificed (see the previous verse).

The second half of our verse then tells us that the 'bronze altar that was before the Lord was too small' (for the function of מן after קטן, cf. König

§406h; Ges-K §133c; GD §44, rem. 1; Williams §§76, 318) to receive all the sacrifices (for כול hiph., see comments on 7:26). The par. 2 Chr. 7:7 restructures this statement as follows: 'the bronze altar which Solomon had made could not hold ...' In this way the predicament of a YHWH-altar that was too small and therefore humiliating to YHWH is turned into a tribute to Solomon's greatness! We pointed out earlier that the statement that Hiram had made an altar on orders of Solomon (as 2 Chr. 4:1 reports) may have dropped out in 1 Kgs. 7. We are speaking of a bronze or copper altar (for נחשת, cf. comments on 7:14), which undoubtedly had to be built in the open air (cf. 9:25; 2 Kgs. 16:14f.). Pedersen, III-IV, 241; 686f., believes the altar was constructed on top of the 'holy rock' and points out that good arguments have been advanced by certain scholars for the belief that that rock was located in the 'holy of holies' (cf. the rock in and underneath the present-day Dome of the Rock mosque (*Kubbet eṣ-Ṣaḥra*] on the former temple square [*Ḥaram-eš-Šarif*] of Jerusalem; Kittel, *SHARG*, 1-96, offers a lengthy exposition on 'Der heilige Fels auf dem Moria. Seine Geschichte und seine Altäre').

The dearth of precise information in our sources makes it particularly difficult, however, to determine the place and size of the altar referred to in our verse. Some time ago De Groot, *Altäre*, attempted, in part on the basis of a statement in 2 Kgs. 12:10, to make a case for the presence in the temple court up until the time of King Ahaz of 2 altars, one in the center of the court and the other the altar referred to in 2 Kgs. 12:10. In his day De Groot found little support for his suggestion (on this subject see: Wiener, *Altars*, 31f.; Busink, 322f.). But not too long ago Gadegaard expressed agreement with him.[2] The stone *bamah*-type is said to have served as the altar for burnt offerings, while the bronze altar was intended for other sacrifices. K. Galling, *BRL*[1], 20, is of the opinion that, in the case of normal use, the 'copper altar' as the only altar in the forecourt had sufficient capacity for the sacrifices (so also A. Reichert, *BRL*[2], 9).

The dimensions of the altar which Solomon built, as cited in 2 Chr. 4:1, are a surface of 20x20 cubits and a height of 10 cubits. But Kittel, *SHARG*, 53, is of the opinion that the chronicler here cites the dimensions of the altar in the second temple, which again agree with the statement by Hekataeus in Josephus, *c.Ap.* I §198. Only the altar described there is not made of bronze (or copper) but of unhewn stones, in keeping with the instruction in Exod. 20:25 (cf. vs. 24). The dimensions of the altar by the so-called tabernacle, as cited in Exod. 27:1ff., are a surface of 5x5 cubits and 3 cubits in height, while it is at the same time stated that this altar is made of acacia wood overlaid with bronze.

---

[2] N.H. Gadegaard, "On the So-Called Burnt Offering Altar in the Old Testament," *PEQ* 110 (1978), 35-45.

Generally scholars agree that the information about the dimensions (etc.) of the tabernacle stem from the postexilic era and have little value for the dimensions (etc.) of the Solomonic temple (see, for example, Kittel's discussion of the altar of burnt offerings in *SHARG*, 51-67; also *RE*³, XIX, 490).

According to Galling and Reichert, 'copper' in our verse means that this material relates to a portable table-altar, 'dessen Leisten und Decken mit Bronzeblech verkleidet sind.' Wiener, 15, on the other hand, believes that the bronze altar of Solomon (as, for that matter, also the tabernacle altar) 'is in the form of a hollow box with no bottom,' a view which Busink, 324, endorses. A. Baumann, *TWAT*, IV, 92, basing himself on the statements that the altar was too small to hold the different kinds of sacrifices, concludes 'daß die Oberfläche dieses Altars Vertiefungen aufwies, die das Ganze einem Gefäß vergleichbar machten.' This is reminiscent of the description as Ezekiel offers it (Ezek. 43:13-17; for this, see also De Groot, *Altäre*, 45-52). But despite the often most ingenious and energetic attempts at reconstruction, it is no longer very well possible to say more about the shape and place of the altar in the temple court than we find reported in our verse, and that is exceedingly little.

In this connection it is worthwhile once more to call attention to the opinion of Gadegaard, art. cit., who again takes a position that is closer to that of De Groot. According to him, neither the altars of burnt offering mentioned in OT, nor the so-called pre-Israelite altars of Ṣar'a by *'Artuf*, the limestone block of Hazor, etc., can be called 'altars of burnt offering' in the true sense. And this not only because they are too small for that purpose, but also because they could not withstand temperatures between 800-1000 degrees Celsius. The altars in question, according to him, were intended only for libations of blood and depositing gifts. In answer to the question where the 'real' offerings could be brought, Gadegaard supposes that in Jerusalem, among other places, there must have been a second altar in the shape of a *bamah*, an elevation, round or square in form and with a diameter of more than 10 m (as, e.g., the platform of Dan shows). The reference here is to an altar described by Vaughan as *bamah*-type II.[3] This *bamah* serves both as an altar by itself and as the base for an ordinary altar (also cf. C. Dohmen, *TWAT*, IV, 796). According to Dohmen, it is possible that for the building of a temple there already was a *bamah*-type I which was then expanded to a type II, and provided with a 'bronze altar.' Whether the 2 kinds, the *bamah* and the altar superimposed on it, were described without differentiation in the OT texts as מזבח is possible but can no longer be clearly determined (so, correctly, Dohmen, a.l.).

8:65 *Around the same time Solomon and all Israel with him – a vast*

---

[3] P.A. Vaughan, *The Meaning of 'bamâ' in the Old Testament*, Cambridge 1974.

assembly coming from the entrance to Hamath to the brook of Egypt – organized a feast for YHWH, our God, lasting seven days [and again seven days, fourteen days (in all)].

In this verse there is mention simply of 'the feast.' Earlier, in the discussion of vs. 2, we already pointed to the problems which crop up in the attempt to determine the time of this feast. Was it 'the Feast of the dedication of the Temple' or 'the Feast of Tabernacles,' which also took place in the fall? Or does the redundant conclusion of our verse (with its 2x7 days) point, at least in the opinion of the dtr. author, to a Dedication Feast which lasted 7 days and subsequently to a Feast of Tabernacles which similarly lasted 7 days (so, e.g., Noth)?

It has often been pointed out that the autumn festival was the most important feast in ancient Israel, in part also because Jeroboam in the northern kingdom introduced an autumn festival at Bethel as counterpart to the Jerusalem pilgrim-festival (1 Kgs. 12:32; see Pedersen, III-IV, 446f.). B. Kedar-Kopfstein, *TWAT*, II, 737, cautions us against saying that originally there were one (our verse and Hos. 9:5), or 2 (Ezek. 45:17-25) or 3 annual festivals (Exod. 23:14-17 E; 34:18, 22f. J; Deut. 16:1-17 D; Lev. 23:4-12; 33-44 H; Num. 28:16-31; 29:12-39 P) because each of these pronouncements has relative value in that it held true for a specific locality at a specific point in time.

As for the time designation in our verse, the author conveys it with the words בעזדההיא, an expression which, along with ביום ההוא (see the previous verse; LXX and Pesh. also in our verse), occurs frequently in dtr. literature (examples in Burney). 'All Israel' is then described as a אהל גדול, which, according to F.-L. Hossfeld, E.-M. Kindl, *TWAT*, VI, 1210, is a 'technical concept' which 'erst durch den Kontext im Hinblick auf den Personenkreis und oder den Zweck der Ansammlung qualifiziert werden muß.' Here the expression refers to Solomon and all Israel as a 'great assembly,' which came together at the time to celebrate the feast of Tabernacles, to distinguish it from a festal gathering as institution. But alongside this quantitative aspect a cultic connotation is clearly present as well (Hossfeld/Kindl, 1213).

The massive extent of Israel's attendance is also indicated by 2 geographical names which describe the northern and southern boundaries of the area in which Israel was thought to dwell. לבוא חמת (cf. also König §406c; Bg. II §11k [p. 57]) occurs a number of times in OT (Num 13:21; 34:8; Josh. 13:5; Judg. 3:3; 2 Kgs. 14:25; Ezek. 47:20; 48:1; Amos 6:14; 1 Chr. 13:5; 2 Chr. 7:8), while Hamath is also repeatedly mentioned without לבוא. Today Hamath is a Syrian city on the Orontes (*nahr al-ʿĀṣī*), the river which originates to the N of present-day Baalbek in the Lebanon, initially flows N between the Lebanon and the Anti-Lebanon, next to the E of the Ansayriya mountain range, and then curves sharply to the W or even SW. Flowing past Antioch, the river shortly thereafter empties into the Mediterranean. The word לבוא has been variously interpreted over the years (for the different explanations see: O. Eißfeldt, *KS*, V, 205-211), but can – with Eissfeldt – best be translated as 'entrance to (Hamath).' In this connection he refers to a note from P. J. Riis, which called attention to the ancient trade route from Jabla (on the Mediterranean) through the mountains to Hamath. In Jabla this road was called 'the entrance to Hamath.' In other words, on this view 'the entrance to Hamath' as geographical term lies on the Mediterranean Sea, nearly S of present-day Latakia, and not, for example, in Coele-Syria between Hermon and Lebanon or elsewhere in the Beqa. Accordingly, this entrance was viewed as the (ideal, to be sure) northern boundary of Israel (otherwise, e.g. Abel, *GP*, I, 300f.: in the neighborhood of Ribla).

The southern boundary was defined by 'the wadi of Egypt' (Num. 34:5; Josh. 15:4, 47; Isa. 27:12). We already encountered the word נחל in 2:37: the wadi of the Kidron. Israel's boundary with Egypt already came up in 5:1. Scholars generally believe the reference here is to the *wadi al-'Ariš*, which empties into the Mediterranean about 70 km SW of Gaza.

After the details added to 'all Israel,' the text continues with the information that Solomon organized the feast before the face of YHWH, 'our God.' LXX further inserts: 'in the house which he had built, while people ate and drank, and rejoiced before the face of YHWH, our God.' It would seem that these words occurred in LXX's 'Vorlage,' and exegetes (Thenius, Oort, Stade-Schwally, Burney, Barthélemy, et al.) surmise, therefore, that MT may have mistakenly (on account of *homoeoteleuton*) omitted them. Benzinger is of the opinion, however, that this omission is intentional in our verse, 'um die Schilderung dem späteren Festcharacter mehr anzupassen.' We think that MT must be maintained, also aside from this last-mentioned opinion (the par. 2 Chr. 7 and the other ancient versions lack this passage as well).

The end of our verse also presents difficulties other than the textcritical ones. It is well for us first to note the par. 2 Chr. 7:8f. The translation of these verses reads as follows: 'At that time Solomon held a feast for 7 days, and all Israel with him, a very great gathering, from the entrance to Hamath to the wadi of Egypt. On the 8th day they held a festive closing gathering (עצרת), for they celebrated the dedication of the altar for 7 days and they celebrated the feast for 7 days.' In Chronicles we are clearly dealing with 2 weeks of feasting, first the feast of the Dedication, then the feast of Tabernacles, with the addition of a closing assembly (cf. Lev. 23:36; Num. 29:35), which is still unknown in the old legislation. Our text in Kings, however, gives the impression that only one feast of 7 days is intended, after which, on the 8th day, Solomon dismissed the people (cf. the following verse). The 5 words at the end, 'and 7 days, 14 days' as such seem redundant. True, Targ. renders this as follows: 7 days for the dedication of the house, and 7 days for the feast (of Tabernacles),' but LXX* does not have these words and, in the opinion of many commentators (Thenius, Klostermann, Benzinger, Kittel, Oort, Ehrlich, Delitzsch, *LSF* §156, et al.), they are redundant in our verse as well. Now Josephus, *Ant.* VIII §123, does mention the '2x7 days' of the feast of Tabernacles. Moreover, Montg.-Gehman (also cf. Barthélemy) refer to 2 Chr. 30:23-26, where we also read of '2x7 days' during passover in the days of king Hezekiah, again because there were so many sacrificial animals (though considerably less than at Solomon's feast of Dedication). Montg.-Gehman, therefore, are of the opinion that 'there may be contained in the Chronicler's report of a double feast a true tradition of annual pre-Exilic feast of Chanukkah or Dedication.' The question here is whether the author of our verse already possessed the mention of '2x7' feast days. According to Barthélemy, not only Josephus but also the author of Chronicles did in fact have this text before him. The latter, however, saw a problem in the fact that the author of Kings offered no reasons for his duplication of the feast of Dedication. The chronicler tried to make this fact clear by adapting the dtr. ritual of the author of Kings to the priestly ritual in vogue in his day, with the result that 2 feasts, each lasting 7 days, were held, with a festive ending on the 8th day. But here again we face a problem which later played a role in the Jewish tradition: if one reserves the first week for the feast of the Dedication of the temple which links up with the feast of Tabernacles, the 'Great Day of Atonement' falls squarely in the middle of the first week of feasting.[4] But the possibility remains, with many commentators, of viewing the last 5 words of MT of our verse as a marginal gloss, derived from the calculation of the chronicler, which was added to the Hebr. text after the origination of LXX. In any case, the author of our book has the feast of the Dedication of the Temple coincide with the feast of Tabernacles.

8:66 *On the eighth day he sent the people away. They blessed the king and went to their tents, joyful and glad of heart for all the great things YHWH had shown David his servant and Israel his people.*
In contrast to the par. section in Chronicles, our verse makes no mention of a 'solemn (closing) feast' (עצרת; 2 Chr. 7:9). But if at the end of the previous verse one omits the last 5 words of MT, then the 8th day is logically the day after the 7 (and not after the 14) preceding days, in which the temple was dedicated and which coincided with the feast of Tabernacles (several ancient versions have the *copula* precede the ביום). But 2 Chr. 7:10 reads: 'on the 23rd day of the 7th month he sent the people away ...,' a reading which is altogether in keeping with the preceding separation of the feasts in Chronicles.

It is reported that the people 'blessed' the king (LXX* reads 'him' in place of king; LXX[B]: 'the king blessed the people'; LXX[Luc.] unites the two; Rahlfs,

---

[4] Cf. P. W. van Boxel, *Rabbijnenbijbel en Contrareformatie*, Hilversum 1983, 79f.

SSt. III, 193f.). According to J. Scharbert, *TWAT*, I, 823, the people at the close of the liturgy utter an 'intercessory prayer' that blessing might be given to the king, a prayer comparable to Ps. 20; 61:7ff.; 63:12. After that the people go 'to their tents,' glad and with a joyful heart, i.e. in a happy mood (Esth. 5:9; Burney; also cf. Pedersen, I-II, 148). The word הטובה occurs, aside from this verse, also elsewhere in OT (e.g. 2 Sam. 7:28). On the basis of older studies and the occurrence of similar concepts in other Near Eastern languages, J.S. Croatto, *AION* NS 18 (1968), 385-389, takes the word to mean 'covenant friendship.'

In the conclusion David is once more mentioned as 'der eigentliche Initiator des Tempelbauwerks' (Noth), to whom the par. text in Chronicles also adds Solomon, so that the trio David-Solomon-Israel is completely present there.

1 KINGS 9:1-9

9:1 *When Solomon had finished building the house of YHWH and the royal palace and all that he found desirable so that he wanted to make it,*
2 YHWH appeared to Solomon a second time as he had appeared to him at Gibeon.
3 YHWH said to him: 'I have heard the prayer and the plea which you have made before me. I have consecrated this house which you have built in order to establish my name there forever; my eyes as well as my heart will always be present there.
4 For your part, if you walk before me with integrity of heart and uprightness, as David your father did, acting according to all that I have commanded you, and observing my statutes and ordinances,
5 I will establish the throne of your royal rule over Israel forever, as I promised your father David with the words: 'There shall not fail you a man on the throne of Israel.'
6 But if you and your children presumptuously turn away from following me and do not observe my commandments and my statutes which I have given you but go off to serve other gods and worship them,
7 I will cut off Israel from the land that I have given them and abandon the house which I have consecrated for my name, so that Israel will become a proverb and a byword among all peoples;
8 and this house will become a heap of ruins. Everyone passing by will shudder and whistle and they will say: "why has YHWH treated this country and this house like this?"
9 Then people will answer: "Because they have forsaken YHWH, their God, who brought their fathers out of the land of Egypt and because they laid hold on other gods, worshiping and serving them: therefore YHWH has brought all this evil upon them".'

INTRODUCTION

According to many scholars this section (par. 2 Chr. 7:12-22) is written in a dtr. vein, and attributed by Kuenen, Wellhausen, Stade, Benzinger, et al., to an editor from the time of the exile, in part because the reference in the vss. 7-9 is obviously to a situation following the destruction of the temple and the deportation of a part of Judah. Although, according to others (Burney among them), this conclusion is not binding, in view of the close of the books of Kings there can be no compelling objection against this view. While some scholars (Skinner et al.) do not wish to rule out the possibility that the vss. 1-5 were written by a pre-exilic redactor and the vss. 6-9 by a later one, in fact the dtr. theological theme clearly runs through the whole composition of the books of Kings and unites the different parts.

On the one hand, 9:1-9 constitutes a response to the prayer in chap. 8, but on the other it is a confirmation of and a cautionary sequel to 3:5-14, in which there is also mention of an appearance at Gibeon. Parker is of the opinion that this chapter forms a turning point in the account of Solomon's conduct: in the chaps. 3-8 he was sketched as an ideal king but beginning with this chapter he becomes 'the ideal's antithesis. His regime is noted for its egregious tyranny, and his wisdom is directed toward his own self-aggrandizement'[1] (cf. Šanda and W. Stark, *ZAW* 55 (1937), 27f.). The right relation between law and wisdom has been broken. It is a question, however, whether the line of division can be drawn as sharply as Parker does.

EXEGESIS

9:1 *When Solomon had finished building the house of YHWH and the royal palace and all that he found desirable so that he wanted to make it,*
The completion of the building of the temple and the palace by Solomon, is here, as repeatedly also in the preceding chapters, highlighted (cf. 3:1; 6:9, 14; 7:1). But before the author goes on to the main clause in vs. 2, he adds a remarkable element to that completed construction. One could ask whether the addition which begins with the third את of our verse also introduces a third object or merely a further description of the splendid way in which the temple and the palace were equipped. The word חשק occurs, aside from here and in vs. 19, also in Isa. 21:4 and 2 Chr. 8:6, where the lastmentioned verse is a par. to vs. 19 of our chapter. The verb חשק occurs somewhat more frequently in various stem-modifications (qal: Gen. 34:8; Deut. 7:7; 10:15; 21:11; 1 Kgs. 9:19 [par. 2 Chr. 8:6]; Isa. 38:17 and Ps. 91:14; pi.: Exod. 38:28; pu.: Exod. 27:17), and means 'to unite with' and then also 'to love' and in a weaker sense 'to desire' (also cf. G. Quell, *TDNT*, I, 22, n. 8). The noun is usually translated by 'pleasure.' The reference here, to cite G. Wallis, *TWAT*, III, 280, is to 'die Lust zu einem Vorhaben, zo Salomos Freude an seiner Bautätigkeit.' Along with the useful and the necessary also 'pleasure' gets its due (Thenius). In our verse this is, perhaps redundantly, again repeated in the last 2 words.

A small textcritical problem arises in this connection from the word חפץ.

---

[1] K.I. Parker, "Solomon as Philosopher King? The Nexus of Law and Wisdom in I Kings 1-11," *JSOT* 53 (1992), 75-91, esp. 86.

According to G.J. Botterweck, *TWAT*, V, 92, this verb occurs 73x in OT, and according to G. Gerleman, *THAT*, I, 624, 86x (but now with the addition of the part. form); in Kings only here and in 10:9, however, and if one adds the part. construction also in 13:33 and 21:6. The meaning is 'to have pleasure in.' In our verse, therefore, חשק and חפץ are not very far apart in meaning. Is this perhaps the reason why Pesh. as well as Tg. translate the words, which in MT have different roots, by words having the same root, so that, on the basis of these translations the textcr. app. in *BHK* as well as in *BHS* propose to read also the second word as חשק? Of course, as the sequel in *BHK* shows, one can also 'correct' the first word in light of the second. Neither LXX, nor Vulg, nor the Hebr. text. itself, however, give us any reason to adopt either of these changes.

Again: are we here dealing in our verse with the 'remaining construction projects' of Solomon, or with a modal or, if you like, a quantitative description of the just-mentioned building of the temple and the palace as 'a pleasure to the eyes'? The par. 2 Chr. 7:11 is completely clear in its choice and renders the last part of our verse as follows: 'and all Solomon had in mind to do in the temple of YHWH and in his palace he successfully accomplished.' But this view by no means has to be normative for the interpretation of our verse. Hentschel correctly remarks that in our verse we are dealing with a dtr. comment which was made long after Solomon's luxurious life and therefore refers to all that – according to tradition – Solomon had built. Also LXX, by using the word πραγματεία, 'work (executed),' seems to take חשק in this direction (also cf. comments on 7:33, further C. Maurer, *TDNT*, VI, 640). In addition, this last part seems to be dependent on vs. 19b (so, correctly, Montg.-Gehman), at least if one does not want to speak of 'borrowing' (so Benzinger). Klostermann even suspected that originally vs. 1a was a protasis for an apodasis which summed up all Solomon's construction projects and hence not at all the protasis of vs. 2 as it is now. The fact that something is really amiss in this sentence is also clear from the double mention of Solomon. The final ואת, in any case, must not be regarded as explicative of the preceding building projects.

Still, the dtr. author apparently placed all of Solomon's building activities in the general context of the building of the temple, as may be evident from what follows. One must therefore agree with Noth that the dtr. author did not have in mind a precise time for the second appearance of YHWH. From vs. 3 one gets the impression that YHWH's appearance was a response to the dedication of the temple (also cf. 6:37f.). It is hard to tell over what period all of Solomon's building activities were extended but one may in any case assume that they also continued after the completion of the building of the temple. These considerations make it the more likely that vs. 1b is to be viewed as a later addition.

9:2 *YHWH appeared to Solomon a second time as he had appeared to him at Gibeon.*
In 3:4-15 we are told of YHWH's first appearance to Solomon, which took place at Gibeon. Now his appearance can be localized in the temple at Jerusalem. The par. 2 Chr. 7:12 only states that YHWH appeared to Solomon at night and omits reference to the first appearance at Gibeon. Taylor, *Sun*, 1243f., 146f., refers, also in connection with our vss. 1-3, to the close links which existed between the sun-cult at Gibeon and Solomon's YHWH cult. In how far this connection in fact existed is something we cannot explore here, though we do not rule it out.

The chronicler, as is explicitly stated in 1 Kgs. 3:5, again has in mind a dream in the night (also Josephus, *Ant.* VIII §125). But in our verse nothing is said about this. In what the comparison with the appearance at Gibeon in fact consisted remains unresolved, unless one would explain it with the aid of motifs from the ancient Near East. Kapelrud cites parallels in Ugar. and Mesopotamian sources, partly of a mythical and partly of a historical nature, in which certain fixed motifs occur which are also said to be applicable to our verses.[2] In conclusion, let it be noted that LXX^B leaves אליך untranslated.

9:3 *YHWH said to him: 'I have heard the prayer and the plea which you have made before me. I have consecrated this house which you have built in order to establish my name there forever; my eyes as well as my heart will always be present there.*
In this verse one encounters a reaction on the part of YHWH to the dedication of the temple. Textcritically it can be noted that LXX^B refers to the 'voice' of the prayer; and in LXX, between לפני and לקדשתי, there is the addition: '(Behold) I have acted completely in accordance with your prayer,' an addition which is also accepted by Thenius, Klostermann, and Oort, among others. The par. 2 Chr. 7:12-16 is even more generous in its additions because here YHWH expressly responds to various elements of Solomon's prayer as it is given in 2 Chr. 6. A third textcritical comment concerns words near the end of our verse, where LXX translates ולבי שם as though the MT read: שם עולם ולבי. None of these deviations from MT in LXX prompt us to make serious changes in the former.

For the words תפלה, 'prayer,' and תחנה, 'plea,' 'entreaty,' see comments on 8:28; for התחנה, see comments on 8:33. Of the 44x it occurs in this modification in OT, the hiph. of קדש is found, in Kings, only again in vs. 7 and 2 Kgs. 12:19 (cf. comments on 8:64, where the verb is found in the pi.-form). In our

---

[2] A. Kapelrud, "Temple Building, a Task for Gods and Kings," *Or* 32 (1963), 56-62; see also the reaction to this position from S. Rummel, *RSP*, III, 277-284; esp. 279.

verse the verb means 'to consecrate,' 'to describe as sanctified (consecrated),' 'to cause to be holy' (cf. W. Staerk, *ZAW* 55 [1937], 27F.). YHWH indicates that he has made the sanctuary built by Solomon his own sanctuary (Jenni, *Piel*, 59f.). In this connection Pedersen, III-IV, 276, comments that formerly people could freely come to draw their strength from the temple but that henceforth people were no longer allowed simply to approach the temple because the power of its holiness was too great. Here the verb indicates that YHWH has really accepted this sanctuary as his own legitimate sanctuary. The pf. of the verb is directed toward the future (König §367y, Burney, et al.). Noth views the pf. as a pf. of coincidence, in which case the pronouncement and the performance of the act coincide (BrSynt. §41d).

Did Solomon build the temple 'to put my name there' (also in 11:36; 14:21; 2 Kgs. 21:4, 7)? This expression differs somewhat from the more usual dtr. expression: לשכן שמי שם, 'to let his name dwell there' (Deut. 12:11; 14:23; etc., see Burney). Our expression occurs only in Deut. 12:5, 21; 14:24. Ehrlich (also Thenius et al.) is of the opinion that in our verse the expression is not dependent on בנתה but on הקדשתי, with a reference to vs. 7. Pedersen, I-II, 245, on the other hand, takes the other position, with reference to 3:2; 5:17, 19 and 8:17, 20, 29, where there is mention of 'building a house for the name of YHWH.' Grammatically both proposals are possible, and commentators as well as translations are divided, though there is a clear preference for the position which Ehrlich et al. take. One could say that the intention of Solomon is realized by the consecration of the temple on the part of YHWH, so that in the end both aspects coincide. In the text itself there is a clear caesura (*atnaḥ*) between this expression and the sequel (vs. 3b), so that Hentschel's translation, for example, which starts an entire new line after בנתה ('Meinen Namen werde ich für immer hierher legen, meine Augen und mein Herz werden allezeit hier weilen') seems hardly warranted.

The second half of our verse is a response to 8:29 and 52 (Burney, Noth et al.) and contains a divine promise. In the dtr. literature 'all the days' often occurs in parallelism with 'forever' (examples in Burney). Thenius here (and in Prov. 23:7) takes the word לב to mean *bona voluntas*. According to Von Meyenfeldt, *Het hart*, 35, he will devote to the temple not merely the observation of the eyes but the actual attention of the heart (for לב also cf. comments on 3:9).

9:4 *For your part, if you walk before me with integrity of heart and uprightness, as David your father did, acting according to all that I have commanded you, and observing my statutes and ordinances,*
In this and the following verse we encounter the conditional promises which are not only dtr. in their wording but strongly resemble what had already been at stake in the preceding verses (for אם תלך לפני and for 'observing my

statutes and ordinances,' cf. comments on 2:4). David had been presented before as one who genuinely walked before YHWH's face (cf. comments on 3:14 above). The word תם, 'perfection,' 'purity,' aside from here, occurs in Kings also in 22:34. In all, the word occurs 23x as noun in this form in OT, and is associated with the verb תמם, 'to be complete, perfect' (K. Koch, *THAT*, II, 1045-1051; B. Kedar-Kopfstein, *TWAT*, VIII, 688-701; cf. comments on 6:22 above). Linked with לבב we also find the expression in Gen. 20:5f.; Ps. 78:72 and 101:2. Pedersen, I-II, 336; cf. 337 and n. 2, takes the word to mean 'innocence,' 'when by that it is understood that no secondary wills have their seat in the soul so as to counteract the main will in which its contents centre.' A related word is ישׁר, 'uprightness' which occurs 14x in this form in OT (G. Liedke, *THAT*, I, 791). In Kings this is the only place. The verb ישׁר, 'to be right,' occurs in qal in Kings also in vs. 12; in pu. we encountered it in 6:35. More frequent is the occurrence of the adjective יָשָׁר (see comments on 1 Kgs. 11:33; also cf. Y. Avishur, UF 8 [1976], 7f. and comments on 3:6 above).

In LXX[B, Luc.] 'all that was commanded' is not viewed as addressed to Solomon ('you') but to David ('him'), but that could be based on a later correction (Burney). LXX is supported by Pesh., Vulg., and the par. 2 Chr. 7:17 when it reads the copula ו before חקי. This seems more correct (so, inter al., Delitzsch, *LSF* §144) than simply omitting the whole (so Stade-Schwally). Asyndetic connections, for that matter, are not unusual.

9:5 *I will establish the throne of your royal rule over Israel forever, as I promised your father David with the words: 'There shall not fail you a man on the throne of Israel.'*
If the condition stated in the previous verse is met, then YHWH's promise of a longlasting royal dynasty will be fulfilled. Here, too, there is linkage with what has been said in 2:2f.; 8:25 (and 2 Sam. 7).

The word ממלכה, 'kingdom,' already occurred in 2:46 and 5:1. In combination with כסא we find it in Deut. 17:18; 2 Sam. 7:13; 2 Chr. 23:20 (cf. Hag. 2:22; see also comment on 1:46 above; Burney). Instead of 'over Israel' LXX[Luc.] reads 'in Jerusalem.' In the reference to 'the throne of Israel' Noth sees a material interpretation of 2 Sam. 7, but thinks that the dtr. here, as also in 2:4; 8:20, 25, may have in mind the Davidic-Solomonic dynasty in general. In any case – this much can be granted Noth – the dtr. author is looking beyond the temporary boundaries of the northern state of Israel.

One finds the word at one time addressed to David in 2:4. Many Hebr. MSS – along with the suggestions of the ancient versions – read אל in place of על, which some commentators accept (Mont.-Gehman; textcr. app. *BHS*). In place of דברתי על־דוד 2 Chr. 7:18 reads כרתי לדוד, evidently referring to an act of covenant-making. Nevertheless there is no reason to deviate from MT if one translates the preposition by 'with regard to' (Burney). Another divergence of our verse in MT from the par. 2 Chr. 7:18 concerns the words מעל כסא. In 2 Chronicles one reads instead the words מושל ב(ישראל) (cf. Mic. 5:1), which agrees with the LXX translation of our verse: 'ruling in (Israel)>' Goettsberger is of the opinion that this translation is 'der messianischen Weissagung von Mic. 5, 1 angeglichen.'

9:6 *But if you and your children presumptuously turn away from following me and do not observe my commandments and my statutes which I have given you but go off to serve other gods and worship them,*
From this verse on the reverse of the salvific promise comes to the fore. It is striking that now there is a jump from the sing. to the pl. (the arguments adduced by Ehrlich for reading the sing. here too – after emendation – are not convincing). Again there is a conditional statement of the things that may lead to disastrous consequences. The root cause of (future) disasters is the departure, the turning away, from following after YHWH. Whereas the verb שוב was used in 8:33, 35, 47f. for indicating a 'return' to YHWH, it is now used to underscore the 'turning away' from him (cf. Num. 14:43; 32:15; Josh. 22:16, 18, 23, 29; etc.). The paranomastic use of the verb (inf. abs. with a form of the finite verb; in the par. 2 Chr. 7:19 only the finite verb is used) only underscores the seriousness of it (for the form cf. Hoftijzer, *Nun Paragogicum*, 33ff.). Again, the par. 2 Chr. 7:19 and the ancient versions have a ו preceding the אם (in the case of חקתי one finds something similar). But our pericope is typically marked by asyndetic connections. Precisely whom the author has in mind with the phrase 'you and your children' (the latter are not mentioned in 2 Chr. 7:19) is not stated but in the framework of this dtr. passage it is certainly imperative to think of the royal dynasty. The sin of 'not keeping the commandments and statutes of YHWH' is understood in 2 Chr. 7:19 as a 'turning away' from them or a 'forsaking' of them. The difference here is not material but gradual.

It is remarkable that LXX departs from MT in identifying the giver of the laws and statutes. In MT this is YHWH (cf. Jer. 9:12; 26:4; 44:10); in LXX it is Moses. The latter must rather be viewed as an expansion made by the author (so, correctly, Stade-Schwally) than as a legitimate translation of the original text (cf. inter alia Böttcher, *Neue Aehrenlese*; Thenius). The failure to keep the commandments and statutes results in 'following and serving other gods.' 'Serving other gods' is a frequently occurring expression (Deut. 7:4; 13:7, 14; 28:36; etc.; see Burney; for עבד in OT cf. the study by Riesener; further C. Westermann, *THAT*, II, 182-200; esp. 195-199; and H. Ringgren, *TWAT*, V, 988-994). Frequently, in connection with the verb עבד, other verbs occur, like הלך, which can refer to festive cultic processions (Riesener, 207) and the hišta'fal of חוה, 'to bow down' (see comments on 1:16 above). 'Serving,' accordingly, clearly has cultic significance.

9:7 *I will cut off Israel from the land that I have given them and abandon the house which I have consecrated for my name, so that Israel will become a proverb and a byword among all peoples;*
This verse ties in, as a threat, with the condition of the previous verse: forsaking YHWH will cost Israel both their land and their temple. Textcritically it is to be noted that, in the interest of clarity, LXX refers to 'this house,' and is supported in this by a Hebr. MS (Kennicott) and the par. 2 Chr. 7:20. Since the addition of the demonstrative pronoun is more probable than its omission, MT needs to be followed. A second textcritical question concerns אשלח which in 2 Chr. 7:20 is reproduced as אשליך. The latter reading seems to be supported by LXX (ἀπορίψω), Vulg. (*proiciam*) and Tg. (ארחיק), while Pesh. has a form of the stem 'qr, 'to eradicate,' 'to pull up.' In meaning Pesh. supports our MT more than LXX (Berlinger). The verb שלח which, both in qal and in pi., occurs numerous times in OT (and also repeatedly in Kings) in the sense of 'to send,' 'to let go' (cf. M. Delcor, E. Jenni, *THAT*, II, 909-916), is also found in Jer. 15:1 in approximately this form (with מעל־פני [Burney]), so that there is no need for textual emendation.

Just as in 8:34, upon forgiveness on the part of YHWH, Israel could again return to the land (to be cultivated and rebuilt), so here we have the threat of expulsion from this cultivated land. We earlier encountered the verb כרת in qal, 'to cut (off)' 'to make (a covenant),' several times (5:20, 26; 8:9, 21); here it occurs in the hiph.-modification in the sense of 'to eradicate' (similarly in 11:16, 14:10, 14; 18:4f.; 21:21; 2 Kgs. 9:8; cf. E. Kutsch, *THAT*, I, 857-860; G.F. Hasel, *TWAT*, IV, 355-367).

In connection with the destruction of the temple there is a reminder of its earlier consecration to the name of YHWH (cf. vs. 3). Since both the expulsion of Israel from its land and the destruction of the temple are events which immediately preceded the exile or were the result of it, this section was clearly recorded after these events.

As a result of these disasters Israel will become an object of ridicule to its enemies. This fact is indicated by the words משל and שנינה, which are found, aside form the par. text in Chr., also in Deut. 28:37 and Jer. 24:9. In 5:12 the word משל was already used in Kings, but then in the positive sense as 'proverb'; here the idea is negative and denigrating: 'a word of ridicule' (cf. König, *Stil.*, 82). The word שנינה only occurs here, parallel to the firstmentioned word, and in the 3 places referred to. The word is connected with the root שנן, 'to sharpen' and means 'sharp ridicule,' 'word of ridicule' (*HAL*, 1483; B. Kedar-Kopfstein, *ZAH* 1 [1988], 150f.). Finally, it may be noted that LXX in its 'rendering' of משל has the word ἀφανισμός, 'disappearance,' 'destruction,' which in LXX is frequently a version of the Hebr. word שמה, 'horror,' that which is 'dreadful' (cf. F. Hauck, *TDNT*, V, 747, n. 14). It is possible that (just as in Ezek. 14:8) LXX misread MT (so also Stade-Schwally).

9:8 *and this house will be a heap of ruins. Everyone passing by will shudder and whistle and they will say: "why has YHWH treated this country and this house like this?"*

The deplorable situation in which the temple will be – and actually already is when the author writes these words – is described in this verse. In this connection it is important to determine the meaning of עליון which also occurs in the par. 2 Chr. 7:21. The word, which in Kings also occurs in 2 Kgs. 15:35, and 18:17, means 'uppermost,' aside from the meaning 'most high' as epithet with (or without) אל (Gen. 14:18ff., 20; Num. 24:16; etc. esp [21x] in the Psalms). Now there are (at least) 2 possibilities (in any case if one does not make a virtue out of necessity and translate the word, for instance, by *ablatio* as Münster did): either the text is intact up to and including this word, but then requires completion (which in the present text has been omitted; so, already, Rashi) to explain the following בהה, or one has to regard עליון as a mistaken rendering of, for instance, עיין, 'heaps of ruins' (Mic. 3:12), a plural form of עי, which occurs, in the sing. as well as in the pl., 6x in OT (Jer. 26:19; Mic. 1:6; 3:12; Ps. 79:1; Job 30:24). It needs to be pointed out that the par. 2 Chr. 7:21 has the same word as our verse but in place of יהיה writes אשר היה, by which the temporal aspect is changed from a future to a perfect. But even then one badly misses a clause in which it is said that the temple has become a ruin. Nor does the translation of the Vulg.: *domus haec erit in exemplum* solve anything (as Amama already very correctly noted), anymore than, for example, the translation of Keil: 'Strafexempel,' adding the explanation: 'weil der Tempel auf einem hohen Berge stand, so daß seine Ruine allen Vorüberziehenden in die Augen fallen mußte' (cf. also Ehrlich, who reads עליון in relation to the abuse threatened in the preceding vs). In this connection Keil even refers to Deut. 26:19 and 28:1 (Keil's view, for that matter, does have some support in the Mechilta; see Barthélemy). Thenius rightly rejects this negative and farfetched translation and explanation of our word, and proposes the reading: והבית הזה אשר היה עליון יהיה לעיין (a reading supported, among others, by Noth). For this reading he can appeal to Tg. ('this house, which was high, will be destroyed'), but not to Böttcher, *Neue Aehrenlese*, who rejects the 'Nothbehelf' of the chronicler and, instead of עיין, prefers עיון, 'little heap of rubble,' analogous to ציון, 'memorial,' or 'monument' (2 Kgs. 23:17). But there is an even simpler solution, as Pesh. shows: 'this house will be destroyed' (cf. Vetus Latina: *deserta*). Berlinger is of the opinion that Pesh. views עליון as a euphemism (with reference to Tg. and Pesh. on 2 Chr. 7:21), but there is a possibility that it read לעיים or עיון in its 'Vorlage' and that an early corrector modified the Hebr. text of Kings for the sake of 'euphemism'³ (also LXX supports the [present] reading of MT; for a reconstruction of a possible course of events, cf. also Barthélemy). In any case, both on the basis of logic as well as of indications for it in the history of the text, we think we may emend the word עליון into לעיי(ם)ן (so also Oort; Brockington; Delitzsch, *LSF* §95a; textcr. app. *BHK* and *BHS*; Van Gelderen; Montg.-Gehman; Hentschel; Robinson; *HAL*, s.v.).

The so-called 'Aramaizing' qal-form ישם (Ges-K §67g; Bg. II, §27o) derives from the verb שמם which is found only here in Kings but otherwise occurs frequently in various modifications elsewhere in OT. The 'basic meaning' of the word is 'to be cut off from life' (F. Stolz, *THAT*, II, 970-974, esp. 971; *HAL*, s.v.) and can on the one hand mean 'to lie fallow,' 'to be solitary,' on the other (as in our verse) 'to shudder,' 'to grow rigid (in fear).' The reference is to one of the many forms of effect which a realized curse can bring about in any passerby, even a non-Israelite (cf. also Pedersen, I-II, 458). The immediately following verb שרק occurs much less often in OT (12x) and means 'to whistle' (the impf. cons. of some Hebr. MSS need not be followed). Aside from here, the word occurs in conjunction with שמם, just mentioned above, also in Jer. 19:8; 49:17; 50:13. Curiously enough, in the par. 2 Chr. 7:21 the word is missing. According to Noth, this 'whistling' serves the 'apotropäische Ziel der Abwehr dämonischer Wirkungen.' Though perhaps this original meaning of whistling cannot be ruled out, still the 2 verbs, in this combination, form a fixed alliterative expression used to describe this kind of situation (cf. also König, *Stil.* 287).

The grammatical sing. in the preceding part of the verse (כל־עבר) is continued by a pl. form (ואמרו), a construction that is not unusual in the Hebr. and, in view of the כל, even understandable (König §346i). The import of the word כבה (see comments on 1:6 above) is usually retrospective or 'anaphoric' (see König, *Stil.* 113). It is assumed that every passerby, Israelite or non-Israelite, knows who YHWH is and what he has done. One can find the same idea conveyed in the vss. 8 and 9 back in Deut. 29:23-27 and Jer. 22:8f.; further in Jer. 5:19; 13:22 and 16:10-13.⁴

9:9 *Then people will answer: "Because they have forsaken YHWH, their God, who brought their fathers out of the land of Egypt and because they laid hold on other gods, worshiping and serving them: therefore YHWH has brought all*

---

³ For 'euphemisms' in the OT, cf. F. Bleek, J. Wellhausen, *Einleitung in das Alte Testament*, Berlin 1886⁵, 593-596.

⁴ Also cf. D.E. Skweres, "Das Motiv der Strafgrunderfragung in biblischen und neu-assyrischen Texte," *BZ* NF 14 (1970), 181-197.

this upon them".'

The answer to the question posed by the passersby is given here, and that by non-Israelites who (according to Noth) 'nunmehr dort wohnen und Auskunft geben könnten.' Apparently also foreigners speak knowledgeably ('kundig,' Böttcher, *Neue Aehrenlese*) about Israel's history (for עזב, see comments on 8:16 above; for חזק qal on 2:2; in 1:50; 2:28 and in our verse the verb occurs in hiph. meaning 'lay hold of' or 'cling to'). The 'laying hold of' other gods only occurs in this combination here and in the par. 2 Chr. 7:22.

In place of 'from the land of Egypt' LXX has 'from Egypt, from the house of bondage,' a reminder of a frequently used expression, e.g. Exod. 13:3, 14; 20:2 and many times more both in and outside of the Pentateuch. LXX, however, has no support in other ancient versions and Hebr. MSS. A second comment concerns the fact that the *qᵉre,* for good reason, wants to read וישתחוו in place of the *kᵉtib*. A third textcritical comment relates to the conclusion of our verse, where LXX adds: 'Then Solomon brought Pharaoh's daughter up from the city of David to his own house which he had built for himself in those days,' an item of information we find in MT in vs. 24.

1 KINGS 9:10-28

9:10 *At the end of twenty years Solomon had finished building the two houses, the house of YHWH and the house of the king.*

11 *Hiram, king of Tyre, had supplied Solomon with all the cedar and cypress timber and gold he wanted. Thereupon king Solomon gave to Hiram twenty towns in Galilee.*

12 *Then Hiram came down from Tyre to see the towns which Solomon had given him, but they were not right in his eyes.*

13 *Then he said: 'What kind of towns are these which you have given me, my brother?' To this day they are called 'the land of Cabul.'*

14 *Thereupon Hiram sent the king one hundred and twenty talents of gold.*

15 *This is an account of the forced labour which king Solomon levied for the building of the house of YHWH, his own house, the fortified tower, the wall of Jerusalem, and Hazor, Megiddo, and Gezer.*

16 *Pharaoh, king of Egypt, went up, conquered Gezer and burnt it with fire. He killed the Canaanites who lived in the city and gave it as dowry to his daughter, Solomon's wife.*

17 *Solomon rebuilt Gezer and Lower Beth-Horon;*

18 *and Baalath and Tamar, which lie in the desert inside the country;*

19 *and all the store-cities he owned, the towns for his chariots and for the horses, as well as an assortment of fine things which Solomon took pleasure in building in Jerusalem, in Lebanon, and in all the land in which he ruled.*

20 *All the people who were left of the Amorites, the Hittites, the Perizzites, the Hivites and the Jebusites, and were not (descended) from the children of Israel,*

21 *their children who were left in the land after them, on whom the children of Israel could not enforce the curse of destruction – these Solomon levied as forced labourers, as they are to this day.*

22 *But of the children of Israel Solomon made no one a slave. They were fighting men, his servants, his officers, his chariot commanders and his horsemen.*

23 *These are the officials in charge of the foremen who were over king Solomon's work: five hundred and fifty men supervising the people who did the work.*

24 *But the daughter of Pharaoh went up from the city of David to her own house which he had built for her. Thereafter he (also) built the fortified tower.*

25 *Three times a year Solomon sacrificed burnt offerings, and peace offerings on the altar which he had built for YHWH, burning incense [...] before*

YHWH. *[He completed the house[1]]*.

26 *King Solomon also built a fleet at Ezion Geber which is near Elath in the land of Edom, on the shore of the Sea of Reeds.*

27 *Hiram sent with the fleet his servants, experienced sailors, along with the servants of Solomon:*

28 *They sailed to Ophir and there took on four hundred and twenty talents of gold which they delivered to king Solomon.*

INTRODUCTION

In this section we find – actually up to the end of chap. 10, interrupted only by the somewhat longer narrative of Solomon's encounter with the queen of Sheba (10:1-13) – miscellaneous items of information which, in a sequence and textual condition which sometimes strike us as chaotic, tell of Solomon's wealth, commercial dealings, building enthusiasm, organizational competence and the like. The section up to the end of the chapter begins with a short narrative concerning Hiram's disappointment with Solomon's 'present' (vss. 10-14), and continues with information about the organization of the forced labour services which were designed to give shape to the construction of various divergent projects (vss. 15-25). In this connection it must be noted that each of the vss. 23, 24, and 25 again broaches a separate topic which arises from these building activities. The chapter ends with a statement about a joint fleet expedition sponsored by Solomon and Hiram.

Merely perusing this and the following chapter in translation suffices to show that there is not much unity in composition and style to be discovered. It is consequently difficult to find 'enough evidence for reconstructing the history of redaction' (so, correctly, Long). All items are arranged under the heading of 'the wealth and prestige of Solomon' (Noth). It is not impossible, indeed it is probable, that also in these summaries we encounter notes from public annals as well as from narrative cycles concerning Solomon, just as this was the case in chaps. 4-7. We may assume that a (final) redactor ordered and united all the material, but it is not certain if he was a dtr. or a post-dtr. redactor. For Noth is right in saying that there are almost no traces of a dtr. redaction to be found in this and the following chapter.

The section 9:10-28 has its parallel in 2 Chr. 8 in which, as usual, both items missing and items added can be found, as well as frequently occurring deviations and expansions.

Special attention is due to LXX, which also here (as in chaps. 4ff.) displays a

---

[1] Alternative translation: *he also used to pay (his vows)*.

sequence in chaps. 9 and 10 which differs from that of MT. The sequence of LXX vis-à-vis MT (reproduced in outline) is as follows: (9b = MT 24a;) 10-14, 26-28; 10:1-22; 9:15, 17b-22; 10:23-25; 26; 5:1a; 10:27-29. In LXX's additions to MT 2:35 and 2:46 we already encountered texts which proved to be translations of verses from MT of our chaps. 9 and 10 (35f-g = MT 9:24f.; 35i-k = MT 10:23ff.; 46d = MT 9:18; 46i-k = MT 10:29f.). We need not pause for long to consider the principle which LXX followed in creating this sequence. It will suffice to refer (inter alia) to the studies of Gooding, who thinks that the LXX translators were guided by a (pedantic) tendency toward 'timetabling' (esp. 1969, 449-463, in which especially our chapters come up for discussion).

EXEGESIS

9:10 *At the end of twenty years Solomon had finished building the two houses, the house of YHWH and the house of the king.*
In the vss. 10-14 Hiram's indemnification by Solomon is dealt with as well as Hiram's reaction to it. Our verse is a kind of introductory time-delimitation to what follows. One could (with Thenius) view our verse as a protasis, vs. 11a as a parenthesis, and vs. 11b as perhaps an apodosis, though it begins with the particle את, which often serves elsewhere as the start of a new sentence (cf. Mulder 1991). The overall style of these verses is rather uneven and artificial.

The beginning of our verse immediately presents some textcritical difficulty. ויהי מקצה is lacking in LXX, but קצה, 'end,' 'edge,' preceded by the prep. מן (cf. BrSynt. §111e; Meyer §87.3a), as a term of time-delimitation ('at the end of,' 'upon the expiration of'), often occurs in OT (further, in Kings, also in 2 Kgs. 8:3; 18:10; *HAL*, 1047; König §416g). It is not immediately necessary, therefore (with Klostermann; Kamphausen; Delitzsch, *LSF* §3a; Benzinger; Ehrlich; textcr. app. of *BHK* and a Hebr. MS of Kennicott) to alter the text to read מקץ העשרים.

In our verse the numbers of 6:38 and 7:1 have been added up, which yields 20 years of building (cf. 2 Chr. 8:1). Noth is of the opinion that by the mention of the 20 years the entire period of Solomon's reign (11:42) can be split into 2 equal halves (without reference to 6:1, 37), so that a dtr. redactor could divide Solomon's reign precisely into a positive and a negative half. Josephus, *Ant.* VIII §130ff., similarly mentions these numbers but, in line with the rabbinical formation of legends (Ginzberg, *Legends*, IV, 155), he stresses the fact that the temple was built with greater zeal and with more miraculous assistance on the part of YHWH than Solomon's palace. The materials used in building the latter, he wrote, were not of the same quality and value as those used for the temple.

9:11 *Hiram, king of Tyre, had supplied Solomon with all the cedar and cypress timber and gold he wanted. Thereupon king Solomon gave to Hiram twenty towns in Galilee.*
This verse has 2 distinct parts, the first of which, a kind of parenthesis, reminds the reader of what the Tyrian king Hiram did for his Israelite colleague in the building of a palace and a temple, while the second indicates what Solomon had in store for Hiram.

We already encountered Hiram, whose name is variously spelled both in the Hebr. and in the translations earlier (in 5:15-32), where there was also mention of his good relations with Solomon. There exists a close connection between the first half of our verse and 5:24, because in these places we read what is materially and often also literally the same information. The only difference is that in our verse 'gold' is added to the other products which Hiram sent Solomon. Kuan suspects that זהב must have been added here because of its mention in chap. 6 in connection with the temple furnishings (also cf. Ehrlich).[2] The fact that our verse is dependent on 5:24 is clear (otherwise: Ehrlich). It is also clear that in this connection one can raise the question whether Solomon's present, viz. the 20 towns, is directly related to Solomon's building activities. We will treat this question further at the end of our discussion of this verse.

The pi.-form of the verb נשא – in pi. only here in the books of Kings – is a 'mixed form' of the verbs ל"ה and ל"א (Böttcher §1083.11; Olsh. §246b; Bg. II §29b; Ges-K §75oo) and means 'to bear,' 'to support (with = ב)' (*HAL*, 686a; Ehrlich, however, thinks that נשא is a qal-form with the prep. את). Montg.-Gehman assume a switch with the root נשא (with *šin*) 'to lend,' but that is not necessary. Cf. comments on 5:13 for 'cedar' and for 'cypress tree' the comments on 5:22.

It is sometimes suspected that the particle אז is an indication of the beginning of the original report, so that what precedes it in vss. 10 and 11 is to be regarded as 'sekundäre Einleitung' (Noth[3]). In any case it is the intent of the redactor of this pericope to link Solomon's gift with Hiram's generosity and the building activities for palace and temple. This gift consisted of 20 towns in the 'land of Galilee.'

הגליל occurs in OT as location also in Josh. 20:7; 21:32; 2 Kgs. 15:29; Isa. 8:23 (גליל הגוים) and 1 Chr. 6:61. The meaning of the Hebr. word is 'district,' 'region' (also cf. גלילה in Josh. 13:2; 22:10f.; Ezek. 47:8; Joel 4:4; *HAL*,

---

[2] J.K. Kuan, "Third Kingdoms 5.1 and Israelite-Tyrian Relations during the Reign of Solomon," *JSOT* 46 (1990), 31-46, esp. 38.

[3] Cf. H. Donner, "Israel und Tyrus im Zeitalter Davids und Salomos," *JNSL* 10 (1982), 43-52, esp. 45.

185f.). As its version of our word LXX has Γαλειλαία, similarly in Josh. 12:23 גלִיל, 2 Chr. 15:29; Isa. 33:9 (בָּשָׁן); Ezek. 47:8; Joel 4:4 as well as in the verse which follows our verse. This term is further found in Jud. 1:8; 15:5(6); Tob. 1:2, 5; 1 Macc. 5:14-23, 55; 10:30; 11:63; 12:47, 49. Roughly speaking, one can describe Galilee geographically as the mountainous region N of the present road from Zephath to Acco on the Mediterranean Sea, running parallel to the coastal strip along the Mediterranean. To the N it borders on the S side of the Lebanon, from which it is separated by the Litanni river. On the E side the Jordan valley plus the former lake Huleh and the present Lake of Tiberias forms a geographical line of separation. On the S side this region passes into the valley of Jezreel. According to Isa. 8:23, the tribal areas of Zebulon and Naphtali at one time belonged to Galilee (cf. Simons, *GTTOT* §§84f.). According to Eusebius, *Onom.* 72, 18f., a distinction is to be made between 'two Galilees,' within the borders of which the abovementioned tribal areas are located. But geographical boundaries are not yet political boundaries. This is also clear from our verse, where we are told that Solomon relinquishes 20 towns from this region to Hiram (according to Ehrlich, the number 20 suggests that Solomon gave Hiram a town for each of the 20 years of Hiram's assistance). The following verse makes clear that these were towns in the Cabul region.

It deserves notice that the par. section of 2 Chr. 8:2 does not have Solomon giving these towns to Hiram but the reverse: Hiram giving them to Solomon. Some exegetes, like Keil and Van Gelderen, have tried to harmonize these data by assuming that Hiram, after disapproving of these towns, returned them to Solomon, but this attempt at resolving a contradiction is far from convincing. Šanda is of the opinion that Solomon mortgaged these towns to Hiram until, after the sea voyage to Ophir, he could pay back the money he had borrowed. It seems clear, however, that the chronicler found such bartering away of what he regarded as Israelite land intolerable. There could well be something else going on here. Donner has pointed out that 'die Territorialtransaktion bereits relativ früh in Salomos Regierungszeit stattfand' (art. cit., 45), and that this was no 'Ruhmesblatt der salomonischen Außenpolitik.' In addition, Hiram's activities in the building of the temple and his trade in the southern regions (vss. 26ff.) betray a certain dependence of Solomon on Tyre. There is a further element here, which we ignored in our comments on 5:15 as more or less irrelevant to MT, viz. the fact that LXX has Hiram send his servants to Hiram 'in order to anoint Solomon in the place of David.' Kuan combines this item, which in his eyes is crucial, with that of our verses and 9:26ff.; 10:11, 22, to underscore Tyrian supremacy over David and Solomon. According to him, there was no such thing as a treaty between Hiram and Solomon as between equals; it must, on the contrary, be considered probable that during Solomon's reign Israel was subject to Tyre: 'Attempts to describe the Solomonic monarchy in terms of Solomonic empire are therefore not only an exaggeration of its international standing but a distortion' (art. cit., 41). Whether this sharp verdict altogether is fairly based on the texts cited, with LXX 5:15 even playing a key role, is doubtful. Certainly it is the case that the tendency we already encountered in the preceding chapters of MT, viz. the aggrandizement of Solomon, is continued in these chapters. But criticism, too, can be read between the lines, at least in the books of Kings. Granted, also the redactor of our book attempts to make an artificial separation between the positive and the negative side of Solomon's reign and activities, so that, strictly speaking, the 'payment' of 20 towns need not be viewed as compensation for services rendered but rather as the loss of territory during a 'neighbour's quarrel' which may have occurred at any time during Solomon's reign.

9:12 *Then Hiram came down from Tyre to see the towns which Solomon had given him, but they were not right in his eyes.*
In this verse we find mention of Hiram's tour of inspection to the region Solomon had ceded to him. LXX adds, redundantly, that Hiram went to Galilee. The result of this inspection is that the towns were not found to be in order, a fact indicated by the use of the verb ישר, a substantive form of which we encountered in vs. 4. In the qal-modification the verb occurs only here in Kings (for the pu.-form, cf. comments on 6:35).

9:13 *Then he said: 'What kind of towns are these which you have given me, my brother?' To this day they are called 'the land of Cabul.'*
Inspection of the towns leaves Hiram disappointed. At the same time we are more precisely told where the towns are located: in the region of Cabul.

Hiram airs his disappointment in a question directly addressed to Solomon, in which he calls him 'my brother' (cf. 20:32; further 1 Macc. 10:18; 11:20; 2 Macc. 11:22). In the ancient Near East such a title was frequently used between rulers of equal status (for examples, aside from several Amarna letters, cf. also the diplomatic contact between Egypt and Cyprus: Mettinger, *King*, 227; Pedersen, I-II, 59).[4]

Hiram's dissatisfaction, which is not explained further, comes to expression in the name he gives to the 20 towns. It is a question whether the 3rd p. sing. in ויקרא refers to Hiram or more generally to 'people' (BrSynt. §36d). With Noth et al. we opt for the latter possibility. Another grammatical question is posed by להם which here goes back to a fem. pl. But this occurs more frequently in Hebr. (see König §§14, 248b, n. 4; Ges-K §135o; Montg.-Gehman).

---

[4] Cf. also Y.L. Holmes, in *Orient and Occident* (Fs C.H. Gordon, ed. H.A. Hoffner; AOAT 22), Neukirchen-Vluyn 1973, 97.

It is evident that we are dealing in this verse with a popular etiological explanation for the name of the place, which is finally given: ארץ כבול, 'the land of Cabul.' LXX here reads 'Ορ(ε)ιον, 'boundary,' possibly a translation of the Hebr. גבול. Josephus, *Ant.* VIII §142, speaks of the land 'Chabalon' (Χαβαλών χῆ), adding: 'for "chabalon," translated from the Phoenician, means "not pleasing"' (see also Eusebius, *Onom.* 174, 13: χωα ὅριον 'Ασηρ). In one of the various translations in the rabbinical tradition (BT Sabb. 54a, Rashi, Redak) the name is explained as 'a land of fetters,' i.e. as quicksand in which one's feet get stuck as though in fetters: 'infertile land.' More modern is the 'witty play of words' thesis which many scholars have adopted: כ + בל, 'as nothing' (Thenius; Burney; et al.; cf. Böttcher, *Neue Aehrenlese*, 'wie ein Klotz, Klumpen [cf. Isa. 44:19]'). Cheyne, *CB*, has still another proposal: he thinks that the name may be popularly associated with a verb גלב, 'to shave,' and that a 'shorn land' could mean treeless land. The region's lack of trees is thought to have displeased Hiram! Worthy of mention is also the view of C.H. Gordon, *IDBS*, 969), who thinks that in this word we are perhaps dealing with a so-called 'Atbash.' 'Atbash' means that the first letter of the alphabet is replaced by the last, the second by the second to the last, etc. One encounters this word game especially in the later rabbinical literature as one of the hermeneutic rules, but scholars believe they find indications of it also in OT (Jer. 25:26; 51:41). In our case, כבול would have to be read as לשפך, 'worthless land,' but this suggestion seems improbable (also cf. Katzenstein, *Tyre*, 104, n. 49).

Right up until the present people still identify a town by the name of *Kabul* approx. 15 km SE of Acco-Ptolemaïs (Simons, *GTTOT* §§826 and 874 [p. 352]). In Josh. 19:27 there is mention of a place named 'Cabul' as belonging to the tribe of Asher (R. Frankl, *ABD*, I, 797). And Josephus (e.g. *Vita* §§213; 227; 234) refers to Χαβωλω, a town on the border near Ptolemais, 40 stadia from Jotapata (cf. *Bell.* III §38[5]). In our discussion of the so-called ninth district of Solomon in 4:16 we already discovered the difficulty of determining, even roughly, the boundaries of this district. It did become clear that the territory of Asher belonged to this district but the precise location of the W boundary remains obscure. It is likely that most of the time the coastal strip was Tyrian or Phoenician. It is, of course, possible that Asher penetrated Tyrian territory (so Abel, *GP*, I, 257), but the reverse cannot be ruled out either. In any case it seems safe to say that the reference is to a number of towns in the region of and around Cabul, hence the SW part of Lower-Galilee, an area of which the Carmel mountain range formed approximately the S

---

[5] See also the explanation of A. Schalit, *Namenwörterbuch zu Flavius Josephus*, Leiden 1968, 48.

border. It is obvious, surely, that Solomon did not give Hiram an enclave inside Israelite territory (Katzenstein, *Tyre*, 105). Donner, art. cit., 45f., offers support for this theory and calls attention to the fact that Phoen. interests possessed ancient rights to this area. From ancient times there were located here not Israelite but Canaanite towns which Solomon could relinquish more readily than Israelite settlements in order to receive financial support for his building policies in exchange. It is likely that the name 'Cabul' had been around for ages but that a popular etiology had played a game with it, linking it to the aversion with which Hiram is said to have accepted these towns.[6]

Here, again (as in 8:8 above), there is mention of 'to this day.'

9:14 *Thereupon Hiram sent the king one hundred and twenty talents of gold.*
This verse is isolated (also in MT where a פ has been placed between vs. 13 and vs. 14) from the immediately preceding passages, inasmuch as it is improbable that Hiram paid, or at least loaned out, so much gold for so little that was of value to him. It is impossible to assume, after all, that Hiram would have given away – שלה can not have this meaning – this gold for no reason at all. LXX[A, B], for that matter, reads ἤνεγκεν (aorist 1 of the verb φέρειν), which in LXX is frequently used to translate the hiph. of בוא (also cf. Rahlfs, *SSt.* III, 247).

Noth links our verse with vs. 11b and explains this thus: Solomon did not give the 20 towns to Hiram for reasons of friendship but ceded them to Hiram to get money, since his treasury was hopelessly depleted. The latter point is almost certain to be true. Solomon had focused so heavily on his domestic politics – which absorbed fortunes – that he had neglected foreign relations, to which his father David had been more attentive. Ultimately not only Damascus in Syria (11:23ff.) and Edom (11:14-22) but also the Tyrians profited from this weakness.

120 talents of gold is a very hefty amount. Earlier, in 7:46, we already encountered the word ככר in the sense of 'neighbourhood.' The word may denote a disk-shaped round loaf of bread (Exod. 29:33; 1 Sam. 2:36; etc.), but also, therefore, a 'disk' of silver or gold as a unit of weight or value (BRL[1], 174-179; H. Weippert, BRL[2], 88ff.; Benzinger, *Arch.* 197-204; De Vaux, *Inst.* I, 309-313; it is translated in LXX by τίλαντον and in Vulg. by *talentum*). One can put a talent at 3,000 shekels (Exod. 38:25f.) or 60,000 *gera* (Lev.

---

[6] See now also Z. Gal, "Khirbet Roš Zayit-biblical Cabul, a Historical-Geographical Case," *BA* 53 (1990), 88-97; "Cabul-A Royal Gift Found," *BARev* 19/2 (1993) 38-44, 84; "A Kernos from Horvat Rosh Zayit in Lower Galilee," *Qad* 23 (1990) 51-52.

27:25; Num. 3:47; 18:16; Ezek. 45:12), 'grain,' the smallest coin unit (cf. Barrois, II, 253-258). But number and value can vary in each era. A talent of gold can be estimated at 35-40 kg, so that the total amount could end up being from 4,200-4,800 kg of gold – an amount that was not only prodigious for that time! Also in 10:10, 16f. we encounter enormous amounts, figures which have frequently prompted the suspicion that on this point Solomon's 'golden' riches have been grossly exaggerated. Millard, however, has called attention to the very large amounts in booty reported also by Assyrian kings like Tiglath-Pileser III, Sargon II, and an Egyptian king like Thut-mose III (cf. e.g. *ANET*, 282b, where there is mention of 150 talents of gold given as tribute by Tyre to Tiglath-Pileser).[7] In any case, if there was exaggeration, it was not peculiar to a particular period or ruler.

INTRODUCTION TO VSS. 15-23

As Mont.-Gehman correctly states, vs. 15a is the introduction to the vss. 20-23, a passage interrupted in the vss. 15b-19 by a list of the cities which were built. LXX[B], the direct translation of which is lacking for the vss. 15-25 MT, has vss. 15, 17b-19, 20-22 for 10:23ff.; vs. 16 for 4:32; vs. 17 for 2:35i and 4:33; vs. 18 for 2:35i and 46d and 23 for 2:35h. Niemann, *Herrschaft*, 19, n. 82, refers to discussions which have recently again ignited concerning what, archaeologically speaking, can be attributed to Solomon in the way of public buildings.[8] It is clear, from a methodological viewpoint, that the comparison of ceramic items found in various places cannot be resolved with a simple ceramic typology, so that the datings are not completely accurate. Dever 1982 offers a fine illustrated overview of architecture in ancient Israel at the time of Israel's first kings, which he dates between approx. 1020-918 BCE.

9:15 *This is an account of the forced labour which king Solomon levied for the building of the house of YHWH, his own house, the fortified tower, the wall of Jerusalem, and Hazor, Megiddo, and Gezer.*
Again, in this verse, there is mention of מס, 'forced labour,' as in 4:6 and 5:27f., introduced by the 'detailing formula': וזה דבר (cf. Deut. 15:2; 19:4; Josh. 5:4; 1 Kgs. 11:27; etc.; see Z. Talshir, *Tarbiz* 51 [1981f.], 23-35). Instead of the more customary φόρος for 'forced labour' or 'payment of tribute' (cf.

---

[7] A.R. Millard, "Does the Bible Exaggerate King Solomon's Golden Wealth?,"*BARev* 15/3 (1989), 20-34; esp. 31.
[8] See, G.J. Wightman, "The Myth of Solomon," *BASOR* 277/278 (1990), 5-22; J. S. Holladay, "Red Slip, Burnish and the Solomonic Gateway at Gezer, ibid., 23-70; and D. Ussishkin, "Notes on Megiddo, Gezer, Ashdod, and Tel Betash in the Tenth to Ninth Centuries," ibid., 71-91.

K. Weiss, *TDNT* IX, 83), LXX has προθομη, 'foraging' but often used, also in LXX, as a translation of the Hebr. word בז, 'booty,' 'plunder.' Though by our modern standards 'forced labour' can be considered virtually identical with the 'plundering' of human freedom, we need not follow LXX's suggestion (cf. also the textcr. app. of *BHK*). Forced labour already came up in 5:27f. in connection with the building of the temple to which the building of the royal palace is linked here. At the same time, probably on the basis of notes in ancient archives, the building of the Millo, the wall of Jerusalem, and even the (re)construction of 3 fairly significant cities is listed in this connection as well.

On the origin, the location, and the character of the so-called 'Millo' there is no agreement among scholars (for an overview cf. Burney; Bussink, 91f.; and esp. Simons, *Jerusalem*, 131-157). Aside from here and in vs. 24, we are also told in 11:27 that Solomon built the Millo. This public building is further mentioned in 2 Sam. 5:9 (par. 1 Chr. 11:8) in the time before David and in 2 Chr. 32:5 in the time of Hezekiah. In 2 Kgs. 12:21 there is reference to the Millo on the way down to Silla, and in Judg. 9:6, 20 to a Beth-millo in or near Shechem. The root of the word מלא means 'to fill (up),' so that scholars often think in this connection of a 'filling,' one or more terraces with a public building erected on top of them (also cf. G. Sauer, *BHHW*, II, 1217). LXX, with its mention of ἄκρα, points in the same direction. Frequently people have thought of it as an (artificially created) fortification, for example, a terracing of an earlier moat in front of the N wall of the ancient city of the Jebusites (Alt, *KS*, III, 308, n. 1) or the filling-up of a *fossa* during the expansion of the city to the north.[9] Steiner proposes, on the basis of an archaeological feature found in Tell el-Hesi, a connection between the Millo and a terrace which had been constructed inside the walls.[10] In general many investigators are agreed that, both in Jerusalem and in other cities referred to here, Solomon sponsored the construction of public buildings and fortifications (so V. Fritz, *ZDPV* 85 [1969], 136-161) and that he also undertook the building of the Millo. Simons thought that the Millo was a component in the defense works of the 'city of David' and represented a particular structure in the walls surrounding the city. In addition, the Millo was built as an exceptionally strong fort at the place where the wall had been broken through. According to him, 2 Sam. 5:9 is a proleptic reference to the place where David began to build (p. 132).[11] Later investigators, however, assume that the terracing on the E slope of the ancient

---

[9] Cf. M. Ottosson, "Fortifikation och Tempel. En studie i Jerusalem Topografi," *Religion och Bibel* 38 (1979), 26-39.

[10] R.C. Steiner, "New Light on the Biblical *Millo* from Hatran Inscriptions," *BASOR* 276 (1989), 15-23. who,

[11] But cf. also M. Görg, "Zur Darstellung Königlicher Baumaßnahmen in Israel und Assur," *BN* 59 (1991) 12-17, esp. 12f..

city of David served a defensive purpose and must be viewed as a 'fill' (see Busink, 92). H. Donner, *BRL*², 160, points out that Solomon extended Jerusalem to the N and NW. The temple eventually came to rest on the *Ḥaram* and, S of the *Ḥaram*, the palace. The area between the S wall of this complex and the N wall of the city of David, the Ophel, was included in the city by the construction of the Millo, while in 11:27b there is the addition that by so doing he had 'closed up the breach of the city of David his father.' In that way the sequence, in our verse, of 'temple, palace, Millo, and wall' makes good sense, says Donner (also cf. K. Galling, *BRL*¹, 300-303).

On the basis of her researches, Kenyon takes the Millo to be terrace constructions on the E side of the city which were ever in danger of sliding down or collapsing.[12] Archaeological investigations have shown that this danger was not imaginary. It is therefore understandable that kings like David, Solomon and Hezekiah did their best, over and over, to restore these constructions or to reinforce them. Still the relation to the more general terrace constructions is not entirely satisfying (so, correctly, Noth in commenting on vs. 24). It is also possible that a stronghold-like fortified tower was designated by the name of Millo.

The reference to the city wall, which – at least in MT – follows the Millo (LXX and Pesh. reverse the order) is vague, but it is probably the wall which Solomon built around the new expansion of the city, hence around the SE and/or SW hill in a N direction (cf. comments on 3:1 above; further, Simons, *Jerusalem*, 242). Josephus, *Ant.* VIII §150, mentions that Solomon believed that the walls of Jerusalem needed towers and other fortifications to enhance the city's security, but also to enhance the dignity of the city! Immediately hereafter, in our verse, follow 3 cities of some importance.

Hazor is the first. The reference is to the city that is mentioned also in Josh. 11:1, 10f., 13; 12:19; 19:36; Judg. 4:2, 17; 1 Sam. 12:9 and 2 Kgs. 15:29. It is situated on the W bank of the Jordan, about 8 km SW of Lake Huleh and 15 km to the N of the Sea of Tiberias, at the foot of the mountains of Galilee, and is to be identified with the hill of ruins, *tell el-Qedah*, also called *tell Waqqas* (LXX here reads Ἀσσοὺρ, cf. Eusebius, *Onom.* 34, 13, who oddly enough adds: 'a city in Judea'; cf. also 90, 9). According to Josh. 11, Hazor was a very important city in the N, in Upper Galilee, certainly before but also still during the 'entry' of the Israelites (cf. V. Fritz, *UF* 5 [1973], 124). In the second millennium before our era the surface area of the city is said to have been the largest in all of Palestine. In 1927 J. Garstang identified the city with the abovementioned *tell* and since then, as a result of a series of successful Israeli excavations and discoveries, the city has become very well known (for

---

[12] K. Kenyon, *Royal Cities of the Old Testament*, London 1971, 35.

an overview of the literature on the archaeological investigations: *HUCA* 42 [1971], 35f.; 52 [1981], 35; 58 [1987], 24f.; also Y. Yadin, *EAEHL*, II, 474-495). Like Megiddo the city was destroyed in the 13th or 12th century BCE and for a long time remained unoccupied until Solomon rebuilt it (Kenyon, op. cit., p. 53). Between 1955 and 1958 and in 1968 Y. Yadin carried out a number of important excavations (Yadin, *IDBS*, 387-391). In stratum X, he found important indications for the reconstruction of the city in the time of Solomon (a casemate wall, for example, and a large gateway with six chambers, which, for that matter, were also found in Megiddo and Gezer[13]; for the acropolis, see the representation in Dever, 274).

Megiddo (*tell el-Mutesellim*), which is situated on the SW rim of the plain of Jezreel, was mentioned already in 4:12 (LXX 2:35i: Μαγαὼ; cf. Eusebius, *Onom.* 132, 20). From 1903-1905 (G. Schumacher), 1908-1910 (G. A. Reisner), then in 1925-1939 (C.S. Fisher, P.L.O. Guy, G. Loud) and, finally, from 1960 on (Yadin) important excavations were carried out here as well, yielding the discovery of public buildings from the days of Solomon (G.W. Van Beek, *IDB*, III, 335-342; Dever 1982, 275, who states that the archaeological investigations have only confirmed that Megiddo was one of the main administrative centers of the Solomonic era; Y. Yadin, *EAEHL*, III, 830-856; idem, *IDBS*, 583ff.; also surveys of the literature in: *HUCA* 42 [1971], 59f.; 52 [1981], 58f.; 58 [1987], 42).

The third city mentioned is Gezer (*tell Ǧazer*; Simons, *GTTOT* §762). It was situated on the coastal strip of the Mediterranean Sea, approx. 15 km SE of Lod (= Lydda) and 8 km SE of Ramleh, somewhat W of the *naḥal Ayyalon,* on the rim of the N Shephelah. The city, which lay on the E boundary of the Philistine region, is mentioned especially in Joshua (10:33; 12:12; 16:3, 10; 21:21), but also in Judg. 1:29; 2 Sam. 5:25 and 1 Chr. 6:52; 7:28; 14:16; and 20:4. As early as 1871 Clermont-Ganneau already identified the city. From 1902-1905 and from 1907-1909 excavations were conducted by R.A.S. Macalister, who published his findings in 1912. More than half a century later, with a brief interruption in 1934 (A. Rowe), the archaeological investigations were continued (1967-1971: Harvard Semitic Museum - Hebrew Union College excavations). Also after that, investigations followed whereupon there was a full discussion of the results (W.G. Dever, *EAEHL*, II, 428-443; idem, *BA* 47 [1984], 206-218; survey of the literature to date: *HUCA* 42 [1971], 30ff.; 52 [1981], 30f.; 58 [1987], 20f.; R.W. Hamilton, *IDB* 2, 388f.; W.G. Dever, *IDBS*, 361ff.). The most striking aspect of all this is that in all 3 cities mentioned similar public buildings were found from the Israelitish period (see the

---

[13] Cf. H. Weippert, *Palästina in vorhellenistischer Zeit* (Handbuch der Archäologie Vorderasiens, II, Bd. 1), München 1988, 428-434.

'casemate-wall' in Hasor above). And as far as Gezer is concerned, Dever, 363, characterizes it as 'a striking confirmation of I Kings 9:15-17, which records an Israelite takeover of the site and its refortification following an Egyptian destruction.'

9:16 *Pharaoh, king of Egypt, went up, conquered Gezer and burnt it with fire. He killed the Canaanites who lived in the city and gave it as dowry to his daughter, Solomon's wife.*
The series of cities which Solomon fortified is now interrupted by a statement about Gezer which one finds in the vss. 16 and 17a. It is going too far to call these verses misplaced (Stade-Schwally) but the statement certainly does not qualify as a glorious page from Solomon's political history (also cf. J. G. McConville, *Bib* 70 [1989], 36f.); for we are told here that an Egyptian pharaoh captured and destroyed by fire the city of Gezer whose inhabitants were Canaanites in order subsequently to give it to Solomon as dowry for his daughter (for the question of the 'dischronologized narrative' at issue in the vss. 15ff.; see W.J. Martin, SVT 17 [1969], 181f.). Albright, *ARI*, 213f. n. 39, was indeed of the opinion that 'Gezer' had to be a corruption of 'Gerar' but this 'corruption' is highly unlikely (McConville, 36, n. 16).

In a sense vs. 16 is a continuation of 3:1. In our comments on this verse we already considered the question which pharaoh was meant here. We mentioned a number of names in that connection without coming to a definite decision. Not long ago Green argued for the choice of pharaoh Siamun, the next-to-the-last king of the 21st Egyptian dynasty.[14] The claim is that his reign was most easily synchronized with that of Solomon. In addition, activities are known of him which fit with what we read in our verse and in 11:14-22. However this may be, along with Green, Noth et al. we are of the opinion that this interpolated notice must be considered historical precisely because it does not add to the glory of Solomon.

It is striking that the pharaoh killed the Canaanites of the city. We would like to know whether there were other inhabitants and to what population group(s) they could have belonged. In any case, while it is possible that in the 12th and 11th century BCE Gezer was inhabited by Canaanites, that does not rule out the presence of 'sojourners' of other ethnic groupings (Israelites; Philistines) (V. Fritz, *BA* 50 [1987], 89).

The word שלחים (a 'plural of intensity,' according to König §261e; an 'Abstract plural,' according to Michel, *Grundlegung*, 88) also occurs in OT in

---

[14] A.R. Green, "Solomon and Siamun: A Synchronism Between Dynastic Israel and the Twenty-First Dynasty of Egypt," *JBL* 97 (1978), 353-367; also cf. A. Malamat, in Ishida, *Studies*, 200f.

Exod. 18:2 and Mic. 1:14. In Exod. 18:2 the word pertains to the 'sending way' of a woman. In Mic. 1:14 it is a 'farewell present' (cf. H.W. Wolff, BK, XIV/4, 32). In our verse, finally, it is a gift which a father sends along to his daughter when she leaves her home and hearth, a 'bridal present' (cf. Ugar.: *tlḥ*, A.F. Rainey, *RSP*, II, iii.2; *HAL*, 1394f.). Pedersen, I-II, 69 and n. 1) sees the gift as a strengthening of the bond between the daughter and her father's house.

9:17 *Solomon rebuilt Gezer and Lower Beth-Horon;*
The first part of this verse again resumes the line of thought with which vs. 1 ended (cf. M. Anbar on 'la reprise,' *VT* 38 [1988], 391). To the cities mentioned in vs. 15 and vs. 17a it now adds 'Lower Beth-Horon' (Josh. 16:3; 18:13f.; 2 Chr. 8:5, a town situated approx. 16 km NW of Jerusalem (for the absence of the article in case of the attributes of proper names: Ges-K §126y [but cf. 2 Chr. 8:5]; and for a masc. attribute in case of a city name combined with בית: König §248c). This city is generally distinguished from 'Upper Beth-Horon' which is situated a few km further to the E on a spur of the Ephraimite mountains (Josh. 16:5; 21:22; 2 Chr. 8:5; also cf. 1 Macc. 3:16, 24; 7:30 and 9:50) (accordingly, the par. 2 Chr. 8:5 mentions both Beth-Horons). The boundary between Ephraim and Benjamin is supposed to have run through or below the 2 cities (cf. Niemann, *Herrschaft*, 118f.). Sometimes one simply reads of 'Beth-Horon' (or of '[Two] Horonim' according to LXX in Josh. 10:10f.; 2 Sam. 13:34), where both places are referred to at once (Josh. 10:10f.; 1 Sam. 13:18; 1 Chr. 6:53; 7:24; 2 Chr. 25:13; cf. Eusebius, *Onom.* 46, 22ff., who also makes a distinction between 2 Beth-Horons: Upper Beth-Horon which is said to have been built by Solomon and Lower Beth-Horon which was given to the Levites to possess). Simons (*GTTOT* §490; cf. Abel, *GP*, II, 274f.) identifies Beth-Horon with *beit 'Ur*; Upper Beth-Horon with *beit 'Ur el-Foqa*, and Lower Beth-Horon with *beit 'Ur et Taḥta*, but this identification is not universally accepted (see J.L. Peterson, *ABD*, I, 688f.). The towns – to the degree there really were two (see Peterson for the opposite viewpoint) – were of strategic importance as the junction of important roads and on either side of a mountain pass.[15] For the time being we must leave unresolved whether the towns were named after a (former) sanctuary (בית) for the deity Horon familiar from Ugar. as well as Egypt. texts (cf. M.H. Pope, W. Röllig, *WbMyth*, I, 288f.).

9:18 *and Baalath and Tamar, which lie in the desert inside the country;*

---

[15] Cf. T. Oelgarte, "Die Bethhoron-Straße," *PJ* 14 (1918), 73-89; W.L. Reed, *IDB*, 1, 393f.; I. Roll, E. Ayalon, "Roman Roads in Western Samaria," *PEQ* 118 (1986), 113-134.

Baalath occurs, aside from in the par. 2 Chr. 8:6, also in Josh. 19:44 (LXX omits this place in our verse). In the lastmentioned text the town is part of the inheritance of Dan, situated in the area around the Philistine city of Ekron. Josephus, *Ant.* VIII §152, localizes the place not far from Beth-Horon. Abel, *GP*, II, 258, indeed makes a distinction between the Baalath of Josh. 19:44 and that of our verse, but immediately adds: 'probablement identique à la précédente.' He localizes the first Baalath on or near 'Mount Baalah' (Josh. 15:11; also cf. R. Greenberg, *ABD*, I, 1955). But Simons, *GTTOT* §336.12, rejecting this identification, simply states that the town is unknown. Rudolph, 218, aside from mentioning a possibility of identification with Josh. 19:44, refers to Baalah (Josh. 15:29) in the S of Judah. S.A. Löwenstam (*EncMiqr.* II, 300f.) calls attention to the order of the cities in Kings and Chronicles. In Kings Baalath, along with the following town of Tamar, should have to be located in the S, whereas in Chronicles, being mentioned after the 2 Beth-Horons, it should rather be found in the area to the N of Jerusalem. For him the opinion of Josephus is decisive, i.e. the identification of Baalath with the place bearing the same name in Josh. 19:44. In our opinion, too, this opinion deserves preference, inasmuch as the addition to the following place ('in the desert') only refers to this town and not to the preceding (also cf. M.C. Astour, D.E. Smith, *RSP*, II, viii.132). Gichon also identifies Baalath with the town of the same name in Josh. 19:44, and associates it with the present-day *el-Morar*, 5 km SE of Javne.[16] On the basis of 1 Chr. 13:6, Niemann, *Herrschaft*, 97, n. 433, identifies Baalath with the name (of a shrine near) Kiriath-Jearim.

In the case of תמר we face a significant $k^e tib$-$q^e re$ question. Are we dealing here with Tamar, a fortress in the S of Judah, or with the well known Tadmor (Palmyra) in the Syrian desert between Homs on the Orontes and Mari on the Euphrates, about 200 km NE of Damascus? LXX$^{Luc.}$, the par. 2 Chr. 8:4, Pesh., Tg., and also Vulg. (Palmyra!) opt simply for the $q^e re$, but also LXX with Ιεθερμαθ can be interpreted as את תמרמר, in which the /r/ is mistakenly written for the /d/ (Burney, cf. Eusebius, *Onom.* 100, 21: Θερμωθ; LXX 2:46d: Thermai). To the Chronicler the idea of Palmyra is not too farfetched, for in 8:3 he reports the conquest of Hamath-Zobah in the vicinity of Palmyra. Rudolph, 219, very correctly notes that the concern here is solely 'zur Erhöhung des Glanzes Salomos' (so already Benzinger). P. Haupt (in Stade-Schwally), despite this, sees an 'etymological connection' between Tadmor and Tamar. The later versions have been blinded by this glitter (but apparently also certain modern scholars, so e.g. C. Hauer, Jr., *JSOT* 18 [1980], 84). Hence the $k^e tib$ of our verse deserves more confidence (so inter al. also Böttcher, *Neue*

---

[16] M. Gichon, "The Defenses of the Salomonic Kingdom," *PEQ* 95 (1963), 113-126.

Aehrenlese, Thenius, Kamphausen, Benzinger).[17]

Also in Ezek. 47:19 and 48:28 Tamar is mentioned as being at the S border of Israel (cf. Num. 34:3ff.). Simons, *GTTOT* §831, who similarly accepts the reading 'Tamar,' for good reason views Tamar as a S counterpart to Hazor in the N. The phrase 'in the steppe,' added to this place, according to him, has the same force as this addition to the place names Beersheba (Gen. 21:14) and Kadesh (Ps. 29:8). That the reference is not to the Syrian desert (where Palmyra is located) but to the Negeb is clear from the following addition: 'inside the country' (viz. Judah of Israel; cf. Hulst, *OTTP*; otherwise: Ehrlich). Even if one were to read the last 2 words as glosses (they are lacking in LXX[x]), they can still be interpreted as indications that identification with Tadmor should be avoided. Pesh. takes these words to mean 'in the steppe land'; cf. Vulg.: *in terra solitudinis.* It has sometimes been suggested that these words should be viewed as a corruption of some place name, but none of these proposals is persuasive (see Burney; Montg.-Gehman). The explanation given by Simons is certainly not implausible.

Further attempts at localizing Tamar have recently yielded 2 proposals (cf. *HAL,* 1617): (1) *'en Ḥusb,* 32 km SW of the S end of the Dead Sea, or (2) עיר התמרים (Judg. 1:16; 3:13: 'City of Palms') = *tell 'en el-Arus,* approx. 10 km SSE of the Dead Sea (Keel, *OLB,* II, 264-270; also cf. Mont.-Gehman, 208; S. Achituv, *EncMiqr.* VIII, 607f.; M.C. Astour, D.E. Smith, *RSP,* II, viii.108; further J.K. Lott, *ABD,* VI, 315f.; Niemann, *Herrschaft,* 97 and n. 434).

9:19 *and all the store-cities he owned, the towns for his chariots and for the horses, as well as an assortment of fine things which Solomon took pleasure in building in Jerusalem, in Lebanon, and in all the land in which he ruled.*

Following the detailed listing of cities which Solomon fortified and formed as a kind of defensive belt around his kingdom and especially also Judah (cf. Niemann, *Herrschaft,* 96-99), we now get a couple of statements about the king's building activities. The words up to the second את are lacking in LXX. In the par. 2 Chr. 8:4 and 6, on the other hand, we find ואת כל־ערי המסכנות even twice מסכנות (Exod. 1:11; 2 Chr. 8:4, 6; 16:4; 17:12 and 32:28) are 'depots,' a word derived from the neo-Assyrian (E. Lipiński, *ZAH* 1 [1988], 69; cf. *HAL,* 573; also cf. W. H. Schmidt in Ishida, *Studies,* 67, who links our

---

[17] See now also M. O'Connor, "The Etymologies of Tadmor and Palmyra," in *A Linguistic Happening in Memory of Ben Schwartz: Studies in Anatolian, Italic, and Other Indo-European Languages* (Bibliotéque des Cahiers de l'Institut de Linguistique de Louvain 42; ed. Y.L. Arbeitman) Louvain-la-Neuve 1988, 235-54; and P.J. Williams, "TMR in 1 Kings IX 18," *VT* 47 (1997), 262-265, suggesting (with H. Ewald) that the *kethib* of 1 Kgs ix 18 was *tammōr* not *tāmār*' and that this *tammōr* is simply a by-form of *tadmōr.*'

text with Exod. 1:11 and considers our verse older than the Yahwist of the exilic and postexilic era). Surely Solomon must have built up supplies and equipment in the cities listed above (Würthwein even thinks that the cities mentioned in the vss. 15, 17f. are described here, which is why he views the first *waw* as *waw explicativum*) but also in other cities (Niemann, 99, n. 443, doubts whether Lower Beth-Horon and Baalah, 'wegen ihrer geomorphologischen Situation,' ever were [large] garrisons). In addition, as Noth rightly observes, further storage locations would have been formed where the goods which were brought in or were exacted as taxes could be laid up.[18] But in the preceding list they were not explicitly mentioned by name.

In addition, there were garrison cities, places where horses and horsemen found their home base. We already encountered the words רכב and פרשים above in 1:5. Just as Noth does here on our verse, so we already indicated there that פרש does not so much mean 'horseman' as 'horse (in harness)'. Accordingly, it is not certain whether Solomon already knew cavalry in our sense of the word. And if we speak of 'cavalry cities,' we may not forget that this word was imported into our text by a later author or redactor in this sense. Haupt (cited in Stade-Schwally) is even of the opinion that 'cities for horsemen' may be a later explicative gloss with 'cities for chariots.'

The beginning of the second part of our verse shows strong resemblance to vs. 1 (see there). Several Hebr. MSS, the par. 2 Chr. 8:6, a number of MSS of the Tg., and Vulg. read כל for חשק but MT deserves preference. It is clear from the preceding text that Jerusalem was the object of Solomon's building activities (vs. 15). The Lebanon as Solomon's building terrain is less obvious. Accordingly, in LXX 10:24 region is not mentioned, but it is in the additions to LXX 2:46 in vs. 46c: 'Solomon began to open up the natural resources of the Lebanon,' as we attempted to translate there. But this translation, as we noted there, is uncertain. Montg.-Gehman, 209, propose that we translate: 'Solomon began to break down the fortifications of the Lebanon' (cf. *JAOS* 56 [1936], 137). In 5:28 we were told that Solomon had a thousand labourers per month working on the Lebanon. Also, there was mention of 'the House of the Forest of the Lebanon' (7:2). All these references make it possible for 'Lebanon' to have crept into the text, perhaps as a gloss.

Nor, in view of the conclusion of our verse, was specific mention of the Lebanon even necessary. Of the 17x the word ממשלה occurs in OT it can be found in the books of Kings, aside from here, also in 2 Kgs. 20:13. It is one of the 3 nouns derived from the verb משל, 'to rule' (cf. H. Groß, *TWAT*, V, 74). It means 'dominions,' 'rule' and is used here to emphasize the extent of

---

[18] Cf. A. Schoors, *Berseba-De opgraving van een bijbelse stad* (Palestina Antiqua 5), Kampen 1986, 48.

Solomon's dominion (Groß, 76). LXX reads the first *mem* of our word as a מן privative (cf. WOC §112.11e) with the infinite of משל + suff., with 'all the people' of the next verse as subject (Montg.-Gehman).

9:20 *All the people who were left of the Amorites, the Hittites, the Perizzites, the Hivites and the Jebusites, and were not (descended) from the children of Israel,*
This verse and the following verses continue the subject with which vs. 15 began: an account of the forced labour and other services. A number of the 'remnant' peoples are listed. The reference is to the so-called 'seven nations' of Palestine which, often in varying composition and order as well as number, are presented whenever the purpose is to describe the pre-Israelite population (cf. e.g. Gen. 15:19ff.; Exod. 3:8, 17; Num. 13:29; Deut. 7:1; Josh. 3:10; 11:3; Judg. 3:5; Ezra 9:1; Neh. 9:8; see also Noth, *Welt*, 70f.).

The Amorites are mentioned approx. 90x in OT (see comments on 4:19 above). From the second half of the third millennium before our era an ethnic group located near the mid-course of the Euphrates was described in cuneiform as *amurru*, 'western,' 'the western land.' Especially the many thousands of personal names but also texts found in Mari show that the Akkadian, in which these people conducted their correspondence, exhibits strong NW Sem. influence. The word 'Amurru' was especially geographic in meaning. The precise birthplace of the Amurru in remote antiquity is disputed (cf. also G.E. Mendenhall, *ABD*, I, 199-202). In the late bronze age there was a kingdom of Amurru in the region of the valley of the Upper Orontes. It is evident from the texts of Alalach but also from Egypt (Amarna Letters) and Hittite texts of the 14th and 13th century BCE that there was a political entity, a state, NW of the Lebanon by the name of Ammuru. In the first half of the first millennium before our era Syria-Palestine is simply denoted 'Amurru' in Assyrian texts. Here, then, the word has a political meaning. In an ethnic sense the word is secondary. Accordingly, in OT the whole pre-Israelite population can be denoted 'Amorite' (Josh. 5:1; 7:7; etc.), but also a certain part of it (e.g. Deut. 7:1; cf. R. Bach, *BHHW*, I, 84f.; *HAL*, 65f.) can be so designated. The cultural and religious legacy of the Amorites in the Ancient Near East must not be underestimated (Mendenhall, 202).

In the second millennium before our era the Hittites formed a great power in Asia Minor and Northern Syria, alongside of Egypt, say, in the S and Assyria in the E (H. Otten, *BHHW*, II, 711-715; Ph.H.J. Houwink ten Cate, *ABD*, III, 219-225). In the 12th century this empire disintegrated and the name Hittite was no longer used in a rigorously political sense but often more generally as a name for the population of Syria and Palestine, especially in Assyrian texts (cf. A. Alt, *KS*, III, 34f.). In the OT the Hittites are mentioned almost 50x (in the books of Kings also in 10:29; 11:1; 15:5; 2 Kgs. 7:6; cf. *HAL*, 349).

The Perizzites, who are mentioned 23x in OT in lists of the pre-Israelite inhabitants of Canaan (in Kings only in our verse), probably belonged to the pre-Canaanite population. It has been conjectured that they were driven from their places of residence by the Canaanites (who are supposed to have lived in 'fortified cities'), so that here and there they were forced to live in 'open' areas (cf. the word p^erazot, 'open land,' Ezek. 38:11 and Zech. 2:8; G. Sauer, *BHHW* 3, 1450; *HAL*, 909a; S.A. Reed, *ABD*, V, 231). But according to T. Ishida (*Bib* 60 [1979], 479f.), the names 'Canaanites' and 'Perizzites' are used 'as terms for a broader division of population groups'; in this connection the Canaanites are representative for the larger (Sem.) nations and the Perizzites for the smaller (non-Semitic) nations. One can infer from Gen. 34:30 and Judg. 1:4f. that before the Israelite conquests at least some of the Perizzites, along with the Canaanites, belonged to the dominant groups.

The Hivites, mentioned 25x in OT (only here in Kings), is a national community belonging to the Canaanites and localized in and around Gibeon (Josh. 9:7; 11:19), but also in more northern regions (Josh. 11:3; Judg. 3:3; 2 Sam. 24:7). Sometimes they were confused with the Horites (cf. Josh. 9:7 MT with LXX; also cf. Isa. 17:9 and Gen. 36:2 with vs. 20). Most striking is that, also in comparison with the Canaanites, they were uncircumcised (Gen. 34:15, 22-25; K.H. Bernhardt, *BHHW* 2, 716; *HAL*, 284f.; D.W. Baker, *ADB*, III, 234).

Finally we encounter the Jebusites, the pre-Israelite inhabitants of Jerusalem and surroundings, who are mentioned 41x in OT, especially in lists of the pre-Israelite inhabitants of Palestine (but in Kings only in our verse). Jebus (the name only occurs 4x in MT: Judg. 19:10f.; 1 Chr. 11:4f.) is the pre-Davidic name for Jerusalem. It is suspected that the Jebusites, following the unrest occasioned by the incursions of the 'sea peoples,' displaced the older Amorite population. It is possible that the Jebusites were of Hittite – i.e. non-Semitic – origin, but this is not certain (Ezek. 16:3 and the name 'Arauna'; cf. G. Molin, *BHHW*, II, 806; S.A. Reed, *ADB*, III, 652f.).

All the peoples mentioned here, who are asyndetically grouped together (cf., on the other hand, the par. 2 Chr. 8:7; Joüon §177o), are presented as the 'remnant' of the pre-Israelite population. The verb יתר occurs in niph. 81 or 82x in OT (in Kings also in 9:21; 15:18; 17:17; 18:22; 19:10, 14; 20:30 (2x); 2 Kgs. 4:7 [Q] and 20:17) in the sense of 'to remain'; in addition, there is the hiph.-form 'to leave over'; 'to have left' (24x; in Kings: 2 Kgs. 4:43f.). A frequently occurring noun (95x; 38x in Kings!) is יתר, 'rest' (see H. Wildberger, *THAT*, II, 846; T. Kronholm, *TWAT*, III, 1079-1090). This 'being left' of the pre-Israelite population of Canaan is linked with the not-fully-completed execution of the ban (curse), as it surfaces in the next verse.

9:21 *their children who were left in the land after them, on whom the* *children of Israel could not enforce the curse of destruction – these Solomon levied as forced labourers, as they are to this day.*

First the grammatical construction of the vss. 20 and 21 requires some attention. The words כל־העם of vs. 20 are picked up again in בניהם. They function as an extended dependent clause (Driver, *Tenses* §197, Burney): 'As it concerns those peoples ... their sons ...'; continued by ויעלם as predicate at the start of the second part of our verse. This predicate is introduced by a *waw consec.*, and thereby acquires emphasis (Driver, §127a; also cf. BrSynt. §123f).

Israel, according to our verse, could not strike all of the people with the ban. The verb חרם in the hiph.-form occurs only here and in 2 Kgs. 19:11 in the books of Kings of the 48x in OT. The root חרם, which occurs in almost all Sem. languages, primarily means 'to devote' (cf. Lev. 27:28; Mi 4:13), but then also 'to ban.' Also the noun חרם, 'ban,' occurs frequently in OT (29x). Originally the חרם meant to indicate that which was prohibited either because it was accursed and had to be destroyed (*res exsecranda*), or because it was holy (*res sacrosancta*). As a rule the verb (in hiph.) is used in connection with war (see C.H.W. Brekelmans, *THAT*, I, 635-639; and N. Lohfink, *TWAT*, V, 180-199).[19] The idea that the חרם was an integral part of the so-called 'holy war,' however, is disputed (cf. P.D. Stern, *Bib* 71 [1990], 43f.). Indeed, in Deut. 20:16ff. almost exactly these peoples of vs. 20 are mentioned whom Israel was to strike with a curse. The reason given is 'that they may not teach you to do according to all their abominable practices which they have done in the service of their gods' (Deut. 20:18). The reference here, says Stern, is to 'offensive warfare under divine aegis against the earlier in habitants of the land.'

As a kind of mitigating execution of the ban, Solomon made these peoples into מס־עבד. Aliens, as long as they were true 'aliens,' like the above-listed peoples, were regarded as pariahs (cf. G. Stählin, *TDNT*, V, 10, n. 62). What is meant by מס־עבד? Earlier already, in our comments on 5:27, we stated that in the case of these words (which are also found in Gen. 49:15 and Josh. 16:10) we are dealing with 'state slavery.' D. Künstlinger, *OLZ* 34 (1931), 611f., has pointed to the varying translation of these words in the ancient versions (LXX: εἰς φόρον; Pesh.: *'bda* [pl.] *msqy* [pl.] *mdata;* Vulg.: *tributarios;* Tg. מסקי מסין פלחין). He believed that עבד could be switched with עבד and translated: 'zum Tribut (zahlen) für ewige Zeiten,' this in contrast to מס as

---

[19] Cf. also C.H.W. Brekelmans, *De Herem in het Oude Testament*, Nijmegen 1959; M. Weinfeld, "The Ban on the Canaanites in the Biblical Codes and Its Historical Development," *History adn Tradition of Early Israel*, (Fs E. Nielsen, ed. A. Lemaire et al.; SVT 50), Leiden 1993, 142-60; and W. Dietrich, "The »Ban« in the Age of the Early Kings," *The Origin of the Ancient Israelite States* (ed. V. Fritz et al., JSOTSup 228), Sheffield 1996, 196-210).

such. But this view would seem to conflict with עבד in the following verse Noth takes עבד to be an attribute with מס and thinks in this connection of a particularly 'niedrige Art der Fron.' The reference was not to slaves but to those who could be regarded as slaves for the duration of their service. It is hard to tell, however, what gradation there is precisely between מס and מס עבד. We therefore translated the expression by 'forced labour.'

9:22 *But of the children of Israel Solomon made no one a slave. They were fighting men, his servants, his officers, his chariot commanders and his horsemen.*

In this verse we are told that the 'children of Israel' were not forced into servitude, a statement which is somewhat hard to reconcile with what was reported in 5:27 (also cf. 11:28 and 12:4; see also Pedersen, I-II, 40). But even from that text one cannot draw the conclusion that Israelites were condemned to lifelong slavery, only that the Judeans in particular were spared.

In place of מס עבד our verse simply reads עבד. The par. 2 Chr. 8:9 reads לעבדים. For מס עבד Klostermann, Ehrlich, Benzinger, et al. choose, for the reading of the Chronicler, the textcr. app. of *BHK* (that of *BHS* refers to 2 Chr. 8:9). LXX reads πρᾶγμα, which probably agrees with עבודה. Along with Šanda, Noth, et al., we need not alter either the text or the vocalization at this point: 'Der Ausdruck ist von der eigentlichen Sklavenfron zu verstehen, von der die Israeliten frei waren' (Šanda).

What Solomon in fact did have in mind for the Israelites is summed up in a series. They are, in the first place, appointed as 'fighting men,' men designated for making war. It is indeed a question here whether these men actually constituted the first category of the series, or whether the now-following categories are further specifications of the main concept of 'fighting men,' so that a colon should be placed after this word. This depends on the meaning of the words which follow. The following category, 'his servants,' is lacking in the par. 2 Chr. 8:9 but the word makes good sense: the reference is to the personal servants of Solomon. Perhaps in time they replaced the 'Cherethites and Pelethites' who, as we saw in connection with 1:38, formed David's special bodyguard.

Now follow 2 separate categories which, in the par. 2 Chr. 8:9 are combined: ושרי שלישיו. In LXX^B this part is lacking and LXX$^{Luc.}$ inserts it later. There is no textcritical reason, however, for departing from MT here. Both the words שר and שליש occur by themselves in OT. In 1:9, 25; 2:5, 32 the former was mentioned in conjunction with הצבא, 'army.' In these cases the reference was to an 'army commander.' According to *HAL*, 1259, the word occurs 421x in OT (and outside of it is found in inscriptions), and can be translated by 'notable,' 'commander,' 'leader' or the like. The word שליש presents more difficulties. Burney offers as his opinion that it is a word of unknown meaning and derivation, but that in commenting on Exod. 14:7 Origen proposes, as a possible meaning, one of the 3 warriors on a chariot. Burney basing himself on the view of Dillmann considers this notion 'purely conjectural.' From within the context (cf. 2 Kgs. 9:25; 10:25; Exod. 14:7) he views these men as 'a class of warriors usually connected with chariots,' and refers to the general terminology in Vulg. (*duces*); Pesh. and Tg. ('heroes'). Noth, however, without mentioning Origen, adopts his view (as well as that of others, e.g., Haupt [in Stade-Schwally]), speaking of 'den dritten Mann' and adding: 'bei einer Dreimannbesetzung eines Streitwagens.' This is said to be customary among the Hittites. The reference, then, aside from the driver and the actual warrior on the chariot, is to the third man present, the 'adjutant.'

שליש occurs in OT in 3 senses: (1) as a term for a 'third' part (Isa. 40:12; Ps. 80:6); (2) as a musical instrument (1 Sam. 18:6); and (3) as the word for a certain category of military (Exod. 14:7; 15:4; 2 Sam. 23:8; 2 Kgs. 7:2, 17, 19; 9:25 [Q]; 10:25; 15:25; Ezek. 23:15, 23; 1 Chr. 11:11 [Q]; 2 Chr. 8:9; and finally in a somewhat obscure sense in Prov. 22:20 [Q]. B.A. Mastin, SVT 30 [1979], 125-154) proposes that we view the last-mentioned as 'men of the third rank,' men who in rank come after the king and the senior offices. He does not believe there is support for the idea of a regular Hittite-Palestinian practice of using chariots with a crew of 3 persons. Certainly in Exod. 14 and 15 it is not a technical term for certain members of a chariot crew. M. Vervenne (*UF* 19 [1987], 355-373) aligns himself with this position after conducting a further study of the Ugar. *tlt* (KTU 1.14.II:2-3 etc.) which is variously interpreted (inter al. by 'bronze'). He reads the Hebr. word to mean 'knight' (so also N. Na'aman, *VT* 38 [1988], 71-79). D.G. Schley, *VT* 40 [1990], 321-326, however, thinks here of a special class of elite warriors who possibly gained fame by some heroic deed and who were directly linked to the king. It is also possible, he writes, that a 'group of three' is meant (cf. 2 Sam. 23:13-17; see also *HAL*, 1412-1413). O. Margalith (*BetM* 72 [1978], 126; *VT* 42 [1992], 266), referring to the Ugar. *tlt*, 'metal,' thinks the reference is to soldiers in armour. If the שרים represent the 'general officers,' the שלישים are perhaps comparable to 'field officers.' But that, of course, reflects a modern view.

The last 2 categories were presented in approximately the same way already in 1:5. Here, too, these men may have been designated for military tasks, though they may also have been qualified for rapid communication in his kingdom.

9:23 *These are the officials in charge of the foremen who were over king Solomon's work: five hundred and fifty men supervising the people who did the work.*

This verse hangs somewhat in the air and is closely related to 5:30. In discussing the latter verse we already dealt with some aspects which come up here as well. It is noteworthy that the verse begins with אלה, after which the reader would expect a list of names (cf. 4:2, 8; so, inter al., also Böttcher, *Neue Aehrenlese*; Benzinger; Ehrlich; Skinner; Noth), which then fails to materialize. If the list has dropped out or been omitted here, this must have happened early. The reference is again to 'the officials in charge of the foremen (or supervisors)' who directed the people who did the work (Pesh. and Vulg. [*et statutis operibus imperabant*] grammatically clearly link the 'execution of the work' with the 'supervisors' and not with 'the people'). Instead of the st. cstr. שרי, LXX^B probably read the st. abs. שרים, 'the foremen (supervisors) who had been put in charge of the work of Solomon.'

The biggest difference with 5:30 concerns the number. Our verse mentions 550 men (so also Josephus, *Ant.* VIII §162); the par. 2 Chr. 8:10 has over 250, which, oddly enough, is a smaller number. I. Benzinger, *Chronik* (KHC 20), suspects that the Chronicler cited another 'Vorlage.' In 5:30 a much higher number of supervisors is mentioned but the ancient versions support MT of our verse. Thenius attempted to resolve the clear difference between our verse and 5:27-30 by pointing out that the levy there pertained to preparatory activities and was requisitioned from among the people as a whole, while here the actual heavy building activities are in view, 'zu der eine Art von Heloten gezwungen ward.' But this explanation hardly seems plausible. Burney looks for an explanation in the consideration that after the building of the temple and the palace fewer supervisors were needed. The construction of this entire verse, however, seems so artificial that it makes little sense to look for an explanation for the difference. Noth is right in observing that the attributive participle 'mit seiner Dependenz' after the number seems 'unpassend und nachhinkend.'

9:24 *But the daughter of Pharaoh went up from the city of David to her own house which he had built for her. Thereafter he (also) built the fortified tower.*

Again we encounter in this verse a stray fragment which contains 2 items: (1) the removal of the daughter of pharaoh and (2) the building of the Millo. Already in 3:1 we learned of Solomon's marriage to pharaoh's daughter and her temporary stay in 'the city of David.' In 7:8 the construction of the new house for this woman was reported. In 9:16 there was mention of a gift from pharaoh for his daughter and now her removal is mentioned.

The verse begins with the particle אך which generally has a restrictive or adversative function (N.H. Snaith, *VT* 14 [1964], 221-225), although there are also known to us cases with an affirmative meaning (*Ges.*^{18}, 52). But the preceding fragment does not warrant such a beginning for our verse. As a solution for this problem it has been suggested that we locate our verse immediately after vs. 14 (textcr. app. *BHK*). Although this transposition does not directly make clearer the linkage with אך, it may help to remind ourselves that LXX located the first part of our verse immediately after vs. 9, which only underscores the uncertain location of our verse here. But LXX has still another version of our verse in LXX 2:35f. The latter verse begins with οὕτως, the former with τότε (which prompts several exegetes to read אז in place of אך; see also the textcr. app. of *BHK* and *BHS*). The fragment in 2:35 is in fact followed by the statement that Solomon built the Millo so that this verse most resembles the 'Vorlage' we have in vs. 24. In addition this verse reports that Solomon had pharaoh's daughter removed to *her* house which he had built for *her*, whereas LXX 9:9 refers to *his* house which he had built for *himself*. But the particles with which both LXX 2:35 and LXX 9:9 begin can hardly be regarded as 'translation' of אך, any more than the ואת of the par. 2 Chr. 8:11. Thenius (followed by Stade-Schwally et al.) has the אז of the second part of our verse refer back to אך and in this connection points to the restrictive meaning which occurs elsewhere as well (e.g. in Gen. 27:30; Judg. 7:19): 'As soon as the daughter ..., he then built the Millo.' By this interpretation a clear (grammatical and temporal) connection is made between the 2 items in our verse without, however, making clear the logic of this connection. True, Thenius suspects that the Millo (a kind of castle) had to serve as a special guardhouse for the royal harem but this is purely hypothetical. Burney, who brings up Thenius's suggestion at some length, himself opts for a text emendation (as do also other exegetes, e.g. Böttcher, *Neue Aehrenlese*; cf. the textcr. app. of *BHK* and *BHS*), basing himself on the readings of LXX: 'and Solomon brought the daughter of pharaoh up from the city of David to her house which he had built for her in those days.'

It is a question, however, whether we need to change the text as we now have it. With Benzinger we are of the opinion that this is 'ein müssiges Unternehmen.' We do not believe אך to be a writer's error, especially since Pesh. (*copula*), Tg. (ברם) and Vulg. (*autem*) seems to agree with MT. We are dealing with a fragment from a longer narrative, which now happens to be located here. As for the content of this notice, we can refer the reader to 3:1. We still wish to point to the curious motivation for the removal of the Egyptian princess in 2 Chr. 8:11. Apart from the fact that Solomon brought her from one location to the other and did not himself 'go up,' he said: 'My wife shall not live in the house of David king of Israel, for the places to which the ark of YHWH has come are holy.'

As for the construction of the Millo, which 'then' (אז; cf. Mulder 1991) took place, see comments on vs. 15 above. Although, in general and also here, אז has temporal significance, this need not mean that we have to make a connection between the removal of the princess and the construction of the Millo (cf. the opinion of Busink, 95, that the old Davidic palace may have been located on the terrace which could only be renovated after the removal of Pharaoh's daughter!) In any case, the chronicler does not make this connection and it is very much a question whether this second part of our verse has anything to do with the first. Possibly what we have here is a gloss which crept into our text at an early stage. The – to our mind – chaotic structure of this chapter, however, prohibits us from drawing more conclusions from dubious data than is strictly necessary.

9:25 *Three times a year Solomon sacrificed burnt offerings, and peace offerings on the altar which he had built for YHWH, burning incense [...] before YHWH. [He completed the house[20]].*
This verse, too, lacks a clear connection with the immediately preceding part, even though it points in the direction of a notice concerning Solomon's building of the temple. The verse reports Solomon's regular sacrificial practices as king in and by his royal court sanctuary. Repeated actions (frequentatives) are more often indicated by the pf. with the *waw cons.* (Ges-K §112dd; Bg. II §9g; GD §72, rem. 1; Driver §120; Burney; et al.). The offerings which Solomon was accustomed to bring 3 times a year (LXX* reads τρεις from τρις [LXX$^{Luc.}$: τριτος], 'three times'; see Rahlfs, *SSt.* I, 3, 240) may relate to the 3 great annual festivals: the 'feast of unleavened bread'; the 'feast of weeks,' and the 'feast of ingathering' at the end of the year (Exod. 23:14-17; 34:18,22f.). Kuenen not only considered this notice credible but he even thought that Solomon laid the foundation for the *trio* of high festivals which was completely established as early as the 7th century BCE.[21] Noth, however, points out that the existence of a cycle of 3 festivals is at the very least doubtful for the ancient cultic tradition of Jerusalem. This, accordingly, could mean that our notice has to be of a late date or a counterpart to what was reported in 3:2f. (so Keil, Rice, et al.). For there we were told of 'sacrificing on the high places,' here of bringing offerings in the newly built temple (for 'burnt offerings' and 'peace offerings,' cf. comments on 3:15 above). With Pedersen, III-IV, 163f.; 350, and many other interpreters (Noth, Würthwein, et al.), however, we must assume that Solomon himself conducted the sacrifices as leader of the temple ritual (cf. 12:33; 2 Kgs. 16:12-15).

The altar here referred to already came up in connection with 8:64.[22] It was not mentioned in connection with the construction and design of the temple. Würthwein believes this happened because this altar was 'certainly' an altar with steps and this was contrary to the instruction in Exod 20:26. But this argument hardly cuts ice because in that case other objects or arrangements (e.g. the pillars Jachin and Boaz), which were inconsistent with later priestly

---

[20] Alternative translation: *he also used to pay (his vows)*.
[21] A. Kuenen, *De Godsdienst van Israel*, I, Leiden 1869, 332.
[22] Now cf. also M. Dijkstra, "The Altar of Ezekiel: Fact or Fiction?," *VT* 42 (1992), 23f.

conventions, would not have been mentioned either. We are not informed in our verse either of the shape or the place of the altar by the temple. The par. 2 Chr. 8:12 reports that it was located before the אולם, the 'fronthall.' In 2 Chr. 8:13-16, for that matter, there is a special expansion to insure that the reader will above all get the impression that Solomon did not 'willfully' arrogate the ministry of offerings — which was later reserved solely for priests and Levites — to himself. He is presented as the executor of a cultic testament left him by his father David by acting publicly as the organizer of the temple ministry! In our verse, however, there is not a trace of all this and Solomon is more or less naively introduced as the priestly king.

This verse is continued by an inf. abs. (König §218a; GD §103; Ges-K §113z; Joüon §123x). In 3:3 we already encountered the verb קטר in hiph. R.E. Clements, *TWAT*, VII, 10-18, points out that the pi.-modification, which occurs 41x in OT, more generally means 'to cause an offering to go up in smoke,' whereas the hiph.-form, which occurs 69x in OT, has a more specific meaning: 'to burn incense' (p. 12).

The 2 words which follow next have given the translators and exegetes numerous headaches: אשר אתו. Both the par. 2 Chr. 8:12, LXX* (2:35g), and Vulg. omit these words. LXX^A has αυτος, with Chronicles omitting the entire statement about the burning of incense. Various interpreters, responding to this omission, use qualifications for the words in question like 'heillos verderbt' (Kittel), 'völlig sinnlos' (Benzinger), 'irrémédiablement corrompu' (De Vaux), or 'unverständlich' (Hentschel). Ewald, §232a, has attempted to make sense of them by translating: 'bei ihm (dem Altare) welcher vor Jhwh war.' In that case the suffix after the particle את refers to the altar just mentioned. But in *GVI*, III, 406, n. 2, he translates: 'er räucherte *bei sich* da wo man ist vor Jahve,' i.e.: 'im Heiligen, אשר als Bezeichnung des Ortes.' Thenius, to mention just one, understands the words as follows: 'Er brachte mit sich (d.i. selbst) Räucheropfer dar vor dem Herrn,' viz. in the sanctuary itself. He assumes that אשר was later intentionally added to the text to conceal the fact that Solomon here performed purely priestly services. Now Tg. and Pesh. also relate אתו to the altar, but Burney has called attention to the fact that אתו is not the same as עליו. Nor can be particle with suffix apply to Solomon himself, as Ewald and Thenius (referring to the use of אתו in Gen. 39:6 and Isa. 44:24) proposed. A more plausible emendation which appeals to him (and many others; cf. Benzinger, textcr. app. *BHK*) is that of Klostermann: את־אשר. The latter translates as follows: 'er räucherte sein Rauchwerk vor Jahwe,' which he views, in contrast to the great festivals which occur 3 times a year, as the daily care of the altar fire. Others, like Stade-Schwallly, Ehrlich, Šanda, and Montg.-Gehman, however, advance serious objections to this emendation. Every interpretation and each emendation contains something unsatisfactory or tortuous. For that reason we, too, will leave these gloss-like words untranslated, and pronounce a verdict of *non liquet*. But that does not mean we are done.

The question is whether שלם in the pi. here has the meaning 'to complete.' How are the last 3 words of our verse connected with the preceding ones? And, in the case of וישלם, are we dealing with a pf. consec. or an ordinary pf. with the copula? This, too, has been a topic of sometimes lengthy discussion by a variety of interpreters. Ehrlich, for example, denies that the pi. of שלם can mean 'to complete.' He thinks its meaning is 'to replace,' 'to restore damage.' Combined with the pf. consec. he translates: 'und er besserte etwaige Schäden im Tempel aus,' i.e. over the years, he had workmen make necessary repairs in the temple. Willi, *Chronik*, 185, agrees with Ehrlich in this matter. Noth attempts to translate the last words of our verse as follows: 'damit erfüllte er den Zweck des Hauses.' He, too, is aware of the difficulties occasioned by these enigmatic words. It is simpler to delete these words, as, e.g., Ehrlich does. Skinner, on the other hand, points to the effect of the periodic offerings: this restores the (ceremonial) integrity of the house. In this manner Skinner maintains the frequentative meaning of the pf. consec. of this verse Gray aligns himself more with Montg.-Gehman, who have proposed an interpretation in the sense of שלם נדר, 'to pay one's vows' (cf. Ps. 76:12) and this in connection with and continuation with the preceding verb. Because this meaning was later misunderstood, someone added 'the house' and heard the Aramaic sense 'to complete' in the verb. Thenius, on the other hand, is one of those who stand by 'to complete': by the regular annual offerings and by his highpriestly offerings of incense Solomon brought the temple ministry to the level of a truly dedicated sanctuary.

It is perhaps to be expected that Tg. and Pesh. as Aram. translations had little difficulty with the meaning 'to complete.' But neither, apparently, did LXX* (LXX$^{B, Luc.}$ a form of συντελέω. LXX^A a form of ἀπαρτίζω which only occurs here in LXX), nor the Vulg. (*perfectumque est templum*). Various modern translations clearly link the last words with the preceding ones. A small anthology of modern translations reads as follows: SV: 'en rookte op dat, hetwelk voor het aangezicht des Heren was, als hij het huis volmaakt had' ('and he turned incense on that which was before the face of the Lord when he had finished the house'); Lutheran translation: 'und räucherte über ihm für dem Herrn, und war also das Haus fertig'; RSV: 'burning incense before the Lord. So he finished his house.' Lexicons like Ges-B (836), BDB, (1022), Zorell (852b) and *HAL* (1420), be it only for our verse and despite the (often undisclosed) odium of its being an Aramaism, all give the meaning 'to complete' and the like for the pi. of שלם.[23] This meaning can no more be ruled

---

[23] M. Wagner, *Die lexikalischen und grammatikalischen Aramaismen im alttestamentlichen Hebräisch* (BZAW 96), Berlin 1966, does not treat this form.

out (for the later Hebr.) than the possibility that the ו before this verb can serve as an ordinary copula. In our opinion, we are dealing in this case with a (late) gloss in which someone noted in the margin that with this act of Solomon the phase of, and the reportage on, '(the building of) the temple was completed.' If one nevertheless wishes to maintain continuity with the preceding words, the suggestion of Montg.-Gehman deserves to be followed. Omitting 'the house' in this case, one may read: 'And he regularly paid (his vows).'

9:26 *King Solomon also built a fleet at Ezion Geber which is near Elath in the land of Edom, on the shore of the Sea of Reeds.*
The last fragment (vss. 26ff.) of this chapter reports the joint trade-voyages of Solomon and Hiram to distant coasts in order, with their ships richly laden with gold, to return again to the home port. It is a striking statement about Israel, a country which was not then or later known as a maritime power or a proud seafaring nation.

The word אני occurs, aside from here and in the next verse, also again in 10:11, 22 (3x) and Isa. 33:21. It is a collective here, denoting 'fleet' (in Hebr. *nomina unitatis* are often fem. : König §255a; GD §18a; Ges-K §122t; see also *HAL*, 69; *Ges.*^{18}, 81; LXX reads sing. ναῦς; also cf. Rahlfs, *SSt.* III, 240f.). The sing. word for ship is אניה: it is already mentioned in the next verse and occurs 30x in OT. Repeatedly the word תרשיש is added to both words. This place name is often identified with a city in Spain on or near the mouth of the Guadalquiver, but this identification is far from certain (cf. the different views listed in *HAL*, 1653f.). In any case a ship or fleet of 'Tarshish' is tantamount to a 'seagoing' vessel or fleet. They were ships built for the long haul on sea or ocean (cf. E. Hilgert, *BHHW*, III, 1694ff.; M. Wüst, *BRL*^{2}, 276-279 [both articles come with depictions of ships]).

We are told that king Solomon built and equipped a fleet at Ezion-geber near Elath on the shore of the 'Sea of Reeds' in the country of Edom (cf. Josephus, *Ant.* VIII §163). This would seem to be a rather precise location. In the par. 2 Chr. 8:17 a couple of details in this verse are conveyed differently: Solomon himself went to Ezion-geber and to Elath on the shore of the sea in the land of Edom. Josephus, *Ant.* VIII §163, refers to 'Gazion-gabel' (cf. LXX) not far from 'Ailane,' 'which is now called Berenice.' Ezion-geber is not disputed as the place where Solomon's fleet was equipped (but cf. 10:11, 22). This city is also mentioned in Num. 33:35f.; Deut. 2:8; 1 Kgs 22:49; 2 Chr. 8:17 and 20:36. Simons, *GTTOT* §832f., informs us that, while the city used to be identified with *('ain) Ghadian,* about 40 km N of the Gulf of Aqabah, it is now (i.e. before 1959) identified with *tell el-Ḥeleifi* (4 km N of Aqabah) approx. half a km from the coast. According to Simons, Eloth, which must have been located close to Ezion-geber, is in that case hidden under the sand of the Nabatean-Roman city Aila (1 km WNW of Aqabah). Now the identification of the archaeological locations of place names mentioned in OT is frequently a difficult matter. B. Mazar (*EI* 12 [1975], 46ff.; 119f.) has proposed identifying *tell el-Ḥeleifi* with Abronah, a town mentioned in Num. 33:35 immediately before Ezion-geber. Bartlett, who made a study of the topography of the towns mentioned in our verse, correctly pointed out that Ezion-geber is described in most texts in which the town is mentioned in OT as a harbor town, or even as a town at which one could suffer shipwreck (1 Kgs. 22:49).[24] But the town does have to be distinguished from Elath which is not linked with the shipping industry (Bartlett, 5). It may, therefore, be useful immediately to note the OT particulars of this last-mentioned town or village.

אילות (pl.) or א(י)לת(sing.) is mentioned, aside from here, also in Deut. 2:8; 2 Kgs. 14:22; 16:6 (3x); 2 Chr. 8:17 and 26:2. Inasmuch as in connection with Ezion-geber the author or glossator refers to Elath, one cannot avoid the conclusion that at the time of the composition of our verse the latter was the better known. According to 2 Kgs. 14:22 king Azariah 'built' Elath. There is a possibility that this notice still applies to his father Amaziah (Bartlett 2), but this does imply that in still earlier times Elath did not yet exist. In his study Bartlett subjects the archaeological findings of *tell el-Ḥeleifi* to further study and comes to the conclusion that this *tell* can be 'tentatively' identified with Elath, though difficulties remain, such as the identification of the town bearing the Hellenistic and Roman name Aila with a group of hills approx. 1 km NNW of Aqabah (Bartlett, 15f.). The uncertainty of whether *tell el-Ḥeleifi* can be identified with Elath or even with Ezion-geber has not yet been fully resolved (cf. E.K. Vogel, *IDB* Suppl. 870; HUCA 42 [1971], 85f.; 52 [1981], 49f.; 58 [1987], 36f.; J.R. Zorn, *ABD* 2, 429f.). Negenman *correctly* points out that in any case the Elath of our verse cannot be equated with the present-day Israeli city of Eilath which is situated some kilometers further to the W. He also mentions the new view which is that the OT Elath was located close to the present Aqabah; and that Ezion-geber must be sought 13 km further to the SW of *Geziret Faraun,* a small island in the Gulf of Agabah, a few hundred m from the mainland (see also *HAL*, 84b).[25] This island is not only said to be a better port than the shallow sandy N coast near present-day Aqabah, but by its natural location is also very well suited for ships with some draft. Finally there is Flinders, who is of the opinion that Ezion-geber functioned as seaport while Eloth served as supply depot and caravanserai, and who in this connection also identifies Eloth with *tell el-Ḥeleifi*[26] (for Ezion-Geber, cf. also M. Lubetski,

---

[24] J.R. Bartlett, "Ezion-Geber, which is near Elath on the Shore of the Red Sea," *OTS* 26 (1990), 1-16.

[25] J. Negenman, *Geografische Gids bij de Bijbel*, Boxtel 1981, 121-126, esp. 122f. (map on p. 123).

[26] A. Flinders, "Is this Solomon's Seaport?," *BARev* 15/4 (1989), 30-43.

ADB, II, 723-726).

In our verse the Gulf of Aqabah is called the 'Sea of Reeds.' This seems strange insofar as this 'sea' is especially familiar from the stories of the exodus from Egypt where it may have been a part of the 'Gulf of Suez' or at least denote the lakes or swamps which must have dotted that area (cf. LXX η ερυθρα θαλασσα. Josephus, *Ant.* VIII §163, speaks of the 'Egyptian Gulf of the Red Sea.' In OT, apart from verse, there is frequent reference to the 'Sea of Reeds' (Exod. 10:19; 13:18; 15:4, 22; 23:31; Num. 14:25; 21:4; 33:10, 11; Deut. 1:40; 2:1; 11:4; Josh. 2:10; 4:23; 24:6; Judg. 11:16; Jer. 49:21; Ps. 106:7, 9, 22; 136:13, 15; Neh. 9:9). It is not always immediately clear, however, which particular sea the author(s) had in mind, because also in Exod. 23:31 and Num. 14:25 the reference has to be to the Gulf of Aqabah (cf. H. Ringgren, *TWAT,* III, 649). C. Houtman, *Exodus,* I, (HCOT), 109f., deals at length with the name 'Sea of Reeds.' He points out, that 'reed' here cannot be taken in the sense of 'papyrus' because this is a sweet-water plant and he suggests that we should return to the LXX interpretation ('Red Sea'). But because the term 'Red Sea' is today used in a more restrictive sense than at the time of the LXX, he decides in the end to maintain the Hebr. term 'Yam Suph.' It is evident that in antiquity the use of the word 'Sea of Reeds' was broader in scope than what we understand by it today. It is striking, however, that the par. 2 Chr. 8:17 omits the word סוף and that LXX refers to ἡ ἐσχατη θαλασση (like Eusebius, *Onom.* 34, 25), in the process reading *sûf* as sôf, 'end' (Vulg. has: *in litore maris rubri*; Pesh. and Tg. the same as MT). Did the LXX consciously have in mind a sea other than the 'Sea of Reeds'? In Exod. 2:3, 5; Isa. 19:6 and Jonah 2:6 the word *sûf* refers to a waterplant (*HAL,* 705); sôf, 'end' occurs in Eccl. 3:11; 7:2; 12:13 and 2 Chr. 20:16 (*HAL,* ibid.) Hence as far as the translation of LXX is concerned, the issue is that of a difference in the vocalization of סוף. In our own rendering we prefer to maintain the translation 'Sea of Reeds,' bearing in mind that the ancient author had an understanding of this word which was broader than one limited to the Gulf of Suez and environs (J. A. Montgomery, *JAOS* 58 [1938], 130-139, in considering the meaning of the *ultimum mare,* thinks of the 'end' of the Indian Ocean).

The particle את here has a locative meaning: 'near' (cf. BrSynt. §117b; Williams §339; WOC §11.2.4a). We already encountered שפה several times before (in 5:9; 7:23f., 26). The word has a broad meaning: 'lip,' 'rim,' 'shore,' but also 'language,' 'speech' (*HAL,* 1255f.). Edom (Pesh. here reads *Arwad*; cf. Berlinger) occurs as the name of a country and a people but also several times in OT as a proper name. As the name of a country it denotes a region S of the Dead Sea, down from the 'wadi Zered' which formed its boundary with Moab and went on in the direction of the Gulf of Aqabah. This name is mentioned for the region also in the Egypt., the cuneiform (*Udumu*) and the

Ugar. It is sometimes said to mean אדום, 'red'.[27] In Gen. 25:30; 32:4, etc. Edom is another name for Esau as well (cf. V. Maag, *BHHW*, I, 366ff.; S. Cohen, *IDB*, II, 24ff.; C.-M. Bennett, *IDBS*, 251f.). Bennett believes that the importance of Edom, also in the time of Solomon, lay not so much in its exploitation of the copper mines which were situated in the environs of the Gulf of Aqabah but in its control over the caravan routes from Arabia going N. Mention in our verse of 'the Land of Edom' does not make clear whether in Solomon's time the Edomites in fact controlled the coast of the Gulf (in 2 Sam. 8:13f., we learn that David 'slew' the Edomites in 'the Valley of Salt' and after that held them in subjection), or that the region had come into Solomon's hands as a legacy from David (or had perhaps fallen under the rule of another power, Egypt for example). Negenman, *Geografische Gids*, 105-110 (map on p. 107), reports that originally Edom (also known in OT by the synonym Seir, a name denoting a landscape already mentioned in the Amarna Letters, at the same time an area that was presumably later added to Edom), was located on the E side of the *wadi al-'Arabah* but may later also have had land on the W side of it (cf. Num. 21:4 and Deut. 2:1-5 with Num. 20:14ff. and Deut. 1:2; Negenman assumes that originally there was a region called Edom on the E side of the Arabah where Semites lived, and a region called Seir on the W side ... where the legendary Horites (Gen. 14:6; Deut. 2:12) played an important role.[28]

9:27 *Hiram sent with the fleet his servants, experienced sailors, along with the servants of Solomon:*
Whereas in the previous verse the building of the fleet was credited to Solomon, in this verse there is explicit mention of the support which Hiram provided him in taking it on the high seas. One may well wonder in how far Hiram, seeing the expertise his country possessed in this area, did not also make major contributions to the building of Solomon's ships (also cf. 10:11 and 22). In any case, this 'joint commercial venture' (Katzenstein, *Tyre*, 110) did not hurt Solomon's good fortune... The par. 2 Chr. 8:17f. is less restrained than our verses in recognizing Hiram's contribution to Solomon when it reports that, on Solomon's going to Ezion-geber, Hiram sent him both ships and sailors who then joined Solomon's servants on their voyage. The Tyrians, accordingly, made use of an Israelite harbour. Groups of sailors made up of men from various nations and going on great voyages were a familiar phenom-

---

[27] Cf., however, A. Brenner, *Colour Terms in the Old Testament* (JSOTSup 21), Sheffield 1982, 58-80.

[28] Cf. M. Weippert, *Edom, Studien und Materialien zur Geschichte der Edomiter auf Grund schriftlicher und archäologischer Quellen*, Tübingen 1971; idem in *TRE*, IX, 291-299 (with lit.!).

phenomenon in antiquity. One may recall in this connection a passage in the travel account of Wen-Amon on a trade mission from Karnak (Egypt) to Byblos (*ANET*, 27) and the treaty between Jehoshaphath of Judah and Ahaziah of Israel (22:49ff.; 2 Chr. 20:35ff.).

In our verse we read that Hiram sent his servants, who were experienced sailors, along on the fleet (Stade-Schwally consider באני a superfluous gloss). But LXX translates: Hiram (also) sent experienced sailors along on the ships of his servants. This suggests (as does the par. 2 Chr. 8:17 to some extent) that from Tyre Hiram sent ships to Ezion-geber. But this immediately raises the question how this could be done. Did those ships have to sail around Africa (granted that the Phoenicians must actually have accomplished this feat in antiquity). Or was there something like a Suez canal, or were the ships transported over land to the Gulf of Aqabah? These questions already occupied various exegetes of earlier times. Thus Vatablus writes that there must have been a Tyre on the Red Sea, a kind of twin city of the familiar Tyre, similarly in Hiram's possession. For this position he can appeal to Strabo (*Geogr.* XVI 3.4 [C766]) who already reported that the cities along the Red Sea bore the same names as their Phoenician counterparts because they were in fact Phoenician colonies. Grotius, in his *Annotata*, similarly refers to this idea. Šanda in his commentary, though he touches on the attempts on the part of the pharaohs Ramses II and Necho to dig a kind of Suez canal in ancient times, according to him only Ptolemaeus Philadelphus (285-247) managed to do it in acceptable fashion. Thenius dismisses as speculation all these attempts to explain the presence and availability of a Phoenician fleet in the Gulf of Aqabah. In any case our verse does not tell us how Hiram's seamen came aboard the fleet at Ezion-geber.

The pl. form of the *nomen regens* (אנשי) often occasions the pl. form of the *nomen rectum* (אניות; Böttcher §727.1; König §267c). The verb ידע, 'to know,' 'to be familiar with,' here has approximately the meaning 'to be skilled in' (so, correctly, R. Bultmann, *TDNT*, I, 697, n. 32): 'to know the sea' is 'to be able to sail the sea' (cf. LXX and Tg.).

9:28 *They sailed to Ophir and there took on four hundred and twenty talents of gold which they delivered to king Solomon.*

A problem presented in our verse is the location of Ophir. Katzenstein, *Tyre*, 109, has correctly pointed out that in any case Ophir cannot have been situated on the Arabian peninsula (as, e.g. Montg.-Gehman and D.W. Baker, *ADB*, V, 26f., suggest, though not without reservations), because in that case caravans could have transported the gold. To equip a fleet of ships with the help of the Tyrians, rather than using such a relatively inexpensive means of transportation, is not cost-effective. Following Albright, *ARI*, 133, he looks for Ophir on the African coast somewhere near Somalia. Carroll mentions a tradition of

Islamic traders who attributed to Solomon the ruins of Great Zimbabwe (approximately 400 km from the E coast of Africa and more than 400 km S of the Zambesi river).[29]

The name Ophir occurs in OT – aside from here – also in Gen. 10:29; 1 Kgs. 10:11 (2x); 22-49; Isa. 13:12; Ps. 45:10; Job 22:24; 28:16; 1 Chr. 1:23; 29:4; 2 Chr. 8:18; 9:10. LXX reads Σωφηρα in our verse, approximately (there is some variation in the spelling) as Josephus did (*Ant.* VIII §164; but cf. Rahlfs, *SSt.* III, 100). To this Josephus adds: 'now called 'the Land of God' which belongs to India' (see also Eusebius, *Onom.* 176, 13-17). But an inscription, found in *tell Qasile* (N of Tel Aviv) mentions the (defective) spelling we find in MT: אפר (B. Maisler, *IEJ* 1 [1950f.], 208ff.; Lemaire, 253ff.). Christidès has tried to demonstrate that the localization of Ophir was not certain because one needs to distinguish 2 cities having the same name: the first Ophir (actually the name of a person: Gen. 10:29), associated with Joktan, lay in S Arabia; the second is said to be found either in India or in E Africa.[30] Lemaire, 254, who also mentions other authors, himself thinks of some part of Kush, i.e. present-day Ethiopia or Somalia.[31] H. von Wissmann, *PW* Suppl. XII, 969-980, notes that in 10:22, where there is a list of various African products, there is no mention of Ophir, so that, according to him, we must look for Ophir in SW Arabia. He rejects the opinion of Christidès. Also the compilers of *Ges.*[18] (p. 25) opt for Von Wissmann's opinion (cf. also *HAL*, 22). It is clear from this brief selection of data and speculations concerning Ophir that up until now we cannot say with certainty where Ophir must be located. But, along with Albright and Katzenstein, we tend to prefer Somalia, 'perhaps in the vicinity of the Land of Punt, where the ships of Queen Hatshepsut brought also gold to Egypt in former times' (Katzenstein, *Tyre*, 109).

Just how the trade worked out between the distant 'Land of Gold' and the 'joint venture' of Solomon and Hiram, a venture in which the latter presumably played the primary role,[32] is something we are not told. In 10:11 and 22 there is mention of products other than the gold which alone is referred to here. In our verse we read of 420 talents of gold, while in the par. 2 Chr. 8:18 there is mention of 450 talents of gold, and in LXX^B of 120 talents. LXX$^{Luc.}$ and the other ancient versions, however, support MT. Whether with Stade-Schwally we have to conclude that the number of LXX^B is the most original because it is the lowest is doubtful. That in antiquity the riches of rulers were often exagger-

---

[29] S.T. Carroll, *International Journal of African Historical Studies* 21 (1988), 233-247.

[30] V. Christidès, "L'énigme d'Ophir," *RB* 77 (1970), 240-247.

[31] See also D.S. Attema, *Woordenboek der Oudheid*, Roermond 1965-, II, 2055f.; and idem, *Arabië en de Bijbel*, Den Haag 1961, 43ff.

[32] See also J. K. Kuan, "Third Kingdoms 5.1 and Israelite-Tyrian Relations During the Reign of Solomon," *JSOT* 46 (1990), 31-46, esp. 39f.

ated, also outside of Israel, cannot be disputed (see A. R. Millard, *BARev* 15/3 [1989], 20-34).

Brettler 1991 reminds us that Solomon's riches in gold, as they are described in our vss. 26ff. and in 10:11f. and elsewhere in this chapter, is diametrically opposed to what is stated in the dtr. law concerning the king in Deut. 17:17b. Also the theme of the 'queen of Sheba,' with which the following chapter begins, focuses more on Solomon's wealth than on his wisdom. Furthermore, in the entire structure of 9:26-11:10, set against the background of Deut. 17:14-17, one can perceive clear criticism by the dtr. redactor of Solomon's conduct, without it being expressly stated in dtr. terminology. The section 9:26-11:10 could be entitled: 'Solomon's violation of Deut. 17:14-17' (p. 97)!

1 KINGS 10:1-29

10:1 *The queen of Sheba heard of Solomon's fame [for the name of YHWH] and came to test him with riddles.*

2 She came to Jerusalem with a most impressive (show of) power: camels laden with balsam oil and an enormous quantity of gold and precious stones. She came to Solomon and discussed with him all the different things she had on her mind.

3 Solomon had an answer for all her questions; not one of them was so obscure that he could not answer her.

4 When the queen of Sheba had seen all the wisdom of Solomon and the palace he had built,

5 as well as the food on his table, the (manner of) seating of his officials, and the attendance of his servants, and the way they were dressed, but also his drinking vessels and his burnt offerings which he used to present in the house of YHWH, she was completely flabbergasted.

6 She said to the king: 'It was true what I heard in my own country concerning your deeds and your wisdom;

7 but I could not believe these things until I came and saw them with my own eyes. Indeed, not even half was told me. Your wisdom and prosperity far surpass the rumours that reached me.

8 How fortunate your people! How fortunate your servants who are continually allowed to wait on you, listening to your wisdom!

9 Praise be to YHWH your God who is showing you his favour by setting you on the throne of Israel, because YHWH loves Israel with an everlasting love and has appointed you to be king to do justice and righteousness.'

10 Thereupon she gave to the king a hundred and twenty talents of gold and large quantities of balsam oil and precious stones. Never again was such a quantity of that balsam oil imported as the queen of Sheba gave to king Solomon.

11 Similarly Hiram's fleet, which imported gold from Ophir, also brought along great quantities of 'almug' wood and precious stones [from Ophir].

12 Of the 'almug' wood the king made material for furnishing the temple of YHWH and the royal palace, as well as harps and lyres for the singers. Never before did 'almug' wood arrive in this manner, nor was it ever seen (in such quantity) to this day.

13 King Solomon gave the queen of Sheba everything she desired, whatever she asked him, even aside from the things Solomon gave her out of his royal bounty. Thereupon she left and returned to her own country, she and her servants.

14 *Now the weight of the gold which Solomon received annually was six hundred and sixty-six talents,*

15 *not including the revenues from (itinerant) merchants and from the traders and from all the kings of Arabia and from the governors of the land.*

16 *In addition king Solomon made two hundred great shields of beaten gold; six hundred (shekels) of gold went into each great shield;*

17 *He also made three hundred small shields of beaten gold, with three minas of gold going into each small shield. The king put them into the House of the Forest of Lebanon.*

18 *King Solomon also made a great ivory throne which he overlaid with the finest gold.*

19 *The throne had six steps, a rounded top at the back of it, and armrests on both sides of the seat, with two lions standing beside the armrests.*

20 *And twelve lions stood on each end of the six steps. Nothing like it had (ever) been made for any other kingdom.*

21 *All the drinking vessels of King Solomon were of gold and all the household articles of the House of the Forest of Lebanon were of pure gold. None was of silver (for) in Solomon's day it was not considered at all valuable.*

22 *For the king had a fleet of Tarshish ships at sea with the fleet of Hiram. Once every three years the fleet returned, laden with gold, silver, ivory, apes and peacocks.*

23 *For riches and for wisdom king Solomon surpassed all other kings on earth.*

24 *The whole world sought out Solomon to hear the wisdom which God had put in his heart.*

25 *And everyone who came brought a present with him: articles of silver and gold, garments, equipment, spices, horses and mules, year after year.*

26 *Solomon, moreover, gathered together in a park both chariots and horsemen. He owned fourteen hundred chariots and twelve thousand horsemen and stationed them in chariot cities and with the king (himself) in Jerusalem.*

27 *The king also made silver as common in Jerusalem as stones, and cedar as plentiful as sycamore in the Lowlands.*

28 *Solomon's horses were imported from Egypt and Cilicia; the king's traders purchased them from Cilicia at the going price;*

29 *a chariot imported from Egypt went for six hundred shekels of silver and a horse for a hundred and fifty; and so, through the king's traders, they were also exported to all the kings of the Hittites and of the Arameans.*

1 KINGS 10:1-29

INTRODUCTION

As already stated in the introduction to 9:10-28, also chap. 10 is part of the 'mixed notices' concerning Solomon's activities. It is only interrupted by the story of the queen of Sheba's encounter with king Solomon in which 'wisdom' and 'riches' form the 2 foci of the ellipse (10:1-13; also the vss. 23f.). The vss. 11 and 12 somewhat interrupt this narrative because the reference here is to the transports of gold and precious stones which Hiram's fleet brought in and which Solomon's people then processed. Many exegetes, accordingly, view these verses as a later insertion which can either be omitted or placed after vs. 13 (as, for example, the modern GNB does). But if one discerns a historical core in the story of the queen of Sheba and Solomon, a story primarily based on the diplomacy, economic advantage and trade relations which Solomon pursued with the distant and wealthy countries of the world, then, in such a context the vss. 12f. are certainly meaningful; and, as it were, provide the key to enable us to read the facts behind the fiction.[1] The close of the previous chapter already, as it were, introduced the story about the queen of Sheba. Again, our narrative, as for that matter the whole of chap. 10, has its parallel in 2 Chr. 9, be it again with a number of variants.

The remainder of the chapter resumes the treatment of the theme of trade in gold and other commodities (vss. 14-25), in the process underscoring Solomon's wealth but also his business acumen, which was ultimately stimulated by his Tyrian colleague Hiram. A few intervening verses (16-21) make plain that Solomon was not only concerned to accumulate gold but also to make it 'practically' useful. This section concludes with an apotheosis of Solomon under the motto: 'to him who has will be given, even if it were the whole world' (vss. 23-25).

The sequel supports this certainly exaggerated and therefore somewhat ironic-feeling 'wisdom' and 'wealth' of Solomon (especially if one looks at all this against the background of chapter 11!) by highlighting a few more 'qualities' of Solomon: his creation of chariot cities (vs. 26); his 'renovating' wealth applied in Jerusalem (vs. 27); and his 'horse-trading' (vs. 28f.). At the end of this chapter Solomon is apparently almost wise enough, rich enough, and powerful enough to dispense with any god ...

In the NT, in Matt. 12:14 (Luke 11:31), we read of the 'queen of the South' in the context of the wisdom of Solomon, to which is added the affirmation that Jesus is 'greater than Solomon,' also in wisdom (cf. U. Wilckens, *TDNT*,

---

[1] Cf. S. Perowne, "Note on 1 Kings, Chapter X, 1-13," *PEQ* 71 (1939), 199-202.

VII, 516f.).[2]

The story of the queen of Sheba's journey to see Solomon is also very well known outside of the OT. Not only, as we just noted, does the NT refer to this story, but it is even an essential component in the sources pertaining to Ethiopian royalty. This story has undergone numerous Arabian, Ethiopian, Jewish, and other 'redactions' and has become the subject of one of the most fruitful and universally familiar cycles of legends in the Near (and more distant) East.[3] In the *kebra negast* ('the glory of the kings' – the national saga of Ethiopia) the 'queen of Sheba' and 'Candace, the queen of the Ethiopians' of Acts 8:27 are equated. We are even told that the birthplace of this queen is Aksum, the ancient capital of Abyssinia. The fusion of the 2 stories has very ancient credentials. The Syrian and Eth. versions of the 'Alexander romance' contain a story of the meeting of Alexander the Great with queen Candace which is reminiscent of Solomon's encounter with the queen of Sheba. Aksum was regarded as the seat of the 'ark of the covenant,' which – at least according to the Ethiopian legend – Menelik I, the son of Solomon and the queen of Sheba, had taken along from Jerusalem, but at the same time as the seat of the Christian queen Candace. Jewish and Christian traditions, accordingly, have clearly merged in the course of time.

Josephus, *Ant.* VIII §§165-175, though he somewhat embellishes the biblical story, nevertheless follows it faithfully. Faber van der Meulen, 93f., suspects that Josephus adopted 2 Chr. 9 as the basis for his paraphrase. It is noteworthy that Josephus speaks of the queen of Sheba as 'the queen of Egypt and Ethiopia,' thus situating the story in an African rather than an Arabian tradition (cf. the reference in the edition by Thackeray, 660f., to Isa. 43:3, where Sheba is also mentioned alongside of Egypt and Nubia).

Ullendorff (op. cit., 135ff.) also cites the Talmudic tradition in which it is even denied that the reference is to 'the queen of Sheba'; it should be to the 'kingdom' of Sheba. In the Tg. on Job 1:15 there is talk of 'Lilith, the queen of Smaragd.' Evidently even in that time legends were developing around a 'diabolical' queen of Sheba, legends which are especially prominent in Islamic

---

[2] For another possible association with the NT, see now also V. Hirth, "Die Königin von Saba und der Kämmerer aus dem Mohrenland oder das Ende menschlicher Weisheit vor Gott," *BN* 83 (1996), 13-15.

[3] Cf. E. Ullendorff, *Ethiopia and the Bible*, Oxford 1967, esp. 131-145. In the brief survey which follows we have borrowed some material from his work. See also R. Bayer, *Die Königin von Saba: Engel oder Dämon. Der Mythos einer Frau*, Bergisch Gladbach 1987; W. Damm, *Die Königin von Saba. Kunst, Legende und Archäologie zwischen Morgenland und Abendland*, Stuttgart 1988; and M. Delcor, "La Reine de Saba et Salomon. Quelques aspects de l'origine de la légende et de sa formation, principalement dans le monde juif et ethiopien, à partir des textes bibliques," *Tradició i Traducció de la Paraula* (Fs G. Camps, ed. F. Raurell et al.), Montserrat 1993, 307-24.

sources. In the Koran (cf. *surah* xxvii, 20-45) there is mention of a hoopoe who had to bring a letter from Solomon to the queen of Sheba. For she and her people were sun-worshippers. First the queen attempts to soften Solomon's heart by sending him expensive gifts but when they are not accepted, the queen herself makes the journey. By a ruse planned by Solomon, upon entering Solomon's palace she had to uncover her legs — because she held the palace floor, made smooth with sheets of glass, to be a pool of water — after which she finally surrenders to Allah, i.e. she joins Solomon in becoming Islamite. This story ties in closely with a fuller version in the Tg *šeni* on Esther. The purpose of the uncovering of the queen's legs is to discover whether she has 'hairy legs' and feet like a donkey's (hence a disguise of the devil). Islamic authors give her the name 'Belqis' (cf. *pallakis*, 'concubine') and some, accordingly, speak of her marriage to Solomon. So far the legends around this story.

From the preceding discussion the reader has already noted that the location of Sheba is uncertain, because, besides the notion that it is in S Arabia (cf. also S.D. Ricks, *ABD*, V, 1170f.), there is also the view that what we have here is an African country (e.g. in 'the horn of Africa'). שְׁבָא, aside from our chapter (vss. 1-13, par. 2 Chr. 9:1-12), also occurs in Gen. 10:7, 28; 25:3; Isa. 60:6; Jer. 6:20; Ezek. 27:22f.; 38:13; Ps. 72:10, 15; Job 1:15, 6:19 and 1 Chr. 1:9, 22, 32. It must be distinguished from סבא in Gen. 10:7; Isa. 43:3 (cf. Isa. 45:14); Ps. 72:10 and 1 Chr. 1:9, where it is mentioned as related to Cush (= Nubia or Ethiopia), and may have led in Josephus to a misunderstanding of its true location. Not only were the gold and incense of Sheba (e.g. Isa. 60:6; Jer. 6:20; Ps. 72:15) known in antiquity but also its location is — be it vaguely — indicated. Thus Dedan (Gen. 10:7; Ezek. 38:13; 1 Chr. 1:9; according to Albright (cf. *HAL*, 206), it is situated in N Hedjaz) is located nearby but also Raamah and other areas (Gen 10:7; Ezek 27:22), from which spices and precious stones were sold. These areas, accordingly, point to N Arabia. In antiquity it was apparently considered a wealthy region, though the prologue of Job tells us that the Sabeans also had rapacious habits. They did not even shy away from trading in people, at least according to Joel 4:8. *HAL*, 1285b, looks for the people and the kingdom in S Arabia, which presumably had trading colonies as far as N Arabia. M. Höfner (*RAAM*, 240f.) reports that Sabah is an ancient Arabian kingdom with which, also by way of inscriptions and discoveries, we are relatively well-acquainted. But of their rulers — their title was *mukarrib* — little is known before 720 CE. After that time we know of (trade) relations with Sargon and Sennacherib of Assyria. But we do know of women rulers from other Arabian tribes. Thus, in his annals, Tiglath-pileser III sometimes mentions the names of queens, e.g. Zabibe, queen of Arabia, from whom he received tribute; and Samsi, queen of Arabia, who was among his enemies (*ANET*, 283a). It is therefore not impossible that in ancient times also

Sheba had queens. Sabeans also occur frequently in the royal lists of Tiglath-pileser and, considering the context in which they occur, they must undoubtedly have belonged to Arabian tribes (*ANET*, 283-286; also cf. Noth). They were settled in N Arabian oases. These observations have prompted scholars (e.g. Šanda, Landersdorfer, Van den Born)[4] to think of the queen of Sheba as having come from the region of N Arabia. Others, however, thought and think rather of SW Arabia, present-day Yemen (cf. G. W. van Beek, *IDB*, IV, 144ff.; Attema, op. cit., 42f.; A.J. Gwinnett, L. Gorelick, *BA* 54 [1991], 196), from which the Sabeans controlled large areas and important trade routes. The ancient capital of their kingdom was situated in Marib,[5] a fairly fertile region. As a result of their activities in trade to distant coasts (India, E Africa), great wealth flowed toward this region. In addition, they lived too far from the great powers Egypt and Assyria to feel threatened. Classical authors, accordingly, not infrequently mention *Arabia Felix,* 'Fortunate Arabia.' It cannot be ruled out that the Sabeans also possessed trade colonies in 'the Horn of Africa' and elsewhere in Africa and that the stories about Solomon and 'the queen of Sheba' later travelled along these routes to present-day Ethiopia, so that Josephus, for example, could easily associate Sheba with Ethiopia, at least with an African region. The notion that the formation of legends on the basis of these stories took place in Ethiopia in the way in which Ullendorff reproduces them is not surprising, and even quite plausible. Nevertheless we cannot say with absolute certainty where the Sheba of our pericope must be located.[6]

EXEGESIS

10:1 *The queen of Sheba heard of Solomon's fame [for the name of YHWH] and came to test him with riddles.*
This verse begins by telling the reader that the queen of Sheba had heard of Solomon's fame. In contrast to the par. 2 Chr. 9:1, where a pf. 3 p. sing. fem. qal of the verb שׁמע is used, we find the part. fem. qal in our verse (not to be confused with 2 p. sing. fem.; see 1:11), which indicates an ongoing action (BrSynt. §44c; cf. WOC §37.6c). Of the 17x the substantive שֵׁמַע, 'rumour,' 'fame,' is used in OT, it occurs only here in Kgs. Hence the queen of Sheba kept hearing over and over of Solomon's fame. The *figura etymologica* even reinforces the – in our case – favorable rumors concerning Solomon. To this

---

[4] Cf. also D. S. Attema, *Arabië en de bijbel*, Den Haag 1961, 41f.
[5] Cf. *Oxford Bible Atlas* (ed. H.G. May), London 1974², 67.
[6] Cf. also the articles of G. W. van Beek; L. H. Silberman; E. Ullendorf and W. M. Watt in *Solomon and Sheba* (ed. J. B. Pritchard), London 1974.

statement is added that this fame is לשם יהוה an expression which is lacking in the par. 2 Chr. 9. LXX here reads 'and the name of the Lord,' after 'the *name of Solomon*' had already gone before. Pesh. only supports LXX in the first-mentioned reading. Tg. is divided, which means that in Sperber's edition the words are omitted but a number of Tiberian and other MSS which support MT. Also Vulg. supports MT (cf. also Barthélemy). Mont.-Gehman (et al.) are right in saying that these words have been added *ad majorem gloriam Dei*. Barthélemy, following a number of modern translations, offers the translator a choice between: 'she heard talk about the fame which Solomon owed to the name of YHWH' or 'she heard what people said of Solomon's fame to the glory of YHWH.' Klostermann, followed by Benzinger, Kamphausen and Skinner (et al.) emended: 'and the fame of the temple which he (i.e. Solomon) had built for the name of YHWH.' The suggestion is, therefore, that a piece of text has dropped out (in vs. 4 a marginal gloss, according to Ehrlich, also cf. 8:44, 48). Though it is certainly a clever emendation, the question is whether it adequately explains this dtr. gloss. Whatever explanation (and translation) one may adopt, the construction remains rather forced. For that reason we have put these words in parentheses in the translation.

The second half of our verse mentions the queen's coming to test Solomon with riddles. The word חידה, 'riddle,' occurs 17x in OT, 8 of which in Judg. 14:12-19 and in the books of Kings only here (cf. H.-P. Müller, *VT* 20 [1970], 465-489; V. Hamp, *TWAT*, II, 870-874). Riddles could be propounded in various forms. König, *Stil*. 12f., distinguishes: (1) common riddles, (2) numerical riddles, and (3) enigmatic statements. In Ezek. 17:2, for example, this word is used alongside of משל, 'proverb' (see comments on 5:12 above). In the Near East, among Arabs for example, 'propounding riddles' is a popular form of entertainment. It is quite possible that already in ancient times 'tournaments of wisdom' were held between rulers, when riddles and enigmatic proverbs were used to test the intelligence of high dignitaries. Josephus, *Ant.* VIII §§ 148f., cites a passage from the Phoen. author Dios who relates how Solomon and Hiram exchanged riddles. The pi.-form of נסה, which occurs 36x in OT, and only here in the books of Kings, means 'to test' (cf. F.J. Helfmeyer, *TWAT*, V, 473-487; G. Gerleman, *THAT*, II, 69ff.). The purpose of the test is to gain insight into what a person can do, what he really has to offer, and who he is (Helfmeyer, 475).

10:2 *She came to Jerusalem with a most impressive (show of) power: camels laden with balsam oil and an enormous quantity of gold and precious stones. She came to Solomon and discussed with him all the different things she had on her mind.*

First we are informed of the queen's coming to Jerusalem, accompanied by much external display. Then, in the second part of our verse, we are told of her coming to Solomon, accompanied only by the inner feelings of her heart. There is clearly a difference between the 2 comings. There have, accordingly, been exegetes who linked the saga of the Ethiopians – the story of how their earlier queen had given birth to a son by Solomon – to that second 'coming' (Thenius). The Hebr. equivalent of 'coming' can indeed have this sexual connotation (e.g. Gen. 16:2; 19:31; 30:3; 38:8; Deut. 22:13). But in that case people are reading more in our text than is really there!

Many Hebr. MSS insert a *yod* between the *lamed* and the *mem* of ירושלמה (Kennicott lists 18 MSS). The word חיל (according to König, *Stil.* 64) is a *synecdoche*: it indicates a broader field of meaning than is denoted by the word 'power': 'goods and personal effects.' These goods are then indicated by asyndetically mentioning the camels which carried a variety of valuables on their back. Now the par. 2 Chr. 9:1 indeed puts the copula *waw* before 'camels,' and is supported in so doing by LXX and Pesh. This need not, however, have much impact on the meaning. But Stade-Schwally point out that the syndetic construction could be a new circumstantial clause. Still the intent is not to say that the queen was arriving on the scene with a powerful army (though Thenius, for example, does not rule out this view). In that case Solomon could be excused from feeling suspicious. It is rather the intent to make clear that the queen was coming to Jerusalem with a great show of her power and riches, i.e. with spectacular gifts. The *beth* before חיל is a so-called *beth comitantiae* (WOC §11.2.5d). The particle refers to the accompanying circumstances (in casu: the goods), and they consist in loaded camels or rather dromedaries (one-humped). The word גמל occurs in the books of Kings only again in 2 Kgs. 8:9, but repeatedly in other books (especially in Gen. 24). The animal was and is particularly loved by bedouins (also cf. O. Michel, *TDNT*, III, 592-593; also *HAL*, 189f.; *Ges.*[18], 223a).

These transport animals, which can travel through deserts for thousands of kilometers, brought with them exotic and especially valuable goods. בשם (sometimes vocalized differently) occurs approx. 36x in OT and is the translation both for the 'balsam tree' (specifically: *commiphora opobalsamum;* so *Ges.*[18], 182; also cf. Josephus, *Ant.* VIII §174; *HAL*, 156) and for the sweet-scented 'balsam oil' an aromatic essence. LXX[B] translates the word by ἥδυσμα, LXX[Luc.] by ἄρομα. Smit, *Planten*, 133, thinks here of the mastic tree (*Pistacia lentiscus*), from which the aromatic balsam oil is derived. Nielsen similarly stresses that the reference is generally to non-specific sweet-smelling aromatic oil.[7] In any case, a present of aromatics, which might also include

---

[7] K. Nielsen, *Incense in Ancient Israel* (SVT 38), Leiden 1986, 67; in this respect agreeing with the view of I. Loew, *Die Flora der Juden*, Wien 1921-1937 (reprint Hildesheim 1967), I, 302.

incense, was not unusual among people of distinction (cf. Gen. 43:11; Matt. 2:11). Also 'gold' was brought along. According to R. de Langhe, *Bib* 40 (1959), 476-494, the Hebr. word זהב can also mean 'spice' and so is a homonym for 'gold,' an opinion based on the S Arabian word *dhb* which is found on altars of incense.[8] But this homonym is hard to prove (so, correctly, also Nielsen). The wisest course of action here, therefore, is to view the word as a designation of 'gold.' The 'valuable stones' (see also comments on 5:31 above) are also non-specific precious stones (for the sing. see: BrSynt. §17).

Thus prepared, the queen of Sheba arrived at king Solomon's palace (added in [MSS of] some ancient version before 'Solomon') in order next to present the things which touched her heart (also cf. comments on 8:17). Von Meyenfeldt, *Het hart*, 37f., translates somewhat more popularly: 'what she had on her mind,' and states that this expression has a twofold meaning: what she was planning to ask' and 'the things she had thought about in her heart. Noth, rejecting the 'popular' translation, agrees with the second viewpoint. Actually the difference between the 2 views is not all that great.

10:3 *Solomon had an answer for all her questions; not one of them was so obscure that he could not answer her.*
Solomon shows himself (as expected!) a perfect and intelligent king. He is not about to be checkmated by a (female) sheik! The part. pass. נֶעְלָם is construed with היה (cf. König §239b; Bg. II §13i; also WOC §37.1c). The verb עלם, 'to be hidden' occurs 28x in OT (5x in Sir.; 6x in Qumran; C. Locher, *TWAT*, VI, 160-167; cf. G. Wehmeier, *THAT*, II, 177), of which in the niph. 11x in OT (in Kings only here). Often the reference is to people for whom something is 'hidden' or 'inaccessible.' But Solomon manages perfectly to resolve all the 'riddles' presented to him by his Arabian colleague (נגד hiph.). Who is to say whether any really intimate secrets of the heart were included?

10:4 *When the queen of Sheba had seen all the wisdom of Solomon and the palace he had built,*
The queen of Sheba not only listened but also 'saw' a lot: the 'extent' of Solomon's wisdom (almost a technical term for his sagacity; cf. G. Fohrer, *TDNT*, VII, 488; also p. 481 where there is mention of the 'Jerusalem school of wisdom') and the 'house' he had built. This is presumably a reference to his palace (also cf. the digression in Josephus, *Ant.* VIII §§168f.), because in the sequel there is mention of certain aspects of the temple (but cf. Ehrlich, who holds another view: '*the* house' is the temple, '*his* house' is his palace; also see comments on vs. 1 above).

---

[8] *Corpus Inscriptionum Semiticorum*, IV, 3. fasc. 1, Paris 1929, 683; cf. Nielsen, 130, n. 519.

10:5 *as well as the food on his table, the (manner of) seating of his officials, and the attendance of his servants, and the way they were dressed, but also his drinking vessels and his burnt offerings which he used to present in the house of YHWH, she was completely flabbergasted.*

This verse continues the series of experiences and objects which totally amazed the queen. The first thing listed is 'the food of his table.' We already encountered the word 'table' earlier (2:7 etc.). Striking is the fact that LXX speaks of 'Solomon' in place of 'table.' The word מאכל occurs 30x in OT, only one of them here in the books of Kings (cf. 5:25; M. Ottosson, *TWAT*, I, 254).

As the second – probably related – point, there is mention of the manner of seating of the officials and the attendance of his servants. The word מושב, 'seat' occurs 44x in OT (in Kings also in 2 Kgs. 2:19; cf. A.R. Hulst, *THAT*, II, 906). Some have thought here of the 'dwellings' of the court officials (so Vulg.: *habitacula*; Thenius et al.), but it is very much a question whether, alongside the buildings which made up Solomon's palace, these would qualify as monuments worthy of the interest of the queen of Sheba. The reference here is obviously to the splendour of the court (Klostermann; Benzinger, etc.) In the translations we have conveyed the distinction between עבדים and משרתים (see comments on 1:4; also H. Strathmann, *TDNT*, IV, 230) as 'official' and 'servants' (with the par. 2 Chr. 9:4 and many Hebr. MSS, one must here follow the *q^{e}re* which indicates a pl.). The word מעמר (H. Ringgren, *TWAT*, VI, 202f.) denotes the 'attendance,' i.e. the 'station' at the table. The word has a fairly broad scale of meanings, as does its Akkad. semantic equivalent *manzaltu* (B.A. Levine, *JJS* 33 [1982], 313). The point of our verse is to describe the position of the many servants at Solomon's court.

The following word מלבוש, 'clothing,' 'robes, occurs only 7x in OT (in Kings again also in 2 Kgs. 10:22), which is considerably less than לבוש. In the ancient Near East there was a variety of types and kinds of clothing in a wide range of qualities (see S. Yeivin, *EncMiqr*. IV, 1034-1045; G. Fohrer, *BHHW*, II, 962-965; H. Weippert, *BRL*^{2} 185-188). The suff. 3 p. pl. denotes the clothing of the court officials and servants. Stade-Schwally, Ehrlich, et al., however, have raised the question whether the clothing of these people was actually of such great importance in the eyes of the queen. Granted, the pl. is maintained in the par. 2 Chr. 9, Josephus, *Ant.* VIII §169, and most of the ancient versions, but LXX* has 'of him' in important MS. In that case, then, we are dealing with Solomon's own wardrobe. Ehrlich even proposes – by way of a slight modification of the text – that we consider 'seine Garderobiers' to be the original reading. Nevertheless all this seems unnecessary. Along with Noth we can agree that the officials and servants wore robes which matched the king's surroundings ('die der Umgebung des Königs angemessen waren').

The last word, which in this verse is formed with a prefigured *mem* (cf.

Burney for these substantives with a preformative *mem* with a preformative *mem*) is the word מַשְׁקָיו. The reference here is to a sing. of מַשְׁקֶה plus suff. (Stade §345a; Ges-K §93ss). The word, which is actually a hiph. part. of the verb שׁקה (most often in a hiph.-modification), 'to give to drink,' can mean both 'butter' (especially in Gen. 40) and 'drink' (*HAL*, 1512f.; also cf. G. Gerleman, *THAT*, II, 1022-1026). The polyvalence of this word also permits it to be translated by 'wine cellar,' 'liquor depot' (*HAL*, 1513a). Faber van der Meulen, 95f., points out that the usual translation here is either 'butler' or 'drink.' The former translation is supported by LXX (LXX^B: οἰθοχοος; LXX^{Luc}: εὐνοῦχος). But why should the 'butlers' be singled out again after the reference to the other officials and servants? Faber van der Meulen opts for Montg.-Gehman's proposal that we translate the word by 'drinking-service' (cf. vs. 21 and Gen. 40:21). We, too, favour this proposal because it fits well in the series of 'objects' listed in this part of our verse. It remains for us to note that 2 Chr. 9:4 and Pesh. (aside from 9a1*fam* again add וּמַלְבּוּשֵׁיתָם, as though the reference here was to the robes of the *butlers*. For this is how the ancient translators must have viewed this word.

The last thing about which the queen of Sheba must have been astonished, at least according to the phrasing of our text, is Solomon's burnt offering. Many ancient translations (minus LXX) here read a pl. (also cf. Delitzsch, *LSF* §53a), but that does not make much material difference in the meaning of this notice. The par. 2 Chr. 9:4, however, reads עֲלִיָּתוֹ, 'his ascent,' although this word usually denotes an 'upper room,' 'space on a top floor' of a house or palace (e.g. 17:19, 23; 2 Kgs. 1:2; 4:10f.; 23:12). But the Chronicler apparently has in mind a splendid royal procession when Solomon brought his burnt offerings. Opinions on this differ also in the Jewish tradition. Rashi, for example, thinks here of a specific route the king took to get from his palace to the temple (cf. 1 Chr. 26:16), which as such is not an unnatural idea. Kimchi viewed it as a stairway of a special architectural style, which led from the palace up to the temple. Ehrlich, too, finds it hard to make sense of the 'burnt offerings.' He makes the point that for a queen who brings with her 120 talents of gold a large sacrifice is hardly something to become ecstatic over. Furthermore, he says, a pagan woman would never have been allowed to witness the sacrificial ceremony. But this last point, however classically rabbinical it may be, is certainly conceived from an overly modern viewpoint. Nor does his assertion stand up that Solomon only sacrificed 3x a year and that it must have been extremely coincidental for the queen of Sheba to be present on one of those days – as if a later Jewish liturgical practice could simply be applied as yardstick to Solomon's conduct with regard to and in his own court temple.

Solomon's 'going up' can also be 'effected' by a slight change in vocalization, as Ehrlich, Montg.-Gehman, et al. have demonstrated: an inf. cstr. with 3 p. sing. suffix of the verb עלה, 'his going up.' It seems best to us, nevertheless, to maintain the somewhat more difficult reading of a later Jewish viewpoint: Solomon as priest-king himself daily offered up his burnt offerings. The impf. indicates the continual repetition in the past (Böttcher §949f.; Driver §30; Bg. II §7d; GD §63a): 'the number of victims offered in a great sacrifice.'

This whole succession of things so affected the queen as to be beside herself. The word רוח, 'breath,' 'wind,' 'spirit' 'life' occurs 378x in the Hebr. and 11x in the Aram. part of OT (HAL, 1117b; cf. R. Albertz, C. Westermann, THAT, II, 726-753; S. Tengström, H.-J. Fabry, TWAT, VII, 385-425), some of them in the books of Kings (also in 18:12, 45; 19:11; 21:5; 22:21-24; 2 Kgs. 2:9, 15f.; 3:17; 19:7). Usually the word is fem., but in our verse (as in a number of other places; cf. K. Albrecht, ZAW 16 [1896], 42ff.; Stade-Schwally) it is masc. Scheepers, following others, translates our verse: 'there was no more breath left in her'[9] (cf. also F. Baumgärtel, TDNT, VI, 359ff.; and E. Jacob, TDNT, IX, 629). This language is, of course, figurative and one could also speak of 'spirit' (Burney). But why the translation of LXX: 'she was altogether beside herself' should 'miss the precise meaning,' as Burney asserts, is not entirely clear, at least to me. The astonishment of the queen is virtually of 'ecstatic' quality.

10:6 *She said to the king: 'It was true what I heard in my own country concerning your deeds and your wisdom;*
Once the queen has recovered from her astonishment, she expresses her admiration in words: 'Truth was the report.' The word אמת (for this word, cf. comments on 2:4) is emphatically positioned first (Jouön §154f.). A substantive used as predicate takes the place of an adjective here (cf. König §206r; Burney). The word היה here is not a simple copula (it is omitted in the par. 2 Chr. 9:5 and in LXX*) but has temporal meaning (Jouön §154m) with the nuance: 'there was something to what they said' (also cf. Mont.-Gehman). We also believe Stade-Schwally to be wrong in saying: 'The nominal clause is more appropriate for a *viva voce* remark and must therefore be considered original in this case.' Did they forget they were looking at a *literary* text?

A Hebr. MS and the LXX read ודבר in place of the pl., as in the text. The textcr. app. of BHK and BHS does not convey that, according to Kennicott, 3 additional Hebr. MSS read עליך in place of this word with the preceding על, an even more farreaching simplification. Stade-Schwally, who with Mont.-Gehman et al. favour the LXX-reading with the argument that the pl. would also include Solomon's wisdom, should, in our opinion, not be followed. In the case of Solomon, after all, many things come up for consideration and, as

---

[9] J. H. Scheepers, *Die Gees van God en die gees van die mens in die Ou Testament*, Kampen 1960, 35.

climax, also his wisdom.

10:7 *but I could not believe these things until I came and saw them with my own eyes. Indeed, not even half was told me. Your wisdom and prosperity far surpass the rumours that reached me.*

It was even more beautiful than she was told, even though rumours, certainly when they travel over long distances, tend to grow and expand. In 8:26 we encountered the niph.-form of אמן (see there) and here we find the hiph.. Construed with the prepositions לְ or בְּ (also cf. Pedersen, I-II, 348, n. 1), it here means 'to believe,' 'to trust,' 'to give credence to'.[10] The 'things' the queen believed are clearly viewed by LXX and Vulg. and possibly so by Pesh. and Tg. (in the Aram. this can no more be established with absolute certainty than in the Hebr.) as 'words.' The intent of the text is of course to say that the queen depended on 'hearsay' in which words and things are materially indivisible.

The phrase עד אשר introduces a temporal clause (see WOC §38.7a). The queen's being an eyewitness led to her conclusion that 'the half' (for the article in contrast to the par. 2 Chr. 9:6 which adds a number of words, cf. König §299d [the article of 'Connexität']) had not been told her. The part (the 'half') that had not been told her consisted of 'wisdom and goodness,' summed up in LXX[B. Luc.], as it were, in the word ἀγαθα. The little word טוב has numerous shades of meaning (see, for example, *HAL*, 355f.; I. Höver-Johag, *TWAT*, III, 315-339; H. J. Stoebe, *THAT*, I, 652-664). It is very much a question, however, whether the ethically good is meant here: Solomon as a 'good person.' Solomon is considered 'wise,' which means that he makes the right choices and has the right insight in the political and economic affairs of and for his country and people. He, therefore, brings about 'good' things. The preposition אל is often exchanged with the preposition על (so a number of Hebr. MSS and the par. 2 Chr. 9:6), but that is not necessary here (cf. Ewald §217i; GD §118, rem. 1; WOC §38.7a; BrSynt. §108b[11]): one can translate 'in relation to' despite the use of the verb יסף (hiph.).

10:8 *How fortunate your people! How fortunate your servants who are continually allowed to wait on you, listening to your wisdom!*

The queen continues – in the words of the dtr. author of course – to pronounce 2 categories of people happy. The nominal exclamation אשרי (see WOC §40.2.3b), a pl. st. cnstr., which at an early stage already hardened into a kind

---

[10] See also J.C.C. van Dorssen, *De derivata van de stam* אמן *in het Hebreeuws van het Oude Testament*, Amsterdam 1951, 23.

[11] See further also A. Noordtzij, *Het Hebreeuwse Voorzetsel* אל, Leiden 1896, 50.

of interjection (cf. Ges-K §931; also König §262e and n. 1), in this form occurs 45x in OT, no fewer than 26 of which in the Psalms and 12 in the (later) wisdom literature (H. Cazelles, *TWAT*, I, 481-485; M. Saebø, *THAT*, I, 257-260). In Kings the word only occurs here. It is a kind of liturgical invocation which seems 'lost' here and which clearly betrays the pen of the dtr.

The first category of fortunate people are – at least in the Hebr. version – the men. LXX, Pesh. and also the Arab. translations here read 'women.' Böttcher (*Neue Aehrenlese*) already makes a plea for the correctness of the latter reading: 'Es wäre zu verwundern, wenn eine Frau das nicht ausgesprochen hätte.' Since then numerous if not most exegetes have adopted this view, recently also Barthélemy. He asserts that the events described in 11:1-4 adequately explain that a 'corrector' of our text wanted to avoid a blessing addressed to Solomon's women because it was they who had lured Solomon's heart away from the true service of YHWH! It is well known that correctors have from time to time made surgical changes in the text in order to correct passages deemed 'offensive'.[12] One need not, therefore, even think of the more innocent solution of a 'writing error' (occasioned by the preceding and following words; so Delitzsch, *LSF* §98c). There are, accordingly, enough modern translations which read 'women' in place of 'men' or the like (LV, Obbink, PVC, JB). Another possibility available to us is to view the words 'men' and 'servants' as a hendiadys. Based on this option, NV arrives at the translation: 'Gelukkig zijn uw mannen, gelukkig deze dienaren van u, die ...' ('Happy are your men, happy these your servants who ...'). For, however natural it is to follow the majority of modern exegetes and translators on the basis of the strong textual witnesses LXX and Pesh., and the logical arguments for their reading, there is still no reason to abstain from saying a good word for the more difficult reading offered by MT. The pl. of איש need not per se mean 'men' but can also have the broader meaning 'people' or 'countrymen' (*HAL*, 42b; *Ges.*[18], 50f.), and that meaning is entirely defensible here (cf. also Šanda, Van Gelderen, Noth, et al., who, sometimes hesitatingly, sometimes with other arguments, e.g. with an appeal to ancient eastern etiquette, maintain MT in this reading). After a somewhat general exclamation, 'your people,' the queen particularizes her congratulations by calling special attention to Solomon's servants who are continually in the privileged position of being able to hear and witness the king's wise words and deeds. With as much cogency as there is for the reverse, one can say that LXX and Pesh. indeed found a Hebr. 'Vorlage' in which the reference was to 'women,' but who guarantees us that this 'Vorlage' was *not* a 'corrected' text?

---

[12] Cf. my "Un euphémisme dans 2 Sam. XII 14?, *VT* 18 (1968), 108-114; and R. Wonneberger, *Leitfaden zur Biblia Hebraica Stuttgartensia*, Göttingen 1986², 44, n. 140.

The demonstrative אלה also occurs after words without an article but with a suffix (König §334y; Driver §209; GD §6).

10:9 *Praise be to YHWH your God who is showing you his favour by setting you on the throne of Israel, because YHWH loves Israel with an everlasting love and has appointed you to be king to do justice and righteousness.'*
Noth is probably correct when he regards the queen of Sheba's eulogy in this verse as a bonus-gift from the dtr., who felt YHWH still had to be mentioned as well, be it *post festum,* as the giver of wisdom to Solomon (for ברוך cf. comments on 2:45, and for חפץ ב on 9:1). The 'love of YHWH' (subj. gen.; Joüon §129d; WOC §9.5.1.b) is described by an infinitive functioning as a noun (cf. BL, 317g; further Böttcher §990 [4B], Bg. II §14p, Lettinga §73b[d], Meyer II §35.1b) of the root אהב (G. Wallis, *TWAT*, I, 108-128; E. Jenni, *THAT*, I, 60-73), which we encountered earlier in 3:3. The word, which occurs approx. 55x in OT (but is often taken as a substantive) occurs only here and in 11:2 in the books of Kings. Another form of the verb occurs only in 11:1 in Kgs as well. Solomon is king on account of YHWH's 'everlasting' love for Israel. The par. 2 Chr. 9:8, evidently supported in this by LXX, reads להעמידו לעולם, that is, YHWH will forever uphold Israel. Stade-Schwally, Burney (et al.) consider this expansion possible also in our verse, though the firstmentioned authors label it a gloss to explain the difficult expression 'forever.' The text, which is somewhat obscure as to the drift of what precisely is happening (the cause and its consequences are repeated in other words in the second half of our verse), has prompted König (*Stil.* 171) to classify our verse as an example of 'palindromy.' There seems to be no end to the queen's praises of Solomon, although in our verse things seem to turn on 'YHWH's love for Israel'! For the combination of 'justice and righteousness,' cf. also J.J. Scullion, *UF* 3 (1971), 342.

10:10 *Thereupon she gave to the king a hundred and twenty talents of gold and large quantities of balsam oil and precious stones. Never again was such a quantity of that balsam oil imported as the queen of Sheba gave to king Solomon.*
The queen now proceeds to act by turning over to Solomon a more-than-royal present. First there are the 120 talents of gold. Earlier, already in 9:14, there was mention of 120 talents of gold, and there too it is an improbably high amount. Second, there is the costly balsam oil already referred to in vs. 2, and third, the precious stones. In reference to the balsam oil there is the comment that never again was so much of it imported into Israel as when the queen of Sheba visited Solomon.

10:11 *Similarly Hiram's fleet, which imported gold from Ophir, also brought*

along great quantities of 'almug' wood and precious stones (from Ophir).
In this and the following verse reference is made to the rich trade which occurred, also by way of the relations with Hiram, in Solomon's days and to the visible results of this trade. True, to our mind these statements somewhat hinder the flow of the narrative about the queen of Sheba but they also indicate, as we said earlier, how important these trade relations were thought to be for the comparatively great wealth of Solomon. Our verse, accordingly, ties in with what was already said in 9:26ff. (see there) and with what is coming in vs. 22, even though Hiram is only here referred to as the 'owner' of the fleet.

A new element in our verse is the question what is meant by the word אלמנים, a word which, aside from here, only occurs again in 2 Chr. 2:7 and the par. 2 Chr. 9:10f., where it is found with the *mem* and the *gimel* transposed (cf. Bg. I §20d). The fact that it is a 'foreign word' is clear (Olsh. §221; Ges-K §35m). Even older exegetes, Jewish as well as non-Jewish, found it hard to translate the word. Rashi and Kimchi, for example, referred to the (Old) French word 'corail,' coral, which they viewed as having petrified, an explanation which is also mentioned by Vatablus in his *Annotata*. In our verse we are told that this kind of wood, for that is what we are dealing with, was transported from Ophir, but this second 'from Ophir' is omitted both in LXX and in the par. 2 Chr. 9. Whereas in 5:20 there is only reference in general to the transportation of timber from the Lebanon, 2 Chr. 2:7 tell us in particular that also 'almug' timber came from the Lebanon. To the Chronicler this kind of wood, then, was not specifically tropical and perhaps well known. Scholars have often thought here of 'sandal wood' (cf. Montg.-Gehman), a kind of hardwood used in the past and still used today for furniture and carving. But this identification is very uncertain (cf. *KBL*, 55). Today some scholars identify it with *Juniperus phoenicia* (*KBL*) or *Juniperus oxycedrus* L (Smit, *Planten*, 98). J.C. Greenfield and M. Mayrhofer, SVT 16 (1967), 83-89, have again brought up for reexamination the extensive literature which exists concerning the 'almug-wood problem.' Already fairly old is the opinion that the word comes from the Sanskrit (*valgu) but the authors (following W.E. Clark, *AJSL* 36 [1920], 103ff.) regard this idea most improbable. The word *'argmn* already occurs in the Ugar. (cf. *DLU*, I, 48f.; also in the Akkad. the word *elammakku(m)* (*AHw*, 196b) is related to the Hebr. Precisely what kind of wood we are dealing with, however, is still unclear. In the Rabbinical tradition[13] there are 2 very different views: (1) a kind of coral; (2) a species of aloe wood (cf. Hochberg-Rosenberg, 114c.). What seems to us, along with numerous other exegetes, the most natural solution is to think in this connection (with the Chronicler) of a kind of wood from the Lebanon (or other mountain ranges

---

[13] Cf. I. Loew, *Die Flora der Juden*, Wien 1921-1937 (reprint Hildesheim 1967), III, 342ff.

further to the N), which is related to the conifers summed up in 2 Chr. 2:7. Accordingly, the second 'from Ophir' in our verse is a gloss which has later crept into the text by mistake. LXX[B] translates the word in question by ξυλα πελετηκα, 'hewn wood.' Pesh. refers to *qesûta*, which Payne Smith, 511b, translates by 'sandalwood', but which Brockelmann, 679b, more cautiously, translates by *'ligni genus.'* Tg. leaves the word untranslated and Vulg. speaks of *ligna thyina*, a translation derived from the Greek (cf. Symmachus's translation of our verse), which can also be found in the NT in Rev. 18:12. There the word is rendered by 'citron wood.' θυον, a tree having aromatic wood, is already mentioned in the Odyssey (5, 60) (Liddell-Scott, 811a). Josephus, *Ant.* VIII §176, speaks of ξυλα πευθικα, 'conifer-like wood.' In view of the context in which the wood is mentioned in 2 Chr. 2:7, this makes sense and is probably the most acceptable solution to the 'almug-wood problem' (cf. Smit, op. cit.). In the translation, however, we will maintain the word which was 'foreign' also to the Hebrews.

10:12 *Of the almug wood the king made material for furnishing the temple of YHWH and the royal palace, as well as harps and lyres for the singers. Never before did 'almug' wood arrive in this manner, nor was it ever seen (in such quantity) to this day.*
Of this special kind of wood objects for the temple and the palace were made. For the first time there is reference to מִסְעָד, a word which in OT only occurs in this verse. In the par. 2 Chr. 9:11 the word מְסִלּוֹת is used, a word which usually means 'roads (raised with stones and dirt).' This word occurs more frequently (27x) in OT, though it is a question whether it has this meaning here (cf. *HAL*, 573b). LXX in our verse translates the word by ὑποστριμα, 'support' (also in 7:24 above), a word used by LXX as the translation for פְּקָעִים, the 'pomegranate-like decorations.' Pesh. has *tasbîta*, 'decoration'; Vulg. *fulchra*, 'buttress,' while Tg. reads: סְעִיד, 'support.' The verb סוּד occurs 12x in OT, especially in the sense of 'support' (G. Warmuth, *TWAT*, V, 889-893), but that does not yet settle the meaning of the word in our verse (cf. Warmuth, 892f.). R. Weiss (*Textus* 6 [1968], 130) thinks the Chronicler read our word as מִצְעָד, 'path,' 'step,' for which, in his version of the story, he then substituted another word with approximately the same meaning. Rashi, also, though not on the same ground, thinks here of pavement, while Kimchi is of the opinion that they were pillars to support the canopy over the road. Warmuth, 893, 'provisionally' translates the word by 'Vertäfelung' ('panelling'). It is certainly possible that certain parts of the building as well as the roads leading to and from the buildings were covered, supported or adorned with woodwork (cf. Ehrlich inter al.). But Noth correctly points out that, in view of the building notices in the chaps. 6 and 7, there is no longer any mention at this point of essential building construction of palace or temple.

Although he considers the translation 'Ausstattungsstücken' ('pieces of equipment') a makeshift solution, it seems to us plausible. Of this high quality wood, various necessary but at the same time ornamental implements and facilities could be made, both inside and outside the buildings.

Aside from pieces of equipment also musical instruments were made of this special wood. The 2 instruments, which in the book of Kings are only mentioned here, occur more frequently elsewhere in OT. כנור occurs over 40x in OT (M. Görg, *TWAT*, IV, 210-216; also cf. Ellenbogen, *Foreign Words*, 1962, 86f.). It is presumably the 'lyre,' and various ancient representations of it have been found (see, e.g.: G. Wallis, *BHHW*, II, 1258-1262). Scholars are not altogether certain of its meaning, anymore than of the meaning of the following word נבל (K. Seybold, *TWAT*, V, 185-188), which occurs 28x in OT (a homonym which occurs 11x in OT means; 'cup,' 'jar') and is usually translated by 'harp,' though 'lyres' and 'harps' are indeed the most widespread musical instruments in the ancient Near East.[14] Ellenbogen, *Foreign Words*, 86f., is of the opinion that כנור, though it occurs in various Semitic languages, was an autochthonous word in use among the pre-Semitic inhabitants of Canaan. This word was borrowed by the Hittites, 'or it may have come from one of the invading non-Semitic peoples such as the Hurrians' (also cf. Görg, 198f.). As for the word נבל, G. Wallis (*BHHW*, II, 648) comments that the resonance chamber of this instrument was probably jar-shaped or covered with skin. Keel, *Bildsymbolik*, 323, reports that, although the harp was already known in Egypt and in Syria-Palestine in the 3rd millennium BCE, up until now no exemplars have come to light, in contrast to the different kinds of lyres of which splendid exemplars have been found. The frequently occurring combination (in OT) of lyres and harps (inter al. in Pss. 57:9; 71:22; 81:3; 92:4; 108:3; 150:3) may certainly also warrant the translation of נבל by 'lyre.' The reason is that on certain representations one can distinguish 2 kinds of 'lyres' (Keel, *Bildsymbolik*, 325, fig. 472). The lyre with curved yoke-arms and a jar-shaped resonance chamber which in a larger design could be strung with ten (or twelve) strings and rested on the floor (fig. 474) is the instrument we call the 'harp,' the smaller, simpler, more angular and portable model, we call the 'lyre' (p. 324).

These musical instruments of fine wood are for (accompanying) the 'singers.' The verb שיר, of which our word can be considered a substantival pl. part., means 'to sing' and occurs 87x in OT (R. Ficker, *THAT*, II, 895-898), but not in the books of Kings (also see comments on 5:12) and in this substantival form only here in Kings. Although we are not told in our verse that musical

---

[14] Cf. M. Wegner, *Die Musikinstrumente des alten Orients* (Orbis Antiquus 2), Münster 1950, 42f.

instruments and singers played a role in the cult, it is likely that the author in fact had this in mind (Tg. expressly adds to this verse that the musical instruments were 'for the Levites'). On the other hand, it is also extremely probable that Solomon employed singers and musicians in his court temple and palace.

At the end of our verse there is a brief comment on the particular quantity and quality of the 'almug' wood. The anaphoric particle כן, used adverbially also here, indicates the manner, quantity and quality (see König §318e; also my article on this particle in *OTS* 21 [1981], 218; further Burney, who [perhaps too easily?] accommodates it to the English idiom: 'there came not *such* almug trees'). The par. 2 Chr. 9:11 omits these words and ends the verse as follows: 'there never was seen the like of them before in the land of Judah' (RSV), a narrowing of the subject which is understandable in the time of the Chronicler.

10:13 *King Solomon gave the queen of Sheba everything she desired, whatever she asked him, even aside from the things Solomon gave her out of his royal bounty. Thereupon she left and returned to her own country, she and her servants.*

The narrator returns to his story about the queen of Sheba and concludes it with a 'happy ending.' The double preposition מלבד means 'aside from' (BrSynt. §119a; Ehrlich). Solomon not only showed himself to be a wealthy oriental ruler but also an excellent and charming host. The words כיד המלך, 'according to the bounty of,' i.e. 'corresponding to' the (abundant) resources and (in this case) the riches of the king, can also be found in Esth. 1:7; 2:18 (*HAL*, 371b; Burney; cf. P. Jouön, *Bib* 14 [1933], 458f., who makes reference to Lev. 5:7; cf. also Tg.: 'according to the wealth of his hand'). The second 'Solomon,' which is omitted by Pesh. and Vulg. and a number of Greek MSS, seems somewhat redundant, but must be maintained in the translation (so inter al. Stade-Schwally). The Chronicler reads: 'besides what she had brought to the king.'

10:14 *Now the weight of the gold which Solomon received annually was six hundred and sixty-six talents,*

From this point on we again find 'mixed items of information' about Solomon's trade relations, economic politics, expenditures of wealth, etc. The vss. 14 and 15 deal with the financial side of the state economy (also cf. O. Eißfeldt, *CAH*, II/2, 592ff.). They link up with 9:28 and the vss. 11 and 12 of our chapter. The annual revenues (Vulg. correctly: *per annos singulos*) of Solomon (and such an eastern potentate could, with good warrant, say: 'l'état, c'est moi') amounted to 666 talents of gold. This figure, which aside from the par. 2 Chr. 9:13 and Ezra 2:13, occurs again (in OT and NT) only in Rev. 13:18, has a particularly distressing meaning in that verse (for משקל, cf.

comments on 7:47). The idea that the number cited in our verse is the result of later exaggeration, as various scholars believe, is indeed likely (cf. comments on 9:14 above) but hard to prove. Šanda (also cf. Noth) has tallied up the talents reported in 9:14; 9:28 and 10:10, plus a few more, and takes this amount to be the final amount for this very particular year, but that is too artificial. The question indeed is: what revenues are we dealing with here?, since the beginning of the following verse expressly excludes the revenues reported in that verse. Pintore is of the opinion that in our verses the reference is to tax levies in Judah (4:7-19, after all, referred to Israel aside from Judah).[15] But this is not information which can simply be inferred from our verses. It *is* possible that the reference here is to the direct taxes which every head of the family (or perhaps even of every adult person in the nation) had to produce to maintain Solomon's costly (state) apparatus. And that is a particularly heavy burden of taxation! It was not for nothing that there later arose sharp protest against the heavy tax pressure which Solomon had imposed (12:4). But other forms of levies and revenues are equally well possible. The statement of our verse, however, is too general to permit farreaching conclusions.

10:15 *not including the revenues from (itinerant) merchants and from the traders and from all the kings of Arabia and from the governors of the land*
Both textcritically and exegetically the categories listed in this verse produce problems. To begin with the former: must we, for example, read מאנשי or מענשי? Granted, on this point the par. 2 Chr. 9:14 agrees textually with MT of our verse but LXX here reads φορος, 'tribute'; Tg.: אגר, 'wages,' while Vulg. explicatively renders the beginning of our verse as follows: *excepto eo quod offerebant viri qui super vectiqalia erant,* 'except that which the men who collected taxes brought in.' Now the genitive combination of 'men' with the following word תרים, which actually denotes 'spies' (qal. part. of the verb תור, 'to spy out,' which occurs especially in Num. 13 and 14), but taken here (in combination with the following רכלים) as 'merchants,' is certainly not, from a grammatical viewpoint, entirely impossible (cf. Ewald §287e; König §337q) but in terms of its meaning apparently redundant. Add to this that also 2 Chr. 9:14 (excepting now LXX) and a number of ancient versions take other approaches in their rendering of the words. Barthélemy demonstrates that Pesh. ('besides the taxes of the cities') there assimilates itself to Tg. of our verse but that the Chronicler in his text only coordinates persons (in the pl.) and describes the syntactical function of those names by making them the subjects of the recurring pl. part. מביאים.

As to this problem in our verse, over the years various modifications of the

---

[15] F. Pintore, "I dodeci intendenti di Salomone," *RSO* 45 (1970), 177-207.

text have been proposed. Thenius (already in the first edition of his work in 1849) proposed the reading מֵעַנְשֵׁי הרדוים, 'from the fines paid by the subject people,' in line with LXX τῶν ὑποτεταγμένων. But Böttcher (*Neue Aehrenlese*) opposed the modification of the second word. He wants to maintain MT at this point and view תרים as 'Reisebeamte, herumziehende Taxatoren und Steuereinnehmer,' but also maintain the first part of Thenius's emendation. The word ענשׁ occurs in 2 Kgs. 23:23 and Prov. 19:19. In these verses there is reference to a 'fine' which was imposed. Klostermann construed the 2 words referred to (אשכר החתרים) as 'the tribute (for this word, cf.: Ezek. 27:15; Ps. 72:10) of the rowers' (see also Oort [LV]). Kittel had still another proposal: 'apart from what came in from the cities' (מאשר בא מן־הערים), inspired by Pesh. on 2 Chr. 9:14 (also cf. Kamphausen [followed inter al. by Burney]), who reads: 'aside from what came in from the business of the merchants,' in the process drawing in the 2 following Hebr. words – somewhat modified textually – and thus smooths out our verse). We will ignore the various other text emendations (see, e.g. Benzinger, Šanda, Montg.-Gehman, as well as the textcr. app. of *BHK* and *BHS*) and with Barthélemey give serious weight to the *lectio difficilior*. We can join him also in raising the question whether LXX really read ענשׁ in MT, the reading on which, after all, so many emendations have been based up until now. The תרים (the word, according to Montg.-Gehman, comes form a second root, related to the Arab.; but also cf. Gray; W. Herrmann, *ZAW* 91 [1979], 334, n. 26; *HAL*, 1574a and b), then, are the 'itinerant traders or merchants.' We possibly indeed have here – as briefly suggested above – an apposition in the form of a genitive: 'people traveling for trade' (Barthélemy). For the word תרים some scholars wish to read תגרים, 'traders' (Dalman, *ANH*, 438b; see Rudolph et al.), but this is unnecessary (also cf. the curious and unwarranted text modification proposed by the textcr. app. of *BHS* on the basis of *ET* 42 [1930f.], 439, and *KBL*: 'the fleet of Tarshish'!). But there seems to be still another possibility both to virtually maintain MT and at the same time to retain the idea of 'taxation' as the basic intent of the statement.

On the basis of Ugar. *'unt*, D. R. Hillers (*HThR* 64 [1971], 257ff.), in nailing down the meaning of the word אנוש in Isa. 33:8 (usually translated by 'man,' 'humanity'; *Ges.*[18], 80a), has proposed the translation 'land tax' (owed to the king). O. Loretz (*UF* 8 [1976], 449) in any case accepts (along with M. Tsevat, mentioned in Hillers' article) this meaning for our verse (although he wants to change תרים into תררים). The advantage of this proposal, accordingly, is that without any appreciable text modification the idea of 'taxation' or 'tribute' can be maintained. It needs to be added that for the levying of taxes by tax collectors the commentaries frequently refer to Palmyra. G. A. Cooke passes on a Palmyran text (probably from the Roman era) in which there is mention of 'tax laws' and tax levies imposed on traders as well as others.[16] Although this method of levying excise and other taxes in the ancient Near East was not unknown (cf. e.g. Matt. 9:9), it is a question whether it can be compared with the method followed in Solomon's time.

The word מסגר occurs in this form only here. It is usually proposed that in its place we read the preposition מן and the substantive סגר, 'business profit' (Isa 23:3, 18; 45:14; Prov. 3:14; 31:18; cf. *HAL*, 708b). The סותר is the 'merchant,' the 'trader' (perhaps in the service of the king, see below, vs. 28), and he is mentioned a number of times in OT, also in the par. 2 Chr. 9:14 (in place of our word). Because the text modification only concerns the punctuation, there is little to be said against this emendation. רכל is also a word for 'merchant' (17x in OT, esp. in Ezek. 27). Josephus, *Ant.* VIII §179, sums up the tributes of the traders and the taxes of the merchants mentioned in our verse as 'that which was brought in by the merchants.'

The following category to be considered is the kings העבר, rendered in many of our translations by 'the kings of Arabia,' probably in imitation of the par. 2 Chr. 9:14, where עֲרָב is read. LXX reads: 'from the kings of τοῦ περαν, which would suggest a Hebr. reading העבר, 'the other side (of the river)' (also cf. comments on 5:4). Tg. reads: 'the kings of the סמכותא, 'auxiliary troops,' i.e. the troops 'of the allied peoples' (Burney). Pesh. and Vulg. support the translation 'Arabia,' as do Aquila, Symmachus, and Josephus, *Ant.* VIII §179. According to *HAL*, 831, the word ערב II (I means 'evening'), only occurs twice: here and in Jer. 25:24. In the case of our verse this dictionary refers to Noth who conforms to the reading of 2 Chr. 9:14 ('Arabia'), and against whose opinion that of Simons, *GTTOT* §8, is cited: 'the term refers to bedouin and other groups without national organization.' In Jer. 25:24, the phrase 'all the kings of הערב' actually expressly follows 'the kings of Arabia,' and is qualified by the clause: 'that dwell in the steppe.' Commentators not infrequently think in this connection of the 'mixed population' (also cf. Jer. 25:20; 50:37; Ezek. 30:5), a term derived from ערב II (*HAL*, 831b). The reference would then be to the kings or sheiks of mixed Arabian tribes from S.E. Arabia (so, for example, Burney).

Some time ago S. Yeivin, *Leš* 38 (1973f.), 33-37 launched another proposal for our כל־מלכי הערב.[17] Noting the place of these kings in our section and the character of the narrative, viz. between the story of the queen of Sheba and the decoration of Solomon's throne, and basing himself on the number 6, he distinguishes in our verse 3 sources of income for Solomon: (1) the unidentified source at the beginning of our verse; (2) the royal trade monopoly; (3) the

---

[16] G.A. Cooke, *A Textbook of North-Semitic Inscriptions*, Oxford 1903, 320-332.
[17] Cf. also *EncMiqr.*, VI, 554f.

kings and governors. He further sums up 3 roots of the word ערב: (1) the 'west'; (2) the 'trade' (Ezek. 27:9, 13, 17; a relatively recent meaning), and (3) 'suretyship.' In the case of subject peoples, the children (inter al.) of the subject parents are pledges for the conquering king. The administration of those subject peoples can be organized in 2 ways; (1) in some countries they may keep their own government; (2) in other countries a governor is appointed. In our verse, says the author, the reference is to (foreign) vassals of king Solomon who vouched for their children and subjects and for this reason had to bring in their assessments as bond money. In the case of the 'governors' of the land we are dealing with the governors of the districts of Israel itself, which were listed in 4:7-19. What we have in 2 Chr. 9:14 is a paraphrase.

However ingenious this explanation may be, still, with the majority of the translations and exegetes, we will stick with 'Arabia' (so, inter al., Benzinger, Gray, Jones, Robinson, Rice, NEB, et al.; otherwise, for instance, Van Gelderen: 'all the kings of the Beduins'; also cf. Šanda). The reference here is possibly to the N part of the Arabian territory, which borders on Israel. Nor can we completely rule out that these words, along with the last 2 words of our verse, are a later addition to our text. For the word פחה, 'governor,' which occurs 28x in the Hebr. part. (and 10x in the Aram. part) of OT (in Kings also again in 20:24 and 2 Kgs. 18:24), is an Akkad. word[18], according to some scholars even a neo-Babylonian loanword (E. Lipiński, *ZAH* 1 [1988], 71; also cf. Ellenbogen, *Foreign Words*, 131). In that language the word *pāḫātu/pīḫātu* occurs in the sense of 'governor' (*AHw,* 862). Also in OT the reference is usually to Assyrian (2 Kgs. 18:24), Babylonian (Jer. 51:23, 28, 57, etc.) or Persian (Esth. 3:12, etc.) dignitaries. After the exile we also hear of these 'governors' in Judah (Zerubbabel: Hag. 1:1, 14, etc.; Nehemiah: Neh. 12:26, etc.). Only in 20:24 do we read of the 'commanders' of the king of Damascus. In 4:7-19 there is mention of נצבים, 'prefects,' and our word does not (yet) occur (see comments on 4:5 above). The correct translation of the word is not as easy as it looks. Petit (art. cit.; also cf. *HAL,* 872b), in an attempt to mark off the precise meaning, has come to the conclusion that one can distinguish 3 different senses of the word (p. 64): (1) satrap, when it concerns the governor of a Persian satrapy; (2) under-satrap (e.g. under Darius I); (3) governor of a specific area (in Syria or Palestine). The last meaning listed seems to us to fit best in the context. We may assume that the word itself was taken over into Hebr. during or after the exile, and was perhaps inserted even later (Noth; Rehm).

---

[18] Cf., inter al., Th. Petit, "L'évolution sémantique des termes hébreux et araméens *phh* et *sgn* et accadiens *pāhatu* et *šaknu,*" *JBL* 107 (1988), 53-67, esp. 53f.

Although, in view of the word פחה, the word 'land' is sometimes understood to refer to 'foreign lands' outside of Israel (cf. Burney, Jones etc.), the last 2 words refer to the revenues which have come in via the governors of the districts mentioned in chap. 4 (so also Thenius, Van Gelderen, Rice, Robinson). Let us note, finally, that the par. 2 Chr. 9:14 adds to the last words of our verse: they 'brought gold and silver to Solomon,' which, though materially correct, is formally redundant.

10:16 *In addition king Solomon made two hundred great shields of beaten gold; six hundred (shekels) of gold went into each great shield;*
The following verses tell us what Solomon did with his wealth. That this was no small matter to the author of this section is immediately apparent from the 2 verses which deal with the 'gold shields' which were stored in the House of the Forest of Lebanon (see comments on 7:2-5 above). The word צנה occurs some 20x in OT, though only here in Kings. It denotes a large, body-covering shield which was often carried by a separate shield bearer (1 Sam. 17:7, 41) and distinguished from the word מגן, a much smaller (round) shield which occurs already in the next verse and with considerable frequency in OT (cf. A. Oepke, *TDNT*, V, 312f.; De Vaux, *Inst.* II, 54; H. Weippert, *BRL*^{2}, 279f.[19]). The difference in the size of the shields can be expressed in 'large shields' and 'small shields' (the KJV distinguishes between 'shields' and 'bucklers'). In our verse the reference is clearly to ornamental shields, though on certain occasions they were also borne by members of the bodyguard (cf. Šanda). It is further added that, as for the gold, it was שחוט (pass. qal part.; cf. also the next verse and the par. 2 Chr. 9:15f.; in Jer. 9:7 [q^ere] it means 'sharpened'). The verb, from which this part. comes, is derived in the newer lexicons (inter al. *KBL*, *HAL*,, Zorell) from a root וחט II (see *HAL*, 1353f.) which is now no longer associated with the synonymous root I ('slaughter'). Two possibilities of translating it are presented and extensively discussed in *HAL*: (1) 'driven,' 'beaten'; (2) 'alloyed,' i.e. mixed with another metal. The first possibility is supported by LXX (χρυσα ελατα), and is accepted in many commentaries, although the other ancient translations seem much less exact here: Vulg. *scuta de auro puro* = Pesh. *dhba onyna,* while Tg. speaks of רהבא טבא. Burney indicates that the translation 'alloyed gold,' obtained from an Arab. verb *sht*, 'delute wine with water' (so, inter al., Gesenius, *Thesaurus*, 1387b) is probably wrong.

We read that Solomon had 200 large shields of gold made. The gold was probably beaten down on a wooden base or frame so that the shields were not

---

[19] See now also A. Millard, "King Solomon's Shields," *Scripture and Other Artifacts* (Fs P.J. King, eds. M.D. Lorgan et al.), Louisville 1994, 286-295.

entirely of pure gold. In the Bronze and Iron Age, according to Weippert (op. cit), wooden shields covered with leather and reinforced with nails were customary in Syria and Palestine. LXX mentions the figure of 300 as the number of the shields, but Josephus, *Ant.* VIII §179, and other ancient versions support MT.

Also in what follows LXX opts for 300 in place of the 600 of MT. The reference is to a unit of value which is not further described in our verse (but see the following verse) as this is the case also elsewhere (see examples in König §314h; GD §47, rem. 2). Usually this is associated here with the שֶׁקֶל, the shekel (but Pesh. here refers to the mina). The shekel is a unit of weight and coinage which tended to fluctuate in weight and value and must have been further defined by the material of which it consisted or by an (officially) fixed standard (e.g. the 'sanctuary shekel' [Exod. 30:13f.; 38:24ff.; etc.]) but of which we can no longer exactly determine the weight and the value (cf. *HAL*, 1515f.; De Vaux, *Inst.* I. 309ff.; H. Weippert, *BRL*², 93f.; M.A. Powell, *ABD*, VI, 905ff.). Earlier we already encountered the כבר, 'talent' (9:14, 28; 10:14), of which a 60th part is the mina. Of this again a 60th part (or sometimes a 50th part: Ezek. 45:12) is the 'shekel' which, in turn, can be divided into 'gerahs.' The 'mina,' which is mentioned in the following verse is presumably an Akkad. loanword (see Ellenbogen, *Foreign Words*, 104f.), and stems from the time of or after the exile (the word occurs in the OT, aside from the next verse, also in Ezek. 45:12; Ezra 2:69; Neh. 7:70f.). If we were to convert the weight given in shekels in our verse into minas, the weight of the large shields would be 10 (or 12 by another calculation) minas a piece. There are commentators who convert this weight into units of weight current among us (Šanda, Van Gelderen, et al.). But in this connection the question is whether we have to deal with the single or the 'heavy' shekel. De Vaux states that the 'common' shekel in Mesopotamia weighed 8.4 g, but in Ugarit 9.5 g. I am happy to leave further exercises in arithmetic to coinage lovers.

It needs to be noted, further, that in the second half of our verse the verb יעלה (for the use of the impf. see: König §153; GD §63, rem. 1; Driver §30; BrSynt. §42b) presented a problem at least to Ehrlich: it is usually translated as a hiph. of the verb עלה (so *HAL*, 785b): 'overlaid with gold' (also cf. Burney). Ehrlich thinks that the shields were of pure gold and therefore takes the verb form to be qal with the added word 'gold' as subject. His translation then reads: 'auf zweihundert Sekel Gold belief sich das Gold für einen Schild.' This correction, however, does not seem to be an improvement on the most common translation which we are following.

10:17 *He also made three hundred small shields of beaten gold, with three minas of gold going into each small shield. The king put them into the House of the Forest of Lebanon.*

In continuity with the previous verse we are now told something about the small shields. Of these shields some 300 were made in the same way as the large shields (for the appositional relation between object and material, cf. among others, König §333c; further, cf. Rahlfs, *SSt.* III, 250f., for the LXX translation of the shields). As stated above, the weight in gold now given for one shield is 3 minas. In view of the occurrence of the word 'mina' (see previous verse), this has to be a specification which was written after the exile. The author – or copyist – of this verse possibly converted the original specification of the weight into the system of weights prevailing in his day. Nevertheless the difference in the specification of the weight in these 2 verses remains striking. In place of '3 minas of gold' the par. 2 Chr. 9:16 writes: '300 (units) of gold,' evidently an attempt to reconcile the 2 versions. The Vetus Latina has: *tres aurei inerant in scuto uno,* whereas the Vulg. speaks of *trecentae minae auri,* as does Pesh. The 'mistaken' specifications of Vulg. and Pesh. would seem capable of explanation (so, correctly, Berlinger).

All these shields were hung in the House of the Forest of Lebanon. In 7:2ff. we were informed at some length about this house. In a representation of the plundering of the temple of Musasir (N.E. of Assyria) by the Assyrians (Sargon II [721-705]), the circular shields in the temple are clearly recognizable (*ANEP*, pl. 370; Keel, *Bildsymboliek,* no. 139 [p. 94]; also cf. *ANEP*, pls. 372f.; for depictions of [Assyrian] shields). The fate of the golden shields is related in 14:26f., where they are mentioned as spoils of war captured by Shishak of Egypt. The golden shields were carried away by the illustrious raider, a fact which prompted Rehoboam to replace them by bronze shields. These shields were entrusted to the care of the officers of the guard, which is not to say that the gold shields were actually used in Solomon's time.

10:18 *King Solomon also made a great ivory throne which he overlaid with the finest gold.*
In this and the following verses we find a description of Solomon's royal throne. First we are told that the throne was made of ivory. The word שׁן is the 'common' word for 'tooth' and occurs repeatedly in OT in this sense. The word has a special meaning when it denotes an elephant's 'tooth': ivory (in Kings again in 22:39). In the Iron Age Syria and Palestine were centers of the ivory industry (H. Weippert, *BRL*^{2}, 67-72). The great demand for ivory in the 9th and 8th century led to the extinction of the Syrian elephants which were eagerly hunted down in earlier times by the kings of Egypt and Syria. Various ivory objects and trinkets from the ancient Near East have been found (depictions in Weippert). D. Ussishkin, *BA* 36 (1973), 90f., finds resemblance between Solomon's throne as described here and a throne from the 13th century BCE found at Megiddo and the throne on the relief of sarcophagus of Ahiram of Byblos. Noth rightly points out that we must not imagine that the

entire throne was made of ivory. Presumably the frame of the throne was made of wood, adorned with 'eingelegten oder aufgesetzten, jedenfalls reliefierten Elfenbeinplatten.'

We are further informed that the throne was overlaid with the 'finest' gold (for the verb צפה, cf. comments on 6:15 above). The word מוּפָז is regarded as a hophal of the verb פזז I (Zorell 645b; *HAL*, 870b) which is only found here in OT. Probably because in later times the word had become unknown or at least obsolete the Chronicler replaced it in the par. 2 Chr. 9:17 by the word טהור, 'pure.' With *HAL*, which follows Noth here, and Zorell, we can perhaps best translate our word by 'fine' or 'pure.' There is a Hebr. MS (Kennicott) which reads מאופז here (perhaps in imitation of Jer. 10:9 and Dan 10:5?). It would then refer to gold from 'Uphaz,' a totally unknown place somewhere far from Israel. This is ultimately no more than a transposition of the difficulty. It remains for us to point out that Pesh. is somewhat more clear on this point with its reading: 'from Ophir.' Ehrlich wants to solve the problem by reading ופז, by which a specification in the quality of the gold is introduced. This Hebr. word, which also means 'pure gold' (according to Ehrlich: 'platinum') indeed occurs a number of times in OT (Isa. 13:12; Ps. 19:11; 21:4; 119:127; Job 28:17; Prov. 8:19; S of S 5:11, 15; and Lam. 4:2; cf. also Stade-Schwally). Kimchi once asserted that the reference is to gold which was imported from a place named Paz (also cf. Tosefta Yoma 44b). The Vulg. speaks of 'exceptionally bright (or pure) gold' (*auro fulvo nimis*); Tg. of 'good gold' and LXX of χρυσιον δοκιμον, 'tested gold,' both of which support our translation.

10:19 *The throne had six steps, a rounded top at the back of it, and armrests on both sides of the seat, with two lions standing beside the armrests.*

Now that the material of the throne has been described, we read in our verse of its shape: it consists of 6 steps, the 7th being the place where the king is seated. On the back the throne appears to be rounded, while it is flanked by 2 armrests and 2 lions. According to Canciani and Pettinato vs. 19b offers suggestions of correspondence between the throne described and the Egyptian throne of the New Kingdom.[20] They refer to murals in the tomb of Ramses III and the rock relief in Silsile. On these depictions the back of the throne runs down from above in a spiral while lion figures are carved into the armrests. It is of course possible that there is Egyptian influence in the description of the throne in our verse (also cf. R.J. Williams, SVT 28 [1975], 234). In any case these representations of a throne help us in taking a closer look at our verse

The word מעלה, 'step,' occurs with some frequency in OT (in Kings: 2 Kgs.

---

[20] F. Canciani, G. Pettinato, "Salomos Thron: philologische und archäologische Erwägungen," *ZDPV* 8 (1965), 88-108.

9:13; 20:9ff.), and is also familiar from the headings of Pss. 120-134, though its meaning in this last case is somewhat controversial. It is further remarkable that the word כסא (twice) in our verse is written in our verse with a final ה, which, aside from another instance in Job 26:9, only occurs in our verse. Are we dealing here with an 'orthographic error' (so, inter al. Delitzsch, *LSF* §14d; BL, 548a), or a simple phonetic variant spelling (Bg. I, §7c; see also Böttcher §429c; Olsh. §182e)? The latter seems most plausible.

The following ורשׁ־עגל presents, also textcritically, some difficulty. We encountered the adj. עגל, 'round,' before (in 7:23). And we noted a moment ago that a rounded upper part on the back of a throne may not be too far from reality. But LXX translates: προτομαι μοσχων, 'calves' heads.' Also Josephus, *Ant.* VIII §140, relates that the seat of the throne rested 'on the head of a calf which faced the back of the throne.' With a small addition to the consonants and a tiny modification in the vocalization MT can also be read that way (see textcr. app. in *BHK* and *BHS*). It is noteworthy that in place of our words the par. 2 Chr. 9:18 here reads (a word which occurs once in OT): צבד (בזהב), 'a (golden) footstool' (*HAL*, 439a), to which is added: 'which was attached to the throne.' It is sometimes suspected that the *šin* must be a *śin* here: כבשׂ, 'a young ram,' which results in a (somewhat modified) adaptation to the words of our verse: a young ram is thought to be more acceptable to the Chronicler than a 'calf' which might be too reminiscent of Canaanite religion (C.R. North, *ZAW* 50 [1932], 28f.). Thenius (and many exegetes after him; Montg.-Gehman even speak of its being 'generally accepted'!) believed he should follow the reading of LXX. It is a question, nevertheless, whether this is necessary: the other ancient versions (Pesh, Vulg., and Tg.) support MT, as do all Hebr. MSS Noth, accordingly, has correctly pointed out that MT can very well be interpreted here to say: 'a rounded top on its back' (eine nach hinten ... gehende Einrollung des oberen Endes der Rückenlehne).

Next we read of armrests (see comment on 7:32f. above; Joüon §91d) on both sides of the seat. The Hebr. word used for 'eat' is a nominalized inf. cstr. (König §24k; Bg. II §11e; Joüon §75m). This, as well as other elements in our text, may point to a more recent linguistic phase in which many of the notes were edited. While lions were depicted as decoration on the wheeled stands (see comments on 7:29 above), they are also mentioned here (W. Michaelis, *TDNT*, IV, 251). Noth suspects that the sphinx-like figures were done in relief (for a rabbinical 'expansion' of the description of the throne, cf. S.R. Shimoff, *JSJ* 18 [1987], 185).

10:20 *And twelve lions stood on each end of the six steps. Nothing like it had (ever) been made for any other kingdom.*
On both sides of the steps of the throne 12 lions were placed. The word שם is lacking in the translations of LXX[B. Luc.] Pesh., and Vulg. It also seems a bit

redundant. Böttcher (*Neue Aehrenlese*), basing himself on the haplography of the *mem* (of the preceding word), prefers to read מִשָּׁם, 'from there [i.e. viewed from the seat of the throne] downward,' but this seems artificial. There is no reason for eliminating the particle in the text.

This is the only time the pl. of ארי occurs in OT with a masc. pl. ending (cf. the par. 2 Chr. 9:19). Various theories have been proposed to explain it (see inter al.: Böttcher (*Neue Aehrenlese*): diminutive form; Stade-Schwally: analogy formation; Delitzsch, *LSF* §97a: idem; Stade §336: metaphorical use, further §114c).

Whether ממלבה (already found in 2:46) has to be written in the pl. is also again disputed. In 2 Chr. 9:19 the word is in the sing. and LXX also supports this reading. The addition 'all,' 'any' indeed renders a plural ending redundant. But we are here speaking about the most beautiful throne of the entire world! Why then should we not maintain our 'exaggerated' Hebr. text?

Greßmann[21] and Montg.-Gehman have called attention to the meaning of the flanking of the 6 steps of the throne by 12 lion figures. The reason is that the seat must have been placed on the 7th step (expanded into a podium) and among the Babylonians heaven was thought of as having 7 steps, the deity dwelling on the top level. But because Solomon's throne was made by Phoen. craftsmen one may well doubt whether Solomon intended or interpreted the original meaning in that light. Still Greßmann does not completely rule out this construal because one can find traces of the deification of the king in OT (Ps. 45:7 and 2:7). Noth does not go this far, though he hardly considers the number 7 accidental. The lions represent the 'strength' and 'power' of Solomon. Ewald, *GVI*, III, 341, considered the lion on Solomon's throne 'das fahnenzeichen Juda's,' and in support of this view refers to texts like Gen 49:9; Isa. 29:1 and Ezek. 19:2ff. But it is doubtful whether one can attribute to the author of this section such a modern insight into heraldry.

The location of the throne in the palace complex is not mentioned in our verses but there is reason to assume that it would be in the 'throne hall' (cf. 7:7) in which the king administered justice.

10:21 *All the drinking vessels of King Solomon were of gold and all the household articles of the House of the Forest of Lebanon were of pure gold. None was of silver (for) in Solomon's day it was not considered at all valuable.*

The riches of Solomon are further enlarged upon in this and the following verse. In the view of the author of these lines, all that glittered in Solomon's

---

[21] Cf. also his *Der Messias*, Göttingen 1929, 43, n. 2; and H. Gunkel, *Die Psalmen*, Göttingen 1926[4], 190 on Ps. 45:7f.

palace and kingdom was literally gold. Is it splendid hyperbole of a kind we tend to recognize with a knowing smile? Or is there perhaps a trace of irony in the wording of the text itself? In any case, we are told that all the drinking vessels (for the LXX here, cf. Rahlfs, *SSt.* III, 200) of the king, say the entire set as well as all other objects in the House of the Forest of Lebanon were of pure gold. We already encountered משקה in vs. 5, the word סגור in 6:20; also cf. Ellenbogen, *Foreign Words,* 119). To the drinking vessels LXX adds: και λουτηρες χρυσοι, 'and golden washing vessels.'

The second half of our verse presents still another peculiar grammatical difficulty. Do we read: 'There was no silver [in the House of the Forest of Lebanon], (for) in the days of Solomon it was not considered of any value'; or is the translation 'in the days of Solomon silver was considered totally worthless' to be preferred? Both translations have their defenders (the former, inter al., Montg.-Gehman; the latter, inter al., Burney). The question is whether we have 2 negations qualifying a single predicate, negations which do not cancel each other out but rather reinforce each other (König §352p, n; Ges-K §152y; BrSynt. §32e), or is it the case that in this respect our verse is somewhat 'suspect' (Driver §162, n. 2; Delitzsch, *LSF* §144). This question is the more pressing when we note that in the par. 2 Chr. 9:20 the negation לא has been omitted (also in Pesh. in our verse). LXX* reads: 'There was no silver, for (οτι) this was ...' etc., thereby marking the caesura in the Hebr. text with a conjunction. Also the Tg. with its translation tends in this direction. There is, therefore, no reason to alter our Hebr. verse in line with 2 Chr. 9:20. Even though, with Burney and other grammars, we recognize the possibility of mutually reinforcing negations in Hebr., still the way pointed out by LXX seems to us the correct translation of our verse fragment: 'in the palace no silver was used for ...' For the verb חשב, also cf. W. Schottroff, *THAT*, I, 641-646; K. Seybold, *TWAT*, III, 243-261. In the niph. modification, as it occurs in this verse, the verb is found 30x in OT. The word מאומה (*HAL*, 511f.) also occurs in Kings in 18:43 and 2 Kgs. 5:20.

10:22 *For the king had a fleet of Tarshish ships at sea with the fleet of Hiram. Once every three years the fleet returned, laden with gold, silver, ivory, apes and peacocks.*

In this verse we are once again reminded of the combined commercial enterprises of Solomon and king Hiram of Tyre (also cf. 9:26f.; 10:11). In our discussion of 9:26 we already remarked that a 'Tarshish fleet' or 'Tarshish ship' does not primarily refer to the destination of such a fleet or ship (as the par. 2 Chr. 9:21 [but also cf. LXX, Pesh. Vulg. and Tg., the last of which has 'from Africa'] apparently suggests), but to the fact that the fleet or ship is intended for the transmarine trade (cf. Isa. 2:16; 23:1, 14; Ezek. 27:25). It is possible that Tarshish refers to a city in SW Spain, though both in antiquity and later numerous other suggestions have been made (so, inter al., Josephus, *Ant.* VIII §181: 'sea of Tarshish' [in Cilicia]; further also Eusebius, *Onom.* 100, 24ff., who besides Josephus's opinion also mentions other ideas such as Carthage and India; Montg.-Gehman and Gray; also cf. S. B. Hoenig, *JQR* 69 [1978], 181f., who states that Tarshish simply means 'sea'; and D.W. Baker, *ABD*, VI, 331-333). Along with Noth we may also accept the idea that the term derives from the nautical vocabulary of the Phoenicians.

Once every 3 years, we are told, the combined fleet (according to 2 Chr. 9: the *fleet* of Solomon with the *servants* of Hiram; cf. LXX$^{Luc.}$ [Rahlfs, *SSt.* III, 251] and also 1 Kgs. 9:27) brought a rich cargo to the shores of Israel (for the distributive element in this phrase, cf. Ewald §217d; BrSynt. §107b; WOC §15.6a: Joüon §142p.; further GD §48, rem. 2). Ehrlich considered such a long seajourney defensible. How one must picture the combination of the 2 fleets (according to Ehrlich a fleet belonging to Hiram and one ship belonging to Solomon); where precisely the home ports were to be located (in Phoenica or by the Red Sea); what the composition of the crews of the different ships (2 Chr. 9:21 mentions אניות in place of the sing.) was — all these questions remain unanswered. Noth even comes to the conclusion 'dass der Verfasser des Begründungssatzes 22 gar keine konkrete Vorstellung hatte.' As a result one might well put a question mark behind these 3-yearly trade expeditions. Still, from antiquity we know of protracted expeditions (cf. Montg.-Gehman 224). It remains a question, of course, whether the author here uses authentic notes or bases himself on experiences from his own time. Stade-Schwally — on good grounds — comment that 'the geographical notions of the ancients were very vague.'

As imported products (for [the vocalization of] the fem. qal part. of נשא, cf. Bg. I §15f.; BL, 612y), 5 different kinds are mentioned. Of these we already know the 'gold' and 'silver,' but the last 3 (combined with the par. 2 Chr. 9:21) constitute *hapax legomena* in the Hebr. Bible (see also S. Powels, *ZAH* 5 [1992], 194ff.).

שנהבים is usually translated by 'ivory,' קפים by 'apes,' and תכיים by 'peacocks.' LXX*, however, translates this section: λιθων τορευτων και πελεκητων, 'with chiselled and hewn stones,' but the hexaplaric recension has: οδοντων ελεφατινων και πιθηκων και ταυνων, 'elephant's teeth and apes and peacocks.' Josephus, *Ant.* VIII §181, reports on πολυς ελεφας Αιθιοπες τε και πιθηκοι, 'much ivory, Ethiopians, and apes.' In his 'Vorlage' Josephus probably mistook תכיים for סכיים, 'Sukkiim' (2 Chron 12:3 = 'cave-dwellers' LXX?), a tribe of people mentioned in between Libyans and Ethiopians as reinforcement of an Egyptian army (Stade-Schwally mention that the word was sometimes taken to mean 'negroes,' among others by C. Niebuhr, *OLZ* 3 [1900], 69; cf. H. Winckler, *OLZ* 4 [1901], 148). Pesh., Tg. and Vulg., however, support the hexapl. translation of LXX and hence the translation we have proposed.

The firstmentioned word 'ivory' (so, inter al., Ges-B, 851b; *HAL*, 148c; cf. also Ellenbogen, *Foreign Words,* 162) is quite transparent. The second קוֹף, as a related word, also occurs in other Sem. languages, e.g. in the Akkad. as *uqupu* (*AHw*, 1427b), but also in Egyptian as *g;f* and Greek (κηπος; Ges-B, 709a; *HAL*, 1018b[22]). Some scholars think here of the *Papio Hamadrias Arabicus,* but where precisely the apes came from remains a matter of conjecture (also cf. E. Firmage, *ABD*, VI, 1154 and 1157, n. 26). They might come from Somalia but also from other parts of Africa. A species of baboon still lives in Yemen and Hadramaut today. As far as that is concerned, the origin of the third animal, the 'peacock,' is more restricted, at least if one reads the Hebr. word this way. For a long time already the translation of the word and the occurrence of the animal have been disputed (see e.g. the discussion between B. Meissner [*OLZ* 16 (1913), 292f.] and B. Laufer [idem, 539f.]). *HAL*, 1594f. (cf. Ges-B, 878a) lists 3 possible translations: (1) peacock; (2) ape; (3) fowl. Not long ago G. Wörpel, *ZAW* 79 (1967), 360f., made a plea for 'turkey,' but K.-H. Bernhardt, *ZAW* 81 (1969), 100, pointed out that this animal is of N American origin. The peacock is of SE Indian, more precisely of Malabar, origin (Tamil: *malajam to kai* = 'the bird with the sparkling train'; also cf. Ellenbogen, *Foreign Words,* 165). The translation 'ape,' 'baboon,' however, also has its modern supporters (see Hulst, *OTTP* 38; S. Powels, *ZAH* [1992], 196; P.J.N. Lawrence, *BiTr* 44 [1993], 348f.). We, however, be it with some hesitation, opt for the usual translation 'peacock' (cf. Vulg.: *pavos*).

10:23 *For riches and for wisdom king Solomon surpassed all other kings on earth.*

By mentioning Solomon's fame, riches, and wealth in this and the following verse, the dtr. author forges a connection with what God had promised him in a dream at Gibeon (3:4-15; spec. 11ff.). In riches (see comments on 3:11, 13; further M. Sæbø, *TWAT*, VI, 446-452) and wisdom, a key word in all of Solomon's public conduct (see comments on 2:6) he surpasses all the kings of the earth (for the use of the *lamed,* cf. Ges-K §119u). In the course of history Solomon's wisdom becomes ever greater and his wealth ever more abundant (E. Lohse, *TDNT*, VII, 461f.).

It remains for me to say that from the vs. 23 to vs. 25 LXX has a section which runs parallel to MT 9:15, 17b-19 and 20-22 (see there). At vs. 26 the LXX text again runs parallel to our MT text (Rahlfs, in his LXX edition, counts that section as the vss. 22a, 22b, and 22c, so that from vs. 23 on the

---

[22] Cf. also H. R. Cohen, *Biblical Hapax Legomena in the Light of Akkadian and Ugaritic,* Missoula 1978, 112, n. 15.

LXX numeration marches along with MT).

10:24 *The whole world sought out Solomon to hear the wisdom which God had put in his heart.*
The result of Solomon's fame and riches is that 'the whole world' comes to him to hear his wisdom. For 'the whole world' the par. 2 Chr. 9:23, supported by LXX and Pesh. has 'all the kings of the world,' which better fits the pl. of the part. Still a masc. pl. occurs more often in the case of a fem. collective (see König §346c; Ges-K §145e; BrSynt. §28b). The part. מבקשים (for the verb, see comments on 1:2) as it were replaces a finite verb (König §239d) and puts a stronger stress on the ongoing condition than the latter (Bg. II §13f.).

10:25 *And everyone who came brought a present with him: articles of silver and gold, garments, (military) equipment, spices, horses and mules, year after year.*
The summary of precious goods in our verse, according to Montg.-Gehman, resembles a list of war booty on the inscriptions of Assyrian kings. Was the author perhaps inspired by such inscriptions, which must have been abundantly available in Mesopotamia? That is a question. In any case, we encounter presents of every kind. We already encountered the word מנחה, 'present,' in 5:1 (cf. K. Weiss, *TDNT*, IX, 79f.). The objects of silver were not mentioned in LXX[B. Luc.], possibly with an eye to vs. 21, where silver is mentioned with disdain. שלמה (with metathesis of the consonants also in the word – which does not occur in Kings – שמלה; see BL, 458s), means 'mantle' and occurs 16x in OT, one of which in Kings again in 11:29f. (*HAL*, 1241b).

The meaning of נשק is disputed. It can mean 'equipment,' 'weaponry' (so e.g. 2 Kgs. 10:2; Isa. 22:8; Ezek. 39:9f.). Pesh., Tg.; Vulg. and many older and newer translations and commentators follow this translation. But LXX here reads the word στακτη, '(dripping) resin,' 'balsam' (cf. LXX Gen. 37:25; 43:11; Exod. 30:34; Ps. 44(45):8; S of S. 1:13; Sir. 24:15; Isa. 39:2 and Ezek. 27:16). Ewald, *GVI*, III, 391 and n. 1, already translated the word by 'wolgerüche,' and believed that the word 'auf keine weise Rüstung bedeuten kann.' Although lexicons like Ges-B (528a), BDB (676b) and *KBL* (640b) opted for 'weaponry' under a single lemma, Zorell (538a) and *HAL* (690b), on the other hand, chose 'fragrant balsam' under a second and separate lemma. J.A. Montgomery, *JAOS* 58 (1938), 137, pointed out the connection of the latter meaning with the Arab. *nsq*, 'to smell' and the Hebr. 'to kiss.' Josephus, *Ant.* VIII §183, speaks of 'various kinds of spices,' thereby (possibly prompted by LXX) also suggesting that our word could mean 'spice' or the like. In how far LXX is influenced by the following word (thus inter al. Burney and Noth; also cf. Stade-Schwally, who speak of a 'misunderstanding') is hard to say. It remains difficult, therefore, to make a choice. Agreement in meaning with the following word is surprising insofar as mention of 2 kinds of fragrant wares in this summary puts a special emphasis on cosmetics. The translation 'equipment,' even though weapons may be included, does not seem incongruous in this summary, all the more when one thinks of the lists of Assyrian war booty. We therefore opt for the traditional translation 'equipment.'

We already encountered the word בשם, 'spice' in vs. 2 of our chapter. The 2 following words belong to the livestock 'given' to Solomon: horses and mules. F.J. Stendebach, *TWAT*, V, 782-791, and also O. Michel, *TDNT*, III, 336f., both devote a study to the horse in the ancient Near East (we already encountered the word סוס in 5:6. It occurs approx. 140x in OT). Solomon's 'horse trading' will come up for discussion later in this chapter.

The fem. form of פרד, 'mule,' was mentioned in chap. 1 (see 1:33). Of the 15x the animal is found in OT, the masc. form occurs again in 18:5 and 2 Kgs. 5:17 (see P. Maiberger, *TWAT*, VI, 738f.).

The concluding words of our verse (see König §306p; further BrSynt. §24e) have the character of an 'annual' (Ewald §209c) payment of tribute, such as also (again) the Assyrian kings demanded from their subject peoples.

10:26 *Solomon, moreover, gathered together in a park both chariots and horsemen. He owned fourteen hundred chariots and twelve thousand horsemen and stationed them in chariot cities and with the king (himself) in Jerusalem.*

In the enumerative description of Solomon's wealth and power we now encounter a passage which we found earlier in a somewhat different form in 5:6. There we read of 4000[0] stalls for Solomon's chariot park and of 12,000 horsemen. Now we read of 1,400 chariots and 12,000 horsemen. If in this connection we compare the par. 2 Chr. 9:25a, we discover that this time the Chronicler does not follow our verse but the par. 1 Kgs. 5:6, whereas it is 2 Chr. 1:14a which turns out to run parallel to our verse. A comparison with LXX* teaches that – aside from LXX[A] – the translation only starts after the first 4 words of MT which then reads: 'Solomon had 4,000 [LXX[Luc.]:40,000) mares for the chariots and 12,000 horsemen ...,' hence a text which more or less corresponds to 5:6. A combination of these rather divergent data prompted Burney (cf. textcr. app. *BHK*) to produce the following reconstruction of our text: 'Solomon gathered chariots and horsemen. He had 4,000 stalls for his chariot horses and 1,400 chariots with 12,000 horsemen ...' etc. Josephus, *Ant.* VIII §183, looks for an even simpler solution by adding the 'new' data to what the king already had earlier. But these and similar reconstructions remain reconstructions. It would appear that something was wrong with these data at an early stage, so that now nothing can be reconstructed with certainty. It is the later writers, after all, whose aim is to magnify Solomon's splendor and power. Montg.-Gehman indeed point out that in the summaries of the Assyrian kings the numbers pertaining to booty in the form of chariots are frequently very high. Since in our comments on 5:6 we have probed this problem, as well as certain Hebr. words, more thoroughly, we take the liberty of referring to that text here.

A small problem in the second part of our verse is the form וַיַּנְחֵם, as it is now vocalized in a hiph.-modification of the verb נחה, 'to lead,' 'to bring.' In the par. 2 Chr. 9:25, as in 2 Chr. 1:14, ויניחם occurs vocalized as a hiph. II-form of נוח, 'to lay,' 'to put' etc. (cf. 7:47). This is a reproduction which also proves to have support in the ancient versions (see further Delitzsch, *LSF* §66b). But Noth correctly remarks that the MT form in our verse can be vocalized without difficulty like the form in Chr. (*scriptio defectiva*).

The 'chariot cities' (a designation given by Solomon himself, according to Josephus, *Ant.* VIII §188) already came up in our discussion of 9:19. Now there is the additional mention of the encampment of horses and horsemen by the king himself in Jerusalem. This makes sense as it stands. But for Josephus, *Ant.* VIII §§ 184ff., this statement is apparently still too simple. He tells us not only that the horses were swifter, more beautiful, and better than other horses but also that their riders, the flower of youth, were splendid tall figures, clothed in Tyrian purple. Every day they sprinkled the hair on their head with gold dust so that their heads glittered like golden globes in the sun. The king, moreover, was accustomed to mount his chariot every day, clothed in a white garment, to drive himself to a little paradise – called Ethan – outside Jerusalem. How the romantic idylls around Solomon could grow![23]

Both in 2 Chr. 9:26 and in LXX there has been added to the words of our verse what is found in MT in 5:1a.

10:27 *The king also made silver as common in Jerusalem as stones, and cedar as plentiful as sycamore in the Lowlands.*
In a kind of 'hyperbole of disdain' (so König, *Stil.* 71) we are again told in this verse how rich Solomon and his age in fact were: silver as stones (see J. Jeremias, *TDNT*, IV, 268ff.) and cedars like sycamore figs. The intent of this verse is clear as such, though textcritically there is still a small problem. This is not so much whether, with LXX and 2 Chr. 1:15 [but not 2 Chr. 9:27!], the silver should be preceded by gold, for this could be a later gloss (Stade-Schwally; Burney) as whether, with numerous MSS and editions, there should not be a *beth* in place of the *kaph* before אבנים. Still, not only on the basis of the parallel passages in Chronicles but especially because of the comparison and the frequently occurring construction of נתן with ב (cf. E. Jenni, *ZAH* 3

---

[23] Also cf. C. Hauer, "The Economics of National Security in Solomonic Israe," *JSOT* 18 (1980), 63-73, esp. 64f., for the problems associated with the horses and chariots.

[1990], 139f.), we opt for maintaining MT.

The word שִׁקְמָה occurs aside from here, also in Isa. 9:9; Amos 7:14; Ps. 78:47; 1 Chr. 27:28 and 2 Chr. 1:15 and 9:27. It is the sycamore fig, also called the mulberry tree, though the latter is different. The sycamore fig tree (*Ficus sycomorus L*) reaches a height of approx. 15 m, while the circumference of the trunk can sometimes even be 7 m. The tree bears much fruit which clusters together both on the branches and on the trunk. These fruits resemble ordinary figs but they are smaller and of lesser quality. Although the tree's wood is soft, it is often used for carpentry and construction (see Smit, *Planten*, 88; further Dalman, *AuS* 1/1, 61f.; Keel, *OLB*, I, 82f.). As the location of these trees ('in great numbers,' see BrSynt. §107i) the שְׁפֵלָה, the 'Lowlands' are mentioned, the hilly area (250-450 m above sealevel) between the coastal strip (the 'land of the Philistines') along the Mediterranean and the mountains of Judea. Of the approx. 20x this word is found in OT it occurs only here in Kings (see Keel, *OLB*, II, 568f.).

It is clear that the subject in this verse as well as in the preceding and following verses is the glorification of Solomon. According to Schley vs. 28 was originally formulated strictly as poetry.[24] But also the 'apparent roughness of 1 Kgs. 10:26-29 in fact derives from the attempt to read as straight prose what is actually a quasipoetic eulogy' (p. 599). The primary purpose of this eulogy, as stated above, was the glorification of Solomon. On this basis he also argues for the retention of the addition which LXX and the par. texts from Chronicles have in the previous verse. With reference to our verse he considers the use of the verb נתן an insertion which serves to convert the originally poetic verse into prose (p. 600, n. 16). He therefore considers Noth's incorrect comment (in *ÜGS*, 71, n. 4). that our verse seems to be a later addition. The Solomon-eulogizing character of the vss. 23-29 blocks the emendation of this section as it was often undertaken, especially in vs. 28, to make it fit a historical account. One can only agree with this final comment.

For another reason A.D. Crown does not believe our verse is a later addition but even 'the key to the whole paragraph'.[25] Reference in our verse to the cedars reminds us that Solomon together with Hiram sponsored commercial expeditions in the area of the Mediterranean Sea at the time when the Phoenicians took the place of the dead city of Ugarit. This view is based in part on the exegesis of the following verse.

10:28 *Solomon's horses were imported from Egypt and Cilicia; the king's traders purchased them from Cilicia at the going price;*

---

[24] D.D. Schley Jr., "1 Kings 10:26-29. A Reconsideration," *JBL* 106 (1987), 595-601, esp. 597.
[25] "Once Again 1 Kings 10:26-29," *Abr-Nahrain* 15 (1974f.), 35-38.

This verse confronts many an exegete with problems (Münster already wrote: '*Locus iste obscurus est in Hebraeo*'). These problems are present not so much on a textcritical as on a geographic and historical level. As a 'simple' rendering of our verse the par. 2 Chr. 9:28 has: 'And horses were imported for Solomon from Egypt and from all lands,' thereby avoiding various difficulties in our verse Virtually identical to our verse is the other par. text from 2 Chr: viz. 1:16, which, for convenience's sake, we reproduce in the translation of RSV: 'And Solomon's import of horses was from Egypt and Kue; the king's traders received them from Kue for a price.' LXX* supports MT practically at all points, though it speaks of θεκουε (instead of Kue) while some LXX MSS, along with the Vetus Latina, still add the name Damascus to the 2 other names. Pesh. translates especially the second part of our verse somewhat differently from the reading of MT. In its translation our entire verse reads approximately as follows: 'Horses were imported for Solomon from Egypt and the king's traders received provision for the goods they purchased.' Also Tg. deviates, though not much, from MT: 'And the horses of Solomon were imported from Egypt and Kue; the king's traders purchased them from Kue for a price.' Vulg., finally, translates: 'And the supply of horses for Solomon occurred from Egypt and from Coa, for the king's traders purchased them from Coa and obtained them for the going price.'

Just what city or country is Kue? Eusebius (*Onom.* 118, 15) mentions Κοα which is situated close to Egypt, a word which Jerome (hence followed by Vulg.) translated by *Coa*. Now in the Akkad. cuneiform texts, inter alia on the so-called 'monolith-inscription' of the Assyr. king Salmanasser III (858-824), there is mention, in a longer enumeration, of '500 soldiers from Que, 1000 soldiers from Musri' (*ANET*, 279a). This region is identified with an area in the Cilician Plain, viz. Cilicia in S.E. Anatolia (see also the article קוה by N. Naman in *EncMiqr.* VII, 87-93, and J. D. Ming, s.v. Cilicia in *ABD*, I, 1022ff.; further M. Görg, *UF* 8 [1976], 53ff.), also mentioned in the Aram. inscription of king Zakkur of Hamath (*KAI*, 202 A, 6; cf. E. Lipiński, *RTAT*, 249).[26] H. Winckler[27] was among the first who thus analyzed and explained this – at least here – rather obscure word מקוה, which elsewhere in OT often means 'hope' or 'collection' (as was often the case in older exegetes like Münster and Vatablus; sometimes it is also rendered 'thread' or 'linen'; but cf. Amama and H. Grotius). Many exegetes (cf. Šanda, Noth, and Katzenstein, *Tyre*, 113f.) have followed him in this interpretation, and also in the view that in our verse,

---

[26] See now also P.T. Crocker, "»Solomon Imported Horses from ...Kue«," *Buried History* 27 (1991), 83-88.

[27] *Alttestamentliche Untersuchungen*, Leipzig 1892, 168ff.; before him also F. Lenormant; cf. Montg.-Gehman; Noth, 205.

in place of מצרים, 'Egypt,' we must read 'Musri' (a region in Cappadocia). In the inscription of Salmanasser III cited above these regions are, in any case, mentioned in one breath. Especially the eastern part of Cilicia, with the adjoining region of Musri but in contrast to Egypt itself, is said to have been an important export and transit country for horses (cf. Simons, *GTTOT* §§69, 835; Benzinger; Burney; Montg.-Gehman; Noth, Gray, et al.).

Still, not all interpreters are persuaded of the correctness of these place-name identifications. Cheyne, *CB,* 334f., looks for these places (also on the basis of the reading 'Tekoue' in LXX) in N Arabia, and, in line with this persuasion, even 'corrects' Ezek. 27:14 — deemed by others to be important for the origin of the horsetrade — where Togarmah, an area in Armenia, is mentioned. H. Tadmor (*IEJ* 11 [1961], 143-150) considers 'Gua' (or Qua), in the monolith-inscription of Salmanasser III, a mistaken spelling for Gubal, i.e. Byblos, while Musri simply means Egypt, so that the areas in Asia Minor disappear from his view. Würthwein offers 2 'Verständnismöglichkeiten,' viz. the one which most exegetes after Winckler have followed and has been mentioned above, but also the possibility simply to maintain Egypt in our text, and with Eusebius et al., to look for Koa somewhere in the neighbourhood of Egypt. For since the time of the Hyksos Egypt proves to have been familiar with horses and chariots and even bred horses.[28] A stele of pharaoh Amen-hotep II (circa 1447-1421 BCE) tells us, among other things, that already as a young man this sports-minded pharaoh loved horses, worked with them and trained them (*ANET*, 244). Nor is the OT lacking in indications that Egypt was famous for its horses (e.g. Deut. 17:16; cf. Isa. 30:16; 31:1), though perhaps cavalry was not a military weapon before the Hellenistic period (S. Mowinckel, *VT* 12 [1962], 280f.). Barthélemy points this out and comes to the conclusion that the redactor of Kings only wanted to designate Egypt as the place from which Solomon received his horses and chariots. Schley, art. cit. p. 595-601, similarly maintains, on the basis of his reconsideration of our pericope, his opinion that the reference is to Egypt. In any case, one has the textual criticism on his side if one clings to the reading 'Egypt' in our verse Before we come to a conclusion, however, we first want to take a closer look at our verse and the next.

Of the 27x מוצא is found in OT it occurs in the books of Kings only here and in 2 Kgs. 2:21. The basic meaning is the 'appearance,' the 'departure,' and in our verse especially the 'export' (of horses from Egypt; *HAL*, 530a; Mowinckel, art. cit., 282, n. 11, wants to read the preposition ל in place of מן but this emendation is too arbitrary to base Solomon's transit-trade on it). The Masoretes placed the *atnaḥ* under מצרים but Stade-Schwally et al. propose that it be

---

[28] Also cf. Y. Ikeda, "Solomon's Trade in Horses and Chariots in Its International Setting," Ishida, *Studies*, 215-238; esp. 227-231.

placed under the next word. W.F. Albright (*JBL* 71 [1952], 249) proposed the deletion of 'Egypt' in vs. 28 (dittography)[29] but this is not advisable. On the basis of suggestions from Eusebius and Jerome, and because of the use of the *aleph* in place of the *he* in the par. 2 Chr. 1:16, Stade-Schwally propose the reading of מקוא, 'from Qoa.' The question then remains unsolved where Qoa is located or what area bears that name.

The second part of our verse mentions the activities of Solomon's traders. In our discussion of vs. 15 we already mentioned certain commercial terms. The word סחר which is used in our verse for 'trader' only occurs in Kings here (elsewhere in OT another 15x). As for the object of the verb, it is often proposed that we attach a 3 p. pl. suff. to the form יקחו (so, inter al. Stade-Schwally: haplography of the [following] *mem*). S. Kogut, *Leš* 34 (1969f.), 320, at one time proposed that we translate the verb itself by 'to buy,' a meaning which may have been attached to לקח in the Mishna Hebr., but from the context it is clear that almost no other meaning can be given to 'receive,' considering also the last word of our verse (also cf. the reaction of T. Muraoka, *Leš* 36 [1971f.], 76f.).

מחיר occurs 15x in OT and, aside from our verse, in Kings only again in 21:2. The meaning is 'purchase price,' the market value of the thing one has purchased. Sometimes the word can be translated by 'money' (e.g. Mic. 3:11; Prov. 17:16; so *HAL*, 539a). It is apparently the intent of this verse to say that the king's traders did their buying in Kue at the going price. Because horses were at issue in the first part, it makes sense to think of them as the object of the purchasing.

10:29 *a chariot imported from Egypt went for six hundred shekels of silver and a horse for a hundred and fifty; and so, through the king's traders, they were also exported to all the kings of the Hittites and of the Arameans.*

Besides horses, chariots come up in this verse as well. The word מרכבה (see comments on 7:33 above; also cf. 5:6), according to some, is used collectively here (König §255a). But Ikeda (art. cit. 223ff.) is of the opinion that precisely in this instance a specific meaning can be attributed to this word (in place of the word רכב see vs. 26). In the context of Egypt this chariot refers to 'an Egyptian royal display chariot' (p. 234). Hence, according to him, Solomon imported from Egypt the royal ceremonial chariot which would be driven in processions and must have been very ornate. This is a possibility, even though the text itself gives us reason to continue to cling to the possibility of a collective. ותעלה is a non-apocopated form of the cons. impf. Such a form can sometimes impart an iterative or durative aspect to the past tense (Joüon §79m;

---

[29] Cf. also J. Bright, *A History of Israel*, London 1972², 212.

further Ges-K §75t; Bg. II §7e). The meaning of the verb is described by *HAL*, 784a (also cf. Šanda) as that of a technical term (with the *beth* of the goods): 'came to' (but Ges-B, 590a [with a question mark]: 'hinaufgebracht werden'). LXX reads the beginning of our vs: καί ἀνέβαινεν ἡ ἔξοδος, so that one may assume that the second verb in our verse was possibly read by LXX as מוצא (see previous verse): 'up came the export from Egypt; a chariot for ...' etc. The par. 2 Chr. 1:17 applies the verb forms to Solomon's traders: 'They arranged and exported ...' etc. With Šanda, Van Gelderen, Noth, Würthwein, *HAL* et al. and essentially also with LXX, we can link the 2 verb forms as follows: 'A chariot, upon being exported, came to be priced at ...,' etc. The 600 shekels of silver, which undoubtedly had to be paid per chariot, and the 150 per horse (for the *beth-pretii*, cf. WOC §11.2.5d), are reduced in LXX to 100 and 50 respectively, but whether this smaller number is more probable (so inter al. Stade-Schwally, textcr. app. *BHK*) is not something which can still be determined (also cf. Ikeda, art. cit., 225-231, who presents a 'comparative chart' of prices charged for chariots and horses in the 2nd and first millennium BCE; see also Van Gelderen who attempts to explain the differences between the 2 versions in terms of the 'large' and the 'small' shekel). Josephus, *Ant.* VIII §189, tailors the text to his own time and explicates it again in a way which diverges from MT: 'He ordered the Egyptian traders to bring him, and to sell to him, a chariot with 2 horses for 600 drachmas; he himself sent them to the kings of Syria and to those beyond the Euphrates.'

The second part of our verse extends Solomon's trade in horses and chariots to 'all the kings of the Hittites and the kings of Aram.' The Hittites were also referred to in 9:20 earlier. In our verse this notice perhaps refers to those states in N Syria in which the so-called 'neo-Hittite' (non-Sem.) culture flourished after the fall of the Hittite kingdom toward the end of the 2nd millennium BCE Information about this culture and these states has been found in royal inscriptions handed down in hieroglyphic Luwian (Ikeda, art. cit., 231f.) according to Ikeda, such states as Gurgum, Carchemish, and Til-Borsip already existed in the days of Solomon.

Aram, often – and understandably – translated in older translations by 'Syria' (so e.g. the KJV) is often mentioned in OT (in Kings, aside from our verse, also in the following vss. 11:25: 15:18; 19:15; 20:1, 20-23, 26-29; 22:1, 3, 11, 31, 35; 2 Kgs. 5:1f., 5; 6:8f., 11, 23f.; 7:4-6, 10, 12, 14ff.; 8:7, 9, 13, 28f.; 9:14f.; 12:18f.; 13:3ff., 7, 17, 19, 22, 24; 15:37; 16:5ff.; 24:2). Rarely is it the name of a person (e.g. in Gen. 10:22f.) or does it refer to the 'Arameans' (e.g. 2 Sam. 10:11; 1 Kgs. 20:20f., 29). But usually the name denotes the region N of Palestine which we call 'Syria' today and which in antiquity consisted of numerous little city-states, of which Aram-Damascus was one of the better-known (e.g. 2 Sam. 8:5f., cf. A. Alt, *KS*, III, 214-232; E. Lipiński, *TRE*, III, 590-599; W.T. Pitard, *ABD*, I, 338-341).

The last 2 words of our verse again present the usual difficulties in translation and interpretation. In the first place it turns out that LXX read בידם, 'by their hand' as though the MT read בים, 'on the sea' (κατὰ θάλασσαν). But the other ancient versions more or less follow MT, so that from a textcritical perspective this will have to be maintained, though Katzenstein, *Tyre*, 114) sees 'another joint venture' of Solomon and Hiram in the LXX-reading. In the second place, there is the vocalization of the last word: must we maintain MT which has a hiph. of יצא; or LXX and Tg. (cf. Vulg. *venumdabant*) which read the qal of the same verb (retaining the consonants)? But 2 Chr. 1:17, even more clearly than our verse, has the hiph.-form of the verb, although this may also be a later reading which may have influenced the Masoretes in their vocalization of Kings. Rudolph wants to read the verb-form in Chronicles as a passive (hophal): 'they were similarly exported by their mediation to all the kings ...' If we maintain MT, the translation reads: 'The traders imported them by their hand to the kings of ...' etc.; if we follow the text modification it may read: 'Similarly for the kings of ..., they (viz. the horses and chariots) were exported by their hand.' An objection to the first translation, noted by Rudolph, is that בידם would then seem to be redundant. In the second half our verse as MT now reads it, however, D. Pardee, *UF* 6 (1974), 282, n. 40, sees a parallel with a Ugar. text on the basis of which one can translate יצא בד ... ל by 'he served as middleman for the export of.' The word ב(י)ד then indicates the intermediary in financial transactions while the preposition ל indicates the destination. But Pardee admits that our verse nevertheless remains hard to interpret (inter al.) by the hiph.-modification used which makes the reading of the qal form 'very attractive' in light of the Ugar.: 'they (the horses and chariots) went out to the kings by their (i.e. Solomon's traders) mediation. Pardee rightly notes that the view of NEB, viz. the translation of the prep. ל here by 'from' ('in the same way the merchants obtained them for export from all the kings ...') is unacceptable.

It is clear that in the vss. 28f. we are dealing with the (profitable) trade relations between Solomon and the great powers of his time, however one may conceive 'Solomon's Trade in Horses and Chariots in Its International Setting' (Ikeda, art. cit.) as a mixture of 'Dichtung und Wahrheit.' Questions do after all arise, like: Did Solomon monopolize the trade in horses between the larger and smaller states of his day? How could that be? What are the patterns in this trade? We can therefore concur with Schley's conclusion (art. cit., 601) that the entire pericope (the vss. 26-29 along with the vss. 23-25) 'comprises a eulogy on Solomon and his glory, and therefore does not give a precise picture of his time.' In this connection it seems safest to let 'Egypt' in vs. 28 remain Egypt!

1 KINGS 11:1-13

11:1 *King Solomon loved many foreign women: the daughter of Pharaoh, Moabite, Ammonite, Edomite, Sidonian, and Hittite women;*
   2 of the peoples of whom YHWH had said: do not have dealings with them and let them have no dealings with you; for surely they will seduce your heart to follow their gods. To them Solomon attached himself in love.
   3 He possessed seven hundred princesses plus three hundred concubines who led him astray.
   4 Now it was especially in Solomon's old age that his wives seduced his heart to follow other gods, so that his heart was not as perfect with YHWH his God as the heart of his father David was.
   5 Thus Solomon followed after Ashtoreth, the goddess of the Sidonians and after Milcom, the abomination of the Ammonites.
   6 So Solomon did things that were evil in the sight of YHWH and did not fully devote himself to YHWH the way his father David did.
   7 Then on the mountain across from Jerusalem, Solomon built a high place for Chemosh, the abomination of Moab, and one for Moloch, the abomination of the Ammonites.
   8 And he did the same for all his foreign wives insofar as they burnt incense and made sacrifices to their gods.
   9 YHWH however, became angry with Solomon since his heart had drawn him away from YHWH the God of Israel, who had twice appeared to him,
   10 and had commanded him in this matter not to go after other gods. But he did not keep to what YHWH had commanded.
   11 Then YHWH said to Solomon: 'Because this was in your mind, namely that you have not kept my covenant and my statutes which I commanded you, I will surely tear the kingship from you and give it to one of your servants.
   12 Only, for the sake of your father David, I will not do it during your lifetime. Out of the hand of your son I will tear it.
   13 Yet I will not tear away the entire kingdom: one tribe will I give to your son, for the sake of David my servant and for the sake of Jerusalem which I have chosen.'

INTRODUCTION TO CHAPTER 11

If we read Deut. 17:16f. against the background of the conclusion of our previous chapter and the beginning of the present chapter, we will immediately have before us, from a dtr. viewpoint, a sketch of the cause of the division of

Solomon's kingdom and of the tragic ending of Solomon's greatness. We learn that the king is not to keep many horses or take the people back to Egypt for the purpose of buying many horses. In addition, he is not to take to himself many wives 'lest his heart turn away,' nor accumulate a great hoard of silver or gold. In the preceding section 2 aspects already came up for consideration: much gold and silver, and a lively horsetrade even with Egypt. This chapter begins with the mention of Solomon's many wives and the consequences of this practice: serious forms of idolatry. This section takes the measure of king Solomon in light of the guidelines sketched in Deut. 17:14-20.

Not only must we take account of Deut. 7 in connection with Solomon's great pool of women, also Deut. 7:3f. and 23:2-9 are in the background. In 23:3f. the Ammonites and Moabites, but also the Edomites and Egyptians, though in a somewhat different capacity, are mentioned. These are 4 of the 6 ethnic groups mentioned in vs. 1 of our chapter (also cf. J. Benkinsopp, *Bib* 72 [1992], 458). Then in Neh. 13:23-27 there is mention of marriages between Israelite men and 'foreign wives,' among whom the Ammonite and Moabite women again play an important role (Blenkinsopp, 458f.; see also the interpolation of these ethnic names in Ezra 9:1). Fishbane even considers Neh. 13:25 a carefully considered reference to our vss. 1 and 2.[1] The vss. 1-5, according to him, reflect a theologically more elaborate statement of Solomon's sins than the vss. 6f., 'which is undoubtedly the primary historical notice.' He shares this last position with Montg.-Gehman et al.

The consequence of the negative assessment especially of Solomon's passion for 'foreign women,' according to the dtr. judgment, is that Solomon's kingdom will fall a prey to division (vss. 1-13).[2] It is not surprising that numerous dtr. phrases can be pointed out in this section (see e.g. the list of such phrases in Burney). Würthwein views even the vss. 1a, 3a and 7 (aside from a small addition) alone as older components and the rest as dtr. cement.

Still chap. 11 does not form a dtr. unit in the sense that it is an unbroken narrative. The vss. 14-25 constitute an intermediate section in which 2 adversaries of Solomon are introduced, apparently without much (chronological) connection with the preceding and following narratives, though in vs. 4a there is a suggestion that by this time Solomon was already an old man. But in vs. 21 we are told that Hadad had already started his revolt against Israel at the time of David's death! Throughout Solomon's entire lifetime, therefore, the deterioration and disintegration of his kingdom had actually already begun.

---

[1] M. Fishbane, *Biblical Interpretation in Ancient Israel*, Oxford 1985, 125.
[2] Cf. also G. N. Knoppers, "Dynastic Secession and Oracle in 1 Kings 11," *Proceedings Eastern Great Lakes and Midwest Biblical Societies* 7 (1987), 159-172; id., "Rehoboam in Chronicles: Villain of Victim," *JBL* 109 (1990), 324-440; esp. 426ff.; id., "Sex, Religion, and Politics: The Deuteronomist on Intermarriage," *HAR* 14 (1994), 121-141.

From vs. 26 on there is a harking back, in a sense, to the vss. 1-13 by presenting the story of the 'calling' of Jeroboam to being the ruler of the ten tribes and the loss of the unity of the kingdom under Solomon as a consequence of the 'sins' of Solomon's old age (vss. 26-40). In the vss. 26-28 and 40 Jeroboam is introduced without much detail of any kind. There is also mention of his flight to Egypt. But this notice is correctly viewed as a torso because in place of a concrete depiction of Jeroboam's conduct, we encounter a prophecy along dtr. lines (also called DtrP; vss. 29-39; Noth; Würthwein).

The vss. 41-43 finally report Solomon's end in a manner stereotypical for the books of Kings.

In the books of Chronicles there is no parallel to the vss. 1-40 (vss. 41ff. = 2 Chr. 9:29ff.). Apparently the Chronicler deviates, as to the negative assessment of Solomon's old age, from his dtr. predecessors and colleagues. Josephus, *Ant.* VIII §§190-211, does not, however, hesitate to reproduce certain features of our chapter in somewhat lurid colours. In his work but also in MT itself the emphasis falls on Solomon's (sexual) passion for women. Josephus, §191, even puts it thus: εἰς δὲ γυναῖκας ἐκμανεὶς, 'he was wild about women' (cf. LXX φιλογύνης). Actually Solomon's choice of foreign women, even supposing he at one time had a thousand of them, was in all likelihood determined by his political preferences. Just the same, Solomon's numerous foreign contacts were bound to have impact on the religious and cultural facets of his domestic policies. Whether this was the case only in Solomon's declining years is very doubtful inasmuch as even the design of Solomon's temple, as we noted above, already revealed many (still) non-Yahwist features.

INTRODUCTION TO VSS. 1-13

In LXX[B. Luc.] one finds the vss. 1-8 in an order that is markedly different from MT (cf. Rahlfs, *SSt.* III, 215f.; Burney). The sequence of the verses in LXX as compared with that in MT is: 1a, 3a, 1b-2; 4aα and b, 3b, 4aβ, 7, 5, 8, 6, while combinations of verse fragments and other modifications occur here and there as well. It turns out that Origen in his Hexapla more than others corrected the text in light of MT, while the usual LXX MSS. subsequently followed him again. Irenaeus, on the other hand, follows LXX[B. Luc.] (Rahlfs, *SSt.* 116f.), a fact by which the antiquity of the lastmentioned text (which deviates from MT) is only confirmed. According to scholars like Stade-Schwally, LXX represents, certainly as it applies to vss. 1-11, 'a subsequent correction' of MT, even though here and there there are 'secondary transpositions' as well. In our discussion of the separate verses we will from time to time pause to note these divergences in LXX.

EXEGESIS

11:1 *King Solomon loved many foreign women: the daughter of Pharaoh, Moabite, Ammonite, Edomite, Sidonian, and Hittite women;*
In the vss. 1-6 we are told not only of Solomon's extended harem, but also of the end to which those many wives of foreign origin seduced him, following which comes a theological appraisal of his conduct. LXX^(B. Luc.) begins vs. 1 as follows: 'Solomon was a lover of women. He had 700 queens and 300 concubines: he took foreign women and the daughter of pharaoh; Moabite, Ammonite, Syrian and Edomite, Hittite and Amorite (women).'

Although this statement does not materially differ very much from MT, there are a couple of things nevertheless which stand out. In the first place MT adds to this matter of 'loving women' the fact that they were 'foreign' and that they were 'many' (on the basis of the specification in the second part of our verse and the 'exact' statement in vs. 3, Ehrlich – rather nicely – would prefer to speak of 'sundry' rather than of 'many' women). In 8:41 we already encountered the word נכרי, which denotes the 'non-citizen.' Whereas this designation is already suspect (cf. Deut. 17:15), even worse is the adjective 'many' (Deut. 17:17). Böttcher (*Neue Aehrenlese*) wants to read this 'loving' as loving 'one after another': 'hatte abwechselnd vielerlei Favoritinnen von vielerlei Herkunft,' a suggestion followed by others as well (e.g. Thenius). But the question of the 'when' of loving all those women seems to us, in light of the intent of our pericope, of secondary importance.

For the 4th time we are informed that 'the daughter of pharaoh' belonged to Solomon's stable of wives (see 3:1; 7:8; 9:24; cf. V. Sasson, *VT* 39 [1989], 408). Many exegetes consider this information superfluous, a gloss which entered the text through a later copyist, since the point here is the presence of the foreign women listed in the second half of our verse In the theological appraisal of Solomon's conduct, however, the redactor may have wished to advance this marriage as an aggravating circumstance, although at this location the statement continues – despite textcritical support – to have an air of redundance, unless (with, say, Ehrlich) one deletes ואת, moves up the *atnaḥ*, and lets 'the daughter of pharaoh' be the first entry in the list of 'foreign women' (for speculations about the name of Solomon's Egyptian father-in-law, see comments on 3:1 above[3]). Another possibility could be to translate ואת 'as supplementary to,' 'in addition to (what has been/can be said)' (see Barthélemy on 11:25; König §270a). P.P. Saydon (*VT* 14 [1964], 207), however, correctly points out that the particle here 'denotes only a series of coordinated accusatives and presents no difficulty.'

---

[3] See also S. H. Horn, "Who was Solomon's Father-in-Law," *BR* 12 (1967), 3-17.

Where LXX^(B. Luc.) differs somewhat from MT, in the second place, is in the listing of the names of the peoples from which the women came (on the connections in which the first 3 [or, counting Egypt, 4] nations occur elsewhere in OT, see the introduction to ch. 11 above). The first 2 are the same in both versions: Moabites and Ammonites. Before the Edomites of MT appear LXX has 'Syrians,' a (possible) translation of ארמיות, at least if this word must not be considered a kind of doublet of the following 'Edomite' (so, inter al., Burney). The Moabites, Ammonites and Edomites, who are often mentioned in OT as Israel's adversaries, all lived on the 'other side' of the Jordan – scanning from north to south we first encounter the Ammonites, then the Moabites (east of the Dead Sea), while the Edomites had settled southeast of the Dead Sea. The northern boundary between Edom and Moab, as is often assumed, was the *wadi el-Ḥesā* (the 'brook of Zered'; cf. Simons *GTTOT* §137), and the southern boundary of Edom the *Wadi Ḥismeh*. The boundary between Moab and Ammon may have been the Arnon (*Seil el-Moğib*), though especially this border is by no means fixed.[4] There was indeed some difference in the degree of appreciation of these 3 peoples by Israel; in Deut. 23:7 Edom, after all, is called 'your brother.' Also the Moabites and Ammonites are occasionally viewed as cognate. The Amorites, mentioned by LXX, must have lived in this area as well.

Further removed from these 'next-door neighbours' of Israel were the Sidonians (for the somewhat divergent form of this word in MT, cf. BL, 501b; Burney). Josephus, *Ant.* VIII §191, additionally makes separate mention of the 'Tyrians' (further only the Ammonites and the Idumeans). We can probably best lump together the 'Sidonians' and 'Tyrians' as 'Phoenicians' (see comments on 5:20 above). Finally, we already encountered the 'Hittites' in 9:2). They primarily lived in the small Aramaean and Syro-Hittite states of Northern Syria and Mesopotamia (cf. E. Lipiński, *TRE*, III, 592; M.C. Astour, *RSP*, II, 290 [viii 46f.]).

11:2 *from the peoples of whom YHWH had said: do not have dealings with them and let them have no dealings with you; for surely they will seduce your heart to follow their gods. To them Solomon attached himself in love.*
In this verse a dtr. 'Verdammungsurteil' (Benzinger) is pronounced on the 'foreign' marriages as an old piece of advice or commandment (cf. Exod. 34:16; Deut. 7:3; Josh. 23:12). In the context of these 'earlier' texts this prohibition does not in the first place apply to 'real' foreigners but primarily to

---

[4] See J. R. Bartlett, "The Moabites and Edomites," *Peoples of Old Testament Times* (ed. D. J. Wiseman), Oxford 1973, 229; further the same in *TRE*, II, 455-463; J.-M. de Tarragon, *ABD*, I, 194ff.

the Canaanites and other inhabitants of Palestine in whose territory the Israelites had settled (Noth).

A difficulty in this verse is posed by the particle אבן which in the books of Kings occurs only here. It is an emphatic, more precisely, an asseverative word at the beginning of a sentence.[5] The meaning is 'indeed, surely' (*Ges.*[18], 55b). Because LXX reads μη (cf. Pesh. and Tg.: רלמה), some scholars believe that instead of the particle mentioned it would be better to read פן, 'that ... not' (Ewald §337b n.; Klostermann; Oort [and LV]; Stade-Schwally; Montg.-Gehman, etc.; also cf. *HAL*, which, though it maintains our particle, enters it as a distinct lemma [p. 46a] meaning: 'so that,' 'in order that,' only in our verse). There is no necessity, however, to conform the text to LXX (Ehrlich proposes that we read כי).

We already encountered the verb נטה hiph. in 8:58 (in qal. 2:28; 8:42). The 'gods' of the foreign peoples are viewed by LXX as 'idols' (εἴδωλον), a reduction which is not infrequently applied in LXX to a variety of words which in the Hebr. text function in a non-Israelitish cultic context (see F. Büchsel, *TDNT* II, 374). The verb דבק, 'to attach oneself to,' 'to stick to' (G. Wallis, *TWAT*, II, 84-89; E. Jenni, *THAT*, I, 431f.), which in Kings also occurs again in 2 Kgs. 3:3, 5:27 and 18:6, sometimes runs parallel with אהב (e.g. Gen. 34:3). In LXX a form of the verb κολλάω is used which in certain cases also strongly connotes 'sexual intercourse' (Gen. 2:24; 34:3; cf. K.L. Schmidt, *TDNT*, III, 822). Also, our text suggests this meaning because following this verse it is again stated *expressis verbis*: לאהבה (for this word, which is essentially an infinitive [but see also Burney] cf. comments on 10:9; also cf. König §226c).

11:3 *He possessed seven hundred princesses plus three hundred concubines who led him astray.*

The number of Solomon's wives is now summed up (for ויהי־לו cf. König §348i, p; Jouön §150j); 700 wives of royal descent and 300 concubines. The word שרה, 'distinguished woman,' 'princess' (*HAL*, 1262) only occurs 5x in OT (aside from here also in Judg. 5:29; Isa. 49:23; Lam. 1:1; Esth. 1:18) in contrast to the masc. equivalent which we encountered several times in 1:19, 25; 2:5, 32; 4:2; 5:30; 9:22f. Noth is of the opinion that the reference here is not so much to 'princesses' hence women of royal descent, as to women who acquired the rank of royal spouse. They, accordingly, are the 'official' wives as opposed to the 'concubines,' who for that matter were less numerous than the official wives. The word פלגש, 'concubine,' of the approx. 37x it is found in

---

[5] Cf. T. Muraoka, *Emphatic Words and Structures in Biblical Hebrew*, Jerusalem/Leiden 1985, 132f.

OT, occurs only here in Kings. According to Ellenborgen the word is of non-Sem. origin, from which also the Greek παλλαξ, παλλακις is derived (cf. Ellenbogen, *Foreign Words,* 134).

According to Hölscher 1923, 174, the 1,000 wives are 'natürlich im wesentlichen Israelitinnen'; it was only the post-dtr. redactor who made these women foreigners. According to Hölscher, the statement concerning the many wives belonged to the few original data he found in our pericpe. But Montg.-Gehman correctly comment that 'chroniclers do not mention such private items, which in the Orient are the gentleman's own business.' They consider the high number of Solomon's harem a product of 'popular "Schwelgerei" of the Solomonic legend.' A moralizing editor has turned the matter into 'an early case of *cherchez la femme.*' In addition, they present a concise overview of harems with the numbers of women specified. David, for example, had 7 wives and 15 sons (1 Chr. 3:1-9; cf. 2 Sam. 3:2-5), plus a number of concubines (2 Sam. 15:16; 20:3). The Song of Solomon (6:8) alludes to 60 'queens' and 80 concubines in Solomon's harem. Rehoboam, Solomon's son, had 18 wives and 60 concubines (2 Chr. 11:21). Spectacular numbers of wives are listed from Israel's 'Umwelt'. Ramses II had an enormous harem with a 100 sons and many daughters; the son and successor of Mohammed had 13 wives and 395 concubines and his son Hasan had 60 and 395 resp. (still more examples in Montg.-Gehman; see also De Vaux, *Inst.,* I, 177-180)! Thus the polygamy of the king by itself was not even that offensive; see also Vatablus: *Regibus Israel licuit ducere uxores usque ad septenarium, Hebraeorum sententia, sed effraenem et immodicum uxorum numerum habere non licuit.* What was offensive is referred to in the remainder of the sentence: these wives led his heart away (from the right way: the Yahwistic way) (for the 3rd p. pl. masc. in place of fem., cf. Ewald §191b, Konig §205d, Joüon §150c).

11:4 *Now it was especially in Solomon's old age that his wives seduced his heart to follow other gods, so that his heart was not as perfect with YHWH his God as the heart of his father David was.*
In his old age – our verse essentially tells us – as a result of the influence of his many wives, Solomon proceeded to worship other gods. We already encountered זקן in 1:1; the noun זקנה occurs 6x in OT (aside from here and in 15:23 also in Gen. 24:36; Isa. 46:4; Ps. 71:9, 18; also cf. J. Conrad, *TWAT,* II, 639-650).

Along with Noth et al. we can agree that the 'geschichtstheologische Konzeption' of the dtr. has played a role in the presentation of a good beginning and a bad ending for Solomon's reign. In reality, considering his 'syncretistic' temple construction and his parity politics in the division of his country, Solomon failed from the start to be the kind of mono-Yahwistic king that the later dtr. theologians thought he should have been. Not only did he retain the 'high places' but he also sought to please his 'foreign' wives (and perhaps even other foreigners insofar as they were subjects in his realm), for whom, as for an Israelite living abroad, the rule was that the power of their country's deity stopped at its borders.

It is noteworthy that in our verse it is again emphasized that the foreign wives had seduced Solomon to go after foreign gods, a statement which is not found in LXX. It was apparently the overruling aim of the redactor or glossator to highlight the aspect of Solomon's 'defection' in his old age (for לבבי ולם, see comments on 8:61 above; for the *scriptio plena* of David: Böttcher §167). Josephus, *Ant*. VIII §195, mentions as Solomon's sins, not the 'idolatrous' altars which he built for his foreign wives, but the casting of the bronze bulls under the brass sea and the sculpturing of the lions around his throne.

11:5 *Thus Solomon followed after Ashtoreth, the goddess of the Sidonians and after Milcom, the abomination of the Ammonites.*
The phrase הלך אחרי is to be understood primarily as a literal 'going after (in procession),' but figuratively means something like 'following and serving cultically and religiously' (also cf. F. Hauck, S. Schulz, *TDNT*, VI, 571). One must not forget that the judgment that Solomon 'followed after other gods' flowed from a much later theological pen. Bertheau and Böttcher, *Neue Aehrenlese*, however, point out with reason that Solomon 'in his wisdom' supported 'foreign' religions from a viewpoint of tolerance, and was not the 'entnervter Sinnensklave' (Thenius) he was later made out to be in certain dtr. theological circles.

Listed, in the first place, is Ashtoreth or Astarte, the 'goddess' of the Sidonians, who in 2 Kgs. 23:13 is described – more contemptuously – as the 'abomination' of the Sidonians. The Hebr. OT, however, has no separate word for 'goddess,' so (as an *epicoenum*) it uses אלהים (Olsh. §114b; König §246c; GD §12c; Ges-K §122f.; Joüon §134d; WOC §6.5.2). Usually the vocalization of עשתרת is considered a *bošet* (= 'shame') vocalization of which the authentic vocalization is 'Astarte.' The explication of this form comes from Th. Nöldeke (*Göttinger Gelehrte Anzeigen* 1 [1884], 1022) and has hardly elicited any resistance, except that recently A. Cooper, *ZAW* 102 (1990), 98ff., has attempted to demonstrate that the masoretic vocalization of the word can be attributed to normal linguistic processes and is therefore in no way disparaging.

In OT the name of the goddess Astarte occurs both in the sing. and in the plur., frequently in conjunction with that of the god Baal (cf. my *Kanaän. goden*, 43-51; H.-P. Müller, *TWAT*, VI, 453-463; A. Cooper, *RSP*, III, iv. 23; and N. Wyatt, *DDD*, 203-213). An equivalent but masc. form of the word already occurs in the Eblaitic as well as in the Akkad., Ugar., and the old S Arabic. The fem. name of the god is formed especially in the NW Sem. Since the time of Amenophis II (15th century BCE) Astarte, who originated in

Canaan, is also known in Egypt. Especially in Phoen. and Punic personal names are known of which the theophorous element is Astarte.[6] Also in the ritual texts and lists of deities of Ugarit Astarte occupied an important place, even though in the well-known Baal-myth the pugnacious Anath is more prominent. It therefore need not surprise us that Astarte is here referred to as the goddess of the Sidonians (i.e. Phoenicians). It may be noted, finally, that LXX in a sense lets our verse merge with vs. 7 (MT), on the understanding that Astarte is there qualified as βδέλυγμα, 'abomination.'

Before Milcom, the 'idol' of the Ammonites, comes up for consideration, Pesh. (except for 9a1*fam*, adapted to MT?), congruently with vs. 7, reads: 'and after Chemosh, the abomination of the Moabites,' supported in this reading by the Arab translation. Thenius takes the reading of Pesh. to be original because in vs. 7 Chemosh himself is listed first and can, therefore, hardly have been overlooked here. In addition he believes the omission of these words to be explicable in terms of the immediately following ואחרי (*homoioarkton*). Others, like Stade-Schwally, take vs. 5 to be a later addition, which renders the problem virtually moot. Vanoni 1984, 64ff., thinks − in part in view of the absence of our verse in LXX − that our verse must be seen as a doubling of vs. 7. It is clear that MT has been subject to redaction.

The second deity mentioned in our verse is Milcom, the 'abomination' of the Ammonites. The word וקוץ occurs some 30x in OT (in Kgs. again in vs. 7 [2x] and in 2 Kgs. 23:13 and 24) and means, cultically, 'idol,' 'abomination.' In OT it is used to designate 'heathen' images or symbols of deities (*HAL* 1513f.). Schroer points out that the word in the first place refers to animals.[7] Often it has come in the place of the 'ordinary' word אלהים, as can be inferred already from its use in the first half of our verse.

The name of the deity in our verse (and vs. 33) is Milcom, whereas in vs. 7 there is mention of Molech. Also in 2 Kgs. 23:13 the reference is to Milcom (cf. also Jer. 49:1, 3). Elsewhere in OT as well, be it on textcritical grounds that are often disputed, one can find instances where Milcom is mentioned (2 Sam. 13:30, par. 1 Chr. 20:2; Amos 1:15; Zeph. 1:5; cf. my *Kanaan. goden*, 57; Barthélemy on vs. 7; and E. Puech, *DDD*, 1076f.). But sometimes one can also translate 'their king' or 'their Molech' because the combination of Hebr. letters מלכם permits both vocalizations. What does remain is the question whether 'Milcom' of the Ammonites is identical with 'Molech' or 'Moloch,' the god who accepts human or child sacrifices, or − according to others − a 'kind of sacrifice,' to which from time to time there is reference in OT as well

---

[6] Cf. F. L. Benz, *Personal Names in the Phoenician and Punic Inscriptions*, Rome 1972, 386f.
[7] S. Schroer, *In Israel gab es Bilder. Nachrichten von darstellender Kunst im Alten Testament* (OBO 74), Freiburg/Göttigne 1987, 351ff.

(cf. my *Kanaän. goden*, 58-64; H.-P. Müller, *TWAT*, IV, 957-968; and G.C. Heider, *DDD*, 1090-1097). In our view 'Molo/ech' was a deity who received sacrifices (with a so-called *bošet*-vocalization), and who, like Astarte, functioned in the vegetation and fertility cult in the area of Syro-Palestine. Whether the Ammonite god Milcom was an appellative for the same god we encounter in OT under the name "Moloch" is something we cannot say with certainty, we wrote some time ago (op. cit., p. 64). Also in vs. 7 we were and are very much inclined to read 'Milcom' instead of 'Molo/ech.' But other voices exist (see A. Cooper, *RSP* III, iv 38, esp. 449) which want to read 'Mole/och' in all 3 verses (5, 7, 33).

We nevertheless believe that Milcom can be maintained as god of the Ammonites, in light also of the (scarce) written material available to us from ancient Ammon. In the so-called 'Amman Citadel Inscription' (S.H. Horn, *BASOR* 193 [1969], 8), it is (probably) said that 'Milcom has built entrances for you all around.' Milcom is also mentioned and venerated as god on seal inscriptions.[8]

11:6 *So Solomon did things that were evil in the sight of YHWH and did not fully devote himself to YHWH the way his father David did.*
The beginning of this verse is a dtr. formula which one can find repeatedly in our books of Kings (14:22; 15:26, 34; 16:19; etc; see also Burney; further König, *Stil.* 217). The adjective רע is here nominalized, with the phrase 'in the eyes of' being dependent on it (BrSynt. §82a; Joüon §132a; also cf. Lettinga §68e2). The reference is to 'that which is evil' in a moral sense (G. Harder, *TDNT*, VI, 550f.). But Ehrlich is of the opinion that the verb מלא here (as also in Gen. 29:27) is used with a view to time. The meaning of this expression would then be: 'He did not fill his entire lifetime with obedience toward YHWH,' which would then be in complete agreement with vs. 4a. Still, in light of corresponding texts, we doubt whether this is the intent of the expression.

The second part of our verse contains an expression which also occurs in Deut. 1:6 and Josh. 14:8f., 14. In Kings we first encountered the verb מלא (pi.) in 1:14, while here it is construed with אחרי יהוה (cf. König §399q for the *positio absoluta verbi* and for more examples). Here it means 'to be completely obedient' (see J. Snijders, *TWAT*, IV, 879f., who, like König, further analyzes the 'supplement' of the verb), or to practice 'restlose Glaubenstreue' (A. Weiser, *TDNT*, VI, 188). In a sense this part is a repetition, in somewhat different words, of vs. 4b.

In conclusion let it be noted that LXX puts our verse after vs. 8 (MT) as a

---

[8] See G. C. Heider, *The Cult of Molek. A Reassessment* (JSOTSup 43), Sheffield 1985, 169f.

kind of conclusion of the pericope, which also contains what is said in the vss. 7f. Though it is logical to treat it as the conclusion of the section on Solomon's 'sin,' we can nevertheless regard the vss. 7f. as an addition from another period, pen, or source, and from a compositional viewpoint insist on maintaining vs. 6 in this location.

11:7 *Then on the mountain across from Jerusalem, Solomon built a high place for Chemosh, the abomination of Moab, and one for Moloch, the abomination of the Ammonites.*
In this verse the author in a sense returns to the subject of vs. 5, be it that this time Chemosh, the god of the Moabites, *is* mentioned in MT but Astarte, the goddess of the Ammonites, is not. As already stated above, LXX has vs. 7 (MT) link up with vs. 3 (MT), as a result of which the text flows more smoothly: in addition all 3 different deities are mentioned here (also cf. 2 Kgs. 23:13). The exegetes are not agreed on the question which part of MT is original and which is a later addition. In LXX, for example, vs. 7aβ ('the mountain across from Jerusalem') is lacking (again cf. 2 Kgs. 23:13 MT). J. H. Wevers, *OTS* 8 (1950), 314, poses the question whether the reason for its omission in LXX might not have been 'that it was too heinous to have the environs of the holy city involved in such heathenism.'
But also the second part of our verse raises problems: do the first 4 words of our verse ('then Solomon built a high place for ...') also apply to what is said in this verse about Chemosh? When we add to this that vs. 8 begins with וכן, the conclusion has to be that Solomon built a *bamah* for all his foreign wives, but only for one of them a high place on the mountain across from Jerusalem. In vs. 5 we already determined that Milcom and not Mole/och has to be regarded as the god of the Ammonites. In our verse LXX seems to have supported this viewpoint (τῷ βασιλεῖ αὐτῶν) Barthélemy is of the opinion that the name of the Ammonite god may sometimes have been with and sometimes without mimation, so that the difference in spelling (and name) from vs. 5 can be explained in terms of this fact. He even wants to maintain this difference in translation (as, e.g., Tg.; cf. Vulg. which has Moloch both times, and Pesh. which has Milcom both times). On the basis of the vss. 5 and 33, we, however, prefer the reading Milcom in both cases (Delitzsch, *LSF* §72b, wants to read מלך, 'king').
The verse begins with the particle אז, we have repeatedly encountered earlier (3:16; 8:1, 12; 9:11, 24; cf. Mulder 1991). As temporal particle it could perhaps refer back to vs. 4a where Solomon's defection is especially attributed to his old age. Noth is of the opinion that the notice in our verse belongs to the tradition material which the dtr. has taken over in his composition, the main reason being that it is much more concrete in content than what vs. 5 managed to report. If his suspicion is correct, then the particle אז need not even refer

back to Solomon's age but may, having been taken over from a chronicle, archive, or some narrative, refer back to a very different item of information from a very different period in Solomon's life. However this may be, we are told that Solomon built a במה for the Moabite deity ('abomination' in the later theological jargon) Chemosh. We already encountered the term 'high place' in 3:2ff. The reference here is to a non-Israelite cult place. We do not know whether also a temple was built on such a high place but the possibility exists. In any case, there must have been an altar and other cultic implements, and of course the requisite personnel. It is interesting that also king Mesha of Moab, in the inscription on the well-known Moabite Stone that was discovered in 1868, speaks of a 'high place' which he had built for Chemosh in Qarchoh (Qeriho) (*KAI* 181, 3; Beyerlin, *RTAT*, 255).

Chemosh is mentioned several more times in OT and the Moabites are called 'the people of Chemosh' (Num. 21:29; Jer. 48:46; on this deity also cf. my *Kanaän. goden*, 76ff., and H.-P. Müller, *DDD*, 356-362).

Especially in inscriptions on the Moabite Stone which dates from the time of king Ahab (cf. 2 Kgs. 3:4), we encounter phrases and expressions which resemble what we find reported about YHWH in OT. The character of this deity seems to be especially associated with war and battle (the Greek name for this god is Ares, and in the Akkad. region he is identified with Nergal, the god of the underworld and infectious diseases). Neither the etymology of his name, nor the origin of the god is clear. He was perhaps of Arabian origin and adapted in the area of Syro-Palestine to the fertility cult. There are certain correspondences in origin and character between Chemosh and YHWH, though in my *Kanaän. goden* I referred to an infinite qualitative difference between the two.

As the location for the *bamah* for Chemosh 'the mountain across from (*or* east of) Jerusalem' is referred to. That can hardly be any mountain other than (the southern part of) the Mount of Olives (Simons, *GTTOT* §184; Abel, *GP*, I, 372ff.; W. Foerster, *TDNT*, V, 484, n. 102), which is so called by name, for instance, in 2 Sam. 15:30 and Zech. 14:4 and also in NT (Matt. 21:1; 24:3; 26:30, etc.). According to 2 Sam. 15:32, the top of the Mount of Olives had a sanctuary already in David's time. That text seems to be saying that this sanctuary was devoted to a god venerated by David but this is not certain. With an allusion to 2 Kgs. 23:13, the Talmud calls the Mount of Olives הר המשחה, 'mount of the anointing,' but 2 Kgs. 23:13, referring to Solomon's building activity on behalf of a foreign cult, speaks of הר־המשחית, 'mount of corruption' (Vulg.: *Mons offensionis*). Traditionally the *Mons scandali* (*Baṭn el-Hawa*) is the southern ridge of the Mount of Olives *(ğebel eṭ-Ṭur)*, on whose western flank the present-day village *Silwan* is located (Simons, a.l.).

Solomon is also said to have built a shrine or *bamah* for Milcom, the Ammonite god. שקץ, again, is a pejorative term for the usual אלהים (Benzinger; D.

Pardee *UF* 5 [1973], 234, n. 54; et al.).

11:8 *And he did the same for all his foreign wives insofar as they burnt incense and made sacrifices to their gods.*
In this verse there is the suggestion that Solomon 'similarly' built 'high places' for all his 'foreign' wives. At least this is how one can without any real difficulty interpret the first part of our verse. In the ancient Near East, we are told, 'high places' were not at all unusual at many locations.[9]

The second part of our verse, however, yields more problems. Must we regard the 2 participles without an article as attributes with the preceding determined noun 'all foreign women'? The grammarians, for good reason, have some difficulty with this (cf. inter al. König §412i; Ges-K §131h, n.; cf. §118p; Joüon §127a; WOC §10.2.2d; also Vanoni, *Literarkritik*, 91f.). It is often observed that the reference here is to an attributive accusative. One could, for example, very well translate: 'insofar as they burned incense and made sacrifices to their gods' (König; also cf. W. Rudolph, *ZAW* 63 [1951], 205, who wants to position והם before the part.: 'obgleich sie ihren Göttern opferten...,' but this emendation is not necessary). LXX even has 3rd p. sing. masc., thereby clearly accusing Solomon of being guilty of idolatrous cult practices.

Not long ago Matty Cohen subjected the second part of our verse to an extensive inquiry (*BetM* 35 [1989f.], 261-269; *VT* 41 [1991], 332-341). In the process, with reference to M. Haran (*VT* 10 [1960], 113-129), she devoted considerable attention to the verb קטר (hiph. and pi.) and זבח (see also comments on 3:2f. above). She pointed out, among other things, that the 2 verbs occur in tandem 13x but then in the reverse order. זבח denotes especially an animal sacrifice, the 'victim'; the other verb the offering up of grain and cereal products mixed with herbs. In the case of this verb the stem modification hiph. (especially) refers to the legitimate cult, the pi. (especially) to the illegitimate (also cf. Zwickel, op. cit., p. 337ff.). In our verse there is a departure from both practices. After a comparison with other OT texts, she proposes that we should not read participles in our verse, but substantives, viz.: *miqṭarôt* (cf. Ezek. 8:11 and 2 Chr. 26:19) and *mizbᵉḥôt*, altars of incense and altars. It cannot be denied, especially because it hardly requires any change in MT, that this proposal is very attractive. Moreover, in that case this verse runs more smoothly than in its present form. But one objection remains: the last phrase 'to their gods' is more redundant than in its present dependence on the

---

[9] See W. Zwickel, *Raucherkult und Räuchergeräte* (OBO 97), Freiburg/Göttingen 1990, 255, n. 14, who refers to *Temples and High Places in Biblical Times: Proceedings of the Colloquium in Honor of the Centennial of Hebrew Union College* (ed. A. Biran), Jerusalem 1981.

verb forms. So we still opt for the *lectio difficilior*, without thereby wanting to say that it is also a *lectio melior* (Zwickel, 338, even questioned with regard to קטר [hiph.] which is otherwise always used for the legitimate cult, whether MT has in fact preserved the right vocalization).

11:9 *YHWH, however, became angry with Solomon since his heart had drawn him away from YHWH, the God of Israel, who had twice appeared to him,*
The result of Solomon's conduct is that YHWH became angry with him. We already encountered the verb אנף, 'be angry,' in 8:46. A deity's anger at his own country is expressed in the same terms on the Moabite Mesha inscription: כי יאנף נפש בארצה, 'for Chemosh was angry at his country' (*KAI* 181, 5f.; for further examples, see Montg.-Gehman). The 'heart,' i.e. the disposition (see F. Baumgärtel, *TDNT*, III, 609f.) of Solomon was turned away from YHWH as the God of Israel.

Expressly added to these words is that YHWH had twice appeared to him. Both in 3:4-15 and 9:1-9 there was mention of an appearance by YHWH to Solomon in Gibeon. Neither in the following (vss. 11ff.) nor in 6:11 is there an actual 'appearance' of YHWH but, at least on the dtr. view, of words of prophetic content, i.e. words spoken by a prophet (so also Josephus, *Ant*. VIII §197). It is remarkable that הנראה (with the article; as a relative pronoun?) is here vocalized as 3rd p. pf., where one would sooner have expected a vocalization as a masc. part. (Burney, also LXX which both here and at the beginning of the following verse translates participially; further cf. the grammars of Böttcher §897 [7]; Ewald §331b, n.; König §52; GD §31, Rem. 3; Ges-K §148k; Joüon §145e; but also cf. *HAL*, 1082a: 'wie öfters in d. bab. Vokalisation,'[10]; otherwise, however, in the case of Ehrlich who, with reference to Gen. 21:3, wants to maintain the pf. here).

11:10 *and had commanded him in this matter not to go after other gods. But he did not keep to what YHWH had commanded.*
This verse is intended as an immediate continuation of the previous verse, as is evident from וצוה. The *waw* with the pf. corresponds to our pluperfect: 'and he had commanded him' (Böttcher §947c; Bg. II §9n; WOC §32.2e; Klostermann and Burney – as does LXX in its translation – consider a participial form more correct here; also cf. Stade-Schwally. In our opinion MT can be maintained).

YHWH's command was not to go after other gods (for לבלתי cf. comments on 6:6). In 9:6 this command was not only addressed to Solomon but also to

---

[10] With reference to Z. Ben-Hayyim. *The Literary and Oral Tradition of Hebr. and Aramaic amongst the Samaritans*, V, Jerusalem 1977, 121.

his 'sons.' With a certain amount of emphasis the expression על־הדבר הזה is used to underscore the importance of this command (König §399f. refers to a 'betonende Anticipation'). The second part of our verse tells us that Solomon did not keep this command. LXX gives the impression that in place of ולא שמר it read לשמר, but MT need not be altered. Nor need one read צוהר in place of the verb without suffix in MT, despite the testimonies of a number of ancient versions. LXX still adds to our verse what we find in 4b (MT).

11:11 *Then YHWH said to Solomon: 'Because this was in your mind, namely that you have not kept my covenant and my statutes which I commanded you, I will surely tear the kingship from you and give it to one of your servants.*
In this verse and the following 2 verses the splitting up of Solomon's kingdom is announced. In the beginning of our verse the words are reminiscent of 2:3. Although our verse gives the impression that YHWH spoke with Solomon without any human meditation, the author probably meant that he brought his word via a prophet (so, for example, also Josephus and Kimchi, who think here of Ahijah the prophet of Shiloh; so too Grotius but also modern exegetes like Keil and Šanda). But Ehrlich is of the opinion that we are dealing here with a 'Selbstgespräch' of YHWH, because there is no response to it. Naturally this is not the intent of the dtr. because the sequel is clear enough (for the particle יען [אשר], cf. my article in *OTS* 18 [1973], 49-83).

The expression זאת עמך also occurs in Job 10:13 and denotes a psychological process that is hidden from others: 'in your consciousness,' 'in your mind,' 'in your heart' (also cf. comments on 8:17 above; further BDB, 768b; D. Vetter, *THAT*, II, 326; Burney; Noth; here, too, Ehrlich has another view: 'because you knew this but despite my covenant have not kept it ...'). In what follows 'covenant' and 'statutes' are mentioned side by side (also cf. vss. 33f., 38). But LXX[B. Luc.] read τὰς ἐντολάς μου, 'my commandments'; Pesh. has an expansion: *wqjmj* (pl.) *wdjnj* (pl.) *wpwqnj* (pl.). But textcritically there is nothing against maintaining 'my covenant' in our verse (otherwise Böttcher, *Neue Aehrenlese,* who wants to alter MT on the basis of LXX). J.W. Wevers, *OTS* 8 (1950), 320, has demonstrated that in LXX's view human beings cannot break God's covenant, on the basis of which LXX has changed MT in its translation. The question remains what the author means by this word or whether the author perhaps uses the word 'reichlich blaß als Ausdruck für gottliche Vorschriften' (Noth). Van Gelderen thinks in this connection of the 'very first requirement of God's covenant' (Exod. 20:2f.), by breaking which Solomon would have undermined the ground on which YHWH's statutes rest. Since the dtr. is a theologian he may perhaps have been able to follow this reasoning.[11]

The transgression will result in the splitting of the kingdom. The text here anticipates the encounter between Jeroboam and the prophet Ahijah (vss. 29-39). In our verse, in a *figura etymologica*, the verb קרא, 'to tear loose,' is used. This verse occurs no fewer than 18x in qal and twice in niph. in the books of Kings (over 60x in OT; cf. W. Thiel, *TWAT*, VII, 189-195). In our chapter the verb also occurs in the vss. 12f., 30f., again in a comparable context in 14:8 (cf. 2 Kgs. 17:21; see also M. Brettler, *VT* 39 [1989], 277f.). Elsewhere in the books of Kings the verb relates more generally to the tearing of clothes (21:27; 2 Kgs. 2:12; 5:7f.; 6:30; 11:14; 18:37; 19:1; 22:11, 19; cf. in niph.: 1 Kgs. 13:3, 5). Aside from in our chapter the act of 'tearing up' is reported both with reference to a king's realm and to the symbolic act of tearing one's clothes also in 1 Sam. 15:27f.; 28:17. In 1 Sam. the reference is to the rejection of Saul as Israel's king. There the tearing off of a piece of a garment is not so much a deliberate act, but in our chapter the tearing off of parts of a garment will soon be such an act. As object of the tearing away the reference here is more generally to the 'kingship' or the 'kingdom' (the word already occurred in 2:46; 5:1; 9:5 and 10:20), without there as yet being any mention of a further division. Also the figure to whom the kingship will then be transferred is indicated in general terms: 'to one of your servants' (for the indefinite meaning of this grammatical construction, see BrSynt. §73a; Joüon §140a).

11:12 *Only, for the sake of your father David, I will not do it during your lifetime. Out of the hand of your son I will tear it.*
The split will not occur in Solomon's days, however, but in the lifetime of his son and successor. In place of the verb 'tearing away' in this and in the following verse LXX probably reads a form of the verb לקח, but MT requires no modification. The fem. suff. can be viewed as neuter (Ges-K §135p). Let it be noted, finally, that Pesh. reads 'my servant' in place of 'your father.' Vanoni, *Literarkritik*, 62, points out that the alternation 'your father' and 'my servant' (following verse) within a single speech of YHWH occurs only here.

11:13 *Yet I will not tear away the entire kingdom: one tribe will I give to your son, for the sake of David my servant and for the sake of Jerusalem which I have chosen.'*
A second restriction on the verdict is the statement that not the entire kingdom will be torn away but that one tribe will be left to his son and successor. The particle רק here has a conjunctional function: 'only' (König §392f.). We

---

[11] See now also V.H. Matthews, "The King's Call to Justice," *BZ* 35 (1991), 204-216.

already encountered the word שבט, 'tribe,' in 8:16. The numeral 'one' is expressly added to the stem here as well as in the vss. 32 and 36 (cf. 12:20). Not until 12:21 do we hear that the tribe of Benjamin joined the one tribe (Judah) (but cf. Munster: *connumeratur tribui Jehuda tribus Benjamin*; so also Clarius and Vatablus; but Grotius says: *Benjaminis tribus non integra fuit Roboami*). Otherwise only the one tribe stands over against the ten other tribes (vss. 31, 35; cf. also U. Holzmeister, *Bib* 20 [1939], 265f.). Cited as the reason why YHWH does this is again the 'election' of David, but this time in conjunction with Jerusalem (cf. vss. 12, 32, 34, 36, in which series Jerusalem is only again mentioned additionally in vs. 32; also cf. comments on 8:16 above). Accordingly, in the view of the dtr., David and Jerusalem (to which LXX and Pesh. minus 9a1*fam* and a few younger MSS still add 'the city'), are jointly proof of divine election (see W. Zimmerli, *TDNT*, V, 664f.; G. Fohrer, *TDNT*, VII, 302, 304).

1 KINGS 11:14-25

11:14 *Then YHWH raised up an adversary to Solomon: Hadad the Edomite who was of the royal family of Edom.*

15 *Once when David was occupied with Edom [Joab, commander of the army, had gone up to bury the casualties] he ordered every male person in Edom to be struck down.*

16 *For Joab and all Israel stayed there no less than six months to cut down every male person in Edom.*

17 *Adad, however, fled to Egypt with a number of Edomites who belonged among his father's servants. Now Hadad was still a little boy.*

18 *Leaving Midian, they went to Paran. They took with them some men from Paran and so came to Pharaoh, king of Egypt, who gave him housing, promised him maintenance, and gave him land;*

19 *for Hadad found so much favour in the sight of pharaoh that he gave him as wife the sister of his own wife: the sister of queen Tahpenes.*

20 *And the sister of Tahpenes bore him a son, Genubath, and after his baby years Tahpenes took him into pharaoh's palace so that Genubath resided in Pharaoh's palace among pharaoh's children.*

21 *When Hadar heard in Egypt that David had gone to rest with his fathers and that Joab, the commander of the army, had died, he said to pharaoh: 'Please give me leave to go to my own country.'*

22 *But pharaoh said to him: 'What do you lack with me that you should want to go to your own country?' But he said: '[Nothing], but do please let me go!'*

23 *And God raised up still another antagonist against him: Rezon, son of Eliada, who had fled from his master, Hadadezer king of Zobah [(24) when David was slaughtering them].*

24 *Gathering men around him he became the leader of a marauding band. They went to Damascus, settled there, and he reigned as king in Damascus.*

25 *And he was an enemy of Israel throughout the entire life of Solomon [add to this the harm done by Hadad]: he loathed Israel and was king in Damascus.*

INTRODUCTION

As a sort of introduction to the revolt of Jeroboam 2 foreign opponents of Solomon are introduced. The first is introduced as Hadad the Edomite (vss. 14-22), the second is Rezon the Syrian (vss. 23ff.). Burney et al. correctly observe that the story of Hadad comes across as somewhat confused. He makes reference to Winckler[1] who believes that 2 stories have been interwoven (also Benzinger follows Winckler). The first consists of the vss. 14, 15aα, bβ, 17b, 17aβ, 19, 20aβ, 20bβ, 21 and 22. In this story the young Edomite Hadad is brought by a servant of his father to the pharaoh of Egypt where he married an Egyptian princess. The second story is composed of the vss. 15aβ, 16a, 17aα, γ, 18, 19b, 20aα, 20bα, in which Joab plays a role and Adad is a Midianite prince who fled to Egypt with his followers, in the process taking with him a number of Edomites from Paran. Pharaoh, who generously favoured him in many respects, gave to him as wife Anoth, the sister of Tahpenes, who bore him a son, Genubath. In both stories modifications are made or glosses identified in MT. Still, such an autonomous unravelling of the present text, however ingenious, does not satisfy.

More deserving of appreciation is the opinion of W.J. Martin, SVT 17 (1969), 184f., who, referring to 'dischronologized narrative,' makes a distinction between the 'narrative order,' which follows the MT, and the 'chronological order,' which, based on MT, may have looked as follows: vss. 17 (Hadad's flight), 18 (Pharaoh's hospitality), 15f. (campaign against Edom and Joab's mass murder), 19 (Hadad's marriage), 21 (David's death), 22 (Hadad's decision to return), 14 (uprising against Solomon). The unity of the 'narrative' pericope is in principle maintained.

That the construction of the pericope was actually more complex than may appear from the immediately preceding discussion is evident, aside from the extended analysis one can find (inter al.) in Vanoni, *Literarkritik*, 72ff., also from the text of LXX which, except for a number of divergent readings, inserts the vss. 23aβ-25aα (MT) after vs. 14a (MT) in its translation. It is Rahlfs' opinion that the cause of this 'transposition' is to be found in the corresponding content (Rahlfs, *SSt.* III, 216f.). According to him, Origen corrected the passage on the model of MT, as a result of which the initial words occur twice (vss. 14 and 23).

We find ourselves agreeing with Noth when he not only considers the Hadad story but also the much shorter Rezon story (vss. 23ff.) inspired by 'Interesse für die Schattenseite der Königherrschaft Salomos, und zwar doch wohl auf Grund sachlich guter Kentnisse.' The dtr. redactor must have taken the notices from a good source. Also from this viewpoint it is not plausible to divide these stories over 2 'sources'.[2]

---

[1] H. Winckler, "Beiträge zur Quellenscheidung der Königsbücher. I. Das elfte Capitel des ersten Königsbuches, seine geschichtlichen Nachrichten und seine Bedeutung für die Quellenscheidung," *Alttestamentliche Untersuchungen*, Leipzig 1892, 1-15.

[2] See now also D. Edelman, "Salomon's Adversaries Hadad, Rezon and Jerobeam: A Trio of »Bad Guy« Characters Illustrating the Theology of Immediate Retribution," *The Pitcher is Broken* (Fs G.W. Ahlström, ed. S.W. Holloway et al.; JSOTSup 190), Sheffield 1995, 166-191.

EXEGESIS

11:14 *Then YHWH raised up an adversary to Solomon: Hadad the Edomite who was of the royal family of Edom.*
Hoftijzer, in a persuasive article, has demonstrated that from a *grammatical* viewpoint our verse is entirely in order as introduction to Hadad's revolt against Solomon.[3] We already encountered the word שָׂטָן, 'adversary' in 5:18 and it recurs in the vss. 23 and 25. G. von Rad, *TDNT*, II, 73-75, was of the opinion that the word has a 'special place in the judicial life of Israel.' Hoftijzer, art. cit., pp. 29ff.; also cf. his n. 9, on the other hand, stresses the intent of an adversary's actually doing evil and causing pain right into a forensic situation as a 'public prosecutor.' This is more than merely being a 'slanderer' at pharaoh's court.[4] YHWH (in vs. 23: *Elohim*) is expressly mentioned as the agitator's instigator, a detail which cannot be said to be without theological significance.

Hadad is the name of the first opponent (for the particle את before proper names, cf. GD §39a). In vs. 17 his name is spelled אדד (for this and the following details, cf. also Bartlett 1976). LXX consistently spells the name as 'Αδερ (Josephus, *Ant.* VIII §199 spells: Αδερος). Also in Gen. 36:35f. and in 1 Chr. 1:46 there is mention of Hadad the Edomite (cf. Gen. 36:39; 1 Chr. 1:50f.). The Mesopotamian and Syrian weather-god Hadad occurs in the Ugar. texts as *hd, hdd, 'add* (cf. F. B. Knutson, RSP III, v. 1 [pp. 474ff.]; my *Kanaän. goden*, 79f.[5]). The occurrence of the theophorous element Hadad (or Adad) in the proper names of Mesopotamians, Syrians, Aramaeans, S Arabians et al. (Ben-Hadad of Damascus, for example, in 15:18), points to the large geographic spread of the Hadad cult. For that reason the words 'Edomite' or 'Edom' in our verse need not be changed into 'Aram,' because also an Edomite may have borne this name (so, correctly, also Montg.-Gehman; otherwise, however A. Lamaire, *BN* 48 [1988], 14-18, who wants to read Edom as Aram).

Although following this statement LXX has the content of the vss. 23-25a, MT continues with the words that Hadad was 'of the king's seed.' LXX here

---

[3] J. Hoftijzer, "Philological-Grammatical Notes on 1 Kings XI 14," *OTS* 25 (1989), 29-37.

[4] Contra: A. Brock-Unte, "»Der Satan«: Die alttestamentliche Satansgestalt im Licht der sozialen Verhältnisse des nahen Orients," *Klio* 28 (1935), 219-227; see now also K.F. de Blois, "How to Deal with Satan?," *BiTr* 37 (1986), 301-309; and C. Breytenbach, P.L. Day, *DDD*, 1369-1380.

[5] See now my article "Der Gott Hadad in nordwestsemitischen Raum," *Interaction and Acculturation in the Mediterranean* (ed. J. G. P. Best et al.), Amsterdam 1980, 69-83; and also J.C. Greenfield, *DDD*, 716-736.

reads ἐκ τοῦ σπέρματος τᾶς βασιλείας (ἐν Ἰδουμαίᾳ), which has prompted various exegetes to propose the word 'kingship' (מלוכה) in place of 'the king' (Klostermann; Benzinger, Ehrlich; Delitzsch, LSF §13d; et al.; cf. 2 Kgs. 25:25; Jer. 41:1; etc.). But this change is unnecessary (so, correctly, Montg.-Gehman; Hoftijzer).

Bartlett 1976, 206f., doubts that Hadad's father was in fact king of Edom and that in David's time Edom had a 'hereditary monarchy.' Our text, however, says no more than that Hadad belonged to a 'royal family.' Hoftijzer (pp. 32f.) takes the word זרע (for this word, which we already encountered in 2:33, cf. H.D. Preuss, TWAT, II, 663-686) to mean the 'descendants' or 'children' of the king. The text means to say, therefore, that Hadad was in fact a direct son of the king, but leaves out of consideration the question whether Edom at this time could have had a king. This position seems to us correct.

The concluding words of our verse are often viewed as a gloss, either belonging to the immediately preceding text or to אח־ארום in the following verse Hoftijzer (p. 33) demonstrates that the words referred to are not 'Frendkörper' in the sentence, but describe the function or status which Hadad had in the land.

Already in 9:26 we encountered the reference to 'Edom.' From an archaeological viewpoint, the inhabitation of Edomite territory must have occurred around the turn of the thirteenth century B.C. (the beginning of the Iron Age). We already mentioned the list of Edomite kings recorded in Gen. 36:31-39 (1 Chr. 1:43, 51a). They speak of 'kings who ruled in the land of Edom' which suggests that the kingship of Edom was not hereditary. In 2 Sam. 8:13f. we read of David's subjugation of Edom after he defeated the Ammonites and a number of Aramean tribes (for more particulars, cf. M. Weippert, TRE, IX, 293f.). It is this event which is recalled in what follows.

11:15 *Once when David was occupied with Edom [Joab, commander of the army, had gone up to bury the casualties] he ordered every male person in Edom to be struck down.*

The beginning of this verse again presents the usual problems. In place of בהיות LXX translates ἐν τῷ ἐξολεθρεῦσαι, 'rooting out.' According to the concordance of Hatch-Redpath, this verb served as the translation of many Hebr. verbs, especially of stem modifications of the verb כרת and שמר. Only once, in 2 Kgs. 9:7 (but disputed: see textcr. app. in BHK and BHS), do we find a rendering of נכה (hiph.). Nevertheless many exegetes opt for a modification of the text in the last-mentioned sense (e.g. Böttcher, *Neue Aehrenlese,* Thenius, Benzinger, Stade-Schwally, Van Gelderen), usually on the basis of the reading of Pesh. (and supported by the Arab. translation) *hrb* 'destroy,' 'eradicate.' In this connection 2 Sam. 8:13 may be supportive as well (Montg.-Gehman). On the other hand, there are those who opt for the firstmentioned

Hebr. verb (e.g., Klostermann, Kamphausen, Oort, Šanda).

Böttcher believed that the word was unclear in all texts and could be read 3 ways: in the way we now have it in MT but also as בהברית or בהכות. The last reading, according to him, was the most fitting and explains the other two. To our mind the difficulty in this solution of the problem, however, is that in that case LXX and Pesh. did not have the same copy of the manuscript as 'Vorlage'! There are also exegetes who attempt to manage the problem with the existing text. So, for example, Keil who considers הָיָה אֶת analogous to הָיָה עִם, 'mit jem. zu schaffen haben aber im feindlichen Sinne.' Brockington (NEB: '... when David reduced Edom') refers (presumably) to a pi.-form of the verb הוה I (HAL, 231b), meaning 'to overthrow' (cf. Prov. 14:35). Materially, indeed, all the proposals pretty much come down to the relative heavy-handedness in David's presence among, or rough conduct against, the Edomites. And this tendency is certainly present in MT. In the case of the verb היה, the *nota accusativi* presents some difficulty at least if the particle את has to function or be construed as such and therefore not as a preposition. Tg. in fact reads the preposition as בְ, which makes the construction flow more smoothly: 'when David was in Edom' (also cf. Vulg. *cum enim esset David in Idumea*). Now it is the case that the prep. את, proceeding from the basic meaning 'on the side of' (*Ges.*¹⁸, 114f.) can have several shades of meaning: 'with,' 'in the case of,' etc. In fact we would rather have expected the prep. בְ (which is perhaps the reason why HAL, 234b inserts a '?' and refers to היה I [HAL, 231b]). Accordingly, the translation: 'And it happened when David was in Edom' retains an air of uncertainty, although this rendering does the least violence to MT.

Next follows, asyndetically, a parenthetical statement in which Joab, who was the commander of the army, is depicted as a kind of funeral undertaker (also cf. Vatablus: *ut curaret sepeliendos Idumaeos interfectos*). Joab is already familiar to us from the first 2 chapters of the books of Kings, though his activities are mostly reported in the books of Samuel (cf. comments on 1:7 and 1:19 for 'commander of the army').

For the verb 'to bury' the pi.-modification of the verb קבר is used here. It is used in this form only 6x (only here in Kings, in other passages it additionally always assumes a part. form), as opposed to the qal-form which we already encountered in 2:31. According to K. Koch, *TWAT*, VI, 1150, the qal-form occurs 86x times and the niph.-form 39x. According to Jenni, *Pi'el*, 145f., in the work of many grammarians of biblical Hebr., the form in our text is a 'prime example' for the 'intensive' function of the piel, in which connection also the performance of an action on various objects can be mentioned (also cf. Ges-K §52f.; Joüon §52d). Jenni himself (p. 150f.) prefers to describe this pi.-form as 'resultative' with an object in the pl.: 'Das Pi'el mit zahlreichen Objecten ist nicht eine selbständige Erscheinung, sondern begegnet immer als Sonderfall des Resultativs.'

The חללים, which in OT occurs in the sing. 92x but only here in the books of Kings, are 'the pierced ones,' 'the slain,' 'the dead' (W. Dommershausen, *TWAT*, II, 981-986; *HAL*, 307b). Since Joab surely did not march out to bury dead Edomites (so, however, Vatablus), the reference here has to be to Israelites who have been killed. The context of this clause must make clear when that took place, as we will see in a moment. Šanda, who also looked carefully at the content of this clause, proposed as interpretation, not to 'have Joab bury the slain' — indeed a fairly futile exercise after the lapse of considerable time — but to have him 'search through the holes.' In that case the text needs some modification: לקבר את־החרים. A number of exegetes have (sometimes hesitantly) followed him (including Van Gelderen, Gray, Bongers). It is truly an ingenious emendation, but one which finds no support in textual criticism (so, correctly, also Bartlett 1976, 208).

The question is to whom the following ויך refers, to Joab or to David (also cf. Vanoni, *Literarkritik*, 94f.). There is something to be said for the former because in the immediately preceding part of the text he is also mentioned as the one who buried the slain and because in the heading of Ps. 60 the same verb form is used: 'Joab slew Edom in the Valley of Salt, 12,000 men.' It is simply a fact that in OT Joab is depicted as a combative general who shrank from almost no challenge of any kind, although he usually acted as the faithful executor of the plans of his boss David (also many translators view Joab as the subject, including the AV, the Lutheran translation, LV, PCV, NV, GNB). But precisely for that reason David must be considered as subject because it was ultimately he who ordered the slaughter of the Edomites by his willing agent Joab. If we were to omit the asyndetic parenthesis in which we observe Joab as undertaker, we would not miss any essential information. Given that omission, vs. 15b would tie in well with the beginning of this verse. Vanoni, *Literarkritik*, 95, is of the opinion that the omission of this intermediate clause would produce a tautology because vs. 15b must be viewed as the continuation of בהכות in the first half of our verse. But we have advanced as our opinion that this part is an emendation, so that his argument does not hold water. Along with Würthwein et al., we are inclined to declare the intermediate clause a later interpolation in the text, which is intended along with vs. 16 to offer a kind of explanation of David's conduct.

The slaying of every male person (זכר occurs 82x in OT; only here and in the following verse in the books of Kings; also cf. R.E. Clements, *TWAT*, II, 593-599) is mentioned repeatedly in OT (Gen. 34:25; Num. 31:7, 17, etc.). If all male persons had really been killed, Edom of course would have been wiped off the map, which was not what happened. Clements thinks it is possible that an exception was made for male children (cf. Deut. 20:13f.) and it is not unlikely that this also crossed the mind of the dtr. redactor. Josephus (*Ant.* VIII §200) speaks of fighting men who were able to bear arms.

11:16 *For Joab and all Israel stayed there no less than six months to cut down every male person in Edom.*

As if to supply further explanation of the preceding notice, the author here refers back to an event in the past in which for a period of no less than 6 months Joab, and 'all Israel,' went on a horrendous rampage in Edom. We concur with Klostermann, Noth et al. that this verse is not a direct reference to 2 Sam. 8:13f., though the 2 events cannot be separated. Precisely what occasioned the punitive expedition mentioned here, a campaign in which (see previous verse) also many Israelites were killed, is not clear. It was possibly a revolt against Israelite overlordship. There is mention of an Edomite revolt also later in the history of Judah and Edom (2 Kgs. 8:20ff.).[6]

For the plupf. after the particle כי cf. König §116; for the form הכרית as inf. cstr., cf. Böttcher §987.7; Ges-K §531 (otherwise: Bg. II §19l).

11:17 *Adad, however, fled to Egypt with a number of Edomites who belonged among his father's servants. Now Hadad was still a little boy.*

Following the intermezzo of the vss. 15f. the text again picks up the name of Hadad mentioned in vs. 14 (for the form of the personal name, see that verse). In response to the raids on Edomite men which were organized by David and his henchmen, he, along with a number of men belonging to the court or the bodyguard of his father, took flight. It was his intent to go to Egypt – frequently an asylum for refugees. It was possibly his father who, in view of his youthful age, sent him, accompanied by a good-sized bodyguard, off on this escape route. After all, he is described here as a 'young boy.' The word קטן, 'small,' having as its second vowel a *qames* occurs alongside the more recent form which has *ḥolem* as its second vowel (formed on the analogy of *gadôl*) (cf. BL, 466, n. 2; see also 5:14 and 1 Sam. 20:35; further J. Conrad, *TWAT*, VII, 3-10). Conrad, 8, correctly points out that the potential pretender to the throne constitutes a latent threat to his opponent. Grammatically our verse follows vs. 15b.

11:18 *Leaving Midian, they went to Paran. They took with them some men from Paran and so came to Pharaoh, king of Egypt, who gave him housing, promised him maintenance and gave him land;*

Reported in this verse are the escape route and the pharaoh's reception. According to MT, the escape route ran via Midian and Paran (where some more men [for the indefinite form, cf. König §74] joined him and his party) to Egypt. At the beginning of our verse LXX[B] has another reading: 'And the men from the city of Madiam arose and the leaders to Pharan; and they took men

---

[6] Cf. J.R. Bartlett, "Edom and the Fall of Jerusalem," *PEQ* 114 (1982), 13-24.

with them and went to pharaoh, the king of Egypt.' In any case this reading is less clear than that of MT. A difference between them is that here Midian is not referred to as a region but as 'the city of Madiam.' From this fact Thenius inferred that originally the reference was probably to the city of Maon (Judg. 10:12), and emended the text accordingly. Some exegetes have followed him (incl. LV, Oort; also cf. the textcr. app. *BHK*). But this emendation is unnecessary. Midian is an ethnic tribe and a region which in its early history is repeatedly mentioned in OT and probably had more power then than later (Exod. 2:15f.; 3:1; 4:19; 18:1; Num. 25:15; 31:37; 22:4, 7; etc.; and esp. in Judg. 6-8).[7] The area lay S of Edom and E of the Gulf of Aqabah (Simons, *GTTOT* §166). It may be that the Midianites provided support to the Edomites in their resistance to Israel.

Paran is mentioned repeatedly in OT, in Deut. 1:1 as well as Gen. 14:6 (here preceded by איל). There is reference also to 'Mount Paran' (Deut. 33:2; Hab. 3:3) and to 'the wilderness of Paran' (Gen. 21:21; Num. 10:12; 12:16; 13:3, 26 and 1 Sam. 25:1). The reference is to a somewhat ill-defined area or oasis on (the N part of) the Sinai-peninsula, to the S of the Arabah and to the E of the *wadi el-Ariš* (Simons, *GTTOT* §358; Abel, *GP*, I, 434). In ancient times the caravan road from the Gulf of Aqabah to Egypt probably ran along the same route (see also Montg.-Gehman and Noth; further K.-H. Bernhardt, *BHHW*, 1445a). Even today there exists a *ğebel Faran,* approx. 80 km W of Petra, but it is not clear that this is precisely the Paran mentioned in our verse (*HAL*, 860a; but also Zorell, 640a).

Reinforced with a number of men from Paran (details about them are again lacking), they arrive at the pharaoh's court. The name of this man, in contrast to vs. 40, is not stated. The young Hadad is received in a way befitting an asylum-seeking prince. He is given a residence, provisions, and land. Because the last 3 words are lacking in LXX[B] some scholars consider them a later addition (inter al. Stade-Schwally) but this is unnecessary. Pharaoh gave Hadad housing and promised him a livelihood. The verb אמר with the preposition l^e means 'to promise,' 'to assign,' 'to allocate' (cf. 2 Chr. 29:24; E. Lipiński, *Phoenix* 28, 2 [1982], 79 and n. 101; *Ges.*[18], 76b). Frequently a connection is made with the Arabic (Burney; L. Kopf., *VT* 8 [1958], 164). The last words of our verse convey the impression of being explicative of the promise of a livelihood: a land grant to enable the recipient to grow his own food. The Pesh., in its translation, has a different verbal rhythm than MT: 'he gave him a house and bread; and he spoke to him: Dwell with me. And he gave him land.'

---

[7] Cf. O. Eißfeldt, "Protektorat der Midianiter über ihre Nachbarn im letzten Viertel des 2. Jt. v. Chr.," *JBL* 87 (1968), 383-393; and G. E. Mendenhall, *ABD*, IV, 815-818.

11:19 *for Hadad found so much favour in the sight of pharaoh that he gave him as wife the sister of his own wife: the sister of queen Tahpenes.*
Evidently Hadad was such a congenial guest in the eyes of pharaoh that he gained for himself an Egyptian princess as wife: the sister of pharaoh's own wife. 'To find favour in the eyes of' is an expression which occurs with relative frequency. In it the subordination of a person vis-à-vis a superior, especially of a subject toward his king, is expressed (see H.J. Stoebe, *THAT*, I, 588ff.; D.N. Freedman, J. Lundblom, *TWAT*, III, 28ff.). In the books of Kings the expression occurs only here.

The sister of his wife, 'sister of Tahpenes, the ruling queen,' becomes Hadad's spouse. However simple this statement sounds, it nevertheless, at one time produced numerous problems for a number of interpreters, which led to a variety of emendations and interventions in the text (Thenius; Böttcher, *Neue Aehrenlese*; Klostermann; etc.). There is first of all the word 'Tahpanes,' which, to be sure, occurs only here and in the following verse, but is virtually indistinguishable from the name of a city (Jer. 2:16; 43:7ff.; 44:1; 46:14; Ezek. 30:18). In any case we are dealing here with an Egyptian name (W.F. Albright, *BASOR* 140 [1955], 32, considers it a proper name). Noth refers to the Egyptian word *t'j ḥm.t nsw*, which means 'the king's consort' Janssen believes, based on the LXX spelling, that the *pe* in the Hebr. word should be a *mem*: Tahmenes.[8] In that case the Hebr. word could be a translation of this Egypt. word. Also Görg interprets this name as the designation of a title which corresponds to the Hebr. designation of a function[9] (also cf. *HAL*, 1584b.). LXX[B] writes the name as θεκεμεινα (Josephus, *Ant.* VIII §201: θαφινη), but adds της μείζω, sometimes viewed as a translation of הגדולה, 'the oldest (sister).'

The word גבירא occurs 15x in OT, 4 of them in the books of Kings (aside from there also in 15:13; 2 Kgs. 5:3 and 10:13). According to Zafrira Ben-Barak, the word has 3 meanings: (1) mother or wife of the ruler; (2) female ruler; (3) mistress.[10] Only in this case the reference is to the most prominent wife of pharaoh; in the other (Israelitish or Judean) cases the reference is to the queen-mother (*Ges.*[18], 194b; *HAL*, 166a; De Vaux, *Inst.* I, 180). It is very likely, therefore, that 'Tahpenes' means nothing other than 'wife of pharaoh.' In that case גבירא is only an apposition with Tahpenes, though Vanoni, *Literarkritik*, 74, for one is not convinced of this.

---

[8] J.M.A. Janssen, *L'Ancien Testament et l'Orient* (Orientalia et Biblica Lovaniensia 1, ed. G. Ryckmans), Leuven 1957, 35; cf. also B. H. Stricker, *Acta Orientalia* 15 (1937), 11f.; P.A. Viviano, *ADB*, VI, 309.

[9] M. Görg, "Namen und Titel in 1 Kön 11:19f.," *BN* 36 (1987), 22-26 (reprinted in M. Görg, *Aegyptiaca-Biblica* [Ägypten und Altes Testament 11], Wiesbaden 1991, 178-191.

[10] Z. Ben-Barak, "The Status and Right of the *Gĕbîrâ*," *JBL* 110 (1991), 23-34; esp. 23.

A curious circumstance is that LXX, in its expansion of 12:24 (d-f), has pharaoh offer to Jeroboam his daughter Ano, the eldest sister of Tahpanes, in marriage.

11:20 *And the sister of Tahpenes bore him a son, Genubath, and after his baby years Tahpenes took him into pharaoh's palace so that Genubath resided in Pharaoh's palace among pharaoh's children.*
The sister of Tahpenes bore Hadad a son named Genubath. This name occurs only here and is often linked with Arab. or (old-) Egyptian (cf. Montg.-Gehman; *HAL*, 191a; *Ges.*^{18}, 224b; Bartlett 1976, 212, n. 22).[11] After a certain period of time the child was 'weaned' by Tahpanes herself. The verb גמל, which in the books of Kings occurs only here, has 2 rather divergent meanings in the qal (34x in OT): (1) 'to affect,' 'prove' (23x); and (2) 'to be finished,' 'to end,' 'to ripen,' 'to bring to maturity,' 'to wean' (11x). In niph. the verb occurs an additional 3x (G. Sauer, *THAT*, I, 426ff.; K. Seybold, *TWAT*, II, 24-35; further *HAL*, 189; *Ges.*^{18}, 222f.). Seybold (*VT* 22 [1972], 112-117), accordingly, believes that it concerns 2 homonymous verbs. In Israel the process of 'weaning from its mother's milk' usually occurred at the end of the child's third year. The event was celebrated with a feast and brought about a change in the legal status of the child: he could now inherit property, be adopted, and begin his training for his future occupation.[12] Clear from the text is still another favour to Hadad: after his years as a baby his son is received and included among the Egyptian princes and princesses and given a solid education at the court (cf. Exod. 2:10; further Bartlett 1976, 213). Although this detail is perhaps unimportant for the progression of the story (so Noth), it does illustrate the close relations between the pharaoh and Hadad.

It is unnecessary, on the basis of LXX, to alter the text into וַתְּנַדְּלֵהוּ, 'and she raised him to adulthood,' as Klostermann, Benzinger, Stade-Schwally, Gray, et al. want. The 'feast of the weaning of the child may very well have been arranged by the sister, the queen' (also cf. Montg.-Gehamn who refer to an expression used by Esharhaddon concerning the Arabian queen Tabua: 'born in my palace').

11:21 *When Hadad heard in Egypt that David had gone to rest with his fathers and that Joab, the commander of the army, had died, he said to pharaoh: Please give me leave to go to my own country.*

---

[11] See now also M. Görg, "Der Name im Kontext: Zur Deutung männlicher Personennamen auf -*at* im Alten Testament," *Text, Methode und Grammatik* (Fs W. Richter, ed. W. Gross et al.), St. Ottilien 1991, 81-95.

[12] For these and other particulars, cf. G. Pfeifer, "Entwöhnung und Entwöhnungsfest im Alten Testament," *ZAW* 84 (1972), 341-347.

On hearing the rumour that David and Joab had died, Hadad again wished to return to his own country. We already encountered the expression 'to go to rest with his fathers' in 1:21.

11:22 *But pharaoh said to him: 'What do you lack with me that you should want to go to your own country?' But he said: '[Nothing], but do please let me go!'*

Consent for Haded's return to his own country was not given without some discussion with pharaoh. The latter was apparently attached to Haded. One can only conjecture about the reason for this. Bartlett 1976, 223, believes that the pharaoh in question, whom he – in line with researches done by K. A. Kitchen – identifies with pharaoh Siamun (circa 978-959 BCE), did not want to get into political trouble with Solomon by openly supporting Hadad's aspirations to liberate Edom.[13]

The particle כי is a *kî*-recitative (Zorell, *Bib* 14 [1933], 466; GD §90b). חסר, which as a verb-form occurs 23x in OT, in qal means both 'to decrease' (thus in 17:14, 16) and 'to lack.' It is used adjectivally here, the only place in Kings of the 17x it is found as such in OT (H.-J. Fabry, *TWAT*, III, 88-98; *HAL*, 325a; also cf. Bg. II §14r). A dozen Hebr. MSS (Kennicott) and LXX read לא as לו. Pesh.'s solution is to maintain the 'no' (as the reply to pharaoh's question whether he lacked anything), meanwhile indicating Hadad's intention to leave by inserting an adversative 'but' (now as translation of כי). This solution seems plausible. The *figura etymologica* more emphatically conveys the will to return to his own country.

Here, aside from a small insertion in vs. 25, the story of Hadad in MT ends. But LXX[B,Luc.] adds to our verse: 'And Ader returned to his own country.' Then LXX, jumping to what vs. 25aβ-b (MT) offers, continues: 'This is the evil Ader did: he was virulently hostile (ἐβαρυθύμησεν; also cf Schleusner, I, 541) toward Israel and became king in Edom.' In vs. 25 (MT) these words are spoken by Solomon's next opponent: Rezon. Various older and more recent exegetes, however, apply these words to Hadad and therefore think that LXX offers the better text here (Klostermann, Benzinger, Oort, Burney, Montg.-Gehman, Gray et al.). Also Josephus (*Ant.* VIII §§203f.) weaves the 2 stories together. He has pharaoh's permission to Hadad to return to 'Idumea' take place at the time when Solomon's fortunes were already beginning to decline. But because he was unable to incite his country to rebel against Solomon, he went to Syria where he found Rezon and allied himself with him against

---

[13] K. A. Kitchen, *The Third Intermediate Period in Egypt (1100-650 B.C.)*, Warminster 1973; cf. also A. Malamat, "Aspects of the Foreign Policy of David and Salomon," *JNES* 22 (1963), 1-17.

Solomon. Josephus also has Hadad instead of Rezon become king over 'a part of Syria'.[14]

Nevertheless, along with Noth and Bartlett, 213f., we reject these or similar 'improvements.' Bartlett stresses that the Edomite Hadad's rebellion was essentially less significant and dangerous to Solomon than that of the Syrian Rezon. Hadad presumably returned to his country (in view of vs. 14) but his rebellion cannot have made a strong impression on Israel. His history ends in silence (Bartlett, 225).

11:23 *And God raised up still another antagonist against him: Rezon, son of Eliada, who had fled from his master, Hadadezer king of Zobah [(24) when David was slaughtering them).*
In this verse and the following verses Solomon's other opponent makes his appearance: Rezon, an Aramaean. The beginning of our verse is almost identical with that of vs. 14a. Perhaps that was the reason why LXX* placed the vss. 23aβ-25aα after the last-mentioned part of the verse (also cf. Rahlfs, *SSt.* III, 216f.). Yet there are 2 – not insignificant – differences between the 4 opening words of the 2 verses. In vs. 14a YHWH is mentioned as the one who raised up the antagonist; in our verse it is Elohim. In vs. 14a Solomon is mentioned by name; in our verse only the pers. pron. 3rd p. sing. is indicated. It is admittedly clear that, despite the relatively long time since Solomon was last mentioned, this reference can only apply to him, but these differences have prompted Vanoni, *Literarkritik*, 72f., to consider the possibility of differing authorship for the 2 sentences. Our verse leaves the impression of being an insertion (so, for example, also Burney, Ehrlich et al.). It should still be noted that אלהים for YHWH is quite rare in the books of Kings (also cf. comments on 3:5 and Vanoni, *Literarkritik*, 73, n. 102), which does not mean that LXX in its rendering has struck the right note.

The antagonist, then, is called Rezon, the son of Eliada. Of him we know only what we read in this pericope. B. Mazar, BA 25 (1962), 104, is of the opinion that the name Rezon is linked with רזן (Judg. 5:3; Isa. 40:23, etc.), a term for a ruler or high dignitary, and that his real name was Hezion, the grandfather of Benhadad (15:18) (also cf. Gray and *HAL*, 1129a; further F.B. Knutson, *RSP*, II, iv, 1g, n. [p. 112]; E. Lipiński, *TRE*, III, 594). But Noth and W.T. Pitard, *ABD*, V, 209, deny this family connection. LXX speaks of 'Εσρωμ, but this need not mean 'a corruption' of Hezron or Hezion (see Ges-B, s.v. [p. 753a]; Josephus, *Ant.* VIII §204, calls him Razos; Pesh. *hdrwn*). Also Rezon's father is unknown to us, although his name (Eliada) occurs

---

[14] See now on *Ant.* VIII §§199-204, C.T. Begg, "Solomon's Two »Satans« According to Josephus," *BN* 85 (1996), 44-55.

repeatedly in OT (inter al. as son of David; 2 Sam. 5:16; 1 Chr. 3:8; cf. 1 Chr. 14:7).

Better known is the name Hadadezer (various Hebr. MSS have Hadarezer; cf. LXX and Josephus), who is mentioned especially in 2 Sam. 8 and the par. 1 Chr. 18 and 19. In 2 Sam. 8 (cf. 1 Chr. 18:1-14), in the context of David's military compaigns, there is reference to the conflict with and defeat of Hadadezer.

Also in 2 Sam. 8 (3, 5, 12; cf. 1 Chr. 18:3, 5, 9) this Hadadezer, son of Rebob, is mentioned as king of Zobah. This area (cf. 2 Sam. 23:36; 1 Chr. 19:6; 2 Chr. 8:3) is sometimes called Aram-Zobah as well (2 Sam. 10:6, 8; Ps. 60:2). The geographic location of the area cannot be indicated with precision but it must probably be sought in the N *Beqâ*-valley, extending as far as the plain of *Ḥoms* and to the borders of Damascus. J. Lewy (*HUCA* 18 [1944], 443-454) thought especially, in this connection, of Baalbek; others, less definitely, of Coele-Syria (K.H. Bernhardt, *BHHW*, 2245; also cf. *HAL*, 947a; A. Haldar, *IDB*, IV, 962f.; W.T. Pitard, *ABD*, VI, 1108).

After Hadadezer's defeat mentioned in 2 Sam. 8, Rezon had fled from the Aramaean army. The words אשר ברח מאת הדדעזר, which as such are clear, have been rendered in LXX^B as follows: τον εν 'Ραεμμαερ 'Αδραζαρ (plus variants in other related LXX traditions). According to Rahlfs (*SSt.* III, 217f.), Origen transcribed MT because he did not understand it (τον βαρα μεεθ Αδαδεζερ): he took the words ברח מאת to be one word and explained it as a proper name: 'in (בְּ) Rachmeath' (cf. also Drusius who calls this '*nimis inscite imperiteque*').

11:24 *Gathering men around him he became the leader of a marauding band. They went to Damascus, settled there, and he reigned as king in Damascus.*

If one relates this verse to Rezon, then the 3rd p. sing. with which this verse begins becomes explicable. LXX and also Pesh. (minus a few MSS) read the pl. here because this includes Hadad. In reality both Hadad and Rezon may have made attempts to gather an army around them. Thenius (and others who followed him) construe the pl. here as a pl. in niph.: 'they were gathered (around him),' i.e. 'they gathered themselves' (cf. 2 Chr. 13:17), but this modification of the text is unnecessary. The verb קבץ, 'to gather' (J.F. Sawyer, *THAT*, II, 583-586; P. Mommer, *TWAT*, VI, 1144-1149) in qal occurs 38x in OT (in Kings also in 18:19f.; 20:1; 22:6; 2 Kgs. 6:24; 10:18), further, in niph. 31x and in pi. 49x (pu. once; hitp. 8x). The word has a somewhat more restricted field of meaning than אסף, which can also mean 'to gather up,' 'to harvest.'

The word גדוד II, 'band,' 'army,' occurs more than 30x in OT (in Kings also in 2 Kgs. 5:2; 6:23; 13:20f.; 24:2 (4x); cf. *HAL*, 170a; *Ges.*[18], 198f.). Of this group of irregulars Rezon became captain. Somewhat hanging in the air now are the following words בהרג דוד אתם (omitted in LXX[B, Luc.] because what is reported here cannot be true of the men around Rezon but only of the men of Hadadezer. There have indeed been a number of exegetes (including Klostermann and Šanda, cf. textcr. app. *BHK*) who wanted to read ארם, 'Syria,' in place of אתם, but from a textcritical viewpoint this is not probable. It is most plausible to view these words as a later gloss which is most appropriate after vs. 23 (so Stade-Schwally, Noth, Vanoni, *Literarkritik*, textcr. app. *BHS* and many others).

The remainder of our verse is intended to make clear that Rezon and his army conquered Damascus and that the captain of the army himself became king there. LXX[B] reads the entire second half of our verse: 'and he captured Damascus.' Pesh. reads the conclusion of our verse: 'and Hadad was king in Damascus' (also Josephus, *Ant.* VIII §204, thinks here of Hadad!); Vulg. *et constituerunt eum regem in Damasco*. However appealing it may be, following LXX, to read 'and he captured' in place of the MT וימלכו, still with Noth we opt for the *lectio difficilior*. The question does remain, however, whether וימלכו should not rather be vocalized as hiph. than as qal. In such a case one indeed expects a 3 p. sing. suff. after the verb (see W. Rudolph, *ZAW* 63 [1951], 205; and *OTTP*). Noth solves the problem of the meaning of the verb 'to be king' by translating '(sie) herrschten ... wie ein König' (p. 240). We do not see why this translation could not be linked to this verb. Rezon is the leader of the band, to be sure; still it was his entire group who staged a coup in Damascus.

11:25 *And he was an enemy of Israel throughout the entire life of Solomon [add to this to the harm done by Hadad]: he abhorred Israel and was king in Damascus.*

At the beginning of our verse something is said of which the reader was given a somewhat different impression in vs. 4ff.: namely, that throughout his entire life and not only in his old age, on account of his evil inclination toward the gods of his many wives, Solomon had at least one adversary (see Vanoni, *Literarkritik*, 125; also cf. the addition in LXX in our comments on 2:46g).

Further, our verse would not produce any special problems were it not for the words ואתהרעה אשר הדד which form a somewhat strange insertion where they stand. In vs. 22 we already noted that LXX adds these words to the story about Hadad which in MT ends in that verse. If we do not wish immediately to regard the added words as a later gloss, we must try to assign a logical meaning to ואת, because this word-combination does not connect in a regular way with the preceding text (so Vanoni, *Literarkritik*, 96, et al.). J. Blau, *VT* 4 (1954), 16, believes that this combination resulted from a contamination of ן and the preposition אֶת. In the comments of König §270a (cf. §283a) et al. (see

Vanoni, *Literarkritik*, 96, n. 77) one finds no special interest in the copula. Also P.P. Saydon (*VT* 14 [1964], 207) is of the opinion that the particle creates a problem. He correctly points out that a change of the particle into זאת (following LXX and Vulg.; Pesh. reads *'al*) does not materially make for much greater clarity. Nor does it help much if, following LXX and Tg., one adds the verb עשה before Hadad: 'and this is the evil which Hadad (sometimes, based on a number of Hebr. MSS, also: "that was with [את] Hadad") did' (also cf. König §§170a, 283a), because in this part the reference is not to Hadad but to Rezon (also cf. the comments in Montg.Gehman). According to Barthélemy, ואת here has the same meaning as in vs. 1: 'en supplément de.' Blau and Saydon concur with this suggestion by writing 'over and above.' But even at that, these words unmistakably remain an (early) elliptical gloss, and though they are not 'unübersetzbar' (so Ehrlich; but also cf. Würthwein and Noth), they are not much to the point here. Noth correctly comments that the purpose of this gloss was to once more call attention to Hadad to whom was applicable the same thing that is said of Rezon, namely that throughout Solomon's reign he was his 'adversary' (also cf. Bartlett 1976, 214f.).

Following this intermezzo, MT continues its report on Rezon. He 'loathed Israel,' i.e. he was nauseated by Israel. The verb קוץ occurs a number of times in OT (aside from here also in Gen 27:46; Lev. 20:23; Num. 21:5; Prov. 3:11; also Sir. 4:9; 6:23; 50:25) in the sense of 'to loathe,' 'to feel abhorrence for.' A second meaning of this verb is 'to shudder at' (Exod. 1:12; Num. 22:3; Isa. 7:16; *HAL*, 1018b). In LXX one finds forms of the verb βαρυθυμέω, 'to be indignant, wrathful,' which still does not warrant the use in MT of a form of the verb קוץ, 'to crowd into a corner,' 'to oppress' (so correctly Noth, Barthélemy et al.; otherwise: textcr. app. *BHK*, for example). In any case, this last rendering would also clash with historical reality: Rezon never really did oppress Israel under Solomon's kingship (also cf. Stade-Schwally). It *is* true that Pesh. uses a form of the aphel of the verb *'wq*: 'to drive into a corner' but applies this action, not to Rezon, but to Hadad (Tg. uses a verb which means 'to rebel'). All in all there is no reason, on textcritical grounds, to alter MT. This word clearly conveys the emotional value of the sense of loathing[15] which Rezon felt toward Israel.

Finally this verse states that Rezon ruled as king in Aram, i.e. Syria. The implication is that Solomon must have lost to Rezon the area of Aram Damascus which David had occupied (see 2 Sam. 8:6). Where the ancient versions (LXX and Pesh.) as well as a few Hebr. MSS (in Kennicott and De Rossi)

---

[15] There is an immediate kinship between the Dutch word 'kotsen' ('vomit') and the Hebr. verb; cf. P.A.F. van Veen, N. van der Sijs, *Etymologish woordenboek. De herkomst van onze woorden*, Utrecht/Antwerpen 1990, 416b.

obviously linked this part of our verse with Hadad, the text has 'Edom' instead of 'Aram.' But this need not distract us from the correctness of MT.

1 KINGS 11:26-43

11:26 *Now Jeroboam, son of Nebat, was an Ephrathite from Zereda, whose mother's name was Zeruah, a widow. He was a servant of Solomon but rebelled against the king.*

27 *Now this was the cause for which he raised his hand against the king: Solomon had built the Millo and closed the gap in the city of David his father.*

28 *Now Jeroboam was a man of valour and Solomon saw how the young man got his work done, so he put him in charge of all the forced labour from the house of Joseph.*

29 *About that time when Jeroboam was going out of Jerusalem, Ahijah the prophet of Shiloh met him on the road, wearing a new cloak, and the two of them were alone in the open country.*

30 *Ahijah took hold of the new cloak he was wearing and tore it into twelve pieces.*

31 *He said to Jeroboam: 'Take for yourself ten pieces, because thus YHWH, the God of Israel, has spoken: "Behold I will tear the kingdom out of Solomon's hand and I will give you the ten tribes;*

32 *but one tribe will be for him, on account of my servant David and on account of Jerusalem, the city which I have chosen above all the tribes of Israel;*

33 *because they have forsaken me and have bowed down before Ashtoreth the deity of the Sidonians, Chemosh the deity of Moab, and Milcom the deity of the Ammonites, but have not walked in my ways, doing what is right in my eyes [and my statutes and ordinances] as David his father did.*

34 *But I will not take the whole kingdom out of his hand, for I have made him ruler all the days of his life for the sake of David my servant, whom I chose because he kept my commandments and my statutes;*

35 *but I will take the kingship out of the hand of his son and give you the ten tribes.*

36 *But to his son I will give one tribe so that David my servant may always have a 'lamp' before me in Jerusalem, the city where I have chosen to establish my name.*

37 *But you I will take and you shall rule in accordance with what your soul wishes, and be king over Israel.*

38 *And if you listen to all that I command you and walk in my ways and do what is right in my eyes by keeping my statutes and my commandments as David my servant did, then I will be with you and build you an enduring house, as I built for David, and I will give Israel to you.*

39 *I will therefore humble David's descendants because of this, but not*

580   1 KINGS 11:26-43

forever".'

40 *Solomon sought to kill Jeroboam, but Jeroboam arose and fled to Egypt, to Shishak king of Egypt. And he remained in Egypt until the death of Solomon.*

41 *Now the rest of the deeds of Solomon, with everything he did and all his wisdom, are they not written in the book of the chronicles of Solomon?*

42 *The time that Solomon reigned in Jerusalem over all Israel was fourty years.*

43 *Then Solomon rested with his fathers and was buried in the city of David his father. And his son Rehoboam succeeded him as king.*

INTRODUCTION

This section of chap. 11 not only continues the report on a series of uprisings which Solomon had to endure during his reign, but at the same time starts the story of the division off the kingdom in which the polar opposite of the Davidic dynasty was to play a prominent role: Jeroboam (11:26-14:20).[1] We are now in a transitional period in which the 'golden age' of (David and) Solomon is definitely concluded and the long succession of rivalries between a northern (Israel) and a southern (Judah) kingdom begins.

The composition of this section, a subdivision of 1 Kgs. 11:26-14:20[2], is itself anything but a unity, although Cohn has called attention to the literary technique of the dtr. historiographer who managed, out of data from a variety of sources, to forge an artistic whole.[3] The vss. 26ff. contain very succinct information about Jeroboam's descent, his position in the administration of Solomon, and his (attempt at an) uprising and flight to Egypt. If we inquire into the cause and background of Jeroboam's rebellion we at most receive an indirect answer. There is indeed a story, in which the prophet Ahijah plays a role vis-à-vis the future division of Solomon's kingdom (vss. 29-32), and which is immediately supplemented by a theological commentary from the pen of the dtr. (vss. 33-39). To this commentary we will pay special attention below. Vs. 40 continues the account of Solomon and Jeroboam, which was abruptly ended in vs. 28 (Debus, op. cit., p. 4, combines the vss. 26 and 40). We are probably not going too far in the assumption − shared for that matter by various other commentators − that between vs. 28 and vs. 40 there may have been a notice about the precise nature and scope of Jeroboam's uprising

---

[1] Cf. J. Debus, *Die Sünde Jerobeams*, Göttingen 1967, esp. 3-7.
[2] Cf. I. Plein, "Erwägungen zur Überlieferung von 1 Reg 11,26-14,20," *ZAW* 78 (1966), 8-24.
[3] R.L. Cohn, "Literary Technique in the Jeroboam Narrative," *ZAW* 97 (1985), 23-25.

against Solomon, a notice which for certain reasons was omitted by the compiler(s) of our chapter and replaced by the prophet story. After all, what took place between Ahijah and Jeroboam (assuming that this prophet story has a historical background) was naturally known only to these 2 men (and not to Solomon).

The history of Jeroboam is continued in chap. 12. From a long supplement following 12:24 in the LXX it is clear that there also existed another version of the course of Jeroboam's life. The assessment of this supplement is very diverse. This is not the place, however, for an extensive discussion and evaluation of it.

EXEGESIS

11:26 *Now Jeroboam, son of Nebat, was an Ephrathite from Zereda, whose mother's name was Zeruah, a widow. He was a servant of Solomon but rebelled against the king.*
In concise formulaic language our verse conveys a lot of information. In the context of our chapter, following Hadar and Rezon, Jeroboam is announced as the third, and ultimately the most dangerous, of Solomon's opponents.

As for the name 'Jeroboam,' it is sometimes rendered by '(May God) increase the nation' (Noth, *IPN*, 206f.); 'Der Onkel(gott) hat Recht geschaft' (J.J. Stamm; cf. *HAL*, 415), or '(my) uncle makes great' (F. B. Knutson, *RSP*, III, 491; for still other interpretations, see Montg.-Gehman on vs. 43). In the postbiblical rabbinical tradition Jeroboam acquired a bad reputation (König, *Stil.* 293f.). He is even listed, along with Ahab and Manasseh, among the 3 kings who will not have a part in the world to come (Mishna Sanh. 10:2).

Jeroboam's father's name was Nebat (Josephus, *Ant.* VIII §205: Ναβαταιος; for the explanation of this name, cf. *HAL*, 625a).[4] This name occurs only in conjunction with Jeroboam. He was an inhabitant of Ephraim. The gentilic אפרתי must not be taken to mean a 'Bethlemite' (so 1 Sam. 17:12; Ruth 1:2), but as an 'inhabitant of Ephraim' (cf. Judg. 12:5; 1 Sam. 1:1; otherwise: F. Willesen, *VT* 8 [1958], 97f., who interprets the word in a general sense: Judean).

As place of origin the text cites Jeredah (with the article; also cf. S. Segert, *ZAH* 1 [1988], 101, on diptotic geographical fem. forms; further 2 Chr. 4:17 where 'Zaretan' should be read; see comments on 7:46). Scholars suspect that

---

[4] For the peculiar explanation of 'ben Nebat' as servant of the goddess Hathor, also called Nebat in Egypt, cf. E. Danelius, "The Sins of Jeroboam Ben-Nabat," *JQR* 57 (1966), 95-114; 58 (1968), 204-223; and Würthwein, 142, n. 8.

this village must be sought near the spring *'ên Serêdâ* in the Samaritan or Ephraimite hill country (cf. LXX 11:43 and 12:24ᵇ), approximately 25 km SW of present-day Nablus (see Würthwein, Noth, Simons, *GTTOT* §839).

The name of Jeroboam's mother is Zeruah 'the leper' (*HAL*, 987a). But LXX^B reads υἱὸς γυναικὸς χήρας, 'the son of a widow' (in LXX^A the name σαρουα is mentioned). Gray, Würthwein, et al. are of the opinion that the original name must have been Zeruah ('one who smelled of mastich'). Würthwein and Debus (op. cit., p. 5) suspect that the name may have been intentionally altered out of hatred against Jeroboam (also cf. Kittel, Šanda). Now this cannot be proved, also because names denoting a physical defect were not uncommon in Israel (Noth, *IPN*, 227). But that there may be something going on with the correct tradition concerning Jeroboam's mother is evident from LXX 12:24b where the name of Jeroboam's father is omitted and his mother's name is spelled Σαρεισά, with the adjoining addition: πορνη, 'harlot' (but cf. the comment of F. Hauck, S. Schultz, *TDNT*, VI, 584, that זונה can also denote 'a woman from another tribe,' i.e. who does not marry within her own tribe). In our verse MT and LXX are unanimous in describing that mother as a 'widow' (cf. comments on 7:14 above; for the apposition: Joüon §131b).

Jeroboam was Solomon's 'servant' (not his father[5]). But this word covers a large semantic field and need not mean that Jeroboam has to be counted as part of the inferior support staff of the court (cf. W. Zimmerli, *TDNT*, V, 658, n. 14). It is more likely that he was a high official. Especially Vanoni, *Literarkritik*, 98f., has referred to the grammatical tension which arises if one understands the term 'servant of Solomon' in apposition with 'Jeroboam' (unless one takes the words 'the name of his mother ... a widow' as a parenthesis). If one grants that the Hebr. construction is not elegant, one will again have an example in which – as, for example, in the description of the temple – (too) much information is pressed into brief formulas.

That Jeroboam enjoyed a high position at Solomon's court is also suggested by the last clause of our verse: '(he) lifted up his hand against' (for the preposition בְּ meaning 'against' see BrSynt. §106h; for the expression itself also U. Dahmen, *TWAT*, VII, 428) is no doubt a figurative saying denoting a rebellion against the king's authority. We are not told how, where, and when this happened. The lack of details on the subject is more or less in accord with the description of the preceding revolts by Hadad and Rezon.

11:27 *Now this was the cause for which he raised his hand against the king: Solomon had built the Millo and closed the gap in the city of David his father.* This verse promises to give the particulars about the revolt. The introductory

---

[5] Contra K. Baltzer, *Die Biographie der Propheten*, Neukirchen-Vluyn 1975, 32, n. 77.

formula for this is הזה דבר, which, according to Tarbiz is a 'detailing formula'[6] we also find elsewhere (see comments on 9:15 above; Debus, op. cit., p. 4). After אשר one would have expected a retrospective pronoun: 'in relation to'; 'as it concerns ...' (Joüon §158i; also cf. Ewald §§331c and 333d, who wants to translate the particle as 'how').

The situation in which this notice places us is the construction of the Millo by Solomon 'by which the breach of the city of his father David was closed' (see comments on 9:15 above). The verb סגר, 'to close,' occurs also in 2 Kgs. 4:4f.; 21, 33 and 6:32 for closing a door (also cf. H. Ringgren, *TWAT*, V, 753-756). The word פרץ, 'breach,' 'rip,' and then also 'accident' only occurs here in the books of Kings (cf. J. Conrad, *TWAT*, VI, 763-770, esp. 768f.). The addition 'his father' does not occur in Pesh., except for 9a1*fam* (for this somewhat 'copious' addition, cf. our discussion below of vs. 43).

11:28 *Now Jeroboam was a man of valour and Solomon saw how the young man got his work done, so he put him in charge of all the forced labour from the house of Joseph.*

Jeroboam's qualities, particularly those which came out in his execution of public works, are here listed. Zeroboam is described, in the first place, as 'a keen fellow.' The combination גבור חיל occurs 14x in the sing. in OT (Judg. 6:12; 11:1; 1 Sam. 9:1; 16:18; 2 Kgs. 5:1; Ruth 2:1; 1 Chr. 12:29; 28:1; 2 Chr. 13:3; 7:16f.; 25:6; 32:21, and in our verse), one of them (in Jdg. 6:12) in the form גבור חיל.[7] In addition one can further find the term 29x in the pl. Van der Ploeg rejected the – often advanced – idea that the גבור חיל was a big landowner who in time of peace contented himself with managing his possessions and in time of war had to use his wealth in the service of this country.[8] The first part of the term especially denotes a 'strong, forceful, and courageous' man (see also comments on 1:18), while חיל denotes 'power,' not in the abstract but concretely, the power which resides in a human being and produces 'actes de force et de vigueur' (also cf. Pedersen, I-II, 230 in approx. the same sense). It seems to us that also in the case of Gideon, Jephthah, Kish, Boaz, et al., who are so described, it is not the idea of a 'big landowner' which plays the primary role but especially a man's striking or still-hidden qualities and potencies (cf. Vatablus: *valebat viribus tam animi quam corporis*). Now this is certainly the case here: Jeroboam was presumably not a large landowner

---

[6] Z. Talshir, "The Detailing Formula וזה הדבר," *Tarbiz* 51 (1981f.), 23-25 (Hebr.).

[7] See my article "Ḥayil in het boek Ruth, een vertaalprobleem," *Verkenningen in een Stroomgebied* (Fs M. A. Beek), Amsterdam 1974, 120-131, esp. 124; also cf. comments on 1:42 above.

[8] J. van der Ploeg, "Le sense du *gibbôr hail*," *Vivre et Penser* 1 (1941) (= *RB* 50), 120-125; cf. idem, in *OTS* 9 (1951), 58f.

but a man endowed with striking qualities which would make him an able administrator (cf. also Burney).

These qualities had not escaped Solomon either. Seeing that Jeroboam did his work well (for the construction, cf. König §414b-c), he promoted him to a high position. It is striking that after referring to האיש Jeroboam the text then uses the word נער, which would seem to be contradictory (so, e.g. Hölscher 1923, 179, who for this reason infers the presence of 'different sources'). Still this contradiction is in fact no more than appearance (cf. the extensive exposition in Vanoni, *Literarkritik*, 148ff.). Vanoni opts for an appositional combination (with Jeroboam) 'mit desemantisierten *ha=îš*' (='jener') because, since Solomon had been mentioned in the preceding verse, the independent pers. pron. הוא in our verse might cause confusion with Solomon. This seems to us a plausible solution to the problem.

נער occurs 239x in OT (in Kings in 3:7 already), 35x in the books of Kings (for these and further data, cf. H.F. Fuhs, *TWAT*, V, 507-518, esp. 511f.). The word offers a variety of semantic nuances: from 'child' to 'young man,' but also 'armourbearer,' 'soldier,' 'servant,' etc. Stähli is of the opinion that the word does not so much denote a 'stage of life' as matters in the sphere of law.[9]

Finally, let us note that Jeroboam was עשה מלאכה. We already several times encountered the first word which means 'work,' 'labour' (see, e.g. comments on 5:30 above). Some scholars (Greßmann with 'Werkführer'; Šanda with 'Bauunternehmer'; Debus, op. cit., p. 6) see in this combination of words a reference to an occupation or official function. Others think of a specific quality or act (examples in Vanoni, *Literarkritik*, 152 n. 463, and most modern translations). LXX reads ἀνὴρ ἔργων; Vulg. (*adulescentem*) *bonae indolis et industrium;* Pesh. repeats the *gnbr ḥyl'* of the beginning of this verse; finally, Tg. translates paronomastically: עביר עבירתא. Vanoni, *Literarkritik*, 152ff., correctly points out that the combination of the 2 words refers rather to the high quality of Jeroboam's work than to an official function or occupation. The latter, after all, is not a ground for promotion, but the former is. And Solomon must undoubtedly have been favourably impressed by his outstanding devotion to his work when he put Jeroboam in charge of the סבל, the 'burden,' of the house of Joseph.

Aside from Ps. 81:7 and Neh. 4:11, this word occurs in this vocalization only in our verse (vocalized as סֹבֶל also in Isa. 9:3; 10:27 and 14:25). In 5:29 we encountered the 'burden bearer.' D. Kellermann, *TWAT*, V, 744-748, esp. 747, regards the word in our verse as the general designation for 'porter service.' Very likely this service must not be equated with the permanent forced labour

---

[9] H.P. Stähli, *Knabe-Jüngling-Knecht. Untersuchungen zum Bergriff* נער *im Alten Testament* (Beiträge zur biblischen Exegese und Theologie 7), Frankfurt am Main 1978, 99f.

mentioned in 9:21f. but with temporary work, probably performed by labourers from the northern tribes of Israel (cf. Mettinger, *Officials*, 138; C.D. Evans, *ABD*, III, 742). Evans believes that, as leader of this northern Israelite labour force, Jeroboam himself experienced the oppression of Solomon's administration and finally, along with his fellow countrymen and fellow members of the tribe, revolted against it. Solomon's surrender of northern Israelite cities to Hiram (9:10-13), says Evans, was the drop which caused the bucket of resentment and hatred against Solomon to run over among these northern Israelites. We cannot, however, get past conjectures here (cf. Munster who mentions as the reason for Jeroboam's rebellion the building of the Millo: '*quae cum displicuisset populo, et nemo audreet quicquam dicere Regi praeter unum filium Nebat, quaesivit eum Rex interficere*'; see also comments on vs. 40 below).

The verb פקד, which occurs here in the hiph.-form and is construed with an acc. and the preposition ל means 'to appoint,' 'charge,' 'entrust' (*HAL*, 902a). The root, in the nominal as well as in the verbal form, occurs in our Hebr. Bible no fewer than 383x (cf. W. Schottroff, *THAT*, II, 466-468; G. André, *TWAT*, VI, 708-723). The verb, which is found in all the usual stem-modifications, enjoys a rather broad spectrum of meanings. For example, in qal it can mean 'to muster,' but also 'to miss' or 'to crave.' On the other hand the verb can mean 'to command,' or 'to charge' (for the data spectrum, see *HAL*, 899b-902b). In the sense of 'to appoint' (hiph.) it occurs here and in 14:27 ('to entrust'; 'to commit') in 1 Kgs. (in 2 Kgs. also in 7:17; 25:22f.).

As the overall term for the labour force of northern Israel of which Jeroboam was put in charge the phrase 'house of Joseph' is used here (see also Gen. 43:17-19, 24; 44:14; 50:8; Josh. 17:17; 18:5; Judg. 1:22f., 35; 2 Sam. 19:21; Amos 5:6; Ob. 18; Zech. 10:6). Noth, too, reckons with the fact that here the expression geographically denotes the 'hill country of Ephraim' (cf. 4:8). Montg.-Gehman see an 'absolute contradiction' here with 9:21f. where it was precisely the Canaanite population which had to perform forced labour and not the Israelites. But the contrast need not be taken so absolutely, inasmuch as also in connection with the division of Solomon's districts (4:7-19) we learned how 'old' tribal areas and 'new' Canaanite areas were put together in a single scheme. Josephus, *Ant.* VIII §206, even thinks that Solomon appointed Jeroboam head of the whole tribe of Joseph instead of over the labour force of this tribe.

De Geus points out that we find mention of 'the house of Joseph' in a context of anti-Judean and anti-Davidic activities, so that the word 'house' does not so much have a primary genealogical content as a political one.[10]

INTRODUCTION TO VSS. 29-39

With vs. 29 an intermezzo prophet story begins which runs to vs. 39 and which, according to Höllscher 1923, 180, 'als junge Einlage auszuschalten ist.' But Noth comments that 'sprachlich und sachlich' this section has immediate links with the vss. 1-13. In saying this, he is proceeding from the assumption of the unity of the vss. 29-39. Now numerous scholars and commentators point to the symbolic act in 1 Sam. 15:27ff. which runs parallel to our vss. 29-31. This is not to say (so, correctly, also Vanoni, *Literarkritik*, 218-23) that the one passage is dependent on the other. There are indeed scholars who assume that the vss. 29-31 may have originated before the redactional composition of the vss. 32-39 (so for example, I. Plein, *ZAW* 78 [1966], 18ff.). But others (Benzinger, Noth et al.) assume the literary unity of the vss. 29-39. Würthwein, 141, traces this entire pericope 'in seinem Grundbestand auf einen zweiten Dtr zurück.'

Seebass takes still another position.[11] According to him, the vss. 30f., 36bα, 40 (along with 12:21-24) belong to the time of Rehoboam; the vss. 26-29, 37, 38bα, on the other hand, to the Ahijah-tradition. As a result of the division of Solomon's kingdom, a sacral form of legitimation of a second kingdom became necessary (vs. 36bα), because originally the institution of kingship was represented as a single kingship for all who served in 'the army of YHWH.'

In conclusion we wish to mention the position of Weippert, who regards the vss. 29ff., 37, 38bαβ, 40abα as a legitimation legend for Jeroboam.[12] According to her, this founding tradition was then adapted to the course of history before the revolt of Baasha by corrections in the vss. 34a, 35a, 40bβ. A redactor in the days of king Josiah – when the text was incorporated in his account of history – then added the vss. 32, 34b, 36b, 38a. bγ, so that the original aetiology of the northern kingdom and of its first dynasty was restructured into an event in the history of Judah. In the vss. 33, 38f., one finds additional material, inserted subsequently, which attempts to explain how it was possible for apostasy to come about also in the northern kingdom.

---

[10] C.H.J. de Geus, *The Tribes of Israel. An Investigation into Some of the Presuppositions of Martin Noth's Amphictyony Hypothesis*, Assen 1976, 87.

[11] H. Seebass, "Zur Teilung der Herrschaft Salomos nach I Reg 11 29-39," *ZAW* 88 (1976), 363-376.

[12] H. Weippert, "Die Ätiologie des Nordreiches und seines Königshauses (1 Reg 11 29-40)," *ZAW* 95 (1983), 344-375.

11:29 *About that time when Jeroboam was going out of Jerusalem, Ahijah the prophet of Shiloh met him on the road, wearing a new cloak, and the two of them were alone in the open country.*
The main figures in the following story are Jeroboam and a prophet from Shiloh named Ahijah (for this prophet cf. G. Fohrer, *TRE*, II, 127f.; K.W. Whitelam, *ABD*, I, 111f.). The name 'Ahijah' (sometimes also spelled 'Ahijahu' when it concerns our prophet: 14:4ff., 18; 2 Chr. 9:29), for that matter, occurs frequently in OT (see comments on 4:3 above; for the extrabiblical occurrence of the name: *Ges.*^{18}, 37a), and is also mentioned in our book, aside from the vss. 29f., in 12:15, 14:2, 4ff., 18; 15:29 (further in 2 Chr. 9:29; 10:15). He came from Shiloh (a town over 20 km S of Shechem [Nablus]; today the *tell* is called *ḫirbet Sēlūn* or: *Seilun*; see *GTTOT* §641; *HAL*, 1371; also the comments on 2:27 where at one time there was an [Israelite] sanctuary). Precisely the fact that in former times Shiloh was an 'amphictyonic' shrine raises the question for researchers whether Ahijah was still associated with the cult at one time practiced there (A. Caquot, *Sem* 11 [1961], 17-27, even identifies him with the Ahijah, great-grandson of Eli, mentioned in 1 Sam. 14:3). Gray points out that the prophet guild in Bethel, mentioned in 2 Kgs. 2f., was similarly a remnant of the old (but ruined) cult-center at Shiloh. He, accordingly, believes that Ahijah's protest, visible in the symbolic act, not only has an anti-Solomonic political background but also contains a religious form of dissent: 'we think it not unlikely that in the protest of Ahijah there was involved a conflict between the old cult of the sacral confederacy at Shechem and Gilgal and the new syncretistic cult of Jerusalem' (p. 294). This view is not implausible.

Our verse begins with a reference to 'at that time.' Bähr, Keil, Thenius, et al. relate 'that time' to what is reported in vs. 28: the appointment of Jeroboam as head of the work project. That would still be before his rebellion against Solomon. Klostermann, on the other hand, thinks of the time after Jeroboam's return from Egypt, but to support that position he has to perform too many surgical operations in the context. It is indeed best to let 'at that time' stand for the time of Jeroboam's promotion, even though we do not believe that 'in his new position (cf. vs. 28) Jeroboam must usually have been active outside Jerusalem,' as Van Gelderen contends. On that point our verse is silent but only states that one day Jeroboam went out of Jerusalem and that he then encountered Ahijah, the prophet of Shiloh (Ahijah 'found' him). LXX adds: 'and he led him off the road,' a statement various commentators then also want to add to our verse because they think that these words may (say, by *homoiotheleuton*) have dropped out of the Hebr. text (so Burney). Stade-Schwally aptly remark that they cannot see why this diversion off the road was so strictly necessary for the staging of the prophet's symbolic act.

Ahijah (and not Jeroboam, as Ewald, *GVI*, III, 417, insists; LXX and Pesh., accordingly, read 'Ahijah' in place of the less definite 'he') was clad in a new cloak (for the word 'cloak,' see comments on 10:25). The hitp.-form of כסה (also in 2 Kgs. 19:1f. in the books of Kings) also has the meaning 'to conceal oneself' 'to hide' (for the verb, cf. also H. Ringgren, *TWAT*, IV, 272-277). The verse ends by stating emphatically that the 2 were 'alone' (this word is lacking in LXX*) in the field. LXX^Luc. adapts the translation to the beginning of the verse by saying they were alone 'on the road.' In conclusion we wish to call attention to the fact that in 12:24° LXX offers another reading of Jeroboam's 'call.'[13]

11:30 *Ahijah took hold of the new cloak he was wearing and tore it into twelve pieces.*
Ahijah, taking a hold of his new cloak, tore it into 12 pieces (for the double accusative, cf. König §327; GD §92c; Ges-K §117ii; Joüon §125w). We already encountered the verb קרא above in 11:11ff.; the noun derived from it occurs in 2 Kgs. 2:12 and Prov. 23:21. The cloak is clearly a symbol of the kingdom. The fact that a cloak can have a special meaning in this connection is not only clear from 1 Sam. 18:4 (inter al.) but also from a Ugar. text (RS 17.159: 22-31), where it is said: 'Utrišarruma is ruler in Ugarit. If Utrišarruma says: "I want to follow my mother," then let him put his cloak on the throne. Let him go' (see F. B. Knutson, *RSP*, II, iv, 5 [p. 120]). It has been pointed out (by Gray et al.) that to take and tear up a cloak is an act of imitative magic, but Knutson (p. 122) is rightly of the opinion that this magic casts but little light either on the symbolic act in Ugarit or on the things narrated in our verse.

The 12 pieces in which the new cloak is divided refer, of course, to the 12 tribes of Israel. The notion is disputed because the precise reference to the 12 varies, even apart from the question of how this number has to function in the context of this story, as will be clear from the rest of the narrative where there is also reference to 10+1 tribes. We can agree with Gray that the 12-tribe confederation was rather a schematization than a historic concept, certainly as it concerns the time of Solomon and his successors. Hölscher 1923, 180, still mentions the fact that what we have here is a 'recent' picture of things which one also finds represented especially in the book of Chronicles.

11:31 *He said to Jeroboam: 'Take for yourself ten pieces, because thus YHWH, the God of Israel, has spoken: "Behold I will tear the kingdom out of Solomon's hand and I will give you the ten tribes;*

---

[13] See now Z. Talshir, *The Alternative Story of the Division of the Kingdom. 3 Kingdoms 12:24 A-Z* (Jerusalem Biblical Studies 6), Jerusalem 1993.

The symbolic act of the prophet Ahijah is coupled with a prophetic message in the form of a messenger-formula which occurs frequently in the prophecies. This is characterized, among other things, by introducing YHWH as speaking. The formula used is הנני with a part. of a verb.[14] Jeroboam is told to take 10 pieces of the torn cloak, with the accompanying prophecy that the kingship will be torn out of Solomon's hand and that *the* 10 tribes will be given 'to you.' LXX and Pesh. (inter al.) avoid this emphasis on 'the' 10 tribes, a fact which in the eyes of Stade-Schwally, Montg.-Gehman et al. is certainly correct because the article in השבטים, according to them, is most likely a dittography. Nevertheless we do not see sufficient reason to modify MT. Nor must we follow the suggestion of Šanda and the textcr. app. of *BHK* et al., which is to correct the number 10 into 11. In this way one introduces harmonizations into the text which attempt to remove irregularities but lack textcritical warrant.

11:32 *but one tribe will be for him, on account of my servant David and on account of Jerusalem, the city which I have chosen above all the tribes of Israel.*
One tribe is explicitly assigned to Solomon, though in vs. 11 there was mention of tearing away the whole kingship from Solomon. In vs. 13, however, he is still given one tribe on account of YHWH's ties with David and, of course, on account of YHWH's election of Jerusalem. Also in our verse this motivation is cited for the allocation of one tribe to Solomon.

The problem in this verse lies of course in the explanation of the 'one' tribe, simply because 10+1 does not add up to 12. LXX, accordingly, has '2 tribes' here (as in vs. 36). Along somewhat the same line, Josephus, *Ant.* VIII §207, writes about 'one tribe and the (tribe) next to it' (μίαν φυλὴν καὶ τὴν ἐξῆς αὐτῇ). Is this an accommodation to logic or the reproduction of the 'Vorlage'? The latter is hard to imagine. But then how do we untangle this puzzle?

In an earlier time Keil sought a solution in the explanation that the numbers must not be understood 'arithmetisch, sondern symbolish': in that case the number 10 is the number of 'Vollständigkeit und Totalität' as opposed to the one tribe of Judah (along this line also Van Gelderen). Klostermann thought in this connection of an original division of the kingdom into 2 tribes (Judah and Ephraim), with reference to Ezek. 37; 15:28. Thenius, Bähr thought that Judah and Benjamin, which bordered on Judah, had to be viewed as a unit, so that little Benjamin had been absorbed into the much bigger Judah. De Vaux, on the other hand, judged that Judah and Simeon had to be counted as a single tribe: 'Benjamin faisait partie des dix tribus et n'a été rattaché que plus tard à

---

[14] Cf. P. Humbert, *Opuscules d'un hebraïsant*, Neuchâtel 1958, 54-59; and my article "Die Partikel יען, *OTS* 18 (1973), 49-83; esp. 77.

Juda.' Van den Born, in looking at the one tribe, explicitly thought of Benjamin: our verse, according to him, was linked with vs. 13 where there was mention of a single tribe which would be left to the house of David. Because this house already was or possessed the tribe of Judah, this simply had to be the tribe of Benjamin (so also Robinson)! Still other exegetes, like Snaith, Würthwein, cling to the one tribe of Judah and simply observe a discrepancy in the calculation, whether this discrepancy originated for textcritical or literary reasons (for a rather extensive list of divergent opinions, cf. Vanoni, *Literarkritik*, 125ff.). Noth points out, however, that even with a literary-critical view of a subsequent correction of the numbers, it cannot be made clear how the 'error in calculation' could arise in MT. According to him, one must proceed from the assumption that the pericope vss. 29-39 is completely dtr. In this context Judah was considered a unity. The tribe which had no landed property in Israel was Levi. But correcting himself with reference to these and other considerations, and referring to 2 Sam. 19:44, Noth writes that in the text the relation between Israel and Judah was possibly considered as a relation between 10 and 1. 'Definitiv wird sich das Problem der in 30ff. angestellten Rechnung nicht klären lassen,' Noth concludes. Also Vanoni, *Literarkritik*, 127, concurs with Noth's last view, so 'daß man allein aufgrund der merkwürdigen Rechnung keine literarkritischen Operationen vornehmen wird.' We need not, therefore, lay an 'error in calculation' or a 'twist in thinking' at the door of the dtr. author: 10 stands for Israel, 1 for Judah, and 12 for the total number of the tribes of Israel.[15]

11:33 *because they have forsaken me and have bowed down before Ashtoreth the deity of the Sidonians, Chemosh the deity of Moab, and Milcom the deity of the Ammonites, but have not walked in my ways, doing what is right in my eyes (and my statutes and ordinances) as David his father did.*
In this verse the reason is stated why YHWH will divide the kingdom. In vs. 31 we learn of the result of what vs. 33 reveals as the cause of the division (cf. my article in *OTS* 18 [1973], 77, 79). This need not yet mean that, as Stade-Schwally insist, vs. 32 is a later addition, but it does mean that it is a parenthetical sentence (so among others Slotki).

The pronominal endings of the first 3 verbs of our verse are in the 3rd p. pl., while LXX, Pesh. and a number of MSS of the Vulg. here read the sing. Ehrlich, Thenius, Delitzsch, *LSF* §37^b, Burney, H. Seebass, *ZAW* 88 (1976), 363, the textcr. app. of *BHK* and *BHS*, and other exegetes want to follow the latter reading because only Solomon is mentioned in the preceding text and

---

[15] Cf. also Z. Kallai, "Judah and Israel. A Study in Israelite Historiography," *IEJ* 28 (1978), 251-261.

because our verse ends with 'as David his father did.' Nevertheless we believe that no textual modification is necessary here because, as Noth puts it: Solomon was 'mit dem Israel seiner Zeit zusammengefaßt.' There exists solidarity in guilt between king and people.

In the vss. 5 and 7 we already encountered the 'idols' mentioned here. It is striking that צדנין (aside from a small number of Hebr. MSS, according to Kennicott) here is written with a final *nun* in place of a final *mem*. This is sometimes referred to as 'Aramaicizing,' although this plural ending is also found in the Moabite (Mesha Stone) and is attested several times in the rest of the OT as well. In the later Hebr. one also finds this ending (cf. Ewald §177a; Stade §323a; BL, 517t; Ges-K §87e; Joüon §90c; WOC §7.4.b; Delitzsch, *LSF* §97b, as so often, again wants to modify the text here; other scholars also consider the spelling incorrect, Stade-Schwally for example). There is not a single reason, however, for changing the orthography.

The gods of the Sidonians, the Moabites, and the Ammonites are successively described in our verse as 'gods' as well. In the vss. 5 and 7 Milcom and Chemosh were still qualified as 'abominations.' In this connection it is interesting to devote some attention to the rendering of LXX. In the first place, LXX renders וישתחוו (for the verb, see comments on 1:16 above) by ἐποίησιν; whereas LXX generally translate it by a form of the verb προσκυνειν, it opts for the word cited only here (see also H. Greeven, *TDNT*, VI, 760, n. 23). In the second place, in LXX[B] the remaining words in the series are different from what our MT-vorlage would lead us to expect: τῇ Ἀστάρτῃ βδελύγματι Σιδωνίων καὶ τῷ Χαμὼς καὶ ἐν τοῖς εἰδώλοις Μωὰβ καὶ τῷ βασιλεῖ αὐτῶν προσοχθίσματι υἱῶν Ἀμμών. Striking there is that the translation uses a spectrum of depreciative words for the uniform word 'god' of MT: βδέλυγμα, 'abomination,' εἴδωλον, 'idol'; and the word προσόχθισμα, 'loathing,' 'abhorrence,' which is rare in the LXX-OT (see LXX Deut. 7:26; 1 Kgs. 16:32; 18:29; 2 Kgs. 23:13, 24; Ezek. 5:11; Sir. 27:13; and 3 Macc. 2:18; also cf. in NT the verb forms in Hebr. 3:10, 17). LXX[Luc.] offers a somewhat more intelligible or corrected translation than LXX*: 'for Chemosh the idol of Moab and for Milcom (Μελχομ) the abhorrence of the sons of Ammon'), without explicit evidence of a direct and literal rendering of MT (also cf. Rahlfs, *SSt.* III, 241; for the LXX translation 'their king' in place of 'Milcom,' see comments on the vss. 5 and 7 above). According to Burney, the terms used for 'idols' in LXX convey deliberate changes to avoid the word 'god' (*Elohim*) for pagan gods, 'in accordance with the feeling of a later time.'

The expression 'עשות הישר בעיני פ, 'doing what is right in the sight of ...,' occurs a number of times in OT, in the books of Kings also in vs. 38; 14:8; 15:5, 11; 22:43; II 12:3; 14:3; 15:3, 34; 16:2; 18:3; 22:2). In 9:4, we encountered the noun ישר in 9:12, the verb with the same radicals. In the words cited we are dealing with 'a stereotypical expression or an idiomatic formula' (see L.

Alonso Schökel, *TWAT*, III, 1061-1069, esp. 1067f.; cf. G. Liedke, *THAT*, I, 792), which, according to Alonso Schökel (p. 1068) can best be translated by 'what pleases God,' 'what God approves,' 'what God disapproves.' The opposite is 'to do evil in the sight of...' (see comments on vs. 6 above; also König, *Stil.* 217).

The following 2 words, the 'statutes and ordinances,' are lacking in LXX and many exegetes therefore propose that these words be omitted as superfluous additions by a later author (so, inter al., Stade-Schwally; Montg.-Gehman; Noth; textcr. app. *BHK*). Pesh. supplements the words by translating: 'he did not keep my statutes and ordinances' (cf. vs. 38¹). Without these 2 words the preceding sentence would indeed have lost none of its meaning or expressiveness. They are explicable as a gloss of a later reader or copyist, the more so since in vs. 38 these words are in fact used more effectively in the context than here. The same is true for the last 2 words of our verse: 'as his father David did' (so also Noth), though, from a textcritical viewpoint, there is no warrant for such an omission.

11:34 *But I will not take the whole kingdom out of his hand, for I have made him ruler all the days of his life for the sake of David my servant, whom I chose because he kept my commandments and my statutes;*
However easily intelligible the content of this verse may be, there nevertheless occur in it a number of difficulties.

There is, in the first place, the expression את־כל־הממלכה. The difficulty lies in the word כל before the determined substantive. There are scholars, accordingly, who want to delete the word (e.g., Noth and Oort). Vanoni, *Literarkritik*, 161-168, has undertaken an extensive study of the function and meaning of the word כל, also in connection with the word ממלכה, 'kingship' or 'kingdom' (a study to which we are happy to refer the reader here). One of his ideas is that the last-mentioned word need not be an expression for a territorial 'area of sovereignty,' but may also be a term for 'the power of kingship.' At the end of his study (p. 167), however, he states: 'Somit ist auch für die einzigen verbleibenden Fälle (*kul ha=mamlakā* in 1 Kön 11, 13a, 34a) das Merkmal [+ teilbar] und folglich konkrete Bedeutung anzusetzen: "Königreich".' But, in our opinion, the first word (כל) does not constitute a difficulty or source of tension even in the abstract sense: 'the whole royal sovereignty.'

In the second place, the words נשיא אשתנו, produce difficulties also in view of the LXX translation. As for MT: the verb שית, 'to make,' 'to place,' 'to appoint,' etc. (with double accusative: Ges-K §117ii; Joüon §125w) occurs, of the approx. 80x it is found in OT, only here in the books of Kings. We already encountered the word נשיא, 'prince,' 'head of tribe,' in 8:1. The conjunction כי, as it were, provides the reason why Solomon is not deprived of the whole kingship. It is not necessary, as some exegetes believe, to understand the word specifically as 'tribal head,' implying the possibility of a 'degradation' of Solomon's position: from being 'king' to being the 'head of a tribe' (see e.g. H. Niehr, *TWAT*, V, 650f.; also cf. Montg.-Gehman; Vanoni, *Literarkritik*, 241, n. 163). The word may be rare in the context of Kings, but it need not by any means be understood in a pejorative sense. Granted, some scholars do consider the words an addition here which is based on Ezekiel's description of a Davidic king (Ezek. 34:24). It is very well possible that the expression was taken over from related theological circles and included in our dtr. exposition. In any case, Solomon remained 'prince' to the end of his life, despite the threat of the contrary. The tension which can be felt (and is felt by many scholars) among the vss. 31, 34, and 35 need not so much be literary in nature as stylistic, i.e. there is here only a stylistic paradox created by the author(s). 'To tear the kingdom away' need not mean: 'to take away the whole kingdom (i.e. the entire kingship).' LXX*, however, seems to entertain a totally different view. Its translation reads: ἀντιτασσόμενος ἀντιταξομαι αὐτῷ. The verb ἀντιτάσσομαι, 'to oppose,' 'to offer resistance,' occurs a number of times in LXX (Hos. 1:6; Prov. 3:15, 34; Esth. 3:14; 4:17 and 4 Macc. 16:23), as for that matter in NT (Acts 18:6; Rom. 13:2; Jam. 4:6; 5:6; 1 Pet. 5:5). So the LXX translation might read: 'because I have firmly resisted him ...' etc. Now in Hos. 1:6 LXX has approximately the same rendering of the Hebr. words: להם נשא אשא, 'I will certainly forgive them.' The question is, whether LXX is also based in our verse 'auf einen hebräischen Schreib- oder Lesefehler' (Rahlfs, *SSt.* III, 202). Rahlfs is correct in finding LXX*'s rendering 'Unsinn,' even while he concedes that LXX^Luc. has attempted, by means of a transposition, to guide the text into proper channels: 'and I am opposed to him all the days of his life, but I will not take the kingship out of his hand during his lifetime for the sake of David my servant.' Burney takes the rendering of Hos. 1:6 as the basis for LXX, so that in our verse LXX might be translated; 'For I will surely *forgive* him during his lifetime ...' But he calls this translation 'inferior to MT.' Some scholars, accordingly, consider the LXX rendering a misconstrual of MT or possibly a rendering of an unreadable 'Vorlage' (so Stade-Schwally). Others, on the other hand, think that, on account of LXX's reading being the *lectio difficilior,* it is original (so, among others, Gray, H. Seebass, *ZAW* 88 [1976], 363; also cf. Ehrlich who 'unbedingt' wants to read נשוא אשאנו, 'ich will allenfalls Nachsicht, eigentlich Geduld, mit ihm haben'), while still others are only inclined to a decision with reservations (so Noth). It has to be granted that the LXX reading is striking and has its own validity. Nevertheless we feel compelled to prefer MT, whose reading is not that much less difficult, all the more since the other ancient versions support it.

The reason why Solomon may retain the royal dignity throughout his entire life is the election of his father David (cf. 8:16). In addition to the election of 'the city' (so 8:44, 48; 11:32, 36) or specifically 'Jerusalem' (11:13), the election of David also plays an important role in our pericope. The last 4 words of MT are lacking in LXX^B. They are not, to be sure, absolutely necessary to the clarity of the sentence, but that is not a reason for omitting them here.

11:35 *but I will take the kingship out of the hand of his son and give you the ten tribes.*
YHWH will take the kingship over the 10 tribes away from Solomon's son. Here the word מלוכה, 'kingship,' is used, a word we encountered earlier in Kings as well (1:46; 2:15, 22; also cf. Vanoni, *Literarkritik*, 175f.). A textcritical difficulty arises from the 3rd p. fem. sing. suff. after 'I will give,' referring back to 'kingship,' and then again the explicit mention of the 10 tribes. Accordingly, the ancient versions, LXX included, do not translate this suffix and so achieve a smoothly running sentence. There are exegetes (cf., e.g., Delitzsch, *LSF* §155; H. Seebass [*ZAW* 88 (1976), 364]; the textcr. app. in *BHK* and *BHS*) who want to delete the last 3 words of our verse as an addition or gloss. Although such additions in MT are often introduced with the particle את, they can also be understood as further explication. The suffix in question seem to us, in light of the ancient versions, to be a gloss.

11:36 *But to his son I will give one tribe so that David my servant may always have a 'lamp' before me in Jerusalem, the city where I have chosen to establish my name.*
Solomon's son – called Rehoboam as will be evident from what follows – is promised 'the one tribe' over which he will be able to rule as king (see e.g. vs. 32). Stated as the reason for the preservation of that one tribe for Solomon's son is that YHWH will be a ניר to his servant David 'before his face.' The Hebr. word occurs, aside from here, also in 15:4; 2 Kgs. 8:19; Prov. 21:4 and 2 Chr. 21:7 (Ges-B 503b; *HAL*, 658a). One finds a homonym, often indicated in lexicon by II, in Jer. 4:3; Hos. 10:12 and Prov. 13:23, a word which denotes the newly cultivated field ('fallow ground'; 'Neubruch'). The former word is usually translated as 'lamp,' or 'light' (e.g.: AV, LV, Obbink, NV, WV; otherwise: GNB: 'herinnering [remembrance]'; NEB: 'a flame [burning before me]'; GoodNB: 'descendant'; RSV: 'lamp'; TOB: 'lampe,' etc.), synonymous with the much more frequently occurring word נר, 'lamp' (which we encountered in 7:49). In how far there is kinship or dependence between the 2 words may be left unresolved for the time being.[16]

---

[16] See the discussions in P.D. Hanson, "The Sonf of Heshbon and David's *nîr*," *HThR* 61 (1968), 297-320; A. van der Kooij, "David, »het licht van Israel«," *Vruchten van de Uithof* (Fs H.A. Brongers), Utrecht 1974, 49-57; and D. Kellermann, *TWAT*, V, 616-626, esp. 618ff.

A glance at the ancient versions shows that Pesh. translates the word by *šerâgâ*, 'light'; Tg. by מלכו, '... (to establish a) kingdom'; Vulg. by *lucerna*, 'lamp'; and LXX, finally, by θέσις, 'thesis,' 'institution' or the like. This is the only time, for that matter, that this Greek word is used in LXX as the translation of MT (also in 1 Ezr. 1:3 and Wisdom 7:19, 29). In other passages LXX translates the Hebr. word in very diverse ways (for this, see also W. Michaelis, *TDNT*, IV, 326, n. 17), inter al.: κατάλειμμα, 'rest,' 'remnant' (15:4): λαμπτήρ, 'candalabrum' (Prov. 21:4); λύχνος, 'lamp' (2 Kgs. 8:19; 2 Chr. 21:7) and φῶς, 'light' (Hos. 10:12; cf. also Montg-Gehman). Schleusner (s.v. θέσις), commenting on the LXX rendering of our verse, writes: *Quomodo haec versio excusanda aut defenda sit, vix apparet*. He suspects that LXX may have read the Hebr. ניר (from גור, 'to sojourn'), so that the word would be: *fixa ac perpetica sedes, aut regia sedes*, with the motivatIon: *si nempe vox haec cum Hierosolyma in sequentibus coniungatur* (also cf. *GELS* 205a). It needs to be noted that LXX^(Luc.) and Theod. read θελήσις, 'will.' According to Rahlfs (*SSt.* III, 202), this is an emendation of the LXX*-text; according to Schleusner (s.v. θέλησις), this would *fortasse per* olectationem, oblectamentum *rectius reddatur*. J. W. Wevers, *OTS* 8 (1950), 315f., translates θέσις in our verse by 'security, pledge' and calls this 'well interpreted.' According to him, LXX sought to avoid 'any possible Messianic connotations by its renderings,' something which Tg., for example, does not do in our verse (and 15:4). In a note (p. 316, n. 13) he believes our Hebr. word is related to the Akkad. *neru*, 'meaning "royal prerogative" in the Assyrian inscriptions.' But Noth points out that, according to written statements made to him by W. von Soden and J. Krecher, this word is not verifiable in the Akkad., so that in the end the 'usual translation is presumably on target.'

Hanson (op. cit., p. 312) interprets our word ניר via a semantic link with the Akkad. word *niru(m)* (*AHw*, 793f.: 'Joch der Herrschaft'), as kingly rule over a subject people or his own subjects. Hanson also wants to interpret texts like Ps. 132:17; 2 Sam. 21:17 and Prov. 21:4 in this sense.[17] M. Görg (*VT* 35 [1985], 363-368) links the word with the Egyptian, where the noun *nîr* has the meaning 'power.' It may be that both the Assyr. and the Egypt. meaning of the word have fused in the Hebr. (see Kellermann, 620). Van der Kooy (art. cit.) shows that in various passages in OT the image of the 'lamp of David' is applied to the Davidic dynasty. On the basis of 1 Kgs. 15:4 but also of 1 Kgs 11:36 and 2 Kgs 8:19 it can be said that ניר denotes the royal successor in the line of David (Van der Kooij, 54). It is clear that 'the light' can be used as

---

[17] See now also E. Ben Zvi, "Once the Lamp has been Kindled ...: A Reconsideration of the Meaning of the MT *nîr* in 1 Kgs 11:36; 15:4; 2 Kgs 8:19; and 2 Chr 21:7," *Australian Biblical Review* 39 (1991), 19-30.

metaphor for the Davidic dynasty (cf. the note in TOB, a.l.: 'la lampe est le signe de la dynastie vivante [2 S 14,7]'). Along with Noth et al. we also hold to the customary understanding of the word, while, in the interest of clarity, in our translation we have put 'lamp' in quotation marks; also cf. Zorell s.v. ניר (2): '*igniculus, qui in domo ... conservatur et exstingui non sinitur (cf. 2 S 14,7), imago prosapiae perpetuandae et ab interitu praeserveandae ...*'; D. Grossberg (*VT* 36 [1986], 484) on the other hand is of the opinion that in our verse 'the agricultural signification is evident.' This meaning, however, is 'eclipsed by the more common meaning "lamp".' Ahijah promises Jeroboam that, though he will become king in Israel, a son of David, i.e. the Davidic dynasty, will also in the future continue to reside in Jerusalem (Kellermann, 624f.; also cf. König, *Stil.* 99).

For לשים שמי שם (also 14:21; 2 Kgs. 21:4, 7), cf. comments on 9:3. As we discover anew in this verse, the Davidic dynasty and Jerusalem are very closely connected.

11:37 *But you I will take and you shall rule in accordance with what your soul wishes, and be king over Israel.*
In this verse Jeroboam is again – after vs. 31 – addressed more explicitly. The verb אול pi, 'to desire,' 'to wish' occurs (of the 11x in pi. in OT) only here in the books of Kings (also cf. *HAL*, 20a; *Ges.*[18], 22b; *DCH*, I, 149; E. Gerstenberger, *THAT*, I, 74ff.; G. Mayer, *TWAT*, I, 145-148). The subject of desire is נפשך, 'your soul,' i.e. 'yourself' (cf., inter al. Deut. 14:26; 1 Sam. 2:16; 2 Sam. 3:21). Expressed here, therefore, is that it has for a long time been Jeroboam's desire to become king. To quote Gerstenberger (p. 76): 'das Wünschen wird als typischer Ausdruck der Lebenskraft, des Ichs, angesehen' (cf. Pedersen, I-II, 147: 'The *desire* comprises everything that may add to the capacity of the soul, both the ideal values and the satisfaction of the claims of the body'). In such a situation we speak of a 'sincere' desire. Whether this can now also be proof that this desire was already known to the Ephramite prophet, as Thenius contends, is – at least to our mind – an overly bold conclusion.

To the preceding words the text adds that Jeroboam will be king 'over Israel.' Vanoni, *Literarkritik*, 170, is of the opinion that 'Israel' most likely refers to 'the people' and not to 'the land,' since of the 46 cases in which a word group with *-al* indicates a king's area of sovereignty this clearly relates 22x to his subjects. Although this cannot be established with certainty, there is much to be said for Vanoni's view (also cf. H.-J. Zobel, *TWAT*, III, 996f. and Vanoni's criticism, p. 171, n. 574). In any case it is clear that here and in the following verse, as well as in many other passages in what follows in 1 and 2 Kings, 'Israel' refers to the so-called 'northern' kingdom, hence to the exclusion of Judah.

11:38 *And if you listen to all that I command you and walk in my ways and do what is right in my eyes by keeping my statutes and my commandments as David my servant did, then I will be with you and build you an enduring house, as I built for David, and I will give Israel to you.*

If Jeroboam remains on the path of obedience to YHWH's commandments, as David did, his dynasty will be established. In place of תשמע, '(if) you listen,' LXX has 'if you keep,' which is perhaps a correction in light of לשמור somewhat further on in our verse (cf. Tg.: תקביל, '[if] you accept'). Still the Hebr. text is not unusual for a dtr. author (Deut. 28:1, 15; with plur. in 11:13 etc.; cf. Burney). The last 4 words in our verse ('and I will give Israel to you') and all of vs. 39 are missing in LXX*. Very often, therefore, this part in MT is considered a gloss (e.g. Benzinger; Stade-Schwally; H. Seebass [ZAW 88 (1976), 363]; cf. textcr. app. in *BHK*), or a section by another author.

We already encountered 'doing what is right in my eyes' in vs. 33. There, too, the words וחקתי ומשפטי were disputed. Then in vs. 34 we found the words מצותי וחקתי, which are repeated in reverse order in our verse. According to Vanoni, *Literarkritik*, 68, these words could be from another author. The dtr. author again explicitly brings David to the fore as the fulfiller of the ordinances and commandments (see comments on 3:14 above).

The expression 'I will be with you' occurs repeatedly in OT (approx. 100x; so H.D. Preuss, *ZAW* 80 [1968], 139-173; esp. [on our verse] 143; see comments on 1:37 and on 8:57 above). According to Preuss, this formula pertains to a fundamental structure of OT belief. Originally this concept arose from the nomadic idea that the deity would travel along with his people; the deity would offer protection and be prepared to fight for them. After the period of David, this formula then entered into more general use.

'To build a sure house' is not just a 'sinnfälliger Ausdruck für die Familie' here (König, *Stil.* 25), but especially a reference to a well-founded dynasty, such as was at one time established for David (cf. 2 Sam. 7:11, 16, 27; see also comments on 2:4 above). The 'sureness' (for the word נאמן, see comments on 8:26; Pedersen, I-II, 339) of David's 'house' 'becomes typical of the Israelites' (Pedersen, I-II, 207; for the use of 'house' in OT, cf. O. Michel *TDNT*, V, 120f.) and is conditionally held out to Jeroboam as well.

11:39 *I will therefore humble David's descendants because of this, but not forever.*
In Mm 898 (cf. also Mm 4069) we find 48x an OT text in which, though the *aleph* is written, it is not read.[18] One of those words is ואענה in our verse. Ehrlich is of the opinion that the masora, by that 'anomale Vokalisation' (the

---

[18] Cf. F. Diaz Esteban, *Sefer 'Oklah we-'Oklah*, Madrid 1975, 137f., noting 47 cases.

quiescence of the *aleph*), sought to signal its doubt about the correctness of the word. He considers that doubt warranted because an impf. here would, from a syntactical viewpoint, be incorrect (see also the discussion of this form in various grammars, e.g. Böttcher §§360, 428; Olsh. §§38b, 79a, 248b; Ewald §88d; Ges-K §23d; BL 425; Joüon §24e; also Vanoni, *Literarkritik*, 102, n. 115). The verb ענה II (*HAL*, 807f.) in the pi. means 'to oppress,' 'to humble,' 'to violate (a woman),' and only occurs here and in 2 Kgs. 17:20 in pi. in the books of Kings (of the 54x the word occurs in the pi. in OT; for another [disputed] form of it, cf. comments on 8:35 above; for the meaning and frequency of the word, cf. E.S. Gerstenberger, *TWAT*, VI, 247-270, with a statistical overview: 249f.; cf. also R. Martin-Achard, *THAT*, II, 342). According to Gerstenberger (pp. 253f.) the verb has a juridical character: the humbling constitutes degradation or loss of status, by which a process of personal or social degradation may begin (cf. LXX^A [in LXX* the verse is lacking, remember], where the verb κακουχέω, 'to torment' is used; in NT, see Hebr. 11:37; 13:3, and cf. W. Michaelis, *TDNT*, V, 907, n. 21). It is presumably best to read a 1st p. sing. impf. of ענה with copula (וָאֲעַנֶּה) and to regard it as a cohortative (in this case, volitive): 'I will humble ...' (cf. e.g. Joüon §114b).

The particle למען here means 'in relation to' (so, correctly, König §396d). For the restrictive or adversative function of the particle אך, cf. comments on 9:24 above. Also in vs. 12 of our chapter the particle introduces a restriction in duration. Older exegetes like Vatablus, believed that the restoration of the kingdom would dawn at the time of the Messiah (*quod adimpletum fuit in Christo Jesu Domino nostro*).

11:40 *So Solomon sought to kill Jeroboam but Jeroboam arose and fled to Egypt, to Shishak king of Egypt. And he remained in Egypt until the death of Solomon.*
After the long intermezzo which began in vs. 29, the first phase of Jeroboam's rise to power is concluded in our verse with the statement that Solomon sought to kill Jeroboam, which was a reason for Jeroboam to escape to Egypt and to the pharaoh's court 'until the death of Solomon' (Debus, op. cit., p. 5, suspects that Jeroboam's rebellion against Solomon failed). In our verse the name of the pharaoh is spelled שישק (Shishak; also cf. 2 Chr. 12:2, 5, 7, 9), but in 14:25 in the k^{e}tib-form: שושק. LXX reads in our verse (as in 14:25 and 12:24): Σουσακείμ. Josephus, *Ant.* VIII §210, speaks of Ἴσακος (in §§ 253ff. of ἴσωκος; in *Ant.* VII §105, however, of Σούσακος; and in *Bell.* VI §436 even of Ἀσωχαῖος). In cuneiform his name is spelled *Susinqu* or *Šusanqu*. In Greek his name is: Σεσώγχις (cf. *HAL*, 1375a). the name derives perhaps from the Lybian word *ššnk* (D.B. Redford, *ABD*, V, 1221). Originating from a Lybian tribe (*Mešweš*), Shishak rose to prominence during the rule of the last king of the 21st Egyptian dynasty, Psusennes II (circa 965-931; also cf. comments on

3:1 above). Originally Shishak was city-king over Heracleopolis until he became the founder of the 22nd dynasty (the so-called Bubastides-dynasty, according to Manetho). It is not certain, however, whether he resided in Bubastis or in Tanis. Various opinions are in circulation about the precise dates of his 21-year rule: some put them at approx. 946-925[19], others at 945-924 (J.A. Wilson, *ANET*, 263 [in *IDB*, IV, 337f., Wilson reports the years 940-915]; S. Morenz, *BHHW*, III, 1810; and M.L. Bierbrier, *LdÄ*, V, 585); Redford, on the other hand, at circa 931-910 (cf. W.F. Albright, *BASOR* 153 [1953], 4-11; 935-914). Although few traces of Shishak's influence remain, there is evidence that he extended his power struggles beyond Egypt's borders. Memorials of him have been found in Megiddo and Byblos. It is not hard to understand, therefore, that Shishak was eager to furnish support to people who, in the region of Syro-Palestine, had initiated rebellion against the rulers of that area. Such persons had potential for strengthening his influence, as could also be inferred from 14:25f.

The picture which Josephus, *Ant.* VIII §§209f., presents in his history is that Jeroboam, encouraged by the words of Ahijah, did not sit still but incited the people to rebel against Solomon and to transfer supreme power to Jeroboam. When Solomon learned of this plot, he sought to arrest and kill him. Josephus may have been influenced the view of LXX 12:24b. We already saw earlier (vss. 26ff.), that no precise reason for Solomon's fury against Jeroboam is provided. We remain caught up here in the realm of hypothesis.

11:41 *Now the rest of the deeds of Solomon, with everything he did and all his wisdom, are they not written in the book of the chronicles of Solomon?*
In this and the following verse we encounter the more or less stereotypical concluding formula used by the dtr. author for the reigns of kings (14:19, 29; 15:7, 23, 31 and *passim* in the books of 1 and 2 Kings; according to T. Kronholm, *TWAT*, III, 1085, the expression יתר דברי occurs in OT 42x in Kings and Chronicles). The noun יתר occurs 95x in OT (Kronholm, 1084) and means that 'which is left over,' 'rest.' In 2 Chr. 9:29, which from this verse on for the time being again runs approximately parallel to Kings, the word אשר is used in about the same sense. The דברים are not only the words but also the deeds, in short, the history in its entire length and breadth (see LXX: ῥήματα in our verse and e.g. in 14:29: λόγοι for the same Hebr. word; cf. O. Procksch, *TDNT*, IV, 91f.). The author is not only aware that the history was broader than he could record but that he himself could not have written anything sensible if he had not had at his disposal 'sources' from which he could draw.

---

[19] Cf. J. von Beckerath, *Abriss der Geschichte des alten Agypten*, Oldenburg 1971, 48.

As we have seen earlier (cf. comments on 2:6, 9, etc.), the 'wisdom of Solomon' was the central theme which ran like a purple thread throughout the composition of the preceding chapters. The only exception to this rule is our chap. 11 – which is perhaps the reason why the Chronicler skipped this episode – but the dtr. could not refrain from once more touching on the חכמה theme here.

As a sort of scholarly account 'avant la lettre' there is a reference here (and in the remainder) to the 'source' or 'sources' where more material can be found: in our case 'the Book of the histories of Solomon' (also cf. Pedersen, III-IV, 573f.). It is possible that in place of דברי שלמה, LXX[Luc.] read the words which also occur in 14:19 etc. דברי הימים לש' the 'chronicles' or 'the annals' of Solomon (see Rahlfs, *SSt.* III, 251; cf. Theod. and Vulg. Clementina: *in libro everborum dierum Salomonis*. Noth, however, correctly observes that it is hard to decide whether the reference in the 'histories of Solomon' is to things other than what can be found in the subsequent 'annals' or 'diaries' of other kings. In any case this book, like the other books, must still have been accessible (to many?) at the time of the composition of Kings. Let it be noted here that in the par. 2 Chr. 9:29, as the rest of the history of Solomon, 'of an earlier and later time' quite different sources are listed: the history of the prophet Nathan; the prophecy of Ahijah the Shilomite; and the visions concerning Jeroboam, son of Nebat, of Iddo the seer. The 'history of Nathan' is also mentioned in 1 Chr. 29:29. The prophecy of Ahijah is unknown to us; there is a reference to it in 12:15 (cf. 2 Chr. 10:15). Perhaps Iddo is the unknown prophet in chap. 13. Josephus, *Ant.* VIII §§231, 235, 240f., 408, calls him Iadoon. Possibly the Chronicler already knew this tradition and in his day there were writings under these names making the rounds.

By הלא, again according to fixed tradition, there is introduced by a question what can only be answered in the affirmative (cf., in the Latin *nonne*). One could translate this composite particle affirmatively as follows: 'as is well known' (see Joüon §161; further König §§351i, 353x; Ges-K §150e), an equivalent of הנה etc. (e.g. 2 Sam. 1:18).

11:42 *The time that Solomon reigned in Jerusalem over all Israel was fourty years.*
As the period of Solomon's reign we are given the round number of 40 years (for the number '40' see inter al. König, *Stil.* 54f.; H. Balz, *TDNT*, VIII, 136; see also comments on 2:11 above). The phrase 'over all Israel' is lacking in LXX[B.] In view of the complicated nature of determining the Judean and Israelitish chronology it is hard to furnish an exact date (cf. my article in *BH*, IIa, 82ff., and the overview on pp. 135-138). Possibly the end of Solomon's reign can be set at approx. 930 BCE.

11:43 *Then Solomon rested with his fathers and was buried in the city of David his father. And his son Rehoboam succeeded him as king.*

For the expression 'to rest with his fathers,' see comments on 1:21 above and 2:10. In the latter verse we also stopped to reflect on 'the city of David.' It is remarkable that in our verse the words 'his father' are added (in 8:1 and 9:24 this addition is lacking). Ehrlich suspects that בעיר should be changed into בקבר, 'in the grave,' but for this textual modification there is no warrant whatever. Also in vs. 27, as we saw earlier, this addition occurred with 'the city of David' (except in the majority of Pesh. MSS). Vanoni, *Literarkritik*, 61, is of the opinion that, if 'the city of David' has to be regarded as a topographical term, the addition 'his father' is inappropriate. But the par. 2 Chr. 9:31 has the addition as well. In 15:24; 22:51 and 2 Kgs. 15:38 we also find it but of these 3 texts the first and the last are textcritically vulnerable as far as the addition is concerned (also the par. vss. in Chr., 2 Chr. 16:14; 21:1 and 27:9 omit it!). Vanoni thinks we may be dealing with additions 'die nicht unbedingt von einer Hand stammen.' To our mind the assessment could be somewhat more 'innocent': the author was so accustomed to put 'his father' after the name David that he simply also added it to the topographically determined 'city of David.' Sometimes the effect of analogies is unconsciously present in authors as well ...

Rehoboam, son of Solomon, succeeds his father. In *HAL*, 1132b, a couple of explanations are given for his name: (1) 'the Uncle (= deity; YHWH?) has caused increase'; (2) 'the people has become larger' (also cf. Noth, *IPN*, 193, n. 4; F. B. Knutson, *RSP*, III, v, 32 [pp. 491f.]; further Montg.-Gehman, 248).

Let it be noted that after 'in the city of his father David' LXX has still a long insertion derived in part from 12:2. The insertion reads: 'And it came to pass when Jeroboam son of Nebat heard (it) – for he was still in Egypt, to which he had fled from the face of Solomon, and he was still residing there – he went on his way and came into his own city, in the land of Sareira, which is situated in Mount Ephraim.'

The verb κατευθύνειν occurs, aside from a number of times in LXX, also in NT (Luke 1:79; 1 Thess. 3:11; 2 Thess. 3:5), and means: 'to make his steps straight,' 'to direct his steps.' We translated it: 'to go on his way.' In LXX 12:24f the reading 'Sareira' is more correct than 'the land of Sareira' (also see Burney). Lxx[Luc.] diverges at a number of points from LXX*, for example, by inserting 'and he resided'; 'in Egypt until Solomon was dead' etc. (cf. Stade-Schwally). Trevolle Barrera devotes an extensive study to the analysis of the parallel texts 1 Kgs. 12:2, 3a and LXX, 11:43.[20] He arrives at the conclusion

---

[20] J.C. Trebolle Barrera, *Salomón y Jeroboán. Historia de la recensión y redacción de 1 Reyes 2-12. 14* (Bibliotheca Salmanticensis. Dissertationes 3), Salamanca/Jerusalem 1980, 49-83; see now also T.M. Willis, "The Text of 1 Kings 11:43-12:3," *CBQ.* 53 (1991), 37-44; and A. Schenker,

that LXX 11:40, 43*, 12:1, 3b best preserves the original continuity.

"Un cas de critique narrative au service de la critique textuelle (1 Rois 11,43-12,2-3.20)," *Bib* 77 (1996), 219-226.

HISTORICAL COMMENTARY ON THE OLD TESTAMENT

PUBLISHED VOLUMES

Exodus I: Exodus 1:1-7:13 (1993)	Cornelis Houtman, Kampen, The Netherlands
Exodus I: Exodus 7:14-19:25 (1996)	Cornelis Houtman, Kampen, The Netherlands
1 Kings I/1: 1 Kings 1-11 (1998)	Martin J. Mulder, Leiden, The Netherlands
Isaiah III/1: Isaiah 40-48 (1997)	Jan L. Koole, Kampen, The Netherlands
Lamentations (1998)	Johan Renkema, Kampen, The Netherlands
Nahum (1997)	Klaas Spronk, Kampen, The Netherlands

FORTHCOMING VOLUMES

Exodus III: Exodus 20-40	Cornelis Houtman, Kampen, The Netherlands
Isaiah 13-39	Willem A.M. Beuken, Louvain, Belgium
Isaiah III/2: Isaiah 49-55	Jan L. Koole, Kampen, The Netherlands
Isaiah III/3: Isaiah 56-66	Jan L. Koole, Kampen, The Netherlands
Zephaniah	Jan Vlaardingerbroek, Rotterdam, The Netherlands
Habakuk	Gert T.M. Prinsloo, Pretoria, South Africa

PROJECTED VOLUMES

Genesis	Erhard Blum, Augsburg, Germany
Leviticus	James W. Watts, Hastings, Nebraska U.S.A.
Numbers	F.A. Gosling, Sheffield, England
Deuteronomy	Cornelis Houtman, Kampen, The Netherlands
Joshua	Hartmut Rösel, Haifa, Israel
Judges	Klaas Spronk, Kampen, The Netherlands
Ruth	Marjo C.A. Korpel, Utrecht, The Netherlands
1 Samuel	Åke Viberg, Lund, Sweden
2 Samuel	Jichan Kim, Seoul, Korea
1 Kings 12-22	Jurie le Roux, Pretoria, South Africa
2 Kings	Kevin J. Cathcart, Dublin, Ireland
1 Chronicles	Peter B. Dirksen, Leiden, The Netherlands
2 Chronicles	Isaac Kalimi, Brookline, MA U.S.A.
Ezra	István Karasszon, Budapest, Hungary
Nehemiah	Edward Noort, Groningen, The Netherlands
Esther	Henk Jagersma, Brussels, Belgium
Job	Richard S. Hess, London, England
Psalms	Phil.J. Botha & Gert T.M. Prinsloo, Pretoria, South Africa
Proverbs	James A. Loader, Vienna, Austria
Ecclesiastes	Anton Schoors, Louvain, Belgium

Song of Songs	Wilfred G.E. Watson, New Castle, England
Isaiah 1-12	Hendrik Leene, Amsterdam, The Netherlands
Jeremiah	Ben J. Oosterhoff† & Erik Peels, Apeldoorn, The Netherlands
Ezekiel 1-24	Herrie F. van Rooy, Potchefstroom, South Africa
Ezekiel 25-48	Corrine Patton, Tallahassee, Florida, U.S.A.
Daniel	Tibor Marjovszki, Debrecen, Hungary
Hosea	Dwight R. Daniels, Glendale, CA U.S.A.
Joel	Willem van der Meer, Kampen, The Netherlands
Amos	Meindert Dijkstra, Utrecht, The Netherlands
Obadaiah	Johan Renkema, Kampen, The Netherlands
Jonah	Johannes H. Potgieter, Pretoria, South Africa
Micah	Johannes C. de Moor, Kampen, The Netherlands
Haggai	William Th. Koopmans, Peterborough, Ont. Canada
Zechariah	Al Wolters, Ancaster, Ont. Canada
Malachi	Raymond C. Van Leeuwen, Ardmore, PA U.S.A.

PRINTED ON PERMANENT PAPER • IMPRIME SUR PAPIER PERMANENT • GEDRUKT OP DUURZAAM PAPIER - ISO 9706

ORIENTALISTE, KLEIN DALENSTRAAT 42, B-3020 HERENT